Scripture Index to the New International Dictionary of New Testament Theology

John and Joo Ling Cuddeford
1821 Peters Road
North Vancouver, B.C.   V7J 1Y7

Scripture Index to the New International Dictionary of New Testament Theology

And Index to Selected Extrabiblical Literature

David Townsley and Russell Bjork

Regency
Reference Library
Zondervan Publishing House
Grand Rapids, Michigan

SCRIPTURE INDEX TO THE NEW INTERNATIONAL DICTIONARY OF NEW
TESTAMENT THEOLOGY AND INDEX TO SELECTED EXTRABIBLICAL LITERATURE

Copyright © 1985 by The Zondervan Corporation
Grand Rapids, Michigan

REGENCY REFERENCE LIBRARY
is an imprint of Zondervan Publishing House
1415 Lake Drive S.E., Grand Rapids, Michigan 49506

Library of Congress Cataloging in Publication Data

Townsley, David.
    Scripture index to the new international dictionary of New Testament theology and index to
selected extrabiblical literature.

    1. The new international dictionary of New Testament theology—Indexes.   2. Bible.
N.T.—Theology—Dictionaries—Indexes.   3. Bible. N.T.—Dictionaries—Indexes.
I. Bjork, Russell.   II. Title.

BS2397.N483T68   1985   225.3   85–14615

ISBN   0–310–44501–9

All rights reserved. No part of this publication may be reproduced, stored in a retrieval system, or
transmitted in any form or by any means—electronic, mechanical, photocopy, recording, or any
other—except for brief quotations in printed reviews, without the prior permission of the
publisher.

Printed in the United States of America

85 86 87 88 89 90 / 10 9 8 7 6 5 4 3 2 1

To

David M. Scholer

We gratefully acknowledge the generosity of Gordon College (Wenham, Massachusetts) in allowing us to use its VAX-11/780 computer system for collating the citations in this index.

Contents

Preface

During my first year in seminary, both the need for this *Scripture Index* and the possibility of producing it as an "extracurricular project" were suggested to me by a good friend and classmate, Paul Mirecki. I began the work almost immediately but soon realized that it would be a long time before I could hope to complete the gargantuan job of manually collating thousands of citations.

The project was ushered into the computer age, however, through the unique talents and generous collaboration of Russell Bjork. I am grateful for his creative and careful work and his willingness to stick with the project despite unforeseen delays and an increasingly demanding teaching schedule.

Two professors, David M. Scholer and J. Ramsey Michaels, whose love of Scripture and other ancient literature and dedication to the highest standards of scholarship provided an inspiration for this work, are due a special thanks. It was in response to an assignment made by David M. Scholer to prepare an extensive collection of extrabiblical passages that parallel Scripture passages that Russ originally developed a program to collate the citations. Thanks to a request by J. Ramsey Michaels for me to prepare a Scripture index for one of his books as part of my responsibility as a student assistant to him, I had the opportunity to approach Russ about developing similar programs for other uses and to pave the way for the present project.

I am particularly indebted to my wife, Daryl, for several suggestions that greatly improved the effeciency of collecting the citations and ensured the accuracy of the data that was entered into the computer. Her help and encouragement were invaluable resources for me.

It has been my good fortune to have an editor who is also a friend and a co-worker. I appreciate the care and patience with which Ed van der Maas has worked to get this ponderous and tedious project into its final form. The work has benefited from his suggestions at several points.

Finally, it is my hope that the *Scripture Index* will achieve its intended purpose: to make *The New International Dictionary of New Testament Theology* both more accessible and more useful to pastors, students, and laypersons everywhere as they endeavor to read, to understand, and to proclaim God's Word.

DAVID L. TOWNSLEY

Introduction

The *Scripture Index* was intended from the outset to be as inclusive as possible. For that reason, the reader should not expect to find a substantive discussion of a given passage every time that passage is cited. Secondary citations can, however, lead the reader to discussions of related passages and provide many "fresh trails."

The *Index to Selected Extrabiblical Literature* also opens the way for the serious reader to benefit from the wealth of background and illustrative material so important to a proper understanding and appreciation of the New Testament. Used in conjunction with the *Scripture Index,* it can provide yet another way of cross-referencing related Scripture passages. Used alone, it facilitates the study of the extrabiblical literature in its own right.

In certain Old Testament passages, the verse numbers of the English versions differ from those of the Septuagint (LXX) and/or the Hebrew Masoretic text. An asterisk (*) following a reference indicates that such a numbering variation was noted in one or more of the articles citing the passage. The asterisks are included as a reminder to the reader that the pursuit of a given verse will be affected at these points, depending upon whether an English or an ancient language text is being consulted.

The preparation of the *Scripture Index* has brought to light a number of citation errors. The *Index* lists the corrected citations. A dagger (†) following an entry alerts the reader to check the Errata on pages 319–20, since on one or more of the pages given for that entry an incorrect reference will be found.

Old Testament

Genesis

1–11	**Vol. 1:** 209
1	**Vol. 1:** 76, 211, 379, 383, 630 **Vol. 2:** 691, 889 **Vol. 3:** 851, 980, 1087, 1100, 1105
1:1 ff	**Vol. 2:** 564, 690 **Vol. 3:** 502
1:1–2:4a	**Vol. 1:** 522 **Vol. 3:** 1153
1:1–2:3	**Vol. 3:** 406
1:1	**Vol. 1:** 380 **Vol. 2:** 70, 190 **Vol. 3:** 1115
1:2	**Vol. 1:** 175, 180, 422 **Vol. 2:** 197, 205 **Vol. 3:** 691, 707, 983, 990, 1177
1:3 ff	**Vol. 2:** 491
1:3–5	**Vol. 1:** 379
1:3	**Vol. 2:** 494, 672, 834
1:4 f	**Vol. 1:** 422
1:5–2:2	**Vol. 2:** 887
1:5	**Vol. 1:** 272 **Vol. 2:** 887, 889
1:6 ff	**Vol. 1:** 523
1:6 f	**Vol. 2:** 613
1:6–8	**Vol. 3:** 1177
1:6	**Vol. 3:** 990
1:7	**Vol. 1:** 379, 523 **Vol. 3:** 984
1:8 f	**Vol. 1:** 272
1:8	**Vol. 2:** 189, 889
1:9 f	**Vol. 3:** 983
1:9	**Vol. 1:** 296, 515 **Vol. 2:** 720 **Vol. 3:** 983, 990
1:11 ff	**Vol. 3:** 524
1:11 f	**Vol. 2:** 502
1:11	**Vol. 1:** 389 **Vol. 2:** 211
1:13 f	**Vol. 2:** 889
1:14 ff	**Vol. 1:** 380 **Vol. 2:** 491
1:14 f	**Vol. 1:** 523
1:14	**Vol. 2:** 189 **Vol. 3:** 835
1:16	**Vol. 1:** 165 **Vol. 2:** 428, 491, 889 **Vol. 3:** 730, 734
1:17	**Vol. 1:** 523 **Vol. 2:** 430
1:18 f	**Vol. 2:** 889
1:18	**Vol. 1:** 165, 422 **Vol. 2:** 99
1:20	**Vol. 3:** 680
1:21	**Vol. 1:** 172, 670
1:22	**Vol. 1:** 211, 732 **Vol. 2:** 128
1:23	**Vol. 2:** 889
1:24 f	**Vol. 1:** 113
1:26 ff	**Vol. 2:** 576
1:26 f	**Vol. 2:** 160–161, 287 **Vol. 3:** 1056
1:26	**Vol. 1:** 522, 670 **Vol. 2:** 189, 287, 498, 502, 505, 564
1:26a	**Vol. 3:** 1056
1:27 f	**Vol. 2:** 576 **Vol. 3:** 1056
1:27	**Vol. 1:** 85, 87, 166, 380 **Vol. 2:** 563, 569–570, 579 **Vol. 3:** 181, 539, 980
1:27a	**Vol. 2:** 564
1:27b	**Vol. 3:** 1056
1:27c	**Vol. 1:** 383
1:28	**Vol. 1:** 180, 211, 288, 522, 560, 617, 732, 734 **Vol. 2:** 128, 564, 576
1:29 f	**Vol. 2:** 268
1:29	**Vol. 1:** 743 **Vol. 2:** 268
1:30	**Vol. 2:** 268
1:31	**Vol. 1:** 523 **Vol. 2:** 103, 889
2 f	**Vol. 1:** 84, 87 **Vol. 3:** 585
2	**Vol. 1:** 379, 383, 434 **Vol. 2:** 564, 761 **Vol. 3:** 980, 1063
2:1	**Vol. 1:** 522 **Vol. 2:** 189 **Vol. 3:** 410
2:2 f	**Vol. 3:** 255–256, 405, 1148
2:2–4a	**Vol. 2:** 889
2:2	**Vol. 2:** 690, 697 **Vol. 3:** 257, 410
2:3	**Vol. 1:** 211 **Vol. 3:** 94, 215
2:4	**Vol. 1:** 181–182, 678 **Vol. 2:** 70 **Vol. 3:** 656
2:4b–3:24	**Vol. 2:** 889
2:4b–25	**Vol. 1:** 522
2:4b	**Vol. 1:** 72 **Vol. 2:** 564, 889
2:5	**Vol. 1:** 743
2:6	**Vol. 1:** 585
2:7 ff	**Vol. 2:** 564
2:7	**Vol. 1:** 85, 520, 665 **Vol. 2:** 478, 564–565, 787 **Vol. 3:** 269, 680, 683–684, 703, 707, 915
2:8	**Vol. 2:** 761
2:9–17	**Vol. 2:** 482
2:9	**Vol. 1:** 389, 562 **Vol. 2:** 268
2:10 ff	**Vol. 2:** 689
2:10–14	**Vol. 2:** 761 **Vol. 3:** 986–988
2:10	**Vol. 1:** 165
2:11 f	**Vol. 2:** 95
2:11	**Vol. 2:** 720
2:13 f	**Vol. 3:** 215
2:15	**Vol. 1:** 522 **Vol. 3:** 1148
2:16 f	**Vol. 2:** 564
2:16	**Vol. 1:** 332 **Vol. 2:** 268 **Vol. 3:** 215
2:17	**Vol. 2:** 103, 272, 478, 889 **Vol. 3:** 578
2:18 ff	**Vol. 2:** 161, 540, 564
2:18–25	**Vol. 1:** 87 **Vol. 3:** 1056
2:18–24	**Vol. 2:** 576
2:18	**Vol. 1:** 385 **Vol. 2:** 103, 724 **Vol. 3:** 539, 542, 1056
2:18b	**Vol. 2:** 576

Genesis *(cont'd)*

2:19 f	**Vol. 2:** 649
2:19	**Vol. 1:** 272, 522
2:20	**Vol. 1:** 84
2:21 ff	**Vol. 2:** 160, 213 **Vol. 3:** 1056
2:21–24	**Vol. 3:** 1056
2:21	**Vol. 1:** 672
2:23 f	**Vol. 2:** 576
2:23	**Vol. 1:** 241, 672 **Vol. 2:** 395
2:24	**Vol. 2:** 349, 564, 570, 579, 722 **Vol. 3:** 181, 251, 329, 505, 534–535, 538–539, 1064, 1069–1070
2:25	**Vol. 3:** 563
3	**Vol. 1:** 78, 86–87, 434, 508–510 **Vol. 2:** 459, 478, 576, 761, 763 **Vol. 3:** 472, 578
3:1 ff	**Vol. 3:** 801
3:1	**Vol. 1:** 168, 510 **Vol. 2:** 616
3:2 f	**Vol. 2:** 271
3:3	**Vol. 3:** 860
3:4	**Vol. 2:** 116 **Vol. 3:** 892
3:5 f	**Vol. 2:** 103 **Vol. 3:** 186
3:5	**Vol. 1:** 76, 562, 565 **Vol. 2:** 99, 498, 729 **Vol. 3:** 892
3:6	**Vol. 2:** 272
3:7	**Vol. 1:** 85, 723 **Vol. 2:** 268, 395, 729 **Vol. 3:** 563
3:8	**Vol. 2:** 214–215 **Vol. 3:** 514, 846, 943
3:10	**Vol. 2:** 214–215 **Vol. 3:** 943
3:13	**Vol. 2:** 458
3:14 f	**Vol. 1:** 113, 168, 208
3:14	**Vol. 1:** 209 **Vol. 2:** 889
3:15	**Vol. 1:** 85, 241 **Vol. 2:** 132 **Vol. 3:** 522
3:16 ff	**Vol. 2:** 420
3:16	**Vol. 1:** 85, 187, 288 **Vol. 2:** 157, 446, 562
3:17 ff	**Vol. 3:** 256, 1148
3:17	**Vol. 1:** 84, 209, 285 **Vol. 2:** 173, 272, 423, 889
3:18	**Vol. 1:** 725–726, 743
3:19	**Vol. 1:** 433 **Vol. 2:** 478, 564 **Vol. 3:** 261, 915
3:20	**Vol. 1:** 87 **Vol. 2:** 649
3:21	**Vol. 1:** 84, 314, 316
3:22	**Vol. 1:** 562, 565 **Vol. 2:** 103 **Vol. 3:** 866
3:24	**Vol. 1:** 101, 280, 453 **Vol. 3:** 395, 866
4	**Vol. 3:** 82, 578
4:1	**Vol. 1:** 87, 343 **Vol. 2:** 395, 649
4:3 ff	**Vol. 3:** 421
4:3–10	**Vol. 3:** 434
4:3–8	**Vol. 3:** 942
4:3	**Vol. 3:** 421
4:4 f	**Vol. 3:** 425
4:4	**Vol. 2:** 41 **Vol. 3:** 425
4:5	**Vol. 1:** 585
4:6 f	**Vol. 3:** 421–422
4:7	**Vol. 1:** 76 **Vol. 3:** 351
4:8 ff	**Vol. 1:** 255
4:8 f	**Vol. 3:** 422
4:8	**Vol. 1:** 181, 429 **Vol. 3:** 430
4:9 ff	**Vol. 2:** 363
4:10 f	**Vol. 2:** 525
4:10	**Vol. 1:** 225, 410 **Vol. 3:** 393, 436, 1014
4:11 f	**Vol. 1:** 209
4:11	**Vol. 1:** 208–209
4:12	**Vol. 3:** 1148
4:13	**Vol. 2:** 138 **Vol. 3:** 574
4:14	**Vol. 2:** 887 **Vol. 3:** 614
4:15	**Vol. 2:** 572, 626, 690 **Vol. 3:** 93
4:16	**Vol. 1:** 321
4:17	**Vol. 1:** 343 **Vol. 2:** 802
4:19	**Vol. 3:** 747
4:22	**Vol. 2:** 97
4:23 f	**Vol. 3:** 578
4:23	**Vol. 2:** 173 **Vol. 3:** 1208
4:24	**Vol. 2:** 697, 770
4:25	**Vol. 1:** 84 **Vol. 3:** 522
4:26	**Vol. 1:** 272, 451 **Vol. 2:** 650
5	**Vol. 1:** 65, 208 **Vol. 2:** 576, 698 **Vol. 3:** 264, 653, 851
5:1 ff	**Vol. 2:** 287
5:1	**Vol. 1:** 181–182, 244 **Vol. 2:** 287 **Vol. 3:** 656
5:2–5	**Vol. 1:** 84
5:2	**Vol. 2:** 569 **Vol. 3:** 539, 1056
5:3	**Vol. 2:** 287
5:18	**Vol. 1:** 531
5:21–24	**Vol. 3:** 264, 266
5:22–24	**Vol. 3:** 615
5:22	**Vol. 2:** 815
5:24	**Vol. 2:** 191, 627, 815, 817 **Vol. 3:** 261–262, 558, 602–603
5:28 f	**Vol. 2:** 681
5:29	**Vol. 1:** 209 **Vol. 2:** 681 **Vol. 3:** 1148
6–9	**Vol. 3:** 578
6–8	**Vol. 3:** 983, 989
6:1 ff	**Vol. 2:** 213, 458 **Vol. 3:** 468, 579
6:1–8:22	**Vol. 3:** 203
6:1–6	**Vol. 1:** 102
6:1–4	**Vol. 1:** 451–452
6:1	**Vol. 1:** 164
6:2	**Vol. 1:** 537 **Vol. 2:** 161 **Vol. 3:** 636
6:3	**Vol. 1:** 679 **Vol. 2:** 478, 887 **Vol. 3:** 705, 828
6:4	**Vol. 3:** 636, 828
6:5	**Vol. 1:** 184, 732 **Vol. 3:** 578
6:6	**Vol. 2:** 103
6:7	**Vol. 2:** 189 **Vol. 3:** 1153
6:8	**Vol. 2:** 117, 681
6:9	**Vol. 1:** 182 **Vol. 2:** 60, 62, 681–682, 815
6:11 f	**Vol. 3:** 578
6:11–9:19	**Vol. 2:** 681
6:11	**Vol. 1:** 468
6:13	**Vol. 2:** 477
6:14	**Vol. 1:** 389
6:15*	**Vol. 2:** 199 **Vol. 3:** 851

Genesis *(cont'd)*

6:17 ff	**Vol. 1:** 672
6:17	**Vol. 3:** 991
6:18	**Vol. 1:** 366
6:19 f	**Vol. 2:** 569
6:22	**Vol. 1:** 332 **Vol. 2:** 682
7:1	**Vol. 2:** 36, 681
7:2 f	**Vol. 2:** 569
7:4 ff	**Vol. 2:** 689
7:4	**Vol. 1:** 420 **Vol. 2:** 696
7:9	**Vol. 2:** 569
7:11 f	**Vol. 3:** 982
7:11	**Vol. 1:** 523 **Vol. 2:** 189 **Vol. 3:** 983
7:11a	**Vol. 2:** 726
7:11b	**Vol. 2:** 726
7:15 f	**Vol. 2:** 569
7:23	**Vol. 1:** 471 **Vol. 3:** 248
8:1	**Vol. 3:** 232, 235, 239, 690
8:2	**Vol. 3:** 983
8:5	**Vol. 2:** 157, 720
8:6–12	**Vol. 1:** 173
8:6	**Vol. 2:** 696
8:7	**Vol. 1:** 515
8:9	**Vol. 3:** 255
8:13	**Vol. 3:** 310
8:20 ff	**Vol. 3:** 150, 425
8:20	**Vol. 1:** 172 **Vol. 3:** 33, 418
8:21 f	**Vol. 1:** 640 **Vol. 2:** 117
8:21	**Vol. 1:** 50, 162, 184, 673 **Vol. 3:** 125, 578, 600–601
8:22	**Vol. 2:** 887 **Vol. 3:** 255
9:1–7	**Vol. 2:** 682
9:1	**Vol. 1:** 734 **Vol. 2:** 128
9:2	**Vol. 1:** 113, 670
9:3	**Vol. 2:** 268
9:4 ff	**Vol. 3:** 159
9:4 f	**Vol. 3:** 680
9:4	**Vol. 1:** 221 **Vol. 2:** 309, 477 **Vol. 3:** 150, 158
9:5	**Vol. 1:** 113, 221–222 **Vol. 3:** 158
9:6	**Vol. 2:** 287, 525, 532, 854 **Vol. 3:** 94, 159
9:7	**Vol. 1:** 180 **Vol. 2:** 128
9:8 ff	**Vol. 1:** 366 **Vol. 2:** 626
9:8–17	**Vol. 2:** 681
9:9	**Vol. 1:** 367 **Vol. 3:** 522
9:11 f	**Vol. 1:** 672
9:12	**Vol. 1:** 366
9:13	**Vol. 3:** 1002
9:15 f	**Vol. 3:** 235
9:19	**Vol. 2:** 34
9:20 f	**Vol. 3:** 918
9:20–27	**Vol. 3:** 919
9:20	**Vol. 2:** 681
9:21	**Vol. 1:** 513
9:22	**Vol. 3:** 45
9:24	**Vol. 2:** 675
9:25	**Vol. 1:** 209
9:26	**Vol. 1:** 208

10	**Vol. 2:** 690, 697, 791
10:5	**Vol. 1:** 472
10:6	**Vol. 1:** 530
10:8–12	**Vol. 1:** 140
10:9	**Vol. 1:** 140
10:11 f	**Vol. 2:** 679, 802
10:11	**Vol. 2:** 679
10:12	**Vol. 2:** 679
10:13	**Vol. 1:** 530
10:19	**Vol. 3:** 93
11–12	**Vol. 2:** 117
11	**Vol. 2:** 791 **Vol. 3:** 578, 653, 782
11:1 ff	**Vol. 1:** 209 **Vol. 2:** 363
11:1–9	**Vol. 1:** 77, 140
11:4 ff	**Vol. 2:** 189
11:4 f	**Vol. 2:** 802
11:4	**Vol. 2:** 34, 157 **Vol. 3:** 787
11:5	**Vol. 2:** 190
11:7	**Vol. 2:** 173 **Vol. 3:** 1079
11:8	**Vol. 2:** 802
11:9	**Vol. 2:** 649
11:10 ff	**Vol. 1:** 208
11:10–30	**Vol. 3:** 851
11:10	**Vol. 1:** 182
11:27–25:11*	**Vol. 1:** 76
11:30	**Vol. 1:** 285
11:31 ff	**Vol. 3:** 241
11:31	**Vol. 2:** 584
11:32	**Vol. 3:** 464
12–50	**Vol. 1:** 65
12–36	**Vol. 1:** 207
12	**Vol. 1:** 210 **Vol. 3:** 464
12:1–8	**Vol. 2:** 180
12:1–3	**Vol. 1:** 53, 80–81, 208–209 **Vol. 3:** 69
12:1	**Vol. 1:** 208 **Vol. 3:** 569
12:2–3	**Vol. 1:** 209
12:2	**Vol. 1:** 209, 411 **Vol. 3:** 740
12:3	**Vol. 1:** 76, 416, 640–641, 695 **Vol. 2:** 794 **Vol. 3:** 69, 329, 491, 871, 1012, 1112
12:3b	**Vol. 1:** 209, 214
12:4 f	**Vol. 3:** 946
12:6 ff	**Vol. 3:** 418
12:6	**Vol. 3:** 786
12:7	**Vol. 2:** 317 **Vol. 3:** 464, 523
12:8	**Vol. 1:** 76, 531, 606 **Vol. 2:** 650 **Vol. 3:** 425, 811
12:10–13:1	**Vol. 1:** 531
12:10–20	**Vol. 1:** 80
12:10	**Vol. 1:** 691 **Vol. 2:** 265
12:13	**Vol. 1:** 255
12:14	**Vol. 2:** 103
12:15 ff	**Vol. 1:** 452
12:15	**Vol. 1:** 99, 165 **Vol. 3:** 816–817
12:16	**Vol. 1:** 415
12:18	**Vol. 3:** 45
13:2	**Vol. 2:** 841
13:3–4	**Vol. 1:** 531
13:3	**Vol. 3:** 811
13:4	**Vol. 1:** 272 **Vol. 3:** 425

Genesis *(cont'd)*

13:6	**Vol. 2:** 845
13:10	**Vol. 2:** 761 **Vol. 3:** 93
13:11	**Vol. 1:** 537
13:12 f	**Vol. 3:** 93
13:13	**Vol. 1:** 565
13:14–17	**Vol. 1:** 76
13:15	**Vol. 2:** 317, 431 **Vol. 3:** 740, 828
13:16	**Vol. 2:** 317
13:18	**Vol. 3:** 418
14	**Vol. 2:** 36 **Vol. 3:** 460, 959
14:3	**Vol. 3:** 983
14:4	**Vol. 1:** 606
14:8	**Vol. 3:** 93
14:10 ff	**Vol. 3:** 93
14:13	**Vol. 2:** 305
14:14	**Vol. 2:** 173
14:17 ff	**Vol. 3:** 41
14:17–20	**Vol. 2:** 694
14:18 ff	**Vol. 1:** 208, 619
14:18 f	**Vol. 2:** 199, 375
14:18–22	**Vol. 2:** 67
14:18–20	**Vol. 1:** 214 **Vol. 2:** 590–591
14:18	**Vol. 2:** 378, 592–593 **Vol. 3:** 36
14:19	**Vol. 1:** 380
14:20	**Vol. 2:** 591, 693 **Vol. 3:** 852
14:22	**Vol. 1:** 380 **Vol. 2:** 149
14:23	**Vol. 2:** 841
14:24	**Vol. 2:** 303
15	**Vol. 1:** 56, 210, 604 **Vol. 3:** 825
15:1	**Vol. 1:** 622 **Vol. 2:** 297 **Vol. 3:** 138, 140, 513, 626, 722, 1120
15:2 ff	**Vol. 1:** 76
15:2	**Vol. 1:** 506
15:4 ff	**Vol. 3:** 425
15:4	**Vol. 1:** 209
15:5	**Vol. 1:** 411, 732 **Vol. 3:** 522, 734
15:6	**Vol. 1:** 77–78, 596–597, 604 **Vol. 2:** 301 **Vol. 3:** 169, 362, 369–370, 490, 823–825, 1112, 1187
15:7	**Vol. 2:** 278
15:9 f	**Vol. 1:** 368
15:10	**Vol. 1:** 534 **Vol. 3:** 739
15:12–21	**Vol. 1:** 80
15:12	**Vol. 1:** 609
15:13 f	**Vol. 3:** 464
15:13–16	**Vol. 1:** 76, 367
15:13–14	**Vol. 1:** 531
15:13	**Vol. 1:** 684, 691 **Vol. 2:** 689
15:14	**Vol. 2:** 363, 425
15:15	**Vol. 1:** 433 **Vol. 2:** 148, 478, 777–778
15:16	**Vol. 1:** 734
15:17–21	**Vol. 2:** 317
15:17	**Vol. 1:** 655 **Vol. 2:** 485
15:18	**Vol. 1:** 76
16	**Vol. 1:** 531–532, 650 **Vol. 3:** 594
16:1 ff	**Vol. 2:** 576
16:1–16	**Vol. 1:** 81
16:1–14	**Vol. 1:** 80
16:1–6	**Vol. 3:** 1057
16:1–4	**Vol. 2:** 582
16:1 f	**Vol. 1:** 498 **Vol. 2:** 576
16:2	**Vol. 2:** 179
16:7–14	**Vol. 3:** 986
16:9	**Vol. 2:** 264
16:12	**Vol. 1:** 255
16:13	**Vol. 1:** 585 **Vol. 2:** 67
16:15	**Vol. 1:** 284 **Vol. 3:** 1014
17	**Vol. 1:** 76 **Vol. 3:** 69
17:1–14	**Vol. 1:** 308
17:1–13	**Vol. 3:** 594
17:1–8	**Vol. 2:** 317
17:1	**Vol. 2:** 67, 139, 278–279, 649–650, 815 **Vol. 3:** 729, 924
17:3	**Vol. 1:** 609
17:4 f	**Vol. 1:** 76
17:4	**Vol. 1:** 411
17:5	**Vol. 1:** 411, 477 **Vol. 2:** 649, 794
17:6	**Vol. 2:** 128
17:7 f	**Vol. 1:** 366 **Vol. 2:** 797
17:7	**Vol. 2:** 596 **Vol. 3:** 522–523, 740
17:8	**Vol. 1:** 691 **Vol. 3:** 522–523
17:9–14	**Vol. 1:** 159
17:10 ff	**Vol. 3:** 499
17:10–14	**Vol. 1:** 154
17:10	**Vol. 2:** 437
17:11 ff	**Vol. 1:** 672
17:11	**Vol. 2:** 626 **Vol. 3:** 499
17:12 f	**Vol. 3:** 608
17:12	**Vol. 1:** 308 **Vol. 2:** 692
17:14	**Vol. 1:** 308, 699 **Vol. 2:** 569
17:15	**Vol. 1:** 80
17:16	**Vol. 1:** 285
17:17–19	**Vol. 1:** 81
17:17	**Vol. 1:** 609 **Vol. 2:** 431, 435, 596, 627, 649
17:19	**Vol. 1:** 531 **Vol. 3:** 1067
17:20	**Vol. 2:** 128
17:23	**Vol. 2:** 569 **Vol. 3:** 835
17:26	**Vol. 3:** 835
17:27	**Vol. 3:** 594
18	**Vol. 1:** 101
18:1 ff	**Vol. 1:** 687, 706
18:1–15	**Vol. 1:** 76, 80
18:1	**Vol. 1:** 332 **Vol. 3:** 846
18:2	**Vol. 2:** 876
18:3	**Vol. 1:** 322, 690 **Vol. 3:** 528
18:4	**Vol. 1:** 153, 239
18:5	**Vol. 2:** 181
18:6	**Vol. 3:** 917
18:7	**Vol. 3:** 946
18:8	**Vol. 3:** 1012
18:10	**Vol. 1:** 209 **Vol. 3:** 835, 846
18:11–14	**Vol. 3:** 1067
18:11	**Vol. 1:** 194 **Vol. 2:** 627
18:12–15	**Vol. 1:** 81
18:12 f	**Vol. 2:** 430
18:12	**Vol. 1:** 504 **Vol. 2:** 431, 435, 513, 562, 649 **Vol. 3:** 1067

Genesis *(cont'd)*

18:14   **Vol. 2:** 627   **Vol. 3:** 835, 846, 1121
18:15   **Vol. 1:** 455   **Vol. 2:** 430
18:16–32   **Vol. 3:** 93
18:17   **Vol. 2:** 214   **Vol. 3:** 639
18:18   **Vol. 1:** 209, 411   **Vol. 2:** 596   **Vol. 3:** 329, 491, 523, 1112
18:19   **Vol. 3:** 937
18:21   **Vol. 3:** 513
18:22–23†   **Vol. 2:** 863
18:23–33   **Vol. 2:** 216
18:25   **Vol. 3:** 357
18:26   **Vol. 1:** 698   **Vol. 3:** 528
18:27   **Vol. 1:** 164
18:28 f   **Vol. 3:** 528
18:33   **Vol. 1:** 321
19   **Vol. 1:** 677   **Vol. 2:** 570, 767   **Vol. 3:** 455
19:1 ff   **Vol. 1:** 687
19:1   **Vol. 2:** 876
19:2 f   **Vol. 1:** 690
19:2   **Vol. 3:** 178
19:3   **Vol. 1:** 250
19:4 ff   **Vol. 1:** 194
19:4   **Vol. 2:** 796
19:7   **Vol. 1:** 255
19:8   **Vol. 2:** 395
19:9   **Vol. 1:** 687, 691
19:11   **Vol. 2:** 426   **Vol. 3:** 448
19:14   **Vol. 3:** 821
19:15   **Vol. 3:** 1169
19:16   **Vol. 3:** 204, 370, 716
19:17   **Vol. 1:** 493
19:19   **Vol. 3:** 354, 528, 748
19:21   **Vol. 2:** 622
19:24 f   **Vol. 3:** 93
19:24   **Vol. 1:** 655, 657   **Vol. 3:** 203
19:26   **Vol. 1:** 493   **Vol. 3:** 93, 240, 1058
19:28   **Vol. 3:** 93
19:29   **Vol. 3:** 204, 235, 370
19:30   **Vol. 3:** 380
19:31   **Vol. 2:** 675
19:32 ff   **Vol. 1:** 442
19:32–35   **Vol. 3:** 919
19:33   **Vol. 1:** 420
19:34 f   **Vol. 2:** 675
19:38†   **Vol. 2:** 675
20:1–17   **Vol. 1:** 80
20:1   **Vol. 1:** 691
20:3 ff   **Vol. 3:** 574, 720
20:3–7   **Vol. 2:** 576
20:3   **Vol. 1:** 420, 512   **Vol. 2:** 898   **Vol. 3:** 1065
20:6   **Vol. 3:** 860
20:7   **Vol. 1:** 76   **Vol. 2:** 862   **Vol. 3:** 77
20:12   **Vol. 2:** 628
20:13   **Vol. 1:** 76   **Vol. 3:** 354
20:16   **Vol. 1:** 415
20:18†   **Vol. 2:** 69

21:1 ff   **Vol. 2:** 627   **Vol. 3:** 846
21:1–7   **Vol. 1:** 80–81
21:1   **Vol. 1:** 189
21:2   **Vol. 1:** 284   **Vol. 3:** 1014, 1067
21:3   **Vol. 2:** 431   **Vol. 3:** 425
21:4   **Vol. 1:** 308
21:6   **Vol. 1:** 81   **Vol. 2:** 431
21:7   **Vol. 1:** 283
21:8–21   **Vol. 1:** 80–81
21:8   **Vol. 3:** 1153
21:9–12   **Vol. 1:** 284
21:9   **Vol. 1:** 81   **Vol. 3:** 1014
21:10 ff   **Vol. 3:** 490
21:10   **Vol. 1:** 453, 531
21:12   **Vol. 1:** 275   **Vol. 3:** 523
21:13   **Vol. 3:** 522
21:14   **Vol. 1:** 283
21:16   **Vol. 2:** 416
21:19   **Vol. 1:** 734   **Vol. 2:** 726
21:20 f   **Vol. 3:** 739
21:21   **Vol. 2:** 578   **Vol. 3:** 1069
21:22 ff   **Vol. 1:** 366
21:22   **Vol. 3:** 835
21:23   **Vol. 3:** 354, 739
21:25   **Vol. 2:** 140
21:33   **Vol. 2:** 67
22   **Vol. 1:** 604   **Vol. 2:** 411   **Vol. 3:** 425, 800
22:1 ff   **Vol. 2:** 543
22:1–19   **Vol. 1:** 81
22:1–14   **Vol. 3:** 370
22:1   **Vol. 1:** 76   **Vol. 3:** 799, 1120
22:2   **Vol. 2:** 76, 725, 819   **Vol. 3:** 421, 863, 946, 1009
22:3 f   **Vol. 3:** 786
22:3   **Vol. 1:** 389   **Vol. 3:** 543
22:5   **Vol. 1:** 283   **Vol. 2:** 876
22:8   **Vol. 3:** 513
22:9 f   **Vol. 3:** 418
22:9   **Vol. 3:** 418, 787
22:12   **Vol. 1:** 283   **Vol. 2:** 76, 725   **Vol. 3:** 643
22:13   **Vol. 3:** 421, 1179
22:16 f   **Vol. 1:** 214   **Vol. 2:** 771   **Vol. 3:** 202
22:16   **Vol. 2:** 76, 596, 725   **Vol. 3:** 643, 740, 1120
22:17   **Vol. 1:** 411, 732   **Vol. 2:** 596   **Vol. 3:** 523, 734
22:18   **Vol. 2:** 179   **Vol. 3:** 522, 1012
23   **Vol. 2:** 847   **Vol. 3:** 464
23:1–2   **Vol. 2:** 417
23:2   **Vol. 2:** 417, 422
23:3 ff   **Vol. 1:** 444
23:4   **Vol. 1:** 264, 684, 690–691   **Vol. 2:** 789
23:6   **Vol. 2:** 222   **Vol. 3:** 238–239
23:7   **Vol. 2:** 876
23:9   **Vol. 1:** 520   **Vol. 3:** 238–239, 380
23:11   **Vol. 2:** 173, 803
23:12   **Vol. 2:** 876
23:15   **Vol. 2:** 96

Genesis *(cont'd)*

23:16   **Vol. 2:** 173   **Vol. 3:** 146
23:20   **Vol. 1:** 664
24   **Vol. 3:** 608, 1072
24:2   **Vol. 2:** 149
24:3   **Vol. 2:** 190, 578   **Vol. 3:** 473
24:5   **Vol. 3:** 1016
24:7   **Vol. 2:** 317
24:9   **Vol. 1:** 207   **Vol. 2:** 148–149
24:10 f   **Vol. 3:** 1057
24:11–20   **Vol. 3:** 988
24:11–18   **Vol. 3:** 986
24:11   **Vol. 1:** 442
24:13   **Vol. 3:** 1072
24:14   **Vol. 3:** 117, 608, 1072
24:16   **Vol. 2:** 876   **Vol. 3:** 1072
24:23   **Vol. 2:** 879   **Vol. 3:** 178
24:25   **Vol. 1:** 743
24:26 f   **Vol. 2:** 864
24:26   **Vol. 2:** 876
24:27   **Vol. 2:** 478   **Vol. 3:** 354, 879
24:28   **Vol. 3:** 1069
24:32   **Vol. 1:** 743
24:34–36   **Vol. 1:** 208
24:35   **Vol. 3:** 608
24:38   **Vol. 3:** 871
24:40   **Vol. 2:** 815
24:43   **Vol. 2:** 87   **Vol. 3:** 1072
24:44   **Vol. 3:** 117
24:47   **Vol. 2:** 879
24:48   **Vol. 2:** 876
24:49   **Vol. 3:** 354, 879
24:52   **Vol. 2:** 876
24:53   **Vol. 2:** 41
24:55   **Vol. 3:** 1072
24:57   **Vol. 2:** 856, 879
24:58   **Vol. 1:** 272   **Vol. 3:** 1057
24:59 ff   **Vol. 2:** 584
24:60   **Vol. 1:** 207   **Vol. 2:** 578, 698   **Vol. 3:** 1055
24:62–67   **Vol. 1:** 81
24:63   **Vol. 2:** 864
24:66   **Vol. 1:** 574
25   **Vol. 1:** 557
25:1   **Vol. 3:** 841
25:6   **Vol. 2:** 576
25:7   **Vol. 2:** 478
25:8   **Vol. 1:** 264   **Vol. 2:** 478, 796
25:15   **Vol. 3:** 841
25:19–28   **Vol. 1:** 81
25:20   **Vol. 2:** 689
25:23   **Vol. 1:** 697   **Vol. 2:** 319, 587
25:24   **Vol. 1:** 734
25:25   **Vol. 1:** 667
25:26   **Vol. 1:** 241, 272   **Vol. 2:** 431
25:27–34   **Vol. 2:** 431
25:27   **Vol. 2:** 395   **Vol. 3:** 811
25:29–34   **Vol. 2:** 782, 847   **Vol. 3:** 869
25:30   **Vol. 1:** 205   **Vol. 2:** 269

26   **Vol. 1:** 210
26:3   **Vol. 1:** 214
26:4   **Vol. 3:** 734, 1012
26:5   **Vol. 3:** 354
26:10   **Vol. 2:** 720
26:11   **Vol. 2:** 142
26:12–13   **Vol. 1:** 81
26:21   **Vol. 2:** 363
26:24   **Vol. 1:** 209
26:25   **Vol. 3:** 418, 425
26:26 ff   **Vol. 1:** 366
26:27   **Vol. 2:** 879
26:29   **Vol. 1:** 81, 207, 565   **Vol. 2:** 777
26:30   **Vol. 2:** 521
26:31   **Vol. 2:** 777
26:34–36   **Vol. 1:** 209
26:35   **Vol. 3:** 691
27   **Vol. 1:** 81, 208, 617
27:1 ff   **Vol. 1:** 208
27:1   **Vol. 2:** 422   **Vol. 3:** 513
27:4 ff   **Vol. 2:** 547
27:4   **Vol. 1:** 207
27:5–17   **Vol. 2:** 317
27:12   **Vol. 1:** 461
27:13   **Vol. 1:** 285
27:16   **Vol. 1:** 241
27:17   **Vol. 2:** 862
27:27 ff   **Vol. 1:** 214
27:27–29   **Vol. 2:** 317
27:27   **Vol. 3:** 600
27:28   **Vol. 3:** 919
27:29   **Vol. 2:** 317, 876
27:30 ff   **Vol. 1:** 214
27:30–40   **Vol. 2:** 847
27:36   **Vol. 2:** 431
27:40   **Vol. 1:** 241   **Vol. 3:** 1161
27:41   **Vol. 3:** 720
27:44   **Vol. 1:** 108   **Vol. 2:** 720
27:45   **Vol. 2:** 720
28   **Vol. 1:** 557
28:3   **Vol. 1:** 293   **Vol. 2:** 67   **Vol. 3:** 729
28:10–22   **Vol. 2:** 778
28:10–17   **Vol. 2:** 317   **Vol. 3:** 630
28:11   **Vol. 1:** 314, 732   **Vol. 2:** 157   **Vol. 3:** 786
28:12 ff   **Vol. 1:** 511
28:12   **Vol. 1:** 140, 512   **Vol. 2:** 185–186, 194
28:13   **Vol. 2:** 278, 317
28:14   **Vol. 1:** 209, 411   **Vol. 2:** 317   **Vol. 3:** 1012
28:17   **Vol. 1:** 140   **Vol. 2:** 29
28:18   **Vol. 2:** 711
28:19   **Vol. 3:** 786
28:20–22   **Vol. 3:** 853
28:21   **Vol. 2:** 778
28:22   **Vol. 2:** 693   **Vol. 3:** 787, 852
29:1–4   **Vol. 3:** 986
29:2 ff   **Vol. 3:** 565
29:2–10   **Vol. 3:** 459
29:2   **Vol. 3:** 255

Genesis *(cont'd)*

29:3	**Vol. 3:** 147
29:6	**Vol. 2:** 170, 778
29:7	**Vol. 3:** 846
29:12 ff	**Vol. 1:** 255
29:13	**Vol. 1:** 574
29:14	**Vol. 1:** 672
29:15–30	**Vol. 2:** 431
29:15	**Vol. 2:** 41, 139 **Vol. 3:** 608
29:17	**Vol. 1:** 704 **Vol. 2:** 103 **Vol. 3:** 993
29:18	**Vol. 3:** 608
29:20	**Vol. 2:** 428
29:21–30:24	**Vol. 3:** 1055
29:21–30	**Vol. 2:** 576
29:22	**Vol. 2:** 576, 578
29:27	**Vol. 2:** 578
29:31 ff	**Vol. 2:** 649
29:31	**Vol. 1:** 555 **Vol. 2:** 726
29:32–35	**Vol. 1:** 272
29:33	**Vol. 1:** 555
29:34	**Vol. 2:** 466 **Vol. 3:** 835
29:35	**Vol. 1:** 61 **Vol. 2:** 305, 319
30:1 ff	**Vol. 1:** 498
30:1–13	**Vol. 3:** 1057
30:1–4	**Vol. 2:** 582
30:1 f	**Vol. 1:** 288
30:1	**Vol. 1:** 285
30:2	**Vol. 1:** 721
30:6–24	**Vol. 1:** 272
30:6	**Vol. 2:** 363
30:13	**Vol. 1:** 216 **Vol. 3:** 872
30:16	**Vol. 2:** 139
30:18	**Vol. 2:** 139 **Vol. 3:** 138
30:20	**Vol. 2:** 41
30:22	**Vol. 3:** 232–233, 246
30:23	**Vol. 3:** 340
30:25 ff	**Vol. 1:** 208
30:27	**Vol. 2:** 554
30:28	**Vol. 3:** 138
30:30	**Vol. 3:** 565
30:31	**Vol. 3:** 1153
30:32 f	**Vol. 3:** 138
30:33	**Vol. 3:** 377
30:36	**Vol. 2:** 687
30:38	**Vol. 2:** 412 **Vol. 3:** 988
30:39	**Vol. 1:** 186
30:41	**Vol. 3:** 835
30:43	**Vol. 2:** 841
31:1	**Vol. 2:** 49, 317
31:2	**Vol. 1:** 585 **Vol. 2:** 317
31:7	**Vol. 2:** 139 **Vol. 3:** 851
31:8a	**Vol. 3:** 138
31:8b	**Vol. 2:** 139
31:10–13	**Vol. 1:** 512
31:11	**Vol. 1:** 512
31:13	**Vol. 1:** 120, 181 **Vol. 2:** 67
31:14	**Vol. 2:** 303
31:15	**Vol. 1:** 684 **Vol. 3:** 823
31:16	**Vol. 2:** 841
31:18	**Vol. 2:** 845
31:19	**Vol. 2:** 284 **Vol. 3:** 377
31:23	**Vol. 2:** 805
31:25 ff	**Vol. 2:** 139
31:27	**Vol. 2:** 578 **Vol. 3:** 673
31:28	**Vol. 3:** 1156
31:30	**Vol. 1:** 456 **Vol. 2:** 317
31:34 f	**Vol. 2:** 284
31:35	**Vol. 3:** 528, 533
31:37	**Vol. 2:** 140–141
31:40	**Vol. 1:** 652
31:41	**Vol. 2:** 139
31:42	**Vol. 1:** 546, 622
31:44 ff	**Vol. 3:** 1041
31:44–50	**Vol. 1:** 366
31:44	**Vol. 3:** 1040
31:46 ff	**Vol. 3:** 1041
31:46	**Vol. 2:** 521
31:50	**Vol. 3:** 739
31:53	**Vol. 1:** 622
31:54	**Vol. 1:** 367 **Vol. 2:** 521 **Vol. 3:** 33, 422, 425
32:1 f*	**Vol. 1:** 101
32:4–6	**Vol. 3:** 1089
32:5	**Vol. 2:** 116
32:6	**Vol. 2:** 116, 318
32:7	**Vol. 1:** 534
32:8	**Vol. 2:** 796
32:9	**Vol. 1:** 181
32:10*	**Vol. 3:** 608, 879
32:11*	**Vol. 2:** 148 **Vol. 3:** 354
32:12	**Vol. 1:** 411
32:13	**Vol. 2:** 41
32:14 f	**Vol. 1:** 415
32:14	**Vol. 3:** 421
32:17*	**Vol. 1:** 665 **Vol. 3:** 564
32:18 f	**Vol. 2:** 41
32:18	**Vol. 1:** 332
32:19	**Vol. 3:** 421
32:20*	**Vol. 3:** 153–154
32:21 f	**Vol. 3:** 421
32:23 ff	**Vol. 1:** 108
32:23–33	**Vol. 3:** 986
32:24 ff	**Vol. 1:** 648
32:24 f	**Vol. 1:** 645
32:25 ff	**Vol. 1:** 108
32:25	**Vol. 3:** 860
32:28	**Vol. 1:** 61 **Vol. 2:** 305, 649
32:30 f	**Vol. 3:** 514
32:30	**Vol. 1:** 585 **Vol. 2:** 317
32:32	**Vol. 1:** 61
33:1–4	**Vol. 2:** 317
33:3	**Vol. 1:** 322 **Vol. 2:** 876
33:5	**Vol. 1:** 288 **Vol. 3:** 608
33:6 f	**Vol. 2:** 876
33:9 f	**Vol. 2:** 876
33:10	**Vol. 3:** 745
33:11	**Vol. 1:** 214 **Vol. 3:** 711
33:14	**Vol. 1:** 241, 322
33:15	**Vol. 2:** 796

Genesis *(cont'd)*

33:18	**Vol. 3:** 458
33:19	**Vol. 1:** 116 **Vol. 2:** 303, 318 **Vol. 3:** 458, 464
33:20	**Vol. 1:** 272 **Vol. 2:** 67, 796 **Vol. 3:** 418, 425
34	**Vol. 2:** 318, 675 **Vol. 3:** 455–456
34:2	**Vol. 2:** 260
34:3	**Vol. 2:** 87 **Vol. 3:** 1072
34:5	**Vol. 3:** 104
34:7	**Vol. 1:** 61
34:12	**Vol. 2:** 578 **Vol. 3:** 1057
34:13–17	**Vol. 1:** 309
34:15	**Vol. 2:** 501
34:21	**Vol. 2:** 593
34:22 f	**Vol. 2:** 501
34:23	**Vol. 2:** 837
34:25	**Vol. 3:** 747
34:29	**Vol. 3:** 590
34:30	**Vol. 2:** 683
35:1–7	**Vol. 3:** 418
35:6	**Vol. 2:** 796
35:7	**Vol. 2:** 67 **Vol. 3:** 318, 425
35:10	**Vol. 1:** 61
35:11	**Vol. 1:** 239, 293, 411 **Vol. 2:** 67, 128, 278 **Vol. 3:** 729
35:14	**Vol. 2:** 711 **Vol. 3:** 423
35:16–20	**Vol. 3:** 872
35:18	**Vol. 2:** 146 **Vol. 3:** 680
35:19	**Vol. 1:** 170
35:20	**Vol. 3:** 239
35:22	**Vol. 3:** 1074
35:23	**Vol. 3:** 872
35:25	**Vol. 1:** 663
35:27	**Vol. 1:** 691
35:29	**Vol. 2:** 318
36:6 f	**Vol. 2:** 845
36:6	**Vol. 3:** 680
36:40	**Vol. 3:** 871
37	**Vol. 1:** 531, 650 **Vol. 2:** 318
37:1–11	**Vol. 2:** 431
37:2 ff	**Vol. 1:** 555
37:2	**Vol. 1:** 182
37:4*	**Vol. 2:** 547
37:5–10	**Vol. 1:** 512
37:5	**Vol. 3:** 45
37:7	**Vol. 3:** 591
37:10	**Vol. 1:** 572
37:14	**Vol. 2:** 169, 778 **Vol. 3:** 513
37:15	**Vol. 1:** 104
37:16	**Vol. 3:** 531
37:17	**Vol. 3:** 1185
37:18	**Vol. 1:** 695
37:20	**Vol. 1:** 113, 565
37:22	**Vol. 2:** 854 **Vol. 3:** 1004
37:23	**Vol. 1:** 314
37:24	**Vol. 1:** 546
37:25	**Vol. 1:** 743 **Vol. 2:** 294
37:26	**Vol. 2:** 319 **Vol. 3:** 137, 159
37:27	**Vol. 1:** 672 **Vol. 2:** 319
37:31	**Vol. 1:** 449
37:33	**Vol. 3:** 601–602
37:34–35	**Vol. 2:** 417
37:34	**Vol. 1:** 239
37:35	**Vol. 1:** 569 **Vol. 3:** 1019
38	**Vol. 1:** 61 **Vol. 2:** 577 **Vol. 3:** 1062
38:6–30	**Vol. 1:** 499
38:6	**Vol. 2:** 578
38:8 ff	**Vol. 2:** 577
38:8	**Vol. 3:** 275, 279
38:11	**Vol. 2:** 584
38:15 f	**Vol. 2:** 582
38:15	**Vol. 1:** 498 **Vol. 2:** 212 **Vol. 3:** 821
38:17 ff	**Vol. 2:** 40
38:24	**Vol. 1:** 655 **Vol. 2:** 582 **Vol. 3:** 538
38:26	**Vol. 3:** 355
38:28	**Vol. 1:** 171
38:29	**Vol. 3:** 950
39–50	**Vol. 1:** 531
39:1	**Vol. 1:** 560
39:2 f	**Vol. 3:** 1030
39:4	**Vol. 2:** 815
39:6	**Vol. 2:** 103
39:14	**Vol. 1:** 410
39:21	**Vol. 2:** 117 **Vol. 3:** 1030
39:22	**Vol. 3:** 591
40:2	**Vol. 1:** 560
40:5 ff	**Vol. 1:** 512
40:8	**Vol. 1:** 512, 577
40:12 ff	**Vol. 2:** 687
40:15	**Vol. 2:** 305 **Vol. 3:** 377
40:16	**Vol. 3:** 351
40:18 f	**Vol. 1:** 393
40:19	**Vol. 1:** 113
40:20	**Vol. 1:** 165 **Vol. 2:** 687
40:23	**Vol. 3:** 232
41	**Vol. 3:** 50
41:1 ff	**Vol. 1:** 512
41:2	**Vol. 1:** 537, 672 **Vol. 2:** 103
41:4	**Vol. 1:** 537 **Vol. 3:** 279
41:5	**Vol. 2:** 185
41:7	**Vol. 3:** 279
41:8	**Vol. 1:** 574, 577 **Vol. 2:** 555 **Vol. 3:** 680, 691, 1027
41:9	**Vol. 3:** 239
41:12	**Vol. 1:** 577
41:13	**Vol. 3:** 147
41:16	**Vol. 2:** 778
41:21	**Vol. 1:** 164
41:24	**Vol. 1:** 574 **Vol. 2:** 555
41:28	**Vol. 3:** 569
41:31	**Vol. 2:** 395
41:35 ff	**Vol. 2:** 268
41:35	**Vol. 2:** 32
41:40–46	**Vol. 3:** 1030
41:40	**Vol. 2:** 612, 796
41:42	**Vol. 2:** 96 **Vol. 3:** 498
41:43	**Vol. 3:** 50
41:45	**Vol. 2:** 576, 649

Genesis *(cont'd)*

41:48	**Vol. 2:** 32
41:49	**Vol. 2:** 683
41:50 ff†	**Vol. 2:** 306
41:53 ff	**Vol. 2:** 265
41:56	**Vol. 1:** 268
41:57	**Vol. 1:** 267
42:1 ff	**Vol. 2:** 265
42:3	**Vol. 2:** 173
42:6–45:4	**Vol. 2:** 432
42:6	**Vol. 2:** 876
42:13	**Vol. 2:** 675
42:15	**Vol. 2:** 675
42:16	**Vol. 3:** 880
42:20	**Vol. 1:** 596 **Vol. 2:** 675
42:21 f	**Vol. 2:** 173
42:21	**Vol. 1:** 322
42:22	**Vol. 3:** 158
42:23	**Vol. 1:** 373, 580
42:24	**Vol. 1:** 322
42:25	**Vol. 1:** 734
42:27	**Vol. 1:** 743 **Vol. 3:** 177
42:28	**Vol. 1:** 527
42:34	**Vol. 1:** 268 **Vol. 2:** 675
43:3–10	**Vol. 2:** 319
43:11	**Vol. 2:** 294
43:14	**Vol. 2:** 116 **Vol. 3:** 729
43:20	**Vol. 2:** 860
43:23	**Vol. 2:** 777 **Vol. 3:** 157, 160
43:24	**Vol. 1:** 743
43:25 ff	**Vol. 2:** 521
43:27 f	**Vol. 2:** 170, 778
43:28	**Vol. 2:** 876
43:29	**Vol. 1:** 285
43:31	**Vol. 1:** 495
43:32	**Vol. 2:** 305
43:33	**Vol. 1:** 193, 527
44	**Vol. 2:** 675
44:4	**Vol. 3:** 377
44:5	**Vol. 2:** 554
44:14	**Vol. 1:** 609
44:15	**Vol. 2:** 554
44:16–34	**Vol. 2:** 319
44:16	**Vol. 3:** 355
44:18	**Vol. 2:** 860
44:20	**Vol. 1:** 255
44:33	**Vol. 3:** 228, 1179–1180
45:1	**Vol. 2:** 765
45:2	**Vol. 2:** 416
45:5 ff	**Vol. 3:** 720
45:5	**Vol. 1:** 532
45:6	**Vol. 3:** 525
45:7–8	**Vol. 1:** 531
45:7	**Vol. 1:** 532
45:9	**Vol. 3:** 224
45:14	**Vol. 1:** 609
45:16	**Vol. 2:** 357
45:17	**Vol. 1:** 743
45:20	**Vol. 2:** 845

46:1	**Vol. 3:** 425
46:2	**Vol. 3:** 513
46:3	**Vol. 1:** 411
46:4	**Vol. 2:** 60
46:27	**Vol. 2:** 690
46:29	**Vol. 1:** 609 **Vol. 2:** 416 **Vol. 3:** 1161
47:2	**Vol. 3:** 604
47:4	**Vol. 1:** 691
47:7–10	**Vol. 1:** 208
47:18	**Vol. 2:** 845
47:23	**Vol. 3:** 521
47:24	**Vol. 2:** 303
47:25	**Vol. 2:** 116 **Vol. 3:** 206
47:28	**Vol. 2:** 478
47:29	**Vol. 1:** 207 **Vol. 2:** 149
47:30	**Vol. 1:** 442
47:31	**Vol. 1:** 408 **Vol. 2:** 876 **Vol. 3:** 739
48:1 ff	**Vol. 1:** 207–208
48:1–6	**Vol. 2:** 318
48:3	**Vol. 2:** 67 **Vol. 3:** 729
48:7	**Vol. 1:** 170
48:8–49:27	**Vol. 2:** 318
48:10	**Vol. 1:** 207
48:12	**Vol. 2:** 876
48:13 ff	**Vol. 1:** 207
48:14	**Vol. 2:** 148
48:15 f	**Vol. 1:** 214
48:15	**Vol. 2:** 815 **Vol. 3:** 565
48:16	**Vol. 3:** 202
48:18	**Vol. 2:** 151
48:20	**Vol. 2:** 649
48:22	**Vol. 1:** 116 **Vol. 2:** 318 **Vol. 3:** 458
49	**Vol. 1:** 208 **Vol. 2:** 695 **Vol. 3:** 461
49:2	**Vol. 2:** 32
49:3	**Vol. 1:** 667
49:4	**Vol. 2:** 587
49:5 ff	**Vol. 3:** 33, 456
49:5	**Vol. 1:** 534
49:6	**Vol. 1:** 108, 230, 293 **Vol. 3:** 1016
49:7	**Vol. 1:** 108
49:8 ff	**Vol. 2:** 335
49:8–12	**Vol. 1:** 61 **Vol. 2:** 374 **Vol. 3:** 461
49:8	**Vol. 1:** 61 **Vol. 2:** 876 **Vol. 3:** 816
49:9 f	**Vol. 3:** 649, 652
49:9	**Vol. 1:** 118 **Vol. 3:** 650, 872
49:10	**Vol. 1:** 407 **Vol. 2:** 319, 791, 899 **Vol. 3:** 650
49:11	**Vol. 1:** 224 **Vol. 3:** 591, 919
49:12	**Vol. 1:** 204
49:14	**Vol. 3:** 255
49:15	**Vol. 3:** 255
49:16	**Vol. 1:** 61 **Vol. 2:** 796
49:17	**Vol. 1:** 241 **Vol. 3:** 872
49:18	**Vol. 2:** 239 **Vol. 3:** 228
49:23	**Vol. 3:** 346
49:24	**Vol. 2:** 104 **Vol. 3:** 381, 565
49:25	**Vol. 1:** 240, 523 **Vol. 2:** 67
49:27	**Vol. 3:** 604
49:28 ff	**Vol. 1:** 207
49:28	**Vol. 1:** 61

Genesis *(cont'd)*

49:29–33	**Vol. 3:** 464
49:30	**Vol. 3:** 239
49:33	**Vol. 2:** 796 **Vol. 3:** 255
50:1–13	**Vol. 2:** 318
50:1	**Vol. 2:** 416
50:2	**Vol. 1:** 120, 264 **Vol. 2:** 167, 305
50:3	**Vol. 1:** 264 **Vol. 2:** 422
50:4	**Vol. 2:** 116
50:5 ff	**Vol. 1:** 531
50:5	**Vol. 3:** 239
50:7	**Vol. 1:** 194 **Vol. 3:** 579
50:10 f	**Vol. 2:** 422
50:13	**Vol. 3:** 239, 464
50:17	**Vol. 1:** 698
50:20	**Vol. 1:** 531 **Vol. 2:** 100 **Vol. 3:** 234, 720
50:24	**Vol. 3:** 720
50:25	**Vol. 1:** 240, 531
50:26	**Vol. 1:** 264

Exodus

1–15	**Vol. 1:** 531 **Vol. 2:** 644
1:1	**Vol. 2:** 305
1:5	**Vol. 3:** 680
1:6	**Vol. 1:** 430 **Vol. 2:** 36
1:7	**Vol. 1:** 732 **Vol. 2:** 130
1:8	**Vol. 2:** 636, 670 **Vol. 3:** 275
1:11	**Vol. 2:** 635–636, 822
1:13 f	**Vol. 3:** 711
1:15–19	**Vol. 2:** 305
1:16 ff	**Vol. 2:** 569
1:16	**Vol. 2:** 636
1:18	**Vol. 1:** 272
1:20	**Vol. 1:** 732
1:22	**Vol. 2:** 569, 636, 796
2	**Vol. 2:** 216
2:1 f	**Vol. 3:** 33
2:1–10	**Vol. 2:** 636
2:1	**Vol. 2:** 636
2:2	**Vol. 2:** 569, 887
2:6	**Vol. 2:** 416
2:8	**Vol. 2:** 87 **Vol. 3:** 1071
2:9 ff	**Vol. 2:** 189
2:9	**Vol. 3:** 138
2:10	**Vol. 1:** 673 **Vol. 2:** 636
2:11–15	**Vol. 2:** 636 **Vol. 3:** 963
2:11–13	**Vol. 2:** 305
2:11	**Vol. 1:** 255
2:12	**Vol. 1:** 165 **Vol. 3:** 345
2:13	**Vol. 1:** 258
2:14	**Vol. 1:** 168 **Vol. 2:** 363, 489 **Vol. 3:** 199
2:15 f	**Vol. 2:** 635 **Vol. 3:** 459
2:15–22	**Vol. 3:** 459
2:15–21	**Vol. 3:** 986
2:15	**Vol. 1:** 691 **Vol. 3:** 531
2:16–22	**Vol. 2:** 636
2:16	**Vol. 3:** 564

2:17	**Vol. 3:** 201
2:18 ff	**Vol. 3:** 33
2:18–26	**Vol. 2:** 636
2:18	**Vol. 2:** 636
2:19	**Vol. 3:** 201
2:21	**Vol. 2:** 576, 578
2:22	**Vol. 1:** 691 **Vol. 2:** 636
2:23 ff	**Vol. 2:** 636
2:23	**Vol. 1:** 410
2:24 f†	**Vol. 3:** 69
2:24	**Vol. 2:** 423 **Vol. 3:** 235, 241
3	**Vol. 2:** 69, 651
3:1 ff	**Vol. 2:** 173 **Vol. 3:** 330, 1005
3:1–4:20	**Vol. 2:** 635
3:1–22	**Vol. 2:** 636
3:1 f	**Vol. 3:** 1014
3:1	**Vol. 2:** 636 **Vol. 3:** 33, 1013
3:2 f	**Vol. 1:** 655
3:2	**Vol. 1:** 656–657
3:3	**Vol. 3:** 513
3:4	**Vol. 1:** 273
3:5	**Vol. 1:** 239 **Vol. 2:** 53, 225 **Vol. 3:** 177, 179
3:6	**Vol. 2:** 91, 215, 318, 650 **Vol. 3:** 263–264, 464–465
3:7	**Vol. 2:** 175, 178, 796 **Vol. 3:** 514
3:8	**Vol. 1:** 683 **Vol. 3:** 1162
3:9	**Vol. 1:** 320 **Vol. 2:** 807
3:10 ff	**Vol. 2:** 68
3:10	**Vol. 2:** 796, 807
3:11	**Vol. 1:** 272
3:12	**Vol. 2:** 350, 626 **Vol. 3:** 464, 550
3:13 ff	**Vol. 2:** 68
3:13	**Vol. 2:** 650, 879
3:14 ff	**Vol. 1:** 383
3:14 f	**Vol. 1:** 56
3:14	**Vol. 2:** 68, 278, 513, 649–651 **Vol. 3:** 969
3:15 f	**Vol. 3:** 263
3:15	**Vol. 2:** 68, 318, 650 **Vol. 3:** 237
3:16	**Vol. 1:** 195 **Vol. 2:** 32 **Vol. 3:** 611
3:18	**Vol. 1:** 195 **Vol. 2:** 305, 687
3:19	**Vol. 3:** 717
3:21	**Vol. 1:** 546 **Vol. 2:** 117
3:22	**Vol. 2:** 96, 856
4 ff	**Vol. 2:** 154
4	**Vol. 2:** 627
4:1 ff	**Vol. 2:** 626
4:1–9	**Vol. 1:** 596 **Vol. 2:** 636
4:1	**Vol. 1:** 272
4:5	**Vol. 3:** 263
4:6	**Vol. 1:** 240
4:10 ff	**Vol. 3:** 730
4:10–17	**Vol. 2:** 636
4:10	**Vol. 1:** 272 **Vol. 2:** 860 **Vol. 3:** 1079
4:11	**Vol. 1:** 218, 428
4:12	**Vol. 2:** 68, 726
4:13–16	**Vol. 3:** 33
4:13	**Vol. 1:** 272, 475–476
4:14	**Vol. 1:** 108

Exodus *(cont'd)*

4:15	**Vol. 2:** 68, 635, 726
4:18	**Vol. 2:** 170
4:19	**Vol. 2:** 640 **Vol. 3:** 531
4:20	**Vol. 2:** 640
4:21	**Vol. 2:** 155 **Vol. 3:** 1185
4:22 f	**Vol. 2:** 68, 71 **Vol. 3:** 636
4:22	**Vol. 1:** 177, 288, 617, 667 **Vol. 2:** 715, 835 **Vol. 3:** 638
4:23	**Vol. 3:** 550, 1016
4:24 ff	**Vol. 1:** 108, 308, 451
4:24	**Vol. 1:** 108 **Vol. 3:** 794
4:27–31†	**Vol. 1:** 596 **Vol. 2:** 636
4:28	**Vol. 1:** 332
4:29	**Vol. 1:** 195 **Vol. 2:** 32
4:31	**Vol. 2:** 876 **Vol. 3:** 1162
5:1–23	**Vol. 2:** 636
5:1	**Vol. 2:** 796
5:2	**Vol. 1:** 273
5:5	**Vol. 3:** 255
5:6	**Vol. 3:** 478
5:9	**Vol. 1:** 277
5:21	**Vol. 3:** 1040
5:22 f	**Vol. 2:** 651
5:22	**Vol. 3:** 342
5:23	**Vol. 2:** 796 **Vol. 3:** 202
6:1–7:7	**Vol. 2:** 637
6:1	**Vol. 3:** 717
6:2 ff	**Vol. 3:** 729
6:2 f	**Vol. 2:** 68
6:2	**Vol. 2:** 649–650
6:3	**Vol. 2:** 67 **Vol. 3:** 316
6:4 f	**Vol. 1:** 366
6:4	**Vol. 1:** 691
6:5	**Vol. 2:** 423 **Vol. 3:** 235, 241
6:6	**Vol. 2:** 200 **Vol. 3:** 192, 201, 1162
6:7	**Vol. 1:** 368 **Vol. 2:** 395, 797 **Vol. 3:** 799, 813
6:8	**Vol. 3:** 235
6:12	**Vol. 2:** 173
6:14 ff	**Vol. 3:** 660
6:16	**Vol. 1:** 691
6:25	**Vol. 1:** 544
6:27	**Vol. 3:** 820
6:30	**Vol. 2:** 173
7 f	**Vol. 2:** 629
7–12	**Vol. 2:** 627
7	**Vol. 3:** 986
7:1	**Vol. 3:** 77
7:2	**Vol. 1:** 332
7:3	**Vol. 2:** 627
7:4	**Vol. 2:** 149
7:5	**Vol. 2:** 395
7:7	**Vol. 2:** 637
7:9–12	**Vol. 1:** 508
7:9	**Vol. 2:** 633
7:10 ff	**Vol. 2:** 219
7:11	**Vol. 2:** 554–555, 642
7:13	**Vol. 1:** 332 **Vol. 2:** 154

7:14 ff	**Vol. 3:** 984
7:14–25	**Vol. 3:** 987
7:14	**Vol. 1:** 261
7:16	**Vol. 2:** 796 **Vol. 3:** 550
7:17 ff	**Vol. 1:** 224
7:17	**Vol. 2:** 395
7:18	**Vol. 1:** 670
7:19–25	**Vol. 2:** 637
7:22	**Vol. 2:** 154, 555
7:23	**Vol. 3:** 125
8:1–14	**Vol. 2:** 637
8:1*	**Vol. 3:** 550
8:3	**Vol. 2:** 555 **Vol. 3:** 917
8:13	**Vol. 1:** 520
8:14 f	**Vol. 2:** 555
8:15	**Vol. 2:** 154
8:16–19	**Vol. 2:** 637
8:19	**Vol. 2:** 150
8:20–32	**Vol. 2:** 637
8:20*	**Vol. 3:** 550
9:1–7	**Vol. 2:** 637
9:1	**Vol. 3:** 550
9:2	**Vol. 3:** 1016
9:3	**Vol. 2:** 149
9:5	**Vol. 1:** 294
9:8–12	**Vol. 2:** 637
9:11	**Vol. 2:** 555
9:13–35	**Vol. 2:** 637
9:16	**Vol. 3:** 45, 48, 329, 490
9:18	**Vol. 1:** 380 **Vol. 3:** 846
9:22	**Vol. 2:** 211
9:24	**Vol. 1:** 655, 657
9:28	**Vol. 3:** 224
9:29	**Vol. 2:** 190
9:33	**Vol. 2:** 190
10	**Vol. 1:** 119
10:1–20	**Vol. 2:** 637
10:1 f	**Vol. 2:** 396 **Vol. 3:** 760
10:3 f	**Vol. 3:** 1016
10:3	**Vol. 3:** 550
10:4	**Vol. 3:** 846
10:5	**Vol. 1:** 729
10:7 f	**Vol. 3:** 550
10:12	**Vol. 1:** 189
10:13	**Vol. 2:** 628, 889 **Vol. 3:** 1001
10:15	**Vol. 3:** 248
10:17	**Vol. 2:** 863
10:19	**Vol. 2:** 628 **Vol. 3:** 248, 1001
10:21–29	**Vol. 2:** 637
10:22	**Vol. 1:** 422
10:23	**Vol. 2:** 586
10:24	**Vol. 3:** 550
10:26	**Vol. 3:** 550
10:27	**Vol. 3:** 1016
11:1–12:30	**Vol. 2:** 637
11:1	**Vol. 1:** 162 **Vol. 3:** 857
11:2	**Vol. 1:** 258
11:3	**Vol. 2:** 117
11:5	**Vol. 3:** 394
11:8	**Vol. 2:** 876

Exodus *(cont'd)*

11:9	**Vol. 2:** 350, 633
11:10	**Vol. 2:** 350
12	**Vol. 2:** 478
12:1 ff	**Vol. 1:** 295 **Vol. 3:** 69
12:1–28	**Vol. 2:** 637
12:1	**Vol. 3:** 1121
12:3 ff	**Vol. 1:** 617
12:3	**Vol. 1:** 294
12:4	**Vol. 2:** 683
12:5	**Vol. 1:** 632 **Vol. 2:** 410, 521, 569, 778 **Vol. 3:** 200, 435
12:6	**Vol. 1:** 292, 294 **Vol. 2:** 521
12:7	**Vol. 1:** 223 **Vol. 2:** 410
12:8 f	**Vol. 2:** 521
12:8	**Vol. 1:** 250, 654 **Vol. 2:** 522
12:11–14	**Vol. 1:** 632
12:11	**Vol. 1:** 250, 632 **Vol. 3:** 121, 1169
12:12 f	**Vol. 1:** 465 **Vol. 2:** 784
12:12	**Vol. 1:** 626
12:13	**Vol. 1:** 162, 223, 632 **Vol. 2:** 410, 626 **Vol. 3:** 159
12:14 ff	**Vol. 3:** 828
12:14–20	**Vol. 1:** 250 **Vol. 2:** 461
12:14	**Vol. 3:** 233, 237
12:15	**Vol. 1:** 699 **Vol. 2:** 461
12:16	**Vol. 1:** 272
12:17	**Vol. 1:** 626 **Vol. 2:** 784, 889
12:18	**Vol. 1:** 665
12:19	**Vol. 1:** 295 **Vol. 2:** 461, 716
12:21 ff	**Vol. 1:** 115
12:21–27	**Vol. 1:** 194
12:21–23	**Vol. 1:** 632
12:21	**Vol. 1:** 272, 632
12:22 f	**Vol. 1:** 221, 223
12:22	**Vol. 2:** 854
12:23–27	**Vol. 2:** 784
12:23	**Vol. 1:** 101, 465, 632 **Vol. 2:** 167, 410
12:24	**Vol. 2:** 134
12:25 f	**Vol. 3:** 550
12:26 f	**Vol. 1:** 617 **Vol. 3:** 777
12:26	**Vol. 1:** 288 **Vol. 2:** 522
12:27 f	**Vol. 2:** 876
12:27	**Vol. 1:** 632 **Vol. 2:** 876
12:31 ff	**Vol. 2:** 637
12:33	**Vol. 3:** 1169
12:34	**Vol. 1:** 250 **Vol. 2:** 461 **Vol. 3:** 917
12:36	**Vol. 2:** 117
12:37	**Vol. 2:** 698
12:38	**Vol. 1:** 252
12:39	**Vol. 1:** 250 **Vol. 2:** 461, 773, 784 **Vol. 3:** 227
12:42	**Vol. 2:** 132
12:43 ff	**Vol. 1:** 684
12:43–48	**Vol. 1:** 308
12:43	**Vol. 2:** 441
12:44	**Vol. 3:** 594, 608
12:45	**Vol. 1:** 691 **Vol. 2:** 139
12:46	**Vol. 1:** 240, 629 **Vol. 2:** 527

12:48	**Vol. 1:** 159, 308, 360
13:1–10	**Vol. 3:** 105, 487
13:2	**Vol. 1:** 474, 667 **Vol. 2:** 570, 729 **Vol. 3:** 430, 660
13:3–10	**Vol. 1:** 250 **Vol. 2:** 892
13:3	**Vol. 3:** 593, 717
13:4	**Vol. 2:** 675
13:5	**Vol. 1:** 683 **Vol. 3:** 550
13:7	**Vol. 2:** 716
13:8	**Vol. 3:** 233
13:9	**Vol. 2:** 136, 149, 440, 864 **Vol. 3:** 237, 717
13:10	**Vol. 3:** 846
13:11–16	**Vol. 3:** 105, 487
13:12	**Vol. 2:** 570, 729 **Vol. 3:** 430, 660
13:13	**Vol. 3:** 190, 192, 857
13:14 ff	**Vol. 1:** 617
13:14	**Vol. 3:** 593, 717
13:15	**Vol. 3:** 190, 192
13:16	**Vol. 1:** 254 **Vol. 2:** 136, 149 **Vol. 3:** 559, 717
13:17 f	**Vol. 2:** 637
13:17	**Vol. 1:** 356 **Vol. 3:** 937
13:19	**Vol. 1:** 531 **Vol. 2:** 637
13:21 f	**Vol. 2:** 491–492
13:21	**Vol. 1:** 420
13:22	**Vol. 1:** 655
14 f	**Vol. 3:** 989
14	**Vol. 2:** 627
14:4	**Vol. 2:** 395
14:6	**Vol. 3:** 1161
14:7	**Vol. 1:** 537
14:11	**Vol. 3:** 238
14:13	**Vol. 1:** 328 **Vol. 3:** 208, 828, 841
14:14	**Vol. 2:** 374
14:15–18	**Vol. 1:** 373
14:17 f	**Vol. 2:** 45
14:18	**Vol. 2:** 395
14:19	**Vol. 1:** 101
14:21	**Vol. 2:** 628 **Vol. 3:** 543
14:23	**Vol. 3:** 983
14:25	**Vol. 3:** 711
14:26 ff	**Vol. 3:** 147
14:27	**Vol. 3:** 560
14:28	**Vol. 3:** 983
14:30	**Vol. 3:** 201
14:31	**Vol. 1:** 598
15	**Vol. 1:** 513 **Vol. 3:** 960, 984
15:1 ff	**Vol. 3:** 69
15:1–18	**Vol. 1:** 245
15:1	**Vol. 1:** 598 **Vol. 3:** 672–674, 983
15:2	**Vol. 1:** 618 **Vol. 2:** 201 **Vol. 3:** 207
15:3	**Vol. 2:** 650
15:4 f	**Vol. 3:** 983
15:5	**Vol. 2:** 197
15:6	**Vol. 2:** 602
15:7	**Vol. 1:** 732
15:8	**Vol. 3:** 691, 988
15:9	**Vol. 2:** 805
15:10	**Vol. 3:** 983, 1001

Exodus *(cont'd)*

15:11   Vol. 2: 720   Vol. 3: 1153
15:13   Vol. 1: 570   Vol. 2: 602   Vol. 3: 192,
           354, 794, 937
15:15   Vol. 3: 747
15:16   Vol. 1: 609   Vol. 3: 192
15:17   Vol. 2: 296   Vol. 3: 117, 350, 866
15:18   Vol. 2: 898   Vol. 3: 841
15:20 f   Vol. 2: 635
15:20   Vol. 3: 77, 1057
15:21   Vol. 3: 672, 983
15:22 ff   Vol. 2: 275
15:23   Vol. 1: 201–203   Vol. 2: 274, 637
15:24   Vol. 2: 836
15:25 f   Vol. 3: 354
15:25   Vol. 3: 799
15:26   Vol. 1: 230   Vol. 2: 167
15:27   Vol. 1: 252   Vol. 2: 637, 754   Vol. 3:
           986

16 ff   Vol. 3: 427
16   Vol. 1: 252   Vol. 2: 637
16:1 ff   Vol. 1: 294–295
16:1   Vol. 3: 1013
16:2 ff   Vol. 3: 804
16:2 f   Vol. 2: 836
16:3 ff   Vol. 2: 265, 267
16:3   Vol. 2: 628
16:4   Vol. 1: 251   Vol. 2: 194, 218   Vol. 3:
           799
16:6 f   Vol. 2: 395
16:6   Vol. 2: 395
16:7   Vol. 2: 45, 175
16:8   Vol. 2: 175
16:9   Vol. 1: 294, 322   Vol. 2: 175
16:10   Vol. 2: 45
16:12   Vol. 2: 175, 395
16:13–15   Vol. 2: 194
16:13   Vol. 1: 173   Vol. 2: 586   Vol. 3: 255
16:14   Vol. 2: 440, 586
16:15   Vol. 1: 252   Vol. 2: 871
16:16   Vol. 2: 158, 683
16:18   Vol. 2: 130–131   Vol. 3: 402
16:20   Vol. 1: 108, 202
16:23   Vol. 1: 626   Vol. 2: 130–131   Vol. 3:
           94, 255–256
16:25   Vol. 1: 626   Vol. 3: 256
16:28   Vol. 2: 440   Vol. 3: 1016
16:29   Vol. 3: 940
16:31   Vol. 1: 459
16:32 ff   Vol. 1: 253
16:33 f   Vol. 3: 815
16:33   Vol. 1: 252
16:35   Vol. 1: 252, 519   Vol. 2: 303,
           696   Vol. 3: 843
17   Vol. 2: 627   Vol. 3: 383
17:1 ff   Vol. 2: 274
17:1–7   Vol. 2: 637   Vol. 3: 459
17:1–6   Vol. 3: 382
17:2   Vol. 3: 799–801

17:3 ff   Vol. 2: 265
17:5 f   Vol. 3: 986, 988
17:5   Vol. 1: 195
17:6   Vol. 2: 276   Vol. 3: 381
17:7   Vol. 1: 203   Vol. 3: 346, 799–801
17:8 ff   Vol. 3: 33
17:8–16   Vol. 2: 331, 637
17:9 ff   Vol. 3: 208
17:9 f   Vol. 3: 1009
17:9   Vol. 1: 537
17:11   Vol. 1: 207
17:12   Vol. 3: 878
17:14   Vol. 1: 243, 471   Vol. 2: 639   Vol. 3:
           236–237, 484
17:15   Vol. 1: 71   Vol. 3: 418
18:1   Vol. 3: 1013
18:3   Vol. 2: 720
18:5   Vol. 3: 1013
18:7   Vol. 2: 778, 876
18:8–11   Vol. 2: 396
18:9   Vol. 2: 99
18:11   Vol. 2: 425
18:12 ff   Vol. 3: 33
18:12   Vol. 2: 521
18:13 ff   Vol. 1: 195
18:13–14   Vol. 3: 588
18:13   Vol. 1: 195
18:16   Vol. 1: 503   Vol. 2: 440
18:17   Vol. 3: 351
18:20   Vol. 1: 59   Vol. 2: 440   Vol. 3: 938,
           1041
18:21   Vol. 3: 29, 137, 880
18:22   Vol. 3: 846
18:23   Vol. 2: 778
18:24 ff   Vol. 2: 637
18:26   Vol. 3: 846, 1120
19–24   Vol. 1: 626   Vol. 3: 1013
19   Vol. 2: 640, 784–785   Vol. 3: 1005,
           1013–1014
19:1–13   Vol. 2: 637
19:1   Vol. 1: 626   Vol. 2: 784   Vol. 3: 937
19:3 ff   Vol. 3: 799, 806
19:3   Vol. 3: 1013
19:4 ff   Vol. 3: 805
19:4   Vol. 1: 173
19:5 f   Vol. 2: 70, 790, 800   Vol. 3: 435
19:5   Vol. 2: 174, 297, 791, 838–840   Vol. 3:
           190
19:6   Vol. 2: 380, 795   Vol. 3: 36–38, 1120
19:7   Vol. 1: 272
19:8   Vol. 2: 174   Vol. 3: 908
19:9 ff   Vol. 1: 108
19:9   Vol. 3: 1001
19:10 ff   Vol. 2: 225
19:10 f   Vol. 3: 117
19:10   Vol. 3: 101, 1013, 1041
19:11   Vol. 3: 1013
19:12 ff   Vol. 1: 656
19:12 f   Vol. 3: 557
19:12   Vol. 1: 430   Vol. 3: 860, 949

23

Exodus *(cont'd)*

19:13	**Vol. 3:** 191
19:14–20:17	**Vol. 2:** 637
19:14	**Vol. 3:** 1013
19:15	**Vol. 2:** 225 **Vol. 3:** 117
19:16–24	**Vol. 3:** 1013
19:16–19	**Vol. 2:** 784
19:16	**Vol. 3:** 112–113, 1013
19:17 f	**Vol. 1:** 195
19:18	**Vol. 1:** 655 **Vol. 2:** 190, 485 **Vol. 3:** 325, 557, 559
19:19	**Vol. 3:** 828
19:20	**Vol. 3:** 1013
19:21	**Vol. 3:** 126, 1041
19:22	**Vol. 3:** 166
19:23	**Vol. 3:** 1013
19:24	**Vol. 3:** 711
20	**Vol. 2:** 640 **Vol. 3:** 464, 1013–1014
20:1 ff	**Vol. 2:** 173
20:1–17	**Vol. 1:** 54 **Vol. 2:** 639
20:1	**Vol. 1:** 531 **Vol. 3:** 1102
20:2 ff	**Vol. 2:** 441
20:2 f	**Vol. 1:** 636
20:2	**Vol. 1:** 367, 716 **Vol. 2:** 68, 278, 797 **Vol. 3:** 1102, 1121
20:3–6	**Vol. 2:** 871 **Vol. 3:** 94
20:3 f	**Vol. 2:** 284
20:3	**Vol. 2:** 68
20:4	**Vol. 1:** 175, 518, 523 **Vol. 2:** 70, 287, 501 **Vol. 3:** 485
20:5	**Vol. 1:** 219, 555 **Vol. 2:** 68, 876 **Vol. 3:** 156, 550, 1166
20:6	**Vol. 2:** 541, 698
20:7	**Vol. 1:** 550 **Vol. 2:** 191, 449, 650, 652, 871 **Vol. 3:** 94, 342, 740
20:8–11	**Vol. 2:** 871 **Vol. 3:** 405–406
20:8	**Vol. 2:** 890 **Vol. 3:** 235
20:9 f	**Vol. 2:** 887 **Vol. 3:** 94, 1148
20:9	**Vol. 3:** 1153
20:10	**Vol. 1:** 115, 360, 688, 691 **Vol. 3:** 256, 406, 594, 608
20:11	**Vol. 2:** 889 **Vol. 3:** 255
20:12–17	**Vol. 2:** 871
20:12	**Vol. 1:** 115, 288, 336, 617, 619 **Vol. 2:** 43, 49, 640 **Vol. 3:** 95, 1057, 1069–1070
20:13	**Vol. 1:** 717 **Vol. 3:** 183
20:14	**Vol. 1:** 717 **Vol. 2:** 576, 580, 583 **Vol. 3:** 95, 183, 536
20:15 f	**Vol. 3:** 70
20:15	**Vol. 1:** 717 **Vol. 3:** 377
20:16	**Vol. 1:** 717 **Vol. 2:** 471 **Vol. 3:** 1041
20:17	**Vol. 1:** 336, 456, 717 **Vol. 3:** 1057
20:18	**Vol. 2:** 485 **Vol. 3:** 1120
20:19	**Vol. 3:** 325
20:20	**Vol. 1:** 328 **Vol. 3:** 799–800
20:21	**Vol. 2:** 215
20:22–23:33	**Vol. 3:** 418, 484
20:22–23:20	**Vol. 2:** 635
20:22–23:19	**Vol. 2:** 822, 841 **Vol. 3:** 1103
20:22	**Vol. 3:** 256
20:23	**Vol. 1:** 115 **Vol. 2:** 96
20:24 ff	**Vol. 3:** 418
20:24	**Vol. 2:** 649 **Vol. 3:** 233
20:25	**Vol. 1:** 203
21	**Vol. 1:** 115
21:1–23:33	**Vol. 2:** 637
21:1–23:19	**Vol. 2:** 441
21:1	**Vol. 3:** 354
21:2 ff	**Vol. 1:** 716 **Vol. 3:** 594
21:2–11	**Vol. 3:** 593
21:2	**Vol. 1:** 716 **Vol. 2:** 41, 96, 306, 822 **Vol. 3:** 593
21:4	**Vol. 3:** 594
21:5 f	**Vol. 3:** 594, 608
21:5	**Vol. 1:** 716
21:6	**Vol. 2:** 572 **Vol. 3:** 434, 594, 827
21:7–11	**Vol. 3:** 594
21:8	**Vol. 1:** 268 **Vol. 2:** 815
21:9	**Vol. 3:** 354
21:10	**Vol. 3:** 379
21:11	**Vol. 2:** 41 **Vol. 3:** 943
21:12	**Vol. 2:** 441 **Vol. 3:** 94
21:15 ff	**Vol. 2:** 441
21:15	**Vol. 1:** 288, 617 **Vol. 3:** 94–95, 1069
21:16 f	**Vol. 1:** 430
21:16	**Vol. 1:** 415 **Vol. 3:** 95, 377, 380, 593, 1070
21:17	**Vol. 1:** 617 **Vol. 3:** 95, 1069
21:18	**Vol. 2:** 586 **Vol. 3:** 346
21:20–27	**Vol. 3:** 594
21:20	**Vol. 1:** 162
21:21	**Vol. 3:** 608
21:22–25	**Vol. 3:** 94
21:22	**Vol. 2:** 96 **Vol. 3:** 963
21:23 ff	**Vol. 2:** 96 **Vol. 3:** 94
21:23–25	**Vol. 3:** 1179
21:23	**Vol. 3:** 196, 680
21:24	**Vol. 3:** 183
21:26 f	**Vol. 3:** 95, 594
21:27	**Vol. 1:** 716
21:30 f	**Vol. 2:** 96
21:30	**Vol. 3:** 190, 192, 196
21:31	**Vol. 3:** 354
21:32	**Vol. 3:** 594
21:33 f	**Vol. 3:** 95
21:33	**Vol. 1:** 609 **Vol. 2:** 726
22	**Vol. 1:** 115 **Vol. 3:** 134
22:1 f	**Vol. 3:** 377
22:1–4	**Vol. 2:** 96
22:1	**Vol. 3:** 95
22:2	**Vol. 2:** 142 **Vol. 3:** 594, 608
22:3	**Vol. 2:** 96 **Vol. 3:** 95
22:4	**Vol. 3:** 95
22:5 f	**Vol. 3:** 95
22:6	**Vol. 1:** 725 **Vol. 3:** 377
22:11–24	**Vol. 3:** 95
22:14*	**Vol. 2:** 139 **Vol. 3:** 138
22:15 f	**Vol. 3:** 1057

Exodus *(cont'd)*

22:16 f	**Vol. 3:** 95
22:16	**Vol. 2:** 578
22:17	**Vol. 2:** 554–555
22:18*	**Vol. 2:** 555 **Vol. 3:** 94
22:20 ff	**Vol. 1:** 410
22:20–23:9	**Vol. 1:** 717
22:20*	**Vol. 1:** 684 **Vol. 2:** 724 **Vol. 3:** 94
22:21 ff*	**Vol. 1:** 360
22:21–24	**Vol. 2:** 257
22:21	**Vol. 1:** 688, 691 **Vol. 2:** 822 **Vol. 3:** 1073
22:22 f	**Vol. 1:** 409 **Vol. 3:** 1074
22:22–27	**Vol. 2:** 822
22:22–24	**Vol. 2:** 738
22:23 f	**Vol. 1:** 109
22:24	**Vol. 2:** 820 **Vol. 3:** 1073
22:25	**Vol. 2:** 254, 856
22:27	**Vol. 1:** 415 **Vol. 3:** 342
22:27b	**Vol. 2:** 822
22:28*	**Vol. 3:** 40, 94, 97, 416
22:30 f	**Vol. 3:** 1103
23	**Vol. 1:** 531
23:1 ff	**Vol. 3:** 1103
23:1	**Vol. 2:** 173 **Vol. 3:** 1041, 1062
23:3–8	**Vol. 3:** 435
23:4 f	**Vol. 1:** 115 **Vol. 2:** 157
23:4	**Vol. 1:** 177, 553
23:6 ff	**Vol. 2:** 822
23:7 f	**Vol. 2:** 41
23:7	**Vol. 1:** 607 **Vol. 3:** 355–357
23:9	**Vol. 1:** 360, 688, 691 **Vol. 2:** 822
23:10 f	**Vol. 2:** 822 **Vol. 3:** 918
23:10	**Vol. 2:** 32
23:11	**Vol. 3:** 191
23:12	**Vol. 1:** 360 **Vol. 3:** 254–255, 405, 409, 594, 686
23:13	**Vol. 3:** 239
23:14 ff	**Vol. 3:** 835
23:14–17	**Vol. 1:** 626 **Vol. 2:** 463
23:14	**Vol. 2:** 687
23:15	**Vol. 2:** 675
23:16	**Vol. 2:** 783 **Vol. 3:** 852
23:17–21	**Vol. 1:** 280
23:17	**Vol. 2:** 562, 687 **Vol. 3:** 1055
23:18	**Vol. 3:** 159
23:19	**Vol. 3:** 415–416, 786, 852
23:20–23	**Vol. 1:** 101
23:20	**Vol. 3:** 117, 119.
23:22	**Vol. 1:** 332, 554 **Vol. 2:** 800, 838 **Vol. 3:** 37
23:24 f	**Vol. 3:** 550
23:24	**Vol. 2:** 876
23:25	**Vol. 3:** 988
23:27	**Vol. 1:** 527
23:31	**Vol. 3:** 983
23:33	**Vol. 2:** 705
24	**Vol. 2:** 540, 637
24:1	**Vol. 1:** 195 **Vol. 2:** 754, 876
24:2	**Vol. 2:** 724
24:3 f	**Vol. 3:** 1103
24:3–8	**Vol. 2:** 533 **Vol. 3:** 425, 1103
24:3	**Vol. 3:** 354
24:4–8	**Vol. 1:** 373
24:4	**Vol. 2:** 639
24:5–8	**Vol. 1:** 222, 369
24:6 ff	**Vol. 1:** 115, 221
24:6	**Vol. 1:** 223
24:7 f	**Vol. 2:** 797
24:7	**Vol. 1:** 243, 245 **Vol. 2:** 173, 639
24:8 ff	**Vol. 1:** 369
24:8	**Vol. 1:** 223–225 **Vol. 2:** 525–526, 533, 854 **Vol. 3:** 28
24:9 ff	**Vol. 1:** 367, 585 **Vol. 2:** 190
24:9–16	**Vol. 3:** 863
24:9–11	**Vol. 2:** 191
24:9 f	**Vol. 2:** 796
24:9	**Vol. 3:** 1013
24:10	**Vol. 1:** 239
24:11	**Vol. 2:** 272, 521
24:12	**Vol. 1:** 485 **Vol. 3:** 484, 631
24:13	**Vol. 2:** 331
24:15 ff	**Vol. 2:** 48
24:15	**Vol. 2:** 212
24:16	**Vol. 1:** 630 **Vol. 3:** 1001, 1013
24:17	**Vol. 1:** 655 **Vol. 2:** 485
24:18	**Vol. 2:** 696 **Vol. 3:** 1013
25 ff	**Vol. 3:** 812
25–31	**Vol. 1:** 66 **Vol. 2:** 637 **Vol. 3:** 484
25:1	**Vol. 3:** 1105
25:2 f	**Vol. 3:** 415
25:2	**Vol. 3:** 821
25:6	**Vol. 2:** 711
25:8–9	**Vol. 3:** 813
25:8	**Vol. 3:** 190, 786
25:9*	**Vol. 1:** 380 **Vol. 2:** 189, 194 **Vol. 3:** 569
25:10 ff	**Vol. 1:** 389
25:10–22	**Vol. 3:** 812
25:11	**Vol. 2:** 95
25:13 ff	**Vol. 2:** 487
25:16	**Vol. 3:** 787, 815
25:17–22*	**Vol. 3:** 153, 156
25:17	**Vol. 3:** 164
25:18–22	**Vol. 3:** 163
25:21 f	**Vol. 3:** 787, 815
25:22	**Vol. 3:** 788
25:23–30	**Vol. 3:** 812
25:26	**Vol. 1:** 239
25:30	**Vol. 1:** 250, 586 **Vol. 3:** 423, 814
25:31 ff	**Vol. 2:** 485 **Vol. 3:** 814
25:31–40	**Vol. 3:** 812
25:31	**Vol. 2:** 95
25:40*	**Vol. 2:** 189 **Vol. 3:** 42, 569, 814, 904–905
26	**Vol. 3:** 851
26:1	**Vol. 1:** 280
26:15–29	**Vol. 3:** 795
26:26 f	**Vol. 2:** 303

25

Exodus *(cont'd)*

26:31–35   **Vol. 3:** 543
26:31   **Vol. 1:** 280   **Vol. 3:** 794
26:33 ff   **Vol. 3:** 794
26:33   **Vol. 3:** 786, 794
26:34   **Vol. 2:** 212
26:36 f   **Vol. 3:** 814
26:37   **Vol. 3:** 794
27:1–8   **Vol. 3:** 812
27:2   **Vol. 3:** 715
27:9–19   **Vol. 3:** 812
27:10–17   **Vol. 3:** 795
27:20   **Vol. 2:** 711
27:21   **Vol. 3:** 794, 828
28–39   **Vol. 3:** 551
28   **Vol. 3:** 35, 396
28:1   **Vol. 2:** 592
28:2 ff   **Vol. 2:** 226
28:3   **Vol. 1:** 735   **Vol. 3:** 1027
28:4   **Vol. 3:** 120–121
28:12   **Vol. 3:** 236
28:15 ff   **Vol. 3:** 966
28:15–21   **Vol. 1:** 205
28:17–20   **Vol. 3:** 396
28:18   **Vol. 3:** 395–396
28:21   **Vol. 3:** 397
28:29   **Vol. 3:** 236, 786
28:30   **Vol. 2:** 296
28:35   **Vol. 3:** 673, 786
28:36   **Vol. 3:** 500
28:38   **Vol. 2:** 232   **Vol. 3:** 38, 150
28:39*   **Vol. 3:** 120
28:40–43   **Vol. 1:** 204
28:40*   **Vol. 3:** 120
28:41   **Vol. 1:** 122   **Vol. 2:** 232   **Vol. 3:** 38
28:42   **Vol. 1:** 672
28:43   **Vol. 3:** 786
29:1–3   **Vol. 1:** 122
29:1   **Vol. 2:** 232   **Vol. 3:** 38, 200, 435, 924
29:2   **Vol. 2:** 711   **Vol. 3:** 36, 917
29:4   **Vol. 1:** 122   **Vol. 3:** 989, 1040
29:5 f   **Vol. 1:** 122
29:7   **Vol. 1:** 122   **Vol. 2:** 711
29:9   **Vol. 2:** 60   **Vol. 3:** 36, 120, 827
29:10 f   **Vol. 3:** 1040
29:10   **Vol. 3:** 169
29:12   **Vol. 1:** 223   **Vol. 3:** 418
29:14   **Vol. 3:** 965
29:16   **Vol. 1:** 221
29:17   **Vol. 1:** 230
29:18   **Vol. 3:** 601
29:19 ff   **Vol. 3:** 435
29:20   **Vol. 1:** 239
29:21   **Vol. 1:** 221, 224   **Vol. 2:** 232, 711   **Vol. 3:** 38
29:22   **Vol. 2:** 61
29:26   **Vol. 1:** 122   **Vol. 2:** 61, 303   **Vol. 3:** 424
29:27   **Vol. 3:** 424

29:29 f   **Vol. 2:** 34
29:29   **Vol. 1:** 122   **Vol. 2:** 60
29:30 f   **Vol. 1:** 221
29:30   **Vol. 3:** 786
29:31   **Vol. 3:** 787
29:33   **Vol. 1:** 684   **Vol. 2:** 742   **Vol. 3:** 152, 159
29:36   **Vol. 3:** 152
29:37   **Vol. 2:** 226   **Vol. 3:** 152
29:38   **Vol. 3:** 924
29:40   **Vol. 2:** 711   **Vol. 3:** 423, 917, 919
29:41   **Vol. 3:** 423
29:42   **Vol. 3:** 421
29:45 f†   **Vol. 1:** 272   **Vol. 3:** 799
29:45   **Vol. 2:** 797
29:46   **Vol. 2:** 395
29:49 ff   **Vol. 3:** 799
30:1–10   **Vol. 3:** 418, 436, 812
30:1–3   **Vol. 2:** 689
30:1   **Vol. 3:** 418
30:5   **Vol. 2:** 746
30:6   **Vol. 3:** 794
30:7   **Vol. 2:** 293–294
30:8   **Vol. 2:** 69, 293–294   **Vol. 3:** 860
30:9   **Vol. 3:** 422
30:10   **Vol. 2:** 716   **Vol. 3:** 152–153, 159, 418, 815
30:11–16   **Vol. 1:** 684   **Vol. 2:** 851   **Vol. 3:** 752, 853
30:12–16   **Vol. 3:** 154
30:12   **Vol. 3:** 190, 192, 196, 1179
30:13–16   **Vol. 3:** 190
30:13   **Vol. 2:** 379, 610   **Vol. 3:** 752
30:15 f   **Vol. 3:** 153
30:15   **Vol. 2:** 841
30:16   **Vol. 3:** 192, 236, 752
30:17 ff   **Vol. 1:** 153   **Vol. 3:** 989
30:17–21   **Vol. 3:** 812
30:18 ff   **Vol. 2:** 149
30:18   **Vol. 2:** 854
30:23   **Vol. 2:** 294
30:24 f   **Vol. 2:** 711
30:24   **Vol. 3:** 1002
30:25   **Vol. 1:** 121   **Vol. 3:** 1153
30:26   **Vol. 1:** 122
30:29   **Vol. 2:** 226
30:31   **Vol. 2:** 711
30:34–35   **Vol. 2:** 293
30:34   **Vol. 2:** 723
30:35   **Vol. 2:** 723   **Vol. 3:** 445
30:36   **Vol. 3:** 788
31:3   **Vol. 1:** 735   **Vol. 3:** 691, 1027
31:7   **Vol. 3:** 153, 156
31:11   **Vol. 2:** 711   **Vol. 3:** 786
31:12–18   **Vol. 1:** 626
31:12–17   **Vol. 3:** 405
31:13–17   **Vol. 3:** 94
31:13   **Vol. 2:** 396, 626
31:14   **Vol. 3:** 405, 407
31:15   **Vol. 2:** 890   **Vol. 3:** 255

Exodus *(cont'd)*

31:17	**Vol. 2:** 626 **Vol. 3:** 255, 406
31:18	**Vol. 3:** 255, 484, 1040
32	**Vol. 1:** 531 **Vol. 2:** 637 **Vol. 3:** 806, 1013
32:1 ff	**Vol. 3:** 33
32:1	**Vol. 1:** 293
32:4	**Vol. 2:** 95, 356 **Vol. 3:** 431
32:5	**Vol. 3:** 51
32:6	**Vol. 2:** 356 **Vol. 3:** 431
32:8	**Vol. 2:** 876 **Vol. 3:** 937
32:10	**Vol. 1:** 109
32:11 f	**Vol. 3:** 155
32:11–14	**Vol. 2:** 307, 863
32:11	**Vol. 2:** 860
32:12	**Vol. 1:** 109, 699 **Vol. 3:** 152, 157, 255
32:13	**Vol. 1:** 732 **Vol. 3:** 235, 608, 734, 828
32:14	**Vol. 1:** 109, 699 **Vol. 3:** 152, 155
32:15	**Vol. 2:** 303 **Vol. 3:** 1040
32:16	**Vol. 2:** 635 **Vol. 3:** 483–484, 488
32:17	**Vol. 2:** 331
32:19	**Vol. 1:** 108 **Vol. 2:** 637 **Vol. 3:** 1013
32:20	**Vol. 2:** 34
32:25 ff	**Vol. 3:** 33
32:26	**Vol. 1:** 322
32:27	**Vol. 1:** 429 **Vol. 2:** 96
32:28	**Vol. 2:** 698
32:30 ff	**Vol. 3:** 159
32:30	**Vol. 3:** 153–154
32:32 f	**Vol. 1:** 243, 471
32:32	**Vol. 2:** 307 **Vol. 3:** 484
32:34	**Vol. 1:** 189
33:7 ff	**Vol. 1:** 294
33:7–11	**Vol. 1:** 373 **Vol. 3:** 787
33:9 f	**Vol. 3:** 257
33:10	**Vol. 2:** 876
33:11	**Vol. 2:** 173, 331
33:12–23	**Vol. 2:** 637
33:12 f	**Vol. 3:** 641
33:12	**Vol. 2:** 117 **Vol. 3:** 316
33:13	**Vol. 2:** 117, 791 **Vol. 3:** 528
33:14 f	**Vol. 1:** 585
33:14	**Vol. 3:** 255
33:16	**Vol. 2:** 117
33:17–23	**Vol. 2:** 45 **Vol. 3:** 1013
33:17	**Vol. 2:** 117
33:18 ff	**Vol. 2:** 281, 478
33:18–34:35	**Vol. 2:** 48
33:18	**Vol. 2:** 45, 489 **Vol. 3:** 514, 890
33:19	**Vol. 2:** 68, 118, 597–598 **Vol. 3:** 912
33:20 ff	**Vol. 3:** 335
33:20	**Vol. 1:** 585 **Vol. 3:** 179, 514
33:21	**Vol. 3:** 381
33:23	**Vol. 3:** 179, 514
34	**Vol. 1:** 54, 366 **Vol. 3:** 418, 862, 882, 889–890
34:1 ff	**Vol. 3:** 1013
34:1–4	**Vol. 2:** 637
34:1	**Vol. 3:** 484, 1120
34:2 ff	**Vol. 3:** 806
34:2	**Vol. 3:** 117
34:4	**Vol. 2:** 185 **Vol. 3:** 484
34:5	**Vol. 1:** 474 **Vol. 3:** 1001
34:6 f	**Vol. 3:** 167
34:6	**Vol. 2:** 71, 119, 351, 769 **Vol. 3:** 879, 882, 889
34:7	**Vol. 2:** 351, 698 **Vol. 3:** 354
34:8	**Vol. 2:** 876
34:9	**Vol. 2:** 595
34:10–27	**Vol. 2:** 637
34:12	**Vol. 2:** 705
34:13	**Vol. 3:** 418
34:14	**Vol. 2:** 876
34:15 f	**Vol. 1:** 492
34:18 ff	**Vol. 3:** 835
34:18	**Vol. 1:** 626 **Vol. 2:** 675
34:20	**Vol. 3:** 190, 192
34:21	**Vol. 3:** 255–256, 405–407, 525
34:22–26	**Vol. 3:** 852
34:22 f	**Vol. 1:** 626
34:22	**Vol. 1:** 296 **Vol. 2:** 783
34:23	**Vol. 2:** 562
34:24	**Vol. 1:** 453
34:26	**Vol. 3:** 786
34:27 f	**Vol. 3:** 484, 1120
34:28–35	**Vol. 2:** 637
34:28†	**Vol. 1:** 612 **Vol. 2:** 640, 893 **Vol. 3:** 1087, 1102
34:29 ff	**Vol. 2:** 641
34:29–36	**Vol. 2:** 45
34:29–35	**Vol. 3:** 861, 864
34:29	**Vol. 3:** 631
34:30	**Vol. 1:** 195 **Vol. 2:** 46, 213
34:31 f	**Vol. 1:** 294
34:32	**Vol. 1:** 195, 332
34:33 ff	**Vol. 3:** 795
34:33–35	**Vol. 2:** 213
34:33	**Vol. 3:** 255
34:34–35	**Vol. 2:** 212
34:34	**Vol. 2:** 213
35–40	**Vol. 2:** 638
35–38	**Vol. 3:** 812
35:1–3	**Vol. 3:** 405
35:1	**Vol. 1:** 293–294
35:2	**Vol. 3:** 255–256
35:3	**Vol. 1:** 654 **Vol. 2:** 890 **Vol. 3:** 405
35:5 f	**Vol. 3:** 416
35:8	**Vol. 2:** 711
35:9	**Vol. 3:** 36
35:10	**Vol. 3:** 1027
35:12	**Vol. 3:** 153, 156, 794
35:13	**Vol. 1:** 586 **Vol. 3:** 423, 814
35:14 f	**Vol. 2:** 711
35:19	**Vol. 3:** 786
35:21 f	**Vol. 3:** 821
35:21	**Vol. 3:** 680
35:22	**Vol. 3:** 125, 497
35:25	**Vol. 3:** 1027
35:26	**Vol. 3:** 821, 1027

Exodus *(cont'd)*

35:28	**Vol. 2:** 711
35:30 ff	**Vol. 1:** 279
35:31–35	**Vol. 3:** 691
35:31	**Vol. 3:** 1027
35:33	**Vol. 3:** 1027, 1153
35:35	**Vol. 3:** 1027
36:1 f	**Vol. 3:** 1028
36:1	**Vol. 3:** 786, 1027
36:2	**Vol. 2:** 181 **Vol. 3:** 1027
36:3 ff	**Vol. 3:** 786
36:4	**Vol. 3:** 1027
36:6	**Vol. 3:** 51
36:7	**Vol. 3:** 728
36:8	**Vol. 3:** 1027
36:18*	**Vol. 3:** 395–396
36:26	**Vol. 3:** 811
36:35*	**Vol. 3:** 794
36:36*	**Vol. 3:** 794–795
36:37 f	**Vol. 3:** 814
36:37*	**Vol. 3:** 794
37:1 ff	**Vol. 3:** 788
37:6*	**Vol. 3:** 153
37:7 ff	**Vol. 3:** 163
37:7–9	**Vol. 1:** 280
37:8 f*	**Vol. 3:** 153
37:17 ff	**Vol. 3:** 814
37:17–24	**Vol. 3:** 812
37:25–28	**Vol. 3:** 812
37:29	**Vol. 2:** 711
37:37 f	**Vol. 2:** 711
38:1–7	**Vol. 3:** 812
38:2	**Vol. 2:** 97
38:5	**Vol. 2:** 97
38:6*	**Vol. 3:** 156
38:8 f*	**Vol. 3:** 156
38:8	**Vol. 3:** 812
38:9–20	**Vol. 3:** 812
38:18*	**Vol. 3:** 794
38:24 ff	**Vol. 3:** 752
38:24*	**Vol. 3:** 416
38:26	**Vol. 1:** 684 **Vol. 2:** 698 **Vol. 3:** 752
38:27*	**Vol. 3:** 786, 794
38:36 f	**Vol. 2:** 651
39:1	**Vol. 3:** 786
39:8 ff	**Vol. 3:** 966
39:10–13	**Vol. 3:** 396
39:19	**Vol. 3:** 36
39:20	**Vol. 1:** 122
39:27 ff	**Vol. 1:** 204
39:29*	**Vol. 3:** 120
39:30	**Vol. 3:** 483
39:36	**Vol. 1:** 586, 696 **Vol. 3:** 423, 814
39:38	**Vol. 2:** 711
39:40*	**Vol. 3:** 794
39:41	**Vol. 3:** 786
40–48	**Vol. 3:** 418
40:2 ff	**Vol. 3:** 1040
40:2	**Vol. 2:** 890
40:3	**Vol. 3:** 794, 1040
40:4	**Vol. 1:** 696
40:5	**Vol. 3:** 418, 794
40:9	**Vol. 1:** 121–122 **Vol. 2:** 711
40:10	**Vol. 1:** 122
40:13	**Vol. 1:** 122
40:15	**Vol. 1:** 120, 122 **Vol. 2:** 711 **Vol. 3:** 36, 828
40:20	**Vol. 3:** 787
40:21	**Vol. 3:** 543, 794
40:22–27	**Vol. 3:** 436
40:22	**Vol. 3:** 794
40:23	**Vol. 3:** 423
40:24	**Vol. 3:** 812
40:26	**Vol. 3:** 794
40:29–32	**Vol. 3:** 812
40:29	**Vol. 3:** 422
40:30 ff	**Vol. 3:** 989
40:34 f	**Vol. 1:** 735 **Vol. 2:** 45 **Vol. 3:** 257, 554
40:38	**Vol. 2:** 305

Leviticus

1–9	**Vol. 1:** 115
1–7	**Vol. 2:** 638
1:1	**Vol. 2:** 638
1:2 f	**Vol. 2:** 41 **Vol. 3:** 423
1:2	**Vol. 2:** 43, 305, 412
1:3	**Vol. 2:** 569 **Vol. 3:** 421, 572, 924
1:4 f	**Vol. 3:** 421
1:4	**Vol. 3:** 159, 421
1:5–10	**Vol. 3:** 421
1:5	**Vol. 1:** 223
1:6	**Vol. 1:** 162 **Vol. 3:** 421
1:7 ff	**Vol. 1:** 655
1:9 ff	**Vol. 3:** 421
1:9	**Vol. 3:** 421, 600–601
1:10	**Vol. 2:** 41, 569 **Vol. 3:** 421, 423, 924
1:11	**Vol. 1:** 223
1:13	**Vol. 3:** 421, 600
1:14 ff	**Vol. 1:** 172 **Vol. 3:** 421
1:14	**Vol. 2:** 41, 379, 610
1:17	**Vol. 3:** 421, 600
2	**Vol. 1:** 250
2:1–16	**Vol. 2:** 711
2:1	**Vol. 2:** 41 **Vol. 3:** 422–423
2:2	**Vol. 2:** 293 **Vol. 3:** 238, 423
2:3	**Vol. 2:** 272
2:4 ff	**Vol. 2:** 41
2:4	**Vol. 3:** 422, 917
2:5	**Vol. 1:** 249 **Vol. 3:** 422–423, 917
2:6	**Vol. 2:** 272
2:7	**Vol. 3:** 422
2:9 ff	**Vol. 2:** 272
2:9	**Vol. 3:** 238, 423
2:11 ff	**Vol. 3:** 422
2:11	**Vol. 2:** 461
2:12	**Vol. 3:** 415, 600
2:13	**Vol. 2:** 746 **Vol. 3:** 444–446

Leviticus *(cont'd)*

2:14 f	**Vol. 3:** 422
2:14	**Vol. 2:** 675
2:16	**Vol. 3:** 238, 423
3	**Vol. 3:** 422–423
3:1	**Vol. 2:** 569 **Vol. 3:** 423, 923–924
3:2	**Vol. 1:** 221 **Vol. 3:** 423
3:3 ff	**Vol. 3:** 423
3:5	**Vol. 1:** 655 **Vol. 3:** 423
3:6–17	**Vol. 3:** 423
3:6	**Vol. 2:** 569 **Vol. 3:** 923–924
3:7	**Vol. 3:** 423
3:9	**Vol. 3:** 924
3:13	**Vol. 3:** 423
3:16 f	**Vol. 3:** 159
3:17	**Vol. 1:** 221 **Vol. 3:** 158
4	**Vol. 3:** 419
4:2–21	**Vol. 3:** 420
4:2	**Vol. 3:** 420, 680
4:3	**Vol. 1:** 122 **Vol. 3:** 924
4:4 ff	**Vol. 3:** 1040
4:5 ff	**Vol. 3:** 419
4:5	**Vol. 2:** 60
4:6	**Vol. 3:** 786, 794
4:7	**Vol. 1:** 223 **Vol. 3:** 418, 436, 686, 715
4:11 f	**Vol. 3:** 419
4:12	**Vol. 3:** 965
4:13 ff	**Vol. 1:** 294
4:13	**Vol. 1:** 294–295 **Vol. 3:** 420
4:14	**Vol. 3:** 924
4:16 ff	**Vol. 3:** 419
4:17	**Vol. 3:** 794
4:18	**Vol. 1:** 223
4:20 ff	**Vol. 1:** 698
4:21	**Vol. 3:** 965
4:22 f	**Vol. 3:** 419
4:22	**Vol. 3:** 420
4:23	**Vol. 2:** 569
4:24	**Vol. 3:** 421
4:25	**Vol. 1:** 223 **Vol. 3:** 419
4:26	**Vol. 3:** 159
4:27 f	**Vol. 3:** 419
4:27	**Vol. 3:** 420
4:28	**Vol. 3:** 924
4:30	**Vol. 1:** 223
4:32	**Vol. 3:** 924
4:33	**Vol. 3:** 421
4:34	**Vol. 1:** 223
5:1–13	**Vol. 3:** 420
5:1	**Vol. 3:** 680
5:2	**Vol. 3:** 680
5:3–6	**Vol. 3:** 740
5:3	**Vol. 3:** 104
5:4	**Vol. 3:** 680
5:5 f	**Vol. 3:** 427
5:5	**Vol. 3:** 420
5:6 ff	**Vol. 1:** 698
5:6	**Vol. 3:** 420
5:7	**Vol. 3:** 421, 728
5:8	**Vol. 3:** 420
5:11 ff	**Vol. 3:** 422
5:11	**Vol. 2:** 293, 711 **Vol. 3:** 1164
5:12	**Vol. 3:** 238, 423
5:14–6:7	**Vol. 3:** 196
5:14	**Vol. 3:** 420
5:15	**Vol. 3:** 420, 680, 752, 924
5:16	**Vol. 3:** 155
5:17 ff	**Vol. 3:** 420
5:17	**Vol. 2:** 664 **Vol. 3:** 420
5:18	**Vol. 2:** 406 **Vol. 3:** 420, 924
5:19	**Vol. 3:** 420
5:24*	**Vol. 3:** 420
5:25*	**Vol. 3:** 924
6	**Vol. 2:** 440
6:1–7*	**Vol. 3:** 420
6:2–7	**Vol. 3:** 95
6:2–6	**Vol. 3:** 421
6:2 f*	**Vol. 2:** 471
6:4*	**Vol. 3:** 420, 601
6:5 f*	**Vol. 3:** 109
6:6*	**Vol. 3:** 420
6:7 f	**Vol. 3:** 422
6:8*	**Vol. 3:** 238, 421, 423
6:9 ff	**Vol. 1:** 655
6:9	**Vol. 3:** 787
6:12*	**Vol. 2:** 569
6:14	**Vol. 3:** 422
6:15*	**Vol. 2:** 440, 711
6:17	**Vol. 2:** 461
6:19 f	**Vol. 3:** 787
6:21	**Vol. 1:** 144 **Vol. 2:** 711 **Vol. 3:** 917
6:23	**Vol. 3:** 786, 1203
6:27	**Vol. 3:** 419
6:28	**Vol. 1:** 144 **Vol. 3:** 419, 914
6:29–30	**Vol. 1:** 612
6:29	**Vol. 3:** 419
6:30	**Vol. 3:** 419
6:37*	**Vol. 2:** 569
7:2	**Vol. 3:** 421, 917
7:8	**Vol. 3:** 421
7:9	**Vol. 3:** 422
7:10 ff	**Vol. 2:** 711
7:11–16	**Vol. 3:** 422–423
7:12–15*	**Vol. 3:** 816
7:12 f	**Vol. 3:** 423, 817
7:13	**Vol. 2:** 461
7:15 f	**Vol. 3:** 423
7:15*	**Vol. 2:** 41 **Vol. 3:** 423
7:18*	**Vol. 3:** 817, 823
7:19 f	**Vol. 3:** 104
7:23 ff	**Vol. 2:** 271
7:26 f	**Vol. 1:** 221 **Vol. 3:** 158
7:33*	**Vol. 2:** 303
7:34	**Vol. 3:** 424
7:37	**Vol. 3:** 422, 1203
7:38	**Vol. 3:** 423, 1013
8–9	**Vol. 2:** 638
8:2	**Vol. 2:** 711
8:3 ff	**Vol. 1:** 294

Leviticus *(cont'd)*

8:3	**Vol. 1:** 293
8:4	**Vol. 1:** 293
8:6	**Vol. 3:** 38
8:7	**Vol. 3:** 120
8:8	**Vol. 2:** 296
8:10	**Vol. 1:** 122 **Vol. 2:** 711
8:12	**Vol. 2:** 711
8:13	**Vol. 3:** 120
8:15	**Vol. 1:** 223 **Vol. 3:** 104
8:21	**Vol. 3:** 421
8:27	**Vol. 3:** 424
8:30	**Vol. 2:** 711 **Vol. 3:** 38
8:33	**Vol. 1:** 734
9:2 f	**Vol. 3:** 420, 924
9:2*	**Vol. 3:** 109, 171
9:3	**Vol. 2:** 410
9:4	**Vol. 2:** 711 **Vol. 3:** 423
9:5 ff	**Vol. 1:** 294
9:7 f	**Vol. 1:** 322
9:7	**Vol. 3:** 421
9:9	**Vol. 1:** 223 **Vol. 3:** 419
9:12	**Vol. 1:** 223 **Vol. 3:** 421
9:15	**Vol. 3:** 420
9:17	**Vol. 3:** 421
9:22 f	**Vol. 1:** 211
9:23 f	**Vol. 1:** 655 **Vol. 2:** 45
9:24	**Vol. 3:** 421
10	**Vol. 2:** 638
10:1–11	**Vol. 2:** 293
10:1	**Vol. 1:** 655, 684
10:2	**Vol. 1:** 655
10:3	**Vol. 1:** 295
10:4 f	**Vol. 3:** 965
10:6	**Vol. 1:** 294
10:7	**Vol. 2:** 711
10:9	**Vol. 3:** 919
10:14 f	**Vol. 3:** 424
10:17 f	**Vol. 3:** 159
10:17	**Vol. 3:** 151, 786
11–15	**Vol. 2:** 34 **Vol. 3:** 989
11	**Vol. 3:** 104
11:7	**Vol. 1:** 117
11:8	**Vol. 3:** 860
11:10	**Vol. 3:** 680
11:13–19	**Vol. 1:** 172
11:14 ff	**Vol. 2:** 501
11:18	**Vol. 1:** 172
11:20 ff	**Vol. 1:** 119
11:20 f	**Vol. 1:** 172
11:27	**Vol. 2:** 638
11:33	**Vol. 3:** 419
11:35	**Vol. 3:** 419, 914
11:36	**Vol. 1:** 296
11:44 f	**Vol. 2:** 307
11:45	**Vol. 1:** 531 **Vol. 2:** 797
12–15	**Vol. 3:** 419
12:1 ff	**Vol. 3:** 989
12:2–8	**Vol. 3:** 430, 790
12:2–5	**Vol. 3:** 1058
12:3	**Vol. 1:** 308, 672 **Vol. 2:** 437, 692 **Vol. 3:** 405
12:4	**Vol. 1:** 320 **Vol. 3:** 786
12:6 ff	**Vol. 1:** 172
12:6	**Vol. 3:** 421, 924
12:7	**Vol. 2:** 569 **Vol. 3:** 104
12:8	**Vol. 3:** 104, 421
13 f	**Vol. 1:** 241 **Vol. 2:** 167 **Vol. 3:** 997
13	**Vol. 1:** 151, 204 **Vol. 2:** 464–465
13:4	**Vol. 1:** 472 **Vol. 2:** 465
13:8	**Vol. 2:** 465
13:10 ff	**Vol. 2:** 169
13:13	**Vol. 2:** 465
13:17	**Vol. 3:** 104
13:18 ff	**Vol. 2:** 465
13:23	**Vol. 3:** 224
13:28	**Vol. 2:** 288
13:40 f	**Vol. 2:** 465
13:44	**Vol. 3:** 104
13:45	**Vol. 2:** 212, 464
13:46	**Vol. 3:** 534
13:47 ff	**Vol. 2:** 465
13:47	**Vol. 2:** 465
13:49	**Vol. 2:** 631 **Vol. 3:** 37, 569, 1043
13:52	**Vol. 1:** 655
13:59	**Vol. 2:** 465
14	**Vol. 1:** 151, 221 **Vol. 3:** 419
14:2–32	**Vol. 3:** 1043
14:2 f	**Vol. 2:** 464 **Vol. 3:** 37
14:5	**Vol. 3:** 914
14:6 f	**Vol. 1:** 225
14:8 f	**Vol. 3:** 989
14:10–32	**Vol. 3:** 420
14:10–29	**Vol. 2:** 711
14:10	**Vol. 2:** 410 **Vol. 3:** 422, 917, 924
14:13	**Vol. 3:** 421, 786–787
14:14	**Vol. 3:** 424
14:18	**Vol. 3:** 159
14:19	**Vol. 3:** 419, 421, 1203
14:20	**Vol. 3:** 421–422, 1196
14:21	**Vol. 3:** 422, 424
14:22	**Vol. 3:** 421
14:24	**Vol. 3:** 424
14:29	**Vol. 3:** 159
14:31	**Vol. 3:** 171, 421
14:34 ff	**Vol. 2:** 465
14:42	**Vol. 1:** 471
14:43	**Vol. 1:** 471
14:44	**Vol. 2:** 465
14:48	**Vol. 1:** 471
14:50	**Vol. 3:** 914
14:51	**Vol. 1:** 225
14:55	**Vol. 2:** 465
14:57	**Vol. 1:** 574
15	**Vol. 1:** 151, 683 **Vol. 3:** 989
15:2 f	**Vol. 1:** 672
15:2	**Vol. 3:** 104
15:11	**Vol. 1:** 233
15:12	**Vol. 3:** 419, 914

Leviticus *(cont'd)*

15:14 f   **Vol. 3:** 421
15:16 f   **Vol. 2:** 586
15:16   **Vol. 1:** 233   **Vol. 2:** 586   **Vol. 3:** 104, 522
15:17   **Vol. 2:** 586
15:18   **Vol. 2:** 586
15:19–31   **Vol. 3:** 1058
15:19–24   **Vol. 3:** 861
15:19   **Vol. 1:** 233   **Vol. 3:** 104, 861
15:21   **Vol. 2:** 587
15:23   **Vol. 2:** 587
15:24   **Vol. 2:** 587   **Vol. 3:** 95, 104, 861
15:25–30   **Vol. 3:** 861
15:25   **Vol. 2:** 890   **Vol. 3:** 104
15:26   **Vol. 2:** 587
15:29 f   **Vol. 3:** 421
15:32   **Vol. 2:** 586
16   **Vol. 1:** 114–115, 221, 223   **Vol. 2:** 151, 199, 598, 718   **Vol. 3:** 38, 41, 94, 104, 151, 156, 192, 198, 243, 366, 419, 433, 579, 788, 794, 812, 941, 947
16:2 f   **Vol. 3:** 786, 812
16:2   **Vol. 3:** 153, 156, 788, 794, 1001, 1040
16:4   **Vol. 1:** 151, 233   **Vol. 3:** 120, 989
16:5   **Vol. 3:** 420, 1203
16:6   **Vol. 1:** 151, 221
16:8   **Vol. 1:** 451   **Vol. 2:** 296
16:10   **Vol. 1:** 451   **Vol. 3:** 159, 1005
16:11–19   **Vol. 1:** 225
16:11   **Vol. 3:** 420
16:12 f   **Vol. 1:** 655   **Vol. 3:** 815
16:12–13   **Vol. 2:** 293–294
16:12   **Vol. 1:** 495   **Vol. 3:** 794
16:13 ff   **Vol. 3:** 153, 156
16:13   **Vol. 1:** 151
16:14 ff   **Vol. 3:** 161
16:14   **Vol. 2:** 690
16:15 ff   **Vol. 1:** 221
16:15   **Vol. 3:** 794, 815
16:16 f   **Vol. 3:** 786
16:16   **Vol. 1:** 380   **Vol. 3:** 153, 419, 574
16:17   **Vol. 2:** 29
16:19   **Vol. 2:** 690
16:20 ff   **Vol. 1:** 699   **Vol. 3:** 150
16:20   **Vol. 1:** 699
16:21 f   **Vol. 3:** 574, 1005
16:21   **Vol. 3:** 164
16:22   **Vol. 1:** 699
16:24   **Vol. 3:** 989
16:26   **Vol. 1:** 451, 698   **Vol. 3:** 989
16:27   **Vol. 3:** 159, 434, 723, 965, 1203
16:28   **Vol. 3:** 419, 989
16:29   **Vol. 1:** 612   **Vol. 2:** 260
16:30   **Vol. 3:** 104
16:31   **Vol. 1:** 495, 612   **Vol. 3:** 255
16:33   **Vol. 3:** 153
17–26   **Vol. 1:** 61   **Vol. 2:** 226
17   **Vol. 1:** 221

17:3 f   **Vol. 3:** 159, 423
17:4   **Vol. 3:** 159, 574, 680, 823
17:7   **Vol. 1:** 451, 551   **Vol. 3:** 200
17:8   **Vol. 1:** 221
17:9   **Vol. 3:** 574
17:10   **Vol. 1:** 221   **Vol. 3:** 158
17:11   **Vol. 1:** 221, 699   **Vol. 2:** 477   **Vol. 3:** 150–151, 158–159, 199, 423, 425, 680
17:12–15   **Vol. 1:** 684
17:12   **Vol. 3:** 158
17:13 f   **Vol. 1:** 226   **Vol. 3:** 422
17:13   **Vol. 1:** 172, 221
17:14   **Vol. 1:** 221   **Vol. 2:** 477   **Vol. 3:** 150, 158, 425, 680
17:15   **Vol. 1:** 221
17:16   **Vol. 3:** 420
18   **Vol. 3:** 538
18:4   **Vol. 2:** 134
18:5   **Vol. 1:** 417   **Vol. 2:** 363, 445, 479
18:6 ff   **Vol. 3:** 104, 310
18:6–18†   **Vol. 1:** 499   **Vol. 2:** 577   **Vol. 3:** 1195
18:6   **Vol. 1:** 673, 675
18:7–18   **Vol. 3:** 95
18:16   **Vol. 3:** 540
18:19–33   **Vol. 2:** 577
18:19   **Vol. 3:** 95, 861
18:20   **Vol. 2:** 576, 586–587   **Vol. 3:** 104, 536
18:21   **Vol. 2:** 375, 649   **Vol. 3:** 421
18:22   **Vol. 2:** 569–570, 587   **Vol. 3:** 95, 104
18:23   **Vol. 2:** 587   **Vol. 3:** 95
18:24–29   **Vol. 3:** 95
18:27 f   **Vol. 3:** 160
18:29   **Vol. 2:** 570   **Vol. 3:** 95, 538
19:2   **Vol. 2:** 226, 230, 307
19:3   **Vol. 1:** 622   **Vol. 3:** 95, 1055, 1057
19:5 ff   **Vol. 3:** 422
19:6   **Vol. 2:** 890
19:8   **Vol. 1:** 337   **Vol. 3:** 545
19:10   **Vol. 2:** 821   **Vol. 3:** 918
19:11   **Vol. 2:** 471   **Vol. 3:** 377
19:12   **Vol. 2:** 471   **Vol. 3:** 94, 183, 740
19:13 ff   **Vol. 3:** 576
19:13   **Vol. 2:** 139   **Vol. 3:** 95, 574, 601
19:14   **Vol. 1:** 218, 622   **Vol. 2:** 707
19:15   **Vol. 1:** 587
19:15a   **Vol. 2:** 451
19:16   **Vol. 2:** 449
19:17 f   **Vol. 1:** 255, 555
19:17   **Vol. 2:** 141
19:18   **Vol. 1:** 111, 257–259, 334, 555, 738   **Vol. 2:** 157, 177, 427, 540–541, 544, 716   **Vol. 3:** 97, 173, 183, 491, 542, 1064
19:19   **Vol. 2:** 441, 742   **Vol. 3:** 1160, 1164
19:20 ff   **Vol. 2:** 582
19:20   **Vol. 1:** 716   **Vol. 2:** 586   **Vol. 3:** 190, 192, 594
19:21   **Vol. 2:** 650
19:26   **Vol. 2:** 554–555   **Vol. 3:** 158

Leviticus *(cont'd)*

19:28	**Vol. 1:** 233 **Vol. 2:** 418, 573 **Vol. 3:** 455, 483, 498
19:29	**Vol. 1:** 499
19:30	**Vol. 3:** 786
19:31	**Vol. 1:** 450 **Vol. 2:** 554–555, 559
19:32	**Vol. 1:** 92, 622 **Vol. 2:** 49
19:33 f	**Vol. 1:** 258, 717
19:34	**Vol. 2:** 540–541
19:35	**Vol. 3:** 402, 1161
19:36	**Vol. 3:** 356, 1160
19:37	**Vol. 2:** 441
20:1–5	**Vol. 3:** 421
20:2 ff	**Vol. 3:** 418
20:2–5	**Vol. 3:** 95
20:2	**Vol. 1:** 655
20:3	**Vol. 1:** 463 **Vol. 3:** 786
20:4	**Vol. 3:** 786
20:5	**Vol. 1:** 463
20:6	**Vol. 1:** 463 **Vol. 2:** 554–555
20:7	**Vol. 2:** 226
20:9–27	**Vol. 2:** 142
20:9	**Vol. 3:** 95, 159, 1070
20:10	**Vol. 2:** 576, 582 **Vol. 3:** 95, 227, 536, 538
20:11 ff	**Vol. 3:** 159, 310
20:11–21	**Vol. 3:** 95
20:11 f	**Vol. 3:** 535
20:13	**Vol. 2:** 569–570, 587 **Vol. 3:** 95
20:14	**Vol. 1:** 655 **Vol. 2:** 96
20:15	**Vol. 3:** 95
20:16	**Vol. 3:** 159
20:18	**Vol. 3:** 95, 786
20:19 ff	**Vol. 2:** 577
20:19	**Vol. 1:** 673
20:21	**Vol. 2:** 576 **Vol. 3:** 540
20:22	**Vol. 2:** 363
20:23	**Vol. 3:** 786
20:24	**Vol. 1:** 683
20:26	**Vol. 2:** 307
20:27	**Vol. 2:** 554–555 **Vol. 3:** 94–95, 159, 786
21	**Vol. 2:** 34
21:1 ff	**Vol. 2:** 415
21:2 f	**Vol. 2:** 53
21:7	**Vol. 1:** 453 **Vol. 2:** 577, 592 **Vol. 3:** 95
21:8	**Vol. 3:** 445
21:9	**Vol. 1:** 655 **Vol. 2:** 96 **Vol. 3:** 95
21:10 ff	**Vol. 2:** 711 **Vol. 3:** 35
21:12	**Vol. 3:** 786
21:13 ff	**Vol. 1:** 619
21:13 f	**Vol. 2:** 577, 592
21:14	**Vol. 3:** 1074
21:17	**Vol. 3:** 424, 445
21:18 ff	**Vol. 1:** 219
21:18	**Vol. 1:** 219
21:20	**Vol. 1:** 520
21:21	**Vol. 2:** 53
21:22	**Vol. 3:** 424
21:23	**Vol. 2:** 53 **Vol. 3:** 786, 794
22:4	**Vol. 2:** 464, 586 **Vol. 3:** 522
22:10	**Vol. 1:** 684, 691 **Vol. 2:** 139, 742
22:11	**Vol. 3:** 594
22:12	**Vol. 3:** 416
22:14	**Vol. 2:** 406
22:17–25	**Vol. 3:** 200, 435
22:18 f	**Vol. 3:** 421
22:18	**Vol. 1:** 344, 534
22:19 ff	**Vol. 2:** 415
22:19–25	**Vol. 3:** 745
22:19	**Vol. 2:** 569 **Vol. 3:** 924
22:21	**Vol. 1:** 534 **Vol. 3:** 422, 924
22:22 f	**Vol. 3:** 1074
22:22	**Vol. 1:** 219
22:23 f	**Vol. 3:** 95
22:23	**Vol. 3:** 423
22:25	**Vol. 1:** 468
22:27	**Vol. 2:** 43
22:29	**Vol. 3:** 423
23	**Vol. 1:** 626
23:1–3	**Vol. 3:** 405, 407
23:2–37	**Vol. 1:** 272
23:3 ff	**Vol. 3:** 918
23:3	**Vol. 3:** 255
23:5	**Vol. 1:** 632
23:6–8	**Vol. 1:** 632
23:6	**Vol. 2:** 690
23:10 f	**Vol. 3:** 1200
23:10	**Vol. 3:** 415
23:12	**Vol. 3:** 421, 924
23:13	**Vol. 3:** 422–423, 919
23:14	**Vol. 2:** 43
23:15 ff	**Vol. 3:** 417
23:15–21	**Vol. 2:** 783
23:15	**Vol. 2:** 890 **Vol. 3:** 424
23:16 f	**Vol. 3:** 422
23:16	**Vol. 2:** 675
23:17	**Vol. 3:** 424
23:18	**Vol. 3:** 924
23:19	**Vol. 3:** 423
23:20	**Vol. 3:** 424
23:22	**Vol. 2:** 821
23:24	**Vol. 3:** 237, 255
23:26–32†	**Vol. 1:** 626
23:27–32	**Vol. 1:** 612
23:27 f	**Vol. 2:** 890 **Vol. 3:** 150, 153
23:27	**Vol. 1:** 495, 612
23:29	**Vol. 1:** 465
23:32	**Vol. 1:** 495, 612
23:34–36	**Vol. 3:** 1005
23:34	**Vol. 2:** 690 **Vol. 3:** 811
23:37	**Vol. 3:** 422–423
23:39–55	**Vol. 3:** 594
23:39	**Vol. 3:** 255
23:42 f	**Vol. 3:** 811, 1005
23:43	**Vol. 1:** 626 **Vol. 2:** 784
24:2	**Vol. 2:** 711
24:3	**Vol. 3:** 794

Leviticus *(cont'd)*

24:5–9	**Vol. 3:** 423
24:7 ff	**Vol. 3:** 792
24:7	**Vol. 2:** 293 **Vol. 3:** 238–239, 423
24:8 f	**Vol. 3:** 239
24:8	**Vol. 2:** 890 **Vol. 3:** 407
24:9	**Vol. 3:** 37, 814
24:10 ff	**Vol. 3:** 342–343
24:10–16	**Vol. 3:** 342
24:11–23	**Vol. 3:** 94
24:14	**Vol. 1:** 294 **Vol. 2:** 29
24:15 f	**Vol. 3:** 95
24:16	**Vol. 1:** 294 **Vol. 2:** 231, 449, 801 **Vol. 3:** 341
24:18	**Vol. 3:** 95
24:19 f	**Vol. 3:** 94
24:20	**Vol. 3:** 183
24:21	**Vol. 3:** 95
25	**Vol. 1:** 698 **Vol. 2:** 298 **Vol. 3:** 191
25:1	**Vol. 3:** 1013
25:3	**Vol. 2:** 32
25:4 f	**Vol. 3:** 255
25:6	**Vol. 1:** 691 **Vol. 2:** 139
25:8	**Vol. 3:** 255
25:9	**Vol. 2:** 890 **Vol. 3:** 150, 156, 873
25:18	**Vol. 3:** 354
25:20	**Vol. 2:** 32
25:22	**Vol. 2:** 713
25:23	**Vol. 1:** 640, 688, 691 **Vol. 3:** 190
25:24	**Vol. 3:** 190
25:25 ff	**Vol. 3:** 728
25:25	**Vol. 3:** 192
25:26	**Vol. 3:** 190
25:28	**Vol. 3:** 256
25:29	**Vol. 3:** 190, 193
25:30	**Vol. 1:** 664 **Vol. 3:** 192
25:31 f	**Vol. 3:** 190, 193
25:31	**Vol. 3:** 823
25:33	**Vol. 3:** 192
25:34	**Vol. 1:** 520
25:35 ff	**Vol. 1:** 690–691 **Vol. 3:** 593
25:35	**Vol. 2:** 540
25:36	**Vol. 2:** 254
25:37	**Vol. 3:** 190
25:38	**Vol. 1:** 531
25:39 ff	**Vol. 2:** 96
25:39–43	**Vol. 3:** 594
25:40	**Vol. 2:** 139
25:44 ff	**Vol. 3:** 593
25:47–55	**Vol. 3:** 594
25:48 f	**Vol. 3:** 190, 192
25:48	**Vol. 3:** 190, 193
25:49	**Vol. 1:** 673
25:50	**Vol. 2:** 139 **Vol. 3:** 191
25:51 f	**Vol. 3:** 190
25:53	**Vol. 2:** 139
25:54	**Vol. 3:** 192
25:55	**Vol. 3:** 190–191
26:1	**Vol. 2:** 876
26:2	**Vol. 1:** 622 **Vol. 3:** 786
26:4	**Vol. 3:** 835, 982, 1001
26:5	**Vol. 1:** 663 **Vol. 3:** 144
26:6	**Vol. 1:** 113 **Vol. 2:** 778
26:8	**Vol. 3:** 962
26:10	**Vol. 2:** 675
26:11 f	**Vol. 2:** 251 **Vol. 3:** 784, 800
26:12	**Vol. 1:** 368 **Vol. 2:** 797, 800 **Vol. 3:** 813, 944–945
26:13	**Vol. 2:** 735 **Vol. 3:** 1161
26:15 f	**Vol. 1:** 367
26:18	**Vol. 3:** 777
26:19	**Vol. 3:** 29–30
26:22	**Vol. 1:** 113
26:25	**Vol. 3:** 93
26:28	**Vol. 3:** 777
26:30	**Vol. 2:** 284
26:31	**Vol. 3:** 600
26:32	**Vol. 2:** 622
26:33	**Vol. 2:** 34
26:34–43	**Vol. 3:** 191
26:36	**Vol. 3:** 249
26:39	**Vol. 3:** 574
26:41	**Vol. 1:** 308
26:42	**Vol. 2:** 596 **Vol. 3:** 235
26:45	**Vol. 3:** 235
26:46	**Vol. 3:** 1013
27	**Vol. 1:** 698 **Vol. 3:** 420
27:3	**Vol. 2:** 569
27:5 ff	**Vol. 2:** 569
27:13	**Vol. 3:** 190, 192
27:15	**Vol. 3:** 190, 192
27:18	**Vol. 1:** 413
27:19 f	**Vol. 3:** 190, 192
27:19	**Vol. 1:** 267, 413
27:23	**Vol. 2:** 683 **Vol. 3:** 756, 823
27:27–31	**Vol. 3:** 192
27:29	**Vol. 1:** 414 **Vol. 3:** 192
27:30–33	**Vol. 2:** 693 **Vol. 3:** 1053
27:30–32	**Vol. 2:** 694 **Vol. 3:** 852
27:30	**Vol. 1:** 116
27:31	**Vol. 3:** 190
27:33	**Vol. 3:** 192

Numbers

1–4	**Vol. 1:** 189
1	**Vol. 2:** 638
1:2	**Vol. 1:** 165, 294 **Vol. 2:** 158
1:3*	**Vol. 2:** 569
1:4–49	**Vol. 2:** 695
1:16	**Vol. 2:** 698
1:21	**Vol. 1:** 190
1:23–46	**Vol. 2:** 698
1:23	**Vol. 1:** 190
1:25	**Vol. 1:** 190
1:44	**Vol. 1:** 189
1:49	**Vol. 2:** 683
2	**Vol. 2:** 638 **Vol. 3:** 397
2:2	**Vol. 3:** 871

Numbers *(cont'd)*

2:3	**Vol. 1:** 165, 665
2:4–32	**Vol. 2:** 698
2:4	**Vol. 1:** 189
2:5	**Vol. 1:** 165
2:7	**Vol. 1:** 165
2:25	**Vol. 3:** 872
3–4	**Vol. 2:** 789
3	**Vol. 2:** 638
3:1	**Vol. 3:** 1013
3:2	**Vol. 1:** 667
3:3	**Vol. 1:** 120 **Vol. 2:** 149
3:4	**Vol. 1:** 655
3:7	**Vol. 1:** 294
3:10	**Vol. 2:** 592 **Vol. 3:** 36, 418, 794, 860
3:26	**Vol. 3:** 794
3:28	**Vol. 3:** 786
3:31 f	**Vol. 3:** 786
3:38	**Vol. 3:** 786, 860
3:39	**Vol. 1:** 189
3:40	**Vol. 2:** 569
3:43	**Vol. 2:** 698
3:46–51	**Vol. 3:** 190
4	**Vol. 2:** 638
4:5	**Vol. 2:** 212 **Vol. 3:** 794, 1040
4:6	**Vol. 2:** 212
4:7	**Vol. 1:** 586 **Vol. 3:** 423
4:8	**Vol. 2:** 212
4:9	**Vol. 2:** 711
4:12	**Vol. 2:** 212 **Vol. 3:** 786
4:15 f	**Vol. 3:** 786
4:15	**Vol. 2:** 212–213, 226 **Vol. 3:** 786
4:16	**Vol. 2:** 711
4:18	**Vol. 2:** 803
4:20	**Vol. 2:** 212–213, 226 **Vol. 3:** 786
4:25 ff	**Vol. 3:** 1040
4:32	**Vol. 3:** 794
4:34	**Vol. 1:** 292
5	**Vol. 2:** 638
5:1 ff	**Vol. 1:** 151
5:2	**Vol. 2:** 464
5:5–8	**Vol. 3:** 196
5:6 ff	**Vol. 3:** 420
5:6 f	**Vol. 3:** 427
5:7 f	**Vol. 3:** 420
5:8	**Vol. 3:** 153, 155–156
5:9	**Vol. 3:** 416
5:11–31	**Vol. 1:** 98 **Vol. 2:** 583
5:11–28	**Vol. 3:** 740
5:12	**Vol. 3:** 583
5:13	**Vol. 1:** 343 **Vol. 2:** 586
5:14	**Vol. 3:** 691
5:15	**Vol. 2:** 41, 711 **Vol. 3:** 236, 239, 243, 422
5:16–28	**Vol. 3:** 208
5:17	**Vol. 2:** 226 **Vol. 3:** 914
5:18 f	**Vol. 2:** 140
5:18	**Vol. 3:** 236, 310, 422
5:19 f	**Vol. 3:** 583
5:19	**Vol. 1:** 98
5:20	**Vol. 2:** 587
5:22	**Vol. 1:** 97
5:23 f	**Vol. 2:** 140 **Vol. 3:** 484
5:25	**Vol. 3:** 422
5:26	**Vol. 3:** 238, 423
5:27	**Vol. 2:** 140
5:29	**Vol. 2:** 440 **Vol. 3:** 583
6	**Vol. 1:** 211 **Vol. 2:** 638
6:1 ff	**Vol. 2:** 225
6:1–21	**Vol. 3:** 431, 793
6:1–12	**Vol. 3:** 420
6:2–21	**Vol. 3:** 101
6:3	**Vol. 3:** 101, 919, 921
6:5	**Vol. 1:** 734 **Vol. 2:** 157
6:6	**Vol. 3:** 680
6:10 f	**Vol. 3:** 421
6:13	**Vol. 2:** 440
6:14 ff	**Vol. 3:** 420
6:14	**Vol. 2:** 41 **Vol. 3:** 421, 423, 923–924
6:15	**Vol. 2:** 711 **Vol. 3:** 422–423
6:17	**Vol. 3:** 423
6:18 f	**Vol. 3:** 422
6:20	**Vol. 3:** 424
6:21	**Vol. 2:** 41, 440
6:22 f	**Vol. 2:** 777
6:23 f	**Vol. 2:** 778
6:23	**Vol. 1:** 211
6:24 ff	**Vol. 2:** 649, 777
6:24–26	**Vol. 1:** 211 **Vol. 2:** 778
6:25 ff	**Vol. 1:** 585
6:25	**Vol. 3:** 318–319
6:27	**Vol. 1:** 211 **Vol. 2:** 649, 778
7	**Vol. 2:** 638
7:1	**Vol. 1:** 122
7:9	**Vol. 3:** 786
7:13 ff	**Vol. 3:** 422
7:13–79	**Vol. 2:** 711
7:25	**Vol. 2:** 43 **Vol. 3:** 155
7:69	**Vol. 3:** 924
7:88	**Vol. 3:** 924
7:89	**Vol. 1:** 280 **Vol. 3:** 153, 156
8	**Vol. 2:** 638
8:4	**Vol. 3:** 569
8:5–22	**Vol. 3:** 989
8:8	**Vol. 3:** 422
8:9	**Vol. 1:** 294–295
8:11	**Vol. 3:** 424, 1148
8:13	**Vol. 3:** 424
8:15	**Vol. 3:** 424
8:18	**Vol. 2:** 711
8:19	**Vol. 3:** 786
8:20	**Vol. 1:** 294
8:21	**Vol. 3:** 101, 424
8:24	**Vol. 3:** 1147
8:25	**Vol. 1:** 606
9:1–10:10	**Vol. 2:** 638
9:2	**Vol. 3:** 835, 846
9:3	**Vol. 2:** 441 **Vol. 3:** 835
9:7	**Vol. 3:** 835, 953

Numbers *(cont'd)*

9:9	**Vol. 1:** 115
9:10 f	**Vol. 2:** 528
9:12	**Vol. 2:** 527
9:13	**Vol. 1:** 699 **Vol. 3:** 835, 953
9:14	**Vol. 2:** 441
9:15	**Vol. 2:** 889
9:17 f	**Vol. 1:** 115
10:4	**Vol. 2:** 698
10:8	**Vol. 3:** 237
10:9	**Vol. 3:** 207, 239
10:10	**Vol. 2:** 890 **Vol. 3:** 237, 239, 873
10:11	**Vol. 2:** 638
10:15−27	**Vol. 2:** 695
10:21	**Vol. 3:** 786
10:29 ff	**Vol. 2:** 99
10:33	**Vol. 3:** 255
10:35 ff	**Vol. 3:** 960
10:35	**Vol. 1:** 555 **Vol. 2:** 34 **Vol. 3:** 279
10:36	**Vol. 2:** 698 **Vol. 3:** 255
11	**Vol. 1:** 252
11:1−3	**Vol. 2:** 638
11:1	**Vol. 1:** 655 **Vol. 2:** 117
11:4 ff	**Vol. 2:** 836 **Vol. 3:** 804
11:4−9	**Vol. 1:** 252 **Vol. 2:** 871
11:4	**Vol. 1:** 456
11:5	**Vol. 2:** 41 **Vol. 3:** 234
11:8	**Vol. 1:** 459 **Vol. 2:** 711 **Vol. 3:** 394
11:10−30	**Vol. 2:** 638 **Vol. 3:** 77
11:11 ff	**Vol. 3:** 342
11:11	**Vol. 3:** 528, 721
11:12 f	**Vol. 3:** 805
11:12	**Vol. 1:** 186, 240 **Vol. 3:** 878
11:16 ff	**Vol. 1:** 195
11:16	**Vol. 2:** 32, 696, 754 **Vol. 3:** 478
11:22	**Vol. 3:** 727
11:24−29	**Vol. 1:** 527
11:25−27	**Vol. 3:** 691
11:25 f	**Vol. 3:** 255
11:25	**Vol. 3:** 256
11:27 ff	**Vol. 2:** 331
11:28	**Vol. 1:** 485 **Vol. 2:** 222
11:29	**Vol. 3:** 78, 699
11:31 f	**Vol. 1:** 173
11:31	**Vol. 3:** 1001
11:32	**Vol. 2:** 32, 889
11:33 f	**Vol. 3:** 804
11:33	**Vol. 1:** 672
11:34 f	**Vol. 3:** 238
11:34	**Vol. 1:** 456
12:1−16	**Vol. 2:** 638
12:1	**Vol. 2:** 576, 578, 684
12:2	**Vol. 2:** 175
12:3	**Vol. 2:** 257
12:6	**Vol. 1:** 512 **Vol. 3:** 87
12:7 f	**Vol. 3:** 608
12:7	**Vol. 1:** 595−596 **Vol. 2:** 248−249
12:8	**Vol. 1:** 704 **Vol. 2:** 745, 756 **Vol. 3:** 345, 514
12:9	**Vol. 1:** 108
12:11 f	**Vol. 3:** 33
12:12	**Vol. 1:** 182 **Vol. 2:** 756
12:13	**Vol. 2:** 860
13 f	**Vol. 3:** 1005
13−14	**Vol. 2:** 638
13:2−15	**Vol. 2:** 695
13:8	**Vol. 2:** 331 **Vol. 3:** 208
13:16	**Vol. 3:** 208
13:18	**Vol. 3:** 713, 993
13:20*	**Vol. 2:** 767
13:24	**Vol. 1:** 723
13:26*	**Vol. 1:** 294 **Vol. 3:** 569
13:29	**Vol. 2:** 802 **Vol. 3:** 985
14	**Vol. 1:** 203
14:1 ff	**Vol. 1:** 294−295
14:1−35	**Vol. 3:** 434
14:2	**Vol. 2:** 666
14:3 f	**Vol. 2:** 180
14:5	**Vol. 1:** 295
14:6−9	**Vol. 2:** 331
14:7 ff	**Vol. 1:** 296
14:8	**Vol. 1:** 683 **Vol. 2:** 818
14:9	**Vol. 1:** 606−607, 622
14:11	**Vol. 2:** 627 **Vol. 3:** 342, 368
14:13−22	**Vol. 2:** 863
14:13	**Vol. 3:** 713
14:14	**Vol. 1:** 655
14:18	**Vol. 2:** 769
14:19	**Vol. 1:** 698 **Vol. 2:** 595 **Vol. 3:** 152, 157
14:20	**Vol. 1:** 165 **Vol. 3:** 157
14:21−23	**Vol. 3:** 742
14:21	**Vol. 1:** 735 **Vol. 2:** 229 **Vol. 3:** 740
14:22	**Vol. 3:** 514, 799−800
14:23	**Vol. 3:** 342
14:27	**Vol. 2:** 175
14:28	**Vol. 3:** 740
14:29	**Vol. 2:** 458
14:30−38	**Vol. 2:** 331
14:30	**Vol. 1:** 321
14:31	**Vol. 1:** 607
14:33	**Vol. 2:** 458 **Vol. 3:** 1195
14:34	**Vol. 3:** 804, 843
14:41	**Vol. 3:** 583
15:2	**Vol. 1:** 321
15:3	**Vol. 3:** 423, 601
15:4−9	**Vol. 2:** 711
15:4	**Vol. 3:** 422, 917
15:5	**Vol. 2:** 410 **Vol. 3:** 423
15:6	**Vol. 3:** 422
15:7	**Vol. 3:** 423, 919
15:9	**Vol. 3:** 422
15:10	**Vol. 3:** 423, 919
15:15 f	**Vol. 1:** 360
15:16	**Vol. 3:** 354
15:17 ff	**Vol. 3:** 416
15:17−21	**Vol. 3:** 416
15:20 f	**Vol. 3:** 415, 917
15:22−26	**Vol. 3:** 420

Numbers *(cont'd)*

15:22   **Vol. 1:** 294
15:24   **Vol. 3:** 423, 924
15:25 f   **Vol. 1:** 698
15:25   **Vol. 3:** 155
15:27–31   **Vol. 3:** 419
15:27   **Vol. 3:** 94
15:28   **Vol. 3:** 416
15:30 f   **Vol. 3:** 94, 342, 1206
15:30   **Vol. 1:** 360   **Vol. 3:** 29, 31
15:32–36   **Vol. 3:** 94–95, 405
15:32   **Vol. 2:** 890   **Vol. 3:** 407
15:35 f   **Vol. 1:** 294
15:35   **Vol. 2:** 29
15:37–41   **Vol. 2:** 174, 177, 864
15:39   **Vol. 3:** 233
16   **Vol. 2:** 638   **Vol. 3:** 1054
16:3   **Vol. 1:** 293
16:5   **Vol. 1:** 295, 537   **Vol. 2:** 395, 400   **Vol. 3:** 500
16:9   **Vol. 1:** 294
16:15   **Vol. 3:** 421
16:16   **Vol. 3:** 117
16:22   **Vol. 1:** 674   **Vol. 3:** 690
16:25   **Vol. 1:** 195
16:28   **Vol. 3:** 630, 645
16:30   **Vol. 3:** 342
16:33   **Vol. 1:** 293, 463
16:35   **Vol. 1:** 655   **Vol. 2:** 485
16:40*   **Vol. 1:** 292, 684   **Vol. 2:** 742   **Vol. 3:** 236
16:41–50   **Vol. 3:** 155
16:46 f   **Vol. 3:** 155
16:46   **Vol. 2:** 294   **Vol. 3:** 159
17   **Vol. 1:** 162   **Vol. 2:** 638
17:1 ff   **Vol. 3:** 484, 815
17:2*   **Vol. 2:** 34
17:5   **Vol. 3:** 236
17:7   **Vol. 1:** 293
17:10   **Vol. 1:** 408   **Vol. 3:** 815
17:12   **Vol. 1:** 295
18:1–7   **Vol. 2:** 34
18:1   **Vol. 2:** 592   **Vol. 3:** 36, 416, 786
18:2   **Vol. 3:** 415
18:3   **Vol. 2:** 34   **Vol. 3:** 786
18:5   **Vol. 3:** 786
18:7   **Vol. 3:** 36, 794
18:8   **Vol. 3:** 416
18:9   **Vol. 2:** 232   **Vol. 3:** 38, 420, 422
18:11   **Vol. 3:** 416
18:12   **Vol. 3:** 416
18:14   **Vol. 1:** 414
18:15   **Vol. 3:** 190, 192, 416
18:17   **Vol. 3:** 192
18:18   **Vol. 3:** 424
18:20–32   **Vol. 2:** 693
18:20–24   **Vol. 2:** 693
18:20   **Vol. 2:** 302
18:21 ff   **Vol. 2:** 693

18:21   **Vol. 2:** 466   **Vol. 3:** 853
18:22 ff   **Vol. 3:** 150
18:22   **Vol. 3:** 1206
18:23 f   **Vol. 2:** 298
18:24   **Vol. 2:** 466
18:26 ff   **Vol. 2:** 466
18:26   **Vol. 2:** 693
18:27   **Vol. 3:** 823
18:28   **Vol. 2:** 693   **Vol. 3:** 853
18:29 f   **Vol. 3:** 416
18:30   **Vol. 3:** 823
18:31   **Vol. 2:** 139
18:32   **Vol. 3:** 416
19   **Vol. 1:** 225   **Vol. 3:** 104
19:2   **Vol. 1:** 203, 205   **Vol. 3:** 924, 1161
19:4   **Vol. 1:** 221
19:8 ff   **Vol. 3:** 419
19:9   **Vol. 2:** 32
19:11 ff   **Vol. 1:** 151
19:11 f   **Vol. 3:** 989
19:11   **Vol. 3:** 860
19:12   **Vol. 3:** 101
19:13   **Vol. 1:** 151
19:14 f   **Vol. 3:** 104
19:14   **Vol. 3:** 811
19:15   **Vol. 2:** 726
19:16   **Vol. 1:** 444   **Vol. 3:** 238, 860
19:17   **Vol. 2:** 854
19:18 f   **Vol. 1:** 144
19:18   **Vol. 3:** 238
19:20   **Vol. 3:** 420, 786
19:21   **Vol. 3:** 419
20   **Vol. 3:** 383
20:1 ff   **Vol. 1:** 294–295
20:1–14   **Vol. 2:** 638
20:1–13   **Vol. 3:** 382
20:1–11   **Vol. 3:** 459
20:1   **Vol. 2:** 638
20:2–5   **Vol. 1:** 203
20:3   **Vol. 2:** 666   **Vol. 3:** 346
20:4   **Vol. 3:** 346
20:6   **Vol. 1:** 293
20:8   **Vol. 1:** 293   **Vol. 3:** 381
20:10 ff   **Vol. 3:** 342
20:11   **Vol. 2:** 276
20:12   **Vol. 2:** 638
20:13   **Vol. 3:** 346
20:16   **Vol. 1:** 410   **Vol. 3:** 1014
20:20   **Vol. 2:** 800
20:22–29   **Vol. 2:** 638
20:27   **Vol. 3:** 939
20:29   **Vol. 1:** 506
21   **Vol. 2:** 638
21:2 f   **Vol. 1:** 415
21:3   **Vol. 1:** 272, 413
21:4 ff   **Vol. 3:** 804
21:4–9   **Vol. 1:** 465   **Vol. 3:** 1005–1006
21:5   **Vol. 3:** 345
21:7   **Vol. 3:** 345
21:8 f   **Vol. 1:** 510

Numbers *(cont'd)*

21:9	**Vol. 1:** 390
21:14	**Vol. 1:** 243
21:16 ff	**Vol. 3:** 459
21:16	**Vol. 2:** 32
21:17	**Vol. 3:** 459, 672–673
21:21	**Vol. 1:** 194
21:22	**Vol. 1:** 520
21:23	**Vol. 2:** 32
21:27	**Vol. 3:** 119
21:29	**Vol. 3:** 590
21:35	**Vol. 3:** 248
22–24	**Vol. 1:** 208, 416 **Vol. 2:** 638 **Vol. 3:** 942, 1054
22	**Vol. 2:** 431
22:1–6	**Vol. 1:** 208
22:4	**Vol. 1:** 293
22:5	**Vol. 1:** 194
22:6–12	**Vol. 1:** 416
22:6	**Vol. 1:** 416
22:7	**Vol. 2:** 554
22:8	**Vol. 3:** 178
22:11	**Vol. 1:** 416
22:12	**Vol. 1:** 208
22:17	**Vol. 1:** 416
22:19	**Vol. 2:** 773
22:20	**Vol. 2:** 898
22:22	**Vol. 1:** 101 **Vol. 3:** 468
22:25	**Vol. 3:** 948
22:28	**Vol. 2:** 726
22:31	**Vol. 1:** 208 **Vol. 2:** 876 **Vol. 3:** 311, 312
22:32	**Vol. 3:** 468
22:38	**Vol. 1:** 208
23:1 f	**Vol. 3:** 418
23:1	**Vol. 3:** 117
23:3–5	**Vol. 1:** 208
23:4	**Vol. 3:** 418
23:5	**Vol. 3:** 1120
23:7–18	**Vol. 2:** 745
23:7–10	**Vol. 1:** 208
23:7	**Vol. 1:** 416 **Vol. 2:** 318
23:9	**Vol. 1:** 688, 694 **Vol. 2:** 307
23:10	**Vol. 2:** 318 **Vol. 3:** 355
23:14	**Vol. 3:** 418
23:16	**Vol. 3:** 1120
23:18–24	**Vol. 1:** 208
23:19	**Vol. 2:** 470 **Vol. 3:** 226, 613, 622
23:23	**Vol. 2:** 318, 554
23:27	**Vol. 2:** 815
23:29 f	**Vol. 3:** 418
23:29	**Vol. 3:** 117
24:1	**Vol. 2:** 103, 554
24:2	**Vol. 2:** 898 **Vol. 3:** 691
24:3–9	**Vol. 1:** 208
24:3	**Vol. 2:** 745
24:4	**Vol. 1:** 527 **Vol. 3:** 311, 1118
24:5 f	**Vol. 1:** 208
24:7	**Vol. 2:** 899 **Vol. 3:** 988
24:9	**Vol. 3:** 255
24:10	**Vol. 2:** 149
24:15–24	**Vol. 1:** 208
24:15	**Vol. 2:** 745
24:16	**Vol. 3:** 311, 1118
24:17	**Vol. 1:** 407 **Vol. 2:** 308, 313, 337, 495, 557, 596, 677 **Vol. 3:** 649–650, 652, 734, 736
24:18	**Vol. 1:** 554
24:20–23	**Vol. 2:** 745
25	**Vol. 2:** 638
25:1–18	**Vol. 2:** 699 **Vol. 3:** 154
25:1–3	**Vol. 2:** 677
25:1–2	**Vol. 2:** 677–678
25:1	**Vol. 3:** 1067
25:2	**Vol. 2:** 876
25:3	**Vol. 1:** 109 **Vol. 2:** 60
25:4	**Vol. 1:** 165 **Vol. 2:** 291
25:5	**Vol. 2:** 60
25:6–11	**Vol. 1:** 109
25:11	**Vol. 3:** 152, 155, 255, 1166
25:12	**Vol. 2:** 778
25:13	**Vol. 3:** 36, 159
26	**Vol. 2:** 638, 789
26:4–63	**Vol. 2:** 695
26:17	**Vol. 1:** 674
26:52–56	**Vol. 2:** 297
27	**Vol. 2:** 638
27:1 f	**Vol. 3:** 1057
27:1–11	**Vol. 3:** 662
27:6	**Vol. 3:** 1057
27:7*	**Vol. 3:** 351
27:11	**Vol. 1:** 673 **Vol. 3:** 354
27:15 ff	**Vol. 2:** 151
27:16	**Vol. 1:** 189, 677
27:17	**Vol. 1:** 191 **Vol. 2:** 412–413, 459
27:18	**Vol. 2:** 151, 331 **Vol. 3:** 691
27:21 ff	**Vol. 2:** 331
27:21	**Vol. 2:** 296
27:23	**Vol. 2:** 151
28 f	**Vol. 2:** 854
28	**Vol. 3:** 421–422
28:1 f	**Vol. 3:** 600
28:2	**Vol. 3:** 424
28:3	**Vol. 3:** 924
28:5 ff	**Vol. 3:** 422
28:5–18	**Vol. 2:** 711
28:7	**Vol. 3:** 208, 423, 786
28:8	**Vol. 3:** 423
28:9–29:39	**Vol. 1:** 626
28:9–24	**Vol. 3:** 423
28:9 f	**Vol. 3:** 37, 792
28:9	**Vol. 2:** 890 **Vol. 3:** 407, 924
28:11	**Vol. 3:** 924
28:13	**Vol. 3:** 421
28:14	**Vol. 3:** 423, 919
28:16	**Vol. 2:** 675
28:19	**Vol. 3:** 924
28:25	**Vol. 1:** 272
28:26–31	**Vol. 2:** 783

Numbers *(cont'd)*

28:26	**Vol. 2:** 675 **Vol. 3:** 422
28:27	**Vol. 3:** 924
28:31	**Vol. 3:** 423, 924
29	**Vol. 3:** 421–422
29:1–11	**Vol. 1:** 626
29:2	**Vol. 3:** 924
29:3–14	**Vol. 2:** 711
29:3	**Vol. 3:** 422
29:6–37	**Vol. 3:** 423
29:7	**Vol. 1:** 495, 612
29:8	**Vol. 3:** 924
29:9	**Vol. 3:** 422
29:11	**Vol. 3:** 153
29:13	**Vol. 3:** 924
29:14	**Vol. 3:** 422
29:17	**Vol. 3:** 924
29:20	**Vol. 3:** 924
29:23	**Vol. 3:** 924
29:26	**Vol. 3:** 924
29:29	**Vol. 3:** 924
29:32	**Vol. 3:** 924
29:36	**Vol. 3:** 924
29:39	**Vol. 3:** 422–423
30	**Vol. 3:** 1057
30:1 ff	**Vol. 2:** 43
30:1*	**Vol. 1:** 165
30:3–12	**Vol. 1:** 472
30:3 f	**Vol. 3:** 740
30:3	**Vol. 3:** 183
30:4*	**Vol. 3:** 224
30:5*	**Vol. 3:** 224
30:9*	**Vol. 3:** 224
30:12*	**Vol. 3:** 224
30:14	**Vol. 1:** 495
30:16†	**Vol. 3:** 354
31	**Vol. 2:** 638
31:1–54	**Vol. 3:** 155
31:2	**Vol. 3:** 93
31:3 ff	**Vol. 1:** 294
31:6	**Vol. 3:** 786
31:7 ff	**Vol. 3:** 593
31:7 f	**Vol. 1:** 429
31:9	**Vol. 3:** 590
31:12 ff	**Vol. 1:** 294
31:16	**Vol. 2:** 677
31:17 f	**Vol. 2:** 569
31:17	**Vol. 2:** 587
31:18	**Vol. 2:** 587
31:21	**Vol. 3:** 354
31:22 f	**Vol. 3:** 419
31:25–41	**Vol. 1:** 252
31:28	**Vol. 3:** 756
31:29	**Vol. 3:** 416
31:32–47	**Vol. 3:** 593
31:32	**Vol. 1:** 655
31:35	**Vol. 2:** 587
31:37–41	**Vol. 3:** 756
31:50	**Vol. 3:** 154, 498

31:54	**Vol. 3:** 236
32	**Vol. 2:** 638
32:2	**Vol. 1:** 294
32:4	**Vol. 1:** 294
32:10	**Vol. 1:** 109 **Vol. 2:** 889
32:18 f	**Vol. 2:** 298
32:23	**Vol. 3:** 574
32:33	**Vol. 3:** 748
32:39	**Vol. 1:** 463
33–36	**Vol. 2:** 638
33:2	**Vol. 2:** 639
33:8 f	**Vol. 1:** 202
33:9	**Vol. 3:** 986
33:10 f	**Vol. 3:** 983
33:16–36	**Vol. 3:** 1013
33:16 f	**Vol. 3:** 238
33:38	**Vol. 3:** 937
33:52	**Vol. 1:** 463
33:55	**Vol. 1:** 726 **Vol. 3:** 268
34:3	**Vol. 3:** 444
34:6	**Vol. 1:** 472
34:11	**Vol. 3:** 983
34:13–28	**Vol. 2:** 695
34:18–28	**Vol. 3:** 871
34:22–15	**Vol. 3:** 94
35	**Vol. 3:** 35
35:5	**Vol. 3:** 940
35:12	**Vol. 1:** 294
35:15	**Vol. 1:** 691
35:19	**Vol. 2:** 96 **Vol. 3:** 94, 159, 190
35:21	**Vol. 2:** 96 **Vol. 3:** 190
35:23	**Vol. 1:** 553
35:24	**Vol. 1:** 294 **Vol. 3:** 190
35:25	**Vol. 2:** 711 **Vol. 3:** 190
35:27	**Vol. 2:** 142 **Vol. 3:** 190
35:29	**Vol. 3:** 354
35:30	**Vol. 1:** 302 **Vol. 2:** 471, 686 **Vol. 3:** 1041
35:31 f	**Vol. 3:** 190, 192
35:31	**Vol. 3:** 94, 190
35:32	**Vol. 3:** 190
35:33	**Vol. 3:** 153–154, 159–160
36	**Vol. 3:** 1057
36:1–12	**Vol. 3:** 662
36:5–9	**Vol. 2:** 577
36:8	**Vol. 3:** 662
36:13	**Vol. 3:** 354

Deuteronomy

1–3	**Vol. 3:** 1103
1	**Vol. 3:** 1013
1:1–31:23	**Vol. 2:** 638
1:1	**Vol. 2:** 638, 830 **Vol. 3:** 1103
1:2	**Vol. 3:** 1013
1:3	**Vol. 1:** 332
1:5	**Vol. 1:** 164
1:8	**Vol. 1:** 77 **Vol. 2:** 367 **Vol. 3:** 522, 740
1:9 ff	**Vol. 1:** 195

Deuteronomy *(cont'd)*

1:9	**Vol. 3:** 836
1:10	**Vol. 3:** 734
1:12	**Vol. 1:** 712
1:13	**Vol. 3:** 1027
1:15	**Vol. 1:** 196 **Vol. 2:** 363 **Vol. 3:** 1027
1:16	**Vol. 3:** 836
1:17	**Vol. 1:** 587 **Vol. 2:** 363, 428 **Vol. 3:** 1120
1:18	**Vol. 3:** 836, 1103
1:19	**Vol. 3:** 946
1:21	**Vol. 1:** 622
1:25	**Vol. 1:** 721
1:26	**Vol. 1:** 589
1:29	**Vol. 1:** 622
1:31	**Vol. 1:** 617 **Vol. 3:** 805, 843
1:32	**Vol. 3:** 878
1:33	**Vol. 3:** 569, 946
1:34 f	**Vol. 3:** 740
1:34	**Vol. 3:** 742
1:35	**Vol. 2:** 36
1:38	**Vol. 3:** 208
1:39	**Vol. 1:** 565
1:43–45	**Vol. 2:** 864
1:43	**Vol. 2:** 175 **Vol. 3:** 583
2:4	**Vol. 1:** 255 **Vol. 2:** 90
2:5	**Vol. 2:** 369 **Vol. 3:** 464, 523
2:7	**Vol. 3:** 804, 1148
2:11	**Vol. 3:** 823
2:14	**Vol. 2:** 458 **Vol. 3:** 740
2:20	**Vol. 3:** 823
2:26	**Vol. 1:** 194
2:33 f	**Vol. 3:** 836
3:3	**Vol. 3:** 836
3:13	**Vol. 3:** 823
3:20	**Vol. 3:** 255–256
3:21	**Vol. 3:** 208
3:24	**Vol. 2:** 602 **Vol. 3:** 569
3:27	**Vol. 3:** 806
3:28	**Vol. 1:** 570 **Vol. 3:** 208
4:1	**Vol. 2:** 258 **Vol. 3:** 354, 760
4:2	**Vol. 3:** 1103
4:3	**Vol. 1:** 481
4:5–10	**Vol. 2:** 307
4:5 f	**Vol. 3:** 354
4:6	**Vol. 3:** 1027
4:7	**Vol. 2:** 53
4:8	**Vol. 3:** 354
4:9–24	**Vol. 3:** 485
4:10	**Vol. 1:** 293, 484 **Vol. 2:** 889 **Vol. 3:** 760, 1013, 1103
4:12	**Vol. 1:** 585, 655, 704
4:13	**Vol. 3:** 484, 1103
4:14	**Vol. 1:** 484 **Vol. 3:** 354, 760, 836
4:15	**Vol. 1:** 655 **Vol. 3:** 485
4:16 ff	**Vol. 2:** 501
4:16	**Vol. 2:** 287
4:17	**Vol. 1:** 172
4:18	**Vol. 1:** 670
4:19	**Vol. 1:** 522 **Vol. 2:** 189, 876 **Vol. 3:** 550, 731, 735
4:20	**Vol. 2:** 98, 797
4:21	**Vol. 3:** 740
4:24	**Vol. 1:** 655
4:25 ff	**Vol. 1:** 688
4:26	**Vol. 3:** 1041
4:27 ff	**Vol. 3:** 249
4:27	**Vol. 2:** 428, 791
4:28	**Vol. 3:** 550
4:29	**Vol. 3:** 531
4:30	**Vol. 1:** 354
4:31	**Vol. 3:** 740
4:32	**Vol. 1:** 379 **Vol. 2:** 194 **Vol. 3:** 1120
4:33	**Vol. 1:** 655
4:34	**Vol. 2:** 627 **Vol. 3:** 799
4:35	**Vol. 2:** 627
4:36	**Vol. 2:** 190 **Vol. 3:** 776, 1103, 1120
4:37	**Vol. 1:** 538
4:39	**Vol. 2:** 190
4:40	**Vol. 3:** 354
4:41	**Vol. 1:** 472
4:43	**Vol. 3:** 1009
4:45	**Vol. 3:** 354
5	**Vol. 3:** 1013
5:1	**Vol. 2:** 134, 173 **Vol. 3:** 354
5:2	**Vol. 3:** 1013
5:4	**Vol. 3:** 409
5:5–21	**Vol. 2:** 639
5:5	**Vol. 3:** 1103
5:6 ff	**Vol. 2:** 173
5:6–21	**Vol. 1:** 54
5:7–10	**Vol. 2:** 871
5:7 f	**Vol. 2:** 284
5:8	**Vol. 1:** 175
5:9	**Vol. 1:** 219, 555 **Vol. 2:** 876 **Vol. 3:** 156, 550
5:10	**Vol. 2:** 698
5:11 ff	**Vol. 3:** 94
5:11	**Vol. 2:** 871 **Vol. 3:** 342
5:12–15	**Vol. 2:** 871, 889 **Vol. 3:** 256, 406
5:13 f	**Vol. 3:** 1148
5:13	**Vol. 2:** 650
5:14	**Vol. 1:** 115 **Vol. 3:** 254, 594
5:15	**Vol. 2:** 890 **Vol. 3:** 232, 235
5:16–21	**Vol. 2:** 871
5:16–20	**Vol. 3:** 379
5:16	**Vol. 2:** 43, 478 **Vol. 3:** 95, 1057, 1070
5:17*	**Vol. 3:** 183, 1041
5:18	**Vol. 2:** 576, 580, 583 **Vol. 3:** 183, 536
5:19	**Vol. 3:** 377
5:21	**Vol. 1:** 336 **Vol. 3:** 1057
5:22	**Vol. 1:** 296 **Vol. 3:** 484
5:24	**Vol. 2:** 45
5:25*	**Vol. 3:** 351
5:28*	**Vol. 3:** 354, 760
5:33	**Vol. 3:** 255, 257
6–8	**Vol. 3:** 804–805
6	**Vol. 3:** 806
6:1 f	**Vol. 3:** 354

Deuteronomy *(cont'd)*

6:1 **Vol. 3:** 760
6:3 **Vol. 1:** 683 **Vol. 3:** 354
6:4 ff **Vol. 2:** 173, 864
6:4–9 **Vol. 2:** 174, 177, 864 **Vol. 3:** 105, 1161
6:4 f **Vol. 2:** 73, 720 **Vol. 3:** 806
6:4 **Vol. 2:** 720–721 **Vol. 3:** 173, 490, 694, 1103
6:5 **Vol. 1:** 259, 334, 456, 622 **Vol. 2:** 68, 177, 181, 427, 541, 544 **Vol. 3:** 131, 542, 685
6:6 **Vol. 3:** 484, 836, 1120
6:7 **Vol. 1:** 288, 617
6:8 f **Vol. 3:** 484
6:8 **Vol. 2:** 136, 149, 864 **Vol. 3:** 484, 490, 559
6:9 **Vol. 3:** 483
6:10–12 **Vol. 1:** 484
6:10 **Vol. 1:** 77 **Vol. 3:** 740
6:11 f **Vol. 2:** 272
6:13 ff **Vol. 1:** 109
6:13 **Vol. 1:** 622 **Vol. 2:** 349, 724, 876, 893 **Vol. 3:** 550, 739, 806–807
6:16 **Vol. 2:** 893 **Vol. 3:** 790, 799–802, 805–806
6:17 **Vol. 3:** 354
6:18 **Vol. 2:** 103 **Vol. 3:** 740
6:20 ff **Vol. 1:** 617 **Vol. 3:** 358
6:20 **Vol. 3:** 354
6:22 **Vol. 2:** 627
6:23 **Vol. 3:** 740
6:24 **Vol. 1:** 332 **Vol. 3:** 354
7:1 f **Vol. 3:** 960
7:1 **Vol. 1:** 96 **Vol. 2:** 300
7:3 f **Vol. 2:** 576
7:4 **Vol. 1:** 607 **Vol. 3:** 550
7:5 **Vol. 3:** 94, 418
7:6–11 **Vol. 2:** 541
7:6 **Vol. 2:** 226, 297, 791, 797, 800, 838, 840
7:7 **Vol. 1:** 538 **Vol. 2:** 307, 798
7:8 **Vol. 1:** 716 **Vol. 2:** 307 **Vol. 3:** 192–193, 717, 740
7:9–11 **Vol. 1:** 555
7:9 **Vol. 1:** 596 **Vol. 2:** 698–699
7:10 **Vol. 1:** 585
7:11 **Vol. 3:** 354
7:12 **Vol. 3:** 354, 740
7:13–16 **Vol. 1:** 209
7:13 **Vol. 1:** 721 **Vol. 2:** 711 **Vol. 3:** 919
7:15 **Vol. 1:** 555 **Vol. 3:** 999
7:16 **Vol. 3:** 550
7:18 **Vol. 3:** 232, 235, 238
7:19–24 **Vol. 3:** 960
7:19 **Vol. 2:** 627 **Vol. 3:** 717, 799
7:21 **Vol. 3:** 716–717
7:25 **Vol. 3:** 94
7:26 **Vol. 1:** 414
8 **Vol. 3:** 806

8:1–6 **Vol. 3:** 777
8:1 **Vol. 3:** 740
8:2 ff **Vol. 3:** 804
8:2 f **Vol. 2:** 871, 893
8:2 **Vol. 3:** 232, 799–800, 804, 937, 1005
8:3 **Vol. 1:** 250, 252 **Vol. 2:** 267–268, 479–480, 893 **Vol. 3:** 329, 805, 1120
8:4–9 **Vol. 3:** 487
8:4 **Vol. 2:** 714 **Vol. 3:** 805
8:5 **Vol. 1:** 617 **Vol. 3:** 776, 778
8:6 **Vol. 3:** 946
8:7 **Vol. 3:** 986, 988
8:8 **Vol. 1:** 723 **Vol. 3:** 806
8:9 **Vol. 2:** 822
8:10 **Vol. 2:** 272
8:11 **Vol. 3:** 354, 806
8:14 ff **Vol. 3:** 805
8:14 **Vol. 3:** 806
8:15 f **Vol. 2:** 893
8:15 **Vol. 1:** 510 **Vol. 3:** 988, 1005
8:16 **Vol. 3:** 799
8:17 **Vol. 1:** 484
8:18 **Vol. 3:** 232, 740
8:19 **Vol. 2:** 876 **Vol. 3:** 806
9:3 **Vol. 1:** 655
9:4–6 **Vol. 1:** 484
9:4 f **Vol. 2:** 93
9:5 **Vol. 1:** 77 **Vol. 2:** 307 **Vol. 3:** 1104
9:7 **Vol. 3:** 232, 235
9:9 **Vol. 1:** 612
9:10 **Vol. 1:** 293, 295 **Vol. 3:** 484
9:14 **Vol. 1:** 471
9:16 **Vol. 3:** 806
9:18 **Vol. 3:** 804
9:19 **Vol. 1:** 318 **Vol. 2:** 893 **Vol. 3:** 324, 836
9:22 **Vol. 1:** 456 **Vol. 3:** 238, 799–800, 804
9:23 f **Vol. 1:** 589
9:24 **Vol. 2:** 889
9:26–29 **Vol. 2:** 297, 863
9:26 **Vol. 2:** 602 **Vol. 3:** 192–193
9:27 **Vol. 1:** 77 **Vol. 3:** 235, 608
9:29 **Vol. 2:** 303, 602
10:1 ff **Vol. 3:** 484
10:1–5 **Vol. 3:** 787
10:4 **Vol. 1:** 293 **Vol. 3:** 1103, 1120
10:8 **Vol. 1:** 474 **Vol. 2:** 649–650
10:9 **Vol. 1:** 636 **Vol. 2:** 297, 302–303 **Vol. 3:** 33
10:10 **Vol. 3:** 1019
10:12 f **Vol. 2:** 42, 541 **Vol. 3:** 550
10:12 **Vol. 1:** 259 **Vol. 2:** 307, 856 **Vol. 3:** 946
10:13 **Vol. 3:** 354
10:14 **Vol. 2:** 189–190
10:16 **Vol. 1:** 154, 241, 308 **Vol. 2:** 184
10:17 f **Vol. 1:** 622
10:17 **Vol. 1:** 587 **Vol. 2:** 41, 622 **Vol. 3:** 713

Deuteronomy *(cont'd)*

10:18   Vol. 1: 688   Vol. 2: 363, 737   Vol. 3: 1073–1074
10:20   Vol. 2: 349, 876   Vol. 3: 739
10:21   Vol. 3: 318
10:22   Vol. 3: 680, 734
11:1   Vol. 3: 354
11:2   Vol. 1: 484   Vol. 2: 425   Vol. 3: 513, 717, 777–778
11:3   Vol. 3: 1148
11:6   Vol. 1: 711
11:9   Vol. 3: 274
11:11   Vol. 3: 988
11:12   Vol. 1: 189
11:13 ff   Vol. 3: 1001
11:13–21   Vol. 2: 174, 177, 864   Vol. 3: 105, 487
11:13   Vol. 3: 550
11:14   Vol. 2: 711   Vol. 3: 846, 919
11:15   Vol. 1: 743
11:16   Vol. 2: 876
11:18   Vol. 2: 136, 149, 864   Vol. 3: 559
11:19   Vol. 3: 760
11:21   Vol. 2: 189
11:22   Vol. 3: 914
11:24   Vol. 2: 369
11:26 ff   Vol. 3: 805
11:26–29   Vol. 1: 416
11:26 f   Vol. 3: 938
11:29   Vol. 1: 210   Vol. 3: 1010
12–26   Vol. 3: 418
12   Vol. 3: 1103–1104
12:1 ff   Vol. 3: 806
12:2–9   Vol. 3: 1010
12:2   Vol. 3: 786
12:3   Vol. 3: 418
12:5–6   Vol. 2: 693
12:5   Vol. 2: 190, 803   Vol. 3: 786
12:6–19   Vol. 2: 693
12:6   Vol. 3: 416, 852
12:7   Vol. 2: 521
12:9   Vol. 3: 256
12:10   Vol. 1: 426, 663   Vol. 3: 255–257
12:11   Vol. 1: 272   Vol. 2: 41, 190, 650, 693   Vol. 3: 415, 852
12:12   Vol. 2: 297, 302–304   Vol. 3: 594
12:13   Vol. 3: 513
12:15–21   Vol. 2: 802
12:16   Vol. 1: 226   Vol. 3: 158
12:17–18   Vol. 2: 693
12:17   Vol. 1: 344   Vol. 2: 711   Vol. 3: 415, 852
12:18   Vol. 3: 594, 608, 805
12:19   Vol. 3: 841
12:20 f   Vol. 1: 456
12:20   Vol. 3: 680
12:21   Vol. 2: 190   Vol. 3: 680, 805
12:23   Vol. 1: 221, 226   Vol. 2: 477   Vol. 3: 151, 158, 425, 680
12:28   Vol. 2: 103   Vol. 3: 1103

12:31   Vol. 1: 655   Vol. 3: 421
13   Vol. 1: 433
13:1–5   Vol. 2: 96   Vol. 3: 95, 800, 806
13:1   Vol. 2: 350   Vol. 3: 1120
13:2 ff   Vol. 2: 629
13:2–6   Vol. 1: 512
13:3   Vol. 3: 680, 800
13:4*   Vol. 1: 492   Vol. 3: 799
13:5*   Vol. 1: 481   Vol. 3: 192–193
13:6 ff   Vol. 1: 556
13:6   Vol. 1: 240, 570   Vol. 2: 458, 498   Vol. 3: 83
13:7   Vol. 1: 518   Vol. 2: 53
13:9   Vol. 1: 196, 665
13:10–16   Vol. 3: 94
13:10   Vol. 1: 607   Vol. 3: 227
13:11   Vol. 1: 622
13:13   Vol. 1: 607
13:14   Vol. 3: 880
13:15   Vol. 1: 415   Vol. 2: 856
13:16*   Vol. 1: 413, 654   Vol. 2: 32   Vol. 3: 828
13:17   Vol. 1: 414
14:1 f   Vol. 1: 617
14:1   Vol. 1: 290   Vol. 2: 418, 782   Vol. 3: 638
14:2   Vol. 1: 538   Vol. 2: 226, 297, 797, 800, 838–840   Vol. 3: 200
14:4   Vol. 2: 271
14:8   Vol. 1: 672
14:11–20   Vol. 1: 172
14:17   Vol. 1: 172
14:19   Vol. 1: 172
14:21   Vol. 1: 684   Vol. 2: 226
14:22–29   Vol. 3: 852, 1053
14:22–27   Vol. 2: 693
14:22–23   Vol. 2: 211, 694
14:23 ff   Vol. 3: 805
14:23 f   Vol. 1: 272
14:23   Vol. 1: 484   Vol. 2: 650, 711, 803   Vol. 3: 786
14:25   Vol. 3: 786
14:27   Vol. 2: 302
14:28–29   Vol. 2: 693
14:28   Vol. 2: 737   Vol. 3: 852
14:29   Vol. 2: 737, 823   Vol. 3: 1074, 1148
15:1 ff   Vol. 1: 255
15:1–18   Vol. 2: 823
15:1–9   Vol. 1: 698
15:1 f   Vol. 2: 667
15:2–18   Vol. 3: 191
15:2   Vol. 1: 272, 698   Vol. 2: 666–667
15:3   Vol. 1: 546, 684
15:6   Vol. 1: 96, 165
15:9   Vol. 2: 667   Vol. 3: 1120
15:10   Vol. 3: 1120
15:12 ff   Vol. 1: 716   Vol. 3: 593
15:12 f   Vol. 1: 716
15:12   Vol. 2: 306   Vol. 3: 594
15:13 ff   Vol. 1: 716

Deuteronomy *(cont'd)*

15:15	**Vol. 3:** 190, 192–193, 232, 235, 1103
15:16 f	**Vol. 2:** 572 **Vol. 3:** 594, 608
15:17	**Vol. 3:** 594, 827
15:18	**Vol. 2:** 139
15:19–23	**Vol. 3:** 852
15:19	**Vol. 1:** 203 **Vol. 3:** 237
15:20	**Vol. 3:** 805
15:21	**Vol. 1:** 219 **Vol. 2:** 415
15:23	**Vol. 3:** 158
16:1 ff	**Vol. 1:** 626
16:1–16	**Vol. 1:** 626
16:1–8	**Vol. 1:** 632
16:1	**Vol. 1:** 632 **Vol. 2:** 675
16:2	**Vol. 1:** 272, 632 **Vol. 3:** 805
16:3 f	**Vol. 2:** 676, 716
16:3	**Vol. 2:** 461, 522 **Vol. 3:** 232
16:5–7	**Vol. 2:** 521
16:6 f	**Vol. 1:** 538
16:6	**Vol. 1:** 272 **Vol. 3:** 805
16:8	**Vol. 3:** 183
16:9–12	**Vol. 2:** 783
16:10	**Vol. 1:** 360 **Vol. 2:** 783
16:11	**Vol. 1:** 272 **Vol. 2:** 737 **Vol. 3:** 594, 805, 1074
16:12	**Vol. 1:** 332 **Vol. 3:** 232, 235
16:13–17	**Vol. 3:** 1005
16:13 f	**Vol. 1:** 360
16:14	**Vol. 2:** 737 **Vol. 3:** 594, 1074
16:16	**Vol. 3:** 155, 805, 813, 835
16:19	**Vol. 1:** 219, 587 **Vol. 2:** 41 **Vol. 3:** 1027
16:20	**Vol. 2:** 258, 806
16:21	**Vol. 3:** 865
17:1	**Vol. 3:** 1087
17:2–7	**Vol. 2:** 96 **Vol. 3:** 95
17:2–6	**Vol. 3:** 28
17:3	**Vol. 2:** 876 **Vol. 3:** 731
17:4	**Vol. 3:** 880
17:6 f	**Vol. 2:** 471 **Vol. 3:** 1041
17:6	**Vol. 2:** 686 **Vol. 3:** 1043, 1062
17:7	**Vol. 3:** 95, 227
17:8–12	**Vol. 3:** 94
17:8	**Vol. 1:** 241 **Vol. 3:** 33, 805
17:9	**Vol. 2:** 440
17:10	**Vol. 3:** 805
17:11 f	**Vol. 2:** 440
17:11	**Vol. 2:** 440
17:12	**Vol. 3:** 29
17:13	**Vol. 1:** 622 **Vol. 2:** 93, 527 **Vol. 3:** 83
17:15	**Vol. 1:** 472
17:17	**Vol. 2:** 576
17:18 ff	**Vol. 1:** 245
17:18	**Vol. 1:** 54, 243 **Vol. 2:** 34 **Vol. 3:** 478, 484
17:19	**Vol. 1:** 484 **Vol. 3:** 354, 1103
18	**Vol. 3:** 418
18:1 f	**Vol. 2:** 297
18:1	**Vol. 2:** 303, 466 **Vol. 3:** 433, 793
18:3	**Vol. 2:** 778
18:4	**Vol. 2:** 711 **Vol. 3:** 415, 919
18:5 f	**Vol. 1:** 538
18:5	**Vol. 1:** 474, 538 **Vol. 2:** 638 **Vol. 3:** 953
18:8	**Vol. 1:** 474 **Vol. 2:** 303
18:9 ff	**Vol. 2:** 189
18:9–14	**Vol. 2:** 296
18:9	**Vol. 2:** 791
18:10–14	**Vol. 2:** 555
18:10 f	**Vol. 2:** 555 **Vol. 3:** 94
18:10	**Vol. 1:** 655 **Vol. 2:** 555, 559 **Vol. 3:** 421
18:11	**Vol. 1:** 444, 450 **Vol. 2:** 206, 559
18:13	**Vol. 2:** 60
18:14	**Vol. 1:** 332
18:15 ff	**Vol. 1:** 66 **Vol. 2:** 337
18:15–18	**Vol. 3:** 80
18:15	**Vol. 1:** 465 **Vol. 2:** 638, 641 **Vol. 3:** 48, 83, 86, 460, 463–465, 624, 643, 696, 864, 1007
18:18 ff	**Vol. 2:** 651
18:18 f	**Vol. 1:** 465 **Vol. 3:** 696
18:18	**Vol. 2:** 641 **Vol. 3:** 48, 86, 460, 463–465
18:19	**Vol. 1:** 465
18:20 ff	**Vol. 3:** 94
18:20	**Vol. 2:** 93, 651 **Vol. 3:** 83
18:21 f	**Vol. 3:** 1104
18:22	**Vol. 2:** 93
19:6	**Vol. 1:** 318 **Vol. 2:** 181
19:10	**Vol. 2:** 142, 525, 854 **Vol. 3:** 159
19:13	**Vol. 3:** 159
19:15 ff	**Vol. 2:** 471 **Vol. 3:** 1041
19:15	**Vol. 1:** 83, 302 **Vol. 2:** 448, 686 **Vol. 3:** 226, 1041, 1043–1045, 1122
19:16 ff	**Vol. 3:** 1041
19:18	**Vol. 3:** 1041
19:19	**Vol. 3:** 95
19:21	**Vol. 3:** 94, 183
20:3	**Vol. 3:** 178
20:4	**Vol. 3:** 207
20:5	**Vol. 2:** 670, 673 **Vol. 3:** 478
20:7	**Vol. 2:** 562, 578
20:10 ff	**Vol. 2:** 802 **Vol. 3:** 593
20:10–20	**Vol. 2:** 699
20:10–14	**Vol. 3:** 593
20:11	**Vol. 2:** 179 **Vol. 3:** 528
20:16 ff	**Vol. 2:** 576
20:17†	**Vol. 1:** 415
20:18	**Vol. 3:** 760
20:19	**Vol. 3:** 951
21:1–9	**Vol. 3:** 94, 151, 154, 159
21:2	**Vol. 1:** 196
21:3	**Vol. 3:** 1161
21:6	**Vol. 2:** 149 **Vol. 3:** 990
21:8 f	**Vol. 3:** 159
21:8	**Vol. 3:** 150–151, 153, 157, 192
21:10 ff	**Vol. 2:** 576 **Vol. 3:** 590

Deuteronomy *(cont'd)*

21:10   **Vol. 3:** 593
21:13   **Vol. 3:** 1065
21:14   **Vol. 1:** 716   **Vol. 2:** 260, 562
21:15 ff   **Vol. 1:** 555, 667
21:17   **Vol. 2:** 317   **Vol. 3:** 266
21:18 ff   **Vol. 3:** 95
21:18   **Vol. 3:** 776
21:19   **Vol. 1:** 343
21:21   **Vol. 2:** 527   **Vol. 3:** 777
21:22 f   **Vol. 1:** 390, 393–394   **Vol. 2:** 96
21:22–23   **Vol. 1:** 265–266
21:23   **Vol. 1:** 233, 264–265, 389–390, 417, 509   **Vol. 2:** 445, 709   **Vol. 3:** 171, 1195
22:1   **Vol. 1:** 115   **Vol. 2:** 458
22:2 ff   **Vol. 3:** 227
22:4   **Vol. 1:** 115
22:9   **Vol. 3:** 918
22:10   **Vol. 1:** 115   **Vol. 2:** 742   **Vol. 3:** 1160
22:13 ff   **Vol. 1:** 555   **Vol. 2:** 562
22:13–21   **Vol. 1:** 505   **Vol. 3:** 1195
22:13–19   **Vol. 2:** 577
22:14   **Vol. 1:** 565   **Vol. 3:** 95
22:18 f   **Vol. 2:** 96
22:18   **Vol. 2:** 96
22:19   **Vol. 3:** 841
22:20 f   **Vol. 2:** 577
22:21   **Vol. 3:** 1024
22:22 ff   **Vol. 2:** 582
22:22–27   **Vol. 2:** 576
22:22 f   **Vol. 2:** 96   **Vol. 3:** 95
22:22   **Vol. 1:** 500, 505   **Vol. 3:** 536, 538, 1065
22:22b   **Vol. 2:** 583
22:23–27   **Vol. 3:** 95
22:23 f   **Vol. 3:** 1058
22:23   **Vol. 2:** 563
22:24   **Vol. 1:** 463
22:25 ff   **Vol. 2:** 577
22:25 f   **Vol. 3:** 1206
22:25   **Vol. 3:** 711
22:27   **Vol. 1:** 520
22:28 f   **Vol. 1:** 505   **Vol. 2:** 577, 582   **Vol. 3:** 95
22:28   **Vol. 3:** 711
22:29   **Vol. 2:** 96   **Vol. 3:** 841
23:1   **Vol. 1:** 560
23:2 ff   **Vol. 1:** 293
23:2   **Vol. 1:** 295
23:3 ff   **Vol. 1:** 295
23:3   **Vol. 1:** 295   **Vol. 3:** 828
23:4   **Vol. 1:** 295
23:5*   **Vol. 2:** 139   **Vol. 3:** 37
23:6*   **Vol. 2:** 778   **Vol. 3:** 828
23:9   **Vol. 1:** 295
23:10   **Vol. 3:** 1120
23:11 f   **Vol. 3:** 989
23:15 f   **Vol. 1:** 717   **Vol. 3:** 594
23:17 f   **Vol. 1:** 499

23:17   **Vol. 1:** 537   **Vol. 2:** 570
23:18 f   **Vol. 1:** 625
23:18   **Vol. 1:** 117
23:19 f   **Vol. 2:** 254
23:19*   **Vol. 2:** 139
23:21 ff   **Vol. 2:** 43
23:21   **Vol. 3:** 183
23:23   **Vol. 3:** 740
23:25   **Vol. 3:** 408
24:1 ff   **Vol. 1:** 505   **Vol. 3:** 189
24:1–14   **Vol. 3:** 660
24:1–4   **Vol. 1:** 500   **Vol. 2:** 576   **Vol. 3:** 172, 181, 183, 534–535, 538–539, 1057
24:1   **Vol. 1:** 243–244, 335, 505, 606   **Vol. 2:** 116   **Vol. 3:** 484, 538, 1065, 1195
24:3   **Vol. 1:** 243–244, 606   **Vol. 3:** 484
24:4   **Vol. 3:** 95
24:5   **Vol. 2:** 562, 578   **Vol. 3:** 1057
24:6   **Vol. 3:** 394
24:7   **Vol. 3:** 377, 380, 593–594
24:7a   **Vol. 2:** 565
24:8   **Vol. 3:** 45
24:9   **Vol. 3:** 235
24:10   **Vol. 2:** 666–667
24:13   **Vol. 3:** 358
24:14–22   **Vol. 2:** 823
24:14 f   **Vol. 2:** 257
24:14   **Vol. 1:** 688   **Vol. 2:** 139   **Vol. 3:** 379
24:15   **Vol. 1:** 410   **Vol. 2:** 139
24:16   **Vol. 2:** 139   **Vol. 3:** 1192
24:17–22   **Vol. 2:** 737
24:17   **Vol. 3:** 1073–1074
24:18   **Vol. 3:** 192–193, 232, 235, 1103, 1120
24:19 ff   **Vol. 3:** 1073–1074
24:20   **Vol. 3:** 232, 1120
24:21   **Vol. 3:** 918
24:22   **Vol. 3:** 232, 235, 1103, 1120
25:1–3   **Vol. 1:** 163   **Vol. 2:** 96
25:1   **Vol. 3:** 355
25:3   **Vol. 2:** 696
25:4   **Vol. 1:** 115, 737   **Vol. 2:** 446, 755   **Vol. 3:** 490–492
25:5 ff   **Vol. 2:** 691   **Vol. 3:** 1074
25:5–10†   **Vol. 1:** 499   **Vol. 2:** 576–577   **Vol. 3:** 95, 487, 1055
25:8   **Vol. 1:** 196
25:12†   **Vol. 2:** 96   **Vol. 3:** 448
25:14 f   **Vol. 3:** 402
25:15   **Vol. 3:** 356
25:17   **Vol. 3:** 235
25:19   **Vol. 3:** 255–256
26   **Vol. 1:** 367
26:1 ff   **Vol. 1:** 210
26:1–15   **Vol. 2:** 693   **Vol. 3:** 852
26:2   **Vol. 1:** 538   **Vol. 3:** 415
26:5–11   **Vol. 1:** 633
26:5   **Vol. 2:** 683
26:6   **Vol. 3:** 1148
26:9   **Vol. 1:** 683
26:10   **Vol. 2:** 876   **Vol. 3:** 415, 852

Deuteronomy *(cont'd)*

26:12–19 **Vol. 2:** 797
26:12–15 **Vol. 2:** 737
26:12 f **Vol. 3:** 1073–1074
26:12 **Vol. 2:** 693, 823 **Vol. 3:** 852
26:15 **Vol. 2:** 190
26:16–19 **Vol. 2:** 797
26:16 f **Vol. 3:** 354
26:18 f **Vol. 2:** 226
26:18 **Vol. 2:** 297, 838, 840
26:19 **Vol. 2:** 226
27 ff **Vol. 3:** 928
27 **Vol. 3:** 1103
27:2–8 **Vol. 2:** 639
27:3 **Vol. 3:** 483–484, 1103
27:4 **Vol. 1:** 67 **Vol. 2:** 878 **Vol. 3:** 451–452
27:5 **Vol. 3:** 418
27:7 **Vol. 3:** 422
27:8 **Vol. 3:** 483
27:9 f **Vol. 3:** 33
27:10 **Vol. 3:** 354
27:12 f **Vol. 3:** 1010
27:14–30:20 **Vol. 3:** 805
27:14–26 **Vol. 3:** 33
27:15 ff **Vol. 1:** 416 **Vol. 3:** 1104
27:15–26 **Vol. 1:** 97–98
27:15 **Vol. 2:** 215, 287
27:18 **Vol. 1:** 218 **Vol. 2:** 458
27:19 **Vol. 2:** 737 **Vol. 3:** 70, 1073–1074
27:20–23 **Vol. 2:** 577
27:25 **Vol. 2:** 41 **Vol. 3:** 159
27:26 **Vol. 1:** 417 **Vol. 2:** 445 **Vol. 3:** 226, 491
28 **Vol. 1:** 208 **Vol. 3:** 135, 740
28:1–15 **Vol. 2:** 139
28:1–14 **Vol. 1:** 210 **Vol. 3:** 800, 804
28:1 f **Vol. 1:** 210
28:1 **Vol. 2:** 174
28:3 ff **Vol. 3:** 140
28:3–7 **Vol. 1:** 209
28:4–11 **Vol. 1:** 288
28:5 **Vol. 1:** 209
28:11 **Vol. 1:** 732
28:12 **Vol. 1:** 96 **Vol. 3:** 835
28:13 **Vol. 2:** 158
28:14 **Vol. 1:** 332 **Vol. 3:** 1103
28:15 ff **Vol. 1:** 219
28:15–68 **Vol. 1:** 210 **Vol. 2:** 139
28:15 f **Vol. 1:** 210
28:15 **Vol. 1:** 332 **Vol. 3:** 382, 1104, 1108
28:16 ff **Vol. 1:** 416
28:20 **Vol. 1:** 463
28:21 **Vol. 2:** 349
28:25 **Vol. 1:** 685
28:26 **Vol. 1:** 264, 444
28:27 **Vol. 1:** 520
28:28 f **Vol. 1:** 218
28:28 **Vol. 1:** 527

28:29 **Vol. 1:** 218 **Vol. 3:** 574
28:30 **Vol. 3:** 382, 1108
28:33 **Vol. 3:** 144
28:40 **Vol. 1:** 121 **Vol. 2:** 711
28:45 **Vol. 3:** 354
28:47 **Vol. 2:** 181
28:48 **Vol. 1:** 312
28:49 **Vol. 1:** 173 **Vol. 2:** 55, 444, 446
28:50 **Vol. 2:** 622
28:51† **Vol. 2:** 711
28:53 **Vol. 2:** 807
28:55 **Vol. 2:** 807
28:56 **Vol. 2:** 735 **Vol. 3:** 799
28:57 **Vol. 2:** 807
28:58–64 **Vol. 2:** 798
28:58 **Vol. 1:** 243 **Vol. 2:** 639 **Vol. 3:** 1103, 1120
28:60 **Vol. 2:** 349
28:61 **Vol. 2:** 440, 639 **Vol. 3:** 999
28:62 **Vol. 3:** 249, 734
28:65 **Vol. 1:** 239 **Vol. 3:** 255
29:2* **Vol. 2:** 627 **Vol. 3:** 799
29:4 **Vol. 2:** 174 **Vol. 3:** 805
29:5 **Vol. 2:** 714 **Vol. 3:** 804
29:12 ff **Vol. 3:** 740
29:13 **Vol. 1:** 77
29:15 **Vol. 2:** 313
29:16* **Vol. 2:** 284
29:17 **Vol. 3:** 687
29:18 ff **Vol. 1:** 108
29:18 **Vol. 1:** 202 **Vol. 2:** 27, 782, 847 **Vol. 3:** 866
29:19 f **Vol. 2:** 639
29:19* **Vol. 2:** 237
29:20 **Vol. 2:** 440 **Vol. 3:** 152, 1166
29:22 **Vol. 1:** 109
29:23 **Vol. 3:** 93, 444, 560
29:25 ff **Vol. 1:** 109
29:25* **Vol. 2:** 876
29:26 **Vol. 2:** 639
29:28* **Vol. 1:** 688 **Vol. 3:** 1103, 1154
29:29 **Vol. 2:** 215 **Vol. 3:** 828
30:1–20 **Vol. 2:** 478
30:1–19 **Vol. 1:** 416
30:3 **Vol. 2:** 32
30:4 **Vol. 1:** 518, 685 **Vol. 2:** 32, 35, 38, 917
30:6 **Vol. 1:** 154 **Vol. 2:** 786
30:7 **Vol. 1:** 555
30:9 **Vol. 3:** 787
30:10 **Vol. 2:** 440, 639 **Vol. 3:** 354
30:11–14 **Vol. 2:** 174
30:12–14 **Vol. 3:** 1122
30:12 **Vol. 2:** 189
30:14 **Vol. 1:** 484 **Vol. 2:** 441 **Vol. 3:** 1103
30:15 ff **Vol. 3:** 938
30:15–20 **Vol. 2:** 297
30:15 f **Vol. 3:** 938
30:15 **Vol. 1:** 434 **Vol. 2:** 99, 478 **Vol. 3:** 140
30:16 **Vol. 3:** 354

Deuteronomy *(cont'd)*

30:17 f	*Vol.* **3**: 938
30:17	*Vol.* **2**: 876
30:18	*Vol.* **1**: 463
30:19	*Vol.* **1**: 210 *Vol.* **2**: 478, 481 *Vol.* **3**: 740, 940
30:20	*Vol.* **1**: 77
31:3 ff	*Vol.* **3**: 208
31:3	*Vol.* **2**: 331
31:4 ff	*Vol.* **3**: 33
31:7	*Vol.* **2**: 331
31:8	*Vol.* **2**: 331
31:9	*Vol.* **2**: 639 *Vol.* **3**: 484
31:10	*Vol.* **2**: 667 *Vol.* **3**: 813
31:11	*Vol.* **2**: 639
31:12 f	*Vol.* **1**: 484
31:12	*Vol.* **3**: 1103
31:14 f	*Vol.* **2**: 331
31:16	*Vol.* **3**: 273
31:17	*Vol.* **1**: 562
31:19	*Vol.* **3**: 484, 673, 760, 1041
31:20	*Vol.* **1**: 367 *Vol.* **3**: 342, 806
31:21 f	*Vol.* **3**: 673
31:21	*Vol.* **3**: 1041
31:22	*Vol.* **3**: 760
31:23	*Vol.* **2**: 331
31:24 ff	*Vol.* **2**: 639 *Vol.* **3**: 33
31:24	*Vol.* **2**: 638
31:26	*Vol.* **2**: 440
31:27	*Vol.* **1**: 203
31:28	*Vol.* **3**: 1041
31:30	*Vol.* **3**: 668, 673
32	*Vol.* **2**: 791 *Vol.* **3**: 263
32:1–43	*Vol.* **2**: 639
32:2 f	*Vol.* **3**: 960
32:4	*Vol.* **2**: 237
32:5 f	*Vol.* **1**: 618
32:5	*Vol.* **2**: 36
32:6	*Vol.* **1**: 538, 617 *Vol.* **2**: 71 *Vol.* **3**: 1025, 1027
32:7	*Vol.* **1**: 617 *Vol.* **3**: 232, 828
32:8 f	*Vol.* **2**: 297, 791
32:8	*Vol.* **3**: 636
32:9	*Vol.* **2**: 303
32:10 ff	*Vol.* **3**: 805
32:11	*Vol.* **1**: 173
32:12	*Vol.* **2**: 724
32:13	*Vol.* **3**: 382
32:14	*Vol.* **1**: 224 *Vol.* **3**: 919
32:15 ff	*Vol.* **3**: 806
32:15	*Vol.* **1**: 239, 607 *Vol.* **2**: 705 *Vol.* **3**: 218
32:16 f	*Vol.* **2**: 284
32:16	*Vol.* **1**: 684
32:17	*Vol.* **1**: 451 *Vol.* **2**: 286 *Vol.* **3**: 806
32:18	*Vol.* **1**: 186
32:20	*Vol.* **2**: 36
32:21	*Vol.* **1**: 112 *Vol.* **2**: 176, 284, 490, 794, 880 *Vol.* **3**: 131–132, 456, 461
32:22	*Vol.* **1**: 661 *Vol.* **3**: 1010
32:24	*Vol.* **1**: 113 *Vol.* **2**: 265
32:26	*Vol.* **3**: 237, 255
32:28	*Vol.* **3**: 1016
32:30	*Vol.* **3**: 962
32:31	*Vol.* **3**: 126
32:32	*Vol.* **1**: 202 *Vol.* **2**: 27 *Vol.* **3**: 93
32:34	*Vol.* **3**: 498, 673
32:35 f	*Vol.* **2**: 230 *Vol.* **3**: 28, 136
32:35	*Vol.* **1**: 111 *Vol.* **2**: 96, 157–158, 513 *Vol.* **3**: 93, 97, 345
32:36	*Vol.* **1**: 569 *Vol.* **2**: 363–364
32:37 f	*Vol.* **3**: 919
32:38	*Vol.* **3**: 344
32:39 ff	*Vol.* **2**: 279
32:39	*Vol.* **2**: 279, 478–479 *Vol.* **3**: 263
32:40	*Vol.* **2**: 190
32:41 ff	*Vol.* **3**: 154
32:41	*Vol.* **3**: 93
32:43	*Vol.* **2**: 96, 356, 799, 876 *Vol.* **3**: 152
32:44	*Vol.* **3**: 760
32:46 f	*Vol.* **3**: 1118
32:46	*Vol.* **1**: 617
32:47	*Vol.* **2**: 479 *Vol.* **3**: 1014, 1103–1104
33	*Vol.* **1**: 208 *Vol.* **2**: 638
33:1–29	*Vol.* **2**: 639
33:1	*Vol.* **3**: 77
33:2	*Vol.* **2**: 190, 376, 735 *Vol.* **3**: 318, 1013–1014
33:3	*Vol.* **3**: 745
33:8 ff	*Vol.* **3**: 33
33:8	*Vol.* **2**: 237, 296 *Vol.* **3**: 346, 799–800
33:9	*Vol.* **2**: 395 *Vol.* **3**: 1118
33:10	*Vol.* **2**: 296, 467 *Vol.* **3**: 33, 354, 421, 478
33:12	*Vol.* **3**: 255, 873
33:13 f	*Vol.* **3**: 845
33:13	*Vol.* **1**: 523
33:16	*Vol.* **3**: 845
33:17	*Vol.* **3**: 212, 715
33:19	*Vol.* **2**: 842 *Vol.* **3**: 356
33:21	*Vol.* **3**: 356, 372, 415
33:26	*Vol.* **2**: 190
33:29	*Vol.* **1**: 227 *Vol.* **3**: 207
34	*Vol.* **1**: 76 *Vol.* **2**: 638
34:1–4	*Vol.* **2**: 893 *Vol.* **3**: 806, 1009
34:4	*Vol.* **1**: 77 *Vol.* **3**: 806
34:6	*Vol.* **1**: 104 *Vol.* **3**: 345
34:8	*Vol.* **2**: 416 *Vol.* **3**: 720
34:9	*Vol.* **1**: 66, 735 *Vol.* **2**: 151, 331
34:10 f	*Vol.* **2**: 638
34:10	*Vol.* **2**: 395 *Vol.* **3**: 77
34:11	*Vol.* **2**: 627

Joshua

1:1–17	*Vol.* **2**: 639
1:1	*Vol.* **3**: 208
1:2	*Vol.* **1**: 430
1:3	*Vol.* **2**: 369

Joshua *(cont'd)*

1:4	**Vol. 3:** 983
1:8	**Vol. 1:** 243 **Vol. 2:** 440
1:9	**Vol. 3:** 423
1:13	**Vol. 3:** 255–256, 423, 1103
1:15	**Vol. 3:** 255–256
1:16	**Vol. 1:** 127
2:1–21	**Vol. 3:** 369, 1067
2:1	**Vol. 3:** 1062
2:12	**Vol. 3:** 1153
2:14	**Vol. 3:** 423
2:18	**Vol. 2:** 303
2:19	**Vol. 2:** 142
2:20	**Vol. 3:** 311
3 f	**Vol. 3:** 788
3	**Vol. 2:** 627
3:3	**Vol. 1:** 492
3:5	**Vol. 3:** 1153
3:7	**Vol. 2:** 69, 639
3:12	**Vol. 1:** 475–476
3:13	**Vol. 3:** 255
3:16	**Vol. 3:** 991
4	**Vol. 3:** 656
4:2	**Vol. 1:** 475
4:6 f	**Vol. 3:** 233, 777
4:7	**Vol. 3:** 237, 316, 828
4:10 ff	**Vol. 2:** 639
4:12	**Vol. 1:** 332
4:21 ff	**Vol. 3:** 777
5:2–7	**Vol. 1:** 308
5:6	**Vol. 1:** 683
5:13 ff	**Vol. 1:** 101
5:14	**Vol. 2:** 189
5:15	**Vol. 2:** 225 **Vol. 3:** 177
6	**Vol. 1:** 208 **Vol. 2:** 627 **Vol. 3:** 788
6:1–8:29	**Vol. 3:** 960
6:1 ff	**Vol. 2:** 691
6:3	**Vol. 2:** 716
6:4–21	**Vol. 3:** 874
6:4–20	**Vol. 3:** 673
6:5	**Vol. 1:** 609
6:6	**Vol. 1:** 322 **Vol. 3:** 469
6:7	**Vol. 1:** 340
6:9	**Vol. 1:** 492
6:10	**Vol. 1:** 322
6:14	**Vol. 2:** 716
6:16	**Vol. 1:** 409
6:17–21	**Vol. 3:** 590
6:17	**Vol. 1:** 413
6:19	**Vol. 2:** 225, 830
6:20	**Vol. 1:** 609
6:21	**Vol. 1:** 415
6:22 f	**Vol. 3:** 590
6:22–25	**Vol. 3:** 1067
6:24	**Vol. 2:** 830 **Vol. 3:** 811
6:25	**Vol. 3:** 206
6:26	**Vol. 3:** 444
7	**Vol. 1:** 109 **Vol. 2:** 847 **Vol. 3:** 720
7:6	**Vol. 1:** 520 **Vol. 3:** 788
7:7	**Vol. 3:** 342
7:8	**Vol. 1:** 554
7:11	**Vol. 3:** 377, 583
7:12	**Vol. 1:** 413
7:13	**Vol. 2:** 797
7:14	**Vol. 3:** 569, 871
7:15	**Vol. 1:** 655
7:19	**Vol. 1:** 345
7:22	**Vol. 3:** 1185
7:25	**Vol. 1:** 264
8:1	**Vol. 3:** 812
8:3	**Vol. 3:** 713
8:6	**Vol. 2:** 636
8:12 ff	**Vol. 3:** 248
8:28	**Vol. 3:** 828
8:29	**Vol. 1:** 393–394
8:30 ff	**Vol. 3:** 787
8:30 f	**Vol. 3:** 418, 788
8:30–35	**Vol. 1:** 367 **Vol. 2:** 639
8:30	**Vol. 2:** 796
8:31–35	**Vol. 2:** 639
8:31*	**Vol. 2:** 440
8:32	**Vol. 3:** 483
8:33	**Vol. 3:** 1010
9:1	**Vol. 3:** 1008
9:4	**Vol. 1:** 412
9:5	**Vol. 2:** 714
9:9	**Vol. 1:** 531 **Vol. 2:** 655
9:11	**Vol. 3:** 608
9:13	**Vol. 2:** 670, 714
9:14 f	**Vol. 2:** 521
9:18 ff	**Vol. 1:** 294
9:18 f	**Vol. 2:** 797
9:23–27	**Vol. 3:** 593
9:24	**Vol. 2:** 639
10	**Vol. 2:** 324, 627–628
10:1–11:43	**Vol. 3:** 960
10:1	**Vol. 2:** 324, 590
10:6	**Vol. 3:** 178
10:11	**Vol. 3:** 1001
10:12	**Vol. 2:** 889
10:16	**Vol. 3:** 380
10:20	**Vol. 3:** 248
10:24	**Vol. 1:** 239, 241
10:26	**Vol. 1:** 390, 393
10:27	**Vol. 2:** 96
10:28 ff	**Vol. 1:** 413–414
10:28	**Vol. 2:** 477
10:30	**Vol. 3:** 1154
10:33	**Vol. 3:** 1154
10:37 f	**Vol. 3:** 1154
11:6	**Vol. 3:** 846
11:12–23	**Vol. 2:** 639
11:12	**Vol. 3:** 248
11:20	**Vol. 2:** 154
11:21	**Vol. 1:** 413
11:23	**Vol. 1:** 332 **Vol. 3:** 255
12:3	**Vol. 3:** 983
12:6	**Vol. 2:** 639
13–19	**Vol. 2:** 298

Joshua *(cont'd)*

13:8–33	**Vol. 2:** 639
13:14	**Vol. 2:** 297
13:19	**Vol. 2:** 297
13:22	**Vol. 2:** 554
13:23	**Vol. 1:** 241
13:27	**Vol. 1:** 472 **Vol. 2:** 303 **Vol. 3:** 983
14:1	**Vol. 2:** 300
14:2–11	**Vol. 2:** 639
14:4	**Vol. 2:** 303
14:7	**Vol. 3:** 594
14:10	**Vol. 3:** 1154
14:12	**Vol. 2:** 856
14:15	**Vol. 2:** 802
15	**Vol. 1:** 61
15:2	**Vol. 2:** 303
15:8	**Vol. 2:** 208
15:9	**Vol. 1:** 366 **Vol. 2:** 802
15:12	**Vol. 1:** 472
15:13	**Vol. 2:** 303, 802
15:15 f	**Vol. 2:** 802
15:18 f	**Vol. 2:** 584
15:21	**Vol. 1:** 665
17:2	**Vol. 2:** 569
17:4	**Vol. 2:** 298, 639
17:13	**Vol. 3:** 713
17:16	**Vol. 2:** 98
18:1 ff	**Vol. 3:** 426
18:1	**Vol. 1:** 293
18:3	**Vol. 3:** 178
18:5	**Vol. 1:** 534
18:7	**Vol. 2:** 639 **Vol. 3:** 36
18:8 f	**Vol. 3:** 484
18:9	**Vol. 1:** 243
18:16	**Vol. 2:** 208
18:19 f	**Vol. 2:** 303
18:20	**Vol. 1:** 472
19:1–22:21	**Vol. 2:** 695
19:15	**Vol. 1:** 170
19:26	**Vol. 3:** 983
19:47	**Vol. 2:** 773
20:2	**Vol. 2:** 639
20:3	**Vol. 3:** 190
20:4	**Vol. 1:** 195
20:5	**Vol. 3:** 190
20:7	**Vol. 2:** 305
21	**Vol. 2:** 34, 789 **Vol. 3:** 565
21:2	**Vol. 2:** 639
21:8	**Vol. 2:** 639
21:9	**Vol. 2:** 650
21:11	**Vol. 2:** 305
21:42	**Vol. 3:** 255
21:43 ff	**Vol. 2:** 297
21:43–45	**Vol. 3:** 69
21:44	**Vol. 3:** 256
21:45	**Vol. 1:** 609 **Vol. 3:** 1104
22	**Vol. 1:** 607
22:1–5	**Vol. 2:** 297
22:2–9	**Vol. 2:** 639
22:4	**Vol. 3:** 255
22:5	**Vol. 2:** 181 **Vol. 3:** 1153
22:10–34	**Vol. 3:** 418
22:10 f	**Vol. 3:** 418
22:12 ff	**Vol. 1:** 294
22:16 ff	**Vol. 1:** 606
22:16	**Vol. 3:** 418
22:19	**Vol. 2:** 296 **Vol. 3:** 418
22:21	**Vol. 2:** 698
22:23	**Vol. 3:** 418
22:24	**Vol. 2:** 91
22:26	**Vol. 3:** 418
22:27 f	**Vol. 3:** 1040
22:27	**Vol. 3:** 550
22:30	**Vol. 2:** 698
22:34	**Vol. 3:** 418
23:1	**Vol. 3:** 255
23:6	**Vol. 2:** 639
23:7	**Vol. 2:** 876
23:10	**Vol. 2:** 374 **Vol. 3:** 962
23:13	**Vol. 2:** 707 **Vol. 3:** 268
23:14	**Vol. 1:** 609 **Vol. 3:** 69, 938, 1104
23:15	**Vol. 3:** 1104
23:16	**Vol. 2:** 876
24	**Vol. 1:** 626 **Vol. 2:** 67, 306
24:1 ff	**Vol. 3:** 787
24:2	**Vol. 1:** 164 **Vol. 3:** 452
24:3	**Vol. 1:** 617
24:5	**Vol. 2:** 639
24:6	**Vol. 2:** 440
24:14–24	**Vol. 3:** 550
24:14	**Vol. 3:** 354, 882
24:15	**Vol. 1:** 537
24:15b	**Vol. 1:** 617
24:17	**Vol. 2:** 796
24:19–24	**Vol. 3:** 113
24:23	**Vol. 1:** 688 **Vol. 2:** 796
24:24†	**Vol. 1:** 367
24:25	**Vol. 1:** 245 **Vol. 2:** 441
24:26	**Vol. 3:** 786–787
24:27	**Vol. 3:** 1040
24:29	**Vol. 3:** 594, 608
24:31	**Vol. 3:** 550
24:32	**Vol. 3:** 459, 464

Judges

1:1–7	**Vol. 2:** 319
1:1	**Vol. 2:** 879
1:3	**Vol. 2:** 298
1:4	**Vol. 2:** 698
1:7	**Vol. 3:** 134
1:14	**Vol. 3:** 557
1:16	**Vol. 2:** 305, 639
1:17	**Vol. 1:** 413
1:19	**Vol. 2:** 98
1:20	**Vol. 2:** 639
1:24	**Vol. 3:** 569
1:27 ff	**Vol. 2:** 802
1:28	**Vol. 3:** 713

Judges *(cont'd)*

2:1 ff	**Vol. 1:** 716
2:1–5	**Vol. 3:** 425
2:1	**Vol. 1:** 531 **Vol. 3:** 788, 828
2:2	**Vol. 1:** 531 **Vol. 2:** 416, 876
2:3	**Vol. 2:** 707 **Vol. 3:** 1069
2:4	**Vol. 2:** 305
2:6 ff	**Vol. 1:** 135
2:6–3:6	**Vol. 3:** 578
2:7	**Vol. 2:** 395 **Vol. 3:** 595
2:9	**Vol. 2:** 298
2:10 f	**Vol. 2:** 396
2:11–22	**Vol. 3:** 1104
2:12 f	**Vol. 1:** 492
2:12	**Vol. 1:** 481 **Vol. 2:** 876
2:14	**Vol. 1:** 109 **Vol. 2:** 148, 367
2:16	**Vol. 3:** 218, 279
2:17	**Vol. 2:** 173, 876
2:18	**Vol. 1:** 356, 569 **Vol. 2:** 423 **Vol. 3:** 218, 279, 594
2:19	**Vol. 2:** 876
2:20	**Vol. 1:** 109
2:22	**Vol. 3:** 799–800
3:1–5	**Vol. 2:** 802
3:1	**Vol. 1:** 698 **Vol. 2:** 791 **Vol. 3:** 799–800
3:2	**Vol. 3:** 760
3:4 ff	**Vol. 3:** 800
3:4	**Vol. 2:** 639 **Vol. 3:** 799
3:9	**Vol. 1:** 409 **Vol. 2:** 363 **Vol. 3:** 218, 462
3:10	**Vol. 3:** 691
3:11	**Vol. 3:** 111
3:15–18	**Vol. 3:** 421
3:15	**Vol. 2:** 41, 363, 414 **Vol. 3:** 218, 462
3:17 f	**Vol. 2:** 41
3:25	**Vol. 2:** 730, 773 **Vol. 3:** 228
3:29	**Vol. 2:** 698 **Vol. 3:** 209
3:30	**Vol. 3:** 111
4:3	**Vol. 2:** 98
4:4	**Vol. 3:** 836, 1057
4:6–23	**Vol. 3:** 960
4:6–14	**Vol. 2:** 698
4:6	**Vol. 3:** 1057
4:10	**Vol. 1:** 239 **Vol. 2:** 139
4:11	**Vol. 2:** 639 **Vol. 3:** 255, 534
4:15	**Vol. 1:** 527
4:17 ff	**Vol. 1:** 687
4:17	**Vol. 2:** 777
4:19	**Vol. 2:** 726
4:23	**Vol. 2:** 260
5	**Vol. 1:** 245
5:1–31	**Vol. 3:** 1057
5:1	**Vol. 3:** 672–673
5:3	**Vol. 2:** 796 **Vol. 3:** 672
5:4 f	**Vol. 2:** 190 **Vol. 3:** 960, 1014
5:4	**Vol. 2:** 898 **Vol. 3:** 556
5:5	**Vol. 2:** 796 **Vol. 3:** 1010, 1013
5:7	**Vol. 3:** 1069
5:9	**Vol. 3:** 87
5:10	**Vol. 1:** 117 **Vol. 2:** 257
5:11	**Vol. 2:** 796 **Vol. 3:** 355–356
5:12	**Vol. 3:** 673
5:13	**Vol. 2:** 796
5:15	**Vol. 1:** 534
5:19	**Vol. 2:** 41 **Vol. 3:** 137
5:20	**Vol. 2:** 189 **Vol. 3:** 735, 1001
5:21	**Vol. 2:** 602
5:25	**Vol. 2:** 856
5:27	**Vol. 1:** 442
5:29	**Vol. 3:** 1027
5:30	**Vol. 3:** 593
5:31	**Vol. 2:** 602 **Vol. 3:** 730, 1068
6	**Vol. 2:** 627
6:2	**Vol. 2:** 139 **Vol. 3:** 1009
6:3	**Vol. 3:** 144
6:4	**Vol. 1:** 711
6:5	**Vol. 2:** 139 **Vol. 3:** 811
6:9	**Vol. 1:** 453 **Vol. 3:** 201
6:11–24	**Vol. 1:** 101
6:11–23	**Vol. 3:** 212
6:12	**Vol. 2:** 69
6:13	**Vol. 1:** 273 **Vol. 2:** 367
6:15 ff	**Vol. 2:** 260 **Vol. 3:** 962
6:15	**Vol. 2:** 428, 698 **Vol. 3:** 993
6:16 ff	**Vol. 2:** 626
6:17	**Vol. 2:** 626 **Vol. 3:** 528
6:18–21	**Vol. 3:** 422
6:18 f	**Vol. 3:** 155
6:18	**Vol. 3:** 421, 534
6:19	**Vol. 1:** 114 **Vol. 2:** 876
6:20	**Vol. 2:** 854 **Vol. 3:** 381, 816
6:21	**Vol. 1:** 655 **Vol. 3:** 381
6:22 f	**Vol. 1:** 585
6:22	**Vol. 3:** 514
6:23	**Vol. 1:** 622
6:24 ff	**Vol. 3:** 418, 425
6:24	**Vol. 2:** 777
6:25a	**Vol. 1:** 116
6:28a	**Vol. 1:** 116
6:33–7:25	**Vol. 3:** 960
6:34	**Vol. 1:** 739 **Vol. 3:** 691
6:36 ff	**Vol. 2:** 626
6:36 f	**Vol. 2:** 626
6:39	**Vol. 3:** 799
7	**Vol. 1:** 650
7:2	**Vol. 3:** 206
7:4	**Vol. 3:** 808
7:5	**Vol. 3:** 1079
7:7	**Vol. 3:** 206
7:10	**Vol. 1:** 283
7:13	**Vol. 1:** 574
7:15	**Vol. 1:** 574–575 **Vol. 2:** 876
7:16	**Vol. 2:** 485 **Vol. 3:** 874
7:18 ff	**Vol. 3:** 673
7:20 ff	**Vol. 3:** 874
7:20	**Vol. 2:** 485
7:22	**Vol. 2:** 374
7:25	**Vol. 3:** 590

Judges *(cont'd)*

8:1	**Vol. 2:** 363	**Vol. 3:** 820
8:3	**Vol. 1:** 165	**Vol. 3:** 255, 691
8:7	**Vol. 1:** 725	**Vol. 3:** 268
8:10	**Vol. 2:** 698	
8:12	**Vol. 1:** 527	**Vol. 3:** 716
8:14	**Vol. 1:** 195, 283	
8:16	**Vol. 1:** 195, 725	
8:19	**Vol. 3:** 739, 1069	
8:20	**Vol. 2:** 675	
8:21	**Vol. 1:** 241	
8:22	**Vol. 3:** 206	
8:23	**Vol. 2:** 374	
8:26	**Vol. 2:** 96	
8:27	**Vol. 2:** 707	
8:33	**Vol. 1:** 367	
8:34	**Vol. 3:** 201–202	
9:1–3	**Vol. 3:** 1069	
9:2	**Vol. 1:** 195	
9:3 f	**Vol. 1:** 492	
9:4	**Vol. 1:** 367, 546	**Vol. 2:** 139
9:7	**Vol. 3:** 1009	
9:8	**Vol. 1:** 121	**Vol. 3:** 866
9:9	**Vol. 1:** 698	
9:10	**Vol. 1:** 723	
9:11	**Vol. 1:** 698	
9:12	**Vol. 1:** 165	
9:13	**Vol. 1:** 698	**Vol. 3:** 919
9:15	**Vol. 1:** 121	
9:16	**Vol. 2:** 61	
9:17	**Vol. 3:** 201	
9:19	**Vol. 2:** 61	
9:23	**Vol. 3:** 720	
9:26–41	**Vol. 2:** 521	
9:27	**Vol. 3:** 673	
9:30	**Vol. 1:** 108	
9:34	**Vol. 1:** 165	
9:36	**Vol. 3:** 554	
9:37	**Vol. 1:** 523	**Vol. 2:** 554
9:45	**Vol. 3:** 444	
9:46	**Vol. 1:** 367	
9:50–54	**Vol. 2:** 431	
9:53	**Vol. 3:** 394	
9:54	**Vol. 1:** 283	
10:1–5	**Vol. 2:** 363	
10:4	**Vol. 1:** 117	**Vol. 2:** 257
10:6	**Vol. 3:** 1069	
10:10	**Vol. 1:** 410	
10:12 ff	**Vol. 3:** 207	
10:16	**Vol. 1:** 262	**Vol. 2:** 815
10:18	**Vol. 1:** 164	**Vol. 2:** 158
11:3	**Vol. 1:** 546	
11:5 ff	**Vol. 1:** 195	
11:6	**Vol. 1:** 165	
11:7	**Vol. 3:** 957	
11:16	**Vol. 3:** 983	
11:18	**Vol. 1:** 609	
11:24	**Vol. 2:** 67	
11:26	**Vol. 3:** 835	

11:27	**Vol. 2:** 363	**Vol. 3:** 356	
11:29	**Vol. 1:** 739	**Vol. 3:** 691	
11:30–40	**Vol. 3:** 425		
11:31	**Vol. 3:** 421		
11:34	**Vol. 3:** 673, 1202		
11:35	**Vol. 1:** 316	**Vol. 2:** 93	
12:1	**Vol. 1:** 272		
12:2 f	**Vol. 3:** 206		
12:3	**Vol. 3:** 218		
12:6	**Vol. 2:** 698		
12:7–15	**Vol. 2:** 363		
12:8–10	**Vol. 1:** 170		
12:14	**Vol. 1:** 117	**Vol. 2:** 257	
13:2	**Vol. 2:** 789		
13:4	**Vol. 3:** 919, 921		
13:5	**Vol. 1:** 203	**Vol. 3:** 206	
13:6	**Vol. 3:** 318		
13:7	**Vol. 2:** 225, 228–229	**Vol. 3:** 919, 921	
13:8	**Vol. 2:** 863		
13:11	**Vol. 3:** 946		
13:14	**Vol. 3:** 919		
13:15 f	**Vol. 3:** 711		
13:16	**Vol. 3:** 422		
13:17 f	**Vol. 1:** 101		
13:19	**Vol. 3:** 381		
13:20	**Vol. 1:** 655		
13:21 f	**Vol. 3:** 212		
14	**Vol. 2:** 584		
14:1	**Vol. 2:** 576		
14:4	**Vol. 3:** 835		
14:6	**Vol. 3:** 691		
14:8	**Vol. 1:** 610		
14:11	**Vol. 2:** 578		
14:12–20	**Vol. 2:** 745		
14:12	**Vol. 2:** 578		
14:15	**Vol. 2:** 458		
14:18	**Vol. 2:** 745		
14:19	**Vol. 1:** 739		
14:20	**Vol. 1:** 258		
15 f	**Vol. 1:** 171		
15:1	**Vol. 1:** 189, 498		
15:4	**Vol. 1:** 343	**Vol. 2:** 485	
15:5	**Vol. 2:** 485		
15:13 f	**Vol. 3:** 591		
15:13	**Vol. 3:** 669		
15:17	**Vol. 2:** 225		
15:18 f	**Vol. 2:** 478		
15:18	**Vol. 2:** 275, 416		
15:19	**Vol. 3:** 686, 690, 694		
16:3	**Vol. 3:** 951		
16:5	**Vol. 2:** 458	**Vol. 3:** 713	
16:7	**Vol. 3:** 993		
16:8	**Vol. 1:** 120		
16:11	**Vol. 3:** 993		
16:17 ff	**Vol. 1:** 203		
16:17	**Vol. 1:** 607	**Vol. 2:** 225, 228	**Vol. 3:** 993
16:19	**Vol. 1:** 607		
16:20	**Vol. 1:** 607	**Vol. 2:** 395	
16:23 ff	**Vol. 3:** 782		

Judges *(cont'd)*

16:24   **Vol. 1:** 99   **Vol. 3:** 668, 816–817
16:26   **Vol. 3:** 255, 716
16:28   **Vol. 2:** 416   **Vol. 3:** 235
16:29   **Vol. 2:** 148
17   **Vol. 3:** 33
17:2   **Vol. 3:** 474
17:3   **Vol. 2:** 96, 225
17:5   **Vol. 3:** 33
17:7   **Vol. 1:** 170   **Vol. 3:** 33
17:8   **Vol. 3:** 1153
17:10   **Vol. 1:** 617   **Vol. 2:** 887   **Vol. 3:** 1161
17:13   **Vol. 2:** 466   **Vol. 3:** 33, 1161
18   **Vol. 3:** 33
18:2   **Vol. 3:** 255
18:4   **Vol. 2:** 139
18:5 f   **Vol. 3:** 33
18:5   **Vol. 2:** 856, 879
18:6   **Vol. 2:** 778
18:7   **Vol. 2:** 437
18:9   **Vol. 3:** 111
18:10   **Vol. 3:** 953
18:11   **Vol. 3:** 120
18:15   **Vol. 2:** 778
18:19   **Vol. 1:** 617
18:29   **Vol. 2:** 650
18:30   **Vol. 3:** 33, 872
18:31   **Vol. 3:** 426, 786
19:1   **Vol. 1:** 170   **Vol. 3:** 33
19:5   **Vol. 2:** 181
19:7   **Vol. 3:** 711
19:10 f   **Vol. 2:** 324
19:15 ff   **Vol. 2:** 521
19:16–30   **Vol. 3:** 872
19:19 f   **Vol. 3:** 953
19:19   **Vol. 1:** 743
19:20   **Vol. 2:** 777
19:22   **Vol. 1:** 687   **Vol. 2:** 511
19:23 f   **Vol. 3:** 1024
19:23   **Vol. 2:** 511
19:25   **Vol. 1:** 420
19:29   **Vol. 1:** 230
19:30   **Vol. 2:** 889
20:1   **Vol. 1:** 293
20:2–46   **Vol. 2:** 698
20:2   **Vol. 1:** 296
20:6   **Vol. 3:** 1024
20:10   **Vol. 3:** 1024
20:15 f   **Vol. 1:** 537
20:16   **Vol. 2:** 414, 690
20:23   **Vol. 2:** 416
20:26   **Vol. 1:** 612   **Vol. 2:** 60, 416   **Vol. 3:** 588
20:27   **Vol. 3:** 788
20:43   **Vol. 3:** 255–256
20:48   **Vol. 1:** 654
21   **Vol. 3:** 872
21:3   **Vol. 2:** 797
21:4   **Vol. 2:** 60

21:5   **Vol. 1:** 295
21:6   **Vol. 1:** 356
21:8   **Vol. 1:** 295
21:10   **Vol. 1:** 414
21:11 f   **Vol. 2:** 569
21:11   **Vol. 1:** 414   **Vol. 2:** 587
21:12 ff   **Vol. 3:** 426
21:12   **Vol. 2:** 587
21:22   **Vol. 2:** 363
21:23   **Vol. 3:** 601
21:24   **Vol. 3:** 943

Ruth

1–4   **Vol. 1:** 499
1:1   **Vol. 1:** 520
1:2   **Vol. 1:** 520
1:4   **Vol. 3:** 656
1:6   **Vol. 1:** 189   **Vol. 2:** 584
1:9   **Vol. 3:** 255
1:12   **Vol. 1:** 710, 712
1:13   **Vol. 1:** 202
1:14   **Vol. 1:** 481
1:19   **Vol. 3:** 112
1:20 f   **Vol. 3:** 729
1:20   **Vol. 1:** 201
1:22   **Vol. 1:** 170
2:2   **Vol. 1:** 520   **Vol. 2:** 116   **Vol. 3:** 1074
2:5 f   **Vol. 1:** 283
2:7   **Vol. 2:** 32   **Vol. 3:** 255
2:8   **Vol. 2:** 349
2:10   **Vol. 1:** 609   **Vol. 2:** 116, 876
2:12   **Vol. 2:** 139
2:13   **Vol. 2:** 116
2:14   **Vol. 1:** 250   **Vol. 3:** 846
2:16   **Vol. 1:** 572
2:20   **Vol. 3:** 191
2:21   **Vol. 2:** 60, 349   **Vol. 3:** 525
3:1   **Vol. 3:** 255
3:2   **Vol. 2:** 34
3:3   **Vol. 1:** 120   **Vol. 3:** 191
3:6 ff   **Vol. 2:** 578
3:6–18   **Vol. 3:** 1062
3:9   **Vol. 3:** 191, 555
3:10   **Vol. 1:** 492, 665   **Vol. 2:** 841
3:12   **Vol. 3:** 191
3:13   **Vol. 3:** 191
4   **Vol. 3:** 95
4:1 ff   **Vol. 2:** 363
4:1–13   **Vol. 2:** 577
4:1   **Vol. 3:** 191
4:3   **Vol. 3:** 191
4:4   **Vol. 3:** 191
4:5   **Vol. 3:** 191, 1057
4:6   **Vol. 3:** 190–191
4:7   **Vol. 3:** 166, 354
4:8   **Vol. 3:** 191
4:9 ff   **Vol. 3:** 1041
4:10   **Vol. 3:** 1057
4:11 f   **Vol. 2:** 578

Ruth *(cont'd)*

4:12	**Vol. 1:** 170
4:13 f	**Vol. 1:** 207
4:14	**Vol. 3:** 178, 191
4:16	**Vol. 1:** 240
4:18 ff	**Vol. 3:** 191, 652

1 Samuel

1 ff	**Vol. 3:** 782
1	**Vol. 2:** 478 **Vol. 3:** 1072
1:3 ff	**Vol. 3:** 426, 1055
1:3–8	**Vol. 3:** 1057
1:3 f	**Vol. 2:** 562 **Vol. 3:** 1058
1:3	**Vol. 2:** 185, 876 **Vol. 3:** 33, 787–788
1:4	**Vol. 1:** 288 **Vol. 2:** 226
1:6	**Vol. 3:** 1055
1:7	**Vol. 2:** 416 **Vol. 3:** 786
1:9 ff	**Vol. 3:** 1055
1:9	**Vol. 3:** 786
1:10 f	**Vol. 2:** 863
1:10	**Vol. 2:** 862
1:11	**Vol. 1:** 288 **Vol. 2:** 260–261 **Vol. 3:** 235
1:12	**Vol. 2:** 862
1:13	**Vol. 3:** 823
1:15	**Vol. 2:** 854
1:16	**Vol. 2:** 260
1:17	**Vol. 2:** 856
1:18	**Vol. 2:** 116 **Vol. 3:** 794
1:19	**Vol. 2:** 876
1:20	**Vol. 1:** 343 **Vol. 2:** 856
1:21	**Vol. 3:** 422
1:22	**Vol. 3:** 827
1:23	**Vol. 3:** 1104
1:25	**Vol. 3:** 1016
1:26 f	**Vol. 2:** 862
1:26	**Vol. 3:** 739
2	**Vol. 3:** 263, 1072
2:1 ff	**Vol. 3:** 1055
2:1–10	**Vol. 2:** 596 **Vol. 3:** 30
2:1	**Vol. 2:** 862 **Vol. 3:** 715
2:2	**Vol. 2:** 225
2:3*	**Vol. 1:** 332
2:5	**Vol. 2:** 265
2:6	**Vol. 3:** 263
2:7 ff	**Vol. 2:** 260
2:7	**Vol. 2:** 201, 262, 596, 841
2:8	**Vol. 1:** 523 **Vol. 2:** 614, 820 **Vol. 3:** 588
2:10	**Vol. 1:** 227 **Vol. 2:** 336, 596, 841–842 **Vol. 3:** 130, 715
2:12–17	**Vol. 3:** 426
2:13–16	**Vol. 3:** 422
2:13	**Vol. 1:** 672 **Vol. 3:** 354, 422
2:15	**Vol. 1:** 672
2:17*	**Vol. 1:** 74 **Vol. 3:** 421
2:19	**Vol. 3:** 1153
2:22	**Vol. 1:** 193
2:24	**Vol. 2:** 173
2:25	**Vol. 2:** 863
2:26	**Vol. 2:** 119
2:27 f	**Vol. 3:** 33
2:27	**Vol. 3:** 311
2:28	**Vol. 1:** 407, 538
2:29	**Vol. 3:** 415, 421, 424
2:30	**Vol. 2:** 797 **Vol. 3:** 828
2:31	**Vol. 1:** 320
2:33	**Vol. 1:** 729
2:35	**Vol. 2:** 181 **Vol. 3:** 162
2:36	**Vol. 2:** 876 **Vol. 3:** 36
3	**Vol. 1:** 511
3:1–4:1	**Vol. 3:** 311
3:1	**Vol. 3:** 311, 1091, 1120
3:2 ff	**Vol. 1:** 442
3:3	**Vol. 3:** 786, 788
3:4–10	**Vol. 1:** 273
3:7	**Vol. 3:** 311, 1091
3:8	**Vol. 3:** 1028
3:9 ff	**Vol. 3:** 311
3:9	**Vol. 1:** 442
3:13 f	**Vol. 3:** 574, 828
3:13	**Vol. 1:** 568 **Vol. 3:** 342
3:14	**Vol. 3:** 153, 155, 423, 740
3:15	**Vol. 2:** 726
3:16	**Vol. 1:** 177, 285
3:17	**Vol. 2:** 214–215
3:18	**Vol. 2:** 214
3:19	**Vol. 1:** 609
3:20	**Vol. 1:** 595–596
3:21	**Vol. 3:** 311–312
4	**Vol. 3:** 788
4:2	**Vol. 2:** 698
4:3 ff	**Vol. 3:** 426
4:3	**Vol. 1:** 195 **Vol. 3:** 207
4:4	**Vol. 1:** 280
4:6	**Vol. 2:** 305
4:7	**Vol. 3:** 1051
4:8	**Vol. 1:** 531 **Vol. 3:** 857
4:9	**Vol. 2:** 305
4:10	**Vol. 2:** 698
4:11	**Vol. 3:** 342
4:13	**Vol. 2:** 803
4:15	**Vol. 3:** 112
4:21 f	**Vol. 2:** 45
5 f	**Vol. 2:** 45
5:1–7:2	**Vol. 3:** 788
5:2	**Vol. 3:** 786
5:5	**Vol. 3:** 787
5:6	**Vol. 2:** 149
5:11	**Vol. 2:** 149
6:2	**Vol. 2:** 554
6:3 f	**Vol. 3:** 420, 856
6:6	**Vol. 1:** 531
6:7	**Vol. 3:** 1161
6:8	**Vol. 3:** 856
6:10	**Vol. 3:** 1161
6:11	**Vol. 2:** 287
6:14 f	**Vol. 3:** 426
6:14	**Vol. 1:** 562 **Vol. 3:** 208

1 Samuel (cont'd)

6:17	**Vol. 3:** 856
6:18	**Vol. 3:** 208
6:19 f	**Vol. 2:** 225
6:19	**Vol. 2:** 698
6:20	**Vol. 2:** 224
7:1	**Vol. 2:** 225 **Vol. 3:** 1010
7:2	**Vol. 2:** 305
7:5	**Vol. 2:** 862
7:6	**Vol. 2:** 854
7:9	**Vol. 3:** 421, 426
7:13	**Vol. 2:** 149, 260
7:17	**Vol. 3:** 426
8–12	**Vol. 2:** 374
8–11	**Vol. 2:** 335
8	**Vol. 1:** 109
8:1–22a	**Vol. 2:** 374
8:1–3	**Vol. 1:** 426
8:1	**Vol. 1:** 472
8:3	**Vol. 1:** 492 **Vol. 3:** 354, 747
8:4 ff	**Vol. 1:** 195
8:5–7	**Vol. 2:** 374
8:6	**Vol. 2:** 862
8:7	**Vol. 1:** 425 **Vol. 2:** 376
8:8	**Vol. 1:** 531 **Vol. 2:** 889
8:9	**Vol. 3:** 354
8:10–18	**Vol. 1:** 716 **Vol. 2:** 432
8:11 f	**Vol. 3:** 608
8:11	**Vol. 3:** 354
8:15	**Vol. 1:** 560 **Vol. 2:** 693 **Vol. 3:** 523
8:17	**Vol. 2:** 693
8:18	**Vol. 1:** 537–538
8:19	**Vol. 1:** 426
8:20	**Vol. 2:** 363
9–12	**Vol. 2:** 306
9:1 ff	**Vol. 2:** 336
9:1–10:16	**Vol. 2:** 374
9:1 f	**Vol. 3:** 872
9:6–20	**Vol. 3:** 77
9:6	**Vol. 2:** 898
9:9	**Vol. 2:** 879
9:11–24	**Vol. 3:** 426
9:12 ff	**Vol. 3:** 1010
9:15	**Vol. 3:** 311–312
9:16 f	**Vol. 2:** 797
9:16	**Vol. 1:** 121, 410 **Vol. 2:** 374
9:19	**Vol. 3:** 45
9:22 ff	**Vol. 2:** 521
9:22	**Vol. 1:** 665 **Vol. 3:** 794
9:24†	**Vol. 3:** 422, 1041
9:25†	**Vol. 3:** 1010
10:1 ff	**Vol. 2:** 626–627
10:1	**Vol. 1:** 121 **Vol. 2:** 711, 797
10:2	**Vol. 1:** 170 **Vol. 3:** 531, 560
10:4	**Vol. 3:** 416
10:5 ff	**Vol. 3:** 77
10:5 f	**Vol. 1:** 527 **Vol. 3:** 77
10:5	**Vol. 3:** 77, 426
10:6	**Vol. 3:** 77
10:8	**Vol. 3:** 426
10:10 ff	**Vol. 3:** 77
10:10	**Vol. 1:** 527
10:12	**Vol. 2:** 745
10:14	**Vol. 3:** 531
10:17–27	**Vol. 2:** 374
10:18	**Vol. 1:** 531
10:19	**Vol. 2:** 698 **Vol. 3:** 218
10:20 f	**Vol. 2:** 296
10:20	**Vol. 2:** 226
10:21	**Vol. 2:** 698 **Vol. 3:** 528
10:24	**Vol. 1:** 538
10:25	**Vol. 3:** 354, 484
10:26	**Vol. 3:** 860
10:27	**Vol. 1:** 415
11:1–11	**Vol. 2:** 374
11:1	**Vol. 1:** 366
11:3	**Vol. 3:** 206
11:5	**Vol. 1:** 574
11:6†	**Vol. 1:** 108, 527 **Vol. 3:** 691
11:7	**Vol. 1:** 492
11:11	**Vol. 1:** 165 **Vol. 2:** 34 **Vol. 3:** 846
11:13†	**Vol. 3:** 207
11:14 f	**Vol. 2:** 374
11:14	**Vol. 2:** 673
11:15	**Vol. 2:** 521 **Vol. 3:** 426
11:16	**Vol. 3:** 691
12:3 ff	**Vol. 3:** 1041
12:3	**Vol. 2:** 336 **Vol. 3:** 153, 192
12:5	**Vol. 2:** 336
12:6–25	**Vol. 3:** 1104
12:6	**Vol. 2:** 639
12:7	**Vol. 3:** 355–356
12:8	**Vol. 1:** 426 **Vol. 2:** 639
12:10	**Vol. 1:** 426
12:12	**Vol. 1:** 426 **Vol. 3:** 748
12:13	**Vol. 2:** 856
12:14 ff	**Vol. 1:** 426
12:14	**Vol. 3:** 113
12:17	**Vol. 2:** 856 **Vol. 3:** 513
12:19	**Vol. 2:** 862
12:22	**Vol. 2:** 257
12:23	**Vol. 2:** 862 **Vol. 3:** 771
12:24	**Vol. 2:** 181
13:3	**Vol. 2:** 305–306, 742
13:6	**Vol. 3:** 381
13:8	**Vol. 1:** 294 **Vol. 3:** 1040
13:9	**Vol. 3:** 426
13:11	**Vol. 1:** 294 **Vol. 2:** 34 **Vol. 3:** 1040
13:12	**Vol. 1:** 495 **Vol. 2:** 860
13:13	**Vol. 3:** 117, 828
13:14	**Vol. 2:** 797
13:19	**Vol. 2:** 98, 305–306
13:20	**Vol. 2:** 98
13:23	**Vol. 1:** 710
14:1	**Vol. 1:** 283
14:2 ff	**Vol. 3:** 150
14:3	**Vol. 3:** 426
14:4	**Vol. 1:** 711
14:6	**Vol. 2:** 428 **Vol. 3:** 962

1 Samuel *(cont'd)*

14:11	**Vol. 2:** 215
14:14	**Vol. 1:** 665
14:15	**Vol. 1:** 527
14:17	**Vol. 1:** 189
14:21	**Vol. 2:** 305
14:23	**Vol. 3:** 207
14:24 ff	**Vol. 2:** 269 **Vol. 3:** 574, 720
14:24	**Vol. 1:** 612
14:29	**Vol. 3:** 166
14:32 ff	**Vol. 1:** 221
14:33	**Vol. 3:** 480
14:34	**Vol. 2:** 34
14:36 – 42	**Vol. 3:** 33
14:37	**Vol. 2:** 296
14:38	**Vol. 2:** 395
14:39	**Vol. 3:** 207
14:41	**Vol. 2:** 296, 299
14:45	**Vol. 1:** 609 **Vol. 2:** 863 **Vol. 3:** 157, 190
14:47*	**Vol. 1:** 478
15:1	**Vol. 1:** 121 **Vol. 2:** 797 **Vol. 3:** 97
15:2 f	**Vol. 2:** 139
15:3 ff	**Vol. 1:** 413
15:3	**Vol. 1:** 281, 429 **Vol. 3:** 590
15:4	**Vol. 1:** 340
15:8 f	**Vol. 3:** 590
15:9	**Vol. 3:** 1016
15:10 ff	**Vol. 2:** 336
15:10	**Vol. 3:** 1090, 1120
15:11	**Vol. 1:** 356 **Vol. 2:** 132 **Vol. 3:** 1104
15:13	**Vol. 3:** 1104
15:17	**Vol. 1:** 121
15:21	**Vol. 1:** 665
15:22	**Vol. 1:** 540 **Vol. 2:** 596 **Vol. 3:** 421, 427
15:23 ff	**Vol. 3:** 578
15:23	**Vol. 2:** 554 **Vol. 3:** 1091
15:24	**Vol. 3:** 583
15:25	**Vol. 2:** 876
15:26	**Vol. 3:** 1091
15:27	**Vol. 3:** 716
15:28	**Vol. 1:** 255
15:29	**Vol. 1:** 357 **Vol. 2:** 470, 564, 830
15:30 f	**Vol. 2:** 876
15:30	**Vol. 1:** 195
15:32	**Vol. 2:** 271
15:35	**Vol. 1:** 356
16:1 ff	**Vol. 2:** 336
16:1	**Vol. 1:** 121, 538 **Vol. 2:** 711
16:2 – 5	**Vol. 3:** 426
16:2	**Vol. 1:** 320
16:3	**Vol. 1:** 121
16:4	**Vol. 1:** 170, 195 **Vol. 3:** 78
16:5	**Vol. 1:** 320 **Vol. 2:** 225
16:6 ff	**Vol. 3:** 673
16:7	**Vol. 2:** 182 – 183 **Vol. 3:** 514, 533
16:7b	**Vol. 2:** 565
16:8 – 10	**Vol. 1:** 538
16:11	**Vol. 2:** 428
16:12 f	**Vol. 1:** 121
16:13	**Vol. 1:** 121 – 122 **Vol. 2:** 711 **Vol. 3:** 691
16:14 ff	**Vol. 1:** 565 **Vol. 3:** 474
16:14 f	**Vol. 1:** 226
16:14	**Vol. 1:** 451 **Vol. 3:** 692
16:15	**Vol. 3:** 692
16:16	**Vol. 2:** 395 **Vol. 3:** 255, 671, 692
16:17	**Vol. 3:** 351
16:18	**Vol. 2:** 395 **Vol. 3:** 671, 1028
16:21	**Vol. 1:** 474
16:22	**Vol. 2:** 1116
16:23	**Vol. 3:** 686, 692
17:12	**Vol. 1:** 170
17:15	**Vol. 1:** 170
17:17	**Vol. 1:** 250
17:18	**Vol. 2:** 778 **Vol. 3:** 957
17:22	**Vol. 2:** 778
17:25	**Vol. 1:** 716 **Vol. 2:** 841
17:28	**Vol. 3:** 29
17:38	**Vol. 2:** 431
17:39	**Vol. 3:** 120, 799, 943
17:45	**Vol. 2:** 69
17:55	**Vol. 3:** 739
18:1	**Vol. 2:** 540 **Vol. 3:** 680
18:3	**Vol. 1:** 365 **Vol. 2:** 540
18:4	**Vol. 3:** 120
18:6	**Vol. 3:** 673
18:8	**Vol. 3:** 1120
18:10	**Vol. 1:** 609 **Vol. 3:** 691
18:13	**Vol. 1:** 606
18:15	**Vol. 2:** 91
18:17 ff	**Vol. 3:** 1057
18:21	**Vol. 2:** 707
18:23 ff	**Vol. 2:** 260
18:25	**Vol. 2:** 578 **Vol. 3:** 823
18:27	**Vol. 2:** 576
18:29	**Vol. 2:** 91
19:1	**Vol. 1:** 534
19:5	**Vol. 2:** 41 **Vol. 3:** 159
19:10 – 17	**Vol. 3:** 209
19:11	**Vol. 3:** 209
19:11b	**Vol. 2:** 565
19:18 ff	**Vol. 3:** 77
19:20 – 24	**Vol. 1:** 527
19:20	**Vol. 3:** 77
20:2	**Vol. 3:** 311, 1087
20:3	**Vol. 2:** 116 **Vol. 3:** 739
20:4	**Vol. 3:** 680, 739
20:5	**Vol. 3:** 426, 588
20:6	**Vol. 1:** 170 **Vol. 3:** 418
20:7	**Vol. 2:** 778
20:8	**Vol. 1:** 365, 367
20:12	**Vol. 3:** 739
20:13	**Vol. 3:** 311, 739
20:17	**Vol. 2:** 540
20:18	**Vol. 3:** 588
20:21	**Vol. 3:** 528
20:24 f	**Vol. 3:** 426

1 Samuel *(cont'd)*

20:25	**Vol. 3:** 588
20:28	**Vol. 1:** 170
20:29	**Vol. 3:** 209, 418, 422
20:30	**Vol. 1:** 108 **Vol. 3:** 310
20:31	**Vol. 2:** 376
20:34	**Vol. 1:** 249
20:35	**Vol. 3:** 1040
20:41	**Vol. 2:** 876
21	**Vol. 3:** 812
21:1 ff	**Vol. 3:** 426
21:1–6	**Vol. 3:** 37, 408, 423, 814
21:1†	**Vol. 3:** 33
21:2–7	**Vol. 3:** 792
21:4 ff*	**Vol. 2:** 225
21:4	**Vol. 2:** 225
21:5 ff	**Vol. 2:** 225
21:5 f	**Vol. 3:** 104
21:6	**Vol. 1:** 586
22:1	**Vol. 3:** 166, 380
22:2	**Vol. 3:** 594
22:8	**Vol. 3:** 311
22:9–23	**Vol. 3:** 33
22:14	**Vol. 1:** 340, 595
22:17	**Vol. 3:** 311, 1016
22:22	**Vol. 2:** 138
23:5	**Vol. 3:** 206
23:8	**Vol. 1:** 340
23:10 f	**Vol. 2:** 797
23:10	**Vol. 1:** 468
23:23	**Vol. 2:** 698
24:2	**Vol. 1:** 537
24:3	**Vol. 3:** 119
24:4	**Vol. 3:** 794
24:5*	**Vol. 2:** 181–182
24:6–11	**Vol. 1:** 122 **Vol. 2:** 336
24:6*	**Vol. 1:** 349 **Vol. 2:** 227 **Vol. 3:** 97
24:9	**Vol. 2:** 876
24:10	**Vol. 3:** 531
24:12*	**Vol. 1:** 177 **Vol. 3:** 93
24:14	**Vol. 2:** 745
24:15	**Vol. 3:** 355
24:16	**Vol. 2:** 363
24:17	**Vol. 3:** 356
24:22	**Vol. 1:** 493
25	**Vol. 2:** 511
25:1†	**Vol. 2:** 417
25:3	**Vol. 1:** 565
25:5	**Vol. 3:** 1024
25:6	**Vol. 2:** 170, 778
25:7*	**Vol. 1:** 332
25:9	**Vol. 2:** 650
25:13	**Vol. 3:** 120–121
25:15*	**Vol. 1:** 332
25:18	**Vol. 3:** 919
25:23	**Vol. 2:** 876
25:25†	**Vol. 2:** 649 **Vol. 3:** 1024
25:26	**Vol. 2:** 222 **Vol. 3:** 206, 740
25:28	**Vol. 1:** 596
25:29	**Vol. 3:** 531
25:31	**Vol. 2:** 41, 181–182, 707, 854 **Vol. 3:** 206
25:33	**Vol. 3:** 206
25:39	**Vol. 2:** 158
25:40 f	**Vol. 1:** 128
25:41	**Vol. 2:** 876
25:42 f	**Vol. 2:** 576
25:44	**Vol. 3:** 1057
26:9–23	**Vol. 1:** 122
26:10	**Vol. 3:** 720
26:17	**Vol. 1:** 285
26:19	**Vol. 1:** 108 **Vol. 2:** 296, 720 **Vol. 3:** 150, 421, 557
26:20	**Vol. 3:** 531
26:23 f	**Vol. 3:** 134
26:23	**Vol. 3:** 879
27:11	**Vol. 3:** 354
27:12	**Vol. 3:** 828
28	**Vol. 3:** 270
28:3†	**Vol. 2:** 417, 554
28:6	**Vol. 1:** 511 **Vol. 2:** 296 **Vol. 3:** 1174
28:7 ff	**Vol. 2:** 206
28:7 f	**Vol. 2:** 554
28:7	**Vol. 2:** 554
28:8	**Vol. 1:** 420, 709 **Vol. 2:** 554
28:9†	**Vol. 1:** 451 **Vol. 2:** 554
28:12 ff	**Vol. 1:** 451 **Vol. 3:** 293
28:13	**Vol. 1:** 450 **Vol. 3:** 270
28:14	**Vol. 2:** 876
28:15	**Vol. 3:** 270
28:17	**Vol. 1:** 255
28:24	**Vol. 3:** 917
29:3	**Vol. 2:** 305–306
29:4	**Vol. 3:** 167, 468
29:6	**Vol. 3:** 937
29:8	**Vol. 1:** 553
30:2	**Vol. 2:** 426
30:11 f	**Vol. 3:** 988
30:11	**Vol. 1:** 520
30:12 f	**Vol. 2:** 226
30:12	**Vol. 2:** 687
30:14	**Vol. 2:** 303
30:15	**Vol. 2:** 226
30:17*	**Vol. 2:** 495 **Vol. 3:** 209
30:25	**Vol. 3:** 354
30:26 ff	**Vol. 1:** 195
31	**Vol. 1:** 433
31:1	**Vol. 2:** 226
31:4	**Vol. 3:** 1016
31:9 f	**Vol. 1:** 393
31:10	**Vol. 1:** 233 **Vol. 3:** 787, 1069
31:12	**Vol. 1:** 233, 264

2 Samuel

1:2	**Vol. 1:** 609 **Vol. 2:** 876
1:4	**Vol. 3:** 1120
1:12	**Vol. 1:** 612 **Vol. 2:** 796
1:14 ff	**Vol. 1:** 122

2 Samuel *(cont'd)*

1:14	**Vol. 3:** 97
1:17 f	**Vol. 3:** 673
1:17–27	**Vol. 2:** 418
1:18	**Vol. 3:** 484, 760
1:21	**Vol. 3:** 416
1:22	**Vol. 3:** 159
1:23	**Vol. 3:** 716
1:26	**Vol. 2:** 355, 540
2–3	**Vol. 3:** 873
2:1	**Vol. 3:** 1089
2:2–5	**Vol. 3:** 1062
2:4 ff	**Vol. 2:** 336
2:4	**Vol. 1:** 61
2:5	**Vol. 2:** 596 **Vol. 3:** 263
2:6	**Vol. 3:** 1153–1154
2:10	**Vol. 1:** 492
2:13	**Vol. 3:** 1194
2:16	**Vol. 2:** 303
2:25 f	**Vol. 3:** 1009
2:32	**Vol. 1:** 170
3	**Vol. 1:** 366
3:1	**Vol. 3:** 994
3:2–5	**Vol. 2:** 576
3:9	**Vol. 2:** 612
3:12 f	**Vol. 1:** 366
3:13	**Vol. 3:** 1057
3:17	**Vol. 1:** 195
3:18	**Vol. 3:** 206, 608–609
3:21	**Vol. 1:** 366
3:24	**Vol. 2:** 777
3:27	**Vol. 3:** 1192
3:29	**Vol. 1:** 324
3:31–34	**Vol. 2:** 417
3:31	**Vol. 3:** 120
3:33 ff	**Vol. 2:** 418
3:39	**Vol. 3:** 134
4:1	**Vol. 3:** 178
4:2	**Vol. 3:** 823
4:3	**Vol. 1:** 690
4:4	**Vol. 2:** 414
4:6	**Vol. 3:** 209
4:8	**Vol. 3:** 531
4:9	**Vol. 3:** 192
4:10	**Vol. 2:** 108
5:1–12	**Vol. 1:** 121
5:1–5	**Vol. 1:** 61
5:1	**Vol. 1:** 241
5:2	**Vol. 2:** 797 **Vol. 3:** 565
5:3	**Vol. 1:** 195 **Vol. 2:** 336
5:6 ff	**Vol. 1:** 218 **Vol. 2:** 324, 335–336, 802
5:6–10	**Vol. 2:** 325 **Vol. 3:** 1010
5:6 f	**Vol. 2:** 186
5:6	**Vol. 2:** 415
5:8 f	**Vol. 2:** 415
5:8	**Vol. 3:** 860
5:9	**Vol. 1:** 272
5:10*	**Vol. 2:** 69
5:14	**Vol. 3:** 659

5:23	**Vol. 2:** 898
6	**Vol. 2:** 325 **Vol. 3:** 782, 788
6:1 ff	**Vol. 2:** 335–336
6:2	**Vol. 1:** 280 **Vol. 2:** 69, 325, 650
6:3	**Vol. 3:** 1010
6:5	**Vol. 3:** 673
6:7	**Vol. 1:** 108
6:11*	**Vol. 1:** 143
6:15 f	**Vol. 2:** 186
6:16 ff	**Vol. 3:** 426
6:16 f	**Vol. 3:** 1057
6:18	**Vol. 2:** 69, 649–651
6:21	**Vol. 1:** 538
7	**Vol. 1:** 122, 177 **Vol. 2:** 378 **Vol. 3:** 426, 828, 1092, 1104
7:1–11b	**Vol. 2:** 374
7:1	**Vol. 1:** 426
7:2	**Vol. 2:** 69 **Vol. 3:** 787
7:4	**Vol. 2:** 898 **Vol. 3:** 1090
7:5 f	**Vol. 2:** 247
7:5	**Vol. 3:** 946
7:6	**Vol. 2:** 889 **Vol. 3:** 794
7:8 ff	**Vol. 1:** 596
7:8*	**Vol. 2:** 69
7:9	**Vol. 1:** 209 **Vol. 3:** 636
7:10	**Vol. 1:** 277 **Vol. 3:** 866
7:11–14	**Vol. 3:** 650
7:11 f	**Vol. 2:** 247
7:11	**Vol. 1:** 426 **Vol. 3:** 254, 787
7:12 ff	**Vol. 3:** 509
7:12–17	**Vol. 3:** 787
7:12–16	**Vol. 1:** 366 **Vol. 3:** 636, 642, 648, 650, 652
7:12	**Vol. 2:** 614 **Vol. 3:** 117, 279, 639
7:13	**Vol. 2:** 612, 650
7:14 f	**Vol. 3:** 778
7:14	**Vol. 1:** 123, 178, 241, 615, 617 **Vol. 2:** 614 **Vol. 3:** 637, 639, 648–650
7:15	**Vol. 1:** 607
7:16	**Vol. 1:** 210, 596 **Vol. 2:** 247, 374, 614 **Vol. 3:** 786
7:18 f	**Vol. 2:** 247
7:18	**Vol. 3:** 588
7:21	**Vol. 3:** 314
7:23	**Vol. 2:** 425 **Vol. 3:** 192–193, 318
7:24	**Vol. 3:** 117
7:25 ff*	**Vol. 2:** 69
7:25–29	**Vol. 2:** 247
7:25	**Vol. 3:** 1104
7:26 f	**Vol. 2:** 69
7:27	**Vol. 2:** 862–863 **Vol. 3:** 311
7:29	**Vol. 1:** 207
8:2	**Vol. 3:** 421
8:6	**Vol. 3:** 207, 421
8:14	**Vol. 3:** 207
8:16–18	**Vol. 3:** 478
8:17	**Vol. 2:** 34 **Vol. 3:** 408, 478
9:3	**Vol. 2:** 414
9:6	**Vol. 2:** 876
9:7	**Vol. 2:** 521

2 Samuel *(cont'd)*

9:8	**Vol. 2:** 876	**Vol. 3:** 595, 608
9:13	**Vol. 2:** 415	
10:4	**Vol. 1:** 128	
10:5	**Vol. 2:** 49	
10:6	**Vol. 1:** 128	**Vol. 2:** 139, 698
10:12	**Vol. 2:** 563	**Vol. 3:** 718
10:17	**Vol. 2:** 32	
10:18	**Vol. 2:** 698	
10:19	**Vol. 3:** 608	
11–12	**Vol. 2:** 336	
11:2	**Vol. 2:** 103	
11:3	**Vol. 1:** 266	**Vol. 2:** 576
11:4	**Vol. 2:** 225	**Vol. 3:** 861
11:7	**Vol. 2:** 777–778	
11:13	**Vol. 2:** 586	
11:14 f	**Vol. 1:** 246	**Vol. 3:** 484
11:14	**Vol. 1:** 243	
11:23	**Vol. 3:** 716	
11:24	**Vol. 3:** 608	
12	**Vol. 3:** 1092	
12:1 ff	**Vol. 3:** 78	
12:1–4	**Vol. 2:** 747	
12:1 f	**Vol. 2:** 841	
12:1	**Vol. 2:** 820	
12:3	**Vol. 1:** 240	**Vol. 2:** 820, 822
12:4	**Vol. 1:** 687	**Vol. 2:** 820, 841
12:5	**Vol. 1:** 108	
12:7	**Vol. 3:** 201	
12:13	**Vol. 1:** 109	**Vol. 3:** 579
12:14	**Vol. 1:** 554	**Vol. 3:** 342
12:15 ff	**Vol. 3:** 997	
12:15	**Vol. 1:** 433	
12:16–23	**Vol. 1:** 612	
12:19	**Vol. 2:** 554	
12:20	**Vol. 1:** 120	**Vol. 2:** 876
12:23	**Vol. 3:** 946	
12:24 f	**Vol. 3:** 605	
12:28	**Vol. 2:** 649	
12:29	**Vol. 2:** 32	
12:30	**Vol. 1:** 405	
12:31	**Vol. 1:** 726	
13	**Vol. 1:** 555	**Vol. 2:** 478
13:1	**Vol. 2:** 103	
13:3	**Vol. 3:** 1027	
13:11	**Vol. 3:** 747	
13:12	**Vol. 2:** 260	
13:13	**Vol. 1:** 258	**Vol. 3:** 1024
13:14	**Vol. 1:** 331	
13:17	**Vol. 1:** 194	
13:19	**Vol. 2:** 157	**Vol. 3:** 94
13:25	**Vol. 3:** 711	
13:27	**Vol. 3:** 711	
13:35	**Vol. 2:** 898	
13:37	**Vol. 2:** 422	
14:2	**Vol. 1:** 120 **Vol. 2:** 711 **Vol. 3:** 480, 1027	
14:4	**Vol. 2:** 876	**Vol. 3:** 206
14:5–7	**Vol. 2:** 747	

14:7	**Vol. 3:** 94, 109	
14:9	**Vol. 2:** 612	
14:11	**Vol. 1:** 609	**Vol. 3:** 94
14:13 f	**Vol. 3:** 823	
14:14	**Vol. 1:** 433	**Vol. 3:** 820, 823–824
14:16	**Vol. 2:** 297	**Vol. 3:** 201
14:20 f	**Vol. 3:** 1120	
14:20	**Vol. 3:** 1027	
14:22	**Vol. 2:** 116, 876	
14:25	**Vol. 3:** 817	
14:26	**Vol. 3:** 752	
14:30	**Vol. 2:** 303	
14:33	**Vol. 2:** 876	
15:1–6	**Vol. 3:** 357	
15:4	**Vol. 2:** 363	**Vol. 3:** 355
15:5	**Vol. 2:** 876	
15:6	**Vol. 2:** 363	
15:7	**Vol. 2:** 60	
15:10	**Vol. 2:** 173	
15:13	**Vol. 3:** 45	
15:14	**Vol. 2:** 803	
15:15	**Vol. 1:** 534, 537	**Vol. 3:** 608
15:16	**Vol. 1:** 698	
15:24 ff	**Vol. 2:** 778	**Vol. 3:** 439
15:24–29	**Vol. 3:** 788	
15:25	**Vol. 2:** 117	
15:30	**Vol. 2:** 157	
15:32	**Vol. 2:** 876	
15:34	**Vol. 3:** 350	
16:1	**Vol. 3:** 919, 1161	
16:2	**Vol. 2:** 257	
16:4	**Vol. 2:** 876	
16:5–13	**Vol. 3:** 872	
16:8	**Vol. 3:** 134, 159	
16:10 ff	**Vol. 1:** 108	
16:10 f	**Vol. 1:** 698	
16:14	**Vol. 3:** 686	
16:20 ff	**Vol. 3:** 1074	
16:21	**Vol. 1:** 331	
16:23	**Vol. 1:** 665	
17:4	**Vol. 1:** 195	**Vol. 3:** 1120
17:8	**Vol. 3:** 178	
17:15	**Vol. 1:** 195	**Vol. 3:** 439
17:23	**Vol. 1:** 117, 433	
18:18	**Vol. 2:** 149, 590, 649 **Vol. 3:** 239	
18:20	**Vol. 2:** 108	
18:21	**Vol. 2:** 876–877	
18:22	**Vol. 2:** 108	
18:28 f	**Vol. 2:** 778	
18:28	**Vol. 2:** 170, 876	
18:31	**Vol. 2:** 363	**Vol. 3:** 356
19:1	**Vol. 2:** 422	**Vol. 3:** 1179
19:6 f	**Vol. 1:** 555	
19:6	**Vol. 3:** 209	
19:9	**Vol. 2:** 363	**Vol. 3:** 201
19:11	**Vol. 3:** 439	
19:12	**Vol. 1:** 195	
19:19	**Vol. 3:** 823	
19:20*	**Vol. 3:** 820, 823	
19:21 f	**Vol. 1:** 122	

2 Samuel *(cont'd)*

19:22	**Vol. 2:** 336
19:26	**Vol. 1:** 117
19:27*	**Vol. 2:** 415
19:29*	**Vol. 3:** 354
19:35*	**Vol. 2:** 395 **Vol. 3:** 672–673
19:39	**Vol. 1:** 537
19:44*	**Vol. 3:** 29, 823
20:2	**Vol. 2:** 349
20:3	**Vol. 1:** 698
20:8	**Vol. 3:** 1161
20:9	**Vol. 2:** 170
20:14	**Vol. 1:** 293
20:16	**Vol. 3:** 1027
20:19	**Vol. 3:** 1069
20:20	**Vol. 3:** 157, 160
20:22	**Vol. 3:** 1027
20:24	**Vol. 3:** 239
21:1–14	**Vol. 3:** 154
21:3 f	**Vol. 3:** 159
21:6	**Vol. 1:** 538
21:10	**Vol. 1:** 113 **Vol. 3:** 255
21:17	**Vol. 3:** 109
22:1	**Vol. 3:** 673
22:2	**Vol. 3:** 381, 673
22:3	**Vol. 3:** 715
22:5	**Vol. 2:** 621
22:6	**Vol. 3:** 180
22:7	**Vol. 3:** 786
22:8	**Vol. 2:** 189
22:9	**Vol. 1:** 657
22:11	**Vol. 1:** 280
22:15	**Vol. 3:** 1001
22:17	**Vol. 2:** 636
22:18	**Vol. 1:** 555 **Vol. 3:** 201
22:20	**Vol. 2:** 817
22:23	**Vol. 3:** 354
22:24	**Vol. 3:** 924
22:26	**Vol. 2:** 60
22:28	**Vol. 2:** 260, 262, 596, 821
22:29	**Vol. 2:** 485
22:31	**Vol. 3:** 924
22:32 ff	**Vol. 2:** 602
22:32	**Vol. 1:** 382
22:33	**Vol. 3:** 924
22:35	**Vol. 3:** 760
22:36	**Vol. 2:** 179
22:43	**Vol. 3:** 915
22:44	**Vol. 3:** 201
22:49	**Vol. 3:** 201
22:50	**Vol. 1:** 344 **Vol. 2:** 655 **Vol. 3:** 672
23:1 f	**Vol. 1:** 122
23:1	**Vol. 2:** 336 **Vol. 3:** 671
23:2	**Vol. 3:** 691
23:4	**Vol. 2:** 491
23:14	**Vol. 1:** 170
23:16 f	**Vol. 3:** 158
23:16	**Vol. 2:** 854
23:17	**Vol. 3:** 157

23:24	**Vol. 1:** 170
24	**Vol. 3:** 1092
24:1	**Vol. 1:** 108, 451, 562 **Vol. 3:** 468, 557
24:3	**Vol. 3:** 1016
24:4	**Vol. 3:** 152
24:9	**Vol. 2:** 698
24:10 ff	**Vol. 3:** 997
24:10	**Vol. 1:** 349 **Vol. 3:** 1025
24:11 ff	**Vol. 3:** 1089
24:12	**Vol. 1:** 537
24:13	**Vol. 2:** 265
24:14	**Vol. 1:** 609 **Vol. 2:** 598
24:15	**Vol. 2:** 698 **Vol. 3:** 846
24:16 f	**Vol. 1:** 101
24:16	**Vol. 1:** 109, 468
24:17–25	**Vol. 3:** 150
24:17	**Vol. 2:** 412 **Vol. 3:** 565
24:18–25	**Vol. 3:** 418, 787
24:20	**Vol. 2:** 876
24:24	**Vol. 2:** 41
24:25	**Vol. 3:** 421

1 Kings

1–11	**Vol. 3:** 606
1	**Vol. 3:** 605
1:8	**Vol. 3:** 78
1:11 ff	**Vol. 3:** 78
1:12	**Vol. 3:** 209
1:14	**Vol. 1:** 734
1:16	**Vol. 2:** 876
1:23	**Vol. 2:** 876
1:25	**Vol. 2:** 521
1:29	**Vol. 3:** 192
1:31	**Vol. 2:** 876
1:33 ff	**Vol. 1:** 122
1:33	**Vol. 2:** 711
1:36	**Vol. 1:** 98
1:39 f	**Vol. 3:** 673
1:39	**Vol. 1:** 121
1:41 ff	**Vol. 2:** 521
1:41	**Vol. 3:** 112
1:42	**Vol. 2:** 109
1:47	**Vol. 2:** 586, 876 **Vol. 3:** 636
1:48	**Vol. 2:** 797
1:53	**Vol. 2:** 876
2	**Vol. 3:** 605
2:2	**Vol. 3:** 938
2:3	**Vol. 2:** 639 **Vol. 3:** 354, 937
2:4	**Vol. 3:** 879, 1104
2:5	**Vol. 1:** 239 **Vol. 3:** 120, 159
2:6	**Vol. 3:** 1027
2:9	**Vol. 3:** 1027
2:12	**Vol. 2:** 376
2:13 ff	**Vol. 3:** 1074
2:13	**Vol. 2:** 876
2:19	**Vol. 2:** 146, 612 **Vol. 3:** 588
2:24	**Vol. 3:** 117
2:26	**Vol. 1:** 520
2:27	**Vol. 1:** 735 **Vol. 3:** 426, 1104

1 Kings *(cont'd)*

2:28	**Vol. 3:** 419
2:29†	**Vol. 1:** 559
2:31	**Vol. 3:** 159
2:32 ff	**Vol. 3:** 159
2:34	**Vol. 3:** 94
2:35	**Vol. 1:** 665 **Vol. 3:** 439
2:42*	**Vol. 3:** 1041
3:1	**Vol. 1:** 531 **Vol. 2:** 357 **Vol. 3:** 240, 605, 1027
3:2	**Vol. 2:** 650 **Vol. 3:** 426
3:4–15	**Vol. 1:** 511–512
3:4	**Vol. 3:** 1010
3:5–14	**Vol. 3:** 1029
3:6	**Vol. 3:** 879
3:7 ff	**Vol. 2:** 336
3:7	**Vol. 2:** 428
3:9	**Vol. 1:** 503 **Vol. 3:** 130–131, 606
3:11 ff	**Vol. 2:** 478
3:11	**Vol. 2:** 841 **Vol. 3:** 130
3:12	**Vol. 2:** 181 **Vol. 3:** 606, 1027
3:13	**Vol. 2:** 841
3:14	**Vol. 1:** 332 **Vol. 3:** 946
3:16–28	**Vol. 3:** 606, 1029
3:16	**Vol. 1:** 498
3:20	**Vol. 1:** 239–240
3:28	**Vol. 3:** 354
4:2 ff	**Vol. 3:** 33
4:3	**Vol. 3:** 239
4:6	**Vol. 2:** 254
4:7–19	**Vol. 3:** 605
4:16	**Vol. 3:** 815
4:20*	**Vol. 3:** 1028
4:25	**Vol. 1:** 724 **Vol. 3:** 256, 866
4:29–34	**Vol. 3:** 606
4:29*	**Vol. 1:** 670 **Vol. 2:** 181
5:9–14*	**Vol. 3:** 1028
5:9 f*	**Vol. 3:** 1027
5:9*	**Vol. 1:** 127 **Vol. 3:** 1027
5:10	**Vol. 3:** 787, 1028
5:11–16*	**Vol. 2:** 698
5:11*	**Vol. 3:** 1028–1029, 1033
5:12 f*	**Vol. 3:** 1029
5:12*	**Vol. 1:** 366 **Vol. 3:** 605, 673, 1029
5:13	**Vol. 3:** 1069
5:14*	**Vol. 3:** 1027, 1029
5:17	**Vol. 2:** 650
5:18*	**Vol. 3:** 254, 787
5:21*	**Vol. 3:** 1029
5:26*	**Vol. 2:** 777 **Vol. 3:** 1027
6 f	**Vol. 3:** 782
6–8	**Vol. 3:** 787
6–7	**Vol. 3:** 783
6	**Vol. 3:** 606
6:1	**Vol. 3:** 937
6:3	**Vol. 3:** 786
6:4	**Vol. 3:** 787
6:5	**Vol. 3:** 786, 948
6:12	**Vol. 3:** 933, 1104
6:15	**Vol. 1:** 389
6:23–28	**Vol. 1:** 280
6:33	**Vol. 3:** 786
6:36	**Vol. 3:** 787, 794
7–9	**Vol. 3:** 426
7:5	**Vol. 2:** 830
7:9 f*	**Vol. 1:** 661
7:12	**Vol. 3:** 787
7:13–47	**Vol. 2:** 97
7:13 f	**Vol. 3:** 787
7:14*	**Vol. 2:** 395
7:15–45	**Vol. 3:** 795
7:21	**Vol. 3:** 786
7:23–26	**Vol. 3:** 418, 787
7:38	**Vol. 1:** 742
7:48	**Vol. 1:** 586 **Vol. 3:** 423
7:50†	**Vol. 3:** 786
7:51	**Vol. 1:** 734
8	**Vol. 1:** 195, 531
8:1 ff	**Vol. 3:** 788
8:1	**Vol. 1:** 293 **Vol. 2:** 324
8:4	**Vol. 3:** 786, 812
8:5	**Vol. 3:** 426, 815
8:8	**Vol. 3:** 786
8:9	**Vol. 2:** 639 **Vol. 3:** 815
8:10 f	**Vol. 1:** 735 **Vol. 2:** 45 **Vol. 3:** 788
8:10	**Vol. 3:** 786
8:12–13	**Vol. 2:** 190
8:12	**Vol. 1:** 422 **Vol. 2:** 215
8:13	**Vol. 2:** 650
8:14 ff	**Vol. 2:** 650
8:14	**Vol. 1:** 210
8:15	**Vol. 1:** 735 **Vol. 3:** 1104
8:16 f	**Vol. 3:** 784
8:16	**Vol. 1:** 538
8:17	**Vol. 2:** 181
8:20	**Vol. 3:** 1104
8:22 ff	**Vol. 2:** 863
8:22	**Vol. 3:** 418, 787
8:24 ff	**Vol. 3:** 608
8:24	**Vol. 1:** 735 **Vol. 3:** 1104
8:25	**Vol. 3:** 946
8:26	**Vol. 1:** 596
8:27	**Vol. 2:** 189–190, 247 **Vol. 3:** 727
8:28 ff	**Vol. 2:** 336, 862
8:28 f	**Vol. 2:** 863
8:28	**Vol. 2:** 860
8:29	**Vol. 3:** 786
8:30	**Vol. 2:** 190, 860 **Vol. 3:** 157, 786
8:31 f	**Vol. 3:** 740
8:32	**Vol. 3:** 355, 357
8:33–47	**Vol. 2:** 860
8:33–36	**Vol. 1:** 345
8:33	**Vol. 2:** 862
8:34	**Vol. 3:** 157
8:35	**Vol. 2:** 260, 862 **Vol. 3:** 1001
8:36	**Vol. 3:** 157, 316
8:37 ff	**Vol. 2:** 265
8:38	**Vol. 2:** 860, 863
8:39	**Vol. 3:** 157, 533

1 Kings *(cont'd)*

8:41 ff	**Vol. 1:** 688
8:42	**Vol. 1:** 320 **Vol. 2:** 862
8:44	**Vol. 2:** 862
8:45	**Vol. 2:** 860, 863 **Vol. 3:** 354
8:46–53	**Vol. 3:** 1104
8:48	**Vol. 2:** 862
8:49	**Vol. 2:** 860, 863
8:50	**Vol. 3:** 157
8:51	**Vol. 2:** 297
8:52	**Vol. 2:** 860
8:53	**Vol. 2:** 297, 639 **Vol. 3:** 673
8:54	**Vol. 1:** 210 **Vol. 2:** 860, 862–863 **Vol. 3:** 418
8:56	**Vol. 2:** 357, 639 **Vol. 3:** 256, 1104
8:58	**Vol. 3:** 937
8:59	**Vol. 3:** 354
8:60	**Vol. 2:** 720
8:61	**Vol. 2:** 60, 593, 778
8:62–65	**Vol. 3:** 426
8:63	**Vol. 2:** 673
8:64	**Vol. 3:** 418, 787
8:65	**Vol. 1:** 293
8:66	**Vol. 2:** 357
9	**Vol. 3:** 828
9:3	**Vol. 2:** 860, 863
9:6–10	**Vol. 3:** 815
9:6–9	**Vol. 1:** 354
9:6	**Vol. 2:** 876
9:9	**Vol. 2:** 876
9:15–19	**Vol. 3:** 605
9:21	**Vol. 3:** 593
9:25	**Vol. 3:** 418, 787
9:26	**Vol. 3:** 983
9:27	**Vol. 3:** 593
10:1–13	**Vol. 2:** 680 **Vol. 3:** 606
10:1–10	**Vol. 2:** 381 **Vol. 3:** 1030
10:1–9	**Vol. 3:** 1029
10:1	**Vol. 2:** 745 **Vol. 3:** 799
10:7	**Vol. 3:** 1027
10:18 ff	**Vol. 2:** 612
10:18	**Vol. 2:** 96
10:21	**Vol. 2:** 96 **Vol. 3:** 823
10:22	**Vol. 3:** 606
10:23 f	**Vol. 3:** 1029
10:23	**Vol. 2:** 841
10:25–29	**Vol. 1:** 117
10:25	**Vol. 1:** 415 **Vol. 3:** 606
10:26	**Vol. 3:** 605
10:28–29	**Vol. 1:** 531
11:1 ff	**Vol. 1:** 492 **Vol. 2:** 791
11:1–11	**Vol. 2:** 576
11:1–10	**Vol. 3:** 606
11:2	**Vol. 2:** 349
11:4	**Vol. 1:** 688 **Vol. 2:** 60, 593, 778 **Vol. 3:** 835
11:5	**Vol. 2:** 67
11:11*	**Vol. 1:** 333
11:13	**Vol. 1:** 538
11:14	**Vol. 3:** 468
11:15	**Vol. 1:** 264
11:23	**Vol. 3:** 468
11:25	**Vol. 3:** 468
11:25b	**Vol. 3:** 468
11:27	**Vol. 3:** 950
11:29 ff	**Vol. 2:** 626
11:29	**Vol. 2:** 670
11:31	**Vol. 2:** 797
11:32	**Vol. 1:** 538
11:34	**Vol. 1:** 538
11:38	**Vol. 1:** 332
11:40	**Vol. 1:** 531
11:41	**Vol. 3:** 1120
12	**Vol. 1:** 61
12:1 ff	**Vol. 1:** 295 **Vol. 2:** 374
12:1–20	**Vol. 3:** 606
12:3 ff	**Vol. 1:** 293
12:3	**Vol. 1:** 295
12:4	**Vol. 3:** 752
12:6 ff	**Vol. 1:** 195
12:8	**Vol. 3:** 1016
12:9 ff	**Vol. 3:** 1161
12:10	**Vol. 1:** 239
12:11	**Vol. 1:** 510
12:14	**Vol. 1:** 510
12:15	**Vol. 3:** 1104
12:21	**Vol. 1:** 293 **Vol. 2:** 305
12:24	**Vol. 2:** 765 **Vol. 3:** 255, 1120
12:26 ff	**Vol. 2:** 325 **Vol. 3:** 33
12:27 f	**Vol. 3:** 426
12:27	**Vol. 2:** 325
12:28 ff	**Vol. 3:** 33, 104
12:28 f	**Vol. 3:** 872
12:28	**Vol. 2:** 325
12:32	**Vol. 1:** 474
13:1 ff	**Vol. 2:** 626
13:1–31	**Vol. 3:** 77
13:2 ff	**Vol. 3:** 426
13:3	**Vol. 2:** 633
13:4	**Vol. 1:** 515 **Vol. 3:** 999
13:5	**Vol. 2:** 633
13:6	**Vol. 2:** 860, 862
13:11	**Vol. 3:** 78
13:17*	**Vol. 1:** 332
13:20	**Vol. 3:** 254, 588
13:22	**Vol. 1:** 264
13:30	**Vol. 3:** 1051
14:2 ff	**Vol. 3:** 426
14:6	**Vol. 1:** 127
14:7	**Vol. 2:** 797
14:8	**Vol. 1:** 481 **Vol. 3:** 608, 946
14:9	**Vol. 1:** 233
14:11	**Vol. 2:** 859
14:16	**Vol. 2:** 116
14:21	**Vol. 1:** 538
14:24	**Vol. 2:** 791
14:25 ff	**Vol. 1:** 531
14:26	**Vol. 2:** 830 **Vol. 3:** 788
15:3	**Vol. 2:** 593, 778

1 Kings *(cont'd)*

15:14	**Vol. 2:** 778
15:18	**Vol. 2:** 830 **Vol. 3:** 788
15:29	**Vol. 3:** 1120
15:31	**Vol. 1:** 243
15:34	**Vol. 3:** 938
16:8	**Vol. 3:** 788
16:9	**Vol. 2:** 254
16:17	**Vol. 3:** 418
16:31	**Vol. 2:** 582, 876 **Vol. 3:** 1067
16:34	**Vol. 3:** 444
17–19	**Vol. 1:** 209
17 f	**Vol. 2:** 627
17	**Vol. 1:** 543 **Vol. 3:** 558
17:1–18:1	**Vol. 2:** 730
17:1	**Vol. 1:** 209, 474, 545 **Vol. 2:** 265, 688, 861 **Vol. 3:** 1091
17:2	**Vol. 3:** 1090, 1120
17:3 f	**Vol. 2:** 274
17:4 ff	**Vol. 1:** 173
17:4	**Vol. 2:** 688
17:7	**Vol. 1:** 515 **Vol. 3:** 786
17:8	**Vol. 3:** 1090, 1120
17:12–16	**Vol. 2:** 711
17:12	**Vol. 1:** 543
17:13	**Vol. 1:** 328
17:14	**Vol. 3:** 1001
17:17–24	**Vol. 2:** 433, 628, 630 **Vol. 3:** 1059, 1067
17:17–22	**Vol. 3:** 261
17:18–16	**Vol. 3:** 1062
17:18	**Vol. 3:** 78, 239
17:19	**Vol. 1:** 240, 442
17:21	**Vol. 1:** 272 **Vol. 2:** 167 **Vol. 3:** 680
17:24	**Vol. 3:** 880
18–22	**Vol. 3:** 1057
18	**Vol. 2:** 724 **Vol. 3:** 426
18:1	**Vol. 1:** 209 **Vol. 2:** 688, 861 **Vol. 3:** 1090, 1120
18:2 ff	**Vol. 2:** 274
18:2a	**Vol. 1:** 209
18:3 ff	**Vol. 3:** 608
18:3	**Vol. 2:** 254
18:4	**Vol. 2:** 582 **Vol. 3:** 988
18:12 ff	**Vol. 3:** 266
18:13	**Vol. 2:** 582 **Vol. 3:** 988
18:16 f	**Vol. 1:** 209
18:17	**Vol. 3:** 1091
18:19–40	**Vol. 3:** 77
18:19	**Vol. 1:** 589
18:24 ff	**Vol. 1:** 272
18:26	**Vol. 2:** 863
18:27	**Vol. 2:** 432
18:28	**Vol. 1:** 527 **Vol. 2:** 437, 573, 854
18:29	**Vol. 2:** 863
18:30 ff	**Vol. 3:** 426
18:31 f	**Vol. 3:** 418
18:36 ff	**Vol. 2:** 627
18:36	**Vol. 3:** 609, 1091
18:38	**Vol. 1:** 655 **Vol. 2:** 628 **Vol. 3:** 266, 421
18:39	**Vol. 1:** 610
18:40	**Vol. 3:** 209
18:41 ff	**Vol. 1:** 210
18:41–46	**Vol. 1:** 209
18:41–45	**Vol. 3:** 988
18:42	**Vol. 3:** 1009
18:44	**Vol. 3:** 1161
18:45	**Vol. 3:** 266
18:46	**Vol. 2:** 898 **Vol. 3:** 946
19	**Vol. 3:** 721
19:1–18	**Vol. 3:** 1013
19:1 f	**Vol. 2:** 582
19:2 ff	**Vol. 3:** 962
19:2	**Vol. 3:** 846
19:3 ff	**Vol. 3:** 1008
19:4–6	**Vol. 3:** 1005
19:8	**Vol. 2:** 893 **Vol. 3:** 804
19:10	**Vol. 1:** 545 **Vol. 2:** 724, 882 **Vol. 3:** 252, 426, 531, 1166
19:11 ff	**Vol. 2:** 281
19:11–18	**Vol. 3:** 1005
19:11–14	**Vol. 3:** 266
19:11 f	**Vol. 1:** 655
19:11	**Vol. 3:** 382, 707
19:12	**Vol. 1:** 280 **Vol. 3:** 1010, 1091
19:14	**Vol. 1:** 545 **Vol. 2:** 724 **Vol. 3:** 531, 1166
19:16 ff	**Vol. 3:** 97
19:16	**Vol. 2:** 337, 711
19:17	**Vol. 3:** 209
19:18	**Vol. 1:** 545 **Vol. 2:** 85, 690–691, 699, 859, 876 **Vol. 3:** 248, 252, 325, 436
19:19 ff	**Vol. 1:** 485
19:19	**Vol. 1:** 116 **Vol. 3:** 121, 1161
19:20 f	**Vol. 1:** 492–493
19:20	**Vol. 1:** 481
19:21	**Vol. 1:** 492 **Vol. 3:** 1161
20	**Vol. 3:** 960
20:6	**Vol. 3:** 533
20:7 f	**Vol. 1:** 195
20:7*	**Vol. 3:** 513
20:8*	**Vol. 3:** 497–498
20:9	**Vol. 1:** 127
20:11	**Vol. 1:** 227
20:13*	**Vol. 2:** 395–396, 800
20:20	**Vol. 1:** 268 **Vol. 3:** 209
20:28	**Vol. 2:** 395–396
20:33	**Vol. 2:** 554
20:34	**Vol. 1:** 366
20:39	**Vol. 3:** 593
20:41	**Vol. 2:** 573
20:42	**Vol. 1:** 414
21	**Vol. 1:** 640 **Vol. 3:** 1091
21:1	**Vol. 3:** 782
21:2*	**Vol. 3:** 166
21:5–25	**Vol. 2:** 582
21:6	**Vol. 3:** 846
21:7	**Vol. 2:** 181

1 Kings *(cont'd)*

21:8	**Vol. 1:** 195, 716 **Vol. 2:** 650
21:9 f	**Vol. 1:** 246
21:9*	**Vol. 1:** 165
21:10*	**Vol. 2:** 686 **Vol. 3:** 1041
21:11*	**Vol. 1:** 127, 165, 195, 716
21:12	**Vol. 2:** 158
21:13*	**Vol. 3:** 342, 1041
21:17 ff	**Vol. 3:** 1090
21:17–19	**Vol. 3:** 1091
21:19 ff	**Vol. 1:** 410
21:27	**Vol. 1:** 612, 672
21:29	**Vol. 2:** 117
22	**Vol. 3:** 960
22:2	**Vol. 2:** 663
22:8	**Vol. 1:** 555
22:10 f	**Vol. 3:** 1099
22:10	**Vol. 3:** 77
22:11	**Vol. 2:** 754 **Vol. 3:** 715
22:12	**Vol. 3:** 77
22:16	**Vol. 3:** 473
22:17	**Vol. 2:** 104, 413, 459
22:19 ff	**Vol. 2:** 190–191 **Vol. 3:** 474
22:19–23	**Vol. 3:** 720
22:19	**Vol. 2:** 189, 613–614 **Vol. 3:** 588
22:21 ff	**Vol. 2:** 458 **Vol. 3:** 693
22:21 f	**Vol. 3:** 692
22:24 ff	**Vol. 3:** 78
22:24	**Vol. 3:** 78
22:25	**Vol. 2:** 891
22:27 f	**Vol. 2:** 778
22:54	**Vol. 2:** 876

2 Kings

1	**Vol. 3:** 1091
1:2 f	**Vol. 3:** 469
1:2	**Vol. 2:** 67
1:3 f	**Vol. 1:** 101 **Vol. 3:** 1090–1091
1:3	**Vol. 1:** 273
1:8	**Vol. 3:** 121
1:9	**Vol. 1:** 273
1:10 ff	**Vol. 2:** 630
1:10	**Vol. 1:** 544, 655, 657
1:12	**Vol. 1:** 544, 654
2	**Vol. 3:** 558, 602
2:1 ff	**Vol. 3:** 78
2:1–15	**Vol. 3:** 266
2:1	**Vol. 3:** 78
2:2	**Vol. 3:** 265
2:3 ff	**Vol. 3:** 78
2:3	**Vol. 3:** 262
2:4	**Vol. 3:** 78
2:5	**Vol. 3:** 78, 262, 265
2:9–12	**Vol. 2:** 82
2:9 f	**Vol. 3:** 265
2:9	**Vol. 3:** 262, 691
2:11 f	**Vol. 3:** 602
2:11	**Vol. 1:** 655 **Vol. 2:** 189, 191 **Vol. 3:** 261, 266, 747
2:12	**Vol. 1:** 177, 617 **Vol. 3:** 602
2:13 f	**Vol. 1:** 116, 207 **Vol. 3:** 121
2:15	**Vol. 2:** 876 **Vol. 3:** 255, 266
2:16 ff	**Vol. 3:** 266
2:19–22	**Vol. 3:** 78, 444
2:23–25	**Vol. 3:** 78
2:24	**Vol. 2:** 651 **Vol. 3:** 584
3:13	**Vol. 3:** 1069
3:15	**Vol. 3:** 78, 673
3:21	**Vol. 3:** 120
3:22	**Vol. 1:** 205
3:27	**Vol. 3:** 421
4	**Vol. 3:** 558
4:1–7	**Vol. 3:** 78
4:1	**Vol. 2:** 96 **Vol. 3:** 594, 608
4:4	**Vol. 1:** 734
4:8–37	**Vol. 3:** 78
4:9	**Vol. 2:** 225
4:10	**Vol. 2:** 487
4:12	**Vol. 1:** 485
4:13 f	**Vol. 2:** 664
4:16 ff	**Vol. 3:** 846
4:16 f	**Vol. 3:** 846
4:17–37	**Vol. 2:** 433
4:18–37	**Vol. 2:** 628 **Vol. 3:** 78, 261
4:23	**Vol. 3:** 407
4:25–37	**Vol. 3:** 1067
4:29	**Vol. 1:** 207 **Vol. 3:** 120
4:32 ff	**Vol. 2:** 206
4:32–37	**Vol. 2:** 630 **Vol. 3:** 1059
4:33	**Vol. 2:** 862
4:34	**Vol. 2:** 167
4:37	**Vol. 2:** 876
4:38	**Vol. 3:** 78
4:42–44	**Vol. 3:** 1007
4:42	**Vol. 3:** 424
5	**Vol. 2:** 628
5:1 ff	**Vol. 2:** 464
5:1–19	**Vol. 3:** 986–987
5:1–14	**Vol. 3:** 78
5:1	**Vol. 2:** 622, 625
5:6	**Vol. 1:** 246
5:7	**Vol. 1:** 316 **Vol. 2:** 167
5:10	**Vol. 3:** 989
5:11–15	**Vol. 3:** 860
5:12	**Vol. 3:** 986
5:13 ff	**Vol. 2:** 167
5:13	**Vol. 1:** 617
5:14	**Vol. 1:** 144 **Vol. 3:** 989, 991
5:15	**Vol. 2:** 396
5:17	**Vol. 3:** 1161
5:18	**Vol. 2:** 876 **Vol. 3:** 152, 156, 255
5:23	**Vol. 3:** 711
5:25	**Vol. 1:** 474
5:27	**Vol. 2:** 349
6 f	**Vol. 2:** 627
6:1	**Vol. 3:** 78
6:3	**Vol. 2:** 257
6:5 ff	**Vol. 2:** 628
6:12	**Vol. 3:** 78

2 Kings *(cont'd)*

6:16	**Vol. 3:** 469
6:17 f	**Vol. 2:** 862
6:17	**Vol. 2:** 189, 729, 919
6:21	**Vol. 1:** 617
6:24 ff	**Vol. 1:** 210
6:26	**Vol. 3:** 206
6:31 ff	**Vol. 3:** 962
6:32	**Vol. 3:** 588
6:33	**Vol. 2:** 773
7:2	**Vol. 2:** 189 **Vol. 3:** 255
7:6	**Vol. 2:** 139
7:7–8	**Vol. 3:** 811
7:10	**Vol. 1:** 171
7:17	**Vol. 3:** 255
8:3	**Vol. 2:** 60
8:5	**Vol. 1:** 574
8:7–15	**Vol. 3:** 78
8:13	**Vol. 3:** 608
9	**Vol. 3:** 1092
9:3	**Vol. 1:** 121 **Vol. 2:** 711
9:6	**Vol. 1:** 121 **Vol. 2:** 711
9:7–37	**Vol. 2:** 582
9:7	**Vol. 3:** 93, 97, 608
9:11	**Vol. 1:** 527
9:13	**Vol. 2:** 379 **Vol. 3:** 873
9:18 ff	**Vol. 1:** 117
9:21	**Vol. 3:** 1161
9:22	**Vol. 2:** 554–555 **Vol. 3:** 1067
9:25	**Vol. 3:** 1161
9:30	**Vol. 3:** 1067
9:34	**Vol. 1:** 416
10:1–6	**Vol. 1:** 246
10:1	**Vol. 3:** 484
10:6	**Vol. 3:** 484
10:10–14	**Vol. 3:** 454
10:10	**Vol. 1:** 609 **Vol. 3:** 1104
10:11	**Vol. 3:** 33
10:19 ff	**Vol. 3:** 33
10:20	**Vol. 2:** 234 **Vol. 3:** 51
10:23	**Vol. 3:** 608
10:24	**Vol. 3:** 196, 209
10:30	**Vol. 2:** 117
10:31	**Vol. 2:** 440
11:1–12	**Vol. 3:** 33
11:4	**Vol. 1:** 366
11:12	**Vol. 1:** 122 **Vol. 2:** 711 **Vol. 3:** 636
11:14	**Vol. 3:** 673
11:18	**Vol. 2:** 287
11:19	**Vol. 1:** 122
12:4–16	**Vol. 3:** 426
12:10	**Vol. 2:** 830 **Vol. 3:** 478, 752
13	**Vol. 3:** 558
13:2	**Vol. 1:** 492
13:5	**Vol. 3:** 218, 462
13:7	**Vol. 3:** 266
13:14 ff	**Vol. 3:** 78
13:14–19	**Vol. 3:** 1099
13:14	**Vol. 1:** 617
13:17	**Vol. 2:** 726
13:20 f	**Vol. 3:** 261
13:23	**Vol. 1:** 366 **Vol. 2:** 117, 318
14:2	**Vol. 2:** 422
14:4	**Vol. 3:** 426
14:6	**Vol. 2:** 639 **Vol. 3:** 484
14:7	**Vol. 1:** 343
14:14	**Vol. 3:** 528
14:15 f	**Vol. 3:** 1120
14:16	**Vol. 1:** 442
14:22	**Vol. 1:** 442
14:26	**Vol. 2:** 117
14:29	**Vol. 1:** 442
15–17	**Vol. 1:** 52 **Vol. 2:** 306 **Vol. 3:** 94
15	**Vol. 3:** 267
15:4	**Vol. 3:** 426
15:5	**Vol. 3:** 860
15:7	**Vol. 1:** 442
15:11–36	**Vol. 3:** 1120
15:16	**Vol. 3:** 1166
15:22	**Vol. 1:** 442
15:30	**Vol. 3:** 208
15:35	**Vol. 3:** 426
15:38	**Vol. 1:** 442
16:3	**Vol. 1:** 655 **Vol. 2:** 208, 791
16:7 f	**Vol. 3:** 608
16:13 ff	**Vol. 3:** 426
16:13	**Vol. 3:** 423
16:15	**Vol. 3:** 421, 423
16:17	**Vol. 3:** 787–788
17	**Vol. 3:** 465
17:1	**Vol. 2:** 887 **Vol. 3:** 208
17:3	**Vol. 3:** 208
17:4	**Vol. 1:** 531 **Vol. 3:** 208
17:6	**Vol. 3:** 208
17:7 ff	**Vol. 3:** 1104
17:7–23	**Vol. 1:** 717 **Vol. 2:** 791
17:7	**Vol. 1:** 531
17:8	**Vol. 3:** 354
17:13 f	**Vol. 3:** 938
17:13	**Vol. 3:** 354, 1041
17:16	**Vol. 2:** 189, 876
17:17	**Vol. 1:** 268, 655 **Vol. 2:** 554–555
17:18	**Vol. 1:** 607
17:19 f	**Vol. 3:** 1104
17:19	**Vol. 3:** 354
17:20 f	**Vol. 3:** 460
17:23	**Vol. 3:** 594
17:24 ff	**Vol. 3:** 451
17:24	**Vol. 3:** 450
17:27 f	**Vol. 2:** 34
17:29	**Vol. 3:** 450
17:30	**Vol. 3:** 450
17:34	**Vol. 3:** 354
17:35 f	**Vol. 2:** 876
17:37	**Vol. 3:** 354
18 ff	**Vol. 2:** 325
18	**Vol. 3:** 267
18:1	**Vol. 3:** 208
18:3	**Vol. 1:** 559

2 Kings *(cont'd)*

18:4	**Vol. 1:** 509 **Vol. 2:** 639 **Vol. 3:** 426
18:6	**Vol. 2:** 349, 639
18:9 ff	**Vol. 1:** 67
18:9 f	**Vol. 3:** 208
18:12	**Vol. 2:** 639
18:13	**Vol. 3:** 866
18:14	**Vol. 2:** 96
18:15 f	**Vol. 3:** 782, 788
18:15	**Vol. 2:** 679
18:16	**Vol. 3:** 786, 878
18:17	**Vol. 3:** 115
18:18	**Vol. 2:** 254 **Vol. 3:** 232, 239
18:19	**Vol. 3:** 1089
18:21	**Vol. 1:** 531
18:22	**Vol. 2:** 876
18:29	**Vol. 3:** 1089
18:30−35	**Vol. 3:** 342
18:30	**Vol. 1:** 596
18:31	**Vol. 3:** 1089
18:32	**Vol. 3:** 201, 919
18:37	**Vol. 2:** 254 **Vol. 3:** 239
19:2	**Vol. 2:** 254 **Vol. 3:** 208
19:3	**Vol. 2:** 890
19:4	**Vol. 1:** 127 **Vol. 2:** 863 **Vol. 3:** 248, 341−342, 436
19:6	**Vol. 3:** 341−342
19:7	**Vol. 3:** 342
19:10−13	**Vol. 1:** 246
19:14	**Vol. 2:** 185
19:15†	**Vol. 1:** 280 **Vol. 2:** 724, 862−863
19:18	**Vol. 2:** 77
19:19	**Vol. 2:** 724
19:20	**Vol. 2:** 862
19:21	**Vol. 2:** 326
19:22	**Vol. 3:** 341−342
19:23	**Vol. 2:** 199 **Vol. 3:** 1009
19:26†	**Vol. 2:** 211
19:29	**Vol. 2:** 626
19:30	**Vol. 3:** 867
19:31	**Vol. 3:** 1166
19:35	**Vol. 1:** 444
19:36	**Vol. 2:** 679
19:37	**Vol. 2:** 876
20	**Vol. 2:** 628
20:1 ff	**Vol. 2:** 478
20:3	**Vol. 3:** 235, 943
20:5	**Vol. 2:** 863
20:7	**Vol. 2:** 167
20:8 ff	**Vol. 2:** 627
20:9 ff	**Vol. 3:** 554
20:9−11	**Vol. 3:** 846
20:12	**Vol. 1:** 246
20:13	**Vol. 2:** 357, 607
20:17	**Vol. 1:** 320
20:18	**Vol. 3:** 782, 786
21:3−6	**Vol. 2:** 555
21:3	**Vol. 2:** 189, 876 **Vol. 3:** 426
21:4	**Vol. 3:** 788
21:6	**Vol. 1:** 655 **Vol. 2:** 208, 554 **Vol. 3:** 94
21:8	**Vol. 1:** 333 **Vol. 2:** 639
21:10−15	**Vol. 1:** 717
21:13	**Vol. 3:** 402
21:14	**Vol. 2:** 297
21:16	**Vol. 2:** 525 **Vol. 3:** 94
21:21	**Vol. 2:** 876
22 f	**Vol. 1:** 55
22:1−23:30	**Vol. 3:** 783
22:3−13	**Vol. 3:** 478
22:4 ff	**Vol. 3:** 788
22:4	**Vol. 2:** 32 **Vol. 3:** 498
22:6	**Vol. 3:** 858
22:7	**Vol. 3:** 878
22:8	**Vol. 2:** 440
22:11	**Vol. 2:** 440
22:14−20	**Vol. 3:** 1057
22:16	**Vol. 3:** 786
22:17	**Vol. 3:** 109
22:19 f	**Vol. 1:** 717
22:20	**Vol. 2:** 32, 778 **Vol. 3:** 111
23−25	**Vol. 1:** 52, 61 **Vol. 3:** 94
23	**Vol. 2:** 306 **Vol. 3:** 783
23:1−12	**Vol. 3:** 788
23:1−3	**Vol. 2:** 797
23:3	**Vol. 3:** 354
23:4	**Vol. 3:** 786
23:5−9	**Vol. 2:** 34 **Vol. 3:** 426
23:5	**Vol. 3:** 731
23:10	**Vol. 2:** 208, 375 **Vol. 3:** 110, 421
23:11	**Vol. 3:** 266, 731, 796
23:12	**Vol. 3:** 787
23:13	**Vol. 3:** 1069
23:21−23	**Vol. 1:** 632 **Vol. 2:** 521
23:24 f	**Vol. 3:** 485
23:24	**Vol. 2:** 554−555
23:25 ff	**Vol. 1:** 717
23:25	**Vol. 1:** 354 **Vol. 2:** 639
23:27	**Vol. 1:** 607
23:33−34	**Vol. 1:** 531
23:33	**Vol. 2:** 96
23:34	**Vol. 2:** 649
24:3 f	**Vol. 3:** 156
24:11−21	**Vol. 1:** 686
24:13	**Vol. 3:** 782, 786
24:14 ff	**Vol. 1:** 686
25	**Vol. 3:** 959
25:4	**Vol. 3:** 948
25:7−30	**Vol. 3:** 1104
25:7	**Vol. 1:** 219
25:9	**Vol. 3:** 185, 788
25:10	**Vol. 3:** 178
25:12	**Vol. 3:** 918
25:13−17	**Vol. 3:** 185, 788
25:17	**Vol. 3:** 389
25:18	**Vol. 2:** 34
25:19	**Vol. 3:** 478
25:27−30	**Vol. 2:** 521
25:27	**Vol. 2:** 158

1 Chronicles

1:1	**Vol. 1:** 84
1:34	**Vol. 2:** 305 **Vol. 3:** 658
2:1 ff	**Vol. 3:** 652
2:21	**Vol. 2:** 578
2:24	**Vol. 3:** 1074
2:34 f	**Vol. 3:** 593
2:55	**Vol. 3:** 478
4:10	**Vol. 1:** 272
4:23	**Vol. 3:** 911
4:27	**Vol. 2:** 131
4:40	**Vol. 2:** 777 **Vol. 3:** 111
5:1	**Vol. 2:** 587
5:12	**Vol. 2:** 157
5:18	**Vol. 3:** 760
5:23	**Vol. 2:** 131
6:3	**Vol. 2:** 639
6:16–33	**Vol. 2:** 34
6:16*	**Vol. 3:** 256
6:31	**Vol. 3:** 673
6:49	**Vol. 2:** 639
6:54–81*	**Vol. 2:** 297
6:61–81†	**Vol. 2:** 695
7:2–40	**Vol. 2:** 698
7:5	**Vol. 2:** 683
7:22	**Vol. 2:** 422
8:6	**Vol. 1:** 165
8:28	**Vol. 1:** 165
9:21	**Vol. 3:** 1040
9:23	**Vol. 3:** 786
9:27	**Vol. 2:** 234, 730 **Vol. 3:** 786
9:29	**Vol. 2:** 293 **Vol. 3:** 786
9:32	**Vol. 1:** 586 **Vol. 3:** 117, 423, 814
10:13	**Vol. 2:** 554, 559
10:14	**Vol. 2:** 559
11–29	**Vol. 1:** 426
11:2	**Vol. 3:** 565
11:4 ff	**Vol. 2:** 324
11:4	**Vol. 2:** 324
11:19	**Vol. 3:** 157, 160
12:17	**Vol. 2:** 777
12:18	**Vol. 2:** 777
12:19	**Vol. 2:** 778
12:20–37	**Vol. 2:** 698
12:23	**Vol. 2:** 376
13:2	**Vol. 1:** 293
13:4	**Vol. 1:** 293
13:5	**Vol. 1:** 293
13:6	**Vol. 1:** 280
14:2	**Vol. 3:** 117
14:14	**Vol. 2:** 898
15:1	**Vol. 3:** 117
15:3	**Vol. 1:** 293
15:15	**Vol. 2:** 639
15:22	**Vol. 3:** 673
15:26	**Vol. 3:** 673
15:27	**Vol. 3:** 672–673
16:2	**Vol. 3:** 426
16:4	**Vol. 1:** 344 **Vol. 3:** 816
16:7	**Vol. 3:** 816, 817
16:9	**Vol. 1:** 574 **Vol. 3:** 668, 672–673
16:10	**Vol. 3:** 816
16:15	**Vol. 3:** 235, 828
16:23	**Vol. 3:** 672
16:24	**Vol. 1:** 574
16:25	**Vol. 1:** 622
16:26	**Vol. 2:** 285
16:28 f	**Vol. 1:** 227
16:29	**Vol. 2:** 876
16:33	**Vol. 3:** 865
16:34	**Vol. 2:** 100 **Vol. 3:** 828
16:35	**Vol. 3:** 218, 816
16:36	**Vol. 1:** 98–99 **Vol. 3:** 816, 828
16:39	**Vol. 3:** 812, 1010
16:40	**Vol. 3:** 426
16:41	**Vol. 1:** 537 **Vol. 3:** 816
16:42	**Vol. 3:** 673
17:5	**Vol. 3:** 794
17:7	**Vol. 2:** 69
17:10	**Vol. 2:** 260
17:11	**Vol. 3:** 117
17:13	**Vol. 1:** 617
17:19	**Vol. 2:** 425
17:21	**Vol. 3:** 192–193
17:23 ff	**Vol. 1:** 596
17:25	**Vol. 2:** 862
18:15–17	**Vol. 3:** 478
18:17	**Vol. 1:** 665
19:6 f	**Vol. 2:** 139
20:1	**Vol. 1:** 468
21	**Vol. 3:** 1092
21:1	**Vol. 1:** 562 **Vol. 3:** 468, 557
21:9	**Vol. 3:** 513
21:12–15	**Vol. 1:** 465
21:15	**Vol. 1:** 356
21:17	**Vol. 3:** 565
21:18–30	**Vol. 3:** 426
21:21	**Vol. 2:** 876
21:25	**Vol. 3:** 787
21:26	**Vol. 1:** 655
21:28 f	**Vol. 3:** 836
21:29	**Vol. 2:** 639 **Vol. 3:** 426, 1010
22:1	**Vol. 3:** 426
22:3	**Vol. 2:** 98 **Vol. 3:** 787
22:8	**Vol. 3:** 787
22:9	**Vol. 2:** 591, 778 **Vol. 3:** 111, 254–255
22:10	**Vol. 1:** 617
22:12	**Vol. 3:** 1027
22:13	**Vol. 2:** 639
22:15	**Vol. 3:** 1027
22:18	**Vol. 3:** 254
22:19	**Vol. 3:** 786
23:4	**Vol. 3:** 478
23:5	**Vol. 3:** 816
23:13 ff	**Vol. 2:** 639
23:23	**Vol. 3:** 255
23:25	**Vol. 2:** 778
23:28–31	**Vol. 3:** 426
23:29†	**Vol. 1:** 586 **Vol. 3:** 402, 423, 917

1 Chronicles *(cont'd)*

23:30	**Vol. 3:** 816
23:32	**Vol. 3:** 786, 1040
24	**Vol. 2:** 34
24:3 ff	**Vol. 1:** 534
24:3	**Vol. 1:** 190 **Vol. 2:** 34
24:5 f	**Vol. 2:** 296
24:6	**Vol. 3:** 478
24:7 ff	**Vol. 1:** 200
24:7	**Vol. 1:** 665
25:3	**Vol. 1:** 344 **Vol. 3:** 208
25:6	**Vol. 3:** 669
25:7	**Vol. 3:** 673, 760
25:8	**Vol. 1:** 485
25:9 ff	**Vol. 1:** 200
25:15	**Vol. 3:** 208
26:14	**Vol. 2:** 299
26:25	**Vol. 3:** 208
26:29	**Vol. 1:** 503
27:1 ff	**Vol. 1:** 534
27:20	**Vol. 3:** 208
27:23	**Vol. 3:** 734
27:24	**Vol. 1:** 243
27:32	**Vol. 3:** 478
27:33	**Vol. 1:** 665
28:1	**Vol. 1:** 293
28:2	**Vol. 3:** 255
28:4	**Vol. 1:** 534
28:5	**Vol. 2:** 612
28:6	**Vol. 1:** 534, 537, 617
28:9	**Vol. 2:** 778
28:10	**Vol. 1:** 534
28:11	**Vol. 3:** 153, 156, 782
28:12	**Vol. 3:** 794
28:13	**Vol. 3:** 550
28:16	**Vol. 1:** 250, 586
28:20	**Vol. 3:** 156
28:21	**Vol. 3:** 1027
29:3	**Vol. 2:** 817, 838
29:4	**Vol. 2:** 234 **Vol. 3:** 786
29:7	**Vol. 2:** 848
29:9	**Vol. 3:** 572
29:10	**Vol. 1:** 293
29:11 ff	**Vol. 2:** 869
29:11	**Vol. 1:** 227, 650 **Vol. 3:** 514
29:12 f	**Vol. 1:** 345
29:12	**Vol. 2:** 841 **Vol. 3:** 713
29:13	**Vol. 1:** 344 **Vol. 3:** 816
29:15	**Vol. 1:** 688, 691 **Vol. 2:** 773 **Vol. 3:** 555
29:17	**Vol. 3:** 572
29:18	**Vol. 1:** 617
29:20	**Vol. 2:** 859, 876
29:21	**Vol. 3:** 423
29:22	**Vol. 3:** 36, 439
29:23	**Vol. 2:** 612
29:28	**Vol. 2:** 841

2 Chronicles

1–9	**Vol. 3:** 606
1:3	**Vol. 2:** 639 **Vol. 3:** 1010
1:4	**Vol. 3:** 117
1:6	**Vol. 3:** 426
1:10 f	**Vol. 3:** 1027
1:11 f	**Vol. 2:** 841, 845
1:12	**Vol. 2:** 845
1:13	**Vol. 3:** 1010
2:2–18*	**Vol. 2:** 698
2:4	**Vol. 1:** 586
2:6 f*	**Vol. 3:** 1027
2:8 ff	**Vol. 3:** 919
2:11 ff*	**Vol. 3:** 1027
2:15	**Vol. 3:** 919
3–5	**Vol. 3:** 787
3–4	**Vol. 3:** 783
3:10–13	**Vol. 1:** 280
3:14	**Vol. 3:** 794
3:17	**Vol. 3:** 786
4:1	**Vol. 3:** 418, 787
4:7 f	**Vol. 3:** 786
4:9	**Vol. 3:** 787
4:19	**Vol. 1:** 586 **Vol. 3:** 423
4:22	**Vol. 3:** 786, 794
5	**Vol. 1:** 195
5:2	**Vol. 2:** 324
5:5	**Vol. 3:** 786, 1040
5:6	**Vol. 1:** 295 **Vol. 3:** 426
5:10	**Vol. 2:** 639
5:11	**Vol. 3:** 786
5:12	**Vol. 3:** 873
5:13	**Vol. 2:** 100 **Vol. 3:** 673, 816
5:14	**Vol. 1:** 735
5:27	**Vol. 3:** 316
6:3	**Vol. 1:** 295
6:6	**Vol. 2:** 878
6:12 f	**Vol. 2:** 149
6:13	**Vol. 2:** 234 **Vol. 3:** 786
6:16	**Vol. 2:** 440
6:19 ff	**Vol. 2:** 862
6:19 f	**Vol. 2:** 863
6:21	**Vol. 3:** 157
6:23	**Vol. 3:** 355
6:24–27	**Vol. 1:** 345
6:24	**Vol. 2:** 862
6:25	**Vol. 3:** 157
6:26	**Vol. 2:** 260, 862
6:27	**Vol. 3:** 157
6:29	**Vol. 2:** 863
6:30	**Vol. 3:** 152
6:32	**Vol. 2:** 862
6:34	**Vol. 1:** 538 **Vol. 2:** 862
6:35	**Vol. 2:** 863 **Vol. 3:** 354
6:36–39	**Vol. 3:** 207
6:38	**Vol. 1:** 538 **Vol. 2:** 803, 862
6:39	**Vol. 2:** 863 **Vol. 3:** 157
6:41	**Vol. 3:** 207, 255
6:42	**Vol. 3:** 235

2 Chronicles (cont'd)

7:1	**Vol. 1:** 655, 735 **Vol. 2:** 862 **Vol. 3:** 421
7:3	**Vol. 2:** 876 **Vol. 3:** 816
7:4–8	**Vol. 3:** 426
7:5	**Vol. 2:** 673
7:6	**Vol. 3:** 669, 673
7:8	**Vol. 3:** 836
7:12	**Vol. 2:** 863 **Vol. 3:** 422
7:13	**Vol. 1:** 119
7:14	**Vol. 2:** 862 **Vol. 3:** 157, 531
7:15	**Vol. 2:** 863
7:19	**Vol. 2:** 876
7:21	**Vol. 2:** 116
7:22	**Vol. 2:** 876
8:11	**Vol. 3:** 1058
8:12	**Vol. 3:** 782
8:13	**Vol. 2:** 639
8:14	**Vol. 3:** 816
8:16	**Vol. 2:** 60
8:18	**Vol. 3:** 593
9:1–12	**Vol. 2:** 381 **Vol. 3:** 1030
9:1	**Vol. 2:** 745 **Vol. 3:** 799
9:3	**Vol. 3:** 1027
9:5	**Vol. 3:** 1027
9:6 f	**Vol. 3:** 1027
9:12	**Vol. 3:** 593
9:20	**Vol. 3:** 823
9:21	**Vol. 1:** 743
9:22 f	**Vol. 3:** 1027
9:22	**Vol. 2:** 841
9:25	**Vol. 3:** 835
9:29	**Vol. 3:** 513
10:4	**Vol. 3:** 1161
10:6 ff	**Vol. 1:** 195
10:7	**Vol. 2:** 817
10:9 ff	**Vol. 3:** 1161
10:9–14	**Vol. 3:** 1161
10:11	**Vol. 1:** 510
10:14	**Vol. 1:** 510 **Vol. 2:** 675 **Vol. 3:** 1161
11:6	**Vol. 1:** 170
11:15	**Vol. 1:** 451, 551 **Vol. 2:** 285
11:16	**Vol. 3:** 531
11:17	**Vol. 2:** 376
12:12	**Vol. 1:** 109 **Vol. 2:** 60
12:13	**Vol. 1:** 538
13:4	**Vol. 3:** 1009
13:6	**Vol. 1:** 606
13:7	**Vol. 2:** 675
13:10 ff	**Vol. 3:** 426
13:11	**Vol. 1:** 586 **Vol. 3:** 423
13:14	**Vol. 3:** 673
14:2*	**Vol. 2:** 103, 199
14:5 f*	**Vol. 3:** 255
15:3	**Vol. 3:** 883
15:5	**Vol. 3:** 835
15:7	**Vol. 2:** 139 **Vol. 3:** 178
15:8	**Vol. 3:** 782
15:10–12	**Vol. 2:** 784
15:10	**Vol. 2:** 784
15:12	**Vol. 3:** 531
15:15	**Vol. 3:** 255
15:17	**Vol. 3:** 426
16:9	**Vol. 2:** 593
16:11	**Vol. 2:** 56
16:12	**Vol. 2:** 167
16:14	**Vol. 1:** 120 **Vol. 3:** 238
17	**Vol. 3:** 478
17:5	**Vol. 2:** 841
17:6	**Vol. 2:** 199
17:7 ff	**Vol. 3:** 761
17:7	**Vol. 3:** 760
17:9	**Vol. 3:** 760
17:14	**Vol. 2:** 684
18:1	**Vol. 2:** 841
18:4	**Vol. 3:** 531
18:7	**Vol. 3:** 531
18:10	**Vol. 2:** 754
19:2	**Vol. 1:** 108
19:7	**Vol. 2:** 622
19:10	**Vol. 3:** 354
20:3	**Vol. 1:** 612 **Vol. 3:** 51
20:4	**Vol. 2:** 32
20:5	**Vol. 1:** 293
20:6	**Vol. 2:** 149
20:7	**Vol. 1:** 77 **Vol. 3:** 369
20:8	**Vol. 3:** 786
20:14	**Vol. 1:** 293
20:15	**Vol. 2:** 800 **Vol. 3:** 962
20:18	**Vol. 2:** 876
20:19	**Vol. 3:** 816
20:21	**Vol. 3:** 816
20:22	**Vol. 1:** 344
20:28	**Vol. 3:** 673
20:30	**Vol. 3:** 255
20:33	**Vol. 3:** 426
20:34	**Vol. 2:** 56
21:8	**Vol. 1:** 606
21:10	**Vol. 1:** 606
21:12–15	**Vol. 1:** 246
23:12	**Vol. 3:** 816
23:13	**Vol. 3:** 668, 672, 817
23:18	**Vol. 2:** 440, 639 **Vol. 3:** 484, 673
24:5	**Vol. 2:** 32
24:6	**Vol. 2:** 639 **Vol. 3:** 752, 1040
24:8	**Vol. 1:** 143
24:9	**Vol. 2:** 639 **Vol. 3:** 51, 752
24:10 f	**Vol. 1:** 143
24:11	**Vol. 1:** 190 **Vol. 2:** 32, 131
24:12	**Vol. 2:** 139
24:13	**Vol. 3:** 478
24:14	**Vol. 3:** 426
24:17	**Vol. 2:** 876
24:18	**Vol. 2:** 284
24:20 ff	**Vol. 3:** 82
24:21	**Vol. 3:** 430
24:22	**Vol. 3:** 514
24:27	**Vol. 1:** 581 **Vol. 3:** 483
25:4	**Vol. 2:** 639

2 Chronicles *(cont'd)*

25:5	**Vol. 1:** 537
25:6	**Vol. 2:** 139
25:14	**Vol. 2:** 876
25:15	**Vol. 1:** 108 **Vol. 2:** 285
25:26	**Vol. 2:** 56
26:2	**Vol. 1:** 442
26:10	**Vol. 3:** 918
26:16	**Vol. 3:** 786
26:18	**Vol. 1:** 606 **Vol. 3:** 786
26:19	**Vol. 2:** 293
26:22	**Vol. 3:** 208
26:23	**Vol. 1:** 442
27:2	**Vol. 3:** 786
27:6	**Vol. 3:** 117
28:6	**Vol. 2:** 889
28:8 ff	**Vol. 3:** 593
28:15	**Vol. 1:** 120
28:18	**Vol. 3:** 426
28:19	**Vol. 1:** 606
28:22	**Vol. 1:** 606
29:5	**Vol. 3:** 786
29:6	**Vol. 1:** 606
29:7	**Vol. 3:** 109, 782, 786
29:17	**Vol. 3:** 782
29:18	**Vol. 1:** 586
29:19	**Vol. 3:** 117
29:21–35	**Vol. 3:** 426
29:21	**Vol. 3:** 786
29:23 f	**Vol. 1:** 221
29:24	**Vol. 3:** 152
29:27–28	**Vol. 3:** 873
29:27	**Vol. 3:** 673
29:28 ff	**Vol. 2:** 876
29:28	**Vol. 3:** 672
29:30	**Vol. 3:** 668
29:31	**Vol. 3:** 423
29:32	**Vol. 3:** 421
29:34	**Vol. 3:** 421
29:35	**Vol. 3:** 423
29:66	**Vol. 3:** 786
30:2 f	**Vol. 2:** 528
30:2	**Vol. 1:** 293, 295
30:4	**Vol. 1:** 293, 295 **Vol. 2:** 815
30:5	**Vol. 3:** 51
30:7	**Vol. 1:** 606
30:8	**Vol. 3:** 595
30:10	**Vol. 2:** 431
30:13	**Vol. 1:** 295 **Vol. 2:** 528
30:15	**Vol. 2:** 528
30:16	**Vol. 1:** 333 **Vol. 2:** 639
30:17	**Vol. 1:** 295
30:18 f	**Vol. 3:** 153
30:18	**Vol. 2:** 862 **Vol. 3:** 152, 154
30:19	**Vol. 3:** 101
30:27	**Vol. 1:** 320 **Vol. 2:** 863
31:1	**Vol. 3:** 418
31:2	**Vol. 1:** 344 **Vol. 3:** 816
31:5–12	**Vol. 2:** 693

31:5 f	**Vol. 3:** 853
31:5	**Vol. 2:** 131, 711 **Vol. 3:** 415
31:10	**Vol. 3:** 415
31:11	**Vol. 3:** 117
31:12	**Vol. 3:** 415
31:14	**Vol. 3:** 415
31:18	**Vol. 1:** 292
32	**Vol. 2:** 325
32:5	**Vol. 3:** 119
32:8	**Vol. 1:** 673, 679
32:12	**Vol. 2:** 876
32:13 ff	**Vol. 3:** 342
32:17	**Vol. 3:** 484
32:20	**Vol. 2:** 862 **Vol. 3:** 208
32:21	**Vol. 1:** 104, 320 **Vol. 3:** 342
32:22	**Vol. 3:** 255
32:24	**Vol. 2:** 633, 862
32:26	**Vol. 1:** 109
32:27	**Vol. 2:** 841
32:28	**Vol. 2:** 711
32:31	**Vol. 1:** 194, 373 **Vol. 2:** 633 **Vol. 3:** 799–800
32:32	**Vol. 3:** 208
33:3 f	**Vol. 3:** 426
33:3	**Vol. 2:** 876
33:6	**Vol. 2:** 208, 554–555
33:7	**Vol. 2:** 287
33:8	**Vol. 2:** 639 **Vol. 3:** 354
33:9	**Vol. 2:** 458
33:13	**Vol. 2:** 862
33:16	**Vol. 2:** 423
33:18 f	**Vol. 2:** 863
33:19	**Vol. 1:** 606
34:1–35:27	**Vol. 3:** 783
34:4	**Vol. 3:** 238
34:8–21	**Vol. 3:** 478
34:12	**Vol. 3:** 673
34:14	**Vol. 2:** 639
34:25	**Vol. 3:** 109
34:28	**Vol. 3:** 238
34:29*	**Vol. 2:** 32
35:3	**Vol. 3:** 788
35:4	**Vol. 3:** 117
35:5	**Vol. 3:** 786
35:6–14	**Vol. 3:** 426
35:6	**Vol. 2:** 639 **Vol. 3:** 117
35:12	**Vol. 2:** 639
35:13	**Vol. 1:** 654
35:14 f	**Vol. 3:** 117
35:16	**Vol. 3:** 117
35:25	**Vol. 3:** 673
36	**Vol. 1:** 52
36:13	**Vol. 1:** 354
36:21 f	**Vol. 1:** 735
36:21	**Vol. 1:** 734, 736 **Vol. 3:** 191
36:22 f	**Vol. 3:** 97
36:22	**Vol. 1:** 340 **Vol. 3:** 51
36:23	**Vol. 1:** 332

Ezra

1	**Vol. 3:** 788
1:1 ff	**Vol. 3:** 97
1:1–8	**Vol. 3:** 451
1:1	**Vol. 3:** 691
1:7*	**Vol. 2:** 284
2:6	**Vol. 3:** 208
2:19	**Vol. 2:** 773
2:21	**Vol. 1:** 170
2:36–39	**Vol. 2:** 466
2:40	**Vol. 2:** 466 **Vol. 3:** 208
2:63	**Vol. 2:** 296
2:69	**Vol. 2:** 848
3:2 f	**Vol. 3:** 788
3:2–7	**Vol. 3:** 427
3:2	**Vol. 2:** 639 **Vol. 3:** 484–485
3:5	**Vol. 3:** 421
3:6	**Vol. 3:** 786
3:8 ff	**Vol. 3:** 788
3:9	**Vol. 2:** 319
3:10	**Vol. 3:** 786, 873
3:12	**Vol. 3:** 788
4	**Vol. 3:** 451
4:1	**Vol. 3:** 873
4:7–6:12	**Vol. 1:** 246
4:7	**Vol. 1:** 580
4:8 f	**Vol. 3:** 478
4:8–6:18	**Vol. 1:** 51
4:12 f	**Vol. 3:** 350
4:12	**Vol. 1:** 606
4:14	**Vol. 3:** 444
4:15	**Vol. 1:** 606
4:16	**Vol. 3:** 350
4:17	**Vol. 2:** 431
4:19	**Vol. 1:** 606
5:3	**Vol. 3:** 350
5:9	**Vol. 3:** 350
5:11 f	**Vol. 2:** 190
5:11	**Vol. 3:** 350
5:12	**Vol. 3:** 177–178
6:2	**Vol. 3:** 236
6:3	**Vol. 2:** 199
6:5	**Vol. 3:** 782
6:9 f	**Vol. 2:** 190 **Vol. 3:** 427
6:11	**Vol. 1:** 393–394
6:14	**Vol. 1:** 196 **Vol. 3:** 350
6:17	**Vol. 2:** 683 **Vol. 3:** 427
6:18	**Vol. 2:** 639
7:6–26	**Vol. 3:** 485
7:6	**Vol. 2:** 149, 639 **Vol. 3:** 478–479
7:10	**Vol. 1:** 580 **Vol. 3:** 478, 760
7:11	**Vol. 3:** 479
7:12–26	**Vol. 1:** 51 **Vol. 3:** 479
7:12*	**Vol. 2:** 190, 441
7:14*	**Vol. 2:** 441
7:17	**Vol. 3:** 427
7:21*	**Vol. 2:** 190, 441 **Vol. 3:** 485
7:22	**Vol. 3:** 444
7:23	**Vol. 2:** 190
7:25*	**Vol. 2:** 441
7:26*	**Vol. 2:** 441
8:1 ff	**Vol. 1:** 196
8:15–20	**Vol. 2:** 466
8:20	**Vol. 2:** 311 **Vol. 3:** 593
8:21–23	**Vol. 1:** 612
8:21	**Vol. 1:** 612
8:22	**Vol. 1:** 109
8:23	**Vol. 1:** 612 **Vol. 2:** 864
8:35	**Vol. 3:** 427
9 f	**Vol. 1:** 688 **Vol. 2:** 576
9–10	**Vol. 1:** 505
9	**Vol. 2:** 174 **Vol. 3:** 658
9:1	**Vol. 2:** 60 **Vol. 3:** 534
9:2	**Vol. 3:** 654
9:3–4	**Vol. 3:** 588
9:8	**Vol. 3:** 250, 787
9:11	**Vol. 2:** 796
9:13	**Vol. 3:** 255
9:15	**Vol. 3:** 250, 357
10:1	**Vol. 1:** 293 **Vol. 2:** 862
10:3	**Vol. 3:** 485
10:8	**Vol. 1:** 295, 414
10:11*	**Vol. 1:** 344–345
10:12	**Vol. 1:** 295
10:14	**Vol. 1:** 196
10:19	**Vol. 2:** 149 **Vol. 3:** 420, 427
10:23	**Vol. 2:** 319

Nehemiah

1:2 f	**Vol. 3:** 250
1:4–11	**Vol. 2:** 863
1:4	**Vol. 1:** 612 **Vol. 2:** 862, 864
1:6	**Vol. 2:** 862–863
1:7 f	**Vol. 2:** 639
1:8	**Vol. 3:** 234
1:9	**Vol. 1:** 685
1:10	**Vol. 3:** 192–193
1:11	**Vol. 2:** 863
1:32*	**Vol. 1:** 332
2:2	**Vol. 1:** 565
2:3	**Vol. 3:** 239
2:4	**Vol. 2:** 862
2:5	**Vol. 3:** 239
2:6	**Vol. 2:** 898
2:8	**Vol. 2:** 761
2:19	**Vol. 1:** 606
3:3	**Vol. 1:** 670
3:5	**Vol. 1:** 241
3:7	**Vol. 2:** 612
3:30	**Vol. 3:** 796
4	**Vol. 3:** 451
4:5*	**Vol. 3:** 255
4:9*	**Vol. 2:** 862
4:10	**Vol. 1:** 520
4:15*	**Vol. 2:** 395
5:1–5	**Vol. 3:** 594
5:3	**Vol. 1:** 98
5:5	**Vol. 2:** 70, 96

Nehemiah *(cont'd)*

5:6	**Vol. 1:** 108
5:8	**Vol. 3:** 111
5:13	**Vol. 1:** 317 **Vol. 3:** 816
5:14 f	**Vol. 3:** 711
5:18	**Vol. 3:** 711
5:19	**Vol. 3:** 235
6:2	**Vol. 3:** 823
6:3	**Vol. 3:** 255
6:6	**Vol. 1:** 606 **Vol. 3:** 823
6:10	**Vol. 1:** 420
6:12	**Vol. 2:** 139
6:14	**Vol. 3:** 235
6:16	**Vol. 2:** 60
6:18	**Vol. 3:** 786
7:1	**Vol. 3:** 672
7:3	**Vol. 2:** 136
7:26	**Vol. 1:** 170
7:44	**Vol. 3:** 672
7:46	**Vol. 3:** 36, 672
7:63 f	**Vol. 1:** 619
7:65	**Vol. 2:** 296
7:70	**Vol. 2:** 848
7:73	**Vol. 3:** 672
8 ff	**Vol. 1:** 333
8	**Vol. 2:** 34, 307, 441 **Vol. 3:** 485
8:1 – 13:28	**Vol. 3:** 485
8:1	**Vol. 2:** 639 **Vol. 3:** 478
8:2	**Vol. 1:** 293, 295
8:3	**Vol. 2:** 440 **Vol. 3:** 846
8:4	**Vol. 2:** 369
8:5	**Vol. 2:** 726
8:6	**Vol. 1:** 98 **Vol. 2:** 876
8:8	**Vol. 1:** 245 **Vol. 3:** 760
8:9	**Vol. 2:** 422, 887
8:10	**Vol. 2:** 355
8:14	**Vol. 2:** 440, 639
8:17	**Vol. 1:** 295 **Vol. 2:** 331
9	**Vol. 2:** 174
9:1	**Vol. 1:** 612
9:2	**Vol. 3:** 534
9:3	**Vol. 2:** 876
9:6	**Vol. 2:** 876 **Vol. 3:** 983
9:9	**Vol. 1:** 531
9:10	**Vol. 2:** 627
9:11	**Vol. 2:** 197
9:12	**Vol. 2:** 491
9:14	**Vol. 2:** 639
9:15	**Vol. 3:** 382
9:16	**Vol. 3:** 29
9:17	**Vol. 3:** 240
9:18	**Vol. 1:** 531
9:21	**Vol. 2:** 714 **Vol. 3:** 804 – 805, 953
9:26	**Vol. 1:** 354, 606 – 607 **Vol. 3:** 1041
9:27	**Vol. 2:** 807 **Vol. 3:** 218
9:28	**Vol. 3:** 202, 254
9:29 f	**Vol. 3:** 1041
9:30	**Vol. 3:** 691
9:34	**Vol. 3:** 1041
10:1	**Vol. 3:** 498
10:3	**Vol. 3:** 415
10:24	**Vol. 3:** 208
10:28	**Vol. 3:** 672
10:29	**Vol. 2:** 639
10:31	**Vol. 1:** 267 **Vol. 3:** 191
10:32 – 39	**Vol. 3:** 853
10:32	**Vol. 3:** 407, 752
10:33 – 37	**Vol. 3:** 427
10:33	**Vol. 1:** 586
10:34	**Vol. 3:** 421, 423 – 424, 484, 841
10:35*	**Vol. 2:** 440
10:37 f	**Vol. 2:** 467, 693
10:37*	**Vol. 2:** 440, 693
10:38 – 39	**Vol. 2:** 693
10:38*	**Vol. 3:** 796
10:39*	**Vol. 3:** 672, 796
10:40*	**Vol. 3:** 416
11:3	**Vol. 1:** 165
11:9	**Vol. 1:** 190 **Vol. 2:** 319
11:14	**Vol. 1:** 190
11:16 f	**Vol. 1:** 165
11:17	**Vol. 2:** 863
11:22	**Vol. 1:** 190 **Vol. 3:** 672
12:8	**Vol. 2:** 319
12:24	**Vol. 3:** 77, 668 – 669, 816
12:27	**Vol. 1:** 344 **Vol. 3:** 673
12:28 f	**Vol. 3:** 672
12:36	**Vol. 2:** 319 **Vol. 3:** 77, 673, 816
12:37	**Vol. 3:** 816
12:42	**Vol. 1:** 190 **Vol. 3:** 672
12:44	**Vol. 2:** 303, 693 **Vol. 3:** 415, 796, 852
12:45 ff	**Vol. 3:** 672
12:46	**Vol. 1:** 665 **Vol. 3:** 669
12:47	**Vol. 2:** 303
13:1 – 10	**Vol. 1:** 688
13:1	**Vol. 2:** 639
13:2	**Vol. 2:** 139
13:4 f	**Vol. 3:** 796
13:4 – 9†	**Vol. 3:** 35, 788
13:5*	**Vol. 1:** 332 **Vol. 2:** 693 **Vol. 3:** 416, 427, 672
13:7	**Vol. 3:** 796
13:8 f	**Vol. 3:** 796
13:9	**Vol. 3:** 427
13:10	**Vol. 2:** 303 **Vol. 3:** 672
13:12	**Vol. 2:** 693 **Vol. 3:** 853
13:13	**Vol. 1:** 670 **Vol. 3:** 823
13:14	**Vol. 3:** 235
13:15 – 22	**Vol. 3:** 407
13:15	**Vol. 3:** 1041
13:17	**Vol. 1:** 716
13:19	**Vol. 1:** 283
13:20	**Vol. 2:** 716
13:21	**Vol. 3:** 1041
13:22	**Vol. 3:** 235
13:23 ff	**Vol. 1:** 505, 688
13:28†	**Vol. 3:** 35, 451
13:29	**Vol. 3:** 36, 235
13:31	**Vol. 3:** 235, 841

Esther

1:1 ff	**Vol. 1:** 512
1:1	**Vol. 2:** 807 **Vol. 3:** 823
1:4	**Vol. 2:** 841–842
1:6	**Vol. 3:** 588
1:7	**Vol. 2:** 96
1:8	**Vol. 2:** 254, 441 **Vol. 3:** 115
1:10	**Vol. 3:** 545
1:13	**Vol. 2:** 441
1:14	**Vol. 1:** 665 **Vol. 2:** 53
1:15	**Vol. 2:** 441
1:18	**Vol. 1:** 364
1:19	**Vol. 2:** 441 **Vol. 3:** 821
1:20	**Vol. 2:** 841
2:2	**Vol. 3:** 545, 1071
2:9	**Vol. 3:** 570
2:12	**Vol. 2:** 294
2:18	**Vol. 2:** 576
2:19	**Vol. 2:** 164 **Vol. 3:** 1071
2:22	**Vol. 2:** 488
2:23	**Vol. 3:** 232
3:2	**Vol. 2:** 876–877
3:4	**Vol. 2:** 895
3:5	**Vol. 2:** 876–877
3:8	**Vol. 2:** 441
3:9	**Vol. 1:** 330 **Vol. 3:** 796, 821
3:10	**Vol. 3:** 498
3:12	**Vol. 2:** 650 **Vol. 3:** 478
3:13	**Vol. 1:** 688 **Vol. 2:** 144 **Vol. 3:** 570, 711, 924
3:15	**Vol. 2:** 803
4:7	**Vol. 3:** 69
4:8	**Vol. 1:** 330
4:13	**Vol. 3:** 234
4:14	**Vol. 3:** 873
4:16	**Vol. 1:** 612 **Vol. 2:** 441
4:17	**Vol. 1:** 637 **Vol. 2:** 291, 876 **Vol. 3:** 29–30, 109, 669, 816
5:1	**Vol. 2:** 863
5:2	**Vol. 3:** 820
5:4	**Vol. 3:** 821
5:10	**Vol. 2:** 839
5:11	**Vol. 1:** 665 **Vol. 2:** 841–842
5:14	**Vol. 1:** 390, 393
6:1	**Vol. 3:** 236, 545, 766
6:3	**Vol. 2:** 116 **Vol. 3:** 545
6:4	**Vol. 1:** 393
6:5	**Vol. 3:** 545
6:9	**Vol. 3:** 51
6:10	**Vol. 2:** 164 **Vol. 3:** 585
6:11	**Vol. 3:** 51
6:12	**Vol. 2:** 839
7:4	**Vol. 3:** 468
7:5	**Vol. 1:** 364
7:7	**Vol. 3:** 279
7:8	**Vol. 3:** 588, 711
7:9 f	**Vol. 1:** 393
8:1	**Vol. 2:** 41 **Vol. 3:** 468, 846
8:3	**Vol. 2:** 860
8:5	**Vol. 2:** 116, 452 **Vol. 3:** 821
8:8	**Vol. 3:** 484, 498, 821
8:9	**Vol. 2:** 254 **Vol. 3:** 478
8:10	**Vol. 3:** 498
8:12	**Vol. 1:** 393 **Vol. 2:** 803
8:13	**Vol. 2:** 735, 876 **Vol. 3:** 29, 818
8:17	**Vol. 2:** 357
9:2	**Vol. 3:** 846
9:13 f	**Vol. 1:** 393
9:16 ff	**Vol. 3:** 254
9:17	**Vol. 3:** 255
9:22	**Vol. 2:** 576 **Vol. 3:** 254
9:23	**Vol. 3:** 484
9:27	**Vol. 2:** 357
9:28	**Vol. 3:** 237
10:1	**Vol. 3:** 756
10:3 ff	**Vol. 1:** 512
10:3†	**Vol. 2:** 842
10:3*	**Vol. 1:** 580

Job

1 f	**Vol. 1:** 83 **Vol. 2:** 191
1	**Vol. 1:** 111
1:1 – 2:10	**Vol. 3:** 720
1:1	**Vol. 1:** 704 **Vol. 2:** 139 **Vol. 3:** 355
1:3	**Vol. 1:** 188 **Vol. 3:** 1161
1:5	**Vol. 3:** 421, 425
1:6 ff	**Vol. 1:** 89 **Vol. 2:** 189–190
1:6	**Vol. 1:** 101, 474 **Vol. 3:** 636
1:7	**Vol. 3:** 943
1:8	**Vol. 1:** 704 **Vol. 2:** 144 **Vol. 3:** 355, 608
1:10	**Vol. 3:** 1148
1:11 f	**Vol. 3:** 801
1:11	**Vol. 3:** 342
1:12	**Vol. 3:** 474, 860
1:20	**Vol. 2:** 876
1:21 f	**Vol. 2:** 771, 775
1:21	**Vol. 3:** 821
1:22	**Vol. 3:** 1024
2	**Vol. 1:** 111
2:1	**Vol. 3:** 232, 636
2:2	**Vol. 3:** 943
2:3 – 10	**Vol. 1:** 467
2:3	**Vol. 2:** 144 **Vol. 3:** 608, 924
2:4	**Vol. 2:** 478
2:5	**Vol. 1:** 240 **Vol. 3:** 342
2:6 f	**Vol. 3:** 801
2:6	**Vol. 3:** 857
2:8	**Vol. 3:** 588
2:9	**Vol. 2:** 767 **Vol. 3:** 255, 342
2:10	**Vol. 2:** 771, 775 **Vol. 3:** 720, 1024–1025
2:11 f	**Vol. 1:** 89
2:11	**Vol. 3:** 908
3:1	**Vol. 2:** 727, 887
3:3	**Vol. 2:** 569
3:5	**Vol. 3:** 554
3:8	**Vol. 1:** 326, 523

Job *(cont'd)*

3:9	**Vol. 2:** 495, 773 **Vol. 3:** 735
3:11 f	**Vol. 2:** 478
3:12–19	**Vol. 3:** 270
3:12	**Vol. 1:** 240
3:13	**Vol. 3:** 254
3:16	**Vol. 1:** 182
3:17	**Vol. 2:** 93 **Vol. 3:** 254, 256
3:18	**Vol. 3:** 908
3:23	**Vol. 3:** 255
3:26	**Vol. 3:** 254
4:3	**Vol. 1:** 568, 570
4:4	**Vol. 3:** 994
4:5	**Vol. 3:** 1169
4:6	**Vol. 3:** 1024
4:7	**Vol. 3:** 103
4:8	**Vol. 3:** 522, 525–526
4:9	**Vol. 1:** 108 **Vol. 3:** 691
4:10	**Vol. 3:** 109
4:14	**Vol. 3:** 557
4:15	**Vol. 1:** 672
4:16	**Vol. 1:** 706 **Vol. 3:** 293
4:17	**Vol. 3:** 924
4:18	**Vol. 1:** 101
4:19	**Vol. 3:** 915
4:21	**Vol. 3:** 815, 1027
5:1	**Vol. 1:** 101
5:6 f	**Vol. 1:** 262
5:9	**Vol. 3:** 1153
5:11	**Vol. 2:** 261–262, 596, 771
5:12	**Vol. 1:** 412 **Vol. 3:** 166
5:13	**Vol. 2:** 616 **Vol. 3:** 747, 1027
5:14	**Vol. 2:** 498
5:17 f	**Vol. 1:** 562
5:17	**Vol. 2:** 141 **Vol. 3:** 717
5:18	**Vol. 2:** 149, 167
5:19	**Vol. 2:** 663
5:20	**Vol. 3:** 166, 201
5:21	**Vol. 3:** 859
5:24	**Vol. 2:** 778
5:25	**Vol. 3:** 846
5:26	**Vol. 3:** 835, 846
6:2	**Vol. 3:** 908, 1160
6:5	**Vol. 1:** 409, 520
6:6	**Vol. 3:** 444, 449
6:10	**Vol. 2:** 765, 773
6:11	**Vol. 2:** 773 **Vol. 3:** 680
6:15	**Vol. 2:** 53
6:19	**Vol. 2:** 93
6:24	**Vol. 3:** 721, 760
6:26	**Vol. 2:** 765
6:27	**Vol. 2:** 737
7:1	**Vol. 2:** 139, 475
7:2	**Vol. 2:** 139
7:3	**Vol. 1:** 420, 547 **Vol. 2:** 773
7:6	**Vol. 1:** 547
7:7–10	**Vol. 3:** 235, 261
7:11	**Vol. 2:** 663
7:12†	**Vol. 1:** 508 **Vol. 3:** 983
7:15	**Vol. 1:** 240 **Vol. 3:** 166
7:16	**Vol. 1:** 547 **Vol. 2:** 475
7:18	**Vol. 1:** 190 **Vol. 3:** 255
8:4–6	**Vol. 3:** 140
8:5	**Vol. 3:** 717
8:7	**Vol. 1:** 665 **Vol. 3:** 134
8:9	**Vol. 2:** 475
8:10	**Vol. 3:** 760, 1027
8:11	**Vol. 3:** 866
8:12	**Vol. 1:** 608 **Vol. 2:** 211, 261
8:13	**Vol. 2:** 93
8:15	**Vol. 2:** 773
8:19 f	**Vol. 2:** 93
8:21	**Vol. 2:** 261, 431
8:22	**Vol. 1:** 314 **Vol. 2:** 93
9:4	**Vol. 2:** 773 **Vol. 3:** 1027
9:5	**Vol. 2:** 714 **Vol. 3:** 1010
9:6	**Vol. 1:** 523, 661
9:7	**Vol. 3:** 498, 731, 735
9:8	**Vol. 2:** 724 **Vol. 3:** 943, 983
9:12–20	**Vol. 3:** 342
9:12	**Vol. 3:** 166
9:13	**Vol. 1:** 670
9:17 ff	**Vol. 2:** 167
9:20 f	**Vol. 2:** 93
9:20	**Vol. 3:** 924
9:23	**Vol. 3:** 355
9:25	**Vol. 1:** 326 **Vol. 3:** 821
9:31	**Vol. 1:** 479
9:32 f	**Vol. 3:** 721
9:33	**Vol. 1:** 373
9:34	**Vol. 3:** 166
10:2 f	**Vol. 2:** 93
10:2	**Vol. 3:** 760
10:3	**Vol. 2:** 735
10:4	**Vol. 1:** 679
10:7	**Vol. 2:** 93
10:8–9	**Vol. 3:** 915
10:11	**Vol. 1:** 672
10:15	**Vol. 2:** 49, 93
10:19	**Vol. 3:** 166, 238
10:20	**Vol. 2:** 428 **Vol. 3:** 254, 842
10:21 f	**Vol. 2:** 206
10:21	**Vol. 1:** 523 **Vol. 3:** 946
10:22	**Vol. 2:** 735
11:4	**Vol. 2:** 144 **Vol. 3:** 924
11:6	**Vol. 3:** 1027
11:8	**Vol. 2:** 197
11:9	**Vol. 3:** 402
11:11	**Vol. 3:** 1149
11:15	**Vol. 1:** 479
11:17	**Vol. 2:** 495
11:18	**Vol. 1:** 277 **Vol. 2:** 777
11:20	**Vol. 3:** 1027
12:2	**Vol. 3:** 1027
12:3	**Vol. 2:** 565
12:4	**Vol. 2:** 431 **Vol. 3:** 924
12:8	**Vol. 1:** 670
12:11	**Vol. 1:** 503 **Vol. 3:** 125
12:12 f	**Vol. 3:** 1027

Job *(cont'd)*

12:13	**Vol. 3:** 130
12:15	**Vol. 2:** 222
12:16†	**Vol. 2:** 458
12:19	**Vol. 2:** 596
12:20	**Vol. 3:** 166
12:22	**Vol. 1:** 423 **Vol. 2:** 197, 212 **Vol. 3:** 554
12:24 ff	**Vol. 2:** 206
12:24	**Vol. 3:** 166
12:25	**Vol. 2:** 491
13:3	**Vol. 3:** 1016
13:5	**Vol. 3:** 1027
13:10	**Vol. 1:** 503 **Vol. 2:** 622
13:11	**Vol. 1:** 609
13:12	**Vol. 3:** 236
13:13	**Vol. 3:** 255
13:22	**Vol. 1:** 272 **Vol. 2:** 766
13:23	**Vol. 3:** 760
13:24	**Vol. 2:** 215
13:25	**Vol. 1:** 743
13:28	**Vol. 2:** 714
14	**Vol. 2:** 565
14:1 ff	**Vol. 1:** 551
14:1	**Vol. 3:** 842
14:2	**Vol. 1:** 609 **Vol. 3:** 555
14:4	**Vol. 1:** 479
14:5	**Vol. 3:** 842
14:6	**Vol. 2:** 139
14:7 ff	**Vol. 3:** 866
14:7	**Vol. 3:** 866
14:9	**Vol. 1:** 503 **Vol. 3:** 599
14:12	**Vol. 1:** 442
14:13–22	**Vol. 2:** 206
14:13	**Vol. 3:** 238, 842
14:14	**Vol. 1:** 184 **Vol. 2:** 773, 890 **Vol. 3:** 261
14:15	**Vol. 3:** 1148
14:17	**Vol. 1:** 142 **Vol. 3:** 498–499
14:18	**Vol. 2:** 714
14:19	**Vol. 2:** 773
14:21 f	**Vol. 2:** 206
15:2–6	**Vol. 3:** 342
15:2	**Vol. 3:** 1027
15:5	**Vol. 1:** 503 **Vol. 3:** 1079
15:6	**Vol. 3:** 1041
15:7 f	**Vol. 2:** 761
15:8	**Vol. 3:** 1027
15:10	**Vol. 1:** 92
15:11	**Vol. 2:** 71
15:12	**Vol. 1:** 364
15:14	**Vol. 2:** 144 **Vol. 3:** 348, 924
15:15	**Vol. 1:** 101 **Vol. 2:** 144, 376 **Vol. 3:** 103, 924
15:18	**Vol. 3:** 1027
15:20	**Vol. 2:** 475
15:21	**Vol. 2:** 778 **Vol. 3:** 821
15:24	**Vol. 2:** 663
15:26 f	**Vol. 3:** 29
15:29	**Vol. 2:** 841 **Vol. 3:** 224
15:31	**Vol. 2:** 773
15:33	**Vol. 1:** 609
15:34	**Vol. 1:** 295 **Vol. 3:** 1040
16:2	**Vol. 1:** 89
16:9	**Vol. 2:** 421
16:11	**Vol. 3:** 574
16:15*	**Vol. 3:** 109, 715
16:16	**Vol. 3:** 554
16:18 ff	**Vol. 1:** 410
16:19	**Vol. 3:** 178, 704
16:20	**Vol. 3:** 1041
16:22	**Vol. 3:** 938, 946
17:1	**Vol. 3:** 691
17:6	**Vol. 2:** 431
17:8	**Vol. 2:** 622 **Vol. 3:** 355
17:9	**Vol. 2:** 149
17:13	**Vol. 2:** 773
18:5 f	**Vol. 2:** 491 **Vol. 3:** 109
18:8 ff	**Vol. 1:** 172
18:14	**Vol. 2:** 138
18:16	**Vol. 3:** 866
18:17	**Vol. 3:** 237
18:20	**Vol. 2:** 622, 890
19:2	**Vol. 2:** 221
19:3	**Vol. 3:** 345–346
19:6–21	**Vol. 3:** 342
19:7	**Vol. 2:** 431
19:8	**Vol. 1:** 422
19:10	**Vol. 3:** 866
19:16	**Vol. 2:** 860
19:21	**Vol. 3:** 860
19:24	**Vol. 2:** 98
19:25 ff	**Vol. 2:** 479
19:25–27	**Vol. 2:** 207
19:25 f	**Vol. 1:** 672 **Vol. 3:** 178, 261
19:25	**Vol. 1:** 433 **Vol. 2:** 479 **Vol. 3:** 178, 704
19:26	**Vol. 3:** 178
20:7	**Vol. 2:** 60 **Vol. 3:** 821
20:8	**Vol. 1:** 512 **Vol. 2:** 622 **Vol. 3:** 324
20:11	**Vol. 1:** 240
20:14	**Vol. 2:** 27
20:15	**Vol. 2:** 842
20:18	**Vol. 1:** 262 **Vol. 2:** 269, 842
20:20 ff	**Vol. 3:** 261
20:20	**Vol. 3:** 209
20:22	**Vol. 2:** 663 **Vol. 3:** 821
20:26	**Vol. 2:** 773 **Vol. 3:** 111
20:28	**Vol. 2:** 890
20:29	**Vol. 1:** 190 **Vol. 2:** 845
21:4	**Vol. 2:** 140
21:5	**Vol. 2:** 622
21:6	**Vol. 3:** 1169
21:7	**Vol. 2:** 714, 842
21:13	**Vol. 3:** 255
21:14	**Vol. 3:** 1016
21:15	**Vol. 3:** 137, 729
21:16	**Vol. 3:** 1149
21:17	**Vol. 3:** 109

Job *(cont'd)*

21:21	**Vol. 3:** 957
21:22	**Vol. 3:** 760, 1028
21:23	**Vol. 3:** 1024
21:32	**Vol. 2:** 137
21:33	**Vol. 1:** 321
21:34	**Vol. 1:** 547 **Vol. 3:** 255
22:2	**Vol. 3:** 760
22:3	**Vol. 2:** 144 **Vol. 3:** 924, 957
22:9	**Vol. 2:** 737 **Vol. 3:** 1074
22:12	**Vol. 3:** 29
22:16	**Vol. 1:** 343
22:19	**Vol. 2:** 430 **Vol. 3:** 924
22:21	**Vol. 2:** 773
22:26	**Vol. 2:** 735
22:28	**Vol. 2:** 491
22:29 f	**Vol. 3:** 209
22:29	**Vol. 2:** 202 **Vol. 3:** 29
22:30	**Vol. 3:** 201 – 202, 209
23:2	**Vol. 2:** 140
23:7	**Vol. 2:** 60
23:12	**Vol. 1:** 240
23:15	**Vol. 1:** 568
24:1	**Vol. 3:** 846
24:3	**Vol. 2:** 737
24:4	**Vol. 2:** 257
24:5	**Vol. 2:** 675
24:9	**Vol. 2:** 737
24:12	**Vol. 2:** 423
24:13	**Vol. 1:** 339
24:14	**Vol. 3:** 1149
24:15	**Vol. 1:** 694
24:16	**Vol. 3:** 498
24:17	**Vol. 3:** 554
24:20	**Vol. 3:** 240
24:21	**Vol. 3:** 1074
25:2	**Vol. 2:** 778
25:3	**Vol. 2:** 491
25:5	**Vol. 2:** 144 **Vol. 3:** 733, 924
26:2	**Vol. 1:** 464
26:3	**Vol. 3:** 1027
26:5	**Vol. 2:** 206
26:6	**Vol. 1:** 312, 463
26:7	**Vol. 1:** 523
26:11	**Vol. 1:** 523 **Vol. 2:** 189
26:12 f	**Vol. 1:** 508
26:12	**Vol. 3:** 255
27:2	**Vol. 1:** 202
27:5	**Vol. 3:** 166
27:6	**Vol. 3:** 1156
27:9	**Vol. 2:** 663
27:10	**Vol. 2:** 735
27:12	**Vol. 1:** 547
27:17	**Vol. 2:** 845
27:18	**Vol. 2:** 842
27:19	**Vol. 2:** 841
27:22	**Vol. 1:** 559
28	**Vol. 3:** 1029
28:1 – 11	**Vol. 2:** 97

28:1	**Vol. 2:** 96
28:3	**Vol. 3:** 554 – 555
28:4	**Vol. 3:** 994
28:8	**Vol. 3:** 30
28:9	**Vol. 3:** 1010
28:12 f	**Vol. 3:** 528
28:12	**Vol. 3:** 1027
28:14	**Vol. 2:** 197
28:15	**Vol. 3:** 166
28:18	**Vol. 3:** 1027
28:18a	**Vol. 3:** 394
28:18b	**Vol. 3:** 395
28:20	**Vol. 3:** 1027
28:22	**Vol. 1:** 463 – 464
28:25 – 28	**Vol. 3:** 641
28:25	**Vol. 3:** 402
28:28	**Vol. 3:** 1027 – 1028
29:3	**Vol. 2:** 485
29:7 – 8	**Vol. 3:** 588
29:10 f	**Vol. 1:** 216
29:10	**Vol. 2:** 349
29:12	**Vol. 2:** 821 **Vol. 3:** 209
29:14	**Vol. 1:** 314
29:15	**Vol. 1:** 218 **Vol. 2:** 415
29:18	**Vol. 3:** 842
29:20	**Vol. 2:** 49
29:21 – 25	**Vol. 2:** 49
29:24	**Vol. 2:** 430 – 431
30:1 – 12	**Vol. 2:** 49
30:1	**Vol. 1:** 568
30:3	**Vol. 3:** 953
30:4	**Vol. 2:** 49 **Vol. 3:** 1006
30:6	**Vol. 3:** 381, 383
30:8	**Vol. 2:** 49 **Vol. 3:** 109, 1024
30:15	**Vol. 3:** 207
30:16	**Vol. 2:** 890 **Vol. 3:** 680
30:17	**Vol. 1:** 240
30:18 – 23	**Vol. 3:** 342
30:21	**Vol. 1:** 652
30:23	**Vol. 3:** 261
30:25	**Vol. 2:** 423
30:26	**Vol. 1:** 422
30:27	**Vol. 2:** 890
30:30	**Vol. 1:** 652
30:31	**Vol. 2:** 416 **Vol. 3:** 720
31:1	**Vol. 3:** 448
31:2	**Vol. 3:** 729
31:6	**Vol. 3:** 1160
31:7*	**Vol. 2:** 663 **Vol. 3:** 860
31:12	**Vol. 1:** 655
31:15	**Vol. 3:** 594
31:22	**Vol. 2:** 730
31:25	**Vol. 2:** 842
31:28	**Vol. 3:** 823
31:30	**Vol. 2:** 856
31:32	**Vol. 1:** 687, 689
31:38	**Vol. 1:** 410 **Vol. 2:** 423
32:1	**Vol. 3:** 111
32:2 f	**Vol. 1:** 108
32:3	**Vol. 2:** 93

Job *(cont'd)*

32:4	**Vol. 2:** 773
32:6	**Vol. 3:** 111
32:7	**Vol. 3:** 1027
32:8	**Vol. 3:** 760
32:9	**Vol. 3:** 1028
32:13	**Vol. 3:** 1027
32:16	**Vol. 2:** 773
32:19	**Vol. 1:** 743
32:20	**Vol. 3:** 255
33:2	**Vol. 2:** 727
33:4	**Vol. 3:** 705, 760
33:5	**Vol. 2:** 773
33:9	**Vol. 2:** 144 **Vol. 3:** 924
33:10	**Vol. 2:** 144
33:11	**Vol. 1:** 389
33:14–18	**Vol. 1:** 511
33:16	**Vol. 2:** 212 **Vol. 3:** 125
33:17	**Vol. 3:** 201
33:19	**Vol. 2:** 586
33:21	**Vol. 3:** 570
33:22	**Vol. 1:** 101 **Vol. 3:** 355
33:23	**Vol. 2:** 144 **Vol. 3:** 125, 704
33:24	**Vol. 3:** 192
33:26	**Vol. 3:** 704
33:30	**Vol. 2:** 479, 492 **Vol. 3:** 816
33:31	**Vol. 3:** 1028
33:33	**Vol. 3:** 760, 1027
34:2	**Vol. 3:** 1027
34:5	**Vol. 3:** 166
34:8	**Vol. 1:** 641 **Vol. 2:** 93
34:10	**Vol. 2:** 93, 513
34:12	**Vol. 2:** 513
34:14 f	**Vol. 2:** 478
34:15	**Vol. 1:** 672
34:19	**Vol. 2:** 49
34:21 f	**Vol. 1:** 423
34:22	**Vol. 2:** 215
34:23 f	**Vol. 1:** 423
34:24	**Vol. 3:** 748
34:25	**Vol. 3:** 1149
34:26	**Vol. 3:** 109
34:27	**Vol. 3:** 354
34:29	**Vol. 2:** 370
34:30	**Vol. 2:** 468
34:32	**Vol. 3:** 760
34:34	**Vol. 3:** 1027
34:35 ff	**Vol. 3:** 342
34:37	**Vol. 3:** 823
35:3	**Vol. 3:** 137
35:12	**Vol. 3:** 29
35:14	**Vol. 3:** 816
35:15	**Vol. 3:** 585
36:2	**Vol. 3:** 224
36:9	**Vol. 3:** 585–586
36:12	**Vol. 1:** 568
36:13	**Vol. 1:** 108 **Vol. 2:** 468
36:15	**Vol. 2:** 257
36:18	**Vol. 1:** 108 **Vol. 3:** 192
36:19	**Vol. 2:** 663
36:22	**Vol. 3:** 716
36:23	**Vol. 3:** 1156
36:27	**Vol. 2:** 189
36:28	**Vol. 1:** 683 **Vol. 3:** 846
37:2	**Vol. 2:** 653
37:4	**Vol. 3:** 29–30
37:5	**Vol. 3:** 1001
37:7	**Vol. 3:** 498
37:8	**Vol. 2:** 586 **Vol. 3:** 111
37:9	**Vol. 2:** 189
37:14	**Vol. 1:** 568
37:15	**Vol. 1:** 387
37:16	**Vol. 1:** 503
37:19	**Vol. 3:** 760
37:24	**Vol. 3:** 1027
38–41	**Vol. 3:** 209
38:1–42:6	**Vol. 3:** 721
38:1	**Vol. 3:** 266, 514
38:2	**Vol. 3:** 342
38:4	**Vol. 1:** 387
38:5	**Vol. 3:** 402
38:7	**Vol. 1:** 101 **Vol. 3:** 636, 669, 816
38:8 ff	**Vol. 3:** 983
38:8–11	**Vol. 3:** 983
38:8	**Vol. 3:** 950
38:12	**Vol. 2:** 495
38:14	**Vol. 3:** 497
38:15	**Vol. 2:** 491 **Vol. 3:** 29
38:17	**Vol. 2:** 29
38:18	**Vol. 1:** 568
38:20	**Vol. 2:** 890
38:22 ff	**Vol. 3:** 846
38:22	**Vol. 2:** 189, 830
38:25 ff	**Vol. 2:** 274
38:25	**Vol. 1:** 683 **Vol. 3:** 117
38:27	**Vol. 1:** 743
38:28	**Vol. 1:** 177
38:30	**Vol. 1:** 683
38:31	**Vol. 3:** 950
38:32	**Vol. 3:** 835
38:36 f	**Vol. 3:** 1027
38:37	**Vol. 2:** 189
38:40	**Vol. 2:** 586
38:41	**Vol. 1:** 173, 409 **Vol. 3:** 117
39:1	**Vol. 3:** 835
39:2	**Vol. 3:** 177, 180
39:5	**Vol. 3:** 177
39:7	**Vol. 2:** 144
39:10	**Vol. 3:** 1161
39:17	**Vol. 3:** 1027
39:24–25	**Vol. 3:** 874
39:27–30	**Vol. 1:** 173
39:28	**Vol. 3:** 381
39:30	**Vol. 1:** 175
39:32*	**Vol. 2:** 468
40:2	**Vol. 3:** 342, 729
40:6 ff	**Vol. 2:** 432
40:7*	**Vol. 2:** 93
40:8	**Vol. 3:** 342

Job *(cont'd)*

40:11*	**Vol. 3:** 29
40:12*	**Vol. 3:** 29, 109
40:14*	**Vol. 1:** 344
40:15–24	**Vol. 3:** 1006
41	**Vol. 3:** 179
41:3*	**Vol. 2:** 773
41:9*	**Vol. 2:** 349, 495
41:10 ff	**Vol. 2:** 485
41:10*	**Vol. 2:** 485
41:15	**Vol. 2:** 349
41:16*	**Vol. 2:** 720
41:19	**Vol. 2:** 485
41:20*	**Vol. 3:** 557
41:21*	**Vol. 3:** 823
41:24*	**Vol. 3:** 823
42	**Vol. 3:** 209
42:4	**Vol. 3:** 760
42:6	**Vol. 1:** 356
42:7 ff	**Vol. 3:** 425
42:7 f	**Vol. 3:** 608
42:8	**Vol. 3:** 421
42:9	**Vol. 3:** 177
42:11	**Vol. 2:** 622
42:12	**Vol. 3:** 1161

Psalms

1	**Vol. 3:** 865, 938
1:1	**Vol. 1:** 216 **Vol. 2:** 93 **Vol. 3:** 938, 1016
1:2	**Vol. 1:** 245 **Vol. 3:** 866
1:3	**Vol. 1:** 389 **Vol. 3:** 835, 866–867
1:4 ff	**Vol. 2:** 93
1:5	**Vol. 1:** 292
1:6	**Vol. 1:** 254 **Vol. 2:** 395 **Vol. 3:** 929
2	**Vol. 1:** 123, 178–179, 408, 426 **Vol. 2:** 336, 644 **Vol. 3:** 639
2:1 f	**Vol. 1:** 168 **Vol. 2:** 793
2:1	**Vol. 2:** 799
2:2 f	**Vol. 3:** 611
2:2	**Vol. 2:** 378 **Vol. 3:** 1194
2:3	**Vol. 3:** 592, 1161
2:4	**Vol. 2:** 431–432 **Vol. 3:** 588
2:5	**Vol. 1:** 108
2:6 ff	**Vol. 2:** 79
2:6	**Vol. 2:** 225, 326
2:7	**Vol. 1:** 123, 177–179, 186, 288, 617, 668 **Vol. 2:** 336, 374, 543, 612, 819 **Vol. 3:** 637, 639, 641–644, 648, 698, 807, 863, 987
2:8 f	**Vol. 2:** 888
2:8	**Vol. 2:** 856 **Vol. 3:** 636, 638
2:9	**Vol. 1:** 111, 164, 407 **Vol. 2:** 98, 570 **Vol. 3:** 649, 911, 913
2:12	**Vol. 1:** 216
3:3	**Vol. 2:** 158
3:4*	**Vol. 2:** 175, 225, 863
3:7	**Vol. 3:** 207
3:8*	**Vol. 3:** 633

4	**Vol. 3:** 673
4:1	**Vol. 2:** 863
4:3	**Vol. 1:** 409
4:5	**Vol. 1:** 111
4:6	**Vol. 2:** 491 **Vol. 3:** 356, 569
4:8	**Vol. 2:** 724, 777–778
5:1*	**Vol. 1:** 230 **Vol. 2:** 175
5:2	**Vol. 2:** 862 **Vol. 3:** 1120
5:3*	**Vol. 1:** 474
5:5	**Vol. 1:** 555
5:6	**Vol. 2:** 471
5:7*	**Vol. 1:** 732 **Vol. 2:** 225, 876 **Vol. 3:** 783, 786
5:8 ff	**Vol. 1:** 554
5:8	**Vol. 1:** 553
5:9	**Vol. 1:** 265 **Vol. 2:** 726–727 **Vol. 3:** 937, 1079
5:10	**Vol. 2:** 93
5:11	**Vol. 1:** 227
5:12	**Vol. 2:** 818
6	**Vol. 3:** 669
6:1*	**Vol. 1:** 318, 373 **Vol. 2:** 141
6:2*	**Vol. 1:** 109 **Vol. 3:** 994
6:4	**Vol. 3:** 201, 207
6:5	**Vol. 1:** 433 **Vol. 2:** 206 **Vol. 3:** 233
6:6	**Vol. 3:** 237
6:7	**Vol. 1:** 420
6:8	**Vol. 1:** 606–607 **Vol. 3:** 1192
6:9	**Vol. 2:** 860, 863
6:10	**Vol. 3:** 562–563
7	**Vol. 3:** 672
7:1*	**Vol. 2:** 806 **Vol. 3:** 201
7:2*	**Vol. 3:** 201, 207
7:3*	**Vol. 3:** 602
7:4 f	**Vol. 3:** 1148
7:5*	**Vol. 2:** 806
7:7–11	**Vol. 3:** 357
7:7*	**Vol. 3:** 633
7:7b	**Vol. 2:** 614
7:9*	**Vol. 2:** 181 **Vol. 3:** 356
7:10	**Vol. 3:** 533, 966
7:11	**Vol. 2:** 71
7:12 ff	**Vol. 2:** 769
7:12	**Vol. 2:** 363
7:13	**Vol. 3:** 966
7:14	**Vol. 1:** 343
7:15	**Vol. 1:** 186 **Vol. 3:** 858
7:16*	**Vol. 3:** 574
7:17*	**Vol. 1:** 344 **Vol. 2:** 649
8	**Vol. 3:** 644
8:2*	**Vol. 1:** 281 **Vol. 3:** 350, 792, 817
8:3–8*	**Vol. 2:** 49
8:3	**Vol. 3:** 350, 733
8:4*	**Vol. 1:** 191 **Vol. 3:** 613, 1148
8:5–8*	**Vol. 2:** 51
8:5–7*	**Vol. 3:** 632
8:5 f	**Vol. 2:** 287
8:5*	**Vol. 1:** 406 **Vol. 2:** 502, 564
8:6–8*	**Vol. 3:** 632
8:6*	**Vol. 3:** 644

Psalms *(cont'd)*

8:7*	**Vol. 1:** 522 **Vol. 3:** 632, 1148
8:9*	**Vol. 1:** 670 **Vol. 2:** 502
9	**Vol. 2:** 257, 823
9:1*	**Vol. 1:** 345
9:2	**Vol. 2:** 622
9:3	**Vol. 3:** 994
9:4 f	**Vol. 3:** 93
9:4	**Vol. 2:** 326
9:5	**Vol. 1:** 572
9:6	**Vol. 3:** 828
9:7	**Vol. 2:** 60 **Vol. 3:** 117, 237
9:8*	**Vol. 1:** 519
9:11	**Vol. 2:** 326
9:12	**Vol. 2:** 820 **Vol. 3:** 159
9:13	**Vol. 1:** 555
9:14	**Vol. 2:** 353 **Vol. 3:** 816
9:16	**Vol. 1:** 343 **Vol. 3:** 673
9:18	**Vol. 2:** 773, 820
9:23*	**Vol. 2:** 93
9:28*	**Vol. 1:** 202, 416
9:34*	**Vol. 2:** 93
10	**Vol. 2:** 257, 823
10:1	**Vol. 1:** 607 **Vol. 2:** 215
10:2*	**Vol. 2:** 737 **Vol. 3:** 29, 820
10:3*	**Vol. 3:** 137, 816–817, 820
10:7	**Vol. 1:** 202, 262, 743
10:8*	**Vol. 2:** 215, 841
10:9*	**Vol. 2:** 821
10:14*	**Vol. 1:** 262 **Vol. 2:** 738 **Vol. 3:** 126
10:17 f*	**Vol. 2:** 260
10:18†	**Vol. 2:** 771
11:1*	**Vol. 3:** 1009
11:4	**Vol. 2:** 596 **Vol. 3:** 784, 786
11:6	**Vol. 2:** 735
12:1*	**Vol. 3:** 207
12:3 f	**Vol. 2:** 468
12:5*	**Vol. 2:** 735, 821
12:6	**Vol. 3:** 101
12:7*	**Vol. 2:** 36, 134
13:2	**Vol. 1:** 585
13:3	**Vol. 1:** 442, 553 **Vol. 2:** 854
13:4	**Vol. 1:** 416
13:5	**Vol. 2:** 355
13:6*	**Vol. 3:** 672
13:10	**Vol. 3:** 940, 1017
14:1*	**Vol. 2:** 430, 860 **Vol. 3:** 1024–1025
14:2	**Vol. 1:** 433 **Vol. 3:** 131–132, 532
14:3*	**Vol. 2:** 27
14:7	**Vol. 2:** 318, 327 **Vol. 3:** 203
15*	**Vol. 3:** 355, 367
15:1	**Vol. 1:** 691 **Vol. 2:** 225
15:2*	**Vol. 3:** 924, 1148
15:5	**Vol. 2:** 41, 302
15:8*	**Vol. 1:** 695
16	**Vol. 3:** 262, 297
16:2	**Vol. 2:** 100
16:3	**Vol. 2:** 227
16:4	**Vol. 3:** 423
16:5 f	**Vol. 2:** 297
16:5	**Vol. 2:** 479 **Vol. 3:** 208
16:6	**Vol. 1:** 609
16:8–11	**Vol. 2:** 356
16:8 f	**Vol. 3:** 491
16:8	**Vol. 1:** 695 **Vol. 3:** 559
16:9 ff	**Vol. 2:** 479
16:9	**Vol. 1:** 230 **Vol. 2:** 353 **Vol. 3:** 859, 1079
16:9c*	**Vol. 3:** 813
16:10*†	**Vol. 1:** 266, 470, 677, 695 **Vol. 2:** 186, 231, 238, 354, 919 **Vol. 3:** 262, 491, 651, 683, 1200
16:11*	**Vol. 2:** 355, 479 **Vol. 3:** 262, 314, 938, 940–941
17*	**Vol. 2:** 863
17:1–5*	**Vol. 3:** 356
17:1*	**Vol. 2:** 860, 863
17:3*	**Vol. 3:** 808
17:4*	**Vol. 3:** 583, 858
17:5*	**Vol. 3:** 350, 858
17:6 f	**Vol. 2:** 863
17:6*	**Vol. 2:** 175 **Vol. 3:** 858, 1120
17:8	**Vol. 2:** 134 **Vol. 3:** 554, 721, 805
17:10*	**Vol. 3:** 29
17:13*	**Vol. 2:** 199 **Vol. 3:** 201
17:14	**Vol. 1:** 698
17:15	**Vol. 1:** 743 **Vol. 3:** 106, 515
17:26*	**Vol. 2:** 116
17:44*	**Vol. 2:** 173
18	**Vol. 1:** 522 **Vol. 2:** 644 **Vol. 3:** 673, 966
18:1*	**Vol. 3:** 713
18:2	**Vol. 3:** 212, 715
18:3*	**Vol. 1:** 636 **Vol. 2:** 596 **Vol. 3:** 816
18:4 ff	**Vol. 3:** 180
18:5 ff	**Vol. 2:** 478
18:5*	**Vol. 1:** 519 **Vol. 3:** 986
18:6*	**Vol. 2:** 863 **Vol. 3:** 783, 786
18:7*	**Vol. 1:** 661 **Vol. 3:** 986
18:9 ff	**Vol. 1:** 422
18:10*	**Vol. 1:** 101, 280 **Vol. 2:** 190 **Vol. 3:** 1001
18:12*	**Vol. 3:** 514
18:15	**Vol. 1:** 661
18:17*	**Vol. 1:** 555 **Vol. 3:** 748, 983
18:18	**Vol. 2:** 889
18:19*	**Vol. 3:** 207, 1019
18:21 ff	**Vol. 3:** 1148
18:21*	**Vol. 3:** 938
18:22–24*	**Vol. 3:** 356
18:22*	**Vol. 3:** 354
18:23*	**Vol. 3:** 924
18:26*	**Vol. 2:** 705
18:27*	**Vol. 2:** 260 **Vol. 3:** 29
18:28	**Vol. 2:** 485
18:29*	**Vol. 3:** 201
18:30*	**Vol. 3:** 924
18:32*	**Vol. 3:** 121, 924
18:33*	**Vol. 3:** 350

Psalms (cont'd)

18:34* **Vol. 3:** 760
18:35* **Vol. 2:** 146   **Vol. 3:** 760
18:39* **Vol. 3:** 121
18:46* **Vol. 2:** 201
18:47 **Vol. 1:** 210
18:49* **Vol. 1:** 344, 346   **Vol. 2:** 791   **Vol. 3:** 672
18:50 **Vol. 2:** 336
18:51* **Vol. 3:** 828
19 **Vol. 2:** 355
19:1 ff **Vol. 3:** 327, 331
19:1* **Vol. 2:** 45, 175, 190   **Vol. 3:** 331
19:2* **Vol. 3:** 45
19:4* **Vol. 1:** 519   **Vol. 2:** 176   **Vol. 3:** 1118
19:5* **Vol. 2:** 353   **Vol. 3:** 1120, 1122
19:6 **Vol. 2:** 175
19:7* **Vol. 1:** 518   **Vol. 2:** 449   **Vol. 3:** 331, 924, 1028
19:8* **Vol. 1:** 281   **Vol. 3:** 101, 354, 1033
19:9* **Vol. 2:** 175   **Vol. 3:** 355
19:10* **Vol. 3:** 358
19:11 **Vol. 3:** 595
19:12* **Vol. 2:** 215   **Vol. 3:** 585–586
19:13* **Vol. 3:** 595, 924
19:14* **Vol. 3:** 178, 193
20:2 **Vol. 2:** 326, 889
20:3 **Vol. 3:** 421
20:4* **Vol. 3:** 235
20:5 **Vol. 3:** 636
20:6* **Vol. 1:** 734   **Vol. 2:** 225, 336
20:7 **Vol. 3:** 266
20:9* **Vol. 2:** 890   **Vol. 3:** 207
21:1 **Vol. 2:** 353
21:2 **Vol. 3:** 636
21:3 **Vol. 3:** 636
21:4* **Vol. 2:** 856   **Vol. 3:** 636
21:5* **Vol. 1:** 409   **Vol. 3:** 828
21:11* **Vol. 1:** 721   **Vol. 3:** 820
21:13* **Vol. 3:** 672
21:22* **Vol. 1:** 295
22 **Vol. 1:** 396   **Vol. 2:** 82, 263   **Vol. 3:** 202, 720
22:1* **Vol. 1:** 411, 544, 615   **Vol. 3:** 585
22:2* **Vol. 1:** 396   **Vol. 3:** 125
22:3* **Vol. 3:** 817
22:4* **Vol. 1:** 617   **Vol. 3:** 202
22:5* **Vol. 3:** 209
22:6 **Vol. 2:** 272
22:7 f **Vol. 1:** 396   **Vol. 2:** 82
22:8 f **Vol. 3:** 287
22:8* **Vol. 3:** 202, 209
22:9 **Vol. 1:** 396
22:10* **Vol. 3:** 1071
22:13* **Vol. 3:** 601
22:15* **Vol. 2:** 349   **Vol. 3:** 491, 713, 914
22:17* **Vol. 3:** 126
22:18* **Vol. 2:** 64, 82, 296, 299   **Vol. 3:** 543, 670

22:19 **Vol. 1:** 396   **Vol. 2:** 299   **Vol. 3:** 287
22:20* **Vol. 3:** 201
22:21* **Vol. 3:** 203, 209
22:22* **Vol. 1:** 255, 304, 396   **Vol. 2:** 82–83, 722   **Vol. 3:** 48, 207, 668, 670
22:23* **Vol. 1:** 293   **Vol. 3:** 816
22:24 **Vol. 1:** 411
22:25* **Vol. 3:** 817
22:26* **Vol. 1:** 295, 411   **Vol. 2:** 181   **Vol. 3:** 816
22:27* **Vol. 2:** 83, 876, 888
22:28 f* **Vol. 3:** 233, 514–515
22:28 **Vol. 2:** 83
22:29* **Vol. 2:** 876
22:30 f* **Vol. 2:** 83   **Vol. 3:** 45
22:30 **Vol. 3:** 522
22:31* **Vol. 3:** 357
23 **Vol. 2:** 104, 412, 479   **Vol. 3:** 565–566
23:1* **Vol. 3:** 255, 804
23:3* **Vol. 2:** 650   **Vol. 3:** 937
23:4* **Vol. 1:** 422, 562   **Vol. 3:** 555
23:5 **Vol. 1:** 120   **Vol. 2:** 711   **Vol. 3:** 208
23:6 **Vol. 2:** 99, 247
24 **Vol. 2:** 186, 613
24:1 **Vol. 1:** 519, 691, 734   **Vol. 2:** 286, 375   **Vol. 3:** 853
24:2* **Vol. 1:** 589   **Vol. 3:** 117, 983, 986, 990
24:3 ff* **Vol. 3:** 355, 357
24:3 f **Vol. 2:** 225   **Vol. 3:** 106
24:3 **Vol. 3:** 787
24:4 **Vol. 2:** 149
24:5* **Vol. 3:** 218, 355
24:6 **Vol. 1:** 586   **Vol. 3:** 531
24:7 ff **Vol. 2:** 44, 898
24:7 **Vol. 1:** 321
24:8* **Vol. 3:** 716, 960
24:9 **Vol. 1:** 321
25:2 **Vol. 3:** 563
25:3* **Vol. 2:** 773
25:4 f* **Vol. 3:** 760
25:5* **Vol. 2:** 773   **Vol. 3:** 218, 220
25:6 f* **Vol. 3:** 234
25:6–9 **Vol. 2:** 364
25:6* **Vol. 2:** 595, 598   **Vol. 3:** 235
25:7 f **Vol. 2:** 105
25:8* **Vol. 3:** 316
25:9* **Vol. 2:** 257   **Vol. 3:** 760, 937
25:10* **Vol. 3:** 879, 937
25:11* **Vol. 1:** 698–699   **Vol. 3:** 152, 156
25:12 **Vol. 1:** 534
25:16 ff* **Vol. 3:** 156
25:16 **Vol. 2:** 823
25:17* **Vol. 2:** 663
25:18* **Vol. 1:** 698   **Vol. 2:** 260, 263
25:20* **Vol. 3:** 201
25:21* **Vol. 2:** 773
25:22* **Vol. 3:** 192–193
25:25 **Vol. 1:** 585
26:1–6* **Vol. 3:** 356
26:1* **Vol. 3:** 924

Psalms *(cont'd)*

26:2*	**Vol. 2:** 181 **Vol. 3:** 799–800, 808
26:3*	**Vol. 2:** 815
26:5	**Vol. 1:** 293, 555
26:6*	**Vol. 2:** 149 **Vol. 3:** 990
26:7*	**Vol. 2:** 622 **Vol. 3:** 816
26:8	**Vol. 2:** 45, 247
26:11*	**Vol. 3:** 192, 924
26:14*	**Vol. 2:** 563
27	**Vol. 1:** 622
27:1*	**Vol. 1:** 636 **Vol. 2:** 479, 491 **Vol. 3:** 218
27:2*	**Vol. 3:** 994
27:4*	**Vol. 1:** 189 **Vol. 2:** 247, 478, 856 **Vol. 3:** 782, 786, 991
27:5*	**Vol. 2:** 201, 215
27:6*	**Vol. 2:** 201 **Vol. 3:** 673
27:8 f	**Vol. 3:** 648
27:8	**Vol. 3:** 531
27:9*	**Vol. 1:** 109 **Vol. 3:** 218, 220
27:10*	**Vol. 3:** 748
27:11*	**Vol. 3:** 938
27:12*	**Vol. 3:** 680, 1041
27:14*	**Vol. 2:** 773
28:2*	**Vol. 2:** 149, 860 **Vol. 3:** 782
28:3	**Vol. 1:** 562
28:6 f	**Vol. 1:** 345
28:6*	**Vol. 1:** 210 **Vol. 2:** 860
28:8	**Vol. 2:** 336
28:9*	**Vol. 3:** 207, 565
29	**Vol. 3:** 1087, 1105
29:1	**Vol. 2:** 44 **Vol. 3:** 636
29:2	**Vol. 2:** 225
29:3 ff	**Vol. 3:** 1105
29:3 f*	**Vol. 3:** 113
29:3*	**Vol. 2:** 44, 876
29:4*	**Vol. 3:** 713
29:8*	**Vol. 2:** 650 **Vol. 3:** 113
29:9*	**Vol. 2:** 190 **Vol. 3:** 350, 783, 786
29:10 ff*	**Vol. 2:** 778
29:10 f*	**Vol. 2:** 778
29:10*	**Vol. 2:** 175, 190 **Vol. 3:** 588, 991
29:11*	**Vol. 3:** 713
30:1*	**Vol. 2:** 201
30:2 f*	**Vol. 3:** 262
30:3	**Vol. 2:** 167–168
30:4*	**Vol. 1:** 344 **Vol. 3:** 233, 238
30:5*	**Vol. 3:** 237
30:6	**Vol. 1:** 109
30:8	**Vol. 2:** 860
30:9*	**Vol. 1:** 433 **Vol. 2:** 206 **Vol. 3:** 45, 880
30:11*	**Vol. 2:** 357, 418 **Vol. 3:** 121, 262, 1192
30:12	**Vol. 1:** 230
30:20*	**Vol. 2:** 115
30:25*	**Vol. 2:** 563
31:1*	**Vol. 3:** 202
31:2	**Vol. 2:** 175
31:4 f	**Vol. 2:** 479
31:4*	**Vol. 1:** 725 **Vol. 3:** 381, 937
31:5*	**Vol. 2:** 212 **Vol. 3:** 192–193
31:6*	**Vol. 3:** 690
31:6a	**Vol. 1:** 554
31:7*	**Vol. 2:** 260, 353
31:8*	**Vol. 2:** 332
31:10*	**Vol. 3:** 713, 994
31:12	**Vol. 2:** 633
31:15*	**Vol. 2:** 806 **Vol. 3:** 835
31:16*	**Vol. 3:** 207, 318
31:17*	**Vol. 2:** 263
31:18*	**Vol. 3:** 29
31:19–20	**Vol. 2:** 215
31:19*	**Vol. 1:** 732 **Vol. 2:** 105
31:21*	**Vol. 1:** 210
31:22*	**Vol. 2:** 860
31:23*	**Vol. 3:** 29
31:24	**Vol. 3:** 718
32:1 ff*	**Vol. 2:** 168 **Vol. 3:** 997
32:1 f*	**Vol. 1:** 79, 216 **Vol. 3:** 169
32:1*	**Vol. 1:** 698, 702 **Vol. 3:** 192
32:2*	**Vol. 2:** 513 **Vol. 3:** 691, 823–824
32:3	**Vol. 2:** 714
32:5	**Vol. 1:** 698 **Vol. 2:** 212, 215
32:6*	**Vol. 2:** 237, 862 **Vol. 3:** 836, 991
32:11	**Vol. 1:** 227 **Vol. 2:** 353
32:16*	**Vol. 1:** 732
33	**Vol. 1:** 383, 523 **Vol. 3:** 1087
33:1*	**Vol. 2:** 668
33:2*	**Vol. 3:** 671
33:3*	**Vol. 2:** 670 **Vol. 3:** 673
33:4	**Vol. 3:** 1105, 1194
33:5*	**Vol. 2:** 364 **Vol. 3:** 357
33:6*	**Vol. 2:** 109, 190 **Vol. 3:** 690, 1105
33:7	**Vol. 2:** 189
33:8	**Vol. 1:** 519
33:9*	**Vol. 1:** 380 **Vol. 3:** 1105
33:10 f*	**Vol. 3:** 823, 1016
33:11*	**Vol. 3:** 224
33:12	**Vol. 1:** 636 **Vol. 2:** 297
33:13 ff	**Vol. 3:** 1105
33:15*	**Vol. 2:** 724
33:16 f*	**Vol. 3:** 206, 209
33:17	**Vol. 1:** 409
33:18 f*	**Vol. 3:** 202, 804
33:18	**Vol. 2:** 240
33:19*	**Vol. 2:** 478 **Vol. 3:** 201
33:20*	**Vol. 2:** 773
33:21	**Vol. 2:** 355
34	**Vol. 2:** 772
34:2*	**Vol. 2:** 257 **Vol. 3:** 816
34:3*	**Vol. 2:** 201–202
34:4*	**Vol. 2:** 735 **Vol. 3:** 201
34:5	**Vol. 1:** 520 **Vol. 2:** 270
34:7*	**Vol. 3:** 202
34:8*	**Vol. 1:** 216 **Vol. 2:** 269–270 **Vol. 3:** 513
34:9*	**Vol. 2:** 227
34:10*	**Vol. 2:** 99, 265, 270, 841 **Vol. 3:** 804, 953

78

Psalms *(cont'd)*

34:11*†   **Vol. 1:** 285   **Vol. 2:** 596, 735   **Vol. 3:** 760
34:12 ff*   **Vol. 1:** 562
34:13–17   **Vol. 2:** 270
34:13*   **Vol. 1:** 240   **Vol. 3:** 1079
34:14*   **Vol. 2:** 806   **Vol. 3:** 531, 1079
34:15*   **Vol. 1:** 230   **Vol. 2:** 778, 782   **Vol. 3:** 1153
34:16   **Vol. 2:** 178, 861   **Vol. 3:** 370
34:17*   **Vol. 2:** 860   **Vol. 3:** 201, 237
34:18*   **Vol. 2:** 260
34:19*   **Vol. 2:** 53, 807–808   **Vol. 3:** 201, 691
34:20   **Vol. 2:** 270
34:21   **Vol. 1:** 555
34:22*   **Vol. 3:** 192
35   **Vol. 2:** 823
35:3*   **Vol. 2:** 806
35:4*   **Vol. 3:** 531, 823
35:7   **Vol. 2:** 41
35:10*   **Vol. 2:** 822
35:11*   **Vol. 2:** 879   **Vol. 3:** 1041
35:13*   **Vol. 1:** 495, 612   **Vol. 2:** 863
35:14*   **Vol. 2:** 815
35:16*   **Vol. 2:** 421   **Vol. 3:** 799–800
35:18*   **Vol. 2:** 863   **Vol. 3:** 816
35:19   **Vol. 2:** 41, 448   **Vol. 3:** 329
35:20*   **Vol. 3:** 820
35:23   **Vol. 3:** 93
35:26   **Vol. 3:** 562–563
35:27*   **Vol. 2:** 353, 778
35:28*   **Vol. 3:** 817, 1079
36:1*   **Vol. 3:** 940
36:4*   **Vol. 3:** 820, 823
36:8 ff   **Vol. 2:** 479
36:8 f   **Vol. 3:** 805
36:9   **Vol. 2:** 478, 486, 492
36:10*   **Vol. 2:** 70, 772   **Vol. 3:** 987
36:11*   **Vol. 3:** 29
36:33*   **Vol. 2:** 370
37   **Vol. 2:** 841
37:2   **Vol. 1:** 743
37:3*   **Vol. 2:** 842
37:4*   **Vol. 1:** 240, 608
37:5*   **Vol. 3:** 938
37:8 f   **Vol. 1:** 108
37:8   **Vol. 2:** 423
37:9*   **Vol. 2:** 298, 773
37:11*   **Vol. 2:** 257–258, 778
37:12   **Vol. 2:** 421
37:13   **Vol. 2:** 431
37:14*   **Vol. 1:** 428   **Vol. 2:** 257, 824
37:16 f*   **Vol. 2:** 428
37:17   **Vol. 1:** 466
37:18*†   **Vol. 2:** 395   **Vol. 3:** 924
37:19*   **Vol. 1:** 743   **Vol. 2:** 890   **Vol. 3:** 804, 835–836
37:20*   **Vol. 1:** 554   **Vol. 2:** 201
37:22   **Vol. 2:** 298

37:28*   **Vol. 3:** 93, 924
37:29   **Vol. 2:** 298
37:30*   **Vol. 3:** 1027, 1079
37:32   **Vol. 3:** 126
37:34*   **Vol. 2:** 773
37:39*   **Vol. 2:** 807   **Vol. 3:** 836
38*   **Vol. 2:** 167   **Vol. 3:** 233, 239
38:1   **Vol. 1:** 318
38:3 ff*   **Vol. 2:** 168   **Vol. 3:** 997
38:3   **Vol. 2:** 777
38:5*   **Vol. 2:** 683   **Vol. 3:** 953, 1024
38:6*   **Vol. 1:** 711
38:8*   **Vol. 1:** 712   **Vol. 2:** 260
38:9   **Vol. 2:** 215, 421
38:10*   **Vol. 2:** 181
38:12*   **Vol. 1:** 690   **Vol. 2:** 175
38:18*   **Vol. 1:** 277
38:19   **Vol. 3:** 233
38:22*   **Vol. 2:** 260
39 f   **Vol. 2:** 168
39*   **Vol. 3:** 673
39:2   **Vol. 3:** 1176
39:3   **Vol. 1:** 318
39:4   **Vol. 3:** 953
39:6*   **Vol. 2:** 287
39:7*   **Vol. 2:** 773   **Vol. 3:** 1203
39:8*   **Vol. 3:** 201–202, 1024
39:9*   **Vol. 3:** 997, 1025
39:11*   **Vol. 1:** 162
39:12*   **Vol. 2:** 789, 860, 863   **Vol. 3:** 997
39:13†   **Vol. 1:** 686, 688, 690–691
40   **Vol. 3:** 783
40:1*   **Vol. 2:** 240, 773, 824, 860
40:3*   **Vol. 1:** 177   **Vol. 2:** 586, 670   **Vol. 3:** 669, 673
40:4*   **Vol. 2:** 471
40:5*   **Vol. 2:** 683   **Vol. 3:** 820
40:6 ff   **Vol. 2:** 818   **Vol. 3:** 433
40:6*   **Vol. 1:** 234   **Vol. 2:** 856   **Vol. 3:** 171, 350, 421
40:7 ff   **Vol. 3:** 1023
40:7 f   **Vol. 3:** 427
40:8*   **Vol. 3:** 1019
40:9*   **Vol. 2:** 109   **Vol. 3:** 357, 1154
40:10*   **Vol. 1:** 241   **Vol. 2:** 222   **Vol. 3:** 357
40:11*   **Vol. 2:** 595, 598
40:13*   **Vol. 2:** 817   **Vol. 3:** 201–202
40:14   **Vol. 3:** 563
40:15   **Vol. 3:** 562
40:17*   **Vol. 2:** 257, 823
41:1*   **Vol. 1:** 216
41:2*   **Vol. 3:** 209, 242
41:4*   **Vol. 3:** 997
41:5   **Vol. 2:** 168
41:7*   **Vol. 3:** 823, 908
41:8   **Vol. 2:** 554
41:9*   **Vol. 2:** 521   **Vol. 3:** 329, 491
41:10   **Vol. 2:** 650   **Vol. 3:** 1192
41:13   **Vol. 2:** 596
41:13*   **Vol. 1:** 98, 210

Psalms *(cont'd)*

42	**Vol. 3:** 236
42:2*	**Vol. 1:** 586 **Vol. 2:** 266 **Vol. 3:** 515
42:3	**Vol. 3:** 106
42:4*	**Vol. 2:** 247
42:5*	**Vol. 2:** 240 **Vol. 3:** 236
42:6*	**Vol. 3:** 683
42:7*	**Vol. 2:** 205
42:8*	**Vol. 2:** 863
43	**Vol. 1:** 544
43:1*	**Vol. 3:** 93, 201, 881
43:3	**Vol. 3:** 881
44:3*	**Vol. 2:** 491 **Vol. 3:** 206
44:4*	**Vol. 2:** 817
44:5*	**Vol. 1:** 332
44:6 f*	**Vol. 3:** 206
44:8*	**Vol. 3:** 816
44:15	**Vol. 2:** 212
44:16*	**Vol. 3:** 345
44:19*	**Vol. 2:** 260 **Vol. 3:** 555
44:22*	**Vol. 3:** 823
44:23	**Vol. 3:** 824
44:24	**Vol. 2:** 215
44:25 f*	**Vol. 2:** 260
44:26*	**Vol. 3:** 192
45	**Vol. 1:** 122 **Vol. 2:** 584–585
45:1*	**Vol. 2:** 602
45:2*	**Vol. 2:** 116
45:4*	**Vol. 2:** 257 **Vol. 3:** 881
45:5*	**Vol. 2:** 622
45:6 f	**Vol. 1:** 123
45:6–7	**Vol. 1:** 408
45:6	**Vol. 1:** 162, 164
45:7 f	**Vol. 1:** 122
45:7*	**Vol. 1:** 122, 239, 427 **Vol. 2:** 71, 354, 374, 448, 602, 711–712 **Vol. 3:** 365, 575, 648, 1061
45:8*	**Vol. 2:** 294
45:9*	**Vol. 2:** 146
45:11*	**Vol. 2:** 602
45:12*	**Vol. 2:** 841, 876
45:15*	**Vol. 3:** 782
45:17*	**Vol. 3:** 233
46	**Vol. 1:** 622 **Vol. 2:** 361, 613 **Vol. 3:** 783
46:3 f*	**Vol. 3:** 983
46:3*	**Vol. 3:** 112
46:4	**Vol. 2:** 803
46:6*	**Vol. 3:** 709
46:10*	**Vol. 2:** 396, 791
47:1*	**Vol. 2:** 149
47:2	**Vol. 2:** 375
47:3	**Vol. 2:** 375
47:5	**Vol. 2:** 644
47:8*	**Vol. 2:** 225, 375, 602
48*	**Vol. 3:** 673, 783, 1068
48:1	**Vol. 2:** 803
48:2	**Vol. 2:** 327, 803
48:5*	**Vol. 1:** 241
48:6	**Vol. 2:** 622
48:7	**Vol. 3:** 1001
48:8	**Vol. 2:** 803
48:9*	**Vol. 3:** 786
49*	**Vol. 2:** 207, 841 **Vol. 3:** 262
49:2*	**Vol. 1:** 519 **Vol. 2:** 841
49:3*	**Vol. 3:** 1027
49:4*	**Vol. 2:** 745
49:5*	**Vol. 2:** 890
49:6*	**Vol. 2:** 841
49:7 f*	**Vol. 3:** 174
49:7*†	**Vol. 3:** 192
49:8*	**Vol. 3:** 153, 192–193
49:10*	**Vol. 2:** 842 **Vol. 3:** 1024, 1027
49:11	**Vol. 2:** 649
49:12*	**Vol. 3:** 126
49:15*	**Vol. 2:** 491 **Vol. 3:** 174, 192, 262, 265
49:16*	**Vol. 2:** 479, 841
49:19	**Vol. 2:** 491
50	**Vol. 1:** 367 **Vol. 2:** 261 **Vol. 3:** 425, 783
50:1–6	**Vol. 2:** 363
50:2	**Vol. 2:** 735 **Vol. 3:** 514
50:3 f	**Vol. 1:** 320
50:3	**Vol. 1:** 655
50:5	**Vol. 2:** 237
50:7*	**Vol. 3:** 1041
50:8–15	**Vol. 3:** 424, 427
50:8*	**Vol. 3:** 316
50:9*	**Vol. 1:** 471
50:10*	**Vol. 1:** 240 **Vol. 3:** 853
50:12 f	**Vol. 3:** 422
50:13*	**Vol. 2:** 93
50:14	**Vol. 3:** 423–424
50:15	**Vol. 1:** 320
50:16*	**Vol. 3:** 354
50:17*	**Vol. 1:** 555 **Vol. 3:** 777
50:18*	**Vol. 2:** 303
50:20*	**Vol. 3:** 345–346, 1069
50:21	**Vol. 1:** 474
50:22*	**Vol. 3:** 601–602
50:23*	**Vol. 3:** 423, 569
51*	**Vol. 1:** 433 **Vol. 2:** 167 **Vol. 3:** 105, 579, 783
51:1*	**Vol. 1:** 732 **Vol. 2:** 595, 598
51:4 ff	**Vol. 2:** 472
51:4*	**Vol. 2:** 724 **Vol. 3:** 320, 355
51:6*	**Vol. 1:** 650 **Vol. 2:** 430 **Vol. 3:** 881, 1027
51:7*	**Vol. 1:** 144, 151, 204, 225
51:10*	**Vol. 1:** 184, 349, 379 **Vol. 2:** 181, 673 **Vol. 3:** 692
51:11*	**Vol. 2:** 227
51:12*	**Vol. 3:** 691, 694
51:13*	**Vol. 3:** 760
51:14*	**Vol. 3:** 201, 357
51:15*	**Vol. 3:** 45
51:16 ff*	**Vol. 2:** 817
51:16*	**Vol. 3:** 1079
51:17*	**Vol. 2:** 181, 260, 865 **Vol. 3:** 691

Psalms *(cont'd)*

51:18 f   **Vol. 3:** 427
51:19*   **Vol. 2:** 818   **Vol. 3:** 421
51:21*   **Vol. 3:** 356, 421
52:1   **Vol. 1:** 227
52:2*   **Vol. 3:** 823
52:3*   **Vol. 3:** 575
52:7*   **Vol. 2:** 841–842   **Vol. 3:** 203
52:8*   **Vol. 2:** 247, 711
52:9 f   **Vol. 2:** 237
52:9*   **Vol. 2:** 239, 772–773
53:1*   **Vol. 2:** 430   **Vol. 3:** 1024
53:2*   **Vol. 3:** 1025
53:5*   **Vol. 2:** 815
54*   **Vol. 3:** 669
54:1*   **Vol. 2:** 650   **Vol. 3:** 207
54:2*   **Vol. 2:** 863
54:3*   **Vol. 1:** 672, 696   **Vol. 2:** 363
54:6   **Vol. 1:** 427   **Vol. 2:** 650
55*   **Vol. 3:** 669
55:1*   **Vol. 2:** 860, 863
55:3   **Vol. 1:** 554
55:5*   **Vol. 1:** 609   **Vol. 3:** 710
55:6*   **Vol. 3:** 255
55:7*   **Vol. 1:** 241
55:13*   **Vol. 2:** 498
55:14*   **Vol. 2:** 479, 653
55:16†   **Vol. 1:** 409
55:17   **Vol. 1:** 575
55:18*   **Vol. 2:** 778   **Vol. 3:** 192
55:19*   **Vol. 3:** 166
55:21   **Vol. 2:** 711
55:22*   **Vol. 1:** 277–278
56:1*   **Vol. 1:** 589
56:3*   **Vol. 3:** 816
56:4   **Vol. 1:** 679
56:5*   **Vol. 3:** 820
56:6*   **Vol. 1:** 672   **Vol. 2:** 773
56:8*   **Vol. 1:** 243
56:10*   **Vol. 3:** 816
56:12   **Vol. 1:** 672   **Vol. 3:** 423
56:13*   **Vol. 1:** 416   **Vol. 2:** 302, 478, 492, 815   **Vol. 3:** 201
57:1*   **Vol. 1:** 174   **Vol. 3:** 554
57:2   **Vol. 3:** 805
57:3   **Vol. 3:** 879
57:4*   **Vol. 3:** 201
57:5*   **Vol. 2:** 201   **Vol. 3:** 1079
57:7*   **Vol. 3:** 117, 673
57:10   **Vol. 3:** 879
57:11*   **Vol. 2:** 201
58:3   **Vol. 2:** 471
58:5*   **Vol. 3:** 1028
58:6   **Vol. 2:** 554
58:7*   **Vol. 3:** 994
58:10*   **Vol. 3:** 93, 159
59:1*   **Vol. 3:** 192, 769
59:2*   **Vol. 3:** 207
59:3*   **Vol. 3:** 201

59:8   **Vol. 2:** 431
59:10*   **Vol. 3:** 569
59:12*   **Vol. 3:** 29
59:15   **Vol. 1:** 743
59:16*   **Vol. 3:** 673
59:17   **Vol. 2:** 889
60   **Vol. 3:** 233
60:3*   **Vol. 2:** 275   **Vol. 3:** 569, 919
60:5*   **Vol. 3:** 207
60:11*   **Vol. 3:** 207
61*   **Vol. 3:** 669
61:1*   **Vol. 2:** 860, 863
61:2*   **Vol. 2:** 201
61:5*   **Vol. 1:** 688, 691   **Vol. 2:** 863   **Vol. 3:** 805, 946
61:7   **Vol. 3:** 879
62:2*   **Vol. 3:** 218
62:3   **Vol. 3:** 950
62:5*   **Vol. 2:** 240, 773
62:6*   **Vol. 3:** 218
62:7   **Vol. 3:** 232, 381
62:9*   **Vol. 2:** 209   **Vol. 3:** 1160
62:10*   **Vol. 1:** 683   **Vol. 3:** 842
62:11*   **Vol. 2:** 716   **Vol. 3:** 716
62:12*   **Vol. 3:** 134, 167
63   **Vol. 3:** 236
63:1*   **Vol. 2:** 266, 305   **Vol. 3:** 680
63:2   **Vol. 1:** 672
63:3*   **Vol. 2:** 117, 479   **Vol. 3:** 816
63:5*   **Vol. 3:** 816
63:6*   **Vol. 2:** 197
63:8   **Vol. 3:** 805
63:9*   **Vol. 1:** 492   **Vol. 2:** 209
63:11*   **Vol. 3:** 574, 816
64:1*   **Vol. 2:** 863
64:4*   **Vol. 3:** 924
64:9*   **Vol. 3:** 45
64:10*   **Vol. 1:** 513   **Vol. 3:** 816
65   **Vol. 1:** 210, 523
65:1*   **Vol. 2:** 668   **Vol. 3:** 669
65:2*   **Vol. 2:** 863
65:3*   **Vol. 1:** 698–699   **Vol. 3:** 153–154, 156
65:4*   **Vol. 3:** 783, 786
65:5 ff   **Vol. 1:** 699
65:5–8*   **Vol. 3:** 207
65:5*   **Vol. 2:** 478   **Vol. 3:** 218, 357, 748
65:6*   **Vol. 3:** 117, 121, 1010
65:7   **Vol. 3:** 560
65:8*   **Vol. 3:** 983
65:9*   **Vol. 2:** 275, 841   **Vol. 3:** 117
65:10*   **Vol. 3:** 986
65:11*   **Vol. 2:** 105
65:13*   **Vol. 3:** 668
66:1*   **Vol. 3:** 671, 986
66:4*   **Vol. 2:** 876
66:5*   **Vol. 1:** 622
66:10*   **Vol. 3:** 808
66:12*   **Vol. 3:** 983
66:19 f*   **Vol. 2:** 863
66:20   **Vol. 1:** 210

Psalms *(cont'd)*

67* **Vol. 2:** 261 **Vol. 3:** 669
67:1 f* **Vol. 3:** 207
67:1* **Vol. 3:** 318
67:2 **Vol. 3:** 221
67:3* **Vol. 3:** 937
67:4* **Vol. 1:** 519
67:5 **Vol. 2:** 363
67:13 **Vol. 2:** 69
67:18* **Vol. 2:** 195
68:1* **Vol. 1:** 555 **Vol. 2:** 34 **Vol. 3:** 671
68:3* **Vol. 1:** 711
68:4–10 **Vol. 1:** 618
68:4* **Vol. 2:** 190 **Vol. 3:** 673
68:5* **Vol. 1:** 617–618 **Vol. 2:** 738 **Vol. 3:** 1073
68:6* **Vol. 1:** 203
68:8 f* **Vol. 3:** 565, 960
68:8 **Vol. 3:** 1013
68:9* **Vol. 2:** 296 **Vol. 3:** 350, 1001
68:11* **Vol. 2:** 109
68:13 **Vol. 2:** 313
68:14* **Vol. 3:** 915
68:17 f **Vol. 3:** 557
68:17* **Vol. 3:** 786
68:18* **Vol. 1:** 99 **Vol. 2:** 186, 209, 698 **Vol. 3:** 203, 494, 591
68:19* **Vol. 1:** 210 **Vol. 2:** 199 **Vol. 3:** 87
68:20* **Vol. 1:** 636 **Vol. 2:** 895
68:24–27* **Vol. 1:** 245
68:24* **Vol. 3:** 786
68:25* **Vol. 2:** 87 **Vol. 3:** 1071
68:28 f* **Vol. 3:** 783
68:28* **Vol. 2:** 602 **Vol. 3:** 350
68:29* **Vol. 3:** 786
68:30* **Vol. 2:** 41 **Vol. 3:** 808
68:31 f* **Vol. 2:** 294
68:32* **Vol. 2:** 41 **Vol. 3:** 673
68:36* **Vol. 2:** 258, 622–623, 625
69:1* **Vol. 3:** 207
69:2 f* **Vol. 3:** 986
69:2* **Vol. 2:** 197 **Vol. 3:** 695
69:4–7 **Vol. 3:** 562–563
69:4 **Vol. 1:** 555 **Vol. 2:** 41
69:5* **Vol. 2:** 215, 449 **Vol. 3:** 1024
69:6* **Vol. 2:** 773, 797
69:8* **Vol. 3:** 1069
69:9* **Vol. 2:** 816, 828, 835 **Vol. 3:** 430, 770, 1013, 1166
69:10 **Vol. 1:** 612
69:12* **Vol. 3:** 671
69:13* **Vol. 2:** 863 **Vol. 3:** 879
69:14* **Vol. 1:** 555 **Vol. 2:** 197 **Vol. 3:** 201, 207
69:15 f* **Vol. 3:** 986
69:15 **Vol. 3:** 695
69:16* **Vol. 2:** 595
69:18* **Vol. 3:** 192
69:19 f **Vol. 3:** 562–563

69:20* **Vol. 2:** 773
69:21* **Vol. 2:** 27–28, 267
69:22* **Vol. 2:** 708
69:23 **Vol. 1:** 424
69:26 **Vol. 3:** 1008
69:27* **Vol. 3:** 357
69:28 f* **Vol. 2:** 824
69:28* **Vol. 3:** 355
69:29* **Vol. 2:** 823
69:30* **Vol. 3:** 816
69:32 f* **Vol. 2:** 824
69:34* **Vol. 3:** 816
69:35 **Vol. 2:** 326
70* **Vol. 3:** 233, 239
70:2 **Vol. 3:** 563
70:4 **Vol. 3:** 233
70:15–17* **Vol. 3:** 233
70:16b* **Vol. 3:** 233
71 **Vol. 2:** 261
71:2* **Vol. 3:** 202, 207, 355
71:4* **Vol. 3:** 201
71:5* **Vol. 2:** 239, 773
71:6* **Vol. 3:** 1071
71:7* **Vol. 2:** 633 **Vol. 3:** 669, 716
71:8* **Vol. 3:** 669
71:9 **Vol. 3:** 835
71:16* **Vol. 2:** 211, 724
71:17*† **Vol. 2:** 622 **Vol. 3:** 45, 760
71:18 **Vol. 1:** 193
71:20* **Vol. 2:** 163, 205, 807 **Vol. 3:** 569
71:22 **Vol. 3:** 880
71:23* **Vol. 3:** 192
71:24 **Vol. 3:** 357, 563
72 **Vol. 1:** 426 **Vol. 2:** 257 **Vol. 3:** 357
72:1 f **Vol. 2:** 363
72:2 **Vol. 2:** 823 **Vol. 3:** 192
72:4* **Vol. 2:** 820, 823 **Vol. 3:** 192, 206–207
72:5* **Vol. 1:** 262 **Vol. 3:** 733
72:6* **Vol. 3:** 461
72:7* **Vol. 1:** 732 **Vol. 3:** 733
72:8* **Vol. 1:** 519 **Vol. 2:** 888 **Vol. 3:** 985
72:10 f* **Vol. 2:** 294, 888
72:10 **Vol. 2:** 41
72:11* **Vol. 2:** 876
72:12 ff **Vol. 2:** 823
72:12 **Vol. 2:** 820 **Vol. 3:** 192
72:13* **Vol. 2:** 820, 822 **Vol. 3:** 192, 206
72:14* **Vol. 3:** 158, 192–193
72:15* **Vol. 2:** 96, 862
72:17* **Vol. 3:** 224
72:18 f* **Vol. 2:** 627
72:18* **Vol. 1:** 210 **Vol. 2:** 596, 724 **Vol. 3:** 1024, 1153
72:19 **Vol. 1:** 98, 735
72:20* **Vol. 3:** 669
72:22* **Vol. 3:** 1024
73 **Vol. 1:** 211 **Vol. 2:** 479, 841 **Vol. 3:** 565, 938
73:1 **Vol. 3:** 659
73:2* **Vol. 2:** 428

Psalms *(cont'd)*

73:3*	**Vol. 2:** 777–778
73:6*	**Vol. 3:** 29
73:11*	**Vol. 1:** 240
73:12*	**Vol. 2:** 842
73:13*	**Vol. 3:** 355, 358, 990
73:17	**Vol. 2:** 61
73:20*	**Vol. 1:** 512 **Vol. 2:** 287
73:21	**Vol. 2:** 167
73:23 ff*	**Vol. 1:** 433 **Vol. 2:** 207 **Vol. 3:** 727
73:23*	**Vol. 1:** 562
73:24*	**Vol. 2:** 191 **Vol. 3:** 262, 748, 1016
73:25 f	**Vol. 2:** 297
73:25	**Vol. 1:** 636
73:26*	**Vol. 1:** 673 **Vol. 2:** 181, 303, 479
74	**Vol. 2:** 416, 823
74:1*	**Vol. 1:** 164 **Vol. 2:** 412 **Vol. 3:** 565
74:2*	**Vol. 2:** 297 **Vol. 3:** 192, 234–235
74:3*	**Vol. 3:** 29, 786
74:8*	**Vol. 3:** 255
74:9	**Vol. 3:** 80
74:12*†	**Vol. 2:** 830 **Vol. 3:** 207
74:13 f*	**Vol. 1:** 508 **Vol. 3:** 983
74:14	**Vol. 1:** 523
74:15*	**Vol. 3:** 986, 988
74:16*	**Vol. 3:** 350
74:18*	**Vol. 1:** 381 **Vol. 3:** 234–235, 1025
74:21*	**Vol. 2:** 260 **Vol. 3:** 816
74:22*	**Vol. 3:** 93, 234–235, 1025
75	**Vol. 2:** 261
75:1	**Vol. 3:** 659
75:4*	**Vol. 2:** 202
75:5*	**Vol. 2:** 202
75:6	**Vol. 1:** 572
75:7*	**Vol. 2:** 202, 262
75:8*	**Vol. 2:** 275 **Vol. 3:** 919, 922
75:9	**Vol. 2:** 276
76*	**Vol. 3:** 669, 783
76:3	**Vol. 2:** 458, 592
76:5*	**Vol. 2:** 842
76:9*	**Vol. 3:** 207
77	**Vol. 3:** 236
77:1–11	**Vol. 2:** 863
77:2–11	**Vol. 3:** 236
77:3	**Vol. 2:** 889
77:4*	**Vol. 3:** 236
77:5*	**Vol. 3:** 820
77:9*	**Vol. 2:** 733
77:12 ff	**Vol. 3:** 236
77:13*	**Vol. 2:** 425
77:14*	**Vol. 2:** 724
77:15*	**Vol. 3:** 192
77:17*	**Vol. 3:** 983
77:18	**Vol. 3:** 1001
77:20*	**Vol. 1:** 683 **Vol. 2:** 412, 639 **Vol. 3:** 565, 937
77:22*	**Vol. 3:** 1212
77:32*	**Vol. 3:** 1212
77:37*	**Vol. 2:** 302
77:61 f*	**Vol. 3:** 590
77:62*	**Vol. 3:** 1187
78*	**Vol. 2:** 627 **Vol. 3:** 451, 578
78:2	**Vol. 1:** 377–378 **Vol. 2:** 217, 753
78:8*	**Vol. 3:** 691
78:9*	**Vol. 2:** 889
78:10*	**Vol. 2:** 134, 440 **Vol. 3:** 1016
78:11*	**Vol. 3:** 569
78:12*	**Vol. 1:** 240, 531
78:15 f*	**Vol. 3:** 382, 988
78:15*	**Vol. 3:** 1005
78:16*	**Vol. 3:** 986, 988
78:17*	**Vol. 3:** 1005
78:18 ff	**Vol. 3:** 804
78:18*	**Vol. 2:** 268, 856 **Vol. 3:** 799, 802
78:19 f*	**Vol. 3:** 117
78:19*	**Vol. 3:** 345, 1005
78:20*	**Vol. 1:** 673 **Vol. 3:** 117
78:21	**Vol. 1:** 109
78:24 f	**Vol. 1:** 252 **Vol. 2:** 871
78:26 ff	**Vol. 3:** 804
78:27	**Vol. 1:** 172, 673
78:30	**Vol. 2:** 268
78:35*	**Vol. 3:** 193
78:38*	**Vol. 1:** 109, 679, 698–699 **Vol. 3:** 153–154, 156
78:39*	**Vol. 1:** 673, 679 **Vol. 2:** 565 **Vol. 3:** 690
78:40 f*	**Vol. 3:** 800
78:40*	**Vol. 3:** 1005
78:41*	**Vol. 3:** 799
78:42*	**Vol. 2:** 889 **Vol. 3:** 192 193
78:43*	**Vol. 1:** 531 **Vol. 2:** 627
78:44*	**Vol. 3:** 986
78:49	**Vol. 1:** 101
78:51*	**Vol. 1:** 531 **Vol. 3:** 415
78:52 f	**Vol. 2:** 104, 412 **Vol. 3:** 565
78:52*	**Vol. 2:** 412 **Vol. 3:** 1005
78:56*	**Vol. 3:** 799
78:60	**Vol. 3:** 426
78:63*	**Vol. 2:** 422
78:67–72	**Vol. 3:** 461
78:71 f	**Vol. 3:** 565
79	**Vol. 2:** 416
79:1	**Vol. 2:** 296 **Vol. 3:** 786
79:2	**Vol. 2:** 237
79:5*	**Vol. 2:** 509
79:6	**Vol. 2:** 650, 854
79:8*	**Vol. 3:** 156, 234
79:9*	**Vol. 1:** 698–699 **Vol. 3:** 154, 161, 201–202, 218
79:10	**Vol. 3:** 93
79:13	**Vol. 3:** 565
79:14*	**Vol. 1:** 117, 520
79:15*	**Vol. 3:** 950
79:19*	**Vol. 3:** 202
80	**Vol. 2:** 416 **Vol. 3:** 233
80:1	**Vol. 1:** 280 **Vol. 2:** 412 **Vol. 3:** 565
80:2*	**Vol. 1:** 320 **Vol. 2:** 735
80:3*	**Vol. 3:** 318

Psalms *(cont'd)*

80:4*	**Vol. 2:** 863
80:5*	**Vol. 3:** 402
80:6	**Vol. 2:** 431
80:7*	**Vol. 3:** 318
80:8 ff*	**Vol. 2:** 248
80:8–19	**Vol. 2:** 747
80:8–15*	**Vol. 3:** 614
80:8–13*	**Vol. 3:** 918
80:8 f*	**Vol. 2:** 313 **Vol. 3:** 866
80:8	**Vol. 1:** 531
80:10 f*	**Vol. 3:** 867
80:14*	**Vol. 1:** 189
80:15*	**Vol. 3:** 350
80:17 f	**Vol. 3:** 614
80:19*	**Vol. 3:** 318
81:7*	**Vol. 2:** 215 **Vol. 3:** 808
81:9*	**Vol. 2:** 876
81:10	**Vol. 2:** 726
81:16*	**Vol. 1:** 743 **Vol. 3:** 382, 836
82	**Vol. 3:** 187–188
82:1 ff	**Vol. 3:** 629
82:1*	**Vol. 1:** 503 **Vol. 2:** 190, 591
82:2	**Vol. 2:** 591 **Vol. 3:** 187
82:3*	**Vol. 2:** 260, 820, 822 **Vol. 3:** 187, 355
82:4*	**Vol. 3:** 187, 201
82:5 ff*	**Vol. 2:** 260
82:5	**Vol. 3:** 187
82:6*	**Vol. 2:** 231, 448 **Vol. 3:** 186, 629, 636
82:8*	**Vol. 2:** 260
83:14*	**Vol. 3:** 1010
83:16–18	**Vol. 3:** 563
83:16	**Vol. 3:** 531
83:17	**Vol. 3:** 563
83:18*	**Vol. 2:** 724
83:24*	**Vol. 3:** 265
84:2*	**Vol. 2:** 181, 212
84:3*	**Vol. 1:** 173–174
84:4*	**Vol. 2:** 247 **Vol. 3:** 816
84:5	**Vol. 2:** 478
84:8*	**Vol. 2:** 863
84:9	**Vol. 2:** 336
84:10*	**Vol. 1:** 537 **Vol. 2:** 247, 698, 887 **Vol. 3:** 811
84:11*	**Vol. 2:** 99, 777 **Vol. 3:** 731
84:12*	**Vol. 1:** 216
85	**Vol. 3:** 356
85:2	**Vol. 1:** 698 **Vol. 2:** 212
85:3*	**Vol. 3:** 255
85:7*	**Vol. 3:** 207, 569
85:8*	**Vol. 2:** 237, 778
85:10	**Vol. 2:** 777 **Vol. 3:** 879
85:11*	**Vol. 3:** 938
85:12	**Vol. 1:** 598
85:13*	**Vol. 2:** 209
86*	**Vol. 2:** 863
86:1*	**Vol. 2:** 175, 820, 822–823
86:2*	**Vol. 2:** 336 **Vol. 3:** 595
86:4*	**Vol. 2:** 336 **Vol. 3:** 595, 680
86:5	**Vol. 2:** 257
86:6*	**Vol. 2:** 860, 863
86:7	**Vol. 2:** 890
86:9*	**Vol. 2:** 876
86:10*	**Vol. 2:** 622, 627, 724
86:11*	**Vol. 3:** 938
86:12 f*	**Vol. 3:** 262
86:13*	**Vol. 3:** 201–202
86:14*	**Vol. 1:** 696
86:15	**Vol. 2:** 769
86:16*	**Vol. 2:** 336 **Vol. 3:** 207, 595, 716
87:3	**Vol. 2:** 803
87:6*	**Vol. 2:** 209
88	**Vol. 2:** 167 **Vol. 3:** 262
88:2*	**Vol. 2:** 860, 863
88:3*	**Vol. 1:** 320 **Vol. 3:** 595
88:4 f	**Vol. 1:** 444
88:5*	**Vol. 1:** 433 **Vol. 2:** 206 **Vol. 3:** 262
88:6*	**Vol. 1:** 295, 422 **Vol. 3:** 555
88:7 f*	**Vol. 3:** 997
88:9*	**Vol. 3:** 559, 994
88:10 f*	**Vol. 3:** 262
88:10	**Vol. 1:** 444
88:11*	**Vol. 2:** 206 **Vol. 3:** 30
88:12	**Vol. 1:** 464
88:13*	**Vol. 2:** 863
88:14*	**Vol. 2:** 863
88:15 ff*	**Vol. 3:** 997
88:48*	**Vol. 1:** 710–711
88:51 f*	**Vol. 2:** 835
89	**Vol. 3:** 356, 649–650
89:1*	**Vol. 3:** 673
89:2*	**Vol. 2:** 190 **Vol. 3:** 117
89:3 ff*	**Vol. 3:** 636
89:3*	**Vol. 3:** 594
89:4*	**Vol. 3:** 117, 522, 648
89:5–7	**Vol. 2:** 376
89:5*	**Vol. 1:** 101
89:6	**Vol. 1:** 293
89:7 ff	**Vol. 2:** 613
89:7*	**Vol. 1:** 101 **Vol. 2:** 498 **Vol. 3:** 636
89:9 f*	**Vol. 3:** 960
89:9*	**Vol. 3:** 153, 716
89:10*	**Vol. 1:** 523 **Vol. 3:** 30
89:11*	**Vol. 3:** 29
89:12*	**Vol. 1:** 379 **Vol. 2:** 353
89:13*	**Vol. 2:** 201
89:14*	**Vol. 3:** 117
89:15	**Vol. 2:** 491
89:16 f	**Vol. 1:** 227
89:16*	**Vol. 2:** 201 **Vol. 3:** 355
89:17*	**Vol. 2:** 818
89:20*	**Vol. 2:** 227, 711
89:21*	**Vol. 2:** 149
89:24	**Vol. 2:** 650
89:26 f	**Vol. 2:** 336
89:26	**Vol. 1:** 617
89:27 ff	**Vol. 1:** 667
89:27 f*	**Vol. 3:** 636
89:27*	**Vol. 1:** 168 **Vol. 2:** 378

Psalms *(cont'd)*

89:29*	**Vol. 2:** 189
89:31*	**Vol. 3:** 354
89:36*	**Vol. 3:** 730, 1068
89:37*	**Vol. 1:** 99 **Vol. 3:** 350, 1041
89:38–45	**Vol. 2:** 644
89:38	**Vol. 1:** 99 **Vol. 2:** 336
89:39	**Vol. 1:** 405 **Vol. 2:** 336
89:47	**Vol. 1:** 379
89:48*	**Vol. 3:** 201, 235, 513
89:49*	**Vol. 3:** 209
89:50 f	**Vol. 2:** 835
89:51*	**Vol. 2:** 336 **Vol. 3:** 235
89:52*	**Vol. 1:** 98, 210
89:57*	**Vol. 3:** 166–167
90*	**Vol. 1:** 433 **Vol. 2:** 639, 863
90:1*	**Vol. 2:** 69, 71 **Vol. 3:** 841
90:2*	**Vol. 3:** 1010
90:3*	**Vol. 2:** 260, 263
90:4*	**Vol. 2:** 697–699, 701, 887
90:5	**Vol. 1:** 512
90:10	**Vol. 2:** 690
90:12*	**Vol. 3:** 1027
90:16*	**Vol. 3:** 1148
90:17*	**Vol. 2:** 485 **Vol. 3:** 1148
91	**Vol. 1:** 210 **Vol. 2:** 893
91:1 f	**Vol. 3:** 729
91:1	**Vol. 3:** 554
91:3*	**Vol. 3:** 201
91:4	**Vol. 1:** 174 **Vol. 3:** 797, 805
91:5	**Vol. 1:** 420 **Vol. 3:** 268
91:6	**Vol. 3:** 268
91:9	**Vol. 3:** 729
91:11 f*	**Vol. 2:** 705–706 **Vol. 3:** 790, 805
91:11*	**Vol. 1:** 332, 335
91:13	**Vol. 1:** 510 **Vol. 3:** 806
91:16*	**Vol. 1:** 433 **Vol. 3:** 207, 569
92	**Vol. 2:** 261, 263 **Vol. 3:** 407
92:2*	**Vol. 3:** 45
92:3*	**Vol. 3:** 673
92:4	**Vol. 2:** 353
92:5*	**Vol. 3:** 820
92:6*	**Vol. 3:** 1024
92:10	**Vol. 2:** 711
92:13*	**Vol. 2:** 247
93	**Vol. 2:** 613
93:1–4*	**Vol. 3:** 960
93:1	**Vol. 2:** 375
93:2*	**Vol. 3:** 117
93:4*	**Vol. 2:** 199
93:5*	**Vol. 2:** 669
93:21*	**Vol. 2:** 370
94:1*	**Vol. 2:** 735
94:2*	**Vol. 3:** 29
94:4	**Vol. 1:** 227
94:6	**Vol. 3:** 1074
94:8*†	**Vol. 3:** 1024–1025
94:9	**Vol. 2:** 175
94:10*†	**Vol. 3:** 760

94:11*	**Vol. 1:** 551 **Vol. 2:** 513 **Vol. 3:** 820
94:12*†	**Vol. 3:** 760
94:13*	**Vol. 2:** 890
94:14	**Vol. 2:** 799
94:20	**Vol. 1:** 262
94:22	**Vol. 2:** 71
95:1*	**Vol. 3:** 218
95:3 ff	**Vol. 2:** 375
95:3 f	**Vol. 2:** 898
95:4*	**Vol. 2:** 199 **Vol. 3:** 1010
95:6*	**Vol. 1:** 609 **Vol. 2:** 859, 876
95:7 f	**Vol. 1:** 372 **Vol. 3:** 227, 434
95:7–11*	**Vol. 1:** 203 **Vol. 2:** 775 **Vol. 3:** 937, 1005
95:7*	**Vol. 2:** 412, 891–892 **Vol. 3:** 565
95:8 ff*	**Vol. 2:** 627
95:8 f*	**Vol. 3:** 802
95:8*	**Vol. 1:** 203 **Vol. 2:** 155, 178, 889 **Vol. 3:** 799–800, 1005
95:9*	**Vol. 3:** 799, 808, 1148
95:10*	**Vol. 2:** 395, 459–460, 696
95:11*†	**Vol. 3:** 73, 256–257
96–99	**Vol. 2:** 613
96	**Vol. 2:** 109 **Vol. 3:** 671
96:1 ff	**Vol. 2:** 888
96:1*	**Vol. 3:** 673
96:2 ff	**Vol. 2:** 109
96:3–9	**Vol. 2:** 45
96:3	**Vol. 2:** 45
96:5	**Vol. 1:** 451
96:8	**Vol. 3:** 421
96:9 f	**Vol. 2:** 888
96:9*	**Vol. 2:** 876
96:10	**Vol. 2:** 375
96:11 ff	**Vol. 2:** 353
96:11	**Vol. 1:** 734 **Vol. 2:** 353, 355
96:13*	**Vol. 1:** 320, 519 **Vol. 3:** 865
97	**Vol. 3:** 356
97:1	**Vol. 2:** 355, 375
97:2 f	**Vol. 2:** 917
97:2	**Vol. 2:** 613 **Vol. 3:** 1001
97:4	**Vol. 2:** 836
97:7*	**Vol. 2:** 876
97:8	**Vol. 2:** 353
97:9*	**Vol. 2:** 201
97:10*	**Vol. 2:** 596 **Vol. 3:** 201
97:12*	**Vol. 3:** 233, 237–238
98:1*	**Vol. 3:** 673, 960
98:2 f*	**Vol. 3:** 311
98:3*	**Vol. 2:** 596 **Vol. 3:** 235
98:4*	**Vol. 3:** 673
98:7	**Vol. 1:** 519, 734
98:8*	**Vol. 3:** 986
98:9	**Vol. 1:** 320, 519
99:1	**Vol. 1:** 280 **Vol. 2:** 375, 613
99:2	**Vol. 2:** 326, 375
99:3	**Vol. 2:** 225
99:4	**Vol. 3:** 357
99:5*	**Vol. 2:** 201, 876
99:6	**Vol. 2:** 639

Psalms *(cont'd)*

99:8	**Vol. 3:** 93
99:9*	**Vol. 2:** 201, 876
100	**Vol. 3:** 423
100:2	**Vol. 1:** 320
100:3	**Vol. 2:** 412 **Vol. 3:** 565
100:4*	**Vol. 1:** 320, 344 **Vol. 3:** 669, 816
101:1*	**Vol. 3:** 673
101:2*	**Vol. 3:** 924
101:3*	**Vol. 1:** 696 **Vol. 2:** 349 **Vol. 3:** 583–584
101:5*	**Vol. 3:** 29, 345–346
101:6*	**Vol. 3:** 514, 924
101:7*	**Vol. 2:** 137 **Vol. 3:** 29
102*	**Vol. 2:** 257, 863
102:1*	**Vol. 2:** 863
102:2	**Vol. 1:** 320
102:3 f	**Vol. 2:** 890
102:3*	**Vol. 2:** 890
102:4*	**Vol. 1:** 743 **Vol. 2:** 211, 272 **Vol. 3:** 836
102:6 f	**Vol. 1:** 173
102:8*	**Vol. 3:** 816
102:9 f	**Vol. 2:** 272
102:11	**Vol. 1:** 743 **Vol. 2:** 211
102:12*	**Vol. 3:** 224
102:13*	**Vol. 3:** 237
102:14	**Vol. 1:** 520
102:15–20*	**Vol. 2:** 261
102:15 f	**Vol. 2:** 888
102:15*	**Vol. 2:** 817
102:17*	**Vol. 2:** 261, 863
102:18*	**Vol. 1:** 379 **Vol. 3:** 816
102:19*	**Vol. 2:** 225
102:20*	**Vol. 2:** 199 **Vol. 3:** 177
102:21 f	**Vol. 2:** 888
102:21*	**Vol. 2:** 602
102:25*	**Vol. 1:** 317
102:26*	**Vol. 2:** 714
102:27 f	**Vol. 2:** 69
103:1*	**Vol. 3:** 262
103:3 ff*	**Vol. 3:** 262
103:3*	**Vol. 2:** 167–168, 610 **Vol. 3:** 943, 997
103:4*	**Vol. 1:** 468 **Vol. 3:** 192–193
103:5*	**Vol. 1:** 173, 663
103:6 ff	**Vol. 2:** 364
103:6–13	**Vol. 1:** 109
103:6*	**Vol. 3:** 355, 357
103:7*	**Vol. 2:** 639 **Vol. 3:** 235, 1019
103:8 ff*	**Vol. 3:** 167
103:8*	**Vol. 2:** 71, 598, 769
103:11	**Vol. 1:** 622
103:13	**Vol. 1:** 617, 622 **Vol. 2:** 596
103:14 ff	**Vol. 1:** 551
103:14*	**Vol. 3:** 235
103:15	**Vol. 1:** 743
103:17 f	**Vol. 1:** 367
103:17	**Vol. 1:** 622 **Vol. 2:** 596
103:18*	**Vol. 1:** 332
103:19*	**Vol. 1:** 522 **Vol. 2:** 376 **Vol. 3:** 117
103:21*	**Vol. 3:** 1019
104–106	**Vol. 1:** 99
104	**Vol. 1:** 99, 383
104:2*	**Vol. 2:** 189, 491 **Vol. 3:** 1068
104:3 f	**Vol. 3:** 1001
104:3*	**Vol. 1:** 523 **Vol. 2:** 189–190, 917 **Vol. 3:** 984
104:4*	**Vol. 1:** 655 **Vol. 3:** 553, 690
104:5	**Vol. 1:** 523
104:6*	**Vol. 3:** 983
104:7*	**Vol. 3:** 113, 983, 1001
104:10 f*	**Vol. 3:** 865, 986
104:11*	**Vol. 3:** 109
104:12*	**Vol. 3:** 113, 813
104:13	**Vol. 1:** 743
104:14 f	**Vol. 2:** 357
104:15*	**Vol. 2:** 711 **Vol. 3:** 919
104:18*	**Vol. 3:** 381
104:19	**Vol. 3:** 835
104:20	**Vol. 1:** 422
104:21*	**Vol. 3:** 601
104:24 ff*	**Vol. 3:** 983
104:24*	**Vol. 1:** 381 **Vol. 3:** 1027
104:27 f	**Vol. 3:** 804
104:29 f	**Vol. 2:** 478
104:29*	**Vol. 1:** 84, 585, 670 **Vol. 3:** 690
104:30*	**Vol. 1:** 84, 379
104:32*	**Vol. 3:** 1010
104:33*	**Vol. 3:** 673
105	**Vol. 1:** 99 **Vol. 2:** 863
105:1–15	**Vol. 3:** 671
105:1–6	**Vol. 1:** 345
105:1–3	**Vol. 2:** 650
105:2*	**Vol. 1:** 574 **Vol. 3:** 673
105:3 f	**Vol. 3:** 531
105:3*	**Vol. 3:** 816
105:4*	**Vol. 1:** 586 **Vol. 3:** 716
105:6*	**Vol. 1:** 77 **Vol. 3:** 867
105:8*	**Vol. 2:** 596 **Vol. 3:** 235, 241
105:9	**Vol. 1:** 572
105:12	**Vol. 3:** 1212
105:15	**Vol. 2:** 835
105:16*	**Vol. 1:** 273
105:20*	**Vol. 3:** 177
105:21*	**Vol. 1:** 381, 472 **Vol. 3:** 1030
105:22*	**Vol. 3:** 1028, 1033
105:26	**Vol. 2:** 639
105:27*	**Vol. 2:** 627
105:28	**Vol. 1:** 422 **Vol. 2:** 60
105:33	**Vol. 3:** 865
105:36*	**Vol. 3:** 415
105:38*	**Vol. 3:** 937
105:40*	**Vol. 1:** 173 **Vol. 2:** 856
105:41*†	**Vol. 1:** 683 **Vol. 3:** 986
105:42*	**Vol. 3:** 235, 594
105:43	**Vol. 1:** 538
105:45*	**Vol. 3:** 354
106	**Vol. 1:** 99 **Vol. 2:** 863
106:3*	**Vol. 3:** 836

Psalms *(cont'd)*

106:4* **Vol. 3:** 234
106:5* **Vol. 1:** 189 **Vol. 3:** 816
106:6 **Vol. 1:** 409
106:7–12* **Vol. 3:** 1005
106:7* **Vol. 1:** 203, 531, 617 **Vol. 3:** 241
106:10* **Vol. 2:** 596 **Vol. 3:** 192
106:12* **Vol. 3:** 673, 816
106:13–33* **Vol. 3:** 1005
106:13* **Vol. 2:** 773
106:14* **Vol. 3:** 799–800
106:16 **Vol. 2:** 231, 639
106:19* **Vol. 2:** 876
106:21* **Vol. 1:** 531 **Vol. 2:** 425
106:22* **Vol. 2:** 622 **Vol. 3:** 318
106:23 **Vol. 2:** 639
106:26* **Vol. 2:** 205
106:30* **Vol. 3:** 152, 155
106:31* **Vol. 3:** 357, 823
106:32 **Vol. 2:** 639
106:36* **Vol. 2:** 707
106:37 f **Vol. 3:** 806
106:37 **Vol. 1:** 451
106:38 **Vol. 2:** 525
106:44* **Vol. 2:** 860 **Vol. 3:** 513
106:45* **Vol. 1:** 356 **Vol. 2:** 596 **Vol. 3:** 235, 241
106:47* **Vol. 1:** 344–345 **Vol. 3:** 207
106:48 **Vol. 1:** 98, 210 **Vol. 2:** 596
107* **Vol. 2:** 261
107:1 **Vol. 1:** 345
107:2* **Vol. 3:** 192
107:5 **Vol. 2:** 265
107:6* **Vol. 2:** 663
107:8 **Vol. 1:** 345
107:9 **Vol. 1:** 743 **Vol. 2:** 266, 596
107:10 f **Vol. 1:** 422
107:10 **Vol. 3:** 555
107:11* **Vol. 1:** 345 **Vol. 3:** 1118
107:12* **Vol. 3:** 994
107:13* **Vol. 2:** 663
107:14 **Vol. 3:** 555, 592
107:15 **Vol. 1:** 345
107:17 ff* **Vol. 3:** 997
107:17 **Vol. 1:** 345
107:18 **Vol. 2:** 29
107:19* **Vol. 2:** 663
107:20* **Vol. 3:** 209
107:21 **Vol. 1:** 345
107:22 **Vol. 3:** 423
107:27* **Vol. 3:** 1027
107:28* **Vol. 2:** 663
107:30* **Vol. 3:** 1019
107:31 **Vol. 1:** 345
107:32* **Vol. 2:** 201 **Vol. 3:** 816
107:33* **Vol. 3:** 986–987
107:35* **Vol. 3:** 992
107:36 ff **Vol. 2:** 265
107:43* **Vol. 3:** 1027

108:1* **Vol. 3:** 117, 673
108:4 **Vol. 3:** 879
108:5* **Vol. 2:** 201
108:6* **Vol. 3:** 207
108:7* **Vol. 2:** 370 **Vol. 3:** 786
108:10 **Vol. 2:** 742
108:14* **Vol. 1:** 471
109:4* **Vol. 2:** 863 **Vol. 3:** 40
109:6* **Vol. 3:** 468
109:7* **Vol. 2:** 863
109:8* **Vol. 2:** 428 **Vol. 3:** 152, 747
109:9 **Vol. 2:** 737
109:10 **Vol. 2:** 737
109:14* **Vol. 3:** 232, 240, 242
109:15* **Vol. 3:** 237
109:18 **Vol. 2:** 711
109:19* **Vol. 3:** 120
109:22 **Vol. 2:** 823
109:23 **Vol. 3:** 560
109:24* **Vol. 1:** 612 **Vol. 3:** 994
109:26* **Vol. 3:** 207
109:30* **Vol. 3:** 816
109:31 **Vol. 1:** 474 **Vol. 2:** 820
110–118 **Vol. 1:** 99
110 **Vol. 1:** 99, 178, 426–427 **Vol. 2:** 336, 590, 644 **Vol. 3:** 41, 297
110:1 ff **Vol. 3:** 643
110:1 f **Vol. 1:** 554 **Vol. 3:** 648
110:1* **Vol. 1:** 239, 477 **Vol. 2:** 80, 146–147, 194, 196, 199, 245, 374, 515, 614, 665 **Vol. 3:** 588, 614, 629, 638, 644, 651, 792
110:2 **Vol. 3:** 636
110:3* **Vol. 1:** 177 **Vol. 2:** 495 **Vol. 3:** 269, 565
110:4* **Vol. 1:** 356 **Vol. 2:** 448, 590–591 **Vol. 3:** 36, 41, 588, 742, 830
110:6 **Vol. 1:** 610
111:1 **Vol. 2:** 863
111:2 **Vol. 3:** 242
111:3* **Vol. 3:** 224
111:4* **Vol. 2:** 598, 771 **Vol. 3:** 237–238
111:5* **Vol. 3:** 235
111:7* **Vol. 1:** 332
111:8 **Vol. 3:** 882
111:9* **Vol. 3:** 193
111:10* **Vol. 1:** 165 **Vol. 3:** 130, 224, 1027–1028
112:3* **Vol. 2:** 841 **Vol. 3:** 224
112:4 **Vol. 1:** 422 **Vol. 2:** 492, 834
112:6* **Vol. 3:** 237
112:7* **Vol. 3:** 117
112:9* **Vol. 2:** 34, 821, 827 **Vol. 3:** 224
112:10 **Vol. 2:** 421
113:1* **Vol. 2:** 740, 822 **Vol. 3:** 816
113:3* **Vol. 3:** 816
113:5 ff **Vol. 2:** 596
113:5–9* **Vol. 2:** 261
113:5 f **Vol. 2:** 190
113:9* **Vol. 3:** 1055

Psalms *(cont'd)*

114–118   **Vol. 3:** 669
114:3*   **Vol. 1:** 419
114:8*   **Vol. 3:** 986, 992
115–118   **Vol. 2:** 522, 528
115   **Vol. 2:** 175
115:1   **Vol. 3:** 879
115:12–15   **Vol. 1:** 210
115:13*   **Vol. 2:** 428
115:15–17   **Vol. 2:** 189
115:15*   **Vol. 3:** 113
115:17*   **Vol. 1:** 444   **Vol. 2:** 206   **Vol. 3:** 816
116:1*   **Vol. 2:** 261, 472, 860
116:3*   **Vol. 1:** 433   **Vol. 3:** 180
116:6*   **Vol. 1:** 281   **Vol. 3:** 209
116:7*   **Vol. 3:** 255
116:8*   **Vol. 1:** 433   **Vol. 2:** 478   **Vol. 3:** 262
116:9*   **Vol. 2:** 815
116:10*   **Vol. 2:** 261
116:11   **Vol. 2:** 471
116:12–19   **Vol. 3:** 436
116:13*   **Vol. 2:** 275   **Vol. 3:** 208
116:15   **Vol. 3:** 158, 436
116:16   **Vol. 3:** 592
116:17   **Vol. 3:** 423
117:1*   **Vol. 2:** 513, 799   **Vol. 3:** 816–817
117:2*   **Vol. 3:** 224, 880
117:7*   **Vol. 1:** 597
117:8*   **Vol. 1:** 589
118*   **Vol. 2:** 479   **Vol. 3:** 669, 1040
118:1–4*   **Vol. 1:** 345   **Vol. 3:** 388
118:1   **Vol. 2:** 100
118:5 ff*   **Vol. 3:** 388
118:5–21*   **Vol. 3:** 388
118:7*   **Vol. 3:** 262
118:10 ff   **Vol. 2:** 650
118:10–21*   **Vol. 3:** 388
118:12*   **Vol. 3:** 109
118:14*   **Vol. 3:** 669
118:15 f   **Vol. 2:** 149
118:15   **Vol. 2:** 146
118:19 f*   **Vol. 3:** 388
118:20   **Vol. 2:** 31, 706
118:21   **Vol. 1:** 345
118:22 ff   **Vol. 2:** 313   **Vol. 3:** 809
118:22 f*   **Vol. 2:** 253   **Vol. 3:** 384
118:22*   **Vol. 1:** 74, 541   **Vol. 2:** 129, 159, 706   **Vol. 3:** 329, 382, 388–391, 393, 624
118:23*   **Vol. 2:** 622–623
118:24*   **Vol. 3:** 1068, 1153
118:25 f   **Vol. 1:** 323
118:25*   **Vol. 1:** 100   **Vol. 3:** 207
118:26 f*   **Vol. 3:** 388
118:26   **Vol. 1:** 100, 174, 213, 321   **Vol. 2:** 328, 379
118:27*   **Vol. 3:** 318, 418–419, 715
118:28 f*   **Vol. 3:** 388
118:28*   **Vol. 2:** 201

118:88*   **Vol. 3:** 1040
118:119*   **Vol. 3:** 1040
118:129*   **Vol. 3:** 1040
118:146*   **Vol. 3:** 1040
118:167 f*   **Vol. 3:** 1040
119*   **Vol. 2:** 261, 355, 439   **Vol. 3:** 938
119:1*   **Vol. 1:** 216   **Vol. 2:** 440   **Vol. 3:** 924, 946
119:5*   **Vol. 3:** 354
119:7 f*   **Vol. 1:** 484
119:8*   **Vol. 3:** 354
119:11   **Vol. 2:** 215
119:12*   **Vol. 1:** 210   **Vol. 3:** 354, 760
119:14*   **Vol. 2:** 355, 842
119:16*   **Vol. 3:** 354
119:17*†   **Vol. 3:** 595
119:18*   **Vol. 3:** 311
119:19   **Vol. 1:** 688, 691   **Vol. 2:** 215
119:20*   **Vol. 3:** 354
119:21*   **Vol. 3:** 29
119:23*   **Vol. 3:** 345, 354, 595
119:24*   **Vol. 3:** 354
119:26*   **Vol. 3:** 354, 760
119:27*   **Vol. 1:** 332   **Vol. 3:** 354
119:28*   **Vol. 1:** 658   **Vol. 3:** 680
119:29   **Vol. 1:** 607   **Vol. 3:** 575
119:30   **Vol. 1:** 534, 537
119:31   **Vol. 2:** 349
119:32*   **Vol. 1:** 254   **Vol. 3:** 946
119:33*   **Vol. 3:** 354
119:34*   **Vol. 2:** 440   **Vol. 3:** 131
119:36   **Vol. 1:** 137   **Vol. 3:** 137
119:38*   **Vol. 3:** 595
119:43   **Vol. 3:** 880
119:44*   **Vol. 2:** 440
119:48*   **Vol. 3:** 354
119:49*   **Vol. 3:** 234–235, 595
119:50   **Vol. 1:** 329, 569   **Vol. 2:** 263
119:51*   **Vol. 3:** 29
119:52*   **Vol. 3:** 236
119:54*   **Vol. 1:** 691   **Vol. 3:** 354
119:55*   **Vol. 3:** 236
119:56*   **Vol. 1:** 332   **Vol. 3:** 354
119:57*   **Vol. 1:** 332   **Vol. 2:** 303
119:59*   **Vol. 3:** 820
119:64*   **Vol. 3:** 354, 760
119:65*   **Vol. 3:** 595
119:66*   **Vol. 1:** 597   **Vol. 3:** 760
119:68*   **Vol. 3:** 354, 760
119:69*   **Vol. 3:** 29, 575
119:71*   **Vol. 1:** 484   **Vol. 3:** 354
119:73*   **Vol. 1:** 484   **Vol. 3:** 117, 131
119:75   **Vol. 3:** 357
119:76*   **Vol. 3:** 595
119:78*   **Vol. 3:** 29
119:79*   **Vol. 2:** 395
119:80*   **Vol. 3:** 354, 924
119:81*   **Vol. 3:** 207
119:83*   **Vol. 3:** 354
119:84*   **Vol. 3:** 595

Psalms *(cont'd)*

119:89	**Vol. 2:** 190
119:93 f*	**Vol. 3:** 354
119:93*	**Vol. 1:** 332
119:94*	**Vol. 3:** 207
119:95*	**Vol. 2:** 773
119:98*	**Vol. 3:** 1028, 1033
119:99*	**Vol. 3:** 760
119:101*	**Vol. 1:** 485 **Vol. 2:** 222
119:104	**Vol. 1:** 555 **Vol. 3:** 574–575
119:105*	**Vol. 2:** 492 **Vol. 3:** 882, 938
119:108*	**Vol. 3:** 760
119:112*	**Vol. 3:** 354
119:117 f*	**Vol. 3:** 354
119:119*	**Vol. 3:** 823
119:121	**Vol. 3:** 574
119:122*	**Vol. 3:** 29, 595
119:124 f*	**Vol. 3:** 595
119:124*	**Vol. 3:** 354, 760
119:125*	**Vol. 3:** 131
119:130	**Vol. 1:** 281
119:134*	**Vol. 3:** 192–193
119:135*	**Vol. 3:** 318, 354, 595, 760
119:139*	**Vol. 1:** 332
119:140*	**Vol. 3:** 595
119:141*	**Vol. 1:** 332 **Vol. 3:** 354
119:142	**Vol. 2:** 232 **Vol. 3:** 881–882, 892
119:143*	**Vol. 2:** 663 **Vol. 3:** 882
119:145*	**Vol. 3:** 354
119:154–169*	**Vol. 3:** 1118
119:154*	**Vol. 3:** 192–193
119:155*	**Vol. 3:** 354
119:162	**Vol. 2:** 355
119:163	**Vol. 3:** 575
119:164*	**Vol. 3:** 816
119:165*	**Vol. 2:** 707, 778
119:169	**Vol. 2:** 53
119:170	**Vol. 1:** 320
119:171*	**Vol. 3:** 354, 669, 760
119:175*	**Vol. 3:** 816
119:176*	**Vol. 1:** 464 **Vol. 2:** 412, 458–459 **Vol. 3:** 595
120:5	**Vol. 1:** 691
121	**Vol. 1:** 210
121:3	**Vol. 3:** 966
121:4	**Vol. 3:** 565
121:6*	**Vol. 3:** 733
121:8*	**Vol. 3:** 937
122:1	**Vol. 2:** 247
122:2*	**Vol. 3:** 595
122:5	**Vol. 2:** 612
122:6 ff*	**Vol. 2:** 778
123	**Vol. 2:** 737
123:4*	**Vol. 3:** 29
123:22*	**Vol. 2:** 511
124:4 f*	**Vol. 3:** 986
124:6	**Vol. 1:** 210
124:7	**Vol. 1:** 172
125:5*	**Vol. 2:** 778

126:1 f	**Vol. 2:** 433
126:1*	**Vol. 2:** 137
126:2*	**Vol. 2:** 353, 431 **Vol. 3:** 1079
126:4	**Vol. 3:** 560
126:5 f	**Vol. 2:** 825 **Vol. 3:** 144
126:5	**Vol. 2:** 353, 357 **Vol. 3:** 526
127:1	**Vol. 2:** 247
127:2	**Vol. 2:** 272
127:3 ff	**Vol. 1:** 288
127:3*	**Vol. 2:** 139 **Vol. 3:** 140
127:4	**Vol. 2:** 746
127:5	**Vol. 1:** 216
127:7 ff*	**Vol. 3:** 1057
128	**Vol. 1:** 210
128:3 ff	**Vol. 3:** 1057
128:3*	**Vol. 1:** 288 **Vol. 2:** 711 **Vol. 3:** 918
129:4 f*	**Vol. 3:** 355
129:8	**Vol. 1:** 210
130:1*	**Vol. 2:** 197
130:2*	**Vol. 2:** 860, 863
130:3	**Vol. 3:** 717
130:4	**Vol. 3:** 156
130:5 ff	**Vol. 2:** 772
130:5*	**Vol. 2:** 239, 773
130:7*†	**Vol. 3:** 193
130:8*	**Vol. 2:** 332, 447 **Vol. 3:** 192–193, 200
131*	**Vol. 2:** 161 **Vol. 3:** 727
131:1*	**Vol. 2:** 201
131:2*	**Vol. 2:** 201, 260–261
132	**Vol. 1:** 210
132:1*	**Vol. 3:** 235, 245
132:4*	**Vol. 3:** 255
132:5	**Vol. 2:** 319 **Vol. 3:** 465
132:7*	**Vol. 2:** 876
132:8*	**Vol. 3:** 255
132:10	**Vol. 2:** 336
132:11	**Vol. 3:** 648
132:12*	**Vol. 3:** 760, 960
132:14*	**Vol. 3:** 256
132:15	**Vol. 1:** 743 **Vol. 2:** 823
132:16*	**Vol. 1:** 314 **Vol. 3:** 207, 960
132:17	**Vol. 2:** 336, 596 **Vol. 3:** 715
132:18*	**Vol. 1:** 405, 554 **Vol. 3:** 960
134	**Vol. 1:** 99 **Vol. 3:** 673
135	**Vol. 1:** 99
135:1*	**Vol. 3:** 816
135:3*	**Vol. 3:** 816
135:4*	**Vol. 2:** 838, 840
135:7	**Vol. 2:** 189
135:9*	**Vol. 2:** 627
135:13*	**Vol. 3:** 237
135:14	**Vol. 1:** 569 **Vol. 2:** 800
135:15	**Vol. 3:** 560
135:17	**Vol. 2:** 175
135:21	**Vol. 2:** 326
136	**Vol. 1:** 523
136:4*	**Vol. 2:** 724
136:7*	**Vol. 2:** 724
136:8	**Vol. 2:** 53 **Vol. 3:** 859
136:12	**Vol. 3:** 717

Psalms *(cont'd)*

136:23*	**Vol. 2:** 261 **Vol. 3:** 235
137	**Vol. 2:** 325 **Vol. 3:** 236, 783
137:1 ff*	**Vol. 3:** 590
137:1*	**Vol. 3:** 236, 588, 986
137:3 f*	**Vol. 3:** 673
137:3*	**Vol. 3:** 668–669, 673
137:4*	**Vol. 3:** 673
137:6*	**Vol. 2:** 157, 349 **Vol. 3:** 236
137:7*	**Vol. 2:** 889 **Vol. 3:** 234
137:9	**Vol. 3:** 716
138:2*	**Vol. 2:** 876 **Vol. 3:** 783, 786
138:3*	**Vol. 1:** 695 **Vol. 2:** 889
138:5*	**Vol. 3:** 673
138:6*	**Vol. 2:** 261
138:8*	**Vol. 3:** 1148
138:15*	**Vol. 1:** 710, 712 **Vol. 2:** 209
139*	**Vol. 1:** 685
139:1*	**Vol. 3:** 808
139:2*	**Vol. 2:** 53 **Vol. 3:** 820
139:3*	**Vol. 3:** 514
139:5*	**Vol. 1:** 165
139:7–12	**Vol. 2:** 215
139:7*	**Vol. 3:** 514, 691
139:8*	**Vol. 1:** 433 **Vol. 2:** 206
139:10	**Vol. 2:** 146
139:11 f	**Vol. 1:** 422 **Vol. 2:** 491
139:13 ff	**Vol. 2:** 478
139:14*	**Vol. 3:** 680
139:15*	**Vol. 2:** 209, 215
139:16*	**Vol. 1:** 243 **Vol. 3:** 514
139:17*	**Vol. 2:** 49
139:19	**Vol. 3:** 583
139:20*	**Vol. 3:** 820
139:21 f	**Vol. 1:** 554–555
139:21	**Vol. 1:** 555
139:23*	**Vol. 3:** 808
140	**Vol. 2:** 823
140:1*	**Vol. 3:** 203
140:2*	**Vol. 3:** 823
140:3*	**Vol. 2:** 27–28 **Vol. 3:** 1079
140:4*	**Vol. 3:** 823, 1079
140:5*	**Vol. 3:** 29
140:6*	**Vol. 2:** 860
140:8	**Vol. 2:** 889
140:9*	**Vol. 3:** 820
140:10	**Vol. 2:** 157
140:12	**Vol. 3:** 93
141:2*	**Vol. 2:** 294, 863
141:3*	**Vol. 3:** 498
141:4	**Vol. 1:** 559
141:5*	**Vol. 2:** 141, 711, 818, 863
141:9*	**Vol. 2:** 707
141:10*	**Vol. 2:** 724
142*	**Vol. 2:** 863
142:2	**Vol. 2:** 854
142:5*	**Vol. 2:** 297, 303
142:6*	**Vol. 2:** 261
142:7*	**Vol. 2:** 478, 773
143:1*	**Vol. 2:** 860, 863 **Vol. 3:** 356
143:2*	**Vol. 2:** 336 **Vol. 3:** 355
143:3	**Vol. 1:** 444
143:4*	**Vol. 3:** 710
143:5*	**Vol. 3:** 236
143:6	**Vol. 2:** 266
143:10*	**Vol. 2:** 100 **Vol. 3:** 760, 1019
143:11*	**Vol. 1:** 700 **Vol. 3:** 355
143:14*	**Vol. 3:** 950
144:1*	**Vol. 3:** 760
144:3*	**Vol. 3:** 823
144:4*	**Vol. 2:** 501 **Vol. 3:** 555
144:6	**Vol. 3:** 1001
144:7*	**Vol. 2:** 199
144:8	**Vol. 3:** 575
144:9*	**Vol. 2:** 670 **Vol. 3:** 673
144:10*	**Vol. 3:** 192, 207
144:11	**Vol. 3:** 575
144:12*	**Vol. 3:** 784
144:15	**Vol. 1:** 636
145 ff	**Vol. 1:** 99
145–150	**Vol. 1:** 99
145	**Vol. 3:** 233
145:2*	**Vol. 3:** 816
145:4*	**Vol. 3:** 816
145:5	**Vol. 1:** 574
145:6*	**Vol. 3:** 318
145:7*	**Vol. 3:** 238, 674
145:9*	**Vol. 2:** 773
145:11–13	**Vol. 2:** 376
145:15	**Vol. 3:** 804
145:16	**Vol. 2:** 149, 726
145:17*	**Vol. 2:** 237 **Vol. 3:** 937
145:18	**Vol. 2:** 53 **Vol. 3:** 882
145:19*	**Vol. 2:** 860
145:20	**Vol. 2:** 134
146	**Vol. 3:** 817
146:1 f*	**Vol. 3:** 816
146:2*	**Vol. 2:** 35
146:3*	**Vol. 3:** 206
146:4*	**Vol. 2:** 565 **Vol. 3:** 820
146:6*	**Vol. 3:** 983
146:7*	**Vol. 2:** 265, 364 **Vol. 3:** 177, 804
146:9*	**Vol. 2:** 71, 737–738 **Vol. 3:** 1073
147:1*	**Vol. 3:** 816
147:2	**Vol. 1:** 685
147:4*	**Vol. 2:** 649 **Vol. 3:** 947
147:5*	**Vol. 3:** 713
147:6	**Vol. 2:** 257, 596
147:7	**Vol. 1:** 344
147:8*	**Vol. 3:** 117, 1009
147:9	**Vol. 1:** 173
147:10*	**Vol. 2:** 817
147:11*	**Vol. 2:** 240, 817
147:12*	**Vol. 3:** 816
147:14	**Vol. 2:** 778
147:15 ff	**Vol. 3:** 1105
147:15–18	**Vol. 3:** 1116
147:15	**Vol. 3:** 1105
147:16	**Vol. 3:** 1105

Psalms *(cont'd)*

147:17   **Vol. 3:** 1105
147:18   **Vol. 1:** 683   **Vol. 3:** 1105
147:19*   **Vol. 3:** 354, 1106
148   **Vol. 1:** 523
148:1–4   **Vol. 3:** 816
148:1   **Vol. 1:** 99
148:3   **Vol. 3:** 735
148:4–6   **Vol. 2:** 189
148:4*   **Vol. 2:** 189   **Vol. 3:** 984
148:5   **Vol. 1:** 379   **Vol. 3:** 1105
148:7   **Vol. 1:** 508   **Vol. 3:** 816
148:8   **Vol. 3:** 1001, 1105
148:10   **Vol. 1:** 113, 172
148:12   **Vol. 3:** 816
148:13   **Vol. 2:** 724
148:14   **Vol. 2:** 202   **Vol. 3:** 669
148:15*   **Vol. 3:** 1118
149:1 ff   **Vol. 2:** 670
149:1   **Vol. 1:** 293   **Vol. 3:** 673
149:2   **Vol. 2:** 326
149:3   **Vol. 3:** 816
149:4   **Vol. 2:** 257, 817
149:9   **Vol. 3:** 484
150   **Vol. 2:** 263   **Vol. 3:** 817
150:1–6   **Vol. 3:** 816
150:1   **Vol. 3:** 786
150:2   **Vol. 1:** 732   **Vol. 2:** 425
150:3   **Vol. 3:** 112

Proverbs

1:1   **Vol. 2:** 745, 757   **Vol. 3:** 606
1:2   **Vol. 2:** 777, 1027
1:3   **Vol. 3:** 125
1:4   **Vol. 1:** 283, 412   **Vol. 2:** 391, 830   **Vol. 3:** 125
1:5 f   **Vol. 3:** 1027
1:5   **Vol. 1:** 194   **Vol. 3:** 1028
1:6   **Vol. 2:** 745
1:7   **Vol. 1:** 622   **Vol. 2:** 93, 391   **Vol. 3:** 130, 777, 1027–1028
1:9   **Vol. 2:** 116
1:10   **Vol. 2:** 93
1:12   **Vol. 2:** 206   **Vol. 3:** 238
1:14   **Vol. 1:** 142
1:18   **Vol. 3:** 159
1:19   **Vol. 2:** 93   **Vol. 3:** 137
1:20 ff   **Vol. 3:** 1029
1:20 f   **Vol. 2:** 735   **Vol. 3:** 1056, 1069
1:20   **Vol. 2:** 735   **Vol. 3:** 668, 1027
1:21   **Vol. 1:** 327   **Vol. 3:** 51
1:22   **Vol. 1:** 281, 555   **Vol. 2:** 93   **Vol. 3:** 29
1:23   **Vol. 3:** 760
1:24–31   **Vol. 2:** 840
1:26   **Vol. 1:** 320   **Vol. 2:** 431
1:27   **Vol. 2:** 621
1:29   **Vol. 1:** 555   **Vol. 3:** 1027
1:31   **Vol. 1:** 281   **Vol. 2:** 93
1:32   **Vol. 2:** 93

2:1 ff   **Vol. 3:** 130
2:2   **Vol. 3:** 1027
2:3 f   **Vol. 2:** 835
2:3   **Vol. 2:** 391   **Vol. 3:** 1027
2:4 ff   **Vol. 2:** 391
2:4 f   **Vol. 2:** 830
2:4   **Vol. 2:** 261   **Vol. 3:** 533
2:5   **Vol. 3:** 130
2:6   **Vol. 2:** 395   **Vol. 3:** 1027
2:8   **Vol. 3:** 354
2:9   **Vol. 3:** 130
2:10   **Vol. 3:** 821, 1027
2:11   **Vol. 3:** 125, 1016
2:12   **Vol. 3:** 938
2:15   **Vol. 1:** 729   **Vol. 3:** 1027
2:16 ff   **Vol. 2:** 583
2:17   **Vol. 2:** 578   **Vol. 3:** 769
2:18 f   **Vol. 2:** 479
2:18   **Vol. 3:** 1027
2:19   **Vol. 2:** 478
2:20   **Vol. 3:** 938
2:22   **Vol. 2:** 93
3:1 f   **Vol. 2:** 478
3:1   **Vol. 2:** 132
3:2   **Vol. 2:** 475, 479, 778
3:3   **Vol. 1:** 241   **Vol. 3:** 484, 880
3:4   **Vol. 1:** 695   **Vol. 2:** 103
3:5   **Vol. 3:** 1027
3:6   **Vol. 3:** 352
3:7   **Vol. 2:** 618
3:10   **Vol. 2:** 690
3:11 f   **Vol. 2:** 141–142, 230, 757   **Vol. 3:** 365, 778, 998
3:11   **Vol. 1:** 462   **Vol. 2:** 549   **Vol. 3:** 189, 776
3:12   **Vol. 1:** 163, 617, 639   **Vol. 2:** 141
3:13   **Vol. 1:** 216   **Vol. 3:** 1027
3:14   **Vol. 1:** 268
3:15   **Vol. 3:** 348
3:16–22   **Vol. 2:** 432
3:16   **Vol. 2:** 475, 478, 841
3:17   **Vol. 2:** 778   **Vol. 3:** 938
3:18   **Vol. 1:** 390, 663   **Vol. 2:** 479   **Vol. 3:** 866
3:19   **Vol. 2:** 616   **Vol. 3:** 117, 1027
3:20   **Vol. 1:** 683
3:21   **Vol. 3:** 125
3:23   **Vol. 2:** 777–778
3:25   **Vol. 2:** 93
3:32   **Vol. 3:** 355
3:33   **Vol. 2:** 93
3:34   **Vol. 2:** 117, 123, 261–262, 618, 757   **Vol. 3:** 29–31, 161
3:35   **Vol. 2:** 93   **Vol. 3:** 1027
4:1   **Vol. 1:** 283   **Vol. 3:** 125
4:2   **Vol. 2:** 41
4:3   **Vol. 2:** 179
4:4   **Vol. 2:** 479   **Vol. 3:** 760
4:5   **Vol. 3:** 1027
4:9   **Vol. 2:** 116

Proverbs *(cont'd)*

4:10	**Vol. 2:** 479 **Vol. 3:** 745
4:11	**Vol. 3:** 760, 938, 1027
4:18 f	**Vol. 2:** 492 **Vol. 3:** 938
4:18	**Vol. 2:** 486, 492 **Vol. 3:** 929
4:19	**Vol. 2:** 486, 491 **Vol. 3:** 929
4:22	**Vol. 2:** 479
4:23	**Vol. 3:** 813
4:26	**Vol. 3:** 351
5:1	**Vol. 3:** 1027
5:2	**Vol. 3:** 125
5:3	**Vol. 2:** 711
5:4	**Vol. 1:** 202 **Vol. 2:** 27
5:5	**Vol. 3:** 1024
5:6	**Vol. 2:** 479 **Vol. 3:** 938
5:11	**Vol. 1:** 673, 675 **Vol. 2:** 421
5:12 f	**Vol. 2:** 141
5:12	**Vol. 1:** 555
5:13	**Vol. 3:** 760, 766
5:15	**Vol. 3:** 813
5:18	**Vol. 2:** 578
5:19	**Vol. 2:** 116
5:20	**Vol. 1:** 239
6:1 ff	**Vol. 2:** 149
6:1	**Vol. 1:** 258
6:5	**Vol. 1:** 172
6:6 – 11	**Vol. 2:** 823
6:6	**Vol. 3:** 1028
6:8	**Vol. 2:** 93 **Vol. 3:** 1027
6:8b	**Vol. 2:** 456
6:9 – 10	**Vol. 2:** 432
6:12	**Vol. 3:** 1024, 1028
6:13	**Vol. 3:** 760
6:15	**Vol. 1:** 320
6:16 ff	**Vol. 1:** 555
6:17	**Vol. 3:** 29, 159, 355, 574, 1079
6:18	**Vol. 3:** 823
6:20 – 35	**Vol. 2:** 583
6:23	**Vol. 2:** 141, 479, 492
6:25	**Vol. 1:** 364, 650 **Vol. 3:** 192
6:27 ff	**Vol. 1:** 655
6:27 – 29	**Vol. 2:** 746
6:27	**Vol. 1:** 240
6:30	**Vol. 3:** 377
6:31	**Vol. 2:** 845 **Vol. 3:** 201
6:34	**Vol. 3:** 1166
6:35	**Vol. 2:** 583, 845 **Vol. 3:** 190, 192
7:4	**Vol. 3:** 1027
7:5 – 27	**Vol. 2:** 583
7:7	**Vol. 3:** 1024
7:9	**Vol. 3:** 111
7:14	**Vol. 3:** 422
7:16	**Vol. 1:** 531
7:17	**Vol. 2:** 587
8	**Vol. 2:** 279 **Vol. 3:** 1032
8:1 ff	**Vol. 3:** 1162
8:1 – 21	**Vol. 3:** 1029
8:1 – 3	**Vol. 3:** 1056, 1069
8:1	**Vol. 3:** 51, 1027
8:3	**Vol. 3:** 668
8:5	**Vol. 1:** 412
8:6	**Vol. 2:** 93 **Vol. 3:** 351
8:7	**Vol. 3:** 880
8:9	**Vol. 3:** 351
8:10	**Vol. 1:** 537 **Vol. 3:** 808
8:11 f	**Vol. 3:** 1027
8:12	**Vol. 3:** 125, 1016, 1027
8:13	**Vol. 3:** 29, 938
8:14	**Vol. 1:** 663 **Vol. 3:** 713
8:15	**Vol. 3:** 97
8:17	**Vol. 2:** 547 **Vol. 3:** 528
8:18 f	**Vol. 2:** 96
8:18	**Vol. 2:** 841, 845 **Vol. 3:** 1028
8:19	**Vol. 1:** 537
8:20	**Vol. 2:** 481 **Vol. 3:** 354, 933, 938
8:21	**Vol. 2:** 547, 845 **Vol. 3:** 1028
8:22 – 36	**Vol. 3:** 1116
8:22 – 31	**Vol. 3:** 1029
8:22 – 30	**Vol. 3:** 641
8:22	**Vol. 1:** 380, 668
8:23	**Vol. 1:** 476, 668 **Vol. 3:** 828
8:27 f	**Vol. 1:** 523
8:27	**Vol. 3:** 117
8:28	**Vol. 1:** 663
8:29	**Vol. 1:** 661 **Vol. 3:** 983
8:32 ff	**Vol. 3:** 1029
8:32 – 36	**Vol. 3:** 1028
8:33	**Vol. 3:** 777, 1027 – 1028
8:35	**Vol. 2:** 479
9:1 ff	**Vol. 3:** 1029
9:1	**Vol. 3:** 1027
9:2	**Vol. 3:** 911
9:3	**Vol. 3:** 51
9:4	**Vol. 3:** 1024
9:5	**Vol. 3:** 911, 1162
9:6*	**Vol. 2:** 481 **Vol. 3:** 1024
9:7 f	**Vol. 2:** 141
9:8 f	**Vol. 3:** 1027
9:9	**Vol. 3:** 1028
9:10	**Vol. 3:** 130, 1027 – 1028
9:11	**Vol. 2:** 479 **Vol. 3:** 842
9:16	**Vol. 3:** 1024
9:18	**Vol. 2:** 479 **Vol. 3:** 842
10:1	**Vol. 2:** 745 **Vol. 3:** 1024, 1027
10:2	**Vol. 2:** 830
10:4	**Vol. 2:** 841 **Vol. 3:** 545, 1024, 1028
10:7	**Vol. 3:** 109, 237 – 238
10:8 f	**Vol. 3:** 572
10:8	**Vol. 3:** 745, 1027
10:10	**Vol. 2:** 735, 782
10:11	**Vol. 3:** 987
10:12	**Vol. 1:** 555, 733 **Vol. 2:** 214
10:13	**Vol. 3:** 1027
10:14	**Vol. 3:** 1027
10:15	**Vol. 2:** 841
10:18	**Vol. 3:** 346, 1024
10:20 f	**Vol. 2:** 181
10:21	**Vol. 3:** 1142
10:22	**Vol. 2:** 841

Proverbs *(cont'd)*

10:23	**Vol. 2:** 431 **Vol. 3:** 1024, 1027, 1156
10:31	**Vol. 3:** 1027
10:32	**Vol. 2:** 116
11:1	**Vol. 2:** 261 **Vol. 3:** 1160
11:2	**Vol. 2:** 261 **Vol. 3:** 29, 1027
11:3	**Vol. 1:** 475 **Vol. 2:** 61 **Vol. 3:** 248
11:4	**Vol. 1:** 110 **Vol. 2:** 890
11:5 f	**Vol. 2:** 93
11:5	**Vol. 1:** 609 **Vol. 3:** 352, 924
11:6	**Vol. 3:** 351
11:7	**Vol. 2:** 239
11:8	**Vol. 1:** 314, 479
11:9	**Vol. 2:** 803
11:12	**Vol. 2:** 803 **Vol. 3:** 111
11:14	**Vol. 1:** 194
11:15	**Vol. 1:** 663
11:16	**Vol. 2:** 841 **Vol. 3:** 818
11:18	**Vol. 2:** 139 **Vol. 3:** 140, 1149
11:20	**Vol. 3:** 924
11:21	**Vol. 2:** 139 **Vol. 3:** 140, 747
11:22	**Vol. 2:** 746
11:25	**Vol. 3:** 572
11:27	**Vol. 2:** 116
11:28	**Vol. 1:** 609 **Vol. 2:** 841, 845
11:30	**Vol. 3:** 525, 866
11:31	**Vol. 3:** 140, 215, 370
12:1	**Vol. 2:** 391 **Vol. 3:** 721, 777, 1024
12:2	**Vol. 2:** 116
12:5	**Vol. 1:** 194 **Vol. 3:** 823
12:7	**Vol. 3:** 228
12:10	**Vol. 2:** 599
12:12	**Vol. 2:** 93
12:13	**Vol. 1:** 609
12:14	**Vol. 3:** 1142
12:15 f	**Vol. 3:** 1024
12:15	**Vol. 2:** 430, 481
12:16	**Vol. 1:** 108, 412
12:17–22	**Vol. 3:** 880
12:17	**Vol. 3:** 1041
12:18	**Vol. 3:** 1142
12:19	**Vol. 3:** 880, 1041
12:22	**Vol. 2:** 841
12:23	**Vol. 3:** 1024
12:25	**Vol. 2:** 158 **Vol. 3:** 1142
12:27	**Vol. 2:** 845
13:1	**Vol. 1:** 412 **Vol. 2:** 179 **Vol. 3:** 721
13:2	**Vol. 3:** 525
13:3	**Vol. 2:** 132
13:5	**Vol. 2:** 735
13:7	**Vol. 2:** 841–842
13:8	**Vol. 2:** 822, 841 **Vol. 3:** 190, 192
13:9	**Vol. 2:** 485, 492 **Vol. 3:** 109
13:10	**Vol. 3:** 29, 1028
13:11	**Vol. 2:** 93
13:12	**Vol. 3:** 866
13:13	**Vol. 1:** 622 **Vol. 3:** 1028
13:14	**Vol. 2:** 440 **Vol. 3:** 459, 987, 1027
13:15	**Vol. 1:** 254
13:16	**Vol. 3:** 1024
13:17	**Vol. 3:** 1028
13:19	**Vol. 2:** 93
13:20	**Vol. 3:** 1024, 1027–1028
13:22	**Vol. 2:** 842
13:24	**Vol. 3:** 776
14:1	**Vol. 3:** 1024, 1027
14:2	**Vol. 3:** 351
14:3	**Vol. 3:** 29, 1024, 1027
14:5	**Vol. 3:** 1041
14:6	**Vol. 3:** 528, 1027
14:7 f	**Vol. 3:** 1024
14:7	**Vol. 3:** 1028
14:8	**Vol. 3:** 125, 1027
14:9	**Vol. 3:** 1024
14:10	**Vol. 3:** 29
14:12	**Vol. 1:** 254 **Vol. 3:** 821
14:13	**Vol. 2:** 357, 420
14:14	**Vol. 3:** 125
14:15	**Vol. 1:** 357
14:16	**Vol. 3:** 1024, 1027
14:17	**Vol. 1:** 555
14:18	**Vol. 3:** 1024
14:20	**Vol. 2:** 822, 841
14:21	**Vol. 2:** 49, 257
14:23	**Vol. 1:** 277, 729
14:24	**Vol. 3:** 1024, 1027
14:25	**Vol. 3:** 1041
14:27	**Vol. 3:** 987
14:29	**Vol. 2:** 769 **Vol. 3:** 691, 1024
14:30	**Vol. 1:** 557 **Vol. 2:** 181
14:31	**Vol. 2:** 49, 823
14:32	**Vol. 2:** 237
14:33	**Vol. 3:** 1024, 1027
15:2	**Vol. 3:** 1024, 1027
15:4	**Vol. 1:** 735 **Vol. 3:** 866, 1079, 1142
15:5	**Vol. 3:** 1024
15:6	**Vol. 2:** 830
15:7	**Vol. 1:** 663 **Vol. 2:** 391 **Vol. 3:** 1024, 1027
15:8	**Vol. 3:** 427, 745
15:9	**Vol. 2:** 806
15:11	**Vol. 1:** 463–464
15:12	**Vol. 2:** 141 **Vol. 3:** 1027
15:14	**Vol. 3:** 351
15:15	**Vol. 2:** 890
15:19	**Vol. 1:** 725
15:20	**Vol. 3:** 1024, 1027
15:21	**Vol. 3:** 126
15:22	**Vol. 3:** 823
15:24	**Vol. 3:** 125
15:25	**Vol. 3:** 29, 1073
15:26	**Vol. 2:** 93 **Vol. 3:** 101, 823
15:28*	**Vol. 3:** 745, 1143
15:32	**Vol. 1:** 555
15:33*	**Vol. 2:** 260–261 **Vol. 3:** 776, 1027–1028
16:2	**Vol. 2:** 261
16:5	**Vol. 3:** 351
16:6	**Vol. 3:** 157, 880

Proverbs *(cont'd)*

16:7	**Vol. 3:** 745
16:9*	**Vol. 3:** 691, 823
16:11	**Vol. 3:** 1160
16:14	**Vol. 3:** 153–154, 1027
16:16	**Vol. 1:** 537 **Vol. 3:** 1027
16:17	**Vol. 2:** 132 **Vol. 3:** 745, 1028, 1033
16:18 f	**Vol. 3:** 29
16:19	**Vol. 2:** 261 **Vol. 3:** 29
16:21	**Vol. 3:** 1027
16:22	**Vol. 3:** 125, 987, 1024
16:23	**Vol. 3:** 125, 1027
16:25	**Vol. 2:** 481 **Vol. 3:** 351, 821
16:27	**Vol. 3:** 1024, 1143
16:28	**Vol. 3:** 1143
16:30	**Vol. 1:** 472 **Vol. 3:** 820, 823
16:31	**Vol. 1:** 227, 229
16:32	**Vol. 2:** 769 **Vol. 3:** 716
16:33	**Vol. 2:** 296, 299
17:1	**Vol. 1:** 459 **Vol. 2:** 777
17:2	**Vol. 2:** 303 **Vol. 3:** 1024
17:3	**Vol. 1:** 656 **Vol. 3:** 808
17:5	**Vol. 2:** 822
17:6	**Vol. 1:** 227
17:7	**Vol. 3:** 1024
17:8	**Vol. 2:** 139
17:10	**Vol. 1:** 572 **Vol. 3:** 1024
17:12	**Vol. 1:** 277 **Vol. 3:** 820, 1024
17:16	**Vol. 3:** 1024, 1027
17:17	**Vol. 2:** 663
17:18	**Vol. 3:** 1024
17:21	**Vol. 3:** 1024
17:23	**Vol. 3:** 354
17:24 f	**Vol. 3:** 1024
17:24	**Vol. 3:** 1028
17:28	**Vol. 3:** 126, 821, 823, 1027
18:2	**Vol. 3:** 957, 1024, 1027
18:4	**Vol. 2:** 197 **Vol. 3:** 459, 987
18:5	**Vol. 2:** 622
18:6 f	**Vol. 3:** 1024
18:7	**Vol. 3:** 1024
18:10 f	**Vol. 2:** 845
18:10	**Vol. 1:** 272 **Vol. 2:** 650
18:11	**Vol. 2:** 841
18:12	**Vol. 2:** 260
18:13	**Vol. 3:** 1024
18:15	**Vol. 3:** 125, 1027
18:18	**Vol. 1:** 472 **Vol. 2:** 296
18:21	**Vol. 3:** 1079, 1142
18:22	**Vol. 2:** 116, 261
19:3*	**Vol. 3:** 1024
19:4*	**Vol. 2:** 822, 842
19:6	**Vol. 2:** 164
19:7	**Vol. 1:** 555 **Vol. 2:** 822 **Vol. 3:** 125
19:10	**Vol. 3:** 29, 1024
19:11	**Vol. 2:** 769
19:12	**Vol. 2:** 421
19:13	**Vol. 2:** 139 **Vol. 3:** 1024
19:15	**Vol. 2:** 265
19:16	**Vol. 1:** 461 **Vol. 2:** 132, 134
19:17	**Vol. 2:** 822 **Vol. 3:** 134
19:18	**Vol. 3:** 29, 776
19:20	**Vol. 3:** 1028
19:21	**Vol. 3:** 823
19:22	**Vol. 2:** 822
19:24	**Vol. 2:** 432
19:25	**Vol. 2:** 141
19:28	**Vol. 3:** 354, 1024
19:29	**Vol. 3:** 1024
20:1	**Vol. 1:** 513 **Vol. 3:** 919, 1024, 1028
20:3†	**Vol. 3:** 346, 1024
20:7	**Vol. 3:** 924, 933
20:9	**Vol. 2:** 735 **Vol. 3:** 101
20:13	**Vol. 3:** 345
20:20	**Vol. 1:** 423 **Vol. 3:** 109
20:22	**Vol. 2:** 157, 773
20:23	**Vol. 3:** 1160
20:24	**Vol. 3:** 125
20:26	**Vol. 3:** 1027
20:28	**Vol. 3:** 354
20:29	**Vol. 1:** 522 **Vol. 3:** 1027
21:1	**Vol. 1:** 412
21:3	**Vol. 3:** 427
21:4	**Vol. 1:** 108 **Vol. 3:** 29
21:5	**Vol. 3:** 953
21:6	**Vol. 3:** 1147
21:8	**Vol. 3:** 101
21:9	**Vol. 1:** 641
21:11	**Vol. 3:** 745, 1027
21:13	**Vol. 3:** 950, 994
21:16	**Vol. 1:** 339 **Vol. 3:** 254
21:17	**Vol. 2:** 711, 842 **Vol. 3:** 919
21:18	**Vol. 1:** 479
21:20	**Vol. 2:** 711 **Vol. 3:** 1024, 1027
21:21	**Vol. 3:** 528
21:22	**Vol. 3:** 963, 1027
21:24	**Vol. 2:** 435 **Vol. 3:** 30
21:27	**Vol. 3:** 427
21:30	**Vol. 3:** 1027
22:1	**Vol. 2:** 841
22:2	**Vol. 2:** 822, 841
22:4	**Vol. 2:** 260, 841
22:5	**Vol. 1:** 726
22:7	**Vol. 2:** 822, 841
22:8	**Vol. 2:** 827 **Vol. 3:** 134, 522
22:9	**Vol. 2:** 49
22:11	**Vol. 3:** 924
22:14a	**Vol. 2:** 664
22:15	**Vol. 1:** 288 **Vol. 3:** 125
22:16	**Vol. 2:** 841
22:17–23:11	**Vol. 3:** 1028
22:17	**Vol. 3:** 1027, 1092
22:21	**Vol. 3:** 760, 880
22:22	**Vol. 2:** 257 **Vol. 3:** 994
22:24	**Vol. 3:** 1027
22:26	**Vol. 2:** 149
23:1	**Vol. 2:** 521
23:4	**Vol. 2:** 841 **Vol. 3:** 125
23:9	**Vol. 3:** 1024

Proverbs *(cont'd)*

23:10–11	**Vol. 2:** 738
23:11	**Vol. 3:** 192, 716
23:12	**Vol. 3:** 117
23:13	**Vol. 1:** 281 **Vol. 3:** 776
23:15	**Vol. 3:** 1028
23:17	**Vol. 1:** 622 **Vol. 2:** 240
23:18	**Vol. 1:** 606 **Vol. 2:** 240
23:19	**Vol. 3:** 125, 1028
23:20 f	**Vol. 3:** 919
23:21	**Vol. 2:** 823
23:22	**Vol. 1:** 461, 617
23:23	**Vol. 3:** 777, 880
23:24	**Vol. 3:** 1027
23:25	**Vol. 2:** 357
23:29	**Vol. 3:** 1051
23:31 ff	**Vol. 3:** 919
23:31	**Vol. 3:** 922
23:32	**Vol. 2:** 27
24:3	**Vol. 3:** 1027
24:4	**Vol. 2:** 842
24:5 f*	**Vol. 3:** 557
24:5	**Vol. 2:** 616 **Vol. 3:** 1027
24:7	**Vol. 3:** 125, 823, 1027–1028
24:11 f	**Vol. 2:** 157
24:12	**Vol. 3:** 167
24:14	**Vol. 3:** 1027
24:16	**Vol. 1:** 608, 610
24:17 f	**Vol. 2:** 157
24:17	**Vol. 1:** 609 **Vol. 2:** 157
24:20	**Vol. 3:** 109
24:21	**Vol. 1:** 622
24:23*	**Vol. 3:** 1027
24:26*	**Vol. 3:** 1028
24:27	**Vol. 3:** 119
24:28*	**Vol. 2:** 803
24:29	**Vol. 2:** 157 **Vol. 3:** 183
24:30*	**Vol. 3:** 1024
25:1	**Vol. 2:** 745, 757
25:4	**Vol. 3:** 808
25:6	**Vol. 3:** 30
25:7	**Vol. 2:** 261–262
25:11–13	**Vol. 2:** 746
25:12 f	**Vol. 1:** 657
25:12	**Vol. 3:** 1027
25:13	**Vol. 1:** 595
25:14 f	**Vol. 3:** 402
25:14	**Vol. 1:** 227
25:15	**Vol. 1:** 240 **Vol. 2:** 769
25:16	**Vol. 3:** 728
25:18	**Vol. 3:** 1041
25:21 f	**Vol. 2:** 268, 757 **Vol. 3:** 97, 183
25:21	**Vol. 2:** 157, 266
25:24	**Vol. 1:** 641 **Vol. 3:** 346
25:26	**Vol. 3:** 950–951
25:27	**Vol. 3:** 957
26:1 ff	**Vol. 2:** 746
26:1	**Vol. 3:** 1024
26:2	**Vol. 1:** 173
26:3	**Vol. 1:** 511
26:4 f	**Vol. 3:** 1024
26:4–11	**Vol. 3:** 1024
26:5	**Vol. 3:** 1027
26:7	**Vol. 2:** 745, 757
26:9	**Vol. 1:** 725 **Vol. 2:** 745
26:11	**Vol. 1:** 117 **Vol. 2:** 757
26:12	**Vol. 3:** 821, 1027
26:16	**Vol. 2:** 690 **Vol. 3:** 1027
26:18	**Vol. 3:** 799
26:20 f	**Vol. 1:** 654
26:21	**Vol. 3:** 346
26:22	**Vol. 2:** 599
26:23	**Vol. 3:** 914
26:27	**Vol. 3:** 720
27:1	**Vol. 1:** 251
27:2	**Vol. 3:** 817
27:3	**Vol. 1:** 108 **Vol. 3:** 1024
27:4	**Vol. 1:** 108
27:9	**Vol. 2:** 711
27:11	**Vol. 3:** 1028
27:13	**Vol. 3:** 29
27:14	**Vol. 3:** 821
27:15	**Vol. 2:** 432 **Vol. 3:** 346
27:20	**Vol. 1:** 463 **Vol. 2:** 206
27:21	**Vol. 1:** 227, 656 **Vol. 3:** 808
27:22	**Vol. 3:** 1024
27:23	**Vol. 2:** 395
28:1	**Vol. 1:** 559
28:2	**Vol. 1:** 412
28:3	**Vol. 2:** 822
28:4	**Vol. 2:** 440
28:6	**Vol. 2:** 822, 841, 845
28:7	**Vol. 2:** 440
28:8	**Vol. 2:** 822, 842
28:9	**Vol. 2:** 440, 863
28:10	**Vol. 2:** 99
28:11	**Vol. 2:** 841, 845 **Vol. 3:** 1028
28:13	**Vol. 1:** 574
28:14	**Vol. 2:** 91, 155
28:15	**Vol. 2:** 421, 820, 822
28:16	**Vol. 3:** 137, 842
28:17	**Vol. 1:** 663 **Vol. 2:** 138 **Vol. 3:** 159
28:22	**Vol. 2:** 841
28:24	**Vol. 3:** 821
28:26	**Vol. 3:** 209, 1024, 1027
28:27	**Vol. 2:** 822
29:1	**Vol. 2:** 155
29:3	**Vol. 2:** 842 **Vol. 3:** 1027
29:5	**Vol. 3:** 119, 1143
29:6	**Vol. 2:** 357
29:7	**Vol. 2:** 820
29:8 f	**Vol. 3:** 1028
29:8	**Vol. 1:** 108
29:10	**Vol. 1:** 555
29:11	**Vol. 3:** 1024, 1028
29:14	**Vol. 3:** 1040
29:15	**Vol. 2:** 141 **Vol. 3:** 1027
29:17	**Vol. 3:** 254, 776
29:18	**Vol. 1:** 574

Proverbs (*cont'd*)

29:20	**Vol. 3:** 1024
29:23	**Vol. 2:** 203, 260–261 **Vol. 3:** 29
29:24	**Vol. 1:** 555 **Vol. 3:** 739
29:25	**Vol. 3:** 218
29:26	**Vol. 2:** 164
30:2*	**Vol. 3:** 1024
30:3*	**Vol. 2:** 395 **Vol. 3:** 760, 1027
30:4	**Vol. 2:** 185
30:7–30	**Vol. 2:** 745
30:7*	**Vol. 2:** 856
30:8*	**Vol. 1:** 251, 597 **Vol. 2:** 841
30:9	**Vol. 3:** 377
30:15	**Vol. 3:** 727
30:17	**Vol. 1:** 175
30:19	**Vol. 2:** 87 **Vol. 3:** 1071
30:20	**Vol. 2:** 583
30:23	**Vol. 3:** 1065
30:24*	**Vol. 3:** 1027
30:26	**Vol. 3:** 381
30:27*	**Vol. 1:** 342, 409
30:28	**Vol. 3:** 786
30:30	**Vol. 3:** 713
30:33	**Vol. 1:** 108
31:1	**Vol. 3:** 325
31:3*	**Vol. 2:** 842
31:5*	**Vol. 3:** 1027
31:6–7	**Vol. 2:** 28
31:9	**Vol. 1:** 503 **Vol. 2:** 257
31:11	**Vol. 1:** 327
31:12	**Vol. 3:** 1147
31:14	**Vol. 2:** 475, 842
31:18	**Vol. 2:** 269, 485
31:20	**Vol. 2:** 257
31:26*	**Vol. 3:** 1028
31:28	**Vol. 2:** 841 **Vol. 3:** 816
31:29	**Vol. 2:** 842
31:30 f	**Vol. 3:** 816
31:30	**Vol. 2:** 815

Ecclesiastes

1:1	**Vol. 3:** 606
1:2	**Vol. 1:** 551
1:3	**Vol. 1:** 262, 728 **Vol. 3:** 137
1:6–20	**Vol. 3:** 1056
1:11	**Vol. 1:** 665 **Vol. 3:** 236, 238
1:13	**Vol. 3:** 1027
1:15	**Vol. 3:** 953
1:16	**Vol. 2:** 830 **Vol. 3:** 1027
1:18	**Vol. 3:** 1027
2:1	**Vol. 1:** 551 **Vol. 3:** 799
2:2	**Vol. 2:** 431, 433
2:3	**Vol. 3:** 1027
2:5	**Vol. 2:** 761
2:8	**Vol. 2:** 838 **Vol. 3:** 673
2:9	**Vol. 3:** 1027
2:11	**Vol. 3:** 137
2:12 f	**Vol. 3:** 1024
2:12	**Vol. 2:** 744 **Vol. 3:** 1027

2:13 f	**Vol. 1:** 728
2:13	**Vol. 3:** 137, 1027
2:14 ff	**Vol. 3:** 1024
2:14	**Vol. 3:** 1028
2:14b	**Vol. 1:** 728
2:15	**Vol. 3:** 1024, 1028
2:16	**Vol. 3:** 236, 238, 1028
2:18 ff	**Vol. 1:** 262
2:18–22	**Vol. 1:** 262
2:19	**Vol. 3:** 1024, 1028
2:21	**Vol. 2:** 830 **Vol. 3:** 1027
2:25	**Vol. 1:** 551
2:26	**Vol. 3:** 1027
3:1 ff	**Vol. 3:** 835
3:1	**Vol. 3:** 835, 842
3:2	**Vol. 3:** 835
3:9	**Vol. 3:** 137
3:10	**Vol. 3:** 799
3:12	**Vol. 2:** 100
3:13	**Vol. 1:** 551
3:16	**Vol. 2:** 93
3:19 f	**Vol. 1:** 434
3:19	**Vol. 1:** 728 **Vol. 3:** 137, 690
3:20	**Vol. 1:** 520
3:21	**Vol. 3:** 690
4:2	**Vol. 3:** 816
4:5	**Vol. 3:** 1024
4:6	**Vol. 3:** 255
4:8	**Vol. 1:** 230 **Vol. 2:** 841 **Vol. 3:** 799
4:9	**Vol. 2:** 139
4:10	**Vol. 1:** 608
4:13	**Vol. 2:** 822 **Vol. 3:** 1024, 1028
4:14	**Vol. 2:** 820
4:17*†	**Vol. 2:** 53 **Vol. 3:** 1024
5:1	**Vol. 1:** 614
5:2 f	**Vol. 3:** 1024
5:2	**Vol. 3:** 799
5:7	**Vol. 1:** 512 **Vol. 2:** 625, 820
5:8	**Vol. 3:** 137
5:11	**Vol. 2:** 841
5:12	**Vol. 2:** 841
5:13	**Vol. 3:** 799
5:15	**Vol. 3:** 137, 690
5:17	**Vol. 2:** 100
5:18	**Vol. 2:** 841
5:19	**Vol. 2:** 845
6:2	**Vol. 1:** 728 **Vol. 2:** 841, 845 **Vol. 3:** 953
6:3	**Vol. 1:** 182
6:8	**Vol. 1:** 728 **Vol. 2:** 257 **Vol. 3:** 137, 1024, 1028
6:9 f	**Vol. 1:** 728
7:2–6	**Vol. 2:** 433
7:4 ff*	**Vol. 3:** 1024
7:4 f*	**Vol. 3:** 1028
7:4*	**Vol. 2:** 431
7:5*	**Vol. 3:** 673
7:6	**Vol. 2:** 431
7:7*	**Vol. 2:** 431 **Vol. 3:** 1028
7:8	**Vol. 3:** 691

Ecclesiastes *(cont'd)*

7:9*   **Vol. 3:** 254, 1024
7:10 ff*   **Vol. 3:** 1027
7:10   **Vol. 1:** 240
7:11 f*   **Vol. 3:** 137
7:12   **Vol. 1:** 728
7:14   **Vol. 1:** 551
7:15   **Vol. 2:** 890
7:16*   **Vol. 3:** 1028, 1033
7:17   **Vol. 1:** 530   **Vol. 3:** 835
7:19*   **Vol. 1:** 728   **Vol. 3:** 1027–1028
7:20   **Vol. 2:** 100
7:23*   **Vol. 3:** 799, 1027–1028
7:25*†   **Vol. 3:** 1024, 1027
7:26   **Vol. 1:** 266
7:27*   **Vol. 1:** 343   **Vol. 3:** 823
7:29*   **Vol. 3:** 823
8:1*   **Vol. 1:** 577, 581   **Vol. 3:** 1027–1028
8:5   **Vol. 2:** 395   **Vol. 3:** 1028
8:8   **Vol. 2:** 222, 887   **Vol. 3:** 209, 842
8:10   **Vol. 3:** 816
8:11 f   **Vol. 3:** 1153
8:14   **Vol. 3:** 140
8:15   **Vol. 3:** 816
8:16   **Vol. 3:** 799, 1027
8:17   **Vol. 2:** 395   **Vol. 3:** 1028
9:1   **Vol. 3:** 1028
9:4   **Vol. 1:** 444, 641
9:5   **Vol. 1:** 444   **Vol. 2:** 139   **Vol. 3:** 237–238, 255
9:6   **Vol. 2:** 139
9:7 ff   **Vol. 1:** 551
9:7   **Vol. 2:** 272
9:9   **Vol. 2:** 478, 890
9:10   **Vol. 3:** 823, 946, 1027
9:11   **Vol. 2:** 116, 841   **Vol. 3:** 1028
9:13   **Vol. 3:** 1024, 1027
9:14   **Vol. 3:** 952
9:15 f   **Vol. 2:** 822   **Vol. 3:** 1027
9:15   **Vol. 3:** 209, 1028
9:17   **Vol. 3:** 255, 1024, 1028
9:18   **Vol. 3:** 1027
10:1   **Vol. 3:** 1024, 1027
10:2   **Vol. 2:** 148   **Vol. 3:** 1024, 1028
10:3   **Vol. 3:** 823, 953, 1024
10:4   **Vol. 3:** 255
10:6   **Vol. 2:** 261, 841   **Vol. 3:** 1024
10:10 f   **Vol. 3:** 137
10:10   **Vol. 3:** 919, 1027
10:11   **Vol. 2:** 554
10:12   **Vol. 3:** 1024, 1028
10:13   **Vol. 3:** 1024
10:14   **Vol. 1:** 493   **Vol. 3:** 1024
10:15   **Vol. 3:** 1024
10:19   **Vol. 2:** 431
10:20   **Vol. 1:** 349   **Vol. 2:** 841
11:5   **Vol. 1:** 240
11:6   **Vol. 2:** 452
11:9†   **Vol. 2:** 355, 890   **Vol. 3:** 924, 943

11:10   **Vol. 3:** 125
12:1   **Vol. 1:** 379   **Vol. 2:** 890   **Vol. 3:** 957
12:2   **Vol. 3:** 733, 735
12:4   **Vol. 1:** 267   **Vol. 3:** 673
12:7   **Vol. 1:** 520   **Vol. 3:** 690
12:9   **Vol. 3:** 760, 1028
12:11   **Vol. 3:** 1028
12:13   **Vol. 1:** 728
12:14   **Vol. 2:** 216

Song of Solomon, or Canticles

1:1   **Vol. 3:** 606, 673
1:3   **Vol. 2:** 87   **Vol. 3:** 1071–1072
1:5   **Vol. 1:** 203
1:7   **Vol. 1:** 259   **Vol. 3:** 680
1:9   **Vol. 1:** 531
1:11   **Vol. 2:** 96, 572
1:13   **Vol. 1:** 240
2:2   **Vol. 1:** 725
2:15   **Vol. 3:** 950
2:17   **Vol. 1:** 559   **Vol. 2:** 501
3:2   **Vol. 1:** 267
3:4   **Vol. 3:** 716
3:6   **Vol. 2:** 293–294
3:8   **Vol. 3:** 760
3:11   **Vol. 2:** 578
4:2   **Vol. 1:** 152
4:6   **Vol. 1:** 559   **Vol. 2:** 293–294
4:10   **Vol. 3:** 600
4:12   **Vol. 3:** 498
4:13   **Vol. 2:** 761
4:14   **Vol. 2:** 293–294
4:16   **Vol. 1:** 683   **Vol. 3:** 600
5:1   **Vol. 2:** 294
5:2   **Vol. 1:** 510   **Vol. 2:** 881
5:3   **Vol. 1:** 449
5:5   **Vol. 2:** 294
5:10   **Vol. 1:** 205
5:13   **Vol. 2:** 294
6:6   **Vol. 1:** 152
6:8*   **Vol. 2:** 87   **Vol. 3:** 816, 1071–1072
6:9*   **Vol. 1:** 510   **Vol. 3:** 385
6:10   **Vol. 3:** 730, 733
7:2*   **Vol. 3:** 950
7:4*   **Vol. 3:** 992
7:5*   **Vol. 1:** 171   **Vol. 3:** 992
7:8   **Vol. 2:** 501
7:10   **Vol. 3:** 273
7:13*   **Vol. 2:** 675
8:5   **Vol. 3:** 858
8:6   **Vol. 2:** 540
8:7   **Vol. 2:** 475   **Vol. 3:** 109
8:9 f   **Vol. 3:** 948
8:10   **Vol. 2:** 735
8:13   **Vol. 1:** 259
8:14   **Vol. 1:** 559

Isaiah

1:1 ff   **Vol. 3:** 155

Isaiah *(cont'd)*

1:1	**Vol. 3:** 208, 311, 1093
1:2–3	**Vol. 2:** 432
1:2	**Vol. 1:** 288 **Vol. 2:** 174, 363
1:3	**Vol. 1:** 173 **Vol. 2:** 395, 797
1:4 ff	**Vol. 3:** 578
1:4	**Vol. 3:** 342, 1051
1:5 f	**Vol. 3:** 997–998
1:5	**Vol. 2:** 181, 420
1:6	**Vol. 1:** 120 **Vol. 2:** 712 **Vol. 3:** 857
1:7	**Vol. 3:** 1005
1:8	**Vol. 2:** 326
1:9 f	**Vol. 3:** 93
1:9	**Vol. 2:** 69, 767 **Vol. 3:** 251–252
1:10 ff	**Vol. 3:** 783
1:10–17	**Vol. 2:** 42 **Vol. 3:** 78
1:10	**Vol. 2:** 174, 440
1:11–31	**Vol. 3:** 427
1:11	**Vol. 1:** 732 **Vol. 3:** 159, 1016
1:13 f	**Vol. 1:** 626
1:13	**Vol. 2:** 765 **Vol. 3:** 407, 421
1:15 ff	**Vol. 2:** 285
1:15–17	**Vol. 2:** 864
1:15 f	**Vol. 2:** 864
1:15	**Vol. 2:** 174 **Vol. 3:** 159, 427
1:16	**Vol. 1:** 699
1:17–23	**Vol. 3:** 1074
1:17	**Vol. 1:** 484–485 **Vol. 2:** 103, 737 **Vol. 3:** 355
1:18	**Vol. 1:** 204–205, 699
1:22	**Vol. 3:** 808
1:23	**Vol. 1:** 717 **Vol. 2:** 363 **Vol. 3:** 1074
1:24	**Vol. 1:** 554 **Vol. 2:** 509
1:25	**Vol. 2:** 96 **Vol. 3:** 29
1:26	**Vol. 2:** 803
1:27	**Vol. 2:** 595
1:28	**Vol. 3:** 908
1:29	**Vol. 3:** 562
1:31	**Vol. 3:** 109
2	**Vol. 3:** 382
2:1	**Vol. 3:** 311, 1094
2:2 ff	**Vol. 1:** 96 **Vol. 2:** 56, 326
2:2–5	**Vol. 2:** 495 **Vol. 3:** 1094
2:2–4	**Vol. 2:** 791 **Vol. 3:** 1010
2:2 f	**Vol. 1:** 661 **Vol. 2:** 325 **Vol. 3:** 791
2:2	**Vol. 2:** 56, 489, 899 **Vol. 3:** 786, 1012
2:3	**Vol. 1:** 321 **Vol. 3:** 1095
2:4	**Vol. 1:** 484 **Vol. 2:** 141
2:5	**Vol. 2:** 302, 492 **Vol. 3:** 1012
2:6	**Vol. 2:** 554, 742
2:7	**Vol. 2:** 257, 683
2:8	**Vol. 2:** 876
2:9	**Vol. 2:** 260
2:10 f	**Vol. 2:** 218
2:10	**Vol. 2:** 215 **Vol. 3:** 714
2:11 f	**Vol. 2:** 887
2:11	**Vol. 2:** 202, 260
2:12–18	**Vol. 2:** 363
2:12	**Vol. 2:** 890 **Vol. 3:** 29
2:17	**Vol. 2:** 199, 202, 260, 887 **Vol. 3:** 29
2:18 ff	**Vol. 2:** 285
2:19	**Vol. 3:** 381, 714
2:20	**Vol. 1:** 551 **Vol. 2:** 876
2:22	**Vol. 1:** 108
2:23	**Vol. 3:** 866
2:24	**Vol. 3:** 70
3:1	**Vol. 2:** 509
3:2	**Vol. 2:** 554
3:3	**Vol. 1:** 279 **Vol. 2:** 175, 554–555 **Vol. 3:** 1028
3:6	**Vol. 3:** 747
3:7	**Vol. 2:** 167
3:8	**Vol. 1:** 589 **Vol. 3:** 1079
3:9	**Vol. 1:** 565 **Vol. 2:** 489 **Vol. 3:** 93
3:10 f	**Vol. 3:** 1149
3:10	**Vol. 2:** 272
3:14 f	**Vol. 2:** 257, 821–822
3:16 f	**Vol. 2:** 326
3:18	**Vol. 1:** 522
3:20	**Vol. 3:** 498
3:24	**Vol. 3:** 120
3:26	**Vol. 2:** 422
4:1	**Vol. 2:** 649 **Vol. 3:** 340
4:2–5	**Vol. 1:** 146
4:2	**Vol. 2:** 201 **Vol. 3:** 867
4:3 f	**Vol. 1:** 699
4:3	**Vol. 1:** 243
4:4	**Vol. 1:** 479 **Vol. 3:** 695, 1178
4:5 f	**Vol. 1:** 653
4:5	**Vol. 1:** 655
5:1 ff	**Vol. 2:** 364
5:1–7	**Vol. 2:** 154, 301, 746 **Vol. 3:** 918, 920
5:1 f	**Vol. 3:** 866
5:1	**Vol. 3:** 673, 866
5:2	**Vol. 1:** 725 **Vol. 3:** 951
5:3	**Vol. 2:** 324
5:4	**Vol. 1:** 725 **Vol. 3:** 867
5:5	**Vol. 3:** 950
5:6	**Vol. 1:** 726 **Vol. 3:** 867
5:7	**Vol. 2:** 248, 305, 432 **Vol. 3:** 357
5:8 ff	**Vol. 2:** 841
5:8 f	**Vol. 2:** 822
5:8	**Vol. 1:** 641
5:9	**Vol. 2:** 178 **Vol. 3:** 1005
5:10	**Vol. 3:** 402, 911, 1161
5:11	**Vol. 3:** 919
5:12	**Vol. 3:** 126, 513, 673
5:13	**Vol. 2:** 275 **Vol. 3:** 590
5:14	**Vol. 2:** 206
5:15	**Vol. 2:** 260
5:18	**Vol. 3:** 1161
5:19	**Vol. 2:** 53 **Vol. 3:** 1016
5:20	**Vol. 1:** 423
5:22	**Vol. 3:** 911, 919
5:23	**Vol. 3:** 355
5:24	**Vol. 2:** 440 **Vol. 3:** 342, 866, 1118
5:25–30	**Vol. 3:** 1094
5:25	**Vol. 1:** 233 **Vol. 2:** 797
5:27	**Vol. 3:** 177

Isaiah (cont'd)

5:28   **Vol. 3:** 823
5:29   **Vol. 2:** 421
5:30   **Vol. 2:** 421
6   **Vol. 3:** 330, 389
6:1 ff   **Vol. 2:** 173, 191 **Vol. 3:** 514
6:1–13   **Vol. 2:** 613
6:1–8   **Vol. 1:** 273
6:1–4   **Vol. 1:** 655
6:1   **Vol. 1:** 54, 509 **Vol. 2:** 613, 632 **Vol. 3:** 786
6:2–6   **Vol. 1:** 280
6:2 f   **Vol. 2:** 689
6:2   **Vol. 1:** 101 **Vol. 2:** 212
6:3 ff   **Vol. 2:** 190
6:3–7   **Vol. 2:** 225
6:3 f   **Vol. 1:** 409
6:3   **Vol. 1:** 735 **Vol. 2:** 45, 70
6:4   **Vol. 3:** 559
6:5 ff   **Vol. 3:** 860
6:5   **Vol. 1:** 108, 585 **Vol. 2:** 375 **Vol. 3:** 104, 514
6:6   **Vol. 1:** 655
6:7   **Vol. 1:** 368, 699 **Vol. 3:** 154
6:8   **Vol. 1:** 127–128
6:8b   **Vol. 3:** 1095
6:9 ff   **Vol. 2:** 174, 178
6:9–11   **Vol. 3:** 1094
6:9 f   **Vol. 2:** 155–156, 630, 753, 799 **Vol. 3:** 128, 131–132, 313, 1094
6:9   **Vol. 2:** 175
6:10   **Vol. 1:** 219, 230, 261 **Vol. 2:** 154, 168, 632, 753, 799 **Vol. 3:** 125
6:11   **Vol. 2:** 154 **Vol. 3:** 1006
6:13   **Vol. 3:** 249, 867
7   **Vol. 1:** 178 **Vol. 3:** 267
7:1–25   **Vol. 1:** 504
7:1–9   **Vol. 2:** 306
7:3   **Vol. 2:** 649 **Vol. 3:** 79
7:7   **Vol. 3:** 226
7:9   **Vol. 1:** 596 **Vol. 3:** 389, 1211
7:10 ff   **Vol. 2:** 626
7:10   **Vol. 2:** 351
7:11 f   **Vol. 2:** 856
7:11   **Vol. 2:** 198–199
7:12   **Vol. 3:** 799–800
7:14 ff   **Vol. 2:** 627
7:14   **Vol. 1:** 186, 737 **Vol. 2:** 86, 649, 715 **Vol. 3:** 662, 697, 1072
7:18   **Vol. 3:** 985
7:19   **Vol. 3:** 254
7:20   **Vol. 2:** 139, 418 **Vol. 3:** 985
7:21   **Vol. 2:** 412
8   **Vol. 3:** 267
8:1 ff   **Vol. 2:** 626
8:1   **Vol. 1:** 368 **Vol. 3:** 483
8:2   **Vol. 1:** 595 **Vol. 3:** 1041
8:3 f   **Vol. 3:** 79
8:3   **Vol. 2:** 649 **Vol. 3:** 1057

8:5–8   **Vol. 3:** 1090
8:6   **Vol. 1:** 543, 581
8:7   **Vol. 3:** 713, 985
8:8   **Vol. 2:** 86
8:9 f   **Vol. 3:** 185
8:9   **Vol. 2:** 791
8:10   **Vol. 3:** 226
8:11–15   **Vol. 3:** 391
8:11   **Vol. 3:** 1054
8:12   **Vol. 3:** 709
8:13 ff   **Vol. 3:** 382
8:13   **Vol. 1:** 622
8:14 f   **Vol. 2:** 706
8:14   **Vol. 1:** 609 **Vol. 2:** 705–706, 708–709 **Vol. 3:** 382–384, 389, 391–393
8:15   **Vol. 1:** 610, 663
8:16 ff   **Vol. 3:** 1094
8:16   **Vol. 2:** 763
8:17   **Vol. 1:** 592, 596 **Vol. 2:** 240
8:18   **Vol. 2:** 190, 325, 627, 633
8:19   **Vol. 1:** 450 **Vol. 2:** 554, 559
8:20   **Vol. 2:** 559
8:22   **Vol. 1:** 422 **Vol. 2:** 807
9   **Vol. 1:** 178
9:1 f   **Vol. 2:** 596
9:1†   **Vol. 1:** 422, 435 **Vol. 2:** 793 **Vol. 3:** 555
9:2–7*   **Vol. 2:** 335, 374 **Vol. 3:** 637
9:2   **Vol. 1:** 422–423 **Vol. 3:** 198, 212, 555, 569, 940
9:3*   **Vol. 2:** 889 **Vol. 3:** 1161
9:4*   **Vol. 3:** 166
9:5 f   **Vol. 2:** 778
9:5   **Vol. 2:** 779 **Vol. 3:** 722
9:6 f*   **Vol. 1:** 210 **Vol. 3:** 648
9:6*   **Vol. 1:** 326, 427 **Vol. 2:** 86, 779 **Vol. 3:** 637, 649, 1016, 1068
9:7–20   **Vol. 3:** 1094
9:7*   **Vol. 1:** 426–427 **Vol. 2:** 376, 448 **Vol. 3:** 841–842, 1094, 1166–1167
9:9*   **Vol. 3:** 29
9:12*   **Vol. 2:** 124
9:13   **Vol. 2:** 889 **Vol. 3:** 531
9:14*   **Vol. 2:** 158 **Vol. 3:** 760
9:17*   **Vol. 1:** 565
9:18 f   **Vol. 1:** 109
10:1–4   **Vol. 1:** 717
10:2   **Vol. 2:** 822 **Vol. 3:** 601, 1074
10:4   **Vol. 1:** 368
10:5 ff   **Vol. 3:** 97
10:5   **Vol. 1:** 111 **Vol. 2:** 791 **Vol. 3:** 549
10:6   **Vol. 1:** 332 **Vol. 3:** 209
10:7 ff   **Vol. 3:** 234
10:7–11   **Vol. 3:** 32
10:7   **Vol. 3:** 125, 823
10:7b   **Vol. 3:** 125
10:8 ff   **Vol. 3:** 342
10:10   **Vol. 2:** 887

Isaiah *(cont'd)*

10:11	**Vol. 2:** 285
10:13	**Vol. 3:** 1027
10:14	**Vol. 1:** 519 **Vol. 3:** 747
10:16	**Vol. 2:** 49
10:19	**Vol. 3:** 248
10:20 ff	**Vol. 3:** 249
10:20	**Vol. 1:** 589
10:21	**Vol. 2:** 86
10:22 f	**Vol. 2:** 513 **Vol. 3:** 251
10:22	**Vol. 2:** 684 **Vol. 3:** 251
10:23	**Vol. 1:** 519
10:25	**Vol. 1:** 109
10:27	**Vol. 2:** 891 **Vol. 3:** 1161
10:33 f	**Vol. 2:** 260
10:33	**Vol. 2:** 509 **Vol. 3:** 29
10:34	**Vol. 3:** 867
11	**Vol. 1:** 210 **Vol. 2:** 333 **Vol. 3:** 637, 692
11:1 ff	**Vol. 1:** 185, 210 **Vol. 2:** 335, 614, 830 **Vol. 3:** 79, 649
11:1–10	**Vol. 3:** 639, 649
11:1–9	**Vol. 1:** 426 **Vol. 2:** 374 **Vol. 3:** 637
11:1–8	**Vol. 3:** 692
11:1–5	**Vol. 3:** 650
11:1–4	**Vol. 3:** 650
11:1 f	**Vol. 2:** 376
11:1	**Vol. 1:** 321, 407, 427 **Vol. 2:** 333, 715 **Vol. 3:** 649–650, 652, 869
11:2 ff	**Vol. 3:** 650
11:2	**Vol. 1:** 122 **Vol. 2:** 93, 654 **Vol. 3:** 130, 254–257, 639, 691, 1016, 1027, 1029
11:3 f	**Vol. 2:** 141
11:4	**Vol. 2:** 257, 686 **Vol. 3:** 192, 639, 690
11:5	**Vol. 1:** 239 **Vol. 3:** 121, 207, 879, 966
11:6–9	**Vol. 2:** 779
11:6 f	**Vol. 3:** 515
11:6	**Vol. 2:** 428, 888 **Vol. 3:** 951
11:8	**Vol. 1:** 281, 510 **Vol. 2:** 586
11:9	**Vol. 2:** 229
11:10	**Vol. 1:** 427 **Vol. 2:** 554 **Vol. 3:** 255, 649, 652, 867, 869
11:11 ff	**Vol. 3:** 249
11:11	**Vol. 1:** 531
11:12	**Vol. 1:** 297 **Vol. 2:** 689
11:13	**Vol. 3:** 1161
11:15	**Vol. 3:** 985
11:16	**Vol. 2:** 889
12:1*	**Vol. 1:** 368
12:2	**Vol. 3:** 218
12:3	**Vol. 3:** 208, 986, 988
12:4	**Vol. 2:** 650 **Vol. 3:** 668
12:5	**Vol. 3:** 46, 668
12:6	**Vol. 2:** 425
13–23	**Vol. 3:** 960
13	**Vol. 1:** 141–142, 519
13:1	**Vol. 3:** 325
13:2	**Vol. 3:** 1009
13:3	**Vol. 1:** 109
13:4	**Vol. 1:** 332
13:6	**Vol. 2:** 53, 888, 890 **Vol. 3:** 729
13:7	**Vol. 3:** 178
13:8	**Vol. 1:** 186 **Vol. 3:** 858
13:9	**Vol. 2:** 363, 890
13:10	**Vol. 1:** 203, 425 **Vol. 2:** 38, 484, 916 **Vol. 3:** 559, 731, 733, 735
13:11	**Vol. 1:** 332 **Vol. 3:** 29
13:13	**Vol. 1:** 108 **Vol. 2:** 189 **Vol. 3:** 29
13:14	**Vol. 2:** 458
13:17	**Vol. 3:** 823, 957
13:19	**Vol. 3:** 93, 560
13:20 f	**Vol. 3:** 255
13:20	**Vol. 3:** 828, 842
13:21 f	**Vol. 3:** 1005
13:21	**Vol. 1:** 451 **Vol. 3:** 255
13:22	**Vol. 3:** 782
14	**Vol. 1:** 142, 519
14:1–23	**Vol. 1:** 141
14:1	**Vol. 1:** 688 **Vol. 3:** 254
14:2	**Vol. 3:** 590
14:3–21	**Vol. 2:** 432
14:3	**Vol. 2:** 890 **Vol. 3:** 254, 256
14:4–21	**Vol. 1:** 141
14:4	**Vol. 2:** 745 **Vol. 3:** 255
14:5	**Vol. 3:** 1161
14:6	**Vol. 3:** 254
14:8	**Vol. 1:** 389
14:9 ff	**Vol. 2:** 206
14:12	**Vol. 1:** 610 **Vol. 2:** 495 **Vol. 3:** 468, 734
14:13 f	**Vol. 3:** 622
14:13	**Vol. 2:** 613
14:16	**Vol. 3:** 557
14:17	**Vol. 3:** 177
14:20	**Vol. 3:** 842
14:21	**Vol. 3:** 117
14:22	**Vol. 3:** 633
14:24	**Vol. 3:** 224
14:25	**Vol. 3:** 1161
14:26	**Vol. 2:** 201 **Vol. 3:** 1016
14:29	**Vol. 3:** 1161
14:30	**Vol. 2:** 777 **Vol. 3:** 255
14:32	**Vol. 1:** 661 **Vol. 2:** 260
15:2–3	**Vol. 2:** 418
15:2 f	**Vol. 2:** 416
15:2	**Vol. 2:** 418 **Vol. 3:** 418
15:5	**Vol. 3:** 557
15:6	**Vol. 1:** 743
16:2	**Vol. 2:** 746
16:4	**Vol. 1:** 690
16:5	**Vol. 3:** 880
16:6	**Vol. 3:** 29
16:8	**Vol. 2:** 422
16:9	**Vol. 3:** 525
16:10	**Vol. 3:** 673
16:12	**Vol. 2:** 862 **Vol. 3:** 418, 786
17:2	**Vol. 2:** 586 **Vol. 3:** 255
17:4	**Vol. 2:** 44

Isaiah *(cont'd)*

17:5   **Vol. 2:** 32   **Vol. 3:** 526
17:6   **Vol. 3:** 867
17:7 f   **Vol. 1:** 589
17:8   **Vol. 3:** 418
17:10   **Vol. 2:** 705   **Vol. 3:** 207, 218, 275
17:11   **Vol. 3:** 525
17:12   **Vol. 3:** 112
17:13   **Vol. 1:** 520   **Vol. 3:** 711
18:1   **Vol. 3:** 836
18:2   **Vol. 1:** 419
18:4   **Vol. 1:** 663   **Vol. 3:** 526
18:5   **Vol. 3:** 526
18:7   **Vol. 2:** 41   **Vol. 3:** 155, 786
19   **Vol. 1:** 531
19:1   **Vol. 2:** 38, 190, 917   **Vol. 3:** 1001
19:3   **Vol. 2:** 554–555, 879   **Vol. 3:** 691
19:4   **Vol. 3:** 1025
19:5–8   **Vol. 3:** 985
19:5   **Vol. 1:** 515
19:6   **Vol. 1:** 515
19:8   **Vol. 2:** 422–423
19:10   **Vol. 3:** 820, 1161
19:11 f   **Vol. 3:** 1028
19:11   **Vol. 1:** 531   **Vol. 3:** 1016, 1025
19:12   **Vol. 3:** 482
19:13 f   **Vol. 2:** 458
19:13   **Vol. 3:** 870
19:14   **Vol. 1:** 513   **Vol. 3:** 911, 913
19:17   **Vol. 1:** 622
19:20   **Vol. 3:** 462
19:25   **Vol. 2:** 297
20   **Vol. 1:** 531
20:1 ff   **Vol. 2:** 626
20:2 ff   **Vol. 2:** 754
20:2   **Vol. 3:** 79, 121
20:3   **Vol. 2:** 633, 741
20:4   **Vol. 1:** 193
20:5   **Vol. 3:** 562
20:6   **Vol. 3:** 209
21:1–10   **Vol. 1:** 141   **Vol. 3:** 1091
21:3   **Vol. 1:** 239   **Vol. 3:** 1169
21:4   **Vol. 1:** 144
21:9   **Vol. 1:** 610
21:16   **Vol. 2:** 139
22:4   **Vol. 1:** 201
22:10   **Vol. 3:** 948
22:11   **Vol. 1:** 380
22:13   **Vol. 2:** 272
22:14   **Vol. 1:** 698
22:16   **Vol. 3:** 239
22:19   **Vol. 2:** 254
22:21   **Vol. 2:** 254   **Vol. 3:** 120
22:22   **Vol. 2:** 726–727, 730, 732–733   **Vol. 3:** 387, 652
22:23   **Vol. 3:** 878
22:25   **Vol. 3:** 878
23   **Vol. 1:** 519   **Vol. 2:** 767   **Vol. 3:** 1052
23:4   **Vol. 2:** 201   **Vol. 3:** 858

23:7   **Vol. 3:** 29
23:9   **Vol. 3:** 29
23:12   **Vol. 3:** 29, 255
23:13   **Vol. 3:** 255
23:15   **Vol. 2:** 690   **Vol. 3:** 673, 842
23:16   **Vol. 3:** 673
23:18   **Vol. 2:** 139
24–28   **Vol. 2:** 306
24–27   **Vol. 1:** 50   **Vol. 3:** 80, 829, 961
24:2   **Vol. 2:** 666
24:4   **Vol. 2:** 422   **Vol. 3:** 203, 1071
24:5   **Vol. 1:** 322, 368
24:7   **Vol. 2:** 422–423
24:8 f   **Vol. 3:** 673
24:8   **Vol. 2:** 842
24:16   **Vol. 2:** 93
24:18   **Vol. 1:** 609, 661
24:21   **Vol. 2:** 888
24:23   **Vol. 1:** 195   **Vol. 2:** 326, 376, 495   **Vol. 3:** 733
25:1–5   **Vol. 2:** 261
25:1   **Vol. 3:** 668, 673, 1016, 1157
25:4   **Vol. 3:** 201
25:5   **Vol. 3:** 554
25:6 ff   **Vol. 2:** 727
25:6–8   **Vol. 2:** 522, 791
25:6   **Vol. 1:** 210   **Vol. 2:** 532, 580, 632   **Vol. 3:** 951
25:8   **Vol. 2:** 631   **Vol. 3:** 267–268, 1112
25:9   **Vol. 2:** 240, 353, 773   **Vol. 3:** 218
25:10   **Vol. 3:** 255–256
25:11   **Vol. 3:** 29
26   **Vol. 1:** 124
26:1   **Vol. 3:** 673
26:2   **Vol. 2:** 726
26:6   **Vol. 2:** 257, 260, 778
26:7   **Vol. 2:** 93
26:8   **Vol. 2:** 650   **Vol. 3:** 237
26:9   **Vol. 1:** 484   **Vol. 3:** 673
26:11   **Vol. 2:** 395   **Vol. 3:** 28, 1167
26:12   **Vol. 1:** 210   **Vol. 2:** 778
26:13   **Vol. 3:** 238
26:14   **Vol. 1:** 444   **Vol. 2:** 569   **Vol. 3:** 237
26:16 ff **Vol. 3:** 1068
26:16–21 **Vol. 3:** 722
26:17 f   **Vol. 1:** 186
26:17   **Vol. 1:** 409
26:19   **Vol. 1:** 434, 444   **Vol. 2:** 479   **Vol. 3:** 268, 273
26:20   **Vol. 1:** 109   **Vol. 2:** 429   **Vol. 3:** 367, 843
26:21   **Vol. 1:** 410   **Vol. 3:** 786
27:1   **Vol. 1:** 205, 210, 508, 523   **Vol. 2:** 891   **Vol. 3:** 1153
27:5   **Vol. 2:** 782   **Vol. 3:** 1153
27:9   **Vol. 3:** 153–154, 203, 418, 865
27:10   **Vol. 3:** 255
27:12   **Vol. 2:** 720   **Vol. 3:** 526, 985
27:13   **Vol. 2:** 38, 876, 917   **Vol. 3:** 874
28:1   **Vol. 1:** 513   **Vol. 2:** 139   **Vol. 3:** 29

Isaiah *(cont'd)*

28:2	**Vol. 3:** 255, 711
28:3	**Vol. 2:** 139 **Vol. 3:** 29
28:5 f	**Vol. 3:** 249
28:6	**Vol. 3:** 238
28:7	**Vol. 1:** 513, 527 **Vol. 2:** 458 **Vol. 3:** 919
28:9 ff	**Vol. 3:** 483
28:9–10	**Vol. 2:** 432
28:9	**Vol. 3:** 771
28:11 f	**Vol. 2:** 444, 446, 513, 740 **Vol. 3:** 1079–1080
28:11	**Vol. 2:** 175
28:12	**Vol. 2:** 154 **Vol. 3:** 255–256, 389, 530
28:13	**Vol. 1:** 419 **Vol. 3:** 1118
28:14–18	**Vol. 1:** 366
28:15	**Vol. 1:** 368 **Vol. 2:** 471, 479 **Vol. 3:** 388–389
28:16	**Vol. 1:** 477, 541, 596, 661 **Vol. 2:** 327, 706, 709 **Vol. 3:** 382, 384, 388–393, 490–491, 500, 563, 1211–1212
28:17	**Vol. 2:** 471
28:17a	**Vol. 3:** 389
28:18	**Vol. 1:** 368 **Vol. 3:** 226
28:21	**Vol. 1:** 202, 688 **Vol. 3:** 1148
28:22*	**Vol. 3:** 713, 1157
28:23–25	**Vol. 2:** 747
28:25	**Vol. 2:** 211
28:27	**Vol. 2:** 211
28:28	**Vol. 1:** 202
29:2	**Vol. 2:** 842
29:3	**Vol. 3:** 951–952
29:4	**Vol. 2:** 554
29:5	**Vol. 2:** 842
29:6	**Vol. 3:** 557
29:7 f	**Vol. 2:** 842
29:8	**Vol. 1:** 546
29:9 f	**Vol. 1:** 219
29:9	**Vol. 3:** 178
29:10	**Vol. 3:** 692
29:11	**Vol. 3:** 498, 500
29:13	**Vol. 1:** 552 **Vol. 2:** 43, 53, 93, 150, 181, 469, 799, 813, 864 **Vol. 3:** 184, 427, 760, 769–770, 807
29:14	**Vol. 1:** 74, 463 **Vol. 3:** 130–132, 504, 1027–1028
29:15	**Vol. 1:** 422 **Vol. 3:** 1149
29:16 f	**Vol. 3:** 823
29:16	**Vol. 2:** 434, 609 **Vol. 3:** 911–912, 915–917
29:17–24	**Vol. 2:** 779
29:18–20	**Vol. 3:** 697
29:18 f	**Vol. 2:** 379
29:18	**Vol. 1:** 218–219
29:19	**Vol. 2:** 257, 823, 891
29:20	**Vol. 3:** 29
29:21	**Vol. 2:** 141
29:23	**Vol. 2:** 653 **Vol. 3:** 1148
29:24	**Vol. 2:** 777 **Vol. 3:** 691–692
30–31	**Vol. 1:** 531
30:1	**Vol. 1:** 607
30:4	**Vol. 2:** 926
30:6	**Vol. 2:** 807, 842 **Vol. 3:** 1005
30:7	**Vol. 1:** 546
30:8	**Vol. 1:** 245 **Vol. 3:** 484, 1094
30:10	**Vol. 2:** 432 **Vol. 3:** 77
30:12	**Vol. 3:** 1094
30:13	**Vol. 2:** 898
30:14	**Vol. 3:** 914
30:15 ff	**Vol. 3:** 249
30:15	**Vol. 2:** 320 **Vol. 3:** 206, 249, 389
30:17	**Vol. 3:** 1009
30:18	**Vol. 1:** 216 **Vol. 2:** 364 **Vol. 3:** 224
30:19	**Vol. 2:** 416
30:20	**Vol. 3:** 766
30:23–25	**Vol. 3:** 986
30:24	**Vol. 2:** 34 **Vol. 3:** 444
30:25	**Vol. 1:** 609
30:26	**Vol. 2:** 690, 890 **Vol. 3:** 731, 733
30:27 f	**Vol. 1:** 108
30:27	**Vol. 1:** 109
30:28	**Vol. 1:** 241 **Vol. 3:** 695, 1178
30:30	**Vol. 2:** 836 **Vol. 3:** 711
30:33	**Vol. 3:** 117
31:1	**Vol. 2:** 257 **Vol. 3:** 531
31:2	**Vol. 3:** 1028, 1094
31:3 f	**Vol. 2:** 602
31:3	**Vol. 1:** 673, 677, 679 **Vol. 3:** 691
31:7	**Vol. 1:** 455
31:9	**Vol. 2:** 208
32:1	**Vol. 2:** 591
32:3	**Vol. 1:** 589
32:4	**Vol. 2:** 777
32:5 f	**Vol. 3:** 1025
32:6	**Vol. 3:** 1025
32:7	**Vol. 2:** 257
32:8	**Vol. 2:** 93
32:9 ff	**Vol. 2:** 326
32:9	**Vol. 2:** 841
32:10	**Vol. 3:** 238
32:11	**Vol. 1:** 239, 314
32:13	**Vol. 1:** 240, 743 **Vol. 2:** 841
32:14	**Vol. 2:** 842
32:15 ff	**Vol. 3:** 355
32:15–20	**Vol. 3:** 692
32:15 f	**Vol. 3:** 1006
32:15	**Vol. 1:** 322 **Vol. 2:** 199, 854 **Vol. 3:** 823
32:16	**Vol. 3:** 255
32:17	**Vol. 3:** 255
32:18†	**Vol. 2:** 803, 842 **Vol. 3:** 254
33:1–24	**Vol. 3:** 78
33:1	**Vol. 3:** 859
33:2	**Vol. 3:** 836
33:3	**Vol. 2:** 34 **Vol. 3:** 207
33:5	**Vol. 2:** 199
33:6	**Vol. 2:** 93, 830 **Vol. 3:** 1027
33:7–10	**Vol. 1:** 91
33:7	**Vol. 1:** 201

Isaiah *(cont'd)*

33:8	**Vol. 1:** 368 **Vol. 3:** 823
33:9	**Vol. 2:** 422
33:13	**Vol. 2:** 53
33:14	**Vol. 1:** 655
33:15 f	**Vol. 3:** 367
33:15	**Vol. 3:** 924, 946
33:16	**Vol. 2:** 199
33:18	**Vol. 3:** 482
33:19	**Vol. 2:** 740
33:20	**Vol. 2:** 841 **Vol. 3:** 842
33:23	**Vol. 2:** 415
33:24	**Vol. 1:** 698
34:1	**Vol. 1:** 519
34:2	**Vol. 1:** 414 **Vol. 2:** 684
34:4	**Vol. 1:** 610, 724 **Vol. 2:** 38, 189, 916 **Vol. 3:** 180, 557, 559, 735–736
34:5	**Vol. 1:** 414, 513 **Vol. 2:** 189
34:6	**Vol. 3:** 159
34:7	**Vol. 1:** 513
34:10	**Vol. 3:** 109, 842
34:11	**Vol. 1:** 173
34:13–15	**Vol. 3:** 1005
34:13	**Vol. 1:** 726
34:14	**Vol. 1:** 451 **Vol. 3:** 255
34:15*	**Vol. 1:** 663 **Vol. 2:** 32
34:17	**Vol. 3:** 255, 842
35	**Vol. 1:** 124 **Vol. 2:** 110
35:1	**Vol. 2:** 266
35:2–7	**Vol. 1:** 91
35:2	**Vol. 2:** 44
35:3–6	**Vol. 2:** 168
35:3–5	**Vol. 3:** 697
35:3	**Vol. 2:** 859
35:4 ff	**Vol. 2:** 170
35:4	**Vol. 1:** 320 **Vol. 3:** 125
35:5–6	**Vol. 1:** 429
35:5 f†	**Vol. 1:** 445 **Vol. 2:** 379 **Vol. 3:** 1006
35:5	**Vol. 1:** 218–219 **Vol. 2:** 726 **Vol. 3:** 56
35:6 f	**Vol. 2:** 266
35:6	**Vol. 2:** 415
35:7	**Vol. 3:** 986
35:8	**Vol. 1:** 272 **Vol. 2:** 458
35:9	**Vol. 1:** 113 **Vol. 3:** 192
35:10	**Vol. 2:** 355, 420 **Vol. 3:** 193
36 ff	**Vol. 2:** 325
36:3	**Vol. 2:** 254
36:6	**Vol. 1:** 589
36:13	**Vol. 1:** 410
36:14–20	**Vol. 3:** 202
36:15	**Vol. 3:** 201
36:18 ff	**Vol. 3:** 342
36:19 f	**Vol. 2:** 285
36:19	**Vol. 3:** 202
36:22	**Vol. 2:** 254
37:2	**Vol. 2:** 254
37:3	**Vol. 2:** 140, 890 **Vol. 3:** 858
37:10 ff	**Vol. 3:** 342
37:15	**Vol. 2:** 862
37:16	**Vol. 1:** 280 **Vol. 2:** 70, 724
37:17	**Vol. 2:** 726
37:20*	**Vol. 3:** 1040
37:21	**Vol. 2:** 862
37:23	**Vol. 2:** 201
37:24	**Vol. 3:** 1009
37:25	**Vol. 3:** 1005
37:26	**Vol. 1:** 165
37:27	**Vol. 1:** 743
37:28	**Vol. 3:** 255
37:32	**Vol. 3:** 1167
37:33	**Vol. 3:** 951
37:36 ff	**Vol. 3:** 342
37:37	**Vol. 2:** 679
37:38	**Vol. 2:** 876
38	**Vol. 2:** 628
38:2	**Vol. 2:** 862
38:3	**Vol. 3:** 235
38:5	**Vol. 2:** 863 **Vol. 3:** 842
38:7 ff	**Vol. 2:** 627
38:8	**Vol. 3:** 554, 846
38:9	**Vol. 2:** 863 **Vol. 3:** 673, 999
38:10	**Vol. 2:** 29–30
38:11	**Vol. 1:** 433
38:12	**Vol. 3:** 811
38:13	**Vol. 1:** 240 **Vol. 3:** 342
38:17	**Vol. 1:** 233 **Vol. 3:** 262, 997
38:18	**Vol. 3:** 226, 816, 880
38:19	**Vol. 1:** 617 **Vol. 3:** 354
38:21	**Vol. 2:** 169
39:2	**Vol. 2:** 357, 607
39:6	**Vol. 2:** 890
39:7	**Vol. 3:** 786
39:8	**Vol. 2:** 100 **Vol. 3:** 354
40–66	**Vol. 1:** 52, 686
40–55	**Vol. 1:** 54, 699 **Vol. 2:** 226 **Vol. 3:** 1101, 1105
40	**Vol. 1:** 383 **Vol. 2:** 326 **Vol. 3:** 828
40:1–31	**Vol. 3:** 69
40:1–8	**Vol. 3:** 1101
40:1–7	**Vol. 3:** 257
40:1–5	**Vol. 3:** 1101
40:1	**Vol. 1:** 569
40:2	**Vol. 1:** 109 **Vol. 3:** 177, 668, 960
40:3 ff	**Vol. 1:** 409 **Vol. 2:** 262
40:3–5	**Vol. 3:** 1011
40:3	**Vol. 1:** 410–412 **Vol. 2:** 715 **Vol. 3:** 53, 55, 118–119, 937, 939–940, 1005–1007
40:4	**Vol. 3:** 392, 1010, 1012
40:5 f	**Vol. 1:** 672 **Vol. 2:** 799
40:5	**Vol. 2:** 45 **Vol. 3:** 221
40:6 ff	**Vol. 1:** 273 **Vol. 2:** 844
40:6 f	**Vol. 3:** 1101
40:6–8	**Vol. 1:** 678
40:6	**Vol. 1:** 411, 673, 743 **Vol. 2:** 211 **Vol. 3:** 1101
40:7	**Vol. 1:** 516, 609, 743–744 **Vol. 2:** 211, 746 **Vol. 3:** 690

Isaiah *(cont'd)*

40:8	**Vol. 1:** 411, 673, 744 **Vol. 3:** 224, 1101, 1122
40:9	**Vol. 2:** 109, 111, 327, 803
40:10 f	**Vol. 1:** 320 **Vol. 3:** 565
40:10	**Vol. 2:** 139, 279
40:11	**Vol. 2:** 32, 34, 412 **Vol. 3:** 565
40:12	**Vol. 3:** 1010, 1160
40:13 f	**Vol. 3:** 129, 1032
40:13	**Vol. 1:** 363 **Vol. 2:** 279, 513, 772 **Vol. 3:** 125, 129
40:15	**Vol. 3:** 823, 1160
40:18 ff	**Vol. 2:** 285
40:18	**Vol. 2:** 502
40:19 f	**Vol. 2:** 287
40:19	**Vol. 3:** 119
40:20	**Vol. 1:** 390, 537
40:22	**Vol. 2:** 189
40:25	**Vol. 2:** 70, 71, 226
40:26	**Vol. 1:** 273, 380 **Vol. 2:** 199 **Vol. 3:** 1102
40:27–31	**Vol. 2:** 266
40:27	**Vol. 2:** 215
40:28	**Vol. 1:** 262 **Vol. 2:** 616 **Vol. 3:** 119, 841
40:29	**Vol. 2:** 215
40:30 f	**Vol. 1:** 262
40:30	**Vol. 1:** 262
40:31	**Vol. 1:** 173 **Vol. 2:** 240, 773
41 f	**Vol. 2:** 309
41–45	**Vol. 3:** 1153
41:1 ff	**Vol. 2:** 364
41:2	**Vol. 1:** 273 **Vol. 3:** 357, 746
41:4	**Vol. 1:** 273, 665 **Vol. 2:** 59, 64, 69–70, 157
41:8 ff	**Vol. 3:** 1102
41:8	**Vol. 1:** 77, 273, 538 **Vol. 2:** 596 **Vol. 3:** 369, 867
41:10 f	**Vol. 3:** 355
41:10	**Vol. 1:** 623
41:11	**Vol. 3:** 562
41:13	**Vol. 1:** 622–623 **Vol. 2:** 149 **Vol. 3:** 716
41:14	**Vol. 3:** 192
41:15	**Vol. 3:** 392, 1010
41:16	**Vol. 2:** 34
41:17 ff	**Vol. 3:** 79
41:17 f	**Vol. 2:** 266
41:17	**Vol. 2:** 257, 823
41:18	**Vol. 3:** 986, 1006
41:19	**Vol. 2:** 266, 711
41:20	**Vol. 1:** 380 **Vol. 2:** 395
41:21	**Vol. 2:** 375–376
41:22	**Vol. 3:** 125
41:23	**Vol. 2:** 56
41:25	**Vol. 3:** 911, 915–916
41:26 f	**Vol. 3:** 1101
41:27	**Vol. 1:** 665 **Vol. 2:** 109
41:28	**Vol. 2:** 879
41:29	**Vol. 2:** 720
42	**Vol. 3:** 110
42:1–9	**Vol. 3:** 609
42:1–4	**Vol. 1:** 374, 651 **Vol. 3:** 48, 69, 110, 609, 612, 692, 1041, 1163
42:1	**Vol. 1:** 534, 538 **Vol. 2:** 543, 819, 888 **Vol. 3:** 258, 609–611, 638–641, 685, 698, 807, 864, 987
42:2 f	**Vol. 2:** 258
42:2	**Vol. 1:** 409
42:3 f	**Vol. 3:** 609
42:3	**Vol. 2:** 888 **Vol. 3:** 109–110
42:4	**Vol. 2:** 240–241, 654 **Vol. 3:** 109
42:5	**Vol. 2:** 77, 164, 190 **Vol. 3:** 690
42:6 ff	**Vol. 1:** 688 **Vol. 2:** 333
42:6	**Vol. 1:** 273 **Vol. 2:** 492, 494, 728, 799, 888 **Vol. 3:** 313, 716
42:7	**Vol. 1:** 422 **Vol. 2:** 596, 726 **Vol. 3:** 592, 609
42:8	**Vol. 2:** 44, 70 **Vol. 3:** 926
42:9	**Vol. 2:** 670, 672 **Vol. 3:** 45, 704
42:10	**Vol. 3:** 669, 675
42:12	**Vol. 2:** 44 **Vol. 3:** 926
42:13	**Vol. 3:** 1167
42:14	**Vol. 2:** 765, 767 **Vol. 3:** 908
42:15	**Vol. 1:** 515 **Vol. 3:** 986
42:16	**Vol. 1:** 422
42:17	**Vol. 2:** 728
42:18	**Vol. 3:** 519
42:21	**Vol. 3:** 140, 355
42:24	**Vol. 2:** 440
42:25	**Vol. 1:** 109
43:1 ff	**Vol. 2:** 337 **Vol. 3:** 79
43:1	**Vol. 1:** 273 **Vol. 2:** 649 **Vol. 3:** 192
43:2	**Vol. 3:** 695, 983, 986
43:3 ff	**Vol. 3:** 623
43:3 f	**Vol. 1:** 479 **Vol. 3:** 192
43:3	**Vol. 2:** 367 **Vol. 3:** 153, 192, 1196
43:4	**Vol. 2:** 541
43:5 ff	**Vol. 3:** 208
43:5	**Vol. 1:** 297 **Vol. 2:** 32
43:6	**Vol. 3:** 718
43:7	**Vol. 1:** 380 **Vol. 2:** 777 **Vol. 3:** 119
43:8 ff	**Vol. 2:** 307
43:8	**Vol. 1:** 428–429
43:9 f	**Vol. 3:** 1101
43:9	**Vol. 3:** 355, 881
43:10 ff	**Vol. 2:** 70
43:10	**Vol. 1:** 273, 538 **Vol. 2:** 720, 888 **Vol. 3:** 130, 1041
43:11	**Vol. 2:** 279
43:12	**Vol. 3:** 1041
43:14	**Vol. 2:** 226 **Vol. 3:** 192
43:15	**Vol. 1:** 382 **Vol. 2:** 226
43:16–21	**Vol. 2:** 670
43:16	**Vol. 3:** 937
43:17	**Vol. 1:** 442 **Vol. 3:** 109
43:18 ff	**Vol. 2:** 671
43:18 f	**Vol. 2:** 670, 672
43:18	**Vol. 3:** 236

Isaiah *(cont'd)*

43:19–21   **Vol. 3:** 986
43:19 f   **Vol. 3:** 1006
43:19   **Vol. 3:** 180, 937, 1006
43:20   **Vol. 2:** 266   **Vol. 3:** 986
43:21   **Vol. 3:** 926–927
43:22–25   **Vol. 3:** 150
43:22–24   **Vol. 3:** 625
43:22   **Vol. 1:** 262
43:23   **Vol. 2:** 221
43:24   **Vol. 1:** 194
43:25   **Vol. 1:** 471   **Vol. 3:** 167, 235, 631
43:26   **Vol. 3:** 355
43:28   **Vol. 1:** 414
44   **Vol. 3:** 828
44:1   **Vol. 3:** 1102
44:2   **Vol. 1:** 622   **Vol. 3:** 807
44:3   **Vol. 2:** 266   **Vol. 3:** 490, 692, 986–989
44:4   **Vol. 1:** 743
44:5   **Vol. 2:** 572   **Vol. 3:** 498
44:6   **Vol. 1:** 665, 667   **Vol. 2:** 59, 64, 70, 279, 282, 375–376   **Vol. 3:** 201–202
44:7 ff   **Vol. 3:** 45
44:7   **Vol. 2:** 498   **Vol. 3:** 704, 1101
44:8   **Vol. 2:** 720   **Vol. 3:** 1041
44:9–20   **Vol. 2:** 285, 432
44:9   **Vol. 3:** 1153
44:12 ff   **Vol. 1:** 654
44:13 ff   **Vol. 1:** 390
44:13   **Vol. 1:** 706
44:15   **Vol. 1:** 654   **Vol. 2:** 876
44:17   **Vol. 2:** 862, 876   **Vol. 3:** 248
44:19   **Vol. 2:** 876   **Vol. 3:** 248, 823
44:21   **Vol. 3:** 236
44:22 ff   **Vol. 3:** 192
44:23   **Vol. 2:** 356
44:24   **Vol. 1:** 95, 522   **Vol. 2:** 189, 279
44:25   **Vol. 2:** 554–555   **Vol. 3:** 1025, 1101
44:26   **Vol. 3:** 1101
44:27   **Vol. 3:** 986, 1005, 1101
44:28   **Vol. 1:** 111   **Vol. 3:** 97, 566, 786, 1019, 1154
45–48   **Vol. 2:** 285
45   **Vol. 3:** 218, 960
45:1 ff   **Vol. 2:** 791
45:1   **Vol. 1:** 111   **Vol. 2:** 335–336   **Vol. 3:** 97, 218, 716
45:2   **Vol. 3:** 1010
45:3   **Vol. 1:** 273   **Vol. 2:** 70, 215, 396, 830, 835
45:5   **Vol. 2:** 279
45:6 f   **Vol. 2:** 396
45:6   **Vol. 2:** 70
45:7   **Vol. 1:** 379, 422   **Vol. 2:** 491, 778   **Vol. 3:** 119
45:9 ff   **Vol. 3:** 1102
45:9   **Vol. 2:** 434, 609   **Vol. 3:** 119, 911–912, 916–917
45:10   **Vol. 3:** 858

45:11   **Vol. 2:** 226
45:13   **Vol. 3:** 190, 192, 590
45:13a   **Vol. 3:** 279
45:14 ff   **Vol. 1:** 688
45:14   **Vol. 2:** 862, 876
45:15   **Vol. 2:** 215   **Vol. 3:** 218
45:17   **Vol. 3:** 218, 828
45:19   **Vol. 3:** 502
45:20   **Vol. 2:** 32, 862   **Vol. 3:** 206, 250
45:21 f   **Vol. 3:** 218
45:21   **Vol. 3:** 218, 355, 1101
45:22   **Vol. 2:** 279, 888   **Vol. 3:** 208
45:23 f   **Vol. 2:** 514
45:23   **Vol. 1:** 321   **Vol. 2:** 369, 513, 650, 859, 925   **Vol. 3:** 1079, 1101
45:24   **Vol. 3:** 355
45:25*   **Vol. 3:** 355
46:1 f   **Vol. 2:** 285
46:2   **Vol. 3:** 209
46:3 f   **Vol. 3:** 250, 805
46:3   **Vol. 2:** 305
46:4   **Vol. 2:** 765   **Vol. 3:** 250
46:5   **Vol. 2:** 501
46:6   **Vol. 2:** 139, 876   **Vol. 3:** 1153, 1161
46:7   **Vol. 3:** 206
46:9   **Vol. 3:** 236
46:10   **Vol. 3:** 45
46:12 f   **Vol. 3:** 357
46:13   **Vol. 2:** 53, 326
47   **Vol. 1:** 141
47:1   **Vol. 3:** 588
47:2   **Vol. 3:** 394
47:3   **Vol. 2:** 212
47:4   **Vol. 3:** 192, 202
47:6   **Vol. 1:** 448   **Vol. 2:** 297   **Vol. 3:** 1161
47:7   **Vol. 3:** 125, 232
47:8 f   **Vol. 3:** 1074
47:8   **Vol. 2:** 395
47:9   **Vol. 2:** 554
47:10   **Vol. 2:** 830   **Vol. 3:** 1028
47:11   **Vol. 1:** 320   **Vol. 2:** 395   **Vol. 3:** 152, 154
47:12   **Vol. 2:** 554
47:13   **Vol. 2:** 189, 555   **Vol. 3:** 735
47:14   **Vol. 3:** 206
48:1 ff   **Vol. 2:** 364
48:1   **Vol. 3:** 232
48:2   **Vol. 2:** 325, 803
48:4   **Vol. 1:** 241
48:6   **Vol. 2:** 670
48:10   **Vol. 1:** 268
48:11   **Vol. 2:** 70
48:12–16a   **Vol. 1:** 141
48:12   **Vol. 1:** 665, 667   **Vol. 2:** 59, 64, 69–70, 279
48:13   **Vol. 2:** 149
48:14 f   **Vol. 1:** 273
48:14   **Vol. 2:** 32   **Vol. 3:** 1101
48:16   **Vol. 3:** 202, 258, 502
48:17   **Vol. 3:** 201–202

Isaiah *(cont'd)*

48:18 f   **Vol. 3:** 355
48:18   **Vol. 2:** 777–778   **Vol. 3:** 987
48:20–22   **Vol. 1:** 141
48:20   **Vol. 2:** 55–56, 318   **Vol. 3:** 202, 594
48:21   **Vol. 1:** 683   **Vol. 2:** 266   **Vol. 3:** 543
48:22   **Vol. 2:** 357, 777–778
49   **Vol. 2:** 309
49:1 ff   **Vol. 2:** 279, 337
49:1 f   **Vol. 3:** 609
49:1–11   **Vol. 3:** 609
49:1–6   **Vol. 1:** 374   **Vol. 3:** 69, 609, 692, 1041
49:1   **Vol. 3:** 612
49:2   **Vol. 2:** 686   **Vol. 3:** 554, 609, 967, 1102
49:3   **Vol. 3:** 609
49:4   **Vol. 1:** 262, 551
49:5 f   **Vol. 3:** 609
49:6 ff   **Vol. 2:** 333
49:6   **Vol. 1:** 477, 544, 641, 685   **Vol. 2:** 34, 55–56, 69, 492, 494–495, 888   **Vol. 3:** 69, 208, 218, 613
49:7   **Vol. 2:** 876   **Vol. 3:** 201–202
49:8   **Vol. 2:** 175, 178, 297, 890   **Vol. 3:** 214, 746, 838
49:9 f   **Vol. 2:** 266
49:9   **Vol. 1:** 422   **Vol. 3:** 565, 592, 609
49:10   **Vol. 2:** 267, 825   **Vol. 3:** 986
49:11   **Vol. 3:** 1012
49:13   **Vol. 2:** 71, 193, 257, 260, 356, 823
49:14 ff   **Vol. 3:** 1102
49:15   **Vol. 3:** 1069
49:16   **Vol. 2:** 149
49:18   **Vol. 2:** 32, 585
49:21   **Vol. 2:** 724   **Vol. 3:** 1068
49:22   **Vol. 1:** 240
49:23   **Vol. 2:** 396, 773, 876
49:24 f   **Vol. 2:** 631   **Vol. 3:** 209, 713
49:25 f   **Vol. 3:** 202
49:25   **Vol. 3:** 201
49:26   **Vol. 1:** 513   **Vol. 2:** 69, 396
50:1 ff   **Vol. 2:** 364
50:1   **Vol. 1:** 268, 505   **Vol. 2:** 307, 576–577   **Vol. 3:** 594, 1068–1069
50:2   **Vol. 1:** 272, 670   **Vol. 2:** 140, 179   **Vol. 3:** 202, 983, 986
50:3   **Vol. 1:** 203   **Vol. 2:** 189   **Vol. 3:** 1102
50:4 ff   **Vol. 2:** 279, 337
50:4–9   **Vol. 3:** 69, 609, 1041
50:4 f   **Vol. 3:** 609
50:4   **Vol. 3:** 1027, 1102
50:5   **Vol. 2:** 178, 726
50:7   **Vol. 3:** 382
50:8   **Vol. 2:** 53   **Vol. 3:** 355
50:9   **Vol. 1:** 316   **Vol. 2:** 714   **Vol. 3:** 357
50:11   **Vol. 1:** 442
51:1 f   **Vol. 3:** 393
51:1   **Vol. 3:** 382, 520
51:2   **Vol. 1:** 80   **Vol. 2:** 720   **Vol. 3:** 369, 382, 520, 858, 867

51:3   **Vol. 2:** 761
51:4   **Vol. 2:** 492
51:5 f   **Vol. 3:** 355
51:5–8   **Vol. 3:** 357
51:5   **Vol. 2:** 53, 239–240, 773
51:6   **Vol. 1:** 316   **Vol. 2:** 189, 714   **Vol. 3:** 520
51:7   **Vol. 2:** 181
51:8   **Vol. 1:** 316, 508   **Vol. 3:** 842
51:9 ff   **Vol. 2:** 672
51:9 f   **Vol. 3:** 983
51:10   **Vol. 2:** 197   **Vol. 3:** 202, 937, 1005
51:11   **Vol. 2:** 420   **Vol. 3:** 192–193
51:12   **Vol. 1:** 743   **Vol. 3:** 613
51:15   **Vol. 2:** 650
51:16   **Vol. 3:** 554, 1102
51:17 f   **Vol. 2:** 276
51:17   **Vol. 1:** 109   **Vol. 2:** 275   **Vol. 3:** 208, 357, 922
51:21 ff   **Vol. 2:** 823
51:22   **Vol. 1:** 109   **Vol. 3:** 922
52   **Vol. 3:** 610
52:1   **Vol. 1:** 154, 314   **Vol. 2:** 325, 803
52:2   **Vol. 3:** 560
52:3   **Vol. 3:** 192, 196, 200, 435
52:4   **Vol. 3:** 711
52:5   **Vol. 2:** 891   **Vol. 3:** 341–343
52:6   **Vol. 2:** 891   **Vol. 3:** 341
52:7   **Vol. 1:** 239   **Vol. 2:** 70, 100, 109, 111, 375–376, 778, 782   **Vol. 3:** 48, 612, 966
52:8   **Vol. 2:** 201
52:9   **Vol. 3:** 202
52:10   **Vol. 3:** 55, 118, 311
52:11   **Vol. 1:** 607   **Vol. 2:** 513   **Vol. 3:** 860
52:12   **Vol. 2:** 355
52:13 ff   **Vol. 2:** 337
52:13–53:12   **Vol. 1:** 374, 426   **Vol. 2:** 307   **Vol. 3:** 69, 269, 357, 609–610, 1041
52:13   **Vol. 3:** 196, 593, 607, 611, 624, 630, 632
52:14 f   **Vol. 1:** 96
52:15   **Vol. 3:** 48, 131–132, 613
53   **Vol. 1:** 96–97, 437, 549, 581, 699, 707   **Vol. 2:** 313, 411, 540   **Vol. 3:** 195–196, 435, 567, 578, 582, 597, 610–612, 621, 638, 697, 723, 748, 825
53:1 ff   **Vol. 2:** 258
53:1–3   **Vol. 1:** 427
53:1   **Vol. 2:** 173, 175, 513, 632   **Vol. 3:** 311–312, 314, 321, 613
53:2 f   **Vol. 1:** 704
53:2   **Vol. 3:** 867
53:3–8   **Vol. 2:** 51
53:3 f   **Vol. 1:** 163   **Vol. 3:** 823
53:3   **Vol. 1:** 162   **Vol. 2:** 49   **Vol. 3:** 999
53:4–6   **Vol. 3:** 721, 1200
53:4   **Vol. 1:** 162, 390   **Vol. 2:** 165   **Vol. 3:** 748, 998–999, 1195
53:5–12   **Vol. 3:** 491

Isaiah *(cont'd)*

53:5   **Vol. 2:** 368, 778   **Vol. 3:** 723, 777–778
53:6   **Vol. 2:** 412, 458–459   **Vol. 3:** 170, 938
53:7 f   **Vol. 2:** 263, 381   **Vol. 3:** 66, 609
53:7–12   **Vol. 1:** 581   **Vol. 2:** 263
53:7   **Vol. 1:** 548   **Vol. 2:** 410, 728   **Vol. 3:** 200, 347, 435
53:8   **Vol. 1:** 548, 576   **Vol. 2:** 38, 260   **Vol. 3:** 624
53:9   **Vol. 2:** 841   **Vol. 3:** 529, 723
53:10 ff   **Vol. 3:** 269
53:10–12   **Vol. 3:** 195, 1200
53:10 f   **Vol. 3:** 293, 420
53:10   **Vol. 3:** 171, 196, 522, 611, 624, 1016
53:10b   **Vol. 3:** 1200
53:11 f   **Vol. 1:** 96   **Vol. 2:** 532   **Vol. 3:** 195
53:11   **Vol. 2:** 854   **Vol. 3:** 196, 355, 1180
53:11a   **Vol. 3:** 1200
53:12   **Vol. 1:** 390, 548   **Vol. 2:** 62, 445, 525, 854   **Vol. 3:** 379, 491, 611–612, 625, 638, 823–826, 967, 1184, 1195
54:1 ff   **Vol. 3:** 1057
54:1   **Vol. 1:** 288, 321, 411   **Vol. 3:** 858, 1065, 1068, 1070
54:2   **Vol. 3:** 713
54:3   **Vol. 3:** 1005–1006
54:4 ff   **Vol. 3:** 1102
54:4–8   **Vol. 2:** 541
54:5 f   **Vol. 3:** 1068
54:5   **Vol. 3:** 201–202, 1068
54:6 f   **Vol. 2:** 541
54:7 ff   **Vol. 3:** 167
54:7 f   **Vol. 1:** 109   **Vol. 3:** 827
54:7   **Vol. 3:** 842, 1200
54:8–10   **Vol. 1:** 109
54:8   **Vol. 2:** 71, 215   **Vol. 3:** 201–202
54:9 f   **Vol. 2:** 672, 681
54:9   **Vol. 3:** 841
54:10   **Vol. 1:** 367   **Vol. 2:** 778–779   **Vol. 3:** 152, 1012
54:11 ff   **Vol. 2:** 823
54:11 f   **Vol. 3:** 397–398
54:11   **Vol. 1:** 661   **Vol. 2:** 260
54:12   **Vol. 3:** 395–396
54:13   **Vol. 2:** 778   **Vol. 3:** 764
54:14†   **Vol. 3:** 161
54:16   **Vol. 1:** 379, 468
54:17   **Vol. 2:** 142, 164   **Vol. 3:** 355, 609
55:1 ff   **Vol. 1:** 210
55:1   **Vol. 2:** 266–267, 275, 277   **Vol. 3:** 490, 813, 986, 988, 1051
55:2   **Vol. 2:** 735
55:3   **Vol. 1:** 367, 426   **Vol. 2:** 237–238   **Vol. 3:** 649, 828
55:5   **Vol. 2:** 226
55:6–13   **Vol. 1:** 699
55:6   **Vol. 3:** 528, 531
55:7   **Vol. 1:** 698   **Vol. 3:** 528, 938
55:8 f   **Vol. 3:** 937
55:8   **Vol. 3:** 528
55:9   **Vol. 3:** 125
55:10 f   **Vol. 2:** 626
55:10   **Vol. 1:** 186, 513, 733   **Vol. 2:** 189, 274   **Vol. 3:** 522
55:11   **Vol. 3:** 1094, 1101
55:12   **Vol. 2:** 778   **Vol. 3:** 761
55:13   **Vol. 2:** 650
56–66   **Vol. 1:** 54   **Vol. 3:** 451
56–59   **Vol. 3:** 357
56:1–8   **Vol. 1:** 688
56:1   **Vol. 2:** 53   **Vol. 3:** 311, 355, 357, 367
56:2   **Vol. 3:** 407
56:3 ff   **Vol. 1:** 560   **Vol. 2:** 117
56:3   **Vol. 1:** 515   **Vol. 3:** 866
56:5   **Vol. 2:** 149
56:6–11   **Vol. 3:** 1101
56:6   **Vol. 3:** 609
56:7   **Vol. 1:** 272   **Vol. 2:** 236, 248, 325, 379, 610, 863   **Vol. 3:** 378, 380, 421, 430, 791
56:8   **Vol. 2:** 32
56:10   **Vol. 2:** 547, 586
56:11 f   **Vol. 3:** 919
56:11   **Vol. 3:** 137, 566
57:2   **Vol. 2:** 778
57:3   **Vol. 2:** 554–555
57:4   **Vol. 2:** 735
57:5   **Vol. 3:** 865
57:6   **Vol. 2:** 298, 854   **Vol. 3:** 423, 919
57:7   **Vol. 2:** 587
57:8   **Vol. 3:** 237
57:9   **Vol. 1:** 194
57:15   **Vol. 2:** 199, 825   **Vol. 3:** 255
57:17 f   **Vol. 1:** 329
57:17   **Vol. 3:** 137
57:18   **Vol. 2:** 777
57:19   **Vol. 2:** 53, 778   **Vol. 3:** 515
57:20   **Vol. 3:** 255
57:21   **Vol. 2:** 357, 777
58:2   **Vol. 1:** 456   **Vol. 2:** 856
58:3 ff   **Vol. 3:** 161
58:3–10   **Vol. 2:** 864
58:3–7   **Vol. 1:** 612
58:3   **Vol. 1:** 495, 612   **Vol. 2:** 260
58:5   **Vol. 1:** 495
58:6–7   **Vol. 2:** 104
58:6   **Vol. 3:** 177
58:7   **Vol. 1:** 250, 312   **Vol. 2:** 265–266, 272
58:8 ff   **Vol. 3:** 357
58:10   **Vol. 1:** 250   **Vol. 2:** 265–266, 492
58:11   **Vol. 3:** 490, 813, 986–988
58:12   **Vol. 3:** 1006
58:13   **Vol. 2:** 890   **Vol. 3:** 1102
58:14   **Vol. 2:** 735
58:23   **Vol. 3:** 407
59:1 f   **Vol. 2:** 175, 864
59:3   **Vol. 1:** 449
59:4   **Vol. 1:** 186
59:6   **Vol. 3:** 1149

Isaiah *(cont'd)*

59:7	**Vol. 3:** 159, 820, 859, 966
59:8	**Vol. 2:** 778
59:9	**Vol. 1:** 606
59:10	**Vol. 1:** 218
59:11	**Vol. 1:** 607 **Vol. 2:** 423
59:13	**Vol. 2:** 471 **Vol. 3:** 881
59:14	**Vol. 1:** 607 **Vol. 3:** 881
59:15	**Vol. 3:** 881
59:17	**Vol. 3:** 966
59:19	**Vol. 3:** 987
59:20 f	**Vol. 2:** 329 **Vol. 3:** 203
59:20	**Vol. 1:** 320, 355 **Vol. 2:** 319, 327 **Vol. 3:** 202–203
59:21	**Vol. 3:** 692
60	**Vol. 1:** 686
60:1 ff	**Vol. 2:** 45, 302, 585
60:1 f	**Vol. 2:** 596
60:1	**Vol. 1:** 320 **Vol. 2:** 45, 495 **Vol. 3:** 634, 1068
60:2	**Vol. 1:** 422 **Vol. 2:** 212
60:3	**Vol. 2:** 492, 793
60:4	**Vol. 2:** 32
60:5 f	**Vol. 1:** 320
60:5	**Vol. 2:** 793, 842
60:6	**Vol. 2:** 294
60:7	**Vol. 2:** 863
60:9	**Vol. 2:** 773
60:10 ff	**Vol. 2:** 888
60:10	**Vol. 1:** 474
60:12	**Vol. 3:** 1005
60:13	**Vol. 3:** 786
60:15	**Vol. 1:** 555
60:16	**Vol. 2:** 842
60:17	**Vol. 1:** 190 **Vol. 2:** 777–778 **Vol. 3:** 357
60:19 f	**Vol. 2:** 491 **Vol. 3:** 731
60:19†	**Vol. 2:** 495 **Vol. 3:** 733
60:20 ff	**Vol. 3:** 836
60:20	**Vol. 2:** 422 **Vol. 3:** 720, 733
60:21†	**Vol. 1:** 184 **Vol. 3:** 357, 722, 866–867
60:22	**Vol. 1:** 297 **Vol. 2:** 428, 698, 887
61	**Vol. 2:** 109, 353 **Vol. 3:** 520
61:1 ff	**Vol. 1:** 445
61:1–4	**Vol. 2:** 823
61:1–3	**Vol. 3:** 612
61:1–2	**Vol. 1:** 429 **Vol. 3:** 639
61:1 f	**Vol. 1:** 91, 738 **Vol. 2:** 168, 379 **Vol. 3:** 56, 71, 612, 639, 696–697, 762, 1108
61:1	**Vol. 1:** 122, 698, 717 **Vol. 2:** 109–110, 257, 279, 337, 779, 824–825 **Vol. 3:** 51, 258, 591, 698, 1061
61:2	**Vol. 1:** 272 **Vol. 2:** 779, 890 **Vol. 3:** 746
61:3	**Vol. 1:** 120 **Vol. 2:** 711, 891
61:4	**Vol. 3:** 1006
61:5	**Vol. 2:** 742, 888 **Vol. 3:** 918

61:6	**Vol. 1:** 272 **Vol. 2:** 380, 625, 842 **Vol. 3:** 37, 1175
61:7	**Vol. 3:** 354
61:8	**Vol. 3:** 354
61:10	**Vol. 1:** 316–317, 522 **Vol. 2:** 584 **Vol. 3:** 207–208, 357
62:1–9	**Vol. 2:** 779
62:1	**Vol. 2:** 485, 779 **Vol. 3:** 355
62:2	**Vol. 2:** 649, 779
62:4	**Vol. 1:** 519 **Vol. 3:** 1006
62:5	**Vol. 2:** 578, 584–585 **Vol. 3:** 1065
62:8	**Vol. 1:** 554
62:9	**Vol. 2:** 32 **Vol. 3:** 816
62:11	**Vol. 2:** 139, 327, 379 **Vol. 3:** 218
62:12	**Vol. 3:** 192
63:1 ff	**Vol. 1:** 109
63:1 f	**Vol. 1:** 111
63:1	**Vol. 3:** 711, 820
63:2 f	**Vol. 1:** 224
63:2–6	**Vol. 3:** 919
63:3	**Vol. 3:** 919
63:4	**Vol. 2:** 890 **Vol. 3:** 193
63:5	**Vol. 3:** 202
63:7	**Vol. 3:** 926
63:7b	**Vol. 2:** 595
63:9	**Vol. 3:** 192
63:10 f	**Vol. 2:** 227
63:11–14	**Vol. 3:** 692
63:11 f	**Vol. 2:** 639
63:11	**Vol. 2:** 412
63:15–64:11	**Vol. 1:** 77
63:15	**Vol. 2:** 598, 765 **Vol. 3:** 1166–1167
63:16	**Vol. 1:** 77, 164, 617 **Vol. 2:** 71 **Vol. 3:** 202
63:17	**Vol. 2:** 458
63:19 f	**Vol. 3:** 1010
63:19	**Vol. 1:** 164 **Vol. 2:** 649
64:1*	**Vol. 2:** 189–190 **Vol. 3:** 543
64:2	**Vol. 3:** 318
64:3*	**Vol. 2:** 773 **Vol. 3:** 504
64:4*	**Vol. 2:** 219, 773 **Vol. 3:** 533
64:6 f	**Vol. 3:** 578
64:7	**Vol. 1:** 272
64:8*	**Vol. 1:** 617 **Vol. 3:** 234, 638
64:12	**Vol. 2:** 765
65:1 f	**Vol. 2:** 176
65:1	**Vol. 1:** 112 **Vol. 2:** 489, 636, 879–880 **Vol. 3:** 528
65:2	**Vol. 1:** 492 **Vol. 2:** 490, 880
65:3	**Vol. 1:** 451
65:4	**Vol. 1:** 117, 449 **Vol. 3:** 238
65:6	**Vol. 1:** 243
65:8	**Vol. 3:** 919
65:10	**Vol. 3:** 255
65:11	**Vol. 1:** 451 **Vol. 2:** 175, 518 **Vol. 3:** 919
65:12	**Vol. 1:** 272 **Vol. 2:** 367 **Vol. 3:** 1016
65:13	**Vol. 2:** 265, 522, 532 **Vol. 3:** 1053
65:15	**Vol. 1:** 272
65:16	**Vol. 1:** 98–99

Isaiah *(cont'd)*

65:17 f	**Vol. 1:** 380 **Vol. 2:** 670
65:17–25	**Vol. 1:** 210
65:17–19	**Vol. 2:** 779
65:17	**Vol. 1:** 185 **Vol. 2:** 189, 219, 888 **Vol. 3:** 180, 533
65:19	**Vol. 2:** 353, 355
65:20	**Vol. 3:** 842
65:21	**Vol. 2:** 888
65:22	**Vol. 1:** 538 **Vol. 3:** 866
65:23	**Vol. 1:** 262, 546
65:23b	**Vol. 1:** 215
65:24	**Vol. 2:** 179
65:25	**Vol. 1:** 250
66	**Vol. 3:** 786
66:1 f	**Vol. 3:** 465, 785, 793
66:1	**Vol. 1:** 518 **Vol. 2:** 193, 247, 252, 613 **Vol. 3:** 256, 258, 741
66:2	**Vol. 1:** 185 **Vol. 2:** 257, 414
66:2b	**Vol. 2:** 260
66:3	**Vol. 1:** 117 **Vol. 3:** 341
66:4	**Vol. 2:** 179 **Vol. 3:** 1016
66:7 ff	**Vol. 3:** 732
66:7–11	**Vol. 3:** 1068
66:7	**Vol. 1:** 186 **Vol. 2:** 569–570
66:8	**Vol. 1:** 186 **Vol. 2:** 717
66:9	**Vol. 3:** 637
66:10–19	**Vol. 1:** 91
66:10	**Vol. 2:** 356–357
66:11	**Vol. 1:** 240 **Vol. 2:** 735
66:12	**Vol. 2:** 778 **Vol. 3:** 987
66:13	**Vol. 3:** 1069
66:14	**Vol. 1:** 91, 240 **Vol. 2:** 357 **Vol. 3:** 269
66:15 f	**Vol. 1:** 655 **Vol. 2:** 836
66:15	**Vol. 1:** 657 **Vol. 2:** 96
66:18 ff	**Vol. 3:** 250
66:18	**Vol. 1:** 320 **Vol. 2:** 32 **Vol. 3:** 823
66:19	**Vol. 1:** 688 **Vol. 2:** 48, 124, 888
66:20	**Vol. 3:** 38, 431
66:22	**Vol. 2:** 48 **Vol. 3:** 180, 224
66:23	**Vol. 2:** 876
66:24	**Vol. 1:** 655, 657 **Vol. 2:** 208 **Vol. 3:** 109–110, 447–448

Jeremiah

1–25	**Vol. 3:** 1095
1:1	**Vol. 3:** 311, 1092–1093, 1120
1:3	**Vol. 3:** 590
1:4–10	**Vol. 3:** 1088, 1095
1:5	**Vol. 2:** 226, 395 **Vol. 3:** 1095
1:6	**Vol. 1:** 272 **Vol. 3:** 1095
1:8	**Vol. 3:** 1095
1:9 f	**Vol. 2:** 252
1:9	**Vol. 3:** 1088, 1095
1:10	**Vol. 2:** 252 **Vol. 3:** 1095
1:11 ff	**Vol. 2:** 173
1:11–12	**Vol. 2:** 432
1:12	**Vol. 3:** 1096, 1153

1:16	**Vol. 2:** 876
1:18	**Vol. 2:** 98
2–4:5†	**Vol. 3:** 1095
2	**Vol. 3:** 263
2:1 ff	**Vol. 2:** 541
2:2	**Vol. 2:** 576, 583, 585 **Vol. 3:** 235
2:3	**Vol. 1:** 565 **Vol. 3:** 420, 987
2:4–9	**Vol. 2:** 364
2:4	**Vol. 2:** 174
2:5	**Vol. 1:** 481, 492, 551–552
2:6	**Vol. 1:** 531 **Vol. 2:** 206, 275 **Vol. 3:** 1005
2:7	**Vol. 2:** 296 **Vol. 3:** 104
2:8	**Vol. 2:** 440 **Vol. 3:** 78, 565
2:10	**Vol. 2:** 576 **Vol. 3:** 125
2:11	**Vol. 2:** 70, 720
2:12	**Vol. 2:** 363
2:13	**Vol. 2:** 479 **Vol. 3:** 1153
2:15	**Vol. 3:** 1005
2:18	**Vol. 1:** 531
2:19	**Vol. 1:** 607 **Vol. 2:** 141
2:20	**Vol. 3:** 592, 1161–1162
2:21	**Vol. 2:** 248, 313 **Vol. 3:** 918
2:23	**Vol. 1:** 492 **Vol. 3:** 104
2:24	**Vol. 3:** 680
2:25	**Vol. 2:** 540, 576
2:26	**Vol. 3:** 562
2:27 f	**Vol. 3:** 206
2:27	**Vol. 3:** 865
2:29	**Vol. 3:** 578
2:30	**Vol. 1:** 551 **Vol. 3:** 745
2:31	**Vol. 2:** 206
2:32	**Vol. 1:** 522
2:36	**Vol. 1:** 531
2:37	**Vol. 2:** 149
3:1–25	**Vol. 2:** 576
3:1–10	**Vol. 2:** 583
3:1–9	**Vol. 1:** 499
3:2	**Vol. 3:** 1098
3:3	**Vol. 3:** 1098
3:4 f	**Vol. 1:** 618
3:4	**Vol. 1:** 618
3:6–10	**Vol. 2:** 541 **Vol. 3:** 1068
3:8	**Vol. 2:** 576
3:9	**Vol. 1:** 390
3:10	**Vol. 3:** 578
3:11 ff	**Vol. 2:** 306
3:11	**Vol. 3:** 355
3:12	**Vol. 1:** 245 **Vol. 2:** 595
3:13	**Vol. 2:** 179
3:14	**Vol. 1:** 607 **Vol. 2:** 519
3:15	**Vol. 3:** 565–566
3:16	**Vol. 2:** 128 **Vol. 3:** 788
3:17	**Vol. 1:** 492, 709 **Vol. 2:** 325–326, 612, 888 **Vol. 3:** 836
3:19	**Vol. 1:** 537, 618 **Vol. 2:** 69 **Vol. 3:** 717
3:20	**Vol. 3:** 1068
3:23	**Vol. 3:** 206
3:25	**Vol. 2:** 179

Jeremiah *(cont'd)*

4:2	**Vol. 3:** 816
4:3 f	**Vol. 2:** 326
4:3	**Vol. 3:** 522
4:4	**Vol. 1:** 109, 154, 308–309 **Vol. 2:** 184 **Vol. 3:** 109
4:5–6:30	**Vol. 3:** 1095
4:7	**Vol. 3:** 1006
4:9	**Vol. 2:** 622
4:10	**Vol. 2:** 509
4:11 f	**Vol. 3:** 695
4:11	**Vol. 2:** 34 **Vol. 3:** 836
4:13	**Vol. 3:** 859
4:14	**Vol. 3:** 820, 823
4:16	**Vol. 3:** 240
4:19–21	**Vol. 3:** 1091, 1096, 1099
4:19	**Vol. 2:** 181, 391 **Vol. 3:** 1097
4:20	**Vol. 3:** 859
4:22	**Vol. 3:** 1024, 1028
4:23–26	**Vol. 2:** 189
4:24	**Vol. 3:** 1010
4:26 f	**Vol. 3:** 1005
4:28	**Vol. 1:** 356 **Vol. 2:** 422
4:29	**Vol. 2:** 218 **Vol. 3:** 381, 383
4:30	**Vol. 1:** 522
4:31	**Vol. 3:** 178, 1068
5:1 ff	**Vol. 1:** 124
5:1	**Vol. 3:** 157
5:3	**Vol. 3:** 382, 514, 745, 777
5:4	**Vol. 3:** 937
5:5	**Vol. 3:** 592, 908, 1161–1162
5:6	**Vol. 1:** 465 **Vol. 2:** 136
5:7 ff	**Vol. 1:** 499
5:7	**Vol. 1:** 743 **Vol. 2:** 583 **Vol. 3:** 157
5:12	**Vol. 2:** 471
5:13	**Vol. 3:** 1095
5:14	**Vol. 3:** 1096
5:17	**Vol. 1:** 724 **Vol. 3:** 865
5:19	**Vol. 1:** 688
5:21	**Vol. 3:** 131, 1025
5:22	**Vol. 2:** 91
5:24	**Vol. 3:** 1001
5:26 ff	**Vol. 2:** 841
5:26	**Vol. 1:** 343
5:27	**Vol. 1:** 172 **Vol. 2:** 841
5:28	**Vol. 2:** 363, 737
5:30	**Vol. 1:** 527
5:31	**Vol. 2:** 470 **Vol. 3:** 574
6:4	**Vol. 3:** 119
6:10	**Vol. 3:** 1016
6:11	**Vol. 1:** 108, 288
6:13	**Vol. 2:** 778 **Vol. 3:** 137
6:14	**Vol. 2:** 778
6:15	**Vol. 2:** 49 **Vol. 3:** 836
6:16	**Vol. 3:** 530, 938
6:18	**Vol. 1:** 293
6:19	**Vol. 1:** 721 **Vol. 2:** 440
6:20	**Vol. 3:** 421, 427, 745
6:21	**Vol. 3:** 994
6:22 ff	**Vol. 2:** 326
6:22*	**Vol. 2:** 55, 841
6:24	**Vol. 3:** 858
6:27	**Vol. 3:** 808
6:29	**Vol. 1:** 654
7:1 ff	**Vol. 3:** 1103
7:1–15	**Vol. 3:** 78
7:1–7	**Vol. 2:** 297
7:1	**Vol. 3:** 1096
7:2	**Vol. 2:** 174
7:3 ff	**Vol. 3:** 82
7:3	**Vol. 3:** 786
7:4	**Vol. 1:** 589 **Vol. 2:** 325 **Vol. 3:** 783, 786, 788, 1096
7:5 ff	**Vol. 3:** 1096
7:5 f	**Vol. 1:** 717
7:6	**Vol. 1:** 492 **Vol. 2:** 525, 737, 862 **Vol. 3:** 1074
7:8	**Vol. 3:** 1096
7:9	**Vol. 1:** 492 **Vol. 3:** 377, 1103
7:10	**Vol. 2:** 650
7:11	**Vol. 2:** 236, 379, 610 **Vol. 3:** 377–378, 380–381, 427, 430, 788, 791
7:12 ff	**Vol. 3:** 426
7:12	**Vol. 3:** 786
7:13	**Vol. 1:** 272 **Vol. 2:** 174
7:14	**Vol. 1:** 227, 272 **Vol. 3:** 1096
7:17 f	**Vol. 3:** 427
7:18	**Vol. 1:** 586, 654 **Vol. 2:** 854 **Vol. 3:** 423, 465, 919
7:20	**Vol. 1:** 109 **Vol. 3:** 109
7:21 f	**Vol. 3:** 427
7:22	**Vol. 2:** 889 **Vol. 3:** 427
7:23 f	**Vol. 3:** 938
7:23	**Vol. 1:** 368 **Vol. 2:** 797 **Vol. 3:** 946
7:24	**Vol. 1:** 562
7:28	**Vol. 3:** 745
7:30	**Vol. 3:** 104
7:31	**Vol. 1:** 655 **Vol. 3:** 110, 418, 426
7:32	**Vol. 2:** 208, 890
7:33	**Vol. 1:** 444 **Vol. 2:** 268
7:34	**Vol. 2:** 578, 584 **Vol. 3:** 394, 1006
8:1	**Vol. 3:** 836
8:2	**Vol. 2:** 876 **Vol. 3:** 731, 735
8:3	**Vol. 1:** 534
8:4	**Vol. 1:** 609–610
8:6	**Vol. 1:** 357
8:7	**Vol. 1:** 173 **Vol. 2:** 395 **Vol. 3:** 835
8:8 f	**Vol. 3:** 1028, 1096
8:8	**Vol. 2:** 440 **Vol. 3:** 478
8:9	**Vol. 3:** 563, 1027
8:10	**Vol. 3:** 137
8:11	**Vol. 2:** 778
8:13	**Vol. 1:** 724 **Vol. 3:** 866–867
8:15	**Vol. 2:** 778
8:16	**Vol. 3:** 557
8:17	**Vol. 2:** 554
8:18–23	**Vol. 3:** 1096
8:19	**Vol. 1:** 551 **Vol. 3:** 200
8:20	**Vol. 3:** 526

Jeremiah *(cont'd)*

8:22	**Vol. 2:** 167
9:2	**Vol. 3:** 1079
9:4	**Vol. 2:** 431 **Vol. 3:** 881
9:5	**Vol. 3:** 881
9:6*	**Vol. 3:** 808
9:7	**Vol. 3:** 1079
9:10 f	**Vol. 3:** 1008
9:10	**Vol. 2:** 249, 418
9:13 – 16	**Vol. 2:** 285
9:13*	**Vol. 3:** 760
9:14*	**Vol. 2:** 663
9:15*	**Vol. 1:** 202 **Vol. 2:** 27, 29
9:16 – 21	**Vol. 2:** 418
9:16*	**Vol. 3:** 1028
9:18	**Vol. 1:** 683 **Vol. 2:** 418
9:19*	**Vol. 3:** 760
9:20*	**Vol. 2:** 174 **Vol. 3:** 745
9:22*	**Vol. 2:** 32, 841 **Vol. 3:** 1027 – 1028
9:23 f	**Vol. 1:** 227
9:23	**Vol. 3:** 130, 1019
9:24	**Vol. 1:** 228 **Vol. 2:** 890 **Vol. 3:** 130, 357
9:25	**Vol. 1:** 308
10:1	**Vol. 2:** 305
10:2	**Vol. 2:** 189, 555 **Vol. 3:** 735
10:6	**Vol. 2:** 498
10:7	**Vol. 2:** 375, 791
10:10 – 15	**Vol. 2:** 285
10:10	**Vol. 3:** 892
10:11	**Vol. 1:** 51
10:12	**Vol. 2:** 616 **Vol. 3:** 1027
10:13	**Vol. 3:** 1001
10:14	**Vol. 3:** 690, 1025
10:15	**Vol. 1:** 551 **Vol. 3:** 836
10:16	**Vol. 1:** 522 **Vol. 2:** 297, 650
10:17	**Vol. 1:** 711
10:19	**Vol. 3:** 857, 1051
10:20	**Vol. 3:** 859
10:21	**Vol. 2:** 104 **Vol. 3:** 125, 531, 565 – 566
10:22	**Vol. 2:** 173, 586 **Vol. 3:** 557
10:24	**Vol. 3:** 777
10:25	**Vol. 1:** 272
11:1 ff	**Vol. 3:** 1095
11:3 ff	**Vol. 2:** 797
11:4	**Vol. 1:** 368 **Vol. 2:** 797, 889
11:5	**Vol. 1:** 98, 683
11:6	**Vol. 1:** 245
11:7	**Vol. 2:** 889
11:12	**Vol. 3:** 206
11:13	**Vol. 3:** 418
11:14	**Vol. 2:** 860, 862 – 863
11:16	**Vol. 2:** 711
11:19	**Vol. 3:** 237, 823
11:20	**Vol. 2:** 181, 183 **Vol. 3:** 357, 808
11:21	**Vol. 3:** 531
11:23	**Vol. 1:** 190
12:1 – 5	**Vol. 3:** 342
12:2	**Vol. 2:** 468
12:3	**Vol. 3:** 808
12:5	**Vol. 2:** 746
12:6	**Vol. 3:** 1212
12:8	**Vol. 1:** 555
12:9	**Vol. 1:** 113
12:12	**Vol. 1:** 518 **Vol. 2:** 778
12:14 ff	**Vol. 2:** 252
12:15 ff	**Vol. 2:** 252
12:16	**Vol. 3:** 760
13:1 ff	**Vol. 3:** 121
13:1 – 11	**Vol. 2:** 754 **Vol. 3:** 1099
13:9	**Vol. 3:** 29 – 30
13:10	**Vol. 1:** 272 **Vol. 2:** 876
13:11	**Vol. 2:** 349
13:14	**Vol. 1:** 685 **Vol. 2:** 34
13:17	**Vol. 3:** 29, 565
13:19	**Vol. 1:** 357 **Vol. 2:** 60, 778 **Vol. 3:** 1099
13:21	**Vol. 1:** 485 **Vol. 3:** 760, 1068
13:22	**Vol. 2:** 212, 583
13:23	**Vol. 1:** 184
13:26	**Vol. 2:** 583
14 ff	**Vol. 2:** 307
14	**Vol. 1:** 210
14:1 – 15:4	**Vol. 3:** 1096
14:2 – 12	**Vol. 3:** 235
14:3	**Vol. 1:** 546
14:5†	**Vol. 1:** 520 **Vol. 2:** 211
14:7	**Vol. 3:** 1096
14:8	**Vol. 2:** 239, 772 – 773 **Vol. 3:** 207, 836
14:9	**Vol. 1:** 272 **Vol. 3:** 206, 1096
14:10	**Vol. 3:** 1096
14:11 – 12	**Vol. 1:** 612
14:11	**Vol. 2:** 862 **Vol. 3:** 1097
14:12	**Vol. 1:** 612 **Vol. 2:** 817, 864
14:13	**Vol. 2:** 777 – 778
14:14 f	**Vol. 2:** 651
14:14	**Vol. 2:** 181, 554
14:19 – 22	**Vol. 3:** 1096
14:19	**Vol. 1:** 538 **Vol. 2:** 326, 773, 778 **Vol. 3:** 836
14:21	**Vol. 2:** 612 **Vol. 3:** 234 – 235
14:22	**Vol. 2:** 285, 773
15:1 – 4	**Vol. 3:** 1096
15:1	**Vol. 2:** 636, 639 **Vol. 3:** 1097
15:2	**Vol. 3:** 590 – 591
15:3	**Vol. 1:** 113 **Vol. 2:** 268
15:4	**Vol. 2:** 663
15:5 – 9	**Vol. 3:** 1068
15:7	**Vol. 1:** 685 **Vol. 2:** 34
15:9	**Vol. 3:** 680, 731, 1068
15:10	**Vol. 3:** 721
15:11	**Vol. 2:** 509 **Vol. 3:** 836
15:13	**Vol. 3:** 166
15:15 – 18	**Vol. 3:** 235
15:15	**Vol. 2:** 769, 806 **Vol. 3:** 134
15:16 – 21	**Vol. 3:** 342
15:16	**Vol. 2:** 355, 357, 830 **Vol. 3:** 1097 – 1098
15:17	**Vol. 2:** 724 **Vol. 3:** 1097

Jeremiah *(cont'd)*

15:19	**Vol. 3:** 81
15:20	**Vol. 3:** 207
15:21	**Vol. 3:** 192
16:1–9	**Vol. 3:** 1097
16:2	**Vol. 3:** 79
16:5–7	**Vol. 2:** 417
16:5 f	**Vol. 2:** 417
16:5	**Vol. 2:** 777–778 **Vol. 3:** 79
16:6	**Vol. 2:** 573
16:8	**Vol. 3:** 79
16:9	**Vol. 2:** 578, 584 **Vol. 3:** 394
16:11	**Vol. 2:** 876, 890
16:12	**Vol. 1:** 492
16:15	**Vol. 3:** 147
16:17	**Vol. 3:** 574, 938
16:19 ff	**Vol. 2:** 888
16:19	**Vol. 1:** 320
16:21	**Vol. 3:** 316
17:1–4	**Vol. 1:** 686
17:3	**Vol. 3:** 426
17:5	**Vol. 1:** 607, 673, 679
17:6	**Vol. 3:** 444
17:7	**Vol. 3:** 866
17:8	**Vol. 1:** 652 **Vol. 3:** 866
17:9 f	**Vol. 2:** 183
17:9	**Vol. 2:** 183
17:10	**Vol. 1:** 721 **Vol. 2:** 181 **Vol. 3:** 648, 808
17:11	**Vol. 2:** 841 **Vol. 3:** 1024–1025
17:12	**Vol. 1:** 668
17:13	**Vol. 1:** 607 **Vol. 2:** 239, 478–479, 754, 772–773
17:14	**Vol. 3:** 207
17:15	**Vol. 3:** 1097
17:16 ff	**Vol. 2:** 890
17:22	**Vol. 2:** 890
17:24	**Vol. 2:** 890
17:26	**Vol. 3:** 423, 1009
17:27	**Vol. 2:** 890 **Vol. 3:** 94, 109
18	**Vol. 1:** 93
18:1–12	**Vol. 3:** 916
18:1–6	**Vol. 2:** 747
18:2	**Vol. 3:** 911–912
18:3	**Vol. 3:** 911
18:6	**Vol. 2:** 609 **Vol. 3:** 911–912, 915–916
18:8	**Vol. 1:** 354, 357 **Vol. 3:** 823
18:11	**Vol. 3:** 823
18:13	**Vol. 3:** 1071
18:15	**Vol. 1:** 546 **Vol. 3:** 994
18:18	**Vol. 3:** 721, 823
18:20	**Vol. 3:** 98, 235
18:22	**Vol. 3:** 377
18:23	**Vol. 3:** 152, 154, 836, 994
19	**Vol. 1:** 93 **Vol. 2:** 754
19:1 ff	**Vol. 2:** 626
19:1–20:6	**Vol. 3:** 1097
19:1	**Vol. 3:** 914
19:2	**Vol. 3:** 912
19:3	**Vol. 3:** 786
19:5	**Vol. 2:** 199 **Vol. 3:** 421
19:6 f	**Vol. 2:** 208
19:6	**Vol. 2:** 890
19:7	**Vol. 1:** 444 **Vol. 2:** 268
19:11	**Vol. 3:** 249, 914
19:13	**Vol. 2:** 854 **Vol. 3:** 423, 465, 919
20:7–10	**Vol. 3:** 342
20:7–9	**Vol. 3:** 1097
20:7	**Vol. 2:** 431 **Vol. 3:** 341, 716
20:8 ff	**Vol. 3:** 235
20:8	**Vol. 2:** 431 **Vol. 3:** 1097
20:9	**Vol. 3:** 1054
20:9a	**Vol. 3:** 1097
20:10	**Vol. 2:** 132, 777
20:11	**Vol. 1:** 485 **Vol. 2:** 806
20:12	**Vol. 2:** 181 **Vol. 3:** 808
20:13	**Vol. 3:** 673, 816
20:14 ff	**Vol. 2:** 478 **Vol. 3:** 721
20:15	**Vol. 2:** 109, 569
21:8	**Vol. 1:** 434 **Vol. 2:** 479, 481 **Vol. 3:** 929, 940
21:8b	**Vol. 3:** 926
21:12	**Vol. 3:** 109
22:3	**Vol. 2:** 737 **Vol. 3:** 1073–1074
22:6	**Vol. 1:** 165
22:7	**Vol. 1:** 465
22:9	**Vol. 2:** 876
22:10	**Vol. 2:** 416
22:13	**Vol. 2:** 41, 139
22:14	**Vol. 2:** 334
22:15 f	**Vol. 2:** 396
22:17	**Vol. 1:** 137 **Vol. 3:** 137
22:18	**Vol. 2:** 418
22:22	**Vol. 3:** 566
22:24–30	**Vol. 3:** 655
22:28 f	**Vol. 1:** 505
22:28	**Vol. 3:** 957
23:1 ff	**Vol. 2:** 412
23:1 f	**Vol. 2:** 104
23:1–5	**Vol. 3:** 566
23:2	**Vol. 3:** 565
23:3	**Vol. 2:** 128 **Vol. 3:** 745
23:4	**Vol. 3:** 566
23:5 ff	**Vol. 2:** 337
23:5 f	**Vol. 2:** 374
23:5	**Vol. 2:** 591, 890 **Vol. 3:** 649–650, 867
23:6	**Vol. 2:** 591
23:7	**Vol. 2:** 890
23:8	**Vol. 3:** 147
23:9–40	**Vol. 3:** 1097
23:9	**Vol. 1:** 527
23:10	**Vol. 2:** 422
23:11	**Vol. 1:** 449
23:12	**Vol. 1:** 190
23:14	**Vol. 3:** 93
23:15	**Vol. 1:** 201–202, 449 **Vol. 2:** 27, 29, 468
23:16 ff	**Vol. 1:** 550–551 **Vol. 3:** 1097
23:16 f	**Vol. 1:** 527

Jeremiah *(cont'd)*

23:17	**Vol. 2:** 778
23:18	**Vol. 3:** 1097
23:19	**Vol. 3:** 557
23:20	**Vol. 2:** 56
23:22	**Vol. 1:** 712 **Vol. 3:** 1097
23:23	**Vol. 2:** 53
23:24	**Vol. 1:** 735 **Vol. 2:** 214–215 **Vol. 3:** 465
23:25	**Vol. 2:** 651
23:26	**Vol. 3:** 1019
23:27	**Vol. 3:** 823
23:28	**Vol. 3:** 1097
23:29	**Vol. 1:** 655 **Vol. 3:** 382, 1097
23:30	**Vol. 3:** 377
23:32	**Vol. 1:** 512 **Vol. 2:** 458
23:34	**Vol. 2:** 796
23:40	**Vol. 2:** 49
24	**Vol. 1:** 724
24:1 f	**Vol. 3:** 866
24:1	**Vol. 2:** 841 **Vol. 3:** 786
24:2 f	**Vol. 2:** 105
24:5	**Vol. 2:** 105
24:6	**Vol. 2:** 252 **Vol. 3:** 147
24:7	**Vol. 1:** 184, 354 **Vol. 2:** 797
24:8	**Vol. 3:** 249
24:9	**Vol. 1:** 416
25:3 ff	**Vol. 3:** 1104
25:5	**Vol. 3:** 938
25:6	**Vol. 2:** 876
25:9	**Vol. 1:** 141 **Vol. 3:** 608
25:10	**Vol. 2:** 485, 578 **Vol. 3:** 394
25:11	**Vol. 2:** 696
25:12	**Vol. 1:** 734
25:14	**Vol. 3:** 134
25:15 ff	**Vol. 1:** 109 **Vol. 2:** 275–276
25:15–28	**Vol. 1:** 106
25:15 f	**Vol. 3:** 922
25:15	**Vol. 1:** 111 **Vol. 3:** 208
25:16	**Vol. 1:** 529
25:27 f	**Vol. 3:** 922
25:28	**Vol. 3:** 745
25:29*	**Vol. 1:** 273 **Vol. 2:** 650
25:30*	**Vol. 3:** 324
25:34 ff	**Vol. 3:** 566
25:34	**Vol. 3:** 566
25:36	**Vol. 1:** 465
25:37 f	**Vol. 1:** 109
25:37	**Vol. 2:** 778
25:38*	**Vol. 3:** 794
26	**Vol. 2:** 363 **Vol. 3:** 1096
26:1 ff	**Vol. 3:** 82
26:1	**Vol. 3:** 1096
26:2 ff	**Vol. 3:** 1104
26:2*	**Vol. 2:** 876 **Vol. 3:** 324
26:3*	**Vol. 3:** 823–824
26:6	**Vol. 1:** 416 **Vol. 3:** 426
26:8 f	**Vol. 3:** 94
26:9	**Vol. 1:** 485 **Vol. 3:** 426
26:16*	**Vol. 2:** 124
26:17	**Vol. 1:** 196
26:19	**Vol. 1:** 699 **Vol. 2:** 860
26:21*	**Vol. 3:** 836
26:23*	**Vol. 3:** 238–239
27:1 ff	**Vol. 2:** 626
27:2–11	**Vol. 3:** 1161
27:4*	**Vol. 3:** 836
27:5*	**Vol. 3:** 821
27:6 f	**Vol. 1:** 141 **Vol. 2:** 148
27:8*	**Vol. 3:** 1161
27:9 f	**Vol. 2:** 555
27:9	**Vol. 1:** 512 **Vol. 2:** 554
27:11*	**Vol. 3:** 1161
27:16*	**Vol. 2:** 124
27:20*	**Vol. 3:** 836
27:22	**Vol. 2:** 890
27:27*	**Vol. 3:** 836
27:29*	**Vol. 1:** 340
28 f	**Vol. 3:** 1099
28:2 ff	**Vol. 3:** 79, 1097
28:2–11	**Vol. 3:** 1161
28:2*	**Vol. 3:** 1161
28:4*	**Vol. 3:** 1161
28:6*	**Vol. 1:** 98 **Vol. 3:** 836
28:9	**Vol. 2:** 778, 891 **Vol. 3:** 1098
28:11*	**Vol. 3:** 1098, 1161
28:12 ff	**Vol. 3:** 1098
28:12	**Vol. 3:** 1098
28:13–17	**Vol. 3:** 1161
28:14*	**Vol. 3:** 1161
28:15	**Vol. 3:** 117
28:27*	**Vol. 1:** 340
28:36*	**Vol. 1:** 515
29:1 ff	**Vol. 2:** 240
29:1	**Vol. 1:** 196
29:3*	**Vol. 3:** 557
29:4–23	**Vol. 1:** 246
29:8*	**Vol. 3:** 842
29:9	**Vol. 2:** 651
29:11*	**Vol. 1:** 562 **Vol. 2:** 240, 777–778 **Vol. 3:** 528–529, 823–824
29:11c	**Vol. 1:** 562
29:12 ff	**Vol. 2:** 864
29:12*	**Vol. 2:** 862–863 **Vol. 3:** 528
29:13 f	**Vol. 3:** 531
29:13*	**Vol. 2:** 881 **Vol. 3:** 528
29:14*	**Vol. 3:** 318
29:17	**Vol. 1:** 724
29:23*	**Vol. 2:** 803 **Vol. 3:** 324
29:26*	**Vol. 1:** 529
29:27*	**Vol. 3:** 346
30 f	**Vol. 2:** 307
30–32	**Vol. 3:** 1095
30:2*	**Vol. 3:** 324
30:3	**Vol. 2:** 890
30:8*	**Vol. 3:** 1161
30:9	**Vol. 3:** 649
30:12 f	**Vol. 3:** 997
30:19*	**Vol. 2:** 131 **Vol. 3:** 673

Jeremiah *(cont'd)*

30:22	**Vol. 1:** 368 **Vol. 2:** 797
30:23 f	**Vol. 1:** 108
30:24	**Vol. 2:** 56
31	**Vol. 3:** 576, 578
31:2*	**Vol. 3:** 1005
31:3	**Vol. 2:** 541
31:4 f	**Vol. 3:** 673
31:4	**Vol. 2:** 252, 541 **Vol. 3:** 1071
31:5*	**Vol. 3:** 816
31:6*	**Vol. 1:** 272 **Vol. 2:** 326
31:7	**Vol. 3:** 208, 673
31:8*	**Vol. 1:** 218, 292, 297 **Vol. 2:** 800
31:9	**Vol. 1:** 617 **Vol. 2:** 71 **Vol. 3:** 636
31:10*	**Vol. 2:** 32 **Vol. 3:** 565
31:11*	**Vol. 3:** 192
31:12	**Vol. 2:** 266, 711 **Vol. 3:** 919
31:15–20	**Vol. 3:** 235
31:15	**Vol. 1:** 170, 737 **Vol. 2:** 417, 715
31:16	**Vol. 2:** 139
31:17	**Vol. 2:** 240
31:18*	**Vol. 1:** 184, 354 **Vol. 3:** 760
31:19	**Vol. 1:** 356 **Vol. 2:** 418
31:20*	**Vol. 1:** 617 **Vol. 3:** 238
31:21	**Vol. 3:** 1071
31:22	**Vol. 1:** 380
31:26*	**Vol. 2:** 431
31:27	**Vol. 2:** 890 **Vol. 3:** 522
31:29 ff	**Vol. 1:** 434
31:31 ff*	**Vol. 1:** 354 **Vol. 2:** 78, 248, 364, 525–526, 533, 536, 661, 670–671 **Vol. 3:** 167, 327, 765
31:31–35	**Vol. 2:** 716
31:31–34	**Vol. 1:** 224, 248, 366, 368–369, 371 **Vol. 2:** 145, 240, 306, 320, 533, 671, 786, 854 **Vol. 3:** 69, 74, 160, 702
31:31–33	**Vol. 2:** 797 **Vol. 3:** 493
31:31	**Vol. 1:** 367 **Vol. 2:** 890
31:32	**Vol. 2:** 889 **Vol. 3:** 227, 747
31:33 f	**Vol. 2:** 127, 155 **Vol. 3:** 74, 701
31:33	**Vol. 1:** 184, 368 **Vol. 2:** 42, 177, 872, 923 **Vol. 3:** 127, 484, 490
31:34*	**Vol. 1:** 701 **Vol. 2:** 448, 596, 803–804 **Vol. 3:** 157, 203, 235, 241, 575, 760
31:34b	**Vol. 2:** 526, 533, 536
31:35*	**Vol. 2:** 491 **Vol. 3:** 733
31:36*	**Vol. 2:** 441
31:38 ff	**Vol. 2:** 325
31:38	**Vol. 2:** 803, 890
31:39	**Vol. 2:** 431
32:4*	**Vol. 2:** 367 **Vol. 3:** 209, 772
32:6 ff	**Vol. 2:** 240, 626
32:7 ff	**Vol. 2:** 754
32:7–9	**Vol. 1:** 93
32:7	**Vol. 3:** 190
32:8	**Vol. 3:** 190
32:10 ff	**Vol. 3:** 484
32:10–12	**Vol. 3:** 478
32:10*	**Vol. 3:** 1041, 1160
32:12 f	**Vol. 1:** 485
32:14	**Vol. 3:** 914
32:15*	**Vol. 1:** 380
32:16*	**Vol. 2:** 862
32:19	**Vol. 3:** 938
32:20 f	**Vol. 2:** 627
32:25*	**Vol. 3:** 1041
32:29*	**Vol. 1:** 203 **Vol. 3:** 423
32:31*	**Vol. 3:** 166
32:33*	**Vol. 3:** 760
32:35*	**Vol. 2:** 208 **Vol. 3:** 110, 418, 421
32:38–40	**Vol. 2:** 797
32:38	**Vol. 1:** 368 **Vol. 2:** 797 **Vol. 3:** 813
32:40	**Vol. 2:** 181
32:41	**Vol. 2:** 100
33:6	**Vol. 2:** 778
33:7	**Vol. 2:** 252
33:8	**Vol. 1:** 606, 701 **Vol. 3:** 105
33:9*	**Vol. 2:** 425, 778
33:10–12*	**Vol. 3:** 1006
33:11	**Vol. 3:** 423
33:12*	**Vol. 3:** 794
33:14	**Vol. 2:** 890
33:15 f	**Vol. 2:** 591
33:15	**Vol. 3:** 649–650, 867
33:21	**Vol. 1:** 366
33:24	**Vol. 1:** 262 **Vol. 3:** 513
33:25	**Vol. 1:** 366
34:1*	**Vol. 1:** 165
34:2*	**Vol. 3:** 772
34:3*	**Vol. 1:** 127
34:5*	**Vol. 2:** 418, 602
34:8 ff	**Vol. 1:** 366, 716 **Vol. 3:** 608
34:8–11	**Vol. 2:** 841
34:8	**Vol. 1:** 698
34:9	**Vol. 2:** 306
34:11	**Vol. 1:** 716
34:13	**Vol. 2:** 889
34:14–22	**Vol. 3:** 191
34:14	**Vol. 2:** 306
34:15	**Vol. 1:** 698
34:17*	**Vol. 1:** 272, 685, 698, 716
34:18 ff	**Vol. 3:** 425
34:18	**Vol. 1:** 368
34:22	**Vol. 2:** 215
35	**Vol. 3:** 565
35:6 f	**Vol. 3:** 919
35:6–10	**Vol. 3:** 811
35:7	**Vol. 3:** 1005
35:9 f	**Vol. 3:** 1005
36	**Vol. 3:** 1097
36:2 f	**Vol. 3:** 1104
36:2*	**Vol. 1:** 716
36:3*	**Vol. 3:** 157, 823–824
36:4	**Vol. 3:** 478, 484
36:5 ff	**Vol. 1:** 245
36:7	**Vol. 1:** 109
36:11	**Vol. 3:** 478
36:12	**Vol. 3:** 478

Jeremiah *(cont'd)*

36:18	**Vol. 3:** 478
36:19	**Vol. 3:** 962
36:23*	**Vol. 3:** 1041, 1097
36:26	**Vol. 3:** 962
36:32	**Vol. 3:** 478, 1097
37:3*	**Vol. 2:** 862
37:5	**Vol. 1:** 531
37:6*	**Vol. 2:** 569
37:7 ff	**Vol. 2:** 306
37:7	**Vol. 1:** 531
37:10	**Vol. 3:** 811–812
37:15 f	**Vol. 2:** 96
37:15	**Vol. 3:** 478
38:1*	**Vol. 2:** 800
38:7	**Vol. 3:** 816
38:9	**Vol. 3:** 351
38:28*	**Vol. 2:** 136
39:10 f*	**Vol. 3:** 498
39:13	**Vol. 3:** 115
39:17*	**Vol. 2:** 602
39:18*	**Vol. 1:** 596 **Vol. 2:** 698 **Vol. 3:** 115
39:24*	**Vol. 1:** 343
39:44*	**Vol. 3:** 498
40:4*	**Vol. 3:** 177, 951
40:8	**Vol. 3:** 232
40:10	**Vol. 2:** 711
40:11–15	**Vol. 3:** 249
40:11*	**Vol. 2:** 105
41:1 f	**Vol. 2:** 521
41:1	**Vol. 3:** 115
41:5	**Vol. 2:** 325, 573 **Vol. 3:** 426, 788
41:8	**Vol. 2:** 711
41:17	**Vol. 1:** 531
42–44	**Vol. 1:** 531
42:2*	**Vol. 2:** 862
42:4*	**Vol. 2:** 862
42:5*	**Vol. 3:** 1041
42:10*	**Vol. 3:** 255
42:18	**Vol. 1:** 109
42:20*	**Vol. 2:** 862
43:7	**Vol. 2:** 613
43:30*	**Vol. 1:** 652
44:3 f	**Vol. 1:** 555
44:3*	**Vol. 1:** 203
44:7	**Vol. 1:** 288
44:8*	**Vol. 1:** 203
44:15–19	**Vol. 2:** 285
44:15	**Vol. 1:** 293
44:17–25	**Vol. 3:** 423
44:23*	**Vol. 2:** 441
44:25*	**Vol. 1:** 344 **Vol. 3:** 226
44:28*	**Vol. 1:** 531 **Vol. 3:** 226
45:3*	**Vol. 3:** 255
45:28*	**Vol. 3:** 841
46–51	**Vol. 3:** 960
46	**Vol. 1:** 531
46:1	**Vol. 3:** 1095
46:6	**Vol. 3:** 209

46:9*	**Vol. 3:** 119
46:10	**Vol. 2:** 363
46:10b	**Vol. 3:** 160
46:18	**Vol. 2:** 375
46:21*	**Vol. 1:** 688 **Vol. 2:** 139, 890 **Vol. 3:** 908
46:27*	**Vol. 3:** 111, 208
46:28	**Vol. 3:** 777
47:1	**Vol. 3:** 1095
47:4	**Vol. 2:** 890
47:5	**Vol. 2:** 573
47:6*	**Vol. 3:** 255
48:2*	**Vol. 3:** 823
48:6	**Vol. 3:** 209
48:8	**Vol. 3:** 209
48:11*	**Vol. 3:** 255, 600
48:12	**Vol. 2:** 890 **Vol. 3:** 911
48:15	**Vol. 2:** 375
48:19	**Vol. 3:** 209
48:29*	**Vol. 3:** 29
48:32	**Vol. 3:** 866
48:33	**Vol. 3:** 673
48:35*	**Vol. 3:** 418
48:37	**Vol. 2:** 573
48:38	**Vol. 3:** 957
48:39*	**Vol. 3:** 166
48:42*	**Vol. 2:** 800
48:44	**Vol. 1:** 609
49:2	**Vol. 2:** 890
49:7*	**Vol. 3:** 1027
49:9	**Vol. 1:** 420
49:11	**Vol. 3:** 1073
49:16	**Vol. 1:** 173
49:18	**Vol. 3:** 93, 560
49:19	**Vol. 2:** 498
49:20*	**Vol. 3:** 823–824
49:22	**Vol. 1:** 173
49:23*	**Vol. 3:** 255
49:30*	**Vol. 3:** 823
49:34	**Vol. 2:** 376 **Vol. 3:** 1095
49:36	**Vol. 2:** 189, 689 **Vol. 3:** 389
49:39	**Vol. 2:** 56
50	**Vol. 1:** 141
50:5	**Vol. 1:** 366
50:6*	**Vol. 2:** 586 **Vol. 3:** 454, 566
50:12	**Vol. 3:** 1069
50:13	**Vol. 1:** 109
50:19	**Vol. 3:** 565
50:20*	**Vol. 3:** 157
50:21	**Vol. 1:** 414
50:25*	**Vol. 2:** 830
50:26	**Vol. 1:** 414
50:27	**Vol. 3:** 835
50:28	**Vol. 3:** 786
50:29	**Vol. 3:** 134
50:30	**Vol. 3:** 835
50:32*	**Vol. 3:** 29
50:34*	**Vol. 3:** 192
50:35	**Vol. 3:** 1028
50:40	**Vol. 3:** 93, 560

Jeremiah *(cont'd)*

50:42*	**Vol. 3:** 119
50:45*	**Vol. 3:** 820, 823–824
50:46*	**Vol. 3:** 557
51	**Vol. 1:** 141
51:2*	**Vol. 3:** 29
51:6	**Vol. 3:** 209
51:7	**Vol. 1:** 111
51:8	**Vol. 1:** 120, 610
51:9*	**Vol. 2:** 349
51:10	**Vol. 2:** 363
51:11*	**Vol. 3:** 119, 786
51:13	**Vol. 3:** 137
51:15*	**Vol. 3:** 1027
51:17*	**Vol. 3:** 1025
51:18	**Vol. 1:** 551
51:19	**Vol. 2:** 297
51:20*	**Vol. 3:** 823
51:23*	**Vol. 2:** 34
51:25	**Vol. 3:** 1010, 1013
51:26	**Vol. 1:** 661
51:33	**Vol. 3:** 526
51:34 f	**Vol. 1:** 673
51:35 f	**Vol. 1:** 221
51:36*	**Vol. 3:** 1005
51:39	**Vol. 1:** 442
51:42	**Vol. 3:** 983
51:45	**Vol. 2:** 800 **Vol. 3:** 209
51:47	**Vol. 2:** 890
51:48	**Vol. 2:** 356
51:52	**Vol. 2:** 423, 890
51:57*	**Vol. 2:** 375 **Vol. 3:** 1028
51:60–63	**Vol. 3:** 394
52	**Vol. 1:** 61 **Vol. 3:** 1087
52:16	**Vol. 3:** 918
52:25	**Vol. 3:** 478

Lamentations

1:3	**Vol. 3:** 255
1:5	**Vol. 1:** 281
1:5b	**Vol. 2:** 261
1:6	**Vol. 3:** 255
1:7	**Vol. 2:** 430, 890
1:8	**Vol. 2:** 423
1:8b	**Vol. 2:** 261
1:10	**Vol. 3:** 786
1:12	**Vol. 2:** 888–889
1:12c	**Vol. 2:** 261
1:13	**Vol. 2:** 199
1:14	**Vol. 2:** 136
1:15	**Vol. 3:** 1071
1:16	**Vol. 2:** 416
1:18	**Vol. 3:** 357, 1071
1:20	**Vol. 2:** 261, 888
1:21	**Vol. 2:** 423
2:1	**Vol. 2:** 888–889
2:5c	**Vol. 2:** 261
2:7	**Vol. 3:** 560, 948
2:8	**Vol. 2:** 422 **Vol. 3:** 402, 908

2:10	**Vol. 1:** 520
2:11	**Vol. 1:** 230
2:12	**Vol. 3:** 178, 680
2:13	**Vol. 3:** 1071
2:14	**Vol. 1:** 550 **Vol. 3:** 1024
2:16	**Vol. 2:** 421
2:18	**Vol. 2:** 261
2:19	**Vol. 3:** 178
2:20	**Vol. 2:** 261 **Vol. 3:** 786
2:21 f	**Vol. 2:** 888–889
3:4	**Vol. 2:** 190
3:8	**Vol. 2:** 863
3:9	**Vol. 3:** 951
3:10 f	**Vol. 3:** 342
3:10	**Vol. 2:** 214–215
3:11	**Vol. 3:** 255
3:13	**Vol. 2:** 27
3:14	**Vol. 2:** 431
3:15	**Vol. 1:** 202, 743 **Vol. 2:** 27, 29
3:17	**Vol. 2:** 777
3:19	**Vol. 1:** 202 **Vol. 2:** 29
3:20	**Vol. 3:** 680
3:21	**Vol. 2:** 773
3:24	**Vol. 2:** 297, 773
3:25	**Vol. 2:** 773
3:26	**Vol. 2:** 773
3:27	**Vol. 3:** 1161
3:29	**Vol. 1:** 743
3:31	**Vol. 2:** 261
3:32–34	**Vol. 2:** 261
3:34 ff	**Vol. 3:** 514
3:36	**Vol. 2:** 370
3:37 f	**Vol. 2:** 261
3:40	**Vol. 3:** 533
3:42 f	**Vol. 1:** 109
3:42	**Vol. 3:** 155
3:44	**Vol. 2:** 863
3:56	**Vol. 2:** 215
3:57	**Vol. 2:** 889
3:58	**Vol. 3:** 192
3:60 f	**Vol. 3:** 820
4:2	**Vol. 3:** 823, 914
4:3	**Vol. 1:** 240
4:4	**Vol. 2:** 349
4:6	**Vol. 3:** 93
4:11	**Vol. 1:** 661
4:12	**Vol. 1:** 519
4:14	**Vol. 1:** 218
4:16	**Vol. 1:** 109
4:18	**Vol. 2:** 898
4:19	**Vol. 1:** 173
4:20	**Vol. 2:** 336
4:21	**Vol. 2:** 357
5:1	**Vol. 3:** 234
5:2	**Vol. 1:** 688
5:5	**Vol. 3:** 254
5:8	**Vol. 3:** 192
5:13	**Vol. 1:** 393–394
5:14	**Vol. 3:** 255
5:21	**Vol. 1:** 354

Ezekiel

1 f	**Vol. 2:** 191
1	**Vol. 2:** 615 **Vol. 3:** 398, 618, 1089
1:1 f	**Vol. 3:** 502, 590
1:1–3:15	**Vol. 3:** 1100
1:1	**Vol. 3:** 311, 514, 986
1:3	**Vol. 3:** 986
1:4 ff	**Vol. 2:** 688
1:4–28	**Vol. 2:** 613
1:4	**Vol. 2:** 97, 501
1:5 ff	**Vol. 1:** 280
1:5–22	**Vol. 2:** 689
1:5–12	**Vol. 1:** 101
1:5	**Vol. 2:** 501
1:7	**Vol. 2:** 45
1:10	**Vol. 1:** 116, 173, 585
1:11	**Vol. 1:** 233 **Vol. 3:** 1162
1:13	**Vol. 2:** 45, 485
1:15 ff	**Vol. 2:** 688
1:16	**Vol. 2:** 501
1:20 f	**Vol. 2:** 479
1:22 f	**Vol. 1:** 523
1:22	**Vol. 2:** 501, 613
1:23	**Vol. 1:** 233 **Vol. 3:** 1162
1:24	**Vol. 3:** 255, 729, 990
1:26–28	**Vol. 3:** 398
1:26	**Vol. 2:** 501
1:27	**Vol. 1:** 655–656 **Vol. 2:** 97
1:28	**Vol. 1:** 610 **Vol. 3:** 514
2:1 ff	**Vol. 1:** 273
2:1*	**Vol. 2:** 501
2:2	**Vol. 3:** 691
2:4	**Vol. 3:** 1098
2:5	**Vol. 3:** 1100
2:6	**Vol. 1:** 510
2:8 ff	**Vol. 1:** 243
2:8	**Vol. 2:** 726
2:9–3:3	**Vol. 3:** 1098
2:9 f	**Vol. 1:** 244 **Vol. 3:** 500
2:10	**Vol. 3:** 1098
3:1 ff	**Vol. 2:** 273
3:1	**Vol. 3:** 1098
3:3	**Vol. 1:** 169
3:4	**Vol. 3:** 1099
3:7	**Vol. 2:** 174
3:9	**Vol. 1:** 203 **Vol. 3:** 382
3:12 f	**Vol. 3:** 557
3:12	**Vol. 3:** 691
3:14	**Vol. 1:** 108
3:15 ff	**Vol. 3:** 986
3:15	**Vol. 3:** 986
3:17 ff	**Vol. 1:** 222
3:18 ff	**Vol. 2:** 479
3:20	**Vol. 3:** 585–586, 856
3:23	**Vol. 3:** 986
3:25–5:4	**Vol. 3:** 1099
3:26	**Vol. 2:** 141
4–5	**Vol. 2:** 626
4:1–5:4	**Vol. 3:** 1099
4:1	**Vol. 2:** 573
4:2	**Vol. 3:** 951
4:4–8	**Vol. 3:** 1099
4:5 f	**Vol. 3:** 804
4:8	**Vol. 2:** 124
4:11	**Vol. 3:** 402
4:16	**Vol. 3:** 402
5	**Vol. 3:** 960
5:2	**Vol. 2:** 34, 687
5:5	**Vol. 2:** 529
5:6 f	**Vol. 3:** 354
5:10	**Vol. 2:** 34
5:11	**Vol. 1:** 74 **Vol. 3:** 786
5:12	**Vol. 2:** 687
5:14	**Vol. 3:** 1005
5:15 f	**Vol. 2:** 265
5:17	**Vol. 1:** 113
6:3	**Vol. 2:** 199 **Vol. 3:** 426
6:4 ff	**Vol. 2:** 284–285
6:5	**Vol. 1:** 610 **Vol. 2:** 34
6:6	**Vol. 3:** 426
6:7	**Vol. 2:** 395
6:9	**Vol. 3:** 236
6:10	**Vol. 2:** 41 **Vol. 3:** 236
6:11 ff	**Vol. 1:** 109
6:11	**Vol. 2:** 149
6:12	**Vol. 2:** 53
6:13	**Vol. 2:** 284–285, 395 **Vol. 3:** 865
6:14	**Vol. 1:** 465 **Vol. 2:** 395
7:3	**Vol. 1:** 110
7:4	**Vol. 2:** 395
7:7	**Vol. 2:** 53, 888 **Vol. 3:** 836
7:8	**Vol. 2:** 854
7:10	**Vol. 1:** 320 **Vol. 3:** 29–30
7:12	**Vol. 1:** 320 **Vol. 3:** 836
7:13	**Vol. 3:** 601
7:17	**Vol. 3:** 178
7:18	**Vol. 2:** 157, 212, 621
7:19	**Vol. 1:** 110 **Vol. 3:** 856
7:20	**Vol. 2:** 287 **Vol. 3:** 29–30
7:23	**Vol. 2:** 803
7:26	**Vol. 2:** 440
7:27†	**Vol. 1:** 165, 314
8	**Vol. 1:** 74 **Vol. 2:** 285 **Vol. 3:** 427
8:1 ff	**Vol. 1:** 196
8:1	**Vol. 3:** 588
8:2	**Vol. 2:** 45, 97, 501
8:3	**Vol. 3:** 691, 794
8:5	**Vol. 2:** 287
8:6	**Vol. 3:** 786
8:10	**Vol. 2:** 285, 502
8:11	**Vol. 2:** 293
8:13 f	**Vol. 3:** 275
8:16	**Vol. 2:** 876 **Vol. 3:** 731, 783
8:17 f	**Vol. 2:** 285
8:17	**Vol. 2:** 558
8:18	**Vol. 2:** 174
9:2	**Vol. 3:** 478
9:3	**Vol. 1:** 280
9:4 ff	**Vol. 3:** 498

Ezekiel *(cont'd)*

9:4   **Vol. 2:** 423, 572–573   **Vol. 3:** 483, 500
9:6   **Vol. 1:** 281   **Vol. 3:** 786
9:7   **Vol. 1:** 444
9:8–10   **Vol. 1:** 109
9:8   **Vol. 3:** 249
9:10   **Vol. 2:** 158
10   **Vol. 1:** 280   **Vol. 2:** 502
10:1   **Vol. 2:** 501–502   **Vol. 3:** 398
10:10   **Vol. 2:** 501–502
10:15   **Vol. 3:** 986
10:17   **Vol. 2:** 479
10:19–22   **Vol. 1:** 101
10:20   **Vol. 3:** 986
10:21 f   **Vol. 2:** 501–502
10:22   **Vol. 1:** 674
11:1   **Vol. 3:** 691
11:2   **Vol. 3:** 823
11:5   **Vol. 1:** 609   **Vol. 3:** 691
11:6   **Vol. 1:** 444
11:7   **Vol. 1:** 444
11:10   **Vol. 2:** 395
11:11 f   **Vol. 2:** 395
11:13   **Vol. 1:** 609   **Vol. 3:** 249
11:15   **Vol. 3:** 190
11:19 f   **Vol. 3:** 692
11:19   **Vol. 1:** 184, 248, 354   **Vol. 2:** 565, 670
11:20   **Vol. 2:** 134, 797   **Vol. 3:** 354
11:22   **Vol. 1:** 101
11:24   **Vol. 3:** 691
12:1 ff   **Vol. 3:** 1099
12:1–16   **Vol. 3:** 1099
12:3 ff   **Vol. 2:** 627
12:6   **Vol. 2:** 633
12:9   **Vol. 1:** 203
12:11   **Vol. 2:** 529, 633
12:14 f   **Vol. 2:** 395
12:15   **Vol. 1:** 686
12:16   **Vol. 2:** 395   **Vol. 3:** 249
12:17 ff   **Vol. 2:** 627
12:17–20   **Vol. 3:** 1099
12:21 ff   **Vol. 3:** 1099
12:22   **Vol. 2:** 53
12:24   **Vol. 2:** 116
12:25   **Vol. 3:** 1099
12:27   **Vol. 2:** 53   **Vol. 3:** 1099
13:5   **Vol. 2:** 890
13:6 ff   **Vol. 1:** 550
13:6   **Vol. 2:** 554
13:8   **Vol. 2:** 471
13:9   **Vol. 2:** 554
13:10 ff   **Vol. 1:** 205
13:10–16   **Vol. 1:** 120   **Vol. 3:** 948
13:10   **Vol. 2:** 779
13:13   **Vol. 3:** 1001
13:14   **Vol. 3:** 310
13:16   **Vol. 2:** 779
13:18 f   **Vol. 2:** 565
13:18   **Vol. 1:** 92

13:19   **Vol. 2:** 470
13:21   **Vol. 3:** 201
13:23   **Vol. 2:** 554   **Vol. 3:** 201
14:3 ff   **Vol. 3:** 687
14:3 f   **Vol. 3:** 125
14:3   **Vol. 3:** 98
14:4   **Vol. 2:** 285   **Vol. 3:** 98
14:7   **Vol. 3:** 98
14:9   **Vol. 2:** 458
14:11   **Vol. 1:** 448   **Vol. 2:** 797   **Vol. 3:** 585–586
14:13   **Vol. 1:** 609   **Vol. 3:** 585
14:14   **Vol. 2:** 681
14:16   **Vol. 1:** 465   **Vol. 2:** 724
14:20   **Vol. 2:** 479, 681   **Vol. 3:** 202
14:21   **Vol. 1:** 113
14:22   **Vol. 3:** 249
15:1–8   **Vol. 3:** 918
15:4   **Vol. 2:** 60
15:8   **Vol. 1:** 609   **Vol. 3:** 585
16   **Vol. 1:** 499   **Vol. 2:** 349, 576, 747   **Vol. 3:** 263
16:1–63   **Vol. 2:** 583
16:2 ff   **Vol. 2:** 324
16:4 f   **Vol. 2:** 889
16:4   **Vol. 3:** 444, 447
16:5   **Vol. 3:** 720
16:8–14   **Vol. 3:** 1068
16:8   **Vol. 1:** 344, 366   **Vol. 2:** 212, 578   **Vol. 3:** 1068
16:9   **Vol. 1:** 121–122   **Vol. 2:** 711
16:10–13   **Vol. 2:** 349
16:12   **Vol. 1:** 229
16:13   **Vol. 2:** 711
16:15   **Vol. 3:** 1069
16:17   **Vol. 2:** 287
16:18 f   **Vol. 2:** 711
16:22   **Vol. 1:** 312   **Vol. 3:** 236
16:23   **Vol. 3:** 1051
16:26   **Vol. 1:** 672
16:31   **Vol. 2:** 139
16:32   **Vol. 2:** 139
16:33   **Vol. 2:** 139
16:34   **Vol. 2:** 139
16:36 f†   **Vol. 3:** 310, 563
16:37   **Vol. 1:** 555   **Vol. 2:** 540
16:38 ff   **Vol. 3:** 538
16:38   **Vol. 3:** 154, 1167
16:40   **Vol. 1:** 292   **Vol. 2:** 582, 800
16:41   **Vol. 2:** 139
16:42   **Vol. 3:** 154, 255
16:46–56   **Vol. 3:** 93
16:49   **Vol. 3:** 29
16:51 f   **Vol. 3:** 355
16:52   **Vol. 3:** 356, 856
16:54   **Vol. 3:** 856
16:55   **Vol. 3:** 147
16:56   **Vol. 3:** 29–30
16:57†   **Vol. 3:** 310
16:59–63   **Vol. 2:** 307

Ezekiel *(cont'd)*

16:59	**Vol. 3:** 583
16:60	**Vol. 3:** 235
16:61	**Vol. 3:** 236
16:62	**Vol. 3:** 236
16:63	**Vol. 2:** 49, 727 **Vol. 3:** 153–154
17	**Vol. 2:** 747
17:1–10	**Vol. 3:** 918
17:2	**Vol. 2:** 745
17:5 ff	**Vol. 3:** 866
17:6	**Vol. 3:** 866
17:8	**Vol. 3:** 866
17:12–21	**Vol. 2:** 747
17:15 ff	**Vol. 3:** 583
17:15	**Vol. 1:** 531, 606 **Vol. 3:** 209
17:17	**Vol. 1:** 292–293 **Vol. 2:** 800
17:18	**Vol. 3:** 209
17:21	**Vol. 3:** 249
17:22 ff	**Vol. 2:** 374
17:22 f	**Vol. 2:** 337
17:23	**Vol. 1:** 531 **Vol. 3:** 255, 554, 867–868
17:24	**Vol. 1:** 515 **Vol. 2:** 260 **Vol. 3:** 866
18	**Vol. 3:** 135, 720
18:1 ff	**Vol. 3:** 1104
18:1–32	**Vol. 3:** 69
18:2	**Vol. 1:** 434 **Vol. 2:** 745
18:4	**Vol. 1:** 221 **Vol. 2:** 479
18:7	**Vol. 2:** 266, 666
18:9	**Vol. 2:** 479 **Vol. 3:** 354
18:12	**Vol. 2:** 820
18:13	**Vol. 2:** 479
18:16	**Vol. 2:** 266
18:17	**Vol. 2:** 479 **Vol. 3:** 354
18:19	**Vol. 3:** 354
18:20 ff	**Vol. 2:** 479
18:20	**Vol. 2:** 139
18:21 ff	**Vol. 1:** 434
18:21 f	**Vol. 1:** 333
18:21	**Vol. 3:** 354
18:22	**Vol. 3:** 585–586
18:23	**Vol. 3:** 1019
18:24	**Vol. 1:** 609 **Vol. 3:** 585
18:26	**Vol. 3:** 585–586
18:27	**Vol. 3:** 368
18:30	**Vol. 3:** 98
18:31 f	**Vol. 1:** 434
18:31	**Vol. 1:** 354 **Vol. 2:** 670 **Vol. 3:** 692
19	**Vol. 2:** 418, 747
19:3	**Vol. 1:** 484
19:4	**Vol. 1:** 531
19:5	**Vol. 1:** 712
19:6	**Vol. 1:** 484
19:10–14	**Vol. 3:** 918
19:10	**Vol. 3:** 866
19:11	**Vol. 3:** 867
19:12 f	**Vol. 3:** 867
19:13	**Vol. 3:** 1005
19:14	**Vol. 3:** 867
20	**Vol. 1:** 531 **Vol. 3:** 1005

20:6	**Vol. 3:** 117
20:9	**Vol. 2:** 307
20:10–26	**Vol. 3:** 1005
20:11	**Vol. 3:** 354
20:12–20	**Vol. 2:** 396
20:13	**Vol. 3:** 354
20:14	**Vol. 2:** 307
20:16	**Vol. 1:** 492 **Vol. 3:** 354
20:18	**Vol. 3:** 354
20:19	**Vol. 3:** 354
20:21	**Vol. 3:** 354
20:22	**Vol. 2:** 307
20:24 f	**Vol. 3:** 354
20:25 f	**Vol. 3:** 421
20:27	**Vol. 1:** 609 **Vol. 3:** 585
20:28	**Vol. 2:** 43 **Vol. 3:** 423
20:29	**Vol. 3:** 426
20:31	**Vol. 3:** 416
20:32	**Vol. 1:** 390 **Vol. 3:** 549
20:33–38	**Vol. 2:** 364
20:33	**Vol. 1:** 503
20:34	**Vol. 3:** 745
20:35	**Vol. 3:** 1006
20:36	**Vol. 3:** 1005
20:37 f	**Vol. 3:** 772
20:38	**Vol. 1:** 537, 606
20:40	**Vol. 3:** 415–416
20:43	**Vol. 3:** 236
20:44	**Vol. 3:** 236
21:3 f*	**Vol. 3:** 109
21:6 f*	**Vol. 2:** 423
21:11 f	**Vol. 2:** 627
21:18*	**Vol. 3:** 355
21:21*	**Vol. 2:** 296
21:22*	**Vol. 3:** 951
21:23	**Vol. 3:** 1099
21:26 ff	**Vol. 2:** 554
21:26*	**Vol. 2:** 260, 262
21:28 f*	**Vol. 3:** 240
21:29*	**Vol. 1:** 241 **Vol. 3:** 310
21:31	**Vol. 2:** 596
21:37*	**Vol. 3:** 238
22	**Vol. 3:** 1103
22:2–4	**Vol. 2:** 803
22:2	**Vol. 3:** 159
22:4	**Vol. 3:** 585
22:7	**Vol. 1:** 415 **Vol. 2:** 737 **Vol. 3:** 1074
22:10 f	**Vol. 2:** 260
22:10	**Vol. 3:** 310, 861, 1074
22:13	**Vol. 3:** 137
22:26	**Vol. 1:** 74 **Vol. 2:** 440
22:27	**Vol. 1:** 118, 137
22:28	**Vol. 2:** 470, 555
22:29	**Vol. 2:** 823
22:30	**Vol. 3:** 933
22:31	**Vol. 1:** 109
23	**Vol. 1:** 499 **Vol. 2:** 576, 747 **Vol. 3:** 263
23:10	**Vol. 1:** 429 **Vol. 3:** 310, 563
23:11–32	**Vol. 1:** 141

Ezekiel *(cont'd)*

23:14	**Vol. 2:** 287
23:15	**Vol. 2:** 501–502 **Vol. 3:** 120
23:18	**Vol. 1:** 607 **Vol. 3:** 310, 563
23:19	**Vol. 3:** 236, 240
23:20	**Vol. 1:** 672 **Vol. 3:** 561
23:21	**Vol. 3:** 794
23:24	**Vol. 2:** 796, 800–801
23:27	**Vol. 3:** 236, 1167
23:28	**Vol. 1:** 555
23:29	**Vol. 2:** 926 **Vol. 3:** 310
23:31–35	**Vol. 3:** 922
23:32†	**Vol. 2:** 431
23:33†	**Vol. 1:** 513
23:37–45	**Vol. 2:** 583
23:41	**Vol. 2:** 711
23:46 f	**Vol. 2:** 800
24:6	**Vol. 2:** 27, 296 **Vol. 3:** 159
24:7 f	**Vol. 2:** 212
24:9	**Vol. 3:** 159
24:11 f	**Vol. 2:** 27
24:15 ff	**Vol. 2:** 626
24:15–24	**Vol. 3:** 1099
24:17	**Vol. 2:** 423
24:18	**Vol. 2:** 689
24:24	**Vol. 2:** 627, 633
24:27	**Vol. 2:** 627, 633
25–32	**Vol. 1:** 688 **Vol. 3:** 960
25:3	**Vol. 3:** 786
25:5	**Vol. 2:** 395
25:10	**Vol. 3:** 238
25:12	**Vol. 3:** 93
25:17	**Vol. 2:** 650
26:2 ff†	**Vol. 2:** 767 **Vol. 3:** 1099
26:8	**Vol. 3:** 951
26:10	**Vol. 3:** 557
26:11	**Vol. 1:** 712
26:12	**Vol. 2:** 842
26:15	**Vol. 2:** 423
26:16	**Vol. 1:** 527
26:18	**Vol. 2:** 890
26:19 f	**Vol. 3:** 989, 1006
26:19	**Vol. 3:** 1006
26:20	**Vol. 2:** 197 **Vol. 3:** 1006
27	**Vol. 1:** 142
27:6	**Vol. 3:** 785
27:7	**Vol. 1:** 531
27:8 ff	**Vol. 3:** 1028
27:8	**Vol. 1:** 194
27:11	**Vol. 2:** 60
27:12–22	**Vol. 1:** 267
27:13	**Vol. 2:** 124
27:15	**Vol. 2:** 139
27:17	**Vol. 2:** 711
27:26	**Vol. 3:** 786
27:27 f	**Vol. 1:** 194
27:27	**Vol. 1:** 293 **Vol. 2:** 139, 890
27:28	**Vol. 3:** 786
27:29 ff	**Vol. 3:** 1054
27:30–34	**Vol. 2:** 418
27:33	**Vol. 2:** 139, 841
27:35	**Vol. 1:** 527
28	**Vol. 1:** 142 **Vol. 3:** 396
28:2	**Vol. 2:** 201, 279
28:3	**Vol. 3:** 1028
28:5	**Vol. 2:** 201
28:9	**Vol. 2:** 279
28:13 ff	**Vol. 2:** 761
28:13	**Vol. 1:** 380 **Vol. 3:** 395–396
28:14–16	**Vol. 1:** 280
28:15	**Vol. 3:** 924
28:17	**Vol. 2:** 291
28:18	**Vol. 3:** 785
28:22	**Vol. 2:** 226
28:24	**Vol. 1:** 725–726
28:25	**Vol. 3:** 608
28:26	**Vol. 2:** 395
29–32	**Vol. 1:** 531
29:3	**Vol. 1:** 205, 508
29:4	**Vol. 1:** 670
29:5	**Vol. 2:** 32
29:7	**Vol. 1:** 239 **Vol. 3:** 255
29:10	**Vol. 3:** 1005
29:16	**Vol. 1:** 492 **Vol. 3:** 240
29:18 f	**Vol. 2:** 139
29:21	**Vol. 2:** 727
30:3 ff	**Vol. 2:** 363
30:3	**Vol. 2:** 53, 888, 890
30:6	**Vol. 3:** 29
30:12	**Vol. 3:** 1005
30:13	**Vol. 3:** 255
30:15	**Vol. 1:** 109
30:18	**Vol. 3:** 29
30:21	**Vol. 3:** 713
30:24 f	**Vol. 1:** 141
30:24	**Vol. 3:** 713
30:26	**Vol. 2:** 34
31	**Vol. 2:** 747
31:3 f	**Vol. 3:** 866
31:4	**Vol. 2:** 201
31:5	**Vol. 3:** 867
31:6	**Vol. 3:** 554, 867–868
31:8 f	**Vol. 2:** 761
31:10	**Vol. 2:** 201
31:12	**Vol. 2:** 796 **Vol. 3:** 867
31:13	**Vol. 3:** 255
31:14	**Vol. 2:** 197, 199
31:15 ff	**Vol. 1:** 91
31:15	**Vol. 2:** 222, 422, 889
31:18	**Vol. 2:** 197
32:1 ff	**Vol. 3:** 1104
32:1–16	**Vol. 2:** 418
32:2	**Vol. 1:** 508 **Vol. 3:** 709
32:7	**Vol. 1:** 203, 425 **Vol. 2:** 38, 916 **Vol. 3:** 109, 559, 731, 733, 735
32:10	**Vol. 2:** 890
32:12	**Vol. 3:** 29
32:13	**Vol. 3:** 709
32:14	**Vol. 2:** 711

Ezekiel (*cont'd*)

32:18 f	**Vol. 2:** 197
32:19 ff	**Vol. 1:** 442
32:20 ff	**Vol. 2:** 206
32:22	**Vol. 1:** 293
32:23 f	**Vol. 3:** 238
32:23	**Vol. 1:** 292
32:24	**Vol. 2:** 197 **Vol. 3:** 856
32:26	**Vol. 3:** 238
32:30	**Vol. 3:** 856
33:1–9	**Vol. 3:** 1100
33:4	**Vol. 2:** 158
33:5	**Vol. 3:** 209
33:7	**Vol. 3:** 1100
33:8	**Vol. 1:** 607 **Vol. 3:** 1100
33:9	**Vol. 1:** 354
33:10	**Vol. 3:** 269, 823
33:11	**Vol. 1:** 354 **Vol. 2:** 479
33:13	**Vol. 3:** 232, 240
33:14 ff	**Vol. 1:** 354
33:16	**Vol. 3:** 240
33:28	**Vol. 3:** 29
33:29	**Vol. 2:** 278
33:30	**Vol. 2:** 720
33:31	**Vol. 1:** 492 **Vol. 3:** 137
33:33	**Vol. 2:** 891
34	**Vol. 2:** 459, 747 **Vol. 3:** 567
34:1 ff	**Vol. 3:** 564–565
34:2–10	**Vol. 3:** 566
34:5 f	**Vol. 2:** 104, 412
34:5	**Vol. 2:** 34, 412–413 **Vol. 3:** 567
34:6	**Vol. 2:** 412
34:11 f	**Vol. 3:** 565
34:12–16	**Vol. 3:** 531
34:12	**Vol. 2:** 887, 889
34:13	**Vol. 2:** 34
34:14 f	**Vol. 3:** 255
34:15	**Vol. 3:** 567
34:16	**Vol. 2:** 34
34:17	**Vol. 1:** 503–504
34:23 f	**Vol. 2:** 337 **Vol. 3:** 609
34:23	**Vol. 2:** 412 **Vol. 3:** 566, 649
34:25	**Vol. 1:** 113, 185 **Vol. 2:** 778 **Vol. 3:** 1005–1006
34:27	**Vol. 2:** 777 **Vol. 3:** 1161
34:29	**Vol. 2:** 266, 825
34:30†	**Vol. 2:** 650
34:31	**Vol. 3:** 565
35:4	**Vol. 3:** 1005
35:9	**Vol. 3:** 1005
35:12 f	**Vol. 3:** 341–342
36 f	**Vol. 2:** 297
36–48	**Vol. 2:** 701
36	**Vol. 2:** 240
36:6	**Vol. 3:** 1166
36:9	**Vol. 3:** 522
36:10	**Vol. 3:** 1006
36:17 f	**Vol. 2:** 284
36:23	**Vol. 2:** 226, 229, 653 **Vol. 3:** 236

36:24 f	**Vol. 1:** 185
36:24	**Vol. 1:** 225
36:25 ff†	**Vol. 3:** 989
36:25–27	**Vol. 3:** 987–988
36:25	**Vol. 1:** 144, 151–152, 225 **Vol. 2:** 284
36:26 ff	**Vol. 2:** 797
36:26–37	**Vol. 3:** 69
36:26 f	**Vol. 1:** 184, 354 **Vol. 2:** 155, 184, 786 **Vol. 3:** 692
36:26	**Vol. 1:** 225 **Vol. 2:** 670
36:27	**Vol. 1:** 225 **Vol. 3:** 354
36:29	**Vol. 1:** 699
36:31	**Vol. 3:** 236
36:33 ff	**Vol. 3:** 1006
36:33	**Vol. 1:** 699 **Vol. 2:** 890
36:36	**Vol. 2:** 278
37–48	**Vol. 1:** 124
37	**Vol. 2:** 240 **Vol. 3:** 269, 578
37:1–14	**Vol. 3:** 692, 1100
37:3	**Vol. 3:** 269
37:4 ff	**Vol. 3:** 269
37:4–6	**Vol. 3:** 1100
37:4	**Vol. 3:** 1100
37:5	**Vol. 2:** 479
37:6	**Vol. 1:** 672 **Vol. 2:** 278, 395
37:7–11	**Vol. 3:** 269
37:7	**Vol. 3:** 557
37:8	**Vol. 1:** 672 **Vol. 3:** 690
37:9–10	**Vol. 3:** 1100
37:9	**Vol. 1:** 444 **Vol. 2:** 787 **Vol. 3:** 690, 703, 1100
37:10	**Vol. 1:** 296 **Vol. 2:** 479 **Vol. 3:** 690, 1185
37:11–14	**Vol. 3:** 269, 1100
37:11	**Vol. 3:** 1100
37:12	**Vol. 3:** 238
37:13	**Vol. 2:** 278
37:14	**Vol. 1:** 354 **Vol. 2:** 786
37:16	**Vol. 3:** 483
37:21	**Vol. 1:** 297
37:22	**Vol. 1:** 534 **Vol. 3:** 566
37:23	**Vol. 2:** 284–285 **Vol. 3:** 200
37:24 f	**Vol. 2:** 337 **Vol. 3:** 609
37:24	**Vol. 2:** 376 **Vol. 3:** 566, 649
37:25 f	**Vol. 1:** 185
37:25	**Vol. 2:** 448 **Vol. 3:** 608
37:26	**Vol. 2:** 778
37:27	**Vol. 2:** 800 **Vol. 3:** 784, 813
38 f	**Vol. 3:** 80, 389
38–39	**Vol. 3:** 962
38:4	**Vol. 1:** 296
38:7	**Vol. 1:** 296
38:8	**Vol. 2:** 777 **Vol. 3:** 1006
38:10	**Vol. 3:** 823
38:11	**Vol. 2:** 777 **Vol. 3:** 111
38:12	**Vol. 1:** 523 **Vol. 3:** 1006
38:14	**Vol. 2:** 777
38:16	**Vol. 2:** 56, 296
38:17	**Vol. 2:** 307
38:18	**Vol. 2:** 890

Ezekiel *(cont'd)*

38:19 f	**Vol. 3:** 557
38:19	**Vol. 3:** 557, 1166
38:20	**Vol. 1:** 610, 670 **Vol. 3:** 1010
38:22	**Vol. 1:** 655
38:23	**Vol. 2:** 56
39:6	**Vol. 1:** 655 **Vol. 2:** 777
39:8	**Vol. 2:** 890
39:11	**Vol. 3:** 239
39:13	**Vol. 2:** 890
39:17	**Vol. 2:** 32
39:21 f	**Vol. 2:** 45
39:24	**Vol. 3:** 105
39:26	**Vol. 2:** 777
39:27	**Vol. 1:** 96
39:28	**Vol. 2:** 278 **Vol. 3:** 318
39:29	**Vol. 2:** 854 **Vol. 3:** 692
40 ff	**Vol. 3:** 784
40–48	**Vol. 2:** 226 **Vol. 3:** 402, 404, 509
40–46	**Vol. 3:** 551
40–43	**Vol. 3:** 783, 787–788
40:3	**Vol. 1:** 101
40:5–9	**Vol. 2:** 498
40:5	**Vol. 3:** 436
40:17	**Vol. 3:** 796
40:38	**Vol. 3:** 421
40:39	**Vol. 3:** 421
40:42	**Vol. 3:** 421
40:43	**Vol. 2:** 43
40:46	**Vol. 2:** 53
41:1	**Vol. 3:** 783, 786
41:4	**Vol. 3:** 783
41:6	**Vol. 3:** 860
41:7 ff	**Vol. 3:** 786
41:15	**Vol. 3:** 783
41:21	**Vol. 3:** 783, 786
41:23	**Vol. 3:** 783, 786
41:25	**Vol. 3:** 783
42:13 f	**Vol. 3:** 786
42:15	**Vol. 2:** 290
42:16–20	**Vol. 3:** 690
42:19	**Vol. 3:** 783
42:20	**Vol. 3:** 436
43:2	**Vol. 2:** 45 **Vol. 3:** 990
43:11	**Vol. 1:** 712 **Vol. 3:** 98, 354
43:13–17	**Vol. 3:** 419
43:14	**Vol. 3:** 156
43:17	**Vol. 3:** 156
43:20	**Vol. 3:** 149, 156, 419
43:22 ff	**Vol. 3:** 200
43:22 f	**Vol. 3:** 435, 924
43:22	**Vol. 3:** 149
43:23–26	**Vol. 3:** 419
43:23	**Vol. 3:** 149, 152
43:24	**Vol. 2:** 746 **Vol. 3:** 445
43:25	**Vol. 3:** 924
43:26	**Vol. 3:** 152, 419
44:7 ff	**Vol. 3:** 593, 786
44:7	**Vol. 1:** 154, 309, 672
44:9	**Vol. 1:** 308, 672
44:11	**Vol. 3:** 421, 786
44:12	**Vol. 3:** 98, 552
44:13	**Vol. 2:** 53
44:15 f	**Vol. 3:** 786
44:15	**Vol. 2:** 34
44:16	**Vol. 1:** 322 **Vol. 3:** 424
44:17 ff	**Vol. 1:** 204
44:18	**Vol. 3:** 711
44:19	**Vol. 3:** 786
44:21	**Vol. 3:** 919
44:22	**Vol. 2:** 592
44:23†	**Vol. 3:** 760
44:24	**Vol. 3:** 354–355
44:27	**Vol. 3:** 156, 786
44:28	**Vol. 1:** 636 **Vol. 2:** 297
44:29	**Vol. 1:** 414
44:30 ff	**Vol. 3:** 853
44:30	**Vol. 3:** 415–416
45:1–6	**Vol. 2:** 698
45:1	**Vol. 2:** 297 **Vol. 3:** 416, 1160
45:2	**Vol. 3:** 786
45:3 f	**Vol. 3:** 786
45:6 f	**Vol. 3:** 416
45:10	**Vol. 3:** 356, 1160
45:11	**Vol. 3:** 1160
45:13	**Vol. 3:** 416
45:14	**Vol. 2:** 711
45:15	**Vol. 3:** 152, 423
45:16	**Vol. 3:** 416
45:17	**Vol. 3:** 152–153, 159, 423
45:18	**Vol. 3:** 786, 924
45:19	**Vol. 3:** 152, 786
45:20	**Vol. 3:** 152–153
45:21	**Vol. 1:** 632 **Vol. 2:** 463
45:23	**Vol. 3:** 421, 924
45:24 f	**Vol. 2:** 711
46:1	**Vol. 2:** 890
46:2 f	**Vol. 2:** 876
46:2	**Vol. 3:** 423
46:4	**Vol. 2:** 410, 890 **Vol. 3:** 421, 924
46:5	**Vol. 2:** 711
46:6	**Vol. 3:** 924
46:7	**Vol. 2:** 711
46:9	**Vol. 2:** 876
46:11	**Vol. 2:** 410, 711
46:12	**Vol. 1:** 344 **Vol. 2:** 890 **Vol. 3:** 423
46:13	**Vol. 3:** 421, 924
46:14 f	**Vol. 2:** 711
46:15	**Vol. 3:** 421
46:17	**Vol. 1:** 698
46:18	**Vol. 2:** 34
46:19	**Vol. 3:** 786
46:24	**Vol. 3:** 422
47:1 ff	**Vol. 2:** 326 **Vol. 3:** 813
47:1–12	**Vol. 3:** 962, 986, 987
47:1	**Vol. 3:** 988
47:6 ff	**Vol. 2:** 685
47:9	**Vol. 1:** 670
47:11	**Vol. 3:** 444

Ezekiel *(cont'd)*

47:12 f	**Vol. 3:** 865
47:12	**Vol. 3:** 786
47:13 f	**Vol. 2:** 297
47:22 f	**Vol. 1:** 688, 691 **Vol. 2:** 297
48:8 ff	**Vol. 3:** 416
48:8–35	**Vol. 2:** 698
48:10	**Vol. 3:** 786
48:12	**Vol. 3:** 416
48:18	**Vol. 3:** 416
48:20 f	**Vol. 3:** 416
48:28	**Vol. 3:** 983
48:29	**Vol. 2:** 297
48:30–34	**Vol. 3:** 871
48:30	**Vol. 3:** 397

Daniel

1:2	**Vol. 3:** 786
1:3	**Vol. 3:** 115
1:4	**Vol. 1:** 140 **Vol. 2:** 557, 616 **Vol. 3:** 760, 924, 1027
1:8	**Vol. 2:** 521
1:9	**Vol. 2:** 116
1:10	**Vol. 2:** 370
1:12 ff	**Vol. 2:** 692
1:12	**Vol. 3:** 799
1:13	**Vol. 2:** 521
1:14	**Vol. 3:** 799
1:15	**Vol. 1:** 672 **Vol. 2:** 521
1:16	**Vol. 2:** 521
1:17	**Vol. 1:** 140 **Vol. 3:** 1027
1:19	**Vol. 3:** 528
1:20	**Vol. 2:** 555 **Vol. 3:** 1035
2	**Vol. 1:** 141, 512 **Vol. 2:** 745 **Vol. 3:** 316
2:1	**Vol. 2:** 808
2:2 f	**Vol. 2:** 557
2:2	**Vol. 2:** 479, 554–555
2:3 ff	**Vol. 2:** 56
2:4–7:28	**Vol. 1:** 51
2:5 ff	**Vol. 3:** 316
2:5	**Vol. 2:** 291
2:8	**Vol. 1:** 267
2:10	**Vol. 3:** 1028
2:11	**Vol. 1:** 679
2:12	**Vol. 3:** 1028
2:13	**Vol. 1:** 330
2:18 f	**Vol. 2:** 190
2:18	**Vol. 1:** 340
2:20–23	**Vol. 3:** 640
2:20 f	**Vol. 3:** 1027
2:20	**Vol. 2:** 555
2:21	**Vol. 2:** 607 **Vol. 3:** 131, 835, 1028
2:22	**Vol. 2:** 215, 491
2:23	**Vol. 3:** 816, 1027
2:27–30	**Vol. 3:** 311
2:27–28	**Vol. 1:** 512
2:27	**Vol. 2:** 555 **Vol. 3:** 1028
2:28 f	**Vol. 2:** 808 **Vol. 3:** 502

2:28	**Vol. 2:** 56, 190, 665, 808, 912 **Vol. 3:** 316, 502
2:29 f	**Vol. 3:** 820
2:29	**Vol. 2:** 665 **Vol. 3:** 316
2:30	**Vol. 3:** 316, 1027
2:31 f	**Vol. 2:** 158
2:31	**Vol. 2:** 287
2:33	**Vol. 3:** 914
2:34 f	**Vol. 2:** 287 **Vol. 3:** 392, 394
2:34	**Vol. 1:** 610 **Vol. 3:** 384, 393, 914
2:37	**Vol. 2:** 49, 190
2:38	**Vol. 2:** 96
2:41	**Vol. 3:** 914
2:42	**Vol. 3:** 914
2:44 f	**Vol. 3:** 392
2:44	**Vol. 1:** 610 **Vol. 2:** 190, 888
2:45	**Vol. 2:** 56, 665, 808
2:46	**Vol. 2:** 876
2:47	**Vol. 2:** 514 **Vol. 3:** 311
2:48	**Vol. 3:** 1029
3	**Vol. 2:** 628 **Vol. 3:** 669
3:1–18	**Vol. 2:** 287
3:4	**Vol. 1:** 340 **Vol. 2:** 799–800 **Vol. 3:** 48, 50–51
3:5 ff	**Vol. 2:** 876
3:5	**Vol. 3:** 594
3:6	**Vol. 1:** 235 **Vol. 3:** 846
3:10 ff	**Vol. 2:** 876
3:14	**Vol. 2:** 876
3:15	**Vol. 3:** 846
3:18	**Vol. 2:** 876 **Vol. 3:** 962
3:19	**Vol. 1:** 706
3:22	**Vol. 1:** 476 **Vol. 2:** 628, 815
3:24 f	**Vol. 2:** 863
3:27	**Vol. 3:** 860
3:28*	**Vol. 2:** 876
3:29*	**Vol. 3:** 341
3:54*	**Vol. 3:** 669
3.56*	**Vol. 3:** 669
3:88*	**Vol. 3:** 201
3:92*	**Vol. 3:** 177
4	**Vol. 2:** 431, 745
4:1–7*	**Vol. 1:** 246
4:3	**Vol. 2:** 376
4:6	**Vol. 3:** 502
4:7*	**Vol. 2:** 555
4:10 f	**Vol. 3:** 866
4:13–33	**Vol. 1:** 113
4:13*	**Vol. 1:** 101
4:15	**Vol. 3:** 866
4:16	**Vol. 1:** 527 **Vol. 3:** 820, 845
4:17*	**Vol. 1:** 101
4:18	**Vol. 3:** 502
4:19	**Vol. 3:** 29
4:21 f	**Vol. 3:** 867–868
4:23	**Vol. 2:** 191
4:24	**Vol. 3:** 192, 585
4:26	**Vol. 3:** 866
4:27	**Vol. 2:** 594
4:30*	**Vol. 1:** 142 **Vol. 3:** 846

Daniel *(cont'd)*

4:31	**Vol. 2:** 607
4:32	**Vol. 3:** 200, 823
4:33 f	**Vol. 3:** 147
4:34*	**Vol. 2:** 791 **Vol. 3:** 29, 193, 601
5:1	**Vol. 2:** 521 **Vol. 3:** 745, 816
5:2 ff	**Vol. 3:** 788
5:4	**Vol. 2:** 77
5:5	**Vol. 2:** 485 **Vol. 3:** 846
5:6	**Vol. 1:** 239 **Vol. 3:** 820
5:7	**Vol. 2:** 555
5:10	**Vol. 3:** 232, 820
5:11 f	**Vol. 3:** 1029
5:11	**Vol. 2:** 555
5:12	**Vol. 1:** 729 **Vol. 2:** 616 **Vol. 3:** 177
5:14	**Vol. 1:** 729 **Vol. 3:** 1027
5:20	**Vol. 3:** 29
5:21	**Vol. 1:** 113
5:23	**Vol. 3:** 788, 816, 938
5:27	**Vol. 3:** 953, 1160
6	**Vol. 2:** 628
6:3	**Vol. 3:** 691
6:5*	**Vol. 3:** 585–586
6:6*	**Vol. 2:** 441
6:11*	**Vol. 2:** 863 **Vol. 3:** 550
6:13*	**Vol. 2:** 882 **Vol. 3:** 98, 226
6:16	**Vol. 1:** 327 **Vol. 3:** 550
6:18	**Vol. 3:** 498–499
6:19	**Vol. 1:** 694
6:20	**Vol. 3:** 203
6:22	**Vol. 2:** 628 **Vol. 3:** 951
6:23*	**Vol. 3:** 585
6:24	**Vol. 3:** 1212
6:25*	**Vol. 3:** 1041
6:26	**Vol. 1:** 732 **Vol. 3:** 224
6:27*	**Vol. 2:** 876
6:28*	**Vol. 2:** 876 **Vol. 3:** 192
7–12	**Vol. 1:** 124
7	**Vol. 1:** 113–114, 118, 141 **Vol. 2:** 80, 604, 607, 745, 891 **Vol. 3:** 196, 510, 616–618, 620, 622, 627, 632, 697, 983, 1114
7:1–8	**Vol. 1:** 119
7:1	**Vol. 3:** 513
7:2	**Vol. 1:** 420 **Vol. 2:** 189
7:3	**Vol. 3:** 984
7:4	**Vol. 1:** 665
7:6	**Vol. 2:** 124
7:7 ff	**Vol. 1:** 126
7:7 f	**Vol. 1:** 508
7:7	**Vol. 2:** 98, 621, 808 **Vol. 3:** 715
7:9 ff	**Vol. 2:** 190
7:9–28	**Vol. 2:** 731
7:9–10	**Vol. 3:** 588
7:9 f	**Vol. 2:** 191 **Vol. 3:** 615
7:9	**Vol. 1:** 204 **Vol. 2:** 613
7:10	**Vol. 1:** 101, 243 **Vol. 2:** 698, 700 **Vol. 3:** 630, 695
7:12	**Vol. 2:** 376, 607 **Vol. 3:** 835
7:13 ff	**Vol. 2:** 190, 337
7:13 f	**Vol. 2:** 376, 912 **Vol. 3:** 614, 863
7:13	**Vol. 1:** 321, 323 **Vol. 2:** 38, 147, 194, 313, 503, 808, 917–918 **Vol. 3:** 195, 384, 513, 613, 615, 621, 627–629, 633, 638
7:14	**Vol. 2:** 376, 448, 607, 610 **Vol. 3:** 615, 630
7:15	**Vol. 2:** 279 **Vol. 3:** 820
7:16	**Vol. 3:** 316
7:17 ff	**Vol. 2:** 56
7:18	**Vol. 2:** 227, 731 **Vol. 3:** 614, 638
7:19–22	**Vol. 3:** 695
7:19	**Vol. 2:** 98
7:21 ff	**Vol. 2:** 227
7:21	**Vol. 3:** 126, 962
7:22	**Vol. 1:** 321 **Vol. 2:** 202
7:22a	**Vol. 3:** 614
7:24	**Vol. 2:** 693 **Vol. 3:** 715
7:25	**Vol. 2:** 441, 688, 700 **Vol. 3:** 614
7:26	**Vol. 3:** 588
7:27	**Vol. 1:** 165, 321, 589 **Vol. 2:** 376, 425, 607, 888 **Vol. 3:** 614
7:28	**Vol. 2:** 279 **Vol. 3:** 820
8	**Vol. 2:** 745
8:3	**Vol. 3:** 715
8:10	**Vol. 2:** 687 **Vol. 3:** 28, 735
8:12	**Vol. 3:** 881, 885
8:13	**Vol. 3:** 786, 1006
8:14	**Vol. 2:** 688
8:16	**Vol. 1:** 101, 103
8:17*	**Vol. 1:** 103, 610 **Vol. 3:** 613, 847
8:18	**Vol. 3:** 279, 860
8:19 ff	**Vol. 2:** 56
8:19*	**Vol. 1:** 110 **Vol. 2:** 61 **Vol. 3:** 847
8:21	**Vol. 2:** 124
8:23 ff	**Vol. 1:** 125
8:23	**Vol. 1:** 734
8:24	**Vol. 2:** 789
8:25	**Vol. 3:** 1161
8:26 f†	**Vol. 3:** 614
8:26	**Vol. 3:** 950
8:27	**Vol. 2:** 622, 625 **Vol. 3:** 993
9	**Vol. 2:** 892
9:1	**Vol. 2:** 376
9:2	**Vol. 1:** 243 **Vol. 3:** 87
9:3–19	**Vol. 1:** 345
9:3	**Vol. 1:** 612 **Vol. 2:** 863
9:4	**Vol. 2:** 132, 134, 622, 862
9:5	**Vol. 1:** 606
9:6	**Vol. 2:** 791
9:8	**Vol. 2:** 509
9:9–11	**Vol. 1:** 607
9:9	**Vol. 1:** 606 **Vol. 3:** 152, 156
9:11	**Vol. 2:** 440, 639
9:13	**Vol. 2:** 639, 860 **Vol. 3:** 881
9:14	**Vol. 2:** 136 **Vol. 3:** 87
9:15 ff	**Vol. 2:** 509
9:15 f	**Vol. 1:** 109
9:15	**Vol. 1:** 531 **Vol. 2:** 406

Daniel *(cont'd)*

9:16   **Vol. 2:** 789   **Vol. 3:** 156, 355
9:17   **Vol. 2:** 863   **Vol. 3:** 318
9:18   **Vol. 2:** 863   **Vol. 3:** 356
9:19   **Vol. 2:** 509   **Vol. 3:** 155–156
9:20   **Vol. 2:** 862–863
9:21*   **Vol. 1:** 101, 103, 164   **Vol. 2:** 863   **Vol. 3:** 847
9:22   **Vol. 1:** 103   **Vol. 3:** 125
9:24   **Vol. 2:** 696   **Vol. 3:** 152–154, 498, 786
9:26   **Vol. 3:** 786
9:27   **Vol. 1:** 74, 125   **Vol. 2:** 912   **Vol. 3:** 255, 1006
10:3   **Vol. 1:** 120, 672
10:5 f **Vol. 1:** 101   **Vol. 2:** 45   **Vol. 3:** 629, 861
10:5   **Vol. 3:** 120, 633
10:6   **Vol. 1:** 233   **Vol. 2:** 485, 800
10:9   **Vol. 1:** 610
10:13   **Vol. 1:** 102, 104, 165
10:14   **Vol. 2:** 56
10:16   **Vol. 2:** 502, 727
10:20   **Vol. 1:** 104   **Vol. 2:** 124
10:21   **Vol. 1:** 102
11:2   **Vol. 2:** 124, 841–842
11:3   **Vol. 3:** 1019
11:4   **Vol. 3:** 761
11:10–13   **Vol. 2:** 800
11:11   **Vol. 2:** 800
11:13   **Vol. 2:** 845
11:14   **Vol. 3:** 994
11:17   **Vol. 3:** 228, 711
11:18   **Vol. 3:** 255
11:19   **Vol. 3:** 994
11:24 f **Vol. 3:** 823
11:24   **Vol. 2:** 845   **Vol. 3:** 820
11:25   **Vol. 3:** 125
11:26   **Vol. 1:** 277
11:27   **Vol. 2:** 61, 521   **Vol. 3:** 836
11:28   **Vol. 2:** 845
11:31   **Vol. 1:** 74   **Vol. 3:** 786, 1006
11:33 ff   **Vol. 3:** 994
11:35   **Vol. 1:** 204
11:37   **Vol. 1:** 694
11:39   **Vol. 3:** 140
11:40–12:3 **Vol. 3:** 961
11:40* **Vol. 3:** 847
11:41   **Vol. 2:** 707–708
11:43   **Vol. 2:** 215
11:45* **Vol. 3:** 847
12   **Vol. 3:** 270
12:1 f **Vol. 3:** 836
12:1   **Vol. 1:** 101, 104, 243   **Vol. 2:** 807–808, 912, 916   **Vol. 3:** 209, 270, 803, 836
12:2   **Vol. 1:** 254, 434, 685   **Vol. 2:** 49, 928   **Vol. 3:** 270, 275, 303, 558, 832
12:3   **Vol. 1:** 586   **Vol. 2:** 486   **Vol. 3:** 196, 270, 734, 861

12:4   **Vol. 1:** 244   **Vol. 2:** 763   **Vol. 3:** 498, 500, 760
12:5 ff **Vol. 2:** 56
12:5–7 **Vol. 3:** 742
12:7   **Vol. 2:** 700   **Vol. 3:** 841
12:9 f **Vol. 3:** 362
12:9   **Vol. 1:** 244   **Vol. 3:** 498, 500, 836
12:10   **Vol. 1:** 204   **Vol. 3:** 799
12:11   **Vol. 1:** 74, 125   **Vol. 2:** 688, 912   **Vol. 3:** 1006
12:12   **Vol. 1:** 216   **Vol. 2:** 688, 772–774   **Vol. 3:** 226
12:13   **Vol. 1:** 734   **Vol. 2:** 298   **Vol. 3:** 254, 845

Hosea

1 ff   **Vol. 2:** 576
1–3   **Vol. 2:** 626   **Vol. 3:** 721
1:1   **Vol. 3:** 311, 1090, 1092–1093
1:2 ff **Vol. 2:** 754   **Vol. 3:** 1093
1:2–9   **Vol. 3:** 1093
1:2   **Vol. 1:** 492   **Vol. 2:** 577   **Vol. 3:** 208, 1093
1:4   **Vol. 3:** 79, 134, 159, 255, 1093
1:6 ff **Vol. 2:** 581
1:6   **Vol. 3:** 79
1:7   **Vol. 3:** 206
1:9   **Vol. 2:** 541, 797   **Vol. 3:** 79, 1103
1:10 ff*   **Vol. 1:** 288
1:10–2:1*   **Vol. 1:** 272, 275   **Vol. 2:** 782, 800   **Vol. 3:** 251, 718
1:10*   **Vol. 1:** 272, 275   **Vol. 2:** 782, 800   **Vol. 3:** 251, 718
2   **Vol. 2:** 240   **Vol. 3:** 263, 578
2:1–5   **Vol. 2:** 746
2:1   **Vol. 1:** 290
2:2 ff* **Vol. 2:** 583
2:2   **Vol. 1:** 240
2:4   **Vol. 3:** 1069
2:5*   **Vol. 1:** 186   **Vol. 2:** 711   **Vol. 3:** 147
2:6*   **Vol. 3:** 950–951
2:7*   **Vol. 1:** 481, 492   **Vol. 3:** 1069
2:8   **Vol. 1:** 726   **Vol. 2:** 711
2:9   **Vol. 3:** 835, 846
2:10*   **Vol. 1:** 498
2:11   **Vol. 3:** 407
2:12*   **Vol. 1:** 724   **Vol. 3:** 865, 1040
2:13 ff **Vol. 3:** 427
2:13   **Vol. 3:** 267
2:14*   **Vol. 2:** 139
2:15   **Vol. 1:** 492   **Vol. 2:** 887   **Vol. 3:** 918
2:16–25 **Vol. 3:** 1005
2:16*   **Vol. 2:** 511   **Vol. 3:** 1006
2:17   **Vol. 1:** 281   **Vol. 2:** 889
2:18   **Vol. 2:** 511   **Vol. 3:** 1093
2:19 f **Vol. 2:** 541   **Vol. 3:** 1068
2:20   **Vol. 1:** 113
2:21*   **Vol. 2:** 595
2:22   **Vol. 2:** 711
2:23 f **Vol. 3:** 1093

Hosea *(cont'd)*

2:23*	**Vol. 1:** 275, 369 **Vol. 2:** 541, 581, 597, 797 **Vol. 3:** 251, 422, 522
3	**Vol. 3:** 1093
3:1–5	**Vol. 3:** 1093
3:1	**Vol. 1:** 258 **Vol. 2:** 540
3:2	**Vol. 2:** 139
3:4	**Vol. 2:** 374 **Vol. 3:** 36
3:5	**Vol. 1:** 354 **Vol. 2:** 56, 583
4–14	**Vol. 3:** 1093
4:1 ff	**Vol. 2:** 285
4:1 f	**Vol. 2:** 396 **Vol. 3:** 70
4:1	**Vol. 2:** 364 **Vol. 3:** 880, 1093
4:2	**Vol. 3:** 159, 1103
4:3	**Vol. 1:** 113, 670 **Vol. 2:** 422
4:4–19	**Vol. 1:** 499
4:4	**Vol. 2:** 141 **Vol. 3:** 78
4:5	**Vol. 3:** 994, 1068
4:6 ff	**Vol. 2:** 797
4:6	**Vol. 2:** 396, 440 **Vol. 3:** 1052
4:9	**Vol. 3:** 134
4:10	**Vol. 2:** 272
4:11 ff	**Vol. 3:** 427
4:11	**Vol. 3:** 745, 919
4:12 ff	**Vol. 2:** 583
4:12	**Vol. 3:** 691–692
4:13 ff	**Vol. 3:** 1069
4:14	**Vol. 2:** 60 **Vol. 3:** 134
4:16	**Vol. 2:** 312
4:18	**Vol. 2:** 540
5:1	**Vol. 2:** 305
5:3	**Vol. 2:** 395
5:4	**Vol. 1:** 354 **Vol. 2:** 396
5:5	**Vol. 3:** 29–30, 994
5:6	**Vol. 3:** 78
5:7 ff	**Vol. 2:** 583
5:8	**Vol. 3:** 50–51
5:9	**Vol. 2:** 141
5:10	**Vol. 2:** 312
5:13	**Vol. 3:** 997
5:14–6:2	**Vol. 2:** 807
5:14	**Vol. 3:** 601
5:15	**Vol. 3:** 786
6:1–7:2	**Vol. 3:** 235
6:1–3	**Vol. 3:** 267
6:1 f	**Vol. 3:** 784
6:1	**Vol. 3:** 601
6:2 ff	**Vol. 3:** 168
6:2	**Vol. 2:** 687, 893 **Vol. 3:** 283, 287, 297, 1200
6:3	**Vol. 3:** 514
6:4	**Vol. 2:** 541 **Vol. 3:** 267, 269
6:5	**Vol. 3:** 1093
6:6	**Vol. 1:** 259, 622 **Vol. 2:** 227, 396, 596, 813 **Vol. 3:** 37, 267, 427, 429, 792, 1022
6:7	**Vol. 1:** 461 **Vol. 3:** 267, 583
6:9	**Vol. 2:** 746
6:10	**Vol. 3:** 267
6:11*	**Vol. 1:** 448 **Vol. 3:** 526
7:2	**Vol. 1:** 230 **Vol. 3:** 673
7:3	**Vol. 2:** 374
7:4	**Vol. 1:** 249
7:5	**Vol. 3:** 919
7:6 f	**Vol. 1:** 249
7:7	**Vol. 1:** 318
7:10	**Vol. 3:** 29–30
7:11	**Vol. 1:** 175, 531
7:12	**Vol. 1:** 172, 293 **Vol. 3:** 776
7:13	**Vol. 3:** 192, 345
7:15	**Vol. 3:** 823
7:16	**Vol. 1:** 531
8:1	**Vol. 1:** 173 **Vol. 2:** 440 **Vol. 3:** 583
8:2	**Vol. 2:** 396
8:4 f	**Vol. 2:** 285
8:7	**Vol. 2:** 432 **Vol. 3:** 526
8:8	**Vol. 3:** 235
8:10	**Vol. 2:** 791 **Vol. 3:** 745
8:11 ff	**Vol. 3:** 235
8:12	**Vol. 1:** 70 **Vol. 3:** 823
8:13	**Vol. 1:** 531 **Vol. 3:** 134
8:14†	**Vol. 3:** 78, 786
9:1 ff	**Vol. 2:** 583
9:2	**Vol. 3:** 267
9:3	**Vol. 1:** 531
9:6	**Vol. 3:** 859
9:7	**Vol. 1:** 320, 527 **Vol. 2:** 890 **Vol. 3:** 77, 93, 134
9:9	**Vol. 1:** 468 **Vol. 3:** 235
9:10	**Vol. 1:** 724 **Vol. 3:** 919, 1005
9:14	**Vol. 1:** 515
9:15	**Vol. 1:** 555
9:17	**Vol. 2:** 174
10:1	**Vol. 2:** 248 **Vol. 3:** 918
10:2	**Vol. 3:** 355
10:6	**Vol. 3:** 421
10:8	**Vol. 1:** 610, 726 **Vol. 2:** 218 **Vol. 3:** 382, 418
10:10	**Vol. 3:** 268, 776
10:11	**Vol. 3:** 760
10:12	**Vol. 1:** 733 **Vol. 2:** 480 **Vol. 3:** 522, 526
10:13	**Vol. 1:** 596, 721, 732 **Vol. 2:** 471 **Vol. 3:** 574
10:14	**Vol. 2:** 889
11:1 ff	**Vol. 1:** 617 **Vol. 2:** 541
11:1	**Vol. 1:** 281, 290, 531–532, 737 **Vol. 2:** 71, 540, 640, 715 **Vol. 3:** 69, 642, 1005, 1007
11:3	**Vol. 3:** 805
11:4	**Vol. 3:** 592
11:5	**Vol. 1:** 354, 531
11:6	**Vol. 3:** 255
11:8 f	**Vol. 2:** 541
11:8	**Vol. 1:** 617
11:9	**Vol. 2:** 70–71, 225
11:11	**Vol. 1:** 531 **Vol. 3:** 147
12	**Vol. 3:** 578
12:1	**Vol. 1:** 531, 596 **Vol. 2:** 711

Hosea *(cont'd)*

12:3 f	**Vol. 1:** 61
12:4	**Vol. 2:** 305, 860
12:6*	**Vol. 2:** 69, 797 **Vol. 3:** 237, 717
12:7*	**Vol. 2:** 53, 240
12:8 f	**Vol. 3:** 727
12:8*	**Vol. 3:** 1160
12:9*	**Vol. 1:** 531 **Vol. 2:** 841
12:10*	**Vol. 3:** 1005–1006
12:11	**Vol. 2:** 432
12:13	**Vol. 1:** 531
12:14	**Vol. 2:** 636
13:1	**Vol. 3:** 354
13:2	**Vol. 2:** 285, 287 **Vol. 3:** 427
13:4 f	**Vol. 3:** 1005
13:4	**Vol. 2:** 396
13:5–9	**Vol. 2:** 364
13:6	**Vol. 3:** 727
13:7	**Vol. 1:** 119
13:8	**Vol. 1:** 520
13:10 f	**Vol. 2:** 374
13:10	**Vol. 3:** 206
13:11	**Vol. 1:** 109
13:12	**Vol. 3:** 498
13:14	**Vol. 1:** 511 **Vol. 2:** 215 **Vol. 3:** 192, 201, 267
13:15	**Vol. 3:** 1005
14:3	**Vol. 2:** 738 **Vol. 3:** 206–207
14:4	**Vol. 1:** 109 **Vol. 3:** 206
14:5 ff*	**Vol. 1:** 354
14:5–10	**Vol. 3:** 1006
14:5 f	**Vol. 3:** 866
14:5	**Vol. 3:** 269
14:6	**Vol. 2:** 711
14:8 f	**Vol. 3:** 357
14:8*	**Vol. 2:** 285 **Vol. 3:** 866
14:9	**Vol. 3:** 940, 942
14:10	**Vol. 3:** 1028

Joel

1:1	**Vol. 3:** 1093
1:2–12	**Vol. 1:** 724
1:5	**Vol. 1:** 513
1:6	**Vol. 2:** 296
1:8	**Vol. 3:** 1071
1:10	**Vol. 2:** 711
1:11	**Vol. 3:** 525
1:12	**Vol. 1:** 515
1:14	**Vol. 2:** 864 **Vol. 3:** 51
1:15	**Vol. 2:** 53, 887–888, 890 **Vol. 3:** 729
1:19	**Vol. 3:** 865
2	**Vol. 1:** 425 **Vol. 3:** 829
2:1 ff	**Vol. 3:** 828
2:1–2	**Vol. 3:** 874
2:1	**Vol. 2:** 53, 888, 890, 898 **Vol. 3:** 50–51
2:2	**Vol. 1:** 423 **Vol. 2:** 887 **Vol. 3:** 1001
2:10 f	**Vol. 1:** 425

2:10	**Vol. 1:** 203, 423 **Vol. 2:** 916 **Vol. 3:** 731, 733, 735
2:11	**Vol. 2:** 890 **Vol. 3:** 318
2:12 ff	**Vol. 1:** 423
2:12	**Vol. 2:** 181, 864
2:13 f	**Vol. 1:** 357
2:13	**Vol. 2:** 769
2:15–17	**Vol. 2:** 864
2:15	**Vol. 3:** 51
2:16	**Vol. 1:** 295
2:17 f	**Vol. 2:** 297
2:19–24	**Vol. 2:** 711
2:19	**Vol. 2:** 711
2:21	**Vol. 2:** 357
2:22	**Vol. 1:** 724 **Vol. 3:** 865
2:23	**Vol. 1:** 286 **Vol. 2:** 357 **Vol. 3:** 355, 766
2:24	**Vol. 2:** 711 **Vol. 3:** 919
2:25–28	**Vol. 2:** 740
2:25	**Vol. 1:** 119 **Vol. 2:** 124
2:26	**Vol. 3:** 816
2:28 ff	**Vol. 2:** 42 **Vol. 3:** 87
2:28–32	**Vol. 2:** 38, 58, 916 **Vol. 3:** 699, 707, 732, 1079
2:28–29*	**Vol. 2:** 854–855 **Vol. 3:** 693
2:28 f	**Vol. 3:** 692
2:28*	**Vol. 1:** 198 **Vol. 2:** 117, 785–786
2:29*	**Vol. 3:** 594
2:30–31	**Vol. 3:** 732
2:30*	**Vol. 1:** 224, 655 **Vol. 2:** 629
2:31*	**Vol. 1:** 203, 224, 320 **Vol. 3:** 318–319, 731, 733–734
2:32*	**Vol. 2:** 329, 654 **Vol. 3:** 209, 213, 250
3–4	**Vol. 2:** 916
3:1*	**Vol. 1:** 512 **Vol. 3:** 836, 986
3:2†	**Vol. 1:** 503 **Vol. 2:** 363
3:2*	**Vol. 2:** 297
3:3*	**Vol. 2:** 296, 633
3:4	**Vol. 2:** 767, 890
3:6*	**Vol. 2:** 124, 324
3:9	**Vol. 3:** 51
3:13	**Vol. 1:** 111 **Vol. 3:** 526, 919
3:14†	**Vol. 2:** 890
3:14*	**Vol. 2:** 887–888
3:15	**Vol. 3:** 731, 735
3:17*	**Vol. 1:** 684 **Vol. 2:** 326, 803 **Vol. 3:** 160
3:18	**Vol. 1:** 683 **Vol. 3:** 813, 919, 986–987, 1010
3:19†	**Vol. 1:** 531 **Vol. 3:** 355
4:2	**Vol. 1:** 503 **Vol. 2:** 363
4:14	**Vol. 2:** 890

Amos

1–2	**Vol. 3:** 960
1	**Vol. 3:** 93
1:1	**Vol. 3:** 311, 557, 1092
1:2	**Vol. 2:** 190, 363
1:3–16	**Vol. 2:** 139

Amos *(cont'd)*

1:3	**Vol. 2:** 98 **Vol. 3:** 1092
1:4 ff	**Vol. 1:** 661
1:4	**Vol. 1:** 654–655
1:5	**Vol. 3:** 1092
1:6	**Vol. 3:** 1092
1:7	**Vol. 1:** 655
1:8	**Vol. 3:** 1092
1:9 f	**Vol. 2:** 767
1:9	**Vol. 3:** 1092
1:11	**Vol. 3:** 1040, 1092
1:13	**Vol. 3:** 1092
1:14	**Vol. 3:** 1092
1:15	**Vol. 1:** 165 **Vol. 3:** 908
2	**Vol. 3:** 93
2:1	**Vol. 1:** 264 **Vol. 3:** 1092
2:3	**Vol. 3:** 1092
2:4	**Vol. 2:** 440, 458, 471 **Vol. 3:** 1092
2:5	**Vol. 1:** 661
2:6 ff	**Vol. 2:** 841
2:6–16	**Vol. 1:** 716
2:6–14	**Vol. 3:** 960
2:6 f	**Vol. 1:** 717 **Vol. 3:** 357
2:6	**Vol. 2:** 96, 260, 820 **Vol. 3:** 594, 1092
2:7 f	**Vol. 3:** 1103
2:7	**Vol. 2:** 225, 257, 260, 649, 822
2:9	**Vol. 3:** 866
2:10	**Vol. 1:** 531
2:11	**Vol. 3:** 1092
2:13 ff	**Vol. 2:** 260
2:13	**Vol. 1:** 743
2:14 f	**Vol. 3:** 209
2:16	**Vol. 3:** 1092
3–5	**Vol. 3:** 1092
3:1 ff	**Vol. 2:** 364
3:2	**Vol. 1:** 538 **Vol. 2:** 395 **Vol. 3:** 135
3:4	**Vol. 3:** 601
3:5	**Vol. 1:** 172, 609 **Vol. 2:** 707
3:6	**Vol. 3:** 113, 720, 874
3:7 f	**Vol. 3:** 502
3:7	**Vol. 3:** 311
3:8	**Vol. 2:** 746 **Vol. 3:** 1092
3:9 f	**Vol. 3:** 1103
3:12	**Vol. 3:** 1092
3:13†	**Vol. 2:** 69, 318 **Vol. 3:** 717, 1041
3:14	**Vol. 3:** 78, 93, 134
3:15	**Vol. 3:** 1092
4:1 ff	**Vol. 1:** 717 **Vol. 3:** 93
4:1–3	**Vol. 3:** 1090
4:1	**Vol. 2:** 820, 822
4:2	**Vol. 2:** 225
4:3	**Vol. 3:** 1092
4:4 f	**Vol. 3:** 427
4:4	**Vol. 1:** 732 **Vol. 2:** 693 **Vol. 3:** 185
4:5 f	**Vol. 3:** 1092
4:5	**Vol. 1:** 344 **Vol. 3:** 423
4:6–8	**Vol. 1:** 354
4:6	**Vol. 1:** 357
4:7	**Vol. 2:** 765 **Vol. 3:** 1001

4:8–11	**Vol. 3:** 1092
4:9	**Vol. 1:** 119
4:10	**Vol. 1:** 429
4:11	**Vol. 3:** 93, 560
4:12	**Vol. 3:** 117
4:13	**Vol. 1:** 379, 523 **Vol. 2:** 69, 650 **Vol. 3:** 690
5:1–2	**Vol. 2:** 418
5:1	**Vol. 2:** 305
5:2	**Vol. 1:** 610 **Vol. 3:** 1071
5:3 f	**Vol. 3:** 1092
5:3	**Vol. 2:** 698
5:4	**Vol. 1:** 357 **Vol. 2:** 442, 479 **Vol. 3:** 355, 367
5:5	**Vol. 3:** 426
5:6 f	**Vol. 1:** 622
5:6	**Vol. 3:** 109, 355
5:7	**Vol. 1:** 717 **Vol. 3:** 355
5:8	**Vol. 1:** 422, 523 **Vol. 3:** 902
5:10 ff	**Vol. 2:** 841
5:10	**Vol. 1:** 555 **Vol. 2:** 141
5:11 ff	**Vol. 1:** 717
5:11	**Vol. 2:** 822
5:12–15	**Vol. 3:** 357
5:12	**Vol. 2:** 820 **Vol. 3:** 166, 192
5:13	**Vol. 3:** 836
5:14 ff	**Vol. 3:** 717
5:14 f	**Vol. 1:** 565 **Vol. 2:** 285 **Vol. 3:** 249
5:14	**Vol. 2:** 69, 479 **Vol. 3:** 355
5:15	**Vol. 1:** 555 **Vol. 3:** 147
5:16–17	**Vol. 2:** 418
5:16	**Vol. 2:** 418, 422 **Vol. 3:** 720
5:17	**Vol. 3:** 1092
5:18	**Vol. 2:** 364, 887, 890, 926
5:19	**Vol. 3:** 948
5:20	**Vol. 1:** 423 **Vol. 2:** 887, 890
5:21 ff	**Vol. 3:** 783
5:21–27	**Vol. 3:** 427
5:21	**Vol. 1:** 626 **Vol. 3:** 600
5:22	**Vol. 3:** 422
5:23 f	**Vol. 2:** 864
5:23	**Vol. 3:** 673
5:25 ff†	**Vol. 3:** 964
5:25–27	**Vol. 2:** 248
5:25	**Vol. 3:** 427, 431
5:26	**Vol. 2:** 85 **Vol. 3:** 735, 904–905
5:27	**Vol. 3:** 465
6:1	**Vol. 1:** 165, 357
6:2	**Vol. 3:** 717
6:3	**Vol. 2:** 53, 888, 890
6:5	**Vol. 3:** 823
6:6	**Vol. 1:** 121, 665 **Vol. 2:** 711 **Vol. 3:** 720
6:7	**Vol. 3:** 590
6:8	**Vol. 3:** 29–30, 740
6:10	**Vol. 1:** 194
6:11	**Vol. 2:** 428
6:12	**Vol. 1:** 202 **Vol. 2:** 746 **Vol. 3:** 355, 525
7–9	**Vol. 2:** 173

Amos *(cont'd)*

7	**Vol. 1:** 699
7:1 ff	**Vol. 1:** 210
7:1–8	**Vol. 3:** 1092
7:1	**Vol. 3:** 569
7:2	**Vol. 3:** 152
7:3	**Vol. 1:** 357 **Vol. 3:** 1092
7:4	**Vol. 3:** 93, 569, 695
7:6	**Vol. 1:** 357
7:7	**Vol. 3:** 569
7:8	**Vol. 2:** 797
7:9	**Vol. 1:** 81 **Vol. 2:** 431 **Vol. 3:** 418, 786
7:10	**Vol. 3:** 1092
7:13	**Vol. 3:** 786, 1092
7:15	**Vol. 2:** 412, 797 **Vol. 3:** 1092
7:17	**Vol. 3:** 104
8	**Vol. 2:** 364
8:1 ff	**Vol. 1:** 716
8:1 f	**Vol. 2:** 432
8:1–2	**Vol. 3:** 1092
8:2	**Vol. 2:** 797 **Vol. 3:** 1090, 1092
8:3	**Vol. 2:** 891
8:4	**Vol. 2:** 257, 820, 822
8:5	**Vol. 2:** 370, 830 **Vol. 3:** 402, 407, 1160
8:6	**Vol. 1:** 268 **Vol. 2:** 260, 820, 822
8:7 f	**Vol. 2:** 260
8:7	**Vol. 3:** 29–30
8:8	**Vol. 1:** 531
8:9	**Vol. 1:** 203, 423 **Vol. 2:** 38, 887, 916 **Vol. 3:** 559, 731
8:10	**Vol. 1:** 626 **Vol. 2:** 422, 890 **Vol. 3:** 673
8:11–13	**Vol. 2:** 266
8:11 f	**Vol. 3:** 1092
8:11	**Vol. 2:** 275
8:13	**Vol. 3:** 1071
8:14	**Vol. 1:** 610 **Vol. 3:** 152, 156
9	**Vol. 2:** 364
9:1 ff	**Vol. 2:** 307
9:1–4	**Vol. 3:** 1092
9:1	**Vol. 1:** 429 **Vol. 3:** 157, 209
9:2	**Vol. 2:** 206
9:3	**Vol. 1:** 508, 523
9:5 f	**Vol. 1:** 523
9:5	**Vol. 1:** 531
9:6	**Vol. 2:** 189
9:7 ff	**Vol. 3:** 82
9:7	**Vol. 1:** 531, 688
9:8	**Vol. 3:** 514
9:9	**Vol. 2:** 791
9:10	**Vol. 1:** 430 **Vol. 2:** 888
9:11 ff	**Vol. 3:** 514
9:11 f	**Vol. 3:** 651
9:11–15	**Vol. 2:** 374
9:11–12	**Vol. 3:** 812
9:11	**Vol. 2:** 248, 252 **Vol. 3:** 650, 828
9:12	**Vol. 1:** 276 **Vol. 3:** 251, 532, 1010
9:13	**Vol. 2:** 890 **Vol. 3:** 144, 522, 919
9:15	**Vol. 3:** 1092

Obadiah

1	**Vol. 3:** 311
3	**Vol. 3:** 29
8	**Vol. 3:** 1028
4	**Vol. 1:** 173 **Vol. 3:** 734
5	**Vol. 3:** 377, 728
11	**Vol. 2:** 296, 889
14	**Vol. 2:** 889
15	**Vol. 2:** 888, 890
17	**Vol. 3:** 250
21	**Vol. 2:** 376

Jonah

1:2	**Vol. 2:** 351, 679
1:3 ff	**Vol. 2:** 350
1:3	**Vol. 2:** 215
1:4	**Vol. 2:** 680
1:6	**Vol. 3:** 115
1:7	**Vol. 1:** 609 **Vol. 2:** 296
1:9	**Vol. 1:** 515
1:10	**Vol. 2:** 680
1:12	**Vol. 2:** 680
1:13	**Vol. 3:** 711
1:14	**Vol. 3:** 355
1:15	**Vol. 2:** 680 **Vol. 3:** 559
1:17*	**Vol. 1:** 169, 420 **Vol. 2:** 687
2	**Vol. 3:** 297
2:1*	**Vol. 1:** 670
2:2	**Vol. 2:** 351, 862
2:3	**Vol. 3:** 673
2:4*	**Vol. 2:** 197 **Vol. 3:** 786
2:5*	**Vol. 1:** 314
2:6	**Vol. 2:** 351
2:7*	**Vol. 2:** 185 **Vol. 3:** 786
2:8	**Vol. 2:** 863 **Vol. 3:** 236
2:9	**Vol. 1:** 551
2:11*	**Vol. 1:** 670
2:23*	**Vol. 2:** 268
3:1–10	**Vol. 2:** 680
3:2	**Vol. 2:** 679 **Vol. 3:** 51
3:3	**Vol. 2:** 679
3:4–10	**Vol. 1:** 612
3:4	**Vol. 2:** 351, 679 **Vol. 3:** 51
3:5	**Vol. 2:** 679 **Vol. 3:** 51, 209
3:6	**Vol. 2:** 679 **Vol. 3:** 588
3:7–10	**Vol. 1:** 109
3:7	**Vol. 2:** 269, 679 **Vol. 3:** 50–51
3:8 ff	**Vol. 3:** 1104
3:9 f	**Vol. 1:** 354, 356
3:10 ff	**Vol. 2:** 351
3:10	**Vol. 1:** 354 **Vol. 2:** 679
4:2	**Vol. 2:** 351, 769, 862
4:3	**Vol. 2:** 509
4:5	**Vol. 3:** 554
4:6	**Vol. 2:** 356 **Vol. 3:** 554
4:11	**Vol. 2:** 395, 679

Micah

1	Vol. 2: 364
1:1	Vol. 3: 1093
1:2	Vol. 2: 174, 888 Vol. 3: 786
1:3	Vol. 2: 925 Vol. 3: 786
1:4	Vol. 3: 1010
1:5	Vol. 2: 305
1:7	Vol. 2: 139, 285
1:8	Vol. 2: 418, 926
1:10	Vol. 2: 431
2:1 f	Vol. 2: 841
2:1	Vol. 1: 562 Vol. 2: 586 Vol. 3: 823
2:2	Vol. 2: 822
2:3	Vol. 3: 351, 823
2:4	Vol. 3: 859
2:5	Vol. 1: 295
2:10	Vol. 3: 255
2:11	Vol. 2: 470 Vol. 3: 919
2:12 f	Vol. 3: 250
2:12*	Vol. 2: 32, 586
3:1–4	Vol. 2: 864
3:1–3	Vol. 1: 717
3:2 ff	Vol. 2: 822
3:2 f	Vol. 1: 673
3:2	Vol. 3: 357, 601
3:4	Vol. 1: 409 Vol. 3: 836
3:5	Vol. 3: 51
3:6 f	Vol. 2: 554
3:6	Vol. 3: 731
3:7	Vol. 3: 345
3:8	Vol. 3: 713
3:9–12	Vol. 3: 78
3:11	Vol. 2: 139, 554 Vol. 3: 78, 255
3:12	Vol. 3: 82, 786
4:1 ff	Vol. 2: 56
4:1 f	Vol. 1: 661 Vol. 2: 325
4:1–3	Vol. 2: 791 Vol. 3: 70, 1010, 1012, 1094
4:1	Vol. 2: 56, 489
4:2	Vol. 2: 440
4:3 f	Vol. 1: 210
4:3	Vol. 1: 484 Vol. 2: 141
4:4	Vol. 1: 724 Vol. 2: 888 Vol. 3: 254–255, 866
4:6 f	Vol. 1: 185 Vol. 3: 565
4:6	Vol. 2: 32 Vol. 3: 745
4:7	Vol. 3: 828
4:8	Vol. 1: 165
4:9 f	Vol. 3: 1068
4:10	Vol. 3: 192, 201
4:12	Vol. 2: 32 Vol. 3: 823, 1016
4:13	Vol. 2: 98 Vol. 3: 650, 715
5	Vol. 3: 649
5:2 ff	Vol. 2: 374
5:2–6*	Vol. 2: 335
5:2*	Vol. 1: 164, 170, 321 Vol. 2: 320, 715, 888 Vol. 3: 490, 828
5:3*	Vol. 3: 567, 827, 835
5:4*	Vol. 2: 649, 888
5:5*	Vol. 2: 778 Vol. 3: 201
5:6	Vol. 3: 269
5:7 f	Vol. 3: 250
5:9	Vol. 1: 554
5:11	Vol. 2: 554
5:12	Vol. 2: 555
5:13	Vol. 2: 876
5:14	Vol. 1: 109
5:15	Vol. 1: 109
6:1	Vol. 2: 363
6:2	Vol. 1: 661
6:4	Vol. 2: 636, 639 Vol. 3: 192
6:5	Vol. 2: 396 Vol. 3: 236, 355–356
6:6 ff	Vol. 3: 155, 427
6:6–8	Vol. 2: 42
6:7	Vol. 1: 721 Vol. 2: 711 Vol. 3: 421
6:8	Vol. 1: 116, 261 Vol. 2: 100, 103, 174, 307 Vol. 3: 46, 70, 117, 367
6:10	Vol. 3: 29
6:11	Vol. 3: 355, 1160
6:12	Vol. 2: 842
6:15	Vol. 2: 711 Vol. 3: 144
6:16	Vol. 3: 354
7:1–6	Vol. 1: 724–725
7:1	Vol. 1: 724 Vol. 3: 866
7:2	Vol. 2: 91
7:3	Vol. 1: 717
7:4	Vol. 2: 416, 890 Vol. 3: 399, 950
7:6	Vol. 1: 725 Vol. 2: 250
7:7	Vol. 2: 240, 773 Vol. 3: 218
7:8	Vol. 1: 422, 609 Vol. 3: 1040
7:9	Vol. 3: 355
7:10	Vol. 3: 650
7:14	Vol. 1: 162 Vol. 3: 565
7:15	Vol. 1: 531
7:18	Vol. 1: 699 Vol. 2: 297 Vol. 3: 250
7:19	Vol. 1: 699 Vol. 2: 197
7:20	Vol. 2: 596 Vol. 3: 523

Nahum

1:1	Vol. 2: 679
1:3	Vol. 2: 769 Vol. 3: 514
1:5	Vol. 3: 1010
1:6	Vol. 2: 836 Vol. 3: 382
1:7	Vol. 2: 91
1:9 ff	Vol. 3: 823
1:9	Vol. 3: 823
1:11	Vol. 3: 823
1:13	Vol. 3: 592
1:15	Vol. 2: 111
2:1*	Vol. 2: 778
2:2*	Vol. 3: 29
2:4*	Vol. 2: 485–486
2:5	Vol. 3: 994
2:6	Vol. 2: 679
2:7	Vol. 1: 710 Vol. 2: 418
2:12	Vol. 1: 226
3:1	Vol. 3: 159
3:2	Vol. 3: 557

Nahum (cont'd)

3:3	**Vol. 3:** 994
3:4	**Vol. 2:** 554–555
3:7	**Vol. 2:** 423, 679
3:10	**Vol. 2:** 296
3:11	**Vol. 1:** 553
3:12	**Vol. 1:** 724
3:13	**Vol. 1:** 553
3:14	**Vol. 3:** 916
3:17	**Vol. 3:** 478
3:18	**Vol. 3:** 566

Habakkuk

1:2	**Vol. 2:** 69
1:4	**Vol. 2:** 60
1:5	**Vol. 1:** 461–462 **Vol. 2:** 625
1:6	**Vol. 1:** 201
1:7	**Vol. 3:** 318
1:8	**Vol. 1:** 173, 175
1:11	**Vol. 3:** 152
1:12	**Vol. 1:** 164
1:14	**Vol. 1:** 670
2:2	**Vol. 3:** 484
2:3 f	**Vol. 1:** 597, 604 **Vol. 3:** 366–367
2:3	**Vol. 2:** 240, 772–773 **Vol. 3:** 953
2:4	**Vol. 1:** 598 **Vol. 2:** 442, 817–818 **Vol. 3:** 359, 365, 367, 685, 1177, 1189
2:5	**Vol. 1:** 461 **Vol. 2:** 435 **Vol. 3:** 30, 919
2:6	**Vol. 1:** 575 **Vol. 2:** 745
2:9	**Vol. 1:** 137
2:11	**Vol. 3:** 393
2:14	**Vol. 1:** 735 **Vol. 2:** 229
2:16	**Vol. 3:** 922
2:18 f	**Vol. 2:** 285
2:18	**Vol. 1:** 428, 596 **Vol. 3:** 766
2:20	**Vol. 3:** 786
3:1	**Vol. 2:** 863 **Vol. 3:** 673
3:2	**Vol. 1:** 108–109
3:3–6	**Vol. 3:** 960
3:3	**Vol. 2:** 71, 190 **Vol. 3:** 926
3:4	**Vol. 2:** 491 **Vol. 3:** 514
3:5	**Vol. 2:** 167 **Vol. 3:** 1116
3:6	**Vol. 3:** 711, 1010
3:8	**Vol. 3:** 983
3:11	**Vol. 3:** 731, 733
3:12	**Vol. 1:** 109
3:13	**Vol. 1:** 241 **Vol. 2:** 336 **Vol. 3:** 207
3:16	**Vol. 2:** 807, 863, 890 **Vol. 3:** 254
3:17	**Vol. 1:** 724 **Vol. 2:** 711 **Vol. 3:** 153
3:18	**Vol. 2:** 353 **Vol. 3:** 218–220
3:19	**Vol. 2:** 60 **Vol. 3:** 673

Zephaniah

1:1	**Vol. 3:** 311, 1090, 1093
1:3	**Vol. 2:** 708 **Vol. 3:** 994
1:5	**Vol. 2:** 876

1:7–18	**Vol. 2:** 363
1:7 f	**Vol. 3:** 117, 160
1:7	**Vol. 2:** 53, 890
1:14–16	**Vol. 3:** 874
1:14	**Vol. 2:** 53, 888
1:15	**Vol. 1:** 110, 425 **Vol. 2:** 663, 887
1:18	**Vol. 2:** 836
2:2 f	**Vol. 1:** 110
2:2	**Vol. 1:** 110
2:3	**Vol. 1:** 110 **Vol. 2:** 257, 260 **Vol. 3:** 355, 1148
2:7	**Vol. 1:** 189 **Vol. 3:** 250
2:9†	**Vol. 3:** 93, 250, 444, 560
2:10	**Vol. 2:** 69 **Vol. 3:** 29–30
2:11	**Vol. 2:** 876
2:13	**Vol. 2:** 679
2:14	**Vol. 1:** 173 **Vol. 2:** 680 **Vol. 3:** 113
3	**Vol. 2:** 472
3:2	**Vol. 3:** 745
3:3	**Vol. 1:** 118
3:4	**Vol. 1:** 461 **Vol. 2:** 440
3:5	**Vol. 3:** 357
3:6	**Vol. 3:** 29
3:7	**Vol. 3:** 745
3:8	**Vol. 2:** 773, 836 **Vol. 3:** 1040
3:10	**Vol. 2:** 888 **Vol. 3:** 155, 421
3:11	**Vol. 3:** 29
3:12	**Vol. 2:** 91, 257, 260
3:13	**Vol. 1:** 551 **Vol. 2:** 471
3:14	**Vol. 3:** 50–51
3:16	**Vol. 1:** 328 **Vol. 3:** 836
3:17	**Vol. 3:** 207
3:18	**Vol. 2:** 772
3:19 f	**Vol. 3:** 745, 836

Haggai

1:6	**Vol. 2:** 139
1:8	**Vol. 3:** 786
1:10	**Vol. 2:** 765
1:11	**Vol. 2:** 711
1:12	**Vol. 3:** 208
1:13	**Vol. 3:** 46
1:14	**Vol. 3:** 208
2:3	**Vol. 2:** 44
2:5	**Vol. 1:** 328, 531 **Vol. 3:** 692
2:6 ff	**Vol. 1:** 686
2:6	**Vol. 2:** 717 **Vol. 3:** 317, 560
2:7	**Vol. 1:** 320, 537 **Vol. 3:** 257
2:9	**Vol. 1:** 380, 735 **Vol. 2:** 778
2:10–14	**Vol. 3:** 451
2:10	**Vol. 3:** 1090
2:11 ff	**Vol. 2:** 226
2:11*	**Vol. 2:** 441
2:12	**Vol. 2:** 711
2:15	**Vol. 2:** 889 **Vol. 3:** 786
2:16	**Vol. 3:** 557
2:18 f	**Vol. 2:** 889
2:18	**Vol. 3:** 786
2:20–23	**Vol. 2:** 307

Haggai *(cont'd)*

2:20	**Vol. 3:** 1090
2:21	**Vol. 1:** 515
2:22	**Vol. 1:** 465
2:23	**Vol. 1:** 534 **Vol. 2:** 336, 891 **Vol. 3:** 609

Zechariah

1:1	**Vol. 3:** 82, 311, 430
1:3–17	**Vol. 3:** 717
1:4	**Vol. 1:** 354
1:7–6:8	**Vol. 3:** 80
1:8	**Vol. 1:** 118, 204–205, 420, 657
1:9	**Vol. 1:** 101
1:11 ff	**Vol. 1:** 101
1:12	**Vol. 2:** 509
1:14	**Vol. 1:** 558
1:15	**Vol. 2:** 807
1:16	**Vol. 3:** 402
1:18 ff	**Vol. 2:** 689
2 f	**Vol. 2:** 190
2:1	**Vol. 3:** 436
2:2–5*	**Vol. 1:** 101
2:5–11*	**Vol. 2:** 45
2:6*	**Vol. 2:** 38, 189, 194, 917
2:8*	**Vol. 3:** 860
2:11 f	**Vol. 2:** 797
2:11	**Vol. 2:** 888 **Vol. 3:** 209
3:1 f	**Vol. 3:** 468
3:1	**Vol. 2:** 146 **Vol. 3:** 192, 569
3:2	**Vol. 1:** 572 **Vol. 3:** 345
3:3 f	**Vol. 1:** 556
3:4 f	**Vol. 1:** 479
3:6*	**Vol. 3:** 1041
3:7	**Vol. 1:** 503
3:8–10	**Vol. 1:** 426
3:8 f	**Vol. 3:** 392
3:8	**Vol. 2:** 336 **Vol. 3:** 609, 649, 867
3:9	**Vol. 3:** 1161
3:10	**Vol. 1:** 724 **Vol. 3:** 866
4:1 ff	**Vol. 2:** 335
4:1	**Vol. 2:** 485
4:2–14	**Vol. 2:** 712
4:2–3	**Vol. 2:** 686
4:3	**Vol. 2:** 487
4:6	**Vol. 2:** 712 **Vol. 3:** 392, 692
4:7–10	**Vol. 3:** 391
4:7	**Vol. 2:** 116 **Vol. 3:** 392
4:9	**Vol. 3:** 392
4:10	**Vol. 2:** 690, 889 **Vol. 3:** 392
4:11 ff	**Vol. 2:** 335
4:11–14	**Vol. 2:** 487, 686
5:6 ff	**Vol. 3:** 402
6:1–8	**Vol. 1:** 118
6:2 ff	**Vol. 1:** 657
6:2	**Vol. 1:** 203, 205
6:5	**Vol. 2:** 189, 689
6:8	**Vol. 3:** 254
6:9 ff	**Vol. 3:** 782
6:9–15	**Vol. 2:** 307
6:10	**Vol. 2:** 891
6:12–15	**Vol. 3:** 786
6:12	**Vol. 1:** 426 **Vol. 2:** 649 **Vol. 3:** 649, 867
6:13	**Vol. 1:** 426 **Vol. 2:** 778 **Vol. 3:** 926
6:14	**Vol. 2:** 773 **Vol. 3:** 237
7:2	**Vol. 3:** 149, 152, 155
7:3–5	**Vol. 1:** 612
7:8–14	**Vol. 2:** 174
7:9	**Vol. 2:** 595
7:10†	**Vol. 2:** 257, 737 **Vol. 3:** 1074
8:1–23	**Vol. 3:** 717
8:3	**Vol. 3:** 250
8:4 f	**Vol. 3:** 79
8:7	**Vol. 3:** 208
8:8	**Vol. 2:** 797 **Vol. 3:** 813, 880
8:9	**Vol. 2:** 889 **Vol. 3:** 786
8:10 ff	**Vol. 2:** 778
8:10	**Vol. 2:** 139
8:11 f	**Vol. 3:** 250
8:13	**Vol. 1:** 328
8:15	**Vol. 1:** 328 **Vol. 2:** 326
8:16	**Vol. 2:** 777 **Vol. 3:** 881, 886
8:17	**Vol. 1:** 555 **Vol. 3:** 823, 825, 881
8:19	**Vol. 1:** 612
8:20 ff	**Vol. 1:** 686
8:20–23	**Vol. 2:** 791
8:21 f	**Vol. 1:** 586
8:21	**Vol. 2:** 860
8:22 f	**Vol. 2:** 888
8:22	**Vol. 3:** 149, 152, 155
9:2 ff	**Vol. 2:** 767
9:5	**Vol. 3:** 585
9:6	**Vol. 3:** 29
9:7	**Vol. 2:** 698 **Vol. 3:** 250
9:9 f	**Vol. 1:** 210, 623 **Vol. 2:** 888, 899
9:9	**Vol. 1:** 100, 117, 321 **Vol. 2:** 257–258, 324–327, 379, 754 **Vol. 3:** 50–51, 218, 462, 509–510, 557
9:10	**Vol. 2:** 257, 591, 778
9:11	**Vol. 2:** 533
9:13	**Vol. 1:** 286 **Vol. 2:** 124
9:14	**Vol. 3:** 559
9:17	**Vol. 1:** 210
10:1	**Vol. 3:** 846
10:2	**Vol. 1:** 512, 550 **Vol. 2:** 554–555
10:3	**Vol. 3:** 565–566
10:7	**Vol. 2:** 357 **Vol. 3:** 919
10:8	**Vol. 3:** 192
10:9	**Vol. 3:** 522
10:10	**Vol. 1:** 531
10:11	**Vol. 2:** 197 **Vol. 3:** 29
11–14	**Vol. 3:** 961
11:5 f	**Vol. 3:** 566
11:5	**Vol. 2:** 841 **Vol. 3:** 720
11:12	**Vol. 1:** 93 **Vol. 2:** 139
11:13	**Vol. 1:** 93, 520 **Vol. 3:** 808
11:14	**Vol. 3:** 451
11:16 f	**Vol. 3:** 566

Zechariah *(cont'd)*

12:3	**Vol. 3:** 28, 803
12:4	**Vol. 1:** 527
12:5 f	**Vol. 2:** 698
12:6	**Vol. 2:** 485
12:8	**Vol. 3:** 649, 966
12:10 ff	**Vol. 2:** 917
12:10–14	**Vol. 1:** 518 **Vol. 2:** 38
12:10	**Vol. 2:** 117, 324, 854 . **Vol. 3:** 566, 629, 649
12:11	**Vol. 3:** 275, 962
13:1 f	**Vol. 3:** 986–987, 989
13:1	**Vol. 1:** 151 **Vol. 3:** 649, 813
13:2	**Vol. 3:** 238
13:4	**Vol. 1:** 116 **Vol. 3:** 121
13:7	**Vol. 1:** 163 **Vol. 2:** 34, 413, 459, 803 **Vol. 3:** 329, 564, 566–567
13:8 f	**Vol. 3:** 250
13:9	**Vol. 2:** 96 **Vol. 3:** 808
13:14	**Vol. 1:** 119
14:1	**Vol. 1:** 320 **Vol. 2:** 926
14:2	**Vol. 3:** 250, 962
14:3	**Vol. 2:** 889–890
14:4	**Vol. 2:** 713 **Vol. 3:** 543, 558, 1010, 1012
14:5 ff	**Vol. 1:** 320
14:5	**Vol. 1:** 101 **Vol. 2:** 376 **Vol. 3:** 557
14:7	**Vol. 1:** 420 **Vol. 2:** 887
14:8	**Vol. 3:** 813, 962, 986–987
14:9	**Vol. 2:** 376, 650
14:10 f	**Vol. 1:** 185
14:11	**Vol. 1:** 413–414
14:12	**Vol. 1:** 683
14:13	**Vol. 3:** 747
14:16	**Vol. 1:** 185, 688 **Vol. 2:** 797, 876 **Vol. 3:** 813
14:18–19	**Vol. 1:** 531
14:18	**Vol. 3:** 813
14:19	**Vol. 3:** 813
14:21	**Vol. 2:** 891

Malachi

1:1	**Vol. 3:** 311
1:2 f	**Vol. 1:** 556
1:2	**Vol. 2:** 318–319
1:3	**Vol. 2:** 318–319
1:4–14	**Vol. 3:** 717
1:6	**Vol. 1:** 617–618 **Vol. 3:** 636
1:7 ff	**Vol. 2:** 415

1:9	**Vol. 1:** 586 **Vol. 3:** 149, 152, 155
1:10	**Vol. 2:** 41 **Vol. 3:** 1019
1:11	**Vol. 2:** 650
1:14	**Vol. 2:** 569 **Vol. 3:** 318
2:2	**Vol. 1:** 416
2:3	**Vol. 2:** 34
2:4	**Vol. 1:** 544
2:5 f	**Vol. 2:** 778
2:5	**Vol. 2:** 478
2:7	**Vol. 2:** 141
2:8	**Vol. 3:** 937
2:10	**Vol. 1:** 379, 617–618 **Vol. 2:** 720
2:14 ff	**Vol. 2:** 583
2:14–16	**Vol. 1:** 505
2:14	**Vol. 2:** 578 **Vol. 3:** 1041
2:16	**Vol. 1:** 555
2:17	**Vol. 2:** 103, 817 **Vol. 3:** 354
3:1 ff	**Vol. 1:** 151 **Vol. 3:** 430
3:1 f	**Vol. 3:** 695
3:1–6	**Vol. 1:** 146
3:1	**Vol. 1:** 102, 544 **Vol. 2:** 38, 596, 891 **Vol. 3:** 46, 80, 119, 121, 212, 786, 937, 940
3:2 ff	**Vol. 2:** 363
3:2	**Vol. 2:** 773
3:3	**Vol. 2:** 96, 891
3:4	**Vol. 2:** 815
3:5†	**Vol. 1:** 410 **Vol. 2:** 139, 554–555 **Vol. 3:** 379, 1073–1074
3:7	**Vol. 1:** 354
3:8	**Vol. 2:** 693 **Vol. 3:** 416, 853
3:10	**Vol. 2:** 693 **Vol. 3:** 853
3:11	**Vol. 1:** 721 **Vol. 2:** 831
3:13	**Vol. 3:** 345
3:14	**Vol. 1:** 551
3:15	**Vol. 3:** 209, 800
3:16–4:3	**Vol. 2:** 833, 838
3:16	**Vol. 2:** 91 **Vol. 3:** 236, 345
3:17	**Vol. 1:** 534 **Vol. 2:** 838
3:19–21*	**Vol. 2:** 891
3:22*	**Vol. 3:** 354
3:23*	**Vol. 3:** 318
3:24*	**Vol. 1:** 414
4:1–6*	**Vol. 3:** 80
4:1	**Vol. 1:** 655 **Vol. 2:** 890 **Vol. 3:** 695
4:2*	**Vol. 2:** 591 **Vol. 3:** 198, 212, 731
4:4	**Vol. 2:** 639
4:5 f*	**Vol. 1:** 354, 543–544 **Vol. 3:** 147
4:5	**Vol. 1:** 320, 323, 593 **Vol. 2:** 443, 596, 890 **Vol. 3:** 86, 121, 198, 212, 863
4:6	**Vol. 1:** 544 **Vol. 3:** 147

New Testament

Matthew

1	**Vol. 2:** 36, 685 **Vol. 3:** 656
1:1 ff	**Vol. 1:** 427
1:1–17	**Vol. 1:** 77 **Vol. 2:** 79, 314 **Vol. 3:** 654–655
1:1	**Vol. 1:** 177, 182, 244 **Vol. 3:** 63
1:2–27	**Vol. 1:** 182
1:2–16	**Vol. 3:** 656
1:2	**Vol. 1:** 81, 182 **Vol. 2:** 318, 320 **Vol. 3:** 658
1:3	**Vol. 1:** 178 **Vol. 2:** 320 **Vol. 3:** 1062
1:5 f	**Vol. 1:** 178
1:5	**Vol. 3:** 1062
1:6 f	**Vol. 3:** 606–607
1:6	**Vol. 1:** 177 **Vol. 2:** 378 **Vol. 3:** 656, 1062
1:7	**Vol. 3:** 659
1:10	**Vol. 3:** 659
1:11	**Vol. 1:** 141
1:12	**Vol. 3:** 655
1:15 f	**Vol. 2:** 318
1:15	**Vol. 2:** 318, 640
1:16	**Vol. 1:** 177, 187 **Vol. 2:** 318 **Vol. 3:** 652, 658, 662, 1073
1:17 f	**Vol. 2:** 691
1:17	**Vol. 1:** 141 **Vol. 2:** 35 **Vol. 3:** 63, 657
1:18 ff	**Vol. 3:** 642, 656, 1062
1:18–25	**Vol. 1:** 506 **Vol. 3:** 697
1:18	**Vol. 1:** 181–182, 322 **Vol. 3:** 1188
1:19	**Vol. 1:** 506 **Vol. 2:** 291, 563 **Vol. 3:** 189, 360, 570, 660
1:20	**Vol. 1:** 102, 106, 177, 288, 512 **Vol. 2:** 488, 513, 585 **Vol. 3:** 517, 652, 658, 660, 1058, 1073
1:21	**Vol. 1:** 273 **Vol. 2:** 332, 654, 799 **Vol. 3:** 212, 221, 580
1:22 f	**Vol. 2:** 715 **Vol. 3:** 82, 1072, 1163
1:22	**Vol. 1:** 736 **Vol. 3:** 489, 657, 1198
1:23	**Vol. 1:** 186, 581, 737 **Vol. 2:** 86–87, 654 **Vol. 3:** 1058, 1072, 1163
1:24	**Vol. 1:** 442, 476 **Vol. 2:** 585 **Vol. 3:** 280, 1058, 1073
1:25	**Vol. 2:** 398 **Vol. 3:** 660
2	**Vol. 3:** 317
2:1 ff	**Vol. 2:** 378, 630
2:1–23	**Vol. 2:** 640 **Vol. 3:** 83, 1068, 1071
2:1–16	**Vol. 2:** 557
2:1–12	**Vol. 3:** 735
2:1	**Vol. 1:** 170, 178
2:2	**Vol. 1:** 321 **Vol. 2:** 315, 877
2:3	**Vol. 3:** 710
2:4	**Vol. 1:** 178 **Vol. 2:** 32, 799 **Vol. 3:** 480
2:5 f	**Vol. 2:** 715 **Vol. 3:** 82
2:5	**Vol. 1:** 170, 736 **Vol. 2:** 320
2:6	**Vol. 1:** 270, 321, 518 **Vol. 2:** 320 **Vol. 3:** 567, 1163
2:7	**Vol. 1:** 110, 274 **Vol. 2:** 488 **Vol. 3:** 844
2:8	**Vol. 1:** 170 **Vol. 3:** 46
2:9	**Vol. 2:** 175
2:10	**Vol. 2:** 356
2:11	**Vol. 1:** 266, 609 **Vol. 2:** 41, 96, 248, 294, 728, 831
2:12 ff	**Vol. 2:** 630
2:12	**Vol. 1:** 421, 512 **Vol. 3:** 324
2:13 ff	**Vol. 3:** 603
2:13 f	**Vol. 3:** 604
2:13–15	**Vol. 3:** 1007
2:13	**Vol. 1:** 102, 326, 421, 463, 512, 532, 559 **Vol. 2:** 513 **Vol. 3:** 517
2:14	**Vol. 3:** 280
2:15	**Vol. 1:** 290, 532, 736–737 **Vol. 2:** 715 **Vol. 3:** 82, 489, 642, 657, 1005, 1007, 1163
2:16	**Vol. 1:** 106, 109 **Vol. 3:** 341, 844
2:17–18	**Vol. 1:** 170
2:17 f	**Vol. 2:** 715 **Vol. 3:** 82, 1163
2:17	**Vol. 1:** 736 **Vol. 3:** 81, 489, 503
2:18	**Vol. 1:** 737 **Vol. 2:** 417 **Vol. 3:** 113
2:19–21	**Vol. 3:** 1007
2:19	**Vol. 1:** 102, 430, 512, 532 **Vol. 3:** 517
2:20 f	**Vol. 3:** 604
2:20	**Vol. 1:** 288, 518 **Vol. 2:** 640
2:22	**Vol. 1:** 421, 512 **Vol. 2:** 303, 381 **Vol. 3:** 324, 1179, 1193
2:23	**Vol. 2:** 333, 715 **Vol. 3:** 81–82, 489, 503, 1163
3:1 ff	**Vol. 3:** 82
3:1	**Vol. 1:** 150, 156 **Vol. 3:** 55, 1007
3:2	**Vol. 1:** 358, 599 **Vol. 2:** 54, 193, 382, 384 **Vol. 3:** 55, 580
3:3	**Vol. 1:** 411, 736 **Vol. 2:** 715 **Vol. 3:** 53, 118, 503, 940
3:4	**Vol. 1:** 116, 119, 240
3:5	**Vol. 1:** 94
3:6	**Vol. 2:** 533 **Vol. 3:** 987, 991, 1208, 1210
3:7 ff	**Vol. 1:** 358
3:7–12	**Vol. 3:** 695
3:7–9	**Vol. 3:** 439
3:7	**Vol. 1:** 111, 327, 509, 559 **Vol. 2:** 311 **Vol. 3:** 439, 644
3:8	**Vol. 1:** 358, 722 **Vol. 3:** 869
3:9	**Vol. 1:** 77, 286, 599 **Vol. 3:** 281, 360, 393, 822

Matthew *(cont'd)*

3:10 **Vol. 1:** 156, 358, 656, 722 **Vol. 2:** 104, 749 **Vol. 3:** 868–869

3:11 **Vol. 1:** 144, 146, 323, 358, 493, 653 **Vol. 2:** 785–786 **Vol. 3:** 55, 110, 447, 714, 1178, 1187, 1208–1210

3:12 **Vol. 1:** 156 **Vol. 2:** 32, 411 **Vol. 3:** 111, 527, 695, 804, 1210

3:13–17 **Vol. 3:** 113, 170, 990

3:13 **Vol. 3:** 987, 991, 1208

3:14 f **Vol. 3:** 170

3:14 **Vol. 3:** 1208

3:15 **Vol. 1:** 549, 738 **Vol. 2:** 669, 715 **Vol. 3:** 360

3:16 f **Vol. 2:** 194

3:16 **Vol. 1:** 175, 704 **Vol. 2:** 75, 185, 193, 314, 726, 728 **Vol. 3:** 258, 543, 987, 1180

3:17 **Vol. 1:** 290 **Vol. 2:** 193, 543, 725, 819 **Vol. 3:** 114, 611, 697, 807, 1070

4:1 ff **Vol. 2:** 630

4:1–11 **Vol. 1:** 125, 384 **Vol. 3:** 83, 470, 657, 797, 800,

4:1 f **Vol. 2:** 640 **Vol. 3:** 1007 804, 979, 1007, 1011

4:1 **Vol. 3:** 469, 602, 697, 1197

4:2 **Vol. 1:** 421, 613 **Vol. 2:** 267, 689, 696, 887, 893 **Vol. 3:** 954

4:3 **Vol. 1:** 290 **Vol. 3:** 643

4:4 **Vol. 1:** 250, 252 **Vol. 2:** 267, 480, 872, 893 **Vol. 3:** 329, 805, 807, 1181, 1193

4:5 ff **Vol. 2:** 631 **Vol. 3:** 790, 796

4:5 **Vol. 2:** 235, 327, 803 **Vol. 3:** 469

4:6 f **Vol. 1:** 290

4:6 **Vol. 1:** 239, 335 **Vol. 2:** 706 **Vol. 3:** 643, 805

4:7 **Vol. 2:** 893 **Vol. 3:** 802, 805, 809

4:8 f **Vol. 3:** 806

4:8 **Vol. 1:** 524 **Vol. 2:** 46, 199, 381 **Vol. 3:** 469, 569, 1010

4:9 **Vol. 1:** 609 **Vol. 2:** 877

4:10 **Vol. 2:** 877, 893 **Vol. 3:** 469, 550, 806

4:11 **Vol. 3:** 469, 517, 546

4:12 **Vol. 2:** 333, 368

4:13–26 **Vol. 3:** 1163

4:13 **Vol. 3:** 251, 1052

4:14 **Vol. 1:** 736 **Vol. 3:** 489, 657

4:15 **Vol. 2:** 793 **Vol. 3:** 757

4:16 **Vol. 1:** 423, 435 **Vol. 3:** 555, 658

4:17 **Vol. 1:** 167, 358, 482, 599, 720 **Vol. 2:** 54, 193, 381, 384 **Vol. 3:** 55, 1163

4:18–22 **Vol. 2:** 825 **Vol. 3:** 985

4:18 **Vol. 3:** 983–984

4:19 **Vol. 2:** 433, 565

4:20 **Vol. 3:** 838

4:21 **Vol. 1:** 274 **Vol. 3:** 350

4:22 **Vol. 3:** 838

4:23 f **Vol. 2:** 164

4:23 **Vol. 2:** 110, 112, 164, 630–631, 750, 799 **Vol. 3:** 52, 56–57, 197, 761, 785, 999, 1110

4:24 **Vol. 2:** 165, 175, 415 **Vol. 3:** 475, 734, 856, 999

4:25 **Vol. 1:** 482 **Vol. 2:** 327, 801

5–9 **Vol. 3:** 1110

5–7 **Vol. 2:** 164, 449 **Vol. 3:** 1011, 1109–1110

5 **Vol. 2:** 583 **Vol. 3:** 184, 1009

5:1 ff **Vol. 3:** 83

5:1–12 **Vol. 2:** 203

5:1 f **Vol. 2:** 110

5:1 **Vol. 1:** 322 **Vol. 2:** 185, 640, 801 **Vol. 3:** 589

5:2 ff **Vol. 3:** 580

5:2 f **Vol. 3:** 763

5:2 **Vol. 2:** 726–727 **Vol. 3:** 761, 763

5:3 ff **Vol. 1:** 495 **Vol. 2:** 640

5:3–11 **Vol. 2:** 543

5:3–10 **Vol. 1:** 217 **Vol. 2:** 386, 388

5:3–6 **Vol. 3:** 696

5:3 **Vol. 1:** 216, 285, 358 **Vol. 2:** 258, 300, 381, 386, 824 **Vol. 3:** 693, 978

5:4 **Vol. 1:** 571 **Vol. 2:** 381, 420, 422

5:5 ff **Vol. 1:** 453

5:5 **Vol. 2:** 258, 300, 311, 380 **Vol. 3:** 807

5:6 **Vol. 1:** 744 **Vol. 2:** 267, 433 **Vol. 3:** 360

5:7 **Vol. 2:** 595

5:8 **Vol. 1:** 587 **Vol. 2:** 183, 756 **Vol. 3:** 106, 335, 515, 518

5:9 **Vol. 1:** 274, 288, 290 **Vol. 2:** 780, 782 **Vol. 3:** 1155

5:10 ff **Vol. 2:** 806

5:10 **Vol. 2:** 193, 300 **Vol. 3:** 360

5:11 ff **Vol. 3:** 142

5:11 f **Vol. 1:** 217 **Vol. 2:** 359, 806

5:11 **Vol. 1:** 556, 567 **Vol. 3:** 257, 340, 627

5:12 **Vol. 2:** 193, 353–354, 358, 806 **Vol. 3:** 83, 311

5:13 **Vol. 2:** 46, 749–750, 757 **Vol. 3:** 445, 447–448, 713, 944, 1012, 1025

5:14 f **Vol. 2:** 217, 749

5:14 **Vol. 2:** 313, 493, 746 **Vol. 3:** 445

5:14b **Vol. 3:** 1012

5:15 ff **Vol. 2:** 487

5:15 f **Vol. 2:** 486

5:15 **Vol. 2:** 750, 757

5:16 **Vol. 2:** 47, 101, 104, 193, 493 **Vol. 3:** 343, 1012, 1150

5:17 ff **Vol. 3:** 184

5:17–20 **Vol. 2:** 640 **Vol. 3:** 181

5:17–19 **Vol. 2:** 443

5:17 f **Vol. 2:** 450, 715, 721, 872 **Vol. 3:** 185, 327, 329, 428–429, 541, 584, 807, 1163

5:17 **Vol. 1:** 322, 335, 719, 737–738 **Vol. 2:** 281, 313–314, 382, 443–444, 714 **Vol. 3:** 81, 181–183, 189, 311, 313, 492

Matthew *(cont'd)*

5:18 ff   **Vol. 1:** 488, 738
5:18 f   **Vol. 1:** 719
5:18   **Vol. 1:** 322, 518   **Vol. 2:** 192, 437, 443–444, 720   **Vol. 3:** 181–183, 484, 742
5:19–20   **Vol. 2:** 426, 443   **Vol. 3:** 184
5:19   **Vol. 1:** 334   **Vol. 3:** 183, 187, 482, 763
5:20   **Vol. 1:** 729   **Vol. 2:** 101, 133, 385, 443   **Vol. 3:** 183, 360, 763, 941, 1162
5:21 ff   **Vol. 1:** 738   **Vol. 3:** 183, 360, 762–763, 1107
5:21–48   **Vol. 1:** 335   **Vol. 2:** 281, 443   **Vol. 3:** 1163
5:21 f   **Vol. 1:** 364   **Vol. 2:** 143
5:21   **Vol. 1:** 167   **Vol. 2:** 177, 365, 437, 443
5:22   **Vol. 1:** 110, 417–418   **Vol. 2:** 443   **Vol. 3:** 696, 742, 1025
5:23 ff   **Vol. 2:** 366
5:23–24   **Vol. 1:** 702   **Vol. 2:** 41, 443, 868   **Vol. 3:** 173, 428–429, 435–436
5:24   **Vol. 1:** 666   **Vol. 3:** 167, 173
5:25 f   **Vol. 3:** 173, 1157
5:25   **Vol. 1:** 554   **Vol. 2:** 136, 365, 368   **Vol. 3:** 547, 939
5:26   **Vol. 2:** 850
5:27 ff   **Vol. 3:** 183, 539
5:27–32   **Vol. 3:** 172
5:27–31   **Vol. 2:** 580
5:27 f   **Vol. 2:** 580, 583
5:27   **Vol. 1:** 167   **Vol. 2:** 443
5:28   **Vol. 1:** 457   **Vol. 2:** 443   **Vol. 3:** 515, 742, 1058, 1175
5:29 f   **Vol. 1:** 138, 231, 561   **Vol. 2:** 708, 710   **Vol. 3:** 448
5:29   **Vol. 1:** 234   **Vol. 2:** 710   **Vol. 3:** 516
5:30   **Vol. 2:** 149, 385, 710
5:31 ff   **Vol. 3:** 183
5:31 f   **Vol. 1:** 506   **Vol. 2:** 580, 583   **Vol. 3:** 188–189, 980, 1058
5:31   **Vol. 1:** 606   **Vol. 2:** 443
5:32   **Vol. 1:** 500, 506   **Vol. 2:** 443, 580, 583   **Vol. 3:** 535, 538, 540, 742, 1155, 1195
5:33–37   **Vol. 3:** 183, 429, 740, 792
5:33   **Vol. 2:** 443   **Vol. 3:** 135, 738, 740
5:34–36   **Vol. 3:** 741
5:34 f   **Vol. 1:** 518   **Vol. 2:** 192
5:34   **Vol. 2:** 74, 193, 443, 614   **Vol. 3:** 740–742
5:35   **Vol. 1:** 50, 239   **Vol. 2:** 74, 327, 803   **Vol. 3:** 741
5:36   **Vol. 1:** 203   **Vol. 2:** 159, 175   **Vol. 3:** 1155
5:37   **Vol. 1:** 730   **Vol. 3:** 741, 1106
5:38 ff   **Vol. 3:** 979
5:38–48   **Vol. 1:** 702
5:38–42   **Vol. 2:** 386   **Vol. 3:** 97, 183
5:38   **Vol. 2:** 443   **Vol. 3:** 94, 1179

5:39 ff   **Vol. 3:** 380
5:39   **Vol. 2:** 443, 739   **Vol. 3:** 742
5:39a   **Vol. 1:** 566
5:40   **Vol. 2:** 365, 433
5:41   **Vol. 2:** 720   **Vol. 3:** 183
5:42   **Vol. 2:** 43, 856–857
5:43 ff   **Vol. 1:** 258, 556   **Vol. 2:** 366, 542   **Vol. 3:** 183
5:43–48   **Vol. 1:** 258, 701   **Vol. 2:** 544   **Vol. 3:** 576
5:43 f   **Vol. 1:** 554, 556
5:43   **Vol. 2:** 443
5:44 ff   **Vol. 1:** 620
5:44 f   **Vol. 3:** 360
5:44   **Vol. 1:** 417   **Vol. 2:** 443, 543, 806, 868   **Vol. 3:** 97, 742, 755
5:45 ff   **Vol. 1:** 556
5:45†   **Vol. 1:** 620   **Vol. 2:** 100, 193   **Vol. 3:** 331, 360, 575, 731, 1002
5:46 f   **Vol. 3:** 580, 757
5:46   **Vol. 2:** 118, 443
5:47   **Vol. 1:** 729   **Vol. 2:** 724, 795
5:48   **Vol. 1:** 335, 492, 730   **Vol. 2:** 63, 65, 77, 101, 192, 229, 443, 566, 778, 782   **Vol. 3:** 185, 927
6:1 ff   **Vol. 3:** 141, 184, 402
6:1–18   **Vol. 3:** 657
6:1–4   **Vol. 2:** 596   **Vol. 3:** 874
6:1   **Vol. 2:** 193   **Vol. 3:** 141, 360, 1198
6:2 ff   **Vol. 2:** 462, 469
6:2 f   **Vol. 3:** 1155
6:2–18   **Vol. 3:** 1162
6:2   **Vol. 1:** 99   **Vol. 2:** 47, 433   **Vol. 3:** 141, 674, 785, 874
6:3   **Vol. 3:** 142
6:4   **Vol. 2:** 76, 214, 216   **Vol. 3:** 517
6:5 ff   **Vol. 2:** 469
6:5–15   **Vol. 2:** 868
6:5   **Vol. 1:** 99   **Vol. 2:** 433, 488, 548, 813   **Vol. 3:** 141, 389, 785
6:6–9   **Vol. 2:** 867
6:6   **Vol. 2:** 30, 76, 214, 216, 730, 869
6:7 ff   **Vol. 3:** 402
6:7   **Vol. 2:** 178, 795   **Vol. 3:** 822, 1175, 1190, 1192
6:8   **Vol. 1:** 620   **Vol. 2:** 726, 857
6:9 ff   **Vol. 2:** 868
6:9–15   **Vol. 2:** 561
6:9–13   **Vol. 2:** 832, 869
6:9   **Vol. 1:** 618, 621   **Vol. 2:** 74, 76, 193, 229, 653, 871
6:10   **Vol. 1:** 323   **Vol. 2:** 74, 194, 267, 382, 921   **Vol. 3:** 1022
6:11   **Vol. 1:** 250–251   **Vol. 2:** 871, 895
6:12   **Vol. 1:** 701–702   **Vol. 2:** 566, 668
6:13   **Vol. 1:** 567   **Vol. 2:** 868   **Vol. 3:** 204, 470, 803
6:13a   **Vol. 1:** 567   **Vol. 3:** 1198
6:13b   **Vol. 1:** 566–567   **Vol. 2:** 878   **Vol. 3:** 1176

Matthew *(cont'd)*

6:14 ff   **Vol. 2:** 668   **Vol. 3:** 402
6:14 f   **Vol. 1:** 701   **Vol. 2:** 770   **Vol. 3:** 586
6:14   **Vol. 1:** 702   **Vol. 2:** 192
6:15   **Vol. 2:** 301   **Vol. 3:** 142
6:16 ff   **Vol. 3:** 331
6:16 f   **Vol. 1:** 586
6:16 – 18   **Vol. 1:** 613
6:16   **Vol. 1:** 99   **Vol. 2:** 433, 488, 813   **Vol. 3:** 141
6:17   **Vol. 1:** 120   **Vol. 2:** 159, 712
6:18   **Vol. 2:** 76, 214, 216, 488   **Vol. 3:** 142
6:19 ff   **Vol. 2:** 749, 831
6:19 f   **Vol. 1:** 119   **Vol. 3:** 378
6:19 – 34   **Vol. 3:** 402
6:19   **Vol. 2:** 268
6:20   **Vol. 2:** 193   **Vol. 3:** 1149
6:21   **Vol. 2:** 757, 832
6:22 f   **Vol. 1:** 423   **Vol. 2:** 706, 749 – 750, 757   **Vol. 3:** 516
6:22   **Vol. 1:** 234   **Vol. 2:** 487   **Vol. 3:** 572
6:23   **Vol. 1:** 565
6:24 ff   **Vol. 1:** 384
6:24   **Vol. 1:** 138, 461   **Vol. 2:** 73, 286, 686, 749 – 750, 832, 838   **Vol. 3:** 595
6:25 ff   **Vol. 2:** 275, 480
6:25 – 34   **Vol. 1:** 277, 642
6:25 – 33   **Vol. 1:** 251   **Vol. 2:** 386
6:25 – 32   **Vol. 2:** 843
6:25   **Vol. 1:** 234, 277   **Vol. 2:** 272   **Vol. 3:** 683
6:26 ff   **Vol. 2:** 749   **Vol. 3:** 331
6:26 – 32   **Vol. 2:** 76
6:26   **Vol. 1:** 173, 278   **Vol. 2:** 32, 192   **Vol. 3:** 520, 526
6:26a   **Vol. 1:** 384
6:26b   **Vol. 2:** 566
6:27   **Vol. 1:** 92, 277
6:28   **Vol. 1:** 263   **Vol. 2:** 129
6:29   **Vol. 2:** 46 – 47   **Vol. 3:** 606 – 607
6:30   **Vol. 1:** 278, 744   **Vol. 2:** 211
6:31   **Vol. 2:** 275
6:32   **Vol. 1:** 142, 278, 620   **Vol. 2:** 192, 793   **Vol. 3:** 532, 958
6:33   **Vol. 1:** 278, 384, 666   **Vol. 2:** 267, 275, 387, 832   **Vol. 3:** 360, 372, 517, 530 – 532
6:34   **Vol. 1:** 251, 277, 563   **Vol. 2:** 757, 832   **Vol. 3:** 727 – 728
7:1 ff   **Vol. 2:** 365
7:1 – 5   **Vol. 2:** 366, 449
7:1 f   **Vol. 2:** 364
7:1   **Vol. 2:** 366   **Vol. 3:** 402
7:2   **Vol. 1:** 572   **Vol. 3:** 402, 1173
7:3 ff   **Vol. 2:** 469
7:3   **Vol. 1:** 116   **Vol. 2:** 433, 749   **Vol. 3:** 129
7:4   **Vol. 1:** 453   **Vol. 2:** 757
7:5   **Vol. 1:** 667   **Vol. 2:** 749   **Vol. 3:** 944

7:6   **Vol. 1:** 117   **Vol. 2:** 746, 749   **Vol. 3:** 395, 944
7:7 – 12   **Vol. 2:** 178
7:7 – 11   **Vol. 2:** 857
7:7 f   **Vol. 2:** 857, 881   **Vol. 3:** 529, 532
7:7   **Vol. 2:** 42, 728, 856, 881   **Vol. 3:** 530
7:8   **Vol. 2:** 856 – 857
7:9 – 11   **Vol. 2:** 857
7:9   **Vol. 3:** 805
7:10   **Vol. 1:** 509
7:11   **Vol. 1:** 286, 565, 620   **Vol. 2:** 41 – 42, 193, 565, 857   **Vol. 3:** 698
7:12 f   **Vol. 2:** 513
7:12   **Vol. 2:** 442   **Vol. 3:** 183, 762
7:13 ff   **Vol. 3:** 603
7:13 f   **Vol. 2:** 29, 31, 481, 746, 749, 881   **Vol. 3:** 940
7:13   **Vol. 1:** 254, 464   **Vol. 2:** 387, 728, 807 – 808
7:14   **Vol. 3:** 530
7:15 – 20   **Vol. 2:** 749
7:15   **Vol. 1:** 114, 118   **Vol. 2:** 472   **Vol. 3:** 81, 84, 604
7:16 ff   **Vol. 1:** 722
7:16 f   **Vol. 3:** 869
7:16   **Vol. 1:** 722, 726   **Vol. 2:** 33, 398   **Vol. 3:** 896, 1174
7:17 – 19   **Vol. 1:** 722
7:17 f   **Vol. 1:** 565   **Vol. 2:** 104
7:17   **Vol. 3:** 868
7:18   **Vol. 2:** 757
7:19   **Vol. 1:** 656, 722   **Vol. 3:** 869
7:20   **Vol. 1:** 722
7:21 ff   **Vol. 1:** 97   **Vol. 2:** 272, 276
7:21   **Vol. 2:** 193, 385, 514, 750   **Vol. 3:** 1022, 1155
7:22 f   **Vol. 2:** 358   **Vol. 3:** 84
7:22   **Vol. 1:** 453   **Vol. 3:** 81, 475 – 476
7:23   **Vol. 1:** 347   **Vol. 2:** 383, 398   **Vol. 3:** 476, 1150
7:24 ff   **Vol. 2:** 177   **Vol. 3:** 1155
7:24 – 27†   **Vol. 2:** 248, 383, 386, 749   **Vol. 3:** 1025
7:24 f   **Vol. 1:** 662   **Vol. 3:** 382
7:24   **Vol. 2:** 175, 619 – 620   **Vol. 3:** 1108
7:25   **Vol. 1:** 610   **Vol. 3:** 707, 982, 984, 987, 1001
7:26   **Vol. 2:** 620
7:27   **Vol. 1:** 610   **Vol. 3:** 707, 982, 984, 987, 1001
7:28 ff   **Vol. 2:** 177
7:28 f   **Vol. 3:** 1163
7:28   **Vol. 2:** 63   **Vol. 3:** 769
7:29   **Vol. 2:** 610, 623   **Vol. 3:** 83, 480 – 481, 1108
8 f   **Vol. 3:** 1110
8 – 9   **Vol. 2:** 164   **Vol. 3:** 851
8:1 – 15   **Vol. 3:** 657
8:1   **Vol. 1:** 482
8:2 – 4   **Vol. 2:** 631   **Vol. 3:** 106
8:2   **Vol. 2:** 860, 877   **Vol. 3:** 758

Matthew *(cont'd)*

8:3   **Vol. 2:** 150, 466   **Vol. 3:** 1022
8:4   **Vol. 2:** 41   **Vol. 3:** 37, 569, 1043
8:5–15 **Vol. 3:** 106
8:5–13 **Vol. 3:** 456, 980
8:5   **Vol. 1:** 570   **Vol. 3:** 964
8:6   **Vol. 1:** 283   **Vol. 2:** 415   **Vol. 3:** 856, 999
8:7   **Vol. 2:** 165
8:8 f   **Vol. 3:** 758
8:8–10 **Vol. 2:** 165
8:8   **Vol. 2:** 168–169   **Vol. 3:** 729, 964, 1108, 1110
8:9   **Vol. 1:** 290   **Vol. 2:** 608   **Vol. 3:** 595, 964
8:10 f **Vol. 2:** 793
8:10   **Vol. 1:** 99, 599   **Vol. 2:** 624, 631   **Vol. 3:** 530, 964
8:11 f **Vol. 1:** 78   **Vol. 2:** 57
8:11   **Vol. 1:** 81, 321, 667   **Vol. 2:** 319, 385, 727   **Vol. 3:** 922
8:12   **Vol. 1:** 289, 424–425   **Vol. 2:** 382, 385, 421, 877
8:13   **Vol. 2:** 165, 168–169   **Vol. 3:** 847–848, 964
8:14 f **Vol. 3:** 1059
8:14   **Vol. 1:** 656
8:15   **Vol. 3:** 546
8:16   **Vol. 1:** 453–454   **Vol. 2:** 165   **Vol. 3:** 475, 694, 1108, 1110
8:17   **Vol. 1:** 736   **Vol. 2:** 165   **Vol. 3:** 489, 748, 998–999
8:18   **Vol. 1:** 341   **Vol. 2:** 630
8:19–26 **Vol. 1:** 489
8:19–22 **Vol. 1:** 464
8:19   **Vol. 3:** 481, 767
8:20 f **Vol. 1:** 488
8:20   **Vol. 1:** 118, 173   **Vol. 2:** 192, 825   **Vol. 3:** 620, 623, 813
8:21–22 **Vol. 1:** 265, 482
8:22   **Vol. 1:** 439, 444, 446, 482
8:23–37 **Vol. 2:** 630
8:23–27 **Vol. 1:** 419   **Vol. 3:** 984–985
8:23   **Vol. 3:** 984
8:24   **Vol. 2:** 212   **Vol. 3:** 557
8:25   **Vol. 3:** 115, 211, 767
8:26 f **Vol. 3:** 1002
8:26   **Vol. 1:** 181   **Vol. 3:** 280
8:27   **Vol. 2:** 179, 623
8:28 ff **Vol. 3:** 475
8:28–34 **Vol. 2:** 631
8:28   **Vol. 1:** 66, 325, 420   **Vol. 3:** 247
8:29   **Vol. 1:** 290, 409, 452–453   **Vol. 2:** 208, 559   **Vol. 3:** 474, 856
8:30–34 **Vol. 1:** 117
8:30   **Vol. 2:** 631   **Vol. 3:** 1011
8:31   **Vol. 1:** 570   **Vol. 3:** 293
8:32   **Vol. 3:** 475, 984–985, 990, 1199
8:34   **Vol. 1:** 325   **Vol. 2:** 803

9   **Vol. 3:** 558
9:2–8   **Vol. 2:** 610, 631
9:2   **Vol. 1:** 286, 328   **Vol. 2:** 415   **Vol. 3:** 999
9:3   **Vol. 2:** 182, 728   **Vol. 3:** 342, 481
9:4   **Vol. 1:** 106, 567
9:5   **Vol. 2:** 434
9:6   **Vol. 2:** 415   **Vol. 3:** 999
9:7   **Vol. 2:** 248
9:8   **Vol. 3:** 622
9:9–13 **Vol. 2:** 523, 630   **Vol. 3:** 758
9:9   **Vol. 1:** 482   **Vol. 2:** 754   **Vol. 3:** 275, 757, 759
9:10 f **Vol. 3:** 580
9:10   **Vol. 3:** 580, 757
9:11   **Vol. 2:** 813   **Vol. 3:** 481, 767
9:12 ff **Vol. 2:** 813
9:12 f **Vol. 3:** 428, 998
9:12   **Vol. 2:** 386   **Vol. 3:** 758
9:13   **Vol. 1:** 274, 322, 486   **Vol. 2:** 566, 596, 757   **Vol. 3:** 360, 427, 492, 580, 1022
9:14 ff **Vol. 1:** 495
9:14–17 **Vol. 2:** 754   **Vol. 3:** 921
9:14 f **Vol. 2:** 359
9:14   **Vol. 1:** 487   **Vol. 3:** 481
9:15   **Vol. 1:** 321   **Vol. 2:** 358, 383, 422, 585
9:16 f **Vol. 2:** 714
9:16   **Vol. 3:** 543
9:17   **Vol. 2:** 670, 675–676, 854
9:18–26 **Vol. 2:** 168, 630   **Vol. 3:** 1059
9:18   **Vol. 1:** 168, 430   **Vol. 2:** 151, 877
9:20 ff **Vol. 2:** 560
9:20 f **Vol. 1:** 316   **Vol. 3:** 860
9:20   **Vol. 2:** 696   **Vol. 3:** 1058
9:21   **Vol. 2:** 714, 724
9:22   **Vol. 1:** 328   **Vol. 2:** 714   **Vol. 3:** 212, 846–848
9:23 ff **Vol. 1:** 445
9:23   **Vol. 1:** 168   **Vol. 2:** 418, 623   **Vol. 3:** 674
9:24   **Vol. 1:** 283, 443   **Vol. 2:** 433, 510
9:25   **Vol. 3:** 280, 717, 1110
9:26   **Vol. 1:** 322
9:27 ff **Vol. 2:** 165
9:27–31 **Vol. 1:** 219
9:27   **Vol. 1:** 409   **Vol. 2:** 595   **Vol. 3:** 652
9:28 f **Vol. 2:** 631
9:29   **Vol. 2:** 630
9:30   **Vol. 2:** 726
9:32 ff **Vol. 3:** 475
9:32   **Vol. 1:** 429   **Vol. 2:** 631
9:33   **Vol. 1:** 429   **Vol. 2:** 488, 623, 801
9:34   **Vol. 1:** 168, 429, 453   **Vol. 2:** 510   **Vol. 3:** 472, 481, 802, 1190, 1198, 1210
9:35–10:42 **Vol. 2:** 733
9:35–38 **Vol. 2:** 750
9:35   **Vol. 2:** 110, 112, 164, 630–631   **Vol. 3:** 52, 56–57, 761, 785, 999, 1110
9:36   **Vol. 2:** 413, 599   **Vol. 3:** 567

Matthew *(cont'd)*

9:37 f	**Vol. 2:** 746 **Vol. 3:** 144, 1150
9:37	**Vol. 1:** 204 **Vol. 3:** 526
9:38	**Vol. 1:** 453 **Vol. 2:** 514, 861 **Vol. 3:** 526
10	**Vol. 2:** 57 **Vol. 3:** 1109
10:1–16	**Vol. 1:** 213 **Vol. 2:** 825 **Vol. 3:** 453
10:1–5	**Vol. 1:** 131
10:1	**Vol. 1:** 274, 454, 500 **Vol. 2:** 165, 610, 695 **Vol. 3:** 475, 999
10:2 ff	**Vol. 2:** 652
10:2–4	**Vol. 1:** 136
10:2	**Vol. 1:** 129, 134, 136 **Vol. 2:** 695 **Vol. 3:** 384
10:3	**Vol. 2:** 550
10:4	**Vol. 1:** 299 **Vol. 2:** 321 **Vol. 3:** 1167
10:5 f	**Vol. 1:** 482 **Vol. 2:** 314 **Vol. 3:** 453–454, 626
10:5	**Vol. 1:** 340 **Vol. 2:** 695, 793 **Vol. 3:** 454, 940
10:6 f	**Vol. 3:** 946
10:6	**Vol. 2:** 248, 315, 385, 413, 459, 695 **Vol. 3:** 567
10:7 ff	**Vol. 3:** 57
10:7 f	**Vol. 2:** 632
10:7–8a	**Vol. 1:** 213
10:7	**Vol. 1:** 482 **Vol. 2:** 54 **Vol. 3:** 55–56
10:8	**Vol. 1:** 446, 454 **Vol. 2:** 41, 165, 184 **Vol. 3:** 281, 475, 994
10:8b	**Vol. 2:** 43
10:9	**Vol. 1:** 142 **Vol. 2:** 96–97 **Vol. 3:** 121
10:10	**Vol. 1:** 143, 407 **Vol. 2:** 272 **Vol. 3:** 349, 794, 855
10:11 ff	**Vol. 1:** 689
10:11	**Vol. 3:** 349
10:12–15	**Vol. 1:** 171
10:12 f	**Vol. 3:** 258
10:12	**Vol. 1:** 213
10:13 ff	**Vol. 2:** 223
10:13	**Vol. 1:** 213, 355 **Vol. 2:** 780–781 **Vol. 3:** 349
10:14	**Vol. 1:** 239 **Vol. 2:** 413 **Vol. 3:** 560
10:15	**Vol. 2:** 203, 366, 767, 894 **Vol. 3:** 93
10:16	**Vol. 1:** 118, 175, 510 **Vol. 2:** 413, 619, 746 **Vol. 3:** 447
10:17 ff	**Vol. 1:** 489 **Vol. 2:** 386
10:17	**Vol. 1:** 163, 364 **Vol. 2:** 368 **Vol. 3:** 785
10:18	**Vol. 1:** 270 **Vol. 2:** 169 **Vol. 3:** 1043
10:19 f	**Vol. 3:** 257
10:19	**Vol. 1:** 278 **Vol. 3:** 849
10:20	**Vol. 1:** 90 **Vol. 2:** 75
10:21	**Vol. 1:** 286–287, 725
10:22	**Vol. 1:** 556 **Vol. 2:** 62, 654, 773, 806 **Vol. 3:** 257
10:23 ff	**Vol. 2:** 450
10:23	**Vol. 1:** 99, 559 **Vol. 2:** 63, 382, 806, 930 **Vol. 3:** 454, 620, 626
10:24 ff	**Vol. 1:** 486
10:24 f	**Vol. 1:** 482, 488–489 **Vol. 2:** 513 **Vol. 3:** 767
10:24	**Vol. 1:** 404, 549 **Vol. 2:** 510 **Vol. 3:** 629
10:25 f	**Vol. 1:** 305
10:25	**Vol. 1:** 168 **Vol. 2:** 509 **Vol. 3:** 472, 727
10:26 f	**Vol. 3:** 314
10:26	**Vol. 1:** 623 **Vol. 2:** 212, 216–217 **Vol. 3:** 312, 657
10:27	**Vol. 1:** 423 **Vol. 2:** 212, 217, 493 **Vol. 3:** 54
10:28	**Vol. 1:** 436, 464, 623 **Vol. 2:** 208–209, 366, 480 **Vol. 3:** 304, 657, 686
10:29–31	**Vol. 2:** 76
10:29 f	**Vol. 2:** 566
10:29	**Vol. 1:** 173, 609
10:30 f	**Vol. 1:** 623
10:30	**Vol. 1:** 203 **Vol. 2:** 159
10:31	**Vol. 3:** 657
10:32 f	**Vol. 1:** 323, 347 **Vol. 2:** 193, 565 **Vol. 3:** 625–626
10:32	**Vol. 1:** 205 **Vol. 2:** 383 **Vol. 3:** 62, 86, 142, 621
10:33	**Vol. 2:** 76
10:34–37	**Vol. 1:** 159
10:34–36	**Vol. 3:** 697
10:34	**Vol. 2:** 780 **Vol. 3:** 181, 967, 978, 1070
10:35 f	**Vol. 1:** 725 **Vol. 2:** 250
10:35	**Vol. 2:** 585
10:37 ff	**Vol. 2:** 544, 825
10:37	**Vol. 1:** 289, 488, 619 **Vol. 2:** 386, 548 **Vol. 3:** 349
10:38	**Vol. 1:** 324, 402, 404, 482, 489, 493 **Vol. 3:** 60, 349, 748
10:39	**Vol. 1:** 464 **Vol. 3:** 529, 682, 1163
10:40 ff	**Vol. 1:** 130
10:40	**Vol. 1:** 91, 285 **Vol. 2:** 176, 920 **Vol. 3:** 56, 314, 326, 629, 746
10:41	**Vol. 2:** 652 **Vol. 3:** 360
10:42	**Vol. 1:** 318 **Vol. 2:** 429 **Vol. 3:** 141–142, 980, 989
11:1	**Vol. 2:** 63, 695 **Vol. 3:** 56, 761
11:2 ff	**Vol. 2:** 631
11:2–6	**Vol. 2:** 314, 379
11:2	**Vol. 1:** 487 **Vol. 2:** 686 **Vol. 3:** 1150
11:3	**Vol. 1:** 323 **Vol. 2:** 245, 379, 739 **Vol. 3:** 367, 378
11:4	**Vol. 2:** 176, 351
11:5 f	**Vol. 2:** 110
11:5	**Vol. 1:** 217–219, 428, 445 **Vol. 2:** 110, 118, 358, 379, 415, 464, 824–825 **Vol. 3:** 281, 519, 696–697, 1110
11:6	**Vol. 1:** 358 **Vol. 2:** 110, 708 **Vol. 3:** 697
11:7–19	**Vol. 2:** 443
11:7	**Vol. 1:** 167 **Vol. 3:** 559, 1007
11:8 ff	**Vol. 3:** 82
11:8	**Vol. 2:** 565

Matthew *(cont'd)*

11:9   **Vol. 1:** 729   **Vol. 3:** 83
11:10–14   **Vol. 1:** 545
11:10   **Vol. 1:** 102   **Vol. 3:** 80, 119, 329, 940
11:11–15   **Vol. 2:** 443
11:11 f   **Vol. 3:** 82
11:11   **Vol. 2:** 427   **Vol. 3:** 184
11:12 f   **Vol. 2:** 383
11:12   **Vol. 3:** 603, 711–712, 1180
11:13   **Vol. 2:** 443   **Vol. 3:** 183
11:14   **Vol. 1:** 323, 545   **Vol. 2:** 443
11:15   **Vol. 2:** 178, 750
11:16   **Vol. 1:** 259, 267, 283
11:17   **Vol. 2:** 418   **Vol. 3:** 674
11:18 f   **Vol. 2:** 276   **Vol. 3:** 623, 921
11:18   **Vol. 1:** 323, 637   **Vol. 2:** 272   **Vol. 3:** 921
11:19   **Vol. 1:** 286, 384, 495, 561   **Vol. 2:** 272, 549   **Vol. 3:** 360, 580, 623, 758, 1030, 1174
11:20 ff   **Vol. 2:** 366
11:20–24   **Vol. 1:** 358
11:20   **Vol. 1:** 167   **Vol. 2:** 803   **Vol. 3:** 340
11:21 ff   **Vol. 2:** 383
11:21   **Vol. 1:** 181   **Vol. 2:** 714   **Vol. 3:** 1052
11:22   **Vol. 2:** 767
11:23 f   **Vol. 3:** 93
11:23   **Vol. 2:** 207   **Vol. 3:** 224
11:24   **Vol. 2:** 767
11:25 ff   **Vol. 1:** 290, 615   **Vol. 3:** 313, 640
11:25–30   **Vol. 1:** 375
11:25–27   **Vol. 1:** 619   **Vol. 3:** 640
11:25 f   **Vol. 1:** 620   **Vol. 2:** 76
11:25   **Vol. 1:** 282, 284, 345–346   **Vol. 2:** 192–193, 216, 354, 514   **Vol. 3:** 533, 821, 837
11:26   **Vol. 2:** 818–819   **Vol. 3:** 1017, 1175
11:27 ff   **Vol. 3:** 326
11:27   **Vol. 1:** 90, 95, 375   **Vol. 2:** 193, 313, 368, 404, 610, 653   **Vol. 3:** 313, 639–640, 642, 645, 1017, 1107, 1163
11:28 ff   **Vol. 1:** 262, 335, 339   **Vol. 2:** 118–119, 262   **Vol. 3:** 256
11:28–30   **Vol. 2:** 281, 443   **Vol. 3:** 1162
11:28 f   **Vol. 3:** 640
11:28   **Vol. 1:** 263, 729   **Vol. 3:** 411, 580, 1162
11:29 f   **Vol. 3:** 1162, 1164
11:29   **Vol. 1:** 486, 570   **Vol. 2:** 106, 258, 262, 281   **Vol. 3:** 529–530, 683
11:30   **Vol. 2:** 106
12   **Vol. 3:** 1109
12:1–12   **Vol. 1:** 631
12:1–8   **Vol. 2:** 267, 754   **Vol. 3:** 37, 408, 423, 1163
12:1   **Vol. 3:** 837, 1163
12:2 ff   **Vol. 2:** 813
12:2   **Vol. 3:** 516
12:3–7   **Vol. 3:** 792
12:3   **Vol. 1:** 427   **Vol. 3:** 329

12:4   **Vol. 1:** 586   **Vol. 2:** 248, 724   **Vol. 3:** 792
12:5   **Vol. 2:** 139, 444
12:6   **Vol. 2:** 426   **Vol. 3:** 380, 429, 658, 792
12:7 f   **Vol. 3:** 429
12:7   **Vol. 2:** 139, 370, 596, 813   **Vol. 3:** 427, 429, 1022
12:8   **Vol. 3:** 792
12:9–16   **Vol. 3:** 1163
12:9–14   **Vol. 3:** 409
12:9   **Vol. 3:** 785
12:10   **Vol. 2:** 165, 610
12:11 f   **Vol. 2:** 459
12:11   **Vol. 1:** 115, 516, 609   **Vol. 2:** 413   **Vol. 3:** 717
12:12   **Vol. 2:** 434, 565, 610
12:13   **Vol. 2:** 150, 170, 739   **Vol. 3:** 147, 442
12:14   **Vol. 1:** 363   **Vol. 2:** 812–813
12:15   **Vol. 2:** 165
12:16   **Vol. 3:** 320
12:17–21   **Vol. 3:** 1163
12:17   **Vol. 1:** 736   **Vol. 3:** 489
12:18 ff   **Vol. 3:** 48
12:18†   **Vol. 1:** 534   **Vol. 2:** 75, 365, 543, 819   **Vol. 3:** 110, 442, 610, 685, 698
12:19   **Vol. 1:** 409
12:20   **Vol. 1:** 421, 651   **Vol. 3:** 109
12:21†   **Vol. 2:** 241, 654   **Vol. 3:** 110
12:22–32   **Vol. 3:** 1163
12:22–30   **Vol. 2:** 603
12:22–28   **Vol. 1:** 454
12:22   **Vol. 1:** 219, 429, 718   **Vol. 3:** 515
12:23 ff   **Vol. 3:** 474
12:23   **Vol. 1:** 427   **Vol. 3:** 652
12:24–37   **Vol. 2:** 177
12:24–32   **Vol. 2:** 813   **Vol. 3:** 481
12:24–29   **Vol. 3:** 696
12:24   **Vol. 1:** 168   **Vol. 2:** 510, 631   **Vol. 3:** 472, 481, 802, 869, 1210
12:25–37   **Vol. 2:** 560   **Vol. 3:** 83, 472
12:25–29   **Vol. 3:** 695
12:25   **Vol. 1:** 106   **Vol. 3:** 128, 1008
12:26 f   **Vol. 1:** 453
12:26   **Vol. 2:** 381   **Vol. 3:** 474
12:27–29   **Vol. 3:** 470
12:27 f   **Vol. 3:** 695
12:27   **Vol. 1:** 487   **Vol. 2:** 365   **Vol. 3:** 472, 474, 476, 696
12:28   **Vol. 1:** 453   **Vol. 2:** 75, 150, 381–382, 921   **Vol. 3:** 475, 696, 985, 1163, 1193–1194, 1210
12:29   **Vol. 1:** 53, 508, 651, 666   **Vol. 2:** 382, 603, 631, 702, 733   **Vol. 3:** 602, 913
12:30 ff   **Vol. 1:** 703
12:30   **Vol. 1:** 297   **Vol. 2:** 32, 34   **Vol. 3:** 568
12:31 f   **Vol. 3:** 696
12:31   **Vol. 3:** 343, 628
12:32 f   **Vol. 1:** 347
12:32   **Vol. 1:** 327, 701   **Vol. 3:** 343–344, 658, 831, 1106

Matthew (cont'd)

12:33 ff   Vol. 2: 749
12:33–37   Vol. 3: 1163
12:33 f   Vol. 3: 869
12:33   Vol. 1: 722   Vol. 3: 868
12:34   Vol. 1: 565, 729
12:35–37   Vol. 1: 427
12:35   Vol. 1: 453, 566–567   Vol. 2: 100, 831
12:36   Vol. 2: 894   Vol. 3: 1121, 1142–1143
12:37   Vol. 2: 370   Vol. 3: 360
12:38 ff   Vol. 2: 629
12:38–42   Vol. 2: 750   Vol. 3: 481, 1163
12:38–41   Vol. 2: 350
12:38   Vol. 3: 481
12:39 f   Vol. 2: 680   Vol. 3: 628
12:39   Vol. 1: 565   Vol. 2: 36, 351, 582, 584   Vol. 3: 532, 579
12:40   Vol. 1: 169, 421, 518, 671   Vol. 2: 207, 351, 687
12:41 f   Vol. 2: 366   Vol. 3: 658, 1163
12:41   Vol. 1: 358   Vol. 2: 352, 365, 680   Vol. 3: 52–53, 83, 275, 516, 1187
12:42   Vol. 1: 517   Vol. 2: 381, 385, 680   Vol. 3: 606–607, 1003, 1030
12:43 ff   Vol. 2: 691   Vol. 3: 475
12:43–45   Vol. 3: 1163
12:43   Vol. 3: 256, 529–530, 1006
12:44   Vol. 1: 477, 524   Vol. 3: 474
12:45   Vol. 2: 251   Vol. 3: 474, 579, 657
12:45c   Vol. 3: 256
12:46 ff   Vol. 3: 1070
12:46–50   Vol. 1: 488   Vol. 2: 750   Vol. 3: 1062
12:46 49   Vol. 3: 1163
12:49   Vol. 2: 150
12:50   Vol. 2: 193   Vol. 3: 1022, 1163
13   Vol. 2: 691, 749   Vol. 3: 1109
13:1–58   Vol. 3: 1163
13:1–9   Vol. 2: 748, 750   Vol. 3: 522
13:1–2   Vol. 3: 589
13:1   Vol. 3: 984
13:2   Vol. 1: 297   Vol. 2: 32
13:3   Vol. 1: 464
13:4–8   Vol. 1: 609
13:4   Vol. 1: 174
13:5   Vol. 1: 464, 517   Vol. 2: 197, 739   Vol. 3: 382
13:6   Vol. 1: 516, 653   Vol. 3: 731
13:7 f   Vol. 2: 739
13:7   Vol. 1: 226, 726   Vol. 2: 185
13:8–23   Vol. 3: 522
13:8   Vol. 1: 722
13:9   Vol. 2: 178, 750
13:10–17   Vol. 2: 750
13:10–15   Vol. 2: 752
13:11   Vol. 1: 742   Vol. 2: 178, 401   Vol. 3: 314, 503, 533
13:12   Vol. 1: 730
13:13 ff   Vol. 2: 178   Vol. 3: 313
13:13 f   Vol. 3: 517

13:13   Vol. 3: 131
13:14   Vol. 1: 736   Vol. 2: 175   Vol. 3: 81, 515
13:15   Vol. 1: 261   Vol. 2: 156, 799   Vol. 3: 131
13:16 f   Vol. 1: 217, 742   Vol. 2: 176, 630
13:16   Vol. 2: 110   Vol. 3: 313
13:17   Vol. 1: 457   Vol. 3: 360, 1163
13:18–23   Vol. 2: 748, 750   Vol. 3: 868
13:19   Vol. 1: 174, 566, 742   Vol. 3: 470, 712
13:20 f   Vol. 3: 382
13:20   Vol. 2: 358   Vol. 3: 382, 837
13:21   Vol. 1: 608   Vol. 2: 708, 808
13:22   Vol. 1: 460, 726   Vol. 2: 459–460, 842–843, 845
13:23   Vol. 1: 742   Vol. 2: 104, 177, 773   Vol. 3: 868
13:24 ff   Vol. 1: 554   Vol. 3: 527
13:24–43   Vol. 1: 299
13:24–30   Vol. 2: 708, 750   Vol. 3: 470, 523
13:24 f   Vol. 3: 868
13:24   Vol. 1: 520   Vol. 2: 104, 502
13:26   Vol. 1: 744   Vol. 2: 211, 488
13:27   Vol. 2: 104, 510   Vol. 3: 115
13:28   Vol. 2: 33
13:29   Vol. 2: 33
13:30 f   Vol. 2: 364
13:30   Vol. 1: 171   Vol. 2: 32–33   Vol. 3: 526
13:31 f   Vol. 2: 385, 429, 747, 750   Vol. 3: 523
13:31   Vol. 2: 502
13:32   Vol. 1: 174   Vol. 2: 129   Vol. 3: 813, 868–869
13:33   Vol. 2: 216, 385, 433, 461 462, 502, 747, 750   Vol. 3: 1058, 1178
13:34 f   Vol. 2: 750, 753
13:34   Vol. 2: 801
13:35   Vol. 1: 377–378, 736   Vol. 2: 217, 727   Vol. 3: 489
13:36–51   Vol. 2: 833, 838
13:36–43   Vol. 2: 750   Vol. 3: 831
13:36   Vol. 1: 489, 701
13:37–43   Vol. 3: 627
13:37   Vol. 2: 104   Vol. 3: 868
13:38   Vol. 1: 289, 566   Vol. 2: 104, 709   Vol. 3: 868
13:39 f   Vol. 2: 62   Vol. 3: 658
13:39   Vol. 1: 566   Vol. 3: 526, 829
13:40 ff   Vol. 1: 289
13:40 f   Vol. 2: 364, 917
13:40   Vol. 2: 33
13:41   Vol. 2: 33, 387, 708–709
13:42   Vol. 1: 657   Vol. 2: 208, 421
13:43   Vol. 2: 486, 750   Vol. 3: 360, 732
13:44 ff   Vol. 1: 647   Vol. 2: 750   Vol. 3: 530
13:44–46   Vol. 2: 386, 749
13:44   Vol. 1: 268   Vol. 2: 216, 502, 832–833, 846   Vol. 3: 528–529
13:45 f   Vol. 2: 833   Vol. 3: 395
13:45   Vol. 2: 502   Vol. 3: 529, 532
13:46   Vol. 2: 846   Vol. 3: 395

Matthew *(cont'd)*

13:47–50	**Vol. 2:** 750
13:47	**Vol. 2:** 32, 502
13:48	**Vol. 2:** 33
13:49 f	**Vol. 1:** 566
13:49	**Vol. 1:** 102, 473 **Vol. 2:** 62, 364 **Vol. 3:** 360, 658, 831
13:50	**Vol. 2:** 208, 421
13:51 f	**Vol. 2:** 750
13:51	**Vol. 3:** 132, 503
13:52	**Vol. 1:** 453 **Vol. 2:** 509, 670, 714, 834 **Vol. 3:** 184, 482
13:53–58	**Vol. 2:** 631 **Vol. 3:** 88
13:53	**Vol. 2:** 63
13:54	**Vol. 1:** 616 **Vol. 3:** 761, 785, 1030
13:55	**Vol. 1:** 279 **Vol. 2:** 320 **Vol. 3:** 660
13:56	**Vol. 3:** 1204
13:57	**Vol. 2:** 248, 708, 757 **Vol. 3:** 696
13:58	**Vol. 3:** 1163
14:1 f	**Vol. 2:** 342
14:1	**Vol. 1:** 418 **Vol. 2:** 175 **Vol. 3:** 39
14:2 ff	**Vol. 3:** 82
14:2	**Vol. 1:** 283 **Vol. 3:** 1152
14:3	**Vol. 1:** 171 **Vol. 2:** 136 **Vol. 3:** 540, 717
14:4	**Vol. 1:** 637
14:5	**Vol. 1:** 430, 623 **Vol. 2:** 801
14:7	**Vol. 1:** 346 **Vol. 2:** 856 **Vol. 3:** 742
14:8	**Vol. 2:** 159, 378 **Vol. 3:** 1071
14:9	**Vol. 1:** 341
14:10	**Vol. 2:** 136
14:11	**Vol. 2:** 159 **Vol. 3:** 1071
14:12	**Vol. 1:** 265, 610
14:13–21	**Vol. 1:** 250, 729 **Vol. 2:** 272, 523, 630
14:13	**Vol. 2:** 839 **Vol. 3:** 1007
14:14	**Vol. 1:** 321 **Vol. 2:** 165, 459, 599, 750
14:15	**Vol. 2:** 268 **Vol. 3:** 189, 847
14:17	**Vol. 1:** 670
14:18	**Vol. 2:** 192
14:19	**Vol. 1:** 341, 744 **Vol. 2:** 211, 801 **Vol. 3:** 519
14:20	**Vol. 1:** 743
14:21	**Vol. 1:** 283 **Vol. 2:** 563, 699
14:22–33	**Vol. 2:** 630 **Vol. 3:** 985, 990
14:22–23	**Vol. 2:** 281 **Vol. 3:** 984
14:22	**Vol. 2:** 663 **Vol. 3:** 189
14:23	**Vol. 2:** 185, 839, 869 **Vol. 3:** 1010
14:24 ff	**Vol. 3:** 1002
14:24	**Vol. 1:** 517 **Vol. 3:** 856
14:25	**Vol. 1:** 420 **Vol. 2:** 136
14:26	**Vol. 1:** 409 **Vol. 2:** 559 **Vol. 3:** 324, 474, 710
14:27	**Vol. 1:** 328, 623
14:28–31	**Vol. 3:** 990
14:30	**Vol. 1:** 409 **Vol. 3:** 211, 990
14:31	**Vol. 1:** 504 **Vol. 3:** 750, 1187
14:33	**Vol. 1:** 290 **Vol. 2:** 550, 877 **Vol. 3:** 132
14:34	**Vol. 3:** 1059
14:36	**Vol. 3:** 211, 860
15	**Vol. 3:** 572, 584
15:1 ff	**Vol. 2:** 813 **Vol. 3:** 584
15:1–20	**Vol. 2:** 715, 813 **Vol. 3:** 481, 763, 990
15:1–11	**Vol. 3:** 183
15:2 ff	**Vol. 2:** 469
15:2 f	**Vol. 3:** 584
15:2	**Vol. 1:** 199 **Vol. 3:** 481, 774
15:3–9	**Vol. 3:** 184
15:3	**Vol. 1:** 335 **Vol. 3:** 868
15:4 f	**Vol. 1:** 730
15:4	**Vol. 1:** 415, 430 **Vol. 3:** 95, 1070
15:5 f	**Vol. 3:** 1070
15:5	**Vol. 1:** 415 **Vol. 2:** 42–43
15:6	**Vol. 1:** 415 **Vol. 2:** 715 **Vol. 3:** 184
15:7 ff	**Vol. 2:** 469 **Vol. 3:** 807
15:7	**Vol. 1:** 736 **Vol. 2:** 43 **Vol. 3:** 81
15:8 ff	**Vol. 2:** 150
15:8	**Vol. 2:** 183, 799
15:9	**Vol. 1:** 552 **Vol. 2:** 93 **Vol. 3:** 57, 184, 770
15:10–20	**Vol. 1:** 169 **Vol. 2:** 150
15:10	**Vol. 1:** 274 **Vol. 2:** 177–178
15:11	**Vol. 1:** 384, 448, 642 **Vol. 3:** 106, 860
15:12	**Vol. 2:** 708 **Vol. 3:** 1106, 1108
15:13	**Vol. 2:** 192, 708, 746 **Vol. 3:** 523, 869
15:14	**Vol. 1:** 220, 424, 609–610 **Vol. 2:** 709, 757 **Vol. 3:** 184, 942
15:15	**Vol. 2:** 746 **Vol. 3:** 384
15:16 f	**Vol. 3:** 106
15:17	**Vol. 1:** 742
15:18 f	**Vol. 1:** 322
15:18	**Vol. 1:** 448, 642 **Vol. 2:** 568
15:19	**Vol. 1:** 169, 564, 566 **Vol. 2:** 182, 472, 568 **Vol. 3:** 820
15:20	**Vol. 1:** 448
15:21 ff	**Vol. 2:** 165 **Vol. 3:** 475
15:21–28	**Vol. 3:** 106, 1059
15:21	**Vol. 1:** 169 **Vol. 2:** 170, 303
15:22 f	**Vol. 1:** 409
15:22	**Vol. 1:** 427 **Vol. 2:** 595 **Vol. 3:** 652
15:23	**Vol. 2:** 880 **Vol. 3:** 189
15:24 f	**Vol. 2:** 315
15:24	**Vol. 1:** 482 **Vol. 2:** 248, 314, 413, 695, 793 **Vol. 3:** 454, 567
15:25	**Vol. 2:** 877
15:26	**Vol. 1:** 117 **Vol. 2:** 434
15:27	**Vol. 1:** 117, 609 **Vol. 2:** 513
15:28	**Vol. 2:** 168–169 **Vol. 3:** 758, 846–848, 1058
15:29	**Vol. 2:** 185
15:30–31	**Vol. 1:** 429 **Vol. 2:** 414–415
15:30	**Vol. 1:** 219 **Vol. 2:** 165
15:31	**Vol. 2:** 73, 170, 623
15:32–39	**Vol. 1:** 250, 729 **Vol. 2:** 272, 523, 630
15:32	**Vol. 2:** 599 **Vol. 3:** 189, 228, 939, 1022
15:33	**Vol. 1:** 743 **Vol. 3:** 1007
15:34	**Vol. 2:** 692 **Vol. 3:** 657
15:35	**Vol. 1:** 340–341
15:36	**Vol. 1:** 670 **Vol. 2:** 692 **Vol. 3:** 819

Matthew *(cont'd)*

15:37   **Vol. 1:** 729   **Vol. 2:** 692   **Vol. 3:** 657
15:38   **Vol. 1:** 283   **Vol. 2:** 699
15:39   **Vol. 3:** 189
16:1 ff   **Vol. 2:** 629
16:1–16 **Vol. 3:** 439
16:1–4   **Vol. 2:** 631, 750 **Vol. 3:** 867
16:1   **Vol. 2:** 192, 351, 629, 680, 880 **Vol. 3:** 439, 442, 804
16:2 f   **Vol. 1:** 656
16:2   **Vol. 2:** 192 **Vol. 3:** 1002
16:3 f   **Vol. 3:** 393
16:3   **Vol. 1:** 503, 586 **Vol. 2:** 398 **Vol. 3:** 848
16:4   **Vol. 1:** 220 **Vol. 2:** 350–351, 582, 584, 687 **Vol. 3:** 532
16:5–12 **Vol. 3:** 132
16:6   **Vol. 3:** 184, 439, 442
16:7 f   **Vol. 3:** 820
16:7   **Vol. 2:** 182
16:8   **Vol. 2:** 398
16:9   **Vol. 3:** 240
16:10   **Vol. 2:** 692
16:11 f   **Vol. 2:** 462
16:11   **Vol. 3:** 184, 439
16:12   **Vol. 3:** 439, 769
16:13 ff **Vol. 2:** 680
16:13–23 **Vol. 2:** 341 **Vol. 3:** 1061
16:13   **Vol. 2:** 550, 879 **Vol. 3:** 623
16:14   **Vol. 1:** 736 **Vol. 3:** 82–83
16:15 ff **Vol. 1:** 200, 489
16:16 ff **Vol. 3:** 132
16:16–19 **Vol. 3:** 386
16:16 f   **Vol. 3:** 387
16:16   **Vol. 1:** 290 **Vol. 2:** 231, 480 **Vol. 3:** 385
16:17 ff **Vol. 2:** 733
16:17   **Vol. 1:** 217, 222, 677–678 **Vol. 2:** 75–76 **Vol. 3:** 314, 330, 336, 384, 533
16:18 f   **Vol. 2:** 207, 786
16:18   **Vol. 1:** 297–298, 302–304, 662 **Vol. 2:** 30, 38, 207, 252, 433 **Vol. 3:** 382–385, 390, 713, 763
16:19   **Vol. 1:** 171, 702–703 **Vol. 2:** 194, 727, 732 **Vol. 3:** 188, 387, 482, 717
16:21   **Vol. 1:** 167 **Vol. 2:** 327, 665, 893 **Vol. 3:** 39, 276, 294, 480, 569, 723
16:22 ff **Vol. 1:** 489
16:22 f   **Vol. 3:** 455, 804
16:22   **Vol. 2:** 708 **Vol. 3:** 160, 751
16:23   **Vol. 1:** 111, 493 **Vol. 2:** 618, 708 **Vol. 3:** 384, 470, 807
16:24 f   **Vol. 1:** 489 **Vol. 3:** 1022
16:24   **Vol. 1:** 324, 394, 402, 455, 464, 493, 718
16:25 f   **Vol. 3:** 174
16:25   **Vol. 1:** 489, 718 **Vol. 2:** 433 **Vol. 3:** 212, 530, 682

16:26   **Vol. 3:** 136–137, 167, 174
16:27   **Vol. 1:** 102, 323, 327 **Vol. 2:** 46, 369 **Vol. 3:** 136, 1158, 1200
16:28   **Vol. 1:** 323 **Vol. 2:** 271, 382, 386–387 **Vol. 3:** 627, 863
17:1–8   **Vol. 2:** 48 **Vol. 3:** 114, 330
17:1 f   **Vol. 3:** 604
17:1   **Vol. 2:** 199, 686 **Vol. 3:** 384, 751, 862–863, 1010, 1012
17:2–5   **Vol. 2:** 47
17:2   **Vol. 1:** 204, 587, 704, 706, 708 **Vol. 2:** 486, 493 **Vol. 3:** 731, 861–862
17:3   **Vol. 2:** 559
17:4   **Vol. 2:** 514 **Vol. 3:** 384
17:5 ff   **Vol. 3:** 132
17:5   **Vol. 2:** 176, 493, 543, 725, 819 **Vol. 3:** 114, 555, 611, 864, 1003
17:6   **Vol. 1:** 290, 586, 610
17:7   **Vol. 1:** 623
17:8   **Vol. 2:** 724
17:9   **Vol. 1:** 335 **Vol. 3:** 276, 294, 515, 862, 1012
17:10–13 **Vol. 2:** 443
17:10   **Vol. 1:** 323, 544 **Vol. 3:** 480
17:11   **Vol. 3:** 80, 147, 480
17:12 f   **Vol. 3:** 658
17:12   **Vol. 1:** 326 **Vol. 2:** 399 **Vol. 3:** 723
17:13   **Vol. 3:** 82
17:14 ff **Vol. 3:** 475
17:14   **Vol. 2:** 860
17:15   **Vol. 1:** 609 **Vol. 2:** 595, 600 **Vol. 3:** 475, 734, 990
17:16 ff **Vol. 2:** 165
17:16   **Vol. 2:** 165
17:17   **Vol. 2:** 36, 766 **Vol. 3:** 1204
17:18   **Vol. 1:** 718 **Vol. 2:** 165 **Vol. 3:** 846–848
17:19   **Vol. 1:** 453
17:20   **Vol. 1:** 504, 600 **Vol. 3:** 1012
17:21   **Vol. 1:** 613
17:22   **Vol. 1:** 326 **Vol. 2:** 150, 368 **Vol. 3:** 984
17:23   **Vol. 1:** 162 **Vol. 3:** 276, 294, 1122
17:24 ff **Vol. 1:** 525
17:24–27 **Vol. 2:** 630, 851 **Vol. 3:** 753, 792, 985
17:24   **Vol. 2:** 62 **Vol. 3:** 384, 767, 853, 1179
17:25   **Vol. 1:** 684 **Vol. 2:** 62, 378, 742 **Vol. 3:** 822
17:26   **Vol. 1:** 717
17:27   **Vol. 1:** 666, 671 **Vol. 2:** 708, 728, 851 **Vol. 3:** 1179–1180
18   **Vol. 2:** 770–771 **Vol. 3:** 1109
18:1 ff   **Vol. 1:** 489
18:1–25 **Vol. 3:** 1071
18:1–6   **Vol. 2:** 429 **Vol. 3:** 1052
18:1–5   **Vol. 2:** 262, 427
18:1   **Vol. 3:** 847
18:2   **Vol. 1:** 274
18:3 f   **Vol. 1:** 285

Matthew *(cont'd)*

18:3   **Vol. 1:** 284, 321, 355, 358   **Vol. 2:** 385   **Vol. 3:** 746
18:4   **Vol. 2:** 262, 427
18:5   **Vol. 2:** 176, 772   **Vol. 3:** 746
18:6   **Vol. 1:** 241, 489   **Vol. 2:** 708–709   **Vol. 3:** 1212
18:7   **Vol. 2:** 664, 708   **Vol. 3:** 1052, 1180
18:7b   **Vol. 2:** 709
18:8 f   **Vol. 1:** 657   **Vol. 2:** 385, 710   **Vol. 3:** 941
18:8   **Vol. 1:** 239   **Vol. 2:** 149, 414–415   **Vol. 3:** 99, 394, 830, 832
18:10   **Vol. 1:** 102, 358, 462, 586   **Vol. 2:** 192, 194, 429   **Vol. 3:** 518, 1052
18:11   **Vol. 3:** 628
18:12 ff   **Vol. 3:** 566
18:12–14   **Vol. 3:** 567–568
18:12 f   **Vol. 2:** 459
18:12   **Vol. 2:** 459–460   **Vol. 3:** 822
18:13   **Vol. 3:** 530
18:14   **Vol. 1:** 358   **Vol. 2:** 429, 818   **Vol. 3:** 1175
18:15 ff   **Vol. 1:** 535   **Vol. 2:** 142, 897
18:15–20   **Vol. 1:** 466   **Vol. 2:** 769, 898
18:15   **Vol. 2:** 724   **Vol. 3:** 138, 579
18:16   **Vol. 1:** 302   **Vol. 2:** 686   **Vol. 3:** 1043, 1122
18:17   **Vol. 1:** 297–298, 302–303   **Vol. 2:** 175, 731, 795   **Vol. 3:** 757–758
18:18   **Vol. 1:** 171, 702–703   **Vol. 2:** 481, 733, 897   **Vol. 3:** 188, 387, 482, 717
18:19   **Vol. 2:** 192, 194, 857–858, 869, 897   **Vol. 3:** 1158
18:20   **Vol. 1:** 90, 285   **Vol. 2:** 32, 895, 897–898, 901
18:21 f   **Vol. 2:** 513   **Vol. 3:** 657
18:21–35   **Vol. 2:** 769, 898
18:21–34   **Vol. 2:** 118
18:21   **Vol. 1:** 701   **Vol. 2:** 691   **Vol. 3:** 384
18:23 ff   **Vol. 3:** 135
18:23–35   **Vol. 2:** 301, 596, 600, 667, 749–750   **Vol. 3:** 173, 758
18:23   **Vol. 2:** 502, 667
18:24   **Vol. 2:** 770
18:25   **Vol. 1:** 268, 286, 341   **Vol. 2:** 513, 846
18:26   **Vol. 1:** 609   **Vol. 2:** 769–770, 772, 877
18:27   **Vol. 1:** 505, 700   **Vol. 2:** 513, 596, 600   **Vol. 3:** 189, 595
18:28   **Vol. 1:** 226   **Vol. 2:** 667   **Vol. 3:** 717
18:29   **Vol. 1:** 570, 609   **Vol. 2:** 769–770
18:30   **Vol. 2:** 136
18:32–35   **Vol. 1:** 702
18:32   **Vol. 1:** 565, 700
18:33 f   **Vol. 2:** 597
18:33   **Vol. 2:** 595–596, 667
18:34   **Vol. 1:** 111   **Vol. 2:** 600, 770   **Vol. 3:** 595, 856
18:35   **Vol. 2:** 192, 596, 770

19:1–12   **Vol. 3:** 538
19:1–9   **Vol. 3:** 980
19:1   **Vol. 2:** 63   **Vol. 3:** 456, 540, 991
19:2   **Vol. 2:** 165
19:3–12   **Vol. 3:** 172
19:3–9   **Vol. 2:** 580   **Vol. 3:** 188, 534
19:3   **Vol. 1:** 506   **Vol. 2:** 138, 563, 580   **Vol. 3:** 189, 534, 539
19:4 f   **Vol. 2:** 579   **Vol. 3:** 329
19:4   **Vol. 1:** 166, 384   **Vol. 2:** 563, 570   **Vol. 3:** 329
19:5 ff   **Vol. 3:** 539
19:5 f   **Vol. 2:** 580   **Vol. 3:** 1175
19:5   **Vol. 2:** 349, 565, 570, 722   **Vol. 3:** 251, 1070
19:5b   **Vol. 1:** 678
19:6–9   **Vol. 2:** 581
19:6   **Vol. 1:** 678   **Vol. 2:** 570   **Vol. 3:** 534–535, 542, 1164
19:7 ff   **Vol. 3:** 189
19:7–9   **Vol. 1:** 506
19:7   **Vol. 1:** 244, 335, 506, 606
19:8   **Vol. 1:** 166   **Vol. 2:** 156   **Vol. 3:** 538, 763, 1204
19:9–12   **Vol. 2:** 580
19:9   **Vol. 1:** 500, 506, 742   **Vol. 2:** 563, 580, 583   **Vol. 3:** 183, 535, 538, 540, 542, 1171, 1195
19:10 ff   **Vol. 3:** 541
19:10   **Vol. 1:** 742   **Vol. 2:** 139   **Vol. 3:** 541–542
19:11 f   **Vol. 1:** 742
19:11   **Vol. 3:** 541–542
19:12   **Vol. 1:** 178, 560, 742   **Vol. 2:** 385, 580–581, 710   **Vol. 3:** 541–542, 1071
19:13 ff   **Vol. 1:** 283–284   **Vol. 3:** 861
19:13   **Vol. 2:** 151
19:14   **Vol. 1:** 284   **Vol. 2:** 222
19:15   **Vol. 1:** 284   **Vol. 2:** 151, 578
19:16–30   **Vol. 1:** 335   **Vol. 2:** 301
19:16–22   **Vol. 2:** 825, 844
19:16–20   **Vol. 3:** 1163
19:16   **Vol. 2:** 480–481   **Vol. 3:** 832
19:17   **Vol. 1:** 336   **Vol. 2:** 100, 133, 879   **Vol. 3:** 1022
19:18 f   **Vol. 2:** 583
19:18   **Vol. 3:** 377, 379, 755
19:20   **Vol. 2:** 135   **Vol. 3:** 954
19:21   **Vol. 1:** 482, 495   **Vol. 2:** 63, 65, 720, 824, 833, 845–846   **Vol. 3:** 141, 1022
19:22   **Vol. 2:** 845–846
19:23 ff   **Vol. 1:** 489
19:23–30   **Vol. 2:** 750
19:23 f   **Vol. 2:** 385, 842–843
19:23   **Vol. 2:** 845
19:24†   **Vol. 1:** 116, 730   **Vol. 2:** 381, 843
19:25   **Vol. 1:** 730   **Vol. 2:** 623, 843
19:26   **Vol. 1:** 730   **Vol. 2:** 603, 606, 843   **Vol. 3:** 213, 519, 1121
19:27   **Vol. 2:** 840   **Vol. 3:** 384, 920

Matthew *(cont'd)*

19:28†   **Vol. 1:** 99, 153, 179, 185–186, 482 **Vol. 2:** 48, 313, 365, 385, 387, 613–614, 695, 786 **Vol. 3:** 180, 454, 588, 629, 871, 920, 1177

19:29   **Vol. 2:** 250, 300–301 **Vol. 3:** 142, 832, 920

19:30   **Vol. 1:** 666 **Vol. 2:** 57

20   **Vol. 3:** 572

20:1–16   **Vol. 2:** 118, 749, 751 **Vol. 3:** 141, 920

20:1–15   **Vol. 2:** 386

20:1–6   **Vol. 3:** 1150

20:1   **Vol. 2:** 315, 502, 510 **Vol. 3:** 1150

20:2 ff   **Vol. 2:** 770

20:2–13   **Vol. 2:** 711

20:2   **Vol. 2:** 851 **Vol. 3:** 1150

20:3   **Vol. 1:** 267 **Vol. 2:** 739 **Vol. 3:** 847

20:4   **Vol. 3:** 360

20:5 f   **Vol. 3:** 847

20:5   **Vol. 3:** 847

20:6   **Vol. 2:** 739 **Vol. 3:** 847

20:8 ff   **Vol. 1:** 666

20:8   **Vol. 1:** 274 **Vol. 3:** 135, 1150

20:9   **Vol. 3:** 847

20:11 ff   **Vol. 3:** 1155

20:11   **Vol. 2:** 510

20:12   **Vol. 1:** 261 **Vol. 2:** 499 **Vol. 3:** 141, 847

20:13–16   **Vol. 3:** 920

20:13–15   **Vol. 3:** 360

20:13   **Vol. 1:** 260 **Vol. 3:** 575

20:14   **Vol. 2:** 846

20:15   **Vol. 3:** 141, 516

20:16   **Vol. 1:** 540, 667 **Vol. 2:** 57, 566

20:17   **Vol. 2:** 695 **Vol. 3:** 751

20:18   **Vol. 2:** 365, 368 **Vol. 3:** 39

20:19   **Vol. 1:** 162, 394 **Vol. 2:** 368 **Vol. 3:** 276, 340

20:20   **Vol. 2:** 276 **Vol. 3:** 1071

20:21   **Vol. 2:** 148, 386, 388 **Vol. 3:** 1019

20:22   **Vol. 1:** 326 **Vol. 2:** 276

20:23   **Vol. 2:** 148 **Vol. 3:** 118, 1178

20:25–28   **Vol. 3:** 979

20:25   **Vol. 1:** 168 **Vol. 2:** 519, 793

20:26   **Vol. 1:** 285 **Vol. 2:** 427 **Vol. 3:** 546–547

20:27 f   **Vol. 1:** 667

20:27   **Vol. 3:** 596, 598

20:28–32   **Vol. 3:** 920

20:28   **Vol. 1:** 96–97, 322, 369 **Vol. 2:** 262 **Vol. 3:** 195, 197, 420, 429, 546–547, 611, 682–683, 1180

20:29–34   **Vol. 1:** 49 **Vol. 2:** 754

20:30   **Vol. 3:** 652, 658, 939

20:31 f   **Vol. 3:** 920

20:32   **Vol. 3:** 1022

20:33   **Vol. 2:** 726, 728

20:34   **Vol. 2:** 599, 631

21:1–9   **Vol. 2:** 379, 754 **Vol. 3:** 791

21:1   **Vol. 2:** 54, 315, 686, 713

21:2   **Vol. 1:** 116–117 **Vol. 3:** 179

21:3   **Vol. 2:** 488

21:4   **Vol. 1:** 736 **Vol. 3:** 489

21:5   **Vol. 2:** 258, 327

21:6   **Vol. 1:** 477

21:7   **Vol. 1:** 117

21:9   **Vol. 1:** 100, 281, 323, 482 **Vol. 3:** 652

21:10–17   **Vol. 1:** 281 **Vol. 3:** 429, 791

21:10   **Vol. 2:** 803 **Vol. 3:** 557

21:11   **Vol. 2:** 333 **Vol. 3:** 83

21:12–17   **Vol. 3:** 1168

21:12 f   **Vol. 2:** 379, 610, 754 **Vol. 3:** 39

21:12   **Vol. 1:** 111, 175

21:13 f   **Vol. 2:** 584

21:13   **Vol. 2:** 248 **Vol. 3:** 329, 378, 380, 430, 788

21:14   **Vol. 1:** 219 **Vol. 2:** 415 **Vol. 3:** 792

21:15 f   **Vol. 1:** 284, 724 **Vol. 3:** 792

21:15   **Vol. 1:** 281, 427 **Vol. 2:** 623 **Vol. 3:** 480–481, 652

21:16   **Vol. 1:** 281 **Vol. 3:** 329, 350, 817

21:17   **Vol. 2:** 528

21:18 f   **Vol. 2:** 267, 630, 750, 754 **Vol. 3:** 793, 868–869

21:18–22   **Vol. 1:** 724

21:19   **Vol. 1:** 181, 515, 722 **Vol. 2:** 488 **Vol. 3:** 528, 829–830

21:20   **Vol. 1:** 515

21:21   **Vol. 1:** 504 **Vol. 2:** 724, 871 **Vol. 3:** 984

21:22   **Vol. 2:** 856–857

21:23–24:1 **Vol. 2:** 236

21:23–27   **Vol. 3:** 792, 1154

21:23   **Vol. 1:** 174, 199 **Vol. 2:** 799 **Vol. 3:** 481, 761, 791, 869

21:24   **Vol. 2:** 879 **Vol. 3:** 1106

21:25   **Vol. 1:** 599 **Vol. 2:** 182, 434

21:26   **Vol. 2:** 801

21:28–32   **Vol. 1:** 356 **Vol. 2:** 751 **Vol. 3:** 869

21:28   **Vol. 1:** 286 **Vol. 2:** 686 **Vol. 3:** 822, 1150

21:29 ff   **Vol. 2:** 514

21:29   **Vol. 1:** 356 **Vol. 3:** 954

21:31 f   **Vol. 1:** 499 **Vol. 3:** 1062

21:31   **Vol. 2:** 381 **Vol. 3:** 757, 953, 1022, 1155

21:32   **Vol. 1:** 339, 356, 599 **Vol. 3:** 360, 517, 758, 940, 954

21:33–46   **Vol. 2:** 746, 751 **Vol. 3:** 641, 869, 920

21:33–41   **Vol. 2:** 301

21:33 f   **Vol. 3:** 868

21:33   **Vol. 2:** 510, 790 **Vol. 3:** 951

21:34   **Vol. 1:** 722 **Vol. 3:** 837

21:35 ff   **Vol. 3:** 748

21:35 f   **Vol. 1:** 547

21:35   **Vol. 1:** 163

21:37 f   **Vol. 1:** 290

21:37   **Vol. 2:** 720 **Vol. 3:** 954

21:38   **Vol. 2:** 182, 543

Matthew *(cont'd)*

21:41 ff   **Vol. 1:** 723
21:41   **Vol. 1:** 564   **Vol. 3:** 920
21:42   **Vol. 2:** 129, 159, 253, 313, 622–623, 706   **Vol. 3:** 329, 389–390, 490, 492, 809, 1175
21:43   **Vol. 2:** 381, 385
21:45 f   **Vol. 3:** 39
21:46   **Vol. 2:** 801   **Vol. 3:** 83
22:1 ff   **Vol. 2:** 339
22:1–14   **Vol. 1:** 324   **Vol. 2:** 580, 727, 750–751   **Vol. 3:** 869, 922
22:1–13   **Vol. 3:** 253
22:1–10   **Vol. 2:** 386, 388, 578
22:1   **Vol. 2:** 748
22:2–10   **Vol. 1:** 274   **Vol. 2:** 747
22:2 f   **Vol. 2:** 358
22:2   **Vol. 2:** 502
22:4   **Vol. 1:** 116   **Vol. 3:** 118
22:6   **Vol. 3:** 28, 252, 717
22:7   **Vol. 1:** 111, 464   **Vol. 3:** 964
22:8   **Vol. 3:** 118, 349
22:9   **Vol. 3:** 528–529, 940
22:10   **Vol. 1:** 566   **Vol. 2:** 32, 100
22:11 ff   **Vol. 1:** 317
22:11 f   **Vol. 1:** 316   **Vol. 2:** 579
22:11   **Vol. 3:** 516
22:12 ff   **Vol. 2:** 236
22:12   **Vol. 1:** 260
22:13 f   **Vol. 1:** 171, 566
22:13   **Vol. 1:** 425   **Vol. 2:** 149, 421   **Vol. 3:** 546
22:14   **Vol. 1:** 96–97, 274, 540
22:15 ff   **Vol. 3:** 378
22:15–40   **Vol. 3:** 657
22:15–22   **Vol. 3:** 549, 754, 1168
22:15   **Vol. 1:** 363   **Vol. 3:** 884, 1108
22:16   **Vol. 1:** 304, 487   **Vol. 2:** 343   **Vol. 3:** 441–442, 940
22:17   **Vol. 3:** 754, 822
22:18   **Vol. 2:** 469
22:19   **Vol. 3:** 754
22:20   **Vol. 2:** 288   **Vol. 3:** 489
22:21   **Vol. 2:** 79
22:22–33   **Vol. 2:** 578
22:22   **Vol. 2:** 624
22:23–40   **Vol. 2:** 516
22:23–33   **Vol. 2:** 580   **Vol. 3:** 263, 792
22:23–32   **Vol. 3:** 439
22:23   **Vol. 1:** 174   **Vol. 3:** 277, 439
22:24–40   **Vol. 3:** 455
22:24   **Vol. 3:** 275, 1074
22:25   **Vol. 1:** 430, 666
22:27   **Vol. 3:** 252, 954
22:28   **Vol. 3:** 277
22:29   **Vol. 2:** 459–460   **Vol. 3:** 305, 490, 492
22:30 f   **Vol. 1:** 290
22:30   **Vol. 1:** 103   **Vol. 2:** 578, 581   **Vol. 3:** 278

22:31 f   **Vol. 2:** 481   **Vol. 3:** 263, 277
22:31   **Vol. 3:** 329, 489
22:32   **Vol. 1:** 78, 81, 445   **Vol. 2:** 73, 319, 480, 578
22:33   **Vol. 2:** 623   **Vol. 3:** 769
22:34–40   **Vol. 1:** 334   **Vol. 2:** 543, 813, 870   **Vol. 3:** 173, 791
22:34–39   **Vol. 2:** 443
22:34   **Vol. 2:** 32   **Vol. 3:** 439, 1194
22:35   **Vol. 3:** 480, 657, 804
22:36 ff   **Vol. 2:** 544   **Vol. 3:** 1155
22:36   **Vol. 1:** 334   **Vol. 2:** 426   **Vol. 3:** 127
22:37 ff   **Vol. 1:** 259
22:37–40   **Vol. 2:** 42
22:37 f   **Vol. 3:** 542
22:37   **Vol. 2:** 73, 147   **Vol. 3:** 685, 763
22:38   **Vol. 1:** 334   **Vol. 2:** 426
22:39 f   **Vol. 1:** 335
22:39   **Vol. 1:** 738   **Vol. 2:** 177, 503   **Vol. 3:** 378, 1064
22:40   **Vol. 2:** 174, 177   **Vol. 3:** 183, 185
22:41–46   **Vol. 2:** 147, 515   **Vol. 3:** 651
22:41–45   **Vol. 1:** 427
22:41   **Vol. 2:** 32   **Vol. 3:** 481
22:42–44   **Vol. 3:** 653
22:42   **Vol. 3:** 652, 658, 822
22:43 f   **Vol. 1:** 177
22:43   **Vol. 3:** 671
22:44   **Vol. 1:** 239, 554   **Vol. 2:** 515   **Vol. 3:** 1178
22:45   **Vol. 3:** 652, 658
22:46   **Vol. 1:** 365   **Vol. 2:** 880
23   **Vol. 1:** 111   **Vol. 2:** 327, 434   **Vol. 3:** 253, 480–481, 657, 1109, 1162
23:1 ff   **Vol. 2:** 261
23:1–25:46   **Vol. 2:** 469
23:1–39   **Vol. 2:** 715   **Vol. 3:** 183
23:1–36   **Vol. 2:** 813   **Vol. 3:** 580
23:1   **Vol. 1:** 174   **Vol. 2:** 799
23:2 f   **Vol. 2:** 640
23:2   **Vol. 1:** 297   **Vol. 2:** 640   **Vol. 3:** 87, 184, 482, 589, 883
23:3   **Vol. 2:** 133   **Vol. 3:** 184, 883, 1149
23:4 ff   **Vol. 3:** 184
23:4   **Vol. 1:** 261, 335   **Vol. 2:** 150   **Vol. 3:** 883, 1162
23:5   **Vol. 1:** 254   **Vol. 2:** 136, 864   **Vol. 3:** 559, 1149–1150
23:6 f   **Vol. 3:** 481
23:6   **Vol. 1:** 666   **Vol. 2:** 548   **Vol. 3:** 785
23:7 ff   **Vol. 1:** 489
23:7–12   **Vol. 3:** 1152
23:7 f   **Vol. 1:** 273
23:7   **Vol. 3:** 115
23:8 ff   **Vol. 2:** 721–722
23:8–12   **Vol. 3:** 482
23:8–10   **Vol. 2:** 84
23:8   **Vol. 3:** 115, 767–768
23:9   **Vol. 1:** 274, 619   **Vol. 2:** 73, 192

Matthew *(cont'd)*

23:11	**Vol. 1:** 285 **Vol. 2:** 427 **Vol. 3:** 546–547, 1152
23:12	**Vol. 1:** 285 **Vol. 2:** 202, 262
23:13 ff	**Vol. 2:** 470, 640, 691 **Vol. 3:** 1052
23:13–36	**Vol. 3:** 482
23:13–16	**Vol. 2:** 443
23:13	**Vol. 2:** 222, 311, 385, 462, 730, 732, 813 **Vol. 3:** 253, 387, 1052
23:15	**Vol. 1:** 289, 361, 516, 688 **Vol. 2:** 208, 720, 732, 792, 813 **Vol. 3:** 360, 480, 984, 1052
23:16 ff	**Vol. 2:** 470 **Vol. 3:** 785
23:16–22	**Vol. 3:** 183, 741, 792, 1052
23:16 f	**Vol. 1:** 220 **Vol. 3:** 429
23:16	**Vol. 3:** 942
23:17	**Vol. 2:** 228–229 **Vol. 3:** 1025
23:18 ff	**Vol. 3:** 435–436
23:18 f	**Vol. 2:** 41
23:18–22	**Vol. 3:** 429
23:19	**Vol. 1:** 220 **Vol. 2:** 228–229
23:22	**Vol. 2:** 74 **Vol. 3:** 588
23:23 f	**Vol. 1:** 116 **Vol. 3:** 1053
23:23	**Vol. 1:** 261 **Vol. 2:** 211, 365, 443, 596, 694, 813 **Vol. 3:** 883
23:24	**Vol. 1:** 116 **Vol. 3:** 883, 942
23:25 f	**Vol. 3:** 106, 990, 1053
23:25	**Vol. 1:** 495, 743 **Vol. 2:** 443, 532, 813 **Vol. 3:** 604
23:26	**Vol. 1:** 220 **Vol. 2:** 813
23:27 ff	**Vol. 2:** 813
23:27 f	**Vol. 2:** 488 **Vol. 3:** 360, 1053
23:27	**Vol. 1:** 205, 241, 265 **Vol. 2:** 443, 501–502 **Vol. 3:** 197
23:28 f	**Vol. 3:** 360
23:29–36	**Vol. 1:** 174
23:29–33	**Vol. 3:** 1053
23:29–31	**Vol. 1:** 265
23:29	**Vol. 2:** 443 **Vol. 3:** 247, 360
23:30	**Vol. 1:** 222, 643
23:31 f	**Vol. 3:** 83
23:31	**Vol. 1:** 288 **Vol. 3:** 82, 1043
23:32	**Vol. 1:** 740 **Vol. 3:** 403, 1053
23:33	**Vol. 1:** 509, 559 **Vol. 2:** 208 **Vol. 3:** 854
23:34 ff	**Vol. 3:** 1030
23:34–36	**Vol. 3:** 83
23:34	**Vol. 1:** 163, 174, 395 **Vol. 2:** 352, 714 **Vol. 3:** 184, 482, 785
23:35 ff	**Vol. 1:** 75
23:35	**Vol. 1:** 163, 221–222 **Vol. 2:** 525, 854 **Vol. 3:** 82, 360, 430, 435–436, 789
23:37 ff	**Vol. 1:** 174 **Vol. 2:** 328 **Vol. 3:** 229
23:37–39	**Vol. 2:** 37 **Vol. 3:** 83, 1052
23:37 f	**Vol. 3:** 1008
23:37	**Vol. 1:** 174, 286, 430 **Vol. 2:** 33, 328, 754, 803 **Vol. 3:** 82
23:38	**Vol. 2:** 328 **Vol. 3:** 1008
23:39	**Vol. 1:** 174, 213 **Vol. 2:** 328, 653
24 f	**Vol. 3:** 831, 844
24	**Vol. 1:** 125 **Vol. 2:** 904, 911 **Vol. 3:** 560, 984, 1109
24:1–3	**Vol. 2:** 713 **Vol. 3:** 1011
24:1	**Vol. 1:** 174 **Vol. 2:** 236 **Vol. 3:** 791–792
24:2 ff	**Vol. 2:** 803
24:2	**Vol. 2:** 450 **Vol. 3:** 185, 189, 1177, 1184
24:3	**Vol. 2:** 37, 62, 629, 900 **Vol. 3:** 658, 831
24:4 ff	**Vol. 2:** 460
24:4 f	**Vol. 2:** 459, 461, 808
24:4–36	**Vol. 2:** 702
24:4–35	**Vol. 2:** 915
24:5	**Vol. 2:** 281
24:6	**Vol. 1:** 326 **Vol. 2:** 62–63, 665, 808, 918 **Vol. 3:** 962
24:7	**Vol. 2:** 266, 793 **Vol. 3:** 280, 558
24:8	**Vol. 2:** 244, 808 **Vol. 3:** 858
24:9–12	**Vol. 1:** 608
24:9	**Vol. 1:** 430 **Vol. 2:** 368, 654, 773, 793, 808
24:10 ff	**Vol. 2:** 773
24:10	**Vol. 1:** 556 **Vol. 2:** 708–709
24:11	**Vol. 2:** 459, 461, 472, 808 **Vol. 3:** 280
24:12	**Vol. 1:** 96, 318, 733 **Vol. 2:** 447, 911 **Vol. 3:** 56
24:13	**Vol. 2:** 62, 773
24:14	**Vol. 1:** 519 **Vol. 2:** 62, 110, 112, 665 **Vol. 3:** 52, 56
24:15–22	**Vol. 3:** 793
24:15	**Vol. 1:** 74 **Vol. 2:** 228 **Vol. 3:** 128, 489, 792, 1008
24:16	**Vol. 1:** 559 **Vol. 3:** 1011
24:17	**Vol. 2:** 845
24:19	**Vol. 3:** 1053
24:20	**Vol. 1:** 559 **Vol. 3:** 410, 698
24:21 f	**Vol. 3:** 803
24:21	**Vol. 2:** 426, 808, 916
24:22	**Vol. 1:** 678 **Vol. 2:** 916
24:23–27	**Vol. 1:** 175
24:24	**Vol. 1:** 323 **Vol. 2:** 426, 459, 461, 472, 629, 633, 808 **Vol. 3:** 84, 280
24:26	**Vol. 3:** 1007
24:27	**Vol. 1:** 610 **Vol. 2:** 488, 900–901 **Vol. 3:** 620, 1001
24:28	**Vol. 1:** 175, 610 **Vol. 2:** 32, 695, 746, 757
24:29 ff	**Vol. 2:** 916
24:29	**Vol. 1:** 203, 425, 610 **Vol. 2:** 37, 192, 484 **Vol. 3:** 559, 732, 734, 736
24:30 f	**Vol. 2:** 900
24:30	**Vol. 1:** 323, 518 **Vol. 2:** 46, 48, 194, 488, 604, 630, 808, 917 **Vol. 3:** 633–634, 1003
24:31	**Vol. 1:** 517, 686, 725 **Vol. 2:** 33, 194, 364, 426, 689, 911, 917 **Vol. 3:** 674, 874

147

Matthew *(cont'd)*

24:32–36 **Vol. 2:** 751
24:32 f **Vol. 1:** 725 **Vol. 2:** 382
24:32 **Vol. 2:** 54, 604 **Vol. 3:** 867
24:33 **Vol. 2:** 30
24:34 **Vol. 1:** 99 **Vol. 2:** 36, 38, 271, 911–912, 916
24:35 **Vol. 1:** 322, 518 **Vol. 2:** 192–193
24:36 ff **Vol. 1:** 725
24:36–25:46 **Vol. 2:** 915
24:36 **Vol. 1:** 323 **Vol. 2:** 192, 901, 916 **Vol. 3:** 847–848
24:37 ff **Vol. 2:** 382 **Vol. 3:** 833
24:37–44 **Vol. 2:** 751 **Vol. 3:** 628
24:37–39 **Vol. 2:** 682 **Vol. 3:** 618
24:37 f **Vol. 2:** 901
24:37 **Vol. 2:** 900 **Vol. 3:** 620
24:38 ff **Vol. 2:** 275
24:38 f **Vol. 3:** 991
24:38 **Vol. 2:** 272, 580–581 **Vol. 3:** 278
24:39 **Vol. 2:** 900–901 **Vol. 3:** 604
24:40 ff **Vol. 2:** 364
24:40–41 **Vol. 2:** 686, 720 **Vol. 3:** 604
24:40 **Vol. 3:** 751, 1058
24:41 **Vol. 3:** 394
24:42–25:13 **Vol. 2:** 749
24:42 f **Vol. 1:** 323
24:42 **Vol. 2:** 137, 894
24:43 f **Vol. 2:** 382 **Vol. 3:** 618
24:43 **Vol. 2:** 136, 400, 433, 509–510, 831, 926 **Vol. 3:** 202, 378
24:44 **Vol. 1:** 323 **Vol. 3:** 118, 604, 822, 848
24:45 ff **Vol. 2:** 254, 382
24:45–51 **Vol. 2:** 751
24:45 **Vol. 1:** 472 **Vol. 2:** 619 **Vol. 3:** 595, 837
24:46 **Vol. 1:** 217 **Vol. 3:** 529–530
24:48 ff **Vol. 2:** 275
24:48 **Vol. 1:** 564 **Vol. 3:** 843
24:49 **Vol. 1:** 513–514 **Vol. 3:** 903
24:50 **Vol. 2:** 245 **Vol. 3:** 847–848
24:51 **Vol. 2:** 304, 421
25 **Vol. 2:** 912
25:1 ff **Vol. 2:** 619
25:1–46 **Vol. 2:** 917
25:1–13 **Vol. 2:** 382, 581, 585, 751 **Vol. 3:** 529, 1025
25:1–12 **Vol. 3:** 253, 1072
25:1–3 **Vol. 3:** 1059
25:1 **Vol. 1:** 325 **Vol. 2:** 486, 502, 585 **Vol. 3:** 1072
25:2 f **Vol. 2:** 620
25:3 ff **Vol. 2:** 711
25:3 f **Vol. 2:** 486
25:3–7 **Vol. 3:** 481
25:5 **Vol. 3:** 843, 1072
25:6 **Vol. 2:** 578, 585
25:7 f **Vol. 2:** 486
25:7 **Vol. 1:** 524 **Vol. 2:** 578 **Vol. 3:** 280

25:8 **Vol. 2:** 620 **Vol. 3:** 109
25:9 **Vol. 2:** 711 **Vol. 3:** 727
25:10 **Vol. 2:** 30–31, 730 **Vol. 3:** 118
25:11 **Vol. 2:** 513, 728 **Vol. 3:** 252–253, 954, 1072
25:13 ff **Vol. 2:** 751
25:13 **Vol. 1:** 323 **Vol. 2:** 137, 894 **Vol. 3:** 847–848
25:14 ff **Vol. 2:** 255
25:14–40 **Vol. 2:** 751
25:14–30 **Vol. 2:** 749, 751, 838 **Vol. 3:** 529
25:14 f **Vol. 2:** 499, 916
25:14 **Vol. 2:** 746, 790, 845
25:15 **Vol. 2:** 790, 839 **Vol. 3:** 1019
25:16 ff **Vol. 3:** 137–138
25:18 **Vol. 2:** 216
25:19 **Vol. 2:** 513 **Vol. 3:** 843
25:20 ff **Vol. 2:** 513
25:20 **Vol. 2:** 689
25:21 ff **Vol. 2:** 255
25:21 **Vol. 2:** 100, 358, 428, 751 **Vol. 3:** 941, 1193
25:23 **Vol. 2:** 358, 428 **Vol. 3:** 941
25:24 **Vol. 2:** 32, 34, 155 **Vol. 3:** 141, 526
25:25 **Vol. 2:** 216, 846
25:26 **Vol. 2:** 32, 34 **Vol. 3:** 526
25:27 **Vol. 2:** 846
25:30 **Vol. 1:** 425 **Vol. 2:** 421 **Vol. 3:** 595
25:31 ff **Vol. 2:** 146, 339, 364, 481, 544, 614, 894, 928
25:31–46 **Vol. 1:** 91, 299, 689 **Vol. 2:** 301, 369, 751, 826 **Vol. 3:** 135, 277
25:31–45 **Vol. 2:** 101
25:31 **Vol. 1:** 102 **Vol. 2:** 339, 383, 614 **Vol. 3:** 197, 589, 620, 629
25:32 f **Vol. 2:** 413
25:32 **Vol. 1:** 115, 297, 473 **Vol. 2:** 32 **Vol. 3:** 565, 567
25:33 **Vol. 2:** 148
25:34 ff **Vol. 1:** 495
25:34–40 **Vol. 2:** 144
25:34 **Vol. 1:** 215, 378 **Vol. 2:** 300, 339, 382, 385, 388, 894 **Vol. 3:** 118, 832
25:35–45 **Vol. 1:** 285
25:35 f **Vol. 3:** 359, 547
25:35 **Vol. 2:** 32, 268, 766 **Vol. 3:** 989
25:36 **Vol. 1:** 190–191, 313
25:37 **Vol. 2:** 268, 275 **Vol. 3:** 360
25:38 **Vol. 1:** 313 **Vol. 2:** 32
25:40 **Vol. 1:** 99 **Vol. 2:** 104, 339, 429, 597 **Vol. 3:** 142, 547, 1155
25:41 **Vol. 1:** 103, 417, 452, 657 **Vol. 2:** 208, 272, 276, 894 **Vol. 3:** 99, 118, 469–471, 830, 832, 947
25:42 **Vol. 2:** 268, 275 **Vol. 3:** 989
25:43 f **Vol. 1:** 313
25:43 **Vol. 1:** 190–191 **Vol. 2:** 32
25:44 **Vol. 3:** 546
25:45 **Vol. 2:** 429, 597 **Vol. 3:** 142, 1155

Matthew *(cont'd)*

25:46	**Vol. 2:** 208, 480–481 **Vol. 3:** 98–99, 303, 360, 830, 832
26	**Vol. 1:** 633
26:1	**Vol. 2:** 63
26:2	**Vol. 1:** 394, 633 **Vol. 2:** 368 **Vol. 3:** 627
26:3	**Vol. 1:** 199, 297 **Vol. 2:** 32 **Vol. 3:** 39, 480
26:4	**Vol. 1:** 363
26:5	**Vol. 2:** 623, 799
26:6 ff	**Vol. 2:** 549
26:6–13	**Vol. 3:** 980, 1060
26:6	**Vol. 2:** 464, 528 **Vol. 3:** 1061
26:7	**Vol. 2:** 159, 295.
26:10	**Vol. 3:** 1149–1150
26:11	**Vol. 2:** 824
26:12	**Vol. 1:** 265 **Vol. 2:** 295
26:13	**Vol. 2:** 110, 112 **Vol. 3:** 52, 242, 244
26:14	**Vol. 1:** 299 **Vol. 2:** 695, 720
26:15	**Vol. 2:** 96, 851
26:16	**Vol. 3:** 532
26:17 ff	**Vol. 2:** 527
26:17	**Vol. 1:** 633 **Vol. 2:** 277 **Vol. 3:** 118, 1019
26:18	**Vol. 1:** 633 **Vol. 3:** 837, 1204
26:19	**Vol. 1:** 633 **Vol. 3:** 118
26:20–25	**Vol. 2:** 531 **Vol. 3:** 804
26:20	**Vol. 2:** 528, 623, 695 **Vol. 3:** 954
26:22	**Vol. 1:** 167 **Vol. 2:** 720
26:24	**Vol. 3:** 329, 1053
26:25	**Vol. 1:** 299 **Vol. 3:** 115
26:26–29	**Vol. 1:** 237 **Vol. 2:** 523
26:26 f	**Vol. 1:** 213 **Vol. 2:** 530
26:26	**Vol. 2:** 533
26:27	**Vol. 3:** 819, 857
26:27b	**Vol. 2:** 533
26:28	**Vol. 1:** 96 97, 154, 223, 369, 438, 701–702 **Vol. 2:** 535, 543, 671, 854 **Vol. 3:** 166, 429, 580, 611, 1174
26:28b	**Vol. 2:** 533
26:29	**Vol. 1:** 251 **Vol. 2:** 526, 581, 894, 896 **Vol. 3:** 922
26:30–35	**Vol. 3:** 386, 803
26:30†	**Vol. 2:** 528 **Vol. 3:** 669
26:31 f	**Vol. 3:** 567
26:31	**Vol. 1:** 163 **Vol. 2:** 34, 413, 459, 708 **Vol. 3:** 188, 329
26:33–75	**Vol. 3:** 384
26:33	**Vol. 2:** 708
26:34	**Vol. 1:** 173, 421 **Vol. 3:** 114
26:36 ff	**Vol. 1:** 420
26:36–46	**Vol. 2:** 178, 561, 868
26:37	**Vol. 1:** 167 **Vol. 2:** 420, 686 **Vol. 3:** 751
26:38	**Vol. 2:** 420 **Vol. 3:** 224, 683
26:39–44	**Vol. 3:** 657
26:39	**Vol. 1:** 335, 609, 620 **Vol. 2:** 83, 276, 869, 871 **Vol. 3:** 1022
26:40	**Vol. 1:** 442 **Vol. 3:** 713, 847
26:41	**Vol. 2:** 137, 871 **Vol. 3:** 694, 994
26:42	**Vol. 1:** 620 **Vol. 2:** 222 **Vol. 3:** 1022
26:43	**Vol. 1:** 261
26:45	**Vol. 2:** 54, 150, 543 **Vol. 3:** 252, 256, 580
26:46	**Vol. 2:** 54
26:47 ff	**Vol. 1:** 299
26:47	**Vol. 1:** 199, 390 **Vol. 3:** 967
26:48 f	**Vol. 2:** 549
26:48	**Vol. 2:** 629 **Vol. 3:** 717
26:49	**Vol. 2:** 358 **Vol. 3:** 115
26:50	**Vol. 1:** 260
26:51 ff.	**Vol. 2:** 630
26:51 f	**Vol. 3:** 967
26:52	**Vol. 1:** 464 **Vol. 3:** 591
26:53–56	**Vol. 3:** 329
26:53	**Vol. 1:** 260, 570 **Vol. 3:** 822
26:54	**Vol. 2:** 666 **Vol. 3:** 188, 490, 492
26:55	**Vol. 2:** 895 **Vol. 3:** 379, 589, 761, 791, 846, 967, 1204
26:56	**Vol. 1:** 736 **Vol. 3:** 490, 492
26:57–75	**Vol. 2:** 379 **Vol. 3:** 386, 803
26:57–68	**Vol. 3:** 409
26:57	**Vol. 1:** 297 **Vol. 2:** 32 **Vol. 3:** 39, 481, 1204
26:58	**Vol. 2:** 62–63 **Vol. 3:** 547
26:59	**Vol. 1:** 364 **Vol. 2:** 472
26:60	**Vol. 2:** 472, 686
26:61	**Vol. 2:** 252, 450, 687, 732 **Vol. 3:** 185, 189, 343, 509, 784, 792
26:62	**Vol. 3:** 39, 275, 1042
26:63 f	**Vol. 3:** 712, 742
26:63	**Vol. 1:** 290 **Vol. 2:** 480 **Vol. 3:** 473, 738
26:64	**Vol. 1:** 323 **Vol. 2:** 147, 194, 380, 515, 930 **Vol. 3:** 457, 1003
26:65	**Vol. 1:** 317 **Vol. 3:** 342, 1043
26:66	**Vol. 2:** 143 **Vol. 3:** 822
26:67	**Vol. 1:** 162–163
26:68	**Vol. 3:** 81, 83
26:69	**Vol. 2:** 333
26:70	**Vol. 1:** 455
26:71	**Vol. 2:** 30, 333
26:72	**Vol. 1:** 455
26:73	**Vol. 3:** 316
26:74	**Vol. 1:** 415, 455 **Vol. 2:** 565 **Vol. 3:** 114, 742
26:75	**Vol. 1:** 201 **Vol. 2:** 417 **Vol. 3:** 240, 1122
27	**Vol. 1:** 633 **Vol. 2:** 378
27:1 f	**Vol. 1:** 394
27:1	**Vol. 1:** 199, 363
27:2	**Vol. 1:** 270 **Vol. 2:** 368, 379
27:3–10	**Vol. 1:** 93 **Vol. 3:** 804, 912, 1008
27:3	**Vol. 1:** 93, 299, 356 **Vol. 2:** 365
27:4	**Vol. 1:** 222 **Vol. 3:** 360
27:5	**Vol. 1:** 94 **Vol. 2:** 321 **Vol. 3:** 793
27:6	**Vol. 1:** 222 **Vol. 2:** 43
27:7 f	**Vol. 1:** 520

149

Matthew *(cont'd)*

27:7	**Vol. 1:** 93, 363, 689 **Vol. 3:** 912
27:8	**Vol. 1:** 93, 222, 265
27:9	**Vol. 1:** 93, 736 **Vol. 2:** 49 **Vol. 3:** 489
27:10	**Vol. 1:** 520 **Vol. 3:** 912
27:11–61	**Vol. 1:** 394
27:11	**Vol. 1:** 270 **Vol. 2:** 315, 378
27:12	**Vol. 1:** 199
27:13	**Vol. 3:** 1042
27:14 f	**Vol. 1:** 270
27:14	**Vol. 2:** 624 **Vol. 3:** 1121
27:15–26	**Vol. 1:** 396 **Vol. 3:** 189
27:15 f	**Vol. 3:** 592
27:16 f	**Vol. 2:** 331
27:17	**Vol. 2:** 32, 339, 378
27:18	**Vol. 1:** 396
27:19	**Vol. 1:** 395 **Vol. 2:** 369 **Vol. 3:** 360–361, 723
27:20	**Vol. 1:** 199, 395, 463, 589 **Vol. 2:** 801, 856
27:21	**Vol. 1:** 270
27:23	**Vol. 1:** 409, 564
27:24 f	**Vol. 1:** 395
27:24	**Vol. 1:** 222 **Vol. 2:** 149–150, 623 **Vol. 3:** 360, 990
27:25 f	**Vol. 2:** 799
27:25	**Vol. 1:** 222, 286 **Vol. 2:** 158–159
27:26	**Vol. 1:** 162
27:27	**Vol. 1:** 270 **Vol. 2:** 32 **Vol. 3:** 964
27:28	**Vol. 1:** 314
27:29 f	**Vol. 2:** 159
27:29	**Vol. 1:** 406, 726 **Vol. 2:** 315, 358, 378, 859 **Vol. 3:** 340, 1188
27:30	**Vol. 3:** 903
27:31	**Vol. 1:** 314–316 **Vol. 3:** 340
27:32	**Vol. 2:** 740
27:34	**Vol. 2:** 27–28, 269 **Vol. 3:** 922
27:35	**Vol. 1:** 396 **Vol. 2:** 82, 299
27:36	**Vol. 2:** 133
27:37	**Vol. 2:** 139, 159, 315, 339, 379 **Vol. 3:** 509
27:38	**Vol. 2:** 148 **Vol. 3:** 379
27:39 ff.	**Vol. 2:** 630
27:39–44	**Vol. 3:** 347
27:39–43	**Vol. 1:** 397
27:39 f	**Vol. 3:** 211, 343
27:39	**Vol. 1:** 396 **Vol. 2:** 82, 159
27:40	**Vol. 1:** 290 **Vol. 2:** 687 **Vol. 3:** 185, 189, 509, 784, 792
27:41	**Vol. 1:** 199 **Vol. 3:** 340
27:42	**Vol. 1:** 323 **Vol. 2:** 315, 379 **Vol. 3:** 1212
27:43	**Vol. 1:** 290, 396, 592 **Vol. 2:** 82
27:44	**Vol. 3:** 340, 379
27:45	**Vol. 1:** 423 **Vol. 3:** 732, 847
27:46 ff	**Vol. 1:** 544
27:46	**Vol. 1:** 396, 411, 620 **Vol. 2:** 82 **Vol. 3:** 113, 253, 670
27:47	**Vol. 3:** 114
27:48	**Vol. 2:** 28 **Vol. 3:** 947
27:49	**Vol. 3:** 211, 253
27:50	**Vol. 1:** 409 **Vol. 2:** 426 **Vol. 3:** 113, 694
27:51–54	**Vol. 3:** 558
27:51	**Vol. 2:** 328 **Vol. 3:** 382, 543, 793, 795
27:52–54	**Vol. 3:** 558
27:52–53	**Vol. 1:** 266
27:52 f	**Vol. 2:** 328 **Vol. 3:** 247
27:52	**Vol. 1:** 234, 443 **Vol. 2:** 728
27:53	**Vol. 2:** 228, 327, 489, 803 **Vol. 3:** 280
27:54	**Vol. 1:** 290 **Vol. 3:** 557, 964
27:55 f	**Vol. 3:** 1059, 1070
27:55	**Vol. 3:** 516, 546
27:56	**Vol. 3:** 662, 1071
27:57	**Vol. 2:** 842–843 **Vol. 3:** 1053
27:58	**Vol. 1:** 234, 341 **Vol. 3:** 135
27:60	**Vol. 2:** 30, 670 **Vol. 3:** 247, 382, 393
27:62–66	**Vol. 3:** 283
27:62	**Vol. 2:** 32 **Vol. 3:** 120, 408, 410
27:63 f	**Vol. 3:** 499
27:63	**Vol. 2:** 459–460, 513, 687 **Vol. 3:** 281
27:64 ff	**Vol. 1:** 663
27:64	**Vol. 1:** 341, 445 **Vol. 2:** 459, 799 **Vol. 3:** 285, 378
27:65	**Vol. 2:** 136
27:66	**Vol. 3:** 499
28	**Vol. 3:** 518
28:1 ff	**Vol. 3:** 1059
28:1–20	**Vol. 3:** 294
28:1	**Vol. 2:** 518, 720 **Vol. 3:** 412, 1060
28:2 f	**Vol. 2:** 486, 493
28:2	**Vol. 1:** 102 **Vol. 2:** 193, 513 **Vol. 3:** 393, 517, 557
28:3	**Vol. 1:** 204 **Vol. 2:** 624 **Vol. 3:** 1001, 1004
28:4	**Vol. 1:** 446, 622 **Vol. 3:** 277, 283, 557
28:5	**Vol. 1:** 102, 623 **Vol. 2:** 624 **Vol. 3:** 517
28:7†	**Vol. 1:** 445, 504 **Vol. 3:** 515, 1174
28:8	**Vol. 2:** 358, 624, 721 **Vol. 3:** 48, 247, 276, 947
28:9	**Vol. 2:** 358, 877 **Vol. 3:** 717
28:10 f	**Vol. 3:** 48
28:10	**Vol. 1:** 623 **Vol. 2:** 721 **Vol. 3:** 48, 276
28:11–17	**Vol. 3:** 288
28:11–15	**Vol. 3:** 283
28:11	**Vol. 3:** 46
28:12	**Vol. 1:** 363 **Vol. 2:** 32 **Vol. 3:** 964
28:13	**Vol. 1:** 442 **Vol. 3:** 285, 291, 378
28:14	**Vol. 1:** 270, 590
28:15	**Vol. 2:** 315 **Vol. 3:** 748, 1106
28:16 ff	**Vol. 3:** 286
28:16–20	**Vol. 1:** 136 **Vol. 2:** 83, 282
28:16	**Vol. 3:** 1011
28:17	**Vol. 2:** 877 **Vol. 3:** 518
28:18 ff	**Vol. 1:** 95, 146 **Vol. 2:** 176, 461 **Vol. 3:** 807
28:18–20	**Vol. 2:** 611

Matthew *(cont'd)*

28:18   **Vol. 1:** 95, 258, 720   **Vol. 2:** 81, 194,
282, 368, 610, 653   **Vol. 3:** 1163
28:19 f   **Vol. 1:** 90
28:19   **Vol. 1:** 145, 290   **Vol. 2:** 84, 653, 655,
687, 793   **Vol. 3:** 327, 648, 698, 946,
1186, 1209
28:20   **Vol. 1:** 214, 335   **Vol. 2:** 62, 133, 895,
901   **Vol. 3:** 57, 763, 829

Mark

1:1   **Vol. 1:** 165   **Vol. 2:** 110,
112–113   **Vol. 3:** 63, 213, 652
1:2   **Vol. 1:** 102, 545, 586, 736   **Vol. 3:** 80,
119, 940
1:3–8   **Vol. 1:** 111
1:3   **Vol. 1:** 411   **Vol. 3:** 53, 118, 940
1:4 f   **Vol. 1:** 701
1:4   **Vol. 1:** 146, 358, 599, 701   **Vol. 2:**
533   **Vol. 3:** 52, 55–56, 212, 580,
1007, 1178, 1208, 1210
1:5 f   **Vol. 2:** 275
1:5   **Vol. 1:** 346   **Vol. 2:** 325, 327   **Vol. 3:**
987, 991, 1208, 1210
1:6   **Vol. 1:** 116, 482, 520   **Vol. 2:**
272   **Vol. 3:** 121
1:7   **Vol. 1:** 323, 493   **Vol. 3:** 55–56, 179,
714, 729
1:8 ff   **Vol. 3:** 990
1:8   **Vol. 1:** 158   **Vol. 2:** 603, 785   **Vol. 3:**
697, 714, 1210
1:9 ff   **Vol. 3:** 170
1:9–11   **Vol. 3:** 113
1:9   **Vol. 1:** 146   **Vol. 3:** 987, 991, 1174,
1208–1210
1:10 f   **Vol. 3:** 987
1:10   **Vol. 1:** 175, 704   **Vol. 2:** 185, 193,
314   **Vol. 3:** 543, 697, 1070, 1180
1:11   **Vol. 2:** 193, 543, 819   **Vol. 3:** 114,
611–612, 621, 639–641, 643, 651, 697,
807
1:12 f   **Vol. 2:** 267   **Vol. 3:** 470, 804,
1007–1008
1:12   **Vol. 1:** 453, 739   **Vol. 3:** 602, 697
1:13   **Vol. 1:** 114   **Vol. 2:** 689, 696, 893
1:14 ff   **Vol. 3:** 762, 1108
1:14 f   **Vol. 3:** 762
1:14   **Vol. 2:** 110, 112   **Vol. 3:** 37, 52
1:15   **Vol. 1:** 358, 482, 599, 702, 738   **Vol. 2:**
54, 110, 112, 381–382, 384, 387,
566   **Vol. 3:** 762, 837, 1212–1213
1:16 ff   **Vol. 1:** 482, 488
1:16–20   **Vol. 2:** 825   **Vol. 3:** 985
1:16   **Vol. 3:** 983–984
1:17   **Vol. 1:** 181, 488–489, 493
1:18   **Vol. 1:** 701   **Vol. 3:** 838
1:19   **Vol. 3:** 350
1:20   **Vol. 1:** 274, 321, 324, 493, 701
1:21 ff   **Vol. 2:** 228

1:21–38   **Vol. 3:** 1108
1:21 f   **Vol. 3:** 761
1:21   **Vol. 1:** 628   **Vol. 3:** 88, 761, 785
1:22   **Vol. 1:** 530   **Vol. 2:** 36, 177, 610, 623,
671   **Vol. 3:** 83, 313, 480, 769
1:23 ff   **Vol. 3:** 506
1:23 f   **Vol. 3:** 998
1:23   **Vol. 1:** 409   **Vol. 3:** 694, 785
1:24   **Vol. 1:** 454, 464   **Vol. 2:** 228, 231, 333,
559   **Vol. 3:** 474, 503
1:25–28   **Vol. 3:** 508
1:25 f   **Vol. 1:** 322   **Vol. 3:** 1108
1:25   **Vol. 1:** 572   **Vol. 3:** 475
1:26 f   **Vol. 3:** 694
1:26   **Vol. 3:** 113–114, 475
1:27   **Vol. 2:** 36, 179, 610, 623–624,
670–671   **Vol. 3:** 313, 769
1:28   **Vol. 3:** 508
1:29 ff   **Vol. 3:** 1059
1:29   **Vol. 1:** 689   **Vol. 3:** 785
1:30   **Vol. 1:** 656
1:31   **Vol. 2:** 630   **Vol. 3:** 546, 717
1:32   **Vol. 1:** 314   **Vol. 3:** 731
1:33   **Vol. 2:** 30, 33, 803
1:34   **Vol. 1:** 701   **Vol. 2:** 165   **Vol. 3:** 474,
506, 860
1:35 ff   **Vol. 3:** 1108
1:35–39   **Vol. 2:** 868
1:35   **Vol. 1:** 321   **Vol. 2:** 869   **Vol. 3:** 275,
509, 1007
1:36   **Vol. 2:** 806, 911
1:38 f   **Vol. 1:** 322   **Vol. 2:** 630   **Vol. 3:** 56
1:38   **Vol. 1:** 322   **Vol. 3:** 54, 509, 1108
1:39   **Vol. 1:** 454   **Vol. 2:** 631   **Vol. 3:** 56,
475, 785
1:40 ff   **Vol. 3:** 860
1:40   **Vol. 2:** 860
1:41 f   **Vol. 2:** 464
1:41   **Vol. 2:** 599, 630   **Vol. 3:** 1022
1:42   **Vol. 2:** 466
1:43 ff   **Vol. 3:** 506, 508
1:44   **Vol. 1:** 476   **Vol. 2:** 631, 640   **Vol. 3:**
507, 569, 1043, 1106
1:45   **Vol. 3:** 56, 320, 508, 1007, 1106,
1108–1109
2   **Vol. 1:** 317   **Vol. 3:** 507
2:1–3:6   **Vol. 3:** 510, 1109
2:1–12   **Vol. 1:** 701
2:2   **Vol. 1:** 297, 742   **Vol. 2:** 30   **Vol. 3:**
1109
2:3 ff   **Vol. 3:** 999–1000
2:3–12   **Vol. 2:** 610, 631
2:3–5   **Vol. 2:** 415
2:3   **Vol. 2:** 689
2:4   **Vol. 3:** 912
2:5 ff   **Vol. 3:** 998
2:5   **Vol. 1:** 286, 599, 701   **Vol. 2:**
631   **Vol. 3:** 1108
2:6   **Vol. 3:** 820

Mark *(cont'd)*

2:7   **Vol. 1:** 701   **Vol. 2:** 720   **Vol. 3:** 342, 481
2:8   **Vol. 3:** 694
2:9 f   **Vol. 2:** 415
2:9   **Vol. 2:** 415, 434
2:10   **Vol. 1:** 518, 701   **Vol. 3:** 508, 622
2:11   **Vol. 3:** 1108
2:12   **Vol. 1:** 528   **Vol. 3:** 508
2:13–17   **Vol. 2:** 523, 630   **Vol. 3:** 106, 428
2:13   **Vol. 3:** 761–762
2:14   **Vol. 1:** 488, 493   **Vol. 2:** 467, 754   **Vol. 3:** 275, 759, 1061, 1108
2:15 ff   **Vol. 1:** 689
2:15 f   **Vol. 3:** 580
2:16 f   **Vol. 2:** 272, 276
2:16   **Vol. 2:** 272, 276, 813   **Vol. 3:** 480–481
2:17   **Vol. 1:** 274, 322   **Vol. 2:** 170, 386, 434, 746, 757, 813   **Vol. 3:** 360, 492, 508, 580, 713, 758, 958, 998
2:18 ff   **Vol. 1:** 384   **Vol. 2:** 630, 732
2:18–22   **Vol. 2:** 585, 754   **Vol. 3:** 921
2:18 f   **Vol. 1:** 495   **Vol. 2:** 359
2:18   **Vol. 1:** 487, 612   **Vol. 2:** 272   **Vol. 3:** 481
2:19 f   **Vol. 2:** 585
2:19   **Vol. 1:** 612   **Vol. 2:** 272, 358, 383, 746   **Vol. 3:** 844
2:20   **Vol. 1:** 321
2:21 f   **Vol. 1:** 317, 613   **Vol. 2:** 671, 714
2:21   **Vol. 1:** 316   **Vol. 2:** 670   **Vol. 3:** 543
2:22   **Vol. 1:** 114   **Vol. 2:** 675–676
2:23 ff   **Vol. 2:** 437
2:23–28   **Vol. 2:** 267, 442, 754   **Vol. 3:** 37, 423, 429
2:23–27   **Vol. 1:** 335   **Vol. 3:** 1168
2:23–26   **Vol. 3:** 408
2:24   **Vol. 3:** 516
2:25 f   **Vol. 3:** 812, 814
2:25   **Vol. 1:** 245, 427   **Vol. 3:** 329, 957
2:26   **Vol. 1:** 586   **Vol. 2:** 248
2:27 f   **Vol. 3:** 623
2:27   **Vol. 1:** 384   **Vol. 3:** 410–411, 1184
2:28 f   **Vol. 2:** 514
2:28   **Vol. 3:** 508
3   **Vol. 3:** 507
3:1 ff   **Vol. 3:** 1168
3:1–6   **Vol. 3:** 409
3:1   **Vol. 1:** 516   **Vol. 3:** 785
3:2 ff   **Vol. 2:** 437
3:2   **Vol. 1:** 83   **Vol. 2:** 133, 165
3:3 ff   **Vol. 1:** 256   **Vol. 3:** 508
3:4   **Vol. 1:** 500, 563   **Vol. 2:** 434, 610
3:5   **Vol. 1:** 111   **Vol. 2:** 150, 156, 568   **Vol. 3:** 147
3:6   **Vol. 1:** 463   **Vol. 2:** 343, 812–813   **Vol. 3:** 441–443
3:7–6:6   **Vol. 3:** 1109
3:7   **Vol. 1:** 733

3:8   **Vol. 3:** 1174
3:9   **Vol. 2:** 768, 807–808
3:10 f   **Vol. 2:** 165   **Vol. 3:** 860
3:10   **Vol. 1:** 163   **Vol. 2:** 165   **Vol. 3:** 860
3:11 f   **Vol. 3:** 506
3:11   **Vol. 3:** 474, 643
3:12 f   **Vol. 1:** 256
3:12   **Vol. 1:** 572   **Vol. 3:** 320, 474
3:13 ff   **Vol. 2:** 630
3:13–19   **Vol. 3:** 453
3:13   **Vol. 1:** 274   **Vol. 2:** 185   **Vol. 3:** 1010
3:14 f   **Vol. 1:** 482   **Vol. 2:** 632, 695   **Vol. 3:** 57
3:14   **Vol. 1:** 136   **Vol. 2:** 695   **Vol. 3:** 54, 56
3:15   **Vol. 2:** 610   **Vol. 3:** 473, 475
3:16 ff   **Vol. 2:** 652
3:16–19   **Vol. 1:** 136
3:16   **Vol. 3:** 383
3:17   **Vol. 1:** 289   **Vol. 2:** 652   **Vol. 3:** 1002
3:18   **Vol. 2:** 550   **Vol. 3:** 1061, 1167
3:19   **Vol. 2:** 321
3:20 ff   **Vol. 1:** 452
3:20 f   **Vol. 2:** 750
3:20   **Vol. 1:** 322   **Vol. 3:** 508
3:21   **Vol. 1:** 528   **Vol. 3:** 1109
3:22–30   **Vol. 1:** 563   **Vol. 2:** 603   **Vol. 3:** 481
3:22–29   **Vol. 3:** 696
3:22   **Vol. 1:** 168, 637   **Vol. 2:** 327, 631   **Vol. 3:** 472, 481, 507, 1109
3:23–30   **Vol. 2:** 560   **Vol. 3:** 83, 472
3:23–27   **Vol. 3:** 695
3:23   **Vol. 3:** 1109
3:26   **Vol. 2:** 62   **Vol. 3:** 275
3:27   **Vol. 1:** 53, 508, 651   **Vol. 2:** 382, 603, 631, 702, 733, 900   **Vol. 3:** 473, 508, 696, 713, 913, 998
3:28 ff   **Vol. 3:** 580
3:28–30   **Vol. 3:** 1206
3:28 f   **Vol. 3:** 628, 696
3:28   **Vol. 1:** 289   **Vol. 3:** 343, 579, 1107
3:29   **Vol. 1:** 327   **Vol. 2:** 143   **Vol. 3:** 99, 343, 473, 579, 658, 830, 832
3:30   **Vol. 1:** 637   **Vol. 3:** 696
3:31 ff   **Vol. 3:** 1070
3:31–35   **Vol. 1:** 256, 488   **Vol. 2:** 750
3:31   **Vol. 1:** 274
3:32   **Vol. 3:** 516
3:33 ff   **Vol. 1:** 256
3:34 f   **Vol. 3:** 1062
3:35   **Vol. 3:** 503, 1022
4   **Vol. 2:** 36, 749
4:1 f   **Vol. 3:** 761
4:1–34   **Vol. 2:** 748
4:1–9   **Vol. 2:** 748, 750   **Vol. 3:** 522
4:1   **Vol. 1:** 297   **Vol. 2:** 36   **Vol. 3:** 984, 1201
4:2   **Vol. 2:** 36   **Vol. 3:** 762
4:4   **Vol. 1:** 174   **Vol. 3:** 1201
4:5   **Vol. 2:** 197   **Vol. 3:** 382
4:6   **Vol. 1:** 516, 653   **Vol. 3:** 731

Mark *(cont'd)*

4:7	**Vol. 1:** 226
4:8	**Vol. 2:** 129
4:9	**Vol. 2:** 178, 750 **Vol. 3:** 510
4:10 ff	**Vol. 2:** 750, 752
4:10–12	**Vol. 3:** 131
4:10 f	**Vol. 1:** 489
4:10	**Vol. 2:** 695, 724, 879
4:11 ff	**Vol. 3:** 507
4:11–12	**Vol. 2:** 434
4:11	**Vol. 1:** 578 **Vol. 2:** 178, 401 **Vol. 3:** 314, 503, 507
4:11b	**Vol. 2:** 753
4:12	**Vol. 1:** 261, 355 **Vol. 2:** 178, 753 **Vol. 3:** 131, 517
4:13–20	**Vol. 1:** 737 **Vol. 2:** 748, 750 **Vol. 3:** 522, 868, 1106
4:14 ff	**Vol. 3:** 1114
4:14–20	**Vol. 1:** 577–578
4:15	**Vol. 1:** 174, 566 **Vol. 3:** 470, 868
4:16–20	**Vol. 3:** 868
4:16 f	**Vol. 3:** 869
4:16	**Vol. 2:** 177, 358 **Vol. 3:** 382, 748
4:17	**Vol. 1:** 608 **Vol. 2:** 808
4:19	**Vol. 1:** 278, 457, 460, 723 **Vol. 2:** 459–460, 842–843, 845 **Vol. 3:** 252, 829
4:20	**Vol. 2:** 104, 773 **Vol. 3:** 868
4:21	**Vol. 2:** 749–750
4:22	**Vol. 1:** 181 **Vol. 2:** 212, 216 **Vol. 3:** 312, 320
4:23	**Vol. 2:** 750
4:24	**Vol. 2:** 178, 499 **Vol. 3:** 402, 822
4:25	**Vol. 2:** 750
4:26–29	**Vol. 2:** 385, 750 **Vol. 3:** 523
4:28	**Vol. 1:** 723, 744
4:29	**Vol. 3:** 526–527
4:30 ff	**Vol. 2:** 385, 429, 750 **Vol. 3:** 523
4:30 f	**Vol. 2:** 502
4:30	**Vol. 3:** 868
4:31	**Vol. 2:** 502
4:32	**Vol. 1:** 174 **Vol. 2:** 192 **Vol. 3:** 555, 813, 869
4:33 f	**Vol. 2:** 750, 753 **Vol. 3:** 1109
4:33	**Vol. 3:** 1109
4:34	**Vol. 1:** 577 **Vol. 3:** 507–508
4:35 ff	**Vol. 3:** 984
4:35–51	**Vol. 3:** 984
4:35–41	**Vol. 2:** 630 **Vol. 3:** 985
4:36–41	**Vol. 1:** 419
4:37	**Vol. 3:** 1002–1003
4:38	**Vol. 1:** 464 **Vol. 3:** 115, 767
4:39	**Vol. 1:** 572 **Vol. 3:** 989, 1002
4:40 f	**Vol. 3:** 131
4:41	**Vol. 1:** 384 **Vol. 2:** 179, 623 **Vol. 3:** 989
5:1 ff	**Vol. 2:** 168 **Vol. 3:** 475, 998
5:1–17	**Vol. 2:** 631
5:2	**Vol. 3:** 247, 1175

5:3–7	**Vol. 1:** 481
5:3	**Vol. 3:** 246
5:4	**Vol. 3:** 714
5:5	**Vol. 1:** 409
5:6 f	**Vol. 3:** 506
5:6	**Vol. 2:** 877 **Vol. 3:** 947
5:7	**Vol. 2:** 74 **Vol. 3:** 113, 474, 643, 737, 856
5:9	**Vol. 2:** 653
5:11	**Vol. 3:** 1011
5:12	**Vol. 1:** 570
5:13	**Vol. 2:** 398, 699 **Vol. 3:** 984–985, 990
5:14	**Vol. 1:** 559 **Vol. 3:** 46
5:15	**Vol. 1:** 502
5:16	**Vol. 1:** 576
5:18 ff	**Vol. 2:** 631
5:19 f	**Vol. 3:** 508
5:19	**Vol. 1:** 701 **Vol. 2:** 595
5:20	**Vol. 2:** 623 **Vol. 3:** 56
5:21–43	**Vol. 2:** 168, 630 **Vol. 3:** 1059
5:21	**Vol. 1:** 297
5:22	**Vol. 1:** 239, 609
5:23	**Vol. 2:** 151, 480
5:25 ff	**Vol. 2:** 170
5:25–34	**Vol. 2:** 560
5:25	**Vol. 1:** 221, 683 **Vol. 2:** 696 **Vol. 3:** 1175
5:26 ff	**Vol. 2:** 168
5:26	**Vol. 2:** 846 **Vol. 3:** 723
5:27–30	**Vol. 3:** 860
5:27	**Vol. 3:** 860
5:29 f	**Vol. 2:** 398
5:29	**Vol. 1:** 163, 234, 516 **Vol. 3:** 987
5:30 ff	**Vol. 2:** 169
5:30	**Vol. 3:** 860
5:31	**Vol. 3:** 861
5:33	**Vol. 1:** 610, 622 **Vol. 3:** 884
5:34	**Vol. 1:** 599 **Vol. 2:** 165, 631, 780 **Vol. 3:** 212, 861
5:35 ff	**Vol. 2:** 480
5:36	**Vol. 1:** 439, 599, 623 **Vol. 3:** 1211
5:37 ff	**Vol. 3:** 508
5:37	**Vol. 1:** 701 **Vol. 3:** 508
5:38 f	**Vol. 2:** 623 **Vol. 3:** 1174, 1185
5:38	**Vol. 1:** 329 **Vol. 2:** 416, 418, 623
5:39	**Vol. 1:** 283 **Vol. 2:** 623 **Vol. 3:** 280
5:40	**Vol. 2:** 433 **Vol. 3:** 280, 507, 751, 1071
5:41	**Vol. 1:** 581 **Vol. 2:** 630 **Vol. 3:** 280, 717
5:42	**Vol. 1:** 528 **Vol. 2:** 696
5:43	**Vol. 2:** 398, 631 **Vol. 3:** 506, 1109
6:1–6	**Vol. 2:** 631 **Vol. 3:** 88, 507
6:2 f	**Vol. 3:** 508
6:2	**Vol. 1:** 96, 488, 530 **Vol. 2:** 149, 603, 624 **Vol. 3:** 761–762, 785, 1030
6:3	**Vol. 1:** 256, 279, 668 **Vol. 2:** 320, 333, 708 **Vol. 3:** 660, 1204
6:4	**Vol. 2:** 248, 757 **Vol. 3:** 83, 696
6:5 f	**Vol. 1:** 600 **Vol. 2:** 165
6:5	**Vol. 2:** 151, 165, 603–604

153

Mark *(cont'd)*

6:6	**Vol. 2:** 165, 624, 631, 750 **Vol. 3:** 761
6:7 ff	**Vol. 2:** 632
6:7–13	**Vol. 1:** 130, 489 **Vol. 2:** 733
6:7–11	**Vol. 1:** 131
6:7	**Vol. 1:** 129, 167, 274 **Vol. 2:** 610, 686, 695 **Vol. 3:** 475
6:8–11	**Vol. 3:** 453
6:8	**Vol. 1:** 142–143, 340, 407 **Vol. 2:** 97 **Vol. 3:** 120–121
6:11	**Vol. 1:** 239, 520 **Vol. 2:** 767 **Vol. 3:** 93, 560, 1043
6:12 f	**Vol. 3:** 57
6:12	**Vol. 1:** 359 **Vol. 3:** 54, 56
6:13	**Vol. 1:** 120–121 **Vol. 2:** 165, 169, 712 **Vol. 3:** 475
6:14 ff	**Vol. 2:** 342 **Vol. 3:** 508
6:14 f	**Vol. 3:** 507
6:14	**Vol. 1:** 446 **Vol. 2:** 603, 652 **Vol. 3:** 320
6:15	**Vol. 1:** 545 **Vol. 3:** 83
6:17–20	**Vol. 1:** 156
6:17	**Vol. 2:** 136, 550, 579 **Vol. 3:** 717
6:18	**Vol. 3:** 540
6:19	**Vol. 1:** 430
6:20	**Vol. 2:** 229 **Vol. 3:** 361
6:21	**Vol. 1:** 666 **Vol. 2:** 699, 887
6:23	**Vol. 2:** 381 **Vol. 3:** 742
6:24–28	**Vol. 2:** 159
6:24	**Vol. 3:** 1071
6:25	**Vol. 3:** 82
6:26	**Vol. 1:** 74
6:27	**Vol. 2:** 136
6:28	**Vol. 3:** 1071
6:29	**Vol. 1:** 265, 487 **Vol. 3:** 247
6:30–44	**Vol. 1:** 729 **Vol. 2:** 523 **Vol. 3:** 508
6:30	**Vol. 1:** 129, 134, 136, 297 **Vol. 3:** 763
6:31	**Vol. 3:** 256, 508
6:32–14	**Vol. 2:** 630
6:32	**Vol. 3:** 1007
6:33	**Vol. 2:** 398 **Vol. 3:** 947
6:34 ff	**Vol. 2:** 272
6:34	**Vol. 2:** 413, 459, 599, 750 **Vol. 3:** 567, 761–762
6:35	**Vol. 3:** 847
6:36	**Vol. 1:** 505 **Vol. 3:** 189
6:37	**Vol. 2:** 711
6:39	**Vol. 1:** 744
6:41	**Vol. 1:** 213, 250 **Vol. 2:** 192 **Vol. 3:** 519
6:42–52	**Vol. 3:** 985
6:42	**Vol. 1:** 743
6:44	**Vol. 2:** 699
6:45–52	**Vol. 2:** 630 **Vol. 3:** 984–985, 990
6:45	**Vol. 1:** 505 **Vol. 3:** 189, 951
6:46	**Vol. 1:** 321 **Vol. 3:** 509, 1010
6:47 ff	**Vol. 3:** 1002
6:48	**Vol. 1:** 322 **Vol. 2:** 136 **Vol. 3:** 856
6:48c	**Vol. 2:** 281

6:49	**Vol. 1:** 409 **Vol. 2:** 281, 559 **Vol. 3:** 293, 324, 822
6:50	**Vol. 1:** 623 **Vol. 2:** 281 **Vol. 3:** 710
6:51	**Vol. 1:** 729
6:52	**Vol. 2:** 155 **Vol. 3:** 131–132
6:53	**Vol. 3:** 1059
6:55	**Vol. 3:** 860
6:56	**Vol. 1:** 267 **Vol. 3:** 860, 994
7	**Vol. 3:** 774
7:1 ff	**Vol. 2:** 272
7:1–23	**Vol. 2:** 715, 813 **Vol. 3:** 481, 763
7:1–4	**Vol. 2:** 150
7:1	**Vol. 1:** 297 **Vol. 2:** 327
7:2–23	**Vol. 3:** 990
7:2	**Vol. 1:** 153, 448 **Vol. 2:** 139, 144
7:3 f	**Vol. 1:** 225 **Vol. 3:** 105, 717, 990
7:3	**Vol. 1:** 153, 199 **Vol. 2:** 150, 315, 813 **Vol. 3:** 774
7:4	**Vol. 1:** 144, 149 **Vol. 3:** 748, 990
7:5 ff	**Vol. 1:** 153 **Vol. 2:** 469
7:5	**Vol. 1:** 199, 448 **Vol. 2:** 813 **Vol. 3:** 481, 774
7:6 ff	**Vol. 2:** 150
7:6–13	**Vol. 3:** 181, 184
7:6 f	**Vol. 2:** 43, 469
7:6	**Vol. 1:** 736 **Vol. 2:** 183
7:7	**Vol. 1:** 552 **Vol. 2:** 93 **Vol. 3:** 770
7:8 f	**Vol. 1:** 336
7:8	**Vol. 1:** 335, 701 **Vol. 3:** 717, 774–775
7:9–13	**Vol. 1:** 289, 619
7:9	**Vol. 1:** 74, 335 **Vol. 2:** 133
7:10 f	**Vol. 2:** 640
7:10	**Vol. 1:** 415, 430 **Vol. 3:** 95, 1070
7:11 f	**Vol. 3:** 1070
7:11	**Vol. 2:** 41–43
7:13	**Vol. 2:** 43, 503 **Vol. 3:** 773–774
7:14 ff	**Vol. 1:** 153
7:14–23	**Vol. 1:** 169 **Vol. 2:** 150
7:14 f	**Vol. 2:** 437, 640
7:14	**Vol. 1:** 274, 448
7:15	**Vol. 1:** 448, 642 **Vol. 3:** 106, 762, 1168
7:17–23	**Vol. 3:** 507–508
7:17	**Vol. 2:** 746 **Vol. 3:** 507
7:18 f	**Vol. 2:** 268
7:18	**Vol. 1:** 448, 642 **Vol. 3:** 106, 131
7:19	**Vol. 2:** 268
7:19c	**Vol. 3:** 106
7:20	**Vol. 1:** 448 **Vol. 3:** 106
7:21 ff	**Vol. 3:** 31
7:21–23	**Vol. 3:** 106
7:21 f	**Vol. 1:** 563
7:21	**Vol. 1:** 499, 564 **Vol. 2:** 182 **Vol. 3:** 820
7:22	**Vol. 1:** 138 **Vol. 3:** 30, 516
7:23	**Vol. 1:** 448
7:24 ff	**Vol. 3:** 475
7:24–30	**Vol. 3:** 980, 1059
7:24	**Vol. 3:** 275, 506–508
7:25	**Vol. 1:** 609, 637
7:26	**Vol. 2:** 126

Mark *(cont'd)*

7:27 f	**Vol. 1:** 117
7:27	**Vol. 1:** 666–667, 744 **Vol. 2:** 434
7:28	**Vol. 1:** 117, 283, 744
7:29	**Vol. 2:** 631
7:30	**Vol. 2:** 248
7:31–37	**Vol. 3:** 508
7:31 f	**Vol. 3:** 475
7:32 ff	**Vol. 2:** 560
7:32	**Vol. 1:** 428 **Vol. 2:** 151
7:33 f	**Vol. 3:** 860
7:33	**Vol. 3:** 507, 751, 1079
7:34	**Vol. 1:** 429 **Vol. 2:** 192, 423, 729 **Vol. 3:** 519
7:35	**Vol. 1:** 428 **Vol. 2:** 175, 726, 728–729 **Vol. 3:** 180, 592, 1079
7:36 f	**Vol. 3:** 508
7:36	**Vol. 1:** 729 **Vol. 2:** 631 **Vol. 3:** 56, 506, 1109
7:37	**Vol. 1:** 428, 729 **Vol. 2:** 170, 623, 632 **Vol. 3:** 56
8:1 ff	**Vol. 2:** 272
8:1–21	**Vol. 3:** 508
8:1–10	**Vol. 1:** 729 **Vol. 2:** 523, 630
8:2	**Vol. 2:** 599 **Vol. 3:** 228
8:3	**Vol. 1:** 505 **Vol. 3:** 189, 939
8:4	**Vol. 1:** 743 **Vol. 3:** 1007
8:5	**Vol. 2:** 692, 879
8:6 f	**Vol. 1:** 213
8:6	**Vol. 1:** 250, 340, 517 **Vol. 3:** 819
8:8	**Vol. 1:** 729, 743 **Vol. 2:** 692
8:9	**Vol. 1:** 505 **Vol. 2:** 699 **Vol. 3:** 189
8:11 f	**Vol. 2:** 192, 631, 750
8:11	**Vol. 2:** 629 **Vol. 3:** 83, 480, 804
8:12 ff	**Vol. 2:** 630
8:12	**Vol. 3:** 531, 694, 1107
8:14–21	**Vol. 3:** 132
8:15–21	**Vol. 3:** 508
8:15	**Vol. 2:** 462 **Vol. 3:** 442
8:16 f	**Vol. 3:** 820
8:17–21	**Vol. 3:** 510
8:17–18	**Vol. 2:** 434
8:17 f	**Vol. 2:** 178 **Vol. 3:** 131
8:17	**Vol. 2:** 155 **Vol. 3:** 131, 503
8:18	**Vol. 3:** 131, 240, 517
8:19	**Vol. 2:** 696, 699
8:20	**Vol. 2:** 692, 699
8:21	**Vol. 3:** 131
8:22–26	**Vol. 3:** 508
8:22–25	**Vol. 1:** 219
8:22	**Vol. 3:** 507
8:23	**Vol. 2:** 151, 170, 560, 803 **Vol. 3:** 749
8:24	**Vol. 3:** 519
8:25	**Vol. 3:** 147, 519
8:26	**Vol. 3:** 506–507, 1174
8:27 ff	**Vol. 1:** 708 **Vol. 2:** 680
8:27–9:1	**Vol. 3:** 864
8:27–33	**Vol. 2:** 341 **Vol. 3:** 508, 1061
8:27–30	**Vol. 3:** 509

8:27	**Vol. 2:** 550
8:28	**Vol. 1:** 545 **Vol. 3:** 82–83, 507–508
8:29–31	**Vol. 3:** 629
8:29	**Vol. 2:** 76, 231 **Vol. 3:** 384
8:30	**Vol. 1:** 572 **Vol. 3:** 506
8:31 ff	**Vol. 3:** 508
8:31 f	**Vol. 1:** 545
8:31	**Vol. 1:** 74, 198, 430 **Vol. 2:** 327, 526, 665, 687, 893 **Vol. 3:** 39, 276, 294, 507, 509, 623–624, 723, 761, 809, 1109, 1198
8:32 f	**Vol. 3:** 455
8:32	**Vol. 1:** 572 **Vol. 3:** 751, 1109
8:33†	**Vol. 1:** 111, 572 **Vol. 2:** 618 **Vol. 3:** 197, 394, 470, 509, 807
8:34	**Vol. 1:** 324, 394, 402, 455, 482, 493 **Vol. 3:** 60
8:35 f	**Vol. 3:** 174
8:35	**Vol. 1:** 464 **Vol. 2:** 110, 112, 433 **Vol. 3:** 212–213, 530, 682
8:36	**Vol. 1:** 524 **Vol. 3:** 137, 142
8:37	**Vol. 2:** 480 **Vol. 3:** 167, 174, 196
8:38 f	**Vol. 2:** 654
8:38	**Vol. 1:** 205, 323, 347 **Vol. 2:** 36, 46, 228, 582, 584 **Vol. 3:** 135, 508, 563, 579–580, 618, 620–621, 625, 1108
9:1	**Vol. 2:** 38, 271, 382, 386–387, 604, 910, 930 **Vol. 3:** 627, 863, 1107
9:2 ff	**Vol. 1:** 708
9:2–8	**Vol. 2:** 48 **Vol. 3:** 114
9:2–7	**Vol. 2:** 47 Sr 9:2 f **Vol. 2:** 486
9:2	**Vol. 1:** 704, 706 **Vol. 2:** 199, 686 **Vol. 3:** 508, 861–863, 1010, 1012
9:3	**Vol. 1:** 204
9:4 f	**Vol. 1:** 545 **Vol. 2:** 640
9:4	**Vol. 2:** 559 **Vol. 3:** 474
9:5	**Vol. 1:** 488 **Vol. 2:** 514 **Vol. 3:** 115, 555, 767
9:7	**Vol. 2:** 176, 543, 725 **Vol. 3:** 114, 611, 621, 639, 643, 651, 864, 1003
9:8	**Vol. 2:** 724
9:9	**Vol. 1:** 335, 576 **Vol. 3:** 276, 294, 506, 862, 1012
9:10	**Vol. 3:** 131, 717, 1106
9:11 ff	**Vol. 1:** 545
9:11	**Vol. 1:** 323, 544–545, 667 **Vol. 3:** 624
9:12 f	**Vol. 1:** 545 **Vol. 3:** 188, 329
9:12	**Vol. 1:** 74, 581 **Vol. 3:** 80, 147, 623–624, 723
9:13	**Vol. 1:** 545 **Vol. 3:** 489
9:14 ff	**Vol. 3:** 475
9:14	**Vol. 3:** 1010
9:15	**Vol. 2:** 623–624
9:17	**Vol. 1:** 428 **Vol. 2:** 595 **Vol. 3:** 475, 767
9:18	**Vol. 1:** 516 **Vol. 3:** 750
9:19	**Vol. 2:** 36, 766 **Vol. 3:** 1204
9:20	**Vol. 1:** 609 **Vol. 3:** 506
9:22	**Vol. 1:** 463, 656 **Vol. 2:** 600 **Vol. 3:** 990

Mark *(cont'd)*

9:23 f   **Vol. 2:** 631   **Vol. 3:** 1211
9:23   **Vol. 1:** 600   **Vol. 2:** 604
9:24   **Vol. 1:** 283
9:25   **Vol. 1:** 428–429, 572   **Vol. 3:** 475, 507,
          694, 1108
9:26   **Vol. 1:** 96, 446   **Vol. 3:** 475
9:28–32   **Vol. 1:** 130
9:28 f   **Vol. 3:** 507
9:29   **Vol. 1:** 613   **Vol. 3:** 474
9:30 ff   **Vol. 3:** 508
9:30 f   **Vol. 3:** 507
9:30   **Vol. 3:** 946, 1010
9:31 f   **Vol. 3:** 508
9:31   **Vol. 1:** 162, 430   **Vol. 2:** 150, 368,
          526–527, 893   **Vol. 3:** 276, 294, 507,
          623–624
9:32   **Vol. 2:** 216, 406, 880   **Vol. 3:** 131, 507,
          1122
9:33–37   **Vol. 1:** 285   **Vol. 2:** 427
9:33–34   **Vol. 2:** 429   **Vol. 3:** 821
9:34   **Vol. 3:** 447
9:35   **Vol. 2:** 57, 695   **Vol. 3:** 114, 447, 761,
          979
9:36   **Vol. 1:** 239
9:37   **Vol. 1:** 285   **Vol. 2:** 176, 429   **Vol. 3:**
          746
9:38   **Vol. 2:** 653   **Vol. 3:** 475, 767
9:39   **Vol. 1:** 415
9:40   **Vol. 2:** 34, 813
9:41   **Vol. 1:** 285   **Vol. 3:** 141, 980, 989, 1107
9:42–50   **Vol. 3:** 446, 448
9:42–48   **Vol. 2:** 387   **Vol. 3:** 1052
9:42 f   **Vol. 3:** 447
9:42   **Vol. 2:** 429, 652   **Vol. 3:** 394, 984, 1212
9:43 ff   **Vol. 2:** 385
9:43–48   **Vol. 2:** 385, 710   **Vol. 3:** 99
9:43   **Vol. 1:** 657   **Vol. 2:** 208, 387, 414–415,
          481   **Vol. 3:** 111, 447
9:45   **Vol. 1:** 239, 657   **Vol. 2:** 208, 415, 481
9:46   **Vol. 2:** 387
9:47 f   **Vol. 2:** 208
9:47   **Vol. 1:** 453, 657   **Vol. 2:** 387
9:48   **Vol. 1:** 430, 657   **Vol. 2:** 709   **Vol. 3:**
          109–110, 447–448
9:49 f   **Vol. 2:** 749–750
9:49   **Vol. 1:** 657   **Vol. 2:** 746   **Vol. 3:**
          446–447, 697
9:50   **Vol. 2:** 757, 781   **Vol. 3:** 445, 447
9:50a   **Vol. 3:** 447
10:1 ff   **Vol. 3:** 762
10:1–12† **Vol. 1:** 506   **Vol. 2:** 442   **Vol. 3:**
          181–182, 538
10:1   **Vol. 3:** 275, 540, 761, 991
10:2 ff   **Vol. 1:** 737
10:2–12† **Vol. 1:** 500   **Vol. 2:** 580   **Vol. 3:** 172,
          188
10:2–9   **Vol. 3:** 534, 980

10:2   **Vol. 1:** 506   **Vol. 2:** 563   **Vol. 3:** 189,
          539, 804
10:3   **Vol. 1:** 335
10:4   **Vol. 1:** 243–244, 506, 606   **Vol. 3:** 189
10:5   **Vol. 1:** 335   **Vol. 2:** 156, 184   **Vol. 3:**
          182, 538
10:6 ff   **Vol. 1:** 500
10:6–9   **Vol. 3:** 539
10:6 f   **Vol. 2:** 579
10:6   **Vol. 1:** 166, 384   **Vol. 2:** 563,
          570   **Vol. 3:** 1058, 1154
10:7 f   **Vol. 2:** 570   **Vol. 3:** 1070
10:7   **Vol. 3:** 251
10:8 f   **Vol. 2:** 570
10:8   **Vol. 2:** 583, 722
10:9 ff   **Vol. 2:** 581
10:9   **Vol. 2:** 565   **Vol. 3:** 1164
10:10   **Vol. 3:** 507
10:11 f   **Vol. 1:** 506   **Vol. 2:** 580, 583
10:11   **Vol. 1:** 500, 506   **Vol. 2:** 564   **Vol. 3:**
          189, 540
10:12   **Vol. 1:** 506   **Vol. 2:** 563   **Vol. 3:** 189,
          540
10:13 ff **Vol. 1:** 283, 489
10:13–16 **Vol. 1:** 160, 213, 284   **Vol. 3:** 861
10:13   **Vol. 1:** 572
10:14 f   **Vol. 1:** 284
10:14   **Vol. 1:** 149   **Vol. 2:** 222–223
10:15   **Vol. 1:** 213, 284   **Vol. 2:** 262,
          385   **Vol. 3:** 746, 1107
10:16   **Vol. 1:** 74, 212, 239, 284   **Vol. 2:** 151
10:17 ff **Vol. 1:** 482   **Vol. 3:** 978
10:17–31 **Vol. 1:** 335   **Vol. 2:** 301
10:17–22 **Vol. 2:** 844
10:17 f   **Vol. 2:** 100
10:17   **Vol. 2:** 388, 480–481, 860   **Vol. 3:** 832
10:18   **Vol. 1:** 565
10:19   **Vol. 1:** 619   **Vol. 2:** 583   **Vol. 3:** 377,
          379, 755
10:20   **Vol. 2:** 135, 675
10:21   **Vol. 1:** 268   **Vol. 2:** 720, 824, 833,
          846   **Vol. 3:** 141, 519, 954
10:22   **Vol. 2:** 845–846   **Vol. 3:** 1108
10:23 ff **Vol. 2:** 843
10:23–31 **Vol. 2:** 750
10:23   **Vol. 2:** 845, 910
10:24   **Vol. 1:** 286, 591   **Vol. 2:** 623
10:25   **Vol. 1:** 116   **Vol. 2:** 842
10:26 ff **Vol. 2:** 118
10:26   **Vol. 1:** 730   **Vol. 2:** 623   **Vol. 3:** 213
10:27   **Vol. 2:** 74, 603, 606   **Vol. 3:** 213, 519
10:28 ff **Vol. 1:** 256
10:28–31 **Vol. 2:** 57
10:28   **Vol. 1:** 701   **Vol. 2:** 840   **Vol. 3:** 516
10:29 f   **Vol. 1:** 287, 619   **Vol. 2:** 250
10:29   **Vol. 2:** 110, 112, 301, 387   **Vol. 3:** 213,
          1107
10:30   **Vol. 2:** 480, 840   **Vol. 3:** 142, 748, 832,
          837–839
10:31   **Vol. 2:** 57

Mark *(cont'd)*

10:32 ff   **Vol. 3:** 507–508
10:32   **Vol. 1:** 482, 489   **Vol. 2:** 623–624, 695
10:33 f   **Vol. 2:** 327, 526
10:33   **Vol. 2:** 368   **Vol. 3:** 39, 516, 623
10:34   **Vol. 1:** 162, 430   **Vol. 2:** 893   **Vol. 3:** 276, 340, 967
10:35–45   **Vol. 2:** 385
10:35–37   **Vol. 2:** 276
10:35   **Vol. 2:** 858
10:37–40   **Vol. 3:** 588
10:37   **Vol. 2:** 41, 148, 386, 388
10:38 f   **Vol. 1:** 144   **Vol. 3:** 697
10:38   **Vol. 1:** 394   **Vol. 2:** 63, 276
10:39   **Vol. 3:** 118
10:40   **Vol. 1:** 730   **Vol. 2:** 148   **Vol. 3:** 1198
10:42–45   **Vol. 3:** 979
10:42   **Vol. 1:** 167–168   **Vol. 2:** 519   **Vol. 3:** 822
10:43 f   **Vol. 2:** 427   **Vol. 3:** 1022
10:43   **Vol. 3:** 546–547
10:44   **Vol. 3:** 611
10:45   **Vol. 1:** 96–97, 322, 369, 398, 437–438, 492, 549, 701–702   **Vol. 2:** 42, 262, 532, 543   **Vol. 3:** 195–197, 508, 546–547, 611–612, 625, 682–683, 1064, 1180
10:45b   **Vol. 2:** 525
10:46 ff   **Vol. 3:** 507–508
10:46–52   **Vol. 1:** 219
10:46†   **Vol. 1:** 288   **Vol. 3:** 589, 939–940, 1201
10:47 f   **Vol. 2:** 341   **Vol. 3:** 507
10:47   **Vol. 2:** 333, 595
10:48   **Vol. 1:** 489, 572   **Vol. 2:** 595   **Vol. 3:** 651
10:49   **Vol. 1:** 328
10:51   **Vol. 3:** 115, 519
10:52   **Vol. 1:** 599   **Vol. 2:** 631   **Vol. 3:** 212, 508, 519, 939
11:1–11   **Vol. 3:** 509
11:1–10   **Vol. 2:** 379, 754   **Vol. 3:** 791
11:1   **Vol. 1:** 725   **Vol. 2:** 54, 713   **Vol. 3:** 1174
11:2   **Vol. 1:** 117, 171   **Vol. 3:** 179
11:3   **Vol. 3:** 1154
11:4 f   **Vol. 1:** 117
11:4   **Vol. 2:** 30   **Vol. 3:** 179
11:5   **Vol. 2:** 869   **Vol. 3:** 179, 1154
11:7 f   **Vol. 1:** 317
11:7   **Vol. 1:** 117   **Vol. 3:** 378
11:9 f   **Vol. 1:** 323
11:9   **Vol. 1:** 100, 213   **Vol. 3:** 378
11:10   **Vol. 1:** 213
11:11–17   **Vol. 2:** 610
11:11   **Vol. 2:** 528, 695   **Vol. 3:** 429, 792, 847
11:12 ff   **Vol. 1:** 724   **Vol. 2:** 267, 750, 754   **Vol. 3:** 793
11:12–25   **Vol. 3:** 784

11:12 f   **Vol. 3:** 868–869
11:13   **Vol. 1:** 724   **Vol. 3:** 837, 958
11:15 ff   **Vol. 1:** 111   **Vol. 2:** 236, 754   **Vol. 3:** 429, 784
11:15–19   **Vol. 2:** 379   **Vol. 3:** 181, 791, 1168
11:15–17   **Vol. 2:** 327
11:15   **Vol. 1:** 175   **Vol. 2:** 236
11:16   **Vol. 3:** 913
11:17   **Vol. 1:** 274   **Vol. 2:** 248, 793   **Vol. 3:** 329, 380, 430, 761–762, 788, 791
11:18   **Vol. 1:** 463   **Vol. 2:** 36, 327, 623, 799   **Vol. 3:** 39, 531, 769
11:19 f   **Vol. 2:** 653
11:19   **Vol. 2:** 528
11:20–26   **Vol. 3:** 1012
11:20   **Vol. 1:** 515
11:21   **Vol. 1:** 417, 488, 515   **Vol. 3:** 115, 767
11:22 ff   **Vol. 1:** 600
11:22   **Vol. 1:** 600
11:23   **Vol. 1:** 504, 600   **Vol. 3:** 984, 1107
11:24 f   **Vol. 1:** 600
11:24   **Vol. 2:** 858, 868
11:25 f   **Vol. 1:** 701   **Vol. 2:** 871
11:25   **Vol. 1:** 620, 702   **Vol. 2:** 868
11:27 ff   **Vol. 3:** 1154
11:27–13:1   **Vol. 2:** 236
11:27–33   **Vol. 3:** 792
11:27   **Vol. 1:** 199   **Vol. 3:** 789, 791
11:29   **Vol. 2:** 880
11:30   **Vol. 2:** 193, 434
11:31   **Vol. 3:** 821, 1211
12:1 f   **Vol. 3:** 868
12:1–12   **Vol. 2:** 301, 746, 751   **Vol. 3:** 641, 869, 920
12:1   **Vol. 2:** 790   **Vol. 3:** 951
12:2   **Vol. 1:** 724   **Vol. 3:** 837
12:3   **Vol. 1:** 163, 547
12:4 ff   **Vol. 2:** 236
12:4   **Vol. 2:** 50, 157
12:5 ff   **Vol. 1:** 430
12:5   **Vol. 1:** 163
12:6   **Vol. 2:** 58, 543, 720
12:9   **Vol. 1:** 464   **Vol. 2:** 513
12:10 f   **Vol. 2:** 129, 313, 622
12:10   **Vol. 1:** 245   **Vol. 2:** 159, 253, 706   **Vol. 3:** 329, 390, 393, 490, 492, 809
12:11   **Vol. 2:** 623
12:12   **Vol. 1:** 724   **Vol. 3:** 508, 717
12:13–17   **Vol. 1:** 269   **Vol. 3:** 549, 754, 979, 1168
12:13   **Vol. 2:** 343, 812   **Vol. 3:** 441, 1108
12:14 ff   **Vol. 3:** 762
12:14–17   **Vol. 3:** 979
12:14   **Vol. 1:** 586–587   **Vol. 3:** 754, 757, 884, 940
12:15   **Vol. 2:** 469   **Vol. 3:** 804
12:16   **Vol. 2:** 288   **Vol. 3:** 489
12:17   **Vol. 2:** 623–624   **Vol. 3:** 978
12:18 ff   **Vol. 1:** 488   **Vol. 2:** 691   **Vol. 3:** 767
12:18–27   **Vol. 2:** 578, 580   **Vol. 3:** 263, 439, 792

Mark (*cont'd*)

12:19	**Vol. 2:** 640
12:24	**Vol. 2:** 459–460, 603 **Vol. 3:** 304, 490, 492, 1174
12:25 f	**Vol. 1:** 290, 446
12:25	**Vol. 1:** 103 **Vol. 2:** 192, 578, 581
12:26 f	**Vol. 1:** 78 **Vol. 2:** 481 **Vol. 3:** 263
12:26	**Vol. 1:** 81, 244 **Vol. 2:** 73, 319, 640 **Vol. 3:** 329
12:27	**Vol. 1:** 445 **Vol. 2:** 460, 480, 578
12:28 ff	**Vol. 1:** 259, 339
12:28–34	**Vol. 2:** 516, 543, 813, 870 **Vol. 3:** 173, 455, 791
12:28	**Vol. 1:** 334 **Vol. 2:** 177, 426, 544 **Vol. 3:** 439
12:29 f	**Vol. 1:** 334 **Vol. 2:** 73, 177
12:29	**Vol. 2:** 720–721
12:30 f	**Vol. 3:** 542
12:30	**Vol. 3:** 127, 685, 713
12:31	**Vol. 1:** 334–335 **Vol. 2:** 177 **Vol. 3:** 1064
12:32	**Vol. 2:** 721, 739 **Vol. 3:** 884
12:33	**Vol. 1:** 730 **Vol. 3:** 131, 431
12:34	**Vol. 2:** 54
12:35 ff	**Vol. 2:** 147 **Vol. 3:** 508, 791
12:35–37	**Vol. 2:** 515 **Vol. 3:** 651
12:35 f	**Vol. 2:** 79 **Vol. 3:** 762
12:35	**Vol. 3:** 481, 761, 791
12:36	**Vol. 1:** 239, 477, 554 **Vol. 2:** 515 **Vol. 3:** 697
12:37–40	**Vol. 2:** 469 **Vol. 3:** 580
12:37	**Vol. 2:** 516
12:38–40	**Vol. 3:** 481
12:38	**Vol. 1:** 267, 312 **Vol. 2:** 36 **Vol. 3:** 769, 1019
12:39	**Vol. 1:** 666 **Vol. 3:** 589, 785
12:40	**Vol. 2:** 738 **Vol. 3:** 482, 748, 1074
12:41–44	**Vol. 2:** 43, 751, 824 **Vol. 3:** 789, 791, 1062, 1074
12:41	**Vol. 2:** 97, 842 **Vol. 3:** 796
12:42	**Vol. 2:** 821, 850
12:43	**Vol. 1:** 274 **Vol. 3:** 796, 1107
12:44	**Vol. 1:** 729 **Vol. 2:** 475, 846 **Vol. 3:** 791, 955
13	**Vol. 1:** 125, 541 **Vol. 2:** 65, 894, 909–915 **Vol. 3:** 65, 490, 560, 844, 984
13:1 ff	**Vol. 2:** 39, 236
13:1–36	**Vol. 2:** 36
13:1–4	**Vol. 2:** 36–37, 713 **Vol. 3:** 1011
13:1	**Vol. 3:** 791
13:2 ff	**Vol. 2:** 803
13:2 f	**Vol. 3:** 792
13:2	**Vol. 1:** 75 **Vol. 2:** 426, 450 **Vol. 3:** 185, 211, 275, 343, 393, 1177
13:3 ff	**Vol. 3:** 507
13:3 f	**Vol. 3:** 508
13:4–23	**Vol. 2:** 915
13:4	**Vol. 2:** 37, 629, 892, 904, 912
13:5–37	**Vol. 2:** 702
13:5–31	**Vol. 2:** 904
13:5–27	**Vol. 3:** 956
13:5–13	**Vol. 2:** 904, 915
13:5 f	**Vol. 2:** 459, 461
13:5	**Vol. 2:** 911, 914
13:5b–23	**Vol. 2:** 913
13:5b	**Vol. 2:** 914
13:6	**Vol. 2:** 281, 913–914
13:7	**Vol. 2:** 62, 665, 892, 912, 918 **Vol. 3:** 962
13:7a	**Vol. 2:** 914
13:7b	**Vol. 2:** 913–914
13:8	**Vol. 1:** 165 **Vol. 2:** 266, 793, 913–914 **Vol. 3:** 558, 858, 956
13:9–13	**Vol. 2:** 904, 911
13:9	**Vol. 1:** 163, 270, 364 **Vol. 2:** 913–914 **Vol. 3:** 785, 1043
13:10	**Vol. 2:** 110, 665 **Vol. 3:** 52, 56, 213
13:11	**Vol. 1:** 90, 277 **Vol. 2:** 913 **Vol. 3:** 83, 697–698, 704, 849
13:12	**Vol. 1:** 286–287, 289, 725 **Vol. 2:** 368
13:13	**Vol. 1:** 556 **Vol. 2:** 38, 62, 773, 806, 916 **Vol. 3:** 257
13:13a	**Vol. 2:** 773, 913
13:13b–17	**Vol. 2:** 913
13:13b	**Vol. 2:** 914
13:14 f	**Vol. 2:** 916
13:14–23	**Vol. 2:** 904
13:14–20	**Vol. 2:** 37, 914 **Vol. 3:** 793
13:14–19	**Vol. 2:** 914
13:14	**Vol. 1:** 74–75 **Vol. 2:** 373, 911–912 **Vol. 3:** 792, 1011
13:15 f	**Vol. 2:** 910
13:16 f	**Vol. 2:** 911
13:17	**Vol. 3:** 1053
13:18	**Vol. 2:** 913
13:19 f	**Vol. 3:** 803
13:19	**Vol. 1:** 166 **Vol. 2:** 664, 808, 912–913, 916
13:20	**Vol. 1:** 539, 542 **Vol. 2:** 916
13:20a	**Vol. 2:** 913
13:21 ff	**Vol. 2:** 904
13:21	**Vol. 2:** 914 **Vol. 3:** 1211
13:22 f	**Vol. 1:** 323
13:22	**Vol. 2:** 472, 629, 633, 911, 913–914 **Vol. 3:** 84, 803
13:23	**Vol. 2:** 911, 914
13:24 f	**Vol. 2:** 916
13:24–31	**Vol. 2:** 904
13:24–30	**Vol. 2:** 38
13:24–27	**Vol. 2:** 913–914, 916
13:24	**Vol. 1:** 203, 425 **Vol. 2:** 37–38, 484, 892 **Vol. 3:** 732, 734
13:25	**Vol. 1:** 610 **Vol. 2:** 192, 603 **Vol. 3:** 559, 736
13:26 f	**Vol. 2:** 252, 911
13:26	**Vol. 1:** 323 **Vol. 2:** 46, 385, 604, 912, 917 **Vol. 3:** 527, 620, 622, 629, 1003

Mark *(cont'd)*

13:27	**Vol. 1:** 102, 518, 725 **Vol. 2:** 33, 194, 313, 689, 911, 917 **Vol. 3:** 527
13:28 ff	**Vol. 2:** 904
13:28–37	**Vol. 2:** 913
13:28–32	**Vol. 2:** 751
13:28 f	**Vol. 2:** 382, 398, 912, 914
13:28	**Vol. 1:** 486, 725 **Vol. 2:** 604 **Vol. 3:** 867
13:28b	**Vol. 2:** 913
13:29	**Vol. 2:** 30, 387, 727, 911
13:30	**Vol. 2:** 36–38, 382, 910–912, 917, 930 **Vol. 3:** 1107
13:31	**Vol. 2:** 193, 911, 913 **Vol. 3:** 1108
13:32 ff	**Vol. 2:** 912
13:32 f	**Vol. 2:** 911, 930
13:32	**Vol. 1:** 323, 548 **Vol. 2:** 75, 192, 894, 904, 910, 913, 916–917 **Vol. 3:** 642, 844, 847–848
13:33–37	**Vol. 2:** 751, 914, 916
13:33 f	**Vol. 2:** 913
13:33	**Vol. 2:** 137, 911, 914 **Vol. 3:** 515, 517, 838
13:34–37	**Vol. 1:** 725
13:34	**Vol. 2:** 502, 732, 751, 913–914
13:35 f	**Vol. 2:** 911
13:35	**Vol. 2:** 136–137, 751, 914
13:36	**Vol. 1:** 489
13:37	**Vol. 2:** 137, 911, 914
14	**Vol. 1:** 633
14:1	**Vol. 1:** 199, 633 **Vol. 3:** 531, 717
14:2	**Vol. 2:** 623, 799
14:3 ff	**Vol. 2:** 295, 549
14:3–9	**Vol. 3:** 1060
14:3	**Vol. 2:** 159, 464, 528 **Vol. 3:** 408, 1061
14:4	**Vol. 1:** 464 **Vol. 3:** 1060
14:5	**Vol. 2:** 112
14:6–9	**Vol. 3:** 1060
14:6	**Vol. 2:** 104 **Vol. 3:** 1149–1150
14:7	**Vol. 2:** 824
14:8	**Vol. 1:** 265 **Vol. 3:** 243, 750
14:9	**Vol. 2:** 110 **Vol. 3:** 52, 213, 242–244, 547
14:10 f	**Vol. 2:** 526
14:10	**Vol. 1:** 299 **Vol. 2:** 695
14:11	**Vol. 3:** 70–71, 531–532
14:12–26	**Vol. 1:** 633
14:12	**Vol. 1:** 633–634 **Vol. 2:** 277, 463, 527 **Vol. 3:** 118, 1019
14:13	**Vol. 1:** 325 **Vol. 3:** 911, 990
14:14	**Vol. 2:** 510, 527, 549 **Vol. 3:** 767–768
14:15	**Vol. 3:** 569
14:16	**Vol. 2:** 527 **Vol. 3:** 118
14:17–21	**Vol. 2:** 531 **Vol. 3:** 804
14:17	**Vol. 2:** 528, 695
14:18–25	**Vol. 2:** 526 **Vol. 3:** 1107
14:18	**Vol. 2:** 272, 521, 526
14:19	**Vol. 2:** 720
14:20	**Vol. 2:** 695
14:21	**Vol. 2:** 526–527 **Vol. 3:** 329, 1053
14:22–25	**Vol. 1:** 237 **Vol. 2:** 523–524 **Vol. 3:** 508
14:22–24	**Vol. 1:** 634
14:22 f	**Vol. 1:** 213
14:22	**Vol. 1:** 251 **Vol. 2:** 523–525, 535
14:22c	**Vol. 2:** 524, 532
14:23	**Vol. 2:** 533 **Vol. 3:** 819
14:24	**Vol. 1:** 96–97, 223, 369, 437–438 **Vol. 2:** 523–526, 530, 532–533, 535–536, 543, 671, 854 **Vol. 3:** 166, 611–612
14:25	**Vol. 2:** 382, 385, 524, 531–532, 535, 727, 882, 894, 896 **Vol. 3:** 180, 922
14:26–31	**Vol. 3:** 386, 803
14:26	**Vol. 2:** 528, 713 **Vol. 3:** 245, 669
14:27 f	**Vol. 3:** 567
14:27	**Vol. 2:** 34, 413, 459 **Vol. 3:** 188, 329, 697, 1122
14:28	**Vol. 2:** 732 **Vol. 3:** 281
14:30	**Vol. 1:** 173, 455 **Vol. 3:** 114, 1107, 1122
14:31	**Vol. 1:** 435
14:32 ff	**Vol. 2:** 526
14:32–42	**Vol. 2:** 178, 561, 868
14:32	**Vol. 2:** 713
14:33	**Vol. 2:** 623–624, 686
14:34	**Vol. 3:** 683
14:35 ff	**Vol. 3:** 804
14:35 f	**Vol. 3:** 509
14:35	**Vol. 1:** 322 **Vol. 2:** 603
14:36	**Vol. 1:** 335, 614–615, 620 **Vol. 2:** 76, 83, 276, 871, 896 **Vol. 3:** 639, 697, 1022
14:37	**Vol. 1:** 442 **Vol. 3:** 713
14:38	**Vol. 1:** 677 **Vol. 2:** 137, 871 **Vol. 3:** 694, 802–803, 994
14:39	**Vol. 1:** 321 **Vol. 2:** 222 **Vol. 3:** 980
14:41 f	**Vol. 3:** 516
14:41	**Vol. 2:** 150, 527, 543 **Vol. 3:** 252, 256, 580
14:42	**Vol. 2:** 54
14:43 ff	**Vol. 1:** 395
14:43	**Vol. 1:** 299, 390 **Vol. 2:** 695, 801 **Vol. 3:** 967
14:44 f	**Vol. 2:** 549
14:44	**Vol. 1:** 663 **Vol. 2:** 526 **Vol. 3:** 717
14:45	**Vol. 3:** 115
14:46	**Vol. 3:** 717
14:47 f	**Vol. 3:** 967
14:47	**Vol. 1:** 489 **Vol. 3:** 978
14:48	**Vol. 1:** 343 **Vol. 3:** 379
14:49	**Vol. 1:** 736 **Vol. 2:** 895 **Vol. 3:** 329, 490, 761, 791, 1204
14:50	**Vol. 1:** 559
14:51	**Vol. 1:** 481 **Vol. 3:** 717
14:52	**Vol. 1:** 313, 559
14:53 ff	**Vol. 1:** 395
14:53–72	**Vol. 2:** 379 **Vol. 3:** 386, 803–804
14:53–65	**Vol. 3:** 409

Mark *(cont'd)*

14:54   **Vol. 1:** 318   **Vol. 2:** 493
14:55   **Vol. 1:** 364   **Vol. 3:** 1043
14:56   **Vol. 2:** 499   **Vol. 3:** 1043
14:57 f   **Vol. 3:** 792
14:57   **Vol. 3:** 275
14:58   **Vol. 2:** 150, 236, 252, 450, 687, 732   **Vol. 3:** 185, 211, 343, 509, 784
14:59   **Vol. 2:** 499   **Vol. 3:** 1043
14:60   **Vol. 3:** 39, 275, 1042
14:61 f   **Vol. 2:** 282   **Vol. 3:** 712
14:61†   **Vol. 1:** 212   **Vol. 3:** 509
14:62   **Vol. 1:** 323   **Vol. 2:** 147, 194, 380, 385, 515, 603, 731–732, 917   **Vol. 3:** 457, 509, 588, 620, 627, 629, 1003
14:63   **Vol. 3:** 958, 1043
14:64   **Vol. 2:** 143, 175, 282, 365, 488   **Vol. 3:** 342
14:65   **Vol. 1:** 162–163   **Vol. 3:** 83, 347, 857
14:67   **Vol. 1:** 318   **Vol. 2:** 333   **Vol. 3:** 520
14:68   **Vol. 1:** 455
14:70 ff   **Vol. 1:** 455
14:70   **Vol. 1:** 455
14:71   **Vol. 1:** 415   **Vol. 2:** 398, 565   **Vol. 3:** 742
14:72   **Vol. 1:** 173   **Vol. 3:** 114, 240
15   **Vol. 2:** 378
15:1 ff   **Vol. 2:** 630
15:1–47   **Vol. 1:** 394
15:1–15   **Vol. 1:** 395
15:1   **Vol. 1:** 199, 363–364   **Vol. 2:** 526
15:2   **Vol. 2:** 315, 378–379   **Vol. 3:** 509
15:3 f   **Vol. 1:** 83
15:3   **Vol. 1:** 199
15:5   **Vol. 2:** 624
15:6–15   **Vol. 1:** 396, 505   **Vol. 3:** 189
15:6   **Vol. 2:** 858
15:7   **Vol. 1:** 633   **Vol. 2:** 331
15:8   **Vol. 1:** 411
15:9   **Vol. 2:** 315, 378   **Vol. 3:** 509
15:10   **Vol. 1:** 396, 558   **Vol. 2:** 526
15:11   **Vol. 1:** 199   **Vol. 3:** 558
15:12   **Vol. 2:** 315   **Vol. 3:** 509
15:13 f   **Vol. 1:** 409
15:14   **Vol. 3:** 189
15:15   **Vol. 1:** 162   **Vol. 2:** 526, 801   **Vol. 3:** 1017
15:16–19   **Vol. 3:** 347
15:16   **Vol. 3:** 964
15:17   **Vol. 1:** 205, 406, 726
15:18   **Vol. 2:** 315, 358, 378
15:19   **Vol. 2:** 159, 859, 877   **Vol. 3:** 903
15:20   **Vol. 1:** 205, 314   **Vol. 3:** 341
15:20b   **Vol. 1:** 396
15:21   **Vol. 1:** 396, 520   **Vol. 2:** 740
15:22   **Vol. 1:** 581
15:23   **Vol. 2:** 28, 295   **Vol. 3:** 922
15:24   **Vol. 1:** 396   **Vol. 2:** 82, 299   **Vol. 3:** 287, 670

15:25   **Vol. 3:** 847
15:26   **Vol. 2:** 139, 315, 339, 379   **Vol. 3:** 489, 509
15:27   **Vol. 2:** 148   **Vol. 3:** 379
15:28   **Vol. 1:** 736   **Vol. 2:** 445   **Vol. 3:** 379, 490, 824
15:29 ff   **Vol. 2:** 630   **Vol. 3:** 211
15:29–32   **Vol. 1:** 395, 397   **Vol. 3:** 347
15:29 f   **Vol. 3:** 792
15:29   **Vol. 1:** 396   **Vol. 2:** 82, 159, 339, 687   **Vol. 3:** 185, 287, 343, 509, 785
15:31 f   **Vol. 3:** 965
15:31   **Vol. 1:** 199, 323   **Vol. 3:** 341
15:32   **Vol. 2:** 379   **Vol. 3:** 340, 509
15:33 f   **Vol. 3:** 847
15:33   **Vol. 1:** 423   **Vol. 3:** 732
15:34 f   **Vol. 1:** 544
15:34   **Vol. 1:** 396, 411, 581, 615, 620   **Vol. 2:** 82   **Vol. 3:** 113, 1187
15:35   **Vol. 3:** 114
15:36   **Vol. 2:** 28   **Vol. 3:** 947
15:37   **Vol. 2:** 426   **Vol. 3:** 113, 708
15:38   **Vol. 2:** 328   **Vol. 3:** 543, 793, 795
15:39   **Vol. 3:** 503, 508, 708, 964–965
15:40 f   **Vol. 3:** 1059–1060, 1070
15:40   **Vol. 3:** 1071
15:41   **Vol. 3:** 546
15:42   **Vol. 3:** 120, 408, 410
15:43   **Vol. 1:** 234, 365   **Vol. 2:** 387
15:44 f   **Vol. 3:** 964
15:44   **Vol. 1:** 274   **Vol. 2:** 624, 714
15:45   **Vol. 1:** 610   **Vol. 2:** 41
15:46 ff   **Vol. 3:** 296
15:46   **Vol. 3:** 246–247, 382, 393
16   **Vol. 1:** 633
16:1 ff   **Vol. 3:** 1059
16:1 f   **Vol. 3:** 288
16:1–8a   **Vol. 3:** 286
16:1–8   **Vol. 3:** 294
16:1   **Vol. 1:** 120   **Vol. 2:** 295   **Vol. 3:** 1060
16:2 f   **Vol. 3:** 247
16:2   **Vol. 3:** 246, 412, 731
16:3   **Vol. 2:** 30
16:4   **Vol. 3:** 519
16:5 f   **Vol. 2:** 623
16:5   **Vol. 1:** 204   **Vol. 2:** 146, 624   **Vol. 3:** 247
16:6 ff   **Vol. 3:** 294
16:6   **Vol. 2:** 333   **Vol. 3:** 281, 285
16:7   **Vol. 1:** 136   **Vol. 3:** 289, 515
16:8   **Vol. 2:** 358–359   **Vol. 3:** 247, 296
16:9–20   **Vol. 1:** 510   **Vol. 2:** 632
16:9–19   **Vol. 3:** 294
16:9   **Vol. 2:** 488   **Vol. 3:** 412, 1059
16:10   **Vol. 2:** 422   **Vol. 3:** 48
16:12   **Vol. 1:** 706, 708   **Vol. 2:** 739   **Vol. 3:** 320
16:13   **Vol. 3:** 48, 251–252
16:14   **Vol. 2:** 183–184   **Vol. 3:** 320, 340
16:15 ff   **Vol. 2:** 632

Mark *(cont'd)*

16:15	**Vol. 1:** 95, 384 **Vol. 2:** 110, 176
16:16	**Vol. 1:** 489 **Vol. 2:** 366
16:17 ff	**Vol. 1:** 446
16:17 f	**Vol. 2:** 560
16:17	**Vol. 3:** 475
16:18	**Vol. 1:** 510
16:19	**Vol. 2:** 515 **Vol. 3:** 749
16:20	**Vol. 1:** 658–659 **Vol. 2:** 632 **Vol. 3:** 1152

Luke

1–2	**Vol. 3:** 700
1	**Vol. 2:** 624 **Vol. 3:** 931, 1072
1:1–4	**Vol. 2:** 113, 787 **Vol. 3:** 773
1:1	**Vol. 1:** 576, 737 **Vol. 3:** 772, 1158
1:2	**Vol. 1:** 166 **Vol. 2:** 718 **Vol. 3:** 546, 773–774
1:3 f	**Vol. 1:** 247 **Vol. 3:** 489
1:3	**Vol. 2:** 86 **Vol. 3:** 718, 822
1:4	**Vol. 1:** 663 **Vol. 2:** 920 **Vol. 3:** 771
1:5–80	**Vol. 3:** 790
1:5–25	**Vol. 2:** 327 **Vol. 3:** 1071
1:5	**Vol. 2:** 34, 378 **Vol. 3:** 37
1:6	**Vol. 1:** 335 **Vol. 2:** 144 **Vol. 3:** 361, 947
1:7	**Vol. 2:** 139, 400
1:8–23	**Vol. 3:** 790
1:8	**Vol. 2:** 34 **Vol. 3:** 37
1:9–11	**Vol. 2:** 294
1:9	**Vol. 1:** 321, 478 **Vol. 2:** 437 **Vol. 3:** 785
1:10	**Vol. 1:** 733 **Vol. 2:** 294, 799 **Vol. 3:** 847
1:11–20	**Vol. 1:** 104
1:11	**Vol. 2:** 294, 513 **Vol. 3:** 436
1:12	**Vol. 1:** 609, 622 **Vol. 3:** 710
1:13	**Vol. 1:** 178, 187, 274, 288, 623 **Vol. 2:** 178, 860
1:14	**Vol. 1:** 181 **Vol. 2:** 353–354, 358
1:15	**Vol. 1:** 739 **Vol. 3:** 457, 698, 921, 1071
1:16–28	**Vol. 1:** 129
1:16 f	**Vol. 1:** 355, 545
1:17	**Vol. 1:** 128, 322–323, 593 **Vol. 2:** 443, 620 **Vol. 3:** 80, 118–119, 361, 694, 698, 940
1:18	**Vol. 1:** 197
1:19	**Vol. 1:** 102–103, 474 **Vol. 3:** 57
1:20	**Vol. 1:** 736 **Vol. 3:** 1211
1:21 f	**Vol. 2:** 624 **Vol. 3:** 785
1:21	**Vol. 3:** 843
1:22	**Vol. 1:** 429 **Vol. 3:** 515
1:23	**Vol. 1:** 737 **Vol. 3:** 552
1:24	**Vol. 1:** 343 **Vol. 2:** 214
1:25	**Vol. 3:** 340
1:26 ff	**Vol. 3:** 1071
1:26–38	**Vol. 1:** 104
1:26	**Vol. 3:** 324
1:27	**Vol. 1:** 427, 668 **Vol. 2:** 248 **Vol. 3:** 652, 1072
1:28	**Vol. 2:** 119, 358
1:30	**Vol. 1:** 104, 623 **Vol. 2:** 118 **Vol. 3:** 530
1:31	**Vol. 1:** 274, 343 **Vol. 2:** 332
1:32 ff	**Vol. 3:** 642
1:32–35	**Vol. 3:** 637
1:32	**Vol. 1:** 274, 427 **Vol. 2:** 74, 200, 513, 614 **Vol. 3:** 457, 652
1:33	**Vol. 2:** 62, 248, 319, 381 **Vol. 3:** 662
1:33b	**Vol. 1:** 177
1:34 f	**Vol. 1:** 85 **Vol. 3:** 662
1:34	**Vol. 1:** 668 **Vol. 2:** 398 **Vol. 3:** 660, 662
1:35	**Vol. 1:** 187, 274, 322 **Vol. 2:** 87, 200, 228, 603 **Vol. 3:** 555, 660, 697–698, 1073
1:35b	**Vol. 1:** 177
1:36	**Vol. 1:** 343 **Vol. 3:** 1073
1:37	**Vol. 3:** 1121
1:38	**Vol. 1:** 607 **Vol. 2:** 119, 262 **Vol. 3:** 30, 1121
1:39	**Vol. 2:** 320 **Vol. 3:** 275, 456, 1008, 1169
1:41 f	**Vol. 3:** 84
1:41	**Vol. 1:** 283, 739 **Vol. 3:** 698, 700
1:42	**Vol. 1:** 213, 411, 722
1:44	**Vol. 1:** 283 **Vol. 2:** 353, 358
1:45	**Vol. 1:** 216–217 **Vol. 2:** 63 **Vol. 3:** 1198, 1211
1:46–55	**Vol. 2:** 596 **Vol. 3:** 30, 674, 1071
1:46–48	**Vol. 3:** 30
1:46	**Vol. 2:** 596 **Vol. 3:** 683
1:47	**Vol. 2:** 353, 358 **Vol. 3:** 219, 693
1:48	**Vol. 1:** 216 **Vol. 2:** 35, 262, 596, 603
1:49–50	**Vol. 3:** 30
1:49	**Vol. 2:** 228, 426
1:50 ff	**Vol. 2:** 543
1:50	**Vol. 2:** 35, 596
1:51–53	**Vol. 3:** 30
1:51	**Vol. 2:** 34 **Vol. 3:** 30, 127, 718
1:52	**Vol. 2:** 203, 262, 596
1:53	**Vol. 1:** 128, 735 **Vol. 2:** 266–267, 596, 842–843
1:54 f	**Vol. 3:** 30
1:54	**Vol. 2:** 596 **Vol. 3:** 241, 612
1:55	**Vol. 2:** 358, 596 **Vol. 3:** 523, 829–830
1:57	**Vol. 1:** 737 **Vol. 3:** 834, 843
1:58	**Vol. 2:** 595
1:59	**Vol. 1:** 284, 309 **Vol. 2:** 692
1:63	**Vol. 2:** 624, 858 **Vol. 3:** 489
1:64	**Vol. 1:** 213 **Vol. 2:** 726, 728 **Vol. 3:** 1079
1:65	**Vol. 3:** 1008
1:66	**Vol. 2:** 149, 513
1:67	**Vol. 1:** 739 **Vol. 3:** 84, 698, 700
1:68 ff	**Vol. 2:** 358
1:68–79	**Vol. 2:** 596 **Vol. 3:** 674, 715

Luke *(cont'd)*

1:68	**Vol. 1:** 191, 212 **Vol. 2:** 73, 358, 596, 799 **Vol. 3:** 198
1:69	**Vol. 1:** 427 **Vol. 2:** 248, 596 **Vol. 3:** 198, 212, 612, 652, 715
1:70	**Vol. 2:** 228, 358 **Vol. 3:** 830
1:71	**Vol. 1:** 554, 557 **Vol. 2:** 596 **Vol. 3:** 198, 212
1:72	**Vol. 2:** 228, 596 **Vol. 3:** 241
1:73	**Vol. 3:** 198, 742
1:74	**Vol. 1:** 554, 566 **Vol. 2:** 596 **Vol. 3:** 550
1:75	**Vol. 2:** 237, 480 **Vol. 3:** 361
1:76	**Vol. 1:** 545 **Vol. 2:** 200, 332, 596 **Vol. 3:** 80, 86, 118, 198, 940
1:77	**Vol. 1:** 701 **Vol. 2:** 596, 799 **Vol. 3:** 198, 212, 580
1:78 f	**Vol. 3:** 212
1:78	**Vol. 2:** 78, 199, 495, 596, 599 **Vol. 3:** 198
1:79	**Vol. 1:** 423 **Vol. 2:** 596, 780–781 **Vol. 3:** 198, 319, 555, 940
1:80	**Vol. 1:** 92 **Vol. 2:** 129 **Vol. 3:** 570, 694, 718, 1007
2	**Vol. 2:** 624 **Vol. 3:** 317, 931, 1073
2:1 ff	**Vol. 3:** 642
2:1–52	**Vol. 3:** 1071
2:1–3	**Vol. 1:** 171
2:1–2	**Vol. 1:** 669
2:1	**Vol. 1:** 269, 322, 330, 519
2:2	**Vol. 1:** 666
2:4	**Vol. 1:** 427, 616 **Vol. 2:** 185, 248, 803 **Vol. 3:** 63, 652, 1174, 1180
2:5	**Vol. 3:** 1073
2:6 f	**Vol. 1:** 187
2:6	**Vol. 1:** 737
2:7	**Vol. 1:** 668 **Vol. 3:** 189
2:8–14	**Vol. 3:** 1007
2:8 f	**Vol. 1:** 421 **Vol. 3:** 566
2:8	**Vol. 2:** 135–136
2:9	**Vol. 1:** 102, 622 **Vol. 2:** 46, 486, 513
2:10	**Vol. 1:** 623 **Vol. 2:** 799 **Vol. 3:** 57
2:11	**Vol. 1:** 427 **Vol. 2:** 332, 358 **Vol. 3:** 219, 652, 838
2:12	**Vol. 1:** 283 **Vol. 2:** 629
2:13	**Vol. 1:** 102, 733 **Vol. 2:** 191 **Vol. 3:** 517, 817, 964
2:14	**Vol. 1:** 288 **Vol. 2:** 46, 358, 566, 780–781, 819 **Vol. 3:** 219
2:15	**Vol. 1:** 169, 171 **Vol. 2:** 193, 358 **Vol. 3:** 314, 1121–1122
2:16	**Vol. 1:** 283 **Vol. 3:** 1169
2:17	**Vol. 3:** 314, 1121
2:18	**Vol. 2:** 624
2:19	**Vol. 3:** 1121–1122
2:20	**Vol. 2:** 176 **Vol. 3:** 817
2:21 f	**Vol. 1:** 737
2:21	**Vol. 1:** 98, 169, 309, 343 **Vol. 2:** 692
2:22 ff	**Vol. 2:** 327
2:22–52	**Vol. 3:** 790
2:22	**Vol. 1:** 474 **Vol. 2:** 444 **Vol. 3:** 409, 1058
2:23	**Vol. 1:** 736 **Vol. 2:** 228, 444, 570, 729 **Vol. 3:** 660
2:24	**Vol. 1:** 172, 175 **Vol. 2:** 41, 444 **Vol. 3:** 430, 790, 1164
2:25–38	**Vol. 3:** 1059
2:25–27	**Vol. 3:** 698
2:25 f	**Vol. 3:** 790
2:25	**Vol. 1:** 329, 570 **Vol. 2:** 91, 245 **Vol. 3:** 84, 361
2:26	**Vol. 3:** 517
2:27	**Vol. 2:** 444
2:28 f	**Vol. 1:** 213
2:28	**Vol. 1:** 239
2:29–32	**Vol. 3:** 674, 790
2:29	**Vol. 1:** 505 **Vol. 2:** 509 **Vol. 3:** 189, 1121–1122
2:30–32	**Vol. 2:** 314
2:30 f	**Vol. 3:** 118
2:30	**Vol. 3:** 221, 515
2:31 f	**Vol. 2:** 799
2:31	**Vol. 1:** 586
2:32	**Vol. 2:** 494, 799 **Vol. 3:** 313
2:33	**Vol. 2:** 624
2:34	**Vol. 1:** 207, 213, 471, 610 **Vol. 2:** 367, 629, 706, 708–709 **Vol. 3:** 276, 516, 821
2:35	**Vol. 3:** 312, 684, 821, 967
2:36	**Vol. 3:** 81, 84, 872–873, 1072
2:37	**Vol. 1:** 607 **Vol. 3:** 550
2:38	**Vol. 2:** 245, 314 **Vol. 3:** 198, 790, 846
2:39	**Vol. 2:** 63, 444
2:40	**Vol. 1:** 92 **Vol. 2:** 118, 129 **Vol. 3:** 718, 1030, 1194
2:41–51	**Vol. 1:** 256
2:41	**Vol. 1:** 169, 632–633 **Vol. 3:** 409
2:42	**Vol. 1:** 169 **Vol. 2:** 437, 696
2:43	**Vol. 1:** 283, 737 **Vol. 2:** 63, 773
2:44	**Vol. 3:** 489, 940
2:46	**Vol. 2:** 236, 327, 880 **Vol. 3:** 767, 789
2:47	**Vol. 3:** 132
2:48	**Vol. 1:** 530
2:49	**Vol. 2:** 327, 665 **Vol. 3:** 698, 1070
2:50	**Vol. 3:** 132, 1122
2:51	**Vol. 3:** 931, 1070
2:52	**Vol. 1:** 92 **Vol. 2:** 118, 130 **Vol. 3:** 1030
3	**Vol. 2:** 36
3:1 ff	**Vol. 2:** 262
3:1	**Vol. 1:** 269 **Vol. 2:** 550
3:2–17	**Vol. 1:** 111
3:2	**Vol. 3:** 39–40, 1007, 1107, 1121, 1193
3:3	**Vol. 3:** 52, 55, 580, 1208
3:4–6	**Vol. 3:** 1011
3:4	**Vol. 1:** 244, 411, 736 **Vol. 3:** 53, 118, 940
3:5	**Vol. 2:** 262
3:6	**Vol. 3:** 118, 221, 1011

Luke *(cont'd)*

3:7–9   **Vol. 3:** 695
3:7   **Vol. 1:** 559   **Vol. 2:** 801   **Vol. 3:** 1208
3:8   **Vol. 1:** 77, 167, 286   **Vol. 3:** 393, 822, 869
3:9   **Vol. 1:** 156, 656, 722   **Vol. 2:** 104, 749   **Vol. 3:** 869
3:10   **Vol. 2:** 801   **Vol. 3:** 869
3:11   **Vol. 2:** 41   **Vol. 3:** 1155
3:12 f   **Vol. 3:** 758
3:12   **Vol. 3:** 767
3:13   **Vol. 3:** 1022, 1157
3:14   **Vol. 3:** 144, 558, 727, 965
3:15–18   **Vol. 3:** 695
3:15   **Vol. 3:** 820
3:16 f   **Vol. 2:** 921
3:16   **Vol. 1:** 323   **Vol. 2:** 785–786, 921   **Vol. 3:** 55, 110, 179, 447, 714, 1210
3:17   **Vol. 1:** 156   **Vol. 2:** 32, 411   **Vol. 3:** 111, 804
3:18   **Vol. 1:** 571   **Vol. 2:** 113   **Vol. 3:** 57, 87
3:19   **Vol. 2:** 141   **Vol. 3:** 540
3:20   **Vol. 2:** 136   **Vol. 3:** 1193
3:21 f   **Vol. 2:** 873   **Vol. 3:** 113
3:21   **Vol. 2:** 193, 728, 799   **Vol. 3:** 170, 543, 990
3:22   **Vol. 1:** 175, 179, 704   **Vol. 2:** 193, 314, 543, 566, 819   **Vol. 3:** 114, 499, 611, 639, 641, 659, 697–698, 807, 987, 1070
3:23 ff   **Vol. 2:** 691
3:23–38   **Vol. 1:** 77, 177–178   **Vol. 2:** 79, 314   **Vol. 3:** 654
3:23   **Vol. 1:** 167   **Vol. 2:** 333   **Vol. 3:** 655, 658–659, 662, 1073
3:24   **Vol. 2:** 467
3:26   **Vol. 2:** 320   **Vol. 3:** 397
3:27   **Vol. 3:** 655
3.29   **Vol. 2:** 331, 467
3:31   **Vol. 1:** 427   **Vol. 3:** 63, 652
3:33   **Vol. 2:** 320
3:34   **Vol. 1:** 77, 81   **Vol. 2:** 318, 320
3:36   **Vol. 3:** 543
3:37   **Vol. 2:** 236
3:38   **Vol. 1:** 85   **Vol. 2:** 920   **Vol. 3:** 659
4:1 f   **Vol. 3:** 1007
4:1–14   **Vol. 3:** 698
4:1–13   **Vol. 3:** 470, 804, 979, 1007
4:1–4   **Vol. 2:** 630
4:1   **Vol. 1:** 739   **Vol. 3:** 602, 697–698, 700, 991
4:2   **Vol. 2:** 267, 689, 696, 893
4:3   **Vol. 3:** 659
4:4   **Vol. 2:** 267, 872   **Vol. 3:** 805
4:5 f   **Vol. 3:** 806
4:5   **Vol. 1:** 519, 524   **Vol. 2:** 381   **Vol. 3:** 569, 843
4:6   **Vol. 2:** 42, 46, 368, 610
4:7   **Vol. 2:** 877, 893   **Vol. 3:** 806–807

4:8   **Vol. 2:** 877, 893   **Vol. 3:** 550
4:9–12   **Vol. 2:** 631   **Vol. 3:** 790, 796, 1011
4:9   **Vol. 2:** 235   **Vol. 3:** 659
4:10 f   **Vol. 3:** 805
4:10   **Vol. 1:** 335
4:11   **Vol. 2:** 706
4:12   **Vol. 2:** 893   **Vol. 3:** 802, 805
4:13   **Vol. 1:** 607   **Vol. 2:** 728   **Vol. 3:** 804
4:14 ff   **Vol. 2:** 631   **Vol. 3:** 762
4:14   **Vol. 2:** 603   **Vol. 3:** 698
4:15 f   **Vol. 3:** 785
4:15   **Vol. 3:** 761
4:16 ff   **Vol. 3:** 88, 761–762, 764
4:16–30   **Vol. 2:** 631
4:16–27   **Vol. 2:** 379
4:16–21   **Vol. 3:** 589, 821
4:16 f   **Vol. 1:** 245
4:16   **Vol. 1:** 245, 321, 628   **Vol. 2:** 333, 437, 887   **Vol. 3:** 56, 275, 409
4:17   **Vol. 1:** 244, 736   **Vol. 2:** 728   **Vol. 3:** 485
4:18 ff   **Vol. 1:** 701
4:18–21   **Vol. 1:** 701
4:18 f   **Vol. 1:** 738   **Vol. 2:** 118   **Vol. 3:** 612, 639, 696
4:18   **Vol. 1:** 122–123, 701   **Vol. 2:** 110, 113, 712, 825   **Vol. 3:** 499, 591, 698, 733, 1061, 1108
4:19   **Vol. 3:** 744, 746
4:20   **Vol. 3:** 135, 520, 785
4:21   **Vol. 1:** 167, 736, 738   **Vol. 2:** 118   **Vol. 3:** 71, 329, 490, 492, 762–763, 1178
4:22   **Vol. 1:** 96   **Vol. 2:** 118, 333, 757   **Vol. 3:** 660
4:22a   **Vol. 2:** 624
4:23   **Vol. 1:** 616   **Vol. 2:** 164, 746, 757
4:24   **Vol. 2:** 231, 641   **Vol. 3:** 83, 86, 746
4:25 f   **Vol. 1:** 544   **Vol. 3:** 1062
4:25   **Vol. 1:** 98   **Vol. 2:** 31, 193, 266, 688, 730   **Vol. 3:** 883
4:27   **Vol. 2:** 464
4:28   **Vol. 1:** 106, 110, 739   **Vol. 3:** 785
4:29   **Vol. 2:** 624   **Vol. 3:** 275
4:30   **Vol. 3:** 1178
4:31   **Vol. 3:** 88
4:32   **Vol. 2:** 610, 623   **Vol. 3:** 83, 532, 1106
4:33   **Vol. 1:** 637   **Vol. 2:** 426   **Vol. 3:** 113, 785
4:34   **Vol. 2:** 228, 333, 559
4:35 f   **Vol. 3:** 1059
4:36   **Vol. 2:** 610, 623–624   **Vol. 3:** 475, 694, 1106
4:37   **Vol. 3:** 112
4:38   **Vol. 1:** 656   **Vol. 2:** 880   **Vol. 3:** 785
4:39   **Vol. 1:** 572   **Vol. 3:** 275, 546
4:40 f   **Vol. 2:** 165
4:40   **Vol. 1:** 314   **Vol. 3:** 731
4:42   **Vol. 3:** 1007
4:43   **Vol. 2:** 113, 665   **Vol. 3:** 54

Luke *(cont'd)*

4:44   **Vol. 1:** 297   **Vol. 2:** 631   **Vol. 3:** 56, 785, 1174
5:1–11   **Vol. 2:** 630, 825   **Vol. 3:** 985
5:1   **Vol. 1:** 181   **Vol. 3:** 315, 984, 992, 1114
5:2   **Vol. 3:** 992
5:3   **Vol. 3:** 761
5:4   **Vol. 2:** 197   **Vol. 3:** 803
5:5–8   **Vol. 3:** 1122
5:5   **Vol. 1:** 263   **Vol. 2:** 595   **Vol. 3:** 115, 1193
5:6   **Vol. 1:** 671, 733   **Vol. 3:** 543
5:7   **Vol. 1:** 344, 736   **Vol. 2:** 739
5:8   **Vol. 1:** 610   **Vol. 2:** 563, 859   **Vol. 3:** 580
5:9   **Vol. 1:** 344   **Vol. 2:** 623–624
5:10   **Vol. 1:** 489, 623, 642
5:11   **Vol. 1:** 482
5:12–16   **Vol. 2:** 631
5:12 f   **Vol. 2:** 466
5:12   **Vol. 1:** 586, 609   **Vol. 2:** 860   **Vol. 3:** 1022
5:13   **Vol. 2:** 150   **Vol. 3:** 1022
5:14   **Vol. 1:** 340   **Vol. 3:** 37, 569, 1043
5:15   **Vol. 3:** 1106
5:16   **Vol. 2:** 869   **Vol. 3:** 1007
5:17   **Vol. 2:** 170   **Vol. 3:** 480, 761, 768
5:18 ff   **Vol. 3:** 1000
5:18–26   **Vol. 2:** 610, 631
5:18   **Vol. 3:** 999
5:19   **Vol. 3:** 912
5:21 ff   **Vol. 2:** 170
5:21   **Vol. 2:** 170, 720, 724   **Vol. 3:** 342, 481
5:22   **Vol. 3:** 820
5:23 f   **Vol. 2:** 920   **Vol. 3:** 280
5:23   **Vol. 2:** 193, 434
5:24   **Vol. 2:** 415   **Vol. 3:** 999
5:26   **Vol. 1:** 528   **Vol. 3:** 748
5:27–32   **Vol. 2:** 523   **Vol. 3:** 428, 980
5:27   **Vol. 2:** 467, 754   **Vol. 3:** 759
5:28   **Vol. 3:** 251, 275, 757
5:29 f   **Vol. 2:** 630
5:29   **Vol. 2:** 467   **Vol. 3:** 757
5:30   **Vol. 2:** 170, 276, 813
5:31   **Vol. 2:** 170, 386, 757   **Vol. 3:** 758, 998
5:32   **Vol. 1:** 274, 322, 358   **Vol. 2:** 276   **Vol. 3:** 361, 492, 580
5:33 ff   **Vol. 1:** 495
5:33–39   **Vol. 2:** 754
5:33–38   **Vol. 3:** 921
5:33 f   **Vol. 2:** 359
5:33   **Vol. 1:** 487, 637   **Vol. 2:** 170, 276
5:34   **Vol. 2:** 358, 383, 585, 799
5:35   **Vol. 2:** 585
5:36 f†   **Vol. 2:** 714
5:36   **Vol. 2:** 670   **Vol. 3:** 543
5:37   **Vol. 2:** 854
5:38   **Vol. 2:** 675–676
5:39   **Vol. 2:** 105, 714   **Vol. 3:** 921

6   **Vol. 1:** 217   **Vol. 3:** 1009
6:1–5   **Vol. 2:** 267, 754   **Vol. 3:** 37, 408, 423, 429
6:2   **Vol. 2:** 170
6:3   **Vol. 1:** 427   **Vol. 3:** 329
6:4   **Vol. 1:** 586   **Vol. 2:** 248   **Vol. 3:** 792
6:5   **Vol. 1:** 216
6:6–11   **Vol. 3:** 409, 442
6:6   **Vol. 1:** 129, 516   **Vol. 3:** 761–762, 785
6:7   **Vol. 1:** 83   **Vol. 2:** 133, 165, 170, 813
6:8   **Vol. 3:** 275, 820
6:9   **Vol. 1:** 463   **Vol. 2:** 102, 434, 880
6:10   **Vol. 2:** 150   **Vol. 3:** 147
6:11   **Vol. 1:** 739   **Vol. 2:** 813   **Vol. 3:** 128
6:12–16   **Vol. 1:** 135   **Vol. 3:** 453, 980
6:12 f   **Vol. 2:** 873
6:12   **Vol. 1:** 420   **Vol. 2:** 869   **Vol. 3:** 1009–1010
6:13   **Vol. 1:** 128, 136, 540, 542   **Vol. 2:** 655, 695   **Vol. 3:** 54
6:14 ff   **Vol. 1:** 136   **Vol. 2:** 652
6:14   **Vol. 2:** 550, 655
6:15   **Vol. 1:** 274, 488   **Vol. 3:** 1167
6:16   **Vol. 1:** 299   **Vol. 2:** 320–321   **Vol. 3:** 1011
6:17–49   **Vol. 2:** 150
6:17   **Vol. 1:** 733   **Vol. 2:** 327, 801   **Vol. 3:** 1009
6:18   **Vol. 2:** 164   **Vol. 3:** 475
6:19   **Vol. 2:** 169, 757   **Vol. 3:** 860, 1201
6:20 ff   **Vol. 1:** 216–217, 495   **Vol. 2:** 386, 388, 449, 543
6:20–49   **Vol. 2:** 598
6:20 f   **Vol. 3:** 696
6:20   **Vol. 2:** 300, 381, 824   **Vol. 3:** 978
6:21   **Vol. 1:** 217, 744   **Vol. 2:** 266–267, 416
6:21b   **Vol. 2:** 433
6:22 ff   **Vol. 2:** 544
6:22   **Vol. 1:** 453, 473, 566   **Vol. 3:** 257, 340, 627
6:23   **Vol. 2:** 353, 426, 894   **Vol. 3:** 83
6:24 ff   **Vol. 2:** 824–825, 843
6:24–26   **Vol. 3:** 1053
6:24   **Vol. 1:** 571   **Vol. 2:** 842
6:25 f   **Vol. 2:** 416
6:25   **Vol. 1:** 735   **Vol. 2:** 267, 417, 422
6:25b   **Vol. 2:** 433
6:26   **Vol. 2:** 472   **Vol. 3:** 83, 1155
6:27 ff   **Vol. 3:** 979
6:27 f   **Vol. 1:** 215   **Vol. 2:** 386, 544   **Vol. 3:** 183
6:27   **Vol. 1:** 556   **Vol. 2:** 543   **Vol. 3:** 97
6:28   **Vol. 1:** 417   **Vol. 3:** 755
6:29 f   **Vol. 3:** 183
6:29   **Vol. 2:** 222   **Vol. 3:** 903
6:30   **Vol. 2:** 846
6:30b   **Vol. 2:** 858
6:32 ff   **Vol. 3:** 580
6:32–36   **Vol. 2:** 386, 544   **Vol. 3:** 183
6:32–34   **Vol. 2:** 118

Luke *(cont'd)*

6:32   **Vol. 2:** 366
6:33   **Vol. 2:** 102 **Vol. 3:** 757
6:34   **Vol. 2:** 241, 498–499 **Vol. 3:** 751
6:35   **Vol. 1:** 556, 566 **Vol. 2:** 102, 106, 426, 929
6:36†   **Vol. 1:** 620 **Vol. 2:** 63, 543, 598
6:37   **Vol. 1:** 505, 702 **Vol. 2:** 370 **Vol. 3:** 189
6:38   **Vol. 1:** 240 **Vol. 2:** 43 **Vol. 3:** 402, 559, 1173
6:39   **Vol. 1:** 220, 610 **Vol. 2:** 757 **Vol. 3:** 942
6:40   **Vol. 1:** 404, 486
6:41 f   **Vol. 2:** 469, 749
6:41   **Vol. 1:** 116 **Vol. 3:** 129
6:42   **Vol. 2:** 757
6:43 ff   **Vol. 2:** 104, 749 **Vol. 3:** 868
6:43 f   **Vol. 3:** 869
6:43   **Vol. 1:** 722 **Vol. 2:** 757
6:44   **Vol. 2:** 33 **Vol. 3:** 1174
6:45   **Vol. 2:** 100, 831
6:45b   **Vol. 1:** 567
6:46   **Vol. 1:** 274 **Vol. 2:** 272, 276, 513–514 **Vol. 3:** 1155
6:47 ff   **Vol. 2:** 383, 749 **Vol. 3:** 1155
6:48 f   **Vol. 1:** 661 **Vol. 3:** 987
6:48   **Vol. 3:** 559
7   **Vol. 3:** 558, 1061
7:1 ff   **Vol. 3:** 999
7:1–10   **Vol. 3:** 456
7:1   **Vol. 2:** 799
7:2 f   **Vol. 3:** 611
7:2   **Vol. 1:** 326 **Vol. 3:** 964
7:3   **Vol. 1:** 197, 199 **Vol. 2:** 315 **Vol. 3:** 211
7:4   **Vol. 1:** 570 **Vol. 3:** 1169
7:5   **Vol. 1:** 297 **Vol. 2:** 793 **Vol. 3:** 785
7:6   **Vol. 2:** 549 **Vol. 3:** 964
7:7 f   **Vol. 3:** 611
7:7   **Vol. 1:** 283 **Vol. 2:** 169 **Vol. 3:** 348
7:8   **Vol. 2:** 608 **Vol. 3:** 964
7:9 f   **Vol. 2:** 245
7:9   **Vol. 2:** 624 **Vol. 3:** 964
7:10   **Vol. 2:** 170
7:11 ff   **Vol. 1:** 445 **Vol. 2:** 168
7:11–17   **Vol. 2:** 630 **Vol. 3:** 303, 1059
7:11 f   **Vol. 2:** 480
7:12   **Vol. 1:** 329 **Vol. 2:** 29 **Vol. 3:** 1071, 1202
7:13   **Vol. 2:** 416, 419, 600 **Vol. 3:** 280
7:14 f   **Vol. 3:** 1108
7:14   **Vol. 3:** 280
7:15   **Vol. 1:** 167, 445 **Vol. 3:** 1071
7:16   **Vol. 1:** 191 **Vol. 2:** 632, 641, 799 **Vol. 3:** 83, 86, 457, 748
7:18 ff   **Vol. 2:** 631
7:19 f   **Vol. 2:** 379
7:19   **Vol. 3:** 367, 378

7:20   **Vol. 3:** 82
7:21 ff   **Vol. 3:** 848
7:21   **Vol. 1:** 163, 219 **Vol. 3:** 475, 515, 847
7:22 f   **Vol. 3:** 1122
7:22   **Vol. 1:** 428, 445 **Vol. 2:** 110, 176, 358, 379, 415, 464, 825 **Vol. 3:** 519, 696–697, 733
7:23   **Vol. 2:** 170, 708
7:24   **Vol. 1:** 102 **Vol. 2:** 799 **Vol. 3:** 559, 1007, 1022, 1198
7:25   **Vol. 2:** 47
7:26 f   **Vol. 3:** 1122
7:26   **Vol. 3:** 83, 86–87
7:27   **Vol. 1:** 102 **Vol. 3:** 80, 119, 329, 940
7:28   **Vol. 2:** 427, 429
7:29   **Vol. 2:** 799 **Vol. 3:** 361, 758
7:30   **Vol. 1:** 74 **Vol. 2:** 170 **Vol. 3:** 480, 1017, 1208
7:31   **Vol. 2:** 433
7:32   **Vol. 2:** 416, 418 **Vol. 3:** 674
7:33 f   **Vol. 3:** 921
7:33   **Vol. 1:** 250 **Vol. 3:** 82, 623, 921
7:34   **Vol. 2:** 276, 549 **Vol. 3:** 628, 758
7:35   **Vol. 1:** 286 **Vol. 3:** 1030, 1180, 1198
7:36 ff   **Vol. 1:** 689 **Vol. 2:** 549 **Vol. 3:** 475, 580
7:36–50   **Vol. 1:** 701 **Vol. 2:** 118 **Vol. 3:** 1059, 1061
7:36 f   **Vol. 2:** 812
7:36   **Vol. 2:** 170, 272, 880 **Vol. 3:** 1061
7:37 f   **Vol. 2:** 295
7:38 ff   **Vol. 1:** 120
7:38–46   **Vol. 1:** 239
7:38   **Vol. 1:** 120, 167 **Vol. 2:** 417 **Vol. 3:** 1002
7:39 f   **Vol. 3:** 88
7:39   **Vol. 3:** 83, 86–87, 860
7:40   **Vol. 3:** 767, 1061
7:41 ††   **Vol. 2:** 750
7:41–43   **Vol. 2:** 386, 668
7:41   **Vol. 2:** 502
7:43 f   **Vol. 3:** 1061
7:43   **Vol. 2:** 364 **Vol. 3:** 749
7:44 ff   **Vol. 3:** 545, 547
7:44 f   **Vol. 2:** 812
7:44   **Vol. 3:** 989, 1002
7:45   **Vol. 3:** 251
7:46   **Vol. 1:** 120 **Vol. 2:** 159, 295, 712
7:47 ff   **Vol. 1:** 701
7:47   **Vol. 1:** 97 **Vol. 2:** 544
7:49   **Vol. 1:** 167, 701
7:50   **Vol. 3:** 212
8   **Vol. 2:** 749
8:1–3   **Vol. 1:** 642 **Vol. 3:** 1059
8:1   **Vol. 2:** 113, 695, 750 **Vol. 3:** 52, 54
8:2   **Vol. 1:** 274 **Vol. 2:** 691 **Vol. 3:** 475, 1059
8:3   **Vol. 2:** 845–846 **Vol. 3:** 546–547, 1053
8:4–8   **Vol. 2:** 748, 750 **Vol. 3:** 522

Luke *(cont'd)*

8:5   **Vol. 1:** 174   **Vol. 2:** 192   **Vol. 3:** 944
8:6 ff   **Vol. 2:** 739
8:6   **Vol. 1:** 516   **Vol. 3:** 382
8:7   **Vol. 1:** 226
8:8   **Vol. 2:** 178, 750   **Vol. 3:** 114
8:9 f   **Vol. 2:** 750, 753   **Vol. 3:** 132
8:9   **Vol. 1:** 340
8:10   **Vol. 2:** 178   **Vol. 3:** 251–253, 313–314, 503
8:11–15   **Vol. 2:** 748, 750   **Vol. 3:** 522, 868
8:11   **Vol. 3:** 746
8:12   **Vol. 1:** 174, 566   **Vol. 3:** 470
8:13   **Vol. 1:** 607–608   **Vol. 2:** 177, 358, 708, 808   **Vol. 3:** 382, 746, 803, 837–838
8:14   **Vol. 1:** 459, 726   **Vol. 2:** 475, 842–843, 846
8:15   **Vol. 2:** 104, 178, 183, 773   **Vol. 3:** 868
8:16   **Vol. 2:** 212, 487, 493, 749   **Vol. 3:** 860, 913
8:17   **Vol. 2:** 212, 216   **Vol. 3:** 312, 320
8:18   **Vol. 2:** 750   **Vol. 3:** 822
8:19 ff   **Vol. 2:** 750   **Vol. 3:** 1062, 1070
8:20   **Vol. 3:** 46
8:21   **Vol. 2:** 733   **Vol. 3:** 315
8:22 ff   **Vol. 3:** 992
8:22–25   **Vol. 2:** 630   **Vol. 3:** 984–985
8:22   **Vol. 3:** 984
8:23 ff   **Vol. 3:** 1002
8:23   **Vol. 1:** 419, 736   **Vol. 3:** 1003
8:24 f   **Vol. 3:** 989
8:24   **Vol. 2:** 595   **Vol. 3:** 115, 767
8:25   **Vol. 2:** 179, 623
8:26 ff   **Vol. 3:** 475
8:26–37   **Vol. 2:** 631
8:27   **Vol. 1:** 325   **Vol. 3:** 246, 729, 843
8:28   **Vol. 2:** 860   **Vol. 3:** 856
8:29   **Vol. 3:** 592, 843, 1008
8:31   **Vol. 2:** 205   **Vol. 3:** 474
8:32   **Vol. 1:** 570   **Vol. 3:** 1011
8:33   **Vol. 1:** 226   **Vol. 3:** 984–985, 990
8:35   **Vol. 1:** 239, 502   **Vol. 2:** 433
8:37   **Vol. 1:** 733
8:39   **Vol. 1:** 576   **Vol. 3:** 56
8:40–56   **Vol. 2:** 168, 630   **Vol. 3:** 1059
8:40   **Vol. 3:** 746
8:41   **Vol. 1:** 168   **Vol. 3:** 785
8:42   **Vol. 1:** 226   **Vol. 2:** 696, 799   **Vol. 3:** 1202
8:43 ff   **Vol. 2:** 165
8:43–48   **Vol. 1:** 77
8:43 f   **Vol. 1:** 683
8:43   **Vol. 2:** 164, 696, 846   **Vol. 3:** 714
8:44 f   **Vol. 3:** 860
8:45 f   **Vol. 3:** 860
8:45   **Vol. 2:** 595   **Vol. 3:** 115, 767
8:47   **Vol. 2:** 138, 168, 799
8:48   **Vol. 1:** 328   **Vol. 3:** 212
8:50   **Vol. 1:** 623

8:51   **Vol. 1:** 284   **Vol. 3:** 1071
8:52   **Vol. 2:** 418
8:54 f   **Vol. 3:** 280
8:54   **Vol. 3:** 114, 717
8:55   **Vol. 2:** 919   **Vol. 3:** 694
8:56   **Vol. 1:** 340   **Vol. 2:** 631
9   **Vol. 3:** 862
9:1 f   **Vol. 2:** 632
9:1–6   **Vol. 2:** 733, 825
9:1   **Vol. 2:** 165, 169, 609–610, 695   **Vol. 3:** 475
9:2–5   **Vol. 3:** 453
9:2   **Vol. 2:** 168–169   **Vol. 3:** 52
9:3   **Vol. 1:** 143, 407
9:5   **Vol. 1:** 239   **Vol. 3:** 560, 946
9:6   **Vol. 2:** 113, 165, 632   **Vol. 3:** 54, 57
9:7 f   **Vol. 2:** 342
9:8   **Vol. 1:** 167   **Vol. 2:** 488   **Vol. 3:** 83, 86
9:10–17   **Vol. 1:** 729   **Vol. 2:** 150, 272, 523
9:10   **Vol. 1:** 131, 136, 576   **Vol. 2:** 401   **Vol. 3:** 131
9:11–17   **Vol. 2:** 630
9:11   **Vol. 2:** 168, 459, 630
9:12   **Vol. 1:** 520   **Vol. 2:** 695   **Vol. 3:** 189, 1007
9:14   **Vol. 2:** 381, 699
9:15   **Vol. 3:** 1043
9:16   **Vol. 2:** 192, 801   **Vol. 3:** 519
9:17   **Vol. 1:** 743
9:18 ff   **Vol. 2:** 680
9:18–22   **Vol. 2:** 341   **Vol. 3:** 1061
9:18   **Vol. 2:** 724, 869, 873
9:19   **Vol. 1:** 167   **Vol. 3:** 82–83, 86
9:20   **Vol. 2:** 76, 231   **Vol. 3:** 384, 809
9:21   **Vol. 1:** 340
9:22   **Vol. 2:** 63, 665, 893   **Vol. 3:** 39, 276, 294, 723
9:23   **Vol. 1:** 324, 394, 402–403, 455   **Vol. 2:** 895   **Vol. 3:** 683
9:24 f   **Vol. 3:** 174
9:24   **Vol. 2:** 433, 919   **Vol. 3:** 212, 530, 682
9:25   **Vol. 3:** 137, 174
9:26   **Vol. 1:** 323   **Vol. 2:** 228   **Vol. 3:** 135, 563
9:27   **Vol. 1:** 98   **Vol. 2:** 271, 382   **Vol. 3:** 863, 883
9:28 ff   **Vol. 2:** 873
9:28–36   **Vol. 2:** 48   **Vol. 3:** 114
9:28   **Vol. 1:** 181   **Vol. 2:** 185, 686, 692   **Vol. 3:** 604, 862, 1010–1012
9:29–35   **Vol. 2:** 47
9:29   **Vol. 1:** 204, 704, 708   **Vol. 2:** 486, 739   **Vol. 3:** 862
9:30 f   **Vol. 2:** 559
9:31   **Vol. 1:** 326, 545   **Vol. 2:** 46, 327   **Vol. 3:** 863, 940, 1011
9:32   **Vol. 1:** 261, 442   **Vol. 2:** 46, 48
9:33   **Vol. 2:** 514, 595   **Vol. 3:** 115, 812
9:34–38   **Vol. 2:** 560
9:34 f   **Vol. 3:** 1003

Luke *(cont'd)*

9:34   **Vol. 3:** 555
9:35   **Vol. 1:** 541   **Vol. 2:** 176, 543   **Vol. 3:** 611
9:36   **Vol. 3:** 48
9:37 ff   **Vol. 3:** 475
9:37   **Vol. 1:** 325   **Vol. 3:** 862, 1010, 1012
9:38   **Vol. 1:** 411   **Vol. 2:** 595, 860   **Vol. 3:** 1202
9:39   **Vol. 1:** 409   **Vol. 3:** 748
9:40   **Vol. 3:** 174
9:41   **Vol. 2:** 766   **Vol. 3:** 1204
9:42   **Vol. 2:** 168
9:43   **Vol. 1:** 530   **Vol. 2:** 426, 623
9:44   **Vol. 1:** 326   **Vol. 2:** 150, 368   **Vol. 3:** 624
9:45   **Vol. 1:** 657   **Vol. 2:** 216, 406, 879–880   **Vol. 3:** 1122
9:46 ff   **Vol. 1:** 285   **Vol. 2:** 427, 429
9:46 f   **Vol. 3:** 821
9:47   **Vol. 3:** 749, 1201
9:48   **Vol. 2:** 176   **Vol. 3:** 746, 821, 979
9:49   **Vol. 3:** 115, 475, 767
9:50   **Vol. 2:** 34
9:51 ff   **Vol. 2:** 337, 630
9:51–56   **Vol. 3:** 454–455, 980
9:51†   **Vol. 1:** 586, 737   **Vol. 3:** 455, 749, 762
9:52 f   **Vol. 3:** 454
9:52   **Vol. 1:** 102
9:53†   **Vol. 3:** 455
9:54 f   **Vol. 3:** 454–455
9:54   **Vol. 1:** 544   **Vol. 2:** 653   **Vol. 3:** 454, 697
9:55   **Vol. 1:** 572   **Vol. 3:** 455, 694
9:56   **Vol. 1:** 464   **Vol. 3:** 455, 628
9:58   **Vol. 1:** 118, 173   **Vol. 2:** 825   **Vol. 3:** 628, 813
9:59–62   **Vol. 1:** 488
9:59–60   **Vol. 1:** 265
9:59 f   **Vol. 1:** 482
9:59   **Vol. 1:** 666–667
9:60   **Vol. 1:** 446   **Vol. 3:** 46
9:61   **Vol. 1:** 666–667   **Vol. 3:** 1174
9:62   **Vol. 1:** 493   **Vol. 2:** 385
10   **Vol. 2:** 920
10:1 ff   **Vol. 2:** 690–691
10:1–24   **Vol. 2:** 733
10:1–20   **Vol. 2:** 150
10:1–16   **Vol. 1:** 129
10:1–13   **Vol. 1:** 489
10:1–12   **Vol. 2:** 754, 825   **Vol. 3:** 453
10:1 f   **Vol. 3:** 144
10:1   **Vol. 1:** 129, 326   **Vol. 2:** 641, 697, 739   **Vol. 3:** 569
10:2   **Vol. 2:** 513, 750   **Vol. 3:** 526
10:3   **Vol. 1:** 118   **Vol. 2:** 411, 413   **Vol. 3:** 455
10:4   **Vol. 1:** 142–143
10:5 ff   **Vol. 1:** 689

10:5 f   **Vol. 2:** 781   **Vol. 3:** 258, 455
10:6   **Vol. 1:** 355   **Vol. 3:** 258
10:7 f   **Vol. 3:** 794
10:7   **Vol. 2:** 272, 275   **Vol. 3:** 349, 492, 855
10:8 ff   **Vol. 3:** 454
10:9   **Vol. 2:** 54, 632, 920   **Vol. 3:** 56, 1194
10:10 f   **Vol. 3:** 455
10:11   **Vol. 2:** 54, 349, 400, 920
10:12   **Vol. 2:** 203, 767, 894   **Vol. 3:** 93, 455
10:13 ff   **Vol. 2:** 383
10:13   **Vol. 2:** 714   **Vol. 3:** 589, 1052
10:14   **Vol. 2:** 767
10:15   **Vol. 2:** 203, 207
10:16   **Vol. 1:** 91, 130, 285   **Vol. 2:** 176, 920   **Vol. 3:** 314, 326, 746
10:17 ff   **Vol. 2:** 641
10:17–20   **Vol. 3:** 455
10:17 f   **Vol. 2:** 702   **Vol. 3:** 695
10:17   **Vol. 2:** 358, 654   **Vol. 3:** 470, 475
10:18   **Vol. 1:** 83, 610   **Vol. 2:** 38, 193, 382, 631, 920   **Vol. 3:** 470, 733, 1001
10:19   **Vol. 1:** 510–511, 554   **Vol. 2:** 603, 610   **Vol. 3:** 575, 806, 944
10:20   **Vol. 1:** 244   **Vol. 2:** 193, 358, 560   **Vol. 3:** 475, 490
10:21 f   **Vol. 1:** 620   **Vol. 3:** 313
10:21   **Vol. 1:** 282, 346, 620   **Vol. 2:** 216, 354, 514, 653, 818   **Vol. 3:** 640, 698, 847
10:22   **Vol. 1:** 90   **Vol. 2:** 368, 404, 610   **Vol. 3:** 313, 326, 639–640, 645, 1017
10:23 f   **Vol. 2:** 176, 630   **Vol. 3:** 313
10:24   **Vol. 3:** 83, 733
10:25 ff   **Vol. 1:** 334, 338   **Vol. 2:** 427
10:25–40   **Vol. 2:** 177
10:25–38   **Vol. 1:** 334
10:25–37   **Vol. 1:** 259, 335   **Vol. 2:** 301, 444   **Vol. 3:** 173, 539, 980
10:25–29   **Vol. 2:** 170
10:25–28   **Vol. 2:** 443, 543, 813, 870   **Vol. 3:** 455, 542, 791
10:25   **Vol. 2:** 481   **Vol. 3:** 275, 480, 767, 802, 804, 832
10:26   **Vol. 2:** 444
10:27   **Vol. 1:** 335   **Vol. 2:** 73   **Vol. 3:** 127, 713, 1064
10:28   **Vol. 2:** 442   **Vol. 3:** 351
10:29–37   **Vol. 1:** 67, 257–258   **Vol. 2:** 750
10:29   **Vol. 1:** 335   **Vol. 3:** 361, 455
10:30 ff   **Vol. 2:** 104
10:30–37   **Vol. 2:** 600, 747, 749   **Vol. 3:** 455–456
10:30–35   **Vol. 3:** 545
10:30   **Vol. 1:** 314   **Vol. 2:** 327, 502   **Vol. 3:** 378, 749, 857
10:31 f   **Vol. 2:** 467
10:31   **Vol. 2:** 600   **Vol. 3:** 37
10:32   **Vol. 2:** 600
10:33 f   **Vol. 1:** 335
10:33b   **Vol. 1:** 259
10:34 f   **Vol. 1:** 689

Luke *(cont'd)*

10:34   **Vol. 1:** 114, 688   **Vol. 2:** 712   **Vol. 3:** 922

10:35   **Vol. 1:** 453

10:36 f   **Vol. 3:** 455

10:36   **Vol. 3:** 378, 822

10:37 f   **Vol. 2:** 600

10:37   **Vol. 1:** 258–259, 335   **Vol. 2:** 444, 544, 595–596, 747   **Vol. 3:** 455

10:37a   **Vol. 2:** 600

10:38 ff   **Vol. 1:** 689

10:38–42   **Vol. 1:** 278   **Vol. 3:** 1059–1060

10:38   **Vol. 3:** 1061

10:39   **Vol. 1:** 239   **Vol. 3:** 589, 1106

10:40   **Vol. 2:** 724   **Vol. 3:** 546

10:42   **Vol. 1:** 540   **Vol. 2:** 304

11   **Vol. 2:** 868

11:1–13   **Vol. 2:** 768, 868

11:1   **Vol. 1:** 487   **Vol. 2:** 873   **Vol. 3:** 762

11:2 ff   **Vol. 1:** 615   **Vol. 2:** 868–869   **Vol. 3:** 204

11:2–4   **Vol. 2:** 561

11:2   **Vol. 1:** 323, 621   **Vol. 2:** 76, 229, 795, 867, 871   **Vol. 3:** 696

11:3   **Vol. 1:** 251   **Vol. 2:** 871, 895

11:4   **Vol. 2:** 668

11:5 ff   **Vol. 1:** 689

11:5–13   **Vol. 2:** 178

11:5–8   **Vol. 2:** 747, 750, 881

11:5 f   **Vol. 2:** 549

11:7   **Vol. 1:** 284   **Vol. 2:** 30, 587, 730   **Vol. 3:** 1174

11:8   **Vol. 2:** 881   **Vol. 3:** 958

11:9 f   **Vol. 2:** 728, 881   **Vol. 3:** 532

11:9   **Vol. 2:** 881   **Vol. 3:** 530

11:11   **Vol. 1:** 509   **Vol. 3:** 1179

11:12   **Vol. 1:** 511

11:13   **Vol. 1:** 286   **Vol. 2:** 41–42, 728, 857, 881   **Vol. 3:** 698

11:14–26   **Vol. 2:** 728

11:14   **Vol. 1:** 429   **Vol. 2:** 623   **Vol. 3:** 475

11:15–23   **Vol. 3:** 696

11:15–22   **Vol. 3:** 481

11:15   **Vol. 1:** 168   **Vol. 2:** 631   **Vol. 3:** 472

11:16   **Vol. 2:** 629, 750   **Vol. 3:** 481, 804

11:17–23   **Vol. 2:** 560   **Vol. 3:** 83, 472

11:17   **Vol. 3:** 128, 1008

11:18 f   **Vol. 3:** 472

11:19–32   **Vol. 2:** 750

11:19 f   **Vol. 3:** 695

11:19   **Vol. 3:** 476, 696

11:20   **Vol. 1:** 358, 651   **Vol. 2:** 74, 150, 382, 631, 920   **Vol. 3:** 475, 696, 985, 998

11:21 f   **Vol. 1:** 508

11:21   **Vol. 2:** 135, 382, 780, 845

11:22   **Vol. 1:** 322, 591, 651   **Vol. 2:** 603

11:23 ff   **Vol. 1:** 739

11:23   **Vol. 2:** 32, 34   **Vol. 3:** 568

11:24 ff   **Vol. 3:** 475

11:24   **Vol. 3:** 128, 256, 530, 694, 1006, 1008

11:25 f   **Vol. 3:** 586

11:25   **Vol. 3:** 474

11:26   **Vol. 1:** 666   **Vol. 2:** 251, 691   **Vol. 3:** 474, 604, 694, 1059

11:27 f   **Vol. 3:** 1062, 1070

11:27   **Vol. 1:** 169, 240

11:28   **Vol. 2:** 177

11:29 ff   **Vol. 2:** 629

11:29–32   **Vol. 2:** 350, 687   **Vol. 3:** 481

11:29 f   **Vol. 3:** 628

11:29   **Vol. 1:** 565   **Vol. 2:** 33, 36, 351, 631, 680

11:29b–30   **Vol. 3:** 628

11:30   **Vol. 2:** 351, 680

11:31 f   **Vol. 2:** 921

11:31   **Vol. 2:** 381, 385, 563   **Vol. 3:** 86, 606, 1003, 1030

11:32   **Vol. 2:** 352, 680   **Vol. 3:** 52–53, 83, 275, 303, 1187

11:33 f   **Vol. 2:** 486

11:33   **Vol. 2:** 214, 484, 487, 493, 749–750, 757   **Vol. 3:** 860

11:34 ff   **Vol. 2:** 706, 749–750

11:34–46   **Vol. 1:** 423

11:34 f   **Vol. 2:** 757

11:34   **Vol. 1:** 565   **Vol. 3:** 572

11:36   **Vol. 2:** 303   **Vol. 3:** 1001

11:37–54   **Vol. 2:** 170

11:37–41   **Vol. 3:** 990

11:37   **Vol. 2:** 812, 880

11:38–42   **Vol. 2:** 813

11:38   **Vol. 1:** 666   **Vol. 2:** 623, 812

11:39   **Vol. 1:** 743   **Vol. 3:** 184, 604, 990, 1053

11:40   **Vol. 3:** 1025

11:41   **Vol. 2:** 596

11:42 ff   **Vol. 2:** 443

11:42–52   **Vol. 2:** 470   **Vol. 3:** 1052

11:42   **Vol. 2:** 211, 665, 693–694   **Vol. 3:** 197, 854

11:43–54   **Vol. 2:** 813

11:43   **Vol. 2:** 543, 548   **Vol. 3:** 785

11:44   **Vol. 1:** 205, 265   **Vol. 2:** 746   **Vol. 3:** 247, 1053

11:45–52   **Vol. 1:** 174   **Vol. 3:** 181

11:45 f   **Vol. 3:** 480

11:45†   **Vol. 3:** 28, 767

11:46 f   **Vol. 2:** 443

11:46   **Vol. 1:** 261, 335   **Vol. 2:** 150   **Vol. 3:** 883

11:47 f   **Vol. 3:** 1053

11:47   **Vol. 3:** 247

11:48   **Vol. 3:** 1043

11:49   **Vol. 1:** 128, 136, 174   **Vol. 3:** 84, 86, 492, 1030

11:50 f   **Vol. 1:** 222   **Vol. 3:** 532

11:50   **Vol. 1:** 378   **Vol. 2:** 854

11:51   **Vol. 1:** 464   **Vol. 2:** 248   **Vol. 3:** 82, 430, 436

11:52   **Vol. 2:** 222, 443, 730   **Vol. 3:** 480, 1052

Luke *(cont'd)*

11:53	**Vol. 3:** 480
12	**Vol. 2:** 832
12:1	**Vol. 2:** 33, 170, 462 **Vol. 3:** 944
12:2	**Vol. 2:** 212, 216 **Vol. 3:** 312
12:3	**Vol. 1:** 423 **Vol. 2:** 493 **Vol. 3:** 54
12:4 f	**Vol. 1:** 623
12:4	**Vol. 1:** 623, 731 **Vol. 2:** 549
12:5	**Vol. 1:** 623 **Vol. 2:** 209, 609 **Vol. 3:** 686
12:6	**Vol. 1:** 173
12:7	**Vol. 1:** 203 **Vol. 2:** 159
12:8 f	**Vol. 1:** 347, 490 **Vol. 3:** 618, 622, 625–626, 628
12:8	**Vol. 1:** 205 **Vol. 2:** 383 **Vol. 3:** 621, 633
12:9	**Vol. 1:** 455
12:10	**Vol. 3:** 343, 472, 580, 628, 658, 696
12:11	**Vol. 1:** 166 **Vol. 2:** 608 **Vol. 3:** 785
12:12	**Vol. 3:** 762–763, 849
12:13 ff	**Vol. 1:** 142
12:13–21	**Vol. 2:** 825
12:13 f	**Vol. 1:** 488 **Vol. 3:** 767
12:13	**Vol. 2:** 300 **Vol. 3:** 767
12:14 f	**Vol. 2:** 833
12:14	**Vol. 2:** 365
12:15	**Vol. 1:** 138, 729 **Vol. 2:** 135, 480, 845–846
12:16–21	**Vol. 2:** 747, 750, 833, 846 **Vol. 3:** 978
12:16–20	**Vol. 2:** 749, 843
12:16	**Vol. 2:** 502, 842
12:17 f	**Vol. 3:** 1155
12:17	**Vol. 1:** 722 **Vol. 2:** 32 **Vol. 3:** 820
12:18	**Vol. 2:** 32
12:19	**Vol. 2:** 272, 275, 355, 846, 919 **Vol. 3:** 683
12:20 f	**Vol. 2:** 833
12:20	**Vol. 2:** 382, 430, 480, 858, 918–919 **Vol. 3:** 1025
12:21	**Vol. 2:** 842
12:22–31	**Vol. 1:** 277 **Vol. 2:** 386
12:22 f	**Vol. 2:** 919
12:22	**Vol. 2:** 831
12:24–28	**Vol. 2:** 749
12:24	**Vol. 1:** 98, 173
12:25	**Vol. 1:** 92
12:26	**Vol. 3:** 252
12:27	**Vol. 2:** 47 **Vol. 3:** 606
12:28	**Vol. 1:** 744
12:29	**Vol. 2:** 275
12:30	**Vol. 1:** 620 **Vol. 2:** 793 **Vol. 3:** 532, 958
12:31	**Vol. 2:** 275 **Vol. 3:** 532
12:32	**Vol. 1:** 620, 623 **Vol. 2:** 382–383, 385, 429, 818–819, 832
12:33 f	**Vol. 2:** 749–750, 831 **Vol. 3:** 378
12:33	**Vol. 1:** 119, 142, 268, 468, 495 **Vol. 2:** 596, 757, 832, 845–846 **Vol. 3:** 1149
12:34 ff	**Vol. 2:** 727
12:34	**Vol. 2:** 832
12:35–38	**Vol. 2:** 751
12:35	**Vol. 1:** 240 **Vol. 2:** 487, 493 **Vol. 3:** 121
12:36–40	**Vol. 2:** 581
12:36 f	**Vol. 2:** 513
12:36	**Vol. 2:** 728, 881 **Vol. 3:** 85, 626
12:37 f	**Vol. 1:** 217
12:37	**Vol. 1:** 322 **Vol. 3:** 546
12:38	**Vol. 2:** 136
12:39 f	**Vol. 2:** 382, 751 **Vol. 3:** 848
12:39	**Vol. 1:** 323 **Vol. 2:** 831 **Vol. 3:** 85, 378, 1157
12:40	**Vol. 3:** 118, 822
12:41–48	**Vol. 2:** 469
12:41–46	**Vol. 2:** 751
12:42 ff	**Vol. 2:** 254
12:42–46	**Vol. 2:** 382
12:42	**Vol. 2:** 164, 254–255, 619, 732
12:43 ff	**Vol. 3:** 472
12:44	**Vol. 2:** 845 **Vol. 3:** 883, 1193
12:45	**Vol. 1:** 284, 513–514 **Vol. 3:** 843, 903
12:46 ff	**Vol. 2:** 398
12:46	**Vol. 2:** 255, 304, 513 **Vol. 3:** 847–848
12:47	**Vol. 3:** 118, 1204
12:48	**Vol. 1:** 730 **Vol. 2:** 858
12:49 f	**Vol. 3:** 697
12:49–50	**Vol. 3:** 697
12:49	**Vol. 1:** 322, 656–657
12:50	**Vol. 1:** 144 **Vol. 2:** 63
12:51 ff	**Vol. 2:** 781
12:51–53	**Vol. 3:** 697
12:51	**Vol. 3:** 822, 967, 978
12:52	**Vol. 2:** 689
12:53	**Vol. 1:** 725 **Vol. 2:** 250, 585 **Vol. 3:** 1070
12:54 ff	**Vol. 3:** 173
12:54	**Vol. 3:** 1003
12:55	**Vol. 3:** 707, 1003
12:56	**Vol. 2:** 192, 469 **Vol. 3:** 808, 838, 848, 1187
12:57	**Vol. 2:** 365 **Vol. 3:** 361
12:58 f	**Vol. 3:** 173–174
12:58	**Vol. 1:** 168, 554 **Vol. 2:** 136, 365, 368 **Vol. 3:** 167, 1150
12:59	**Vol. 2:** 850
13:1 ff	**Vol. 1:** 75 **Vol. 3:** 998
13:1–9	**Vol. 2:** 750
13:1–8	**Vol. 1:** 725
13:1–5	**Vol. 1:** 564 **Vol. 2:** 366
13:1–3	**Vol. 1:** 633
13:1	**Vol. 1:** 221 **Vol. 3:** 430, 788, 837
13:2	**Vol. 3:** 723, 822
13:3–6	**Vol. 2:** 813
13:3	**Vol. 1:** 286, 464 **Vol. 3:** 173, 430
13:4	**Vol. 1:** 609 **Vol. 2:** 327 **Vol. 3:** 822
13:5	**Vol. 1:** 464, 725 **Vol. 3:** 173, 869
13:5b	**Vol. 3:** 920
13:6 ff	**Vol. 1:** 722 **Vol. 2:** 366

Luke *(cont'd)*

13:6–9   **Vol. 1:** 417   **Vol. 2:** 630, 749   **Vol. 3:** 174, 868–869, 919
13:6–8   **Vol. 2:** 118
13:6 f   **Vol. 3:** 868
13:6   **Vol. 1:** 722, 725   **Vol. 3:** 532, 918
13:7   **Vol. 1:** 73
13:8   **Vol. 1:** 480   **Vol. 2:** 513
13:9   **Vol. 1:** 326
13:10–17   **Vol. 3:** 409
13:10   **Vol. 3:** 761, 785
13:11   **Vol. 1:** 452, 637   **Vol. 2:** 168   **Vol. 3:** 994, 998, 1058, 1142
13:12   **Vol. 1:** 505   **Vol. 3:** 189
13:13   **Vol. 2:** 151   **Vol. 3:** 86
13:14   **Vol. 2:** 165, 665, 692   **Vol. 3:** 1150
13:15   **Vol. 1:** 115, 117   **Vol. 3:** 180
13:16   **Vol. 1:** 452, 718   **Vol. 2:** 665, 920   **Vol. 3:** 179, 470, 592, 857, 998
13:17   **Vol. 2:** 47, 358
13:18–21   **Vol. 2:** 749
13:18 f   **Vol. 2:** 429, 750   **Vol. 3:** 523, 868
13:19   **Vol. 1:** 174   **Vol. 2:** 129   **Vol. 3:** 813, 869
13:20 f   **Vol. 2:** 502, 750   **Vol. 3:** 1058
13:20   **Vol. 2:** 747
13:21   **Vol. 2:** 216, 461–462
13:22–30   **Vol. 3:** 174
13:22   **Vol. 3:** 761
13:23 f   **Vol. 2:** 481, 749
13:23   **Vol. 1:** 607
13:24   **Vol. 1:** 646–647   **Vol. 2:** 29, 31
13:25 ff   **Vol. 2:** 510
13:25–28   **Vol. 2:** 751
13:25   **Vol. 2:** 31, 728, 881   **Vol. 3:** 280
13:26 ff   **Vol. 2:** 272
13:26   **Vol. 1:** 607   **Vol. 2:** 272, 276   **Vol. 3:** 761–762
13:27   **Vol. 1:** 607   **Vol. 2:** 276, 383   **Vol. 3:** 575
13:28 ff   **Vol. 2:** 57
13:28–30   **Vol. 1:** 667
13:28 f   **Vol. 1:** 78
13:28   **Vol. 1:** 81   **Vol. 2:** 385, 421
13:29   **Vol. 1:** 689   **Vol. 3:** 1003
13:30   **Vol. 2:** 57
13:31   **Vol. 2:** 812   **Vol. 3:** 847
13:32 f   **Vol. 3:** 979
13:32   **Vol. 1:** 118, 453   **Vol. 2:** 63, 630, 688   **Vol. 3:** 475, 838
13:33   **Vol. 1:** 163, 464   **Vol. 2:** 170, 328, 641, 665, 803, 825   **Vol. 3:** 83, 696, 723
13:34 ff   **Vol. 2:** 328
13:34 f   **Vol. 1:** 174   **Vol. 2:** 754   **Vol. 3:** 230
13:34   **Vol. 1:** 286   **Vol. 2:** 33, 37, 757   **Vol. 3:** 82, 1008
13:35   **Vol. 1:** 174   **Vol. 2:** 37   **Vol. 3:** 392, 1008
14:1 ff   **Vol. 2:** 170

14:1–6   **Vol. 3:** 409
14:1   **Vol. 1:** 168   **Vol. 2:** 133, 812
14:3   **Vol. 2:** 610   **Vol. 3:** 480
14:4   **Vol. 3:** 111, 749–750
14:5   **Vol. 1:** 115, 117
14:6   **Vol. 3:** 714
14:7–10   **Vol. 3:** 589
14:7   **Vol. 1:** 540, 666
14:8   **Vol. 1:** 666   **Vol. 2:** 578
14:9   **Vol. 2:** 57
14:10   **Vol. 2:** 549
14:11   **Vol. 2:** 202, 262
14:12 ff   **Vol. 2:** 825, 844
14:12   **Vol. 2:** 549, 842   **Vol. 3:** 114, 135
14:13 f   **Vol. 2:** 203
14:13   **Vol. 1:** 219   **Vol. 2:** 415
14:14   **Vol. 1:** 129, 217, 495   **Vol. 3:** 277, 361
14:15–24   **Vol. 2:** 750
14:15   **Vol. 1:** 250   **Vol. 2:** 272
14:16 ff   **Vol. 1:** 689
14:16–25   **Vol. 1:** 274
14:16–24   **Vol. 1:** 324   **Vol. 2:** 747
14:17–20   **Vol. 3:** 695
14:17   **Vol. 3:** 118
14:18 f   **Vol. 2:** 858, 880
14:18   **Vol. 1:** 520, 666   **Vol. 2:** 663
14:19   **Vol. 2:** 689   **Vol. 3:** 1164
14:20   **Vol. 2:** 579
14:21   **Vol. 1:** 110–111, 219   **Vol. 2:** 415, 510, 825
14:23   **Vol. 2:** 663   **Vol. 3:** 951
14:24   **Vol. 2:** 270
14:25–34   **Vol. 3:** 448
14:25–33   **Vol. 2:** 825
14:26 f   **Vol. 1:** 289, 305, 488
14:26   **Vol. 1:** 256, 287, 556, 619   **Vol. 3:** 682–683
14:27   **Vol. 1:** 324, 394, 402, 404   **Vol. 2:** 203   **Vol. 3:** 60
14:28–33   **Vol. 2:** 747, 750
14:28–32   **Vol. 2:** 386, 752
14:28   **Vol. 1:** 667
14:29   **Vol. 1:** 661   **Vol. 3:** 341, 516, 714
14:31   **Vol. 1:** 667   **Vol. 2:** 699   **Vol. 3:** 1190
14:32   **Vol. 1:** 197   **Vol. 2:** 780
14:33   **Vol. 1:** 305, 358, 495   **Vol. 2:** 845
14:34 f   **Vol. 2:** 749–750
14:34   **Vol. 2:** 757   **Vol. 3:** 445, 447, 1025
14:35   **Vol. 1:** 480   **Vol. 2:** 750
15   **Vol. 2:** 118, 332, 443, 566   **Vol. 3:** 920
15:1 ff   **Vol. 3:** 580, 762
15:1–32   **Vol. 3:** 213, 314
15:1–7   **Vol. 2:** 750
15:1–6   **Vol. 3:** 529
15:1 f   **Vol. 2:** 524, 754
15:1   **Vol. 2:** 790
15:2 ff   **Vol. 1:** 129
15:2   **Vol. 2:** 170
15:4 ff   **Vol. 2:** 460
15:4–10   **Vol. 2:** 747

Luke *(cont'd)*

15:4–7   **Vol. 2:** 386, 388   **Vol. 3:** 567
15:4–6   **Vol. 3:** 566
15:4 f   **Vol. 3:** 530, 566
15:4   **Vol. 1:** 463   **Vol. 2:** 413, 459   **Vol. 3:** 565, 1008
15:5   **Vol. 3:** 530
15:6   **Vol. 1:** 463   **Vol. 2:** 358, 549   **Vol. 3:** 529
15:7   **Vol. 2:** 358, 416, 720   **Vol. 3:** 361, 529
15:8 ff   **Vol. 2:** 750   **Vol. 3:** 1058
15:8–10   **Vol. 2:** 386, 388   **Vol. 3:** 529
15:8 f   **Vol. 2:** 851
15:8   **Vol. 1:** 463   **Vol. 2:** 487, 493   **Vol. 3:** 531–532, 860
15:9   **Vol. 2:** 358, 549
15:10   **Vol. 1:** 103   **Vol. 2:** 358   **Vol. 3:** 529
15:11 ff   **Vol. 1:** 556, 701   **Vol. 2:** 76
15:11–32   **Vol. 2:** 386, 388, 600, 749–750   **Vol. 3:** 580, 920, 1061
15:12 f   **Vol. 2:** 846
15:12   **Vol. 1:** 535   **Vol. 2:** 303, 475, 675, 846, 871
15:13   **Vol. 2:** 32, 34, 480, 790
15:14   **Vol. 1:** 167   **Vol. 2:** 266   **Vol. 3:** 713, 954
15:15 f   **Vol. 1:** 117
15:15   **Vol. 2:** 349, 804   **Vol. 3:** 920
15:16   **Vol. 1:** 169, 457   **Vol. 3:** 1174
15:17   **Vol. 1:** 250, 464, 729   **Vol. 2:** 266, 566
15:18   **Vol. 2:** 193
15:19   **Vol. 3:** 348
15:20 ff   **Vol. 1:** 701
15:20   **Vol. 1:** 241, 609   **Vol. 2:** 549, 600   **Vol. 3:** 529, 947
15:21   **Vol. 2:** 193   **Vol. 3:** 348, 529
15:22–24   **Vol. 3:** 529
15:22   **Vol. 1:** 666
15:23   **Vol. 1:** 116   **Vol. 2:** 272, 356, 358   **Vol. 3:** 529
15:24   **Vol. 1:** 359, 436, 446, 463   **Vol. 2:** 170, 480   **Vol. 3:** 278, 529
15:25   **Vol. 1:** 198   **Vol. 3:** 674
15:26   **Vol. 1:** 284
15:27   **Vol. 1:** 116   **Vol. 2:** 170   **Vol. 3:** 751
15:28–32   **Vol. 2:** 170
15:28   **Vol. 1:** 110, 570   **Vol. 2:** 600
15:29   **Vol. 1:** 114, 322   **Vol. 2:** 356, 549
15:30   **Vol. 1:** 116   **Vol. 2:** 475, 846
15:31   **Vol. 1:** 286   **Vol. 2:** 846
15:32   **Vol. 1:** 359, 446, 463   **Vol. 2:** 356, 358, 480   **Vol. 3:** 529
16:1 ff   **Vol. 2:** 254, 732   **Vol. 3:** 576
16:1–17   **Vol. 2:** 254
16:1–14   **Vol. 2:** 832
16:1–9   **Vol. 2:** 750
16:1–8   **Vol. 2:** 749, 837
16:1   **Vol. 2:** 34, 842, 845   **Vol. 3:** 468
16:2   **Vol. 2:** 254   **Vol. 3:** 114

16:3   **Vol. 2:** 513   **Vol. 3:** 1155
16:5–7   **Vol. 2:** 668
16:5   **Vol. 2:** 513
16:6 f   **Vol. 3:** 489
16:6   **Vol. 2:** 711   **Vol. 3:** 492–493
16:8 f   **Vol. 3:** 575
16:8   **Vol. 1:** 289   **Vol. 2:** 495, 619, 837
16:9   **Vol. 2:** 255, 381–382, 549, 749, 832, 837, 844   **Vol. 3:** 811–812, 832, 1180
16:10 f   **Vol. 2:** 255
16:11   **Vol. 1:** 684   **Vol. 2:** 837, 844   **Vol. 3:** 884, 1211
16:12   **Vol. 1:** 684   **Vol. 2:** 742, 846
16:13   **Vol. 1:** 138, 461   **Vol. 2:** 749–750, 838
16:14 f   **Vol. 3:** 603
16:14   **Vol. 2:** 170, 550, 843   **Vol. 3:** 341, 712
16:15   **Vol. 2:** 183, 200   **Vol. 3:** 361, 1010
16:16   **Vol. 2:** 113, 383, 443   **Vol. 3:** 603, 711–712, 1107
16:17   **Vol. 1:** 609   **Vol. 2:** 443–444   **Vol. 3:** 182
16:18   **Vol. 1:** 500, 506   **Vol. 2:** 580–581, 583   **Vol. 3:** 172, 188–189, 534, 538
16:18a   **Vol. 1:** 506   **Vol. 3:** 540
16:18b   **Vol. 1:** 506   **Vol. 2:** 564   **Vol. 3:** 540
16:19–31   **Vol. 2:** 267, 747, 750, 843, 846   **Vol. 3:** 99, 978, 1061
16:19 f   **Vol. 2:** 272
16:19   **Vol. 2:** 355, 486, 842, 895
16:20   **Vol. 2:** 30, 466, 825   **Vol. 3:** 1061
16:21 f   **Vol. 2:** 842
16:21   **Vol. 1:** 117, 744
16:22 ff   **Vol. 1:** 78
16:22   **Vol. 1:** 78, 103, 240   **Vol. 2:** 825
16:23–31†   **Vol. 2:** 433
16:23   **Vol. 1:** 240   **Vol. 2:** 85, 207   **Vol. 3:** 682, 856
16:24 f   **Vol. 2:** 597
16:24   **Vol. 1:** 145   **Vol. 2:** 150, 595–596   **Vol. 3:** 114, 989, 1079
16:25   **Vol. 1:** 286, 564, 571   **Vol. 2:** 843   **Vol. 3:** 240, 751
16:26   **Vol. 2:** 207
16:27 ff   **Vol. 2:** 630
16:28   **Vol. 2:** 689   **Vol. 3:** 856
16:29–31   **Vol. 2:** 641
16:29   **Vol. 2:** 174
16:31   **Vol. 1:** 591   **Vol. 2:** 352   **Vol. 3:** 1061
17   **Vol. 2:** 904, 918   **Vol. 3:** 430
17:1 f   **Vol. 2:** 429   **Vol. 3:** 394
17:1   **Vol. 1:** 136   **Vol. 2:** 709   **Vol. 3:** 1052
17:2   **Vol. 2:** 429   **Vol. 3:** 393
17:3 f   **Vol. 3:** 579
17:3   **Vol. 1:** 572
17:4   **Vol. 2:** 691
17:5 f   **Vol. 1:** 600
17:5   **Vol. 1:** 136, 489, 600
17:6   **Vol. 1:** 600   **Vol. 3:** 984, 1012
17:7–10   **Vol. 2:** 747, 750, 838   **Vol. 3:** 595
17:7 f   **Vol. 2:** 271

Luke *(cont'd)*

17:8   **Vol. 3:** 121, 546
17:9 f   **Vol. 3:** 1155
17:9   **Vol. 2:** 118
17:10   **Vol. 3:** 141, 1149–1150
17:11 ff   **Vol. 2:** 631
17:11–19   **Vol. 3:** 106, 455–456, 980
17:11   **Vol. 3:** 449
17:12 ff   **Vol. 2:** 466
17:12   **Vol. 1:** 325   **Vol. 2:** 464   **Vol. 3:** 997
17:13   **Vol. 2:** 595, 838   **Vol. 3:** 115
17:14–17   **Vol. 3:** 106
17:14   **Vol. 3:** 37
17:15 f   **Vol. 3:** 456
17:15–16   **Vol. 3:** 113
17:16–18   **Vol. 1:** 67
17:16   **Vol. 1:** 609   **Vol. 3:** 818
17:17 ff   **Vol. 2:** 566
17:18   **Vol. 1:** 685   **Vol. 2:** 46, 742   **Vol. 3:** 455, 529
17:19   **Vol. 3:** 212
17:19c   **Vol. 3:** 106
17:20 f   **Vol. 2:** 37, 170, 340, 382, 384, 921   **Vol. 3:** 762
17:20   **Vol. 2:** 133, 382, 385
17:21 ff   **Vol. 2:** 921
17:21   **Vol. 1:** 358   **Vol. 3:** 844
17:22 ff   **Vol. 3:** 605
17:22–37   **Vol. 3:** 628
17:22 f   **Vol. 2:** 918
17:22   **Vol. 2:** 930   **Vol. 3:** 620, 628, 633
17:23 ff   **Vol. 1:** 175
17:23 f   **Vol. 2:** 900   **Vol. 3:** 618
17:23   **Vol. 2:** 806
17:24   **Vol. 2:** 486, 894   **Vol. 3:** 633, 1001
17:25   **Vol. 1:** 74, 667   **Vol. 2:** 665   **Vol. 3:** 623–624, 723
17:26 ff   **Vol. 2:** 382   **Vol. 3:** 633
17:26–36   **Vol. 2:** 751
17:26 f   **Vol. 2:** 682
17:26   **Vol. 2:** 385, 580
17:27 ff   **Vol. 2:** 275
17:27   **Vol. 2:** 581   **Vol. 3:** 991
17:29   **Vol. 1:** 657   **Vol. 2:** 193, 767   **Vol. 3:** 93, 1002
17:30   **Vol. 3:** 620
17:31 f   **Vol. 1:** 493
17:31   **Vol. 3:** 913
17:32   **Vol. 3:** 93, 240, 1058
17:33   **Vol. 1:** 464   **Vol. 2:** 203, 838–839, 920   **Vol. 3:** 682
17:34 f   **Vol. 2:** 920   **Vol. 3:** 604
17:34   **Vol. 1:** 421   **Vol. 2:** 918
17:35   **Vol. 3:** 1058, 1194
17:37   **Vol. 1:** 175, 234   **Vol. 2:** 33, 746, 757   **Vol. 3:** 1054
18:1 ff   **Vol. 3:** 576, 1074
18:1–8   **Vol. 2:** 750, 768   **Vol. 3:** 1059
18:1–6   **Vol. 2:** 771

18:1   **Vol. 1:** 563   **Vol. 2:** 666, 771   **Vol. 3:** 1204
18:2 ff   **Vol. 2:** 747
18:2   **Vol. 1:** 623   **Vol. 2:** 365
18:3 ff   **Vol. 2:** 96   **Vol. 3:** 97
18:3   **Vol. 1:** 554
18:4   **Vol. 1:** 623
18:5   **Vol. 2:** 62
18:6   **Vol. 3:** 575
18:7 f   **Vol. 3:** 93, 199
18:7   **Vol. 1:** 411, 541   **Vol. 2:** 771
18:8   **Vol. 2:** 37   **Vol. 3:** 529–530, 620, 626–627
18:9 ff   **Vol. 2:** 366   **Vol. 3:** 580
18:9–27   **Vol. 2:** 443
18:9–14   **Vol. 2:** 261, 442, 584, 694, 750   **Vol. 3:** 253, 361
18:9   **Vol. 1:** 591   **Vol. 3:** 161, 252–253, 361
18:10–14   **Vol. 2:** 747   **Vol. 3:** 790
18:10   **Vol. 2:** 185, 236, 868   **Vol. 3:** 837
18:11 f   **Vol. 3:** 819
18:11   **Vol. 2:** 869   **Vol. 3:** 252–253, 575, 604, 757
18:12   **Vol. 2:** 693   **Vol. 3:** 854
18:13   **Vol. 2:** 192, 869   **Vol. 3:** 160, 903
18:14   **Vol. 2:** 202, 262, 868   **Vol. 3:** 161, 361, 1202
18:15 ff   **Vol. 1:** 284   **Vol. 2:** 223   **Vol. 3:** 861
18:15–17   **Vol. 1:** 160
18:15   **Vol. 1:** 283
18:16 f   **Vol. 1:** 283
18:16   **Vol. 2:** 222
18:17   **Vol. 1:** 284–285   **Vol. 2:** 385, 757   **Vol. 3:** 746
18:18–30   **Vol. 1:** 335   **Vol. 2:** 301
18:18–24   **Vol. 2:** 825
18:18–23   **Vol. 2:** 844
18:18 f   **Vol. 2:** 100
18:18   **Vol. 1:** 168   **Vol. 2:** 300, 480–481   **Vol. 3:** 832
18:20   **Vol. 2:** 583   **Vol. 3:** 377, 379, 755
18:21   **Vol. 2:** 135, 675, 871
18:22   **Vol. 2:** 368, 720, 824, 833, 846   **Vol. 3:** 141, 251, 253
18:23   **Vol. 2:** 842, 845–846
18:24–30   **Vol. 2:** 750
18:24   **Vol. 2:** 845
18:25   **Vol. 1:** 116   **Vol. 2:** 842
18:26 f   **Vol. 3:** 546
18:26   **Vol. 1:** 730   **Vol. 3:** 213, 546
18:27   **Vol. 2:** 603, 606
18:28   **Vol. 2:** 840, 846
18:29 f   **Vol. 2:** 250, 840
18:29   **Vol. 2:** 112–113, 301, 387
18:30   **Vol. 3:** 142, 751, 832
18:31 ff   **Vol. 3:** 329
18:31   **Vol. 2:** 63–64, 695   **Vol. 3:** 39, 488
18:32   **Vol. 3:** 28, 340
18:33   **Vol. 1:** 162   **Vol. 2:** 63   **Vol. 3:** 276

Luke *(cont'd)*

18:34   **Vol. 1:** 489   **Vol. 2:** 216, 398   **Vol. 3:** 132, 1122
18:35   **Vol. 3:** 455
18:37   **Vol. 1:** 322   **Vol. 2:** 333
18:38   **Vol. 1:** 411
18:40   **Vol. 1:** 341
18:41   **Vol. 3:** 519
18:42   **Vol. 3:** 212
18:43   **Vol. 2:** 631   **Vol. 3:** 817
19:1 ff   **Vol. 3:** 580
19:1–10   **Vol. 1:** 701   **Vol. 3:** 980
19:1–6   **Vol. 2:** 434
19:1   **Vol. 3:** 455
19:2   **Vol. 2:** 842   **Vol. 3:** 758
19:3   **Vol. 1:** 92   **Vol. 2:** 428   **Vol. 3:** 1180
19:4   **Vol. 1:** 326
19:5 f   **Vol. 2:** 524, 754   **Vol. 3:** 1169
19:5   **Vol. 3:** 224, 519, 838
19:6   **Vol. 2:** 358
19:7†   **Vol. 2:** 563, 630   **Vol. 3:** 189
19:8   **Vol. 2:** 825, 844–846   **Vol. 3:** 758
19:9 f   **Vol. 2:** 118   **Vol. 3:** 213
19:9   **Vol. 1:** 77   **Vol. 3:** 212, 838
19:10 ff   **Vol. 2:** 813
19:10   **Vol. 1:** 322, 464   **Vol. 2:** 513   **Vol. 3:** 532, 567, 628
19:11 ff   **Vol. 2:** 255
19:11–27   **Vol. 2:** 751, 838
19:11   **Vol. 1:** 326   **Vol. 2:** 920   **Vol. 3:** 455, 822
19:12 27   **Vol. 3:** 809
19:12 f   **Vol. 2:** 916
19:12   **Vol. 1:** 188   **Vol. 2:** 381
19:13   **Vol. 1:** 274   **Vol. 3:** 1158
19:14   **Vol. 1:** 197   **Vol. 2:** 804
19:15   **Vol. 2:** 381   **Vol. 3:** 1158
19:16   **Vol. 2:** 739
19:17 ff   **Vol. 2:** 255
19:17   **Vol. 2:** 100, 428, 608, 751   **Vol. 3:** 141
19:18   **Vol. 2:** 739
19:19 f   **Vol. 2:** 751
19:19   **Vol. 3:** 141
19:20   **Vol. 2:** 739
19:21   **Vol. 3:** 526
19:22   **Vol. 2:** 365   **Vol. 3:** 526
19:23   **Vol. 3:** 1157
19:24   **Vol. 1:** 190
19:28–40   **Vol. 2:** 754
19:28–38   **Vol. 2:** 379   **Vol. 3:** 791
19:28   **Vol. 2:** 713   **Vol. 3:** 455
19:29–44   **Vol. 2:** 713
19:29   **Vol. 1:** 274   **Vol. 2:** 54
19:30 f   **Vol. 3:** 179
19:30   **Vol. 1:** 117
19:33   **Vol. 1:** 117   **Vol. 2:** 513   **Vol. 3:** 179
19:35   **Vol. 1:** 117
19:37–38   **Vol. 3:** 113, 817
19:37   **Vol. 1:** 733   **Vol. 2:** 603   **Vol. 3:** 817

19:38   **Vol. 1:** 323   **Vol. 2:** 46, 781   **Vol. 3:** 652
19:39   **Vol. 1:** 572   **Vol. 2:** 170
19:40   **Vol. 1:** 409–410, 724   **Vol. 3:** 393
19:41 ff   **Vol. 1:** 75, 725
19:41–44   **Vol. 2:** 37
19:42   **Vol. 1:** 600   **Vol. 2:** 216, 328, 780–781
19:43 f   **Vol. 2:** 328
19:43   **Vol. 1:** 554   **Vol. 3:** 952, 965
19:44   **Vol. 1:** 286   **Vol. 3:** 838
19:45 ff   **Vol. 2:** 236, 327
19:45–48   **Vol. 3:** 791
19:45 f   **Vol. 1:** 111   **Vol. 2:** 610, 754   **Vol. 3:** 429, 784, 789, 1168
19:46   **Vol. 2:** 248   **Vol. 3:** 329, 378, 380, 430, 788
19:47 f   **Vol. 2:** 379   **Vol. 3:** 784
19:47   **Vol. 2:** 799   **Vol. 3:** 39, 761, 789, 791
19:48   **Vol. 2:** 799
20 f   **Vol. 3:** 762
20–21   **Vol. 3:** 785
20:1–21:38   **Vol. 2:** 236
20:1–8   **Vol. 3:** 792, 1154
20:1   **Vol. 1:** 199   **Vol. 2:** 113, 799   **Vol. 3:** 791
20:3   **Vol. 2:** 879
20:4   **Vol. 2:** 434
20:6   **Vol. 1:** 591   **Vol. 3:** 86
20:7   **Vol. 2:** 129
20:9–19   **Vol. 2:** 301, 746, 751   **Vol. 3:** 641, 869, 920
20:9 f   **Vol. 3:** 843, 868
20:9   **Vol. 2:** 790, 799
20:10 f   **Vol. 1:** 128, 163, 547
20:10   **Vol. 1:** 722–723   **Vol. 3:** 837
20:11   **Vol. 2:** 50
20:13   **Vol. 2:** 543, 720
20:14   **Vol. 1:** 181   **Vol. 3:** 820
20:17 f   **Vol. 2:** 920   **Vol. 3:** 393
20:17   **Vol. 2:** 159, 253, 313, 622, 706   **Vol. 3:** 188, 329, 390, 492, 519, 809
20:18   **Vol. 1:** 610   **Vol. 2:** 706   **Vol. 3:** 393
20:19   **Vol. 3:** 39, 846–847
20:20–26   **Vol. 3:** 442, 549, 754, 1168
20:20   **Vol. 1:** 166, 270   **Vol. 2:** 133, 469, 608   **Vol. 3:** 361, 749, 1106, 1108
20:21   **Vol. 3:** 351, 940
20:22   **Vol. 3:** 754
20:23   **Vol. 1:** 239, 413   **Vol. 3:** 129, 361
20:24   **Vol. 2:** 288   **Vol. 3:** 489
20:26   **Vol. 2:** 624   **Vol. 3:** 714, 1122
20:27–40   **Vol. 3:** 263, 792
20:27–39   **Vol. 3:** 439
20:27–38   **Vol. 3:** 578, 580
20:27   **Vol. 3:** 439, 685
20:34 f†   **Vol. 2:** 581
20:34   **Vol. 1:** 289
20:35   **Vol. 3:** 349
20:36 f   **Vol. 2:** 481

Luke *(cont'd)*

20:36   **Vol. 1:** 103, 289–290   **Vol. 2:** 578, 920, 929   **Vol. 3:** 278
20:37 f   **Vol. 1:** 78   **Vol. 3:** 263
20:37   **Vol. 1:** 81   **Vol. 2:** 73, 319
20:38   **Vol. 1:** 445   **Vol. 2:** 480, 578, 920
20:39 f   **Vol. 1:** 334
20:41–44   **Vol. 1:** 427   **Vol. 2:** 147   **Vol. 3:** 651–652, 791–792
20:41   **Vol. 2:** 79, 515
20:42 f   **Vol. 1:** 177   **Vol. 2:** 515
20:42   **Vol. 1:** 244   **Vol. 3:** 671, 675
20:43   **Vol. 1:** 477, 554
20:44   **Voi. 2:** 515–516
20:45 ff   **Vol. 2:** 469–470   **Vol. 3:** 580
20:45   **Vol. 2:** 799
20:46 f   **Vol. 3:** 481
20:46   **Vol. 1:** 297   **Vol. 2:** 548   **Vol. 3:** 785, 1019
20:47–48   **Vol. 1:** 265
20:47   **Vol. 1:** 730   **Vol. 3:** 482, 1074
21   **Vol. 1:** 125   **Vol. 2:** 904, 911   **Vol. 3:** 65, 430
21:1–4   **Vol. 2:** 41, 43, 751, 824   **Vol. 3:** 791, 1062, 1074
21:1   **Vol. 2:** 41, 842   **Vol. 3:** 519, 796
21:2   **Vol. 1:** 564–565   **Vol. 2:** 821, 850
21:3   **Vol. 1:** 98   **Vol. 3:** 883
21:4   **Vol. 2:** 41, 475, 846   **Vol. 3:** 955
21:5–7   **Vol. 2:** 713   **Vol. 3:** 1011
21:5 f   **Vol. 3:** 792
21:5   **Vol. 1:** 414   **Vol. 2:** 236   **Vol. 3:** 791
21:6 ff   **Vol. 2:** 803
21:6   **Vol. 3:** 185, 189
21:7   **Vol. 1:** 320, 326
21:8–36   **Vol. 2:** 702
21:8 f   **Vol. 2:** 920
21:8   **Vol. 1:** 493   **Vol. 2:** 281, 459, 461, 911   **Vol. 3:** 838
21:9   **Vol. 1:** 667   **Vol. 2:** 62, 665, 918   **Vol. 3:** 962
21:10   **Vol. 2:** 266, 793
21:11   **Vol. 1:** 622   **Vol. 2:** 426, 629   **Vol. 3:** 558
21:12   **Vol. 1:** 270, 297   **Vol. 2:** 136, 368   **Vol. 3:** 785
21:13   **Vol. 3:** 1043
21:15 f   **Vol. 2:** 629
21:15   **Vol. 1:** 91   **Vol. 3:** 1030
21:16   **Vol. 1:** 287   **Vol. 2:** 549
21:17   **Vol. 1:** 556   **Vol. 2:** 773, 806   **Vol. 3:** 257
21:18   **Vol. 1:** 203   **Vol. 2:** 159
21:19   **Vol. 2:** 773
21:20 ff   **Vol. 2:** 54
21:20–24   **Vol. 2:** 37   **Vol. 3:** 793
21:20   **Vol. 1:** 75   **Vol. 2:** 328, 664   **Vol. 3:** 792, 964, 1008
21:21   **Vol. 1:** 559   **Vol. 3:** 1011

21:22   **Vol. 1:** 736   **Vol. 3:** 97, 329, 488–489
21:23 f   **Vol. 3:** 1062
21:23   **Vol. 1:** 111   **Vol. 2:** 664   **Vol. 3:** 1053
21:24–35   **Vol. 2:** 911
21:24   **Vol. 1:** 610, 737   **Vol. 2:** 328–329, 664, 793   **Vol. 3:** 591, 803, 837, 944, 967
21:25–28   **Vol. 2:** 916
21:25   **Vol. 2:** 192   **Vol. 3:** 112, 560, 732, 734, 736, 984
21:26   **Vol. 1:** 322, 519, 622   **Vol. 2:** 244   **Vol. 3:** 559, 736
21:27–30   **Vol. 2:** 912
21:27   **Vol. 1:** 323   **Vol. 2:** 46, 604, 920   **Vol. 3:** 629, 1003
21:28   **Vol. 1:** 725   **Vol. 2:** 54, 388, 894   **Vol. 3:** 199, 633
21:29 ff   **Vol. 2:** 382
21:29–33   **Vol. 2:** 751
21:29   **Vol. 1:** 725   **Vol. 2:** 604   **Vol. 3:** 867
21:31   **Vol. 2:** 54, 382, 387–388
21:32   **Vol. 2:** 36, 38, 193, 911–912, 916
21:33   **Vol. 2:** 193
21:34 ff   **Vol. 2:** 751
21:34–36   **Vol. 2:** 37
21:34 f   **Vol. 1:** 725   **Vol. 2:** 894
21:34   **Vol. 1:** 261, 278, 513–514   **Vol. 2:** 182   **Vol. 3:** 922
21:35   **Vol. 1:** 322, 586
21:36   **Vol. 2:** 137, 861, 911   **Vol. 3:** 620, 627, 839
21:37 f   **Vol. 3:** 791
21:37   **Vol. 2:** 713   **Vol. 3:** 761
22   **Vol. 1:** 633
22:1   **Vol. 1:** 633   **Vol. 2:** 463
22:2   **Vol. 2:** 799   **Vol. 3:** 39
22:3   **Vol. 1:** 299   **Vol. 2:** 684, 695   **Vol. 3:** 470, 473
22:4   **Vol. 3:** 964
22:6   **Vol. 1:** 346   **Vol. 3:** 532
22:7   **Vol. 1:** 633   **Vol. 2:** 277, 527
22:8   **Vol. 1:** 633
22:9   **Vol. 3:** 118
22:10   **Vol. 3:** 911, 990
22:11   **Vol. 1:** 633   **Vol. 2:** 510, 527   **Vol. 3:** 189
22:12   **Vol. 2:** 527   **Vol. 3:** 569
22:13   **Vol. 1:** 633   **Vol. 3:** 118
22:14   **Vol. 1:** 136, 634   **Vol. 2:** 528   **Vol. 3:** 804
22:15–20   **Vol. 2:** 523, 531, 534
22:15   **Vol. 1:** 457, 633   **Vol. 2:** 277, 527–528   **Vol. 3:** 670
22:16   **Vol. 2:** 534, 894
22:17   **Vol. 2:** 523   **Vol. 3:** 819
22:18   **Vol. 2:** 382, 531, 534
22:19 f†   **Vol. 1:** 237, 439, 634
22:19   **Vol. 1:** 641   **Vol. 2:** 42, 523, 530, 534, 536   **Vol. 3:** 243
22:20   **Vol. 1:** 223, 369   **Vol. 2:** 312, 523, 529–530, 534, 536, 671, 854   **Vol. 3:** 166, 1174

Luke *(cont'd)*

22:21 ff	**Vol. 3:** 804
22:21–23	**Vol. 2:** 531 **Vol. 3:** 624
22:21	**Vol. 3:** 470
22:22	**Vol. 1:** 473 **Vol. 3:** 946, 1053
22:23	**Vol. 1:** 326 **Vol. 3:** 1157
22:24 ff	**Vol. 2:** 276
22:24	**Vol. 2:** 550 **Vol. 3:** 822
22:25–27	**Vol. 3:** 979
22:25 f	**Vol. 2:** 339
22:25	**Vol. 1:** 143, 274 **Vol. 2:** 378, 518 **Vol. 3:** 1152
22:26 f	**Vol. 2:** 427, 518 **Vol. 3:** 546
22:26	**Vol. 1:** 197 **Vol. 2:** 675 **Vol. 3:** 547, 1152
22:27	**Vol. 1:** 549 **Vol. 2:** 262 **Vol. 3:** 195, 546–547, 625
22:28 ff	**Vol. 2:** 385, 727, 882, 920–921
22:28–34	**Vol. 3:** 803
22:28	**Vol. 1:** 185 **Vol. 3:** 804
22:29 f	**Vol. 1:** 323 **Vol. 3:** 85
22:29	**Vol. 1:** 369 **Vol. 2:** 382, 385 **Vol. 3:** 697, 871
22:30	**Vol. 1:** 251 **Vol. 2:** 48, 272, 276, 313, 365, 387, 581, 695 **Vol. 3:** 180, 629, 871
22:31 ff	**Vol. 2:** 731
22:31–34	**Vol. 3:** 386
22:31	**Vol. 2:** 858
22:32	**Vol. 1:** 355, 359, 489 **Vol. 2:** 857, 861
22:33	**Vol. 2:** 136 **Vol. 3:** 118
22:34	**Vol. 1:** 173 **Vol. 3:** 114
22:35–38	**Vol. 3:** 978
22:35 f	**Vol. 1:** 142
22:35	**Vol. 1:** 142, 384 **Vol. 3:** 729, 954
22:36 ff	**Vol. 3:** 977
22:36	**Vol. 1:** 143, 268 **Vol. 3:** 967
22:37 f	**Vol. 1:** 489
22:37	**Vol. 1:** 581 **Vol. 2:** 62–64, 445 **Vol. 3:** 612, 824–826, 967
22:38	**Vol. 3:** 729, 967
22:39	**Vol. 2:** 437
22:40–46	**Vol. 2:** 178, 561, 868
22:41	**Vol. 2:** 859
22:42	**Vol. 1:** 335, 620 **Vol. 2:** 83, 276, 871 **Vol. 3:** 1017–1018, 1022
22:43	**Vol. 1:** 102 **Vol. 2:** 193 **Vol. 3:** 517
22:44	**Vol. 1:** 646 **Vol. 2:** 861, 873
22:45	**Vol. 1:** 305, 442 **Vol. 2:** 420 **Vol. 3:** 275
22:46	**Vol. 2:** 871
22:47	**Vol. 1:** 299 **Vol. 2:** 549, 695
22:48	**Vol. 3:** 624
22:49 ff	**Vol. 3:** 729
22:49	**Vol. 3:** 967, 1175, 1190
22:51	**Vol. 2:** 168
22:52	**Vol. 3:** 379, 964, 967
22:53	**Vol. 1:** 423 **Vol. 2:** 150, 610, 895 **Vol. 3:** 470, 791
22:54–71	**Vol. 2:** 379 **Vol. 3:** 386, 409, 804
22:54	**Vol. 1:** 343
22:55	**Vol. 1:** 656
22:56	**Vol. 2:** 493 **Vol. 3:** 519–520
22:57 ff	**Vol. 1:** 455
22:60	**Vol. 3:** 114, 742
22:61	**Vol. 1:** 201–202 **Vol. 3:** 240, 519
22:62	**Vol. 3:** 1122
22:63	**Vol. 1:** 162 **Vol. 3:** 341
22:64	**Vol. 3:** 83
22:65	**Vol. 3:** 343
22:66	**Vol. 1:** 199, 297, 364 **Vol. 2:** 32
22:67	**Vol. 3:** 1211
22:69	**Vol. 1:** 323 **Vol. 2:** 147, 194, 380, 515 **Vol. 3:** 457, 621, 627, 629, 838
22:71	**Vol. 3:** 1043
23	**Vol. 1:** 633 **Vol. 2:** 378 **Vol. 3:** 1174
23:1–56	**Vol. 1:** 394
23:1	**Vol. 1:** 733
23:2	**Vol. 1:** 269, 395 **Vol. 2:** 222, 378, 793 **Vol. 3:** 652, 754
23:3	**Vol. 2:** 315, 378–379
23:4	**Vol. 2:** 139 **Vol. 3:** 529
23:5	**Vol. 1:** 395 **Vol. 2:** 799 **Vol. 3:** 558, 762
23:7	**Vol. 2:** 608
23:8	**Vol. 2:** 241 **Vol. 3:** 517, 843
23:10	**Vol. 1:** 83, 395
23:11	**Vol. 2:** 486 **Vol. 3:** 341, 964
23:12	**Vol. 1:** 554 **Vol. 2:** 549
23:13 ff	**Vol. 1:** 395
23:13	**Vol. 1:** 168
23:14	**Vol. 1:** 83 **Vol. 2:** 139, 365 **Vol. 3:** 529
23:15	**Vol. 3:** 1157
23:16–25	**Vol. 3:** 189
23:16	**Vol. 1:** 162 **Vol. 3:** 778
23:17–25	**Vol. 1:** 396
23:17	**Vol. 2:** 378
23:18	**Vol. 1:** 409
23:19	**Vol. 2:** 136 **Vol. 3:** 1191
23:21	**Vol. 1:** 409
23:22	**Vol. 2:** 139 **Vol. 3:** 529, 778
23:22b	**Vol. 1:** 395
23:23	**Vol. 2:** 856 **Vol. 3:** 113, 7i3
23:24	**Vol. 2:** 76, 858
23:25	**Vol. 2:** 136
23:25b	**Vol. 1:** 395
23:26–31	**Vol. 3:** 980
23:26	**Vol. 1:** 493 **Vol. 2:** 740 **Vol. 3:** 749
23:27	**Vol. 1:** 733 **Vol. 2:** 418
23:28 ff	**Vol. 1:** 75 **Vol. 2:** 328
23:28–32	**Vol. 2:** 37
23:28–31	**Vol. 1:** 395
23:28	**Vol. 1:** 286, 395 **Vol. 3:** 1062
23:29	**Vol. 1:** 240
23:30	**Vol. 1:** 610 **Vol. 2:** 212, 216, 218
23:31	**Vol. 1:** 390, 515 **Vol. 2:** 382
23:32 ff	**Vol. 3:** 725
23:32	**Vol. 1:** 564

Luke *(cont'd)*

23:33   **Vol. 1:** 564   **Vol. 2:** 148   **Vol. 3:** 379
23:34   **Vol. 1:** 620   **Vol. 2:** 82, 299, 543, 871, 873
23:34b   **Vol. 1:** 396
23:35 ff **Vol. 1:** 397
23:35–39 **Vol. 3:** 347
23:35   **Vol. 1:** 168, 323, 396, 539, 541   **Vol. 2:** 82, 379, 630–631   **Vol. 3:** 341
23:36   **Vol. 2:** 28, 339   **Vol. 3:** 341
23:37 f   **Vol. 2:** 315
23:37   **Vol. 2:** 379, 418
23:38   **Vol. 2:** 379   **Vol. 3:** 489, 492, 509
23:39   **Vol. 1:** 564   **Vol. 3:** 211
23:40   **Vol. 1:** 572   **Vol. 2:** 739
23:41   **Vol. 3:** 361, 725, 751, 1157
23:42   **Vol. 1:** 320   **Vol. 2:** 763   **Vol. 3:** 241
23:43   **Vol. 1:** 701   **Vol. 2:** 543, 761, 918, 921   **Vol. 3:** 211, 302, 504, 682, 838
23:44   **Vol. 1:** 423   **Vol. 3:** 847
23:45   **Vol. 1:** 203   **Vol. 3:** 543, 732, 793, 795
23:46   **Vol. 1:** 409, 620   **Vol. 2:** 149, 426, 871, 919   **Vol. 3:** 113, 694, 708
23:47   **Vol. 3:** 361, 964–965
23:48   **Vol. 3:** 903
23:49   **Vol. 1:** 481   **Vol. 3:** 1059, 1070
23:50–56 **Vol. 3:** 980
23:50   **Vol. 2:** 563   **Vol. 3:** 361
23:51   **Vol. 2:** 315, 385   **Vol. 3:** 1017, 1158
23:52   **Vol. 1:** 234
23:53   **Vol. 3:** 246, 1190
23:54   **Vol. 3:** 408, 410
23:55–24:11 **Vol. 3:** 1060
23:55   **Vol. 1:** 234, 322   **Vol. 3:** 247, 516
23:56†   **Vol. 1:** 335   **Vol. 2:** 295   **Vol. 3:** 111
24   **Vol. 3:** 287–288, 297, 518
24:1–53 **Vol. 3:** 294
24:1   **Vol. 2:** 198, 295   **Vol. 3:** 246, 412, 1059
24:2   **Vol. 3:** 247, 393
24:4   **Vol. 1:** 204
24:5   **Vol. 1:** 445   **Vol. 3:** 277
24:6 ff   **Vol. 3:** 48
24:7   **Vol. 2:** 63, 663, 665
24:8   **Vol. 3:** 1122
24:9   **Vol. 2:** 358   **Vol. 3:** 48, 247, 252
24:10   **Vol. 1:** 136   **Vol. 3:** 252, 1060
24:11   **Vol. 2:** 359, 488, 911   **Vol. 3:** 296, 1060
24:12   **Vol. 2:** 624, 724   **Vol. 3:** 247, 947
24:13   **Vol. 2:** 686
24:16   **Vol. 2:** 398, 739   **Vol. 3:** 276, 717
24:18   **Vol. 1:** 691   **Vol. 3:** 1061
24:19 ff **Vol. 2:** 340
24:19   **Vol. 2:** 333, 341, 603, 641, 799   **Vol. 3:** 83, 86, 1149–1150
24:20   **Vol. 1:** 168, 394–395   **Vol. 2:** 365, 368
24:21   **Vol. 1:** 326   **Vol. 2:** 241, 313–314   **Vol. 3:** 198–200, 296
24:22   **Vol. 1:** 528   **Vol. 3:** 247
24:23   **Vol. 3:** 515

24:24   **Vol. 2:** 314   **Vol. 3:** 247
24:25 ff **Vol. 3:** 329
24:25   **Vol. 2:** 183   **Vol. 3:** 129, 188, 492, 1212
24:26   **Vol. 2:** 46, 339–340, 663, 665   **Vol. 3:** 503–504, 723–724
24:27   **Vol. 1:** 167, 581   **Vol. 2:** 444, 641   **Vol. 3:** 490, 492, 830
24:29 f   **Vol. 3:** 276
24:29   **Vol. 3:** 224
24:30 f   **Vol. 2:** 524
24:30   **Vol. 1:** 213   **Vol. 2:** 48, 524
24:31 f   **Vol. 2:** 729
24:31   **Vol. 2:** 726, 729   **Vol. 3:** 276, 518
24:32   **Vol. 1:** 581   **Vol. 2:** 183, 342, 729   **Vol. 3:** 490, 492
24:33   **Vol. 2:** 33   **Vol. 3:** 846
24:34–40 **Vol. 3:** 297
24:34   **Vol. 3:** 285, 297
24:35   **Vol. 1:** 576   **Vol. 2:** 524, 897
24:36 ff **Vol. 1:** 128
24:36–49 **Vol. 3:** 295, 297
24:36 f   **Vol. 3:** 518
24:37 ff **Vol. 3:** 474
24:37–41 **Vol. 2:** 559
24:37   **Vol. 2:** 624   **Vol. 3:** 324, 694, 822
24:38   **Vol. 2:** 185, 282   **Vol. 3:** 710
24:39 f   **Vol. 1:** 239
24:39   **Vol. 1:** 241, 393, 677, 679   **Vol. 2:** 282   **Vol. 3:** 276, 323, 694
24:41–43 **Vol. 3:** 449
24:41   **Vol. 2:** 282, 359, 624
24:43   **Vol. 2:** 524, 920
24:44–47 **Vol. 3:** 329
24:44   **Vol. 1:** 736   **Vol. 2:** 314, 444, 641, 665   **Vol. 3:** 485, 671, 675
24:45   **Vol. 3:** 132, 490
24:46 ff **Vol. 1:** 136   **Vol. 2:** 176
24:46 f   **Vol. 1:** 702
24:46   **Vol. 2:** 63, 359   **Vol. 3:** 723
24:47   **Vol. 1:** 359, 701, 720   **Vol. 2:** 328, 359   **Vol. 3:** 56
24:48 f   **Vol. 1:** 90
24:48   **Vol. 3:** 1044
24:49   **Vol. 2:** 200, 328, 786   **Vol. 3:** 70–71, 229, 698
24:50–51 **Vol. 1:** 214   **Vol. 2:** 713
24:51   **Vol. 1:** 607
24:52 f   **Vol. 3:** 793
24:52   **Vol. 2:** 328, 359, 877
24:53   **Vol. 1:** 213   **Vol. 2:** 236, 327–328

John

1:1 ff   **Vol. 1:** 63, 175, 549   **Vol. 2:** 405, 546, 840, 927   **Vol. 3:** 462, 1116–1117
1:1–18 **Vol. 1:** 628   **Vol. 3:** 791, 1114–1115
1:1–14 **Vol. 3:** 582
1:1–12 **Vol. 1:** 66
1:1–4   **Vol. 3:** 1114–1115
1:1–3   **Vol. 3:** 1115

John *(cont'd)*

1:1 f   **Vol. 3:** 1116
1:1   **Vol. 1:** 166, 383–384   **Vol. 2:** 81, 654   **Vol. 3:** 61, 326, 1106, 1114–1115, 1176, 1186
1:1a   **Vol. 3:** 1204
1:1b   **Vol. 3:** 1172, 1185, 1204–1205
1:2   **Vol. 3:** 1115
1:3 f   **Vol. 3:** 1115
1:3   **Vol. 1:** 95, 181, 384, 524   **Vol. 3:** 1182
1:4–9   **Vol. 3:** 916
1:4 f   **Vol. 3:** 314, 1115
1:4   **Vol. 1:** 168   **Vol. 2:** 80, 482, 494   **Vol. 3:** 314
1:5 ff   **Vol. 3:** 1115
1:5–13   **Vol. 3:** 1115
1:5   **Vol. 1:** 424   **Vol. 2:** 488   **Vol. 3:** 723, 750, 1114–1115
1:6 ff   **Vol. 1:** 111   **Vol. 2:** 494   **Vol. 3:** 82
1:6–8   **Vol. 3:** 1115
1:6   **Vol. 3:** 1201, 1203
1:7   **Vol. 1:** 323, 603   **Vol. 3:** 1045, 1211
1:8 f   **Vol. 2:** 80
1:8   **Vol. 3:** 697, 1045
1:9–11   **Vol. 3:** 1114–1115
1:9   **Vol. 1:** 323, 524   **Vol. 2:** 280, 494   **Vol. 3:** 893, 1115
1:10 f   **Vol. 3:** 1116
1:10   **Vol. 1:** 303, 524–525   **Vol. 2:** 400   **Vol. 3:** 1182
1:11   **Vol. 2:** 839, 846   **Vol. 3:** 321, 460, 723, 750–751
1:12 f   **Vol. 1:** 158, 179, 256, 287, 290, 303, 526   **Vol. 2:** 928   **Vol. 3:** 1115
1:12   **Vol. 1:** 599   **Vol. 2:** 610, 929   **Vol. 3:** 646–647, 748, 1213
1:13   **Vol. 1:** 148, 159, 221, 678   **Vol. 2:** 76   **Vol. 3:** 647, 661, 1188
1:14 f   **Vol. 3:** 1117
1:14–18   **Vol. 3:** 890, 1115
1:14   **Vol. 1:** 347, 678–679, 739–740   **Vol. 2:** 47–48, 75–76, 80, 119, 122, 176, 185, 404, 567, 632, 725, 928   **Vol. 3:** 313, 323, 326, 516, 630, 697, 813, 889–890, 1106, 1114–1115, 1117, 1202
1:15   **Vol. 1:** 323, 409, 493   **Vol. 3:** 1045, 1115, 1176
1:16 f   **Vol. 2:** 120
1:16   **Vol. 1:** 739   **Vol. 3:** 749, 1115, 1179
1:17 f   **Vol. 3:** 1115
1:17   **Vol. 1:** 374   **Vol. 2:** 80, 119, 232, 339, 443, 448, 641–642, 673   **Vol. 3:** 631, 889–890, 1022, 1116
1:18   **Vol. 1:** 240, 573, 575–576, 620   **Vol. 2:** 75, 79, 81, 404, 505, 725   **Vol. 3:** 314, 462, 517, 646, 1174, 1176, 1185–1186
1:19 ff   **Vol. 3:** 1045
1:19–34   **Vol. 3:** 697, 791

1:19–28   **Vol. 1:** 111
1:19 f   **Vol. 2:** 339
1:19   **Vol. 2:** 315, 467, 879   **Vol. 3:** 455
1:20   **Vol. 1:** 346–347, 455   **Vol. 2:** 282
1:21   **Vol. 1:** 544–545   **Vol. 2:** 443, 640, 879
1:23   **Vol. 1:** 411, 736   **Vol. 3:** 940
1:25 ff   **Vol. 1:** 487
1:25   **Vol. 1:** 544–545   **Vol. 2:** 640, 879
1:26 f   **Vol. 3:** 55
1:26   **Vol. 3:** 990, 1210
1:27   **Vol. 1:** 323, 493   **Vol. 3:** 179, 348
1:28   **Vol. 3:** 991
1:29 ff   **Vol. 1:** 629
1:29–36   **Vol. 1:** 629
1:29–34   **Vol. 3:** 170
1:29   **Vol. 1:** 525, 701–702   **Vol. 2:** 411, 527, 927   **Vol. 3:** 516, 582, 611, 1117, 1196
1:30   **Vol. 1:** 493   **Vol. 3:** 1174, 1176
1:31   **Vol. 2:** 315   **Vol. 3:** 312, 314, 321, 323, 990, 1210
1:32 ff   **Vol. 3:** 516
1:32–34   **Vol. 2:** 411
1:32 f   **Vol. 2:** 878   **Vol. 3:** 460, 704, 987
1:32   **Vol. 1:** 175   **Vol. 3:** 225, 258, 516, 1045
1:33   **Vol. 1:** 158   **Vol. 2:** 231   **Vol. 3:** 697, 704, 990, 1070, 1210
1:34   **Vol. 1:** 539, 541   **Vol. 3:** 611, 1045
1:35 ff   **Vol. 2:** 686
1:35–51   **Vol. 2:** 825   **Vol. 3:** 791, 985
1:35–43   **Vol. 1:** 136
1:35   **Vol. 1:** 487
1:36   **Vol. 2:** 80, 411, 434   **Vol. 3:** 520, 611
1:37   **Vol. 1:** 487
1:38–40   **Vol. 2:** 311
1:38   **Vol. 1:** 488, 581   **Vol. 3:** 115, 224, 516, 767
1:39 ff   **Vol. 2:** 231
1:39   **Vol. 1:** 321   **Vol. 3:** 847, 1205
1:41   **Vol. 2:** 334, 338–339   **Vol. 3:** 462, 528, 530
1:42   **Vol. 1:** 273, 581   **Vol. 3:** 382–383, 386, 520
1:43 ff   **Vol. 1:** 483
1:43   **Vol. 1:** 482, 488, 581
1:44–47   **Vol. 2:** 550
1:44   **Vol. 3:** 1180
1:45   **Vol. 2:** 333, 339   **Vol. 3:** 489, 528–529
1:46   **Vol. 2:** 101, 334
1:47 ff   **Vol. 2:** 339
1:47   **Vol. 1:** 321   **Vol. 2:** 310, 314   **Vol. 3:** 516, 894
1:48   **Vol. 2:** 398   **Vol. 3:** 114, 460, 517
1:49 ff   **Vol. 2:** 231
1:49   **Vol. 2:** 315, 550   **Vol. 3:** 115, 460, 652
1:51   **Vol. 1:** 102   **Vol. 2:** 185–186, 194, 319, 726–728   **Vol. 3:** 543, 620, 630, 632
2:1 ff   **Vol. 2:** 630, 632
2:1–11   **Vol. 2:** 580, 676   **Vol. 3:** 791, 922, 990
2:1 f   **Vol. 2:** 579
2:2   **Vol. 1:** 274   **Vol. 2:** 578

John (cont'd)

2:4   **Vol. 1:** 321, 738   **Vol. 2:** 927   **Vol. 3:** 848, 890, 1058, 1070
2:5   **Vol. 3:** 546
2:6   **Vol. 1:** 742   **Vol. 3:** 105, 990
2:9   **Vol. 2:** 269, 585   **Vol. 3:** 546, 922
2:10   **Vol. 1:** 513   **Vol. 2:** 133, 428
2:11   **Vol. 1:** 489   **Vol. 2:** 47–48, 629, 632   **Vol. 3:** 312, 314, 516–517
2:12–22   **Vol. 1:** 629
2:13 ff   **Vol. 2:** 328
2:13–22   **Vol. 3:** 430
2:13–17   **Vol. 2:** 610, 754   **Vol. 3:** 39, 429, 791, 1168
2:13   **Vol. 1:** 629, 633–634   **Vol. 2:** 54, 315, 927
2:14 ff   **Vol. 1:** 111   **Vol. 3:** 789
2:14   **Vol. 1:** 175   **Vol. 2:** 413
2:15   **Vol. 2:** 854
2:16 f   **Vol. 2:** 248
2:16   **Vol. 2:** 236   **Vol. 3:** 430, 516
2:17   **Vol. 3:** 430, 1167
2:18 ff   **Vol. 3:** 784
2:18–22   **Vol. 3:** 791–792
2:18†   **Vol. 2:** 434, 629   **Vol. 3:** 569
2:19 ff   **Vol. 2:** 252
2:19–22   **Vol. 2:** 434   **Vol. 3:** 813
2:19–21   **Vol. 2:** 450   **Vol. 3:** 784
2:19–20   **Vol. 2:** 687
2:19   **Vol. 2:** 236, 252, 732   **Vol. 3:** 180, 185, 211, 343, 509
2:20   **Vol. 2:** 434, 685   **Vol. 3:** 185, 788
2:21   **Vol. 1:** 234   **Vol. 3:** 185, 890
2:22   **Vol. 3:** 185, 491–492
2:23 ff   **Vol. 2:** 632   **Vol. 3:** 791
2:23†   **Vol. 1:** 633   **Vol. 2:** 629, 927   **Vol. 3:** 1213
2:24   **Vol. 3:** 1211, 1213
2:25   **Vol. 2:** 879   **Vol. 3:** 517, 1044
3   **Vol. 1:** 284, 510
3:1–36   **Vol. 2:** 751
3:1–15   **Vol. 3:** 791
3:1   **Vol. 1:** 168   **Vol. 2:** 812
3:2   **Vol. 1:** 420, 488   **Vol. 2:** 79, 604, 629   **Vol. 3:** 115, 768
3:3 ff   **Vol. 1:** 303   **Vol. 2:** 567
3:3–8   **Vol. 3:** 460
3:3–7   **Vol. 3:** 1132
3:3 f   **Vol. 1:** 180   **Vol. 3:** 185
3:3   **Vol. 1:** 179   **Vol. 2:** 385, 604, 661, 787, 928   **Vol. 3:** 518, 647, 1178
3:4   **Vol. 1:** 179   **Vol. 2:** 434, 812   **Vol. 3:** 1071
3:5–8   **Vol. 1:** 179   **Vol. 2:** 878   **Vol. 3:** 703, 705
3:5   **Vol. 1:** 147–148, 154, 158, 160, 179–180, 185, 290, 526   **Vol. 2:** 385, 604, 661, 929   **Vol. 3:** 459, 647, 704, 1178

3:6   **Vol. 1:** 179, 678–679   **Vol. 2:** 567, 928
3:7   **Vol. 1:** 179   **Vol. 2:** 625, 666   **Vol. 3:** 1178
3:8   **Vol. 1:** 147, 179, 656   **Vol. 3:** 113, 703, 708, 1022
3:9   **Vol. 2:** 625, 812
3:10   **Vol. 3:** 767
3:11   **Vol. 3:** 516, 1045
3:12 f   **Vol. 2:** 196
3:13   **Vol. 2:** 185, 787, 928   **Vol. 3:** 622, 629–631, 646
3:14 ff   **Vol. 2:** 642
3:14 f   **Vol. 1:** 147, 510
3:14   **Vol. 1:** 390, 509   **Vol. 2:** 202, 204, 339, 665   **Vol. 3:** 630–631, 1007
3:15 ff   **Vol. 2:** 42
3:15 f†   **Vol. 1:** 638   **Vol. 2:** 80   **Vol. 3:** 832
3:15   **Vol. 2:** 388   **Vol. 3:** 832, 1178, 1212
3:16 ff   **Vol. 1:** 525, 603   **Vol. 2:** 367
3:16–21   **Vol. 1:** 290   **Vol. 2:** 928   **Vol. 3:** 791
3:16   **Vol. 1:** 287, 338, 464, 638, 702   **Vol. 2:** 42, 75, 78–79, 122, 404, 542, 546, 548, 610, 725   **Vol. 3:** 321, 643, 646, 825, 1202
3:17 f   **Vol. 2:** 365
3:17   **Vol. 1:** 525   **Vol. 3:** 216, 445, 643, 646, 1022
3:18 f   **Vol. 1:** 424   **Vol. 2:** 894, 928
3:18   **Vol. 1:** 599   **Vol. 2:** 75, 654, 702, 725   **Vol. 3:** 646, 1202, 1213
3:18b   **Vol. 3:** 1211
3:19–21   **Vol. 3:** 1150
3:19   **Vol. 1:** 323, 424, 524–525, 566   **Vol. 2:** 366, 494, 543, 928   **Vol. 3:** 1150
3:20   **Vol. 1:** 556, 564, 603   **Vol. 2:** 141   **Vol. 3:** 1158
3:21   **Vol. 1:** 490   **Vol. 2:** 232   **Vol. 3:** 312, 314, 321, 891, 1149–1150
3:22–26   **Vol. 1:** 487
3:22   **Vol. 3:** 1205
3:23   **Vol. 2:** 592   **Vol. 3:** 1210
3:25 f   **Vol. 3:** 1205
3:25   **Vol. 1:** 487   **Vol. 3:** 532
3:26   **Vol. 3:** 115, 991, 1045
3:27   **Vol. 2:** 193, 359
3:28   **Vol. 3:** 1044
3:29 f   **Vol. 2:** 585
3:29   **Vol. 1:** 741   **Vol. 2:** 356, 549, 585, 751   **Vol. 3:** 113
3:31 f   **Vol. 2:** 196   **Vol. 3:** 1045
3:31   **Vol. 2:** 928   **Vol. 3:** 629
3:32   **Vol. 3:** 314, 516, 1045
3:33   **Vol. 2:** 77   **Vol. 3:** 499, 749, 1046
3:34   **Vol. 2:** 878   **Vol. 3:** 403, 697, 704, 1114, 1122
3:35   **Vol. 1:** 620   **Vol. 2:** 81, 149, 542, 546, 610, 653   **Vol. 3:** 313, 645–646, 1122, 1174, 1185
3:36   **Vol. 1:** 111–113, 593, 638   **Vol. 2:** 388, 404, 546   **Vol. 3:** 226, 832, 837

John *(cont'd)*

4	**Vol. 3:** 143, 459, 461
4:1 ff	**Vol. 1:** 146
4:1 – 45	**Vol. 3:** 455
4:1 – 42	**Vol. 1:** 67 **Vol. 2:** 751 **Vol. 3:** 456, 458, 980
4:1 f	**Vol. 1:** 160
4:1	**Vol. 2:** 398
4:2	**Vol. 1:** 179
4:3	**Vol. 3:** 115
4:4	**Vol. 3:** 449
4:5 ff	**Vol. 3:** 987
4:5	**Vol. 1:** 258 **Vol. 2:** 318 **Vol. 3:** 454, 457 – 458
4:6	**Vol. 1:** 263 **Vol. 2:** 318 **Vol. 3:** 459, 847, 1180
4:6b	**Vol. 3:** 458
4:7 ff	**Vol. 3:** 459
4:7 – 27	**Vol. 3:** 1059
4:7	**Vol. 3:** 989
4:8	**Vol. 3:** 454, 458
4:9	**Vol. 2:** 315 **Vol. 3:** 460, 1058
4:10 ff	**Vol. 2:** 277 **Vol. 3:** 185
4:10 – 15	**Vol. 3:** 459, 991
4:10 – 14	**Vol. 2:** 928
4:10	**Vol. 1:** 683 **Vol. 2:** 41 – 42 **Vol. 3:** 459, 1132
4:11 f	**Vol. 3:** 459
4:11	**Vol. 2:** 198, 277, 434
4:12	**Vol. 1:** 116 **Vol. 2:** 318, 426 **Vol. 3:** 461
4:13 ff	**Vol. 2:** 80
4:13 f	**Vol. 3:** 459, 987, 989
4:13	**Vol. 2:** 267, 277
4:14 f	**Vol. 2:** 267, 514
4:14	**Vol. 2:** 277, 482, 787 **Vol. 3:** 459, 462, 703, 830, 832
4:16 – 19	**Vol. 3:** 460
4:17 f	**Vol. 3:** 460
4:18	**Vol. 3:** 460, 890
4:19	**Vol. 1:** 66 **Vol. 3:** 83, 460, 462, 516 – 517
4:20 ff	**Vol. 2:** 927
4:20	**Vol. 2:** 878 **Vol. 3:** 459 – 460, 789
4:21 – 24	**Vol. 3:** 460
4:21	**Vol. 2:** 878, 927 **Vol. 3:** 460 – 461, 1211 – 1212
4:22 ff	**Vol. 2:** 878
4:22 f	**Vol. 3:** 458
4:22	**Vol. 2:** 314 **Vol. 3:** 212, 216, 219, 460 – 463
4:23 f	**Vol. 2:** 80, 873, 927 **Vol. 3:** 460 – 461, 551, 705
4:23	**Vol. 1:** 324 **Vol. 2:** 280, 878 **Vol. 3:** 532, 890 – 891, 893
4:24	**Vol. 2:** 66, 75, 666 **Vol. 3:** 891
4:25 f	**Vol. 2:** 339, 927 **Vol. 3:** 462
4:25	**Vol. 2:** 231, 334, 338 **Vol. 3:** 47 – 48, 461 – 462
4:26	**Vol. 3:** 462
4:27	**Vol. 3:** 1058 – 1059
4:29	**Vol. 3:** 462
4:31 – 34	**Vol. 3:** 1132
4:31	**Vol. 1:** 488 **Vol. 2:** 879
4:32 f	**Vol. 3:** 185
4:32	**Vol. 2:** 268 – 269, 434
4:34	**Vol. 1:** 128 **Vol. 2:** 64, 268 – 269, 359, 561 **Vol. 3:** 1022, 1150
4:35 – 38	**Vol. 2:** 927
4:35 f	**Vol. 2:** 359
4:35	**Vol. 1:** 204 **Vol. 2:** 750 **Vol. 3:** 516, 526
4:36 ff	**Vol. 3:** 144
4:36 – 38	**Vol. 3:** 526
4:36	**Vol. 1:** 723 **Vol. 2:** 32 **Vol. 3:** 832
4:37	**Vol. 2:** 280 **Vol. 3:** 893
4:38	**Vol. 1:** 263 **Vol. 3:** 458
4:39 – 42	**Vol. 3:** 462
4:39	**Vol. 3:** 1046
4:40	**Vol. 2:** 879 **Vol. 3:** 454, 1205
4:41	**Vol. 3:** 1106
4:42	**Vol. 1:** 525, 603 **Vol. 3:** 219, 460, 462
4:43 f	**Vol. 3:** 460
4:44	**Vol. 1:** 616 **Vol. 3:** 83, 696
4:45	**Vol. 2:** 927
4:46	**Vol. 3:** 994
4:47 ff	**Vol. 2:** 480, 632
4:47	**Vol. 1:** 326 **Vol. 2:** 879
4:48	**Vol. 2:** 629
4:49	**Vol. 1:** 284
4:50	**Vol. 1:** 284 **Vol. 2:** 631 **Vol. 3:** 280, 1211
4:51	**Vol. 1:** 284 **Vol. 3:** 46
4:52 f	**Vol. 3:** 848
4:53	**Vol. 2:** 248, 250
5	**Vol. 3:** 630
5:1 ff	**Vol. 2:** 328, 632
5:1 – 9	**Vol. 3:** 409
5:1	**Vol. 1:** 629 **Vol. 2:** 927
5:2	**Vol. 2:** 309
5:3	**Vol. 1:** 516 **Vol. 2:** 415
5:4	**Vol. 3:** 709, 990, 998
5:5	**Vol. 2:** 685
5:6	**Vol. 3:** 843, 1022
5:7	**Vol. 1:** 637 **Vol. 2:** 514 **Vol. 3:** 709, 990, 994
5:8 ff	**Vol. 2:** 168
5:9 ff	**Vol. 2:** 170
5:10	**Vol. 2:** 610
5:12	**Vol. 2:** 879
5:13 f	**Vol. 2:** 169
5:14	**Vol. 2:** 236 **Vol. 3:** 792, 998
5:16	**Vol. 2:** 806 **Vol. 3:** 409, 533
5:17 – 47	**Vol. 1:** 704
5:17 – 30	**Vol. 3:** 646
5:17	**Vol. 2:** 74, 499 **Vol. 3:** 186, 409, 604, 1150
5:18	**Vol. 2:** 449, 500 **Vol. 3:** 186 – 187, 532, 604

179

John *(cont'd)*

5:19 ff	**Vol. 2:** 500
5:19–47	**Vol. 2:** 751
5:19	**Vol. 1:** 549 **Vol. 2:** 313, 604 **Vol. 3:** 645–646
5:20	**Vol. 2:** 426, 542, 548, 625, 653 **Vol. 3:** 569, 646
5:21	**Vol. 3:** 304, 647, 1022
5:21a	**Vol. 3:** 303
5:22	**Vol. 2:** 365 **Vol. 3:** 645
5:23	**Vol. 2:** 50 **Vol. 3:** 645–646
5:24 ff	**Vol. 3:** 848
5:24–25	**Vol. 3:** 114
5:24	**Vol. 1:** 436, 439, 637 **Vol. 2:** 186, 366, 482, 567, 702, 929 **Vol. 3:** 277, 517, 832, 1114, 1212
5:25–28	**Vol. 2:** 929
5:25	**Vol. 1:** 324 **Vol. 2:** 178 **Vol. 3:** 113, 837
5:26	**Vol. 3:** 304, 645, 1183
5:27	**Vol. 2:** 610 **Vol. 3:** 618, 630–631
5:28 f	**Vol. 1:** 440 **Vol. 2:** 625 **Vol. 3:** 303, 839
5:28–29	**Vol. 3:** 113
5:28	**Vol. 2:** 178 **Vol. 3:** 247
5:29 f	**Vol. 2:** 365
5:29	**Vol. 1:** 324, 564 **Vol. 2:** 101, 366 **Vol. 3:** 303, 1157–1158
5:30	**Vol. 2:** 366, 561, 604 **Vol. 3:** 362, 532
5:30a	**Vol. 3:** 1022
5:30b	**Vol. 3:** 1022
5:31 f	**Vol. 3:** 890
5:31	**Vol. 3:** 890, 1045
5:32	**Vol. 2:** 739 **Vol. 3:** 1045
5:33	**Vol. 3:** 1045
5:34	**Vol. 3:** 216
5:35 f	**Vol. 2:** 494
5:35	**Vol. 2:** 353, 487–488 **Vol. 3:** 848
5:36	**Vol. 1:** 128 **Vol. 2:** 64, 313, 426 **Vol. 3:** 1045, 1149–1150
5:37	**Vol. 1:** 704 **Vol. 3:** 461, 1045
5:38 ff	**Vol. 1:** 638
5:38	**Vol. 1:** 704 **Vol. 3:** 1212
5:39–47	**Vol. 3:** 329
5:39 f	**Vol. 2:** 399
5:39	**Vol. 1:** 246, 737 **Vol. 2:** 314, 448, 641, 927 **Vol. 3:** 188, 215, 429, 490, 492, 499, 517, 533, 822, 832, 1045, 1212
5:40	**Vol. 1:** 324 **Vol. 3:** 1212
5:41	**Vol. 2:** 46–47
5:42	**Vol. 3:** 461
5:43	**Vol. 1:** 323 **Vol. 3:** 748
5:44	**Vol. 2:** 46–47, 724 **Vol. 3:** 532
5:45 ff	**Vol. 2:** 641
5:45	**Vol. 1:** 83 **Vol. 2:** 241 **Vol. 3:** 533, 631, 822
5:46	**Vol. 3:** 489, 1212
5:47	**Vol. 3:** 493, 1212

6	**Vol. 1:** 629–630 **Vol. 2:** 534–535 **Vol. 3:** 631
6:1 ff	**Vol. 2:** 267, 339, 632 **Vol. 3:** 499
6:1–13	**Vol. 1:** 729 **Vol. 2:** 272, 523
6:1	**Vol. 3:** 984
6:2	**Vol. 3:** 994
6:4	**Vol. 1:** 633–634 **Vol. 2:** 927
6:5–13	**Vol. 2:** 630
6:5	**Vol. 2:** 274, 550, 801
6:6	**Vol. 1:** 326
6:7	**Vol. 2:** 550, 711 **Vol. 3:** 727
6:9	**Vol. 1:** 284
6:10	**Vol. 1:** 744 **Vol. 2:** 684
6:11	**Vol. 1:** 670
6:12	**Vol. 1:** 464 **Vol. 2:** 32
6:13	**Vol. 1:** 729 **Vol. 2:** 32
6:14 f	**Vol. 3:** 509
6:14	**Vol. 2:** 641 **Vol. 3:** 80, 83
6:15–21	**Vol. 2:** 281, 630
6:15	**Vol. 1:** 326, 629, 633 **Vol. 2:** 379 **Vol. 3:** 602
6:16 ff	**Vol. 3:** 984
6:16–21	**Vol. 3:** 985, 990
6:17	**Vol. 1:** 423
6:18	**Vol. 3:** 707
6:20	**Vol. 2:** 434
6:22–66	**Vol. 2:** 751
6:22	**Vol. 1:** 321
6:25	**Vol. 2:** 736 **Vol. 3:** 115
6:26	**Vol. 1:** 743
6:27–59	**Vol. 2:** 58
6:27 f	**Vol. 3:** 1202
6:27†	**Vol. 1:** 464 **Vol. 2:** 268–269, 273, 482, 928–929 **Vol. 3:** 499, 631, 832, 1022
6:28	**Vol. 3:** 1149
6:29	**Vol. 2:** 736 **Vol. 3:** 136, 144, 1150, 1212
6:30	**Vol. 2:** 629, 750, 894 **Vol. 3:** 1211–1212
6:31–35	**Vol. 3:** 1132
6:31–34	**Vol. 1:** 253
6:31 f	**Vol. 2:** 194
6:31	**Vol. 3:** 1007
6:32 ff	**Vol. 3:** 185
6:32–35	**Vol. 2:** 642
6:32	**Vol. 2:** 273, 280 **Vol. 3:** 893
6:33 ff	**Vol. 2:** 218
6:33	**Vol. 2:** 185, 482 **Vol. 3:** 1176
6:34	**Vol. 1:** 250 **Vol. 2:** 514
6:35 ff	**Vol. 2:** 727, 882
6:35–58	**Vol. 3:** 383
6:35	**Vol. 1:** 251 **Vol. 2:** 80, 267, 269, 273, 279–280, 482, 535 **Vol. 3:** 1212
6:36	**Vol. 1:** 678
6:37	**Vol. 1:** 324, 453 **Vol. 3:** 1204, 1212
6:38	**Vol. 2:** 185, 194 **Vol. 3:** 1022, 1176
6:39 ff	**Vol. 2:** 900
6:39 f	**Vol. 2:** 58, 929 **Vol. 3:** 277
6:39	**Vol. 1:** 324, 464 **Vol. 2:** 894 **Vol. 3:** 304, 529, 1022

John *(cont'd)*

6:40   **Vol. 2:** 482   **Vol. 3:** 304, 517, 645, 832, 1022
6:41 f   **Vol. 2:** 185, 194
6:41   **Vol. 2:** 269, 279–280   **Vol. 3:** 1176
6:42   **Vol. 2:** 333   **Vol. 3:** 1176
6:44 f   **Vol. 3:** 1212
6:44   **Vol. 1:** 303, 324   **Vol. 2:** 58, 567, 604, 929   **Vol. 3:** 304
6:45   **Vol. 1:** 486   **Vol. 3:** 81, 764
6:46   **Vol. 2:** 505   **Vol. 3:** 516, 518, 1185, 1202
6:47   **Vol. 2:** 280, 482, 535   **Vol. 3:** 832
6:48–51   **Vol. 2:** 642
6:48   **Vol. 2:** 80, 273, 279–280, 482
6:49 f   **Vol. 2:** 273
6:49–51a   **Vol. 1:** 253
6:49   **Vol. 3:** 1007
6:50 f   **Vol. 2:** 194
6:50   **Vol. 2:** 186
6:51 ff   **Vol. 2:** 80, 273, 277, 535   **Vol. 3:** 323
6:51–58   **Vol. 1:** 678   **Vol. 2:** 523, 534   **Vol. 3:** 704
6:51–56   **Vol. 1:** 679
6:51   **Vol. 1:** 253   **Vol. 2:** 279–280   **Vol. 3:** 445, 611, 830
6:51c–58   **Vol. 2:** 534
6:51c   **Vol. 2:** 523, 535
6:52   **Vol. 3:** 963
6:53 ff   **Vol. 1:** 701   **Vol. 2:** 727, 882
6:53–58   **Vol. 3:** 704
6:53–56   **Vol. 1:** 224
6:53   **Vol. 3:** 631
6:54   **Vol. 1:** 324   **Vol. 2:** 58, 535, 929   **Vol. 3:** 277, 304, 832
6:55†   **Vol. 2:** 268–269   **Vol. 3:** 891
6:56   **Vol. 2:** 535   **Vol. 3:** 226, 1192
6:57   **Vol. 1:** 620   **Vol. 2:** 929   **Vol. 3:** 226, 1022, 1185
6:57a   **Vol. 3:** 1183
6:58   **Vol. 2:** 186   **Vol. 3:** 830
6:59   **Vol. 3:** 764, 785
6:60 f   **Vol. 2:** 709
6:60   **Vol. 1:** 490   **Vol. 2:** 155
6:61   **Vol. 2:** 708   **Vol. 3:** 1117
6:62 f   **Vol. 2:** 787   **Vol. 3:** 704
6:62   **Vol. 1:** 678   **Vol. 2:** 185   **Vol. 3:** 629, 631
6:63   **Vol. 1:** 679   **Vol. 2:** 80, 535, 709, 878, 928–929   **Vol. 3:** 244, 459–460, 703–704, 1114, 1117, 1122
6:64   **Vol. 1:** 166
6:65   **Vol. 2:** 567   **Vol. 3:** 1045, 1180, 1212
6:66†   **Vol. 1:** 321, 490, 493, 608   **Vol. 2:** 268, 709
6:67   **Vol. 2:** 695
6:68 f   **Vol. 2:** 76
6:68   **Vol. 2:** 482   **Vol. 3:** 114, 384, 462, 832, 1114, 1122

6:69†   **Vol. 1:** 489, 603   **Vol. 2:** 231, 404   **Vol. 3:** 384
6:70 f   **Vol. 3:** 582
6:70   **Vol. 1:** 540, 542   **Vol. 2:** 695   **Vol. 3:** 470, 472
6:71   **Vol. 2:** 695
7   **Vol. 2:** 57
7:1–52   **Vol. 2:** 751
7:1   **Vol. 1:** 430   **Vol. 3:** 532
7:2 ff   **Vol. 2:** 217
7:2   **Vol. 2:** 927   **Vol. 3:** 813
7:3–9   **Vol. 3:** 813
7:4   **Vol. 2:** 736   **Vol. 3:** 312, 314, 321
7:5   **Vol. 1:** 256   **Vol. 3:** 321
7:6 f   **Vol. 3:** 837
7:6   **Vol. 2:** 899   **Vol. 3:** 118, 321
7:7   **Vol. 1:** 525, 556, 603   **Vol. 3:** 1150
7:8 ff   **Vol. 2:** 185
7:8–10   **Vol. 2:** 217
7:8   **Vol. 1:** 738   **Vol. 2:** 217, 927
7:10 ff   **Vol. 2:** 328
7:10 f   **Vol. 2:** 927
7:10   **Vol. 2:** 217   **Vol. 3:** 320
7:11   **Vol. 2:** 315
7:12   **Vol. 2:** 101, 460, 739, 801
7:13   **Vol. 1:** 622   **Vol. 2:** 736
7:14   **Vol. 2:** 236, 927   **Vol. 3:** 764, 792, 813
7:15–36   **Vol. 3:** 813
7:15 f   **Vol. 2:** 641
7:15   **Vol. 1:** 488   **Vol. 2:** 624   **Vol. 3:** 481, 493
7:16 f   **Vol. 3:** 769
7:16   **Vol. 1:** 128, 549   **Vol. 2:** 624
7:17   **Vol. 2:** 641   **Vol. 3:** 1022, 1155, 1188
7:18   **Vol. 2:** 46   **Vol. 3:** 532, 575–576, 645
7:19 ff   **Vol. 1:** 430
7:19   **Vol. 2:** 448, 450, 641   **Vol. 3:** 532
7:20   **Vol. 1:** 453, 529, 637
7:21   **Vol. 2:** 624   **Vol. 3:** 1149
7:22 f   **Vol. 1:** 309
7:22   **Vol. 3:** 405, 409
7:23   **Vol. 2:** 170, 448, 625   **Vol. 3:** 186–187
7:24   **Vol. 1:** 678, 680   **Vol. 2:** 365   **Vol. 3:** 362
7:25   **Vol. 2:** 325
7:26   **Vol. 1:** 168   **Vol. 2:** 736
7:27   **Vol. 3:** 652
7:28   **Vol. 1:** 409   **Vol. 2:** 280   **Vol. 3:** 461, 764, 792
7:29   **Vol. 1:** 128   **Vol. 2:** 236, 279, 653   **Vol. 3:** 1202
7:30   **Vol. 1:** 738   **Vol. 3:** 848
7:31   **Vol. 2:** 801
7:33   **Vol. 2:** 429   **Vol. 3:** 843
7:34 ff   **Vol. 3:** 185
7:34   **Vol. 3:** 529
7:35   **Vol. 1:** 326, 686   **Vol. 2:** 35, 126   **Vol. 3:** 764
7:36   **Vol. 2:** 277
7:37 ff   **Vol. 2:** 787   **Vol. 3:** 83

John *(cont'd)*

7:37 f	**Vol. 1:** 409 **Vol. 3:** 459, 813, 988, 991
7:37	**Vol. 1:** 324, 629, 683 **Vol. 2:** 277, 894, 927 **Vol. 3:** 383, 748, 1212
7:38 f	**Vol. 2:** 785, 787, 929 **Vol. 3:** 703–704
7:38	**Vol. 1:** 169, 683 **Vol. 2:** 80 **Vol. 3:** 490, 492, 704
7:39	**Vol. 1:** 147, 326 **Vol. 2:** 46, 878 **Vol. 3:** 459, 749, 813, 988, 991
7:40	**Vol. 3:** 80, 83
7:41 f	**Vol. 3:** 1176
7:42	**Vol. 1:** 170, 427 **Vol. 2:** 399, 803 **Vol. 3:** 490, 492, 652
7:43	**Vol. 2:** 801 **Vol. 3:** 543
7:44	**Vol. 3:** 1019
7:47	**Vol. 2:** 459–460
7:48 f	**Vol. 2:** 801
7:48	**Vol. 1:** 168
7:49	**Vol. 1:** 417 **Vol. 2:** 399, 448, 801
7:50	**Vol. 2:** 812
7:51	**Vol. 1:** 666 **Vol. 2:** 399, 448 **Vol. 3:** 1062
7:52	**Vol. 2:** 448 **Vol. 3:** 83, 533
7:53 ff	**Vol. 2:** 754
7:53–8:11	**Vol. 1:** 506 **Vol. 2:** 448, 580 **Vol. 3:** 480
8	**Vol. 3:** 463
8:1–11	**Vol. 3:** 536, 538, 541
8:2	**Vol. 3:** 764, 792, 796
8:3–11	**Vol. 2:** 584
8:3	**Vol. 3:** 480
8:5 ff	**Vol. 2:** 448
8:5	**Vol. 2:** 448, 582
8:6	**Vol. 2:** 150 **Vol. 3:** 489, 804
8:7 ff	**Vol. 3:** 539
8:7	**Vol. 2:** 96, 879 **Vol. 3:** 227, 579, 1062
8:8	**Vol. 2:** 150 **Vol. 3:** 489
8:9	**Vol. 1:** 167, 198, 350
8:10	**Vol. 2:** 365
8:11	**Vol. 1:** 701 **Vol. 2:** 365 **Vol. 3:** 536, 1062
8:12–59	**Vol. 2:** 751
8:12	**Vol. 1:** 323, 424, 483, 638 **Vol. 2:** 80, 217, 279–280, 482, 494, 749 **Vol. 3:** 314, 814, 916, 945
8:13–58	**Vol. 3:** 890
8:13	**Vol. 2:** 187 **Vol. 3:** 1045
8:14	**Vol. 1:** 689 **Vol. 3:** 1045
8:15	**Vol. 1:** 678, 680 **Vol. 3:** 890
8:16	**Vol. 2:** 280, 724–725 **Vol. 3:** 893
8:17	**Vol. 2:** 448, 686 **Vol. 3:** 890, 1043–1045, 1123
8:18	**Vol. 3:** 890, 1044
8:19	**Vol. 1:** 689
8:20	**Vol. 1:** 738 **Vol. 2:** 236, 927 **Vol. 3:** 764, 792, 796, 848
8:23	**Vol. 1:** 179 **Vol. 2:** 187, 928
8:24	**Vol. 3:** 582
8:25 ff	**Vol. 1:** 689

8:25	**Vol. 1:** 166
8:26–29	**Vol. 1:** 620
8:26	**Vol. 2:** 178 **Vol. 3:** 314
8:28	**Vol. 2:** 202, 204 **Vol. 3:** 631, 764
8:29	**Vol. 2:** 725, 816 **Vol. 3:** 646
8:30–40	**Vol. 1:** 79
8:30	**Vol. 1:** 742 **Vol. 3:** 1212
8:31 ff	**Vol. 2:** 567
8:31–36	**Vol. 1:** 718
8:31 f	**Vol. 1:** 719 **Vol. 2:** 63
8:31	**Vol. 1:** 490, 720, 742 **Vol. 3:** 226, 1149, 1211–1212
8:32–36	**Vol. 1:** 717
8:32	**Vol. 1:** 717, 742 **Vol. 2:** 80
8:33	**Vol. 1:** 717 **Vol. 3:** 1163
8:34 ff	**Vol. 1:** 720
8:34–44	**Vol. 3:** 1155
8:34	**Vol. 1:** 742 **Vol. 3:** 596
8:35	**Vol. 2:** 751 **Vol. 3:** 225, 830
8:36	**Vol. 1:** 719 **Vol. 3:** 596
8:37	**Vol. 1:** 742 **Vol. 3:** 532
8:38	**Vol. 1:** 720 **Vol. 3:** 516, 1201, 1205
8:39 f	**Vol. 1:** 79
8:39	**Vol. 1:** 286, 718
8:40	**Vol. 2:** 175, 178
8:41–47	**Vol. 2:** 473, 567
8:41–44	**Vol. 2:** 312
8:41	**Vol. 1:** 637 **Vol. 3:** 661, 1150
8:42–47	**Vol. 2:** 403
8:42 f	**Vol. 2:** 405
8:42	**Vol. 1:** 179, 322–323 **Vol. 2:** 505, 546 **Vol. 3:** 1203
8:43	**Vol. 1:** 529 **Vol. 2:** 604
8:44 f	**Vol. 3:** 582
8:44	**Vol. 1:** 166, 458, 567 **Vol. 2:** 472 **Vol. 3:** 470, 472, 890, 892, 1150
8:45 f	**Vol. 3:** 1212
8:45	**Vol. 3:** 517, 892
8:46	**Vol. 2:** 141 **Vol. 3:** 170
8:47	**Vol. 2:** 567 **Vol. 3:** 1114, 1122, 1188
8:48–59	**Vol. 1:** 79 **Vol. 3:** 472
8:48 f	**Vol. 1:** 453 **Vol. 3:** 462
8:48	**Vol. 1:** 637 **Vol. 3:** 456, 462–463, 465
8:49	**Vol. 1:** 453 **Vol. 2:** 50, 314 **Vol. 3:** 463
8:50	**Vol. 2:** 46–47 **Vol. 3:** 532
8:50b	**Vol. 3:** 531
8:51 f	**Vol. 1:** 337 **Vol. 3:** 830
8:51	**Vol. 1:** 79, 436, 439 **Vol. 2:** 133 **Vol. 3:** 517, 832, 1114
8:52	**Vol. 1:** 79, 453, 529 **Vol. 2:** 271
8:53	**Vol. 2:** 426
8:54 f	**Vol. 3:** 461
8:55	**Vol. 1:** 337 **Vol. 2:** 503
8:56	**Vol. 1:** 80 **Vol. 2:** 354, 359, 630
8:58	**Vol. 1:** 80
8:59	**Vol. 2:** 217 **Vol. 3:** 792
9–12	**Vol. 1:** 384
9	**Vol. 3:** 409
9:1 ff	**Vol. 1:** 219 **Vol. 2:** 632

John (cont'd)

9:1 **Vol. 3:** 1180
9:2 ff **Vol. 2:** 169 **Vol. 3:** 998
9:2 f **Vol. 2:** 366
9:2 **Vol. 1:** 219 **Vol. 2:** 879 **Vol. 3:** 115, 409, 997
9:3 **Vol. 1:** 163, 219 **Vol. 3:** 312, 314, 321
9:4 **Vol. 1:** 421 **Vol. 2:** 79 **Vol. 3:** 1149–1150
9:5 **Vol. 1:** 629 **Vol. 2:** 80, 494 **Vol. 3:** 916
9:6–15 **Vol. 3:** 916
9:7 **Vol. 1:** 581, 629
9:8 **Vol. 3:** 516, 589·
9:10 **Vol. 2:** 726, 728 **Vol. 3:** 519
9:11 **Vol. 3:** 519
9:14 **Vol. 2:** 726, 728 **Vol. 3:** 519
9:15 **Vol. 2:** 879 **Vol. 3:** 519
9:16–41 **Vol. 3:** 582
9:16 **Vol. 2:** 133, 604 **Vol. 3:** 543
9:17 **Vol. 2:** 726, 728 **Vol. 3:** 83, 519
9:18 **Vol. 3:** 519, 1211
9:19 **Vol. 2:** 879
9:21 **Vol. 1:** 92 **Vol. 2:** 726, 728, 879 **Vol. 3:** 519
9:22 **Vol. 1:** 347 **Vol. 2:** 312
9:23 **Vol. 1:** 92 **Vol. 2:** 879
9:25 **Vol. 2:** 720
9:26 **Vol. 2:** 726, 728 **Vol. 3:** 519
9:28 **Vol. 1:** 487 **Vol. 2:** 642 **Vol. 3:** 347
9:29 f **Vol. 1:** 689
9:30 **Vol. 1:** 487 **Vol. 2:** 623, 726, 728 **Vol. 3:** 519
9:31 **Vol. 2:** 85, 94 **Vol. 3:** 1022
9:32 **Vol. 2:** 726, 728 **Vol. 3:** 519, 830
9:33 **Vol. 3:** 1202–1203
9:34 f **Vol. 1:** 453
9:34 **Vol. 1:** 178 **Vol. 3:** 764
9:35–39 **Vol. 3:** 631
9:38 **Vol. 2:** 859, 877
9:39 **Vol. 1:** 525 **Vol. 2:** 217, 279, 365, 750
9:41 **Vol. 3:** 582, 890
10 f **Vol. 3:** 1115
10 **Vol. 1:** 303 **Vol. 2:** 459 **Vol. 3:** 187, 567
10:1–42 **Vol. 2:** 751
10:1–30 **Vol. 3:** 567
10:1–11 **Vol. 2:** 413
10:1–5 **Vol. 2:** 751
10:1–3 **Vol. 2:** 31
10:1 f **Vol. 2:** 30
10:1 **Vol. 3:** 378
10:2 f **Vol. 3:** 314
10:3 f **Vol. 2:** 839 **Vol. 3:** 566
10:3 **Vol. 2:** 652, 728 **Vol. 3:** 114, 314
10:4 **Vol. 1:** 453, 483 **Vol. 3:** 568
10:5 **Vol. 1:** 559, 684 **Vol. 2:** 742
10:6 **Vol. 2:** 757
10:7–9 **Vol. 1:** 303

10:7 **Vol. 2:** 31, 279–280
10:8 **Vol. 2:** 280 **Vol. 3:** 378
10:9 **Vol. 2:** 31, 80, 279–280 **Vol. 3:** 216
10:10 ff **Vol. 2:** 80
10:10 **Vol. 1:** 323, 464, 729 **Vol. 2:** 482 **Vol. 3:** 378, 445, 728
10:11 ff **Vol. 1:** 464
10:11 **Vol. 1:** 398 **Vol. 2:** 101, 104, 279–280 **Vol. 3:** 611, 683
10:12 **Vol. 1:** 118, 559 **Vol. 2:** 34 **Vol. 3:** 602
10:14 ff **Vol. 2:** 721, 723
10:14 f **Vol. 2:** 403–404
10:14 **Vol. 2:** 101, 104, 279–280
10:15 **Vol. 1:** 438 **Vol. 2:** 610, 653, 747 **Vol. 3:** 313, 611, 640
10:15a **Vol. 1:** 620
10:15b **Vol. 2:** 42
10:16 **Vol. 1:** 338 **Vol. 2:** 177, 413, 928 **Vol. 3:** 114, 463, 567
10:17 f **Vol. 1:** 260 **Vol. 3:** 611
10:17 **Vol. 1:** 337 **Vol. 2:** 217, 546 **Vol. 3:** 683
10:18 **Vol. 1:** 337 **Vol. 2:** 217, 610 **Vol. 3:** 567, 748
10:19 **Vol. 3:** 543
10:20 f **Vol. 1:** 453, 637
10:20 **Vol. 1:** 529
10:21 **Vol. 2:** 604, 726, 728 **Vol. 3:** 1122
10:22–29 **Vol. 1:** 629
10:22 **Vol. 3:** 366
10:23 **Vol. 2:** 236 **Vol. 3:** 789, 792
10:24 f **Vol. 2:** 653, 736
10:24 **Vol. 2:** 736 **Vol. 3:** 683
10:25 **Vol. 3:** 1045, 1150
10:26 ff **Vol. 1:** 304
10:27–29 **Vol. 2:** 101
10:27–28 **Vol. 3:** 114
10:27 f **Vol. 3:** 568, 837
10:27 **Vol. 1:** 483 **Vol. 2:** 177 **Vol. 3:** 114
10:28 f **Vol. 2:** 42
10:28 **Vol. 1:** 440, 464 **Vol. 2:** 80, 149, 482 **Vol. 3:** 602, 830, 832
10:29 **Vol. 2:** 149, 426 **Vol. 3:** 602
10:30 **Vol. 1:** 620 **Vol. 2:** 79, 217, 505, 721–722, 725
10:32 **Vol. 3:** 187, 1045
10:33–36 **Vol. 3:** 629
10:33 **Vol. 2:** 231, 565 **Vol. 3:** 187
10:34–38 **Vol. 3:** 622
10:34–36 **Vol. 3:** 187
10:34† **Vol. 2:** 448 **Vol. 3:** 187
10:35 f **Vol. 3:** 186, 329
10:35 **Vol. 3:** 188, 491–492
10:36 **Vol. 2:** 231 **Vol. 3:** 187, 342, 611
10:37 **Vol. 3:** 187, 1149, 1212
10:38 **Vol. 3:** 187, 1192
10:38a **Vol. 3:** 1212
10:39 **Vol. 3:** 187
10:40 **Vol. 3:** 991

John *(cont'd)*

10:41 f   **Vol. 3:** 1197
10:41   **Vol. 3:** 890
10:42   **Vol. 1:** 702
11   **Vol. 1:** 265, 445   **Vol. 2:** 630   **Vol. 3:** 558, 980
11:1 ff   **Vol. 2:** 168, 480, 632
11:1 – 12:8   **Vol. 3:** 1060
11:1 – 44   **Vol. 3:** 303, 1059
11:1   **Vol. 3:** 1174, 1176, 1180
11:2   **Vol. 1:** 120, 239   **Vol. 2:** 295
11:3   **Vol. 2:** 548
11:4   **Vol. 2:** 46, 48, 632   **Vol. 3:** 998, 1206
11:6   **Vol. 1:** 265
11:7 – 10   **Vol. 2:** 706
11:8   **Vol. 3:** 115
11:9 f   **Vol. 2:** 706, 751   **Vol. 3:** 945
11:9   **Vol. 3:** 847
11:10   **Vol. 1:** 421   **Vol. 2:** 493
11:11 – 14   **Vol. 1:** 443
11:11   **Vol. 2:** 549   **Vol. 3:** 280
11:12   **Vol. 3:** 216
11:13   **Vol. 1:** 442   **Vol. 3:** 822
11:14   **Vol. 2:** 736, 873
11:15   **Vol. 3:** 911
11:16   **Vol. 1:** 488
11:17   **Vol. 1:** 265   **Vol. 2:** 418, 689   **Vol. 3:** 247
11:19   **Vol. 1:** 329   **Vol. 2:** 418
11:20 ff   **Vol. 3:** 1060
11:24   **Vol. 2:** 57 – 58, 894, 900   **Vol. 3:** 277, 280
11:25 ff   **Vol. 2:** 546
11:25 f   **Vol. 1:** 324   **Vol. 2:** 42, 367, 567   **Vol. 3:** 832
11:25   **Vol. 1:** 436, 603   **Vol. 2:** 81, 279 – 280, 388, 482, 928 – 929   **Vol. 3:** 277, 280, 647
11:26   **Vol. 2:** 900   **Vol. 3:** 830
11:26b   **Vol. 3:** 1211
11:27 f   **Vol. 3:** 768
11:27   **Vol. 3:** 646
11:28   **Vol. 2:** 899
11:30   **Vol. 2:** 418
11:31 ff   **Vol. 3:** 1060
11:31   **Vol. 1:** 329   **Vol. 2:** 416, 418   **Vol. 3:** 247, 822
11:32   **Vol. 1:** 609
11:33   **Vol. 2:** 416, 418, 878   **Vol. 3:** 694, 710
11:35   **Vol. 2:** 418
11:36   **Vol. 2:** 542, 548
11:37   **Vol. 3:** 280
11:38   **Vol. 2:** 418   **Vol. 3:** 247, 381
11:39   **Vol. 1:** 430   **Vol. 3:** 1060
11:40   **Vol. 2:** 631 – 632   **Vol. 3:** 280, 313 – 314
11:41 f   **Vol. 3:** 819
11:41   **Vol. 1:** 620   **Vol. 2:** 76, 178, 187   **Vol. 3:** 646
11:42   **Vol. 3:** 1184

11:43   **Vol. 2:** 178   **Vol. 3:** 113, 280
11:44   **Vol. 1:** 265, 489   **Vol. 2:** 149   **Vol. 3:** 179
11:46 f   **Vol. 2:** 812
11:47 ff   **Vol. 3:** 440
11:47   **Vol. 1:** 364   **Vol. 2:** 32
11:48   **Vol. 2:** 793   **Vol. 3:** 39
11:49 ff   **Vol. 2:** 399
11:49   **Vol. 1:** 397   **Vol. 3:** 39
11:49b – 53   **Vol. 3:** 39
11:50 ff   **Vol. 2:** 793
11:50 f   **Vol. 3:** 611
11:50   **Vol. 1:** 398   **Vol. 2:** 434, 721, 723, 799   **Vol. 3:** 824, 826, 1174, 1197
11:51 f   **Vol. 3:** 1197
11:51   **Vol. 1:** 326   **Vol. 3:** 39
11:52   **Vol. 1:** 297   **Vol. 2:** 32, 34, 722 – 723, 928
11:53   **Vol. 1:** 430
11:54   **Vol. 2:** 217
11:55 f   **Vol. 2:** 927
11:55   **Vol. 1:** 265, 629, 632 – 634   **Vol. 3:** 101
11:56   **Vol. 3:** 792, 822
11:57   **Vol. 1:** 337   **Vol. 2:** 812
12 ff   **Vol. 1:** 629
12   **Vol. 1:** 630
12:1 ff   **Vol. 1:** 630
12:1 – 11   **Vol. 3:** 980
12:1   **Vol. 1:** 445, 630, 633   **Vol. 3:** 1061
12:2 – 11   **Vol. 1:** 265
12:2   **Vol. 3:** 546, 1060
12:3   **Vol. 1:** 120, 239, 736   **Vol. 2:** 295   **Vol. 3:** 600, 1060
12:4 ff   **Vol. 1:** 642   **Vol. 3:** 1060
12:5   **Vol. 2:** 295
12:6   **Vol. 1:** 143   **Vol. 3:** 378
12:7 f   **Vol. 3:** 1060
12:7   **Vol. 1:** 265   **Vol. 2:** 133, 434
12:8   **Vol. 2:** 824
12:9   **Vol. 1:** 445   **Vol. 2:** 801
12:10   **Vol. 3:** 39
12:12 ff   **Vol. 1:** 630   **Vol. 2:** 328, 339
12:12 – 19   **Vol. 2:** 379   **Vol. 3:** 791
12:12 – 15   **Vol. 1:** 629
12:12   **Vol. 2:** 927
12:13   **Vol. 1:** 100, 212, 409   **Vol. 2:** 231   **Vol. 3:** 652
12:14   **Vol. 1:** 117   **Vol. 3:** 188
12:15   **Vol. 1:** 117, 623, 718   **Vol. 2:** 327
12:16   **Vol. 2:** 46, 546   **Vol. 3:** 1122
12:17   **Vol. 3:** 114, 247, 1044
12:19   **Vol. 1:** 493
12:20 ff   **Vol. 2:** 126
12:20   **Vol. 2:** 877, 927
12:21 f   **Vol. 2:** 550
12:21   **Vol. 2:** 513, 879
12:23 ff   **Vol. 2:** 546
12:23 – 28   **Vol. 2:** 48
12:23   **Vol. 2:** 927   **Vol. 3:** 631
12:24 – 26   **Vol. 1:** 441

John *(cont'd)*

12:24   **Vol. 1:** 609, 722   **Vol. 2:** 724, 751   **Vol. 3:** 524
12:25 f   **Vol. 2:** 433   **Vol. 3:** 530
12:25   **Vol. 1:** 464, 556   **Vol. 2:** 135, 482   **Vol. 3:** 174, 212, 682, 832, 843
12:26 ff   **Vol. 1:** 482
12:26   **Vol. 1:** 483   **Vol. 2:** 50   **Vol. 3:** 546
12:27 f   **Vol. 1:** 620   **Vol. 2:** 873   **Vol. 3:** 646
12:27   **Vol. 2:** 83, 927   **Vol. 3:** 211, 216, 710, 848
12:28   **Vol. 2:** 193, 653   **Vol. 3:** 114, 848
12:29   **Vol. 3:** 1002
12:30   **Vol. 3:** 1184
12:31   **Vol. 1:** 83, 168, 525–526   **Vol. 2:** 38, 193, 609, 631, 702   **Vol. 3:** 470, 582, 802
12:32   **Vol. 1:** 483, 510   **Vol. 2:** 202, 204, 567, 928
12:33   **Vol. 1:** 326, 438, 738
12:34   **Vol. 2:** 202, 204, 339, 448   **Vol. 3:** 631, 830
12:35 f   **Vol. 1:** 638   **Vol. 3:** 945
12:35   **Vol. 1:** 424   **Vol. 2:** 80, 429   **Vol. 3:** 750, 945
12:36   **Vol. 1:** 289   **Vol. 2:** 494   **Vol. 3:** 1213
12:37 ff   **Vol. 2:** 632   **Vol. 3:** 460
12:37–43 **Vol. 2:** 632
12:37–41 **Vol. 3:** 131
12:38 f   **Vol. 1:** 736
12:38   **Vol. 1:** 736   **Vol. 3:** 312, 314, 321
12:39 ff   **Vol. 1:** 261   **Vol. 3:** 313
12:40   **Vol. 1:** 355   **Vol. 2:** 155, 178, 753   **Vol. 3:** 128, 132
12:41   **Vol. 1:** 736   **Vol. 2:** 46, 48
12:42   **Vol. 1:** 168, 181, 347   **Vol. 2:** 312
12:43   **Vol. 2:** 543
12:44 ff   **Vol. 1:** 409
12:44   **Vol. 1:** 483   **Vol. 3:** 314
12:44c   **Vol. 3:** 1214
12:45   **Vol. 1:** 587   **Vol. 2:** 79, 404   **Vol. 3:** 517
12:46 f   **Vol. 1:** 323
12:46   **Vol. 1:** 424   **Vol. 2:** 494
12:47 f   **Vol. 1:** 171   **Vol. 3:** 1114
12:47   **Vol. 1:** 525   **Vol. 2:** 135   **Vol. 3:** 216
12:48   **Vol. 1:** 74, 637   **Vol. 2:** 58, 929   **Vol. 3:** 136, 748–749, 1114
12:49 f   **Vol. 1:** 337, 620   **Vol. 2:** 930
12:49   **Vol. 1:** 337   **Vol. 3:** 645
12:50   **Vol. 1:** 337   **Vol. 2:** 482   **Vol. 3:** 832
13–17   **Vol. 1:** 490   **Vol. 2:** 911
13   **Vol. 2:** 434
13:1 ff   **Vol. 2:** 754
13:1–17:26 **Vol. 2:** 751
13:1–30   **Vol. 2:** 526, 534
13:1–20   **Vol. 3:** 226, 990
13:1–15   **Vol. 3:** 547

13:1   **Vol. 1:** 630, 633, 738   **Vol. 2:** 64, 186, 217, 528, 927   **Vol. 3:** 848
13:2 ff   **Vol. 3:** 804
13:2   **Vol. 1:** 299   **Vol. 2:** 526   **Vol. 3:** 470
13:3   **Vol. 1:** 322   **Vol. 2:** 79, 149, 610, 653, 738   **Vol. 3:** 1174
13:4 ff   **Vol. 3:** 611
13:4–16   **Vol. 1:** 549
13:4 f   **Vol. 3:** 121
13:4   **Vol. 2:** 264
13:5–14   **Vol. 1:** 239
13:5   **Vol. 1:** 167, 239   **Vol. 3:** 989
13:6   **Vol. 2:** 514
13:7   **Vol. 1:** 154   **Vol. 2:** 398
13:8   **Vol. 1:** 241   **Vol. 2:** 304   **Vol. 3:** 829–830
13:9   **Vol. 2:** 159
13:10   **Vol. 1:** 152–153   **Vol. 3:** 107, 704
13:13 ff   **Vol. 1:** 154
13:13 f   **Vol. 3:** 768
13:13   **Vol. 3:** 116
13:14   **Vol. 2:** 535   **Vol. 3:** 116, 945
13:15   **Vol. 1:** 492   **Vol. 2:** 291   **Vol. 3:** 547, 597, 905, 1155
13:16   **Vol. 1:** 129, 134, 404   **Vol. 3:** 629
13:17   **Vol. 1:** 217
13:18   **Vol. 1:** 540, 542, 736   **Vol. 3:** 188, 329, 490, 492
13:20   **Vol. 1:** 91, 285   **Vol. 2:** 176, 535, 920   **Vol. 3:** 314, 326, 629, 746, 748
13:21   **Vol. 2:** 878   **Vol. 3:** 694
13:23   **Vol. 1:** 78, 240   **Vol. 3:** 589, 1174, 1186
13:25   **Vol. 3:** 589
13:26–30 **Vol. 2:** 321
13:26   **Vol. 1:** 145   **Vol. 2:** 528
13:27   **Vol. 3:** 470, 473
13:29   **Vol. 1:** 143, 642   **Vol. 2:** 927   **Vol. 3:** 822
13:30   **Vol. 1:** 421   **Vol. 2:** 528
13:31 ff   **Vol. 1:** 630
13:31 f   **Vol. 2:** 46   **Vol. 3:** 631
13:31   **Vol. 3:** 631
13:33   **Vol. 1:** 286   **Vol. 2:** 429
13:34 f   **Vol. 1:** 303, 490, 526, 719
13:34   **Vol. 1:** 335, 337–338, 738   **Vol. 2:** 43, 546, 671, 673
13:35 f   **Vol. 1:** 483
13:35   **Vol. 1:** 338, 490   **Vol. 2:** 398, 404
13:36   **Vol. 3:** 954
13:37 f   **Vol. 3:** 683
13:38   **Vol. 1:** 702
14–16   **Vol. 2:** 339, 780   **Vol. 3:** 697
14:1–6   **Vol. 3:** 941
14:1   **Vol. 1:** 355   **Vol. 3:** 710
14:1a   **Vol. 3:** 1214
14:2 ff   **Vol. 2:** 751
14:2 f   **Vol. 1:** 440   **Vol. 2:** 727, 929   **Vol. 3:** 118, 946
14:2   **Vol. 2:** 250   **Vol. 3:** 229
14:3   **Vol. 3:** 751

185

John (*cont'd*)

14:4 f	**Vol. 3:** 185
14:6–10	**Vol. 3:** 326
14:6	**Vol. 1:** 355, 375, 489, 620 **Vol. 2:** 31, 48, 80–81, 279, 281, 460, 482, 610, 751 **Vol. 3:** 163, 395, 647, 742, 832, 890–891, 893, 941, 1114
14:7 ff	**Vol. 3:** 185
14:7	**Vol. 1:** 620 **Vol. 2:** 404 **Vol. 3:** 314
14:8 f	**Vol. 2:** 550 **Vol. 3:** 569
14:8	**Vol. 3:** 728
14:9	**Vol. 1:** 338, 587, 620 **Vol. 2:** 79, 288, 404, 722, 766 **Vol. 3:** 314, 517, 891
14:10 f	**Vol. 1:** 620 **Vol. 3:** 1192
14:10	**Vol. 2:** 79, 505 **Vol. 3:** 224–225, 1114, 1122, 1149
14:10b	**Vol. 3:** 1193
14:11	**Vol. 3:** 1150, 1212
14:12 ff	**Vol. 3:** 1155
14:12	**Vol. 3:** 946, 1149–1150, 1155
14:13 f	**Vol. 2:** 654, 857–858
14:14	**Vol. 3:** 1114
14:15 ff	**Vol. 1:** 630
14:15–17	**Vol. 1:** 490
14:15	**Vol. 1:** 337–338, 526 **Vol. 2:** 133
14:16 ff	**Vol. 1:** 324
14:16–28	**Vol. 3:** 704
14:16 f	**Vol. 1:** 89 **Vol. 2:** 787
14:16	**Vol. 1:** 90, 324 **Vol. 2:** 359, 857, 878–879 **Vol. 3:** 704, 830
14:17	**Vol. 1:** 89–90, 303 **Vol. 2:** 403, 604, 878 **Vol. 3:** 225, 892, 1114, 1205
14:18–24	**Vol. 2:** 787
14:18	**Vol. 2:** 359, 738
14:19	**Vol. 2:** 359, 429
14:19b	**Vol. 1:** 701
14:20	**Vol. 2:** 359 **Vol. 3:** 1192
14:21 ff	**Vol. 2:** 546
14:21 f	**Vol. 2:** 489 **Vol. 3:** 314
14:21	**Vol. 1:** 337–338 **Vol. 2:** 133
14:22 ff	**Vol. 3:** 185
14:22	**Vol. 1:** 326
14:23 f	**Vol. 2:** 133, 546
14:23	**Vol. 1:** 337, 526 **Vol. 2:** 727 **Vol. 3:** 229, 1205
14:24	**Vol. 1:** 128, 337 **Vol. 3:** 229, 1114
14:25	**Vol. 3:** 764, 1205
14:26	**Vol. 1:** 89–90, 123, 324 **Vol. 2:** 231, 359, 654, 687, 878 **Vol. 3:** 242, 314, 403, 704, 763–764, 942–943, 1203
14:27	**Vol. 1:** 622 **Vol. 2:** 359, 780–781 **Vol. 3:** 710
14:28	**Vol. 2:** 426, 500 **Vol. 3:** 946
14:30	**Vol. 1:** 168 **Vol. 2:** 609 **Vol. 3:** 470, 802
14:31	**Vol. 1:** 337 **Vol. 2:** 404, 546 **Vol. 3:** 280
15	**Vol. 3:** 567
15:1 ff	**Vol. 1:** 303
15:1 f	**Vol. 3:** 868–869
15:1–16	**Vol. 2:** 751
15:1–11	**Vol. 3:** 921
15:1–8	**Vol. 2:** 313 **Vol. 3:** 226
15:1	**Vol. 2:** 279–281 **Vol. 3:** 893
15:2 ff	**Vol. 1:** 722 **Vol. 2:** 449
15:2	**Vol. 1:** 723 **Vol. 3:** 102
15:3	**Vol. 3:** 107, 1114
15:4 ff	**Vol. 1:** 285 **Vol. 2:** 546
15:4 f	**Vol. 3:** 225, 1192
15:4	**Vol. 2:** 359 **Vol. 3:** 226
15:5 ff	**Vol. 2:** 101
15:5	**Vol. 1:** 723 **Vol. 2:** 279, 281 **Vol. 3:** 226, 1155
15:6	**Vol. 1:** 515, 608, 656 **Vol. 2:** 32 **Vol. 3:** 226
15:7 ff	**Vol. 1:** 290
15:7	**Vol. 2:** 359, 857–858 **Vol. 3:** 226, 921, 1114, 1122
15:8	**Vol. 1:** 490, 723
15:9 ff	**Vol. 1:** 526, 630
15:9–17	**Vol. 2:** 482 **Vol. 3:** 226
15:9 f	**Vol. 2:** 546
15:9	**Vol. 2:** 359, 404, 546 **Vol. 3:** 226, 921
15:10	**Vol. 1:** 337–338, 549 **Vol. 2:** 133 **Vol. 3:** 226, 921
15:11	**Vol. 1:** 741 **Vol. 2:** 359 **Vol. 3:** 921
15:12 ff	**Vol. 1:** 338
15:12	**Vol. 1:** 337–338 **Vol. 2:** 546
15:13	**Vol. 1:** 257 **Vol. 2:** 359, 549, 673
15:14	**Vol. 2:** 750 **Vol. 3:** 1062
15:15	**Vol. 2:** 178 **Vol. 3:** 314, 613
15:16	**Vol. 1:** 540, 542, 723 **Vol. 2:** 359, 654, 857–858 **Vol. 3:** 226
15:17	**Vol. 1:** 338 **Vol. 2:** 546
15:18 ff	**Vol. 1:** 525, 556 **Vol. 2:** 806
15:18–27	**Vol. 2:** 709
15:18	**Vol. 1:** 603 **Vol. 2:** 398, 403
15:19	**Vol. 1:** 525–526, 540, 542 **Vol. 2:** 359, 542, 548 **Vol. 3:** 1171, 1188
15:20	**Vol. 1:** 337, 404, 549 **Vol. 2:** 806
15:21	**Vol. 3:** 257
15:22 ff	**Vol. 3:** 1150
15:22–24	**Vol. 3:** 582
15:23	**Vol. 1:** 603
15:24	**Vol. 3:** 1149–1150
15:25	**Vol. 1:** 556, 736 **Vol. 2:** 41, 448 **Vol. 3:** 329, 489
15:26 f	**Vol. 1:** 490, 683
15:26	**Vol. 1:** 89–90, 123, 324 **Vol. 2:** 687, 878 **Vol. 3:** 314, 403, 704, 892, 1046, 1202–1203
15:27	**Vol. 1:** 166 **Vol. 3:** 1046
16:1 ff	**Vol. 3:** 849
16:1	**Vol. 2:** 708–709
16:2 ff	**Vol. 2:** 751
16:2 f	**Vol. 2:** 403
16:2	**Vol. 2:** 359 **Vol. 3:** 551, 822, 848
16:4	**Vol. 1:** 166
16:5–15	**Vol. 2:** 895

John *(cont'd)*

16:5   **Vol. 1:** 630   **Vol. 2:** 879
16:6   **Vol. 1:** 297
16:7 ff   **Vol. 1:** 91
16:7   **Vol. 1:** 89–90, 324   **Vol. 2:** 878,
        929   **Vol. 3:** 890, 946
16:8 ff   **Vol. 2:** 141
16:8–11   **Vol. 1:** 270   **Vol. 2:** 48   **Vol. 3:** 705
16:8 f   **Vol. 3:** 582
16:8   **Vol. 1:** 89   **Vol. 2:** 141, 927   **Vol. 3:**
        362
16:9 ff   **Vol. 1:** 89
16:9   **Vol. 3:** 136
16:10   **Vol. 2:** 359, 699   **Vol. 3:** 362
16:11   **Vol. 1:** 168, 525–526   **Vol. 2:** 365,
        609   **Vol. 3:** 470, 582, 802
16:12 ff   **Vol. 1:** 90, 324
16:12 f   **Vol. 3:** 704
16:13 f   **Vol. 1:** 89, 123
16:13   **Vol. 1:** 90   **Vol. 2:** 878   **Vol. 3:** 47,
        258, 314–315, 892, 942
16:14   **Vol. 2:** 84   **Vol. 3:** 47, 704
16:15a   **Vol. 1:** 620
16:16 ff   **Vol. 2:** 895
16:16–19   **Vol. 2:** 429
16:16 f   **Vol. 3:** 515
16:16   **Vol. 1:** 741
16:17 f   **Vol. 3:** 185
16:19   **Vol. 2:** 879
16:20–24   **Vol. 2:** 482
16:20–22   **Vol. 2:** 420
16:20   **Vol. 1:** 741   **Vol. 2:** 417–419
16:21   **Vol. 1:** 178, 187, 284   **Vol. 2:** 751,
        809   **Vol. 3:** 848
16:22   **Vol. 1:** 91, 741   **Vol. 2:** 359, 421, 809
16:23–26   **Vol. 2:** 857
16:23 f   **Vol. 2:** 178, 857
16:23   **Vol. 2:** 857, 879
16:24   **Vol. 1:** 741   **Vol. 2:** 357, 858
16:25   **Vol. 2:** 757–758   **Vol. 3:** 47
16:26 f   **Vol. 2:** 857
16:26   **Vol. 2:** 857–858
16:27 f   **Vol. 2:** 79   **Vol. 3:** 1202
16:27   **Vol. 2:** 542, 548   **Vol. 3:** 1174
16:28   **Vol. 1:** 323   **Vol. 3:** 946, 1174
16:29   **Vol. 2:** 757–758
16:30   **Vol. 2:** 879   **Vol. 3:** 1174, 1192
16:32   **Vol. 2:** 34, 725, 839   **Vol. 3:** 516, 646,
        848
16:33   **Vol. 1:** 328, 526, 638, 651   **Vol. 2:** 359,
        780–781, 809, 911   **Vol. 3:** 1212
17   **Vol. 2:** 653, 723   **Vol. 3:** 38
17:1 ff   **Vol. 1:** 290
17:1   **Vol. 1:** 620, 738   **Vol. 2:** 46, 74, 76,
        192, 217, 873, 927   **Vol. 3:** 646
17:2 f   **Vol. 2:** 80   **Vol. 3:** 832
17:2   **Vol. 1:** 303, 678   **Vol. 2:** 482, 610
17:3   **Vol. 2:** 42, 73, 280, 339, 403–404, 482,
        724   **Vol. 3:** 630, 643, 645, 893

17:4 f   **Vol. 2:** 46
17:4   **Vol. 1:** 549   **Vol. 2:** 64, 79   **Vol. 3:**
        1150
17:5   **Vol. 1:** 620   **Vol. 2:** 46, 76,
        204   **Vol. 3:** 1205
17:6   **Vol. 1:** 304, 337   **Vol. 2:** 42, 217,
        653   **Vol. 3:** 312, 314, 321
17:8   **Vol. 1:** 603   **Vol. 2:** 404   **Vol. 3:**
        748–749, 1114, 1122, 1202
17:9   **Vol. 2:** 879
17:11 f   **Vol. 2:** 135, 653   **Vol. 3:** 645
17:11   **Vol. 1:** 620   **Vol. 2:** 76, 79, 133, 228,
        231, 721–722   **Vol. 3:** 1188
17:12   **Vol. 1:** 299, 464, 736   **Vol. 2:** 135,
        653   **Vol. 3:** 188, 329, 491, 529
17:13   **Vol. 1:** 741   **Vol. 2:** 359
17:14   **Vol. 1:** 526, 556   **Vol. 3:** 1114, 1171,
        1188
17:14b   **Vol. 3:** 1188
17:15   **Vol. 1:** 526, 566   **Vol. 2:** 133,
        879   **Vol. 3:** 472, 1188
17:16   **Vol. 1:** 526   **Vol. 3:** 1171, 1188
17:17   **Vol. 2:** 232   **Vol. 3:** 890, 892, 1114
17:18   **Vol. 1:** 526   **Vol. 3:** 892
17:19   **Vol. 2:** 232   **Vol. 3:** 38, 40
17:20 ff   **Vol. 1:** 338
17:20 f   **Vol. 2:** 413
17:20   **Vol. 1:** 158   **Vol. 2:** 879, 928   **Vol. 3:**
        1106
17:21 ff   **Vol. 2:** 404, 721
17:21   **Vol. 1:** 128, 304, 620   **Vol. 2:** 64, 79,
        722–723   **Vol. 3:** 1192
17:22   **Vol. 2:** 46–47   **Vol. 3:** 529
17:23 ff   **Vol. 2:** 546
17:23   **Vol. 2:** 64, 404, 722   **Vol. 3:** 1192
17:24 f   **Vol. 1:** 620
17:24   **Vol. 1:** 377–378   **Vol. 2:** 46, 482,
        929   **Vol. 3:** 518
17:25 f   **Vol. 1:** 620
17:25   **Vol. 1:** 128   **Vol. 2:** 610, 653   **Vol. 3:**
        362
17:26   **Vol. 2:** 404, 546, 653   **Vol. 3:** 314
18 f   **Vol. 2:** 378
18–21   **Vol. 1:** 305
18   **Vol. 1:** 633
18:1 ff   **Vol. 1:** 630
18:1–2   **Vol. 2:** 713
18:2–11   **Vol. 2:** 526
18:2   **Vol. 2:** 32
18:3 f   **Vol. 3:** 39
18:3   **Vol. 2:** 486   **Vol. 3:** 40, 547, 964
18:5   **Vol. 3:** 333
18:6   **Vol. 1:** 610
18:7   **Vol. 2:** 333
18:9   **Vol. 1:** 464, 736   **Vol. 3:** 529
18:10 f   **Vol. 3:** 967
18:11   **Vol. 2:** 276
18:12   **Vol. 1:** 343   **Vol. 2:** 315, 699   **Vol. 3:**
        547
18:13–24   **Vol. 3:** 409

John *(cont'd)*

18:13	**Vol. 1:** 630 **Vol. 3:** 39
18:14	**Vol. 1:** 363 **Vol. 3:** 611, 1197
18:15	**Vol. 1:** 321
18:16 ff	**Vol. 3:** 1122
18:16	**Vol. 2:** 30
18:17	**Vol. 3:** 804
18:18 ff	**Vol. 1:** 318
18:18	**Vol. 1:** 318 **Vol. 3:** 547
18:19	**Vol. 2:** 879 **Vol. 3:** 769
18:20	**Vol. 2:** 217 **Vol. 3:** 761, 764, 785, 791
18:21	**Vol. 2:** 879
18:22 ff	**Vol. 1:** 299
18:22 f	**Vol. 2:** 451
18:22	**Vol. 3:** 547
18:23	**Vol. 3:** 1044
18:24	**Vol. 1:** 630 **Vol. 3:** 39–40
18:25 ff	**Vol. 1:** 455 **Vol. 3:** 804, 1122
18:27	**Vol. 1:** 173
18:28–19:24	**Vol. 1:** 394
18:28	**Vol. 1:** 265, 448, 630, 633–634 **Vol. 2:** 527–528, 927 **Vol. 3:** 39
18:29	**Vol. 1:** 83
18:31	**Vol. 1:** 364, 395 **Vol. 2:** 365, 449, 451
18:32	**Vol. 1:** 326, 438, 736
18:33 ff	**Vol. 2:** 339
18:33	**Vol. 2:** 315
18:35	**Vol. 2:** 315, 793
18:36 f	**Vol. 2:** 339
18:36–37	**Vol. 3:** 977
18:36	**Vol. 1:** 646 **Vol. 2:** 387, 641 **Vol. 3:** 1188
18:37	**Vol. 1:** 304, 323, 427, 603 **Vol. 3:** 114, 462, 652, 892, 1045
18:37d	**Vol. 3:** 890
18:38	**Vol. 1:** 270 **Vol. 2:** 139 **Vol. 3:** 529, 893
18:38b	**Vol. 1:** 395
18:39	**Vol. 1:** 633 **Vol. 2:** 315, 927 **Vol. 3:** 189
18:40	**Vol. 1:** 409 **Vol. 3:** 378
19	**Vol. 1:** 630, 633
19:1	**Vol. 1:** 162
19:2	**Vol. 1:** 205, 316, 406 **Vol. 2:** 159 **Vol. 3:** 964
19:3	**Vol. 1:** 162 **Vol. 2:** 315, 358
19:4	**Vol. 1:** 395 **Vol. 2:** 139, 398 **Vol. 3:** 529
19:5	**Vol. 1:** 205, 406, 726 **Vol. 2:** 565
19:6 f	**Vol. 1:** 395
19:6	**Vol. 2:** 139 **Vol. 3:** 39, 529, 916
19:7	**Vol. 2:** 443, 448–449
19:10	**Vol. 3:** 189
19:11	**Vol. 1:** 179 **Vol. 3:** 97, 582, 916
19:12–16	**Vol. 1:** 270
19:12 f	**Vol. 1:** 395
19:12	**Vol. 1:** 409 **Vol. 2:** 549 **Vol. 3:** 189, 1154
19:13	**Vol. 2:** 309, 369 **Vol. 3:** 588–589, 1185
19:14	**Vol. 1:** 629–630, 633–634 **Vol. 2:** 463, 527–528, 927 **Vol. 3:** 120, 410, 847, 916
19:15	**Vol. 3:** 39, 916
19:15b	**Vol. 1:** 395
19:17	**Vol. 2:** 309
19:19 ff	**Vol. 1:** 323 **Vol. 2:** 315, 339
19:19	**Vol. 2:** 315, 333–334, 379 **Vol. 3:** 509, 652
19:20	**Vol. 2:** 54, 126, 309
19:21 f	**Vol. 2:** 339
19:21	**Vol. 2:** 315
19:23	**Vol. 2:** 303, 689
19:24	**Vol. 1:** 396, 478, 736 **Vol. 2:** 299 **Vol. 3:** 490, 492, 543, 670
19:25	**Vol. 2:** 82 **Vol. 3:** 662, 1060–1061, 1201, 1205
19:26 f	**Vol. 3:** 1070
19:26	**Vol. 3:** 1058
19:27	**Vol. 2:** 839 **Vol. 3:** 846
19:28	**Vol. 1:** 736 **Vol. 2:** 64, 267 **Vol. 3:** 491–492
19:29 f	**Vol. 2:** 28
19:29	**Vol. 3:** 913
19:30	**Vol. 1:** 335 **Vol. 2:** 64, 159, 368, 787, 929 **Vol. 3:** 704
19:31	**Vol. 1:** 234 **Vol. 2:** 463, 879–880 **Vol. 3:** 120, 408, 410
19:32–36	**Vol. 1:** 629
19:32	**Vol. 1:** 393, 666
19:34	**Vol. 1:** 221 **Vol. 2:** 787 **Vol. 3:** 704, 990
19:35	**Vol. 2:** 280 **Vol. 3:** 517–518
19:36 f	**Vol. 3:** 490
19:36	**Vol. 1:** 241, 634, 720, 736 **Vol. 2:** 527 **Vol. 3:** 492
19:37†	**Vol. 2:** 739
19:38	**Vol. 2:** 217, 879
19:39	**Vol. 1:** 265 **Vol. 2:** 295, 812 **Vol. 3:** 294
19:40	**Vol. 2:** 295, 437 **Vol. 3:** 296
19:41 f	**Vol. 3:** 247
19:41	**Vol. 2:** 670
19:42	**Vol. 3:** 120, 408, 410
20	**Vol. 2:** 780 **Vol. 3:** 276, 283
20:1 ff	**Vol. 1:** 630
20:1–21:25	**Vol. 3:** 294
20:1–18	**Vol. 3:** 1060
20:1–4	**Vol. 3:** 247
20:1	**Vol. 1:** 423 **Vol. 3:** 393, 412
20:2	**Vol. 3:** 288, 296, 947
20:3–6	**Vol. 3:** 1185
20:3	**Vol. 3:** 1174
20:4	**Vol. 1:** 666 **Vol. 3:** 947
20:6	**Vol. 3:** 247
20:7 f	**Vol. 3:** 297
20:7	**Vol. 2:** 159
20:8	**Vol. 3:** 247, 517, 1185

John *(cont'd)*

20:9	**Vol. 1:** 445 **Vol. 2:** 666 **Vol. 3:** 490, 492
20:11	**Vol. 3:** 247
20:12	**Vol. 1:** 204 **Vol. 2:** 159 **Vol. 3:** 294
20:13	**Vol. 3:** 285
20:14 ff	**Vol. 3:** 287
20:14–29	**Vol. 3:** 518
20:15	**Vol. 2:** 513, 739 **Vol. 3:** 822
20:16	**Vol. 2:** 309 **Vol. 3:** 115, 767
20:17	**Vol. 2:** 185 **Vol. 3:** 276, 860, 941
20:18	**Vol. 3:** 46, 48, 1060
20:19–23	**Vol. 3:** 286, 295
20:19	**Vol. 1:** 622 **Vol. 2:** 30, 730, 780 **Vol. 3:** 297
20:20	**Vol. 1:** 393 **Vol. 2:** 359, 624 **Vol. 3:** 569
20:21 ff	**Vol. 1:** 136
20:21–29	**Vol. 3:** 295
20:21	**Vol. 1:** 526 **Vol. 2:** 176, 654, 733, 780, 787, 927 **Vol. 3:** 286
20:22 f	**Vol. 3:** 705
20:22	**Vol. 2:** 231, 787, 878, 929 **Vol. 3:** 460, 694, 698, 703–704, 749
20:23	**Vol. 1:** 303, 702–703 **Vol. 2:** 733, 787 **Vol. 3:** 387, 580, 717
20:24–29	**Vol. 3:** 289
20:24	**Vol. 2:** 695
20:25 ff	**Vol. 1:** 393
20:25	**Vol. 2:** 150 **Vol. 3:** 518
20:25a	**Vol. 3:** 904
20:26	**Vol. 2:** 692, 730, 780 **Vol. 3:** 297
20:27	**Vol. 1:** 602 **Vol. 2:** 150 **Vol. 3:** 276
20:28	**Vol. 2:** 81, 513–515, 725
20:29	**Vol. 1:** 217, 603 **Vol. 3:** 517
20:30 f	**Vol. 1:** 136, 244 **Vol. 3:** 489
20:30	**Vol. 1:** 244 **Vol. 2:** 632
20:31	**Vol. 1:** 148, 287, 290, 599 **Vol. 2:** 80, 231, 339 **Vol. 3:** 646, 1213
20:31a	**Vol. 3:** 1211
21	**Vol. 3:** 276, 283
21:1–23	**Vol. 3:** 295
21:1–19	**Vol. 2:** 630
21:1–11	**Vol. 3:** 985
21:1	**Vol. 3:** 312, 314, 321, 984
21:3–10	**Vol. 3:** 295
21:3	**Vol. 3:** 757
21:6	**Vol. 1:** 671, 733 **Vol. 2:** 146, 303
21:7	**Vol. 1:** 313 **Vol. 3:** 121
21:9	**Vol. 1:** 670
21:11–17	**Vol. 3:** 295
21:11	**Vol. 2:** 684–685 **Vol. 3:** 543
21:12 f	**Vol. 3:** 276
21:12	**Vol. 1:** 365 **Vol. 2:** 624
21:13	**Vol. 2:** 524
21:14	**Vol. 1:** 445 **Vol. 3:** 312, 314, 321
21:15 ff	**Vol. 1:** 136 **Vol. 2:** 542, 548, 928
21:15–17	**Vol. 3:** 568
21:15	**Vol. 2:** 411, 548 **Vol. 3:** 386
21:16 ff	**Vol. 3:** 387
21:16	**Vol. 2:** 548 **Vol. 3:** 568
21:17	**Vol. 2:** 398, 548 **Vol. 3:** 386
21:18	**Vol. 2:** 150, 675 **Vol. 3:** 121
21:19 ff	**Vol. 1:** 482
21:20	**Vol. 3:** 589
21:22 f	**Vol. 2:** 930
21:24	**Vol. 1:** 136 **Vol. 3:** 489
21:25	**Vol. 1:** 244, 742

Acts

1–12	**Vol. 3:** 1114
1–7	**Vol. 3:** 1114
1–5	**Vol. 2:** 314
1	**Vol. 1:** 90 **Vol. 3:** 387
1:1 ff	**Vol. 2:** 787
1:1	**Vol. 1:** 167, 247 **Vol. 2:** 86 **Vol. 3:** 88, 764, 1106
1:2–16	**Vol. 2:** 921
1:2	**Vol. 1:** 335 **Vol. 3:** 276, 698, 749
1:3	**Vol. 1:** 128, 474 **Vol. 2:** 689, 696 **Vol. 3:** 516, 723, 1181
1:4	**Vol. 1:** 128, 340 **Vol. 2:** 245, 328, 786 **Vol. 3:** 70–71, 228, 296, 449, 534
1:5	**Vol. 1:** 158, 303 **Vol. 2:** 786 **Vol. 3:** 697–698, 990, 1210
1:6 ff	**Vol. 2:** 921 **Vol. 3:** 147
1:6–8	**Vol. 2:** 610
1:6 f	**Vol. 3:** 844
1:6	**Vol. 2:** 313, 315, 786, 879–880, 920
1:7	**Vol. 1:** 477 **Vol. 2:** 75, 609 **Vol. 3:** 838
1:8	**Vol. 1:** 129, 136, 303, 322, 335, 517 **Vol. 2:** 57, 176, 603, 632, 740, 786 **Vol. 3:** 87, 449, 456, 698, 700, 909, 1044, 1114
1:9 ff	**Vol. 2:** 918
1:9	**Vol. 3:** 276, 749, 1003, 1114
1:10 f	**Vol. 2:** 194 **Vol. 3:** 947
1:10	**Vol. 1:** 102, 204 **Vol. 3:** 520
1:11	**Vol. 2:** 192, 333, 713, 920 **Vol. 3:** 520, 749
1:12	**Vol. 2:** 54, 713 **Vol. 3:** 940–941
1:13–26	**Vol. 1:** 135
1:13	**Vol. 1:** 136, 488 **Vol. 2:** 320, 550 **Vol. 3:** 1167
1:14	**Vol. 1:** 256 **Vol. 2:** 768, 873 **Vol. 3:** 908, 1065
1:15	**Vol. 2:** 652, 740, 801 **Vol. 3:** 1194
1:16	**Vol. 1:** 343, 427, 736 **Vol. 2:** 663 **Vol. 3:** 490, 699, 942
1:17 ff	**Vol. 1:** 299
1:17	**Vol. 1:** 478 **Vol. 2:** 299 **Vol. 3:** 546
1:18–20	**Vol. 3:** 1008
1:18	**Vol. 1:** 93–94 **Vol. 2:** 600, 854 **Vol. 3:** 912
1:19	**Vol. 1:** 93
1:20	**Vol. 1:** 190, 244 **Vol. 3:** 671, 675, 1008

Acts *(cont'd)*

1:21 f   **Vol. 1:** 183   **Vol. 2:** 299, 786   **Vol. 3:** 764

1:21   **Vol. 1:** 322   **Vol. 2:** 663   **Vol. 3:** 769, 843–844

1:22   **Vol. 1:** 136   **Vol. 3:** 276–277, 660, 749, 1044

1:24 f   **Vol. 2:** 299, 873

1:24   **Vol. 1:** 540, 542   **Vol. 2:** 183   **Vol. 3:** 569

1:25   **Vol. 1:** 299   **Vol. 3:** 584

1:26   **Vol. 1:** 609   **Vol. 2:** 299, 787

2–5   **Vol. 3:** 699, 785

2   **Vol. 1:** 90, 129, 528   **Vol. 2:** 732, 784–785   **Vol. 3:** 387, 704, 1080

2:1 ff   **Vol. 2:** 328   **Vol. 3:** 86

2:1–13   **Vol. 2:** 784–785

2:1   **Vol. 1:** 737   **Vol. 2:** 784, 786   **Vol. 3:** 1194

2:2 f   **Vol. 2:** 632

2:2   **Vol. 1:** 736   **Vol. 2:** 193, 310   **Vol. 3:** 112, 559, 589, 707, 711

2:3 f   **Vol. 3:** 110

2:3   **Vol. 1:** 656   **Vol. 3:** 109, 571

2:4 ff   **Vol. 1:** 303

2:4–38   **Vol. 2:** 921

2:4   **Vol. 1:** 739   **Vol. 2:** 739, 786   **Vol. 3:** 699–700, 1080

2:5–11   **Vol. 3:** 700

2:5   **Vol. 2:** 91, 563, 786   **Vol. 3:** 197

2:6   **Vol. 2:** 786

2:7 f   **Vol. 2:** 740

2:7   **Vol. 2:** 625, 740

2:8   **Vol. 2:** 786

2:9–11   **Vol. 2:** 309, 786

2:9   **Vol. 1:** 427

2:10   **Vol. 1:** 532   **Vol. 2:** 740

2:11   **Vol. 1:** 361   **Vol. 2:** 426, 740, 786   **Vol. 3:** 1079–1080

2:13   **Vol. 2:** 739–740   **Vol. 3:** 700, 922

2:14–39   **Vol. 3:** 62

2:14–36   **Vol. 3:** 87

2:14   **Vol. 2:** 175   **Vol. 3:** 1070, 1080, 1122

2:15–21   **Vol. 2:** 38

2:15   **Vol. 1:** 514   **Vol. 3:** 749, 847

2:16 f   **Vol. 3:** 1191

2:16–21   **Vol. 3:** 1079

2:17 ff   **Vol. 3:** 699

2:17–36   **Vol. 2:** 315

2:17–21   **Vol. 2:** 654, 740, 916   **Vol. 3:** 71, 707, 732

2:17–18   **Vol. 2:** 855

2:17 f   **Vol. 2:** 42, 194, 785–786   **Vol. 3:** 86–87, 699–700, 1194

2:17   **Vol. 1:** 198, 512   **Vol. 2:** 58, 785, 787   **Vol. 3:** 87, 515, 700

2:18   **Vol. 2:** 786

2:19–20   **Vol. 3:** 732

2:19   **Vol. 1:** 224   **Vol. 2:** 187, 629   **Vol. 3:** 700

2:20   **Vol. 1:** 203–204, 224, 425   **Vol. 3:** 213, 318–319, 732, 734

2:21   **Vol. 3:** 732

2:22   **Vol. 2:** 333, 603, 629   **Vol. 3:** 570–571, 1154, 1198

2:23–32   **Vol. 3:** 1200

2:23 f   **Vol. 3:** 299

2:23   **Vol. 1:** 473, 693   **Vol. 3:** 1017

2:24   **Vol. 2:** 78   **Vol. 3:** 180, 717, 793, 858

2:25–35   **Vol. 2:** 186

2:25–28   **Vol. 3:** 262

2:25   **Vol. 1:** 427, 695   **Vol. 3:** 559

2:26 f   **Vol. 3:** 297

2:26   **Vol. 2:** 354, 356   **Vol. 3:** 813, 1079

2:27 ff   **Vol. 1:** 266

2:27   **Vol. 1:** 468, 470   **Vol. 2:** 207, 238, 919   **Vol. 3:** 651, 683

2:28   **Vol. 2:** 356   **Vol. 3:** 314, 940–941

2:29 f   **Vol. 1:** 66

2:29   **Vol. 1:** 65, 430   **Vol. 2:** 736   **Vol. 3:** 246

2:30   **Vol. 1:** 240, 722   **Vol. 2:** 79   **Vol. 3:** 742

2:31   **Vol. 1:** 468, 470, 677, 695   **Vol. 2:** 207, 340, 919   **Vol. 3:** 262, 276, 491, 515

2:32–36   **Vol. 2:** 194   **Vol. 3:** 71

2:32 f   **Vol. 3:** 298

2:32   **Vol. 2:** 78   **Vol. 3:** 56, 1044

2:33   **Vol. 1:** 153   **Vol. 2:** 148, 176, 202–203, 785–786, 855, 921   **Vol. 3:** 87–88, 698, 700, 705, 748

2:34   **Vol. 1:** 427   **Vol. 2:** 148, 185, 515   **Vol. 3:** 276

2:35   **Vol. 1:** 239, 477, 554

2:36   **Vol. 1:** 168, 394–395, 663   **Vol. 2:** 81, 203, 248, 315, 340, 386, 400, 515   **Vol. 3:** 65, 299, 658, 698

2:37   **Vol. 2:** 183   **Vol. 3:** 252

2:38–40   **Vol. 3:** 71

2:38 f   **Vol. 1:** 159   **Vol. 2:** 786   **Vol. 3:** 71, 699

2:38   **Vol. 1:** 146, 148, 152, 154, 157–158, 185, 359, 701–702   **Vol. 2:** 41–42, 533, 611, 655, 785–786   **Vol. 3:** 56, 499, 580, 732, 990, 1187, 1208–1210

2:39   **Vol. 1:** 159, 286   **Vol. 2:** 73, 786

2:40   **Vol. 1:** 571   **Vol. 2:** 36, 860   **Vol. 3:** 87, 213, 732

2:41   **Vol. 1:** 149   **Vol. 2:** 699, 786   **Vol. 3:** 686, 746

2:42   **Vol. 1:** 251, 642   **Vol. 2:** 523, 530, 768, 786   **Vol. 3:** 769, 964

2:43–47   **Vol. 2:** 786

2:43   **Vol. 2:** 169, 629   **Vol. 3:** 683, 700

2:44 f   **Vol. 1:** 496   **Vol. 2:** 499

2:44   **Vol. 3:** 545, 1194, 1211, 1213

2:45   **Vol. 2:** 845–846   **Vol. 3:** 957

2:46 f   **Vol. 2:** 869, 895   **Vol. 3:** 908

Acts *(cont'd)*

2:46   **Vol. 1:** 369   **Vol. 2:** 236, 250, 272, 328, 354, 523, 768, 895   **Vol. 3:** 750, 793, 1201
2:47   **Vol. 2:** 119, 354, 895   **Vol. 3:** 817, 1194
3 f   **Vol. 3:** 611
3   **Vol. 1:** 214
3:1 ff   **Vol. 2:** 328, 632   **Vol. 3:** 785
3:1–10   **Vol. 3:** 793
3:1–8   **Vol. 2:** 597
3:1   **Vol. 2:** 185   **Vol. 3:** 101, 847
3:2 ff   **Vol. 2:** 415
3:2   **Vol. 1:** 169   **Vol. 2:** 29–30, 415, 895   **Vol. 3:** 1071
3:3   **Vol. 1:** 326
3:4   **Vol. 3:** 520
3:6–8   **Vol. 3:** 520
3:6   **Vol. 2:** 333, 597, 654   **Vol. 3:** 61, 213
3:7   **Vol. 2:** 415
3:8   **Vol. 3:** 817
3:9   **Vol. 2:** 799   **Vol. 3:** 817
3:10   **Vol. 1:** 528   **Vol. 2:** 29, 623, 625
3:11   **Vol. 2:** 236, 623   **Vol. 3:** 717, 789, 947
3:12–26   **Vol. 3:** 87
3:12 f   **Vol. 1:** 78
3:12   **Vol. 2:** 310, 625   **Vol. 3:** 520
3:13 ff   **Vol. 3:** 299
3:13–26   **Vol. 3:** 62
3:13 f   **Vol. 1:** 455   **Vol. 3:** 793
3:13   **Vol. 1:** 81   **Vol. 2:** 73, 319, 364   **Vol. 3:** 189, 610–611, 624
3:14 f   **Vol. 2:** 808
3:14   **Vol. 1:** 261   **Vol. 2:** 116, 119, 229, 563   **Vol. 3:** 361
3:15   **Vol. 1:** 168, 445, 669   **Vol. 3:** 199, 723, 1044
3:16   **Vol. 3:** 1193, 1211
3:17   **Vol. 1:** 168, 455   **Vol. 2:** 407   **Vol. 3:** 1157
3:18   **Vol. 1:** 736   **Vol. 3:** 46, 48, 81, 699, 723
3:19 ff   **Vol. 3:** 148
3:19–21   **Vol. 3:** 66
3:19 f   **Vol. 2:** 785
3:19†   **Vol. 1:** 355, 359, 471   **Vol. 3:** 732
3:20 f   **Vol. 2:** 614
3:20   **Vol. 3:** 658, 686
3:21   **Vol. 1:** 186   **Vol. 2:** 194, 665, 920   **Vol. 3:** 81, 147–148, 830
3:22–26   **Vol. 2:** 315
3:22 f   **Vol. 2:** 638   **Vol. 3:** 80, 83, 86, 1007
3:22   **Vol. 2:** 641   **Vol. 3:** 88
3:23†   **Vol. 1:** 465   **Vol. 3:** 683, 732
3:24   **Vol. 3:** 48
3:25 f   **Vol. 1:** 214
3:25   **Vol. 1:** 78, 212, 288, 616   **Vol. 2:** 786   **Vol. 3:** 1012
3:26   **Vol. 1:** 355   **Vol. 3:** 213, 610–611, 624
4   **Vol. 1:** 364
4:1 ff   **Vol. 2:** 827

4:1   **Vol. 3:** 439, 964
4:2   **Vol. 3:** 47, 56, 440, 763–764, 1191
4:4   **Vol. 2:** 684, 699   **Vol. 3:** 686, 941, 1114
4:5   **Vol. 1:** 168, 297   **Vol. 2:** 32   **Vol. 3:** 481
4:6   **Vol. 3:** 39–40
4:7   **Vol. 2:** 253, 603, 654
4:8 ff   **Vol. 3:** 387
4:8–12   **Vol. 3:** 87
4:8   **Vol. 1:** 168, 739   **Vol. 2:** 786, 921   **Vol. 3:** 699–700
4:9 f   **Vol. 3:** 213
4:9   **Vol. 2:** 365, 799   **Vol. 3:** 1152
4:10 ff   **Vol. 3:** 62, 793
4:10 f   **Vol. 3:** 393
4:10   **Vol. 1:** 394, 445   **Vol. 2:** 170, 333, 799   **Vol. 3:** 56, 61, 212
4:11   **Vol. 1:** 74   **Vol. 2:** 129, 159, 249, 313, 622, 706   **Vol. 3:** 389
4:12   **Vol. 2:** 654, 666, 722   **Vol. 3:** 213, 732, 1210
4:13   **Vol. 2:** 456, 625, 736   **Vol. 3:** 516, 699, 750
4:15   **Vol. 1:** 341
4:16   **Vol. 2:** 629, 632   **Vol. 3:** 320
4:18   **Vol. 1:** 340   **Vol. 3:** 763–764
4:19   **Vol. 2:** 364   **Vol. 3:** 361
4:20   **Vol. 2:** 176   **Vol. 3:** 313, 1044
4:21   **Vol. 3:** 98, 529
4:22   **Vol. 2:** 629, 632
4:23   **Vol. 3:** 189
4:24   **Vol. 2:** 192–193, 509   **Vol. 3:** 908, 984, 1154
4:25 ff   **Vol. 2:** 799
4:25 f   **Vol. 1:** 168
4:25   **Vol. 1:** 177, 427   **Vol. 2:** 793, 921   **Vol. 3:** 611–612, 699
4:26   **Vol. 2:** 33, 378   **Vol. 3:** 1194
4:27 f   **Vol. 1:** 696
4:27   **Vol. 1:** 122–123   **Vol. 2:** 33, 229, 712   **Vol. 3:** 611, 1061
4:28   **Vol. 3:** 1017
4:29–31   **Vol. 3:** 699
4:29 f   **Vol. 2:** 632
4:29   **Vol. 2:** 736   **Vol. 3:** 1113–1114
4:30 f   **Vol. 3:** 700
4:30   **Vol. 2:** 149–150, 629   **Vol. 3:** 611
4:31 ff   **Vol. 1:** 303
4:31   **Vol. 1:** 297, 739   **Vol. 2:** 32, 736, 786, 921   **Vol. 3:** 559, 699–700, 1114
4:32 ff   **Vol. 1:** 642
4:32   **Vol. 1:** 496, 504, 733   **Vol. 2:** 722, 845–846   **Vol. 3:** 685, 1213
4:33   **Vol. 2:** 119, 603   **Vol. 3:** 276, 1044
4:34   **Vol. 1:** 268
4:35   **Vol. 3:** 957, 1201
4:36 f   **Vol. 2:** 499, 846
4:36   **Vol. 1:** 276, 289, 571, 581, 642   **Vol. 2:** 467   **Vol. 3:** 87
4:37   **Vol. 1:** 520   **Vol. 2:** 845

Acts *(cont'd)*

5:1–11   **Vol. 1:** 466, 642, 703   **Vol. 3:** 387
5:1–10   **Vol. 3:** 700, 1206
5:1 f   **Vol. 2:** 846
5:1   **Vol. 2:** 845
5:2   **Vol. 1:** 350
5:3   **Vol. 1:** 739   **Vol. 2:** 473, 845, 847, 921   **Vol. 3:** 87, 471
5:4   **Vol. 1:** 567   **Vol. 2:** 473   **Vol. 3:** 547, 1158
5:5 ff   **Vol. 1:** 265   **Vol. 3:** 471
5:5   **Vol. 1:** 610
5:6   **Vol. 2:** 675
5:7   **Vol. 3:** 847
5:8   **Vol. 2:** 845   **Vol. 3:** 135
5:9   **Vol. 2:** 30, 513, 921   **Vol. 3:** 802
5:10   **Vol. 1:** 446, 610
5:11   **Vol. 1:** 303
5:12   **Vol. 2:** 149, 236, 629, 632   **Vol. 3:** 789, 793, 908
5:13   **Vol. 1:** 365   **Vol. 2:** 349   **Vol. 3:** 252
5:14   **Vol. 1:** 603, 733   **Vol. 2:** 517   **Vol. 3:** 686, 1058
5:15 f   **Vol. 2:** 168
5:15   **Vol. 1:** 340   **Vol. 3:** 387, 555
5:16   **Vol. 1:** 733   **Vol. 2:** 165, 921   **Vol. 3:** 475
5:17 ff   **Vol. 2:** 827
5:17–32   **Vol. 2:** 434
5:17 f   **Vol. 1:** 364   **Vol. 2:** 654
5:17   **Vol. 1:** 535, 739   **Vol. 3:** 439, 1167
5:18   **Vol. 2:** 790, 839
5:19   **Vol. 1:** 103, 421   **Vol. 2:** 30, 136, 513, 630, 726, 729
5:20 f   **Vol. 2:** 328   **Vol. 3:** 793
5:20   **Vol. 3:** 61, 1122
5:21   **Vol. 1:** 363   **Vol. 2:** 236   **Vol. 3:** 39, 764
5:22   **Vol. 2:** 136   **Vol. 3:** 934
5:23   **Vol. 1:** 663   **Vol. 2:** 30, 136, 729–730
5:24   **Vol. 3:** 39, 964
5:25   **Vol. 2:** 136, 236, 328   **Vol. 3:** 764
5:26   **Vol. 3:** 711
5:27   **Vol. 3:** 39
5:28   **Vol. 1:** 222, 340   **Vol. 2:** 654   **Vol. 3:** 763–764
5:29   **Vol. 1:** 593   **Vol. 2:** 565   **Vol. 3:** 387
5:30 ff   **Vol. 3:** 62
5:30 f   **Vol. 3:** 298
5:30   **Vol. 1:** 266, 390   **Vol. 2:** 73   **Vol. 3:** 793, 868
5:31   **Vol. 1:** 168, 359, 669, 701–702   **Vol. 2:** 148, 202–203   **Vol. 3:** 199, 219, 580
5:32   **Vol. 1:** 593   **Vol. 2:** 921   **Vol. 3:** 700, 704, 1122
5:33   **Vol. 2:** 183
5:34   **Vol. 1:** 341   **Vol. 2:** 799, 812   **Vol. 3:** 480, 768
5:35   **Vol. 1:** 326   **Vol. 2:** 310   **Vol. 3:** 1157

5:36 f   **Vol. 1:** 591   **Vol. 2:** 339   **Vol. 3:** 378
5:36   **Vol. 2:** 34, 689   **Vol. 3:** 275
5:37 f   **Vol. 3:** 768
5:37   **Vol. 1:** 493, 607, 717   **Vol. 2:** 34, 320
5:38 f   **Vol. 3:** 189
5:38   **Vol. 1:** 607   **Vol. 3:** 1017, 1149
5:39   **Vol. 1:** 179, 590, 646   **Vol. 2:** 74   **Vol. 3:** 529, 763, 963
5:40   **Vol. 1:** 163, 340, 590   **Vol. 2:** 654   **Vol. 3:** 189
5:41   **Vol. 2:** 50, 359, 361, 654   **Vol. 3:** 349
5:42   **Vol. 2:** 113, 236, 250, 328   **Vol. 3:** 57, 763–764, 1201
6   **Vol. 1:** 305   **Vol. 3:** 548, 1066–1067
6:1 ff   **Vol. 2:** 547, 740, 827   **Vol. 3:** 909, 1075
6:1–7   **Vol. 2:** 847
6:1–6   **Vol. 3:** 548
6:1 f   **Vol. 1:** 490
6:1   **Vol. 1:** 181, 490   **Vol. 2:** 126, 310–311   **Vol. 3:** 465–466, 546–547, 1201
6:2 ff   **Vol. 1:** 135
6:2   **Vol. 1:** 274, 733   **Vol. 2:** 695, 816   **Vol. 3:** 251, 546, 1113
6:3 ff   **Vol. 2:** 785
6:3   **Vol. 1:** 174, 191, 472, 735, 739   **Vol. 2:** 563, 921   **Vol. 3:** 88, 700, 958, 1030, 1043
6:4   **Vol. 2:** 768   **Vol. 3:** 546
6:5   **Vol. 1:** 361, 540, 733, 735, 739   **Vol. 2:** 114, 550, 563, 677, 921   **Vol. 3:** 65, 700
6:6   **Vol. 2:** 152, 873   **Vol. 3:** 66
6:7   **Vol. 1:** 490   **Vol. 2:** 130, 179   **Vol. 3:** 37, 1113–1114
6:8 ff   **Vol. 3:** 88, 548
6:8–15   **Vol. 3:** 65
6:8–10   **Vol. 2:** 603
6:8 f   **Vol. 1:** 364
6:8   **Vol. 1:** 739   **Vol. 2:** 119, 603, 629, 632   **Vol. 3:** 700, 1067
6:9 ff   **Vol. 3:** 87
6:9   **Vol. 1:** 297   **Vol. 2:** 740   **Vol. 3:** 275, 598, 785, 1180
6:10   **Vol. 1:** 739   **Vol. 2:** 365, 632, 786, 921   **Vol. 3:** 700, 714, 1030
6:11 ff   **Vol. 2:** 641
6:11   **Vol. 1:** 739   **Vol. 2:** 450   **Vol. 3:** 342, 345, 1122
6:12 ff   **Vol. 2:** 827
6:12   **Vol. 2:** 799   **Vol. 3:** 481
6:13 f   **Vol. 1:** 174
6:13   **Vol. 2:** 450   **Vol. 3:** 1043, 1122, 1199
6:14   **Vol. 2:** 236, 333, 437, 920   **Vol. 3:** 167, 185, 189, 343, 464, 509, 773–774, 792
6:15   **Vol. 3:** 257, 520, 588
7   **Vol. 1:** 532   **Vol. 3:** 65, 431, 464–465, 607
7:1–60   **Vol. 3:** 1067
7:2–53   **Vol. 2:** 315   **Vol. 3:** 87, 464, 466

Acts *(cont'd)*

7:2	**Vol. 2:** 46, 76 **Vol. 3:** 71
7:4	**Vol. 3:** 464–465
7:5 ff	**Vol. 3:** 464
7:5 f	**Vol. 3:** 523
7:5	**Vol. 1:** 286 **Vol. 2:** 300, 369 **Vol. 3:** 71, 464, 1043
7:6	**Vol. 1:** 684 **Vol. 2:** 689, 742
7:7	**Vol. 2:** 793 **Vol. 3:** 464, 550
7:8 f	**Vol. 1:** 65
7:8	**Vol. 1:** 81, 154, 309 **Vol. 2:** 318, 695
7:9	**Vol. 3:** 1167
7:10	**Vol. 2:** 378 **Vol. 3:** 1030
7:11	**Vol. 1:** 744 **Vol. 2:** 266
7:12	**Vol. 2:** 318
7:13	**Vol. 3:** 314, 320
7:14	**Vol. 2:** 318 **Vol. 3:** 683
7:15 f	**Vol. 3:** 458, 464
7:15	**Vol. 1:** 430
7:17†	**Vol. 1:** 346, 732, 733 **Vol. 2:** 130 **Vol. 3:** 71
7:18	**Vol. 3:** 275
7:20	**Vol. 3:** 837
7:22	**Vol. 2:** 641 **Vol. 3:** 197, 778, 1149
7:23	**Vol. 1:** 191, 737 **Vol. 2:** 636, 696 **Vol. 3:** 843
7:24	**Vol. 3:** 97, 575
7:25 ff	**Vol. 2:** 641
7:25	**Vol. 2:** 149
7:26	**Vol. 1:** 251 **Vol. 2:** 780 **Vol. 3:** 575, 963
7:27	**Vol. 1:** 168, 258 **Vol. 3:** 575
7:29	**Vol. 1:** 518, 559, 691 **Vol. 3:** 1175, 1192
7:30 ff	**Vol. 3:** 1007
7:30	**Vol. 1:** 656, 737 **Vol. 2:** 636, 696 **Vol. 3:** 465, 1014
7:31	**Vol. 2:** 625 **Vol. 3:** 862
7:32	**Vol. 1:** 81, 365 **Vol. 2:** 73 **Vol. 3:** 464–465
7:33	**Vol. 3:** 179
7:34	**Vol. 2:** 178, 424
7:35	**Vol. 2:** 149, 641 **Vol. 3:** 199, 465
7:36	**Vol. 1:** 518 **Vol. 2:** 629, 636, 696 **Vol. 3:** 80, 984
7:37	**Vol. 2:** 638, 641 **Vol. 3:** 83, 86, 464, 1007
7:38	**Vol. 1:** 303 **Vol. 3:** 465, 1014, 1106, 1118
7:39	**Vol. 1:** 532 **Vol. 2:** 179–180
7:41–43	**Vol. 3:** 1008
7:41	**Vol. 2:** 356 **Vol. 3:** 431
7:42 f	**Vol. 2:** 164 **Vol. 3:** 465
7:42–43	**Vol. 2:** 248
7:42	**Vol. 2:** 193, 368, 696 **Vol. 3:** 465, 550
7:43	**Vol. 1:** 141 **Vol. 2:** 85 **Vol. 3:** 736, 749, 905
7:44–50	**Vol. 3:** 793
7:44	**Vol. 3:** 811, 905

7:45 f	**Vol. 3:** 465
7:45	**Vol. 1:** 427 **Vol. 2:** 331
7:46–50	**Vol. 2:** 248
7:46	**Vol. 2:** 248, 319 **Vol. 3:** 530, 815
7:47–58	**Vol. 1:** 174
7:47–50	**Vol. 3:** 465
7:47	**Vol. 2:** 248, 315 **Vol. 3:** 606
7:48 ff	**Vol. 3:** 785
7:48 f	**Vol. 2:** 450
7:48	**Vol. 2:** 74, 150, 200, 248, 920 **Vol. 3:** 461, 793
7:49	**Vol. 1:** 239, 518 **Vol. 2:** 74, 193 **Vol. 3:** 258, 465
7:50	**Vol. 2:** 149 **Vol. 3:** 607
7:51 f	**Vol. 2:** 229
7:51	**Vol. 1:** 309, 311 **Vol. 2:** 155, 178, 921 **Vol. 3:** 700
7:52	**Vol. 1:** 320 **Vol. 2:** 806 **Vol. 3:** 46, 82, 199, 361, 793
7:53	**Vol. 1:** 103 **Vol. 2:** 135, 450 **Vol. 3:** 345, 465, 1174, 1187
7:54 ff	**Vol. 1:** 440 **Vol. 2:** 827
7:54	**Vol. 2:** 183, 421
7:55 ff	**Vol. 1:** 303
7:55 f	**Vol. 2:** 148 **Vol. 3:** 287
7:55	**Vol. 1:** 739 **Vol. 2:** 46, 192, 359, 921 **Vol. 3:** 257, 504, 520, 699–700
7:56	**Vol. 2:** 729, 919, 921 **Vol. 3:** 543, 621, 633
7:57 ff	**Vol. 2:** 450
7:57 f	**Vol. 3:** 909
7:57	**Vol. 2:** 96, 178 **Vol. 3:** 113, 908
7:58	**Vol. 2:** 762 **Vol. 3:** 1043
7:59	**Vol. 1:** 276 **Vol. 2:** 921 **Vol. 3:** 694
7:60	**Vol. 1:** 410, 443 **Vol. 2:** 859 **Vol. 3:** 113, 292
8–12	**Vol. 3:** 1114
8	**Vol. 3:** 456
8:1	**Vol. 1:** 303, 686 **Vol. 2:** 34, 381 **Vol. 3:** 449, 456, 909
8:2	**Vol. 2:** 91, 418
8:3	**Vol. 1:** 303 **Vol. 2:** 136, 368
8:4 ff	**Vol. 3:** 57, 1067
8:4–25	**Vol. 3:** 453, 456–457
8:4–13	**Vol. 3:** 456
8:4	**Vol. 1:** 686 **Vol. 3:** 1113
8:5 ff	**Vol. 2:** 114
8:5–40	**Vol. 2:** 550
8:5	**Vol. 3:** 52, 56, 456
8:6 ff	**Vol. 2:** 632
8:6 f	**Vol. 3:** 457
8:6	**Vol. 2:** 629 **Vol. 3:** 908
8:7–29	**Vol. 2:** 921
8:7	**Vol. 1:** 411 **Vol. 2:** 165, 415 **Vol. 3:** 113, 475, 999
8:8	**Vol. 2:** 359 **Vol. 3:** 456
8:9 ff	**Vol. 3:** 457
8:9–24	**Vol. 3:** 88
8:9–13	**Vol. 3:** 700

Acts *(cont'd)*

8:9 **Vol. 1:** 528 **Vol. 2:** 74, 558 **Vol. 3:** 457, 463
8:10 **Vol. 2:** 426, 428 **Vol. 3:** 457, 462
8:11 **Vol. 1:** 528 **Vol. 2:** 558 **Vol. 3:** 457
8:12 ff **Vol. 3:** 699
8:12 **Vol. 1:** 160 **Vol. 2:** 387, 654 **Vol. 3:** 1211
8:13 **Vol. 2:** 603, 768 **Vol. 3:** 457
8:14 ff **Vol. 1:** 135, 146, 148
8:14–17 **Vol. 2:** 785
8:14 f **Vol. 2:** 114
8:14 **Vol. 1:** 136 **Vol. 2:** 328 **Vol. 3:** 746, 1114
8:15–19 **Vol. 3:** 699
8:15–17 **Vol. 1:** 158
8:16 **Vol. 1:** 609 **Vol. 2:** 655, 724 **Vol. 3:** 61, 1209
8:17 ff **Vol. 2:** 152
8:17 **Vol. 2:** 42
8:18 ff **Vol. 2:** 152
8:18–24 **Vol. 3:** 458
8:18–20 **Vol. 2:** 605
8:18 **Vol. 2:** 845, 847
8:19–24 **Vol. 2:** 557
8:19 **Vol. 2:** 611
8:20 **Vol. 1:** 464 **Vol. 2:** 845
8:21 ff **Vol. 3:** 87
8:21 **Vol. 2:** 302, 304 **Vol. 3:** 1106
8:22 **Vol. 1:** 563 **Vol. 2:** 861
8:23 **Vol. 1:** 202 **Vol. 2:** 28 **Vol. 3:** 575
8:24 **Vol. 2:** 860–861 **Vol. 3:** 1174
8:25 **Vol. 2:** 113, 513 **Vol. 3:** 1044, 1113
8:26–40 **Vol. 3:** 65
8:26 **Vol. 1:** 103 **Vol. 2:** 513 **Vol. 3:** 275, 941, 1008
8:27 **Vol. 1:** 560 **Vol. 2:** 381, 511, 877
8:28 **Vol. 1:** 245, 736
8:29 **Vol. 2:** 349, 847 **Vol. 3:** 700
8:30–35 **Vol. 3:** 87
8:30 **Vol. 1:** 736
8:31 **Vol. 1:** 570 **Vol. 3:** 943
8:32 f **Vol. 2:** 381
8:32 **Vol. 1:** 581 **Vol. 2:** 410–411, 413, 728 **Vol. 3:** 490
8:33 **Vol. 1:** 576, 581 **Vol. 2:** 38, 365
8:34 **Vol. 3:** 609
8:35 **Vol. 2:** 263, 410, 726–728 **Vol. 3:** 490
8:36 **Vol. 2:** 223 **Vol. 3:** 941, 990
8:37 **Vol. 3:** 639, 646, 1211
8:38 f **Vol. 3:** 990, 1180
8:38 **Vol. 1:** 341
8:39 **Vol. 2:** 359, 513 **Vol. 3:** 602, 700, 941
8:40 **Vol. 3:** 529
9 **Vol. 1:** 305
9:1–19 **Vol. 1:** 136
9:1 f **Vol. 2:** 827 **Vol. 3:** 380, 1199
9:1 **Vol. 1:** 490 **Vol. 3:** 708

9:2 **Vol. 1:** 171 **Vol. 2:** 856 **Vol. 3:** 785, 941
9:3–9 **Vol. 3:** 330
9:3–6 **Vol. 1:** 183
9:3 **Vol. 2:** 193, 493
9:4 ff **Vol. 3:** 85
9:4 f **Vol. 2:** 806
9:4 **Vol. 1:** 174, 358, 610 **Vol. 2:** 155 **Vol. 3:** 114
9:5 **Vol. 1:** 511 **Vol. 2:** 513 **Vol. 3:** 88
9:6 **Vol. 2:** 623, 666 **Vol. 3:** 275
9:7 **Vol. 3:** 114
9:8 **Vol. 2:** 726, 728 **Vol. 3:** 520
9:9 **Vol. 2:** 272
9:10 f **Vol. 3:** 85
9:10–16 **Vol. 2:** 867
9:10 **Vol. 1:** 490 **Vol. 3:** 87, 515, 517, 700, 862
9:11 **Vol. 2:** 320, 861, 867, 873 **Vol. 3:** 275
9:12 **Vol. 3:** 515, 517, 519, 862
9:13 **Vol. 1:** 305
9:14 **Vol. 1:** 276 **Vol. 2:** 654
9:15 **Vol. 1:** 136, 540 **Vol. 3:** 38, 912, 1065
9:16 **Vol. 2:** 654, 666 **Vol. 3:** 257, 725
9:17 **Vol. 1:** 739 **Vol. 2:** 152, 921 **Vol. 3:** 285, 458, 519, 699–700, 941, 1191
9:18 **Vol. 3:** 519
9:19 **Vol. 1:** 490 **Vol. 2:** 523
9:20 ff **Vol. 3:** 87
9:20 **Vol. 3:** 52, 56, 62, 639, 644, 785
9:22 **Vol. 3:** 1199
9:23 **Vol. 1:** 363, 737
9:24 **Vol. 2:** 29, 133
9:25 f **Vol. 1:** 490
9:25 **Vol. 1:** 420 **Vol. 3:** 948
9:26–30 **Vol. 3:** 65
9:26 **Vol. 2:** 349 **Vol. 3:** 802
9:27 f **Vol. 2:** 736
9:27 **Vol. 1:** 136, 576 **Vol. 2:** 736 **Vol. 3:** 749, 941, 1191
9:29 **Vol. 2:** 126, 311 **Vol. 3:** 908
9:30 **Vol. 2:** 328
9:31 **Vol. 1:** 303, 623, 733 **Vol. 2:** 252, 921 **Vol. 3:** 87, 449, 456, 699, 947
9:32 ff **Vol. 2:** 632
9:32 **Vol. 3:** 387
9:33 **Vol. 3:** 999
9:34 f **Vol. 2:** 867
9:34 **Vol. 2:** 654 **Vol. 3:** 275
9:35 **Vol. 1:** 355
9:36–42 **Vol. 2:** 433
9:36 **Vol. 1:** 581, 735 **Vol. 2:** 596 **Vol. 3:** 1065
9:37 **Vol. 2:** 596 **Vol. 3:** 994
9:38 **Vol. 1:** 490
9:39 **Vol. 1:** 316 **Vol. 2:** 416 **Vol. 3:** 1065, 1154
9:40 **Vol. 2:** 726, 728, 859
9:42 **Vol. 3:** 1212
10 f **Vol. 3:** 456

Acts *(cont'd)*

10   **Vol. 1:** 90   **Vol. 2:** 732   **Vol. 3:** 387, 793
10:1 ff   **Vol. 3:** 66
10:1–11:18 **Vol. 1:** 361   **Vol. 3:** 106
10:1   **Vol. 1:** 274   **Vol. 3:** 85, 964
10:2   **Vol. 1:** 361, 623   **Vol. 2:** 94, 596, 800, 861
10:3–8   **Vol. 1:** 103
10:3   **Vol. 3:** 320, 515, 517, 700, 847, 862
10:4   **Vol. 2:** 185, 513, 596   **Vol. 3:** 242, 520
10:6   **Vol. 1:** 689   **Vol. 3:** 984
10:7   **Vol. 2:** 768   **Vol. 3:** 700, 964
10:8   **Vol. 1:** 576
10:9 ff   **Vol. 2:** 873
10:9–16   **Vol. 2:** 434   **Vol. 3:** 113
10:9   **Vol. 2:** 873   **Vol. 3:** 847, 941
10:10–16 **Vol. 3:** 700
10:10   **Vol. 1:** 528   **Vol. 2:** 269   **Vol. 3:** 87, 119, 410, 1193
10:11   **Vol. 1:** 166   **Vol. 2:** 689, 729   **Vol. 3:** 543, 913
10:12   **Vol. 1:** 175   **Vol. 2:** 192
10:13–14 **Vol. 3:** 113
10:13   **Vol. 3:** 88
10:14 f   **Vol. 2:** 268
10:14   **Vol. 1:** 448, 642   **Vol. 2:** 275
10:15   **Vol. 1:** 448, 642   **Vol. 3:** 106
10:16   **Vol. 3:** 749, 913
10:17   **Vol. 2:** 30   **Vol. 3:** 862
10:18   **Vol. 3:** 114
10:19–47 **Vol. 2:** 921
10:19   **Vol. 3:** 700, 862
10:20   **Vol. 1:** 504
10:21   **Vol. 2:** 138
10:22   **Vol. 1:** 361, 623   **Vol. 2:** 228, 793   **Vol. 3:** 325, 361, 964, 1043, 1122
10:23   **Vol. 1:** 690
10:24   **Vol. 2:** 549, 663
10:25 f   **Vol. 2:** 877
10:25   **Vol. 1:** 325, 609
10:28   **Vol. 1:** 448, 685   **Vol. 2:** 349, 563, 742   **Vol. 3:** 569
10:29   **Vol. 3:** 1106
10:30 ff **Vol. 2:** 873
10:30   **Vol. 2:** 486   **Vol. 3:** 847
10:31   **Vol. 2:** 178, 596   **Vol. 3:** 242
10:32   **Vol. 3:** 984
10:33   **Vol. 1:** 477   **Vol. 2:** 899   **Vol. 3:** 1198
10:34   **Vol. 1:** 587   **Vol. 2:** 726–728   **Vol. 3:** 750
10:35   **Vol. 2:** 794   **Vol. 3:** 361, 746
10:36 ff **Vol. 3:** 660
10:36–43 **Vol. 3:** 62, 66
10:36 f   **Vol. 3:** 1113
10:36   **Vol. 1:** 239   **Vol. 2:** 780, 782   **Vol. 3:** 1113
10:37–41 **Vol. 3:** 62
10:37 f   **Vol. 3:** 499

10:37   **Vol. 1:** 167   **Vol. 3:** 52, 1113
10:38   **Vol. 1:** 122, 453   **Vol. 2:** 168–169, 333, 603, 632, 712   **Vol. 3:** 470, 698, 713, 1061, 1152
10:39   **Vol. 1:** 266, 390   **Vol. 2:** 328   **Vol. 3:** 793, 868
10:40 f   **Vol. 1:** 445
10:40   **Vol. 2:** 489, 687
10:41   **Vol. 1:** 478   **Vol. 2:** 272, 524, 799, 897   **Vol. 3:** 283, 449
10:42 f   **Vol. 1:** 701
10:42   **Vol. 1:** 340–341, 445, 473   **Vol. 2:** 365, 480
10:43   **Vol. 2:** 654   **Vol. 3:** 213, 580, 748, 1212
10:44 ff **Vol. 1:** 148   **Vol. 3:** 286, 699
10:44–48 **Vol. 1:** 158   **Vol. 2:** 611, 785
10:44–47 **Vol. 3:** 699
10:44 f   **Vol. 1:** 146   **Vol. 2:** 596
10:44   **Vol. 1:** 528, 609   **Vol. 3:** 1122
10:45   **Vol. 1:** 310   **Vol. 2:** 785, 794, 855   **Vol. 3:** 1194
10:46   **Vol. 1:** 528   **Vol. 2:** 740, 786   **Vol. 3:** 1080
10:47 f   **Vol. 2:** 596
10:47   **Vol. 2:** 42, 223   **Vol. 3:** 499, 990
10:48   **Vol. 1:** 160, 476   **Vol. 2:** 655, 880, 895   **Vol. 3:** 227, 1210
11:1 ff   **Vol. 1:** 135, 302
11:1   **Vol. 2:** 794   **Vol. 3:** 746
11:2   **Vol. 1:** 310, 504
11:3   **Vol. 1:** 309–310
11:4   **Vol. 1:** 167
11:5   **Vol. 1:** 528   **Vol. 2:** 689   **Vol. 3:** 862, 913
11:6   **Vol. 1:** 114, 175   **Vol. 2:** 192   **Vol. 3:** 520
11:7–9   **Vol. 3:** 113
11:8   **Vol. 1:** 448
11:9   **Vol. 1:** 448
11:12–28 **Vol. 2:** 921
11:12   **Vol. 1:** 503   **Vol. 3:** 85, 700
11:14   **Vol. 1:** 148   **Vol. 2:** 250
11:15–18 **Vol. 3:** 699
11:15 f   **Vol. 3:** 699
11:15   **Vol. 1:** 166–167, 528, 609
11:16   **Vol. 1:** 158   **Vol. 2:** 514, 786   **Vol. 3:** 241, 990, 1122, 1210
11:17   **Vol. 1:** 528   **Vol. 2:** 223, 499   **Vol. 3:** 61, 1212, 1214
11:18   **Vol. 1:** 359   **Vol. 2:** 794   **Vol. 3:** 111
11:19 f   **Vol. 3:** 458
11:19   **Vol. 1:** 686   **Vol. 2:** 34, 809   **Vol. 3:** 941, 1113–1114
11:20   **Vol. 2:** 113, 126, 740   **Vol. 3:** 61
11:21   **Vol. 1:** 355   **Vol. 2:** 149, 513
11:22   **Vol. 1:** 303   **Vol. 2:** 328   **Vol. 3:** 1106
11:23   **Vol. 1:** 571, 697   **Vol. 2:** 119, 359   **Vol. 3:** 87, 228
11:24   **Vol. 1:** 739   **Vol. 3:** 700, 729
11:25   **Vol. 2:** 328

Acts *(cont'd)*

11:26	**Vol. 1:** 123, 199, 490 **Vol. 2:** 32, 333, 343, 523, 654 **Vol. 3:** 764
11:26c	**Vol. 3:** 325
11:27 ff	**Vol. 2:** 827
11:27 f	**Vol. 3:** 86–87, 700
11:27	**Vol. 2:** 328 **Vol. 3:** 458
11:28 ff	**Vol. 2:** 268
11:28–30	**Vol. 2:** 694
11:28	**Vol. 1:** 326, 519 **Vol. 2:** 266 **Vol. 3:** 86–87, 1183
11:29 f	**Vol. 2:** 827
11:29	**Vol. 1:** 473, 490 **Vol. 2:** 694 **Vol. 3:** 546–547
11:30	**Vol. 1:** 199 **Vol. 2:** 149 **Vol. 3:** 1155
12	**Vol. 3:** 387
12:1 ff	**Vol. 2:** 827
12:1–3	**Vol. 1:** 343
12:1	**Vol. 1:** 303 **Vol. 2:** 378 **Vol. 3:** 837, 1180
12:2	**Vol. 3:** 292, 967
12:3 ff	**Vol. 2:** 630
12:3	**Vol. 2:** 816
12:4 f	**Vol. 2:** 136
12:4	**Vol. 1:** 633 **Vol. 2:** 135, 368, 689, 799
12:5	**Vol. 1:** 303 **Vol. 2:** 868
12:6–11	**Vol. 2:** 919
12:6	**Vol. 1:** 326, 442 **Vol. 2:** 30, 136
12:7–10	**Vol. 1:** 103
12:7	**Vol. 1:** 421 **Vol. 2:** 486, 493, 513
12:8	**Vol. 3:** 121
12:9	**Vol. 3:** 822, 862
12:10	**Vol. 1:** 607, 666 **Vol. 2:** 29, 136, 726, 729
12:11 f	**Vol. 2:** 244
12:11	**Vol. 2:** 150
12:12–16	**Vol. 2:** 434
12:12	**Vol. 1:** 276, 642 **Vol. 2:** 33, 847, 869 **Vol. 3:** 1065, 1071
12:13	**Vol. 2:** 30, 179, 881
12:14	**Vol. 2:** 30, 726, 729 **Vol. 3:** 113, 1180
12:15	**Vol. 1:** 102, 529
12:16	**Vol. 2:** 729, 881 **Vol. 3:** 227
12:17	**Vol. 1:** 576 **Vol. 3:** 558
12:18	**Vol. 1:** 181 **Vol. 3:** 709–710
12:19	**Vol. 1:** 341 **Vol. 2:** 136, 365 **Vol. 3:** 532
12:20	**Vol. 1:** 589 **Vol. 2:** 378, 780 **Vol. 3:** 908
12:21–22	**Vol. 3:** 113
12:21	**Vol. 2:** 369 **Vol. 3:** 588
12:22	**Vol. 1:** 410 **Vol. 2:** 789
12:23	**Vol. 1:** 103, 181 **Vol. 2:** 46, 168 **Vol. 3:** 998
12:24	**Vol. 1:** 733 **Vol. 2:** 130, 513 **Vol. 3:** 1113–1114
12:25	**Vol. 2:** 827 **Vol. 3:** 546–547
13–28	**Vol. 3:** 1114
13	**Vol. 3:** 64–65
13:1–4	**Vol. 1:** 135
13:1	**Vol. 1:** 303 **Vol. 2:** 740 **Vol. 3:** 86–87, 700, 767–768
13:2	**Vol. 1:** 274, 474 **Vol. 2:** 873, 921 **Vol. 3:** 85, 552, 700
13:3	**Vol. 1:** 613 **Vol. 2:** 152, 873 **Vol. 3:** 55
13:4–12	**Vol. 2:** 467, 557
13:4	**Vol. 2:** 921 **Vol. 3:** 700
13:5	**Vol. 1:** 297 **Vol. 2:** 113 **Vol. 3:** 47, 87, 410, 785, 1113–1114
13:6 ff	**Vol. 3:** 88
13:6	**Vol. 1:** 623 **Vol. 2:** 74, 331, 472, 557
13:7 f	**Vol. 1:** 270
13:7	**Vol. 2:** 176 **Vol. 3:** 532, 1113–1114
13:8	**Vol. 1:** 581 **Vol. 2:** 557
13:9–11	**Vol. 3:** 700
13:9	**Vol. 1:** 739 **Vol. 2:** 786, 921 **Vol. 3:** 520, 699–700
13:10	**Vol. 1:** 289, 554 **Vol. 3:** 197, 361, 471, 941–942
13:11	**Vol. 1:** 219, 424, 466, 609 **Vol. 2:** 149 **Vol. 3:** 87, 731
13:12	**Vol. 1:** 270, 530 **Vol. 3:** 769, 942, 1214
13:13	**Vol. 3:** 1203
13:14–52	**Vol. 3:** 203
13:14	**Vol. 2:** 314 **Vol. 3:** 410, 589, 785
13:15	**Vol. 1:** 245 **Vol. 2:** 799 **Vol. 3:** 87, 485
13:16 ff	**Vol. 1:** 691
13:16–41	**Vol. 3:** 62, 65, 87
13:16	**Vol. 1:** 361 **Vol. 2:** 310 **Vol. 3:** 558
13:17	**Vol. 1:** 532, 541 **Vol. 2:** 73, 200, 202, 799 **Vol. 3:** 1010
13:18	**Vol. 2:** 696 **Vol. 3:** 843, 1007
13:19	**Vol. 2:** 300, 793
13:20	**Vol. 2:** 41, 689
13:21	**Vol. 2:** 696 **Vol. 3:** 872
13:22	**Vol. 1:** 427 **Vol. 2:** 378 **Vol. 3:** 1018
13:23–31	**Vol. 3:** 62
13:23	**Vol. 2:** 786 **Vol. 3:** 71, 219, 523
13:24	**Vol. 1:** 358 **Vol. 3:** 660, 940, 1208
13:25	**Vol. 2:** 62 **Vol. 3:** 179, 348, 947
13:26	**Vol. 1:** 78, 257, 361, 623 **Vol. 3:** 213, 1113
13:27 ff	**Vol. 3:** 793
13:27	**Vol. 1:** 168, 245, 736 **Vol. 2:** 328, 407 **Vol. 3:** 114
13:28	**Vol. 2:** 139 **Vol. 3:** 529
13:29	**Vol. 1:** 266 **Vol. 2:** 63 **Vol. 3:** 247, 488–489
13:30	**Vol. 1:** 445
13:31	**Vol. 2:** 328, 799 **Vol. 3:** 285, 1044, 1181
13:32 f	**Vol. 3:** 71
13:32	**Vol. 2:** 786 **Vol. 3:** 71
13:33 ff	**Vol. 3:** 523
13:33	**Vol. 1:** 177–179, 286, 736 **Vol. 3:** 639, 641, 644, 671, 675, 698
13:34 ff	**Vol. 3:** 1017

Acts *(cont'd)*

13:34–37 **Vol. 3:** 1200
13:34 f **Vol. 1:** 468
13:34 **Vol. 1:** 427, 445 **Vol. 2:** 238 **Vol. 3:** 303
13:35 ff **Vol. 1:** 470
13:35–37 **Vol. 1:** 266
13:35 **Vol. 2:** 238 **Vol. 3:** 491
13:36 f **Vol. 3:** 1017
13:36 **Vol. 1:** 427, 443 **Vol. 2:** 35 **Vol. 3:** 547, 1017
13:37 **Vol. 2:** 919 **Vol. 3:** 651
13:38 f **Vol. 1:** 158 **Vol. 3:** 361, 1113
13:38 **Vol. 1:** 701 **Vol. 2:** 113, 451, 641 **Vol. 3:** 47, 213
13:41 **Vol. 1:** 462 **Vol. 2:** 625 **Vol. 3:** 1148–1149
13:42 **Vol. 1:** 570 **Vol. 3:** 1122
13:43 **Vol. 1:** 361, 589 **Vol. 2:** 85, 94, 119 **Vol. 3:** 179–180, 228, 785
13:44 **Vol. 2:** 33, 176 **Vol. 3:** 410, 1113–1114
13:45 **Vol. 1:** 739 **Vol. 3:** 343, 1167
13:46 **Vol. 2:** 315, 364, 663, 736, 794 **Vol. 3:** 832, 1113–1114
13:47† **Vol. 1:** 341, 477 **Vol. 2:** 57, 495 **Vol. 3:** 613
13:48 f **Vol. 2:** 513
13:48 **Vol. 1:** 476 **Vol. 2:** 359 **Vol. 3:** 832, 1114, 1186
13:49 **Vol. 3:** 1113
13:50 **Vol. 1:** 361 **Vol. 2:** 94
13:51 **Vol. 1:** 239 **Vol. 3:** 561
13:52 **Vol. 1:** 490, 739 **Vol. 2:** 359, 921 **Vol. 3:** 699
14 **Vol. 3:** 327
14:1–20 **Vol. 3:** 203
14:1† **Vol. 1:** 297, 361, 733 **Vol. 2:** 126, 314 **Vol. 3:** 410, 785
14:2 **Vol. 1:** 563, 593 **Vol. 3:** 685
14:3 f **Vol. 2:** 736
14:3 **Vol. 2:** 119, 629, 632, 736 **Vol. 3:** 843
14:4 **Vol. 1:** 136, 733 **Vol. 3:** 544
14:5 **Vol. 3:** 27
14:6 **Vol. 2:** 606
14:8–18 **Vol. 2:** 85
14:8 **Vol. 2:** 415
14:9 **Vol. 3:** 212, 520
14:10 **Vol. 2:** 654 **Vol. 3:** 113, 351
14:11 f **Vol. 3:** 457
14:11 **Vol. 2:** 503
14:13 **Vol. 1:** 116, 405 **Vol. 2:** 30
14:14 **Vol. 1:** 128, 130, 136, 317, 410
14:15 **Vol. 1:** 355, 551 **Vol. 2:** 73, 193, 503 **Vol. 3:** 200, 984
14:16 **Vol. 2:** 35, 407, 793 **Vol. 3:** 940–941, 947
14:17 **Vol. 1:** 701 **Vol. 2:** 77, 102, 182, 193, 356 **Vol. 3:** 310, 331, 837, 1004

14:18 **Vol. 2:** 839 **Vol. 3:** 258, 1071
14:19 **Vol. 1:** 322, 589 **Vol. 3:** 558
14:20 **Vol. 1:** 490
14:22 **Vol. 1:** 490, 571 **Vol. 2:** 809, 920 **Vol. 3:** 87, 226
14:23 **Vol. 1:** 199–200, 303, 478, 613 **Vol. 2:** 150 **Vol. 3:** 1201, 1212
14:25 **Vol. 3:** 1113
14:26 **Vol. 2:** 119, 368
14:27 **Vol. 1:** 303 **Vol. 2:** 31–32, 726–727, 729 **Vol. 3:** 47
14:28–29 **Vol. 3:** 101
14:28 **Vol. 1:** 490
15 **Vol. 1:** 62, 129 **Vol. 2:** 795 **Vol. 3:** 387, 1164
15:1 ff **Vol. 2:** 328
15:1–21 **Vol. 2:** 641
15:1 **Vol. 1:** 310 **Vol. 2:** 437 **Vol. 3:** 458, 764
15:2 **Vol. 1:** 136, 199, 310 **Vol. 3:** 458, 532
15:3 **Vol. 1:** 355 **Vol. 2:** 359 **Vol. 3:** 449, 458, 1174
15:4 **Vol. 1:** 199 **Vol. 3:** 47, 1174, 1198
15:5 **Vol. 1:** 310, 341, 535 **Vol. 2:** 450, 812 **Vol. 3:** 804
15:6 **Vol. 1:** 199, 297 **Vol. 2:** 32
15:7–11 **Vol. 1:** 157
15:7 **Vol. 1:** 158, 168, 541 **Vol. 2:** 110, 112, 563 **Vol. 3:** 1114
15:8 **Vol. 2:** 183, 921 **Vol. 3:** 699
15:9 **Vol. 1:** 158, 503 **Vol. 3:** 106
15:10 f **Vol. 2:** 119 **Vol. 3:** 213
15:10 **Vol. 1:** 241, 490 **Vol. 3:** 802, 1164
15:11 **Vol. 3:** 909, 1211
15:12 **Vol. 1:** 131, 576, 733 **Vol. 2:** 629, 632
15:13–21 **Vol. 3:** 812
15:13 **Vol. 2:** 563
15:14 **Vol. 1:** 191, 576 **Vol. 2:** 73, 800
15:16 f **Vol. 3:** 651
15:16 **Vol. 1:** 355, 427 **Vol. 2:** 248, 252, 920 **Vol. 3:** 650, 934
15:17 ff **Vol. 3:** 387
15:17–18 **Vol. 3:** 812
15:17 **Vol. 1:** 276 **Vol. 3:** 251, 532
15:18 **Vol. 2:** 451 **Vol. 3:** 830
15:19 ff **Vol. 3:** 387
15:19 f **Vol. 1:** 310
15:19 **Vol. 1:** 355 **Vol. 2:** 364 **Vol. 3:** 812
15:20 **Vol. 1:** 221, 226 **Vol. 2:** 286, 678, 682, 826 **Vol. 3:** 538, 931, 1195
15:21 **Vol. 1:** 245 **Vol. 2:** 35, 286 **Vol. 3:** 56, 785
15:22 f **Vol. 1:** 199
15:22 **Vol. 1:** 540 **Vol. 2:** 321 **Vol. 3:** 87, 822
15:23–29 **Vol. 1:** 247
15:23 **Vol. 1:** 247, 256 **Vol. 2:** 358 **Vol. 3:** 458
15:24 **Vol. 3:** 710
15:25 **Vol. 1:** 540 **Vol. 3:** 822, 908

Acts *(cont'd)*

15:26   **Vol. 2:** 368   **Vol. 3:** 257, 683
15:27   **Vol. 3:** 1106
15:28 ff   **Vol. 2:** 309
15:28 f   **Vol. 1:** 261   **Vol. 2:** 450–451, 921
15:28   **Vol. 3:** 700, 822
15:29   **Vol. 1:** 226   **Vol. 2:** 284–286, 678,
          682   **Vol. 3:** 106, 432, 538, 931, 1157,
          1195
15:30   **Vol. 1:** 297, 733   **Vol. 2:** 32   **Vol. 3:**
          189
15:31   **Vol. 1:** 245   **Vol. 2:** 359
15:32   **Vol. 1:** 570–571   **Vol. 3:** 86–87, 700
15:33   **Vol. 3:** 189, 843, 1198
15:34   **Vol. 3:** 822
15:35 f   **Vol. 3:** 1113
15:35   **Vol. 2:** 513   **Vol. 3:** 763–764
15:36–40   **Vol. 1:** 129
15:36   **Vol. 1:** 191   **Vol. 2:** 113   **Vol. 3:**
          1113–1114
15:37 ff   **Vol. 3:** 909
15:37   **Vol. 1:** 274
15:38   **Vol. 1:** 607
15:39   **Vol. 1:** 110   **Vol. 2:** 467
15:40   **Vol. 2:** 119
15:41   **Vol. 1:** 303
16:1 ff   **Vol. 3:** 491
16:1–5   **Vol. 3:** 203
16:1–3   **Vol. 1:** 159
16:1   **Vol. 1:** 324, 490   **Vol. 2:** 126
16:2   **Vol. 3:** 1043
16:3   **Vol. 1:** 310   **Vol. 2:** 451, 641   **Vol. 3:**
          431
16:4   **Vol. 1:** 136, 199, 330–331   **Vol. 2:** 135,
          451, 718   **Vol. 3:** 773–774
16:5   **Vol. 1:** 303   **Vol. 2:** 895
16:6–18   **Vol. 2:** 921
16:6 f   **Vol. 2:** 786   **Vol. 3:** 700
16:6   **Vol. 2:** 222–223
16:7   **Vol. 3:** 88, 700, 802
16:8   **Vol. 1:** 341
16:9 f   **Vol. 1:** 476, 570   **Vol. 3:** 700
16:9   **Vol. 1:** 421, 512   **Vol. 3:** 87, 515, 862
16:10–17   **Vol. 1:** 490
16:10   **Vol. 1:** 274   **Vol. 3:** 862
16:12   **Vol. 2:** 304, 550, 895
16:13   **Vol. 1:** 628   **Vol. 2:** 29, 875   **Vol. 3:**
          410, 987, 990, 1063
16:14 f   **Vol. 3:** 1065
16:14   **Vol. 1:** 205, 361   **Vol. 2:** 94, 183
16:15   **Vol. 1:** 159, 689   **Vol. 2:** 250,
          364   **Vol. 3:** 1063, 1065
16:16 ff   **Vol. 3:** 475
16:16–18   **Vol. 3:** 474
16:16   **Vol. 2:** 558, 875   **Vol. 3:** 81, 88
16:17   **Vol. 1:** 410   **Vol. 2:** 74, 113   **Vol. 3:**
          47, 213, 941–942
16:18   **Vol. 1:** 340   **Vol. 2:** 609, 654   **Vol. 3:**
          475, 846

16:19   **Vol. 1:** 168, 267   **Vol. 3:** 749
16:20   **Vol. 3:** 964
16:21   **Vol. 2:** 438
16:22 ff   **Vol. 3:** 87
16:22   **Vol. 1:** 163, 341, 407   **Vol. 3:** 964
16:23 f   **Vol. 1:** 340
16:23   **Vol. 1:** 163, 663   **Vol. 2:** 133,
          136   **Vol. 3:** 857
16:24   **Vol. 1:** 663   **Vol. 2:** 136   **Vol. 3:** 794
16:25 ff   **Vol. 2:** 630   **Vol. 3:** 592
16:25   **Vol. 1:** 420   **Vol. 2:** 175   **Vol. 3:**
          669–670, 675
16:26 f   **Vol. 2:** 30, 729
16:26   **Vol. 1:** 661   **Vol. 3:** 558–559
16:27   **Vol. 1:** 326   **Vol. 2:** 136   **Vol. 3:** 967
16:28   **Vol. 1:** 564   **Vol. 3:** 1157
16:29   **Vol. 1:** 610   **Vol. 2:** 493, 858
16:30   **Vol. 1:** 663   **Vol. 2:** 513   **Vol. 3:** 252
16:31–34   **Vol. 1:** 159
16:31   **Vol. 1:** 604   **Vol. 2:** 250   **Vol. 3:** 61,
          213, 1212
16:32 f   **Vol. 2:** 176
16:32   **Vol. 3:** 1113
16:33   **Vol. 1:** 148–149, 152, 163   **Vol. 2:** 250
16:34   **Vol. 1:** 603   **Vol. 2:** 250, 354   **Vol. 3:**
          1211, 1214
16:35 f   **Vol. 3:** 189, 964
16:35   **Vol. 1:** 407
16:37   **Vol. 1:** 163, 453   **Vol. 2:** 136, 139, 790
16:38   **Vol. 1:** 407   **Vol. 3:** 46, 964
16:39   **Vol. 1:** 571
16:40   **Vol. 1:** 570   **Vol. 2:** 136   **Vol. 3:** 87,
          1063
17–24   **Vol. 3:** 821
17   **Vol. 3:** 65, 327
17:1–9   **Vol. 1:** 269
17:1   **Vol. 1:** 297   **Vol. 3:** 785
17:2   **Vol. 1:** 590   **Vol. 2:** 437   **Vol. 3:** 87,
          410, 490, 492, 821
17:3   **Vol. 2:** 729   **Vol. 3:** 48, 723–724, 1199
17:4   **Vol. 1:** 361, 590   **Vol. 2:** 126, 300,
          302   **Vol. 3:** 1063, 1065
17:5   **Vol. 1:** 267, 566   **Vol. 2:** 623,
          789   **Vol. 3:** 750–751, 1167
17:6   **Vol. 1:** 411, 519, 691   **Vol. 2:** 285, 804
17:7   **Vol. 1:** 269, 330–331   **Vol. 2:** 380,
          804   **Vol. 3:** 1157
17:8   **Vol. 2:** 804   **Vol. 3:** 710
17:9   **Vol. 3:** 252
17:10 f   **Vol. 3:** 87
17:10   **Vol. 1:** 297   **Vol. 3:** 785
17:11   **Vol. 1:** 188   **Vol. 2:** 364   **Vol. 3:** 490,
          492, 746, 1114
17:12   **Vol. 2:** 126   **Vol. 3:** 1063, 1065
17:13   **Vol. 3:** 559, 710, 1113–1114
17:14   **Vol. 3:** 984
17:15   **Vol. 1:** 337, 472
17:16   **Vol. 1:** 110   **Vol. 2:** 74, 245   **Vol. 3:**
          694

Acts *(cont'd)*

17:17   **Vol. 1:** 267, 361   **Vol. 3:** 87, 410, 785, 821
17:18   **Vol. 1:** 689   **Vol. 2:** 550   **Vol. 3:** 46, 261, 277, 822, 1036
17:19   **Vol. 2:** 85, 574, 670   **Vol. 3:** 749, 769
17:20   **Vol. 1:** 689   **Vol. 2:** 175
17:21   **Vol. 1:** 689   **Vol. 2:** 670
17:22–31   **Vol. 3:** 87
17:22   **Vol. 1:** 257, 453   **Vol. 2:** 85   **Vol. 3:** 431
17:23   **Vol. 1:** 689   **Vol. 2:** 74, 77, 93–94, 113, 406–407, 503   **Vol. 3:** 460–461, 489
17:24 f   **Vol. 2:** 73, 164
17:24   **Vol. 1:** 524   **Vol. 2:** 74, 77, 150, 193, 514, 721, 920   **Vol. 3:** 784–785, 793
17:25   **Vol. 2:** 149, 164, 480, 861   **Vol. 3:** 461, 707
17:26–29   **Vol. 3:** 331
17:26   **Vol. 1:** 221, 473, 477, 586   **Vol. 2:** 721, 921
17:27 f   **Vol. 2:** 85
17:27   **Vol. 3:** 529, 532
17:28 f   **Vol. 2:** 565
17:28   **Vol. 1:** 85   **Vol. 2:** 77, 480, 919–920   **Vol. 3:** 927, 1155
17:29   **Vol. 1:** 106, 175, 279   **Vol. 2:** 86, 96, 503   **Vol. 3:** 331
17:30   **Vol. 1:** 340–341   **Vol. 2:** 407   **Vol. 3:** 47, 844, 1113
17:31 f   **Vol. 3:** 261
17:31   **Vol. 1:** 326, 473   **Vol. 2:** 238, 365, 894, 920   **Vol. 3:** 361, 1210
17:32   **Vol. 3:** 277
17:32a   **Vol. 3:** 303
17:34   **Vol. 2:** 349
18–25   **Vol. 2:** 785
18:1   **Vol. 3:** 534, 1174
18:2   **Vol. 1:** 476   **Vol. 2:** 847   **Vol. 3:** 240, 534, 1065
18:3   **Vol. 1:** 279   **Vol. 3:** 812
18:4   **Vol. 1:** 361, 589   **Vol. 3:** 87, 410, 785, 821
18:5 ff   **Vol. 3:** 203
18:5   **Vol. 3:** 1044
18:6   **Vol. 1:** 222, 317   **Vol. 2:** 158, 794   **Vol. 3:** 343, 561
18:7   **Vol. 1:** 297, 361   **Vol. 2:** 85, 94   **Vol. 3:** 785
18:8   **Vol. 1:** 148, 159–160, 603   **Vol. 2:** 176, 250, 517
18:9   **Vol. 1:** 421, 512, 623   **Vol. 3:** 85, 515, 862
18:10   **Vol. 2:** 800
18:11   **Vol. 2:** 895   **Vol. 3:** 764, 1113
18:12 f   **Vol. 3:** 908
18:12–17   **Vol. 1:** 270
18:12   **Vol. 1:** 270   **Vol. 2:** 369
18:13   **Vol. 1:** 361   **Vol. 2:** 450   **Vol. 3:** 909

18:14   **Vol. 1:** 326   **Vol. 2:** 726, 728, 766   **Vol. 3:** 575
18:15   **Vol. 2:** 451
18:16 f   **Vol. 2:** 369
18:17   **Vol. 3:** 749, 903
18:18   **Vol. 1:** 203   **Vol. 2:** 157, 159, 162, 641, 867, 895   **Vol. 3:** 228, 431
18:19   **Vol. 1:** 297, 324   **Vol. 3:** 251, 785, 821
18:20   **Vol. 2:** 880   **Vol. 3:** 843
18:21   **Vol. 3:** 1021
18:23   **Vol. 1:** 490   **Vol. 3:** 843
18:24–28   **Vol. 3:** 87
18:24   **Vol. 1:** 324   **Vol. 3:** 490, 492, 1106, 1117
18:25 f   **Vol. 3:** 941
18:25   **Vol. 1:** 318   **Vol. 2:** 921   **Vol. 3:** 110, 694, 699–700, 763–764, 771, 942, 1117
18:26   **Vol. 2:** 736   **Vol. 3:** 751, 785, 942, 1065
18:27   **Vol. 1:** 261, 490   **Vol. 2:** 119   **Vol. 3:** 489, 746
18:28   **Vol. 2:** 790   **Vol. 3:** 490, 492, 764
19:1 ff   **Vol. 1:** 146, 148   **Vol. 3:** 699
19:1–21   **Vol. 2:** 921
19:1–7   **Vol. 2:** 785   **Vol. 3:** 458
19:1 f   **Vol. 3:** 699
19:1   **Vol. 1:** 490   **Vol. 3:** 1017
19:2   **Vol. 3:** 941
19:4 f   **Vol. 1:** 157–158
19:4   **Vol. 1:** 359   **Vol. 3:** 1208, 1212
19:5   **Vol. 2:** 176   **Vol. 3:** 61, 1209
19:6   **Vol. 1:** 528   **Vol. 2:** 42, 152, 611, 740, 786   **Vol. 3:** 86–87, 699–700, 1080
19:7   **Vol. 2:** 696   **Vol. 3:** 458
19:8 f   **Vol. 3:** 821
19:8   **Vol. 1:** 590   **Vol. 2:** 736   **Vol. 3:** 87, 410, 785
19:9   **Vol. 1:** 415, 473, 490, 593, 607, 733   **Vol. 2:** 155, 794, 895   **Vol. 3:** 941
19:10   **Vol. 2:** 126   **Vol. 3:** 1113–1114
19:11   **Vol. 2:** 603
19:12 f   **Vol. 3:** 694
19:12   **Vol. 3:** 167, 174, 475
19:13 ff   **Vol. 2:** 74   **Vol. 3:** 476
19:13 f   **Vol. 3:** 473
19:13–20   **Vol. 3:** 88
19:13–16   **Vol. 2:** 654   **Vol. 3:** 476
19:13   **Vol. 1:** 322   **Vol. 3:** 52, 473, 475, 737–738
19:15 f   **Vol. 3:** 694
19:15   **Vol. 2:** 655   **Vol. 3:** 475
19:16   **Vol. 1:** 313   **Vol. 2:** 519
19:17   **Vol. 1:** 609
19:18   **Vol. 1:** 346, 702   **Vol. 2:** 556–557
19:19   **Vol. 1:** 243, 267   **Vol. 2:** 74, 556–557   **Vol. 3:** 1157
19:20   **Vol. 2:** 130, 557   **Vol. 3:** 714, 718, 1113–1114
19:21–21:16   **Vol. 2:** 827
19:21–41   **Vol. 2:** 85

Acts *(cont'd)*

19:21   **Vol. 1:** 737   **Vol. 2:** 328, 666   **Vol. 3:** 700, 1183
19:22   **Vol. 3:** 843
19:23 ff   **Vol. 2:** 623
19:23–41   **Vol. 2:** 74
19:23–40   **Vol. 3:** 203
19:23   **Vol. 3:** 709–710, 837, 941
19:24   **Vol. 1:** 279   **Vol. 2:** 96   **Vol. 3:** 784–785
19:25–27   **Vol. 2:** 568
19:26 f   **Vol. 2:** 235
19:26   **Vol. 1:** 589   **Vol. 2:** 73, 801   **Vol. 3:** 784
19:27   **Vol. 1:** 419, 519   **Vol. 2:** 94, 235, 303, 426   **Vol. 3:** 824, 826, 1175
19:28   **Vol. 1:** 106, 110, 410, 739   **Vol. 3:** 947
19:29   **Vol. 3:** 521
19:30   **Vol. 1:** 490   **Vol. 2:** 789
19:31   **Vol. 2:** 549
19:32   **Vol. 1:** 303   **Vol. 3:** 521
19:33   **Vol. 2:** 789   **Vol. 3:** 558
19:34   **Vol. 3:** 114, 847
19:35–41   **Vol. 1:** 270
19:35   **Vol. 3:** 480, 796
19:36   **Vol. 3:** 1157
19:37   **Vol. 2:** 235
19:38   **Vol. 1:** 84, 267, 270, 279
19:39 f   **Vol. 1:** 303
19:39   **Vol. 1:** 577–578   **Vol. 2:** 789   **Vol. 3:** 521, 532
19:40   **Vol. 1:** 84, 419   **Vol. 2:** 139   **Vol. 3:** 189
19:41   **Vol. 3:** 521
20   **Vol. 1:** 364
20:1   **Vol. 1:** 490   **Vol. 2:** 623
20:2   **Vol. 2:** 126   **Vol. 3:** 87, 164
20:3   **Vol. 1:** 326   **Vol. 2:** 398, 827
20:4   **Vol. 1:** 656
20:5–15   **Vol. 1:** 490
20:5   **Vol. 1:** 322   **Vol. 3:** 224
20:6   **Vol. 1:** 634   **Vol. 2:** 550, 692
20:7 ff   **Vol. 2:** 632
20:7 f   **Vol. 1:** 297
20:7   **Vol. 1:** 326, 631   **Vol. 2:** 32, 518, 523   **Vol. 3:** 410, 412, 821
20:8   **Vol. 2:** 32, 486
20:9–12   **Vol. 1:** 446
20:9   **Vol. 1:** 609   **Vol. 2:** 198   **Vol. 3:** 589, 821, 1198
20:10   **Vol. 2:** 623, 919
20:11   **Vol. 2:** 289, 523
20:13 f   **Vol. 3:** 749
20:13   **Vol. 1:** 326
20:15   **Vol. 2:** 739
20:16   **Vol. 2:** 785   **Vol. 3:** 843
20:17–37   **Vol. 3:** 65
20:17   **Vol. 1:** 199   **Vol. 3:** 568
20:18 ff   **Vol. 3:** 844

20:18   **Vol. 3:** 843
20:19   **Vol. 2:** 263   **Vol. 3:** 802
20:20   **Vol. 2:** 250, 790   **Vol. 3:** 764
20:21   **Vol. 1:** 359   **Vol. 3:** 1213
20:22 f   **Vol. 2:** 921   **Vol. 3:** 1183
20:22   **Vol. 1:** 171, 325   **Vol. 3:** 700
20:23   **Vol. 2:** 809, 827   **Vol. 3:** 87, 224, 592, 700
20:24   **Vol. 2:** 62, 110, 112, 119, 359, 827   **Vol. 3:** 546, 947, 1044
20:25   **Vol. 3:** 52, 56, 87, 517
20:26 ff   **Vol. 3:** 1018
20:26   **Vol. 1:** 222
20:27   **Vol. 2:** 77   **Vol. 3:** 1017–1018
20:28   **Vol. 1:** 191–192, 199, 223, 303, 477   **Vol. 2:** 73, 83, 838, 921   **Vol. 3:** 166, 395, 568, 700, 1018
20:29   **Vol. 1:** 118, 261
20:30   **Vol. 1:** 490, 493
20:31   **Vol. 1:** 568   **Vol. 2:** 137
20:32   **Vol. 2:** 119, 230, 249, 252, 302   **Vol. 3:** 1114
20:33   **Vol. 2:** 96
20:34   **Vol. 3:** 547, 958
20:35   **Vol. 2:** 41, 514, 694   **Vol. 3:** 967, 994
20:36   **Vol. 2:** 859
20:37   **Vol. 1:** 241, 609   **Vol. 2:** 549
21:1–18   **Vol. 1:** 490
21:3   **Vol. 2:** 148
21:4   **Vol. 1:** 490   **Vol. 2:** 692, 827, 921   **Vol. 3:** 227, 700, 1022, 1183
21:5   **Vol. 1:** 286   **Vol. 2:** 859, 869   **Vol. 3:** 351
21:6   **Vol. 2:** 839
21:8   **Vol. 2:** 114, 550   **Vol. 3:** 548, 1067
21:9 ff   **Vol. 3:** 86
21:9–11   **Vol. 3:** 700
21:9   **Vol. 2:** 212, 689   **Vol. 3:** 81, 87, 1072
21:10 ff   **Vol. 2:** 827, 900
21:10 f   **Vol. 3:** 86
21:10   **Vol. 3:** 87, 227
21:11   **Vol. 2:** 149–150, 921   **Vol. 3:** 85–87, 121, 1183
21:12–14   **Vol. 3:** 1183
21:12   **Vol. 3:** 1183
21:13   **Vol. 2:** 416, 623   **Vol. 3:** 118, 257, 546
21:14   **Vol. 1:** 591   **Vol. 3:** 111
21:15–20   **Vol. 2:** 451
21:15   **Vol. 2:** 328
21:16   **Vol. 1:** 167, 490
21:17–26   **Vol. 1:** 310
21:17   **Vol. 3:** 746
21:18 ff   **Vol. 3:** 592
21:18–26   **Vol. 3:** 101
21:18   **Vol. 1:** 199   **Vol. 2:** 328
21:19   **Vol. 1:** 576
21:20 ff   **Vol. 2:** 641
21:20   **Vol. 2:** 450   **Vol. 3:** 686
21:21   **Vol. 1:** 310, 607   **Vol. 2:** 450, 795   **Vol. 3:** 764, 771, 944

Acts (*cont'd*)

21:22	**Vol. 1:** 733
21:23	**Vol. 2:** 689, 867
21:24 ff	**Vol. 2:** 641
21:24–26	**Vol. 3:** 101
21:24	**Vol. 1:** 203 **Vol. 2:** 135, 450, 452 **Vol. 3:** 771
21:25	**Vol. 1:** 226 **Vol. 2:** 135, 284–286, 682 **Vol. 3:** 432, 931
21:26 ff	**Vol. 2:** 236
21:26	**Vol. 2:** 451 **Vol. 3:** 46–47, 101, 431, 793
21:27 f	**Vol. 2:** 451
21:28 f	**Vol. 3:** 949
21:28	**Vol. 1:** 641–642 **Vol. 2:** 126, 310, 438, 450, 799 **Vol. 3:** 764
21:29	**Vol. 1:** 695 **Vol. 3:** 515
21:30 ff	**Vol. 2:** 623
21:30	**Vol. 2:** 30, 730 **Vol. 3:** 749
21:31 ff	**Vol. 2:** 699
21:31–35	**Vol. 3:** 788
21:31	**Vol. 1:** 430
21:32	**Vol. 3:** 903, 964
21:33	**Vol. 1:** 341 **Vol. 3:** 749
21:34	**Vol. 1:** 410 **Vol. 2:** 623 **Vol. 3:** 965
21:35	**Vol. 3:** 711
21:36	**Vol. 2:** 799
21:37–40	**Vol. 2:** 434
21:37	**Vol. 2:** 126, 699 **Vol. 3:** 965
21:38 ff	**Vol. 3:** 729
21:38	**Vol. 1:** 532, 717 **Vol. 2:** 699 **Vol. 3:** 1007
21:39	**Vol. 2:** 328, 804, 860
21:40	**Vol. 2:** 309 **Vol. 3:** 558
22:1–21	**Vol. 1:** 136
22:2	**Vol. 2:** 309 **Vol. 3:** 111
22:3	**Vol. 2:** 315, 328, 451 **Vol. 3:** 778, 873, 1167, 1178
22:4–16	**Vol. 1:** 183
22:4	**Vol. 2:** 136, 368, 806 **Vol. 3:** 941–942
22:5	**Vol. 1:** 197 **Vol. 3:** 1043
22:6–11	**Vol. 3:** 330
22:6	**Vol. 2:** 193, 493 **Vol. 3:** 1203
22:7 f	**Vol. 2:** 806
22:7	**Vol. 3:** 114
22:8	**Vol. 2:** 333, 513
22:9	**Vol. 2:** 493 **Vol. 3:** 114
22:10	**Vol. 1:** 476 **Vol. 2:** 513
22:11	**Vol. 2:** 46, 493 **Vol. 3:** 520, 1180
22:12	**Vol. 2:** 91, 451 **Vol. 3:** 1043
22:13	**Vol. 3:** 519, 846
22:14	**Vol. 1:** 476 **Vol. 2:** 73, 176 **Vol. 3:** 114, 361, 1022, 1191
22:15	**Vol. 2:** 176 **Vol. 3:** 1044
22:16	**Vol. 1:** 146, 148, 152, 154, 157–158, 276 **Vol. 3:** 990, 1210
22:17 ff	**Vol. 3:** 87
22:17–21	**Vol. 1:** 476
22:17 f	**Vol. 3:** 700
22:17	**Vol. 1:** 528 **Vol. 2:** 236 **Vol. 3:** 793, 913
22:18	**Vol. 3:** 88
22:19	**Vol. 1:** 163 **Vol. 2:** 136 **Vol. 3:** 785, 1212
22:20	**Vol. 2:** 854 **Vol. 3:** 1044
22:21	**Vol. 1:** 136 **Vol. 3:** 38
22:23	**Vol. 1:** 449
22:24	**Vol. 1:** 163, 341, 410 **Vol. 2:** 139, 699 **Vol. 3:** 965
22:25 f	**Vol. 3:** 964
22:26–29	**Vol. 2:** 699
22:28	**Vol. 2:** 157, 804
22:29	**Vol. 1:** 607
22:30–23:10	**Vol. 1:** 364 **Vol. 3:** 40
22:30	**Vol. 1:** 83, 341 **Vol. 3:** 179, 1198
23:1 ff	**Vol. 3:** 39
23:1	**Vol. 1:** 353 **Vol. 2:** 101, 804 **Vol. 3:** 520
23:2 f	**Vol. 3:** 903
23:3 ff	**Vol. 3:** 40
23:3	**Vol. 1:** 205, 265, 341 **Vol. 2:** 365, 451 **Vol. 3:** 588, 948
23:4 f	**Vol. 3:** 35, 347
23:5	**Vol. 1:** 168
23:6–9	**Vol. 3:** 440
23:6	**Vol. 1:** 288, 446 **Vol. 2:** 242, 303, 365 **Vol. 3:** 439
23:7	**Vol. 1:** 733 **Vol. 3:** 439, 544
23:8 ff	**Vol. 1:** 346
23:8 f	**Vol. 3:** 695
23:8	**Vol. 1:** 101 **Vol. 2:** 812 **Vol. 3:** 439
23:9	**Vol. 1:** 564 **Vol. 2:** 303, 812 **Vol. 3:** 482, 529
23:10	**Vol. 1:** 341, 623 **Vol. 2:** 91, 699 **Vol. 3:** 602, 964–965
23:11	**Vol. 1:** 328, 421, 476, 512 **Vol. 2:** 666 **Vol. 3:** 85, 88, 1043
23:12–14	**Vol. 1:** 430
23:12	**Vol. 2:** 689
23:14	**Vol. 1:** 415
23:15	**Vol. 1:** 326 **Vol. 2:** 489, 699
23:16	**Vol. 3:** 965
23:17 ff	**Vol. 2:** 699
23:17	**Vol. 3:** 964
23:18	**Vol. 3:** 592
23:19	**Vol. 3:** 749
23:21	**Vol. 1:** 591
23:22	**Vol. 1:** 340 **Vol. 2:** 489, 699
23:23	**Vol. 3:** 964
23:24	**Vol. 1:** 270 **Vol. 3:** 211
23:25	**Vol. 3:** 489, 904
23:26–30	**Vol. 1:** 247
23:26	**Vol. 1:** 247, 270 **Vol. 2:** 358 **Vol. 3:** 718
23:27	**Vol. 1:** 344, 486 **Vol. 3:** 964
23:28	**Vol. 1:** 84 **Vol. 2:** 139
23:29	**Vol. 1:** 84 **Vol. 2:** 450–451 **Vol. 3:** 592
23:30	**Vol. 1:** 83, 340

Acts *(cont'd)*

23:31   **Vol. 3:** 749, 1181
23:32   **Vol. 3:** 965
23:33   **Vol. 1:** 270
23:34   **Vol. 1:** 114   **Vol. 3:** 1188
23:35   **Vol. 1:** 83, 341   **Vol. 2:** 135
24   **Vol. 3:** 65
24:1   **Vol. 1:** 270   **Vol. 2:** 489   **Vol. 3:** 40
24:2   **Vol. 1:** 83   **Vol. 2:** 780
24:3   **Vol. 1:** 695   **Vol. 3:** 718, 818
24:4   **Vol. 2:** 221, 258
24:5   **Vol. 1:** 519, 535   **Vol. 2:** 333, 438
24:6   **Vol. 2:** 365   **Vol. 3:** 717, 793, 802
24:7   **Vol. 2:** 699
24:8   **Vol. 1:** 341   **Vol. 2:** 365
24:10   **Vol. 1:** 270
24:11   **Vol. 2:** 696, 877
24:12   **Vol. 1:** 297   **Vol. 2:** 236   **Vol. 3:** 785, 793, 821
24:13   **Vol. 1:** 83
24:14   **Vol. 1:** 535, 604   **Vol. 2:** 451   **Vol. 3:** 550, 941, 1211
24:15   **Vol. 1:** 326   **Vol. 2:** 73, 242, 245   **Vol. 3:** 303, 361, 575
24:16   **Vol. 1:** 350, 353, 495   **Vol. 2:** 707   **Vol. 3:** 1175, 1192
24:17 f   **Vol. 3:** 431
24:17   **Vol. 2:** 597
24:18   **Vol. 2:** 236, 623   **Vol. 3:** 101, 793
24:19   **Vol. 1:** 83   **Vol. 2:** 899
24:20   **Vol. 1:** 364   **Vol. 3:** 529, 575
24:21   **Vol. 3:** 114
24:22   **Vol. 2:** 699   **Vol. 3:** 941
24:23   **Vol. 2:** 222   **Vol. 3:** 547, 717, 964
24:24   **Vol. 3:** 1213
24:25   **Vol. 1:** 495   **Vol. 2:** 365   **Vol. 3:** 361, 750, 821
24:26   **Vol. 2:** 845
24:27   **Vol. 1:** 737   **Vol. 2:** 119
25–28   **Vol. 1:** 276
25:2   **Vol. 2:** 489   **Vol. 3:** 39
25:3   **Vol. 2:** 119   **Vol. 3:** 941
25:5   **Vol. 1:** 83
25:6   **Vol. 1:** 341   **Vol. 2:** 369
25:7   **Vol. 1:** 261   **Vol. 3:** 570–571
25:8   **Vol. 1:** 269   **Vol. 2:** 236, 450   **Vol. 3:** 793
25:9   **Vol. 2:** 119
25:10 f   **Vol. 3:** 575
25:10   **Vol. 2:** 369
25:11   **Vol. 1:** 83, 269   **Vol. 2:** 116, 119, 858   **Vol. 3:** 349, 1157
25:12   **Vol. 1:** 363
25:13 f   **Vol. 2:** 378
25:14   **Vol. 3:** 592
25:15   **Vol. 2:** 370, 489
25:16   **Vol. 1:** 83–84   **Vol. 2:** 116, 119, 438
25:17   **Vol. 1:** 341   **Vol. 2:** 369
25:18   **Vol. 1:** 83   **Vol. 2:** 139

25:19   **Vol. 1:** 453
25:20   **Vol. 3:** 532
25:21   **Vol. 1:** 269, 341   **Vol. 2:** 93
25:22   **Vol. 3:** 1017
25:23   **Vol. 1:** 341   **Vol. 2:** 699
25:24   **Vol. 1:** 411, 733   **Vol. 2:** 882
25:25   **Vol. 2:** 93   **Vol. 3:** 750, 1157
25:26   **Vol. 3:** 349, 489
25:27   **Vol. 2:** 139   **Vol. 3:** 592, 822, 1118
26   **Vol. 3:** 65
26:1   **Vol. 2:** 150
26:2–18   **Vol. 1:** 136
26:2   **Vol. 1:** 84
26:3   **Vol. 2:** 437, 860
26:4   **Vol. 1:** 166   **Vol. 2:** 675
26:5   **Vol. 1:** 535, 693   **Vol. 2:** 451   **Vol. 3:** 551, 1043
26:6   **Vol. 2:** 786   **Vol. 3:** 71, 550
26:7   **Vol. 1:** 84   **Vol. 2:** 139, 695   **Vol. 3:** 550, 871
26:8   **Vol. 2:** 364   **Vol. 3:** 304
26:9–18   **Vol. 1:** 183
26:9–11   **Vol. 3:** 1199
26:9   **Vol. 2:** 333   **Vol. 3:** 822, 1157
26:10   **Vol. 1:** 305   **Vol. 2:** 136   **Vol. 3:** 482
26:11   **Vol. 1:** 730   **Vol. 3:** 785
26:12–18   **Vol. 3:** 330
26:13   **Vol. 2:** 193, 486, 493   **Vol. 3:** 732, 941
26:14 f   **Vol. 2:** 806
26:14   **Vol. 1:** 511   **Vol. 2:** 155, 309   **Vol. 3:** 114
26:15–18   **Vol. 2:** 302
26:15   **Vol. 2:** 513
26:16 f   **Vol. 1:** 136
26:16   **Vol. 1:** 476   **Vol. 3:** 285, 515, 546, 1044, 1191
26:17 f   **Vol. 3:** 38
26:18   **Vol. 1:** 355, 359, 424   **Vol. 2:** 230, 654, 726, 728, 920   **Vol. 3:** 213, 471, 1213
26:19   **Vol. 1:** 593   **Vol. 3:** 1191
26:20   **Vol. 1:** 355, 359   **Vol. 3:** 47, 1150
26:21   **Vol. 3:** 793, 802
26:22   **Vol. 1:** 326   **Vol. 2:** 426, 641
26:23   **Vol. 1:** 326, 667–668   **Vol. 2:** 113, 793   **Vol. 3:** 304, 722, 724, 1113
26:24   **Vol. 1:** 529   **Vol. 3:** 113, 493
26:25   **Vol. 1:** 502, 529   **Vol. 3:** 718, 884, 1122
26:26   **Vol. 1:** 591   **Vol. 2:** 736   **Vol. 3:** 389
26:27   **Vol. 1:** 604
26:27a   **Vol. 3:** 1211
26:28   **Vol. 1:** 123, 590   **Vol. 2:** 343
26:29   **Vol. 2:** 867
26:30   **Vol. 1:** 270   **Vol. 3:** 588
26:31   **Vol. 3:** 592, 1157
26:32   **Vol. 1:** 269   **Vol. 3:** 189
27:1–28:16   **Vol. 1:** 490
27:1   **Vol. 2:** 93   **Vol. 3:** 964
27:3   **Vol. 2:** 549–550, 739
27:4   **Vol. 3:** 1002
27:6   **Vol. 3:** 964

Acts (*cont'd*)

27:7   **Vol. 3:** 1002
27:9   **Vol. 3:** 843
27:10   **Vol. 3:** 27
27:11   **Vol. 1:** 198, 591, 593   **Vol. 3:** 964
27:12   **Vol. 3:** 1017
27:13   **Vol. 1:** 697   **Vol. 3:** 822, 1003
27:14   **Vol. 3:** 1002, 1199
27:15   **Vol. 3:** 1002
27:20   **Vol. 3:** 211, 252, 317, 319, 731, 735
27:21   **Vol. 1:** 593   **Vol. 3:** 27, 136
27:22   **Vol. 3:** 87, 683
27:23 – 24   **Vol. 1:** 512
27:23   **Vol. 1:** 421, 474   **Vol. 3:** 87
27:24   **Vol. 1:** 269, 474, 623   **Vol. 2:** 116, 119, 666
27:25   **Vol. 3:** 1211
27:27 f   **Vol. 1:** 103
27:29   **Vol. 2:** 689, 867
27:30   **Vol. 1:** 326, 559   **Vol. 3:** 984
27:31   **Vol. 3:** 211, 964
27:33   **Vol. 3:** 717, 750 – 751
27:34   **Vol. 1:** 203, 609   **Vol. 3:** 211, 1204
27:35   **Vol. 3:** 819
27:36   **Vol. 3:** 751
27:37   **Vol. 3:** 683
27:38   **Vol. 3:** 984
27:39   **Vol. 1:** 240
27:40   **Vol. 3:** 984
27:41   **Vol. 3:** 180, 560, 711
27:42   **Vol. 3:** 1017
27:43   **Vol. 1:** 341   **Vol. 2:** 222   **Vol. 3:** 211, 964, 1017
27:44   **Vol. 3:** 211, 252
28   **Vol. 1:** 364
28:1 – 6   **Vol. 1:** 510
28:1   **Vol. 3:** 211
28:2 f   **Vol. 1:** 656
28:2   **Vol. 1:** 318   **Vol. 2:** 550   **Vol. 3:** 860, 1004
28:3   **Vol. 2:** 33
28:4   **Vol. 2:** 96   **Vol. 3:** 211, 984
28:5   **Vol. 1:** 564, 656   **Vol. 2:** 921   **Vol. 3:** 561, 723
28:6   **Vol. 1:** 610
28:7   **Vol. 1:** 690   **Vol. 2:** 550
28:8   **Vol. 1:** 656   **Vol. 2:** 151
28:9   **Vol. 3:** 252
28:10   **Vol. 2:** 50   **Vol. 3:** 958
28:12   **Vol. 3:** 227
28:13   **Vol. 1:** 322   **Vol. 3:** 1003
28:14   **Vol. 1:** 570   **Vol. 2:** 692   **Vol. 3:** 227
28:15   **Vol. 1:** 325
28:16   **Vol. 3:** 964
28:17   **Vol. 2:** 437, 799   **Vol. 3:** 592
28:18   **Vol. 2:** 139, 365   **Vol. 3:** 189
28:19   **Vol. 1:** 83, 269   **Vol. 2:** 663
28:20   **Vol. 1:** 570   **Vol. 2:** 314 – 315
28:21   **Vol. 1:** 567   **Vol. 3:** 492
28:22   **Vol. 1:** 535   **Vol. 2:** 617
28:23   **Vol. 2:** 314, 444, 641   **Vol. 3:** 65, 87, 1044
28:24 – 28   **Vol. 2:** 37
28:24   **Vol. 1:** 591
28:25 – 28   **Vol. 3:** 87
28:25   **Vol. 1:** 736   **Vol. 3:** 699
28:26 f   **Vol. 2:** 753, 799   **Vol. 3:** 131 – 132, 313
28:27   **Vol. 1:** 261   **Vol. 2:** 156, 178
28:28   **Vol. 3:** 221
28:30 f   **Vol. 3:** 226, 1114
28:30   **Vol. 3:** 746
28:31   **Vol. 1:** 590   **Vol. 2:** 340, 387, 736   **Vol. 3:** 52, 56, 764

Romans

1 – 11   **Vol. 1:** 65
1 – 8   **Vol. 1:** 370   **Vol. 3:** 251, 368, 580
1 – 7   **Vol. 3:** 38
1 – 4   **Vol. 1:** 436   **Vol. 2:** 800
1 – 3   **Vol. 1:** 112   **Vol. 2:** 366 – 367, 400   **Vol. 3:** 164
1   **Vol. 2:** 570   **Vol. 3:** 372
1:1 ff   **Vol. 2:** 111
1:1 – 7   **Vol. 1:** 247
1:1 – 4   **Vol. 3:** 62
1:1   **Vol. 1:** 276, 474, 638, 718, 720   **Vol. 2:** 111   **Vol. 3:** 596, 601
1:2 – 4   **Vol. 3:** 1122
1:2   **Vol. 2:** 176, 228, 605   **Vol. 3:** 70, 313, 487, 491 – 492
1:3 f   **Vol. 3:** 61, 243, 299, 323, 639, 1110, 1171, 1188
1:3 – 4   **Vol. 3:** 643, 651
1:3   **Vol. 1:** 427, 473, 675   **Vol. 2:** 79, 314, 378   **Vol. 3:** 643 – 644, 661, 1073, 1199
1:4   **Vol. 1:** 323, 675   **Vol. 2:** 79, 81, 203, 230, 340, 604 – 605   **Vol. 3:** 129, 277, 299 – 300, 304, 643, 703, 705, 1073
1:5   **Vol. 1:** 129   **Vol. 2:** 121, 179, 654, 793 – 794   **Vol. 3:** 38, 314, 748 – 749, 1150
1:6 f   **Vol. 1:** 275, 298
1:7   **Vol. 1:** 275, 300, 305, 620   **Vol. 2:** 229, 516, 544, 780 – 781
1:7b   **Vol. 2:** 874
1:8 ff   **Vol. 2:** 874
1:8 – 12   **Vol. 1:** 247
1:8   **Vol. 1:** 599, 601   **Vol. 2:** 73, 873   **Vol. 3:** 611, 818
1:9 f   **Vol. 2:** 874 – 875
1:9   **Vol. 3:** 230, 246, 550 – 551, 643 – 644, 693, 742, 1043
1:10 ff   **Vol. 2:** 826
1:10   **Vol. 2:** 861, 874   **Vol. 3:** 943, 1021
1:11 f   **Vol. 1:** 129
1:11   **Vol. 1:** 458   **Vol. 2:** 41, 43   **Vol. 3:** 703, 706 – 707
1:12 f   **Vol. 1:** 399

Romans *(cont'd)*

1:13   **Vol. 1:** 697, 723 **Vol. 2:** 223, 406 **Vol. 3:** 252, 1022

1:14   **Vol. 2:** 126–127, 668

1:15   **Vol. 2:** 112 **Vol. 3:** 214

1:16 f   **Vol. 2:** 111 **Vol. 3:** 365, 371, 1031

1:16   **Vol. 1:** 397, 601, 666–667 **Vol. 2:** 78, 127, 314, 604–605 **Vol. 3:** 214, 367, 563

1:17   **Vol. 1:** 289 **Vol. 2:** 78, 111, 447 **Vol. 3:** 312, 315, 321, 362, 365, 1171, 1177, 1189–1190

1:18 ff   **Vol. 2:** 460, 566, 682 **Vol. 3:** 315, 332, 576, 1031

1:18–5:21   **Vol. 1:** 401

1:18–4:25   **Vol. 3:** 368

1:18–3:20   **Vol. 1:** 112 **Vol. 2:** 472 **Vol. 3:** 580, 584

1:18–32   **Vol. 2:** 127, 286, 793 **Vol. 3:** 163, 1202

1:18–23   **Vol. 3:** 310

1:18   **Vol. 1:** 112, 417 **Vol. 2:** 76, 94, 193, 399 **Vol. 3:** 197, 575–576, 580, 885, 1199

1:19 ff   **Vol. 2:** 77 **Vol. 3:** 327, 331

1:19–23   **Vol. 3:** 331

1:19 f   **Vol. 2:** 400, 503

1:19   **Vol. 3:** 320–321

1:20 ff   **Vol. 1:** 382

1:20   **Vol. 1:** 385 **Vol. 2:** 77–78, 86, 139, 604 **Vol. 3:** 128, 321, 515, 829, 885, 1154, 1185, 1187

1:20b   **Vol. 1:** 386

1:21 ff   **Vol. 1:** 112 **Vol. 2:** 566

1:21 f   **Vol. 2:** 78 **Vol. 3:** 132

1:21   **Vol. 1:** 424, 551–552 **Vol. 2:** 47, 161, 183, 399, 874 **Vol. 3:** 132, 200, 333, 576, 819, 821, 1192

1:22 f   **Vol. 2:** 400

1:23   **Vol. 1:** 175, 469 **Vol. 2:** 46, 76–77, 503, 874 **Vol. 3:** 167, 304, 331

1:24   **Vol. 1:** 235, 457 **Vol. 2:** 51, 155–156, 182, 368, 567 **Vol. 3:** 1175, 1192

1:25   **Vol. 1:** 99, 385, 461 **Vol. 2:** 93–94, 399, 472, 874 **Vol. 3:** 167, 550, 576, 830, 885

1:25b   **Vol. 1:** 213

1:26 ff   **Vol. 2:** 563

1:26–32   **Vol. 3:** 929

1:26   **Vol. 2:** 50–51, 155, 660 **Vol. 3:** 167, 722

1:27   **Vol. 1:** 460–461, 701 **Vol. 2:** 459–460, 569–570 **Vol. 3:** 197, 751

1:28 ff   **Vol. 3:** 1157

1:28   **Vol. 2:** 155, 399 **Vol. 3:** 28, 808–809

1:29 ff   **Vol. 3:** 31

1:29–32   **Vol. 2:** 597

1:29–31   **Vol. 3:** 31

1:29 f   **Vol. 3:** 28

1:29   **Vol. 1:** 138, 557, 563 **Vol. 3:** 197, 346, 576

1:30   **Vol. 1:** 589, 593 **Vol. 2:** 86, 435 **Vol. 3:** 28, 30, 32, 345–346

1:31   **Vol. 2:** 539, 542 **Vol. 3:** 132

1:32   **Vol. 2:** 77, 399, 446 **Vol. 3:** 332, 349, 363, 581, 1155, 1157

2 f   **Vol. 3:** 168

2   **Vol. 3:** 372

2:1–3:20   **Vol. 3:** 163

2:1   **Vol. 2:** 139, 365, 566, 739

2:2 f   **Vol. 2:** 365

2:2   **Vol. 2:** 449

2:3   **Vol. 2:** 766 **Vol. 3:** 824–825

2:4   **Vol. 1:** 461 **Vol. 2:** 79, 106, 766, 770

2:5 f   **Vol. 3:** 1151

2:5   **Vol. 1:** 106, 112, 358, 417 **Vol. 2:** 76, 155–156, 183–184, 834, 836, 894, 926 **Vol. 3:** 315

2:6 f   **Vol. 2:** 446

2:6   **Vol. 1:** 323 **Vol. 3:** 136, 142, 1200

2:7   **Vol. 1:** 113, 470 **Vol. 2:** 47, 50, 101, 446, 774–775 **Vol. 3:** 142, 302, 368, 832

2:8   **Vol. 1:** 106, 591 **Vol. 3:** 575–576, 885

2:9 f†   **Vol. 1:** 667 **Vol. 2:** 127

2:9   **Vol. 1:** 106, 666 **Vol. 2:** 127, 446, 808 **Vol. 3:** 683

2:10   **Vol. 1:** 666 **Vol. 2:** 47, 50 **Vol. 3:** 1151

2:11 f   **Vol. 2:** 446

2:11   **Vol. 1:** 587

2:12–16   **Vol. 2:** 77 **Vol. 3:** 327

2:12   **Vol. 2:** 365, 445–446 **Vol. 3:** 163

2:13   **Vol. 2:** 176–177, 445–446 **Vol. 3:** 362–363, 1155, 1202

2:14 ff   **Vol. 1:** 350

2:14–16   **Vol. 2:** 127, 660

2:14 f   **Vol. 2:** 794, 905 **Vol. 3:** 584

2:14   **Vol. 2:** 177, 444, 922–923 **Vol. 3:** 927

2:15   **Vol. 1:** 83, 350, 353 **Vol. 2:** 183, 444, 446, 567 **Vol. 3:** 490, 824, 1042

2:16   **Vol. 2:** 111, 113, 218, 365, 446 **Vol. 3:** 61–62, 611

2:17 ff   **Vol. 2:** 566 **Vol. 3:** 1020

2:17–29   **Vol. 3:** 584

2:17–24   **Vol. 2:** 448

2:17–20   **Vol. 2:** 216, 655

2:17   **Vol. 2:** 444, 652, 655 **Vol. 3:** 258

2:18   **Vol. 2:** 399 **Vol. 3:** 771, 808

2:19   **Vol. 1:** 220, 424, 592 **Vol. 3:** 942

2:20   **Vol. 1:** 282, 637, 708 **Vol. 2:** 216, 399 **Vol. 3:** 778, 885

2:21   **Vol. 3:** 54, 764

2:22–24   **Vol. 1:** 282

2:22   **Vol. 2:** 235

2:23 ff   **Vol. 3:** 584

2:23   **Vol. 1:** 228, 637

2:24   **Vol. 2:** 653 **Vol. 3:** 342–343

2:25–29   **Vol. 2:** 573

Romans *(cont'd)*

2:25	**Vol. 1:** 311 **Vol. 3:** 1158
2:26	**Vol. 2:** 135 **Vol. 3:** 363, 824, 1175
2:27	**Vol. 2:** 62, 660 **Vol. 3:** 493, 1183
2:28 f	**Vol. 2:** 786 **Vol. 3:** 702, 1199
2:28	**Vol. 2:** 218 **Vol. 3:** 164, 320
2:29	**Vol. 2:** 218 **Vol. 3:** 142, 320, 493, 701, 817
3 f	**Vol. 3:** 168
3	**Vol. 3:** 165, 432
3:1 f	**Vol. 1:** 311
3:1–4	**Vol. 3:** 320
3:1	**Vol. 1:** 730
3:2	**Vol. 3:** 1106, 1118, 1211
3:3	**Vol. 1:** 73 **Vol. 2:** 77 **Vol. 3:** 378
3:4	**Vol. 1:** 181, 743 **Vol. 2:** 472 **Vol. 3:** 363, 886
3:5 ff	**Vol. 3:** 364
3:5	**Vol. 2:** 565 **Vol. 3:** 362, 372, 575–576
3:6	**Vol. 1:** 524 **Vol. 2:** 365
3:7	**Vol. 1:** 730
3:8	**Vol. 2:** 365
3:9	**Vol. 1:** 202 **Vol. 2:** 127
3:10	**Vol. 3:** 362
3:11	**Vol. 3:** 131–132, 532
3:12	**Vol. 2:** 781
3:13	**Vol. 1:** 265 **Vol. 2:** 28, 726 **Vol. 3:** 1079
3:13a	**Vol. 2:** 727
3:14	**Vol. 1:** 202, 416
3:15	**Vol. 1:** 222, 239 **Vol. 2:** 28, 443, 854
3:16	**Vol. 3:** 859, 940
3:17	**Vol. 2:** 781 **Vol. 3:** 940
3:18	**Vol. 2:** 28
3:19 ff	**Vol. 1:** 719
3:19 f	**Vol. 2:** 450
3:19	**Vol. 1:** 417, 524 **Vol. 2:** 444 **Vol. 3:** 951
3:20–27	**Vol. 3:** 161
3:20	**Vol. 1:** 675, 730 **Vol. 2:** 101, 398, 446 **Vol. 3:** 363–364, 580, 1151, 1178, 1190
3:21 ff	**Vol. 1:** 385, 702 **Vol. 2:** 119 **Vol. 3:** 364, 372, 581
3:21–31	**Vol. 2:** 120
3:21–30	**Vol. 1:** 157
3:21–28	**Vol. 1:** 702
3:21–26	**Vol. 3:** 163, 954
3:21 f	**Vol. 3:** 362
3:21	**Vol. 2:** 282, 446 **Vol. 3:** 81, 312, 315, 321, 365, 831, 837, 1043
3:21b	**Vol. 2:** 444
3:22 ff	**Vol. 1:** 158
3:22 f	**Vol. 3:** 1190
3:22	**Vol. 1:** 601 **Vol. 2:** 566 **Vol. 3:** 1190
3:23 ff	**Vol. 2:** 366
3:23	**Vol. 1:** 719 **Vol. 2:** 46, 161, 446 **Vol. 3:** 954
3:24 ff	**Vol. 2:** 119
3:24	**Vol. 2:** 41–42, 120 **Vol. 3:** 199, 363–364, 576, 701, 1190, 1192
3:25 f	**Vol. 1:** 398, 437 **Vol. 2:** 446 **Vol. 3:** 169, 362, 364, 581, 1176, 1185, 1190
3:25†	**Vol. 1:** 223, 417, 697, 701–702 **Vol. 2:** 339, 407, 766–767 **Vol. 3:** 163, 165, 170, 198–199, 431, 435, 579, 1175, 1184, 1190, 1212
3:25b	**Vol. 3:** 165
3:26	**Vol. 3:** 165, 362–363, 365, 576, 837, 1190
3:27–31	**Vol. 1:** 601
3:27 f	**Vol. 3:** 1151
3:27	**Vol. 1:** 228 **Vol. 2:** 446
3:28	**Vol. 2:** 444, 446 **Vol. 3:** 363, 824–825
3:29 f	**Vol. 2:** 127, 446, 721
3:29	**Vol. 2:** 434, 566, 793
3:30	**Vol. 1:** 309–311, 375 **Vol. 2:** 73 **Vol. 3:** 363, 372, 1171, 1176, 1189
3:31	**Vol. 1:** 73, 719 **Vol. 2:** 445, 450 **Vol. 3:** 185, 320, 580
3:35	**Vol. 3:** 165
4	**Vol. 3:** 366, 825–826, 906
4:1–5:1	**Vol. 1:** 289
4:1–25	**Vol. 3:** 1151
4:1–13	**Vol. 1:** 78
4:1–3	**Vol. 1:** 79
4:1	**Vol. 3:** 529, 1199
4:2	**Vol. 1:** 228 **Vol. 2:** 120 **Vol. 3:** 363
4:3 ff	**Vol. 3:** 168
4:3–8	**Vol. 3:** 169
4:3–6	**Vol. 3:** 825
4:3	**Vol. 1:** 78, 157, 596, 604 **Vol. 2:** 73, 301 **Vol. 3:** 169, 362, 369, 490, 824, 1175, 1187, 1214
4:4–8	**Vol. 1:** 79
4:4	**Vol. 1:** 675 **Vol. 2:** 118, 120 **Vol. 3:** 142, 824
4:5	**Vol. 1:** 157 **Vol. 2:** 94, 388 **Vol. 3:** 362–363, 824, 1212, 1214
4:6	**Vol. 1:** 216, 427 **Vol. 3:** 362, 824, 1151
4:7–12	**Vol. 1:** 311
4:7	**Vol. 1:** 702 **Vol. 3:** 169
4:8	**Vol. 2:** 513 **Vol. 3:** 824–825
4:9 ff	**Vol. 1:** 601 **Vol. 3:** 824
4:9–25	**Vol. 3:** 393
4:9–12	**Vol. 1:** 79
4:9	**Vol. 1:** 216, 596 **Vol. 3:** 362–363, 1187–1188
4:10	**Vol. 1:** 309–310 **Vol. 3:** 825
4:11 f	**Vol. 1:** 311
4:11	**Vol. 1:** 154, 157, 601 **Vol. 3:** 362–364, 368, 499, 1182, 1187, 1190
4:12	**Vol. 2:** 452 **Vol. 3:** 1189
4:13 ff	**Vol. 2:** 300, 312
4:13–16	**Vol. 3:** 584
4:13 f	**Vol. 2:** 302
4:13	**Vol. 1:** 79 **Vol. 2:** 301 **Vol. 3:** 72, 362, 364, 368
4:14–20	**Vol. 3:** 585

Romans *(cont'd)*

4:14	**Vol. 1:** 547 **Vol. 2:** 301 **Vol. 3:** 72, !188
4:15	**Vol. 1:** 112 **Vol. 2:** 444 **Vol. 3:** 584
4:16 ff	**Vol. 3:** 523
4:16 f	**Vol. 2:** 794
4:16	**Vol. 1:** 79, 157, 659 **Vol. 2:** 120 **Vol. 3:** 1184, 1187
4:17 ff	**Vol. 1:** 601
4:17	**Vol. 1:** 275, 384, 436, 440, 445–446, 477 **Vol. 2:** 480, 605 **Vol. 3:** 71, 304, 368, 1214
4:18–22	**Vol. 1:** 79
4:18	**Vol. 2:** 73, 243 **Vol. 3:** 1178, 1187
4:19–25	**Vol. 1:** 157
4:19	**Vol. 1:** 80, 235, 445, 504 **Vol. 3:** 1067
4:20 f	**Vol. 1:** 504
4:20	**Vol. 1:** 504 **Vol. 2:** 46, 874 **Vol. 3:** 1187
4:21	**Vol. 3:** 71, 1154
4:22 ff	**Vol. 3:** 489, 824–825
4:22 f	**Vol. 1:** 596
4:22	**Vol. 1:** 702 **Vol. 3:** 362, 1187
4:23 ff	**Vol. 3:** 825
4:23 f	**Vol. 3:** 906
4:24 f	**Vol. 2:** 343
4:24	**Vol. 1:** 326, 446 **Vol. 3:** 281, 1212, 1214
4:25	**Vol. 1:** 86, 437, 702 **Vol. 2:** 120, 339, 380, 527 **Vol. 3:** 363, 371, 586, 611, 643, 1184
5	**Vol. 1:** 97 **Vol. 2:** 774 **Vol. 3:** 581
5:1 ff	**Vol. 3:** 171, 581
5:1 f	**Vol. 3:** 941
5:1–8:39	**Vol. 3:** 368
5:1	**Vol. 1:** 638 **Vol. 2:** 83, 370, 605, 781 **Vol. 3:** 171, 363, 368, 372, 1190
5:2 f	**Vol. 2:** 874
5:2	**Vol. 1:** 229, 611, 638 **Vol. 2:** 47, 83, 121, 242–243, 774 **Vol. 3:** 40
5:3 ff	**Vol. 2:** 774–775, 809
5:3	**Vol. 1:** 229 **Vol. 2:** 774, 809 **Vol. 3:** 1192
5:4	**Vol. 3:** 809
5:5	**Vol. 1:** 564 **Vol. 2:** 79, 183, 545, 785, 855 **Vol. 3:** 563, 701–702
5:5b	**Vol. 3:** 171
5:6 ff	**Vol. 1:** 437
5:6	**Vol. 2:** 94, 338 **Vol. 3:** 198, 837, 995, 1197
5:7	**Vol. 1:** 365 **Vol. 3:** 362
5:8 ff	**Vol. 3:** 169
5:8–10	**Vol. 3:** 1111
5:8 f	**Vol. 1:** 112 **Vol. 2:** 179
5:8	**Vol. 1:** 435, 438 **Vol. 2:** 94, 338, 544, 604 **Vol. 3:** 581, 995, 1197
5:9 ff	**Vol. 2:** 566
5:9 f	**Vol. 3:** 1184
5:9	**Vol. 1:** 437 **Vol. 3:** 166, 168, 214, 363, 644, 1175, 1182
5:10 f	**Vol. 1:** 398, 702 **Vol. 3:** 168, 1193
5:10	**Vol. 1:** 554 **Vol. 2:** 481 **Vol. 3:** 167–168, 171, 643–644, 1193
5:11	**Vol. 1:** 228 **Vol. 2:** 517, 874 **Vol. 3:** 167–168, 581, 838, 1182, 1193
5:12 ff	**Vol. 1:** 524 **Vol. 2:** 481, 682, 721 **Vol. 3:** 168
5:12–21	**Vol. 1:** 86, 436, 472 **Vol. 2:** 57 **Vol. 3:** 580
5:12–20	**Vol. 2:** 723
5:12	**Vol. 1:** 86, 96, 321, 436 **Vol. 2:** 723 **Vol. 3:** 204, 304, 581, 1194
5:13–18	**Vol. 3:** 165
5:13	**Vol. 2:** 783 **Vol. 3:** 702
5:14 ff	**Vol. 1:** 86
5:14	**Vol. 1:** 71, 86, 327 **Vol. 2:** 380, 504, 641 **Vol. 3:** 378, 585, 906
5:15 ff	**Vol. 2:** 723 **Vol. 3:** 586
5:15–21	**Vol. 1:** 96 **Vol. 2:** 120
5:15–17	**Vol. 2:** 42
5:15 f	**Vol. 2:** 121
5:15	**Vol. 1:** 96, 730 **Vol. 2:** 41, 120, 504, 718, 723 **Vol. 3:** 581, 586
5:16–19	**Vol. 3:** 363
5:16	**Vol. 1:** 97 **Vol. 2:** 41, 365 **Vol. 3:** 363, 371
5:17 f	**Vol. 3:** 586
5:17	**Vol. 1:** 649 **Vol. 2:** 41, 380, 723 **Vol. 3:** 138, 362, 364, 368, 746, 749
5:18 f	**Vol. 3:** 1194
5:18	**Vol. 1:** 96, 398, 738 **Vol. 2:** 365 **Vol. 3:** 363, 365, 368, 371, 586
5:19	**Vol. 1:** 96, 223, 472 **Vol. 2:** 175, 179 **Vol. 3:** 362, 365
5:20 f	**Vol. 2:** 445
5:20	**Vol. 1:** 322, 370, 719, 730 **Vol. 2:** 131, 445 **Vol. 3:** 580, 586
5:20a	**Vol. 3:** 1183
5:20b	**Vol. 2:** 120, 122, 445
5:21	**Vol. 2:** 120, 380, 617 **Vol. 3:** 204, 362, 368, 581, 832
6–8	**Vol. 1:** 717
6	**Vol. 2:** 388, 463 **Vol. 3:** 1210
6:1 ff	**Vol. 1:** 148, 152, 225, 604, 701 **Vol. 2:** 131 **Vol. 3:** 368
6:1 f	**Vol. 2:** 120
6:1–11	**Vol. 2:** 655 **Vol. 3:** 278, 581
6:1	**Vol. 2:** 120, 123, 131, 434, 678, 718 **Vol. 3:** 227
6:2	**Vol. 1:** 400, 718
6:3 ff	**Vol. 1:** 147, 289, 300 **Vol. 2:** 218, 715 **Vol. 3:** 581
6:3–13†	**Vol. 2:** 403
6:3–11	**Vol. 1:** 158
6:3 f	**Vol. 1:** 150, 438 **Vol. 2:** 519
6:3	**Vol. 1:** 146, 181, 186, 401 **Vol. 2:** 406, 718 **Vol. 3:** 1209–1210

Romans *(cont'd)*

6:4 f   **Vol. 1:** 315, 455
6:4   **Vol. 1:** 146–147, 266, 602   **Vol. 2:**
              46–47, 76, 338, 481, 605, 671, 718,
              920   **Vol. 3:** 281, 368, 944
6:5–9   **Vol. 2:** 718
6:5   **Vol. 2:** 504   **Vol. 3:** 277
6:6 ff   **Vol. 2:** 566
6:6   **Vol. 1:** 73, 236, 399, 401–402, 438,
              466, 643, 718   **Vol. 2:** 401, 420, 566,
              715   **Vol. 3:** 581
6:7 ff   **Vol. 2:** 340
6:7   **Vol. 3:** 363–364
6:8   **Vol. 1:** 181, 643   **Vol. 2:** 243   **Vol. 3:**
              1211
6:9   **Vol. 1:** 146   **Vol. 2:** 338, 519   **Vol. 3:**
              281, 303
6:9b   **Vol. 3:** 581
6:10 f   **Vol. 1:** 439   **Vol. 2:** 481
6:10–13   **Vol. 2:** 920
6:10   **Vol. 1:** 400–401, 438   **Vol. 2:**
              717–718   **Vol. 3:** 363, 368, 723, 1209
6:11   **Vol. 1:** 181, 446, 718   **Vol. 2:** 120,
              718   **Vol. 3:** 277, 364, 368, 824
6:12 ff   **Vol. 1:** 457   **Vol. 3:** 581
6:12–23   **Vol. 2:** 120
6:12   **Vol. 1:** 234, 236, 457, 718   **Vol. 2:** 179,
              380
6:13 ff   **Vol. 3:** 372
6:13–19   **Vol. 1:** 475
6:13   **Vol. 1:** 231, 446, 475   **Vol. 3:** 362, 364,
              368, 964, 1070
6:14 f   **Vol. 2:** 120
6:14   **Vol. 1:** 718   **Vol. 2:** 519
6:15   **Vol. 1:** 719   **Vol. 2:** 120
6:16   **Vol. 3:** 362, 581, 596, 854
6:17 f   **Vol. 2:** 874
6:17   **Vol. 2:** 121, 183, 718   **Vol. 3:** 61, 581,
              596, 770, 773, 904
6:18 ff   **Vol. 1:** 720
6:18–22   **Vol. 1:** 718
6:18   **Vol. 1:** 717–718   **Vol. 3:** 362,
              364–365, 596–597
6:19–22   **Vol. 2:** 230
6:19   **Vol. 1:** 231, 718   **Vol. 2:** 565   **Vol. 3:**
              364, 994
6:20–23   **Vol. 1:** 718
6:20   **Vol. 1:** 718
6:21 ff   **Vol. 2:** 120
6:21 f   **Vol. 2:** 61
6:21   **Vol. 1:** 719
6:22 f   **Vol. 3:** 832
6:22   **Vol. 1:** 717–718   **Vol. 2:** 61, 230,
              482   **Vol. 3:** 364, 368, 597
6:23   **Vol. 1:** 86, 436, 470, 719   **Vol. 2:** 101,
              121, 419, 517, 617   **Vol. 3:** 142,
              144–145, 204, 368
7 f   **Vol. 3:** 168

7   **Vol. 1:** 78   **Vol. 2:** 282–283   **Vol. 3:**
              363, 538
7:1 ff   **Vol. 2:** 480
7:1–25   **Vol. 3:** 161
7:1–24   **Vol. 1:** 335
7:1–3   **Vol. 1:** 507   **Vol. 3:** 535
7:1   **Vol. 2:** 399, 406, 444, 519
7:2 ff   **Vol. 3:** 538
7:2–9   **Vol. 3:** 538
7:2 f   **Vol. 2:** 563   **Vol. 3:** 537
7:2   **Vol. 1:** 73, 171
7:2b   **Vol. 2:** 444
7:3–6   **Vol. 1:** 718
7:3   **Vol. 1:** 718   **Vol. 2:** 583
7:3a   **Vol. 3:** 325
7:4 f   **Vol. 1:** 723
7:4   **Vol. 1:** 437   **Vol. 2:** 715
7:5 ff   **Vol. 3:** 581
7:5 f   **Vol. 3:** 839
7:5   **Vol. 1:** 231, 458, 676, 679   **Vol. 3:** 538,
              722, 1152, 1187, 1200
7:6   **Vol. 1:** 438   **Vol. 2:** 446, 519, 671–672,
              675, 714–716, 786   **Vol. 3:** 493,
              596–597, 701–702, 944
7:7 ff   **Vol. 1:** 86, 336   **Vol. 2:** 282   **Vol. 3:**
              580, 964
7:7–13   **Vol. 1:** 719   **Vol. 3:** 1021
7:7–12   **Vol. 3:** 585
7:7–10   **Vol. 1:** 337
7:7 f   **Vol. 1:** 458
7:7   **Vol. 2:** 398, 434, 444, 446   **Vol. 3:** 278
7:8 ff   **Vol. 3:** 278
7:8–13   **Vol. 2:** 445
7:8   **Vol. 1:** 336   **Vol. 3:** 197
7:9 ff   **Vol. 3:** 581
7:9 f   **Vol. 1:** 336, 437   **Vol. 2:** 445
7:9   **Vol. 3:** 278, 538
7:10 ff   **Vol. 2:** 715
7:10 f   **Vol. 1:** 719
7:10   **Vol. 1:** 336, 719   **Vol. 2:** 446   **Vol. 3:**
              368
7:11   **Vol. 1:** 336, 430   **Vol. 2:**
              459–460   **Vol. 3:** 278
7:11c   **Vol. 2:** 446
7:12 ff   **Vol. 2:** 447
7:12   **Vol. 1:** 336, 370, 719   **Vol. 2:** 228,
              443–445, 447   **Vol. 3:** 362, 779
7:13–25   **Vol. 3:** 581
7:13   **Vol. 2:** 446, 488
7:14 ff   **Vol. 1:** 236   **Vol. 2:** 566   **Vol. 3:** 1158
7:14–25   **Vol. 3:** 702
7:14   **Vol. 1:** 236, 268, 336, 719   **Vol. 3:** 706
7:15 ff   **Vol. 3:** 1021
7:15   **Vol. 1:** 556, 564   **Vol. 2:** 398
7:17 ff   **Vol. 1:** 564
7:17   **Vol. 2:** 251, 443
7:18 ff   **Vol. 2:** 101
7:18 f   **Vol. 2:** 446, 566   **Vol. 3:** 1021
7:18   **Vol. 1:** 676   **Vol. 2:** 104, 251
7:19   **Vol. 1:** 564   **Vol. 3:** 1021

Romans *(cont'd)*

7:20   **Vol. 2:** 251
7:21–25   **Vol. 2:** 282
7:21   **Vol. 1:** 564   **Vol. 2:** 104, 446   **Vol. 3:** 529, 1021
7:22 f   **Vol. 3:** 591
7:22   **Vol. 1:** 231
7:23 f   **Vol. 1:** 719
7:23   **Vol. 1:** 231, 564   **Vol. 2:** 444, 741   **Vol. 3:** 127, 515, 597
7:24   **Vol. 1:** 236, 336, 436, 566   **Vol. 2:** 446, 874   **Vol. 3:** 204, 859
7:25   **Vol. 1:** 231, 335–336, 564   **Vol. 2:** 121, 446, 517, 741, 873–874   **Vol. 3:** 127, 204, 596
7:25b   **Vol. 2:** 444
8   **Vol. 1:** 651   **Vol. 2:** 242, 282, 617, 885   **Vol. 3:** 1119
8:1 ff   **Vol. 1:** 336, 398, 719   **Vol. 2:** 566   **Vol. 3:** 581
8:1–17   **Vol. 2:** 566
8:1–11   **Vol. 2:** 883
8:1   **Vol. 1:** 702   **Vol. 2:** 282, 365, 370, 884   **Vol. 3:** 1192
8:2 ff   **Vol. 1:** 718
8:2–27   **Vol. 3:** 38
8:2   **Vol. 1:** 335   **Vol. 2:** 444, 481   **Vol. 3:** 304, 368, 701, 1021, 1178, 1183
8:3   **Vol. 1:** 236, 473, 676, 679, 718, 738   **Vol. 2:** 366, 446, 504, 725   **Vol. 3:** 170–171, 323, 597, 643–644, 1117, 1175, 1203
8:3b   **Vol. 3:** 204
8:4 ff   **Vol. 1:** 602
8:4–14   **Vol. 2:** 75
8:4–6   **Vol. 3:** 702
8:4 f   **Vol. 2:** 816
8:4   **Vol. 1:** 168, 675, 681, 738   **Vol. 2:** 445–446   **Vol. 3:** 161, 204, 363, 944, 995
8:5 ff   **Vol. 1:** 236
8:5–11   **Vol. 2:** 715
8:5–9   **Vol. 1:** 681
8:5–8   **Vol. 1:** 680
8:5   **Vol. 1:** 681   **Vol. 2:** 617–618   **Vol. 3:** 204, 1200
8:6–17   **Vol. 3:** 204
8:6   **Vol. 1:** 719   **Vol. 2:** 481, 617, 781, 816   **Vol. 3:** 368
8:7 f   **Vol. 2:** 605
8:7   **Vol. 1:** 555, 681   **Vol. 2:** 617, 816
8:8 f   **Vol. 1:** 676   **Vol. 3:** 1200
8:8   **Vol. 2:** 816
8:9 ff   **Vol. 1:** 458   **Vol. 3:** 225
8:9–17   **Vol. 3:** 581
8:9 f   **Vol. 1:** 147, 168
8:9   **Vol. 1:** 638, 679, 681   **Vol. 2:** 251, 424, 785, 816   **Vol. 3:** 701, 703
8:10 f   **Vol. 2:** 481

8:10   **Vol. 1:** 446   **Vol. 2:** 338   **Vol. 3:** 362, 368, 702, 1192
8:11   **Vol. 1:** 638   **Vol. 2:** 78, 83, 243, 251, 605, 816   **Vol. 3:** 281, 304, 699, 702–703, 1183
8:12–17   **Vol. 1:** 256
8:12 f   **Vol. 1:** 299, 719   **Vol. 3:** 702
8:12   **Vol. 1:** 236, 681   **Vol. 2:** 668
8:13–17   **Vol. 1:** 286
8:13   **Vol. 1:** 235, 286, 326–327, 681   **Vol. 2:** 816   **Vol. 3:** 368, 581, 702, 1158
8:14 ff   **Vol. 1:** 615   **Vol. 2:** 605   **Vol. 3:** 613
8:14–17   **Vol. 1:** 620   **Vol. 3:** 698
8:14–16   **Vol. 3:** 701
8:14 f   **Vol. 2:** 785
8:14   **Vol. 1:** 256, 289, 638   **Vol. 2:** 230, 873   **Vol. 3:** 645, 702–703
8:15 ff   **Vol. 2:** 218
8:15–17   **Vol. 3:** 701
8:15 f   **Vol. 1:** 289   **Vol. 2:** 786, 874   **Vol. 3:** 702–703
8:15   **Vol. 1:** 410, 614–615, 621, 623, 681   **Vol. 2:** 76, 867, 871, 873, 883, 896   **Vol. 3:** 597, 639, 694, 705, 749
8:16 f   **Vol. 1:** 256
8:16   **Vol. 2:** 76, 424, 567, 816, 873   **Vol. 3:** 693–694, 1042
8:17   **Vol. 1:** 643, 669   **Vol. 2:** 46–47, 300, 360–361, 419, 482, 809, 926   **Vol. 3:** 724–725
8:18 ff   **Vol. 2:** 671   **Vol. 3:** 725
8:18–25   **Vol. 3:** 702
8:18–23   **Vol. 1:** 720
8:18 f   **Vol. 3:** 316
8:18   **Vol. 1:** 327   **Vol. 2:** 46, 48, 419   **Vol. 3:** 349, 722, 725, 824–825, 837–839
8:19 ff   **Vol. 1:** 384
8:19–23   **Vol. 1:** 286
8:19–22   **Vol. 1:** 437   **Vol. 3:** 180
8:19   **Vol. 1:** 552   **Vol. 2:** 244–245   **Vol. 3:** 645
8:20–23   **Vol. 2:** 243
8:20–22   **Vol. 1:** 524
8:20   **Vol. 1:** 385, 552   **Vol. 3:** 1193
8:21   **Vol. 1:** 385, 470, 518, 552, 717–718   **Vol. 2:** 46, 48   **Vol. 3:** 595, 597, 884
8:22 f   **Vol. 2:** 883   **Vol. 3:** 204
8:22   **Vol. 1:** 385, 552   **Vol. 2:** 424
8:23   **Vol. 1:** 289, 315, 385, 440, 638, 669   **Vol. 2:** 40, 243, 245, 423–424, 774, 785–786, 874, 884, 926   **Vol. 3:** 199, 320, 417, 701–702
8:24 ff   **Vol. 2:** 243
8:24 f   **Vol. 3:** 563
8:24   **Vol. 1:** 601   **Vol. 2:** 241, 245, 774   **Vol. 3:** 61, 214
8:25   **Vol. 2:** 243, 245, 774–775
8:26 f   **Vol. 2:** 874, 882, 884   **Vol. 3:** 702

Romans (cont'd)

8:26   **Vol. 1:** 90   **Vol. 2:** 424, 666, 873–874, 884   **Vol. 3:** 995
8:27   **Vol. 2:** 183, 424, 885   **Vol. 3:** 533, 1200
8:28 ff   **Vol. 1:** 697
8:28–39   **Vol. 1:** 173
8:28–30   **Vol. 3:** 529
8:28   **Vol. 1:** 275, 696–697   **Vol. 2:** 101, 121–122   **Vol. 3:** 701–702, 1018, 1152, 1201
8:29 f   **Vol. 1:** 275, 298, 542
8:29   **Vol. 1:** 256, 668–669, 693, 695, 707   **Vol. 2:** 288, 725   **Vol. 3:** 214, 303, 305, 643, 645
8:30   **Vol. 1:** 696   **Vol. 2:** 46, 48   **Vol. 3:** 363
8:31 ff   **Vol. 2:** 121
8:31–39   **Vol. 2:** 102
8:31–32   **Vol. 2:** 411
8:31 f   **Vol. 2:** 360
8:31   **Vol. 2:** 83   **Vol. 3:** 1199
8:32   **Vol. 1:** 702   **Vol. 2:** 78, 119, 122, 242, 368, 527, 725   **Vol. 3:** 643–644, 1197
8:33 f   **Vol. 1:** 83   **Vol. 3:** 925, 1199
8:33   **Vol. 1:** 84, 542   **Vol. 2:** 229, 882   **Vol. 3:** 363
8:34   **Vol. 1:** 90   **Vol. 2:** 80, 147, 338, 365, 874, 883   **Vol. 3:** 40, 61–62, 281, 287, 303, 612
8:35 ff   **Vol. 2:** 544
8:35–39   **Vol. 2:** 806   **Vol. 3:** 534
8:35–36   **Vol. 3:** 534
8:35   **Vol. 1:** 313, 419, 564   **Vol. 2:** 267, 808–809   **Vol. 3:** 967
8:35a   **Vol. 3:** 534
8:36 ff   **Vol. 1:** 440
8:36   **Vol. 2:** 413   **Vol. 3:** 824
8:37 ff   **Vol. 1:** 564   **Vol. 2:** 545
8:37   **Vol. 1:** 651   **Vol. 2:** 545, 809
8:38 f   **Vol. 1:** 103, 719   **Vol. 2:** 605
8:38–39   **Vol. 3:** 534
8:38   **Vol. 1:** 103, 167, 326, 441, 591, 718   **Vol. 2:** 243, 518, 603, 895
8:39   **Vol. 1:** 385   **Vol. 2:** 198, 200   **Vol. 3:** 534, 1192
9–11   **Vol. 1:** 159, 256, 370, 467, 540, 593, 619   **Vol. 2:** 156, 314–316, 340, 794, 800   **Vol. 3:** 38, 168, 251, 1112
9   **Vol. 2:** 545
9:1–11:36   **Vol. 3:** 320
9:1–3   **Vol. 2:** 874
9:1   **Vol. 1:** 350, 353   **Vol. 3:** 702, 742, 885, 1042
9:2   **Vol. 1:** 370   **Vol. 2:** 425   **Vol. 3:** 229
9:3   **Vol. 1:** 414, 675   **Vol. 2:** 867, 874–875   **Vol. 3:** 229, 1199
9:4 f   **Vol. 1:** 286, 370, 637   **Vol. 2:** 122, 794, 800
9:4   **Vol. 2:** 285, 310, 445   **Vol. 3:** 551

9:5   **Vol. 1:** 99, 213, 675   **Vol. 2:** 80–81, 195, 314, 725, 874   **Vol. 3:** 1188, 1193, 1199
9:6 ff   **Vol. 2:** 77
9:6–29   **Vol. 1:** 159
9:6–13   **Vol. 2:** 319
9:6 f   **Vol. 1:** 286, 299   **Vol. 3:** 524
9:6   **Vol. 1:** 609   **Vol. 3:** 1112
9:7 f   **Vol. 1:** 286, 557
9:7   **Vol. 1:** 79, 81, 275   **Vol. 3:** 523
9:8   **Vol. 1:** 286, 675   **Vol. 3:** 824–825, 1175
9:9   **Vol. 1:** 80   **Vol. 3:** 846, 1067, 1112
9:10   **Vol. 1:** 81, 619   **Vol. 2:** 587
9:11 f   **Vol. 1:** 541, 557
9:11   **Vol. 1:** 275, 540, 564, 697   **Vol. 2:** 319   **Vol. 3:** 225, 251, 1018
9:12   **Vol. 2:** 428, 587   **Vol. 3:** 1151
9:13 ff   **Vol. 2:** 544
9:13   **Vol. 1:** 556
9:14 ff   **Vol. 3:** 1020
9:14   **Vol. 3:** 576
9:15–18   **Vol. 3:** 912
9:15 f   **Vol. 2:** 641
9:15   **Vol. 2:** 118, 597–598
9:16   **Vol. 1:** 469   **Vol. 2:** 597, 807   **Vol. 3:** 947
9:17   **Vol. 3:** 46, 48, 329, 490, 492
9:18   **Vol. 2:** 155, 597   **Vol. 3:** 1018
9:19 ff   **Vol. 3:** 912
9:19–33   **Vol. 3:** 912
9:19   **Vol. 1:** 416   **Vol. 2:** 139, 144–145   **Vol. 3:** 912, 1017–1018
9:20–23   **Vol. 2:** 434
9:20–21   **Vol. 3:** 917
9:20   **Vol. 3:** 912
9:21 ff   **Vol. 3:** 913, 1065
9:21   **Vol. 2:** 609   **Vol. 3:** 912, 917
9:22 ff   **Vol. 3:** 912
9:22–33   **Vol. 3:** 917
9:22   **Vol. 1:** 112, 464   **Vol. 2:** 76, 770   **Vol. 3:** 350, 1020, 1187
9:23 f   **Vol. 2:** 597   **Vol. 3:** 314
9:23   **Vol. 1:** 112   **Vol. 2:** 842, 844   **Vol. 3:** 118, 1187
9:24 ff   **Vol. 3:** 1020
9:24   **Vol. 2:** 800   **Vol. 3:** 251
9:25 f   **Vol. 2:** 581, 597   **Vol. 3:** 251
9:25   **Vol. 1:** 275, 369
9:26   **Vol. 1:** 274–275, 290   **Vol. 3:** 645
9:27   **Vol. 1:** 410, 736   **Vol. 2:** 684   **Vol. 3:** 251
9:28 f   **Vol. 2:** 513
9:29   **Vol. 1:** 736   **Vol. 2:** 69, 767   **Vol. 3:** 93, 251
9:30 f   **Vol. 2:** 807   **Vol. 3:** 362
9:30   **Vol. 2:** 78, 794   **Vol. 3:** 364, 368, 383, 750, 1188, 1190
9:31 f   **Vol. 3:** 383
9:31   **Vol. 3:** 363

209

Romans *(cont'd)*

9:32 f	**Vol. 3:** 393
9:32	**Vol. 2:** 706 **Vol. 3:** 363, 1151, 1190
9:33	**Vol. 1:** 477 **Vol. 2:** 327, 706, 708–709 **Vol. 3:** 382–383, 390, 563, 1020, 1212
10:1–4	**Vol. 3:** 1200
10:1	**Vol. 2:** 818, 861, 874 **Vol. 3:** 1174
10:2	**Vol. 1:** 637 **Vol. 2:** 400, 570 **Vol. 3:** 1043, 1167
10:3	**Vol. 2:** 78, 407 **Vol. 3:** 362–363, 372, 532, 581
10:4 ff	**Vol. 3:** 362
10:4	**Vol. 1:** 311, 370, 719, 730 **Vol. 2:** 61, 445, 451 **Vol. 3:** 363–364, 779, 1150, 1177, 1187
10:5	**Vol. 1:** 719 **Vol. 2:** 641 **Vol. 3:** 323, 363, 368, 1177
10:6–10	**Vol. 2:** 183
10:6 f	**Vol. 2:** 185
10:6	**Vol. 3:** 364, 368, 613, 1188
10:7	**Vol. 1:** 719 **Vol. 2:** 205
10:8 ff	**Vol. 1:** 347 **Vol. 3:** 55
10:8 f	**Vol. 3:** 62
10:8	**Vol. 2:** 719 **Vol. 3:** 1122
10:9 ff	**Vol. 1:** 205
10:9–11	**Vol. 3:** 1213
10:9	**Vol. 1:** 147, 153, 599 **Vol. 2:** 75, 78 **Vol. 3:** 61, 1142, 1199, 1211
10:9a	**Vol. 2:** 514
10:10	**Vol. 3:** 362, 364, 1187
10:11	**Vol. 2:** 186, 706 **Vol. 3:** 490, 1212
10:12 ff	**Vol. 1:** 276 **Vol. 2:** 874
10:12 f	**Vol. 3:** 1199
10:12	**Vol. 1:** 730 **Vol. 2:** 126–127, 566, 842
10:13	**Vol. 2:** 654
10:14 ff	**Vol. 1:** 719 **Vol. 2:** 176
10:14	**Vol. 3:** 1142, 1212
10:15	**Vol. 1:** 129, 239 **Vol. 2:** 111 **Vol. 3:** 55
10:16 ff	**Vol. 3:** 1020
10:16	**Vol. 1:** 736 **Vol. 2:** 175, 513
10:17	**Vol. 1:** 158 **Vol. 2:** 175 **Vol. 3:** 1020, 1122, 1190
10:18	**Vol. 1:** 519 **Vol. 3:** 1020, 1122
10:19	**Vol. 1:** 110, 112 **Vol. 2:** 641, 794 **Vol. 3:** 131–132
10:20	**Vol. 1:** 736 **Vol. 2:** 489, 880 **Vol. 3:** 528
10:21	**Vol. 1:** 593 **Vol. 2:** 490, 880
11	**Vol. 1:** 541 **Vol. 2:** 598
11:1–32	**Vol. 1:** 159
11:1 f	**Vol. 2:** 799–800
11:1	**Vol. 1:** 79, 370 **Vol. 2:** 310 **Vol. 3:** 505, 872
11:2 ff	**Vol. 1:** 545
11:2–5	**Vol. 2:** 874
11:2	**Vol. 1:** 667, 693 **Vol. 2:** 882 **Vol. 3:** 490
11:3	**Vol. 2:** 513, 724 **Vol. 3:** 252, 436
11:4 ff	**Vol. 3:** 436
11:4	**Vol. 2:** 85, 690–691, 699, 859 **Vol. 3:** 252, 325
11:5 f	**Vol. 2:** 120
11:5	**Vol. 1:** 159, 181, 540–541 **Vol. 2:** 699 **Vol. 3:** 251–252, 325, 837
11:6	**Vol. 2:** 699 **Vol. 3:** 1151
11:7	**Vol. 1:** 159, 540–541 **Vol. 2:** 156 **Vol. 3:** 251–253, 532
11:8	**Vol. 2:** 178 **Vol. 3:** 313, 694
11:9 f	**Vol. 3:** 505
11:9	**Vol. 1:** 427 **Vol. 2:** 708 **Vol. 3:** 135
11:10	**Vol. 1:** 424
11:11–16	**Vol. 1:** 370
11:11 f	**Vol. 2:** 794 **Vol. 3:** 586
11:11	**Vol. 1:** 611, 730 **Vol. 2:** 794
11:12	**Vol. 1:** 739 **Vol. 2:** 794, 844 **Vol. 3:** 252
11:13 f	**Vol. 2:** 451, 794
11:13	**Vol. 1:** 129 **Vol. 2:** 794 **Vol. 3:** 546, 548
11:14	**Vol. 1:** 675 **Vol. 3:** 214
11:15	**Vol. 1:** 702 **Vol. 3:** 167–168, 581, 751, 1189
11:16 ff	**Vol. 1:** 79
11:16 f	**Vol. 3:** 869
11:16	**Vol. 2:** 691 **Vol. 3:** 869–870, 917
11:17–24	**Vol. 1:** 311 **Vol. 2:** 712, 747 **Vol. 3:** 921
11:17 f	**Vol. 1:** 228 **Vol. 3:** 868–869
11:17	**Vol. 1:** 644 **Vol. 2:** 794 **Vol. 3:** 870
11:18	**Vol. 3:** 869–870
11:19	**Vol. 3:** 869
11:20	**Vol. 2:** 200, 617–618 **Vol. 3:** 505, 1010
11:21	**Vol. 2:** 660
11:22 f	**Vol. 3:** 227
11:22	**Vol. 1:** 611 **Vol. 2:** 106
11:24	**Vol. 2:** 660 **Vol. 3:** 869
11:25 ff	**Vol. 1:** 667
11:25 f	**Vol. 2:** 800 **Vol. 3:** 84, 214
11:25	**Vol. 1:** 321, 370, 739 **Vol. 2:** 37, 156, 304, 406, 620, 794 **Vol. 3:** 505
11:26 f	**Vol. 1:** 370
11:26	**Vol. 2:** 37, 313, 315, 319, 327, 329 **Vol. 3:** 202, 205, 871
11:28 ff	**Vol. 1:** 541
11:28	**Vol. 1:** 540–541, 554 **Vol. 2:** 544 **Vol. 3:** 1184
11:29	**Vol. 1:** 275, 356–357, 370 **Vol. 2:** 77, 122
11:30	**Vol. 1:** 593 **Vol. 2:** 597
11:31	**Vol. 2:** 597
11:32–36	**Vol. 2:** 101
11:32	**Vol. 1:** 96, 593, 730 **Vol. 2:** 499, 597, 800 **Vol. 3:** 1187
11:33 ff	**Vol. 3:** 505
11:33–36	**Vol. 1:** 370–371 **Vol. 2:** 926 **Vol. 3:** 168

Romans (cont'd)

11:33 f   **Vol. 3:** 1032
11:33   **Vol. 2:** 75, 198, 365–366, 400   **Vol. 3:** 533, 940, 1032
11:34   **Vol. 1:** 363   **Vol. 3:** 129
11:36   **Vol. 1:** 94–95, 99, 238   **Vol. 2:** 46, 73, 874   **Vol. 3:** 830, 1182–1183
12–16   **Vol. 2:** 883
12–15   **Vol. 1:** 65
12   **Vol. 1:** 232, 301   **Vol. 2:** 885   **Vol. 3:** 1119
12:1 ff   **Vol. 1:** 300, 604
12:1 f   **Vol. 2:** 816
12:1   **Vol. 1:** 234–235, 475, 570   **Vol. 2:** 42, 78, 230, 263, 568, 597–598, 885   **Vol. 3:** 38, 368, 432, 447, 550–551, 746, 838, 1106, 1118
12:2   **Vol. 1:** 185, 708–709   **Vol. 2:** 62, 567–568, 673   **Vol. 3:** 130, 702, 808, 810, 831, 861, 864, 931, 970, 1020–1021, 1187
12:3 ff   **Vol. 2:** 42   **Vol. 3:** 1119
12:3–5   **Vol. 2:** 121
12:3   **Vol. 1:** 502, 570   **Vol. 2:** 121, 499, 617–618   **Vol. 3:** 403, 703, 928, 1183
12:4 ff   **Vol. 1:** 300
12:4–8   **Vol. 3:** 702–703, 1067
12:4 f   **Vol. 1:** 231, 235   **Vol. 2:** 884
12:4   **Vol. 3:** 572, 1158
12:5   **Vol. 1:** 96, 237
12:6 ff   **Vol. 2:** 499   **Vol. 3:** 1119
12:6–8   **Vol. 2:** 121   **Vol. 3:** 703
12:6   **Vol. 1:** 50   **Vol. 2:** 121   **Vol. 3:** 81, 707
12:7   **Vol. 3:** 546–547, 764, 770
12:8   **Vol. 1:** 197, 570–571   **Vol. 2:** 41, 43, 597   **Vol. 3:** 572, 1169
12:9   **Vol. 1:** 567   **Vol. 2:** 350, 470   **Vol. 3:** 927
12:10   **Vol. 1:** 257   **Vol. 2:** 51, 539, 542, 549–550   **Vol. 3:** 928
12:11   **Vol. 1:** 318   **Vol. 3:** 110, 596–597, 694, 1169
12:12 f   **Vol. 2:** 774
12:12   **Vol. 2:** 241, 244, 359–360, 768
12:12c   **Vol. 2:** 874
12:13   **Vol. 1:** 690   **Vol. 2:** 230, 550, 617, 807   **Vol. 3:** 752, 958
12:14   **Vol. 1:** 215, 417   **Vol. 2:** 806, 874   **Vol. 3:** 755
12:15   **Vol. 2:** 361, 416
12:16   **Vol. 2:** 200, 263, 617–618, 620   **Vol. 3:** 1010
12:17 f   **Vol. 2:** 816
12:17   **Vol. 1:** 564, 695   **Vol. 3:** 136, 183, 755, 1179
12:18   **Vol. 2:** 781
12:19 ff   **Vol. 1:** 702
12:19–21   **Vol. 3:** 929
12:19 f   **Vol. 3:** 97

12:19   **Vol. 1:** 111, 417   **Vol. 2:** 157, 513   **Vol. 3:** 345
12:20   **Vol. 1:** 554, 657   **Vol. 2:** 157, 268, 757
12:21   **Vol. 1:** 564, 651   **Vol. 3:** 755
13   **Vol. 2:** 885, 903, 905, 924–925   **Vol. 3:** 549
13:1 ff   **Vol. 3:** 97
13:1–11   **Vol. 2:** 922
13:1–7   **Vol. 2:** 609   **Vol. 3:** 930
13:1–4   **Vol. 2:** 101
13:1   **Vol. 1:** 476, 564   **Vol. 2:** 158, 608   **Vol. 3:** 97, 683, 755
13:2 ff   **Vol. 3:** 755
13:3 f   **Vol. 1:** 564   **Vol. 3:** 817
13:3   **Vol. 1:** 168, 564, 622   **Vol. 2:** 609
13:4 f   **Vol. 3:** 755
13:4   **Vol. 1:** 111, 564   **Vol. 3:** 97, 546, 549, 967, 1157
13:5   **Vol. 1:** 350, 353   **Vol. 2:** 664   **Vol. 3:** 1184
13:6 f   **Vol. 3:** 754
13:6   **Vol. 2:** 62, 768   **Vol. 3:** 553
13:7   **Vol. 2:** 50, 62, 668
13:8 ff   **Vol. 2:** 546   **Vol. 3:** 755
13:8–10   **Vol. 2:** 481
13:8   **Vol. 1:** 738   **Vol. 2:** 668, 739   **Vol. 3:** 377, 752
13:9 f   **Vol. 3:** 378
13:9   **Vol. 1:** 259, 336, 338   **Vol. 2:** 163, 544, 583   **Vol. 3:** 755
13:10   **Vol. 1:** 564, 738–739   **Vol. 3:** 755
13:10b   **Vol. 2:** 445   **Vol. 3:** 779
13:11 ff   **Vol. 3:** 849
13:11–14   **Vol. 1:** 563   **Vol. 2:** 922
13:11   **Vol. 2:** 925   **Vol. 3:** 214, 838–839, 848
13:12   **Vol. 1:** 315–316, 421, 424   **Vol. 2:** 54, 130, 495, 894, 922, 925
13:13   **Vol. 1:** 513   **Vol. 2:** 587, 894, 925–926   **Vol. 3:** 31, 945, 1167
13:14   **Vol. 1:** 316, 676, 695   **Vol. 2:** 587, 926
14 f   **Vol. 2:** 273
14:1–15:13 **Vol. 3:** 995
14:1   **Vol. 1:** 350, 504, 602   **Vol. 2:** 130   **Vol. 3:** 821, 995
14:2   **Vol. 2:** 211   **Vol. 3:** 996, 1211
14:3 ff   **Vol. 2:** 364
14:3   **Vol. 3:** 751
14:4   **Vol. 1:** 610, 684   **Vol. 2:** 450, 742
14:5 ff   **Vol. 1:** 631
14:5   **Vol. 2:** 364   **Vol. 3:** 107, 130, 996, 1202
14:6   **Vol. 2:** 874   **Vol. 3:** 819
14:7 ff   **Vol. 3:** 944
14:7   **Vol. 2:** 481
14:8   **Vol. 1:** 441   **Vol. 2:** 481, 517
14:9   **Vol. 1:** 445, 702   **Vol. 2:** 81, 204, 207, 481, 514, 519
14:10 ff   **Vol. 2:** 369
14:10   **Vol. 1:** 323, 474   **Vol. 3:** 369, 925–926   **Vol. 3:** 1151
14:11 ff   **Vol. 2:** 481

Romans *(cont'd)*

14:11   **Vol. 2:** 513, 859, 874, 925   **Vol. 3:** 1079
14:12   **Vol. 3:** 854, 1106
14:13   **Vol. 2:** 364, 706–708, 710   **Vol. 3:** 996
14:14   **Vol. 1:** 448, 591   **Vol. 2:** 517   **Vol. 3:** 824–825, 996
14:15   **Vol. 1:** 464   **Vol. 2:** 268   **Vol. 3:** 944, 1197
14:17   **Vol. 1:** 300   **Vol. 2:** 268, 277, 360, 482, 781   **Vol. 3:** 362, 701–702
14:18   **Vol. 2:** 817   **Vol. 3:** 596–597, 808, 931
14:19   **Vol. 2:** 781, 807   **Vol. 3:** 189
14:20   **Vol. 2:** 268, 710   **Vol. 3:** 107, 189, 996
14:21   **Vol. 2:** 272, 275, 706, 710   **Vol. 3:** 107, 922, 996, 1192
14:22   **Vol. 1:** 217   **Vol. 3:** 809
14:23   **Vol. 1:** 504, 602   **Vol. 2:** 366, 446, 618   **Vol. 3:** 581, 996
15   **Vol. 3:** 553
15:1 ff **Vol. 2:** 668
15:1–3   **Vol. 2:** 815
15:1   **Vol. 2:** 606, 815   **Vol. 3:** 995–996
15:2   **Vol. 2:** 101, 815
15:3–6   **Vol. 2:** 774
15:3   **Vol. 1:** 492   **Vol. 2:** 619, 815, 828, 835   **Vol. 3:** 340, 770
15:4 f   **Vol. 3:** 87
15:4   **Vol. 1:** 571   **Vol. 3:** 489–490, 492, 770
15:5 ff **Vol. 1:** 311   **Vol. 3:** 909
15:5 f   **Vol. 2:** 874
15:5   **Vol. 2:** 121, 618–619
15:6   **Vol. 1:** 620   **Vol. 2:** 76, 722, 874   **Vol. 3:** 908
15:7   **Vol. 1:** 492   **Vol. 2:** 46   **Vol. 3:** 751
15:8 f   **Vol. 3:** 38
15:8   **Vol. 1:** 311, 659   **Vol. 2:** 179   **Vol. 3:** 72, 546, 1118
15:9 ff **Vol. 2:** 874
15:9   **Vol. 1:** 346   **Vol. 2:** 111, 597, 874   **Vol. 3:** 671–672, 675
15:10   **Vol. 2:** 186, 356, 799
15:11   **Vol. 2:** 513, 793, 799   **Vol. 3:** 817
15:12   **Vol. 1:** 167, 736   **Vol. 3:** 869
15:13   **Vol. 1:** 730   **Vol. 2:** 241, 243, 360, 781, 874   **Vol. 3:** 38, 702
15:14   **Vol. 1:** 569, 591   **Vol. 2:** 101
15:15   **Vol. 1:** 365   **Vol. 2:** 304   **Vol. 3:** 38, 489, 1183
15:16–19 **Vol. 3:** 703
15:16   **Vol. 2:** 78, 111, 235   **Vol. 3:** 38, 431, 552, 746
15:17 ff **Vol. 2:** 874
15:17   **Vol. 1:** 228   **Vol. 2:** 388
15:18 f **Vol. 2:** 632
15:18   **Vol. 1:** 130, 365   **Vol. 3:** 314
15:19   **Vol. 1:** 129   **Vol. 2:** 328, 605, 629, 903   **Vol. 3:** 752
15:20 f **Vol. 3:** 400
15:20   **Vol. 1:** 662, 684   **Vol. 2:** 550, 742

15:21   **Vol. 3:** 48, 131–132, 613
15:22   **Vol. 2:** 220–221
15:23 f **Vol. 3:** 400
15:23   **Vol. 1:** 458   **Vol. 2:** 903   **Vol. 3:** 730
15:24   **Vol. 2:** 826   **Vol. 3:** 516
15:25–28 **Vol. 3:** 854
15:25   **Vol. 2:** 826   **Vol. 3:** 546
15:26 ff **Vol. 2:** 818
15:26   **Vol. 1:** 642   **Vol. 2:** 826   **Vol. 3:** 854
15:27   **Vol. 2:** 328, 668, 826   **Vol. 3:** 552, 707, 752
15:28   **Vol. 2:** 826   **Vol. 3:** 499
15:29   **Vol. 1:** 214, 739
15:30 ff **Vol. 2:** 874
15:30–33 **Vol. 2:** 874
15:30   **Vol. 1:** 570, 646–647   **Vol. 2:** 517, 545, 868   **Vol. 3:** 702
15:31   **Vol. 1:** 593   **Vol. 2:** 329, 826   **Vol. 3:** 546, 746, 752, 1176
15:32   **Vol. 3:** 1021
15:33   **Vol. 1:** 99   **Vol. 2:** 78, 780, 874
16   **Vol. 3:** 1063
16:1 f   **Vol. 3:** 1063
16:1   **Vol. 1:** 301   **Vol. 3:** 546, 549, 1065
16:2   **Vol. 1:** 474   **Vol. 2:** 517   **Vol. 3:** 958, 1158
16:3 f   **Vol. 3:** 1065
16:3   **Vol. 3:** 548, 1063
16:4   **Vol. 1:** 241, 398   **Vol. 3:** 683, 818
16:5   **Vol. 1:** 301   **Vol. 2:** 550   **Vol. 3:** 416
16:6   **Vol. 1:** 263   **Vol. 3:** 1063
16:7   **Vol. 1:** 130   **Vol. 3:** 591, 601, 1192
16:8   **Vol. 2:** 517
16:9   **Vol. 3:** 548
16:10 f **Vol. 2:** 550
16:10   **Vol. 3:** 808, 810
16:12   **Vol. 1:** 263   **Vol. 3:** 1063
16:13   **Vol. 1:** 539   **Vol. 2:** 517
16:15   **Vol. 2:** 550   **Vol. 3:** 378, 1063
16:16   **Vol. 1:** 299   **Vol. 2:** 530, 547, 549   **Vol. 3:** 701
16:17   **Vol. 1:** 486, 535   **Vol. 2:** 708, 710, 719   **Vol. 3:** 770
16:18   **Vol. 1:** 169, 212, 563   **Vol. 2:** 460   **Vol. 3:** 596
16:19   **Vol. 1:** 564   **Vol. 2:** 101, 179   **Vol. 3:** 1022
16:20   **Vol. 1:** 239   **Vol. 2:** 78, 780–781, 874   **Vol. 3:** 471
16:21   **Vol. 2:** 517   **Vol. 3:** 548
16:22   **Vol. 1:** 247   **Vol. 2:** 517
16:23   **Vol. 1:** 689   **Vol. 2:** 254
16:25 ff **Vol. 2:** 724, 874   **Vol. 3:** 322
16:25 f **Vol. 3:** 832, 837
16:25   **Vol. 2:** 112, 217   **Vol. 3:** 52–53, 61, 314, 504, 844
16:26   **Vol. 2:** 77, 179   **Vol. 3:** 81, 314, 491–492, 1150
16:27   **Vol. 1:** 99   **Vol. 2:** 46, 77, 724   **Vol. 3:** 1032

1 Corinthians

1–3   **Vol. 3:** 1030
1:1 ff   **Vol. 1:** 247
1:1–9   **Vol. 3:** 1165
1:1   **Vol. 1:** 129, 276   **Vol. 3:** 1020
1:2   **Vol. 1:** 275–276, 298–300, 305   **Vol. 2:** 229, 654, 874
1:3   **Vol. 1:** 620   **Vol. 2:** 516, 780–781, 874   **Vol. 3:** 1178
1:4 ff   **Vol. 2:** 121, 874
1:4–7   **Vol. 3:** 701
1:4   **Vol. 2:** 73, 119   **Vol. 3:** 818
1:5   **Vol. 2:** 400, 828, 842, 844   **Vol. 3:** 197, 954
1:6   **Vol. 1:** 659–660   **Vol. 3:** 905, 1043
1:7   **Vol. 2:** 518   **Vol. 3:** 315, 707, 954
1:8   **Vol. 1:** 467, 660   **Vol. 2:** 61, 140, 517, 874, 894   **Vol. 3:** 169, 924
1:9   **Vol. 1:** 275, 643   **Vol. 2:** 77   **Vol. 3:** 643, 924, 1182
1:10 ff   **Vol. 1:** 535
1:10–4:21   **Vol. 1:** 400
1:10   **Vol. 1:** 570   **Vol. 2:** 398, 654   **Vol. 3:** 130, 350, 482, 544
1:11   **Vol. 3:** 316, 544, 905
1:12   **Vol. 2:** 311   **Vol. 3:** 297, 383, 387, 544, 1117, 1209
1:13–17   **Vol. 1:** 146
1:13   **Vol. 1:** 398   **Vol. 2:** 655   **Vol. 3:** 387, 544, 1209
1:14 ff   **Vol. 1:** 147
1:14–17   **Vol. 1:** 179
1:14   **Vol. 1:** 160   **Vol. 2:** 874   **Vol. 3:** 819
1:15   **Vol. 2:** 655   **Vol. 3:** 1209
1:16   **Vol. 1:** 159, 675   **Vol. 2:** 248, 250   **Vol. 3:** 252
1:17 f   **Vol. 1:** 397
1:17   **Vol. 1:** 129, 147, 399–400, 547, 602, 638   **Vol. 2:** 111   **Vol. 3:** 1031
1:18 ff   **Vol. 2:** 171   **Vol. 3:** 1031
1:18–3:20   **Vol. 3:** 1111
1:18–2:16   **Vol. 2:** 401
1:18–31   **Vol. 2:** 430   **Vol. 3:** 581
1:18–25   **Vol. 1:** 397
1:18–24   **Vol. 1:** 400
1:18   **Vol. 1:** 397, 399, 464   **Vol. 2:** 78, 338, 604   **Vol. 3:** 61, 169, 214, 714, 1026
1:19 ff   **Vol. 1:** 397, 399
1:19   **Vol. 1:** 74, 463   **Vol. 3:** 131–132, 504, 1031
1:20   **Vol. 3:** 831, 1026, 1030
1:21–25   **Vol. 3:** 820
1:21   **Vol. 1:** 397, 601   **Vol. 2:** 400, 819   **Vol. 3:** 52–53, 214, 1031
1:22 ff   **Vol. 3:** 1111
1:22 f   **Vol. 2:** 127
1:22–24   **Vol. 2:** 127
1:22   **Vol. 1:** 398   **Vol. 2:** 629, 680, 858   **Vol. 3:** 532, 1031

1:23 f   **Vol. 1:** 439
1:23   **Vol. 1:** 399–400, 638   **Vol. 2:** 706, 708, 794   **Vol. 3:** 52, 55, 504, 1025, 1031
1:24 ff   **Vol. 3:** 1111
1:24   **Vol. 1:** 174, 275, 551   **Vol. 2:** 78, 126, 604   **Vol. 3:** 1030–1032
1:25 f   **Vol. 3:** 714
1:25   **Vol. 3:** 995, 1026
1:26 ff   **Vol. 3:** 1031
1:26–29   **Vol. 1:** 248, 399   **Vol. 2:** 605
1:26 f   **Vol. 3:** 504
1:26   **Vol. 1:** 188, 275, 680   **Vol. 3:** 515
1:27 f   **Vol. 1:** 542
1:27   **Vol. 2:** 605   **Vol. 3:** 563, 995
1:28   **Vol. 1:** 73
1:29 ff   **Vol. 2:** 874
1:29   **Vol. 1:** 228, 675   **Vol. 3:** 1031
1:30 f   **Vol. 2:** 119–120
1:30   **Vol. 1:** 417   **Vol. 2:** 78, 217, 229, 591, 605   **Vol. 3:** 163, 199, 258, 326, 362, 364, 372, 1031–1032
1:31   **Vol. 1:** 228   **Vol. 3:** 504, 1031
2   **Vol. 1:** 183
2:1–16   **Vol. 3:** 967
2:1–5   **Vol. 1:** 400
2:1 f   **Vol. 1:** 248, 397
2:1   **Vol. 3:** 47, 504, 1031, 1043, 1112
2:2 f   **Vol. 3:** 995
2:2   **Vol. 1:** 248, 399   **Vol. 2:** 364   **Vol. 3:** 55, 504, 1031, 1111
2:3   **Vol. 1:** 183, 622   **Vol. 2:** 434   **Vol. 3:** 504
2:4–16   **Vol. 3:** 336
2:4 f   **Vol. 3:** 701, 703, 1031
2:4   **Vol. 1:** 588, 592, 602   **Vol. 2:** 605, 632   **Vol. 3:** 52–53, 570–571, 963, 1112, 1125
2:5   **Vol. 1:** 601   **Vol. 2:** 78
2:6–16   **Vol. 3:** 327, 1031
2:6–13   **Vol. 2:** 569
2:6–8   **Vol. 2:** 435
2:6 f   **Vol. 3:** 1031
2:6   **Vol. 1:** 73, 168, 675   **Vol. 2:** 62   **Vol. 3:** 185, 504, 802, 829
2:7–16   **Vol. 3:** 345
2:7   **Vol. 1:** 696   **Vol. 2:** 46, 217   **Vol. 3:** 504, 830
2:8   **Vol. 1:** 167, 169   **Vol. 2:** 46, 513   **Vol. 3:** 802, 1111
2:9–16   **Vol. 2:** 874
2:9   **Vol. 2:** 176, 183, 185, 219   **Vol. 3:** 118, 492, 504, 515, 533
2:10–16   **Vol. 1:** 680   **Vol. 2:** 567   **Vol. 3:** 1031
2:10–12   **Vol. 3:** 701
2:10 f   **Vol. 2:** 217
2:10   **Vol. 1:** 465   **Vol. 2:** 75, 198, 217   **Vol. 3:** 314, 533
2:11 ff   **Vol. 2:** 883
2:11   **Vol. 2:** 75, 400   **Vol. 3:** 694
2:12–3:4   **Vol. 3:** 705

1 Corinthians *(cont'd)*

2:12–14	**Vol. 3:** 703
2:12 f	**Vol. 2:** 605
2:12	**Vol. 2:** 75, 122 **Vol. 3:** 129, 504, 694, 701, 749, 1203
2:12a	**Vol. 3:** 1174, 1188
2:12b	**Vol. 3:** 1174
2:13–3:1	**Vol. 3:** 706
2:13–15	**Vol. 3:** 707
2:13 f	**Vol. 3:** 703
2:13	**Vol. 2:** 364, 605 **Vol. 3:** 707, 764, 1031, 1112
2:14 f	**Vol. 2:** 75
2:14	**Vol. 1:** 246 **Vol. 2:** 365, 400 **Vol. 3:** 504, 684
2:15 ff	**Vol. 1:** 248
2:15	**Vol. 2:** 605 **Vol. 3:** 504, 707, 1200
2:16	**Vol. 1:** 638, 739 **Vol. 2:** 900 **Vol. 3:** 129
3:1–3	**Vol. 1:** 679
3:1	**Vol. 1:** 282 **Vol. 2:** 605 **Vol. 3:** 707, 963, 1200
3:2	**Vol. 2:** 268–269
3:3	**Vol. 1:** 535, 681 **Vol. 2:** 565 **Vol. 3:** 944–945, 1167, 1200
3:4–10	**Vol. 1:** 301
3:4	**Vol. 1:** 681 **Vol. 2:** 311 **Vol. 3:** 544
3:5 ff	**Vol. 1:** 400
3:5–17	**Vol. 2:** 252
3:5–11	**Vol. 2:** 129
3:5	**Vol. 2:** 517 **Vol. 3:** 548, 809, 1117, 1211
3:6 ff	**Vol. 2:** 248
3:6 f	**Vol. 2:** 129
3:6	**Vol. 3:** 164, 868
3:8	**Vol. 1:** 263 **Vol. 2:** 839 **Vol. 3:** 1200
3:9 ff	**Vol. 3:** 390
3:9	**Vol. 1:** 248, 300 **Vol. 2:** 252 **Vol. 3:** 1152
3:10 ff	**Vol. 1:** 279 **Vol. 3:** 500
3:10–14†	**Vol. 2:** 253
3:10–13	**Vol. 2:** 747
3:10–12	**Vol. 2:** 249
3:10	**Vol. 1:** 662 **Vol. 2:** 121, 249 **Vol. 3:** 143, 1032
3:11 f	**Vol. 3:** 1151
3:11	**Vol. 1:** 662 **Vol. 2:** 129, 739 **Vol. 3:** 387, 390
3:12 ff	**Vol. 1:** 662
3:12–15	**Vol. 3:** 387
3:12	**Vol. 1:** 390, 744 **Vol. 2:** 96, 211, 249, 756
3:13 ff	**Vol. 2:** 370 **Vol. 3:** 136
3:13	**Vol. 1:** 467, 657 **Vol. 2:** 756, 894 **Vol. 3:** 315, 317, 320, 446, 808–809, 1178
3:14	**Vol. 2:** 249 **Vol. 3:** 142, 224
3:15	**Vol. 1:** 467, 662 **Vol. 3:** 99, 143, 214, 1181
3:16 f	**Vol. 2:** 249 **Vol. 3:** 387, 784
3:16	**Vol. 1:** 638 **Vol. 2:** 83, 249, 251–252 **Vol. 3:** 701, 809
3:17	**Vol. 1:** 467–468 **Vol. 3:** 84, 86
3:18 ff	**Vol. 3:** 1031
3:18–23	**Vol. 3:** 1032
3:18 f	**Vol. 3:** 1031
3:18	**Vol. 2:** 460 **Vol. 3:** 822, 831, 1026, 1032
3:19 f	**Vol. 3:** 1031
3:19	**Vol. 1:** 413, 524 **Vol. 3:** 1026, 1030, 1036, 1202
3:20	**Vol. 1:** 551 **Vol. 2:** 513 **Vol. 3:** 821
3:21 ff	**Vol. 1:** 525
3:21	**Vol. 1:** 228, 718 **Vol. 3:** 504
3:22 f	**Vol. 1:** 441
3:22	**Vol. 1:** 95, 326 **Vol. 3:** 383
3:23	**Vol. 1:** 718 **Vol. 2:** 160
4:1	**Vol. 1:** 129 **Vol. 2:** 75, 255, 732 **Vol. 3:** 504, 546, 824–825
4:2	**Vol. 2:** 255 **Vol. 3:** 252, 529, 532
4:3 ff	**Vol. 3:** 810
4:3	**Vol. 2:** 365
4:4	**Vol. 1:** 350, 352 **Vol. 3:** 363, 365, 432, 1192
4:5	**Vol. 1:** 425 **Vol. 2:** 183, 218, 364, 495, 518 **Vol. 3:** 321, 817, 838–839, 1017
4:6 ff	**Vol. 1:** 399
4:6	**Vol. 1:** 400, 486, 709 **Vol. 3:** 864, 1196, 1199
4:7	**Vol. 1:** 228, 504, 639 **Vol. 3:** 749
4:8	**Vol. 1:** 638 **Vol. 2:** 267, 380, 668, 828, 842, 844 **Vol. 3:** 143, 305, 1111
4:9 ff	**Vol. 3:** 143
4:9–13	**Vol. 1:** 129 **Vol. 2:** 57
4:9	**Vol. 1:** 103 **Vol. 2:** 434, 565 **Vol. 3:** 521, 570–571, 600, 822
4:10	**Vol. 1:** 183, 281, 638 **Vol. 2:** 47, 51, 620 **Vol. 3:** 432, 714, 995, 1026
4:11	**Vol. 1:** 163 **Vol. 3:** 847, 857
4:12	**Vol. 1:** 215, 263 **Vol. 2:** 766, 806, 839 **Vol. 3:** 347
4:13	**Vol. 1:** 479 **Vol. 3:** 102
4:14 ff	**Vol. 1:** 619
4:14 f	**Vol. 1:** 180
4:14	**Vol. 1:** 286, 568 **Vol. 3:** 489
4:15	**Vol. 1:** 180 **Vol. 2:** 692, 697, 834
4:16 f	**Vol. 1:** 571
4:16	**Vol. 1:** 129, 400, 491
4:17	**Vol. 1:** 180, 286, 491 **Vol. 2:** 517 **Vol. 3:** 241–242, 764, 940, 942
4:19 f	**Vol. 2:** 605–606
4:19	**Vol. 2:** 399, 517 **Vol. 3:** 1021, 1106, 1125
4:20	**Vol. 1:** 300 **Vol. 3:** 1125
4:21	**Vol. 1:** 407 **Vol. 2:** 258 **Vol. 3:** 694, 1175
5 ff	**Vol. 2:** 581
5–7	**Vol. 3:** 802
5	**Vol. 3:** 535

1 Corinthians (cont'd)

5:1 ff	**Vol. 1:** 500
5:1–13	**Vol. 3:** 214
5:1–8	**Vol. 1:** 628
5:1–6	**Vol. 2:** 676
5:1–5	**Vol. 1:** 703
5:1	**Vol. 2:** 794 **Vol. 3:** 1195
5:2	**Vol. 1:** 466 **Vol. 2:** 422 **Vol. 3:** 1157
5:3 ff	**Vol. 2:** 874
5:3–5	**Vol. 1:** 466
5:3	**Vol. 1:** 235 **Vol. 2:** 364, 875, 899 **Vol. 3:** 694
5:4	**Vol. 1:** 466 **Vol. 2:** 33, 605, 654
5:5	**Vol. 1:** 466–467 **Vol. 2:** 368, 517 **Vol. 3:** 214, 470–471, 535, 694
5:6 ff	**Vol. 2:** 755
5:6–8	**Vol. 2:** 716
5:6	**Vol. 1:** 228 **Vol. 2:** 428, 462 **Vol. 3:** 489, 917
5:7–8	**Vol. 1:** 634 **Vol. 2:** 463, 716 **Vol. 3:** 417, 431
5:7	**Vol. 1:** 437, 629, 633–634 **Vol. 2:** 338, 463, 527, 534, 675–676, 714 **Vol. 3:** 102, 917
5:8	**Vol. 1:** 563, 630 **Vol. 2:** 676 **Vol. 3:** 886
5:9 ff	**Vol. 1:** 500 **Vol. 3:** 536
5:9–12	**Vol. 2:** 576
5:9 f	**Vol. 3:** 1165
5:9	**Vol. 2:** 922 **Vol. 3:** 489
5:10 f	**Vol. 1:** 138 **Vol. 2:** 286 **Vol. 3:** 31, 604
5:10	**Vol. 1:** 524–525 **Vol. 2:** 926
5:11	**Vol. 1:** 138, 257, 513 **Vol. 2:** 273, 655 **Vol. 3:** 347, 489
5:12 f	**Vol. 3:** 1199
5:12	**Vol. 2:** 365–366
5:13	**Vol. 1:** 566 **Vol. 2:** 463 **Vol. 3:** 535
5:14	**Vol. 1:** 720 **Vol. 2:** 604
6	**Vol. 3:** 380
6:1 f	**Vol. 2:** 230
6:1–11	**Vol. 1:** 400 **Vol. 3:** 576
6:1–6	**Vol. 3:** 1165
6:1	**Vol. 1:** 365 **Vol. 3:** 576, 1158, 1204
6:2 f	**Vol. 1:** 649 **Vol. 2:** 365 **Vol. 3:** 1165
6:2	**Vol. 1:** 440 **Vol. 2:** 366, 613
6:4	**Vol. 3:** 588
6:5	**Vol. 1:** 373, 504 **Vol. 3:** 1032
6:6	**Vol. 2:** 365
6:7 f	**Vol. 3:** 575
6:7	**Vol. 2:** 365 **Vol. 3:** 380
6:8	**Vol. 3:** 380
6:9 ff	**Vol. 2:** 584 **Vol. 3:** 536–537, 1165
6:9–10	**Vol. 2:** 583 **Vol. 3:** 31, 832, 929
6:9–20	**Vol. 1:** 500
6:9–11	**Vol. 3:** 701
6:9	**Vol. 2:** 300, 459–460, 570 **Vol. 3:** 576, 929
6:10 f	**Vol. 1:** 138
6:10	**Vol. 1:** 138, 513 **Vol. 3:** 347, 377, 604, 929
6:11	**Vol. 1:** 152 **Vol. 2:** 75, 230, 463, 654 **Vol. 3:** 61, 363, 499, 536, 701, 990
6:12–20	**Vol. 2:** 402, 576
6:12	**Vol. 2:** 611
6:13–20	**Vol. 1:** 235
6:13	**Vol. 1:** 73, 169, 500 **Vol. 2:** 268, 517 **Vol. 3:** 718
6:14	**Vol. 2:** 606, 923 **Vol. 3:** 304
6:15 ff	**Vol. 1:** 500
6:15–19	**Vol. 1:** 501
6:15 f	**Vol. 1:** 507
6:15	**Vol. 1:** 231, 235 **Vol. 2:** 273
6:16	**Vol. 1:** 232 **Vol. 2:** 350, 579, 722
6:17	**Vol. 2:** 350, 722 **Vol. 3:** 694, 701, 703
6:18 f	**Vol. 1:** 718
6:18	**Vol. 1:** 500, 559 **Vol. 2:** 273 **Vol. 3:** 197, 535, 579, 1165
6:19 f	**Vol. 1:** 235 **Vol. 2:** 463 **Vol. 3:** 701
6:19	**Vol. 1:** 638 **Vol. 2:** 249, 566 **Vol. 3:** 784
6:20	**Vol. 1:** 268 **Vol. 2:** 47, 49, 874 **Vol. 3:** 198, 200, 854
6:25 ff	**Vol. 3:** 535
7–16	**Vol. 3:** 1203
7–10	**Vol. 1:** 717
7	**Vol. 2:** 903, 923 **Vol. 3:** 188, 534–537, 1072
7:1–24	**Vol. 3:** 535
7:1–16	**Vol. 2:** 563
7:1–9	**Vol. 2:** 580 **Vol. 3:** 541–542
7:1–7	**Vol. 3:** 1072
7:1–2	**Vol. 3:** 534
7:1	**Vol. 1:** 496 **Vol. 2:** 104, 565, 581 **Vol. 3:** 536, 1203
7:2 ff	**Vol. 3:** 1058, 1065
7:2–7	**Vol. 3:** 189, 539
7:2	**Vol. 1:** 501 **Vol. 2:** 923 **Vol. 3:** 536
7:3–7	**Vol. 3:** 534
7:3–5	**Vol. 3:** 1201
7:3 f	**Vol. 1:** 338 **Vol. 3:** 536
7:3	**Vol. 2:** 579, 668
7:4	**Vol. 1:** 235 **Vol. 2:** 273 **Vol. 3:** 1064, 1067
7:5	**Vol. 1:** 322, 495–496 **Vol. 3:** 380, 471, 536, 802, 837, 1067, 1194
7:7	**Vol. 1:** 496 **Vol. 2:** 121, 273, 581 **Vol. 3:** 536, 1022, 1188
7:7b	**Vol. 3:** 536
7:8 f	**Vol. 2:** 564 **Vol. 3:** 225
7:8–9	**Vol. 3:** 534
7:8	**Vol. 2:** 104 **Vol. 3:** 536, 1075
7:9	**Vol. 1:** 495–496, 656 **Vol. 3:** 536 188, 535–536
7:10–16	**Vol. 2:** 580
7:10–11	**Vol. 3:** 534–535
7:10 f	**Vol. 1:** 507 **Vol. 2:** 580 **Vol. 3:** 172, 183,

1 Corinthians *(cont'd)*

7:10   **Vol. 1:** 130   **Vol. 2:** 514, 581,
900   **Vol. 3:** 85, 534, 931, 967

7:10b   **Vol. 3:** 535

7:11–13   **Vol. 1:** 701

7:11   **Vol. 3:** 167, 535–537

7:12–16   **Vol. 2:** 581   **Vol. 3:** 173, 534, 536, 1165

7:12 f   **Vol. 2:** 250

7:12   **Vol. 1:** 130   **Vol. 2:** 900   **Vol. 3:** 85, 252, 535

7:13–16   **Vol. 3:** 173

7:14   **Vol. 1:** 149, 159   **Vol. 2:** 230   **Vol. 3:** 1175, 1192

7:15–24   **Vol. 1:** 275

7:15   **Vol. 1:** 275   **Vol. 2:** 781   **Vol. 3:** 535, 537, 540, 1191

7:16   **Vol. 3:** 214, 535

7:17 ff   **Vol. 1:** 299

7:17–24   **Vol. 3:** 932

7:17   **Vol. 1:** 301   **Vol. 2:** 517

7:18   **Vol. 1:** 310

7:19   **Vol. 1:** 311, 336, 338, 602   **Vol. 2:** 133

7:20 ff   **Vol. 1:** 525

7:20–24   **Vol. 3:** 596

7:20   **Vol. 1:** 275

7:21 ff   **Vol. 3:** 582, 1162

7:21   **Vol. 3:** 225, 596, 860

7:22 ff   **Vol. 3:** 596

7:22 f   **Vol. 2:** 51

7:22   **Vol. 1:** 638, 717–718, 720   **Vol. 3:** 598, 613, 854

7:23   **Vol. 1:** 268   **Vol. 3:** 198, 200

7:24   **Vol. 3:** 1202

7:25 ff   **Vol. 3:** 1072

7:25–38   **Vol. 3:** 1072

7:25–28   **Vol. 3:** 537

7:25   **Vol. 1:** 341   **Vol. 2:** 398, 597   **Vol. 3:** 85, 535–536, 1066, 1072, 1203

7:26–35   **Vol. 3:** 537

7:26–29   **Vol. 2:** 580

7:26   **Vol. 1:** 496   **Vol. 2:** 104, 664   **Vol. 3:** 536

7:27 f   **Vol. 3:** 173, 537, 540

7:27   **Vol. 1:** 171   **Vol. 3:** 188, 537

7:28   **Vol. 1:** 496, 675   **Vol. 3:** 189, 536, 1072

7:29 ff   **Vol. 1:** 525, 639, 675   **Vol. 2:** 581   **Vol. 3:** 188, 536, 1165

7:29–31   **Vol. 3:** 121

7:29   **Vol. 1:** 278   **Vol. 2:** 62, 922   **Vol. 3:** 252, 838

7:30   **Vol. 2:** 361, 416

7:31   **Vol. 1:** 278, 325, 525, 709   **Vol. 2:** 62

7:32 ff   **Vol. 1:** 278   **Vol. 3:** 536

7:32   **Vol. 2:** 816   **Vol. 3:** 536, 1022

7:34   **Vol. 1:** 235   **Vol. 3:** 536, 694

7:36 ff   **Vol. 2:** 581, 588   **Vol. 3:** 536, 538, 541

7:36   **Vol. 2:** 588   **Vol. 3:** 1021, 1072

7:37   **Vol. 1:** 661   **Vol. 2:** 133, 364, 663   **Vol. 3:** 1019

7:38   **Vol. 2:** 581, 588

7:39 f   **Vol. 2:** 564

7:39   **Vol. 1:** 171, 443   **Vol. 2:** 517   **Vol. 3:** 173, 535, 537, 843, 1165, 1191

7:40   **Vol. 1:** 217   **Vol. 2:** 398   **Vol. 3:** 85, 224, 703, 822, 967

8   **Vol. 3:** 802

8:1 ff   **Vol. 1:** 352   **Vol. 3:** 996

8:1–11:1   **Vol. 1:** 400

8:1–13   **Vol. 3:** 433

8:1–7   **Vol. 2:** 74

8:1–6   **Vol. 2:** 286

8:1 f   **Vol. 3:** 432

8:1   **Vol. 1:** 638   **Vol. 2:** 253, 284–285, 401–402, 546   **Vol. 3:** 432, 996, 1203

8:2   **Vol. 2:** 402   **Vol. 3:** 822

8:3   **Vol. 2:** 400, 402–403, 545

8:4 ff   **Vol. 2:** 721–722   **Vol. 3:** 433

8:4–6   **Vol. 1:** 628

8:4   **Vol. 2:** 73, 268–269, 284–286, 721–722, 831   **Vol. 3:** 432, 996

8:5 f   **Vol. 2:** 73, 515

8:5   **Vol. 2:** 895

8:6   **Vol. 1:** 95, 384, 620   **Vol. 2:** 73, 84, 160, 195, 515–516, 671, 721–722   **Vol. 3:** 61, 996, 1063, 1182, 1198

8:7 ff   **Vol. 1:** 350

8:7   **Vol. 1:** 352, 449   **Vol. 2:** 284–285, 402   **Vol. 3:** 432, 995–996

8:8†   **Vol. 1:** 475, 731   **Vol. 2:** 268

8:9 ff   **Vol. 2:** 273

8:9–13   **Vol. 2:** 286

8:9   **Vol. 2:** 402, 706   **Vol. 3:** 996

8:10 ff   **Vol. 3:** 433

8:10 f   **Vol. 3:** 1165

8:10   **Vol. 1:** 352   **Vol. 2:** 284–285   **Vol. 3:** 432, 995–996, 1208

8:11   **Vol. 1:** 257   **Vol. 3:** 996, 1197

8:12   **Vol. 1:** 352   **Vol. 3:** 903

8:13   **Vol. 1:** 352   **Vol. 2:** 268, 708, 710   **Vol. 3:** 829–830, 996

9   **Vol. 3:** 854, 1053

9:1 ff   **Vol. 1:** 136

9:1   **Vol. 1:** 183, 229, 528   **Vol. 3:** 284, 314, 1151

9:2   **Vol. 3:** 499

9:3–18   **Vol. 3:** 771

9:3 f   **Vol. 3:** 855

9:3   **Vol. 2:** 365

9:4–6   **Vol. 2:** 611

9:4   **Vol. 2:** 223, 275

9:5   **Vol. 1:** 131–132, 256   **Vol. 2:** 121   **Vol. 3:** 252, 383, 387

9:7 ff   **Vol. 2:** 223

9:7   **Vol. 1:** 723   **Vol. 2:** 816   **Vol. 3:** 144, 525, 568, 868, 964

9:8 ff   **Vol. 1:** 49   **Vol. 2:** 446

9:8–18   **Vol. 3:** 854

9:8   **Vol. 2:** 444

1 Corinthians *(cont'd)*

9:9   **Vol. 1:** 115, 737   **Vol. 2:** 641, 746, 755
9:10   **Vol. 3:** 489, 492, 1193
9:11   **Vol. 3:** 525, 707, 752
9:12 f   **Vol. 2:** 706
9:12   **Vol. 2:** 111, 221   **Vol. 3:** 142
9:13 f   **Vol. 3:** 794
9:13   **Vol. 2:** 235, 694   **Vol. 3:** 433, 436, 793
9:14   **Vol. 2:** 111, 272   **Vol. 3:** 47, 349, 773, 1053
9:15–18   **Vol. 2:** 435
9:15   **Vol. 1:** 229   **Vol. 3:** 142, 1053
9:16   **Vol. 1:** 229   **Vol. 2:** 112, 664   **Vol. 3:** 142, 504
9:17 f   **Vol. 3:** 142
9:17   **Vol. 2:** 255   **Vol. 3:** 1158
9:18   **Vol. 2:** 111   **Vol. 3:** 964
9:19 ff   **Vol. 1:** 720   **Vol. 2:** 451   **Vol. 3:** 137
9:19–23   **Vol. 3:** 793
9:19 f   **Vol. 2:** 706
9:19   **Vol. 1:** 718, 720   **Vol. 3:** 137, 596
9:20 f   **Vol. 3:** 431
9:20   **Vol. 1:** 310   **Vol. 2:** 314, 445
9:21 f   **Vol. 3:** 1165
9:21   **Vol. 2:** 445–446   **Vol. 3:** 1151
9:22   **Vol. 1:** 310   **Vol. 2:** 816   **Vol. 3:** 137, 214, 431
9:23   **Vol. 1:** 644   **Vol. 2:** 112
9:24 ff   **Vol. 1:** 648   **Vol. 3:** 838, 947
9:24–27   **Vol. 1:** 469, 647   **Vol. 3:** 214
9:24   **Vol. 1:** 649   **Vol. 3:** 142, 750
9:25   **Vol. 1:** 406, 495–496, 645   **Vol. 2:** 244
9:26   **Vol. 1:** 449
9:27   **Vol. 1:** 163, 235, 647   **Vol. 3:** 54, 808, 810
10   **Vol. 3:** 806, 984
10:1 ff   **Vol. 1:** 149
10:1–13   **Vol. 1:** 467   **Vol. 3:** 1007
10:1–5   **Vol. 2:** 719
10:1–4   **Vol. 3:** 706
10:1 f   **Vol. 3:** 990, 1003
10:1   **Vol. 1:** 619   **Vol. 2:** 406   **Vol. 3:** 984, 1022
10:2–5   **Vol. 2:** 641
10:2   **Vol. 1:** 144   **Vol. 3:** 1209–1210
10:3 f   **Vol. 2:** 276   **Vol. 3:** 382–383, 706–707
10:3   **Vol. 2:** 268–269
10:4   **Vol. 1:** 677   **Vol. 2:** 276, 755   **Vol. 3:** 459
10:5   **Vol. 2:** 819   **Vol. 3:** 1007–1008
10:6   **Vol. 1:** 71, 564   **Vol. 2:** 277   **Vol. 3:** 724
10:7–10   **Vol. 2:** 286
10:7 f   **Vol. 3:** 802
10:7   **Vol. 2:** 286
10:8   **Vol. 1:** 501, 610   **Vol. 2:** 699
10:9 f   **Vol. 1:** 464
10:9   **Vol. 3:** 802, 809
10:10   **Vol. 1:** 467

10:11   **Vol. 1:** 325, 568–569, 581   **Vol. 3:** 489, 759, 829, 831, 906, 1204
10:12   **Vol. 1:** 610   **Vol. 3:** 822
10:13   **Vol. 2:** 77, 565, 611   **Vol. 3:** 802–803, 809
10:14 ff   **Vol. 2:** 273
10:14–22   **Vol. 2:** 286
10:14   **Vol. 1:** 500, 559   **Vol. 2:** 286
10:15   **Vol. 2:** 364, 620
10:16 f   **Vol. 1:** 237   **Vol. 2:** 277
10:16   **Vol. 1:** 213, 223, 251, 643   **Vol. 2:** 273, 521, 523, 529, 536   **Vol. 3:** 166, 819
10:16b   **Vol. 1:** 369
10:17   **Vol. 1:** 96, 639   **Vol. 2:** 277, 534
10:18   **Vol. 1:** 257, 643, 675   **Vol. 2:** 218, 312, 339   **Vol. 3:** 433, 436
10:19 ff.   **Vol. 3:** 433
10:19†   **Vol. 2:** 284–285   **Vol. 3:** 432–433
10:20 ff   **Vol. 2:** 273
10:20 f   **Vol. 1:** 452   **Vol. 3:** 1208
10:20   **Vol. 2:** 74, 85, 520   **Vol. 3:** 310, 1008
10:21   **Vol. 1:** 639   **Vol. 2:** 516, 518, 520, 522   **Vol. 3:** 1165
10:22   **Vol. 2:** 516, 522   **Vol. 3:** 714
10:23–30   **Vol. 3:** 433
10:23 f   **Vol. 1:** 352, 638   **Vol. 2:** 611
10:23   **Vol. 1:** 300   **Vol. 2:** 253, 611
10:24   **Vol. 2:** 739
10:25 ff   **Vol. 1:** 352
10:25–30   **Vol. 2:** 286
10:25   **Vol. 2:** 273, 364
10:27 ff   **Vol. 3:** 1165
10:27   **Vol. 1:** 275, 299, 352   **Vol. 2:** 269, 364
10:28   **Vol. 1:** 352   **Vol. 2:** 235, 284–285, 611
10:29   **Vol. 1:** 352   **Vol. 2:** 364
10:30   **Vol. 2:** 121, 874   **Vol. 3:** 819
10:31 ff   **Vol. 1:** 352   **Vol. 2:** 235, 611   **Vol. 3:** 433
10:31   **Vol. 2:** 46–47, 272, 874   **Vol. 3:** 1155, 1187
10:32   **Vol. 2:** 126–127, 159, 273, 286, 707   **Vol. 3:** 1165
10:33–11:1   **Vol. 2:** 160
10:33   **Vol. 2:** 816   **Vol. 3:** 214, 531–532
11   **Vol. 2:** 530, 547   **Vol. 3:** 1066
11:1–6   **Vol. 2:** 212
11:1   **Vol. 1:** 400, 491   **Vol. 3:** 60, 724, 729
11:2 ff   **Vol. 2:** 51
11:2–16   **Vol. 3:** 1063
11:2–15   **Vol. 2:** 159
11:2   **Vol. 2:** 718–719   **Vol. 3:** 241, 773–774, 817
11:3 ff   **Vol. 2:** 563
11:3   **Vol. 2:** 160, 579   **Vol. 3:** 1022, 1063
11:4–6   **Vol. 2:** 160
11:4–5   **Vol. 2:** 212
11:4 f   **Vol. 2:** 869, 874
11:4   **Vol. 2:** 160   **Vol. 3:** 1199
11:5   **Vol. 2:** 160–161, 212, 883   **Vol. 3:** 1066

1 Corinthians *(cont'd)*

11:6–7   **Vol. 2:** 212
11:6   **Vol. 3:** 564
11:7–9   **Vol. 2:** 160
11:7   **Vol. 2:** 46, 51, 160–161, 288, 563, 668
11:8   **Vol. 2:** 213
11:9   **Vol. 1:** 385   **Vol. 2:** 161, 213   **Vol. 3:** 1177, 1183
11:10   **Vol. 1:** 102   **Vol. 2:** 160–161, 213, 668, 874
11:11 f   **Vol. 1:** 385
11:11   **Vol. 3:** 1183
11:12   **Vol. 2:** 160   **Vol. 3:** 1063, 1177
11:12b   **Vol. 3:** 1188
11:13 ff   **Vol. 2:** 563
11:13 f   **Vol. 2:** 365
11:13–15   **Vol. 2:** 162
11:13   **Vol. 2:** 212–213, 669, 874, 883   **Vol. 3:** 1066
11:14   **Vol. 2:** 50–51, 162, 661   **Vol. 3:** 764
11:15   **Vol. 2:** 162   **Vol. 3:** 1066, 1179
11:16   **Vol. 1:** 299, 301   **Vol. 2:** 162, 213, 550   **Vol. 3:** 822
11:17 ff   **Vol. 1:** 322
11:17–34   **Vol. 3:** 349, 547
11:17–22   **Vol. 3:** 544
11:17   **Vol. 1:** 341   **Vol. 3:** 817, 1187
11:18 f   **Vol. 1:** 535
11:18   **Vol. 1:** 299   **Vol. 3:** 544, 1194, 1211
11:19   **Vol. 3:** 320, 808, 1052
11:20 ff   **Vol. 2:** 272
11:20–29   **Vol. 2:** 221
11:20   **Vol. 1:** 514   **Vol. 2:** 516, 518, 522, 534   **Vol. 3:** 411, 1194
11:21   **Vol. 1:** 514   **Vol. 2:** 267, 273, 534   **Vol. 3:** 750
11:22   **Vol. 1:** 299, 461   **Vol. 2:** 846   **Vol. 3:** 817
11:23 ff   **Vol. 3:** 62
11:23–26   **Vol. 1:** 131, 237   **Vol. 2:** 277
11:23–25   **Vol. 2:** 523–524
11:23   **Vol. 1:** 129, 251, 630   **Vol. 2:** 368, 523, 527–528, 719   **Vol. 3:** 61, 322, 611, 751, 773–774, 1171, 1181
11:24 f   **Vol. 1:** 398, 437   **Vol. 2:** 523   **Vol. 3:** 243
11:24   **Vol. 1:** 237, 437–439   **Vol. 2:** 368, 524, 530, 536, 874   **Vol. 3:** 819
11:25   **Vol. 1:** 223, 369–370   **Vol. 2:** 312, 316, 524–525, 529–530, 533, 536, 671, 786   **Vol. 3:** 166, 819
11:26 ff   **Vol. 2:** 530
11:26   **Vol. 1:** 237, 437   **Vol. 2:** 273, 516, 523, 530–531, 894, 896   **Vol. 3:** 47, 245–246
11:27–32   **Vol. 1:** 369
11:27 f   **Vol. 2:** 523
11:27   **Vol. 1:** 223, 237   **Vol. 2:** 143, 516, 522, 531   **Vol. 3:** 349

11:28   **Vol. 1:** 414   **Vol. 3:** 808
11:29   **Vol. 1:** 301, 504   **Vol. 2:** 273
11:30–32   **Vol. 3:** 1206
11:30 f   **Vol. 1:** 163
11:30   **Vol. 1:** 467   **Vol. 3:** 730, 998
11:31 f   **Vol. 2:** 522
11:31   **Vol. 1:** 503
11:32   **Vol. 2:** 366, 516   **Vol. 3:** 778, 998
11:32b   **Vol. 3:** 779
11:33–34   **Vol. 3:** 544
11:33   **Vol. 2:** 245
11:34   **Vol. 2:** 267   **Vol. 3:** 252
12–14   **Vol. 2:** 176   **Vol. 3:** 707
12   **Vol. 1:** 232, 238, 301   **Vol. 2:** 168–169, 566, 723   **Vol. 3:** 1079
12:1 ff   **Vol. 2:** 42
12:1   **Vol. 2:** 406   **Vol. 3:** 84, 706–707, 1203
12:2   **Vol. 2:** 793   **Vol. 3:** 1079
12:3   **Vol. 1:** 205, 369, 414   **Vol. 2:** 75, 402, 514, 516   **Vol. 3:** 61, 314, 475, 703, 780, 967
12:4 ff   **Vol. 1:** 535   **Vol. 2:** 84
12:4–31   **Vol. 3:** 1067
12:4   **Vol. 3:** 297
12:5   **Vol. 2:** 517   **Vol. 3:** 546–548
12:6   **Vol. 3:** 1021, 1151–1152
12:7   **Vol. 1:** 232   **Vol. 3:** 323, 1210
12:8 ff   **Vol. 2:** 632
12:8–11   **Vol. 3:** 703
12:8   **Vol. 1:** 602   **Vol. 3:** 1031, 1210
12:9 ff   **Vol. 2:** 121
12:9   **Vol. 1:** 601   **Vol. 2:** 721   **Vol. 3:** 1210
12:10   **Vol. 1:** 452, 504, 581–582   **Vol. 2:** 605, 740   **Vol. 3:** 475, 695, 1080, 1152
12:11–27   **Vol. 2:** 121
12:11   **Vol. 1:** 535   **Vol. 2:** 721, 839   **Vol. 3:** 1017–1018, 1021, 1152, 1210
12:12 ff   **Vol. 1:** 231, 467   **Vol. 2:** 499
12:12–30   **Vol. 1:** 237
12:12–27   **Vol. 1:** 300
12:12–26   **Vol. 1:** 235   **Vol. 3:** 544
12:12 f   **Vol. 1:** 237   **Vol. 2:** 722   **Vol. 3:** 1062
12:13   **Vol. 1:** 96, 147–148, 152, 237, 720   **Vol. 2:** 51, 126–127, 309, 721, 785, 800   **Vol. 3:** 499, 701–702, 1187, 1209–1210
12:14 ff   **Vol. 1:** 300
12:14–26   **Vol. 1:** 237   **Vol. 2:** 434   **Vol. 3:** 703
12:17   **Vol. 2:** 175
12:18 f   **Vol. 2:** 720
12:18   **Vol. 1:** 477   **Vol. 3:** 1021
12:22 f   **Vol. 3:** 822
12:23 f   **Vol. 2:** 51
12:23   **Vol. 2:** 50
12:24   **Vol. 3:** 955, **1021**
12:25–38   **Vol. 1:** 129
12:25   **Vol. 1:** 278   **Vol. 2:** 514   **Vol. 3:** 544
12:26   **Vol. 2:** 722   **Vol. 3:** 724
12:27   **Vol. 1:** 237, 300, 535   **Vol. 2:** 273, 304
12:28 ff   **Vol. 2:** 121, 499

1 Corinthians *(cont'd)*

12:28 f	**Vol. 3:** 84
12:28†	**Vol. 1:** 198, 667 **Vol. 2:** 605, 632 **Vol. 3:** 88, 703, 767–768
12:29 ff	**Vol. 1:** 66
12:30	**Vol. 1:** 581 **Vol. 2:** 740
12:31	**Vol. 2:** 121, 123, 425 **Vol. 3:** 88, 569, 1167
12:31b	**Vol. 3:** 942
13	**Vol. 1:** 300, 720 **Vol. 2:** 79, 499, 544–545, 723
13:1–14:1	**Vol. 1:** 352
13:1	**Vol. 1:** 103 **Vol. 2:** 97, 221, 565, 786, 884 **Vol. 3:** 112, 674
13:2	**Vol. 1:** 602, 638 **Vol. 2:** 545 **Vol. 3:** 84, 505
13:3	**Vol. 1:** 235–236 **Vol. 2:** 845, 847
13:4	**Vol. 2:** 106, 771 **Vol. 3:** 1167
13:5	**Vol. 1:** 110, 564 **Vol. 3:** 532, 824–825
13:6	**Vol. 3:** 576, 887
13:7	**Vol. 2:** 243, 545, 774 **Vol. 3:** 887, 1211
13:8	**Vol. 1:** 73, 609 **Vol. 2:** 400, 545 **Vol. 3:** 225
13:9 f	**Vol. 2:** 304
13:9	**Vol. 2:** 62, 546
13:10	**Vol. 1:** 73 **Vol. 2:** 62, 304
13:11	**Vol. 1:** 73, 282 **Vol. 2:** 563, 617 **Vol. 3:** 824
13:12 f	**Vol. 2:** 401
13:12	**Vol. 1:** 282, 587 **Vol. 2:** 218, 304, 400, 402–403, 482, 503, 546, 746 **Vol. 3:** 335
13:13†	**Vol. 1:** 236, 282, 601, 609 **Vol. 2:** 242, 425, 545–546, 687 **Vol. 3:** 225
14	**Vol. 2:** 884 **Vol. 3:** 77, 89, 505, 967, 1032, 1066, 1079
14:1–6	**Vol. 1:** 582
14:1–5	**Vol. 3:** 703
14:1–4	**Vol. 2:** 740
14:1	**Vol. 2:** 546, 807, 868 **Vol. 3:** 88, 706–707, 942, 967, 1167
14:2–19	**Vol. 2:** 741
14:2–6	**Vol. 1:** 582
14:2 f	**Vol. 3:** 87
14:2	**Vol. 1:** 582 **Vol. 2:** 786 **Vol. 3:** 505, 1080
14:3–5	**Vol. 2:** 253
14:3 f	**Vol. 1:** 329
14:3	**Vol. 3:** 81, 84
14:4 f	**Vol. 1:** 300
14:4	**Vol. 2:** 253
14:5–12	**Vol. 3:** 112
14:5	**Vol. 1:** 581–582 **Vol. 3:** 748, 1022, 1080
14:6 f	**Vol. 2:** 874 **Vol. 3:** 819
14:6	**Vol. 2:** 400 **Vol. 3:** 81, 315, 770, 962
14:7–12	**Vol. 2:** 883
14:7 f	**Vol. 2:** 434, 883 **Vol. 3:** 674
14:7	**Vol. 2:** 398
14:8–9	**Vol. 3:** 874
14:8	**Vol. 3:** 119, 410, 874, 962
14:9	**Vol. 1:** 449 **Vol. 3:** 1113
14:11 f	**Vol. 3:** 962
14:11	**Vol. 3:** 1191
14:12	**Vol. 1:** 300, 731 **Vol. 2:** 253 **Vol. 3:** 390, 695, 703, 707, 1167
14:13 ff	**Vol. 2:** 883
14:13–16:26	**Vol. 2:** 869
14:13–19	**Vol. 3:** 703
14:13	**Vol. 1:** 581–582 **Vol. 2:** 874, 884 **Vol. 3:** 505
14:14 ff	**Vol. 3:** 1080
14:14–17	**Vol. 3:** 702
14:14–16	**Vol. 2:** 873
14:14 f	**Vol. 2:** 874 **Vol. 3:** 672
14:14	**Vol. 1:** 582, 723 **Vol. 3:** 129, 694
14:15 f	**Vol. 3:** 84
14:15	**Vol. 3:** 671–672, 675, 705
14:16–19	**Vol. 3:** 672
14:16	**Vol. 1:** 99, 213, 582 **Vol. 2:** 456, 874 **Vol. 3:** 505
14:17	**Vol. 2:** 253
14:18	**Vol. 1:** 528 **Vol. 2:** 121, 874 **Vol. 3:** 819, 1080
14:19	**Vol. 1:** 300, 528, 582 **Vol. 2:** 253, 567, 692, 873 **Vol. 3:** 112, 129, 771, 1080, 1113
14:20	**Vol. 1:** 282, 284 **Vol. 2:** 62
14:21	**Vol. 2:** 175, 444, 446, 513, 740 **Vol. 3:** 1079
14:22	**Vol. 2:** 741, 883 **Vol. 3:** 1080
14:23 f	**Vol. 2:** 741 **Vol. 3:** 84, 962
14:23	**Vol. 1:** 300, 322, 528–529, 582 **Vol. 2:** 402, 456–457 **Vol. 3:** 1080
14:24 f	**Vol. 3:** 84, 703, 705, 1080
14:24	**Vol. 2:** 141, 364, 456–457 **Vol. 3:** 129, 1165
14:25 f	**Vol. 3:** 671
14:25	**Vol. 1:** 610 **Vol. 2:** 218, 874 **Vol. 3:** 47, 320
14:26 ff	**Vol. 2:** 884 **Vol. 3:** 1080
14:26	**Vol. 1:** 322, 581 **Vol. 2:** 253 **Vol. 3:** 110, 315, 671, 703, 770
14:27 ff	**Vol. 3:** 962
14:27	**Vol. 1:** 581–582 **Vol. 2:** 304, 400
14:28	**Vol. 1:** 300, 581–582 **Vol. 2:** 874
14:28b	**Vol. 3:** 1080
14:29	**Vol. 1:** 503
14:30 f	**Vol. 1:** 570
14:30	**Vol. 1:** 667 **Vol. 3:** 84, 315, 589
14:31	**Vol. 1:** 571 **Vol. 3:** 81, 84
14:32	**Vol. 3:** 84, 694
14:33 f	**Vol. 1:** 301
14:33–38	**Vol. 3:** 932
14:33	**Vol. 1:** 300, 667 **Vol. 2:** 78, 780
14:33a	**Vol. 3:** 84
14:33b–36	**Vol. 3:** 1066
14:34 f	**Vol. 3:** 1063
14:34	**Vol. 2:** 446

1 Corinthians *(cont'd)*

14:35	**Vol. 2:** 880 **Vol. 3:** 564, 1066
14:36	**Vol. 1:** 322, 325 **Vol. 2:** 517 **Vol. 3:** 61, 1110
14:37	**Vol. 1:** 337 **Vol. 2:** 403, 407, 605 **Vol. 3:** 706–707, 822
14:38	**Vol. 2:** 403, 407 **Vol. 3:** 84
14:39	**Vol. 2:** 222 **Vol. 3:** 1167
14:39b	**Vol. 3:** 1080
14:40	**Vol. 1:** 667
15	**Vol. 1:** 236, 266, 445, 651 **Vol. 2:** 208, 903, 905, 923–925 **Vol. 3:** 276–277, 280–281, 287, 304
15:1 ff	**Vol. 1:** 394–395 **Vol. 2:** 111, 338
15:1–8	**Vol. 3:** 1047
15:1–7	**Vol. 1:** 131 **Vol. 3:** 62
15:1–5	**Vol. 3:** 61
15:1–3	**Vol. 2:** 719 **Vol. 3:** 1110
15:1 f	**Vol. 3:** 55, 1111
15:1	**Vol. 3:** 61, 314
15:2	**Vol. 1:** 601 **Vol. 2:** 111 **Vol. 3:** 214, 1106
15:3 ff	**Vol. 1:** 298, 437, 445 **Vol. 3:** 61, 773–774
15:3–4:11	**Vol. 1:** 601
15:3–10	**Vol. 3:** 283
15:3–8	**Vol. 3:** 55, 288, 297
15:3–7	**Vol. 3:** 62
15:3–5	**Vol. 2:** 338 **Vol. 3:** 286, 612, 1110
15:3 f	**Vol. 1:** 150 **Vol. 2:** 380 **Vol. 3:** 491, 1200
15:3	**Vol. 1:** 398, 435, 438, 680 **Vol. 2:** 532, 926 **Vol. 3:** 166, 196, 322, 581, 751, 773, 1184, 1197
15:4–7	**Vol. 3:** 285
15:4	**Vol. 1:** 266 **Vol. 2:** 340, 481, 687, 893 **Vol. 3:** 283, 292
15:5 ff	**Vol. 2:** 524 **Vol. 3:** 518
15:5–9	**Vol. 1:** 136
15:5–8	**Vol. 2:** 786 **Vol. 3:** 281
15:5–7	**Vol. 3:** 285
15:5	**Vol. 2:** 695 **Vol. 3:** 285, 383–384
15:6 f	**Vol. 3:** 286
15:6	**Vol. 1:** 443 **Vol. 2:** 717, 925 **Vol. 3:** 224, 285
15:7	**Vol. 1:** 129–130, 133, 256 **Vol. 3:** 285
15:8 ff	**Vol. 2:** 171
15:8	**Vol. 1:** 86, 130, 182–183, 528 **Vol. 2:** 57 **Vol. 3:** 284–285, 314
15:9 ff	**Vol. 3:** 288
15:9	**Vol. 1:** 183, 274–275, 301 **Vol. 2:** 176, 429, 806 **Vol. 3:** 184, 581, 729
15:10 f	**Vol. 3:** 581
15:10	**Vol. 1:** 263 **Vol. 2:** 121 **Vol. 3:** 701
15:11	**Vol. 1:** 131, 601 **Vol. 3:** 55, 314
15:12 ff	**Vol. 1:** 440, 446 **Vol. 2:** 338, 924 **Vol. 3:** 831
15:12–24	**Vol. 2:** 926
15:12	**Vol. 1:** 638 **Vol. 2:** 402, 924 **Vol. 3:** 52, 55, 277–278, 304–305
15:13–17	**Vol. 3:** 281
15:14–17	**Vol. 3:** 281
15:14	**Vol. 1:** 547, 551, 601 **Vol. 2:** 242 **Vol. 3:** 52–53, 284, 417
15:15	**Vol. 2:** 472 **Vol. 3:** 529, 1043
15:16 f	**Vol. 2:** 338
15:17–19	**Vol. 2:** 559
15:17	**Vol. 1:** 86, 551, 601, 702 **Vol. 2:** 242 **Vol. 3:** 281
15:18	**Vol. 1:** 443 **Vol. 2:** 925 **Vol. 3:** 1207
15:19	**Vol. 2:** 597, 724 **Vol. 3:** 417
15:20 ff	**Vol. 2:** 242, 481–482, 895 **Vol. 3:** 831
15:20–28	**Vol. 2:** 702
15:20–22	**Vol. 1:** 86
15:20	**Vol. 1:** 86, 443, 731 **Vol. 2:** 48, 338, 786, 925 **Vol. 3:** 303, 417, 558, 1189
15:21 f	**Vol. 1:** 436 **Vol. 2:** 57, 566
15:21	**Vol. 3:** 1198
15:22 ff	**Vol. 1:** 467
15:22 f	**Vol. 3:** 1191
15:22	**Vol. 1:** 86, 96, 440 **Vol. 2:** 481, 721 **Vol. 3:** 304, 1192, 1194
15:23 ff	**Vol. 2:** 58, 924
15:23–28	**Vol. 2:** 665 **Vol. 3:** 644
15:23 f	**Vol. 3:** 277
15:23	**Vol. 1:** 446, 649 **Vol. 2:** 338, 786, 839, 900, 924, 926 **Vol. 3:** 297, 303–304, 417, 1189
15:24 ff	**Vol. 2:** 926
15:24–28	**Vol. 1:** 238 **Vol. 2:** 388
15:24–27	**Vol. 1:** 467
15:24	**Vol. 1:** 73, 103, 167, 718 **Vol. 2:** 62, 74, 195, 368, 518, 603, 609
15:25 f	**Vol. 3:** 276
15:25	**Vol. 1:** 177, 239, 477, 554 **Vol. 2:** 147, 339, 381, 514–515, 665
15:26 ff	**Vol. 2:** 58
15:26†	**Vol. 1:** 73, 440, 719 **Vol. 2:** 482–483, 631, 874, 926
15:27	**Vol. 1:** 239 **Vol. 3:** 148, 316, 632
15:28	**Vol. 2:** 74, 80, 242, 482, 514, 926 **Vol. 3:** 643–644, 839, 1191
15:29	**Vol. 1:** 147, 398, 400 **Vol. 2:** 874 **Vol. 3:** 990, 1197, 1207–1208
15:30 ff	**Vol. 1:** 129, 400
15:30–32	**Vol. 3:** 1208
15:30	**Vol. 1:** 419 **Vol. 3:** 848
15:31 f	**Vol. 2:** 895
15:31	**Vol. 1:** 228 **Vol. 2:** 895
15:32	**Vol. 1:** 431 **Vol. 2:** 272, 275, 565 **Vol. 3:** 674
15:33	**Vol. 1:** 468–469, 564 **Vol. 2:** 437–438, 459–460, 757
15:34	**Vol. 1:** 515 **Vol. 2:** 402, 924 **Vol. 3:** 304, 363
15:35 ff	**Vol. 1:** 722 **Vol. 2:** 482, 566 **Vol. 3:** 286
15:35–42a	**Vol. 1:** 470

1 Corinthians *(cont'd)*

15:35   **Vol. 3:** 684
15:36 ff   **Vol. 2:** 923   **Vol. 3:** 524
15:37   **Vol. 1:** 313   **Vol. 3:** 252
15:38   **Vol. 1:** 236   **Vol. 3:** 278, 1020
15:39 ff   **Vol. 2:** 739
15:39   **Vol. 1:** 114, 670, 674, 679   **Vol. 2:** 565
15:40 f   **Vol. 2:** 46
15:40   **Vol. 1:** 518
15:41   **Vol. 3:** 731, 735
15:42 ff   **Vol. 1:** 470
15:42 – 50   **Vol. 3:** 694, 701
15:42 – 44   **Vol. 3:** 281
15:42   **Vol. 1:** 236   **Vol. 3:** 302 – 305
15:42b   **Vol. 1:** 470
15:43 f   **Vol. 2:** 789
15:43   **Vol. 2:** 48, 50 – 51
15:44 ff   **Vol. 3:** 684
15:44 – 49   **Vol. 3:** 702
15:44 – 46   **Vol. 3:** 706
15:44   **Vol. 1:** 236, 470   **Vol. 2:** 566 – 567   **Vol. 3:** 297, 303, 305, 706, 1195
15:44b   **Vol. 1:** 87
15:45 ff†   **Vol. 1:** 86   **Vol. 2:** 566
15:45 – 49   **Vol. 1:** 86
15:45 – 48   **Vol. 3:** 661
15:45   **Vol. 1:** 179, 665   **Vol. 2:** 57, 242, 481, 504   **Vol. 3:** 632, 683 – 684, 703, 705, 1175, 1178, 1183
15:46 – 49   **Vol. 2:** 160
15:46   **Vol. 3:** 303, 706
15:47 f   **Vol. 3:** 632
15:47 – 49   **Vol. 1:** 520
15:47   **Vol. 1:** 518   **Vol. 2:** 57
15:48 – 53   **Vol. 2:** 789
15:48 f   **Vol. 2:** 196
15:49   **Vol. 2:** 288   **Vol. 3:** 283, 303, 305
15:50 – 54   **Vol. 3:** 304
15:50   **Vol. 1:** 222, 236, 290, 470, 675, 679   **Vol. 2:** 566   **Vol. 3:** 301 – 303, 305
15:50a   **Vol. 2:** 300 – 301
15:50b   **Vol. 2:** 300
15:51 ff   **Vol. 2:** 482
15:51 f   **Vol. 2:** 925   **Vol. 3:** 84, 167
15:51   **Vol. 1:** 443   **Vol. 2:** 922, 924 – 925   **Vol. 3:** 305, 505
15:52 ff   **Vol. 2:** 242   **Vol. 3:** 304
15:52 f   **Vol. 2:** 665
15:52   **Vol. 1:** 470   **Vol. 2:** 894, 924   **Vol. 3:** 281, 305, 874
15:53 f   **Vol. 1:** 435   **Vol. 2:** 923   **Vol. 3:** 302
15:53   **Vol. 1:** 316, 440   **Vol. 3:** 283, 305
15:54 f   **Vol. 1:** 440, 651   **Vol. 3:** 267, 304
15:54   **Vol. 1:** 470   **Vol. 3:** 267, 1106, 1112
15:55 ff   **Vol. 2:** 545
15:55   **Vol. 1:** 511, 719   **Vol. 3:** 267

15:56   **Vol. 1:** 437, 511, 719   **Vol. 2:** 605   **Vol. 3:** 581
15:56b   **Vol. 2:** 445
15:57   **Vol. 1:** 440, 470, 651   **Vol. 2:** 121, 517, 874
15:58   **Vol. 1:** 257, 602, 661 – 662, 730   **Vol. 2:** 517, 924   **Vol. 3:** 1151
16:1 – 4   **Vol. 2:** 826
16:1 – 3   **Vol. 3:** 854
16:1 – 2   **Vol. 3:** 752
16:1 f   **Vol. 3:** 854
16:1   **Vol. 1:** 301, 305   **Vol. 2:** 826   **Vol. 3:** 1155, 1203
16:2   **Vol. 1:** 631   **Vol. 2:** 329, 518, 694, 826, 834   **Vol. 3:** 410, 412, 854, 943
16:3   **Vol. 2:** 121, 826   **Vol. 3:** 752, 809, 854
16:4   **Vol. 2:** 826
16:5 – 9   **Vol. 1:** 247
16:6 f   **Vol. 3:** 1204
16:6   **Vol. 3:** 228
16:7 f   **Vol. 3:** 227
16:7   **Vol. 2:** 517   **Vol. 3:** 843
16:8   **Vol. 3:** 417
16:9   **Vol. 2:** 30, 726 – 727
16:10   **Vol. 1:** 181   **Vol. 3:** 1149, 1151
16:11   **Vol. 2:** 245, 780
16:12   **Vol. 3:** 1019
16:13   **Vol. 1:** 421   **Vol. 2:** 137, 563
16:14   **Vol. 2:** 546
16:15   **Vol. 2:** 248   **Vol. 3:** 416, 546 – 547
16:16   **Vol. 1:** 263
16:17   **Vol. 1:** 741   **Vol. 2:** 899 – 900   **Vol. 3:** 955
16:18   **Vol. 2:** 399, 785   **Vol. 3:** 256, 694
16:19   **Vol. 1:** 301, 718   **Vol. 2:** 517   **Vol. 3:** 1065
16:20 – 22   **Vol. 2:** 530
16:20   **Vol. 2:** 523, 530, 549
16:20a   **Vol. 2:** 531
16:21   **Vol. 1:** 247   **Vol. 2:** 62, 148   **Vol. 3:** 489
16:22 f   **Vol. 2:** 874
16:22   **Vol. 1:** 323, 414   **Vol. 2:** 229, 515 – 516, 523, 531, 543, 548, 895 – 896   **Vol. 3:** 84, 319
16:22a   **Vol. 2:** 530, 874
16:22b   **Vol. 2:** 530
16:23   **Vol. 2:** 516, 874

2 Corinthians

1 – 9   **Vol. 2:** 922
1:1   **Vol. 1:** 129, 299   **Vol. 2:** 83, 229
1:2   **Vol. 1:** 299, 620   **Vol. 2:** 83, 780, 874   **Vol. 3:** 934
1:3 ff   **Vol. 1:** 571   **Vol. 2:** 874
1:3   **Vol. 1:** 212, 620   **Vol. 2:** 73, 76, 78, 516, 598
1:4   **Vol. 2:** 808 – 809
1:5 ff   **Vol. 3:** 722, 998

2 Corinthians *(cont'd)*

1:5	**Vol. 1:** 639 **Vol. 2:** 808 **Vol. 3:** 724
1:6 f	**Vol. 3:** 724
1:6	**Vol. 2:** 774, 808–809
1:7 f	**Vol. 3:** 1174
1:7	**Vol. 1:** 643 **Vol. 2:** 243, 874–875 **Vol. 3:** 725
1:8–11	**Vol. 2:** 924
1:8	**Vol. 1:** 261 **Vol. 2:** 406, 809, 924
1:9	**Vol. 1:** 591–592 **Vol. 3:** 304
1:10	**Vol. 3:** 203
1:11	**Vol. 1:** 586 **Vol. 2:** 121, 861, 874 **Vol. 3:** 818, 1174
1:12 ff	**Vol. 2:** 874
1:12	**Vol. 1:** 229, 350, 353, 524, 731 **Vol. 2:** 120, 739 **Vol. 3:** 504, 934, 1031, 1043
1:13 f	**Vol. 1:** 592
1:13	**Vol. 1:** 245 **Vol. 2:** 61
1:14	**Vol. 1:** 228, 742 **Vol. 2:** 304, 517, 874, 894 **Vol. 3:** 1180
1:15 f	**Vol. 3:** 1184
1:15	**Vol. 1:** 592
1:17	**Vol. 1:** 675 **Vol. 3:** 963
1:18	**Vol. 2:** 77 **Vol. 3:** 1112
1:19 f	**Vol. 3:** 1112, 1116
1:19	**Vol. 1:** 130 **Vol. 3:** 52, 55, 643, 1198
1:20	**Vol. 1:** 99 **Vol. 2:** 874 **Vol. 3:** 55, 72, 742
1:21 f	**Vol. 3:** 499
1:21	**Vol. 1:** 123, 660
1:22	**Vol. 1:** 123, 147, 372, 638, 669 **Vol. 2:** 40, 42, 183 **Vol. 3:** 304, 499, 701
1:23	**Vol. 1:** 276 **Vol. 2:** 874 **Vol. 3:** 683, 742, 1043
1:24	**Vol. 2:** 360, 519 **Vol. 3:** 1152
2:1 ff	**Vol. 2:** 420
2:1	**Vol. 2:** 182 **Vol. 3:** 471, 1020
2:2	**Vol. 2:** 356
2:3	**Vol. 1:** 591 **Vol. 2:** 360
2:4	**Vol. 2:** 360, 546, 809 **Vol. 3:** 489
2:5–11	**Vol. 1:** 467
2:5	**Vol. 1:** 261 **Vol. 2:** 304, 420 **Vol. 3:** 1180
2:6	**Vol. 1:** 572
2:7	**Vol. 1:** 467 **Vol. 2:** 122
2:8	**Vol. 1:** 664
2:9	**Vol. 2:** 179 **Vol. 3:** 809–810, 1113
2:10	**Vol. 2:** 122 **Vol. 3:** 214
2:11	**Vol. 1:** 138, 467, 718 **Vol. 3:** 128, 471, 591
2:12 f	**Vol. 2:** 924
2:12	**Vol. 2:** 30, 111, 517, 726–727 **Vol. 3:** 1177
2:13	**Vol. 3:** 694
2:14 ff	**Vol. 3:** 170, 600
2:14–17	**Vol. 1:** 650
2:14	**Vol. 1:** 649–650 **Vol. 2:** 121, 403, 874 **Vol. 3:** 322, 600–601
2:15 f	**Vol. 1:** 248 **Vol. 3:** 601
2:15	**Vol. 1:** 464 **Vol. 3:** 214, 600
2:16	**Vol. 1:** 439 **Vol. 3:** 729
2:17	**Vol. 1:** 96, 138, 248 **Vol. 3:** 1110, 1112
3	**Vol. 2:** 786 **Vol. 3:** 495
3:1–3	**Vol. 3:** 499
3:1	**Vol. 1:** 248 **Vol. 3:** 958
3:2 f	**Vol. 1:** 247–248
3:2	**Vol. 1:** 245 **Vol. 3:** 490, 935
3:3	**Vol. 1:** 203, 248, 592 **Vol. 3:** 493, 546, 701–702
3:4–18	**Vol. 2:** 312 **Vol. 3:** 327
3:4–6	**Vol. 3:** 703
3:4	**Vol. 1:** 592 **Vol. 2:** 73
3:5 f	**Vol. 1:** 592 **Vol. 3:** 729
3:5	**Vol. 1:** 130, 248 **Vol. 3:** 729, 824, 914, 1176
3:5b	**Vol. 3:** 1188
3:6 ff	**Vol. 2:** 316
3:6–4:15	**Vol. 3:** 336
3:6–8	**Vol. 3:** 701
3:6	**Vol. 1:** 154, 248, 430 **Vol. 2:** 312, 446, 605, 671, 715 **Vol. 3:** 493, 546, 548, 702, 729, 1178, 1183
3:7 ff	**Vol. 1:** 737
3:7–18	**Vol. 3:** 706, 795
3:7–11	**Vol. 2:** 47 **Vol. 3:** 225
3:7 f	**Vol. 3:** 546
3:7	**Vol. 1:** 73 **Vol. 2:** 46, 641 **Vol. 3:** 493, 520, 547
3:8 f	**Vol. 2:** 482 **Vol. 3:** 546–547
3:9 f	**Vol. 1:** 730
3:9†	**Vol. 2:** 365, 641 **Vol. 3:** 362, 364–365, 372, 547
3:10	**Vol. 2:** 303
3:11 f	**Vol. 2:** 736
3:11	**Vol. 1:** 73 **Vol. 2:** 213 **Vol. 3:** 1176
3:12–18	**Vol. 3:** 861
3:12	**Vol. 2:** 242
3:13–18	**Vol. 3:** 701
3:13–16	**Vol. 2:** 213
3:13	**Vol. 1:** 73, 587 **Vol. 2:** 46, 61, 214 **Vol. 3:** 520
3:14 ff	**Vol. 1:** 245 **Vol. 3:** 313
3:14–17	**Vol. 3:** 701
3:14 f	**Vol. 1:** 245, 587 **Vol. 2:** 182–183, 213
3:14	**Vol. 1:** 73, 666 **Vol. 2:** 156, 213, 716 **Vol. 3:** 128, 215, 591, 1192
3:15	**Vol. 1:** 587 **Vol. 2:** 641
3:16 f	**Vol. 3:** 1178
3:16	**Vol. 1:** 245, 355, 587 **Vol. 2:** 213, 641 **Vol. 3:** 1204
3:17 f	**Vol. 2:** 641
3:17	**Vol. 1:** 147, 246, 248, 717, 719 **Vol. 2:** 81, 84, 213, 516, 873 **Vol. 3:** 493, 701
3:18	**Vol. 1:** 707 **Vol. 2:** 46–48, 213–214, 288, 756 **Vol. 3:** 303–304, 701–703, 861, 864, 1178, 1183, 1189, 1198
4	**Vol. 2:** 834
4:1	**Vol. 1:** 563 **Vol. 2:** 597 **Vol. 3:** 546, 548

2 Corinthians *(cont'd)*

4:2	**Vol. 1:** 130, 350, 413 **Vol. 2:** 217 **Vol. 3:** 323, 564, 885–886, 945, 1110, 1112
4:3	**Vol. 1:** 464 **Vol. 2:** 112, 214
4:4 ff	**Vol. 2:** 161
4:4	**Vol. 1:** 466, 587 **Vol. 2:** 46–47, 213–214, 288–289, 493–495, 609 **Vol. 3:** 128, 591, 694, 831, 1191
4:5	**Vol. 2:** 112 **Vol. 3:** 55, 596
4:6	**Vol. 1:** 175, 384, 424, 587 **Vol. 2:** 46–47, 183, 213, 402, 486, 493–495, 567, 672, 834 **Vol. 3:** 701, 914
4:7 ff	**Vol. 2:** 806
4:7–15	**Vol. 3:** 278
4:7–12	**Vol. 1:** 129, 400 **Vol. 3:** 601
4:7	**Vol. 1:** 638 **Vol. 2:** 78, 605, 830, 834 **Vol. 3:** 912, 914
4:8 ff	**Vol. 2:** 420
4:8	**Vol. 2:** 51, 808–809
4:9 f	**Vol. 2:** 481
4:9	**Vol. 1:** 464
4:10 ff	**Vol. 1:** 479, 638 **Vol. 3:** 322
4:10 f	**Vol. 2:** 566, 808
4:10	**Vol. 1:** 438, 445, 639, 679 **Vol. 2:** 47, 481, 655, 808
4:11 f	**Vol. 1:** 440
4:11	**Vol. 1:** 679 **Vol. 2:** 420, 668
4:12	**Vol. 2:** 922 **Vol. 3:** 1152
4:13	**Vol. 3:** 694, 1211
4:14	**Vol. 1:** 474 **Vol. 2:** 606, 925 926 **Vol. 3:** 281
4:14b	**Vol. 3:** 304
4:15	**Vol. 1:** 94 **Vol. 2:** 121, 131, 874 **Vol. 3:** 819, 1187
4:16	**Vol. 1:** 185, 467, 470 **Vol. 2:** 566, 671, 673, 895
4:17 f	**Vol. 3:** 832
4:17	**Vol. 1:** 261 **Vol. 2:** 46, 48, 51, 809 **Vol. 3:** 257
4:18	**Vol. 1:** 602 **Vol. 2:** 789 **Vol. 3:** 839
5	**Vol. 2:** 923–925 **Vol. 3:** 825, 1032
5:1 ff	**Vol. 2:** 482
5:1–10	**Vol. 1:** 236, 440 **Vol. 2:** 903 **Vol. 3:** 283, 304
5:1–7	**Vol. 3:** 814
5:1–5	**Vol. 1:** 470 **Vol. 3:** 702
5:1 f	**Vol. 2:** 193
5:1	**Vol. 1:** 518, 638 **Vol. 2:** 252–253, 925 **Vol. 3:** 189, 305, 814, 832, 1188
5:2 f	**Vol. 2:** 207, 925
5:2	**Vol. 1:** 313, 316, 458 **Vol. 2:** 423, 925 **Vol. 3:** 814, 1195
5:3	**Vol. 1:** 313, 316
5:4 f	**Vol. 3:** 304
5:4	**Vol. 1:** 261, 315–316, 467 **Vol. 2:** 423, 922, 925 **Vol. 3:** 302, 814, 1194–1195
5:5	**Vol. 1:** 638 **Vol. 2:** 40, 42, 605, 789 **Vol. 3:** 499, 701, 1195
5:6–9	**Vol. 2:** 789
5:6–8	**Vol. 3:** 814
5:6	**Vol. 1:** 315, 328 **Vol. 2:** 517 **Vol. 3:** 814, 1205
5:7 ff	**Vol. 3:** 945
5:7	**Vol. 1:** 601–602, 704 **Vol. 2:** 243, 482, 789 **Vol. 3:** 1031, 1182
5:8 f	**Vol. 2:** 244
5:8	**Vol. 1:** 328 **Vol. 2:** 207, 244, 482, 517, 762, 789, 818, 925–926 **Vol. 3:** 302, 1172, 1204–1205, 1207
5:9	**Vol. 2:** 550, 789, 816 **Vol. 3:** 931
5:10 f	**Vol. 3:** 322, 324
5:10	**Vol. 1:** 112, 248, 323, 564 **Vol. 2:** 102, 365, 369, 665, 789, 894 **Vol. 3:** 136, 142, 214, 277, 322, 584, 1151, 1182, 1204
5:11–21	**Vol. 2:** 398
5:11	**Vol. 1:** 350, 590, 623 **Vol. 2:** 398 **Vol. 3:** 322
5:12	**Vol. 2:** 182, 398–399 **Vol. 3:** 1199
5:13	**Vol. 1:** 502, 528 **Vol. 2:** 398
5:14 ff	**Vol. 1:** 437
5:14–20	**Vol. 3:** 572
5:14 f	**Vol. 1:** 437–438 **Vol. 2:** 398, 672 **Vol. 3:** 1197
5:14	**Vol. 1:** 375, 492 **Vol. 2:** 364, 399, 545, 721, 723 **Vol. 3:** 169, 225, 1111, 1197
5:15	**Vol. 1:** 248, 718 **Vol. 2:** 481
5:15b	**Vol. 1:** 702
5:16	**Vol. 1:** 675, 680 **Vol. 2:** 398–399, 672 **Vol. 3:** 276, 1178, 1200
5:16b	**Vol. 2:** 399 **Vol. 3:** 1199
5:17 ff	**Vol. 3:** 171
5:17	**Vol. 1:** 168, 186, 248, 299, 384–385, 440, 602, 666, 680, 702 **Vol. 2:** 83, 399, 545, 566, 671–672, 714, 781 **Vol. 3:** 831, 1192, 1207
5:18 ff	**Vol. 2:** 544 **Vol. 3:** 54, 547
5:18–21	**Vol. 3:** 168, 198
5:18–20	**Vol. 3:** 167
5:18 f	**Vol. 1:** 702 **Vol. 3:** 167, 581
5:18	**Vol. 1:** 702 **Vol. 2:** 83 **Vol. 3:** 167–169, 171, 546, 1182, 1188, 1193
5:19 ff	**Vol. 1:** 398, 525 **Vol. 2:** 545, 605
5:19 f	**Vol. 1:** 299
5:19	**Vol. 1:** 477, 524, 702 **Vol. 2:** 80, 83 **Vol. 3:** 167–169, 171–172, 586, 824, 1111–1112, 1193
5:19a	**Vol. 3:** 1192
5:20 f	**Vol. 1:** 719 **Vol. 2:** 370
5:20	**Vol. 1:** 129, 197, 398, 570 **Vol. 2:** 860 **Vol. 3:** 87, 169, 171
5:21	**Vol. 1:** 390, 417, 437, 702 **Vol. 2:** 78, 83, 366, 398, 445 **Vol. 3:** 168–171, 362–363, 576, 581, 825, 1192, 1197
6:1 ff	**Vol. 2:** 771
6:1–9	**Vol. 2:** 121
6:1	**Vol. 1:** 547, 571 **Vol. 2:** 121 **Vol. 3:** 701, 746, 1152

2 Corinthians *(cont'd)*

6:2 ff   **Vol. 2:** 894
6:2   **Vol. 1:** 638 **Vol. 2:** 178, 186, 894 **Vol. 3:** 214, 744, 746, 838
6:3–10   **Vol. 2:** 420
6:3–7a   **Vol. 3:** 1190
6:3   **Vol. 2:** 705 **Vol. 3:** 546
6:4–10   **Vol. 2:** 605, 809
6:4–7   **Vol. 3:** 886
6:4   **Vol. 2:** 664, 774, 808 **Vol. 3:** 546, 548
6:5   **Vol. 1:** 263, 613 **Vol. 2:** 136–137 **Vol. 3:** 857
6:6   **Vol. 2:** 470 **Vol. 3:** 702, 1177
6:7 f   **Vol. 2:** 51
6:7   **Vol. 2:** 148, 605 **Vol. 3:** 362, 886, 963
6:8 f   **Vol. 2:** 481
6:8   **Vol. 2:** 47, 50, 459–460
6:9   **Vol. 2:** 407 **Vol. 3:** 779, 808
6:10   **Vol. 1:** 479, 639 **Vol. 2:** 360–361, 420, 828, 842, 844
6:11   **Vol. 1:** 254 **Vol. 2:** 726–727
6:12   **Vol. 1:** 742 **Vol. 2:** 567, 600, 807–808
6:13   **Vol. 1:** 286, 742 **Vol. 3:** 197
6:14 ff   **Vol. 2:** 800 **Vol. 3:** 471, 934, 1165
6:14–7:1   **Vol. 2:** 922
6:14–18   **Vol. 1:** 563
6:14   **Vol. 1:** 424, 639 **Vol. 2:** 494, 741–742 **Vol. 3:** 362, 1160, 1164
6:15   **Vol. 1:** 125 **Vol. 2:** 304 **Vol. 3:** 471
6:16 ff   **Vol. 1:** 256
6:16   **Vol. 1:** 254, 368 **Vol. 2:** 73, 83, 249, 251 **Vol. 3:** 471, 784, 813, 944–945
6:16a   **Vol. 3:** 1165
6:17   **Vol. 1:** 473 **Vol. 2:** 513 **Vol. 3:** 745, 860
6:18   **Vol. 1:** 256, 615 **Vol. 2:** 69 **Vol. 3:** 645, 718, 1175
7:1   **Vol. 1:** 449, 623 **Vol. 3:** 72, 197, 694
7:2   **Vol. 1:** 138, 468, 742 **Vol. 3:** 575
7:3   **Vol. 1:** 435, 643 **Vol. 2:** 365
7:4 ff   **Vol. 1:** 571
7:4 f   **Vol. 2:** 809
7:4   **Vol. 1:** 228 **Vol. 2:** 727, 874
7:5 f   **Vol. 2:** 263
7:5   **Vol. 1:** 647, 674 **Vol. 2:** 179, 360, 924
7:6 f   **Vol. 2:** 899–900
7:7   **Vol. 1:** 458 **Vol. 3:** 47, 1167
7:8–11   **Vol. 2:** 420
7:8–10   **Vol. 1:** 356
7:8   **Vol. 1:** 356
7:9 f   **Vol. 1:** 359 **Vol. 3:** 1187
7:9   **Vol. 3:** 1174, 1200
7:10   **Vol. 1:** 356, 467 **Vol. 2:** 360, 420 **Vol. 3:** 1200
7:11 f   **Vol. 3:** 1169
7:11   **Vol. 1:** 458 **Vol. 2:** 360 **Vol. 3:** 97, 101, 1158, 1167, 1200
7:12   **Vol. 3:** 322, 575

7:13   **Vol. 2:** 360 **Vol. 3:** 256, 694, 1174, 1193, 1198
7:14   **Vol. 1:** 228 **Vol. 3:** 563, 885, 1174
7:15   **Vol. 1:** 622 **Vol. 2:** 567, 600 **Vol. 3:** 746
7:16   **Vol. 1:** 328 **Vol. 2:** 360
8 f   **Vol. 2:** 311
8–9   **Vol. 3:** 854
8   **Vol. 1:** 138 **Vol. 2:** 826 **Vol. 3:** 553
8:1–5   **Vol. 3:** 854
8:1–3   **Vol. 2:** 694
8:1   **Vol. 1:** 301 **Vol. 2:** 121 **Vol. 3:** 314
8:2   **Vol. 1:** 731 **Vol. 2:** 197, 809, 842, 844 **Vol. 3:** 572, 809–810, 1199
8:3 f   **Vol. 3:** 547
8:3   **Vol. 3:** 1043
8:4   **Vol. 2:** 860 **Vol. 3:** 546, 548, 854
8:5   **Vol. 2:** 42 **Vol. 3:** 547, 1021
8:6   **Vol. 2:** 121, 826 **Vol. 3:** 1169, 1187
8:7 f   **Vol. 2:** 329
8:7   **Vol. 2:** 121, 400, 546, 694 **Vol. 3:** 752, 1169, 1188
8:8–9   **Vol. 1:** 731 **Vol. 2:** 694
8:8   **Vol. 2:** 694, 826 **Vol. 3:** 1169
8:9 ff   **Vol. 2:** 400
8:9   **Vol. 1:** 492, 547 **Vol. 2:** 824, 826, 828, 842, 844 **Vol. 3:** 547, 810, 854
8:10 f   **Vol. 3:** 1021
8:10   **Vol. 2:** 826 **Vol. 3:** 1021, 1174
8:11   **Vol. 2:** 846 **Vol. 3:** 1021
8:12   **Vol. 3:** 746, 1180
8:13   **Vol. 2:** 499
8:14 f   **Vol. 2:** 329
8:14   **Vol. 2:** 499 **Vol. 3:** 837, 955
8:15 f   **Vol. 2:** 826
8:15   **Vol. 2:** 131
8:16 f   **Vol. 2:** 874
8:16   **Vol. 2:** 121 **Vol. 3:** 1169, 1190
8:18 f   **Vol. 2:** 826
8:18   **Vol. 2:** 111 **Vol. 3:** 817
8:19 ff   **Vol. 2:** 47
8:19   **Vol. 1:** 301, 478 **Vol. 2:** 121, 150, 694 **Vol. 3:** 546, 752
8:21   **Vol. 1:** 695
8:22 f   **Vol. 2:** 826
8:22   **Vol. 1:** 592 **Vol. 3:** 809, 1213
8:23   **Vol. 1:** 130, 642 **Vol. 2:** 826 **Vol. 3:** 548, 1174
8:24   **Vol. 1:** 228 **Vol. 3:** 752
9   **Vol. 2:** 826 **Vol. 3:** 553
9:1–5   **Vol. 3:** 547
9:1–4   **Vol. 2:** 826
9:1   **Vol. 3:** 546, 548, 752, 854
9:2 f   **Vol. 3:** 119, 410
9:2   **Vol. 3:** 1167, 1174
9:3   **Vol. 1:** 547 **Vol. 2:** 303
9:4   **Vol. 1:** 712 **Vol. 3:** 563
9:5–14   **Vol. 3:** 752
9:5–10   **Vol. 2:** 694
9:5 f   **Vol. 1:** 214

2 Corinthians *(cont'd)*

9:5 **Vol. 1:** 138, 322 **Vol. 2:** 694, 826 **Vol. 3:** 70, 350, 752, 854
9:6–13 **Vol. 1:** 347
9:6–11 **Vol. 2:** 129
9:6–9 **Vol. 3:** 854
9:6 f **Vol. 2:** 827
9:6 **Vol. 3:** 525, 854
9:7 **Vol. 2:** 43, 329, 567, 663, 694 **Vol. 3:** 547, 854, 1180
9:8 **Vol. 1:** 731 **Vol. 2:** 121 **Vol. 3:** 197, 727–728
9:9 f **Vol. 3:** 362
9:9 **Vol. 2:** 34, 821, 827
9:10 ff **Vol. 2:** 844
9:10 **Vol. 1:** 733 **Vol. 2:** 129, 268, 831
9:11 f **Vol. 2:** 874 **Vol. 3:** 819
9:11 **Vol. 2:** 842 **Vol. 3:** 572
9:12–15 **Vol. 3:** 547
9:12–13 **Vol. 2:** 694 **Vol. 3:** 752
9:12 f **Vol. 3:** 546, 548
9:12 **Vol. 1:** 731, 741 **Vol. 2:** 329 **Vol. 3:** 552, 854, 955
9:13 ff **Vol. 2:** 827
9:13 **Vol. 1:** 346–347, 642 **Vol. 2:** 874 **Vol. 3:** 547, 572, 809
9:14 **Vol. 1:** 458 **Vol. 2:** 121, 861, 874–875
9:15 **Vol. 2:** 41–42, 121, 694
10–13 **Vol. 2:** 111, 923–924, 927 **Vol. 3:** 1190
10–12 **Vol. 2:** 874
10:1–13:10 **Vol. 2:** 922
10:1–13:4 **Vol. 2:** 435
10:1 f **Vol. 3:** 1190
10:1 **Vol. 1:** 328, 492, 570 **Vol. 2:** 258, 263 **Vol. 3:** 914, 929
10:2 f **Vol. 1:** 675
10:2 **Vol. 1:** 328, 365, 592 **Vol. 2:** 860, 899 **Vol. 3:** 824–825
10:3 f **Vol. 2:** 927
10:3 **Vol. 1:** 646, 676, 679 **Vol. 3:** 944, 963, 1188, 1200
10:4 f **Vol. 3:** 824, 963
10:4 **Vol. 3:** 963
10:5 f **Vol. 2:** 179
10:5 **Vol. 2:** 179, 200, 399 **Vol. 3:** 128, 197, 591, 824
10:6 **Vol. 2:** 175 **Vol. 3:** 97, 118
10:7 **Vol. 3:** 515, 824–825
10:8 **Vol. 1:** 228, 731 **Vol. 2:** 252, 517, 611
10:9 **Vol. 3:** 822
10:10 f **Vol. 3:** 1190
10:10 **Vol. 1:** 261 **Vol. 2:** 899–900 **Vol. 3:** 714, 914, 994, 1106, 1113
10:11 **Vol. 2:** 899 **Vol. 3:** 824, 1149
10:12 **Vol. 1:** 365 **Vol. 2:** 364 **Vol. 3:** 131, 403
10:13–16 **Vol. 2:** 112 **Vol. 3:** 400
10:13 **Vol. 3:** 400, 403–404

10:15 f **Vol. 1:** 684 **Vol. 2:** 130, 742
10:15 **Vol. 1:** 602 **Vol. 2:** 129, 425 **Vol. 3:** 404
10:16 **Vol. 1:** 662
10:17 f **Vol. 1:** 228
10:18 **Vol. 2:** 112 **Vol. 3:** 808
10:27 **Vol. 1:** 592
10:32 **Vol. 2:** 83
11 **Vol. 2:** 311 **Vol. 3:** 1026, 1072
11:1–12:10 **Vol. 3:** 170
11:1 **Vol. 2:** 429, 668, 765 **Vol. 3:** 1026
11:2 f **Vol. 3:** 572
11:2 **Vol. 1:** 87, 475 **Vol. 2:** 563, 581, 585 **Vol. 3:** 101, 1072, 1167
11:3 **Vol. 1:** 87, 413, 468–469, 510 **Vol. 2:** 459–460, 585 **Vol. 3:** 128
11:4 **Vol. 2:** 112, 741, 766 **Vol. 3:** 52, 55, 694–695, 701, 746, 885
11:5 **Vol. 2:** 765 **Vol. 3:** 824–825, 955
11:6 **Vol. 2:** 456 **Vol. 3:** 322, 914
11:7 **Vol. 2:** 41, 111, 263
11:8 **Vol. 3:** 144, 379, 546
11:9 **Vol. 1:** 741 **Vol. 2:** 899 **Vol. 3:** 953, 955, 1204
11:10 **Vol. 3:** 951
11:12 ff **Vol. 1:** 228
11:12–15 **Vol. 2:** 927
11:13 ff **Vol. 1:** 710
11:13–15 **Vol. 1:** 710
11:13 **Vol. 2:** 472 **Vol. 3:** 864
11:14 **Vol. 2:** 495, 622, 625 **Vol. 3:** 471, 864
11:15 **Vol. 1:** 710 **Vol. 2:** 61 **Vol. 3:** 362, 364, 546, 864
11:16 ff **Vol. 1:** 229, 727
11:16–12:10 **Vol. 2:** 809
11:16 f **Vol. 3:** 1026
11:16 **Vol. 2:** 83, 429 **Vol. 3:** 822
11:17 **Vol. 1:** 712
11:18 **Vol. 1:** 228, 675
11:19 f **Vol. 2:** 766
11:19 **Vol. 2:** 620 **Vol. 3:** 1026
11:20 f **Vol. 3:** 1190
11:20 **Vol. 1:** 586
11:21–12:10 **Vol. 3:** 601
11:21 **Vol. 1:** 365 **Vol. 3:** 1026
11:22 **Vol. 1:** 79, 370 **Vol. 2:** 83, 310, 315
11:23 ff **Vol. 2:** 420 **Vol. 3:** 724, 998
11:23–30 **Vol. 1:** 727
11:23–29 **Vol. 1:** 129 **Vol. 2:** 263
11:23 **Vol. 1:** 163, 263, 731 **Vol. 2:** 136 **Vol. 3:** 546, 548, 857, 1172
11:24 **Vol. 1:** 163 **Vol. 2:** 96, 696
11:25 **Vol. 1:** 163, 407 **Vol. 2:** 717
11:26 **Vol. 1:** 257, 419 **Vol. 2:** 472 **Vol. 3:** 379, 984, 987, 1007–1008
11:27 **Vol. 1:** 263, 313, 318, 613 **Vol. 2:** 137, 267
11:28 **Vol. 1:** 278 **Vol. 2:** 895
11:29 **Vol. 1:** 656 **Vol. 2:** 708

2 Corinthians (cont'd)

11:30   **Vol. 1:** 183, 229   **Vol. 2:** 762   **Vol. 3:** 995, 1026, 1190
11:31   **Vol. 1:** 213, 620   **Vol. 2:** 472, 516, 874
11:32   **Vol. 2:** 135, 378
11:33   **Vol. 2:** 150   **Vol. 3:** 948
12   **Vol. 1:** 528   **Vol. 3:** 1026
12:1 ff   **Vol. 2:** 176, 900   **Vol. 3:** 315
12:1   **Vol. 1:** 133, 727   **Vol. 2:** 517   **Vol. 3:** 297, 515, 517
12:2 ff   **Vol. 1:** 528   **Vol. 3:** 602
12:2–4   **Vol. 2:** 192   **Vol. 3:** 694
12:2 f   **Vol. 3:** 602
12:2   **Vol. 2:** 688, 762   **Vol. 3:** 602, 1192
12:4   **Vol. 1:** 528   **Vol. 2:** 176, 688, 762–763   **Vol. 3:** 602, 1121
12:5–10   **Vol. 2:** 884
12:5   **Vol. 1:** 229   **Vol. 2:** 762   **Vol. 3:** 995, 1192
12:6 ff   **Vol. 3:** 571
12:6   **Vol. 1:** 228, 727   **Vol. 2:** 175   **Vol. 3:** 824–825
12:7 ff   **Vol. 1:** 183   **Vol. 3:** 728, 998
12:7–10   **Vol. 2:** 263
12:7   **Vol. 1:** 102–103, 163, 467, 674, 726–727   **Vol. 2:** 221   **Vol. 3:** 203, 469–471, 474, 714, 802, 857, 998
12:8 f   **Vol. 2:** 867
12:8   **Vol. 1:** 607   **Vol. 2:** 874   **Vol. 3:** 1174
12:9–10   **Vol. 3:** 914
12:9 f   **Vol. 1:** 399, 727   **Vol. 2:** 605, 762   **Vol. 3:** 995, 1190
12:9   **Vol. 1:** 163, 229, 467, 731   **Vol. 2:** 62, 121   **Vol. 3:** 315, 714, 814, 857, 971, 995, 1026, 1190, 1192, 1194
12:10   **Vol. 2:** 435, 664, 806, 808, 818   **Vol. 3:** 27, 998
12:11   **Vol. 3:** 955, 1026
12:12   **Vol. 1:** 129   **Vol. 2:** 605, 629, 632, 774   **Vol. 3:** 571
12:13   **Vol. 2:** 122   **Vol. 3:** 252
12:14   **Vol. 2:** 668, 834   **Vol. 3:** 118
12:15   **Vol. 1:** 731   **Vol. 2:** 567
12:16   **Vol. 1:** 261, 413
12:17 f   **Vol. 1:** 138
12:17   **Vol. 1:** 138
12:18   **Vol. 3:** 694
12:19   **Vol. 2:** 252, 714   **Vol. 3:** 822
12:20   **Vol. 1:** 106   **Vol. 2:** 263   **Vol. 3:** 31, 346, 928, 1167
12:21   **Vol. 1:** 359, 500   **Vol. 2:** 73, 263, 422   **Vol. 3:** 1157
12:24 ff   **Vol. 1:** 235
13:1   **Vol. 2:** 686   **Vol. 3:** 1043, 1123
13:2   **Vol. 2:** 899   **Vol. 3:** 252
13:3 f   **Vol. 2:** 605
13:3–4   **Vol. 3:** 914
13:3   **Vol. 2:** 179   **Vol. 3:** 314, 809–810

13:4   **Vol. 1:** 400   **Vol. 2:** 481, 604, 606   **Vol. 3:** 995, 1171, 1190
13:5   **Vol. 2:** 402   **Vol. 3:** 802, 808, 810, 1192
13:7   **Vol. 1:** 564   **Vol. 2:** 104, 488, 867, 874–875
13:8   **Vol. 3:** 885–886, 1199
13:9 f   **Vol. 3:** 1190
13:9   **Vol. 2:** 867, 874–875   **Vol. 3:** 350, 995
13:10   **Vol. 2:** 252, 517, 611, 899
13:11   **Vol. 1:** 571   **Vol. 2:** 79, 360, 544, 618, 780–781, 874   **Vol. 3:** 252, 350
13:12   **Vol. 2:** 549
13:13   **Vol. 1:** 643   **Vol. 2:** 84, 119, 516, 544, 687
13:14   **Vol. 2:** 874   **Vol. 3:** 327, 702
15:9   **Vol. 2:** 83
15:12   **Vol. 1:** 228
20:19   **Vol. 2:** 263

Galatians

1 f   **Vol. 2:** 311
1:1–5   **Vol. 1:** 247
1:1   **Vol. 1:** 129, 133   **Vol. 2:** 328   **Vol. 3:** 1110
1:2   **Vol. 1:** 301
1:3 f   **Vol. 3:** 62
1:3   **Vol. 2:** 516, 780, 874
1:4   **Vol. 1:** 566   **Vol. 2:** 42   **Vol. 3:** 61, 198, 611, 831, 1019, 1174, 1197
1:5   **Vol. 1:** 99   **Vol. 2:** 46, 874
1:6 ff   **Vol. 1:** 399   **Vol. 2:** 741   **Vol. 3:** 774
1:6–10   **Vol. 2:** 112
1:6–9   **Vol. 1:** 247   **Vol. 2:** 112
1:6   **Vol. 1:** 275   **Vol. 2:** 625
1:7   **Vol. 2:** 221   **Vol. 3:** 710
1:8 f   **Vol. 1:** 719   **Vol. 2:** 874   **Vol. 3:** 1201
1:8   **Vol. 1:** 103, 415   **Vol. 2:** 193, 741
1:9   **Vol. 1:** 415
1:10   **Vol. 1:** 590   **Vol. 2:** 112   **Vol. 3:** 596
1:11–17   **Vol. 3:** 55
1:11   **Vol. 2:** 111   **Vol. 3:** 314
1:12–17   **Vol. 1:** 136
1:12   **Vol. 1:** 129   **Vol. 2:** 217, 565, 900   **Vol. 3:** 322, 384, 701, 764
1:13 ff   **Vol. 2:** 282
1:13 f   **Vol. 2:** 310
1:13   **Vol. 1:** 299, 301   **Vol. 2:** 83, 806   **Vol. 3:** 934, 963
1:14   **Vol. 1:** 730   **Vol. 2:** 130   **Vol. 3:** 312, 764, 774, 1167
1:15 f   **Vol. 3:** 701, 1110
1:15   **Vol. 1:** 275, 474   **Vol. 2:** 819   **Vol. 3:** 284, 612, 701, 1071
1:16   **Vol. 1:** 129, 183, 222, 528, 675   **Vol. 2:** 111–112, 126, 794   **Vol. 3:** 643, 773, 1191
1:17 f   **Vol. 2:** 328
1:17   **Vol. 1:** 130, 133   **Vol. 2:** 523   **Vol. 3:** 1008

Galatians *(cont'd)*

1:18–20	**Vol. 2:** 328
1:18 f	**Vol. 1:** 130, 132 **Vol. 3:** 288
1:18	**Vol. 2:** 895 **Vol. 3:** 227, 383, 1204
1:19	**Vol. 1:** 130, 256
1:20	**Vol. 2:** 472 **Vol. 3:** 742
1:22 f	**Vol. 3:** 1193
1:22	**Vol. 1:** 299, 301 **Vol. 2:** 407
1:23	**Vol. 2:** 719, 806 **Vol. 3:** 61, 963
1:24	**Vol. 2:** 874
1:33	**Vol. 3:** 934
2–5	**Vol. 1:** 717
2:1 ff	**Vol. 2:** 328
2:1–14	**Vol. 3:** 549
2:1	**Vol. 1:** 129–130 **Vol. 2:** 185
2:2	**Vol. 1:** 469, 547 **Vol. 2:** 111, 328 **Vol. 3:** 52, 54, 61, 315, 563, 822, 947
2:3	**Vol. 1:** 257, 310 **Vol. 2:** 663
2:4	**Vol. 1:** 322, 717–718 **Vol. 2:** 472
2:5	**Vol. 3:** 884
2:6 ff	**Vol. 1:** 310
2:6	**Vol. 1:** 587 **Vol. 3:** 822
2:7 ff	**Vol. 3:** 454
2:7–9	**Vol. 2:** 794
2:7 f	**Vol. 2:** 111
2:7	**Vol. 1:** 132, 310 **Vol. 2:** 112 **Vol. 3:** 1211
2:8 f	**Vol. 3:** 38
2:8	**Vol. 1:** 129 **Vol. 2:** 112 **Vol. 3:** 384, 387
2:9	**Vol. 1:** 129–131, 302, 643 **Vol. 2:** 121, 126, 146 **Vol. 3:** 383, 387, 795, 822, 1184
2:10	**Vol. 2:** 826–828 **Vol. 3:** 241, 246, 1169
2:11 ff	**Vol. 3:** 386, 1066
2:11–21	**Vol. 3:** 387
2:11–14	**Vol. 1:** 310
2:11	**Vol. 2:** 365 **Vol. 3:** 383
2:12	**Vol. 1:** 310, 473 **Vol. 2:** 272, 794
2:13	**Vol. 1:** 130 **Vol. 2:** 469 **Vol. 3:** 252
2:14	**Vol. 2:** 310, 795 **Vol. 3:** 352, 383–384, 1204
2:15 f	**Vol. 3:** 549
2:15	**Vol. 2:** 660, 793 **Vol. 3:** 549
2:16 ff	**Vol. 1:** 158
2:16 f	**Vol. 3:** 363
2:16	**Vol. 1:** 157, 599, 675 **Vol. 3:** 363, 372, 549, 1151, 1178, 1190, 1212–1213
2:17	**Vol. 2:** 434 **Vol. 3:** 365, 529, 532, 546, 549
2:18–21	**Vol. 3:** 549
2:18 f	**Vol. 1:** 719
2:18	**Vol. 3:** 189
2:19 ff	**Vol. 1:** 399
2:19 f	**Vol. 1:** 439
2:19	**Vol. 1:** 397, 400–401
2:20 f	**Vol. 2:** 119, 338, 605
2:20	**Vol. 1:** 148, 235, 289, 676, 679, 727 **Vol. 2:** 368, 481, 544–545, 900 **Vol. 3:** 198, 323, 372, 643–644, 1192, 1197, 1200
2:21	**Vol. 1:** 74, 437, 602 **Vol. 2:** 41, 120 **Vol. 3:** 362–363
3	**Vol. 1:** 311 **Vol. 3:** 372, 906
3:1–4:7	**Vol. 2:** 786
3:1–5	**Vol. 1:** 719 **Vol. 3:** 967
3:1	**Vol. 1:** 301, 397, 399 **Vol. 2:** 559 **Vol. 3:** 55, 62, 129, 463, 490, 1111
3:2 f	**Vol. 3:** 701
3:2	**Vol. 1:** 158, 486 **Vol. 2:** 175 **Vol. 3:** 1151, 1178
3:3	**Vol. 1:** 680 **Vol. 3:** 129
3:4	**Vol. 3:** 723
3:5 ff	**Vol. 1:** 289
3:5	**Vol. 2:** 175, 605, 632 **Vol. 3:** 701, 1178
3:6 ff	**Vol. 1:** 78
3:6–18	**Vol. 3:** 1151
3:6–14	**Vol. 3:** 1112
3:6–9	**Vol. 1:** 78, 702
3:6 f	**Vol. 3:** 869
3:6	**Vol. 1:** 78, 157, 596, 604 **Vol. 2:** 73, 301 **Vol. 3:** 169, 362–363, 824–825, 1187, 1214
3:7	**Vol. 1:** 286, 289, 299 **Vol. 2:** 794 **Vol. 3:** 1188
3:8–14	**Vol. 1:** 214
3:8	**Vol. 1:** 157, 212, 214, 695 **Vol. 2:** 793 **Vol. 3:** 329, 363, 491–492, 515, 1012
3:9	**Vol. 3:** 1188
3:10 ff	**Vol. 1:** 601 **Vol. 2:** 101 **Vol. 3:** 161, 491
3:10–14	**Vol. 3:** 581, 1164
3:10–13	**Vol. 1:** 417 **Vol. 2:** 312
3:10	**Vol. 1:** 78, 244, 417, 719 **Vol. 2:** 102, 445, 449 **Vol. 3:** 226, 1151, 1178
3:11	**Vol. 2:** 447 **Vol. 3:** 316, 362–363, 365, 367, 369, 1177
3:12–19	**Vol. 1:** 375
3:12	**Vol. 3:** 1022
3:12b	**Vol. 2:** 445
3:13 f	**Vol. 2:** 794 **Vol. 3:** 171
3:13	**Vol. 1:** 214–215, 266, 268, 389–390, 398, 438, 509, 719 **Vol. 2:** 83, 366, 445, 504, 709 **Vol. 3:** 597, 868, 1197
3:14	**Vol. 1:** 158, 181, 214, 417 **Vol. 3:** 72, 701, 749
3:15 ff	**Vol. 2:** 445
3:15–18	**Vol. 3:** 72, 366
3:15	**Vol. 1:** 74, 369–370, 664
3:16 f	**Vol. 1:** 79
3:16–19	**Vol. 3:** 523
3:16	**Vol. 1:** 370 **Vol. 2:** 186, 338, 755 **Vol. 3:** 73, 400
3:17 ff	**Vol. 1:** 601 **Vol. 2:** 641

Galatians *(cont'd)*

3:17   **Vol. 1:** 73, 370, 664   **Vol. 2:** 445, 689   **Vol. 3:** 1187
3:18   **Vol. 2:** 122, 302   **Vol. 3:** 72
3:19–29   **Vol. 2:** 445
3:19 f   **Vol. 1:** 374–375
3:19   **Vol. 1:** 103, 719   **Vol. 2:** 445   **Vol. 3:** 345, 465, 585, 1182
3:20   **Vol. 2:** 73
3:21 f   **Vol. 3:** 72
3:21   **Vol. 2:** 445, 605   **Vol. 3:** 362–363
3:22 ff   **Vol. 3:** 585
3:22 f   **Vol. 2:** 445
3:22   **Vol. 3:** 492, 580
3:23 ff   **Vol. 1:** 289, 601   **Vol. 3:** 580
3:23–39   **Vol. 2:** 302
3:23   **Vol. 1:** 321, 326   **Vol. 2:** 135   **Vol. 3:** 315
3:24 ff   **Vol. 3:** 779
3:24   **Vol. 1:** 78, 370   **Vol. 2:** 445   **Vol. 3:** 363
3:25   **Vol. 1:** 321   **Vol. 2:** 445   **Vol. 3:** 779
3:26 ff   **Vol. 1:** 371   **Vol. 2:** 800
3:26–29   **Vol. 1:** 601   **Vol. 2:** 127, 794   **Vol. 3:** 1200
3:26 f   **Vol. 1:** 157–158, 289   **Vol. 2:** 445
3:26   **Vol. 1:** 146, 256   **Vol. 3:** 645, 1190, 1212
3:27 ff   **Vol. 1:** 147, 300
3:27–29   **Vol. 3:** 932
3:27   **Vol. 1:** 146, 148, 158, 186, 315–316   **Vol. 3:** 1209
3:28†   **Vol. 1:** 385, 718, 720   **Vol. 2:** 126, 309, 563, 566, 570, 722   **Vol. 3:** 1062, 1067, 1190, 1192, 1209
3:29   **Vol. 1:** 289   **Vol. 2:** 301, 570   **Vol. 3:** 523–524, 869
4   **Vol. 2:** 452
4:1 ff   **Vol. 1:** 289, 620
4:1–11   **Vol. 2:** 453
4:1–7   **Vol. 2:** 828   **Vol. 3:** 613
4:1   **Vol. 2:** 301   **Vol. 3:** 779, 843
4:2   **Vol. 1:** 477   **Vol. 2:** 254
4:3 ff   **Vol. 3:** 839
4:3   **Vol. 1:** 103, 282, 718–719   **Vol. 2:** 452–453, 828   **Vol. 3:** 596
4:4 ff   **Vol. 2:** 84
4:4–7   **Vol. 1:** 615
4:4 f   **Vol. 1:** 738   **Vol. 2:** 828   **Vol. 3:** 643, 843
4:4   **Vol. 1:** 181, 187, 268, 282, 321, 374, 549   **Vol. 2:** 78–79   **Vol. 3:** 198, 597, 661, 831, 834, 1058, 1073, 1198
4:5 ff   **Vol. 1:** 417
4:5 f   **Vol. 1:** 286
4:5   **Vol. 1:** 283, 289   **Vol. 2:** 453, 672   **Vol. 3:** 751
4:6 ff   **Vol. 2:** 605

4:6 f   **Vol. 1:** 289   **Vol. 2:** 183   **Vol. 3:** 645, 698, 701
4:6   **Vol. 1:** 410, 614–615, 621, 623, 681   **Vol. 2:** 76, 218, 605, 786, 867, 871, 873–874, 883, 896   **Vol. 3:** 62, 639, 643, 701, 703
4:7   **Vol. 2:** 301
4:8 ff   **Vol. 2:** 73
4:8–11   **Vol. 1:** 631
4:8 f   **Vol. 2:** 73, 400   **Vol. 3:** 596, 838, 1164
4:8   **Vol. 2:** 453   **Vol. 3:** 597
4:9 ff   **Vol. 3:** 837
4:9   **Vol. 1:** 718   **Vol. 2:** 400, 402, 452–453, 545, 645, 828   **Vol. 3:** 994
4:10   **Vol. 2:** 133, 828, 887   **Vol. 3:** 410
4:11   **Vol. 1:** 263, 623
4:12   **Vol. 2:** 860   **Vol. 3:** 575
4:13 f   **Vol. 3:** 998
4:13–15   **Vol. 1:** 727
4:13   **Vol. 1:** 674, 679   **Vol. 3:** 994
4:14   **Vol. 1:** 674   **Vol. 2:** 176, 559   **Vol. 3:** 746, 802
4:15   **Vol. 1:** 163, 216   **Vol. 3:** 802, 857, 1043
4:16   **Vol. 1:** 554   **Vol. 3:** 887
4:17   **Vol. 2:** 221
4:18   **Vol. 2:** 899   **Vol. 3:** 1167, 1204
4:19   **Vol. 1:** 178, 180, 286, 708   **Vol. 3:** 858, 1070
4:20   **Vol. 2:** 899   **Vol. 3:** 113, 167, 1204
4:21–31   **Vol. 1:** 80–81, 532, 601, 718, 720   **Vol. 2:** 312, 755   **Vol. 3:** 1014, 1200
4:21–26   **Vol. 1:** 49
4:21 f   **Vol. 1:** 286
4:21   **Vol. 1:** 245, 412   **Vol. 2:** 444
4:22 ff   **Vol. 2:** 452
4:22–31   **Vol. 3:** 706
4:22 f   **Vol. 1:** 284, 718
4:22   **Vol. 3:** 491
4:23 f   **Vol. 3:** 661
4:23   **Vol. 1:** 178, 286, 370
4:23a   **Vol. 3:** 1200
4:24 ff   **Vol. 2:** 316
4:24 f   **Vol. 3:** 1014
4:24   **Vol. 1:** 176, 370   **Vol. 2:** 746, 755
4:25 f   **Vol. 2:** 188, 803
4:25   **Vol. 1:** 81, 286, 371   **Vol. 2:** 329, 452
4:26 ff   **Vol. 1:** 371
4:26 f   **Vol. 3:** 1070
4:26   **Vol. 1:** 686, 689, 718   **Vol. 2:** 194, 329, 755   **Vol. 3:** 203, 1014, 1069
4:27   **Vol. 1:** 187, 411   **Vol. 2:** 356   **Vol. 3:** 858
4:28   **Vol. 1:** 81, 286, 412   **Vol. 3:** 1200
4:29   **Vol. 1:** 286   **Vol. 2:** 806   **Vol. 3:** 701, 1189, 1200
4:30 f   **Vol. 1:** 284
4:30   **Vol. 1:** 453   **Vol. 2:** 302   **Vol. 3:** 490, 492
4:31   **Vol. 1:** 286, 718

Galatians *(cont'd)*

5:1–26	**Vol. 3:** 1164
5:1–13	**Vol. 1:** 718
5:1–12	**Vol. 2:** 926
5:1–6	**Vol. 2:** 120
5:1	**Vol. 1:** 717–719 **Vol. 2:** 338 **Vol. 3:** 702, 1164
5:3 f	**Vol. 3:** 1164
5:3	**Vol. 2:** 444, 668
5:4	**Vol. 1:** 73, 611 **Vol. 2:** 120, 123 **Vol. 3:** 363
5:5	**Vol. 2:** 241–242, 245, 924 **Vol. 3:** 362, 365, 702
5:6	**Vol. 1:** 311, 336, 338, 602, 624 **Vol. 2:** 545 **Vol. 3:** 713–714, 1152, 1182
5:7	**Vol. 1:** 469, 591 **Vol. 2:** 221 **Vol. 3:** 884, 947
5:8	**Vol. 1:** 588, 592–593
5:9	**Vol. 1:** 628 **Vol. 2:** 428, 462 **Vol. 3:** 917
5:10	**Vol. 1:** 591–592 **Vol. 2:** 618 **Vol. 3:** 710, 1213
5:11 ff	**Vol. 1:** 719
5:11	**Vol. 1:** 73, 399 **Vol. 2:** 708, 806 **Vol. 3:** 54
5:12	**Vol. 2:** 668
5:13 ff	**Vol. 3:** 581
5:13–22	**Vol. 2:** 546
5:13 f	**Vol. 1:** 719–720
5:13	**Vol. 1:** 718 **Vol. 3:** 596–597, 944, 1193
5:14	**Vol. 1:** 94, 259, 738 **Vol. 2:** 445, 544, 546, 720 **Vol. 3:** 185
5:15–26	**Vol. 1:** 604
5:16 ff	**Vol. 1:** 236, 602
5:16–26	**Vol. 3:** 581
5:16–24	**Vol. 3:** 701, 1200
5:16–21	**Vol. 1:** 457
5:16 f	**Vol. 3:** 702
5:16	**Vol. 1:** 106, 457–458, 676 **Vol. 2:** 62 **Vol. 3:** 702, 944, 1167
5:17	**Vol. 1:** 676 **Vol. 3:** 1021, 1199–1200
5:18–23	**Vol. 3:** 702
5:18	**Vol. 1:** 106, 719 **Vol. 2:** 445 **Vol. 3:** 698, 702, 1164
5:19 ff†	**Vol. 1:** 535, 554 **Vol. 2:** 286 **Vol. 3:** 31, 1157
5:19–24	**Vol. 1:** 557
5:19–23	**Vol. 3:** 31, 928
5:19–21	**Vol. 1:** 681
5:19 f	**Vol. 1:** 106, 496
5:19	**Vol. 1:** 501, 676, 739 **Vol. 3:** 320, 581, 1151, 1158
5:20	**Vol. 1:** 106, 452, 535, 555 **Vol. 2:** 558 **Vol. 3:** 1167
5:21	**Vol. 1:** 513 **Vol. 2:** 300–301, 503, 924 **Vol. 3:** 84, 1158
5:22	**Vol. 1:** 106, 720, 723, 739 **Vol. 2:** 106, 360, 445, 545, 771, 780, 782 **Vol. 3:** 927
5:23	**Vol. 1:** 495–496 **Vol. 2:** 258–259
5:24	**Vol. 1:** 148, 236, 401, 676 **Vol. 3:** 581, 722
5:25	**Vol. 1:** 106, 739 **Vol. 2:** 481, 673 **Vol. 3:** 702
5:25b	**Vol. 2:** 452
5:26	**Vol. 1:** 557 **Vol. 2:** 47, 481
6:1	**Vol. 2:** 258, 605 **Vol. 3:** 350, 586, 694, 702, 707, 750, 802
6:2	**Vol. 1:** 261, 738 **Vol. 2:** 444, 446, 722 **Vol. 3:** 1151
6:3	**Vol. 3:** 822
6:4	**Vol. 1:** 229 **Vol. 2:** 724, 739 **Vol. 3:** 808
6:5	**Vol. 1:** 261
6:6	**Vol. 2:** 101 **Vol. 3:** 61, 771, 1110
6:7 ff	**Vol. 3:** 134
6:7–10	**Vol. 2:** 926–927
6:7 f	**Vol. 1:** 469 **Vol. 3:** 204, 525
6:7	**Vol. 2:** 459–460 **Vol. 3:** 341, 525
6:8	**Vol. 1:** 681, 719 **Vol. 2:** 482, 924 **Vol. 3:** 701–702, 832
6:9	**Vol. 2:** 102, 104 **Vol. 3:** 189, 839, 1155
6:10	**Vol. 1:** 256 **Vol. 2:** 101, 249, 251, 719 **Vol. 3:** 752, 838, 1151, 1199, 1204
6:11	**Vol. 1:** 163, 247, 727 **Vol. 2:** 148 **Vol. 3:** 489, 492, 802
6:12 ff	**Vol. 1:** 310
6:12 f	**Vol. 1:** 310
6:12	**Vol. 1:** 399, 675 **Vol. 2:** 806
6:13 f	**Vol. 1:** 311
6:13	**Vol. 1:** 228, 675, 680 **Vol. 2:** 135 **Vol. 3:** 1158
6:14 f	**Vol. 1:** 385
6:14	**Vol. 1:** 228, 397, 399, 401, 438, 680 **Vol. 2:** 420, 671
6:15	**Vol. 1:** 311, 336, 384, 602 **Vol. 2:** 452, 671–672, 781 **Vol. 3:** 400
6:16	**Vol. 1:** 51, 61, 257 **Vol. 2:** 218, 313, 339, 452, 573, 597, 780, 874 **Vol. 3:** 400, 871
6:17	**Vol. 1:** 163, 235, 399, 727 **Vol. 2:** 573 **Vol. 3:** 252, 1113
6:18	**Vol. 1:** 99 **Vol. 2:** 874 **Vol. 3:** 693

Ephesians

1:1	**Vol. 1:** 130 **Vol. 3:** 1020
1:2	**Vol. 2:** 780, 874
1:3–14	**Vol. 2:** 302
1:3–11	**Vol. 2:** 77
1:3–6	**Vol. 3:** 817
1:3	**Vol. 1:** 212, 214, 620 **Vol. 2:** 73, 76, 196, 516, 874 **Vol. 3:** 72, 197, 706, 967
1:4	**Vol. 1:** 377–378, 542 **Vol. 2:** 302 **Vol. 3:** 925
1:5 ff	**Vol. 2:** 129
1:5	**Vol. 1:** 696 **Vol. 2:** 819 **Vol. 3:** 1019
1:6 f	**Vol. 2:** 122

Ephesians *(cont'd)*

1:6   **Vol. 2:** 122, 874   **Vol. 3:** 504
1:7 ff   **Vol. 1:** 730
1:7 f   **Vol. 3:** 701
1:7   **Vol. 1:** 221, 223–224, 398, 701   **Vol. 2:** 79, 122, 302, 844   **Vol. 3:** 166, 198–200, 586
1:8   **Vol. 3:** 197, 966, 1032
1:9 f   **Vol. 3:** 504
1:9   **Vol. 1:** 697, 738   **Vol. 2:** 620, 819   **Vol. 3:** 314, 1019
1:10–23   **Vol. 2:** 195
1:10   **Vol. 1:** 738   **Vol. 2:** 129, 163, 195, 255, 302   **Vol. 3:** 504, 1019, 1032, 1176
1:11–14   **Vol. 2:** 300
1:11 f   **Vol. 2:** 302   **Vol. 3:** 1018
1:11   **Vol. 1:** 696–697   **Vol. 2:** 299–300, 819   **Vol. 3:** 1017–1019, 1152
1:12   **Vol. 2:** 241, 874
1:13 f   **Vol. 3:** 701
1:13   **Vol. 1:** 147, 158   **Vol. 2:** 113, 176, 302   **Vol. 3:** 214, 499, 701, 1212
1:14   **Vol. 1:** 372   **Vol. 2:** 839, 874   **Vol. 3:** 199, 499, 702
1:15 ff   **Vol. 2:** 874
1:15 f   **Vol. 3:** 818
1:15   **Vol. 2:** 230, 546   **Vol. 3:** 1212
1:16–23   **Vol. 2:** 874–875
1:16   **Vol. 3:** 246
1:17 f   **Vol. 3:** 258, 702
1:17   **Vol. 1:** 437   **Vol. 2:** 46, 400, 516   **Vol. 3:** 315, 694, 701, 1032
1:18   **Vol. 2:** 47, 243, 300, 302, 844   **Vol. 3:** 516
1:19 ff   **Vol. 3:** 287
1:19   **Vol. 2:** 78, 605   **Vol. 3:** 714, 718
1:20–23   **Vol. 2:** 209
1:20 f   **Vol. 1:** 103, 302   **Vol. 2:** 514, 518, 604
1:20   **Vol. 1:** 402, 445   **Vol. 2:** 80–81, 147, 196, 515   **Vol. 3:** 588, 1152
1:21 f   **Vol. 2:** 162
1:21   **Vol. 1:** 103, 326   **Vol. 2:** 603, 609   **Vol. 3:** 197, 795, 831
1:22 f   **Vol. 1:** 237
1:22   **Vol. 1:** 95   **Vol. 2:** 243   **Vol. 3:** 390
1:23   **Vol. 1:** 740   **Vol. 2:** 81, 83, 195   **Vol. 3:** 1191
2 f   **Vol. 2:** 794
2   **Vol. 3:** 185
2:1 ff   **Vol. 3:** 934, 944
2:1–3:6   **Vol. 2:** 302
2:1   **Vol. 1:** 310, 355, 402, 446   **Vol. 3:** 586, 1176
2:2 f   **Vol. 1:** 676
2:2   **Vol. 1:** 169, 289, 449, 452, 524, 593   **Vol. 2:** 193   **Vol. 3:** 471, 694, 802, 944, 1152
2:3   **Vol. 1:** 112, 286, 457   **Vol. 2:** 660, 794   **Vol. 3:** 252, 934

2:4–9   **Vol. 2:** 597
2:4   **Vol. 2:** 597, 842
2:5–10   **Vol. 2:** 660
2:5–8   **Vol. 1:** 157   **Vol. 3:** 204
2:5   **Vol. 1:** 446, 643   **Vol. 2:** 122   **Vol. 3:** 586
2:6   **Vol. 1:** 402, 643, 689   **Vol. 2:** 196, 380   **Vol. 3:** 277, 588, 966
2:7   **Vol. 1:** 322   **Vol. 2:** 106, 122, 844
2:8 f   **Vol. 1:** 228   **Vol. 2:** 122
2:8   **Vol. 1:** 158   **Vol. 2:** 41–42   **Vol. 3:** 214, 701, 1190
2:10   **Vol. 1:** 386   **Vol. 2:** 83, 101, 129   **Vol. 3:** 118, 143, 1154, 1193
2:11 ff   **Vol. 1:** 689
2:11–22   **Vol. 3:** 390, 1018
2:11–21   **Vol. 3:** 1200
2:11 f   **Vol. 1:** 676   **Vol. 2:** 794
2:11   **Vol. 2:** 150
2:12 ff   **Vol. 1:** 301
2:12   **Vol. 1:** 685   **Vol. 2:** 241–242, 742, 804   **Vol. 3:** 73, 172, 837
2:13–16   **Vol. 2:** 722
2:13   **Vol. 1:** 223, 398   **Vol. 3:** 166, 172
2:14 ff   **Vol. 1:** 311   **Vol. 3:** 674
2:14–22   **Vol. 2:** 163
2:14–18   **Vol. 2:** 443, 781   **Vol. 3:** 172
2:14 f   **Vol. 2:** 591   **Vol. 3:** 1154
2:14   **Vol. 1:** 331, 555   **Vol. 2:** 328, 646   **Vol. 3:** 180, 185–186, 323, 795, 949
2:15 f   **Vol. 3:** 186
2:15   **Vol. 1:** 73, 330–331, 336–337, 385, 402, 679   **Vol. 2:** 122, 163, 447, 566, 671   **Vol. 3:** 500, 949
2:16   **Vol. 1:** 402, 430, 555   **Vol. 3:** 167, 171–172, 432, 949
2:17–22   **Vol. 2:** 794
2:17   **Vol. 2:** 113, 780, 782
2:18 f   **Vol. 3:** 941
2:18   **Vol. 1:** 223   **Vol. 2:** 40, 315, 327, 336, 500, 721   **Vol. 3:** 504, 701, 1210
2:19 ff   **Vol. 2:** 253
2:19–22   **Vol. 2:** 249, 251
2:19 f   **Vol. 3:** 387
2:19   **Vol. 1:** 256, 689, 691   **Vol. 2:** 83, 129, 228, 249, 251, 794, 804
2:20 ff   **Vol. 1:** 331   **Vol. 2:** 129
2:20–22   **Vol. 1:** 662   **Vol. 3:** 393
2:20 f   **Vol. 2:** 129   **Vol. 3:** 504
2:20   **Vol. 1:** 661–662   **Vol. 2:** 249, 253, 313   **Vol. 3:** 84, 387, 390, 393, 397, 500
2:21   **Vol. 1:** 623   **Vol. 2:** 83   **Vol. 3:** 186, 784
2:22   **Vol. 2:** 163, 249, 253
2:28   **Vol. 3:** 542
3:1–13   **Vol. 2:** 794
3:1–9   **Vol. 2:** 113

Ephesians *(cont'd)*

3:1–6   **Vol. 1:** 129
3:1   **Vol. 2:** 573, 794   **Vol. 3:** 592
3:2   **Vol. 2:** 255
3:3   **Vol. 2:** 900   **Vol. 3:** 314, 490, 533
3:4   **Vol. 3:** 129, 132
3:5 ff   **Vol. 2:** 217
3:5   **Vol. 1:** 289   **Vol. 2:** 35   **Vol. 3:** 84, 314, 321–322, 533, 701, 967
3:6 f   **Vol. 2:** 126
3:6   **Vol. 2:** 302   **Vol. 3:** 73, 504
3:7   **Vol. 3:** 546, 548, 1152
3:8 ff   **Vol. 1:** 697   **Vol. 3:** 837
3:8–10   **Vol. 2:** 75
3:8   **Vol. 2:** 217, 429, 842   **Vol. 3:** 504, 966
3:9 f   **Vol. 3:** 1032
3:9   **Vol. 2:** 255, 655   **Vol. 3:** 504, 830
3:10   **Vol. 1:** 167, 302   **Vol. 2:** 193, 196, 609   **Vol. 3:** 314
3:11 f   **Vol. 3:** 941
3:12   **Vol. 1:** 592, 638   **Vol. 3:** 966
3:13 f   **Vol. 2:** 856
3:13   **Vol. 1:** 563   **Vol. 2:** 573, 809   **Vol. 3:** 505
3:14 ff   **Vol. 3:** 505
3:14–19   **Vol. 2:** 874
3:14 f   **Vol. 1:** 621   **Vol. 2:** 655, 867
3:14   **Vol. 2:** 859, 869   **Vol. 3:** 1204
3:15   **Vol. 1:** 616   **Vol. 2:** 192, 195, 655   **Vol. 3:** 504, 1133
3:16 f   **Vol. 2:** 605   **Vol. 3:** 701
3:16   **Vol. 2:** 46–47, 76, 78, 844
3:17 ff   **Vol. 2:** 546
3:17   **Vol. 1:** 148, 662   **Vol. 2:** 183, 251   **Vol. 3:** 868
3:18   **Vol. 1:** 254   **Vol. 2:** 198   **Vol. 3:** 750
3:19   **Vol. 1:** 740   **Vol. 2:** 78, 545
3:20 f   **Vol. 2:** 874
3:20   **Vol. 1:** 730   **Vol. 2:** 78
3:21   **Vol. 1:** 99, 662   **Vol. 2:** 35, 46
4   **Vol. 2:** 723
4:1–16   **Vol. 2:** 722   **Vol. 3:** 548
4:1   **Vol. 1:** 275, 571   **Vol. 2:** 263, 517   **Vol. 3:** 349, 592, 945, 965–966
4:2 ff   **Vol. 3:** 927
4:2   **Vol. 2:** 259, 263, 765, 771
4:3 ff   **Vol. 1:** 302
4:3 f   **Vol. 2:** 163   **Vol. 3:** 702
4:3   **Vol. 1:** 602   **Vol. 2:** 133, 669, 721–722, 780, 782   **Vol. 3:** 592, 1169
4:4 ff   **Vol. 2:** 84, 721
4:4–6   **Vol. 1:** 147
4:4   **Vol. 2:** 243, 721–722
4:5 f   **Vol. 2:** 515
4:5   **Vol. 1:** 146–147, 602   **Vol. 2:** 515, 721   **Vol. 3:** 61
4:6   **Vol. 1:** 375, 620   **Vol. 2:** 73
4:7   **Vol. 1:** 93, 638   **Vol. 2:** 41, 122, 517   **Vol. 3:** 403

4:8 ff   **Vol. 1:** 302   **Vol. 2:** 186   **Vol. 3:** 494
4:8   **Vol. 2:** 42, 185–186, 199, 209, 785   **Vol. 3:** 87, 203, 591, 965
4:9   **Vol. 2:** 122, 195, 303
4:10   **Vol. 2:** 195
4:11 ff   **Vol. 3:** 1067
4:11–16   **Vol. 3:** 703
4:11   **Vol. 1:** 66, 129, 302, 486   **Vol. 2:** 114   **Vol. 3:** 84, 568, 703, 767–768
4:12   **Vol. 1:** 92, 237, 302   **Vol. 2:** 249, 253   **Vol. 3:** 350, 546–547
4:13   **Vol. 1:** 92–93, 282, 302, 325, 602, 740   **Vol. 2:** 62, 162–163, 563, 722   **Vol. 3:** 350, 403
4:14 ff   **Vol. 1:** 325
4:14   **Vol. 1:** 92, 238, 282, 413, 740   **Vol. 2:** 459–460   **Vol. 3:** 770, 943, 1002, 1204
4:15 f   **Vol. 1:** 238   **Vol. 2:** 129
4:15   **Vol. 1:** 282   **Vol. 2:** 162, 568   **Vol. 3:** 886–887
4:16   **Vol. 1:** 92, 241   **Vol. 2:** 128, 162, 249, 253, 304, 499, 546, 568   **Vol. 3:** 403, 1152, 1190
4:17   **Vol. 1:** 552   **Vol. 2:** 517, 793   **Vol. 3:** 130
4:18   **Vol. 1:** 424, 685   **Vol. 2:** 183, 567, 742   **Vol. 3:** 127
4:19   **Vol. 1:** 138   **Vol. 2:** 368   **Vol. 3:** 197
4:20 f   **Vol. 2:** 176
4:20   **Vol. 1:** 486–487   **Vol. 3:** 931
4:21   **Vol. 3:** 765, 886
4:22 ff   **Vol. 1:** 457   **Vol. 2:** 566
4:22   **Vol. 1:** 315, 457, 468–469, 718   **Vol. 2:** 460, 473, 675, 715   **Vol. 3:** 886, 934
4:23 f   **Vol. 2:** 673
4:23   **Vol. 1:** 106, 458   **Vol. 2:** 675–676   **Vol. 3:** 130, 694
4:24   **Vol. 1:** 106, 315–316, 386   **Vol. 2:** 237, 473, 671   **Vol. 3:** 362, 365, 886, 1200
4:25 ff   **Vol. 1:** 259
4:25   **Vol. 1:** 231–232, 315   **Vol. 2:** 473   **Vol. 3:** 886, 967
4:26   **Vol. 1:** 110–111   **Vol. 3:** 731
4:27   **Vol. 3:** 470
4:28   **Vol. 1:** 639   **Vol. 2:** 41, 694   **Vol. 3:** 378, 854
4:29   **Vol. 2:** 118, 249, 253   **Vol. 3:** 449, 967
4:30   **Vol. 1:** 147   **Vol. 2:** 894   **Vol. 3:** 499, 701, 703
4:31   **Vol. 1:** 106, 110, 202   **Vol. 3:** 31, 343
4:32–5:2   **Vol. 3:** 927
4:32   **Vol. 1:** 110, 702   **Vol. 2:** 122, 600
5:1   **Vol. 1:** 287, 491–492
5:2   **Vol. 1:** 492   **Vol. 2:** 42, 209, 544   **Vol. 3:** 198, 432, 600–601, 944, 1197
5:3 ff   **Vol. 3:** 31
5:3   **Vol. 1:** 138, 501   **Vol. 2:** 655   **Vol. 3:** 197
5:4   **Vol. 2:** 874   **Vol. 3:** 819, 1026

Ephesians *(cont'd)*

5:5   **Vol. 1:** 138   **Vol. 2:** 286, 300, 388, 400
5:6   **Vol. 1:** 110, 112, 289, 321, 547, 593   **Vol. 2:** 76, 459   **Vol. 3:** 572
5:8 ff   **Vol. 3:** 945
5:8 f   **Vol. 3:** 838
5:8   **Vol. 1:** 286, 355, 424   **Vol. 2:** 493, 495, 517   **Vol. 3:** 446, 839, 944
5:9   **Vol. 1:** 723   **Vol. 2:** 495   **Vol. 3:** 362, 365
5:10   **Vol. 2:** 816   **Vol. 3:** 808, 810, 931
5:11   **Vol. 1:** 424, 644
5:12   **Vol. 2:** 214, 217   **Vol. 3:** 564
5:13   **Vol. 2:** 141   **Vol. 3:** 322, 967
5:14   **Vol. 2:** 186   **Vol. 3:** 276, 492
5:15 f   **Vol. 2:** 256   **Vol. 3:** 446–447
5:15   **Vol. 3:** 133, 945, 1026, 1032
5:16   **Vol. 1:** 268   **Vol. 3:** 838–839
5:17 f   **Vol. 3:** 1020
5:17   **Vol. 3:** 131, 133, 1026
5:18 ff   **Vol. 3:** 671, 674–675
5:18–20   **Vol. 1:** 514
5:18 f   **Vol. 3:** 703, 967
5:18   **Vol. 1:** 514   **Vol. 3:** 922, 1210
5:19   **Vol. 2:** 874   **Vol. 3:** 669–671, 673, 706, 967
5:20   **Vol. 1:** 620   **Vol. 2:** 654, 874   **Vol. 3:** 675, 819
5:21–6:9   **Vol. 1:** 59, 514
5:21–33   **Vol. 1:** 496   **Vol. 2:** 579, 905, 923   **Vol. 3:** 219, 535, 539, 1067
5:21   **Vol. 1:** 623   **Vol. 3:** 929, 1064
5:22 ff   **Vol. 2:** 160, 545, 563, 581
5:22–6:9   **Vol. 3:** 929, 932
5:22–32   **Vol. 2:** 585
5:22   **Vol. 3:** 1064
5:23   **Vol. 2:** 349, 579   **Vol. 3:** 220
5:25 ff   **Vol. 3:** 220
5:25–27   **Vol. 1:** 302
5:25   **Vol. 1:** 492   **Vol. 2:** 209, 368, 563   **Vol. 3:** 1063–1064, 1197
5:26 f   **Vol. 2:** 349
5:26   **Vol. 1:** 147, 153–154, 157–158, 185   **Vol. 3:** 107, 967, 990
5:27   **Vol. 1:** 475   **Vol. 2:** 47   **Vol. 3:** 924–925
5:28–33   **Vol. 2:** 722
5:28   **Vol. 2:** 563   **Vol. 3:** 1064
5:30   **Vol. 1:** 231–232, 241
5:31   **Vol. 2:** 349, 579, 722   **Vol. 3:** 535, 1064, 1070
5:32   **Vol. 2:** 349, 581   **Vol. 3:** 505, 1064, 1068
6:1 ff   **Vol. 1:** 289
6:1–9   **Vol. 2:** 180
6:1–4   **Vol. 1:** 619
6:1–3   **Vol. 1:** 160
6:1   **Vol. 1:** 286   **Vol. 3:** 362
6:2   **Vol. 1:** 336   **Vol. 3:** 95

6:4   **Vol. 1:** 110, 286, 568–569   **Vol. 3:** 777, 779
6:5–8   **Vol. 3:** 582
6:5   **Vol. 1:** 623   **Vol. 2:** 509, 513   **Vol. 3:** 596
6:6   **Vol. 2:** 815–817   **Vol. 3:** 685, 854
6:7   **Vol. 2:** 565
6:8   **Vol. 1:** 718
6:9   **Vol. 1:** 587   **Vol. 2:** 51, 513   **Vol. 3:** 583, 598
6:10 ff   **Vol. 1:** 647, 718
6:10–17   **Vol. 3:** 364, 802, 965
6:10   **Vol. 2:** 517, 604   **Vol. 3:** 252, 714, 718
6:11–17   **Vol. 2:** 925
6:11   **Vol. 1:** 316   **Vol. 3:** 470–471, 943, 965
6:12   **Vol. 1:** 167, 222, 424, 449, 452, 566, 647, 676, 679, 718   **Vol. 2:** 193, 514, 518, 559   **Vol. 3:** 707, 718, 838
6:13   **Vol. 1:** 566   **Vol. 2:** 887   **Vol. 3:** 749, 965
6:14   **Vol. 1:** 240   **Vol. 3:** 121, 362, 365, 886, 966
6:15   **Vol. 1:** 239   **Vol. 2:** 113, 780   **Vol. 3:** 117–118, 966
6:16   **Vol. 1:** 566, 656   **Vol. 3:** 109, 471, 749, 966
6:17–20   **Vol. 2:** 868
6:17   **Vol. 3:** 703, 966–967
6:18 ff   **Vol. 2:** 874   **Vol. 3:** 802
6:18 f   **Vol. 2:** 768   **Vol. 3:** 1174, 1176
6:18   **Vol. 2:** 137, 768, 861, 873, 883   **Vol. 3:** 702, 705, 839
6:19   **Vol. 2:** 726–727, 736   **Vol. 3:** 314, 322
6:20   **Vol. 1:** 197   **Vol. 2:** 736   **Vol. 3:** 169
6:21–33   **Vol. 2:** 51
6:21   **Vol. 3:** 314, 546, 548, 1157
6:23 f   **Vol. 2:** 874
6:23   **Vol. 2:** 545, 780
6:24   **Vol. 1:** 469   **Vol. 3:** 302

Philippians

1   **Vol. 2:** 924–925
1:1   **Vol. 1:** 191, 300, 718, 720   **Vol. 2:** 550   **Vol. 3:** 546, 548, 596, 613
1:2   **Vol. 2:** 516, 780, 874
1:3 ff   **Vol. 2:** 874
1:3–11   **Vol. 1:** 247
1:3   **Vol. 2:** 73   **Vol. 3:** 246
1:4   **Vol. 2:** 861, 874–875
1:5 f   **Vol. 2:** 360
1:5   **Vol. 1:** 643   **Vol. 2:** 360   **Vol. 3:** 818
1:6   **Vol. 2:** 102, 130, 243, 894, 922, 926   **Vol. 3:** 1151
1:7   **Vol. 1:** 637, 644, 658–659   **Vol. 2:** 121, 617   **Vol. 3:** 362, 592
1:8   **Vol. 2:** 567, 600   **Vol. 3:** 1043
1:9 ff   **Vol. 2:** 874–875
1:9   **Vol. 1:** 730   **Vol. 2:** 391, 400, 707   **Vol. 3:** 197

Philippians *(cont'd)*

1:10 f   **Vol. 1:** 467
1:10   **Vol. 2:** 391, 707, 894, 922, 926   **Vol. 3:** 279, 808, 810, 1187
1:11   **Vol. 1:** 723, 739 **Vol. 2:** 874 **Vol. 3:** 362, 365, 817, 1187
1:12 ff   **Vol. 3:** 38, 592
1:12   **Vol. 2:** 398
1:13 f   **Vol. 3:** 592
1:13   **Vol. 3:** 252, 320, 1192
1:14   **Vol. 1:** 592, 731 **Vol. 3:** 61, 1110
1:15 ff   **Vol. 2:** 360
1:15–18   **Vol. 2:** 360
1:15   **Vol. 1:** 558 **Vol. 2:** 818 **Vol. 3:** 52, 55
1:16   **Vol. 1:** 471
1:17–26   **Vol. 3:** 38
1:17   **Vol. 2:** 809 **Vol. 3:** 101, 280, 592
1:18   **Vol. 2:** 360 **Vol. 3:** 54
1:19–26   **Vol. 3:** 432
1:19 f   **Vol. 2:** 874
1:19   **Vol. 2:** 605, 861 **Vol. 3:** 703
1:20 ff   **Vol. 3:** 203
1:20–26   **Vol. 3:** 279
1:20   **Vol. 1:** 440–441 **Vol. 2:** 244–245, 360, 566, 736
1:21   **Vol. 1:** 440 **Vol. 2:** 481 **Vol. 3:** 137, 227, 279
1:22–24   **Vol. 1:** 676
1:22   **Vol. 1:** 534, 723 **Vol. 2:** 925 **Vol. 3:** 314, 323
1:23   **Vol. 1:** 315, 457, 679 **Vol. 2:** 187, 207, 482, 762, 925–926 **Vol. 3:** 302, 1205, 1207
1:24   **Vol. 1:** 679 **Vol. 3:** 227, 323
1:25 f   **Vol. 2:** 130
1:25   **Vol. 1:** 592 **Vol. 2:** 130, 360, 924 **Vol. 3:** 228
1:26   **Vol. 1:** 229, 730 **Vol. 2:** 605, 874, 899–900 **Vol. 3:** 1204
1:27   **Vol. 1:** 646–647 **Vol. 2:** 111, 804 **Vol. 3:** 349, 685, 702
1:28   **Vol. 1:** 464, 623
1:29   **Vol. 2:** 122 **Vol. 3:** 725, 1212–1213
1:30   **Vol. 1:** 648
2   **Vol. 1:** 400, 549, 714 **Vol. 2:** 500, 620
2:1 ff   **Vol. 1:** 400 **Vol. 2:** 187, 546 **Vol. 3:** 942
2:1–18   **Vol. 3:** 687
2:1–4   **Vol. 3:** 597
2:1 f   **Vol. 2:** 360
2:1   **Vol. 1:** 328–329, 570 **Vol. 2:** 598, 600 **Vol. 3:** 702
2:2   **Vol. 2:** 618, 722 **Vol. 3:** 687
2:3   **Vol. 2:** 47, 262, 617 **Vol. 3:** 928
2:4 ff   **Vol. 1:** 301 **Vol. 3:** 929
2:5 ff   **Vol. 1:** 492 **Vol. 2:** 343, 618 **Vol. 3:** 137, 529–530, 597
2:5–11   **Vol. 1:** 472, 483, 706 **Vol. 2:** 203, 504, 514, 844 **Vol. 3:** 603–604, 644

2:5   **Vol. 2:** 179, 262, 504, 619 **Vol. 3:** 1192
2:6 ff   **Vol. 1:** 707 **Vol. 2:** 262, 289, 828
2:6–11   **Vol. 1:** 147, 398, 547, 706–707 **Vol. 2:** 262, 500, 618 **Vol. 3:** 61, 612, 674
2:6–8   **Vol. 2:** 203
2:6 f   **Vol. 2:** 500
2:6   **Vol. 1:** 400, 547, 705 **Vol. 2:** 80–82, 498 **Vol. 3:** 603, 712
2:6b   **Vol. 3:** 604
2:7 f   **Vol. 1:** 437
2:7   **Vol. 1:** 455, 546, 548–549, 709 **Vol. 2:** 187, 262, 504, 565, 855 **Vol. 3:** 583, 596, 604, 661, 748, 1064
2:8 ff   **Vol. 1:** 399 **Vol. 2:** 91, 119
2:8–11   **Vol. 2:** 926 **Vol. 3:** 55
2:8 f   **Vol. 3:** 298
2:8   **Vol. 1:** 223, 335, 398, 549 **Vol. 2:** 80, 179, 187, 445, 500 **Vol. 3:** 165, 364, 529–530, 1190
2:8b   **Vol. 2:** 445 **Vol. 3:** 597
2:8c   **Vol. 2:** 262
2:9 ff   **Vol. 1:** 95, 102–103 **Vol. 2:** 514
2:9–11   **Vol. 2:** 81, 203, 386
2:9 f   **Vol. 2:** 195, 654
2:9   **Vol. 1:** 123, 406 **Vol. 2:** 203, 332
2:10 f   **Vol. 2:** 196, 262, 369, 619, 926 **Vol. 3:** 279
2:10   **Vol. 1:** 518 **Vol. 2:** 187, 194, 859, 925
2:11   **Vol. 1:** 168, 205, 347 **Vol. 2:** 187, 514–515, 874 **Vol. 3:** 1079, 1187
2:12–16   **Vol. 2:** 187, 230
2:12–15   **Vol. 1:** 491
2:12   **Vol. 1:** 299, 622–623 **Vol. 2:** 91, 179, 724, 899–900 **Vol. 3:** 214
2:12b   **Vol. 2:** 566
2:13 f   **Vol. 2:** 819
2:13   **Vol. 1:** 623 **Vol. 2:** 83, 566 **Vol. 3:** 143, 1021, 1152, 1178
2:14   **Vol. 3:** 821, 1155
2:15   **Vol. 1:** 525 **Vol. 2:** 36, 139, 144, 488, 493, 495 **Vol. 3:** 924–925
2:16–17   **Vol. 1:** 649
2:16   **Vol. 1:** 229, 263, 547 **Vol. 2:** 47, 481, 874, 894, 922 **Vol. 3:** 61, 563, 947, 1111
2:17 f   **Vol. 2:** 360
2:17   **Vol. 1:** 479, 648 **Vol. 2:** 42, 360 **Vol. 3:** 38, 431, 552
2:19   **Vol. 1:** 299
2:20 f   **Vol. 2:** 360
2:20   **Vol. 1:** 278, 637 **Vol. 2:** 498–499
2:21   **Vol. 1:** 278 **Vol. 2:** 360, 605 **Vol. 3:** 532
2:22   **Vol. 1:** 286 **Vol. 3:** 596, 809–810
2:24   **Vol. 1:** 591–592
2:25 ff   **Vol. 3:** 1164
2:25–30   **Vol. 2:** 221
2:25   **Vol. 1:** 130 **Vol. 2:** 816 **Vol. 3:** 548, 553, 957
2:26   **Vol. 3:** 1193

Philippians *(cont'd)*

2:27   **Vol. 2:** 597
2:28   **Vol. 3:** 1169
2:29   **Vol. 2:** 51, 517
2:30   **Vol. 1:** 741   **Vol. 3:** 553, 683, 955, 1151
3   **Vol. 3:** 278
3:1   **Vol. 2:** 359–360, 517   **Vol. 3:** 252, 1194
3:2 ff   **Vol. 2:** 401, 924
3:2 f   **Vol. 1:** 117
3:2   **Vol. 1:** 309, 311, 564   **Vol. 3:** 517
3:3–7   **Vol. 1:** 681
3:3 f   **Vol. 1:** 592, 675, 679
3:3   **Vol. 1:** 228, 311   **Vol. 2:** 218, 573, 786, 874   **Vol. 3:** 550, 701–702, 1192
3:4   **Vol. 1:** 592   **Vol. 3:** 822
3:5–11   **Vol. 2:** 444
3:5   **Vol. 1:** 309, 311, 370   **Vol. 2:** 310, 315, 692, 695, 812   **Vol. 3:** 465, 872
3:6   **Vol. 1:** 301, 556, 681   **Vol. 2:** 139, 282, 806   **Vol. 3:** 161, 363, 1167
3:7 ff   **Vol. 1:** 400
3:7 f   **Vol. 3:** 873
3:7   **Vol. 2:** 835   **Vol. 3:** 136
3:8 ff   **Vol. 1:** 638   **Vol. 2:** 605
3:8–11   **Vol. 1:** 675
3:8   **Vol. 1:** 480   **Vol. 2:** 403   **Vol. 3:** 137, 278
3:9   **Vol. 1:** 649, 681   **Vol. 2:** 78   **Vol. 3:** 137, 278, 362–364, 367, 529–530, 1177, 1188
3:10–16   **Vol. 2:** 402
3:10–14   **Vol. 1:** 649
3:10 f   **Vol. 2:** 420   **Vol. 3:** 278
3:10†   **Vol. 1:** 401, 643, 648–649, 707   **Vol. 2:** 402–403, 604, 606, 808   **Vol. 3:** 276–278, 722, 724–725
3:11   **Vol. 1:** 325   **Vol. 3:** 278, 489
3:12 ff   **Vol. 2:** 807   **Vol. 3:** 749
3:12–16   **Vol. 2:** 569   **Vol. 3:** 278
3:12–15   **Vol. 2:** 129
3:12 f   **Vol. 2:** 741   **Vol. 3:** 750
3:12   **Vol. 1:** 491, 649   **Vol. 2:** 62, 806
3:13   **Vol. 1:** 493   **Vol. 3:** 824–825
3:14   **Vol. 1:** 275, 649   **Vol. 2:** 52, 62, 188, 194, 741, 806   **Vol. 3:** 142
3:15   **Vol. 1:** 649   **Vol. 2:** 62, 618, 741   **Vol. 3:** 315
3:16   **Vol. 2:** 144, 452   **Vol. 3:** 400
3:17   **Vol. 1:** 129, 400–401, 491   **Vol. 3:** 905
3:18 f   **Vol. 1:** 400, 464
3:18   **Vol. 1:** 400, 554   **Vol. 2:** 402, 804, 926
3:19 ff   **Vol. 2:** 924
3:19   **Vol. 1:** 518   **Vol. 2:** 61, 65, 73, 402, 619   **Vol. 3:** 564
3:20 f   **Vol. 2:** 48, 926
3:20   **Vol. 1:** 299, 686, 689–690   **Vol. 2:** 194, 245, 387, 518, 804, 903, 922, 925   **Vol. 3:** 219, 221, 279

3:21   **Vol. 1:** 707, 709   **Vol. 2:** 46, 48, 83, 263, 288, 566, 606, 741, 926   **Vol. 3:** 199, 278–279, 297, 864, 1152
4:1   **Vol. 1:** 257, 406   **Vol. 2:** 517, 924
4:2   **Vol. 1:** 570–571   **Vol. 2:** 618–619   **Vol. 3:** 1063
4:3   **Vol. 1:** 244, 344, 646–647   **Vol. 3:** 252, 548, 1164
4:4   **Vol. 2:** 359–360
4:5   **Vol. 1:** 278   **Vol. 2:** 54, 258, 360, 518, 896, 903, 922
4:6 f   **Vol. 2:** 874
4:6   **Vol. 1:** 278   **Vol. 2:** 858, 861, 868, 874   **Vol. 3:** 314, 819
4:7   **Vol. 2:** 135, 182, 780–781   **Vol. 3:** 128
4:8   **Vol. 2:** 95   **Vol. 3:** 101, 252, 362, 824–825, 927–928
4:9   **Vol. 1:** 486   **Vol. 2:** 78, 780, 874   **Vol. 3:** 751, 1158
4:9b   **Vol. 2:** 874
4:10   **Vol. 2:** 359–360, 617   **Vol. 3:** 837, 1194
4:11   **Vol. 3:** 727–728, 955
4:12 f   **Vol. 2:** 263
4:12   **Vol. 1:** 731, 744   **Vol. 2:** 267   **Vol. 3:** 954–955
4:13   **Vol. 2:** 604, 606   **Vol. 3:** 714, 1210
4:14   **Vol. 1:** 644   **Vol. 2:** 360, 809
4:15   **Vol. 1:** 138, 166   **Vol. 2:** 131, 550   **Vol. 3:** 1106
4:16   **Vol. 2:** 360, 717   **Vol. 3:** 957–958
4:17   **Vol. 2:** 42, 131   **Vol. 3:** 532
4:18   **Vol. 1:** 731   **Vol. 2:** 131, 816   **Vol. 3:** 242, 431, 600–601, 746
4:19   **Vol. 2:** 73, 874   **Vol. 3:** 957–958
4:20   **Vol. 1:** 99   **Vol. 2:** 46, 874
4:22   **Vol. 1:** 269
4:23   **Vol. 2:** 874   **Vol. 3:** 693

Colossians

1:1   **Vol. 1:** 130
1:2 f   **Vol. 2:** 874
1:2   **Vol. 2:** 229, 780
1:2b   **Vol. 2:** 874
1:3 ff   **Vol. 2:** 874
1:3 f   **Vol. 3:** 818
1:3†   **Vol. 2:** 76, 516, 875
1:3b   **Vol. 2:** 874
1:4 f   **Vol. 1:** 601
1:4   **Vol. 2:** 243   **Vol. 3:** 1212
1:5   **Vol. 2:** 111, 241, 243
1:5b   **Vol. 2:** 122
1:6   **Vol. 2:** 129, 899
1:7   **Vol. 1:** 257, 486   **Vol. 3:** 546, 548, 1196
1:8   **Vol. 3:** 316, 702
1:9–14†   **Vol. 2:** 874–875
1:9–12   **Vol. 2:** 857
1:9 f   **Vol. 2:** 400
1:9   **Vol. 2:** 856   **Vol. 3:** 133, 706, 1032

Colossians *(cont'd)*

1:10 f   **Vol. 2:** 129
1:10   **Vol. 1:** 723   **Vol. 2:** 101, 817   **Vol. 3:** 349, 945, 1032
1:11   **Vol. 2:** 46–47, 360, 605, 771, 774   **Vol. 3:** 718
1:12   **Vol. 1:** 620   **Vol. 2:** 228, 230, 302, 304, 495   **Vol. 3:** 729, 819
1:13–20   **Vol. 1:** 147
1:13 f   **Vol. 3:** 644
1:13   **Vol. 1:** 301, 424, 566   **Vol. 2:** 609   **Vol. 3:** 204, 831
1:14   **Vol. 1:** 221, 638, 701   **Vol. 3:** 198–199, 204
1:15 ff   **Vol. 1:** 95, 103, 302
1:15–23   **Vol. 2:** 195
1:15–20   **Vol. 1:** 237   **Vol. 2:** 614   **Vol. 3:** 674
1:15–18   **Vol. 1:** 628, 740
1:15–17   **Vol. 3:** 647
1:15 f   **Vol. 1:** 95   **Vol. 2:** 77   **Vol. 3:** 515, 647
1:15   **Vol. 1:** 256, 668–669   **Vol. 2:** 79, 288–289, 834   **Vol. 3:** 518
1:16 ff   **Vol. 1:** 95, 258   **Vol. 3:** 172
1:16 f   **Vol. 1:** 94   **Vol. 2:** 195
1:16   **Vol. 1:** 103, 167, 384, 668   **Vol. 2:** 160, 195, 518, 609, 612   **Vol. 3:** 1182, 1186
1:17   **Vol. 1:** 166, 549, 668   **Vol. 3:** 1177
1:17b   **Vol. 3:** 1186
1:18 ff   **Vol. 3:** 287
1:18 f   **Vol. 2:** 81
1:18   **Vol. 1:** 86, 166, 256, 301, 445, 662, 666, 668–669, 740   **Vol. 2:** 162   **Vol. 3:** 303, 504, 1189
1:18a   **Vol. 1:** 237
1:19–22   **Vol. 3:** 171, 1111, 1193
1:19 f   **Vol. 1:** 95, 237, 402, 669   **Vol. 3:** 169
1:19   **Vol. 1:** 740   **Vol. 2:** 203, 251, 819, 834   **Vol. 3:** 172, 1193
1:20   **Vol. 1:** 167, 224, 301, 740   **Vol. 2:** 195, 203, 781–782, 808   **Vol. 3:** 166–167, 171, 504, 1182, 1193
1:21 ff   **Vol. 3:** 228, 934
1:21 f   **Vol. 3:** 172
1:21   **Vol. 1:** 554, 566, 685   **Vol. 2:** 742   **Vol. 3:** 127, 1175, 1192
1:22   **Vol. 1:** 437, 474–475, 676, 740   **Vol. 2:** 140, 808   **Vol. 3:** 167, 171, 323, 924–925, 1193
1:23   **Vol. 1:** 95, 661–662, 741   **Vol. 2:** 111, 243   **Vol. 3:** 52, 172, 227–228, 546, 548, 925
1:24   **Vol. 1:** 301, 438, 479, 643, 648, 676, 679, 741   **Vol. 2:** 360, 573, 808   **Vol. 3:** 504, 722, 724, 953, 955
1:25 ff   **Vol. 2:** 217
1:25 f   **Vol. 3:** 322
1:25   **Vol. 1:** 741   **Vol. 2:** 255   **Vol. 3:** 315, 546, 548, 1111

1:26   **Vol. 2:** 35, 401   **Vol. 3:** 321–322, 504, 830–831, 837
1:27   **Vol. 2:** 47, 217, 242   **Vol. 3:** 314, 504, 1020, 1192
1:28 f   **Vol. 3:** 956
1:28   **Vol. 1:** 474, 568, 647   **Vol. 2:** 62   **Vol. 3:** 504, 765
1:29–2:3   **Vol. 2:** 874–875
1:29   **Vol. 1:** 263, 647   **Vol. 2:** 874   **Vol. 3:** 1152
2:1–15   **Vol. 1:** 740
2:1–3   **Vol. 2:** 874
2:1 f   **Vol. 1:** 647
2:2 f   **Vol. 2:** 402   **Vol. 3:** 132
2:2   **Vol. 2:** 401, 546, 834   **Vol. 3:** 133
2:3   **Vol. 1:** 174   **Vol. 2:** 216–217, 830, 834   **Vol. 3:** 1032
2:4–23   **Vol. 2:** 401
2:4   **Vol. 1:** 592   **Vol. 2:** 459
2:5   **Vol. 2:** 360, 874–875   **Vol. 3:** 694, 1213
2:6   **Vol. 2:** 514, 517   **Vol. 3:** 61, 751, 775, 944
2:7   **Vol. 1:** 660, 730   **Vol. 2:** 249, 253, 874   **Vol. 3:** 61, 765, 819, 868
2:7c   **Vol. 3:** 1190
2:8–17   **Vol. 1:** 631
2:8   **Vol. 1:** 525   **Vol. 2:** 200, 269, 401, 452–453, 459–460, 550, 559, 828   **Vol. 3:** 379, 774, 1035
2:9   **Vol. 1:** 95, 676, 740   **Vol. 2:** 79, 81, 86, 187, 251, 343   **Vol. 3:** 172, 1193
2:10–15   **Vol. 2:** 453
2:10 f   **Vol. 1:** 167
2:10   **Vol. 1:** 167, 740   **Vol. 2:** 83, 162, 514, 609   **Vol. 3:** 1192
2:11 f   **Vol. 1:** 148, 154, 158, 311   **Vol. 2:** 218   **Vol. 3:** 499
2:11–14   **Vol. 3:** 956
2:11–13   **Vol. 2:** 573
2:11   **Vol. 1:** 315, 676   **Vol. 2:** 786   **Vol. 3:** 204
2:12 ff   **Vol. 1:** 740
2:12–15   **Vol. 3:** 204
2:12 f   **Vol. 1:** 154, 157–158
2:12   **Vol. 1:** 146, 148, 158, 266, 315, 401, 643   **Vol. 2:** 217, 655   **Vol. 3:** 278, 1152
2:13 ff   **Vol. 1:** 224   **Vol. 2:** 366, 783   **Vol. 3:** 172
2:13   **Vol. 1:** 445–446, 643, 676   **Vol. 2:** 122   **Vol. 3:** 204, 277, 586, 825, 1176
2:14 f   **Vol. 1:** 167, 302, 402   **Vol. 3:** 1196
2:14   **Vol. 1:** 330, 471   **Vol. 3:** 410, 994, 1199
2:15   **Vol. 1:** 315, 467, 525, 649   **Vol. 2:** 291, 559, 645, 702, 736   **Vol. 3:** 172, 570
2:16 f   **Vol. 2:** 268
2:16   **Vol. 1:** 648   **Vol. 2:** 268, 277, 304, 364   **Vol. 3:** 410
2:17   **Vol. 1:** 327   **Vol. 3:** 556

Colossians *(cont'd)*

2:18	**Vol. 1:** 103, 648, 676 **Vol. 2:** 263, 559 **Vol. 3:** 551, 1035, 1198
2:19	**Vol. 1:** 241, 302 **Vol. 2:** 128
2:20–4:1	**Vol. 2:** 463
2:20–23	**Vol. 2:** 270
2:20	**Vol. 1:** 302, 330, 401, 438–439, 525 **Vol. 2:** 195, 200, 452–453, 559, 828 **Vol. 3:** 278
2:21 ff	**Vol. 2:** 453
2:21–23	**Vol. 2:** 559
2:21	**Vol. 1:** 330 **Vol. 2:** 269 **Vol. 3:** 860
2:22	**Vol. 1:** 402 **Vol. 3:** 572, 770
2:23	**Vol. 2:** 51, 263 **Vol. 3:** 1204
3:1–4:6	**Vol. 2:** 566
3:1–17	**Vol. 3:** 934
3:1–5	**Vol. 2:** 920
3:1–4	**Vol. 1:** 290 **Vol. 3:** 204
3:1 f	**Vol. 2:** 188
3:1	**Vol. 1:** 402, 643 **Vol. 2:** 147, 263, 453, 515, 619, 702 **Vol. 3:** 278, 298
3:2	**Vol. 1:** 518 **Vol. 2:** 619
3:3 f	**Vol. 1:** 138 **Vol. 2:** 218
3:3	**Vol. 1:** 401 **Vol. 2:** 217, 481, 672, 834
3:4	**Vol. 2:** 48, 481 **Vol. 3:** 163, 257, 322, 956, 1207
3:5–10	**Vol. 2:** 127
3:5–9	**Vol. 1:** 401
3:5	**Vol. 1:** 138, 231, 401, 445, 518, 564 **Vol. 2:** 286 **Vol. 3:** 31, 722, 928–929
3:6	**Vol. 1:** 110, 112
3:8 f	**Vol. 1:** 106
3:8	**Vol. 1:** 106, 110 **Vol. 3:** 31, 343, 564
3:9 ff	**Vol. 1:** 311 **Vol. 2:** 566 **Vol. 3:** 1062
3:9 f	**Vol. 2:** 675
3:9	**Vol. 1:** 315, 718 **Vol. 2:** 473, 673, 715
3:10–12	**Vol. 1:** 386
3:10 f	**Vol. 2:** 51
3:10	**Vol. 1:** 185, 315–316 **Vol. 2:** 161, 288, 400, 473, 671, 673, 675 **Vol. 3:** 303, 1063, 1187, 1200
3:11	**Vol. 1:** 95, 258, 311, 718, 720 **Vol. 2:** 126–127, 800 **Vol. 3:** 1191
3:12 f	**Vol. 2:** 62, 127
3:12	**Vol. 1:** 316, 542 **Vol. 2:** 79, 106, 229, 259, 263, 544, 598, 600, 673, 771, 920 **Vol. 3:** 927–928
3:13	**Vol. 1:** 147, 702 **Vol. 2:** 122, 765
3:14	**Vol. 1:** 110 **Vol. 2:** 62 **Vol. 3:** 592, 1193
3:15 ff	**Vol. 2:** 874
3:15	**Vol. 1:** 275, 648 **Vol. 2:** 183, 722, 781 **Vol. 3:** 818–819
3:16	**Vol. 1:** 568–569 **Vol. 2:** 121, 251, 842, 874 **Vol. 3:** 669–671, 673, 675, 706, 765, 1178
3:17	**Vol. 2:** 654 **Vol. 3:** 819, 1155
3:18 ff	**Vol. 2:** 51 539, 1067
3:18–4:11	**Vol. 1:** 59
3:18–4:1	**Vol. 3:** 929–930
3:18–20	**Vol. 2:** 180
3:18 f	**Vol. 1:** 496 **Vol. 2:** 160, 579, 905, 923 **Vol. 3:**
3:18	**Vol. 3:** 930, 1064
3:19	**Vol. 1:** 202 **Vol. 2:** 563 **Vol. 3:** 1064
3:20 f	**Vol. 1:** 619
3:20	**Vol. 1:** 160, 286 **Vol. 2:** 816 **Vol. 3:** 930, 1191
3:21	**Vol. 1:** 286
3:22 ff	**Vol. 2:** 517
3:22–25	**Vol. 3:** 582
3:22	**Vol. 1:** 587, 623, 680 **Vol. 2:** 509, 513, 817 **Vol. 3:** 596
3:23	**Vol. 3:** 685, 1155
3:24	**Vol. 2:** 302 **Vol. 3:** 135–136, 596–597, 751
3:25	**Vol. 1:** 587 **Vol. 3:** 575, 930
4:1	**Vol. 1:** 637 **Vol. 2:** 499 **Vol. 3:** 362, 583
4:2 ff	**Vol. 2:** 874
4:2 f	**Vol. 2:** 768
4:2	**Vol. 2:** 137, 768, 869, 874 **Vol. 3:** 819
4:2c	**Vol. 3:** 1190
4:3	**Vol. 1:** 171, 647 **Vol. 2:** 30, 726–727 **Vol. 3:** 504
4:4	**Vol. 3:** 322
4:5	**Vol. 1:** 268 **Vol. 2:** 256 **Vol. 3:** 838, 945, 1032
4:6	**Vol. 2:** 118 **Vol. 3:** 449
4:7	**Vol. 1:** 257 **Vol. 3:** 314, 546, 548, 596
4:9	**Vol. 3:** 314
4:10	**Vol. 1:** 337 **Vol. 2:** 467 **Vol. 3:** 591, 601, 746
4:11	**Vol. 1:** 310 **Vol. 2:** 331 **Vol. 3:** 548, 1152
4:12	**Vol. 1:** 647 **Vol. 2:** 62, 868, 874–875 **Vol. 3:** 596, 613
4:13	**Vol. 1:** 319 **Vol. 3:** 1043
4:14	**Vol. 2:** 168
4:15 f	**Vol. 1:** 302
4:15	**Vol. 1:** 301
4:16	**Vol. 1:** 245–246 **Vol. 3:** 489
4:17	**Vol. 2:** 517 **Vol. 3:** 546
4:18	**Vol. 2:** 874

1 Thessalonians

1:1 ff	**Vol. 2:** 874
1:1 f	**Vol. 1:** 298
1:1	**Vol. 1:** 130, 299 **Vol. 2:** 780
1:1b	**Vol. 2:** 874
1:2 ff	**Vol. 2:** 874
1:2–10	**Vol. 1:** 247
1:2 f	**Vol. 2:** 874–875 **Vol. 3:** 242, 818
1:2	**Vol. 3:** 230, 246
1:3	**Vol. 1:** 263 **Vol. 2:** 242–243, 545, 774 **Vol. 3:** 818
1:4	**Vol. 1:** 540–542

1 Thessalonians *(cont'd)*

1:5	**Vol. 2:** 632 **Vol. 3:** 701, 703, 1106
1:6	**Vol. 1:** 491 **Vol. 2:** 360, 809 **Vol. 3:** 60–61, 529, 701, 746, 905, 1110
1:7	**Vol. 3:** 905
1:8	**Vol. 1:** 599 **Vol. 3:** 1110, 1211, 1214
1:9 f	**Vol. 3:** 644, 1112
1:9	**Vol. 1:** 355, 720 **Vol. 2:** 73–74, 285–286 **Vol. 3:** 304, 597, 888, 940
1:10	**Vol. 1:** 112, 445, 566 **Vol. 2:** 76, 194, 245, 544, 925 **Vol. 3:** 62, 205, 214, 643
2:1	**Vol. 1:** 329 **Vol. 3:** 940
2:2	**Vol. 2:** 78, 111, 550, 736 **Vol. 3:** 27, 54
2:3 ff	**Vol. 3:** 50
2:3	**Vol. 1:** 329 **Vol. 2:** 460
2:4	**Vol. 2:** 183, 816 **Vol. 3:** 809, 1211
2:5	**Vol. 1:** 138 **Vol. 3:** 1043, 1112
2:6	**Vol. 2:** 46–47 **Vol. 3:** 1174, 1176
2:7	**Vol. 1:** 261, 282, 286 **Vol. 3:** 1070
2:8	**Vol. 2:** 41, 43, 818 **Vol. 3:** 54, 683
2:9	**Vol. 1:** 138, 261, 263 **Vol. 2:** 111 **Vol. 3:** 52, 54
2:10	**Vol. 2:** 139, 144 **Vol. 3:** 363, 1043
2:11	**Vol. 1:** 286, 329
2:12	**Vol. 1:** 275, 300, 329, 571 **Vol. 2:** 46, 76 **Vol. 3:** 54, 87, 945
2:13 ff	**Vol. 2:** 874
2:13	**Vol. 1:** 325 **Vol. 2:** 175 **Vol. 3:** 230, 314, 329, 746, 751, 819, 888, 1110, 1112
2:14–16	**Vol. 2:** 312
2:14 f	**Vol. 2:** 312
2:14	**Vol. 1:** 299, 491 **Vol. 2:** 83 **Vol. 3:** 724
2:15 f	**Vol. 1:** 394–395 **Vol. 2:** 221 **Vol. 3:** 203
2.15	**Vol. 1:** 430, 740 **Vol. 2:** 806, 816
2:16	**Vol. 1:** 112, 740 **Vol. 2:** 61, 222, 794 **Vol. 3:** 214
2:17–3:13	**Vol. 3:** 955
2:17	**Vol. 1:** 457, 731 **Vol. 2:** 182 **Vol. 3:** 837, 848, 1169
2:18	**Vol. 2:** 221, 901 **Vol. 3:** 471
2:19 f	**Vol. 2:** 47
2:19	**Vol. 1:** 229, 406 **Vol. 2:** 243, 874, 900–901
2:20	**Vol. 2:** 360
3:1	**Vol. 2:** 818
3:2	**Vol. 1:** 570 **Vol. 3:** 87, 548, 1152
3:3	**Vol. 1:** 471 **Vol. 2:** 360, 809
3:4	**Vol. 1:** 326 **Vol. 2:** 809 **Vol. 3:** 84, 1204
3:5	**Vol. 1:** 547, 601, 718 **Vol. 3:** 471, 563, 802, 809
3:6	**Vol. 2:** 545 **Vol. 3:** 246, 1204
3:7	**Vol. 1:** 571 **Vol. 2:** 664, 809
3:8	**Vol. 1:** 601
3:9 f	**Vol. 3:** 819
3:9	**Vol. 2:** 360, 874
3:10–13	**Vol. 2:** 874
3:10	**Vol. 1:** 730 **Vol. 2:** 130, 860, 874–875 **Vol. 3:** 350, 955
3:11 ff	**Vol. 2:** 874
3:12 f	**Vol. 2:** 517
3:12	**Vol. 1:** 730 **Vol. 2:** 131, 144
3:13	**Vol. 2:** 139, 144, 228, 900 **Vol. 3:** 1207
4–5	**Vol. 2:** 924
4	**Vol. 2:** 925
4:1–8	**Vol. 3:** 955
4:1	**Vol. 1:** 570–571, 730 **Vol. 2:** 517, 666, 816 **Vol. 3:** 252, 751, 944, 1192
4:2	**Vol. 1:** 341 **Vol. 2:** 517
4:3–8	**Vol. 3:** 1064
4:3–7	**Vol. 2:** 230
4:3	**Vol. 1:** 501 **Vol. 3:** 1064
4:4	**Vol. 2:** 50, 580 **Vol. 3:** 913, 1064, 1067
4:5	**Vol. 2:** 73, 793 **Vol. 3:** 722, 1064
4:6	**Vol. 1:** 138 **Vol. 3:** 97, 584, 1042, 1064, 1158
4:7	**Vol. 3:** 1191, 1193
4:8	**Vol. 1:** 74 **Vol. 2:** 42, 786 **Vol. 3:** 701
4:9–12	**Vol. 3:** 955
4:9	**Vol. 2:** 549
4:10	**Vol. 1:** 571, 730
4:11	**Vol. 1:** 341 **Vol. 2:** 550 **Vol. 3:** 112, 1157
4:12	**Vol. 3:** 945
4:13 ff	**Vol. 2:** 925 **Vol. 3:** 55
4:13–5:11	**Vol. 3:** 955
4:13–18	**Vol. 2:** 559, 903, 924 **Vol. 3:** 1200
4:13–17	**Vol. 2:** 482
4:13 f	**Vol. 1:** 441
4:13	**Vol. 1:** 443 **Vol. 2:** 242, 406, 794, 901 **Vol. 3:** 251–252
4:14–17	**Vol. 1:** 649
4:14	**Vol. 1:** 443, 599 **Vol. 2:** 925–926 **Vol. 3:** 61, 1178, 1211
4:15 ff	**Vol. 2:** 911, 922, 926
4:15	**Vol. 1:** 443 **Vol. 2:** 514, 900–901, 923–924, 926 **Vol. 3:** 305, 967
4:16 ff	**Vol. 2:** 924–925
4:16	**Vol. 1:** 103, 342, 410, 446, 667 **Vol. 2:** 38, 186, 194, 924–925 **Vol. 3:** 113, 277, 558, 674, 874, 1207
4:17	**Vol. 1:** 325, 449, 643, 649 **Vol. 2:** 482, 517, 923–926 **Vol. 3:** 278, 602, 1003, 1207
4:18	**Vol. 1:** 571 **Vol. 2:** 244, 924
5	**Vol. 2:** 925
5:1 ff	**Vol. 2:** 702, 900 **Vol. 3:** 833, 838, 844
5:1–5	**Vol. 2:** 911
5:1	**Vol. 2:** 922, 924, 926
5:2 f	**Vol. 2:** 360
5:2	**Vol. 1:** 323, 421 **Vol. 2:** 75, 517, 894, 925–926 **Vol. 3:** 378
5:3	**Vol. 1:** 466 **Vol. 3:** 858
5:4–10	**Vol. 2:** 911
5:4–6	**Vol. 1:** 425

1 Thessalonians *(cont'd)*

5:4   **Vol. 2:** 894, 925   **Vol. 3:** 378, 750
5:5–7   **Vol. 1:** 421
5:5   **Vol. 1:** 289, 421   **Vol. 2:** 495, 925
5:6 ff   **Vol. 2:** 911
5:6–8   **Vol. 1:** 514
5:6   **Vol. 1:** 421, 442, 513   **Vol. 2:** 137, 794, 894, 925   **Vol. 3:** 252
5:7   **Vol. 1:** 421, 513   **Vol. 2:** 925
5:8 f   **Vol. 3:** 214
5:8   **Vol. 1:** 316   **Vol. 2:** 242, 244, 545, 925   **Vol. 3:** 965–966
5:9 f   **Vol. 3:** 61
5:9   **Vol. 1:** 112, 477   **Vol. 2:** 839   **Vol. 3:** 214
5:10   **Vol. 1:** 437, 443   **Vol. 2:** 137, 923, 925–926   **Vol. 3:** 1197, 1207
5:11   **Vol. 1:** 571   **Vol. 2:** 253
5:12   **Vol. 1:** 197, 263, 569   **Vol. 3:** 930
5:13   **Vol. 3:** 930
5:14   **Vol. 1:** 329, 569   **Vol. 2:** 771   **Vol. 3:** 687, 955
5:15   **Vol. 2:** 101, 807   **Vol. 3:** 136, 1179
5:16   **Vol. 2:** 360
5:17 f   **Vol. 2:** 874
5:17   **Vol. 3:** 230
5:18   **Vol. 2:** 874   **Vol. 3:** 819
5:19–22   **Vol. 3:** 695, 703
5:19 f   **Vol. 3:** 703
5:19   **Vol. 3:** 109
5:20   **Vol. 3:** 110
5:21   **Vol. 3:** 808, 810
5:22   **Vol. 1:** 567, 704
5:23 f   **Vol. 2:** 874
5:23   **Vol. 1:** 235   **Vol. 2:** 78, 133, 139, 144, 230, 568, 780–781, 874, 900–901   **Vol. 3:** 684, 694
5:24 f   **Vol. 2:** 874
5:24   **Vol. 3:** 1154
5:25   **Vol. 1:** 647   **Vol. 2:** 868, 874
5:26   **Vol. 2:** 549
5:27   **Vol. 1:** 245–247   **Vol. 3:** 489, 738
5:28   **Vol. 2:** 874
6:16 f   **Vol. 2:** 518

2 Thessalonians

1:1 ff   **Vol. 2:** 875
1:1 f   **Vol. 1:** 298
1:1   **Vol. 1:** 130
1:2   **Vol. 2:** 516, 780, 874
1:3 ff   **Vol. 2:** 874, 911
1:3 f   **Vol. 2:** 806
1:3   **Vol. 2:** 129–131, 546, 668   **Vol. 3:** 819
1:4 f   **Vol. 3:** 725
1:4   **Vol. 1:** 228, 299, 301   **Vol. 2:** 83, 766, 774
1:5–12   **Vol. 2:** 903
1:5 f   **Vol. 3:** 362

1:5   **Vol. 1:** 300   **Vol. 2:** 366   **Vol. 3:** 349, 725
1:6 f   **Vol. 2:** 809
1:6–10   **Vol. 2:** 911
1:7   **Vol. 1:** 102   **Vol. 2:** 194   **Vol. 3:** 315
1:8   **Vol. 1:** 657   **Vol. 2:** 96, 179
1:9†   **Vol. 1:** 466–467   **Vol. 2:** 46, 96, 518   **Vol. 3:** 99, 714, 830, 832
1:10   **Vol. 2:** 47, 625   **Vol. 3:** 1043, 1211, 1213
1:11 f   **Vol. 2:** 605, 874, 911
1:11   **Vol. 2:** 101, 819
1:12   **Vol. 2:** 47, 81, 654
2   **Vol. 2:** 461
2:1 ff   **Vol. 3:** 838
2:1–15   **Vol. 2:** 903
2:1–12   **Vol. 2:** 447, 702   **Vol. 3:** 319
2:1–2   **Vol. 3:** 112
2:1 f   **Vol. 2:** 911
2:1   **Vol. 2:** 33, 518, 900   **Vol. 3:** 1174
2:2 f   **Vol. 1:** 247
2:2   **Vol. 2:** 517, 901, 921   **Vol. 3:** 315, 412, 559, 695
2:3 ff   **Vol. 1:** 125   **Vol. 2:** 633
2:3–12   **Vol. 3:** 471
2:3 f   **Vol. 1:** 667   **Vol. 3:** 505
2:3   **Vol. 1:** 464, 607   **Vol. 2:** 447, 459–460, 911, 924   **Vol. 3:** 315
2:4 ff   **Vol. 2:** 911
2:4   **Vol. 1:** 75   **Vol. 2:** 93   **Vol. 3:** 570–571, 784
2:5   **Vol. 1:** 269   **Vol. 3:** 1204
2:6 f   **Vol. 3:** 319
2:6   **Vol. 3:** 315
2:7 ff   **Vol. 2:** 901
2:7   **Vol. 2:** 447, 911   **Vol. 3:** 319, 505
2:8–12   **Vol. 2:** 911
2:8 f   **Vol. 2:** 900
2:8   **Vol. 1:** 73   **Vol. 2:** 74, 447, 518   **Vol. 3:** 315, 319, 694, 703
2:9–12   **Vol. 3:** 576
2:9   **Vol. 2:** 603, 629   **Vol. 3:** 319, 471, 1152
2:10   **Vol. 1:** 464   **Vol. 2:** 459–460   **Vol. 3:** 746, 886
2:11   **Vol. 2:** 459   **Vol. 3:** 1152
2:12   **Vol. 2:** 365, 818   **Vol. 3:** 127, 575
2:13 f   **Vol. 3:** 214
2:13   **Vol. 1:** 166, 534   **Vol. 2:** 230, 544, 668, 874, 911   **Vol. 3:** 214, 416, 701, 818, 885
2:14   **Vol. 1:** 275   **Vol. 2:** 46–47, 839
2:15   **Vol. 1:** 247   **Vol. 2:** 718, 911   **Vol. 3:** 61, 717, 765, 774
2:16 f   **Vol. 2:** 874
2:16   **Vol. 1:** 571   **Vol. 2:** 243–244   **Vol. 3:** 832
2:17   **Vol. 1:** 660   **Vol. 3:** 87, 197, 1149, 1151
3:1–3   **Vol. 2:** 874
3:1   **Vol. 1:** 647   **Vol. 2:** 868   **Vol. 3:** 61, 252, 947

2 Thessalonians *(cont'd)*

3:2	**Vol. 1:** 565 **Vol. 3:** 203, 1176
3:3	**Vol. 1:** 566 **Vol. 2:** 135
3:4	**Vol. 1:** 341, 591 **Vol. 2:** 615
3:5	**Vol. 2:** 183, 775, 874
3:6	**Vol. 1:** 341 **Vol. 2:** 654, 718 **Vol. 3:** 751, 774, 905, 945
3:7	**Vol. 1:** 491 **Vol. 2:** 666
3:8	**Vol. 1:** 250, 261 **Vol. 2:** 41
3:9	**Vol. 1:** 491 **Vol. 2:** 611 **Vol. 3:** 905
3:10 ff	**Vol. 1:** 341
3:10	**Vol. 2:** 272, 901 **Vol. 3:** 1204
3:11	**Vol. 1:** 267 **Vol. 2:** 434
3:12	**Vol. 1:** 341, 571 **Vol. 3:** 112
3:13	**Vol. 1:** 563 **Vol. 2:** 102
3:14	**Vol. 2:** 179
3:15	**Vol. 1:** 554, 569
3:16	**Vol. 2:** 513, 517, 780–781, 874
3:17	**Vol. 2:** 629 **Vol. 3:** 489
3:18	**Vol. 2:** 874

1 Timothy

1:1 ff	**Vol. 2:** 171
1:1	**Vol. 1:** 130 **Vol. 2:** 78 **Vol. 3:** 220
1:2	**Vol. 1:** 180, 286, 619 **Vol. 2:** 516, 597, 780
1:3–7	**Vol. 3:** 380
1:3	**Vol. 1:** 341 **Vol. 2:** 718 **Vol. 3:** 228
1:4	**Vol. 2:** 36, 131, 644 **Vol. 3:** 532, 768, 1119
1:5	**Vol. 1:** 341, 351, 353, 552, 604 **Vol. 2:** 62, 101, 183, 470 **Vol. 3:** 107
1:6 ff	**Vol. 2:** 171
1:6	**Vol. 1:** 552, 608 **Vol. 3:** 903
1:7	**Vol. 2:** 447 **Vol. 3:** 480, 768
1:8	**Vol. 2:** 104, 447, 549
1:9–10	**Vol. 3:** 31
1:9 f	**Vol. 2:** 447 **Vol. 3:** 31, 380
1:9	**Vol. 2:** 94, 237, 447 **Vol. 3:** 362, 365
1:10	**Vol. 2:** 170–171, 570, 584 **Vol. 3:** 738, 770
1:11	**Vol. 1:** 217 **Vol. 2:** 46, 77–78 **Vol. 3:** 1211
1:12 ff	**Vol. 2:** 122
1:12	**Vol. 1:** 477 **Vol. 2:** 121, 604
1:13	**Vol. 2:** 407, 597, 806 **Vol. 3:** 27–28, 343, 345
1:14	**Vol. 2:** 545 **Vol. 3:** 1020
1:15	**Vol. 3:** 214, 581, 744, 765
1:15a	**Vol. 3:** 746
1:16	**Vol. 1:** 326, 666 **Vol. 2:** 597 **Vol. 3:** 832, 1184, 1212
1:17	**Vol. 1:** 469 **Vol. 2:** 46, 50, 73, 77, 724 **Vol. 3:** 515, 518
1:18	**Vol. 1:** 341, 619 **Vol. 2:** 104 **Vol. 3:** 963
1:19	**Vol. 1:** 351, 353, 608 **Vol. 2:** 101 **Vol. 3:** 61
1:20	**Vol. 1:** 415 **Vol. 2:** 368 **Vol. 3:** 470–471, 779
2:1 ff	**Vol. 3:** 930
2:1–15	**Vol. 1:** 59
2:1	**Vol. 2:** 861 **Vol. 3:** 819
2:2	**Vol. 2:** 95, 378, 475, 846 **Vol. 3:** 112
2:3	**Vol. 2:** 78 **Vol. 3:** 745–746, 768
2:4 ff	**Vol. 1:** 375 **Vol. 3:** 197
2:4	**Vol. 2:** 78, 405, 721 **Vol. 3:** 214, 887, 1020
2:5 f	**Vol. 2:** 722 **Vol. 3:** 61
2:5	**Vol. 1:** 374–375 **Vol. 2:** 73, 84, 565, 721
2:6	**Vol. 1:** 398 **Vol. 2:** 42 **Vol. 3:** 195, 197–198, 214, 611, 1180, 1197
2:7	**Vol. 1:** 130, 477 **Vol. 2:** 126 **Vol. 3:** 52, 170, 767–768
2:8	**Vol. 1:** 110 **Vol. 2:** 237, 869 **Vol. 3:** 821, 1017
2:9–15	**Vol. 3:** 929, 932
2:9	**Vol. 1:** 502, 524 **Vol. 2:** 96 **Vol. 3:** 395, 561
2:10	**Vol. 2:** 85, 95, 669 **Vol. 3:** 70, 561
2:11 ff	**Vol. 2:** 160
2:11–15	**Vol. 3:** 1063
2:11	**Vol. 3:** 112
2:12	**Vol. 1:** 87 **Vol. 3:** 112, 349, 765, 1066
2:13 ff	**Vol. 1:** 85
2:13	**Vol. 1:** 87 **Vol. 3:** 401
2:14	**Vol. 2:** 459–460 **Vol. 3:** 585
2:15	**Vol. 1:** 187, 285, 502, 603 **Vol. 3:** 215, 225, 1177
3	**Vol. 3:** 930
3:1–13	**Vol. 3:** 929
3:1–7	**Vol. 3:** 548
3:1	**Vol. 1:** 190, 192, 457, 460–461 **Vol. 2:** 104 **Vol. 3:** 765
3:2	**Vol. 1:** 191, 496, 502, 515, 524, 690 **Vol. 2:** 550, 563, 580–581 **Vol. 3:** 750, 765
3:3	**Vol. 1:** 514, 646 **Vol. 2:** 258 **Vol. 3:** 922
3:4	**Vol. 1:** 197, 286 **Vol. 2:** 95
3:5	**Vol. 1:** 197 **Vol. 2:** 83
3:6 f	**Vol. 3:** 470
3:6	**Vol. 1:** 609
3:7	**Vol. 1:** 198, 609 **Vol. 2:** 104 **Vol. 3:** 340, 471
3:8–13	**Vol. 3:** 546, 548, 1067
3:8	**Vol. 2:** 95 **Vol. 3:** 137, 564, 922
3:9	**Vol. 1:** 351, 353 **Vol. 3:** 107, 505
3:10	**Vol. 2:** 140 **Vol. 3:** 546, 808, 924
3:11	**Vol. 1:** 515 **Vol. 3:** 470, 546, 549, 1065
3:12	**Vol. 1:** 197 **Vol. 2:** 563, 580–581
3:13	**Vol. 2:** 104, 736, 838 **Vol. 3:** 546, 1212
3:15	**Vol. 1:** 300, 661–662 **Vol. 2:** 83, 249 **Vol. 3:** 500, 794–795, 934
3:16	**Vol. 1:** 662, 677, 679 **Vol. 2:** 46, 48, 94, 203, 289, 340 **Vol. 3:** 61, 322, 363, 505, 674, 694, 705, 749

1 Timothy *(cont'd)*

4:1–3   **Vol. 2:** 447
4:1   **Vol. 1:** 452, 607–608   **Vol. 2:** 459–460   **Vol. 3:** 380, 694, 705, 770, 838, 953
4:2   **Vol. 1:** 351–352   **Vol. 2:** 469, 472, 574
4:3 ff   **Vol. 2:** 268
4:3 f   **Vol. 1:** 385
4:3   **Vol. 2:** 579   **Vol. 3:** 750, 819, 1119
4:4   **Vol. 2:** 104, 268
4:6   **Vol. 2:** 104, 718   **Vol. 3:** 61, 546, 770
4:7 f   **Vol. 2:** 95
4:7   **Vol. 1:** 313, 647   **Vol. 2:** 401, 405, 645, 858
4:8   **Vol. 1:** 313, 327, 406   **Vol. 2:** 95, 429, 480
4:9   **Vol. 3:** 744, 746, 765
4:10   **Vol. 1:** 263, 647   **Vol. 2:** 78   **Vol. 3:** 220
4:11 ff   **Vol. 3:** 934
4:11   **Vol. 3:** 765
4:12   **Vol. 1:** 462, 603   **Vol. 2:** 675   **Vol. 3:** 101, 905, 934
4:13   **Vol. 3:** 771
4:14   **Vol. 1:** 199   **Vol. 2:** 122, 152   **Vol. 3:** 705, 1182
4:15   **Vol. 2:** 130   **Vol. 3:** 320
4:16   **Vol. 3:** 215, 228, 770
5:1–21   **Vol. 1:** 59
5:1 f   **Vol. 2:** 675
5:1   **Vol. 3:** 1042
5:2   **Vol. 1:** 198   **Vol. 3:** 101, 1070
5:3–16   **Vol. 3:** 930
5:3   **Vol. 2:** 50, 405   **Vol. 3:** 1075
5:4–16   **Vol. 3:** 1075
5:4   **Vol. 1:** 286   **Vol. 2:** 95   **Vol. 3:** 745–746, 1075
5:5   **Vol. 2:** 861   **Vol. 3:** 228, 1075
5:7   **Vol. 1:** 341   **Vol. 3:** 750
5:8   **Vol. 1:** 455   **Vol. 2:** 251
5:9†   **Vol. 2:** 428, 564   **Vol. 3:** 1065, 1075
5:10   **Vol. 1:** 187, 239, 496, 690   **Vol. 2:** 104   **Vol. 3:** 1075, 1151
5:11   **Vol. 2:** 858
5:12   **Vol. 1:** 74, 712
5:13   **Vol. 1:** 267, 322, 487   **Vol. 2:** 557   **Vol. 3:** 903, 1075
5:14 f   **Vol. 1:** 285, 496
5:14   **Vol. 1:** 187   **Vol. 2:** 510   **Vol. 3:** 347, 1017, 1075
5:15   **Vol. 1:** 493   **Vol. 3:** 470–471, 903
5:16   **Vol. 1:** 261   **Vol. 3:** 1075
5:17   **Vol. 1:** 198–199, 263   **Vol. 2:** 50   **Vol. 3:** 572, 771
5:18†   **Vol. 1:** 115   **Vol. 2:** 755   **Vol. 3:** 349, 490, 492
5:19   **Vol. 1:** 83, 199   **Vol. 2:** 686   **Vol. 3:** 1043, 1193
5:20   **Vol. 2:** 141   **Vol. 3:** 252

5:21   **Vol. 2:** 135, 364   **Vol. 3:** 1044
5:22   **Vol. 1:** 685   **Vol. 2:** 133, 152, 742   **Vol. 3:** 101
5:23   **Vol. 3:** 922
5:24   **Vol. 2:** 366
5:25   **Vol. 2:** 104, 217   **Vol. 3:** 1151
6:1 f   **Vol. 1:** 59   **Vol. 3:** 582
6:1   **Vol. 2:** 50, 509, 653   **Vol. 3:** 342–343, 596, 771, 1162
6:2   **Vol. 1:** 462   **Vol. 3:** 765, 1152
6:3 ff   **Vol. 3:** 1119
6:3–5   **Vol. 3:** 380
6:3   **Vol. 1:** 322   **Vol. 2:** 94, 170–171   **Vol. 3:** 768, 770
6:4   **Vol. 1:** 558   **Vol. 3:** 343, 532, 998
6:5 f   **Vol. 2:** 95
6:5   **Vol. 1:** 607   **Vol. 2:** 859   **Vol. 3:** 127, 887
6:6   **Vol. 3:** 727
6:7   **Vol. 3:** 317
6:8   **Vol. 1:** 318   **Vol. 3:** 727
6:9 f   **Vol. 2:** 845
6:9   **Vol. 1:** 457, 466–467, 609   **Vol. 2:** 842   **Vol. 3:** 802
6:10   **Vol. 1:** 138, 460–461, 564   **Vol. 2:** 459–460, 550, 843   **Vol. 3:** 868
6:11 ff   **Vol. 3:** 838
6:11   **Vol. 1:** 559, 603   **Vol. 2:** 94, 258, 775, 807   **Vol. 3:** 363, 365
6:12–16   **Vol. 2:** 724
6:12 f   **Vol. 1:** 346   **Vol. 3:** 1047
6:12   **Vol. 1:** 346, 647   **Vol. 2:** 104   **Vol. 3:** 319, 750, 832
6:13 f   **Vol. 1:** 341   **Vol. 3:** 61
6:13   **Vol. 3:** 198
6:14   **Vol. 1:** 337, 341   **Vol. 2:** 133, 518   **Vol. 3:** 319, 838
6:15 f   **Vol. 2:** 724   **Vol. 3:** 304
6:15   **Vol. 1:** 217   **Vol. 2:** 77, 381, 514, 519   **Vol. 3:** 198, 569
6:16   **Vol. 1:** 435   **Vol. 2:** 50, 250, 494   **Vol. 3:** 302, 518, 718, 832
6:17 ff   **Vol. 2:** 844
6:17   **Vol. 1:** 341   **Vol. 2:** 198, 842
6:18   **Vol. 1:** 642   **Vol. 2:** 100, 102, 104, 694   **Vol. 3:** 1151
6:19   **Vol. 1:** 326   **Vol. 2:** 104   **Vol. 3:** 1017, 1149
6:20   **Vol. 1:** 337   **Vol. 2:** 135, 401, 405, 652, 655, 677   **Vol. 3:** 61, 770, 903, 1119
6:21   **Vol. 1:** 608   **Vol. 3:** 70, 903

2 Timothy

1:1   **Vol. 1:** 130   **Vol. 3:** 1020
1:2   **Vol. 1:** 286, 619   **Vol. 2:** 516, 597, 780
1:3   **Vol. 1:** 351, 353   **Vol. 2:** 121, 861   **Vol. 3:** 230, 246
1:4   **Vol. 3:** 705

2 Timothy *(cont'd)*

1:5   **Vol. 1:** 159, 591, 604   **Vol. 2:** 251, 470   **Vol. 3:** 241, 247, 1070

1:6   **Vol. 2:** 138, 152   **Vol. 3:** 110, 240, 243, 705, 1182

1:7   **Vol. 1:** 622–623   **Vol. 3:** 258, 705

1:8 f   **Vol. 2:** 604

1:8   **Vol. 3:** 563, 724–725

1:9   **Vol. 1:** 697   **Vol. 2:** 122   **Vol. 3:** 215, 832, 844

1:10   **Vol. 1:** 73, 437, 469   **Vol. 2:** 113, 480–481, 495   **Vol. 3:** 220–221, 302, 304, 312, 319, 323

1:11   **Vol. 1:** 477   **Vol. 2:** 113   **Vol. 3:** 52, 88, 170, 767

1:12   **Vol. 1:** 591   **Vol. 2:** 135, 138, 894, 922   **Vol. 3:** 203, 770, 1211

1:13   **Vol. 2:** 170   **Vol. 3:** 61

1:14   **Vol. 2:** 104, 135, 251   **Vol. 3:** 61, 770

1:16†   **Vol. 2:** 248, 250, 517, 597, 874   **Vol. 3:** 563, 686

1:17   **Vol. 3:** 529, 694, 1169

1:18†   **Vol. 2:** 597, 874, 922   **Vol. 3:** 546, 831

2:1 f   **Vol. 2:** 718

2:1   **Vol. 1:** 180, 286, 619   **Vol. 2:** 122, 604

2:2   **Vol. 2:** 718   **Vol. 3:** 729, 765

2:3 f   **Vol. 3:** 964

2:3   **Vol. 2:** 104   **Vol. 3:** 724

2:4   **Vol. 1:** 646   **Vol. 2:** 475, 816, 846   **Vol. 3:** 1158

2:5   **Vol. 1:** 406, 645–646   **Vol. 2:** 258, 447

2:6   **Vol. 1:** 263, 723   **Vol. 3:** 197, 750

2:7   **Vol. 2:** 405, 517   **Vol. 3:** 132

2:8   **Vol. 1:** 427, 445   **Vol. 2:** 79, 113   **Vol. 3:** 61, 243, 299, 651

2:9   **Vol. 1:** 171, 564   **Vol. 2:** 74, 113   **Vol. 3:** 725

2:10   **Vol. 2:** 47, 775   **Vol. 3:** 215, 832

2:11 ff   **Vol. 2:** 775   **Vol. 3:** 203

2:11 f   **Vol. 1:** 455

2:11   **Vol. 1:** 130, 435, 441   **Vol. 3:** 278, 765, 1063, 1066

2:12   **Vol. 1:** 323, 455, 643   **Vol. 2:** 380, 775

2:13   **Vol. 1:** 455

2:14–19   **Vol. 3:** 915

2:14–18   **Vol. 3:** 1119

2:14   **Vol. 3:** 241, 1042, 1044, 1119

2:15   **Vol. 1:** 309, 475   **Vol. 3:** 352, 809, 1169

2:16   **Vol. 2:** 94, 130

2:17 f   **Vol. 3:** 305

2:17   **Vol. 2:** 550   **Vol. 3:** 999

2:18   **Vol. 1:** 608   **Vol. 2:** 550   **Vol. 3:** 277–278

2:18b   **Vol. 2:** 402

2:19   **Vol. 1:** 299, 662   **Vol. 2:** 249, 400, 655   **Vol. 3:** 500, 576

2:20 f   **Vol. 1:** 662   **Vol. 3:** 913

2:20   **Vol. 2:** 50–51   **Vol. 3:** 915

2:21   **Vol. 2:** 509   **Vol. 3:** 102, 118, 912, 915, 1065

2:22–26   **Vol. 3:** 915

2:22   **Vol. 1:** 559, 603   **Vol. 2:** 782, 807   **Vol. 3:** 107, 363, 365

2:23–26   **Vol. 3:** 903

2:23†   **Vol. 1:** 176   **Vol. 2:** 858   **Vol. 3:** 532, 963, 1026

2:24   **Vol. 3:** 765

2:25   **Vol. 2:** 405, 874   **Vol. 3:** 1187

2:26   **Vol. 1:** 515   **Vol. 3:** 470–471, 1178, 1187

3:1 ff   **Vol. 1:** 496   **Vol. 2:** 58

3:1–5   **Vol. 1:** 460

3:1   **Vol. 1:** 420   **Vol. 2:** 894   **Vol. 3:** 839, 954, 1191

3:2–5   **Vol. 3:** 31

3:2–4   **Vol. 1:** 420   **Vol. 3:** 903

3:2   **Vol. 1:** 593   **Vol. 2:** 237, 435, 550, 843   **Vol. 3:** 30–32, 343, 345

3:3   **Vol. 1:** 495–496   **Vol. 2:** 539, 542   **Vol. 3:** 470

3:4   **Vol. 2:** 550, 605

3:5   **Vol. 1:** 455, 708   **Vol. 2:** 95   **Vol. 3:** 31, 903

3:6   **Vol. 1:** 457   **Vol. 3:** 591, 1058

3:7   **Vol. 1:** 487   **Vol. 2:** 405   **Vol. 3:** 887

3:8   **Vol. 2:** 219, 557–558, 642   **Vol. 3:** 127, 808

3:9   **Vol. 2:** 130   **Vol. 3:** 128

3:10 f   **Vol. 3:** 724

3:10   **Vol. 1:** 697   **Vol. 2:** 770–771, 775   **Vol. 3:** 771, 935

3:11   **Vol. 2:** 806   **Vol. 3:** 203, 722

3:12   **Vol. 2:** 94, 480, 806   **Vol. 3:** 935

3:13   **Vol. 1:** 565   **Vol. 2:** 130, 459–460, 558

3:14 ff   **Vol. 3:** 491

3.14 f   **Vol. 3:** 215, 1033

3:14   **Vol. 1:** 486   **Vol. 3:** 224–225, 935

3:15   **Vol. 1:** 159, 284   **Vol. 2:** 235   **Vol. 3:** 487, 493, 1212

3:16 f   **Vol. 3:** 492

3:16   **Vol. 2:** 141–142   **Vol. 3:** 327, 329, 352, 363, 365, 401, 490–491, 708, 771, 779

3:17   **Vol. 3:** 350

4:1   **Vol. 1:** 327   **Vol. 2:** 365, 387   **Vol. 3:** 61, 1042, 1044

4:2   **Vol. 1:** 572   **Vol. 2:** 141, 770   **Vol. 3:** 770, 838

4:3 f   **Vol. 2:** 171, 718

4:3   **Vol. 2:** 170, 766   **Vol. 3:** 61, 768, 770, 839, 887

4:4   **Vol. 2:** 645   **Vol. 3:** 887, 903

4:5   **Vol. 1:** 514–515, 647, 735   **Vol. 2:** 114   **Vol. 3:** 546, 548, 1149

4:6 ff   **Vol. 3:** 203

4:6-†   **Vol. 1:** 648   **Vol. 2:** 855

4:7 f   **Vol. 1:** 441   **Vol. 3:** 365

4:7   **Vol. 1:** 647   **Vol. 2:** 62, 104, 133   **Vol. 3:** 947

2 Timothy *(cont'd)*

4:8   **Vol. 1:** 406   **Vol. 2:** 365, 894   **Vol. 3:** 252, 319, 362–363
4:9   **Vol. 3:** 1169
4:10   **Vol. 2:** 543
4:11   **Vol. 3:** 546, 749
4:14   **Vol. 3:** 136, 1200
4:15   **Vol. 2:** 135
4:16   **Vol. 2:** 874–875   **Vol. 3:** 824–825
4:17 f   **Vol. 3:** 203
4:17   **Vol. 1:** 118, 474, 735   **Vol. 2:** 604   **Vol. 3:** 52–53
4:18   **Vol. 1:** 566   **Vol. 2:** 46, 196, 387   **Vol. 3:** 203, 215, 1176
4:19   **Vol. 2:** 248, 250   **Vol. 3:** 1065
4:21   **Vol. 3:** 1169
4:22   **Vol. 3:** 693

Titus

1:1–3   **Vol. 2:** 171
1:1   **Vol. 1:** 130, 542   **Vol. 2:** 94, 405   **Vol. 3:** 613
1:2 f   **Vol. 2:** 481
1:2   **Vol. 2:** 77, 242, 472   **Vol. 3:** 71, 73, 832, 844, 1193
1:3   **Vol. 2:** 78   **Vol. 3:** 52–53, 198, 220, 323, 839, 1211
1:4   **Vol. 1:** 286, 619   **Vol. 2:** 138, 597, 780
1:5–9   **Vol. 3:** 929
1:5   **Vol. 1:** 199–200, 472   **Vol. 3:** 251, 253
1:6 ff   **Vol. 3:** 930
1:6 f   **Vol. 2:** 140   **Vol. 3:** 924
1:6   **Vol. 1:** 83, 286, 496   **Vol. 2:** 563, 581
1:7†   **Vol. 1:** 110, 191–192, 199, 514   **Vol. 2:** 255   **Vol. 3:** 137, 564
1:8   **Vol. 1:** 496, 502   **Vol. 2:** 550   **Vol. 3:** 362, 365
1:9   **Vol. 2:** 141, 170, 718   **Vol. 3:** 61, 604, 770
1:10   **Vol. 1:** 309, 552
1:11   **Vol. 3:** 137, 765
1:12   **Vol. 1:** 114, 564   **Vol. 3:** 81, 887
1:13   **Vol. 1:** 604   **Vol. 2:** 141, 170   **Vol. 3:** 61, 887
1:14 ff   **Vol. 3:** 1119
1:14   **Vol. 1:** 336   **Vol. 2:** 310
1:15   **Vol. 1:** 351–352, 448   **Vol. 3:** 107, 127
1:16   **Vol. 1:** 347, 496, 593   **Vol. 3:** 197, 808, 1151
2:1   **Vol. 2:** 170, 669   **Vol. 3:** 770
2:2 ff   **Vol. 3:** 930
2:2–10   **Vol. 3:** 929
2:2 f   **Vol. 1:** 197
2:2   **Vol. 1:** 502, 515, 604   **Vol. 2:** 95, 170–171, 775
2:3 ff   **Vol. 3:** 1065
2:3–5   **Vol. 3:** 112
2:3   **Vol. 2:** 235   **Vol. 3:** 470, 768, 922
2:4 f   **Vol. 3:** 1063

2:4   **Vol. 2:** 549–550, 675
2:5   **Vol. 1:** 502   **Vol. 3:** 101, 342–343
2:6   **Vol. 1:** 502   **Vol. 2:** 675
2:7   **Vol. 2:** 95, 104   **Vol. 3:** 771, 905, 1151
2:8   **Vol. 1:** 564   **Vol. 2:** 170
2:9 f   **Vol. 3:** 582
2:9   **Vol. 2:** 509, 816   **Vol. 3:** 596
2:10   **Vol. 1:** 524   **Vol. 3:** 220, 771
2:11–13   **Vol. 3:** 779
2:11   **Vol. 2:** 78, 122   **Vol. 3:** 220–221, 312, 319
2:12 ff   **Vol. 1:** 457
2:12   **Vol. 1:** 186, 524   **Vol. 2:** 94   **Vol. 3:** 363, 365
2:13 f   **Vol. 3:** 779
2:13   **Vol. 1:** 217   **Vol. 2:** 46, 76, 78, 81–82, 241, 245, 725   **Vol. 3:** 220, 319
2:14   **Vol. 2:** 104, 447, 800, 839   **Vol. 3:** 200, 1151, 1167, 1197
2:15   **Vol. 1:** 462   **Vol. 2:** 141
3:1   **Vol. 1:** 166, 593   **Vol. 2:** 608   **Vol. 3:** 97, 118, 197, 243
3:2   **Vol. 1:** 646   **Vol. 2:** 258
3:3 ff   **Vol. 1:** 459
3:3   **Vol. 1:** 185, 457, 460, 556–557, 593   **Vol. 2:** 459–460   **Vol. 3:** 31, 596, 929, 1193
3:4   **Vol. 1:** 185   **Vol. 2:** 78–79, 106, 550   **Vol. 3:** 220–221, 312, 319
3:5 f   **Vol. 2:** 122   **Vol. 3:** 220
3:5–7   **Vol. 1:** 154, 158   **Vol. 2:** 786
3:5   **Vol. 1:** 147–148, 153, 158, 184–186, 290   **Vol. 2:** 597, 672–673   **Vol. 3:** 215, 363, 365, 705
3:6   **Vol. 2:** 785, 843, 855   **Vol. 3:** 1194
3:7 f   **Vol. 1:** 441
3:7   **Vol. 2:** 122, 242, 300–301   **Vol. 3:** 220, 365, 832
3:8   **Vol. 1:** 197, 277   **Vol. 2:** 73, 104   **Vol. 3:** 765, 1017, 1151, 1211, 1214
3:9   **Vol. 2:** 36, 447, 645   **Vol. 3:** 532, 963, 1119
3:10   **Vol. 1:** 535, 568–569   **Vol. 2:** 858–859
3:11   **Vol. 2:** 365
3:12   **Vol. 2:** 364   **Vol. 3:** 1169
3:13   **Vol. 2:** 447   **Vol. 3:** 251, 253, 480, 1169
3:14   **Vol. 1:** 197, 723   **Vol. 2:** 104, 645   **Vol. 3:** 958, 1151, 1187
3:15   **Vol. 2:** 549

Philemon

1   **Vol. 1:** 192
2   **Vol. 1:** 301   **Vol. 2:** 250, 816
3   **Vol. 2:** 516, 780, 874
3   **Vol. 2:** 416
4 ff   **Vol. 2:** 874–875
4 f   **Vol. 3:** 818
4   **Vol. 2:** 73, 874   **Vol. 3:** 246

Philemon *(cont'd)*

5	**Vol. 3:** 1174, 1176, 1185, 1211
6	**Vol. 1:** 643 **Vol. 2:** 403, 874
7	**Vol. 2:** 567, 600 **Vol. 3:** 256
8	**Vol. 2:** 736
9	**Vol. 1:** 197 **Vol. 3:** 170, 592
10	**Vol. 1:** 180, 619 **Vol. 3:** 1070
11	**Vol. 2:** 434
12	**Vol. 2:** 567, 600
13	**Vol. 1:** 398 **Vol. 3:** 1017, 1174, 1196, 1204
14	**Vol. 2:** 663
15	**Vol. 2:** 179 **Vol. 3:** 534, 832, 848, 1184
16	**Vol. 3:** 583
17	**Vol. 1:** 642 **Vol. 3:** 930
18	**Vol. 3:** 575, 930
19	**Vol. 1:** 247 **Vol. 3:** 489
20	**Vol. 2:** 434, 600 **Vol. 3:** 256
21	**Vol. 1:** 592 **Vol. 3:** 1155
22	**Vol. 1:** 690 **Vol. 2:** 116, 122, 874
23 f	**Vol. 2:** 331
23	**Vol. 3:** 591, 601
25	**Vol. 2:** 516 **Vol. 3:** 693

Hebrews

1:1 ff	**Vol. 2:** 75
1:1–4	**Vol. 3:** 1113
1:1 f	**Vol. 3:** 216, 312
1:1	**Vol. 1:** 576, 619 **Vol. 2:** 675, 714 **Vol. 3:** 82
1:2 ff	**Vol. 2:** 81
1:2 f	**Vol. 3:** 647
1:2	**Vol. 1:** 63, 384, 477, 576 **Vol. 2:** 57–58, 289, 301, 514 **Vol. 3:** 326, 647, 829–831, 1118, 1174, 1191
1:3–4	**Vol. 3:** 588
1:3	**Vol. 1:** 123, 549, 712–713 **Vol. 2:** 64, 147, 195, 199, 288–290, 426, 515 **Vol. 3:** 107, 287, 298, 588, 674, 1010, 1154, 1186
1:4–14	**Vol. 1:** 102
1:4 f	**Vol. 2:** 654
1:4	**Vol. 1:** 123, 659 **Vol. 2:** 301
1:5 ff	**Vol. 1:** 123 **Vol. 3:** 1113
1:5–2:18	**Vol. 3:** 433
1:5–14	**Vol. 3:** 40
1:5	**Vol. 1:** 177–179, 668 **Vol. 2:** 622 **Vol. 3:** 641, 647
1:6	**Vol. 1:** 519, 668
1:7	**Vol. 3:** 553, 695, 1204
1:8 f	**Vol. 3:** 553
1:8	**Vol. 1:** 123, 164, 408 **Vol. 3:** 365, 647, 830
1:9	**Vol. 1:** 122–123, 556 **Vol. 2:** 204, 354, 448, 712 **Vol. 3:** 365, 575, 1061
1:10	**Vol. 1:** 384 **Vol. 2:** 149 **Vol. 3:** 1148
1:11 f	**Vol. 1:** 384
1:11	**Vol. 1:** 316–317, 464
1:12	**Vol. 3:** 167

1:13	**Vol. 1:** 177, 239, 477, 554 **Vol. 2:** 147, 204, 515 **Vol. 3:** 298
1:14	**Vol. 1:** 326 **Vol. 2:** 300 **Vol. 3:** 216, 546, 553, 695
2:1	**Vol. 1:** 683, 731
2:2 f	**Vol. 1:** 658
2:2	**Vol. 1:** 103, 659 **Vol. 2:** 175 **Vol. 3:** 585, 1113, 1180
2:3 ff	**Vol. 2:** 632
2:3 f	**Vol. 3:** 216
2:3	**Vol. 1:** 299, 659 **Vol. 2:** 176 **Vol. 3:** 1113
2:4	**Vol. 1:** 659 **Vol. 2:** 629, 785 **Vol. 3:** 705, 1023
2:5 ff	**Vol. 3:** 632
2:5	**Vol. 1:** 326, 519
2:6 ff	**Vol. 3:** 632
2:6	**Vol. 1:** 190–191, 289
2:7–19	**Vol. 3:** 143
2:7	**Vol. 1:** 406 **Vol. 2:** 204
2:8	**Vol. 1:** 239 **Vol. 3:** 632, 839
2:9 f	**Vol. 1:** 437 **Vol. 3:** 722–723
2:9	**Vol. 1:** 123, 406 **Vol. 2:** 123, 270–271 **Vol. 3:** 515, 723, 1178
2:10	**Vol. 1:** 168, 669 **Vol. 2:** 46–47, 63, 669 **Vol. 3:** 63, 215, 725, 941, 1177, 1183
2:11 f	**Vol. 1:** 256
2:11	**Vol. 1:** 669 **Vol. 2:** 138, 230, 722 **Vol. 3:** 563
2:12	**Vol. 1:** 304, 396 **Vol. 2:** 82, 722 **Vol. 3:** 48, 669–670, 675
2:13	**Vol. 1:** 284, 592
2:14–18	**Vol. 1:** 396
2:14 f	**Vol. 1:** 222, 437–438 **Vol. 2:** 271 **Vol. 3:** 174
2:14	**Vol. 1:** 73, 284, 436–437, 677 **Vol. 2:** 207, 525 **Vol. 3:** 471, 718
2:15	**Vol. 1:** 435, 437, 622–623 **Vol. 2:** 143 **Vol. 3:** 167, 174, 596–597
2:16	**Vol. 1:** 80 **Vol. 3:** 750
2:17	**Vol. 1:** 256 **Vol. 2:** 505, 598, 668, 800 **Vol. 3:** 41, 161
2:18	**Vol. 1:** 63, 724, 801, 804, 1175
3 f	**Vol. 3:** 1007
3	**Vol. 2:** 719 **Vol. 3:** 434
3:1 ff	**Vol. 3:** 433
3:1–4:16	**Vol. 2:** 718
3:1–6	**Vol. 2:** 249, 447 **Vol. 3:** 1007
3:1	**Vol. 1:** 130, 276, 346 **Vol. 2:** 194, 230 **Vol. 3:** 40, 61, 129, 397
3:2 ff	**Vol. 2:** 642
3:2	**Vol. 2:** 248
3:3 f	**Vol. 3:** 120
3:4–6	**Vol. 3:** 198
3:4	**Vol. 1:** 383 **Vol. 2:** 74 **Vol. 3:** 1148
3:5	**Vol. 2:** 164, 248 **Vol. 3:** 198
3:6	**Vol. 1:** 660, 712 **Vol. 2:** 243, 736 **Vol. 3:** 647, 794
3:6b	**Vol. 2:** 249

Hebrews (*cont'd*)

3:7 ff   **Vol. 3:** 954
3:7–4:14   **Vol. 1:** 299
3:7–4:13   **Vol. 3:** 433
3:7–19   **Vol. 1:** 372
3:7–11   **Vol. 2:** 178, 775
3:7   **Vol. 1:** 372   **Vol. 3:** 705, 838
3:8 f   **Vol. 3:** 802
3:8   **Vol. 1:** 203, 473   **Vol. 2:** 155   **Vol. 3:** 1007–1008
3:9   **Vol. 2:** 696   **Vol. 3:** 1148
3:10   **Vol. 2:** 459–460   **Vol. 3:** 940
3:11   **Vol. 1:** 321, 327   **Vol. 3:** 257, 742
3:12 f   **Vol. 3:** 838
3:12   **Vol. 1:** 607–608   **Vol. 2:** 183   **Vol. 3:** 325, 434, 586
3:13   **Vol. 2:** 155, 459–460, 568
3:14   **Vol. 1:** 165, 326, 396, 608, 639, 660, 712   **Vol. 2:** 64
3:15 ff   **Vol. 3:** 227
3:15   **Vol. 1:** 203, 372   **Vol. 2:** 155, 775   **Vol. 3:** 838
3:16   **Vol. 1:** 203, 532   **Vol. 2:** 642
3:17   **Vol. 1:** 610–611   **Vol. 2:** 696   **Vol. 3:** 1007–1008
3:18   **Vol. 1:** 321, 327, 593   **Vol. 3:** 257, 742
4   **Vol. 2:** 719   **Vol. 3:** 434
4:1 ff   **Vol. 3:** 257
4:1–13   **Vol. 1:** 372   **Vol. 3:** 143, 227
4:1–9   **Vol. 3:** 73
4:1   **Vol. 3:** 257, 954, 1113
4:2   **Vol. 2:** 175   **Vol. 3:** 73, 215, 954
4:3 ff   **Vol. 1:** 327
4:3–11   **Vol. 2:** 178, 775
4:3   **Vol. 1:** 375, 378   **Vol. 3:** 257, 742
4:4   **Vol. 2:** 690   **Vol. 3:** 257, 457
4:5   **Vol. 3:** 257
4:6   **Vol. 1:** 593
4:7   **Vol. 1:** 372, 427, 473   **Vol. 2:** 155   **Vol. 3:** 838
4:8   **Vol. 2:** 331   **Vol. 3:** 257
4:9–11   **Vol. 3:** 742
4:9   **Vol. 1:** 372   **Vol. 2:** 800   **Vol. 3:** 74, 410
4:10 f   **Vol. 3:** 257
4:11   **Vol. 1:** 593, 611   **Vol. 2:** 291   **Vol. 3:** 905, 1113, 1169
4:12   **Vol. 1:** 63, 106, 241   **Vol. 2:** 365, 686   **Vol. 3:** 128, 684, 693, 724, 967, 1113, 1152
4:13   **Vol. 1:** 313, 386   **Vol. 3:** 516, 1204
4:14–7:21   **Vol. 3:** 433
4:14–5:10   **Vol. 2:** 447
4:14 f   **Vol. 1:** 396
4:14   **Vol. 1:** 321, 346, 637   **Vol. 2:** 195   **Vol. 3:** 61, 647, 717
4:15 f   **Vol. 2:** 614
4:15   **Vol. 2:** 504–505, 598   **Vol. 3:** 41, 63, 582, 663, 722, 724, 801, 804, 995

4:16   **Vol. 1:** 322   **Vol. 2:** 598, 614, 736   **Vol. 3:** 41, 530, 748
5:1 ff   **Vol. 2:** 42
5:1   **Vol. 1:** 472   **Vol. 2:** 41   **Vol. 3:** 41, 433, 1174, 1197, 1203
5:2   **Vol. 2:** 407, 459–460   **Vol. 3:** 41
5:3   **Vol. 2:** 668, 799   **Vol. 3:** 41, 1174, 1203
5:4 f   **Vol. 2:** 47
5:4   **Vol. 2:** 50   **Vol. 3:** 41
5:5   **Vol. 1:** 178–179   **Vol. 2:** 204
5:6   **Vol. 2:** 591   **Vol. 3:** 41, 830
5:7 ff   **Vol. 3:** 41
5:7–10   **Vol. 1:** 396
5:7–9   **Vol. 3:** 432
5:7 f   **Vol. 2:** 64, 178   **Vol. 3:** 582
5:7   **Vol. 1:** 646, 677, 679   **Vol. 2:** 91, 178, 861   **Vol. 3:** 63, 211, 323, 713, 1171, 1180–1181
5:8   **Vol. 1:** 223, 487   **Vol. 2:** 91, 289   **Vol. 3:** 647, 724
5:9 f   **Vol. 1:** 123   **Vol. 2:** 178
5:9   **Vol. 2:** 63, 138   **Vol. 3:** 215–216
5:10   **Vol. 1:** 168   **Vol. 2:** 591   **Vol. 3:** 42
5:11–6:19   **Vol. 2:** 591
5:11   **Vol. 3:** 1106, 1180
5:12 f   **Vol. 3:** 844
5:12   **Vol. 1:** 166   **Vol. 2:** 64, 452   **Vol. 3:** 765, 768, 1106, 1118
5:13 f   **Vol. 1:** 282
5:13   **Vol. 3:** 365
5:14   **Vol. 1:** 313, 504   **Vol. 2:** 64, 391
6:1 ff   **Vol. 2:** 452   **Vol. 3:** 765
6:1–20   **Vol. 2:** 718
6:1–12   **Vol. 1:** 299
6:1–8   **Vol. 3:** 227
6:1 f   **Vol. 3:** 216
6:1   **Vol. 1:** 166, 446, 599, 662, 702   **Vol. 2:** 64, 73   **Vol. 3:** 1212, 1214
6:2   **Vol. 1:** 146, 149   **Vol. 2:** 152, 365   **Vol. 3:** 61, 99, 277, 830
6:4 ff   **Vol. 2:** 156, 270, 487, 717–718   **Vol. 3:** 582, 705, 750, 809
6:4–10   **Vol. 1:** 417
6:4–8   **Vol. 1:** 359, 372   **Vol. 3:** 143, 434, 1206
6:4   **Vol. 1:** 639, 703   **Vol. 2:** 41, 194, 606   **Vol. 3:** 990
6:5   **Vol. 1:** 187, 327   **Vol. 2:** 632, 785   **Vol. 3:** 830, 832
6:6   **Vol. 1:** 394, 397, 608, 702   **Vol. 2:** 291   **Vol. 3:** 586, 647, 1187
6:7 f   **Vol. 1:** 214
6:7   **Vol. 2:** 211   **Vol. 3:** 750, 1004
6:8   **Vol. 1:** 359, 416, 726   **Vol. 2:** 64   **Vol. 3:** 808–809
6:9–15   **Vol. 2:** 769
6:9   **Vol. 1:** 591   **Vol. 3:** 216
6:10   **Vol. 3:** 546
6:11 f   **Vol. 2:** 771   **Vol. 3:** 74
6:11   **Vol. 1:** 457, 492   **Vol. 2:** 64   **Vol. 3:** 1169

Hebrews *(cont'd)*

6:12 ff **Vol. 3:** 73
6:12 **Vol. 1:** 215, 491–492, 712 **Vol. 2:** 300–301
6:13 ff **Vol. 3:** 366
6:13 **Vol. 1:** 80 **Vol. 3:** 74, 742
6:14 **Vol. 1:** 214, 732 **Vol. 3:** 73
6:15 **Vol. 1:** 215 **Vol. 2:** 771 **Vol. 3:** 73
6:16 ff **Vol. 1:** 659
6:16 f **Vol. 3:** 742
6:16 **Vol. 1:** 658, 660
6:17 **Vol. 1:** 374–375, 731 **Vol. 2:** 300–301, 686 **Vol. 3:** 1017–1018
6:18 f **Vol. 2:** 244
6:18 **Vol. 1:** 571 **Vol. 2:** 77, 301, 472, 606 **Vol. 3:** 713, 717, 1158, 1180
6:19–20 **Vol. 3:** 543
6:19 **Vol. 1:** 372, 658, 660 **Vol. 3:** 684, 794–795
6:20 **Vol. 1:** 168 **Vol. 2:** 301 **Vol. 3:** 795, 830, 941, 947
7–10 **Vol. 3:** 366
7 **Vol. 2:** 693 **Vol. 3:** 228
7:1 ff **Vol. 2:** 378 **Vol. 3:** 41, 1113
7:1–10 **Vol. 2:** 447, 591, 694
7:1–7 **Vol. 1:** 214
7:1–3 **Vol. 2:** 591
7:1 **Vol. 1:** 325 **Vol. 2:** 74, 591 **Vol. 3:** 163, 435
7:2 **Vol. 1:** 49, 80, 581 **Vol. 2:** 59, 694, 781 **Vol. 3:** 365, 448, 854, 1174
7:2b **Vol. 2:** 591, 694
7:3 **Vol. 1:** 166, 616, 619 **Vol. 2:** 36, 64, 480, 505, 591, 694 **Vol. 3:** 41, 647
7:3b **Vol. 2:** 592
7:3c **Vol. 2:** 592
7:4 ff **Vol. 1:** 80
7:4–10 **Vol. 2:** 592, 694
7:4–7 **Vol. 2:** 694
7:4 **Vol. 1:** 65 **Vol. 2:** 694 **Vol. 3:** 1174
7:5 ff **Vol. 3:** 41
7:5 **Vol. 1:** 240, 337 **Vol. 2:** 447, 467, 592, 693 **Vol. 3:** 854
7:6–8 **Vol. 2:** 447
7:6 **Vol. 2:** 36, 592, 694 **Vol. 3:** 73
7:7 **Vol. 2:** 592
7:8 **Vol. 2:** 592, 694
7:9–10 **Vol. 2:** 694
7:9 **Vol. 2:** 467
7:10 **Vol. 1:** 240, 325
7:11–28 **Vol. 2:** 591–592
7:11 **Vol. 2:** 64, 448, 467 **Vol. 3:** 41, 275, 585
7:12 **Vol. 2:** 320, 447, 663
7:13 ff **Vol. 2:** 447
7:13 f **Vol. 1:** 619 **Vol. 3:** 872
7:13 **Vol. 3:** 435–436
7:14 **Vol. 2:** 320, 642 **Vol. 3:** 397, 435

7:15 **Vol. 1:** 731 **Vol. 2:** 447, 505 **Vol. 3:** 275
7:16 **Vol. 1:** 337, 677 **Vol. 2:** 207, 447, 505, 592 **Vol. 3:** 41, 189
7:17 **Vol. 3:** 830
7:18 f **Vol. 3:** 41–42
7:18 **Vol. 1:** 337 **Vol. 2:** 447 **Vol. 3:** 995
7:19 **Vol. 2:** 55, 64, 447, 448 **Vol. 3:** 1113
7:20 ff **Vol. 1:** 375
7:20–22 **Vol. 3:** 742
7:20 f **Vol. 3:** 41, 738
7:21 **Vol. 1:** 356 **Vol. 3:** 830
7:22 **Vol. 1:** 371–372, 375
7:23 f **Vol. 3:** 228
7:23 **Vol. 2:** 222 **Vol. 3:** 41
7:24 **Vol. 2:** 592 **Vol. 3:** 41, 225, 584–585, 830
7:25–27 **Vol. 3:** 582
7:25 **Vol. 1:** 90 **Vol. 2:** 294, 592, 882 **Vol. 3:** 41, 62, 215, 612
7:26–28 **Vol. 2:** 42
7:26 **Vol. 1:** 563 **Vol. 2:** 195, 199, 238, 669 **Vol. 3:** 41, 534, 663, 925, 1010
7:27 f **Vol. 2:** 717
7:27 **Vol. 1:** 372, 448 **Vol. 2:** 717, 799, 895 **Vol. 3:** 41, 162, 433, 723, 1154, 1196–1197
7:28 **Vol. 2:** 63, 65, 592 **Vol. 3:** 41, 647, 738, 830, 995, 1113
7:28b **Vol. 2:** 447
8–9 **Vol. 3:** 814
8:1–2 **Vol. 2:** 195 **Vol. 3:** 814
8:1 **Vol. 1:** 637 **Vol. 2:** 81, 147, 157, 193, 195, 426 **Vol. 3:** 298, 435
8:2 **Vol. 2:** 230 **Vol. 3:** 42, 552, 811, 888–889
8:3 f **Vol. 2:** 41–42
8:3 **Vol. 1:** 472 **Vol. 3:** 41, 433
8:4 f **Vol. 1:** 518 **Vol. 2:** 447
8:5 **Vol. 1:** 326, 371 **Vol. 2:** 194, 291, 642, 804 **Vol. 3:** 42, 550, 555–556, 569, 814, 905
8:5b **Vol. 2:** 447
8:6 ff **Vol. 3:** 42
8:6–13 **Vol. 1:** 154 **Vol. 3:** 227
8:6 **Vol. 1:** 371–372, 374–375, 666 **Vol. 2:** 447–448, 671 **Vol. 3:** 73, 552
8:7–13 **Vol. 3:** 433
8:7 **Vol. 1:** 666 **Vol. 2:** 139, 145, 671 **Vol. 3:** 531
8:8 ff **Vol. 2:** 316
8:8–12 **Vol. 1:** 256, 371 **Vol. 2:** 145 **Vol. 3:** 74
8:8 **Vol. 1:** 666 **Vol. 2:** 139, 144–145, 248, 315, 320, 671
8:9 f **Vol. 2:** 156
8:9 **Vol. 1:** 532 **Vol. 2:** 145 **Vol. 3:** 227, 750

Hebrews *(cont'd)*

8:10   **Vol. 1:** 368 **Vol. 2:** 42, 248 **Vol. 3:** 127, 227, 490

8:11   **Vol. 2:** 428, 804 **Vol. 3:** 765

8:12   **Vol. 3:** 160, 241, 575–576

8:13   **Vol. 1:** 371, 666 **Vol. 2:** 447, 671, 675, 716

9–10   **Vol. 2:** 199

9   **Vol. 3:** 366

9:1–10:39 **Vol. 3:** 433

9:1–10   **Vol. 3:** 120

9:1–5   **Vol. 3:** 163

9:1   **Vol. 1:** 524 **Vol. 3:** 42, 365, 551

9:2–5   **Vol. 3:** 814

9:2–3   **Vol. 2:** 230 **Vol. 3:** 814

9:2   **Vol. 1:** 586, 666 **Vol. 2:** 487 **Vol. 3:** 120

9:4 f   **Vol. 3:** 787

9:4   **Vol. 1:** 252–253, 408 **Vol. 2:** 294

9:5   **Vol. 1:** 280, 371 **Vol. 2:** 304, 614 **Vol. 3:** 163–164

9:5a   **Vol. 3:** 163

9:6–8   **Vol. 3:** 814

9:6   **Vol. 1:** 666 **Vol. 3:** 120, 551

9:7   **Vol. 1:** 222 **Vol. 2:** 406, 717, 724 **Vol. 3:** 41

9:8 ff   **Vol. 3:** 832

9:8   **Vol. 1:** 666 **Vol. 3:** 317, 323, 543, 705, 941

9:9   **Vol. 1:** 351–352 **Vol. 2:** 41, 63, 746, 804 **Vol. 3:** 433, 550, 555, 831

9:10   **Vol. 1:** 146, 149, 677 **Vol. 2:** 268 **Vol. 3:** 351, 365, 831

9:11 ff   **Vol. 3:** 166, 336

9:11 f   **Vol. 3:** 199, 1177

9:11   **Vol. 1:** 327, 386 **Vol. 2:** 64, 102, 150, 195 **Vol. 3:** 42, 317, 814–815, 1178

9:12 ff   **Vol. 1:** 223

9:12 f   **Vol. 1:** 114, 222

9:12   **Vol. 1:** 116, 372 **Vol. 2:** 230, 717–718 **Vol. 3:** 63, 162, 198, 200, 529, 723, 812

9:13 ff   **Vol. 1:** 225, 371

9:13–14   **Vol. 1:** 224, 677 **Vol. 3:** 41, 107

9:13   **Vol. 1:** 115–116, 448

9:14   **Vol. 1:** 116, 223, 351–352, 355, 446 **Vol. 2:** 718 **Vol. 3:** 41, 199–200, 432, 435, 550, 705, 925

9:15 f   **Vol. 3:** 323

9:15   **Vol. 1:** 276, 371, 374–375, 659 **Vol. 2:** 80, 300, 671 **Vol. 3:** 73, 199, 584–585

9:16 f   **Vol. 1:** 371

9:16   **Vol. 1:** 369 **Vol. 2:** 663

9:17   **Vol. 1:** 659 **Vol. 3:** 713

9:18 ff   **Vol. 1:** 224–225

9:18–22   **Vol. 1:** 222

9:18   **Vol. 2:** 673 **Vol. 3:** 366

9:19 ff   **Vol. 1:** 222 **Vol. 2:** 447

9:19 f   **Vol. 1:** 337

9:19   **Vol. 1:** 114, 116, 223, 244

9:20   **Vol. 2:** 533

9:21   **Vol. 3:** 552, 913

9:22   **Vol. 1:** 222, 701–702 **Vol. 2:** 854 **Vol. 3:** 41, 107, 199–200

9:23–28 **Vol. 1:** 115

9:23 f   **Vol. 2:** 194–195

9:23   **Vol. 2:** 291, 663 **Vol. 3:** 433

9:24 ff   **Vol. 2:** 447

9:24 f   **Vol. 3:** 794

9:24   **Vol. 1:** 587 **Vol. 2:** 80, 150, 199, 230, 489 **Vol. 3:** 42, 63, 814, 888–889, 905

9:25 ff   **Vol. 2:** 42

9:25 f   **Vol. 2:** 664 **Vol. 3:** 199, 433

9:25   **Vol. 1:** 222, 685 **Vol. 2:** 742 **Vol. 3:** 1175

9:26 ff   **Vol. 2:** 717

9:26   **Vol. 1:** 325, 378 **Vol. 3:** 41, 162, 323, 829–832

9:27   **Vol. 2:** 366

9:28   **Vol. 1:** 96–97, 438 **Vol. 2:** 194 **Vol. 3:** 199, 215. 612

10   **Vol. 3:** 366, 905

10:1 ff   **Vol. 3:** 41, 588

10:1–4   **Vol. 3:** 107

10:1   **Vol. 1:** 115, 327, 371 **Vol. 2:** 63, 102, 288, 447, 804 **Vol. 3:** 41, 63, 433, 555–556, 905, 1158

10:1c   **Vol. 2:** 448

10:2 f   **Vol. 2:** 717

10:2   **Vol. 1:** 351–352 **Vol. 2:** 315, 717 **Vol. 3:** 550

10:2b   **Vol. 2:** 447

10:3   **Vol. 2:** 717 **Vol. 3:** 243, 245

10:4–10   **Vol. 3:** 582

10:4   **Vol. 1:** 114–116, 222, 225 **Vol. 2:** 606

10:5 ff   **Vol. 3:** 41–42, 434, 1023

10:5–10   **Vol. 3:** 432–433, 1023

10:5–9   **Vol. 3:** 63

10:5   **Vol. 1:** 234 **Vol. 3:** 350, 1023

10:6   **Vol. 2:** 818 **Vol. 3:** 431, 1203

10:7   **Vol. 2:** 157 **Vol. 3:** 1023

10:8   **Vol. 2:** 448, 818 **Vol. 3:** 431, 434, 1023, 1203

10:9 f   **Vol. 3:** 1023

10:9a   **Vol. 2:** 448

10:9b   **Vol. 2:** 447

10:10 ff   **Vol. 2:** 42

10:10   **Vol. 1:** 234, 372 **Vol. 2:** 230, 448, 717 **Vol. 3:** 434, 552, 1023

10:11–13   **Vol. 3:** 588

10:11 f   **Vol. 3:** 433

10:11   **Vol. 2:** 895 **Vol. 3:** 552

10:12 ff   **Vol. 1:** 371

10:12 f   **Vol. 2:** 80, 515

10:12   **Vol. 2:** 147, 204, 717–718, 720 **Vol. 3:** 162, 298

10:13   **Vol. 1:** 239, 477, 554 **Vol. 2:** 245 **Vol. 3:** 252

10:14–18 **Vol. 3:** 227

Hebrews *(cont'd)*

10:14	**Vol. 2:** 64, 230, 717, 720 **Vol. 3:** 433
10:15 ff	**Vol. 3:** 433
10:15–18	**Vol. 1:** 154
10:15 f	**Vol. 2:** 786
10:15	**Vol. 3:** 705
10:16 ff	**Vol. 1:** 371 **Vol. 2:** 316
10:16 f	**Vol. 1:** 371 **Vol. 3:** 42, 74
10:16	**Vol. 3:** 127, 490
10:17	**Vol. 2:** 448 **Vol. 3:** 241
10:18	**Vol. 2:** 448, 736 **Vol. 3:** 42, 433, 582, 1203
10:19 ff	**Vol. 2:** 505 **Vol. 3:** 41
10:19–25	**Vol. 2:** 718, 881
10:19–22	**Vol. 3:** 366
10:19–20	**Vol. 3:** 543, 941
10:19	**Vol. 1:** 223 **Vol. 2:** 230 **Vol. 3:** 41, 166, 366, 812, 832, 940
10:20	**Vol. 1:** 677 **Vol. 2:** 673, 675 **Vol. 3:** 63, 795, 1180
10:21	**Vol. 1:** 637 **Vol. 3:** 794
10:22	**Vol. 1:** 152, 154, 157–158, 223–225, 322, 351–352 **Vol. 2:** 183 **Vol. 3:** 38, 41, 107, 888–889, 941, 990
10:23	**Vol. 1:** 346 **Vol. 2:** 244 **Vol. 3:** 61, 74
10:24	**Vol. 1:** 110 **Vol. 3:** 129
10:25 ff	**Vol. 3:** 434
10:25	**Vol. 1:** 713 **Vol. 2:** 55, 438 **Vol. 3:** 74, 143
10:26 ff	**Vol. 1:** 372
10:26–39	**Vol. 1:** 299 **Vol. 2:** 718
10:26–31	**Vol. 3:** 1206
10:26–30	**Vol. 3:** 136
10:26 f	**Vol. 1:** 359, 703 **Vol. 3:** 582
10:26	**Vol. 2:** 405 **Vol. 3:** 28, 434, 586, 888, 1203
10:27 f	**Vol. 2:** 244
10:27	**Vol. 1:** 326, 623 **Vol. 2:** 366
10:28 f	**Vol. 2:** 598
10:28	**Vol. 1:** 74 **Vol. 2:** 686 **Vol. 3:** 1043
10:29 f	**Vol. 2:** 230
10:29	**Vol. 1:** 223, 371, 448 **Vol. 2:** 123, 533, 786 **Vol. 3:** 28, 166, 434, 647, 705, 944
10:30	**Vol. 1:** 111 **Vol. 2:** 158, 365, 800 **Vol. 3:** 97
10:31	**Vol. 1:** 609, 611, 623 **Vol. 2:** 149
10:32	**Vol. 1:** 646 **Vol. 2:** 495, 775 **Vol. 3:** 240, 722–723, 725
10:33	**Vol. 1:** 644 **Vol. 3:** 340, 521, 934
10:34	**Vol. 2:** 361, 775, 845, 847 **Vol. 3:** 225, 604, 722, 724
10:35 ff	**Vol. 3:** 143
10:35	**Vol. 2:** 736 **Vol. 3:** 74, 143
10:36	**Vol. 2:** 300, 361, 775 **Vol. 3:** 1023
10:37 f	**Vol. 1:** 604 **Vol. 3:** 366
10:37	**Vol. 2:** 429 **Vol. 3:** 74, 843
10:38 f	**Vol. 1:** 372
10:38†	**Vol. 2:** 818 **Vol. 3:** 362, 365, 685
10:39	**Vol. 2:** 775, 839 **Vol. 3:** 685
11	**Vol. 1:** 714 **Vol. 2:** 835 **Vol. 3:** 367, 433, 582, 1047
11:1	**Vol. 1:** 604, 712–713 **Vol. 2:** 142, 243, 768 **Vol. 3:** 1158
11:2	**Vol. 1:** 198 **Vol. 3:** 1047
11:3	**Vol. 1:** 713 **Vol. 2:** 488, 768 **Vol. 3:** 128, 350, 829–831, 1187
11:4	**Vol. 2:** 41 **Vol. 3:** 365, 434, 436, 1047
11:5 f	**Vol. 2:** 817
11:5	**Vol. 2:** 627 **Vol. 3:** 264, 265, 325, 602, 1047
11:6	**Vol. 1:** 322 **Vol. 2:** 606 **Vol. 3:** 73, 143, 532
11:7	**Vol. 2:** 91, 300–301, 365, 682 **Vol. 3:** 120, 211, 365, 1181, 1188
11:8–12	**Vol. 1:** 80
11:8–10	**Vol. 3:** 1007
11:8	**Vol. 1:** 326, 461 **Vol. 2:** 180, 301
11:9–10	**Vol. 1:** 691 **Vol. 3:** 811
11:9	**Vol. 1:** 81, 460, 684 **Vol. 2:** 318 **Vol. 3:** 565, 815
11:10–16	**Vol. 3:** 73
11:10	**Vol. 1:** 279, 327, 387, 661, 690 **Vol. 2:** 245, 803
11:11	**Vol. 1:** 80, 92, 378 **Vol. 3:** 73, 1067
11:12	**Vol. 1:** 241, 445, 732 **Vol. 2:** 435 **Vol. 3:** 735
11:13	**Vol. 1:** 346, 460, 689–691 **Vol. 2:** 630, 790, 804 **Vol. 3:** 565, 815
11:14	**Vol. 1:** 460, 616 **Vol. 2:** 489 **Vol. 3:** 532
11:15 f	**Vol. 1:** 689
11:15	**Vol. 1:** 460 **Vol. 3:** 241
11:16	**Vol. 1:** 327, 460 **Vol. 2:** 73, 194, 725, 803, 847 **Vol. 3:** 563
11:17–19	**Vol. 1:** 80
11:17 18	**Vol. 1:** 81
11:17	**Vol. 1:** 461 **Vol. 2:** 76
11:18	**Vol. 3:** 523
11:19	**Vol. 2:** 604, 746 **Vol. 3:** 304, 824, 826
11:20	**Vol. 1:** 81, 214, 326
11:21	**Vol. 1:** 214, 408 **Vol. 2:** 318
11:22	**Vol. 1:** 337, 430 **Vol. 3:** 940
11:23 ff	**Vol. 2:** 642
11:23	**Vol. 1:** 284, 330, 623 **Vol. 2:** 216, 378 **Vol. 3:** 365
11:24–28	**Vol. 2:** 768
11:24–27	**Vol. 1:** 532
11:24	**Vol. 1:** 455 **Vol. 3:** 457
11:25 f	**Vol. 3:** 839, 1180
11:25	**Vol. 1:** 534 **Vol. 2:** 73
11:26	**Vol. 2:** 830, 835, 844 **Vol. 3:** 143, 340
11:27	**Vol. 1:** 623 **Vol. 2:** 77, 378, 768, 835
11:28	**Vol. 1:** 222–223, 465, 633 **Vol. 2:** 854
11:29	**Vol. 1:** 356, 516 **Vol. 3:** 802, 984
11:30	**Vol. 1:** 609 **Vol. 2:** 690 **Vol. 3:** 948
11:31	**Vol. 1:** 499, 593 **Vol. 3:** 1067
11:32	**Vol. 1:** 427, 576 **Vol. 3:** 843
11:33 f	**Vol. 3:** 365

Hebrews *(cont'd)*

11:33   **Vol. 1:** 118, 646   **Vol. 3:** 70, 951
11:34   **Vol. 1:** 559, 656, 685   **Vol. 2:**
742   **Vol. 3:** 109–110, 713, 961–962,
967
11:35 f   **Vol. 2:** 739
11:35   **Vol. 3:** 200, 277, 1067
11:36   **Vol. 1:** 163   **Vol. 2:** 136   **Vol. 3:** 802
11:37   **Vol. 1:** 114, 322   **Vol. 3:** 967
11:38   **Vol. 2:** 459   **Vol. 3:** 381, 1007
11:39   **Vol. 2:** 64   **Vol. 3:** 70, 73, 1047
11:40   **Vol. 2:** 64
12   **Vol. 1:** 400   **Vol. 2:** 775   **Vol. 3:** 1014
12:1 f   **Vol. 3:** 367
12:1–29   **Vol. 1:** 372   **Vol. 2:** 718
12:1–11   **Vol. 1:** 604
12:1–4   **Vol. 1:** 648   **Vol. 3:** 582
12:1   **Vol. 1:** 406, 712   **Vol. 2:** 775   **Vol. 3:**
73, 947, 1047, 1180
12:2 f   **Vol. 2:** 775
12:2   **Vol. 1:** 168, 394, 400, 461, 604   **Vol. 2:**
51, 60–61, 64, 147, 204, 331, 361, 505,
515, 775   **Vol. 3:** 298, 563, 941, 1180
12:3 ff   **Vol. 3:** 143
12:3 f   **Vol. 1:** 647
12:3   **Vol. 2:** 64, 775   **Vol. 3:** 189, 685
12:4 ff   **Vol. 3:** 998
12:4   **Vol. 1:** 222, 646   **Vol. 3:** 240
12:5–11   **Vol. 3:** 365
12:5 f   **Vol. 2:** 757   **Vol. 3:** 778
12:5   **Vol. 1:** 462, 571   **Vol. 2:** 142   **Vol. 3:**
189, 821
12:6   **Vol. 1:** 163, 639   **Vol. 2:** 549   **Vol. 3:**
778
12:7–11   **Vol. 3:** 778
12:7   **Vol. 2:** 775   **Vol. 3:** 647, 1187
12:8   **Vol. 1:** 188, 639
12:9   **Vol. 1:** 621   **Vol. 3:** 647, 695, 778
12:10   **Vol. 2:** 230   **Vol. 3:** 750, 778
12:11   **Vol. 1:** 313, 723   **Vol. 2:** 361, 780, 782,
899   **Vol. 3:** 363, 365, 778, 822, 954
12:12 ff   **Vol. 3:** 143
12:12–28   **Vol. 1:** 299
12:12   **Vol. 2:** 859
12:13   **Vol. 2:** 415   **Vol. 3:** 351, 903
12:14   **Vol. 2:** 230, 244, 782, 807
12:15 ff   **Vol. 2:** 123, 847   **Vol. 3:** 143
12:15   **Vol. 1:** 96–97, 191, 202, 448   **Vol. 2:**
782   **Vol. 3:** 868, 954
12:16 f   **Vol. 3:** 582
12:16   **Vol. 1:** 501   **Vol. 2:** 268, 318,
782   **Vol. 3:** 869, 1179
12:17   **Vol. 1:** 215, 359   **Vol. 2:** 300, 318,
361   **Vol. 3:** 532, 809
12:18 ff   **Vol. 1:** 656
12:18–29   **Vol. 3:** 433, 1014
12:18–24   **Vol. 3:** 1007
12:18–19   **Vol. 2:** 642   **Vol. 3:** 874
12:19   **Vol. 2:** 785, 858   **Vol. 3:** 112, 674

12:20   **Vol. 3:** 568
12:21   **Vol. 1:** 623   **Vol. 3:** 324
12:22 ff   **Vol. 2:** 803   **Vol. 3:** 550
12:22 f   **Vol. 1:** 689
12:22   **Vol. 1:** 327   **Vol. 2:** 194, 207, 327,
329   **Vol. 3:** 1014
12:23   **Vol. 1:** 304, 669   **Vol. 2:** 64, 193, 354,
365   **Vol. 3:** 38, 365, 694
12:24   **Vol. 1:** 224–225, 371,
374–375   **Vol. 2:** 675   **Vol. 3:** 1014
12:25 ff   **Vol. 3:** 143
12:25   **Vol. 2:** 193, 642, 858   **Vol. 3:** 325, 1014
12:26   **Vol. 2:** 717   **Vol. 3:** 557, 560
12:27   **Vol. 1:** 214   **Vol. 3:** 265, 317, 1154
12:28 f   **Vol. 3:** 1014
12:28   **Vol. 2:** 91, 121   **Vol. 3:** 74, 550,
560–561, 931, 1181
12:29   **Vol. 1:** 656   **Vol. 2:** 91
13:1 ff   **Vol. 2:** 718
13:1   **Vol. 2:** 549
13:2   **Vol. 1:** 690   **Vol. 2:** 550
13:3   **Vol. 3:** 241
13:4   **Vol. 1:** 448   **Vol. 2:** 365, 580, 583–584,
587   **Vol. 3:** 925
13:5   **Vol. 2:** 899   **Vol. 3:** 727–728
13:6   **Vol. 1:** 328, 623
13:7   **Vol. 1:** 491–492   **Vol. 3:** 934
13:8   **Vol. 3:** 830, 839
13:9   **Vol. 1:** 689   **Vol. 2:** 123, 183,
268   **Vol. 3:** 770, 944
13:10 ff   **Vol. 3:** 817
13:10–13   **Vol. 3:** 434
13:10   **Vol. 2:** 273   **Vol. 3:** 38, 433, 435–436,
550, 815
13:11–13   **Vol. 3:** 723
13:11   **Vol. 1:** 222   **Vol. 2:** 476   **Vol. 3:** 794,
965, 1182, 1203
13:12 f   **Vol. 3:** 724
13:12   **Vol. 1:** 223   **Vol. 2:** 230, 800   **Vol. 3:**
166, 723
13:13   **Vol. 3:** 340, 435, 965
13:14   **Vol. 1:** 689, 720   **Vol. 2:** 329,
804   **Vol. 3:** 74, 225, 434, 532, 832,
965, 970
13:15 f   **Vol. 2:** 42   **Vol. 3:** 42, 242, 434
13:15   **Vol. 1:** 346   **Vol. 3:** 817, 965
13:16   **Vol. 2:** 694, 817   **Vol. 3:** 435
13:17   **Vol. 1:** 591   **Vol. 2:** 137, 423   **Vol. 3:**
685, 930
13:18   **Vol. 1:** 223, 351, 591, 647
13:19   **Vol. 3:** 147
13:20 ff   **Vol. 2:** 718   **Vol. 3:** 287
13:20 f   **Vol. 2:** 875
13:20   **Vol. 1:** 223, 371, 437   **Vol. 2:** 78, 413,
533, 671, 780–781   **Vol. 3:** 166, 298
13:21   **Vol. 1:** 99   **Vol. 2:** 46, 817   **Vol. 3:**
197, 350, 830, 1023
13:22   **Vol. 1:** 571   **Vol. 2:** 766   **Vol. 3:** 1113

James

1:1	**Vol. 1:** 55, 247, 686 **Vol. 2:** 34, 358, 695, 804 **Vol. 3:** 370, 613
1:2 f	**Vol. 2:** 809 **Vol. 3:** 810
1:2	**Vol. 1:** 406, 460, 609 **Vol. 2:** 361 **Vol. 3:** 802
1:3 f	**Vol. 2:** 775
1:3	**Vol. 1:** 604 **Vol. 2:** 400 **Vol. 3:** 809
1:4 f	**Vol. 3:** 251
1:4	**Vol. 2:** 63, 65 **Vol. 3:** 253
1:5–7	**Vol. 2:** 868
1:5 f	**Vol. 2:** 857
1:5	**Vol. 2:** 43, 857 **Vol. 3:** 253, 340, 572, 1032
1:6 ff	**Vol. 1:** 604 **Vol. 2:** 435
1:6–8	**Vol. 1:** 504
1:6	**Vol. 3:** 984, 1003
1:7	**Vol. 2:** 565, 857
1:8	**Vol. 1:** 505 **Vol. 3:** 572, 686–687, 940
1:9 f	**Vol. 2:** 263
1:9	**Vol. 2:** 200
1:10 f	**Vol. 2:** 842, 844
1:10	**Vol. 1:** 744 **Vol. 2:** 211 **Vol. 3:** 523
1:10c	**Vol. 2:** 263
1:11	**Vol. 1:** 515, 586, 609, 744 **Vol. 2:** 211 **Vol. 3:** 523, 731
1:12	**Vol. 1:** 217, 406 **Vol. 2:** 775 **Vol. 3:** 802, 809
1:13–16	**Vol. 3:** 888
1:13	**Vol. 1:** 563 **Vol. 3:** 802–803
1:13a	**Vol. 3:** 1198
1:13c	**Vol. 3:** 1198
1:14	**Vol. 1:** 458 **Vol. 3:** 802, 809
1:15	**Vol. 1:** 178, 187, 343, 458 **Vol. 3:** 582
1:16	**Vol. 2:** 459–460
1:17 f	**Vol. 2:** 186
1:17	**Vol. 1:** 621 **Vol. 2:** 41–42, 63, 495 **Vol. 3:** 554, 556, 888, 1018
1:18	**Vol. 1:** 158, 178, 187, 289, 386 **Vol. 3:** 416, 888, 1017
1:19 f	**Vol. 1:** 110
1:19	**Vol. 3:** 1143
1:20	**Vol. 2:** 563 **Vol. 3:** 369–370, 372
1:21	**Vol. 1:** 479, 731 **Vol. 3:** 685, 868, 1118
1:22–25	**Vol. 3:** 1154
1:22 f	**Vol. 2:** 177
1:22	**Vol. 2:** 176, 449, 459 **Vol. 3:** 1155
1:23 f	**Vol. 3:** 228
1:23	**Vol. 1:** 181 **Vol. 2:** 176 **Vol. 3:** 1155
1:25	**Vol. 1:** 717–718, 720 **Vol. 2:** 63, 176, 449 **Vol. 3:** 1150–1151, 1154–1155
1:26 f	**Vol. 3:** 551
1:26	**Vol. 1:** 551–552 **Vol. 2:** 460 **Vol. 3:** 551, 822, 1079
1:27	**Vol. 1:** 190–191, 448 **Vol. 2:** 738 **Vol. 3:** 107, 925, 1074, 1202
2:1 ff	**Vol. 2:** 566
2:1	**Vol. 1:** 587
2:2–4	**Vol. 3:** 589
2:2 f	**Vol. 2:** 486, 825
2:2	**Vol. 1:** 296, 479
2:3	**Vol. 1:** 239 **Vol. 3:** 589
2:4	**Vol. 1:** 505, 566 **Vol. 2:** 365
2:5	**Vol. 1:** 542 **Vol. 2:** 300–301, 380, 826, 842, 844
2:6 f	**Vol. 2:** 825
2:6	**Vol. 2:** 50, 842, 844
2:7	**Vol. 1:** 146, 276 **Vol. 2:** 105, 654
2:8	**Vol. 1:** 259 **Vol. 2:** 63, 449, 544 **Vol. 3:** 490–491
2:9 ff	**Vol. 3:** 584
2:9–11	**Vol. 3:** 584
2:9	**Vol. 1:** 587
2:10 f	**Vol. 2:** 449
2:10	**Vol. 2:** 133, 143, 720 **Vol. 3:** 184
2:11	**Vol. 1:** 607 **Vol. 2:** 583
2:12	**Vol. 1:** 717–718, 720 **Vol. 2:** 449
2:13	**Vol. 1:** 228 **Vol. 2:** 449, 597, 826 **Vol. 3:** 1155
2:14–26	**Vol. 1:** 79 **Vol. 3:** 369, 1182
2:14–18	**Vol. 3:** 369
2:15–16	**Vol. 2:** 694
2:15	**Vol. 3:** 251, 253
2:16	**Vol. 1:** 234, 318, 744 **Vol. 2:** 435
2:17	**Vol. 1:** 446, 605 **Vol. 2:** 63 **Vol. 3:** 1151
2:18	**Vol. 3:** 569
2:19	**Vol. 1:** 453 **Vol. 2:** 73
2:19a	**Vol. 3:** 1211
2:20	**Vol. 2:** 63, 398
2:21	**Vol. 1:** 81 **Vol. 3:** 369–370, 436, 1196
2:22	**Vol. 1:** 604 **Vol. 2:** 63 **Vol. 3:** 228, 362, 370, 1151–1152
2:23	**Vol. 1:** 596, 604, 736 **Vol. 2:** 73, 549 **Vol. 3:** 169, 369, 490, 492, 824–826, 1187
2:24	**Vol. 3:** 369, 1151
2:25	**Vol. 1:** 102, 453, 499 **Vol. 3:** 369
2:26	**Vol. 1:** 446 **Vol. 3:** 370, 694
3:1 ff	**Vol. 3:** 369
3:1–6	**Vol. 2:** 435
3:1	**Vol. 3:** 767–768
3:2	**Vol. 2:** 63, 563
3:3	**Vol. 1:** 118, 591 **Vol. 3:** 1187
3:4	**Vol. 2:** 155
3:5 ff	**Vol. 1:** 231
3:5 f	**Vol. 1:** 656 **Vol. 3:** 1079
3:5	**Vol. 1:** 231 **Vol. 2:** 757 **Vol. 3:** 370, 1143
3:6–10	**Vol. 1:** 564
3:6	**Vol. 1:** 182, 231 **Vol. 3:** 576, 1143
3:7	**Vol. 1:** 114, 175 **Vol. 2:** 661
3:8	**Vol. 2:** 28, 661 **Vol. 3:** 1079, 1143
3:9 f	**Vol. 1:** 213, 417
3:9	**Vol. 2:** 505
3:10	**Vol. 3:** 958
3:11 ff	**Vol. 3:** 369
3:11 f	**Vol. 3:** 988
3:11	**Vol. 1:** 201 **Vol. 3:** 987

James *(cont'd)*

3:12	**Vol. 1:** 725 **Vol. 2:** 711, 757 **Vol. 3:** 449
3:13 ff	**Vol. 3:** 369
3:13	**Vol. 2:** 105, 258 **Vol. 3:** 569, 1032
3:14	**Vol. 1:** 201, 228–229 **Vol. 2:** 567 **Vol. 3:** 888, 1167
3:15 f	**Vol. 3:** 1032
3:15	**Vol. 1:** 452 **Vol. 3:** 684
3:16	**Vol. 1:** 564 **Vol. 3:** 1158, 1167
3:17	**Vol. 1:** 505 **Vol. 2:** 258, 470, 597, 780, 782 **Vol. 3:** 101, 1032
3:18	**Vol. 1:** 723 **Vol. 2:** 780, 782 **Vol. 3:** 363, 365, 369–370, 525
4:1	**Vol. 1:** 231, 459, 646 **Vol. 3:** 962, 964
4:2	**Vol. 1:** 639 **Vol. 3:** 963
4:3	**Vol. 1:** 459 **Vol. 2:** 858
4:4	**Vol. 1:** 257, 472 **Vol. 2:** 548–549, 584
4:5	**Vol. 1:** 558 **Vol. 2:** 251 **Vol. 3:** 491–492, 693, 705, 822
4:6	**Vol. 2:** 123, 757 **Vol. 3:** 30–31
4:6b	**Vol. 2:** 263
4:7	**Vol. 1:** 559 **Vol. 3:** 471
4:8–10	**Vol. 2:** 422
4:8	**Vol. 2:** 55, 422 **Vol. 3:** 101, 572
4:9 f	**Vol. 2:** 361, 417
4:9	**Vol. 2:** 417, 422, 433 **Vol. 3:** 859
4:10	**Vol. 2:** 203, 263
4:11 f	**Vol. 2:** 449 **Vol. 3:** 346
4:11	**Vol. 2:** 365
4:12	**Vol. 1:** 464 **Vol. 2:** 365, 450, 721–722
4:13	**Vol. 1:** 268 **Vol. 3:** 137, 1154
4:14	**Vol. 2:** 480, 488
4:15	**Vol. 2:** 480 **Vol. 3:** 31, 1023, 1179
4:16	**Vol. 1:** 228 **Vol. 3:** 31
4:17	**Vol. 2:** 105 **Vol. 3:** 31, 582
5:1 ff	**Vol. 3:** 369
5:1–6	**Vol. 2:** 844
5:1	**Vol. 1:** 322 **Vol. 3:** 859
5:2	**Vol. 2:** 842
5:3	**Vol. 1:** 119 **Vol. 2:** 28, 96, 836 **Vol. 3:** 1190
5:4	**Vol. 1:** 410–411 **Vol. 2:** 69, 178 **Vol. 3:** 526
5:5	**Vol. 2:** 182
5:6	**Vol. 2:** 370 **Vol. 3:** 369–370
5:7 f	**Vol. 2:** 518, 771, 900–901
5:7–11	**Vol. 2:** 769, 771
5:7	**Vol. 1:** 722 **Vol. 2:** 245, 771 **Vol. 3:** 1003
5:8	**Vol. 2:** 55, 387, 771
5:9	**Vol. 2:** 30, 365, 423, 727, 771
5:10	**Vol. 2:** 291, 513, 771 **Vol. 3:** 724, 905
5:11	**Vol. 1:** 216 **Vol. 2:** 63, 598, 600, 775
5:12	**Vol. 1:** 609 **Vol. 3:** 183, 741
5:13 ff	**Vol. 1:** 121 **Vol. 2:** 875
5:13	**Vol. 3:** 671–672, 722
5:14–18	**Vol. 2:** 868
5:14 f	**Vol. 2:** 632
5:14	**Vol. 1:** 120–121, 198–199, 274, 304 **Vol. 2:** 513, 712
5:15 ff	**Vol. 3:** 582
5:15 f	**Vol. 1:** 703
5:15	**Vol. 2:** 861, 867 **Vol. 3:** 212, 216
5:16	**Vol. 1:** 346, 702 **Vol. 2:** 169, 861, 867 **Vol. 3:** 369–370, 713
5:17 f	**Vol. 2:** 193, 730
5:17	**Vol. 1:** 544 **Vol. 2:** 503, 688, 861 **Vol. 3:** 1002
5:18	**Vol. 3:** 1004
5:19 f	**Vol. 1:** 355 **Vol. 2:** 460
5:19	**Vol. 2:** 459 **Vol. 3:** 888, 942
5:20	**Vol. 1:** 733 **Vol. 2:** 214, 400, 460 **Vol. 3:** 685, 940

1 Peter

1:1–2:10	**Vol. 1:** 180
1:1 f	**Vol. 1:** 305 **Vol. 2:** 230 **Vol. 3:** 1201
1:1	**Vol. 1:** 55, 130, 141, 305, 686, 690 **Vol. 2:** 34, 695, 790, 804 **Vol. 3:** 336, 435, 871
1:2	**Vol. 1:** 223–224, 693, 733 **Vol. 2:** 179, 230, 687, 780–781 **Vol. 3:** 166, 257, 705
1:2a	**Vol. 3:** 435
1:3	**Vol. 1:** 180, 212, 290 **Vol. 2:** 73, 76, 242, 516, 597 **Vol. 3:** 215, 276–277, 1189
1:3a	**Vol. 3:** 1201
1:3b	**Vol. 3:** 1201
1:4 ff	**Vol. 3:** 257
1:4	**Vol. 1:** 290, 469 **Vol. 2:** 193, 300 **Vol. 3:** 925, 1173
1:5 ff	**Vol. 3:** 316
1:5 f	**Vol. 3:** 839
1:5	**Vol. 1:** 180 **Vol. 2:** 135, 605 **Vol. 3:** 118, 215, 838
1:6 f	**Vol. 3:** 810
1:6	**Vol. 2:** 354 **Vol. 3:** 802
1:7	**Vol. 1:** 464, 604, 656 **Vol. 2:** 50–51 **Vol. 3:** 257, 446, 529, 809, 817, 1151
1:8 f	**Vol. 2:** 361
1:8	**Vol. 1:** 603 **Vol. 2:** 354 **Vol. 3:** 1212
1:9	**Vol. 2:** 61, 63 **Vol. 3:** 215, 685
1:10 ff	**Vol. 2:** 630 **Vol. 3:** 257, 837
1:10 f	**Vol. 3:** 83
1:10	**Vol. 2:** 123 **Vol. 3:** 215, 532–533
1:11 f	**Vol. 3:** 313
1:11	**Vol. 3:** 63, 81, 257, 317, 533, 705, 722–723
1:12	**Vol. 2:** 113, 193 **Vol. 3:** 312–313, 316, 546, 705
1:13 ff	**Vol. 1:** 223
1:13–19	**Vol. 1:** 634
1:13	**Vol. 1:** 180, 240, 515, 634 **Vol. 2:** 63, 123, 270 **Vol. 3:** 128, 257, 316
1:14–18	**Vol. 1:** 552

1 Peter *(cont'd)*

1:14 f   **Vol. 2:** 230
1:14   **Vol. 1:** 458, 709   **Vol. 2:** 179   **Vol. 3:** 934
1:15 ff   **Vol. 2:** 270
1:15 f   **Vol. 2:** 228
1:15–18   **Vol. 3:** 935
1:15   **Vol. 1:** 275–276, 305   **Vol. 2:** 76   **Vol. 3:** 934
1:17   **Vol. 1:** 587, 621, 623, 634, 691   **Vol. 2:** 50, 270, 365   **Vol. 3:** 844, 934, 1200
1:18 f   **Vol. 1:** 223, 437   **Vol. 3:** 200, 435, 1175
1:18   **Vol. 1:** 551–552   **Vol. 2:** 96, 270   **Vol. 3:** 215, 435
1:19   **Vol. 1:** 629, 634   **Vol. 2:** 411, 463   **Vol. 3:** 166, 257, 924–925
1:20   **Vol. 1:** 378, 693   **Vol. 2:** 58   **Vol. 3:** 63, 323, 843–844, 1191
1:21   **Vol. 1:** 305   **Vol. 2:** 73   **Vol. 3:** 1214
1:21a   **Vol. 3:** 1211
1:21b   **Vol. 3:** 1213
1:22   **Vol. 1:** 180   **Vol. 2:** 179, 470, 549, 868   **Vol. 3:** 101, 107, 685, 888
1:23 ff   **Vol. 3:** 329
1:23–35   **Vol. 1:** 158
1:23–25†   **Vol. 2:** 113
1:23 f   **Vol. 3:** 1118
1:23   **Vol. 1:** 180, 289–290, 469   **Vol. 2:** 270   **Vol. 3:** 224–225, 1176, 1201
1:24 f   **Vol. 3:** 1122
1:24   **Vol. 1:** 516, 609, 678, 744   **Vol. 2:** 46, 211
1:25   **Vol. 3:** 61, 224
2   **Vol. 2:** 775
2:1–3   **Vol. 3:** 346
2:1   **Vol. 2:** 270, 469
2:2   **Vol. 1:** 284, 558   **Vol. 2:** 270   **Vol. 3:** 215, 1106, 1118
2:3   **Vol. 2:** 270
2:4 ff   **Vol. 1:** 661   **Vol. 2:** 706
2:4–10   **Vol. 2:** 381
2:4–8   **Vol. 3:** 393
2:4 f   **Vol. 2:** 249   **Vol. 3:** 435
2:4   **Vol. 1:** 539, 541   **Vol. 2:** 49, 83, 249, 270   **Vol. 3:** 390, 393, 809
2:5 ff   **Vol. 1:** 305   **Vol. 2:** 732
2:5   **Vol. 1:** 662   **Vol. 2:** 42, 230, 249, 253   **Vol. 3:** 37, 383, 387, 390, 393, 706–707, 746
2:6–8   **Vol. 2:** 313, 706
2:6 f   **Vol. 3:** 393
2:6†   **Vol. 1:** 477, 539, 541   **Vol. 2:** 49, 327, 709   **Vol. 3:** 390, 397, 491, 563, 1212
2:7   **Vol. 1:** 593   **Vol. 2:** 50, 129, 159, 253, 622, 706   **Vol. 3:** 383, 389–390
2:8   **Vol. 1:** 593   **Vol. 2:** 706, 708–709   **Vol. 3:** 382–383, 389–390, 397, 1186
2:9 f   **Vol. 1:** 256

2:9   **Vol. 1:** 276, 305, 424, 539, 541   **Vol. 2:** 73, 83, 380, 623, 800, 839   **Vol. 3:** 37, 46–47, 336, 435, 927
2:10   **Vol. 1:** 369   **Vol. 2:** 597
2:11 f   **Vol. 3:** 934
2:11   **Vol. 1:** 458, 646, 677, 690–691   **Vol. 2:** 790, 804   **Vol. 3:** 336, 685, 964
2:12   **Vol. 1:** 190   **Vol. 2:** 105, 794   **Vol. 3:** 346, 515, 725, 935, 1150–1151
2:13 ff   **Vol. 3:** 97, 755
2:13–3:7   **Vol. 1:** 59
2:13–18   **Vol. 2:** 775
2:13–17   **Vol. 3:** 549, 930
2:13 f   **Vol. 1:** 270
2:13   **Vol. 1:** 386   **Vol. 2:** 378, 517
2:14   **Vol. 1:** 270   **Vol. 2:** 101   **Vol. 3:** 817, 1155
2:15   **Vol. 2:** 102   **Vol. 3:** 1023, 1026
2:16   **Vol. 1:** 718–719   **Vol. 3:** 854
2:17   **Vol. 1:** 257, 305, 623   **Vol. 2:** 50–51
2:18–3:7   **Vol. 3:** 929
2:18   **Vol. 1:** 623   **Vol. 2:** 58, 258, 509   **Vol. 3:** 596
2:19 f   **Vol. 2:** 123   **Vol. 3:** 725
2:19   **Vol. 1:** 350, 353   **Vol. 3:** 183, 575–576, 725
2:20   **Vol. 1:** 163   **Vol. 2:** 102, 775   **Vol. 3:** 857, 1202
2:21 ff   **Vol. 1:** 305
2:21–25   **Vol. 2:** 775   **Vol. 3:** 257, 582
2:21–24   **Vol. 1:** 702
2:21   **Vol. 1:** 276   **Vol. 2:** 291, 338, 809   **Vol. 3:** 490, 723–724, 905
2:22–25   **Vol. 3:** 435
2:22 f   **Vol. 3:** 63
2:22   **Vol. 3:** 435, 529, 723
2:23 f   **Vol. 2:** 51
2:23   **Vol. 3:** 347, 370–371
2:24 ff   **Vol. 3:** 371
2:24   **Vol. 1:** 163, 181, 234, 266, 390   **Vol. 3:** 370–371, 723, 868
2:24a   **Vol. 3:** 1171, 1195
2:25   **Vol. 1:** 191, 355   **Vol. 2:** 413, 459–460   **Vol. 3:** 568, 685
3:1–7   **Vol. 2:** 923   **Vol. 3:** 932, 1067
3:1   **Vol. 1:** 593   **Vol. 2:** 50   **Vol. 3:** 138, 935
3:2   **Vol. 1:** 623   **Vol. 2:** 218   **Vol. 3:** 101, 515
3:3 ff   **Vol. 3:** 346
3:3 f   **Vol. 1:** 469
3:3   **Vol. 1:** 524
3:4   **Vol. 1:** 386   **Vol. 2:** 182, 218, 258   **Vol. 3:** 112, 693
3:5   **Vol. 2:** 73, 218
3:6   **Vol. 1:** 80   **Vol. 2:** 102, 218, 513   **Vol. 3:** 1067
3:7   **Vol. 2:** 50, 221, 223, 301, 400, 563   **Vol. 3:** 913, 994, 1058, 1065, 1067, 1200–1201

1 Peter *(cont'd)*

3:8   **Vol. 1:** 257   **Vol. 2:** 63, 549–550, 600   **Vol. 3:** 257
3:9   **Vol. 1:** 215, 276   **Vol. 2:** 300–301   **Vol. 3:** 136, 183, 347, 1179
3:10 ff   **Vol. 2:** 270
3:10   **Vol. 1:** 564   **Vol. 2:** 887   **Vol. 3:** 1023, 1079
3:11   **Vol. 1:** 564   **Vol. 2:** 782, 807   **Vol. 3:** 531
3:12   **Vol. 2:** 178, 861   **Vol. 3:** 370–371, 516
3:13–17   **Vol. 3:** 964
3:13   **Vol. 2:** 51   **Vol. 3:** 1167
3:14   **Vol. 1:** 623   **Vol. 3:** 370–371, 710, 725
3:15   **Vol. 1:** 51   **Vol. 2:** 244, 858   **Vol. 3:** 118
3:16   **Vol. 1:** 350–351, 353   **Vol. 2:** 102, 258   **Vol. 3:** 257, 346, 934–935
3:17   **Vol. 1:** 563   **Vol. 2:** 51, 102   **Vol. 3:** 1023
3:18 ff   **Vol. 3:** 61
3:18–22   **Vol. 3:** 63, 674, 964
3:18 f   **Vol. 3:** 694
3:18   **Vol. 1:** 437, 479, 677   **Vol. 2:** 338, 717   **Vol. 3:** 40, 257, 323, 370–371, 575–576, 582, 705, 723, 1174, 1203
3:19 ff   **Vol. 2:** 207–208, 682
3:19 f   **Vol. 1:** 103
3:19   **Vol. 1:** 438   **Vol. 2:** 136, 207   **Vol. 3:** 54, 947
3:20 f   **Vol. 3:** 990
3:20   **Vol. 1:** 593, 677   **Vol. 2:** 692, 770, 881   **Vol. 3:** 119, 211, 215, 683, 1177
3:21 f   **Vol. 1:** 290
3:21   **Vol. 1:** 146–148, 158, 350–352, 479, 677   **Vol. 2:** 102, 682, 880–881   **Vol. 3:** 211, 215, 276–277, 906, 990, 1208
3:22   **Vol. 2:** 80–81, 147, 514, 603   **Vol. 3:** 947
4:1–3   **Vol. 1:** 677
4:1   **Vol. 1:** 679   **Vol. 3:** 128, 323, 582, 722, 724, 964
4:2 ff   **Vol. 3:** 964
4:2   **Vol. 1:** 458   **Vol. 2:** 475   **Vol. 3:** 844, 1023
4:3   **Vol. 1:** 322, 458, 514   **Vol. 2:** 274, 475   **Vol. 3:** 31, 727, 922, 929, 947, 1017
4:4 f   **Vol. 1:** 677
4:4   **Vol. 1:** 689   **Vol. 3:** 343, 947
4:5 f   **Vol. 2:** 365
4:5   **Vol. 1:** 445   **Vol. 3:** 118
4:6   **Vol. 1:** 677   **Vol. 2:** 207–208, 565   **Vol. 3:** 694, 705, 1200
4:7   **Vol. 1:** 515, 656   **Vol. 2:** 54–55, 63, 563, 923   **Vol. 3:** 794
4:8   **Vol. 1:** 502, 733   **Vol. 2:** 214
4:9   **Vol. 1:** 690   **Vol. 2:** 550

4:10 f   **Vol. 3:** 546
4:10   **Vol. 1:** 305   **Vol. 2:** 105, 121, 123, 255, 732   **Vol. 3:** 547, 854, 1118
4:11   **Vol. 2:** 46   **Vol. 3:** 718, 1106, 1118
4:12 ff   **Vol. 1:** 141, 305
4:12   **Vol. 1:** 656, 689   **Vol. 3:** 110, 446, 802
4:13   **Vol. 2:** 46, 354, 361, 808   **Vol. 3:** 257, 316, 722, 724
4:14   **Vol. 1:** 286   **Vol. 2:** 75, 654   **Vol. 3:** 257, 340, 705, 1194
4:15   **Vol. 2:** 742   **Vol. 3:** 377, 725
4:16   **Vol. 1:** 123   **Vol. 2:** 343, 654   **Vol. 3:** 563, 724–725
4:17 f   **Vol. 3:** 839
4:17   **Vol. 1:** 167, 593, 667   **Vol. 2:** 63, 78, 249, 365
4:18   **Vol. 2:** 94, 488   **Vol. 3:** 215, 370–371
4:19   **Vol. 1:** 383, 386   **Vol. 2:** 102   **Vol. 3:** 686, 725, 1023, 1155
5:1 ff   **Vol. 1:** 305
5:1   **Vol. 1:** 198, 643   **Vol. 2:** 47–48   **Vol. 3:** 257, 316, 568, 722, 724–725
5:2 f   **Vol. 2:** 519
5:2–4   **Vol. 3:** 568
5:2   **Vol. 1:** 190   **Vol. 3:** 137, 1200
5:3 f   **Vol. 3:** 568
5:3   **Vol. 2:** 302   **Vol. 3:** 905
5:4   **Vol. 1:** 406   **Vol. 2:** 47   **Vol. 3:** 257, 323
5:5 f   **Vol. 3:** 161
5:5   **Vol. 1:** 198   **Vol. 2:** 117, 123, 262–264, 618, 675   **Vol. 3:** 30–31
5:6   **Vol. 2:** 149, 203, 263   **Vol. 3:** 718, 839
5:7   **Vol. 1:** 278
5:8 f   **Vol. 1:** 141, 305
5:8   **Vol. 1:** 118, 421, 515, 554, 718   **Vol. 2:** 137   **Vol. 3:** 203, 469, 471, 531, 802, 944
5:9   **Vol. 1:** 257, 305, 660   **Vol. 3:** 722, 724–725
5:10   **Vol. 1:** 276, 290, 660, 662   **Vol. 2:** 47, 78, 123   **Vol. 3:** 350, 725
5:11   **Vol. 2:** 47   **Vol. 3:** 718
5:12   **Vol. 2:** 78, 123   **Vol. 3:** 489, 824, 826, 888, 1042, 1174
5:13   **Vol. 1:** 141, 180, 619   **Vol. 3:** 388
5:14   **Vol. 2:** 547, 549, 780–781

2 Peter

1:1 f   **Vol. 3:** 221
1:1   **Vol. 1:** 130, 478   **Vol. 2:** 73, 498–499   **Vol. 3:** 370
1:2   **Vol. 1:** 733   **Vol. 2:** 400, 405, 780
1:3 f   **Vol. 1:** 276   **Vol. 2:** 86   **Vol. 3:** 927
1:3–8   **Vol. 2:** 95
1:3   **Vol. 1:** 644   **Vol. 2:** 41–42, 405, 661   **Vol. 3:** 927, 1182

2 Peter *(cont'd)*

1:4   **Vol. 1:** 448, 458, 469, 559, 644   **Vol. 2:** 661   **Vol. 3:** 71, 302, 304, 832, 927, 1177
1:5 ff   **Vol. 3:** 927
1:5 f   **Vol. 2:** 405
1:5   **Vol. 1:** 497   **Vol. 2:** 400   **Vol. 3:** 927, 1169
1:6   **Vol. 1:** 496–497   **Vol. 2:** 775
1:7   **Vol. 2:** 542, 549
1:8   **Vol. 1:** 472, 723   **Vol. 2:** 131, 405, 661
1:9   **Vol. 2:** 714, 899
1:10   **Vol. 1:** 540, 542, 660   **Vol. 2:** 661   **Vol. 3:** 1155, 1169
1:11   **Vol. 2:** 387, 661, 843   **Vol. 3:** 221, 815, 832, 940–941
1:12 f   **Vol. 3:** 241–242
1:12   **Vol. 1:** 326   **Vol. 2:** 899
1:13 f   **Vol. 3:** 815
1:13   **Vol. 3:** 247, 370
1:14   **Vol. 1:** 315   **Vol. 3:** 317, 815
1:15   **Vol. 3:** 240, 815, 940, 1169
1:16–18   **Vol. 3:** 862
1:16   **Vol. 2:** 426, 645, 900–901   **Vol. 3:** 314, 832, 863, 1033
1:17   **Vol. 2:** 46–47, 819   **Vol. 3:** 114, 863
1:19   **Vol. 1:** 659–660   **Vol. 2:** 289, 487–488, 493, 495–496, 558   **Vol. 3:** 81
1:20 f   **Vol. 3:** 329
1:20   **Vol. 1:** 181, 577–578   **Vol. 2:** 839   **Vol. 3:** 490, 492
1:21   **Vol. 1:** 578–579   **Vol. 3:** 705, 1022–1023
2   **Vol. 3:** 862
2:1 f   **Vol. 2:** 449
2:1   **Vol. 1:** 268, 438, 455, 464, 535   **Vol. 2:** 472, 509   **Vol. 3:** 768
2:2   **Vol. 3:** 343, 888, 942
2:3   **Vol. 1:** 138, 268   **Vol. 2:** 365
2:4–10   **Vol. 3:** 832
2:4 f   **Vol. 2:** 682
2:4   **Vol. 1:** 103, 452
2:5 f   **Vol. 2:** 95
2:5   **Vol. 1:** 168, 666   **Vol. 2:** 135, 692   **Vol. 3:** 52, 170, 203, 370, 991
2:6   **Vol. 1:** 326   **Vol. 2:** 291, 366, 767   **Vol. 3:** 93, 203, 905
2:7 f   **Vol. 3:** 240, 370
2:7   **Vol. 3:** 204, 934
2:8   **Vol. 2:** 175, 449   **Vol. 3:** 856, 934
2:9   **Vol. 2:** 95, 366, 700, 894   **Vol. 3:** 98, 203, 576, 802–803, 1176
2:10 ff†   **Vol. 3:** 342
2:10   **Vol. 1:** 365, 448, 458, 462, 493, 677   **Vol. 2:** 46, 518   **Vol. 3:** 947
2:11   **Vol. 2:** 365   **Vol. 3:** 345, 371, 714, 1202
2:12   **Vol. 1:** 468–469   **Vol. 2:** 406, 476, 661   **Vol. 3:** 1118

2:13 ff   **Vol. 1:** 459
2:13   **Vol. 1:** 460   **Vol. 2:** 459–460, 547   **Vol. 3:** 575–576
2:14   **Vol. 1:** 138, 286, 313, 416   **Vol. 2:** 584   **Vol. 3:** 516
2:15   **Vol. 2:** 459–460, 677   **Vol. 3:** 576, 942
2:16   **Vol. 2:** 142
2:17   **Vol. 1:** 425   **Vol. 3:** 987–988, 1003
2:18   **Vol. 1:** 458, 552, 559   **Vol. 2:** 459–460
2:19   **Vol. 1:** 718   **Vol. 3:** 70
2:20 f   **Vol. 3:** 942
2:20   **Vol. 1:** 448, 559   **Vol. 2:** 405   **Vol. 3:** 221
2:21   **Vol. 1:** 339, 355   **Vol. 2:** 405   **Vol. 3:** 221, 370, 774, 942, 1174
2:22   **Vol. 1:** 117, 355   **Vol. 2:** 757   **Vol. 3:** 888, 990
3   **Vol. 2:** 461, 771
3:1   **Vol. 3:** 127, 241, 247, 489
3:2   **Vol. 1:** 339   **Vol. 3:** 221, 241, 1122
3:3–7   **Vol. 2:** 584
3:3   **Vol. 2:** 58, 894   **Vol. 3:** 341, 947
3:4 ff   **Vol. 2:** 769, 901
3:4   **Vol. 1:** 166, 443   **Vol. 2:** 900, 930
3:5–10   **Vol. 3:** 832
3:5–7   **Vol. 2:** 682
3:5   **Vol. 2:** 836   **Vol. 3:** 1019, 1023, 1176
3:6   **Vol. 1:** 464
3:7   **Vol. 1:** 657   **Vol. 2:** 95, 193, 366
3:8   **Vol. 2:** 698–699, 894   **Vol. 3:** 684
3:9 f   **Vol. 2:** 772
3:9   **Vol. 1:** 359, 464, 742   **Vol. 2:** 771   **Vol. 3:** 1017–1018
3:10 ff   **Vol. 2:** 38
3:10–12   **Vol. 3:** 180
3:10   **Vol. 1:** 657   **Vol. 2:** 193, 452, 894   **Vol. 3:** 378
3:11 ff   **Vol. 1:** 441
3:11 f   **Vol. 2:** 95   **Vol. 3:** 832
3:11   **Vol. 3:** 180
3:12   **Vol. 1:** 657   **Vol. 2:** 193, 245, 452, 887, 894, 900   **Vol. 3:** 1169
3:13   **Vol. 1:** 186, 518   **Vol. 2:** 193, 245, 671, 714   **Vol. 3:** 71, 371, 832
3:14   **Vol. 2:** 780   **Vol. 3:** 529, 925, 1169
3:15 f   **Vol. 1:** 693   **Vol. 3:** 401, 492
3:15   **Vol. 2:** 770–771   **Vol. 3:** 215
3:16   **Vol. 1:** 247, 578   **Vol. 3:** 129, 252, 490, 492
3:17   **Vol. 1:** 611, 693   **Vol. 2:** 135, 459–460
3:18   **Vol. 2:** 46, 123, 129–130, 405   **Vol. 3:** 221, 832

1 John

1:1 ff   **Vol. 3:** 276
1:1–10   **Vol. 1:** 338
1:1–4   **Vol. 2:** 404
1:1–3   **Vol. 1:** 638
1:1 f   **Vol. 2:** 482

1 John *(cont'd)*

1:1†   **Vol. 1:** 63, 166   **Vol. 2:** 176   **Vol. 3:** 47, 61, 313, 517, 825, 1114, 1185
1:2 f   **Vol. 3:** 47
1:2   **Vol. 3:** 312, 314, 321, 323, 1046, 1204
1:3   **Vol. 1:** 644   **Vol. 3:** 646
1:4   **Vol. 1:** 741   **Vol. 2:** 359   **Vol. 3:** 582
1:5–10   **Vol. 3:** 162
1:5 f   **Vol. 1:** 126
1:5   **Vol. 1:** 424   **Vol. 2:** 175, 494   **Vol. 3:** 46–47
1:6 f   **Vol. 1:** 638   **Vol. 2:** 494   **Vol. 3:** 945
1:6   **Vol. 1:** 424, 644   **Vol. 2:** 473   **Vol. 3:** 891, 945
1:7 ff   **Vol. 3:** 163
1:7–10   **Vol. 1:** 223
1:7   **Vol. 1:** 223, 644   **Vol. 2:** 183   **Vol. 3:** 47, 107, 163, 166, 582, 646
1:8   **Vol. 2:** 449, 459–460   **Vol. 3:** 362, 582, 890
1:9–2:2   **Vol. 3:** 362
1:9   **Vol. 1:** 148, 346, 602, 702   **Vol. 2:** 449   **Vol. 3:** 107, 163, 362, 576, 582
1:10   **Vol. 2:** 449, 473, 567
2:1 f   **Vol. 1:** 89
2:1–6   **Vol. 2:** 716
2:1   **Vol. 1:** 90–91, 286, 324, 637   **Vol. 2:** 84   **Vol. 3:** 40, 162–163, 362, 704
2:1b   **Vol. 2:** 449
2:2   **Vol. 1:** 525   **Vol. 3:** 162, 582, 1203
2:3 ff   **Vol. 1:** 638
2:3 f   **Vol. 1:** 166, 338
2:3   **Vol. 1:** 638   **Vol. 2:** 133, 398
2:4 f   **Vol. 1:** 126, 338
2:4   **Vol. 2:** 473
2:5   **Vol. 2:** 64, 398
2:6   **Vol. 1:** 638   **Vol. 2:** 668   **Vol. 3:** 226, 945
2:7 ff   **Vol. 2:** 673
2:7–11   **Vol. 2:** 404
2:7 f   **Vol. 1:** 338
2:7   **Vol. 1:** 166, 338–339   **Vol. 2:** 671, 673, 716   **Vol. 3:** 582
2:8 ff   **Vol. 2:** 494
2:8–11   **Vol. 2:** 673
2:8   **Vol. 1:** 338–339, 424   **Vol. 2:** 280, 488, 494, 671
2:9 ff   **Vol. 3:** 98
2:9   **Vol. 1:** 257, 424, 556
2:10   **Vol. 2:** 494, 708–709   **Vol. 3:** 47, 226
2:11   **Vol. 1:** 424   **Vol. 2:** 709   **Vol. 3:** 945
2:12   **Vol. 1:** 286   **Vol. 2:** 654   **Vol. 3:** 582
2:13 f   **Vol. 1:** 651   **Vol. 3:** 472
2:13   **Vol. 1:** 566
2:14   **Vol. 1:** 566   **Vol. 2:** 405
2:15 ff   **Vol. 1:** 603
2:15   **Vol. 1:** 526   **Vol. 2:** 548   **Vol. 3:** 32
2:16   **Vol. 1:** 458, 678   **Vol. 2:** 475, 846   **Vol. 3:** 31

2:17   **Vol. 1:** 458, 526   **Vol. 3:** 226, 830, 1022–1023, 1155
2:18–27   **Vol. 3:** 1206
2:18   **Vol. 1:** 123, 126   **Vol. 2:** 58, 435, 645   **Vol. 3:** 849
2:19   **Vol. 3:** 312, 314, 321
2:20   **Vol. 1:** 123, 638   **Vol. 2:** 228, 231   **Vol. 3:** 703–704
2:21   **Vol. 3:** 489, 764
2:22 ff   **Vol. 2:** 231
2:22 f   **Vol. 1:** 126, 455   **Vol. 3:** 646
2:22   **Vol. 1:** 347, 455   **Vol. 2:** 339, 473, 567   **Vol. 3:** 1206
2:23   **Vol. 1:** 347, 455   **Vol. 2:** 78, 302
2:24   **Vol. 1:** 166   **Vol. 3:** 226
2:26†   **Vol. 2:** 459–460   **Vol. 3:** 1141
2:27   **Vol. 1:** 123, 638   **Vol. 3:** 225, 703–704, 764, 890
2:28   **Vol. 1:** 123, 286   **Vol. 2:** 64, 736–737, 900–901   **Vol. 3:** 312, 314, 321
2:29   **Vol. 1:** 179   **Vol. 2:** 76   **Vol. 3:** 362, 647, 1155
3   **Vol. 2:** 449
3:1–10   **Vol. 3:** 582
3:1 f   **Vol. 1:** 620
3:1   **Vol. 1:** 274   **Vol. 2:** 546   **Vol. 3:** 517, 646–647
3:2 f   **Vol. 2:** 242
3:2   **Vol. 2:** 242, 503   **Vol. 3:** 278, 312, 314, 321, 515
3:3   **Vol. 2:** 244   **Vol. 3:** 101–102
3:5   **Vol. 3:** 312, 314, 321, 323, 582, 1117
3:6 ff   **Vol. 1:** 126
3:6   **Vol. 2:** 404, 449   **Vol. 3:** 226
3:7 ff   **Vol. 3:** 1155
3:7 f   **Vol. 3:** 362
3:7   **Vol. 1:** 286   **Vol. 2:** 459–460   **Vol. 3:** 362
3:8 f   **Vol. 3:** 582
3:8   **Vol. 1:** 166   **Vol. 3:** 312, 314, 321, 323, 362, 471–472, 646, 1150
3:9 f   **Vol. 3:** 647
3:9   **Vol. 1:** 179   **Vol. 2:** 76   **Vol. 3:** 524, 703–704, 1188
3:10   **Vol. 1:** 179, 287   **Vol. 2:** 546   **Vol. 3:** 320, 362, 472, 582, 646
3:11–18   **Vol. 3:** 98
3:11   **Vol. 1:** 166   **Vol. 3:** 46–47
3:12   **Vol. 1:** 566   **Vol. 3:** 362, 472, 1150
3:13   **Vol. 1:** 556   **Vol. 2:** 625
3:14 ff   **Vol. 2:** 546
3:14 f   **Vol. 3:** 226
3:14   **Vol. 1:** 439   **Vol. 2:** 186, 482
3:15   **Vol. 1:** 556
3:16 f   **Vol. 2:** 76   **Vol. 3:** 945
3:16   **Vol. 1:** 257   **Vol. 2:** 404, 546, 668   **Vol. 3:** 163, 547, 1206
3:17   **Vol. 2:** 475, 600, 694, 733, 846   **Vol. 3:** 957
3:18   **Vol. 1:** 286   **Vol. 3:** 1079, 1176

1 John *(cont'd)*

3:19	**Vol. 1:** 590
3:20 f	**Vol. 2:** 365
3:21 ff	**Vol. 1:** 338
3:21 f	**Vol. 3:** 1206
3:21	**Vol. 1:** 590 **Vol. 2:** 736
3:22 ff	**Vol. 2:** 449
3:22	**Vol. 1:** 338–339 **Vol. 2:** 133, 816, 857–858
3:23	**Vol. 1:** 338–339 **Vol. 2:** 654 **Vol. 3:** 1213
3:24	**Vol. 1:** 338 **Vol. 3:** 703–704, 764, 1192
4	**Vol. 2:** 449
4:1 ff	**Vol. 1:** 123
4:1–3	**Vol. 3:** 630, 704
4:1 f	**Vol. 1:** 347
4:1	**Vol. 1:** 452 **Vol. 2:** 472 **Vol. 3:** 81, 475, 695, 808, 810, 988
4:2 f	**Vol. 1:** 126, 347 **Vol. 3:** 1206
4:2	**Vol. 1:** 323, 347, 638, 678–679 **Vol. 2:** 339 **Vol. 3:** 323, 475
4:3	**Vol. 1:** 126 **Vol. 3:** 695
4:4 f	**Vol. 1:** 651
4:4	**Vol. 1:** 286 **Vol. 2:** 76 **Vol. 3:** 1188
4:5	**Vol. 2:** 567
4:6	**Vol. 1:** 603 **Vol. 2:** 404, 459–460 **Vol. 3:** 694–695, 704, 892, 1188
4:7 ff	**Vol. 2:** 546 **Vol. 3:** 162
4:7–12	**Vol. 3:** 98
4:7 f	**Vol. 2:** 404, 546
4:7	**Vol. 1:** 179 **Vol. 2:** 76, 79 **Vol. 3:** 582, 647, 1188
4:8	**Vol. 2:** 79, 404, 542, 546
4:9–14	**Vol. 3:** 646
4:9 f	**Vol. 2:** 404
4:9	**Vol. 2:** 75, 482, 546 **Vol. 3:** 162, 312, 314, 321, 643, 1202
4:10	**Vol. 2:** 78–79 **Vol. 3:** 162–163, 582, 643
4:11	**Vol. 3:** 945
4:12 ff	**Vol. 2:** 546
4:12	**Vol. 2:** 64
4:13 ff	**Vol. 1:** 638
4:13–21	**Vol. 3:** 162
4:13	**Vol. 2:** 41 **Vol. 3:** 703–704, 1192
4:14 f	**Vol. 3:** 225
4:14	**Vol. 3:** 643, 1046
4:15 f	**Vol. 3:** 1192
4:15	**Vol. 1:** 347, 638 **Vol. 3:** 646
4:16	**Vol. 2:** 76, 404, 542, 546 **Vol. 3:** 1211
4:17	**Vol. 2:** 64, 366, 736, 894 **Vol. 3:** 98, 163
4:18	**Vol. 1:** 624 **Vol. 2:** 64 **Vol. 3:** 98
4:19	**Vol. 3:** 98, 945
4:20	**Vol. 1:** 556 **Vol. 2:** 473, 546 **Vol. 3:** 337
4:21	**Vol. 1:** 287, 339 **Vol. 2:** 546
5:1–12	**Vol. 2:** 449
5:1 f	**Vol. 1:** 126
5:1	**Vol. 2:** 339 **Vol. 3:** 647, 1188
5:2 f	**Vol. 1:** 338
5:2	**Vol. 1:** 339 **Vol. 3:** 1155
5:3 f	**Vol. 1:** 339
5:3	**Vol. 1:** 262, 624
5:4 f	**Vol. 1:** 651 **Vol. 3:** 780
5:4	**Vol. 1:** 602, 651 **Vol. 3:** 647, 1188
5:5	**Vol. 3:** 646
5:6–8	**Vol. 3:** 704
5:6	**Vol. 3:** 163, 166, 892, 990, 1046
5:8	**Vol. 2:** 84, 687 **Vol. 3:** 990
5:10	**Vol. 1:** 638 **Vol. 2:** 473, 567 **Vol. 3:** 1046, 1187
5:10b	**Vol. 3:** 1211
5:10c	**Vol. 3:** 1213
5:11	**Vol. 2:** 78 **Vol. 3:** 1046
5:12	**Vol. 1:** 637 **Vol. 2:** 78, 302, 482
5:13	**Vol. 2:** 654 **Vol. 3:** 489, 1213
5:14 ff	**Vol. 3:** 1022, 1205
5:14 f	**Vol. 2:** 857
5:14	**Vol. 2:** 178, 736–737, 857 **Vol. 3:** 1023
5:15	**Vol. 2:** 858
5:16–21	**Vol. 3:** 582
5:16 f	**Vol. 3:** 1172, 1185, 1205–1206
5:16	**Vol. 1:** 703 **Vol. 2:** 856, 879
5:16a	**Vol. 2:** 449 **Vol. 3:** 1206
5:16b	**Vol. 2:** 449
5:17	**Vol. 2:** 449 **Vol. 3:** 575–576
5:18 f	**Vol. 1:** 566
5:18	**Vol. 1:** 525 **Vol. 2:** 133 **Vol. 3:** 647
5:18a	**Vol. 3:** 1188
5:19	**Vol. 1:** 566 **Vol. 3:** 1188
5:20	**Vol. 2:** 82, 280, 403, 482 **Vol. 3:** 127, 646
5:21	**Vol. 1:** 286 **Vol. 2:** 135

2 John

1	**Vol. 1:** 286, 539 **Vol. 2:** 518
2	**Vol. 3:** 830
3	**Vol. 2:** 597, 780
4 ff	**Vol. 1:** 338
4	**Vol. 1:** 286, 338–339 **Vol. 2:** 518 **Vol. 3:** 528, 945
5 f	**Vol. 1:** 339
5	**Vol. 1:** 166 **Vol. 2:** 518, 546, 670, 673, 880
6	**Vol. 1:** 166, 338–339 **Vol. 2:** 518, 880 **Vol. 3:** 945
7–11	**Vol. 3:** 646
7	**Vol. 1:** 126, 638, 678–679 **Vol. 2:** 339, 459–460 **Vol. 3:** 323, 630, 1176, 1206
8	**Vol. 3:** 144, 749, 751
9 f	**Vol. 3:** 770
9	**Vol. 1:** 247, 637–638 **Vol. 2:** 78, 302 **Vol. 3:** 224
10	**Vol. 1:** 535 **Vol. 2:** 358

2 John *(cont'd)*

11	**Vol. 1:** 566
12	**Vol. 1:** 203, 741 **Vol. 2:** 359
13	**Vol. 1:** 286, 539 **Vol. 2:** 518

3 John

2	**Vol. 2:** 170, 867 **Vol. 3:** 684, 943
3 f	**Vol. 3:** 945
3	**Vol. 3:** 1044–1045
4	**Vol. 1:** 286
5	**Vol. 1:** 689
6	**Vol. 1:** 304 **Vol. 3:** 1044–1045
7	**Vol. 2:** 654
8	**Vol. 3:** 751, 1152
9	**Vol. 1:** 304 **Vol. 2:** 550
10	**Vol. 1:** 304, 453, 566 **Vol. 3:** 241, 1149–1150
11	**Vol. 1:** 491, 563–564 **Vol. 2:** 102 **Vol. 3:** 1188
12	**Vol. 3:** 1044–1045
13	**Vol. 1:** 203

Jude

3b	**Vol. 2:** 719
23a	**Vol. 2:** 597
2	**Vol. 1:** 733 **Vol. 2:** 597, 780–781
3	**Vol. 1:** 646 **Vol. 2:** 717–718 **Vol. 3:** 61, 216, 774, 1199
4	**Vol. 1:** 455 **Vol. 2:** 95, 123, 714, 725 **Vol. 3:** 490
5	**Vol. 1:** 532 **Vol. 2:** 717, 719 **Vol. 3:** 216, 241
6	**Vol. 1:** 103, 452 **Vol. 2:** 161, 366, 894
7	**Vol. 1:** 321, 493, 657, 677 **Vol. 2:** 96, 767 **Vol. 3:** 93, 99, 344, 570, 830
8	**Vol. 1:** 74, 448 **Vol. 2:** 46, 518 **Vol. 3:** 344
9	**Vol. 1:** 103–104, 365, 504, 572 **Vol. 2:** 365 **Vol. 3:** 344, 471, 492, 821
10	**Vol. 1:** 468–469 **Vol. 2:** 661 **Vol. 3:** 345, 1118
11	**Vol. 2:** 459, 677 **Vol. 3:** 942, 947, 1054
12	**Vol. 1:** 723 **Vol. 2:** 547 **Vol. 3:** 868–869, 1003
13	**Vol. 1:** 425, 520 **Vol. 2:** 459 **Vol. 3:** 564, 684, 736
14 f	**Vol. 2:** 817, 897 **Vol. 3:** 265, 492
14	**Vol. 1:** 85 **Vol. 2:** 219, 228, 692 **Vol. 3:** 602
15	**Vol. 2:** 95, 141, 155
16	**Vol. 1:** 587 **Vol. 2:** 145, 625 **Vol. 3:** 947
17	**Vol. 2:** 718 **Vol. 3:** 241, 1122
18	**Vol. 2:** 58, 95 **Vol. 3:** 844, 947
19–20	**Vol. 3:** 705
20	**Vol. 2:** 249, 718, 883 **Vol. 3:** 61
21–23	**Vol. 2:** 597
21	**Vol. 2:** 245 **Vol. 3:** 832

22	**Vol. 1:** 504
23	**Vol. 1:** 556 **Vol. 3:** 216, 602
24	**Vol. 2:** 46, 135, 354 **Vol. 3:** 925
25	**Vol. 2:** 46, 73, 426 **Vol. 3:** 221, 830

Revelation

1–3	**Vol. 2:** 691 **Vol. 3:** 85
1	**Vol. 2:** 674
1:1	**Vol. 1:** 103, 247 **Vol. 2:** 665 **Vol. 3:** 85, 88, 312, 316, 569, 613
1:2	**Vol. 3:** 89, 1046
1:3	**Vol. 3:** 85, 489–490, 838
1:4	**Vol. 1:** 114, 304 **Vol. 2:** 687, 691, 780–781 **Vol. 3:** 706, 1171, 1181
1:5	**Vol. 1:** 152, 223, 256, 445, 602, 668 **Vol. 2:** 340, 378, 514 **Vol. 3:** 166, 180, 200, 303, 582, 990, 1046, 1174
1:6	**Vol. 2:** 231, 380 **Vol. 3:** 37, 718, 1154
1:7	**Vol. 1:** 99, 518 **Vol. 3:** 629, 871, 1003
1:8	**Vol. 2:** 59, 64, 69, 80, 282, 513–514, 674 **Vol. 3:** 718
1:9 ff	**Vol. 2:** 826 **Vol. 3:** 287
1:9	**Vol. 1:** 642 **Vol. 2:** 775 **Vol. 3:** 89, 517, 1046
1:10 ff	**Vol. 3:** 490
1:10–12	**Vol. 3:** 113
1:10	**Vol. 1:** 528, 631 **Vol. 2:** 176, 426, 518, 674 **Vol. 3:** 113, 411–412, 706, 874
1:11	**Vol. 1:** 244, 257, 304 **Vol. 2:** 550, 691
1:12–20	**Vol. 2:** 674
1:12 f	**Vol. 2:** 487
1:12	**Vol. 2:** 486
1:13 ff	**Vol. 2:** 80, 482
1:13	**Vol. 1:** 240 **Vol. 2:** 503 **Vol. 3:** 121, 527, 629, 633
1:14	**Vol. 1:** 204 **Vol. 3:** 1004
1:15	**Vol. 1:** 239, 656 **Vol. 2:** 97 **Vol. 3:** 113
1:16	**Vol. 2:** 488, 686 **Vol. 3:** 732, 735, 967
1:17 f	**Vol. 1:** 437–438 **Vol. 2:** 282, 482
1:17	**Vol. 1:** 239, 610, 623, 667 **Vol. 2:** 58, 64, 80 **Vol. 3:** 839
1:18	**Vol. 2:** 207, 340, 727, 733 **Vol. 3:** 387
1:19	**Vol. 1:** 326 **Vol. 3:** 505
1:20	**Vol. 1:** 103, 304 **Vol. 2:** 486–487 **Vol. 3:** 505, 735–736
2 f	**Vol. 2:** 691
2	**Vol. 1:** 651 **Vol. 2:** 42 **Vol. 3:** 88, 490
2:1	**Vol. 1:** 103, 304 **Vol. 2:** 486–487 **Vol. 3:** 718, 735, 944
2:2 f	**Vol. 2:** 775
2:2	**Vol. 1:** 263, 564, 603 **Vol. 2:** 473, 567, 677 **Vol. 3:** 88, 529, 802
2:3	**Vol. 1:** 263 **Vol. 3:** 257
2:4	**Vol. 2:** 388
2:5	**Vol. 1:** 611 **Vol. 2:** 487 **Vol. 3:** 1150
2:6	**Vol. 1:** 556 **Vol. 2:** 388, 676

Revelation *(cont'd)*

2:7   **Vol. 1:** 390, 651   **Vol. 2:** 41, 178,
          763   **Vol. 3:** 706, 868
2:8   **Vol. 1:** 304, 406, 445, 667   **Vol. 2:** 58,
          64
2:9 f   **Vol. 3:** 471
2:9   **Vol. 1:** 296–297   **Vol. 2:** 315, 826, 842,
          844   **Vol. 3:** 343
2:10   **Vol. 1:** 406, 455, 602, 623   **Vol. 2:** 136,
          692, 894   **Vol. 3:** 722, 803
2:11   **Vol. 1:** 441, 651   **Vol. 2:** 178   **Vol. 3:**
          575–576, 706
2:12   **Vol. 1:** 304   **Vol. 2:** 686   **Vol. 3:** 967
2:13   **Vol. 1:** 455, 602   **Vol. 2:** 654   **Vol. 3:**
          717, 1008, 1047
2:14–15   **Vol. 2:** 677
2:14 f   **Vol. 3:** 717
2:14   **Vol. 1:** 253, 471   **Vol. 2:** 284–286, 315,
          708   **Vol. 3:** 432, 765, 770
2:15   **Vol. 2:** 676–677   **Vol. 3:** 770
2:16   **Vol. 2:** 686   **Vol. 3:** 963
2:17   **Vol. 1:** 205, 251, 253   **Vol. 2:** 41, 178,
          218, 653, 671, 674   **Vol. 3:** 490, 706,
          967
2:18   **Vol. 1:** 239, 304, 656   **Vol. 2:**
          503   **Vol. 3:** 648
2:19   **Vol. 1:** 602–603   **Vol. 2:** 775   **Vol. 3:**
          546
2:20 ff   **Vol. 2:** 582
2:20 f   **Vol. 3:** 844
2:20   **Vol. 2:** 284–286, 459, 677   **Vol. 3:** 81,
          432, 765, 1067
2:21 f   **Vol. 1:** 359
2:21   **Vol. 3:** 1023
2:22   **Vol. 2:** 808
2:23   **Vol. 1:** 436   **Vol. 2:** 181, 183,
          399   **Vol. 3:** 533, 648, 1151, 1200
2:24   **Vol. 1:** 261   **Vol. 2:** 198, 401,
          677   **Vol. 3:** 86, 770
2:25   **Vol. 3:** 717
2:26–28   **Vol. 2:** 677
2:26 f   **Vol. 2:** 795   **Vol. 3:** 648
2:26   **Vol. 2:** 64, 133
2:27–28   **Vol. 1:** 407
2:27   **Vol. 1:** 164, 177, 408   **Vol. 2:**
          98   **Vol. 3:** 913
2:28   **Vol. 3:** 736, 748
2:29   **Vol. 2:** 178   **Vol. 3:** 706
3   **Vol. 1:** 651   **Vol. 2:** 42   **Vol. 3:** 88, 490
3:1   **Vol. 1:** 304   **Vol. 2:** 652   **Vol. 3:** 706,
          736
3:2 f   **Vol. 2:** 137
3:2   **Vol. 1:** 326, 436   **Vol. 3:** 252
3:3   **Vol. 2:** 133, 926   **Vol. 3:** 848
3:4 f   **Vol. 1:** 204
3:4   **Vol. 1:** 317, 449, 556   **Vol. 2:**
          652   **Vol. 3:** 349, 944
3:5   **Vol. 1:** 244, 317, 323, 347, 471   **Vol. 2:**
          653

3:6   **Vol. 2:** 178   **Vol. 3:** 706
3:7 f   **Vol. 2:** 727, 733
3:7   **Vol. 1:** 257, 304   **Vol. 2:** 31, 76, 228,
          550, 730   **Vol. 3:** 387, 652, 893
3:8   **Vol. 1:** 427, 455   **Vol. 2:** 30–31, 133,
          654, 727   **Vol. 3:** 257
3:9   **Vol. 1:** 239, 296–297   **Vol. 2:** 312,
          314–315, 399, 474
3:10   **Vol. 1:** 326, 519   **Vol. 2:** 133, 245, 776,
          808   **Vol. 3:** 803, 848
3:11   **Vol. 1:** 406   **Vol. 3:** 717, 748
3:12   **Vol. 2:** 186, 194, 329, 654, 671,
          804   **Vol. 3:** 490, 784, 795, 1154
3:13   **Vol. 2:** 178   **Vol. 3:** 706
3:14   **Vol. 1:** 99, 166, 304, 384   **Vol. 3:** 893,
          1046
3:15–16   **Vol. 1:** 318
3:15   **Vol. 2:** 668
3:17 f   **Vol. 2:** 842, 844
3:17   **Vol. 1:** 313–314   **Vol. 2:** 597, 826,
          842   **Vol. 3:** 519, 859, 958
3:18   **Vol. 1:** 204, 313–314, 317, 363,
          656   **Vol. 3:** 321, 518, 564
3:18b   **Vol. 1:** 319
3:19   **Vol. 1:** 318   **Vol. 2:** 142, 549   **Vol. 3:**
          779
3:20   **Vol. 1:** 319   **Vol. 2:** 31, 726–727,
          881   **Vol. 3:** 85
3:21   **Vol. 2:** 41   **Vol. 3:** 588
3:22   **Vol. 2:** 178   **Vol. 3:** 706
4   **Vol. 3:** 398
4:1–8:2   **Vol. 2:** 691
4:1 f   **Vol. 1:** 528
4:1   **Vol. 2:** 31, 665   **Vol. 3:** 113, 569, 874
4:2–10   **Vol. 2:** 702   **Vol. 3:** 588
4:2   **Vol. 3:** 706, 1193
4:3   **Vol. 2:** 503   **Vol. 3:** 397–398, 515,
          1003
4:4 ff   **Vol. 1:** 200
4:4   **Vol. 1:** 200, 204, 406   **Vol. 2:** 159,
          614–615
4:5   **Vol. 1:** 656   **Vol. 2:** 486, 691   **Vol. 3:**
          706, 1001–1002
4:6–8   **Vol. 1:** 280
4:6   **Vol. 2:** 503, 615, 689   **Vol. 3:** 398, 984
4:7   **Vol. 1:** 116, 118, 173, 175   **Vol. 2:** 503,
          689
4:8–11   **Vol. 2:** 868, 877
4:8   **Vol. 2:** 69, 76, 228–229, 514, 687,
          689   **Vol. 3:** 256, 718
4:9 f   **Vol. 2:** 482   **Vol. 3:** 1193
4:9   **Vol. 2:** 46, 689   **Vol. 3:** 718, 819
4:10 f   **Vol. 1:** 200
4:10   **Vol. 1:** 406, 610   **Vol. 2:** 615
4:11   **Vol. 1:** 386   **Vol. 2:** 50, 73, 513–514,
          604, 615, 878   **Vol. 3:** 349, 1023
5:1 ff   **Vol. 1:** 244   **Vol. 2:** 340
5:1–13   **Vol. 3:** 588
5:1   **Vol. 2:** 691   **Vol. 3:** 490, 500
5:2 ff   **Vol. 2:** 726

257

Revelation *(cont'd)*

5:2–10   **Vol. 3:** 500
5:2–9   **Vol. 2:** 727
5:2   **Vol. 2:** 426, 653   **Vol. 3:** 54, 180, 349, 714
5:3 f   **Vol. 3:** 515
5:3   **Vol. 2:** 194
5:4   **Vol. 3:** 349, 529
5:5 ff   **Vol. 2:** 674
5:5 f   **Vol. 2:** 194
5:5   **Vol. 1:** 114, 118, 200, 427   **Vol. 2:** 320, 340   **Vol. 3:** 180, 397, 652, 869, 872
5:6 ff   **Vol. 1:** 200   **Vol. 2:** 80, 615
5:6–13   **Vol. 2:** 702
5:6   **Vol. 1:** 114, 118, 629, 634   **Vol. 2:** 147, 411, 689, 691   **Vol. 3:** 706, 715
5:8 ff   **Vol. 1:** 114
5:8–14   **Vol. 2:** 868
5:8–10   **Vol. 2:** 877
5:8   **Vol. 1:** 164   **Vol. 2:** 294, 411, 689, 867
5:9 ff   **Vol. 3:** 672
5:9 f   **Vol. 2:** 795
5:9   **Vol. 1:** 223, 268, 629, 634   **Vol. 2:** 411, 671, 674, 878   **Vol. 3:** 166, 181, 200, 349, 672–675, 1079, 1175
5:10   **Vol. 2:** 231, 380, 388, 411   **Vol. 3:** 37
5:11 ff   **Vol. 2:** 194
5:11–12   **Vol. 3:** 113
5:11   **Vol. 1:** 103   **Vol. 2:** 176, 684, 689, 692, 697, 700
5:12 ff   **Vol. 2:** 700
5:12 f   **Vol. 2:** 411   **Vol. 3:** 674
5:12–14   **Vol. 2:** 877
5:12   **Vol. 1:** 213, 629, 634   **Vol. 2:** 426, 844, 878   **Vol. 3:** 113, 349, 714, 748, 1032
5:13   **Vol. 1:** 386   **Vol. 2:** 176, 604, 615   **Vol. 3:** 718
5:13b   **Vol. 1:** 213
5:14   **Vol. 2:** 689
6 f   **Vol. 3:** 180
6–19   **Vol. 1:** 114
6   **Vol. 2:** 911
6:1–8   **Vol. 1:** 657
6:1   **Vol. 2:** 689   **Vol. 3:** 500, 1002
6:2–8   **Vol. 1:** 118
6:2   **Vol. 1:** 118, 205, 651
6:3   **Vol. 2:** 689   **Vol. 3:** 500
6:4   **Vol. 1:** 118, 205, 656   **Vol. 3:** 748, 967, 1174
6:5   **Vol. 1:** 203   **Vol. 2:** 689   **Vol. 3:** 500, 1162
6:6   **Vol. 1:** 118   **Vol. 2:** 689, 711   **Vol. 3:** 575–576, 922, 1162
6:7   **Vol. 2:** 689   **Vol. 3:** 500
6:8   **Vol. 1:** 114, 118, 205, 430   **Vol. 2:** 266, 609, 711, 926   **Vol. 3:** 967, 998, 1175, 1198
6:9–10   **Vol. 3:** 113
6:9 f   **Vol. 3:** 245, 436

6:9   **Vol. 2:** 207   **Vol. 3:** 89, 500, 686, 1046–1047
6:10 f   **Vol. 1:** 222
6:10   **Vol. 1:** 410   **Vol. 2:** 228, 426, 509   **Vol. 3:** 97, 893
6:11   **Vol. 1:** 204, 430   **Vol. 2:** 772   **Vol. 3:** 97, 256
6:12–17   **Vol. 2:** 38
6:12   **Vol. 1:** 204, 224   **Vol. 3:** 500, 558, 732, 734
6:13   **Vol. 1:** 610, 725   **Vol. 2:** 192   **Vol. 3:** 557, 736
6:14   **Vol. 3:** 736, 1013
6:15–17   **Vol. 3:** 382
6:15 f   **Vol. 2:** 844
6:15   **Vol. 1:** 217, 314, 718   **Vol. 2:** 218, 378, 699   **Vol. 3:** 381, 713
6:16   **Vol. 1:** 111, 610   **Vol. 2:** 216, 412   **Vol. 3:** 588
6:17   **Vol. 2:** 76, 426, 894
7:1–8   **Vol. 2:** 314
7:1   **Vol. 1:** 103, 517   **Vol. 2:** 689   **Vol. 3:** 179, 389, 707, 718, 868, 984, 1002
7:2 f   **Vol. 2:** 573   **Vol. 3:** 575–576, 984
7:2   **Vol. 1:** 410   **Vol. 2:** 426   **Vol. 3:** 731
7:3 ff   **Vol. 2:** 574
7:3   **Vol. 3:** 613, 868
7:4 ff   **Vol. 2:** 695
7:4–8   **Vol. 2:** 700   **Vol. 3:** 871
7:4   **Vol. 2:** 315, 684, 696, 700   **Vol. 3:** 871
7:5–8   **Vol. 2:** 700   **Vol. 3:** 397, 872
7:5   **Vol. 2:** 320   **Vol. 3:** 397
7:7   **Vol. 2:** 467
7:9–17   **Vol. 2:** 702, 868
7:9–10   **Vol. 3:** 113
7:9   **Vol. 1:** 204   **Vol. 2:** 207, 695–696, 700, 795, 799, 801   **Vol. 3:** 1079
7:10 ff   **Vol. 3:** 500
7:10–17   **Vol. 3:** 588
7:10–12   **Vol. 2:** 877
7:10   **Vol. 1:** 410   **Vol. 2:** 412, 426, 878   **Vol. 3:** 216
7:11   **Vol. 1:** 103, 200   **Vol. 2:** 689
7:12   **Vol. 1:** 99, 213   **Vol. 2:** 73, 604, 878   **Vol. 3:** 672, 714, 718, 819, 1032
7:13   **Vol. 1:** 200, 204
7:14   **Vol. 1:** 152, 223, 317   **Vol. 2:** 193, 513, 808   **Vol. 3:** 166, 181
7:15   **Vol. 3:** 784, 813
7:16 f   **Vol. 2:** 631
7:16   **Vol. 1:** 653   **Vol. 2:** 267   **Vol. 3:** 731
7:17   **Vol. 1:** 471   **Vol. 2:** 420   **Vol. 3:** 568, 943, 988–990, 1178
8–9   **Vol. 2:** 711
8   **Vol. 2:** 687
8:1   **Vol. 3:** 500
8:2 ff†   **Vol. 2:** 691
8:2–9:21   **Vol. 3:** 874
8:2 f   **Vol. 1:** 103
8:2   **Vol. 1:** 103

Revelation *(cont'd)*

8:3–11:18 **Vol. 2:** 691
8:3 **Vol. 2:** 161, 294, 702 **Vol. 3:** 436
8:4 **Vol. 2:** 294
8:5 **Vol. 2:** 294 **Vol. 3:** 436, 558, 1001–1002
8:7 f **Vol. 1:** 103
8:7 **Vol. 1:** 224, 657, 744 **Vol. 3:** 868, 1004
8:8 f **Vol. 1:** 387
8:8 **Vol. 3:** 984, 1013
8:9 **Vol. 1:** 224 **Vol. 3:** 683
8:10 ff **Vol. 3:** 737, 989
8:10 **Vol. 1:** 103, 610 **Vol. 2:** 192, 486 **Vol. 3:** 984, 987
8:11 **Vol. 1:** 202 **Vol. 2:** 27, 29 **Vol. 3:** 874
8:12 **Vol. 1:** 103, 421, 425 **Vol. 2:** 488 **Vol. 3:** 732, 734, 736
8:13† **Vol. 1:** 165 **Vol. 2:** 687 **Vol. 3:** 1054
9:1 f **Vol. 2:** 205
9:1 **Vol. 1:** 103, 610 **Vol. 2:** 192 **Vol. 3:** 737
9:2 **Vol. 1:** 425 **Vol. 2:** 727 **Vol. 3:** 93, 732
9:3 ff **Vol. 2:** 205
9:3 **Vol. 1:** 118, 511 **Vol. 2:** 609
9:4 **Vol. 1:** 744 **Vol. 2:** 565, 573 **Vol. 3:** 500–501, 575–576, 868
9:5 **Vol. 1:** 511 **Vol. 2:** 690 **Vol. 3:** 856
9:6 **Vol. 1:** 559 **Vol. 2:** 894 **Vol. 3:** 528–529, 531
9:7 ff **Vol. 1:** 119
9:7 **Vol. 1:** 118 **Vol. 2:** 503 **Vol. 3:** 962
9:8 **Vol. 1:** 118 **Vol. 3:** 1067
9:9 **Vol. 1:** 118 **Vol. 2:** 98 **Vol. 3:** 947, 962
9:10 **Vol. 1:** 511 **Vol. 2:** 609, 690 **Vol. 3:** 575–576
9:11 **Vol. 1:** 464 **Vol. 2:** 205, 309
9:12 **Vol. 1:** 204, 321, 449 **Vol. 2:** 159
9:13 **Vol. 1:** 103 **Vol. 2:** 689 **Vol. 3:** 436, 715
9:14 f **Vol. 2:** 689 **Vol. 3:** 179
9:14 **Vol. 3:** 987
9:15–18 **Vol. 1:** 430
9:17 **Vol. 1:** 118 **Vol. 3:** 515
9:18 **Vol. 3:** 857, 1198
9:19 **Vol. 1:** 118, 510 **Vol. 2:** 609 **Vol. 3:** 575–576
9:20 f **Vol. 1:** 163, 452 **Vol. 2:** 286 **Vol. 3:** 179
9:20 **Vol. 1:** 452 **Vol. 2:** 96–97, 178, 286, 794, 877 **Vol. 3:** 251, 857, 1008
9:21 **Vol. 1:** 501 **Vol. 2:** 558
10:1 ff **Vol. 1:** 103
10:1 **Vol. 1:** 239, 656 **Vol. 2:** 193 **Vol. 3:** 714, 732, 1003
10:2 **Vol. 2:** 148
10:3 f **Vol. 3:** 1002
10:3 **Vol. 1:** 118, 410 **Vol. 2:** 426

10:4 ff **Vol. 2:** 691
10:4 **Vol. 1:** 326 **Vol. 2:** 193 **Vol. 3:** 500
10:5 **Vol. 2:** 192
10:6 **Vol. 1:** 387 **Vol. 2:** 74, 193 **Vol. 3:** 742, 844, 984
10:7 **Vol. 1:** 326 **Vol. 2:** 64, 894 **Vol. 3:** 88, 505, 613
10:8 ff **Vol. 1:** 103
10:8 **Vol. 2:** 193 **Vol. 3:** 113
10:9 f **Vol. 1:** 169, 202
10:9 **Vol. 2:** 273
10:11 **Vol. 2:** 793, 799 **Vol. 3:** 1079
11:1 ff **Vol. 2:** 329
11:1 f **Vol. 3:** 404, 784, 948
11:1 **Vol. 3:** 436
11:2 **Vol. 1:** 453 **Vol. 2:** 688, 700, 795, 803 **Vol. 3:** 436, 944
11:3 ff **Vol. 1:** 545
11:3–6 **Vol. 1:** 545
11:3 **Vol. 1:** 545 **Vol. 2:** 688, 700 **Vol. 3:** 1047
11:4–11 **Vol. 2:** 686
11:4 **Vol. 1:** 321 **Vol. 2:** 487, 712
11:5 **Vol. 1:** 554, 657 **Vol. 2:** 665 **Vol. 3:** 575–576
11:6 **Vol. 1:** 163, 224, 544 **Vol. 2:** 31, 193, 686 **Vol. 3:** 81, 987–988, 1002, 1004
11:7 ff **Vol. 2:** 700
11:7 **Vol. 1:** 114, 430, 651 **Vol. 2:** 64, 205 **Vol. 3:** 962, 1047
11:8 f **Vol. 1:** 610
11:8 **Vol. 1:** 394, 532 **Vol. 2:** 329, 365, 803 **Vol. 3:** 93, 706
11:9 **Vol. 1:** 265 **Vol. 2:** 688, 795, 799 **Vol. 3:** 246, 1079
11:10 **Vol. 2:** 41, 356 **Vol. 3:** 88, 856
11:11 **Vol. 1:** 239, 609 **Vol. 3:** 694, 706, 1185
11:12 **Vol. 1:** 554 **Vol. 2:** 193 **Vol. 3:** 113
11:13 **Vol. 1:** 610 **Vol. 2:** 46, 193, 652, 700 **Vol. 3:** 253, 558
11:15–19 **Vol. 3:** 874
11:15–18 **Vol. 2:** 868, 877
11:15 **Vol. 1:** 103 **Vol. 2:** 381, 388, 426, 514 **Vol. 3:** 113, 672, 913
11:16 ff **Vol. 1:** 200
11:16 **Vol. 3:** 857
11:17 f **Vol. 3:** 672
11:17 **Vol. 2:** 69, 229, 381, 514, 604 **Vol. 3:** 718, 819
11:18 **Vol. 1:** 111, 446, 468, 623 **Vol. 2:** 76, 426 **Vol. 3:** 88, 613, 839
11:19–16:1 **Vol. 2:** 691
11:19 **Vol. 2:** 194, 727 **Vol. 3:** 558, 784, 1001–1002, 1004
12 ff **Vol. 2:** 273
12 **Vol. 1:** 508 **Vol. 2:** 653, 918 **Vol. 3:** 732, 737, 1067–1068
12:1 **Vol. 1:** 239 **Vol. 2:** 192, 695 **Vol. 3:** 732, 734, 736, 1067
12:2–6 **Vol. 2:** 700

Revelation *(cont'd)*

12:2	**Vol. 1:** 178, 187, 410 **Vol. 2:** 615 **Vol. 3:** 856, 858
12:3	**Vol. 1:** 187, 205, 405, 657 **Vol. 2:** 192, 691, 693 **Vol. 3:** 715
12:4 f	**Vol. 1:** 326 **Vol. 2:** 653
12:4	**Vol. 2:** 192, 687, 700 **Vol. 3:** 737, 1046, 1067
12:5	**Vol. 1:** 164, 187, 407 **Vol. 2:** 98, 570, 702, 795 **Vol. 3:** 470, 602–603
12:6	**Vol. 1:** 559 **Vol. 2:** 688, 700 **Vol. 3:** 1007–1008, 1067, 1198
12:7 ff	**Vol. 1:** 83, 103, 508
12:7–12	**Vol. 3:** 470
12:7	**Vol. 1:** 103–104 **Vol. 2:** 192, 688 **Vol. 3:** 962–963
12:8	**Vol. 3:** 714
12:9 ff	**Vol. 2:** 702
12:9	**Vol. 1:** 168, 508, 510, 519 **Vol. 2:** 459–461 **Vol. 3:** 470, 472
12:10 ff	**Vol. 3:** 672, 674
12:10 f	**Vol. 2:** 877
12:10	**Vol. 1:** 83 **Vol. 2:** 388, 604 **Vol. 3:** 216, 470
12:11	**Vol. 1:** 164, 223, 629, 634 **Vol. 3:** 166, 471, 683, 1046, 1183
12:12	**Vol. 2:** 193, 356 **Vol. 3:** 471, 813, 839, 1054
12:13 ff	**Vol. 1:** 508 **Vol. 3:** 984
12:13	**Vol. 2:** 570, 806
12:14–17	**Vol. 3:** 1067
12:14	**Vol. 1:** 339 **Vol. 3:** 1007
12:15 f	**Vol. 3:** 987
12:15	**Vol. 3:** 989
12:16 f	**Vol. 3:** 471
12:16	**Vol. 2:** 701
12:17	**Vol. 1:** 111, 339 **Vol. 2:** 133, 653, 695 **Vol. 3:** 89, 253, 523, 962, 1046, 1068
13	**Vol. 1:** 75, 125, 608 **Vol. 2:** 687 **Vol. 3:** 253
13:1 ff	**Vol. 2:** 625
13:1–14	**Vol. 2:** 604
13:1	**Vol. 1:** 114, 405 **Vol. 2:** 159, 381, 653, 693 **Vol. 3:** 715, 983–984
13:2	**Vol. 1:** 114, 118–119, 239, 508 **Vol. 2:** 603–604, 610
13:3	**Vol. 1:** 114, 493 **Vol. 2:** 625 **Vol. 3:** 857
13:4 ff	**Vol. 2:** 615
13:4	**Vol. 1:** 114, 508 **Vol. 2:** 610, 877 **Vol. 3:** 963
13:5	**Vol. 2:** 688, 700
13:6	**Vol. 3:** 342, 813
13:7 ff	**Vol. 1:** 111
13:7 f	**Vol. 1:** 114 **Vol. 2:** 795
13:7	**Vol. 1:** 651 **Vol. 3:** 962, 1079
13:8	**Vol. 1:** 244, 378 **Vol. 2:** 877 **Vol. 3:** 490
13:10	**Vol. 1:** 602 **Vol. 2:** 776 **Vol. 3:** 591, 967
13:11 ff	**Vol. 2:** 633
13:11–18	**Vol. 2:** 574
13:11	**Vol. 1:** 114
13:12	**Vol. 1:** 119 **Vol. 2:** 610, 674, 877
13:13	**Vol. 1:** 114, 657 **Vol. 2:** 192
13:14	**Vol. 1:** 114 **Vol. 2:** 459, 461 **Vol. 3:** 857, 967
13:15	**Vol. 1:** 114 **Vol. 2:** 288, 574 **Vol. 3:** 694, 706
13:16 f	**Vol. 1:** 114 **Vol. 3:** 500
13:16	**Vol. 2:** 428, 826, 842 **Vol. 3:** 490
13:17 ff	**Vol. 2:** 653
13:17 f	**Vol. 2:** 684
13:17	**Vol. 2:** 574, 653 **Vol. 3:** 471
13:18	**Vol. 1:** 119, 126 **Vol. 2:** 574 **Vol. 3:** 129, 1032
14:1	**Vol. 2:** 327, 329, 573, 654, 700 **Vol. 3:** 490, 500
14:2	**Vol. 3:** 990
14:3	**Vol. 1:** 200, 268, 486 **Vol. 2:** 207, 671, 674, 689, 695, 700, 702, 763 **Vol. 3:** 673, 675
14:4	**Vol. 1:** 449, 482 **Vol. 3:** 416, 568, 1067, 1072
14:5	**Vol. 2:** 473, 702 **Vol. 3:** 925
14:6 ff	**Vol. 1:** 103
14:6	**Vol. 2:** 795 **Vol. 3:** 1079
14:7	**Vol. 2:** 193, 366, 877 **Vol. 3:** 113, 848, 984, 987, 989–990, 1154
14:8	**Vol. 1:** 106, 142, 610 **Vol. 2:** 793, 795 **Vol. 3:** 922
14:9 ff	**Vol. 3:** 501
14:9	**Vol. 2:** 574 **Vol. 3:** 113, 500
14:10	**Vol. 1:** 106, 111, 657 **Vol. 2:** 76, 228 **Vol. 3:** 856, 913, 922
14:11	**Vol. 2:** 574 **Vol. 3:** 256, 500, 856
14:12	**Vol. 1:** 602 **Vol. 2:** 133, 776
14:13	**Vol. 1:** 216, 263, 441, 446 **Vol. 2:** 193 **Vol. 3:** 256, 706
14:14 ff	**Vol. 3:** 1003
14:14	**Vol. 1:** 204 **Vol. 2:** 503 **Vol. 3:** 633
14:15 ff	**Vol. 3:** 784
14:15	**Vol. 1:** 103, 410, 516 **Vol. 3:** 527, 633, 848
14:16	**Vol. 3:** 527
14:17 ff	**Vol. 1:** 103
14:18	**Vol. 1:** 657 **Vol. 2:** 33 **Vol. 3:** 114, 436
14:19 f	**Vol. 1:** 224
14:19	**Vol. 1:** 106, 111 **Vol. 2:** 33
14:20	**Vol. 2:** 697, 700 **Vol. 3:** 919
15:1 ff	**Vol. 2:** 58
15:1	**Vol. 1:** 103, 106, 111, 163 **Vol. 2:** 64, 192, 623, 625 **Vol. 3:** 857
15:2 ff	**Vol. 1:** 651 **Vol. 2:** 868
15:2–18:24	**Vol. 2:** 691
15:2	**Vol. 1:** 114, 656 **Vol. 2:** 625, 684 **Vol. 3:** 984

Revelation (cont'd)

15:3 f **Vol. 2:** 793, 877 **Vol. 3:** 672
15:3 **Vol. 2:** 58, 69, 74, 237, 378, 623, 642, 793 **Vol. 3:** 362, 672–675, 718, 893, 940
15:4 **Vol. 2:** 76, 237, 724 **Vol. 3:** 321, 362
15:5–8 **Vol. 3:** 784
15:5 **Vol. 2:** 727 **Vol. 3:** 811
15:6 f **Vol. 1:** 103
15:6 **Vol. 2:** 486 **Vol. 3:** 105, 107, 120, 857
15:7 **Vol. 1:** 106, 743 **Vol. 2:** 689
15:8 **Vol. 2:** 46, 64, 76 **Vol. 3:** 857
16 **Vol. 2:** 855
16:1 **Vol. 1:** 106 **Vol. 2:** 426 **Vol. 3:** 784
16:2 **Vol. 1:** 564 **Vol. 2:** 574 **Vol. 3:** 998
16:3 f **Vol. 1:** 224
16:3 **Vol. 3:** 683, 984
16:4 **Vol. 3:** 984, 987, 989
16:5 ff **Vol. 2:** 868
16:5–7 **Vol. 2:** 877
16:5 **Vol. 2:** 237 **Vol. 3:** 362, 988, 990
16:6 f **Vol. 1:** 222
16:6 **Vol. 2:** 854 **Vol. 3:** 88
16:7 **Vol. 2:** 69, 514 **Vol. 3:** 362, 436, 718, 893
16:8 **Vol. 1:** 653 **Vol. 3:** 731
16:9 **Vol. 1:** 359, 653 **Vol. 2:** 654 **Vol. 3:** 342, 857
16:10–12 **Vol. 3:** 1180
16:10 f **Vol. 3:** 97
16:10 **Vol. 1:** 425 **Vol. 2:** 381, 615 **Vol. 3:** 1079
16:11 **Vol. 2:** 193 **Vol. 3:** 342
16:12 **Vol. 1:** 516 **Vol. 2:** 378 **Vol. 3:** 731, 987
16:13 f **Vol. 1:** 452 **Vol. 3:** 694
16:13 **Vol. 1:** 114 **Vol. 2:** 472, 474 **Vol. 3:** 988
16:14 **Vol. 1:** 519 **Vol. 2:** 33, 69, 378, 633, 894 **Vol. 3:** 718, 962
16:15 **Vol. 1:** 216, 313 **Vol. 2:** 133, 137 **Vol. 3:** 85
16:16 **Vol. 1:** 274 **Vol. 2:** 33, 309 **Vol. 3:** 962
16:17 **Vol. 1:** 449 **Vol. 3:** 113, 784
16:18 **Vol. 3:** 558, 1001–1002
16:19 **Vol. 1:** 106, 111, 142, 610 **Vol. 2:** 795 **Vol. 3:** 241, 246, 922
16:20 **Vol. 1:** 559 **Vol. 3:** 1013
16:21 **Vol. 3:** 342, 857, 1004
17–19 **Vol. 1:** 501
17 f **Vol. 3:** 179
17 **Vol. 1:** 75 **Vol. 3:** 1047
17:1–19:10 **Vol. 1:** 142
17:1–18 **Vol. 3:** 1068
17:1 **Vol. 1:** 103, 142 **Vol. 2:** 365, 582, 653
17:2 ff **Vol. 2:** 378
17:2 **Vol. 1:** 514 **Vol. 3:** 922
17:3 f **Vol. 1:** 142

17:3 **Vol. 1:** 205, 743 **Vol. 2:** 159, 653, 693 **Vol. 3:** 706, 715, 1008, 1067
17:4 **Vol. 1:** 111, 142, 205, 743 **Vol. 3:** 395–396, 1067
17:5 **Vol. 1:** 142, 518 **Vol. 2:** 582, 625, 653 **Vol. 3:** 490, 1069
17:6 ff **Vol. 2:** 625
17:6 f **Vol. 3:** 1067
17:6 **Vol. 1:** 222, 514 **Vol. 2:** 623, 625 **Vol. 3:** 1047
17:7 **Vol. 2:** 625, 693 **Vol. 3:** 505, 715
17:8 **Vol. 1:** 114, 244, 378, 464 **Vol. 2:** 205, 625, 899
17:9 ff **Vol. 2:** 378
17:9 f **Vol. 3:** 1067
17:9 **Vol. 1:** 142 **Vol. 3:** 129, 1013, 1032, 1070
17:10 **Vol. 1:** 610 **Vol. 2:** 665, 692
17:11 **Vol. 1:** 114
17:12 ff **Vol. 3:** 715
17:12 **Vol. 2:** 381, 693 **Vol. 3:** 715
17:13 f **Vol. 2:** 603
17:13 **Vol. 2:** 398, 722
17:14 **Vol. 1:** 652 **Vol. 2:** 378, 514 **Vol. 3:** 963
17:15 **Vol. 2:** 799, 801 **Vol. 3:** 1079
17:16–18 **Vol. 3:** 1008
17:16 **Vol. 1:** 656 **Vol. 2:** 693 **Vol. 3:** 715, 1008
17:17 **Vol. 2:** 64
17:18 **Vol. 3:** 1067
18 **Vol. 3:** 1054
18:1–2 **Vol. 1:** 103 **Vol. 3:** 113
18:1 **Vol. 2:** 38, 46, 193, 486
18:2–24 **Vol. 3:** 1008
18:2 **Vol. 1:** 410, 557, 610 **Vol. 2:** 136, 249, 426 **Vol. 3:** 505, 694, 714, 1008
18:3 ff **Vol. 2:** 378
18:3 **Vol. 1:** 106, 111 **Vol. 2:** 795, 844 **Vol. 3:** 922
18:4 **Vol. 1:** 642, 644 **Vol. 2:** 193, 800 **Vol. 3:** 857
18:5 **Vol. 2:** 349 **Vol. 3:** 241–242, 575
18:6 **Vol. 3:** 572, 913
18:7 ff **Vol. 3:** 856
18:7 f **Vol. 2:** 423
18:7 **Vol. 2:** 381 **Vol. 3:** 588, 1074, 1149
18:8 **Vol. 1:** 656 **Vol. 2:** 266, 720 **Vol. 3:** 714, 857
18:9 **Vol. 1:** 656 **Vol. 2:** 417 **Vol. 3:** 1054
18:10 **Vol. 1:** 321 **Vol. 2:** 426 **Vol. 3:** 714, 848, 856
18:11 **Vol. 2:** 422 **Vol. 3:** 1054
18:12 **Vol. 1:** 390 **Vol. 2:** 97–98 **Vol. 3:** 393, 395, 913
18:13 **Vol. 1:** 114, 234 **Vol. 2:** 294–295, 711 **Vol. 3:** 922
18:14 **Vol. 1:** 457 **Vol. 2:** 486
18:15 **Vol. 2:** 422, 842, 844 **Vol. 3:** 856

Revelation *(cont'd)*

18:16   **Vol. 1:** 205   **Vol. 2:** 426   **Vol. 3:** 393, 395
18:17   **Vol. 1:** 198   **Vol. 2:** 842, 844   **Vol. 3:** 848, 1008, 1054
18:18 f   **Vol. 2:** 426
18:18   **Vol. 1:** 656
18:19   **Vol. 1:** 520   **Vol. 2:** 159, 422, 844   **Vol. 3:** 848, 1008
18:20   **Vol. 2:** 193, 228, 356   **Vol. 3:** 84, 88
18:21   **Vol. 2:** 426   **Vol. 3:** 394, 714, 1013
18:22   **Vol. 1:** 279   **Vol. 3:** 394, 874
18:23   **Vol. 1:** 452   **Vol. 2:** 459–461, 487–488, 493, 558, 578, 585, 795
18:24   **Vol. 1:** 222   **Vol. 3:** 88
19:1 f   **Vol. 3:** 672, 674
19:1–21:8   **Vol. 2:** 692
19:1–8   **Vol. 2:** 868
19:1–7   **Vol. 2:** 877
19:1   **Vol. 1:** 99   **Vol. 2:** 46, 192, 426, 604, 878   **Vol. 3:** 113, 216
19:2   **Vol. 1:** 222, 405, 468–469   **Vol. 3:** 97, 362, 613, 893
19:3   **Vol. 1:** 99   **Vol. 2:** 878
19:4 f   **Vol. 2:** 702
19:4   **Vol. 1:** 99   **Vol. 2:** 689, 878
19:5   **Vol. 2:** 73, 428   **Vol. 3:** 817
19:6 ff   **Vol. 3:** 672
19:6   **Vol. 1:** 99   **Vol. 2:** 381, 514   **Vol. 3:** 505, 674, 718, 990, 1002
19:7 ff   **Vol. 2:** 58, 581   **Vol. 3:** 1068
19:7–9   **Vol. 2:** 354
19:7 f   **Vol. 1:** 657
19:7   **Vol. 1:** 164   **Vol. 2:** 354, 358, 412, 585   **Vol. 3:** 118, 1067
19:8   **Vol. 2:** 486   **Vol. 3:** 107, 362, 714
19:9   **Vol. 1:** 164, 216, 274   **Vol. 2:** 358, 412, 585   **Vol. 3:** 489, 893
19:10   **Vol. 1:** 103, 239, 609   **Vol. 2:** 877   **Vol. 3:** 81, 89, 706
19:11–21   **Vol. 2:** 700
19:11   **Vol. 1:** 118, 205   **Vol. 2:** 727   **Vol. 3:** 362, 963
19:12   **Vol. 1:** 656   **Vol. 2:** 654   **Vol. 3:** 365, 490
19:13   **Vol. 1:** 63, 145, 164, 224   **Vol. 2:** 654, 686   **Vol. 3:** 326, 1114
19:14   **Vol. 1:** 118, 204–205   **Vol. 3:** 107, 964
19:15 f   **Vol. 2:** 514
19:15   **Vol. 1:** 106, 111, 164, 407   **Vol. 2:** 69, 98, 686, 795   **Vol. 3:** 718, 922, 967
19:16   **Vol. 1:** 168   **Vol. 2:** 378, 654   **Vol. 3:** 490, 964
19:17 ff   **Vol. 3:** 716
19:17–21   **Vol. 1:** 118
19:17   **Vol. 1:** 103, 410   **Vol. 2:** 33   **Vol. 3:** 732
19:18 ff   **Vol. 2:** 378
19:18   **Vol. 2:** 428, 699

19:19 f   **Vol. 1:** 114
19:19   **Vol. 2:** 33   **Vol. 3:** 964
19:20   **Vol. 1:** 114, 657   **Vol. 2:** 209, 459, 472, 474, 574, 633   **Vol. 3:** 992
19:21   **Vol. 1:** 430, 744   **Vol. 3:** 252, 967
20   **Vol. 1:** 53   **Vol. 2:** 701–703
20:1 ff   **Vol. 1:** 103   **Vol. 2:** 65, 631
20:1–7   **Vol. 2:** 389, 697
20:1–5   **Vol. 1:** 52
20:1–3   **Vol. 2:** 702
20:1   **Vol. 2:** 205, 734
20:2 f   **Vol. 1:** 508
20:2–7   **Vol. 2:** 700–701
20:2   **Vol. 1:** 168, 508, 510   **Vol. 3:** 718
20:3   **Vol. 1:** 508   **Vol. 2:** 64, 205, 459, 461, 665, 702, 734, 795   **Vol. 3:** 179, 499
20:4 ff   **Vol. 3:** 277, 303
20:4   **Vol. 1:** 205   **Vol. 2:** 207, 365, 380, 574, 613   **Vol. 3:** 89, 278, 490, 686, 1046
20:5 f   **Vol. 3:** 278
20:5   **Vol. 1:** 446   **Vol. 2:** 64, 380   **Vol. 3:** 252
20:6   **Vol. 1:** 649   **Vol. 2:** 231, 304, 380   **Vol. 3:** 37, 304
20:7 ff   **Vol. 1:** 111   **Vol. 3:** 389
20:7–10   **Vol. 3:** 962
20:7   **Vol. 2:** 64, 136, 207   **Vol. 3:** 179, 471, 962
20:8–15   **Vol. 2:** 701
20:8–10   **Vol. 2:** 460
20:8   **Vol. 1:** 508   **Vol. 2:** 33, 459, 461, 684, 689, 795   **Vol. 3:** 962
20:9   **Vol. 1:** 254, 657   **Vol. 2:** 193   **Vol. 3:** 965, 1174
20:10 ff   **Vol. 3:** 992
20:10   **Vol. 1:** 114, 508, 657   **Vol. 2:** 209, 459–460, 472, 474, 631   **Vol. 3:** 99, 471, 856
20:11 ff   **Vol. 3:** 277
20:11–15   **Vol. 3:** 136, 277, 303
20:11   **Vol. 1:** 204, 559   **Vol. 2:** 193   **Vol. 3:** 589, 1013
20:12 f   **Vol. 1:** 446   **Vol. 2:** 365
20:12   **Vol. 1:** 244   **Vol. 2:** 426   **Vol. 3:** 136
20:13 f   **Vol. 1:** 441   **Vol. 2:** 207, 926
20:13   **Vol. 2:** 207   **Vol. 3:** 984
20:14 f   **Vol. 2:** 209   **Vol. 3:** 99
20:14   **Vol. 1:** 437, 657   **Vol. 2:** 207   **Vol. 3:** 304, 471
20:15   **Vol. 3:** 136, 490, 528
21 f   **Vol. 2:** 764
21   **Vol. 2:** 303   **Vol. 3:** 396–398, 948
21:1 ff   **Vol. 1:** 387   **Vol. 2:** 632
21:1–25:5   **Vol. 1:** 142
21:1–5   **Vol. 1:** 185
21:1–4   **Vol. 2:** 779
21:1   **Vol. 1:** 321, 518   **Vol. 2:** 193, 631, 671, 674   **Vol. 3:** 558, 984, 1013
21:2 f   **Vol. 3:** 1068

Revelation *(cont'd)*

21:2   **Vol. 2:** 186, 194, 231, 329, 563, 585, 671, 674, 722, 804   **Vol. 3:** 118

21:3 f   **Vol. 2:** 483

21:3   **Vol. 1:** 368   **Vol. 2:** 193, 426, 800   **Vol. 3:** 518, 784, 813

21:4   **Vol. 1:** 321   **Vol. 2:** 419–420, 423, 631, 674   **Vol. 3:** 872

21:5   **Vol. 1:** 186, 387   **Vol. 2:** 674   **Vol. 3:** 588, 893, 1154, 1193

21:6   **Vol. 1:** 166   **Vol. 2:** 41, 59, 64, 80, 267, 282, 482   **Vol. 3:** 988, 991

21:7   **Vol. 1:** 651   **Vol. 2:** 300

21:8   **Vol. 1:** 452, 657   **Vol. 2:** 74, 286, 304, 473, 495, 558, 584   **Vol. 3:** 304, 992, 1067

21:9 ff   **Vol. 2:** 585

21:9 f   **Vol. 3:** 569

21:9–22:21   **Vol. 2:** 692

21:9   **Vol. 1:** 743   **Vol. 2:** 58, 585   **Vol. 3:** 857, 1068

21:10 ff   **Vol. 2:** 804

21:10 f   **Vol. 2:** 48, 329

21:10   **Vol. 2:** 186, 194, 199, 231   **Vol. 3:** 706, 1010

21:11   **Vol. 2:** 76, 493   **Vol. 3:** 393, 396–398

21:12 ff   **Vol. 1:** 200   **Vol. 2:** 696

21:12 f   **Vol. 2:** 30, 329

21:12   **Vol. 2:** 199, 315, 652   **Vol. 3:** 397, 490, 871, 948, 1010

21:13   **Vol. 2:** 687   **Vol. 3:** 397, 1003

21:14   **Vol. 1:** 130, 134, 661   **Vol. 2:** 412, 652   **Vol. 3:** 88, 387, 395, 397

21:15   **Vol. 3:** 404

21:16   **Vol. 1:** 254   **Vol. 2:** 199, 498, 700

21:17–21   **Vol. 3:** 948

21:17   **Vol. 3:** 404, 948

21:18   **Vol. 2:** 96   **Vol. 3:** 107

21:19–21   **Vol. 3:** 396

21:19 f   **Vol. 3:** 872

21:19   **Vol. 1:** 661   **Vol. 3:** 393, 395, 398

21:21   **Vol. 2:** 30, 96   **Vol. 3:** 107, 395

21:22   **Vol. 2:** 58, 69, 194, 231, 329, 514   **Vol. 3:** 37, 718, 784, 1068

21:23 f   **Vol. 2:** 495

21:23   **Vol. 2:** 76, 412, 487–488   **Vol. 3:** 398, 732, 734

21:24   **Vol. 2:** 378, 793, 795   **Vol. 3:** 944

21:25   **Vol. 1:** 421   **Vol. 2:** 30   **Vol. 3:** 387, 395, 948

21:26   **Vol. 2:** 795

21:27   **Vol. 1:** 448, 641   **Vol. 2:** 74, 473, 495   **Vol. 3:** 490

22:1 f   **Vol. 2:** 763   **Vol. 3:** 962, 988

22:1   **Vol. 2:** 482, 486, 615, 702   **Vol. 3:** 569, 988–989, 991, 1203

22:2–14   **Vol. 2:** 482

22:2   **Vol. 1:** 390, 723   **Vol. 3:** 868

22:3   **Vol. 1:** 415   **Vol. 2:** 495, 665, 702   **Vol. 3:** 613

22:4   **Vol. 1:** 587   **Vol. 2:** 573, 654, 804   **Vol. 3:** 490, 500

22:5   **Vol. 1:** 421   **Vol. 2:** 388, 487, 493, 495   **Vol. 3:** 397, 732

22:6   **Vol. 2:** 514, 665   **Vol. 3:** 88, 569, 694, 893

22:7   **Vol. 3:** 85

22:8 f   **Vol. 1:** 103   **Vol. 2:** 877

22:8   **Vol. 1:** 239, 609   **Vol. 3:** 569

22:9   **Vol. 3:** 88

22:10   **Vol. 3:** 500, 838

22:11   **Vol. 1:** 479   **Vol. 2:** 495   **Vol. 3:** 362, 575–576

22:12   **Vol. 3:** 136

22:13   **Vol. 1:** 166, 667   **Vol. 2:** 58–59, 64, 80, 282, 674

22:14   **Vol. 1:** 339, 390–391   **Vol. 2:** 30, 763   **Vol. 3:** 868

22:15   **Vol. 1:** 452   **Vol. 2:** 286, 473, 558, 584   **Vol. 3:** 99, 948

22:16   **Vol. 1:** 117, 304, 407, 427   **Vol. 2:** 340, 486, 495, 558   **Vol. 3:** 652, 735–737, 869

22:17–21   **Vol. 2:** 516, 523, 530

22:17   **Vol. 2:** 41, 267, 482, 585, 883   **Vol. 3:** 706, 988, 991, 1023

22:18 f   **Vol. 2:** 495   **Vol. 3:** 88, 489–490

22:18   **Vol. 3:** 857

22:19   **Vol. 1:** 390–391   **Vol. 2:** 231, 304, 482   **Vol. 3:** 868

22:20   **Vol. 1:** 99, 323   **Vol. 2:** 229, 530–531, 585, 674, 896   **Vol. 3:** 316, 319

Old Testament Apocrypha and Pseudepigrapha

Addition to Daniel: Susanna
(Ad. Dan. Sus.)

5	**Vol. 3:** 570, 821
13	**Vol. 3:** 943
37	**Vol. 3:** 255

Addition to Daniel: Bel and the Dragon
(Ad. Dan. Bel)

1	**Vol. 3:** 873	
3	**Vol. 2:** 876	
5	**Vol. 1:** 380	
7	**Vol. 2:** 431	
9	**Vol. 2:** 284	**Vol. 3:** 342, 570
11	**Vol. 3:** 911	
12	**Vol. 2:** 730	
14	**Vol. 2:** 285	**Vol. 3:** 557
15	**Vol. 2:** 437	
18	**Vol. 2:** 431	
19	**Vol. 2:** 431	
23	**Vol. 2:** 876	
30	**Vol. 2:** 801	

Additions to Esther (Ad. Est.)

13.1–6	**Vol. 1:** 246
13.12 ff	**Vol. 2:** 310
16.4	**Vol. 3:** 818

Apocalypse of Ezra. *See* 2 Esdras

Aristeas, Letter of (Aristeas)

47–50	**Vol. 2:** 697
84	**Vol. 3:** 229
102	**Vol. 3:** 570
139	**Vol. 3:** 186
178	**Vol. 3:** 908
225	**Vol. 2:** 116

Assumption of Moses (Ass. Mos.)

3.9	**Vol. 3:** 263	
6 ff	**Vol. 1:** 125	
7	**Vol. 2:** 311	
10.1	**Vol. 2:** 602	
10.5	**Vol. 1:** 203	**Vol. 3:** 731, 733
10.7–10	**Vol. 3:** 961	

10.12	**Vol. 2:** 892
11.17	**Vol. 3:** 46
12.10	**Vol. 1:** 334

1 Baruch (Bar.). *See also* Epistle of Jeremy

1–3	**Vol. 1:** 345	
1.10 ff	**Vol. 1:** 700	
1.11	**Vol. 2:** 863	
1.12	**Vol. 3:** 555	
1.13	**Vol. 2:** 863	
1.20	**Vol. 1:** 683	**Vol. 3:** 610
2.6	**Vol. 3:** 1163	
2.8	**Vol. 3:** 125	
2.9	**Vol. 2:** 136	
2.11	**Vol. 2:** 627	
2.12	**Vol. 3:** 354	
2.17	**Vol. 3:** 233, 354	
2.19	**Vol. 3:** 354	
2.20	**Vol. 3:** 610	
2.28	**Vol. 3:** 610	
2.32	**Vol. 3:** 816	
3.6 f	**Vol. 3:** 816	
3.12 f	**Vol. 2:** 840	
3.12	**Vol. 3:** 842	
3.13	**Vol. 3:** 842	
3.14	**Vol. 1:** 485	
3.23	**Vol. 2:** 644	
3.27–28	**Vol. 3:** 641	
3.34	**Vol. 3:** 735	
4.7	**Vol. 1:** 451	
4.8–23	**Vol. 3:** 1068	
4.10	**Vol. 3:** 1194	
4.13	**Vol. 3:** 354	
4.22	**Vol. 3:** 218	
4.24	**Vol. 3:** 209	
4.27	**Vol. 3:** 238	
4.29	**Vol. 3:** 209	
5.5	**Vol. 3:** 238	
5.7	**Vol. 1:** 663	
5.8	**Vol. 3:** 555	
6	**Vol. 2:** 285	
6.18	**Vol. 3:** 379	
6.28	**Vol. 3:** 444–445	

2 Baruch. *See* Syriac Apocalypse of Baruch

3 Baruch. *See* Greek Book of Baruch

Ecclesiasticus. *See* Sirach, Book of

1 Enoch. *See* Ethiopic Book of Enoch

2 Enoch. *See* Slavonic Book of Enoch

3 Enoch. *See* Hebrew Book of Enoch

Epistle of Jeremy (Ep. Jer.)
[appears at end of 1 Baruch
(= Bar. 6)]

5 f	**Vol. 2:** 876
9	**Vol. 3:** 119
12	**Vol. 2:** 27
24	**Vol. 2:** 27
37	**Vol. 2:** 663
45 f	**Vol. 3:** 119
60	**Vol. 3:** 735
65	**Vol. 1:** 416

1 Esdras (1 Esd.) [LXX and English versions, 3 Esd. in Vulgate]

1.5	**Vol. 2:** 425
1.8	**Vol. 3:** 786
1.20	**Vol. 3:** 841
1.48	**Vol. 3:** 583
1.55	**Vol. 3:** 177
1.57	**Vol. 1:** 735
2.2	**Vol. 3:** 51
2.20	**Vol. 3:** 1147
2.28	**Vol. 1:** 694
3.5	**Vol. 3:** 1028
3.7	**Vol. 3:** 1027
3.8	**Vol. 3:** 498
3.9	**Vol. 3:** 1028
4.20	**Vol. 2:** 349
4.22	**Vol. 3:** 241
4.31	**Vol. 2:** 431
4.37	**Vol. 3:** 1149
4.39	**Vol. 2:** 817
4.40	**Vol. 2:** 425
4.42	**Vol. 3:** 1028
4.44	**Vol. 3:** 534
4.56	**Vol. 3:** 144
4.57	**Vol. 3:** 534
4.59 f	**Vol. 3:** 1027
5.6	**Vol. 3:** 1028
5.39	**Vol. 3:** 534
5.43	**Vol. 3:** 786
5.50	**Vol. 3:** 813
5.53	**Vol. 1:** 380
5.60	**Vol. 3:** 669

5.62	**Vol. 3:** 669
5.63	**Vol. 1:** 695
6.13	**Vol. 1:** 380
6.15	**Vol. 2:** 191
6.31	**Vol. 2:** 839
7.13	**Vol. 3:** 534
8 f	**Vol. 3:** 456
8.7	**Vol. 3:** 760
8.11	**Vol. 3:** 821
8.17	**Vol. 3:** 957
8.18	**Vol. 3:** 786
8.23	**Vol. 3:** 760, 1027
8.24	**Vol. 3:** 98
8.46	**Vol. 3:** 820
8.47	**Vol. 3:** 873
8.62	**Vol. 3:** 846
8.64	**Vol. 3:** 786
8.76	**Vol. 3:** 841
8.94	**Vol. 1:** 589
9.3	**Vol. 3:** 51
9.9	**Vol. 3:** 534
9.13	**Vol. 3:** 177
9.36	**Vol. 1:** 505
9.40	**Vol. 3:** 808
9.41	**Vol. 3:** 125
9.42	**Vol. 2:** 369
9.46	**Vol. 3:** 177
9.47	**Vol. 1:** 409
9.48 f	**Vol. 3:** 760
9.53	**Vol. 1:** 341
9.55	**Vol. 3:** 760

2 Esdras (2 Esd.)

3.7	**Vol. 1:** 434	**Vol. 2:** 791
3.10 f	**Vol. 3:** 816	
3.12	**Vol. 2:** 791, 800	
4.5	**Vol. 2:** 139	
4.21	**Vol. 1:** 73	
4.23	**Vol. 1:** 73	
4.28 ff	**Vol. 3:** 522	
4.33	**Vol. 2:** 892	
4.35	**Vol. 2:** 892	
4.36	**Vol. 2:** 925	
4.38	**Vol. 3:** 1148	
4.43	**Vol. 3:** 1148	
4.51 ff	**Vol. 3:** 575	
4.51 f	**Vol. 2:** 629	
5.2 ff	**Vol. 2:** 892	
5.4	**Vol. 2:** 688	**Vol. 3:** 731, 733
5.5	**Vol. 1:** 73	**Vol. 3:** 393
5.8	**Vol. 1:** 124	
5.23 ff	**Vol. 1:** 539	
5.23	**Vol. 2:** 313	
5.26	**Vol. 2:** 314	
5.45	**Vol. 2:** 207	**Vol. 3:** 210
5.50 ff	**Vol. 1:** 124	
6.5 ff	**Vol. 2:** 830	
6.7	**Vol. 2:** 56	
6.8	**Vol. 1:** 73	

2 Esdras (2 Esd.) *(cont'd)*

6.10	**Vol. 2:** 863
6.11 f	**Vol. 2:** 629
6.11	**Vol. 2:** 839
6.15	**Vol. 3:** 559
6.21	**Vol. 1:** 124
6.23–24	**Vol. 3:** 874
6.23	**Vol. 2:** 925
6.26	**Vol. 1:** 545
6.27 f	**Vol. 3:** 462
6.29	**Vol. 3:** 559
6.34	**Vol. 2:** 56
6.55 ff	**Vol. 2:** 798
6.58	**Vol. 2:** 798
7	**Vol. 2:** 364, 842 **Vol. 3:** 271, 293
7.7 ff	**Vol. 2:** 481 **Vol. 3:** 940
7.7 f	**Vol. 3:** 940
7.7	**Vol. 3:** 672
7.11	**Vol. 2:** 310
7.12 f	**Vol. 2:** 928
7.13	**Vol. 2:** 420
7.20	**Vol. 3:** 957
7.24	**Vol. 3:** 673
7.25	**Vol. 3:** 1027
7.26	**Vol. 2:** 803 **Vol. 3:** 772
7.28 f	**Vol. 2:** 701 **Vol. 3:** 610, 637, 642
7.28–31	**Vol. 3:** 271
7.28	**Vol. 3:** 652
7.29	**Vol. 2:** 893
7.31 ff	**Vol. 1:** 434
7.32–38	**Vol. 3:** 303
7.32–36	**Vol. 3:** 271
7.36	**Vol. 2:** 208
7.37 ff	**Vol. 3:** 271
7.38	**Vol. 1:** 656
7.77	**Vol. 2:** 830
7.78 ff	**Vol. 3:** 682
7.78–100	**Vol. 2:** 207
7.88 ff	**Vol. 1:** 435
7.88	**Vol. 2:** 565
7.89	**Vol. 3:** 271
7.97	**Vol. 2:** 486 **Vol. 3:** 271
7.98 ff	**Vol. 2:** 736
7.98	**Vol. 3:** 106
7.100	**Vol. 2:** 565
7.113	**Vol. 2:** 56
7.119	**Vol. 3:** 70, 1149
7.132–139	**Vol. 2:** 651
8.3	**Vol. 3:** 210
8.17	**Vol. 3:** 673
8.25	**Vol. 3:** 416
8.31–33	**Vol. 2:** 118
8.31	**Vol. 3:** 201
8.36	**Vol. 1:** 710 **Vol. 2:** 118
8.41	**Vol. 3:** 210
8.47–54	**Vol. 2:** 261
8.52 ff	**Vol. 2:** 928
8.52	**Vol. 2:** 803
8.59	**Vol. 2:** 265
8.63	**Vol. 2:** 629
9.7 f	**Vol. 3:** 250
9.7	**Vol. 1:** 598 **Vol. 3:** 210
9.13	**Vol. 3:** 210
9.17	**Vol. 3:** 522
9.26–13.56	**Vol. 2:** 745
9.31	**Vol. 3:** 522
9.38–10.59	**Vol. 3:** 1068
9.38–10.27	**Vol. 3:** 509
10.1	**Vol. 2:** 863
10.2	**Vol. 2:** 578, 773
10.6	**Vol. 3:** 796
10.7	**Vol. 3:** 1069
10.19	**Vol. 1:** 569
10.23	**Vol. 3:** 498
10.24	**Vol. 3:** 672
10.27	**Vol. 2:** 326
10.54	**Vol. 2:** 326
12.22	**Vol. 3:** 650
12.31	**Vol. 3:** 650
12.33	**Vol. 3:** 961
12.34	**Vol. 3:** 250
12.36 ff	**Vol. 3:** 502
13.1–13	**Vol. 3:** 616
13.5 ff	**Vol. 3:** 962
13.10 f	**Vol. 1:** 656 **Vol. 2:** 836
13.23	**Vol. 3:** 210
13.25 ff	**Vol. 2:** 326
13.25	**Vol. 3:** 652
13.26	**Vol. 3:** 250, 616
13.32	**Vol. 3:** 610, 616, 637, 642
13.36	**Vol. 2:** 326
13.37	**Vol. 3:** 610, 616, 637, 642
13.48	**Vol. 3:** 250
13.52	**Vol. 3:** 610, 616, 637, 642
13.54	**Vol. 3:** 616
14.5	**Vol. 2:** 56
14.9	**Vol. 2:** 202 **Vol. 3:** 610, 637, 642
14.22	**Vol. 3:** 939
14.23	**Vol. 2:** 696
14.29	**Vol. 3:** 210
14.34	**Vol. 3:** 210
14.35	**Vol. 3:** 210
14.42–47	**Vol. 1:** 243–244
14.49	**Vol. 2:** 202

3 Esdras. *See* 1 Esdras

**Ethiopic Book of Enoch
(Eth. Enoch)**

1–36	**Vol. 3:** 265, 272
1.3–9	**Vol. 2:** 897
1.6–9	**Vol. 2:** 836
1.9	**Vol. 1:** 85 **Vol. 2:** 155, 219, 817, 897 **Vol. 3:** 265, 492
5.4	**Vol. 1:** 607
5.6	**Vol. 3:** 210
5.8 f	**Vol. 2:** 892
6 ff	**Vol. 3:** 636

Ethiopic Book of Enoch
(Eth. Enoch) *(cont'd)*

6–16	**Vol. 1:** 102
6–11	**Vol. 2:** 681
6	**Vol. 2:** 213 **Vol. 3:** 801
6.6	**Vol. 1:** 451
6.7	**Vol. 2:** 651
7.2 ff	**Vol. 1:** 452
7.5–9.3	**Vol. 1:** 410
8.1	**Vol. 1:** 452
9.1	**Vol. 1:** 103
9.3	**Vol. 2:** 882
9.9–10	**Vol. 1:** 103
10.4 ff	**Vol. 2:** 205
10.4	**Vol. 3:** 1006
10.6	**Vol. 2:** 364
10.10	**Vol. 2:** 928
10.17 ff	**Vol. 1:** 729
10.17	**Vol. 2:** 698
10.19	**Vol. 2:** 698
14.9–22	**Vol. 1:** 655
14.11	**Vol. 1:** 280
14.16–20	**Vol. 3:** 789
14.18 ff	**Vol. 2:** 613
14.18 f	**Vol. 2:** 613
14.18	**Vol. 1:** 280
14.22	**Vol. 2:** 698
15.4	**Vol. 3:** 693
15.6–10	**Vol. 3:** 693
15.6	**Vol. 3:** 693
15.7	**Vol. 3:** 229
15.10	**Vol. 3:** 229
17.3	**Vol. 2:** 830
17.6	**Vol. 1:** 423, 674
18.2	**Vol. 2:** 689
18.11 ff	**Vol. 2:** 205
18.13–16	**Vol. 2:** 459
19–21	**Vol. 1:** 102
19	**Vol. 3:** 801
19.1	**Vol. 3:** 459
20.2	**Vol. 1:** 464
20.5	**Vol. 1:** 104
20.7	**Vol. 1:** 103, 280
21.1–10	**Vol. 2:** 459
22	**Vol. 2:** 207
22.7	**Vol. 1:** 410
22.9 ff	**Vol. 3:** 229
22.9	**Vol. 2:** 274
22.12	**Vol. 1:** 410
22.13	**Vol. 3:** 272
24.4	**Vol. 2:** 763
25.3	**Vol. 3:** 789
25.4 f	**Vol. 1:** 389–390 **Vol. 2:** 763
26.1 f	**Vol. 3:** 789
26.1	**Vol. 1:** 523
27.1 ff	**Vol. 2:** 208
37–71	**Vol. 3:** 196, 265, 610, 614, 789
37.4	**Vol. 2:** 928 **Vol. 3:** 640
38.1	**Vol. 2:** 731
38.2	**Vol. 2:** 899
38.3	**Vol. 3:** 502
39.3 f	**Vol. 2:** 762
39.3	**Vol. 2:** 202
39.4 ff	**Vol. 3:** 229, 692
39.4 f	**Vol. 3:** 682
40.1	**Vol. 2:** 698
40.3	**Vol. 1:** 103
40.6	**Vol. 1:** 103
40.9	**Vol. 1:** 103 **Vol. 2:** 602–603, 928
42	**Vol. 3:** 1029
42.1 ff	**Vol. 3:** 1116
42.1 f	**Vol. 2:** 840 **Vol. 3:** 1115
45.3	**Vol. 2:** 250, 614
46	**Vol. 3:** 615, 961
46.3 ff	**Vol. 3:** 615
46.3 f	**Vol. 1:** 321
46.3	**Vol. 2:** 216, 835 **Vol. 3:** 615
46.6	**Vol. 3:** 272
46.7 f	**Vol. 2:** 652
46.8	**Vol. 3:** 615
47.1 f	**Vol. 3:** 242
47.1–4	**Vol. 3:** 956
48.1	**Vol. 1:** 729 **Vol. 3:** 459, 986
48.2 ff	**Vol. 3:** 615
48.2	**Vol. 1:** 321
48.7	**Vol. 2:** 228, 928 **Vol. 3:** 210, 575
48.8 f	**Vol. 2:** 228
49.3	**Vol. 1:** 175
49.4	**Vol. 2:** 899
50.3	**Vol. 3:** 210
51	**Vol. 3:** 961
51.1 f	**Vol. 3:** 272
51.1	**Vol. 2:** 207
51.2	**Vol. 3:** 633
51.3	**Vol. 2:** 216, 613
51.5 f	**Vol. 1:** 729
51.5	**Vol. 2:** 486
52.1	**Vol. 2:** 202, 762
52.6	**Vol. 2:** 836
53	**Vol. 3:** 961
53.6	**Vol. 2:** 731 **Vol. 3:** 615
54.1 ff	**Vol. 2:** 208
54.6	**Vol. 1:** 103 **Vol. 3:** 469
54.7–55.2	**Vol. 2:** 681
55 f	**Vol. 3:** 961
55.4	**Vol. 2:** 613
56.3 f	**Vol. 2:** 208
56.5	**Vol. 3:** 615
58.2	**Vol. 1:** 216
60	**Vol. 2:** 681
60.7	**Vol. 3:** 983
60.8	**Vol. 3:** 1006
60.16	**Vol. 3:** 983
61.8	**Vol. 3:** 1161
61.10	**Vol. 2:** 518, 602–603, 608 **Vol. 3:** 983
62	**Vol. 3:** 961
62.2	**Vol. 2:** 613–614
62.3	**Vol. 2:** 369, 613–614, 926
62.5 ff	**Vol. 2:** 613–614

**Ethiopic Book of Enoch
(Eth. Enoch)** *(cont'd)*

62.5	**Vol. 2:** 369, 926
62.7 ff	**Vol. 3:** 615
62.8	**Vol. 2:** 731 **Vol. 3:** 615
62.11–15	**Vol. 1:** 539
62.12	**Vol. 1:** 110
62.13–16	**Vol. 3:** 272
62.13	**Vol. 3:** 210
62.14 ff	**Vol. 1:** 204
62.14	**Vol. 2:** 532
63.6	**Vol. 1:** 423
63.10	**Vol. 2:** 207
65.1–69.25	**Vol. 2:** 681
66.2	**Vol. 3:** 983
68.1	**Vol. 3:** 502
69.2 f	**Vol. 2:** 655–656
69.4	**Vol. 2:** 195
69.13–21	**Vol. 2:** 652
69.22	**Vol. 3:** 983
70 f	**Vol. 3:** 615, 618
71	**Vol. 3:** 615
71.1	**Vol. 2:** 195
71.11	**Vol. 1:** 409, 527
71.14	**Vol. 2:** 817
71.15 f	**Vol. 3:** 229
71.15	**Vol. 2:** 928
71.16	**Vol. 3:** 682
72–82	**Vol. 2:** 191 **Vol. 3:** 265
72–74	**Vol. 3:** 731
72.7–32	**Vol. 1:** 627
76.1 ff	**Vol. 2:** 695
77.1 ff	**Vol. 2:** 689
77.1	**Vol. 1:** 212
78	**Vol. 3:** 731
80.4 ff	**Vol. 1:** 124
80.4	**Vol. 3:** 733
81.4	**Vol. 1:** 243
82.8	**Vol. 2:** 602–603
82.11 ff	**Vol. 2:** 689
82.11	**Vol. 2:** 695
83–90	**Vol. 3:** 265
83.7	**Vol. 3:** 502
83.8	**Vol. 2:** 731 **Vol. 3:** 250
84.5	**Vol. 2:** 731
85–90	**Vol. 2:** 745 **Vol. 3:** 789
86.1–88.3	**Vol. 3:** 468
89.52	**Vol. 2:** 202
89.59 ff	**Vol. 2:** 696
89.59 f	**Vol. 2:** 690
89.61–64	**Vol. 1:** 243
89.76	**Vol. 3:** 35
90.9	**Vol. 3:** 715
90.19	**Vol. 3:** 961
90.26 f	**Vol. 2:** 208
90.29	**Vol. 3:** 509
90.30	**Vol. 3:** 250
90.31	**Vol. 1:** 545 **Vol. 2:** 202
90.33	**Vol. 2:** 311 **Vol. 3:** 272
90.37 f	**Vol. 3:** 715
91–104	**Vol. 3:** 265
91–94	**Vol. 2:** 892
91.1	**Vol. 3:** 693
91.5 ff	**Vol. 3:** 575
91.9	**Vol. 1:** 655–656
91.10	**Vol. 1:** 442
91.12 f	**Vol. 2:** 701
91.16	**Vol. 2:** 602–603
92.3	**Vol. 1:** 442
93.1–14	**Vol. 2:** 701
93.9	**Vol. 1:** 607
94	**Vol. 3:** 961
94.7	**Vol. 3:** 961
94.9	**Vol. 3:** 961
94.10	**Vol. 3:** 961
95.3 ff	**Vol. 3:** 272
95.3	**Vol. 3:** 961
96.4	**Vol. 2:** 842
98.10	**Vol. 3:** 193–194, 196, 210
98.14	**Vol. 3:** 210
99	**Vol. 1:** 124
99.1	**Vol. 3:** 210
99.7	**Vol. 1:** 452 **Vol. 3:** 806
100.1–5	**Vol. 3:** 961
100.6	**Vol. 2:** 842
100.9	**Vol. 1:** 655–656
102 ff	**Vol. 1:** 435
102.1	**Vol. 1:** 656 **Vol. 3:** 210
102.5	**Vol. 2:** 207
103.2 ff	**Vol. 3:** 502
103.4 f	**Vol. 2:** 842
103.4	**Vol. 3:** 272, 682
103.5	**Vol. 1:** 216
103.7	**Vol. 2:** 207 **Vol. 3:** 682
104.2–6	**Vol. 3:** 272
105.1–2	**Vol. 3:** 637
105.2	**Vol. 2:** 405 **Vol. 3:** 642
106	**Vol. 2:** 681 **Vol. 3:** 642
106.1–19	**Vol. 2:** 681
106.5	**Vol. 2:** 195
106.16	**Vol. 3:** 209
107	**Vol. 2:** 681
108.11 ff	**Vol. 1:** 423
108.12	**Vol. 2:** 279

4 Ezra. *See* 2 Esdras

Greek Book of Baruch (Gr. Bar.)

2 ff	**Vol. 2:** 202
2.2	**Vol. 2:** 762
4	**Vol. 2:** 207
4.17	**Vol. 3:** 31
6–9	**Vol. 3:** 731
8.5	**Vol. 3:** 31
13.2	**Vol. 1:** 554
13.4	**Vol. 3:** 31

Hebrew Book of Enoch (Heb. Enoch)

5.6	**Vol. 2:** 158
11.1	**Vol. 3:** 502
48C.7	**Vol. 3:** 35, 640
48D.1	**Vol. 3:** 35

Jubilees, Book of (Jub.)

1.11	**Vol. 1:** 452
1.16	**Vol. 2:** 158
1.17	**Vol. 3:** 509
1.20	**Vol. 3:** 939
1.22 – 25	**Vol. 3:** 637
1.24 f	**Vol. 1:** 615, 618
1.27 f	**Vol. 3:** 509
1.27	**Vol. 1:** 104
1.28	**Vol. 1:** 618
1.29	**Vol. 1:** 104
2.1	**Vol. 1:** 104
2.2 f	**Vol. 2:** 603
2.4	**Vol. 3:** 984
2.17 – 33	**Vol. 3:** 407
2.18	**Vol. 3:** 623
2.20	**Vol. 3:** 637
3.10	**Vol. 1:** 656
4.17	**Vol. 2:** 817 **Vol. 3:** 265
4.20	**Vol. 2:** 698
4.25	**Vol. 3:** 35
5.1 – 12	**Vol. 3:** 468
5.1	**Vol. 1:** 452
5.6 ff	**Vol. 2:** 205
5.14	**Vol. 1:** 423
6.7	**Vol. 1:** 221
6.12 ff	**Vol. 1:** 221
6.17 – 21	**Vol. 2:** 784
6.23 – 32	**Vol. 1:** 627
6.32 – 38	**Vol. 1:** 627
7.19	**Vol. 3:** 962
7.27	**Vol. 1:** 452
8.19	**Vol. 1:** 523
8.25	**Vol. 3:** 962
9.8	**Vol. 3:** 962
9.15	**Vol. 1:** 656
10.1 ff	**Vol. 1:** 452
10.8	**Vol. 3:** 468
10.17	**Vol. 2:** 817
10.22	**Vol. 2:** 791
11.19	**Vol. 1:** 572
15	**Vol. 1:** 309
15.13	**Vol. 3:** 669
16.13	**Vol. 3:** 669
16.18	**Vol. 3:** 37
16.26	**Vol. 3:** 867
17 – 19	**Vol. 3:** 801
17	**Vol. 3:** 801
19.9	**Vol. 1:** 243
19.28	**Vol. 3:** 468
19.29	**Vol. 1:** 618 **Vol. 3:** 637
22.1	**Vol. 1:** 104
22.17	**Vol. 1:** 452

23	**Vol. 3:** 692
23.26	**Vol. 3:** 939
23.30	**Vol. 3:** 610, 961
24.22	**Vol. 2:** 279
24.28	**Vol. 1:** 110
24.30	**Vol. 1:** 110
26 – 31	**Vol. 3:** 692
30.5	**Vol. 3:** 456
30.19 ff	**Vol. 3:** 486
33.13	**Vol. 1:** 499
33.18	**Vol. 1:** 499
34.19	**Vol. 3:** 243
36.10	**Vol. 2:** 767
45.3	**Vol. 3:** 263
47.5 f	**Vol. 2:** 309
49.6	**Vol. 3:** 919
50.5	**Vol. 3:** 160
50.11	**Vol. 3:** 428

Judith (Jud.)

2.2	**Vol. 3:** 502, 1016
2.15	**Vol. 1:** 341
2.20	**Vol. 2:** 396
3.8	**Vol. 3:** 821
4.9	**Vol. 1:** 612
4.12	**Vol. 3:** 908
4.13	**Vol. 1:** 612
5.8	**Vol. 2:** 876
5.19	**Vol. 1:** 685
6.1	**Vol. 3:** 255
6.14	**Vol. 3:** 177
6.16	**Vol. 1:** 197
6.18	**Vol. 2:** 876
6.19	**Vol. 3:** 30
6.21	**Vol. 1:** 197
7.18	**Vol. 2:** 801
8.1	**Vol. 3:** 873
8.6	**Vol. 1:** 626
8.12	**Vol. 3:** 799
8.14	**Vol. 3:** 125, 533, 823
8.16	**Vol. 3:** 613
8.18	**Vol. 2:** 876
8.25 f	**Vol. 3:** 799
8.25 – 27	**Vol. 3:** 778
8.25	**Vol. 3:** 818
8.26	**Vol. 3:** 800
8.31	**Vol. 2:** 93
9.2	**Vol. 3:** 177, 456, 873
9.6	**Vol. 1:** 693
9.8	**Vol. 3:** 256
9.11	**Vol. 3:** 263
9.12	**Vol. 1:** 381
10.2	**Vol. 1:** 626
10.5	**Vol. 1:** 143
10.8	**Vol. 2:** 876
10.15	**Vol. 3:** 209
10.18	**Vol. 2:** 898
10.23	**Vol. 2:** 876
11.3	**Vol. 3:** 209

Judith (Jud.) *(cont'd)*

11.13	**Vol. 3:** 416
11.17	**Vol. 2:** 863
11.19	**Vol. 1:** 693
12.1	**Vol. 1:** 341
12.6	**Vol. 2:** 863
12.7	**Vol. 1:** 144 **Vol. 3:** 228
12.9	**Vol. 3:** 228
12.10	**Vol. 1:** 272 **Vol. 3:** 957
13.3	**Vol. 2:** 863
13.5	**Vol. 3:** 836
13.6	**Vol. 3:** 399
13.7	**Vol. 3:** 716
13.10	**Vol. 1:** 143 **Vol. 2:** 863
13.13	**Vol. 3:** 860
13.14	**Vol. 3:** 816
13.15	**Vol. 1:** 143
13.17	**Vol. 2:** 876
13.18	**Vol. 1:** 380
13.19	**Vol. 3:** 233
14.7	**Vol. 2:** 876
15.2	**Vol. 3:** 908
15.5	**Vol. 3:** 908
15.9	**Vol. 3:** 908
15.11	**Vol. 3:** 1161
16.2	**Vol. 3:** 672
16.14	**Vol. 1:** 381
16.14b	**Vol. 1:** 381
16.17	**Vol. 3:** 110
16.18 f	**Vol. 1:** 414
16.18	**Vol. 2:** 876

1 Maccabees (1 Macc.)

1.1	**Vol. 2:** 124
1.10	**Vol. 2:** 124 **Vol. 3:** 318
1.11–15	**Vol. 1:** 688
1.13	**Vol. 3:** 354
1.15	**Vol. 1:** 268 **Vol. 2:** 228 **Vol. 3:** 799, 1161
1.17	**Vol. 2:** 801
1.20	**Vol. 2:** 801
1.21	**Vol. 3:** 29, 419, 788
1.22	**Vol. 3:** 794
1.23	**Vol. 2:** 215
1.24	**Vol. 3:** 29
1.29	**Vol. 2:** 801
1.36	**Vol. 3:** 468
1.38	**Vol. 1:** 286
1.39	**Vol. 1:** 626
1.43	**Vol. 3:** 550
1.45	**Vol. 1:** 626 **Vol. 3:** 428
1.46	**Vol. 2:** 227 **Vol. 3:** 418
1.47	**Vol. 1:** 641
1.48 ff	**Vol. 1:** 309
1.49	**Vol. 3:** 354
1.54 ff	**Vol. 1:** 74–75
1.54	**Vol. 3:** 418–419, 788, 1006
1.59	**Vol. 3:** 418
1.60 f	**Vol. 1:** 309

1.62	**Vol. 1:** 448
1.63	**Vol. 2:** 228
2.6	**Vol. 3:** 342
2.19	**Vol. 1:** 607 **Vol. 3:** 550
2.21	**Vol. 3:** 157, 354
2.22	**Vol. 3:** 550
2.23 ff	**Vol. 3:** 418
2.28	**Vol. 3:** 381
2.40	**Vol. 3:** 354
2.42	**Vol. 2:** 237, 810
2.44	**Vol. 3:** 209
2.45	**Vol. 3:** 418
2.47	**Vol. 3:** 29
2.49	**Vol. 3:** 29
2.52	**Vol. 3:** 369, 799, 823, 1188
2.53	**Vol. 2:** 134
2.54	**Vol. 3:** 36
2.57	**Vol. 3:** 649
2.58	**Vol. 3:** 747
2.60	**Vol. 3:** 202, 951
2.63	**Vol. 3:** 820
2.68	**Vol. 3:** 428
3.2	**Vol. 2:** 349
3.6	**Vol. 3:** 209
3.18 f	**Vol. 2:** 191
3.18	**Vol. 3:** 209
3.19	**Vol. 1:** 650
3.20	**Vol. 3:** 29
3.26	**Vol. 1:** 574
3.28	**Vol. 3:** 144, 796
3.30	**Vol. 1:** 729
3.34	**Vol. 2:** 310
3.44	**Vol. 2:** 863
3.45	**Vol. 3:** 794
3.46	**Vol. 2:** 863
3.52	**Vol. 3:** 823
4.9	**Vol. 3:** 209
4.10 f	**Vol. 2:** 191
4.11	**Vol. 3:** 192, 194, 209
4.18	**Vol. 2:** 735
4.23	**Vol. 2:** 842
4.24	**Vol. 3:** 669
4.25	**Vol. 3:** 209
4.30	**Vol. 2:** 863 **Vol. 3:** 218
4.33	**Vol. 3:** 669, 816
4.35	**Vol. 3:** 823
4.36–59	**Vol. 1:** 629 **Vol. 3:** 788
4.36–41	**Vol. 1:** 626
4.42	**Vol. 3:** 924
4.44–49	**Vol. 3:** 419
4.46	**Vol. 3:** 80, 311
4.49 ff	**Vol. 3:** 788
4.51	**Vol. 3:** 794
4.54–59	**Vol. 3:** 366
4.54	**Vol. 3:** 673
4.55	**Vol. 2:** 876
5.19	**Vol. 1:** 194
5.33	**Vol. 2:** 863
5.39	**Vol. 2:** 139
5.49	**Vol. 3:** 51

1 Maccabees (1 Macc.) *(cont'd)*

5.58	**Vol. 1:** 340
5.62	**Vol. 3:** 209
5.68	**Vol. 3:** 418
6.1	**Vol. 2:** 842
6.2	**Vol. 2:** 124, 841
6.9	**Vol. 3:** 823
6.10	**Vol. 1:** 277
6.15	**Vol. 3:** 498
6.17	**Vol. 2:** 675
6.19	**Vol. 3:** 823
6.21	**Vol. 2:** 349
6.29	**Vol. 2:** 139
6.38	**Vol. 3:** 557
6.40	**Vol. 1:** 663
6.44	**Vol. 3:** 209
6.49	**Vol. 3:** 191
6.53	**Vol. 3:** 191
6.60	**Vol. 2:** 776, 815
6.63	**Vol. 3:** 711
7.7	**Vol. 3:** 98
7.12 ff	**Vol. 3:** 479
7.12	**Vol. 3:** 358
7.13	**Vol. 2:** 237, 810
7.16	**Vol. 3:** 479
7.18	**Vol. 3:** 882
7.31	**Vol. 3:** 311
7.37	**Vol. 2:** 863
7.38	**Vol. 3:** 229
7.40	**Vol. 2:** 863
8.9	**Vol. 2:** 124
8.12	**Vol. 3:** 255
8.18	**Vol. 2:** 124 **Vol. 3:** 1161
8.23 ff	**Vol. 2:** 310
8.23	**Vol. 1:** 515
8.26	**Vol. 2:** 134 **Vol. 3:** 821
8.28	**Vol. 2:** 134 **Vol. 3:** 821
8.29	**Vol. 2:** 789
8.31	**Vol. 3:** 1161
8.32	**Vol. 1:** 515
9.9	**Vol. 3:** 209
9.10	**Vol. 2:** 138
9.12–13	**Vol. 3:** 874
9.21	**Vol. 3:** 209
9.27	**Vol. 3:** 80, 311
9.35	**Vol. 2:** 801
9.39	**Vol. 2:** 578
9.46	**Vol. 3:** 209
9.58	**Vol. 3:** 111
9.73	**Vol. 3:** 255
10.3	**Vol. 1:** 246
10.7	**Vol. 1:** 246
10.17–20	**Vol. 1:** 246
10.20 f	**Vol. 3:** 35
10.24	**Vol. 2:** 199
10.26 f	**Vol. 3:** 226
10.29	**Vol. 1:** 406 **Vol. 3:** 444
10.31	**Vol. 3:** 756
10.34	**Vol. 3:** 570
10.37	**Vol. 3:** 957
10.38	**Vol. 2:** 173 **Vol. 3:** 452, 823
10.42	**Vol. 3:** 957
10.43	**Vol. 2:** 667
10.47	**Vol. 2:** 817
10.52	**Vol. 3:** 716
10.63 f	**Vol. 3:** 51
10.83	**Vol. 2:** 284 **Vol. 3:** 209
10.84	**Vol. 3:** 785
10.89	**Vol. 2:** 437
11.4	**Vol. 3:** 785
11.8	**Vol. 3:** 820, 823
11.24	**Vol. 3:** 452
11.28	**Vol. 3:** 70
11.29–37	**Vol. 1:** 246
11.33	**Vol. 3:** 358
11.35	**Vol. 3:** 444, 756, 992
11.48	**Vol. 3:** 209
11.54	**Vol. 2:** 675
11.57	**Vol. 2:** 675 **Vol. 3:** 452
11.58	**Vol. 3:** 545
11.71	**Vol. 2:** 863
12.5–23	**Vol. 1:** 246
12.6	**Vol. 2:** 789
12.9	**Vol. 1:** 243
12.10	**Vol. 3:** 799
12.11	**Vol. 2:** 669, 863 **Vol. 3:** 229
12.15	**Vol. 2:** 191
12.25	**Vol. 2:** 765
12.27	**Vol. 2:** 136
12.29	**Vol. 2:** 227
12.45	**Vol. 3:** 957
13.15	**Vol. 3:** 957
13.31	**Vol. 2:** 675
13.37	**Vol. 1:** 406 **Vol. 3:** 957
13.39	**Vol. 2:** 667 **Vol. 3:** 756
13.45	**Vol. 1:** 410
13.47	**Vol. 2:** 285 **Vol. 3:** 669
13.51	**Vol. 3:** 669, 673, 675
14.9	**Vol. 1:** 314
14.11	**Vol. 2:** 357
14.20–25	**Vol. 2:** 789
14.22	**Vol. 3:** 1016
14.23	**Vol. 3:** 570
14.32	**Vol. 3:** 144
14.36	**Vol. 3:** 101
14.41	**Vol. 2:** 817 **Vol. 3:** 80, 311
14.49	**Vol. 3:** 796
15.3	**Vol. 3:** 147
15.8	**Vol. 2:** 666
15.9	**Vol. 3:** 786
15.17	**Vol. 2:** 789
15.20	**Vol. 3:** 821
15.22 f	**Vol. 2:** 309
16.2	**Vol. 3:** 201

2 Maccabees (2 Macc.)

1.1–9	**Vol. 1:** 246
1.2	**Vol. 2:** 318

2 Maccabees (2 Macc.) *(cont'd)*

1.4	**Vol. 1:** 341
1.5	**Vol. 3:** 166–167
1.6	**Vol. 2:** 863
1.9	**Vol. 3:** 813
1.10–2.18	**Vol. 1:** 246
1.10	**Vol. 3:** 766
1.11	**Vol. 3:** 818
1.13	**Vol. 3:** 821
1.16	**Vol. 2:** 215 **Vol. 3:** 381
1.19 ff	**Vol. 3:** 428
1.20	**Vol. 1:** 341 **Vol. 3:** 821
1.23 f	**Vol. 2:** 863
1.23	**Vol. 1:** 409
1.24 ff	**Vol. 1:** 382
1.24	**Vol. 2:** 105
1.25	**Vol. 3:** 209
1.27	**Vol. 1:** 685
1.28	**Vol. 3:** 29
1.30	**Vol. 3:** 669
1.34	**Vol. 3:** 808
1.36	**Vol. 1:** 580
2.4 ff	**Vol. 1:** 252
2.4	**Vol. 3:** 325
2.7	**Vol. 3:** 157
2.8	**Vol. 3:** 316
2.9	**Vol. 3:** 786
2.10†	**Vol. 2:** 863
2.13	**Vol. 1:** 377, 414, 574
2.17	**Vol. 3:** 37
2.19	**Vol. 3:** 418
2.21	**Vol. 2:** 310
2.22	**Vol. 3:** 157, 178
2.23	**Vol. 3:** 799
2.24	**Vol. 3:** 318
2.25	**Vol. 3:** 238
2.27	**Vol. 3:** 119, 818
2.29	**Vol. 1:** 377 **Vol. 3:** 821
3.1 ff	**Vol. 3:** 428
3.6	**Vol. 3:** 796
3.7	**Vol. 1:** 476
3.8	**Vol. 1:** 696
3.10	**Vol. 3:** 1074
3.12	**Vol. 2:** 93
3.22	**Vol. 1:** 663
3.24	**Vol. 3:** 796
3.26	**Vol. 3:** 229
3.28	**Vol. 3:** 796
3.29	**Vol. 3:** 209, 1147
3.32 ff	**Vol. 3:** 428
3.32	**Vol. 3:** 209
3.33	**Vol. 3:** 156
3.40	**Vol. 3:** 796
4.1	**Vol. 1:** 387
4.2	**Vol. 1:** 415
4.3	**Vol. 3:** 808
4.5	**Vol. 2:** 803
4.6	**Vol. 1:** 694 **Vol. 3:** 125
4.10	**Vol. 2:** 124

4.11	**Vol. 1:** 645 **Vol. 2:** 803
4.12–15	**Vol. 3:** 35
4.13	**Vol. 2:** 311
4.14	**Vol. 3:** 550
4.15	**Vol. 2:** 124
4.18	**Vol. 1:** 645
4.21	**Vol. 1:** 324, 663
4.24	**Vol. 1:** 324
4.27	**Vol. 3:** 716
4.34	**Vol. 3:** 561
4.36	**Vol. 2:** 124
4.38	**Vol. 3:** 98
4.40	**Vol. 3:** 125
4.41	**Vol. 3:** 381
4.42	**Vol. 2:** 138 **Vol. 3:** 796
4.44	**Vol. 1:** 324
4.47	**Vol. 3:** 859
4.50	**Vol. 1:** 137 **Vol. 2:** 803
5.5	**Vol. 3:** 604
5.6	**Vol. 2:** 803 **Vol. 3:** 821
5.8	**Vol. 1:** 607 **Vol. 2:** 803 **Vol. 3:** 933
5.12	**Vol. 1:** 341
5.15	**Vol. 3:** 727
5.18	**Vol. 3:** 796
5.20	**Vol. 3:** 166
5.21	**Vol. 3:** 29
5.23	**Vol. 2:** 803
5.25	**Vol. 2:** 468
6.1 ff	**Vol. 2:** 125
6.1	**Vol. 2:** 803
6.6 f	**Vol. 1:** 626
6.7	**Vol. 2:** 663
6.8	**Vol. 2:** 124
6.9	**Vol. 2:** 124
6.11	**Vol. 2:** 93 **Vol. 3:** 381
6.12–17	**Vol. 3:** 778
6.12–16	**Vol. 1:** 734
6.12	**Vol. 1:** 734 **Vol. 3:** 823
6.13	**Vol. 1:** 734
6.14	**Vol. 1:** 324, 735 **Vol. 3:** 98
6.20	**Vol. 2:** 773
6.21	**Vol. 2:** 468 **Vol. 3:** 119
6.23	**Vol. 2:** 803 **Vol. 3:** 823, 933
6.24	**Vol. 2:** 207, 468
6.28	**Vol. 2:** 93, 290
6.30	**Vol. 3:** 721
6.31	**Vol. 1:** 435 **Vol. 2:** 290 **Vol. 3:** 926
7.5	**Vol. 1:** 341
7.6	**Vol. 3:** 673
7.7	**Vol. 1:** 665
7.8	**Vol. 3:** 1153
7.9	**Vol. 1:** 506 **Vol. 2:** 928 **Vol. 3:** 200, 270–271
7.11 f	**Vol. 3:** 270
7.11	**Vol. 3:** 200, 270–271
7.13 f	**Vol. 3:** 270
7.13	**Vol. 3:** 856
7.14	**Vol. 2:** 928 **Vol. 3:** 200, 271
7.16	**Vol. 3:** 821
7.18	**Vol. 3:** 721

273

2 Maccabees (2 Macc.) *(cont'd)*

7.20	**Vol. 3:** 238, 348
7.21	**Vol. 2:** 569 **Vol. 3:** 823
7.22 f	**Vol. 3:** 271
7.23	**Vol. 1:** 382 **Vol. 3:** 270
7.24	**Vol. 2:** 841 **Vol. 3:** 957
7.25	**Vol. 3:** 209
7.29	**Vol. 3:** 270–271
7.32	**Vol. 3:** 721
7.33	**Vol. 3:** 166–167, 610
7.34	**Vol. 2:** 191
7.36 f	**Vol. 3:** 270
7.36	**Vol. 3:** 29
7.37	**Vol. 1:** 235, 345 **Vol. 3:** 157, 195–196
8.1	**Vol. 2:** 310
8.3	**Vol. 1:** 410
8.4	**Vol. 3:** 341–342
8.9	**Vol. 1:** 476
8.10	**Vol. 1:** 734
8.11	**Vol. 3:** 93
8.12	**Vol. 2:** 898
8.15	**Vol. 2:** 93
8.16	**Vol. 2:** 684
8.17	**Vol. 2:** 803 **Vol. 3:** 29
8.18	**Vol. 2:** 69
8.21	**Vol. 2:** 480
8.23	**Vol. 1:** 245
8.27	**Vol. 3:** 209
8.28	**Vol. 3:** 1074
8.29	**Vol. 3:** 166–167
8.30	**Vol. 2:** 498 **Vol. 3:** 1074
8.33	**Vol. 2:** 139
9.4	**Vol. 3:** 30, 229, 342
9.5	**Vol. 2:** 599
9.6	**Vol. 2:** 599
9.7 f	**Vol. 3:** 29
9.7	**Vol. 1:** 341
9.8	**Vol. 3:** 30, 821
9.10	**Vol. 3:** 734, 821
9.11	**Vol. 3:** 29
9.12	**Vol. 2:** 498, 765 **Vol. 3:** 29–30, 342
9.18	**Vol. 3:** 358
9.19	**Vol. 2:** 170, 803
9.21	**Vol. 1:** 663
9.27	**Vol. 2:** 257
9.28†	**Vol. 3:** 341–342
10.1–8	**Vol. 1:** 626
10.2	**Vol. 1:** 387 **Vol. 3:** 418
10.4	**Vol. 3:** 341–342, 585
10.6	**Vol. 3:** 381
10.7	**Vol. 3:** 669, 818
10.8	**Vol. 1:** 330
10.12	**Vol. 3:** 799
10.19	**Vol. 3:** 534
10.26	**Vol. 3:** 157, 484
10.28	**Vol. 1:** 372
10.34	**Vol. 3:** 341–342
10.35	**Vol. 3:** 342
10.38	**Vol. 3:** 669

11.2	**Vol. 2:** 124 **Vol. 3:** 823
11.6	**Vol. 3:** 209
11.14	**Vol. 3:** 358
11.17	**Vol. 3:** 325
11.19	**Vol. 3:** 799
11.20	**Vol. 3:** 820
11.24	**Vol. 2:** 124
11.25	**Vol. 2:** 437, 803
11.34	**Vol. 2:** 789
12.7	**Vol. 2:** 803
12.12	**Vol. 3:** 534
12.14	**Vol. 3:** 342, 346
12.15	**Vol. 3:** 841
12.16	**Vol. 3:** 992
12.25	**Vol. 3:** 209
12.31	**Vol. 3:** 818
12.32	**Vol. 2:** 783
12.37	**Vol. 3:** 669
12.41	**Vol. 2:** 216
12.43 f	**Vol. 3:** 270
12.43	**Vol. 3:** 271, 820
12.44	**Vol. 2:** 863
13.2	**Vol. 2:** 124
13.3	**Vol. 3:** 209
13.4	**Vol. 2:** 437
13.8	**Vol. 3:** 418
13.9	**Vol. 1:** 261
13.10	**Vol. 1:** 340
13.12	**Vol. 1:** 341 **Vol. 3:** 229
13.14	**Vol. 1:** 382 **Vol. 2:** 803
13.15	**Vol. 1:** 650
13.21	**Vol. 3:** 502
13.22	**Vol. 3:** 358
14.3	**Vol. 3:** 209
14.4	**Vol. 1:** 406
14.5	**Vol. 3:** 125
14.6	**Vol. 2:** 237, 810
14.8	**Vol. 2:** 803
14.9	**Vol. 1:** 694
14.12	**Vol. 1:** 476
14.14	**Vol. 3:** 821
14.15	**Vol. 3:** 318
14.23	**Vol. 2:** 801
14.26	**Vol. 3:** 570
14.27	**Vol. 1:** 341
14.31	**Vol. 1:** 341
14.33	**Vol. 3:** 318
14.36	**Vol. 3:** 923–924
14.38	**Vol. 2:** 310
14.40	**Vol. 3:** 821
14.41	**Vol. 3:** 711
14.42	**Vol. 3:** 29
14.43	**Vol. 2:** 801
14.45 f	**Vol. 2:** 801
14.46	**Vol. 3:** 270–271
15.1	**Vol. 1:** 663 **Vol. 3:** 256
15.2	**Vol. 2:** 224, 663
15.4	**Vol. 1:** 341, 495
15.5	**Vol. 3:** 957
15.6	**Vol. 3:** 30

2 Maccabees (2 Macc.) *(cont'd)*

15.7	**Vol. 3:** 229
15.8 f	**Vol. 1:** 329
15.8	**Vol. 3:** 125
15.10	**Vol. 3:** 584
15.11 ff	**Vol. 1:** 512
15.11	**Vol. 1:** 663
15.14	**Vol. 2:** 863
15.17	**Vol. 3:** 926
15.20	**Vol. 2:** 303
15.21	**Vol. 2:** 898
15.23	**Vol. 2:** 191
15.24	**Vol. 3:** 342
15.27	**Vol. 3:** 318
15.30	**Vol. 2:** 803
15.33	**Vol. 3:** 125
15.34	**Vol. 3:** 318, 923–924
15.36	**Vol. 1:** 330 **Vol. 3:** 411
15.37	**Vol. 3:** 255

3 Maccabees (3 Macc.)

1.3	**Vol. 1:** 330 **Vol. 3:** 98
1.4	**Vol. 3:** 177
1.16	**Vol. 2:** 663
1.19	**Vol. 3:** 561
1.22	**Vol. 1:** 696 **Vol. 2:** 765, 803
1.23	**Vol. 3:** 902
1.25	**Vol. 3:** 799
1.26	**Vol. 3:** 821
1.27	**Vol. 3:** 29
1.29	**Vol. 3:** 821
2.2	**Vol. 2:** 191
2.3	**Vol. 1:** 380 **Vol. 3:** 29
2.5	**Vol. 3:** 29
2.6	**Vol. 3:** 808
2.7	**Vol. 2:** 801
2.8	**Vol. 3:** 816
2.9	**Vol. 1:** 380
2.10	**Vol. 3:** 70
2.17	**Vol. 3:** 29
2.19	**Vol. 3:** 318
2.21	**Vol. 3:** 29
2.22	**Vol. 3:** 113
2.26	**Vol. 1:** 696
2.27	**Vol. 1:** 696
2.28	**Vol. 3:** 711
2.29	**Vol. 2:** 574
2.30	**Vol. 2:** 498 **Vol. 3:** 502
2.32	**Vol. 3:** 201, 799
3.4 ff	**Vol. 2:** 310
3.4	**Vol. 2:** 803
3.7	**Vol. 2:** 876
3.8	**Vol. 2:** 124
3.15	**Vol. 3:** 711
3.16	**Vol. 3:** 125, 786
3.17	**Vol. 2:** 898
3.20	**Vol. 2:** 669 **Vol. 3:** 125
3.21	**Vol. 2:** 233
3.24	**Vol. 1:** 694 **Vol. 3:** 571

3.25	**Vol. 2:** 669 **Vol. 3:** 29
3.26	**Vol. 3:** 98
3.28	**Vol. 2:** 846
3.29	**Vol. 2:** 658
3.30	**Vol. 3:** 904
4.1	**Vol. 2:** 735
4.4	**Vol. 3:** 823, 908
4.5	**Vol. 3:** 561
4.6	**Vol. 3:** 908
4.7	**Vol. 3:** 711
4.9	**Vol. 2:** 663 **Vol. 3:** 1161
4.16	**Vol. 3:** 816
4.20	**Vol. 3:** 570
4.21	**Vol. 3:** 1147
5.2	**Vol. 2:** 684
5.5 f	**Vol. 3:** 821
5.6	**Vol. 2:** 663
5.7	**Vol. 1:** 618
5.11	**Vol. 1:** 382
5.12	**Vol. 1:** 696 **Vol. 3:** 823, 1147
5.13	**Vol. 3:** 29, 816
5.14	**Vol. 1:** 272
5.16	**Vol. 3:** 823
5.22	**Vol. 3:** 821
5.28	**Vol. 3:** 1147
5.29	**Vol. 1:** 696
5.30	**Vol. 1:** 694 **Vol. 3:** 125
5.31	**Vol. 3:** 570, 923
5.35	**Vol. 3:** 318, 816
5.40	**Vol. 3:** 821
5.49	**Vol. 3:** 821
5.51	**Vol. 2:** 30
6.1	**Vol. 2:** 863
6.2	**Vol. 2:** 69
6.3	**Vol. 1:** 618
6.4	**Vol. 3:** 29, 318
6.8	**Vol. 1:** 618
6.9	**Vol. 3:** 29, 318
6.10	**Vol. 3:** 201
6.11	**Vol. 3:** 202
6.12	**Vol. 3:** 29
6.13	**Vol. 3:** 209
6.16	**Vol. 2:** 863
6.19	**Vol. 1:** 622
6.27	**Vol. 2:** 839 **Vol. 3:** 177
6.29	**Vol. 3:** 177, 218
6.30	**Vol. 3:** 166, 821
6.32	**Vol. 3:** 218, 673, 816
6.33	**Vol. 3:** 209, 229
6.34	**Vol. 3:** 109
6.36	**Vol. 3:** 209
6.37	**Vol. 2:** 839
7.3	**Vol. 3:** 98
7.6	**Vol. 1:** 663
7.8	**Vol. 2:** 839
7.12	**Vol. 2:** 735
7.13	**Vol. 1:** 409 **Vol. 2:** 669
7.14	**Vol. 2:** 291 **Vol. 3:** 98
7.16	**Vol. 3:** 209, 218, 263, 669, 818
7.17	**Vol. 3:** 228, 1016

275

3 Maccabees (3 Macc.) *(cont'd)*

7.19	**Vol. 1:** 691 **Vol. 2:** 669
7.20	**Vol. 2:** 863 **Vol. 3:** 209
7.21	**Vol. 3:** 557
7.22	**Vol. 3:** 209

4 Maccabees (4 Macc.)

1.1–35	**Vol. 3:** 823
1.1	**Vol. 2:** 93 **Vol. 3:** 1035
1.2	**Vol. 3:** 926
1.5	**Vol. 3:** 716
1.7	**Vol. 2:** 93
1.8	**Vol. 3:** 570, 926
1.10	**Vol. 2:** 49 **Vol. 3:** 816, 926
1.11	**Vol. 2:** 773 **Vol. 3:** 611
1.14	**Vol. 1:** 503
1.15	**Vol. 2:** 475, 846
1.16	**Vol. 2:** 138
1.17	**Vol. 2:** 93
1.20	**Vol. 2:** 658
1.26	**Vol. 3:** 30
1.29	**Vol. 2:** 437
1.30	**Vol. 3:** 926
1.33	**Vol. 3:** 902
1.35	**Vol. 2:** 765 **Vol. 3:** 125
2.2–24†	**Vol. 3:** 823
2.2	**Vol. 3:** 816
2.3	**Vol. 2:** 675
2.7	**Vol. 2:** 437
2.8	**Vol. 2:** 803 **Vol. 3:** 711
2.11	**Vol. 3:** 98
2.15	**Vol. 3:** 30
2.16	**Vol. 3:** 125
2.21 f	**Vol. 2:** 565
2.21	**Vol. 2:** 437
2.23	**Vol. 2:** 377, 803
3.1–19	**Vol. 3:** 823
3.9	**Vol. 2:** 521
3.11	**Vol. 3:** 177
3.15	**Vol. 3:** 823
3.17	**Vol. 1:** 650 **Vol. 2:** 663 **Vol. 3:** 109
3.19	**Vol. 3:** 570
3.20	**Vol. 2:** 803 **Vol. 3:** 1156
4.3	**Vol. 3:** 786, 796
4.4	**Vol. 3:** 816
4.6	**Vol. 3:** 796
4.11	**Vol. 2:** 191, 863
4.12	**Vol. 3:** 669
4.14	**Vol. 3:** 209
4.15	**Vol. 3:** 29
4.22	**Vol. 2:** 325
4.23	**Vol. 1:** 330 **Vol. 2:** 803
4.26	**Vol. 2:** 310 **Vol. 3:** 856
5.2	**Vol. 2:** 284
5.6	**Vol. 3:** 561, 821, 856, 1035
5.8 f	**Vol. 3:** 126
5.8	**Vol. 2:** 658
5.9	**Vol. 3:** 821
5.10	**Vol. 3:** 823, 1035
5.11	**Vol. 3:** 1035
5.12	**Vol. 2:** 876
5.13	**Vol. 2:** 663
5.16	**Vol. 2:** 663, 803
5.18	**Vol. 2:** 93
5.20	**Vol. 1:** 334
5.22	**Vol. 3:** 1035
5.23	**Vol. 2:** 773
5.24	**Vol. 2:** 93, 437, 498 **Vol. 3:** 761
5.25	**Vol. 1:** 382 **Vol. 2:** 658
5.28	**Vol. 2:** 431
5.29	**Vol. 2:** 134
5.30	**Vol. 2:** 599
5.31	**Vol. 2:** 93 **Vol. 3:** 823
5.34	**Vol. 1:** 495
5.35	**Vol. 3:** 1035
5.36	**Vol. 2:** 93, 475
5.37	**Vol. 2:** 663 **Vol. 3:** 682
5.38	**Vol. 2:** 93 **Voi. 3:** 823
6.2	**Vol. 2:** 93
6.4	**Vol. 3:** 50
6.5	**Vol. 3:** 856
6.7	**Vol. 3:** 823
6.9	**Vol. 1:** 461 **Vol. 2:** 663, 773
6.10 f	**Vol. 3:** 856
6.11	**Vol. 3:** 904
6.15	**Vol. 2:** 468
6.16	**Vol. 1:** 410
6.17	**Vol. 2:** 468
6.18	**Vol. 2:** 134
6.19	**Vol. 2:** 675
6.22	**Vol. 2:** 93
6.24	**Vol. 2:** 663
6.27	**Vol. 3:** 856
6.28 f	**Vol. 3:** 193, 611
6.28	**Vol. 3:** 157, 195–196, 727
6.30–35	**Vol. 3:** 823
6.30	**Vol. 3:** 856
6.31	**Vol. 2:** 93
6.33	**Vol. 1:** 650
7.1–24	**Vol. 3:** 823
7.2	**Vol. 3:** 856
7.7	**Vol. 2:** 475, 846 **Vol. 3:** 1035
7.9	**Vol. 2:** 773 **Vol. 3:** 1035
7.11	**Vol. 2:** 293
7.13	**Vol. 3:** 177
7.15	**Vol. 2:** 93, 475
7.16	**Vol. 1:** 461 **Vol. 2:** 93 **Vol. 3:** 856
7.18	**Vol. 1:** 694
7.19	**Vol. 2:** 480
7.21	**Vol. 2:** 93 **Vol. 3:** 399, 1035
7.22	**Vol. 2:** 773 **Vol. 3:** 926
7.23	**Vol. 3:** 1028
7.24	**Vol. 3:** 1035
8 ff	**Vol. 2:** 690
8.2	**Vol. 3:** 856
8.5	**Vol. 1:** 529 **Vol. 3:** 856
8.6	**Vol. 3:** 98
8.7	**Vol. 1:** 455 **Vol. 2:** 803
8.8	**Vol. 2:** 124, 846

4 Maccabees (4 Macc.) *(cont'd)*

8.9	**Vol. 3:** 98, 856
8.11	**Vol. 3:** 820
8.14	**Vol. 2:** 663 **Vol. 3:** 157
8.16	**Vol. 3:** 823
8.17	**Vol. 3:** 126
8.19	**Vol. 3:** 30, 823, 856
8.22	**Vol. 2:** 663
8.23	**Vol. 2:** 475
8.24†	**Vol. 2:** 663 **Vol. 3:** 711
8.26	**Vol. 3:** 957
8.27	**Vol. 3:** 856
9.4	**Vol. 3:** 209
9.5 f	**Vol. 3:** 856
9.6	**Vol. 2:** 93, 663, 773 **Vol. 3:** 856
9.7	**Vol. 3:** 799, 856
9.8	**Vol. 2:** 773 **Vol. 3:** 926
9.9	**Vol. 2:** 767 **Vol. 3:** 856
9.15	**Vol. 3:** 856
9.16	**Vol. 3:** 166, 856
9.17	**Vol. 3:** 545, 823
9.18	**Vol. 3:** 856, 926
9.20	**Vol. 3:** 109
9.22	**Vol. 1:** 709 **Vol. 2:** 773
9.24	**Vol. 1:** 694 **Vol. 3:** 157
9.27	**Vol. 3:** 856
9.28	**Vol. 2:** 767
9.30	**Vol. 2:** 773 **Vol. 3:** 29, 821, 823, 856
9.32	**Vol. 1:** 491 **Vol. 3:** 856
10.1 f	**Vol. 2:** 767
10.1	**Vol. 1:** 435
10.2	**Vol. 1:** 410
10.5	**Vol. 2:** 735
10.8	**Vol. 2:** 599
10.10	**Vol. 3:** 926
10.11	**Vol. 3:** 856
10.13	**Vol. 1:** 529
10.15	**Vol. 1:** 455 **Vol. 2:** 93 **Vol. 3:** 827
10.16	**Vol. 3:** 856
10.19	**Vol. 3:** 823
10.21	**Vol. 3:** 119, 669
11.1	**Vol. 3:** 856
11.2	**Vol. 3:** 856, 926
11.5	**Vol. 1:** 382 **Vol. 2:** 93 **Vol. 3:** 821
11.6	**Vol. 3:** 856
11.8	**Vol. 2:** 93
11.12	**Vol. 2:** 117
11.16	**Vol. 3:** 821, 856
11.20	**Vol. 1:** 645 **Vol. 3:** 856
11.23	**Vol. 2:** 93 **Vol. 3:** 856
11.25	**Vol. 3:** 711, 823
11.26	**Vol. 3:** 711
11.27	**Vol. 3:** 823
12.3	**Vol. 3:** 799
12.4	**Vol. 3:** 856
12.6	**Vol. 3:** 209
12.8 f	**Vol. 3:** 177
12.12	**Vol. 3:** 856
12.13	**Vol. 2:** 452 **Vol. 3:** 856
12.18	**Vol. 3:** 157
13.1	**Vol. 3:** 823
13.3	**Vol. 3:** 816, 823
13.7	**Vol. 3:** 98
13.9	**Vol. 1:** 491
13.10	**Vol. 3:** 570
13.11	**Vol. 2:** 767
13.12	**Vol. 2:** 773
13.14	**Vol. 3:** 821
13.15	**Vol. 3:** 856
13.16	**Vol. 3:** 823
13.17	**Vol. 3:** 682, 816
13.19	**Vol. 1:** 694
13.24	**Vol. 2:** 542
13.27	**Vol. 2:** 437, 658, 765 **Vol. 3:** 856
14.1	**Vol. 1:** 461
14.2	**Vol. 3:** 823
14.5	**Vol. 3:** 682, 856, 946
14.8	**Vol. 3:** 856
14.9	**Vol. 2:** 767
14.11	**Vol. 3:** 823, 856
15.1	**Vol. 3:** 823
15.2	**Vol. 3:** 209
15.3	**Vol. 2:** 480, 542 **Vol. 3:** 119, 209
15.4	**Vol. 2:** 502
15.8	**Vol. 3:** 209
15.10	**Vol. 2:** 134
15.11	**Vol. 3:** 823, 856
15.12	**Vol. 2:** 480
15.16	**Vol. 3:** 799
15.18–22	**Vol. 3:** 856
15.22	**Vol. 2:** 574, 599 **Vol. 3:** 856
15.23	**Vol. 3:** 823
15.24	**Vol. 1:** 598 **Vol. 3:** 1211
15.25	**Vol. 2:** 658
15.27	**Vol. 3:** 209
15.29	**Vol. 2:** 599, 690
15.30	**Vol. 2:** 569, 773
15.31 f	**Vol. 2:** 773
15.32	**Vol. 3:** 856
16.1 f	**Vol. 3:** 856
16.1	**Vol. 2:** 773 **Vol. 3:** 823
16.2	**Vol. 3:** 570
16.3	**Vol. 2:** 658 **Vol. 3:** 856, 951
16.4	**Vol. 3:** 823
16.8	**Vol. 2:** 773
16.13	**Vol. 1:** 435
16.15	**Vol. 3:** 856
16.16–23	**Vol. 1:** 714
16.17	**Vol. 2:** 773 **Vol. 3:** 856
16.18	**Vol. 3:** 240
16.19	**Vol. 2:** 773
16.21	**Vol. 2:** 773 **Vol. 3:** 951
16.22	**Vol. 1:** 598 **Vol. 3:** 1211
16.25	**Vol. 2:** 480
17.2	**Vol. 1:** 598 **Vol. 3:** 711
17.3	**Vol. 3:** 856
17.4	**Vol. 2:** 773
17.5	**Vol. 2:** 93
17.7	**Vol. 2:** 773 **Vol. 3:** 856

4 Maccabees (4 Macc.) *(cont'd)*

17.9	Vol. 3: 711
17.10	Vol. 2: 773 Vol. 3: 856
17.11	Vol. 1: 645
17.12	Vol. 1: 435 Vol. 2: 480, 773 Vol. 3: 682, 808, 926
17.14 ff	Vol. 1: 646
17.17	Vol. 2: 773 Vol. 3: 926
17.18 ff	Vol. 3: 348
17.18	Vol. 1: 474
17.19	Vol. 2: 803
17.20 f	Vol. 3: 611
17.20	Vol. 2: 49
17.21 f	Vol. 3: 195–196
17.22	Vol. 1: 694 Vol. 3: 157, 164–165, 193, 209
17.23	Vol. 2: 290, 773 Vol. 3: 856, 926
18.2	Vol. 2: 93 Vol. 3: 823
18.3	Vol. 1: 235
18.5	Vol. 2: 437 Vol. 3: 98
18.6	Vol. 3: 354
18.7	Vol. 2: 134
18.10	Vol. 3: 761
18.11 ff	Vol. 3: 1042
18.12	Vol. 3: 761
18.13	Vol. 3: 951
18.15	Vol. 3: 669
18.18	Vol. 3: 673, 761
18.19	Vol. 2: 480
18.20	Vol. 2: 124 Vol. 3: 109, 856
18.22	Vol. 2: 325

Manasses, Prayer of (Man.)

5	Vol. 1: 109
9 f	Vol. 1: 108

Martyrdom of Isaiah (Mart. Isa.)

2.1	Vol. 1: 125
2.3 ff	Vol. 3: 806
2.8–11	Vol. 3: 1006–1007
3.11	Vol. 1: 125

Psalms of Solomon (Pss. Sol.)

2.1 f	Vol. 3: 815
2.6	Vol. 2: 573
2.10	Vol. 3: 358
2.15	Vol. 3: 358
2.18	Vol. 3: 358
2.30 f	Vol. 3: 815
2.32	Vol. 3: 358
2.34	Vol. 3: 358
3.1 ff	Vol. 2: 364
3.3	Vol. 3: 358
3.4–8	Vol. 3: 358
3.4	Vol. 3: 778
3.5	Vol. 3: 210, 358
3.16	Vol. 2: 480, 928
4	Vol. 3: 749

4.7	Vol. 2: 815	
4.8	Vol. 2: 815	
4.9	Vol. 3: 358	
4.19	Vol. 2: 815	
4.21	Vol. 3: 233	
5.1–12	Vol. 2: 266	
5.1	Vol. 3: 358	
5.2	Vol. 2: 824	
5.6	Vol. 2: 811	
5.11	Vol. 2: 824	
6.1	Vol. 3: 210	
8.7	Vol. 3: 358	
8.8	Vol. 3: 358	
8.14	Vol. 3: 913	
8.16 ff	Vol. 1: 125	
8.22	Vol. 2: 818	
8.23	Vol. 3: 358	
8.26	Vol. 3: 358	
8.28	Vol. 1: 685	
9.1	Vol. 3: 193	
9.2	Vol. 3: 358	
9.6 f	Vol. 2: 867	
9.9	Vol. 2: 831	
9.12	Vol. 1: 345	
10.1–6	Vol. 2: 266	
10.2	Vol. 3: 165	
10.4	Vol. 3: 241	
10.5	Vol. 3: 358	
10.6	Vol. 2: 824	
10.7	Vol. 2: 824	
10.8	Vol. 3: 210	
12.6	Vol. 2: 867	Vol. 3: 193, 210
13.2	Vol. 3: 210	
13.7–10	Vol. 2: 266	
13.7	Vol. 3: 210	
13.9	Vol. 3: 778	
14.2	Vol. 3: 946	
14.6 f	Vol. 2: 207	
14.6	Vol. 2: 928	
15.1	Vol. 2: 824	
15.6 ff	Vol. 3: 498, 500	
15.6–9	Vol. 2: 573	
15.6	Vol. 3: 210, 358	
15.8–10	Vol. 2: 574	
15.11	Vol. 2: 207	
15.15	Vol. 2: 480	
16.2	Vol. 2: 30	
16.4 f	Vol. 3: 210	
16.5–13	Vol. 2: 867	
17	Vol. 3: 210, 649	
17.13	Vol. 1: 125	
17.21 ff	Vol. 2: 337 Vol. 3: 961	
17.21–42	Vol. 2: 867	
17.21	Vol. 3: 656	
17.23–18.9	Vol. 2: 812	
17.23	Vol. 1: 178	
17.24	Vol. 1: 710 Vol. 2: 602	
17.29	Vol. 3: 575	
17.30	Vol. 2: 782 Vol. 3: 430	
17.32	Vol. 3: 358	

Psalms of Solomon (Pss. Sol.) *(cont'd)*

17.35 f	**Vol. 3:** 649
17.36	**Vol. 3:** 575
17.37	**Vol. 1:** 175
17.40 f	**Vol. 3:** 170
17.41–46	**Vol. 2:** 498
17.42 f	**Vol. 2:** 602
17.45	**Vol. 3:** 508, 566
17.51	**Vol. 2:** 602
18	**Vol. 3:** 210, 749
18.2	**Vol. 2:** 824
18.4	**Vol. 2:** 310
18.5 ff	**Vol. 2:** 337

Sibylline Oracles (Sib.)

1.20	**Vol. 2:** 405
1.29	**Vol. 1:** 87
1.103	**Vol. 2:** 208
1.125 ff	**Vol. 2:** 682
2.54	**Vol. 2:** 115
2.186 ff	**Vol. 1:** 656
2.187–213	**Vol. 2:** 836
2.230	**Vol. 1:** 705
2.238 ff	**Vol. 1:** 656
3	**Vol. 2:** 364
3.63 ff	**Vol. 1:** 125
3.83–92	**Vol. 2:** 836
3.88 ff	**Vol. 1:** 125
3.256	**Vol. 3:** 1013
3.271	**Vol. 2:** 309
3.319 ff	**Vol. 3:** 962
3.429 f	**Vol. 2:** 396
3.570–579	**Vol. 3:** 428
3.582 ff	**Vol. 3:** 693
3.652–660	**Vol. 2:** 701
3.662 ff	**Vol. 3:** 962
3.663 ff	**Vol. 2:** 326
3.787	**Vol. 2:** 326
3.796 ff	**Vol. 2:** 629
3.801 f	**Vol. 3:** 731
3.811 f	**Vol. 2:** 744
3.812	**Vol. 2:** 756
4.28	**Vol. 1:** 428
4.45–87	**Vol. 2:** 692
4.46	**Vol. 1:** 729
4.165–167	**Vol. 1:** 155
4.171–182	**Vol. 2:** 836
4.173–174	**Vol. 3:** 874
4.178–190	**Vol. 2:** 207
4.189	**Vol. 1:** 729
5.12 ff	**Vol. 2:** 684
5.138 ff	**Vol. 2:** 684
5.155–161	**Vol. 2:** 836
5.249	**Vol. 2:** 310
5.251 f	**Vol. 2:** 326
5.264	**Vol. 3:** 160
5.495	**Vol. 3:** 913
8.14	**Vol. 3:** 394
8.239	**Vol. 3:** 874

Sirach, Book of (Sir.)

Prol. 3	**Vol. 3:** 816
Prol. 4	**Vol. 3:** 1027
Prol. 10	**Vol. 3:** 1027
Prol. 14	**Vol. 3:** 821
Prol. 27	**Vol. 2:** 437
1.1–10	**Vol. 3:** 641
1.1	**Vol. 3:** 1027
1.2	**Vol. 3:** 828
1.3 f	**Vol. 3:** 1027
1.4	**Vol. 1:** 380 **Vol. 3:** 1027
1.6–20	**Vol. 3:** 1069
1.6	**Vol. 1:** 412 **Vol. 3:** 311, 1027
1.8	**Vol. 3:** 1028
1.9 f	**Vol. 1:** 380
1.11 ff	**Vol. 1:** 622
1.12	**Vol. 2:** 357
1.14	**Vol. 1:** 580 **Vol. 3:** 1027
1.16	**Vol. 3:** 1027
1.18	**Vol. 3:** 1027
1.19 f	**Vol. 3:** 130
1.20	**Vol. 3:** 1027
1.21	**Vol. 3:** 355
1.24 ff	**Vol. 3:** 1027
1.25	**Vol. 2:** 835
1.27	**Vol. 2:** 258, 818
1.28	**Vol. 3:** 687
1.29	**Vol. 2:** 468
1.30	**Vol. 1:** 609
2.1	**Vol. 3:** 117, 799
2.2	**Vol. 2:** 767
2.3	**Vol. 2:** 349
2.5	**Vol. 3:** 745, 808
2.7	**Vol. 1:** 609
2.8	**Vol. 2:** 139
2.10	**Vol. 3:** 226
2.14	**Vol. 2:** 773
2.17	**Vol. 2:** 264 **Vol. 3:** 117
2.18	**Vol. 1:** 609
3.3–16	**Vol. 2:** 49
3.3	**Vol. 3:** 150
3.5	**Vol. 2:** 863
3.6	**Vol. 3:** 255
3.15	**Vol. 3:** 240
3.16	**Vol. 3:** 341
3.17	**Vol. 3:** 745
3.18	**Vol. 2:** 203
3.21	**Vol. 1:** 420
3.28	**Vol. 3:** 29
3.29	**Vol. 2:** 175 **Vol. 3:** 1028
3.30	**Vol. 3:** 150, 153, 157
4.1–10	**Vol. 3:** 638
4.8	**Vol. 2:** 258
4.10	**Vol. 3:** 638
4.11	**Vol. 3:** 1027
4.15	**Vol. 2:** 179
4.17	**Vol. 1:** 622 **Vol. 3:** 354
4.23	**Vol. 3:** 209
4.24	**Vol. 3:** 1027

Sirach, Book of (Sir.) *(cont'd)*

4.26	**Vol. 3:** 711
4.27	**Vol. 3:** 1025
4.28	**Vol. 1:** 645
5.5 f	**Vol. 3:** 152
5.6	**Vol. 1:** 732 **Vol. 3:** 150, 255
5.7 ff	**Vol. 1:** 110
5.7	**Vol. 1:** 109 **Vol. 3:** 836
5.13	**Vol. 1:** 609 **Vol. 2:** 49
5.15	**Vol. 1:** 381
6.8	**Vol. 3:** 228
6.10	**Vol. 3:** 228
6.11	**Vol. 2:** 735
6.15	**Vol. 3:** 167
6.16	**Vol. 1:** 329
6.18 f	**Vol. 1:** 322
6.18	**Vol. 3:** 1027
6.20	**Vol. 3:** 226
6.22	**Vol. 3:** 1027
6.24	**Vol. 3:** 1161
6.26	**Vol. 3:** 685, 938, 1161
6.27	**Vol. 1:** 495
6.28	**Vol. 3:** 255–256
6.30	**Vol. 3:** 1161
6.32	**Vol. 1:** 412
6.33 f	**Vol. 3:** 1028
6.34 f	**Vol. 1:** 92
6.35	**Vol. 1:** 575 **Vol. 2:** 757
6.37	**Vol. 3:** 1027
7.2	**Vol. 1:** 607
7.5	**Vol. 3:** 358, 1028, 1033
7.11	**Vol. 2:** 261–262
7.17	**Vol. 3:** 110
7.19	**Vol. 3:** 1028
7.20	**Vol. 2:** 139 **Vol. 3:** 882
7.22	**Vol. 3:** 226
7.29	**Vol. 3:** 479
7.31	**Vol. 3:** 416
7.33	**Vol. 2:** 115
8.1	**Vol. 1:** 609
8.2	**Vol. 2:** 841
8.8	**Vol. 2:** 757 **Vol. 3:** 1027–1028
8.14	**Vol. 2:** 818
8.15	**Vol. 3:** 1024
9.2	**Vol. 3:** 921
9.3	**Vol. 1:** 609
9.5	**Vol. 2:** 707
9.8	**Vol. 1:** 655
9.10	**Vol. 2:** 675
9.12	**Vol. 2:** 818 **Vol. 3:** 355
9.14	**Vol. 3:** 1028
9.15	**Vol. 1:** 575 **Vol. 3:** 820
9.17	**Vol. 3:** 816, 1028
10.1	**Vol. 3:** 1028
10.6	**Vol. 3:** 29
10.7	**Vol. 3:** 29
10.8	**Vol. 3:** 29
10.9	**Vol. 3:** 29
10.11	**Vol. 3:** 271

10.12 f	**Vol. 3:** 29
10.12	**Vol. 1:** 607 **Vol. 3:** 30
10.15 ff	**Vol. 2:** 261
10.17	**Vol. 3:** 255
10.18	**Vol. 1:** 381 **Vol. 3:** 29
10.19	**Vol. 2:** 49
10.22	**Vol. 2:** 841
10.23	**Vol. 2:** 49 **Vol. 3:** 358
10.25	**Vol. 3:** 1028
10.26	**Vol. 3:** 1028
10.28	**Vol. 2:** 258
10.29	**Vol. 3:** 355, 358
10.30	**Vol. 2:** 823, 841
11.1	**Vol. 3:** 1027
11.7	**Vol. 1:** 572
11.11–13	**Vol. 3:** 953
11.12 f	**Vol. 2:** 261
11.12	**Vol. 1:** 729
11.13	**Vol. 2:** 621
11.17	**Vol. 2:** 91, 93, 818 **Vol. 3:** 228
11.18 f	**Vol. 2:** 845
11.18	**Vol. 2:** 139, 841
11.19	**Vol. 3:** 255, 528
11.21	**Vol. 2:** 841 **Vol. 3:** 226
11.22	**Vol. 2:** 93, 139 **Vol. 3:** 847
11.27	**Vol. 3:** 310–311, 847
11.28	**Vol. 3:** 271
11.30	**Vol. 3:** 29
11.32	**Vol. 1:** 655
12.1	**Vol. 2:** 117
12.2	**Vol. 2:** 93
12.4	**Vol. 2:** 93
12.15	**Vol. 2:** 767
13.1	**Vol. 2:** 501
13.2 f	**Vol. 2:** 841
13.11	**Vol. 2:** 498
13.13	**Vol. 1:** 381
13.18–23	**Vol. 2:** 841
13.20	**Vol. 2:** 259–260 **Vol. 3:** 29
13.22	**Vol. 3:** 355, 358
13.26	**Vol. 3:** 820
14.16	**Vol. 3:** 270
14.18 f	**Vol. 1:** 433
14.18	**Vol. 1:** 221, 673
14.20–27	**Vol. 3:** 1029
14.20	**Vol. 1:** 216 **Vol. 3:** 1027
14.25	**Vol. 3:** 794
14.27	**Vol. 1:** 653
15.1	**Vol. 3:** 748
15.3	**Vol. 3:** 459, 1027
15.7	**Vol. 3:** 131
15.8	**Vol. 3:** 29
15.10	**Vol. 3:** 1027
15.12	**Vol. 3:** 957
15.15	**Vol. 2:** 818
15.18	**Vol. 3:** 1027
16.7	**Vol. 1:** 109 **Vol. 3:** 152
16.8	**Vol. 3:** 29
16.10	**Vol. 2:** 184
16.12	**Vol. 1:** 110 **Vol. 3:** 167

Sirach, Book of (Sir.) *(cont'd)*

16.13	**Vol. 2:** 773
16.17	**Vol. 1:** 381
16.22	**Vol. 2:** 773
16.23	**Vol. 3:** 1024–1025
17.1	**Vol. 1:** 381
17.2	**Vol. 3:** 835
17.3 f	**Vol. 2:** 287
17.3	**Vol. 2:** 287
17.10	**Vol. 3:** 816
17.15	**Vol. 2:** 215
17.20	**Vol. 2:** 215
17.22	**Vol. 2:** 117
17.24	**Vol. 2:** 773
17.27 f	**Vol. 3:** 233, 270, 816
17.31	**Vol. 1:** 221
18.2	**Vol. 3:** 355
18.6	**Vol. 2:** 622
18.10	**Vol. 2:** 698
18.13	**Vol. 2:** 141 **Vol. 3:** 565, 761
18.14	**Vol. 3:** 776
18.15	**Vol. 1:** 495
18.16	**Vol. 3:** 255
18.17	**Vol. 2:** 116
18.18	**Vol. 3:** 1025
18.20	**Vol. 3:** 847
18.21	**Vol. 3:** 836
18.22	**Vol. 3:** 355, 358
18.23	**Vol. 3:** 117, 799, 801
18.24	**Vol. 3:** 836
18.25	**Vol. 2:** 842
18.27	**Vol. 2:** 90 **Vol. 3:** 1028
18.28	**Vol. 3:** 271, 1027
18.29	**Vol. 2:** 757 **Vol. 3:** 1028
18.30	**Vol. 1:** 460, 495
18.31	**Vol. 2:** 817
18.33	**Vol. 1:** 142
19.1	**Vol. 2:** 841
19.2	**Vol. 2:** 349
19.11 ff	**Vol. 3:** 1025
19.20	**Vol. 3:** 1027
19.22 f	**Vol. 3:** 1027
19.23	**Vol. 3:** 1024
19.24	**Vol. 1:** 729
19.25	**Vol. 1:** 412
19.30	**Vol. 2:** 369, 431
20.4	**Vol. 3:** 711
20.5	**Vol. 3:** 1028
20.7	**Vol. 3:** 1024, 1028
20.13	**Vol. 3:** 1025, 1028
20.14	**Vol. 3:** 1024
20.15	**Vol. 3:** 50
20.16	**Vol. 3:** 1025
20.19	**Vol. 2:** 644
20.20	**Vol. 3:** 1025
20.21	**Vol. 3:** 255
20.22	**Vol. 3:** 1024
20.26	**Vol. 2:** 437
20.27	**Vol. 3:** 1028
20.28	**Vol. 3:** 150
20.29	**Vol. 3:** 902, 1028
20.30 f	**Vol. 3:** 1027
20.31	**Vol. 3:** 1025
21.2	**Vol. 1:** 559
21.4	**Vol. 2:** 842 **Vol. 3:** 29
21.10	**Vol. 1:** 254
21.11	**Vol. 3:** 125, 1027
21.12	**Vol. 1:** 412
21.13	**Vol. 3:** 991, 1028
21.14	**Vol. 3:** 1025
21.15	**Vol. 3:** 816, 1028
21.16	**Vol. 1:** 574 **Vol. 3:** 1025
21.18	**Vol. 3:** 1025, 1027
21.19	**Vol. 3:** 126
21.20	**Vol. 1:** 412 **Vol. 2:** 431, 433 **Vol. 3:** 1025
21.22	**Vol. 3:** 1025
21.23	**Vol. 3:** 1024
21.25	**Vol. 3:** 1161
21.26	**Vol. 3:** 1025, 1028
22.6	**Vol. 1:** 575 **Vol. 3:** 1027
22.7 f	**Vol. 3:** 1025
22.7	**Vol. 3:** 761, 914
22.11 f	**Vol. 3:** 1025
22.11	**Vol. 3:** 255, 270
22.13	**Vol. 3:** 255, 1024
22.14	**Vol. 3:** 1025
22.18	**Vol. 2:** 773 **Vol. 3:** 1025
22.22	**Vol. 1:** 559 **Vol. 3:** 29, 310–311, 502
22.24	**Vol. 1:** 655 **Vol. 3:** 346
22.27	**Vol. 3:** 498
23.1	**Vol. 1:** 618 **Vol. 2:** 509
23.2	**Vol. 3:** 1027
23.3	**Vol. 1:** 732 **Vol. 2:** 131
23.4	**Vol. 1:** 618
23.6	**Vol. 1:** 460
23.8	**Vol. 2:** 707 **Vol. 3:** 29, 346
23.9 ff	**Vol. 3:** 740
23.11	**Vol. 3:** 355
23.12	**Vol. 1:** 607
23.14	**Vol. 3:** 1025
23.16 ff	**Vol. 1:** 233
23.16	**Vol. 1:** 655, 732 **Vol. 3:** 109
23.18	**Vol. 2:** 586
23.19	**Vol. 3:** 730
23.20	**Vol. 1:** 381
23.21	**Vol. 3:** 98
23.23	**Vol. 3:** 1195
24	**Vol. 3:** 1032
24.1	**Vol. 3:** 816, 1027
24.3–12	**Vol. 3:** 1116
24.6	**Vol. 2:** 840
24.7	**Vol. 3:** 255–256
24.8 ff	**Vol. 3:** 1029
24.8 f	**Vol. 1:** 380
24.8	**Vol. 1:** 382 **Vol. 3:** 255
24.9	**Vol. 3:** 416
24.11	**Vol. 3:** 255
24.12	**Vol. 3:** 808

Sirach, Book of (Sir.) *(cont'd)*

24.15	**Vol. 2:** 294	**Vol. 3:** 600–601
24.17	**Vol. 2:** 842	**Vol. 3:** 919
24.18 ff	**Vol. 3:** 640	
24.22	**Vol. 2:** 179	
24.23 ff	**Vol. 3:** 1029	
24.23	**Vol. 3:** 459	
24.25–34	**Vol. 3:** 459	
24.25	**Vol. 3:** 1027	
24.30–33	**Vol. 3:** 986	
24.33	**Vol. 3:** 769	
25.2	**Vol. 2:** 583, 841	**Vol. 3:** 29, 1025
25.4 ff	**Vol. 1:** 92	
25.5	**Vol. 3:** 125, 1027	
25.7–10	**Vol. 1:** 216	
25.8	**Vol. 1:** 216	
25.10	**Vol. 3:** 1027	
25.18	**Vol. 1:** 504	
25.21	**Vol. 1:** 109	
25.24	**Vol. 1:** 434	
25.25	**Vol. 1:** 565	**Vol. 2:** 735
26.4	**Vol. 2:** 841	
26.5	**Vol. 2:** 90	
26.14	**Vol. 3:** 167	
26.16	**Vol. 3:** 730, 1068	
26.28	**Vol. 3:** 953	
26.29	**Vol. 3:** 355	
27.1 ff	**Vol. 2:** 845	
27.3	**Vol. 3:** 1169	
27.4 f	**Vol. 3:** 823	
27.4	**Vol. 1:** 480	
27.5	**Vol. 3:** 799, 808, 820, 911	
27.7	**Vol. 3:** 799, 816, 823	
27.8	**Vol. 3:** 748	
27.11	**Vol. 1:** 575	**Vol. 3:** 733, 1024, 1027–1028
27.13	**Vol. 2:** 431, 433	**Vol. 3:** 1025
27.15	**Vol. 2:** 854	**Vol. 3:** 29
27.16 f	**Vol. 3:** 502	
27.21	**Vol. 3:** 346, 502	
27.23	**Vol. 2:** 621	
27.28	**Vol. 3:** 29	
27.30	**Vol. 1:** 109	
28.1	**Vol. 3:** 717	
28.2	**Vol. 3:** 177	
28.6	**Vol. 3:** 226	
28.10 f	**Vol. 1:** 654	
28.10	**Vol. 1:** 109	**Vol. 2:** 842
28.12	**Vol. 3:** 109	
28.16	**Vol. 3:** 255	
28.19 f	**Vol. 3:** 1161	
28.23	**Vol. 3:** 109	
28.25	**Vol. 3:** 1161	
29.1 ff	**Vol. 2:** 769	
29.6	**Vol. 3:** 346, 823	
29.15	**Vol. 1:** 372	
30.2	**Vol. 3:** 816	
30.3	**Vol. 3:** 761	
30.9	**Vol. 2:** 621	
30.14	**Vol. 2:** 822, 841	
30.16	**Vol. 2:** 357	
30.17	**Vol. 3:** 255–256, 271	
30.20	**Vol. 3:** 711	
30.21 ff	**Vol. 2:** 420	
30.24	**Vol. 1:** 277	
30.27	**Vol. 3:** 761	
31.3 f	**Vol. 3:** 255	
31.3	**Vol. 2:** 841, 845	
31.5 f	**Vol. 2:** 845	
31.5	**Vol. 3:** 355	
31.7	**Vol. 3:** 1024	
31.8	**Vol. 1:** 492	**Vol. 2:** 841 **Vol. 3:** 924
31.10	**Vol. 3:** 808	
31.11	**Vol. 3:** 1027	
31.18	**Vol. 2:** 41	
31.21	**Vol. 3:** 255, 711	
31.24	**Vol. 2:** 509	
31.26	**Vol. 3:** 808	
31.27	**Vol. 1:** 381	
31.30	**Vol. 3:** 1024, 1079	
32.2	**Vol. 3:** 957	
32.3	**Vol. 2:** 669	
32.4	**Vol. 3:** 1028, 1033	
32.12	**Vol. 3:** 29	
32.17	**Vol. 3:** 1019	
32.18	**Vol. 3:** 125	
32.23	**Vol. 2:** 132	
33.1	**Vol. 2:** 509	**Vol. 3:** 799–800, 1025
33.2	**Vol. 3:** 1028	
33.3	**Vol. 2:** 879	
33.5 f	**Vol. 3:** 1025	
33.5	**Vol. 3:** 820	
33.8	**Vol. 1:** 626	
33.10–13	**Vol. 3:** 916	
33.10	**Vol. 1:** 381	
33.13	**Vol. 2:** 818	**Vol. 3:** 911
33.25	**Vol. 3:** 255	
33.26	**Vol. 2:** 569	**Vol. 3:** 1161
33.28	**Vol. 1:** 589	**Vol. 2:** 669
34.1 f	**Vol. 2:** 137	
34.1	**Vol. 3:** 1024	
34.2	**Vol. 3:** 555	
34.5 ff	**Vol. 1:** 512	
34.8	**Vol. 3:** 1027	
34.10	**Vol. 3:** 799	
34.19	**Vol. 3:** 150	
34.20	**Vol. 2:** 137	
34.22	**Vol. 2:** 139	
34.23 f	**Vol. 3:** 1041	
34.25	**Vol. 1:** 144, 152	
34.26	**Vol. 2:** 863	
35.1	**Vol. 2:** 131	
35.2	**Vol. 2:** 117	
35.3	**Vol. 1:** 607	
35.5 f	**Vol. 3:** 498	
35.6	**Vol. 3:** 479	
35.8	**Vol. 3:** 416	
35.15	**Vol. 2:** 468, 707	
35.17	**Vol. 2:** 863	

Sirach, Book of (Sir.) *(cont'd)*

36.2	**Vol. 2:** 468
36.4 f	**Vol. 2:** 396
36.12 f	**Vol. 2:** 609, 803
36.13	**Vol. 2:** 818
36.15	**Vol. 1:** 381　**Vol. 3:** 255
36.18	**Vol. 2:** 139, 773
36.24	**Vol. 3:** 255
37.11	**Vol. 2:** 139　**Vol. 3:** 818
37.20 f	**Vol. 3:** 1027
37.20	**Vol. 3:** 1028
37.22 ff	**Vol. 3:** 1028
37.26	**Vol. 3:** 1028
37.27	**Vol. 3:** 799
38.1 f	**Vol. 2:** 167
38.1	**Vol. 1:** 381　**Vol. 2:** 50
38.4	**Vol. 1:** 381
38.6	**Vol. 2:** 622
38.9–14	**Vol. 2:** 167
38.12	**Vol. 1:** 381
38.14	**Vol. 3:** 255
38.19	**Vol. 3:** 228
38.21	**Vol. 3:** 271
38.23	**Vol. 3:** 255
38.24 f	**Vol. 3:** 1028
38.24–39.11	**Vol. 3:** 479
38.24–34	**Vol. 3:** 911
38.24	**Vol. 3:** 1027
38.25 ff	**Vol. 3:** 479
38.25	**Vol. 1:** 575
38.27	**Vol. 2:** 773　**Vol. 3:** 497
38.28	**Vol. 1:** 654
38.29–30	**Vol. 3:** 911
38.30	**Vol. 2:** 115
38.31	**Vol. 3:** 1028, 1212
38.34	**Vol. 1:** 382
39.1	**Vol. 3:** 479, 1027
39.2	**Vol. 1:** 575
39.3	**Vol. 2:** 757
39.4	**Vol. 3:** 479, 799
39.5	**Vol. 2:** 863
39.6	**Vol. 3:** 479, 1120
39.7 f	**Vol. 3:** 479
39.7	**Vol. 2:** 863　**Vol. 3:** 1027
39.8	**Vol. 1:** 227, 735　**Vol. 3:** 769
39.9 f	**Vol. 1:** 735
39.9	**Vol. 3:** 271, 816
39.10	**Vol. 3:** 1027
39.11	**Vol. 3:** 226, 255
39.14	**Vol. 3:** 600–601, 673, 816
39.18	**Vol. 2:** 818
39.19	**Vol. 2:** 215
39.21–30	**Vol. 1:** 381
39.22	**Vol. 3:** 991
39.26	**Vol. 3:** 444, 919
39.33 f	**Vol. 3:** 846
39.34	**Vol. 3:** 808
40.1	**Vol. 3:** 937, 1161
40.2	**Vol. 3:** 820

40.5 f	**Vol. 3:** 255
40.7	**Vol. 3:** 209
40.9	**Vol. 2:** 265
40.10	**Vol. 1:** 381　**Vol. 3:** 991
40.14	**Vol. 3:** 381
40.17	**Vol. 2:** 117
40.19	**Vol. 3:** 823, 924
40.20	**Vol. 3:** 1027
40.24	**Vol. 3:** 201–202
40.28	**Vol. 2:** 823
40.29	**Vol. 3:** 820, 823
41.1 f	**Vol. 3:** 232
41.1–4	**Vol. 1:** 433
41.1	**Vol. 2:** 271
41.2	**Vol. 2:** 773
41.11 ff	**Vol. 3:** 271
41.14 f	**Vol. 3:** 1027
41.15	**Vol. 3:** 1025
42.1	**Vol. 3:** 310–311
42.2	**Vol. 3:** 358
42.4	**Vol. 3:** 1161
42.8	**Vol. 2:** 675　**Vol. 3:** 126, 808, 1025
42.9	**Vol. 1:** 277
42.15	**Vol. 3:** 262
42.16	**Vol. 2:** 491
42.17	**Vol. 2:** 622
42.18	**Vol. 1:** 349
42.19	**Vol. 1:** 322　**Vol. 2:** 215
42.21	**Vol. 3:** 1027
43.1 ff	**Vol. 2:** 491
43.2 ff	**Vol. 2:** 491
43.2	**Vol. 2:** 622
43.3	**Vol. 1:** 652
43.5	**Vol. 3:** 255
43.6 ff	**Vol. 2:** 491
43.6–8	**Vol. 3:** 733
43.6	**Vol. 3:** 842
43.8	**Vol. 2:** 128, 622
43.13	**Vol. 3:** 255
43.19	**Vol. 1:** 726
43.23	**Vol. 3:** 823, 983
43.24 f	**Vol. 1:** 381
43.24	**Vol. 1:** 419
43.31	**Vol. 1:** 575–576
43.33	**Vol. 3:** 1027
44–50	**Vol. 1:** 714
44.1 ff	**Vol. 1:** 617
44.2	**Vol. 1:** 381
44.4	**Vol. 3:** 1028
44.6	**Vol. 2:** 841
44.8	**Vol. 3:** 271
44.15	**Vol. 3:** 1027
44.16	**Vol. 2:** 290, 815, 817　**Vol. 3:** 265–266, 602
44.17 ff	**Vol. 3:** 991
44.17 f	**Vol. 2:** 681
44.17	**Vol. 3:** 167, 836
44.19 ff	**Vol. 3:** 369
44.21	**Vol. 2:** 499
44.23	**Vol. 3:** 255

Sirach, Book of (Sir.) *(cont'd)*

45.3	**Vol. 3:** 255
45.4	**Vol. 2:** 257
45.6–26	**Vol. 3:** 479
45.8	**Vol. 3:** 36
45.17	**Vol. 3:** 761
45.20	**Vol. 3:** 416
45.24	**Vol. 3:** 36
45.26	**Vol. 3:** 1027
46.1	**Vol. 3:** 209, 479
46.5	**Vol. 2:** 70
46.6	**Vol. 2:** 70
46.10	**Vol. 1:** 492
46.12	**Vol. 3:** 271
46.19	**Vol. 3:** 270
47.6	**Vol. 1:** 405 **Vol. 3:** 816
47.11	**Vol. 3:** 649
47.12 f	**Vol. 3:** 255
47.13	**Vol. 2:** 655
47.14	**Vol. 3:** 1028
47.17	**Vol. 1:** 580 **Vol. 2:** 757
47.19	**Vol. 1:** 233
47.20 ff	**Vol. 1:** 108–109
47.20	**Vol. 3:** 1024
47.23	**Vol. 3:** 255, 1024
48.3	**Vol. 1:** 544 **Vol. 2:** 765
48.5	**Vol. 1:** 444
48.7	**Vol. 3:** 1013
48.8	**Vol. 3:** 209
48.9	**Vol. 3:** 262, 265, 747
48.10	**Vol. 1:** 544 **Vol. 2:** 337
48.12	**Vol. 1:** 735 **Vol. 3:** 693
48.14	**Vol. 2:** 622 **Vol. 3:** 1148
48.15	**Vol. 1:** 607
48.18	**Vol. 3:** 29
48.19	**Vol. 3:** 1068
48.20	**Vol. 3:** 192, 194
48.25	**Vol. 2:** 215
49.3	**Vol. 2:** 93
49.10	**Vol. 3:** 192, 194
49.12	**Vol. 3:** 117
49.14 f	**Vol. 3:** 265
49.14	**Vol. 3:** 602, 747
49.16	**Vol. 1:** 84
50	**Vol. 1:** 700
50.5	**Vol. 3:** 794
50.6	**Vol. 3:** 733–734
50.15	**Vol. 3:** 919
50.20	**Vol. 1:** 216
50.21	**Vol. 2:** 876
50.24	**Vol. 3:** 192–194
50.25 f	**Vol. 3:** 456, 461
50.26	**Vol. 3:** 1025
50.27	**Vol. 2:** 325, 331, 573 **Vol. 3:** 479, 1027
50.28	**Vol. 3:** 1028, 1033
51.1–12	**Vol. 1:** 345
51.1	**Vol. 1:** 618 **Vol. 2:** 514, 863 **Vol. 3:** 218, 220
51.2 f	**Vol. 3:** 192, 194

51.2	**Vol. 3:** 193
51.3	**Vol. 2:** 421
51.6	**Vol. 3:** 816
51.8	**Vol. 2:** 773
51.10	**Vol. 1:** 618 **Vol. 3:** 29
51.13	**Vol. 2:** 863 **Vol. 3:** 1027
51.17	**Vol. 3:** 1027
51.22	**Vol. 2:** 139
51.23–30	**Vol. 2:** 262
51.23	**Vol. 3:** 479
51.24	**Vol. 2:** 266
51.25 f	**Vol. 3:** 1161–1162
51.26	**Vol. 3:** 1161
51.27	**Vol. 3:** 255–256
51.30	**Vol. 2:** 139 **Vol. 3:** 836

Slavonic Book of Enoch (Sl. Enoch)

2–20	**Vol. 2:** 613
3–21	**Vol. 2:** 688
3.1	**Vol. 2:** 925
3.3	**Vol. 3:** 984
7	**Vol. 2:** 762
8	**Vol. 2:** 762–763
8.1–8	**Vol. 2:** 191
8.1	**Vol. 2:** 761
10.4 f	**Vol. 3:** 31
11–16	**Vol. 3:** 731
11	**Vol. 2:** 762
17	**Vol. 2:** 763
18	**Vol. 2:** 762
19.4	**Vol. 3:** 983
20	**Vol. 2:** 614
21.3	**Vol. 1:** 103
22.4 ff	**Vol. 3:** 35
22.8	**Vol. 1:** 204
24.1	**Vol. 1:** 103
30.15	**Vol. 1:** 254 **Vol. 2:** 493 **Vol. 3:** 939
31	**Vol. 1:** 449
33.1	**Vol. 2:** 698
33.4	**Vol. 2:** 698
39.2	**Vol. 2:** 279
49.2	**Vol. 3:** 1161
52.1 ff	**Vol. 1:** 216
55.2	**Vol. 2:** 326
58.6	**Vol. 1:** 410
61.2	**Vol. 3:** 229
64.5a	**Vol. 3:** 35–36
65.7 f	**Vol. 3:** 836

Syriac Apocalypse of Baruch (Syr. Bar.)

4.2 ff	**Vol. 2:** 326
4.2–6	**Vol. 3:** 789
6	**Vol. 2:** 56
8	**Vol. 2:** 56
13.3	**Vol. 2:** 202
14.12	**Vol. 3:** 1149

**Syriac Apocalypse of Baruch
(Syr. Bar.)** *(cont'd)*

22.1	**Vol. 3:** 543
25–30	**Vol. 3:** 695
25.4	**Vol. 2:** 892
27	**Vol. 2:** 892
27.6	**Vol. 2:** 266
29.3	**Vol. 2:** 701 **Vol. 3:** 652
29.5–8	**Vol. 1:** 729
29.5	**Vol. 2:** 698 **Vol. 3:** 919
29.6 ff	**Vol. 2:** 272
29.6	**Vol. 2:** 842
29.7 f	**Vol. 2:** 892
29.8	**Vol. 1:** 252 **Vol. 2:** 218
30.1–5	**Vol. 2:** 701
30.2	**Vol. 3:** 956
37.1	**Vol. 1:** 656
39.7	**Vol. 3:** 919
40.2 f	**Vol. 3:** 961
40.2	**Vol. 3:** 250
40.3	**Vol. 2:** 701
44.3	**Vol. 3:** 939
44.7	**Vol. 1:** 570
44.15	**Vol. 1:** 656
48.38	**Vol. 3:** 1149
48.39	**Vol. 1:** 656
50–51	**Vol. 3:** 297
50.2	**Vol. 3:** 271
50.3 f	**Vol. 3:** 271
51.1–12	**Vol. 3:** 861
51.1	**Vol. 1:** 706
51.3	**Vol. 3:** 271
51.5	**Vol. 3:** 271
51.12–52	**Vol. 2:** 842
51.15	**Vol. 3:** 174
54.2	**Vol. 3:** 1149
54.5	**Vol. 1:** 598
54.16	**Vol. 1:** 598
54.17 f	**Vol. 2:** 396
54.19	**Vol. 1:** 434
54.21	**Vol. 1:** 598
56	**Vol. 2:** 213
57.2	**Vol. 1:** 77, 598
59.10	**Vol. 2:** 208
66.2	**Vol. 3:** 160
67.6	**Vol. 3:** 601
70.2	**Vol. 3:** 526
70.9	**Vol. 3:** 610
76.4	**Vol. 2:** 696
85.3	**Vol. 3:** 311
85.13	**Vol. 2:** 208

**Testament of Asher
(Test. Ash.)**

1.3	**Vol. 2:** 481 **Vol. 3:** 939–940
1.5	**Vol. 2:** 481 **Vol. 3:** 939–940
1.9	**Vol. 3:** 939
4.3	**Vol. 1:** 491

5.2	**Vol. 2:** 928 **Vol. 3:** 210
6	**Vol. 3:** 693
6.6	**Vol. 3:** 210
7.2†	**Vol. 1:** 685
7.3	**Vol. 3:** 210, 961

**Testament of Benjamin
(Test. Ben.)**

3.1	**Vol. 1:** 491
3.8	**Vol. 3:** 165, 195
4.1	**Vol. 1:** 405, 491 **Vol. 3:** 210
4.5	**Vol. 3:** 1152
5	**Vol. 3:** 807
6	**Vol. 3:** 807
6.4	**Vol. 3:** 963
8.2	**Vol. 3:** 125
8.3	**Vol. 3:** 125–126
9.1	**Vol. 1:** 499
10	**Vol. 2:** 207
10.1	**Vol. 2:** 136
10.3 f	**Vol. 1:** 334
10.5	**Vol. 3:** 210
10.6–9	**Vol. 3:** 272
10.11	**Vol. 2:** 313
11.2	**Vol. 2:** 397
11.5	**Vol. 3:** 953

Testament of Dan (Test. Dan)

5.1	**Vol. 1:** 334
5.10 f	**Vol. 3:** 961
5.10	**Vol. 3:** 210
5.13–6.4	**Vol. 2:** 602
6.2	**Vol. 1:** 104 **Vol. 3:** 35
6.3 f	**Vol. 1:** 554
6.9	**Vol. 3:** 210
6.10	**Vol. 3:** 372

Testament of Gad (Test. Gad)

2.5	**Vol. 3:** 263
4.7	**Vol. 3:** 210, 1152
5.1	**Vol. 3:** 963
5.3	**Vol. 2:** 261
5.4	**Vol. 3:** 346
5.7	**Vol. 3:** 210
7.5	**Vol. 3:** 210

**Testament of Issachar
(Test. Iss.)**

1.11	**Vol. 1:** 742
3.8	**Vol. 3:** 572, 1152
5.2	**Vol. 1:** 334 **Vol. 2:** 427
7	**Vol. 3:** 807

Testament of Joseph (Test. Jos.)

1.6	**Vol. 2:** 116
2.2	**Vol. 3:** 263
2.7	**Vol. 3:** 570

Testament of Joseph (Test. Jos.) *(cont'd)*

4.6 ff	**Vol. 2:** 583
5.1	**Vol. 2:** 583
6.7	**Vol. 3:** 263
8.3	**Vol. 1:** 528
8.5	**Vol. 3:** 670
10.3	**Vol. 3:** 210
12.2 f	**Vol. 2:** 309
13.3	**Vol. 2:** 309
14.5	**Vol. 3:** 570
17.4	**Vol. 1:** 569
19 f	**Vol. 2:** 311
19.11	**Vol. 3:** 210

Testament of Judah (Test. Jud.)

6	**Vol. 1:** 499
11.1	**Vol. 3:** 125
13	**Vol. 1:** 499
14.2 f	**Vol. 3:** 126
14.3	**Vol. 1:** 233
14.4	**Vol. 1:** 514
14.6	**Vol. 1:** 334
14.7	**Vol. 3:** 957
15.4	**Vol. 2:** 272
16.1	**Vol. 3:** 31
16.3 f	**Vol. 1:** 334
16.3	**Vol. 3:** 963
20	**Vol. 3:** 693
20.1	**Vol. 3:** 929
21.2	**Vol. 3:** 35–36
21.4	**Vol. 3:** 36
22.2	**Vol. 2:** 899 **Vol. 3:** 210
24.1–5	**Vol. 2:** 495
24.1	**Vol. 1:** 407 **Vol. 2:** 558 **Vol. 3:** 35, 170
24.4–6	**Vol. 3:** 650
25	**Vol. 2:** 433
25.1–4	**Vol. 3:** 272
25.1	**Vol. 2:** 480
25.4	**Vol. 1:** 442

Testament of Levi (Test. Lev.)

2–5	**Vol. 1:** 512
2	**Vol. 2:** 688
2.4	**Vol. 3:** 210
2.7	**Vol. 3:** 984
2.10	**Vol. 3:** 210
3	**Vol. 2:** 614, 688
3.4 ff	**Vol. 3:** 789
3.8	**Vol. 2:** 608
4.1	**Vol. 1:** 515 **Vol. 3:** 180, 210
4.3	**Vol. 2:** 397
5.1 f	**Vol. 3:** 789
5.6	**Vol. 1:** 104
6	**Vol. 3:** 455
7	**Vol. 3:** 461, 693
8.14 f	**Vol. 2:** 899
8.15	**Vol. 3:** 656

11	**Vol. 3:** 693
13.2	**Vol. 3:** 229
13.5	**Vol. 2:** 831
14.1	**Vol. 3:** 487
14.2	**Vol. 1:** 334
14.3	**Vol. 2:** 313
14.4	**Vol. 2:** 312
14.6	**Vol. 1:** 155, 334
18	**Vol. 3:** 693
18.1–14	**Vol. 1:** 81
18.2	**Vol. 3:** 35
18.3 f	**Vol. 2:** 558
18.3	**Vol. 1:** 407 **Vol. 2:** 397, 495
18.6 ff	**Vol. 1:** 175
18.9 ff	**Vol. 3:** 80
18.9	**Vol. 3:** 170
18.11	**Vol. 2:** 763
19.1	**Vol. 3:** 929, 939

Testament of Naphtali (Test. Naph.)

2.5	**Vol. 3:** 125
4.1	**Vol. 3:** 487
5–7	**Vol. 1:** 512
8.2 f	**Vol. 3:** 210
8.4	**Vol. 3:** 807

Testament of Reuben (Test. Reub.)

1	**Vol. 1:** 499
2	**Vol. 3:** 939
3	**Vol. 3:** 693, 939
3.3–6	**Vol. 3:** 31
3.9	**Vol. 3:** 210
4.1	**Vol. 3:** 1164
4.4	**Vol. 1:** 569
4.10	**Vol. 3:** 263
5	**Vol. 2:** 213
5.5	**Vol. 3:** 98, 210
6	**Vol. 1:** 499
6.8	**Vol. 3:** 35
6.12	**Vol. 3:** 961
7.2	**Vol. 3:** 380

Testament of Simeon (Test. Sim.)

2.8	**Vol. 3:** 263
2.12	**Vol. 1:** 515 **Vol. 2:** 222
4.8	**Vol. 3:** 963
5.5	**Vol. 3:** 961
6.2	**Vol. 2:** 313
6.5	**Vol. 2:** 313
7.1 f	**Vol. 3:** 210
7.2	**Vol. 2:** 313

Testament of Zebulun
(Test. Zeb.)

2.7	**Vol. 1:** 515
3.4	**Vol. 3:** 487
7.3	**Vol. 2:** 599 **Vol. 3:** 957
8.2	**Vol. 2:** 599
8.6	**Vol. 2:** 599
9	**Vol. 2:** 158
10.3	**Vol. 3:** 210
10.4	**Vol. 3:** 272

Tobit (Tob.)

1.1	**Vol. 1:** 243 **Vol. 3:** 873
1.4	**Vol. 2:** 675
1.6	**Vol. 1:** 626 **Vol. 3:** 416
1.11 f	**Vol. 3:** 233
1.14	**Vol. 1:** 142
1.18	**Vol. 2:** 310 **Vol. 3:** 342, 377
1.22	**Vol. 3:** 498
2.1	**Vol. 2:** 783
2.2	**Vol. 3:** 228, 233
2.6	**Vol. 2:** 433
2.8	**Vol. 1:** 444
2.12	**Vol. 2:** 139
2.13	**Vol. 2:** 607
2.14	**Vol. 2:** 139
3.1–6	**Vol. 1:** 345
3.1	**Vol. 2:** 863
3.2	**Vol. 3:** 358
3.6	**Vol. 1:** 506 **Vol. 2:** 663
3.8	**Vol. 3:** 570
3.10	**Vol. 2:** 478 **Vol. 3:** 823
3.13	**Vol. 1:** 506
3.15	**Vol. 3:** 821, 1202
3.16	**Vol. 2:** 863
3.17	**Vol. 3:** 177
4.8 ff	**Vol. 2:** 830
4.9	**Vol. 2:** 663
4.14	**Vol. 2:** 139 **Vol. 3:** 933
4.21	**Vol. 1:** 607
5.3	**Vol. 2:** 139
5.5	**Vol. 3:** 1185
5.6	**Vol. 1:** 688
5.7	**Vol. 2:** 139, 773
5.8	**Vol. 2:** 767
5.9	**Vol. 2:** 139
5.10	**Vol. 1:** 665
5.13	**Vol. 2:** 876
5.14 f	**Vol. 2:** 139
5.15	**Vol. 1:** 663
5.16	**Vol. 1:** 212
5.18	**Vol. 1:** 479
6.1 ff	**Vol. 1:** 670
6.2 f	**Vol. 1:** 283
6.5	**Vol. 1:** 218
6.7	**Vol. 1:** 451
6.9	**Vol. 1:** 218
6.11 f	**Vol. 3:** 355
6.13 f	**Vol. 1:** 451

6.17	**Vol. 2:** 863
7.3	**Vol. 3:** 873
7.6	**Vol. 1:** 212
7.7	**Vol. 1:** 212
7.8	**Vol. 2:** 521
7.10	**Vol. 2:** 577 **Vol. 3:** 882
7.14	**Vol. 3:** 498
7.18	**Vol. 2:** 514
8.1	**Vol. 2:** 521
8.2	**Vol. 1:** 142
8.3	**Vol. 3:** 1005–1007
8.4 f	**Vol. 2:** 863
8.5	**Vol. 1:** 381 **Vol. 2:** 191
8.6	**Vol. 1:** 87
8.13	**Vol. 3:** 860
8.15	**Vol. 1:** 381
8.18	**Vol. 1:** 341
8.19	**Vol. 2:** 578 **Vol. 3:** 119
9.5	**Vol. 3:** 498–499
9.6	**Vol. 1:** 212
10.1	**Vol. 3:** 823
10.8	**Vol. 3:** 316
10.12	**Vol. 1:** 212
11.12 ff	**Vol. 1:** 218
12.1 ff	**Vol. 2:** 139
12.1	**Vol. 1:** 322
12.4	**Vol. 3:** 355
12.5	**Vol. 2:** 139
12.6	**Vol. 3:** 669
12.7	**Vol. 3:** 502
12.8	**Vol. 2:** 863
12.9	**Vol. 3:** 358
12.12	**Vol. 1:** 444 **Vol. 2:** 863 **Vol. 3:** 242
12.14	**Vol. 3:** 799
12.15	**Vol. 2:** 227, 863
12.18	**Vol. 3:** 669
12.22	**Vol. 3:** 669
13.1	**Vol. 2:** 863
13.2	**Vol. 2:** 209
13.4	**Vol. 1:** 618
13.10 f	**Vol. 2:** 326
13.11	**Vol. 3:** 816
13.14 f	**Vol. 1:** 216
13.14	**Vol. 2:** 357
13.16 ff	**Vol. 2:** 326
13.16–18	**Vol. 3:** 397
13.18	**Vol. 3:** 816
14	**Vol. 1:** 737
14.4	**Vol. 1:** 734 **Vol. 3:** 209, 823
14.5	**Vol. 1:** 734, 740
14.7 ff	**Vol. 3:** 233
14.7	**Vol. 3:** 209
14.9	**Vol. 3:** 358
14.10	**Vol. 1:** 609
14.11	**Vol. 3:** 358
14.13	**Vol. 2:** 846

Wisdom of Solomon (Wis.)

1.1 f	**Vol. 3:** 648

287

Wisdom of Solomon (Wis.) *(cont'd)*

1.1	**Vol. 2:** 512		
1.2	**Vol. 1:** 598	**Vol. 3:** 799, 801	
1.3 f	**Vol. 3:** 648		
1.3	**Vol. 3:** 648, 808, 823, 1024		
1.4–6	**Vol. 3:** 1027		
1.5	**Vol. 3:** 823		
1.6	**Vol. 3:** 341, 1041		
1.7	**Vol. 1:** 735	**Vol. 2:** 512	**Vol. 3:** 693
1.8	**Vol. 3:** 93		
1.9	**Vol. 2:** 512		
1.11	**Vol. 3:** 345		
1.14	**Vol. 1:** 380		
1.15	**Vol. 3:** 358		
2–5	**Vol. 3:** 618		
2.1 ff	**Vol. 1:** 598		
2.1	**Vol. 2:** 475	**Vol. 3:** 823	
2.3	**Vol. 3:** 109		
2.4	**Vol. 2:** 475		
2.5	**Vol. 2:** 475	**Vol. 3:** 498, 555	
2.6	**Vol. 1:** 381		
2.9	**Vol. 3:** 29		
2.10–20	**Vol. 2:** 202		
2.10	**Vol. 3:** 358, 1074		
2.13–18	**Vol. 3:** 638		
2.13	**Vol. 2:** 512, 782	**Vol. 3:** 610	
2.14	**Vol. 3:** 125		
2.16 ff	**Vol. 1:** 618		
2.16	**Vol. 3:** 30, 823		
2.17	**Vol. 3:** 624, 799		
2.18 ff	**Vol. 3:** 202		
2.18	**Vol. 1:** 288	**Vol. 2:** 782	
2.19	**Vol. 2:** 257	**Vol. 3:** 808	
2.20	**Vol. 2:** 370	**Vol. 3:** 624	
2.21	**Vol. 3:** 823		
2.22	**Vol. 2:** 139	**Vol. 3:** 502, 924	
2.23	**Vol. 1:** 380	**Vol. 2:** 287	
2.24	**Vol. 1:** 557	**Vol. 3:** 468, 799	
3.1 ff	**Vol. 1:** 598		
3.1	**Vol. 3:** 358, 680, 856		
3.2	**Vol. 3:** 821, 823, 1024		
3.4	**Vol. 1:** 435	**Vol. 3:** 98	
3.5	**Vol. 3:** 799–800		
3.6	**Vol. 3:** 808		
3.7–10	**Vol. 2:** 202		
3.7	**Vol. 3:** 836		
3.9	**Vol. 1:** 598	**Vol. 3:** 228, 882	
3.10	**Vol. 1:** 572	**Vol. 3:** 823	
3.11	**Vol. 3:** 1027		
3.12	**Vol. 3:** 1024		
3.13	**Vol. 2:** 586	**Vol. 3:** 585, 923	
3.14–5.5	**Vol. 2:** 49		
3.14	**Vol. 2:** 117		
3.16	**Vol. 2:** 586		
3.17	**Vol. 3:** 823		
3.18	**Vol. 1:** 329		
3.19	**Vol. 1:** 420		
4.1	**Vol. 1:** 435	**Vol. 3:** 238, 926	
4.2	**Vol. 1:** 491, 645	**Vol. 3:** 923	
4.3	**Vol. 1:** 663		
4.4	**Vol. 3:** 711		
4.7	**Vol. 3:** 255		
4.8 f	**Vol. 2:** 480		
4.9	**Vol. 2:** 846		
4.10 ff	**Vol. 2:** 627, 817	**Vol. 3:** 266	
4.10	**Vol. 2:** 202, 815	**Vol. 3:** 265, 602	
4.11	**Vol. 3:** 601		
4.12	**Vol. 3:** 125		
4.13	**Vol. 3:** 842		
4.17	**Vol. 1:** 663	**Vol. 3:** 1028	
4.18	**Vol. 3:** 29		
4.19	**Vol. 2:** 502	**Vol. 3:** 238	
5.1–5	**Vol. 2:** 202		
5.1	**Vol. 2:** 735		
5.2	**Vol. 3:** 209		
5.3	**Vol. 2:** 431		
5.4	**Vol. 2:** 846	**Vol. 3:** 823, 1024	
5.5	**Vol. 3:** 638		
5.6	**Vol. 3:** 730		
5.8	**Vol. 2:** 842	**Vol. 3:** 29–30	
5.9	**Vol. 1:** 322	**Vol. 3:** 555	
5.11	**Vol. 3:** 571, 711		
5.13	**Vol. 3:** 926		
5.14	**Vol. 3:** 238		
5.15	**Vol. 2:** 139		
5.16	**Vol. 1:** 405		
5.17	**Vol. 1:** 381		
5.18	**Vol. 3:** 358		
5.19	**Vol. 2:** 237	**Vol. 3:** 966	
5.22	**Vol. 3:** 983		
6.2	**Vol. 2:** 801		
6.7	**Vol. 1:** 694	**Vol. 2:** 509	
6.9	**Vol. 1:** 485, 609	**Vol. 3:** 585, 1027	
6.10	**Vol. 3:** 760–761		
6.12	**Vol. 3:** 1027		
6.13	**Vol. 1:** 692		
6.14	**Vol. 2:** 842		
6.15	**Vol. 2:** 61		
6.18	**Vol. 2:** 132		
6.20–23	**Vol. 3:** 1027		
6.20	**Vol. 2:** 377		
6.22	**Vol. 2:** 215	**Vol. 3:** 502, 882	
6.24	**Vol. 3:** 209, 1028		
6.25	**Vol. 3:** 1120		
7.2	**Vol. 1:** 322, 459		
7.3	**Vol. 2:** 498		
7.6†	**Vol. 2:** 498	**Vol. 3:** 937	
7.7	**Vol. 3:** 1027		
7.8	**Vol. 2:** 842		
7.9	**Vol. 3:** 823		
7.11	**Vol. 2:** 842		
7.12–22	**Vol. 3:** 1056, 1069		
7.12	**Vol. 3:** 1027, 1029		
7.13	**Vol. 1:** 485	**Vol. 2:** 842	
7.15	**Vol. 3:** 937, 1027–1028		
7.17	**Vol. 2:** 452	**Vol. 3:** 1147	
7.18	**Vol. 3:** 835		
7.20	**Vol. 2:** 658	**Vol. 3:** 711, 820	
7.22	**Vol. 3:** 760–761, 1027		

Wisdom of Solomon (Wis.) *(cont'd)*

7.23	**Vol. 1:** 663
7.24	**Vol. 3:** 1027
7.25 f	**Vol. 2:** 290, 603 **Vol. 3:** 647
7.25	**Vol. 2:** 506
7.26	**Vol. 2:** 287, 290 **Vol. 3:** 827, 1147
7.27	**Vol. 3:** 1029
7.28	**Vol. 3:** 1027
7.29	**Vol. 3:** 730, 734
7.30	**Vol. 3:** 1027
8.3 f	**Vol. 1:** 641
8.3	**Vol. 2:** 509
8.4	**Vol. 3:** 502
8.5	**Vol. 2:** 841–842 **Vol. 3:** 1027
8.7	**Vol. 1:** 502 **Vol. 3:** 926
8.8	**Vol. 1:** 692 **Vol. 3:** 835
8.12	**Vol. 3:** 228
8.13	**Vol. 3:** 238
8.17	**Vol. 3:** 823, 1027
8.18	**Vol. 2:** 842
8.19 f	**Vol. 2:** 480
8.20	**Vol. 1:** 233 **Vol. 3:** 923
8.21	**Vol. 2:** 882
9.1	**Vol. 3:** 263, 1116
9.2	**Vol. 1:** 381 **Vol. 3:** 1027
9.4 f	**Vol. 3:** 610
9.4	**Vol. 3:** 1027, 1029
9.6	**Vol. 3:** 823, 1027
9.8	**Vol. 1:** 491
9.9	**Vol. 3:** 1027
9.10	**Vol. 2:** 191, 815
9.14	**Vol. 3:** 823
9.15	**Vol. 1:** 233 **Vol. 3:** 680, 811, 814
9.17 f	**Vol. 3:** 1027
9.17	**Vol. 3:** 86
9.18	**Vol. 2:** 452 **Vol. 3:** 209, 760–761
10	**Vol. 1:** 714
10.1	**Vol. 1:** 380 **Vol. 3:** 586
10.2	**Vol. 3:** 585
10.3	**Vol. 1:** 109
10.4	**Vol. 2:** 681 **Vol. 3:** 1027
10.5	**Vol. 2:** 143 **Vol. 3:** 924
10.6 ff	**Vol. 3:** 240
10.7	**Vol. 3:** 1040
10.8 f	**Vol. 3:** 1027
10.8	**Vol. 3:** 238
10.11	**Vol. 2:** 841
10.12	**Vol. 1:** 648, 663 **Vol. 2:** 93
10.15	**Vol. 2:** 143 **Vol. 3:** 924
10.16	**Vol. 2:** 627
10.17	**Vol. 2:** 139
10.18	**Vol. 3:** 1024
10.19	**Vol. 3:** 255
10.20	**Vol. 3:** 669, 816, 908
10.21	**Vol. 1:** 428 **Vol. 3:** 1027
11.2–19.22	**Vol. 3:** 916
11.5	**Vol. 3:** 98
11.8	**Vol. 3:** 98
11.9†	**Vol. 1:** 109 **Vol. 3:** 799–800

11.10	**Vol. 1:** 568 **Vol. 2:** 370 **Vol. 3:** 808
11.12	**Vol. 3:** 238
11.13	**Vol. 3:** 98
11.15	**Vol. 3:** 823
11.16	**Vol. 3:** 98
11.17	**Vol. 1:** 380
11.20	**Vol. 3:** 402
12 f	**Vol. 3:** 331
12.1	**Vol. 1:** 468 **Vol. 3:** 692–693
12.2	**Vol. 1:** 568, 609 **Vol. 3:** 232, 585, 1212–1213
12.5	**Vol. 3:** 502
12.7	**Vol. 3:** 610
12.10	**Vol. 3:** 823
12.14 f	**Vol. 3:** 98
12.15	**Vol. 2:** 370 **Vol. 3:** 358
12.16	**Vol. 3:** 358
12.18	**Vol. 2:** 257
12.19–21	**Vol. 3:** 638
12.19	**Vol. 3:** 721, 760–761
12.20	**Vol. 3:** 610, 721, 842
12.21	**Vol. 3:** 721
12.22	**Vol. 3:** 721, 727
12.23	**Vol. 3:** 1024
12.24	**Vol. 3:** 1024
12.25–27	**Vol. 3:** 721
12.26	**Vol. 1:** 568 **Vol. 3:** 799
12.27	**Vol. 1:** 455 **Vol. 2:** 370 **Vol. 3:** 98, 821
13–15	**Vol. 2:** 287
13	**Vol. 3:** 885
13.1 f	**Vol. 2:** 491
13.1–10	**Vol. 3:** 885
13.1–9	**Vol. 2:** 396
13.1	**Vol. 1:** 387 **Vol. 2:** 400, 658, 660
13.2	**Vol. 3:** 735
13.3	**Vol. 1:** 380
13.4	**Vol. 3:** 128, 1147
13.5	**Vol. 1:** 382, 385
13.6	**Vol. 2:** 144 **Vol. 3:** 528
13.7	**Vol. 2:** 863
13.10	**Vol. 1:** 444 **Vol. 2:** 77
13.13	**Vol. 2:** 287
13.14	**Vol. 3:** 885
13.15	**Vol. 1:** 663
13.16	**Vol. 1:** 694 **Vol. 2:** 287
14	**Vol. 3:** 885
14.1	**Vol. 1:** 520
14.2	**Vol. 3:** 1027
14.3	**Vol. 1:** 618, 663, 694
14.5	**Vol. 3:** 1027
14.6	**Vol. 3:** 29
14.10	**Vol. 3:** 98
14.11	**Vol. 1:** 382 **Vol. 3:** 1024
14.15	**Vol. 2:** 285, 287
14.17	**Vol. 2:** 287 **Vol. 3:** 1169
14.20	**Vol. 3:** 823
14.23–26	**Vol. 3:** 929
14.23	**Vol. 3:** 502
14.25 f	**Vol. 3:** 31

Wisdom of Solomon (Wis.) *(cont'd)*

14.26	**Vol. 3:** 680
14.27 f	**Vol. 1:** 499
14.27	**Vol. 2:** 138
14.31	**Vol. 3:** 584
15.1 ff	**Vol. 2:** 769
15.1	**Vol. 3:** 882
15.2	**Vol. 3:** 823
15.3	**Vol. 1:** 435 **Vol. 3:** 358
15.5	**Vol. 1:** 444 **Vol. 2:** 287 **Vol. 3:** 1024
15.7 – 17	**Vol. 3:** 916
15.7	**Vol. 2:** 609 **Vol. 3:** 912, 916
15.8	**Vol. 3:** 916
15.9	**Vol. 1:** 491 **Vol. 3:** 916
15.10	**Vol. 3:** 916
15.11	**Vol. 2:** 787 **Vol. 3:** 692, 703, 1147
15.12	**Vol. 3:** 823
15.13	**Vol. 1:** 387 **Vol. 3:** 916
15.14	**Vol. 3:** 1024
15.15	**Vol. 2:** 175 **Vol. 3:** 823
15.18	**Vol. 3:** 125
16.1	**Vol. 3:** 98
16.2 f	**Vol. 1:** 460
16.2	**Vol. 3:** 98
16.6	**Vol. 1:** 568 – 569 **Vol. 3:** 209, 239
16.7	**Vol. 3:** 209, 462
16.9	**Vol. 3:** 98, 680
16.11	**Vol. 3:** 867
16.12	**Vol. 2:** 167
16.13	**Vol. 2:** 30
16.16	**Vol. 1:** 455
16.17	**Vol. 1:** 509 **Vol. 3:** 109, 218, 1147
16.20	**Vol. 1:** 459
16.21	**Vol. 1:** 711
16.22	**Vol. 2:** 773
16.24	**Vol. 1:** 381 **Vol. 3:** 98
16.27	**Vol. 3:** 572

16.28	**Vol. 2:** 882 **Vol. 3:** 818
16.29	**Vol. 1:** 683
17.2	**Vol. 1:** 694
17.4	**Vol. 2:** 644
17.5	**Vol. 2:** 773 **Vol. 3:** 711, 735
17.7	**Vol. 3:** 30
17.8	**Vol. 2:** 91
17.9	**Vol. 1:** 622
17.10	**Vol. 1:** 455 **Vol. 3:** 748
17.11	**Vol. 1:** 349, 420 **Vol. 2:** 370
17.12	**Vol. 3:** 823
17.13	**Vol. 2:** 138, 621 **Vol. 3:** 823
17.14 f	**Vol. 1:** 420
17.14	**Vol. 3:** 324
17.18	**Vol. 3:** 711
17.21	**Vol. 2:** 287
18.2	**Vol. 3:** 818
18.5	**Vol. 3:** 209, 908, 1114
18.6	**Vol. 1:** 663, 692
18.7	**Vol. 3:** 209
18.11	**Vol. 3:** 93, 98
18.14 ff	**Vol. 3:** 1116
18.18	**Vol. 2:** 138
18.19	**Vol. 2:** 621
18.20 ff	**Vol. 3:** 36
18.20	**Vol. 1:** 109
18.21	**Vol. 2:** 143, 863 **Vol. 3:** 552, 924
18.22	**Vol. 3:** 98, 1147
18.25	**Vol. 1:** 465
19.1	**Vol. 1:** 109
19.3	**Vol. 3:** 125, 823
19.4	**Vol. 1:** 734 **Vol. 3:** 98
19.5	**Vol. 3:** 799
19.6	**Vol. 1:** 381 **Vol. 3:** 610
19.7	**Vol. 3:** 555
19.9	**Vol. 3:** 816
19.13	**Vol. 1:** 420 **Vol. 3:** 571, 711
19.20b	**Vol. 2:** 658

Qumran Writings (Dead Sea Scrolls)

The Blessings (1QSb)

3.22	**Vol. 2:** 34
3.28	**Vol. 2:** 799
4.23	**Vol. 2:** 298 **Vol. 3:** 35
4.25 f	**Vol. 2:** 298
5.20 ff	**Vol. 3:** 650
5.25	**Vol. 3:** 961
5.27	**Vol. 2:** 558, 799

Commentary on Habakkuk (1QpHab)

1.9	**Vol. 3:** 823
1.13	**Vol. 3:** 359, 766
2.2	**Vol. 3:** 359, 766
2.3	**Vol. 2:** 312
2.5 f	**Vol. 2:** 56
2.5 – 9	**Vol. 3:** 1120
2.6	**Vol. 2:** 893
2.7 ff	**Vol. 3:** 492

Commentary on Habakkuk (1QpHab) *(cont'd)*

2.8 f	**Vol. 2:** 34
2.9	**Vol. 3:** 610
4.29	**Vol. 1:** 679
5.3	**Vol. 2:** 793, 798
5.4 ff	**Vol. 1:** 539
5.4	**Vol. 2:** 793
5.5	**Vol. 2:** 798
5.10	**Vol. 3:** 359, 766
6.14	**Vol. 3:** 484
7.1 ff	**Vol. 3:** 492
7.1–5	**Vol. 3:** 80
7.2	**Vol. 2:** 61 **Vol. 3:** 842
7.4–8	**Vol. 3:** 1120
7.4	**Vol. 3:** 359, 766
7.7 f	**Vol. 3:** 503
7.7	**Vol. 2:** 61
7.12	**Vol. 2:** 61
7.13 f	**Vol. 1:** 627
7.13	**Vol. 3:** 842
7.14	**Vol. 1:** 412
8.1–3	**Vol. 1:** 598 **Vol. 2:** 314 **Vol. 3:** 359, 367
8.3	**Vol. 3:** 766
8.8	**Vol. 2:** 34
9.2	**Vol. 1:** 676
9.6	**Vol. 2:** 893
9.9 ff	**Vol. 2:** 34
9.9	**Vol. 2:** 56 **Vol. 3:** 766
10.7	**Vol. 3:** 484
10.9 f	**Vol. 2:** 312
10.9	**Vol. 3:** 39, 801
10.10	**Vol. 1:** 296
10.14	**Vol. 3:** 484
11.1	**Vol. 2:** 397
11.5	**Vol. 3:** 766
11.8	**Vol. 3:** 801
11.10	**Vol. 3:** 484
11.15	**Vol. 3:** 359
12.3	**Vol. 2:** 824
12.6	**Vol. 2:** 824
12.10	**Vol. 2:** 824
12.13 f	**Vol. 2:** 893
12.13	**Vol. 2:** 792
12.14	**Vol. 3:** 842
13.1 ff	**Vol. 2:** 893
13.2 ff	**Vol. 3:** 842
13.3 f	**Vol. 2:** 792

Community Rule (1QS)

1	**Vol. 1:** 556
1.1	**Vol. 3:** 531
1.2 f	**Vol. 1:** 556
1.3 f	**Vol. 2:** 542
1.3	**Vol. 1:** 333, 554 **Vol. 2:** 640 **Vol. 3:** 610
1.4	**Vol. 1:** 539
1.5	**Vol. 3:** 883

1.6	**Vol. 1:** 499 **Vol. 3:** 934
1.8 f	**Vol. 2:** 782
1.8	**Vol. 2:** 61, 595 **Vol. 3:** 934
1.9 ff	**Vol. 1:** 345
1.9 f	**Vol. 1:** 554
1.9–11	**Vol. 1:** 556
1.9	**Vol. 1:** 627 **Vol. 2:** 492 **Vol. 3:** 637
1.10	**Vol. 2:** 298, 312 **Vol. 3:** 469
1.11 f	**Vol. 1:** 641
1.12	**Vol. 2:** 842
1.14 f	**Vol. 3:** 842
1.15	**Vol. 3:** 882, 934
1.16–2.18	**Vol. 2:** 493, 784
1.17	**Vol. 1:** 333
1.18 f	**Vol. 3:** 210
1.18	**Vol. 1:** 452 **Vol. 2:** 492, 608 **Vol. 3:** 469
1.20	**Vol. 1:** 98
1.21	**Vol. 2:** 599
1.22	**Vol. 2:** 595
1.23 f	**Vol. 2:** 608
1.23	**Vol. 1:** 452
1.24	**Vol. 1:** 345 **Vol. 2:** 492
1.25	**Vol. 3:** 934
2.1	**Vol. 2:** 595, 599 **Vol. 3:** 828
2.2–4	**Vol. 1:** 212
2.2	**Vol. 2:** 61, 298 **Vol. 3:** 934
2.3 f	**Vol. 3:** 828
2.3	**Vol. 2:** 782 **Vol. 3:** 126
2.4 ff	**Vol. 1:** 416, 452
2.4 f	**Vol. 2:** 312
2.4–9	**Vol. 1:** 554 **Vol. 3:** 469
2.4	**Vol. 2:** 595, 779
2.5	**Vol. 2:** 298, 492 **Vol. 3:** 469
2.7 f	**Vol. 2:** 493
2.8	**Vol. 1:** 656, 700 **Vol. 3:** 160, 828
2.11	**Vol. 2:** 285
2.12	**Vol. 2:** 706–707
2.13 f	**Vol. 3:** 28
2.13	**Vol. 3:** 1120
2.14	**Vol. 3:** 934
2.15	**Vol. 1:** 109 **Vol. 3:** 828
2.16	**Vol. 2:** 492 **Vol. 3:** 637
2.17	**Vol. 2:** 285, 298, 706–707 **Vol. 3:** 828
2.18	**Vol. 1:** 98
2.19 f	**Vol. 2:** 34
2.19	**Vol. 2:** 492, 608 **Vol. 3:** 469
2.20	**Vol. 1:** 98, 102
2.21 f	**Vol. 2:** 699
2.21	**Vol. 2:** 799
2.22	**Vol. 2:** 397, 472
2.23	**Vol. 2:** 298
2.24	**Vol. 2:** 105, 261, 595 **Vol. 3:** 926, 928
2.25–3.12	**Vol. 1:** 144
2.25	**Vol. 3:** 828
2.26	**Vol. 1:** 700 **Vol. 3:** 934
3	**Vol. 2:** 364
3.1	**Vol. 3:** 680, 823, 842
3.2	**Vol. 1:** 641
3.3	**Vol. 2:** 493

Community Rule (1QS) *(cont'd)*

3.4 f	**Vol. 1:** 152
3.4–12	**Vol. 3:** 105, 989
3.4	**Vol. 3:** 28, 823
3.6 ff	**Vol. 2:** 878
3.6–12	**Vol. 1:** 700
3.6	**Vol. 2:** 141 **Vol. 3:** 882
3.7 ff	**Vol. 1:** 700
3.7 f	**Vol. 3:** 693
3.7–9	**Vol. 3:** 695
3.7	**Vol. 2:** 480
3.8 f	**Vol. 1:** 152
3.8	**Vol. 2:** 261 **Vol. 3:** 680
3.9	**Vol. 3:** 934
3.10	**Vol. 1:** 627
3.13 ff	**Vol. 1:** 563
3.13–4.26	**Vol. 2:** 565 **Vol. 3:** 126, 693
3.13	**Vol. 2:** 492 **Vol. 3:** 761, 766
3.15	**Vol. 2:** 71–72, 397 **Vol. 3:** 503
3.16	**Vol. 1:** 735
3.17 ff	**Vol. 3:** 939, 964
3.17 f	**Vol. 1:** 382
3.17–25	**Vol. 1:** 452
3.18 ff	**Vol. 1:** 102 **Vol. 3:** 943–944
3.18	**Vol. 2:** 56 **Vol. 3:** 837, 934
3.19 ff	**Vol. 2:** 492
3.19–26	**Vol. 2:** 71
3.20 ff	**Vol. 3:** 940
3.20 f	**Vol. 2:** 493 **Vol. 3:** 934, 944
3.20–23	**Vol. 3:** 469
3.20	**Vol. 2:** 481, 492 **Vol. 3:** 503, 704
3.21 f	**Vol. 3:** 503
3.21–24	**Vol. 1:** 423
3.21	**Vol. 2:** 459, 492 **Vol. 3:** 503, 801
3.23	**Vol. 2:** 56, 608 **Vol. 3:** 842
3.24 ff	**Vol. 3:** 994
3.24 f	**Vol. 1:** 102
3.24	**Vol. 2:** 707–708 **Vol. 3:** 801, 882
3.25	**Vol. 1:** 102, 382 **Vol. 2:** 71
3.26	**Vol. 2:** 492
4	**Vol. 2:** 364 **Vol. 3:** 273
4.1–5.13	**Vol. 3:** 250
4.1	**Vol. 1:** 452
4.3 f	**Vol. 3:** 928
4.3–14	**Vol. 3:** 926
4.3	**Vol. 2:** 105, 261, 824
4.4 f	**Vol. 2:** 595
4.5	**Vol. 2:** 285 **Vol. 3:** 926
4.6 ff	**Vol. 2:** 493
4.6	**Vol. 1:** 333 **Vol. 2:** 216 **Vol. 3:** 926
4.7 f	**Vol. 1:** 423 **Vol. 3:** 273
4.7	**Vol. 2:** 480, 779
4.8	**Vol. 3:** 1025
4.9–11	**Vol. 1:** 452 **Vol. 3:** 31, 1025
4.9	**Vol. 1:** 333 **Vol. 2:** 471 **Vol. 3:** 926
4.10	**Vol. 1:** 109, 499 **Vol. 3:** 926
4.11	**Vol. 2:** 34
4.12 f	**Vol. 2:** 493 **Vol. 3:** 842
4.12	**Vol. 1:** 110, 452

4.13	**Vol. 1:** 656
4.15 ff	**Vol. 2:** 298
4.15	**Vol. 2:** 707
4.16	**Vol. 3:** 939
4.17	**Vol. 2:** 105 **Vol. 3:** 882
4.18 ff	**Vol. 2:** 56 **Vol. 3:** 837
4.18	**Vol. 3:** 126, 1029
4.20 f	**Vol. 1:** 673 **Vol. 2:** 878 **Vol. 3:** 105
4.20–21	**Vol. 3:** 883
4.20	**Vol. 3:** 1029
4.21 f	**Vol. 1:** 225 **Vol. 3:** 639, 989, 1029
4.21	**Vol. 3:** 695
4.22	**Vol. 1:** 102, 288, 539 **Vol. 2:** 71, 782 **Vol. 3:** 1029
4.24	**Vol. 3:** 882, 1025
4.25	**Vol. 2:** 397 **Vol. 3:** 842
4.26	**Vol. 2:** 298
5.1	**Vol. 1:** 333, 357
5.2	**Vol. 1:** 732 **Vol. 2:** 34, 134, 842
5.3 f	**Vol. 3:** 928
5.3	**Vol. 2:** 261, 299 **Vol. 3:** 626
5.4	**Vol. 2:** 105, 595 **Vol. 3:** 801, 883, 926
5.5 f	**Vol. 2:** 312
5.5	**Vol. 1:** 309
5.6	**Vol. 2:** 248 **Vol. 3:** 160
5.7–11	**Vol. 3:** 740
5.7	**Vol. 3:** 1194
5.8	**Vol. 1:** 333, 357 **Vol. 2:** 640
5.9	**Vol. 1:** 732 **Vol. 2:** 34, 134
5.10 f	**Vol. 3:** 939
5.10	**Vol. 3:** 944
5.11	**Vol. 2:** 397 **Vol. 3:** 801, 823
5.12	**Vol. 1:** 110
5.13 f	**Vol. 3:** 989
5.14	**Vol. 3:** 1120
5.15	**Vol. 3:** 487
5.17 f	**Vol. 3:** 823
5.17	**Vol. 3:** 487
5.19	**Vol. 3:** 1120
5.21 ff	**Vol. 2:** 397
5.21	**Vol. 3:** 692
5.22	**Vol. 1:** 333 **Vol. 2:** 842
5.23 f	**Vol. 3:** 486
5.24	**Vol. 2:** 782 **Vol. 3:** 692
5.25	**Vol. 2:** 105, 261, 595 **Vol. 3:** 928
6.1	**Vol. 3:** 1120, 1122
6.3	**Vol. 2:** 34
6.4 f	**Vol. 1:** 630
6.4–6	**Vol. 2:** 522
6.4	**Vol. 3:** 1120
6.7 f	**Vol. 3:** 486
6.8	**Vol. 1:** 197
6.9	**Vol. 2:** 799
6.10 f	**Vol. 3:** 486
6.12	**Vol. 1:** 190
6.14	**Vol. 1:** 190
6.15	**Vol. 3:** 882
6.16 f	**Vol. 3:** 105
6.16	**Vol. 2:** 54, 299 **Vol. 3:** 1120
6.17	**Vol. 2:** 842

Community Rule (1QS) *(cont'd)*

6.18	**Vol. 2:** 299
6.19 f	**Vol. 1:** 641
6.19	**Vol. 1:** 732 **Vol. 2:** 54, 842
6.20	**Vol. 1:** 190
6.21	**Vol. 2:** 299
6.22	**Vol. 2:** 54
6.25	**Vol. 3:** 105
6.26	**Vol. 3:** 486
6.27	**Vol. 3:** 233
7	**Vol. 3:** 842
7.1	**Vol. 3:** 486
7.3	**Vol. 3:** 105
7.6	**Vol. 2:** 842 **Vol. 3:** 1016
7.16	**Vol. 3:** 105
7.18 ff	**Vol. 1:** 607
7.18	**Vol. 3:** 692
7.20	**Vol. 1:** 735
7.22 ff	**Vol. 1:** 607
7.22	**Vol. 1:** 735
7.23	**Vol. 3:** 692
8	**Vol. 3:** 1006
8.1 – 15	**Vol. 1:** 539
8.1	**Vol. 2:** 782
8.2	**Vol. 2:** 105, 595 **Vol. 3:** 883, 926
8.3	**Vol. 2:** 134 **Vol. 3:** 160, 692
8.4 ff	**Vol. 2:** 61
8.4 – 9	**Vol. 2:** 779
8.5 ff	**Vol. 1:** 661 **Vol. 2:** 228
8.5 f	**Vol. 2:** 878
8.5 – 10	**Vol. 3:** 169
8.5 – 9	**Vol. 2:** 312
8.5	**Vol. 2:** 248, 312 **Vol. 3:** 783
8.6	**Vol. 2:** 818 **Vol. 3:** 160, 883
8.7 f	**Vol. 3:** 382, 392
8.9	**Vol. 2:** 248, 782
8.10	**Vol. 3:** 160
8.11 f	**Vol. 3:** 1120
8.12	**Vol. 3:** 692
8.13	**Vol. 2:** 228 **Vol. 3:** 939
8.14	**Vol. 3:** 487
8.15	**Vol. 2:** 640
8.18	**Vol. 2:** 782
8.20	**Vol. 2:** 61, 782
8.21	**Vol. 2:** 228
8.22	**Vol. 2:** 640
8.35	**Vol. 2:** 707
9.2	**Vol. 2:** 782
9.3 ff	**Vol. 2:** 228
9.3 – 6	**Vol. 2:** 878
9.3	**Vol. 1:** 661
9.4 f	**Vol. 2:** 118
9.5 f	**Vol. 2:** 782
9.5	**Vol. 2:** 312
9.6	**Vol. 2:** 248 **Vol. 3:** 783
9.8 f	**Vol. 2:** 782
9.10 f	**Vol. 2:** 899 **Vol. 3:** 35
9.11	**Vol. 1:** 321 **Vol. 3:** 80
9.12 ff	**Vol. 1:** 333 **Vol. 3:** 836
9.12	**Vol. 3:** 766
9.13 f	**Vol. 1:** 627
9.13	**Vol. 3:** 761, 1016
9.14	**Vol. 3:** 359
9.15	**Vol. 3:** 1016
9.17	**Vol. 2:** 216 **Vol. 3:** 883
9.18 ff	**Vol. 3:** 836
9.18	**Vol. 3:** 640
9.19 f	**Vol. 3:** 1006
9.19	**Vol. 2:** 782
9.21 – 23	**Vol. 1:** 556
9.21	**Vol. 2:** 707 **Vol. 3:** 766
9.22	**Vol. 2:** 261
9.23	**Vol. 3:** 1016
9.26	**Vol. 3:** 842
9.27	**Vol. 2:** 707
10.1 ff	**Vol. 3:** 842
10.1 – 8	**Vol. 1:** 627
10.4	**Vol. 2:** 595
10.6	**Vol. 2:** 118
10.9	**Vol. 2:** 397
10.11	**Vol. 2:** 353
10.12	**Vol. 2:** 72, 397
10.16	**Vol. 2:** 72, 595
10.17	**Vol. 3:** 210
10.18 ff	**Vol. 2:** 56
10.18	**Vol. 2:** 72, 707
10.19	**Vol. 1:** 109 **Vol. 2:** 893
10.20	**Vol. 1:** 357 **Vol. 3:** 926
10.22	**Vol. 3:** 926
10.25 f	**Vol. 3:** 926
10.25	**Vol. 3:** 372
10.26	**Vol. 2:** 595
11.1 – 14	**Vol. 3:** 160
11.1	**Vol. 2:** 261 **Vol. 3:** 801
11.2 f	**Vol. 3:** 161
11.2	**Vol. 3:** 359
11.3	**Vol. 1:** 700 **Vol. 3:** 359
11.4	**Vol. 3:** 882
11.5	**Vol. 2:** 71, 493 **Vol. 3:** 161, 359
11.6	**Vol. 2:** 216, 397
11.7 f	**Vol. 2:** 298 **Vol. 3:** 614
11.7	**Vol. 2:** 302
11.8	**Vol. 2:** 228, 302
11.9	**Vol. 1:** 673
11.10	**Vol. 3:** 944
11.11	**Vol. 2:** 72, 782
11.12 f	**Vol. 2:** 118, 595
11.12	**Vol. 1:** 673 **Vol. 2:** 707 **Vol. 3:** 359, 372, 801
11.13 f	**Vol. 2:** 72
11.14	**Vol. 2:** 72
11.15 – 20	**Vol. 3:** 640
11.15	**Vol. 2:** 397
11.17	**Vol. 2:** 72, 782 **Vol. 3:** 1016
11.18	**Vol. 2:** 118 **Vol. 3:** 359
11.19	**Vol. 2:** 72, 197
11.21	**Vol. 3:** 823
12 ff	**Vol. 3:** 1006
14.13	**Vol. 2:** 118

Community Rule (1QS) *(cont'd)*

16.9	**Vol. 3:** 359
16.15	**Vol. 2:** 707
17.4	**Vol. 2:** 707

Damascus Document (CD)

1.3	**Vol. 2:** 312
1.4	**Vol. 2:** 779 **Vol. 3:** 234, 250
1.5 f	**Vol. 1:** 110
1.5–11	**Vol. 3:** 783
1.7	**Vol. 2:** 312
1.11	**Vol. 3:** 359, 766
1.13	**Vol. 3:** 487, 939
1.14	**Vol. 2:** 312
1.15	**Vol. 3:** 801
1.21	**Vol. 1:** 110
2.3 f	**Vol. 1:** 700
2.3	**Vol. 3:** 640
2.4	**Vol. 1:** 412 **Vol. 2:** 397
2.6	**Vol. 3:** 250, 939
2.12 f	**Vol. 2:** 337
2.13	**Vol. 3:** 801
2.14	**Vol. 2:** 279
2.16	**Vol. 1:** 499
2.17	**Vol. 2:** 459 **Vol. 3:** 801
2.18–21	**Vol. 3:** 468
2.18	**Vol. 1:** 102 **Vol. 2:** 134
2.21	**Vol. 1:** 333 **Vol. 2:** 134
3.1	**Vol. 3:** 801
3.2 f	**Vol. 2:** 134
3.3 f	**Vol. 3:** 486
3.4	**Vol. 2:** 459 **Vol. 3:** 801
3.8	**Vol. 1:** 110
3.13 f	**Vol. 3:** 639
3.14 ff	**Vol. 3:** 503
3.14	**Vol. 2:** 459 **Vol. 3:** 801
3.15	**Vol. 3:** 1016
3.16	**Vol. 3:** 459
3.18	**Vol. 1:** 700
3.19	**Vol. 2:** 248, 312
3.20	**Vol. 2:** 45, 480
3.21	**Vol. 2:** 34
4.1	**Vol. 3:** 801
4.2	**Vol. 1:** 357
4.3	**Vol. 2:** 312
4.4	**Vol. 1:** 273 **Vol. 2:** 56
4.6 ff	**Vol. 3:** 160
4.11	**Vol. 2:** 312
4.12b–5.14a	**Vol. 3:** 538
4.13	**Vol. 2:** 314, 779 **Vol. 3:** 469
4.15	**Vol. 3:** 469
4.16	**Vol. 2:** 314
4.17	**Vol. 1:** 499
4.20	**Vol. 1:** 499
4.21	**Vol. 1:** 383
5.1 f	**Vol. 3:** 487
5.2 f	**Vol. 3:** 486
5.2	**Vol. 3:** 499
5.8	**Vol. 2:** 640
5.18	**Vol. 1:** 102 **Vol. 2:** 492, 640 **Vol. 3:** 704
5.19	**Vol. 3:** 210
5.20	**Vol. 3:** 801
5.21	**Vol. 2:** 640
6.1	**Vol. 2:** 312
6.2 f	**Vol. 2:** 312, 314
6.2	**Vol. 3:** 234
6.4	**Vol. 3:** 459
6.11	**Vol. 2:** 56
6.14–7.4	**Vol. 3:** 173, 428
6.14	**Vol. 2:** 134
6.17	**Vol. 2:** 738
6.18 f	**Vol. 1:** 627
6.18	**Vol. 2:** 134
6.19	**Vol. 1:** 368 **Vol. 2:** 312
7.2	**Vol. 2:** 141
7.6	**Vol. 2:** 699
7.10	**Vol. 3:** 1120
7.15 ff	**Vol. 3:** 486
7.15	**Vol. 3:** 650
7.16	**Vol. 3:** 651
7.18 ff	**Vol. 3:** 487
7.18 f	**Vol. 2:** 313
7.18–20	**Vol. 3:** 650
7.18	**Vol. 3:** 531
7.19 f	**Vol. 2:** 558
7.19–20	**Vol. 3:** 735
7.20 f	**Vol. 3:** 961
8.1	**Vol. 2:** 893
8.2 f	**Vol. 2:** 56
8.2	**Vol. 2:** 314
8.3	**Vol. 1:** 109, 333 **Vol. 2:** 312
8.5	**Vol. 3:** 926
8.6	**Vol. 3:** 926
8.8–18	**Vol. 2:** 579
8.14	**Vol. 2:** 640
8.16	**Vol. 2:** 312
8.20	**Vol. 3:** 1120
8.21	**Vol. 2:** 312
8.40	**Vol. 2:** 312
9.1–10.3	**Vol. 3:** 740
9.4	**Vol. 1:** 197
9.10–12	**Vol. 2:** 573
9.11	**Vol. 2:** 640
10.2	**Vol. 1:** 333
10.6	**Vol. 3:** 487
10.14–11.18	**Vol. 3:** 408
10.14	**Vol. 2:** 134
10.16	**Vol. 2:** 134
11.22	**Vol. 1:** 296
12.2	**Vol. 3:** 469
12.3	**Vol. 3:** 801
12.6	**Vol. 1:** 296
12.20	**Vol. 1:** 333
12.21	**Vol. 3:** 766
12.23 f	**Vol. 3:** 35
12.23	**Vol. 1:** 321
13.1 f	**Vol. 2:** 699
13.4	**Vol. 2:** 299

Damascus Document (CD) *(cont'd)*

13.6 f	**Vol. 1:** 190
13.9	**Vol. 1:** 190 **Vol. 3:** 566
13.11	**Vol. 3:** 126
13.12	**Vol. 2:** 298
13.18	**Vol. 2:** 595
13.22	**Vol. 3:** 766
14.3 ff	**Vol. 1:** 360
14.3–6	**Vol. 2:** 311
14.4 ff	**Vol. 3:** 486
14.9–12	**Vol. 1:** 190
14.12 ff	**Vol. 3:** 545
14.14	**Vol. 2:** 738
14.16	**Vol. 3:** 193
15.2	**Vol. 2:** 640 **Vol. 3:** 234
15.5	**Vol. 3:** 740
15.9	**Vol. 2:** 640
15.12	**Vol. 2:** 640
15.15 ff	**Vol. 2:** 161
15.15	**Vol. 3:** 1025
16.1–9	**Vol. 3:** 680
16.2	**Vol. 2:** 640
16.3 f	**Vol. 3:** 487
16.4 f	**Vol. 2:** 605
16.5	**Vol. 1:** 102 **Vol. 2:** 640
16.7	**Vol. 2:** 134
16.8	**Vol. 3:** 194
19.1 f	**Vol. 2:** 134, 699
19.1	**Vol. 2:** 595
19.5–16	**Vol. 2:** 56
19.9	**Vol. 2:** 56, 134
19.15 f	**Vol. 1:** 109
19.16	**Vol. 1:** 357
19.17	**Vol. 3:** 926
19.18	**Vol. 3:** 926
19.26 f	**Vol. 2:** 312
19.26	**Vol. 2:** 640
19.28	**Vol. 2:** 134
19.34	**Vol. 3:** 459
19.35	**Vol. 2:** 798 **Vol. 3:** 823
20.1	**Vol. 1:** 321 **Vol. 3:** 766
20.2	**Vol. 1:** 333
20.3 f	**Vol. 2:** 299
20.9	**Vol. 2:** 285
20.11	**Vol. 2:** 459
20.14 f	**Vol. 3:** 272
20.14	**Vol. 3:** 766
20.17	**Vol. 2:** 134
20.19	**Vol. 3:** 486, 823
20.21	**Vol. 2:** 595
20.22	**Vol. 2:** 134, 699
20.27 f	**Vol. 2:** 56
20.32	**Vol. 3:** 359, 766
20.33 f	**Vol. 2:** 56
20.33	**Vol. 2:** 355
20.34	**Vol. 1:** 288 **Vol. 3:** 160

Florilegium (4Qflor)

1.7 ff	**Vol. 3:** 650

1.8	**Vol. 3:** 801
1.9	**Vol. 3:** 823
1.10 ff	**Vol. 1:** 178
1.11	**Vol. 3:** 531, 650
1.12 f	**Vol. 3:** 651
1.12	**Vol. 3:** 650
1.17	**Vol. 2:** 285
1.19	**Vol. 2:** 56
2.3	**Vol. 2:** 640

Genesis Apocryphon (1QGenAp)

2	**Vol. 2:** 682 **Vol. 3:** 642
2.1	**Vol. 1:** 102
2.4	**Vol. 2:** 71
2.16	**Vol. 1:** 102
20.12	**Vol. 2:** 71
20.13	**Vol. 2:** 71
20.16 ff	**Vol. 1:** 452
20.28 f	**Vol. 1:** 452

Hymns, Hodayot (1QH)

1.3	**Vol. 3:** 828
1.5–39	**Vol. 1:** 700
1.7 f	**Vol. 1:** 382 **Vol. 3:** 828
1.7	**Vol. 2:** 397
1.8	**Vol. 3:** 1016
1.9 ff	**Vol. 3:** 503
1.10	**Vol. 1:** 333
1.12	**Vol. 3:** 52
1.13 f	**Vol. 1:** 382
1.17	**Vol. 2:** 779
1.20	**Vol. 2:** 72
1.21	**Vol. 3:** 312
1.26	**Vol. 2:** 71
1.27 f	**Vol. 1:** 382
1.28 f	**Vol. 3:** 1120
1.30	**Vol. 2:** 622, 651
1.31	**Vol. 2:** 397
1.32	**Vol. 2:** 595
1.33	**Vol. 2:** 622
2.2	**Vol. 1:** 296
2.3	**Vol. 1:** 102
2.7–35	**Vol. 3:** 680
2.9	**Vol. 1:** 357
2.10	**Vol. 1:** 102
2.13 f	**Vol. 3:** 503, 1029
2.13	**Vol. 2:** 818 **Vol. 3:** 359
2.14	**Vol. 2:** 459 **Vol. 3:** 801
2.16 f	**Vol. 3:** 469
2.17	**Vol. 3:** 761
2.18	**Vol. 2:** 397
2.19	**Vol. 2:** 459
2.20	**Vol. 1:** 345 **Vol. 2:** 480
2.23	**Vol. 2:** 118, 595
2.25 f	**Vol. 1:** 656
2.25	**Vol. 2:** 118, 595
2.30	**Vol. 2:** 651
2.31	**Vol. 1:** 345 **Vol. 2:** 480
2.32	**Vol. 3:** 193, 210, 823

Hymns, Hodayot (1QH) *(cont'd)*

2.35	**Vol. 3:** 193		
3.5–18	**Vol. 3:** 722		
3.6	**Vol. 3:** 680, 823		
3.7–10	**Vol. 3:** 1068		
3.12–18	**Vol. 2:** 311		
3.19–23	**Vol. 2:** 161		
3.19	**Vol. 3:** 193, 680		
3.20	**Vol. 3:** 52		
3.21 f	**Vol. 2:** 298		
3.22	**Vol. 2:** 298		
3.23	**Vol. 2:** 622, 651		
3.24 f	**Vol. 2:** 298		
3.24	**Vol. 3:** 823		
3.25 ff	**Vol. 1:** 110, 656		
3.28	**Vol. 1:** 110		
3.29–39	**Vol. 3:** 559		
3.29–36	**Vol. 2:** 836		
3.29	**Vol. 3:** 469		
3.32	**Vol. 3:** 469		
3.34 ff	**Vol. 3:** 272		
3.36	**Vol. 1:** 102	**Vol. 3:** 842	
4.7	**Vol. 2:** 459		
4.8 f	**Vol. 3:** 823		
4.10–16	**Vol. 2:** 314		
4.10	**Vol. 2:** 471		
4.12	**Vol. 2:** 459	**Vol. 3:** 801	
4.14	**Vol. 3:** 687, 823, 883		
4.16	**Vol. 3:** 801		
4.20	**Vol. 2:** 72	**Vol. 3:** 801	
4.23	**Vol. 2:** 602	**Vol. 3:** 823	
4.25	**Vol. 3:** 801		
4.26	**Vol. 2:** 799		
4.27	**Vol. 1:** 96		
4.28 f	**Vol. 2:** 602		
4.28	**Vol. 2:** 622		
4.29	**Vol. 2:** 622	**Vol. 3:** 503	
4.30	**Vol. 1:** 673	**Vol. 3:** 359	
4.31	**Vol. 3:** 693		
4.32 f	**Vol. 2:** 566	**Vol. 3:** 637	
4.32	**Vol. 1:** 288	**Vol. 2:** 72	
4.33	**Vol. 2:** 818		
4.34 f	**Vol. 3:** 234		
4.35	**Vol. 3:** 1120		
4.37	**Vol. 1:** 700	**Vol. 2:** 72, 118, 595	**Vol. 3:** 160
4.38	**Vol. 1:** 382		
5.9	**Vol. 3:** 312		
5.11 f	**Vol. 3:** 210		
5.12–39	**Vol. 3:** 680		
5.12	**Vol. 2:** 808		
5.20 ff	**Vol. 2:** 194		
5.20	**Vol. 2:** 738		
5.21	**Vol. 1:** 102		
5.22	**Vol. 2:** 595		
5.23 f	**Vol. 2:** 521		
5.25	**Vol. 1:** 288	**Vol. 2:** 216	
5.26 f	**Vol. 2:** 312		
5.26	**Vol. 3:** 823		
5.28	**Vol. 2:** 707	**Vol. 3:** 801	
5.36	**Vol. 2:** 707	**Vol. 3:** 801	
5.38	**Vol. 3:** 823		
5.39	**Vol. 3:** 469		
6.4	**Vol. 3:** 312		
6.8	**Vol. 2:** 798		
6.9	**Vol. 2:** 595		
6.11	**Vol. 2:** 622		
6.12 f	**Vol. 2:** 793		
6.13	**Vol. 1:** 102		
6.21	**Vol. 3:** 469		
6.26	**Vol. 3:** 382		
6.28 ff	**Vol. 3:** 961		
6.29 f	**Vol. 3:** 272		
6.30 f	**Vol. 2:** 56		
6.30	**Vol. 1:** 288	**Vol. 2:** 602	
6.34	**Vol. 3:** 273		
7.4	**Vol. 3:** 469		
7.6 f	**Vol. 2:** 602, 878		
7.8 f	**Vol. 2:** 249		
7.8	**Vol. 3:** 382		
7.10	**Vol. 3:** 610		
7.12	**Vol. 2:** 312		
7.15	**Vol. 2:** 779		
7.18	**Vol. 1:** 700	**Vol. 2:** 595	
7.20	**Vol. 1:** 288	**Vol. 2:** 595	**Vol. 3:** 637
7.27	**Vol. 2:** 118, 595		
7.30 f	**Vol. 2:** 72		
7.30	**Vol. 1:** 700		
7.34	**Vol. 1:** 296	**Vol. 2:** 72	
7.35	**Vol. 1:** 700	**Vol. 2:** 118, 595	
8.1–8	**Vol. 3:** 722		
8.4–14	**Vol. 3:** 986		
8.10 f	**Vol. 2:** 216		
8.11	**Vol. 3:** 499, 823		
8.14	**Vol. 3:** 823		
8.36	**Vol. 2:** 707	**Vol. 3:** 610, 801	
9	**Vol. 3:** 722		
9.7 f	**Vol. 3:** 680		
9.7	**Vol. 2:** 595		
9.9	**Vol. 2:** 397		
9.10	**Vol. 2:** 118, 595		
9.11	**Vol. 2:** 779		
9.14	**Vol. 2:** 118, 595		
9.17	**Vol. 2:** 72		
9.24	**Vol. 2:** 357		
9.28 f	**Vol. 3:** 212		
9.28	**Vol. 2:** 808	**Vol. 3:** 680	
9.29 f	**Vol. 1:** 539		
9.30	**Vol. 2:** 72		
9.32 f	**Vol. 2:** 72		
9.33	**Vol. 2:** 780	**Vol. 3:** 680	
9.34	**Vol. 2:** 72		
9.35 f	**Vol. 1:** 618		
9.35	**Vol. 2:** 71		
9.38	**Vol. 2:** 651		
9.66	**Vol. 2:** 480		
10.2	**Vol. 2:** 818	**Vol. 3:** 1016	
10.3	**Vol. 2:** 71		
10.5 f	**Vol. 2:** 72		

Hymns, Hodayot (1QH) *(cont'd)*

10.5	**Vol. 3:** 823
10.6	**Vol. 2:** 818
10.8	**Vol. 2:** 71
10.9	**Vol. 2:** 72, 818 **Vol. 3:** 1016
10.14	**Vol. 2:** 72, 595
10.16	**Vol. 2:** 72, 595
10.20	**Vol. 3:** 52
10.21	**Vol. 1:** 700
10.34 f	**Vol. 1:** 102
11.5	**Vol. 2:** 595
11.6	**Vol. 2:** 651 **Vol. 3:** 52
11.7	**Vol. 2:** 72
11.9 f	**Vol. 2:** 72
11.9	**Vol. 1:** 700 **Vol. 2:** 566, 818
11.11 f	**Vol. 2:** 298
11.12	**Vol. 2:** 228
11.13	**Vol. 1:** 102
11.14	**Vol. 2:** 397
11.17 f	**Vol. 2:** 595
11.17	**Vol. 2:** 72
11.18	**Vol. 2:** 72
11.23 f	**Vol. 3:** 210
11.23	**Vol. 2:** 355
11.24	**Vol. 2:** 397
11.25	**Vol. 2:** 651
11.28	**Vol. 2:** 595 **Vol. 3:** 126
11.29	**Vol. 2:** 72
11.30 f	**Vol. 2:** 595
11.30	**Vol. 2:** 355, 357
11.31	**Vol. 2:** 118
11.33	**Vol. 2:** 72
12.3	**Vol. 2:** 651
12.4–11	**Vol. 1:** 627
12.5	**Vol. 1:** 333
12.10	**Vol. 2:** 72
12.11 ff	**Vol. 3:** 1029
12.11 f	**Vol. 2:** 878
12.11	**Vol. 3:** 693
12.13	**Vol. 2:** 71, 397 **Vol. 3:** 126
12.14	**Vol. 2:** 595
12.21	**Vol. 2:** 595
12.30	**Vol. 3:** 52
13.5	**Vol. 2:** 595
13.6	**Vol. 2:** 357
13.11 f	**Vol. 1:** 383
13.11	**Vol. 3:** 52
13.13 f	**Vol. 1:** 673
13.13	**Vol. 2:** 72 **Vol. 3:** 126
13.16	**Vol. 2:** 633
13.18 f	**Vol. 2:** 878 **Vol. 3:** 610
13.19	**Vol. 2:** 72 **Vol. 3:** 693
14.12 f	**Vol. 3:** 487
14.13	**Vol. 2:** 818 **Vol. 3:** 1016
14.15 ff	**Vol. 2:** 72
14.15	**Vol. 2:** 72, 397
14.17	**Vol. 2:** 397
14.19	**Vol. 2:** 298
14.24	**Vol. 1:** 700
14.25	**Vol. 2:** 878 **Vol. 3:** 610
15.11	**Vol. 1:** 333
15.12	**Vol. 2:** 397
15.14 f	**Vol. 1:** 382
15.15	**Vol. 3:** 211
15.16 f	**Vol. 1:** 673
15.16	**Vol. 2:** 779, 808 **Vol. 3:** 210
15.17	**Vol. 1:** 110, 382 **Vol. 2:** 72, 893
15.18 f	**Vol. 1:** 333
15.20	**Vol. 2:** 397, 633
15.22	**Vol. 3:** 693
15.25	**Vol. 2:** 72 **Vol. 3:** 882
16.1 ff	**Vol. 3:** 487
16.5	**Vol. 2:** 707 **Vol. 3:** 801
16.6 f	**Vol. 2:** 878
16.9	**Vol. 2:** 595
16.10	**Vol. 3:** 610
16.11 f	**Vol. 2:** 878
16.12	**Vol. 2:** 118, 595
16.14	**Vol. 3:** 610
16.16	**Vol. 2:** 595
16.17	**Vol. 3:** 883
16.18	**Vol. 3:** 610
16.20	**Vol. 2:** 459
17.12	**Vol. 2:** 640
17.13	**Vol. 1:** 656
17.15	**Vol. 2:** 45, 298
17.17	**Vol. 3:** 52
17.20	**Vol. 2:** 651 **Vol. 3:** 194
17.22	**Vol. 2:** 261
17.23	**Vol. 2:** 707 **Vol. 3:** 801
17.26	**Vol. 2:** 878
18.5	**Vol. 3:** 211
18.8	**Vol. 2:** 651
18.14 f	**Vol. 3:** 610
18.14	**Vol. 3:** 52
18.15	**Vol. 2:** 355
18.20	**Vol. 1:** 309
18.22	**Vol. 2:** 72
18.26	**Vol. 3:** 823
18.30	**Vol. 2:** 779

Manual of Discipline.
See Community Rule

Messianic Rule (1QSa)

1.1	**Vol. 2:** 56
1.3 f	**Vol. 1:** 296
1.3	**Vol. 3:** 160
1.5	**Vol. 1:** 333
1.6–11	**Vol. 2:** 579
1.7	**Vol. 3:** 761
1.9	**Vol. 1:** 296
1.13	**Vol. 1:** 296
1.14	**Vol. 2:** 699
1.15	**Vol. 3:** 871
1.21	**Vol. 3:** 961
1.26	**Vol. 3:** 961
1.29	**Vol. 2:** 699 **Vol. 3:** 871

Messianic Rule (1QSa) *(cont'd)*

2.4	**Vol. 1:** 296
2.5 ff	**Vol. 1:** 219
2.5–9	**Vol. 2:** 161
2.5	**Vol. 1:** 296
2.7 f	**Vol. 1:** 296
2.8 f	**Vol. 2:** 161, 298 **Vol. 3:** 961
2.9 f	**Vol. 2:** 194
2.11 f	**Vol. 3:** 637
2.11–22	**Vol. 3:** 509
2.11–21	**Vol. 2:** 34, 314
2.11	**Vol. 1:** 178, 273
2.12 ff	**Vol. 3:** 35
2.12	**Vol. 2:** 312
2.17 ff	**Vol. 3:** 545
2.17–22	**Vol. 1:** 630
2.17–21	**Vol. 2:** 522
2.21	**Vol. 1:** 296

Testimonies (4Qtest)

1	**Vol. 2:** 640
5 ff	**Vol. 2:** 640
12 f	**Vol. 2:** 558 **Vol. 3:** 735
12	**Vol. 3:** 650
23	**Vol. 3:** 469

War Scroll (1QM)

1	**Vol. 3:** 961
1.1–7	**Vol. 2:** 793
1.1	**Vol. 2:** 298, 312 **Vol. 3:** 469, 961
1.5	**Vol. 2:** 72, 298
1.6	**Vol. 3:** 250
1.9 f	**Vol. 2:** 71, 779
1.9	**Vol. 2:** 480, 893
1.10 f	**Vol. 1:** 102, 452
1.10	**Vol. 1:** 296
1.11	**Vol. 2:** 298, 779, 893
1.12 f	**Vol. 3:** 193
1.12	**Vol. 2:** 798, 808 **Vol. 3:** 193, 210–211
1.13–15	**Vol. 1:** 452
1.13	**Vol. 3:** 469
2	**Vol. 3:** 961
2.1	**Vol. 2:** 34
2.2 f	**Vol. 3:** 871
2.4	**Vol. 1:** 333
2.5	**Vol. 2:** 118
2.6	**Vol. 2:** 651, 696
2.7	**Vol. 1:** 273
2.10–15	**Vol. 2:** 793
3–9	**Vol. 3:** 961
3	**Vol. 2:** 117
3.2 ff	**Vol. 3:** 486
3.2	**Vol. 1:** 273
3.4	**Vol. 2:** 651
3.5	**Vol. 2:** 780
3.9–19	**Vol. 2:** 364
3.9	**Vol. 1:** 110
3.11	**Vol. 2:** 780

3.12–4.17	**Vol. 3:** 871
3.13 ff	**Vol. 2:** 651 **Vol. 3:** 486
3.14 f	**Vol. 3:** 871
4.1 f	**Vol. 3:** 469
4.1–13	**Vol. 2:** 651
4.1	**Vol. 1:** 110 **Vol. 3:** 828
4.2	**Vol. 2:** 298, 699 **Vol. 3:** 250
4.3	**Vol. 3:** 828
4.6	**Vol. 3:** 372, 882
4.7 f	**Vol. 3:** 828
4.10	**Vol. 1:** 273, 296
4.13	**Vol. 3:** 210
4.14	**Vol. 2:** 780
4.15	**Vol. 2:** 285
4.19	**Vol. 2:** 285
4.32	**Vol. 2:** 842
5.1 ff	**Vol. 2:** 651
5.5	**Vol. 3:** 823
5.14	**Vol. 3:** 823
6.1–6	**Vol. 1:** 646
6.2 f	**Vol. 3:** 486
6.6	**Vol. 2:** 228, 793, 798
6.9	**Vol. 2:** 842
6.12 f	**Vol. 3:** 761
7.4 f	**Vol. 1:** 219
7.5	**Vol. 2:** 893
7.6	**Vol. 1:** 102 **Vol. 2:** 161, 298
7.10–9.9	**Vol. 2:** 34
7.11	**Vol. 3:** 823
7.12	**Vol. 2:** 34
7.27	**Vol. 2:** 842
8.4 ff	**Vol. 3:** 389
8.9	**Vol. 2:** 799
9.1	**Vol. 2:** 798
9.7 f	**Vol. 1:** 321
9.14 f	**Vol. 3:** 486
9.14–16	**Vol. 1:** 103–104
9.34	**Vol. 2:** 842
10–14	**Vol. 3:** 961
10.2	**Vol. 2:** 798 **Vol. 3:** 761
10.4 f	**Vol. 3:** 210
10.6	**Vol. 2:** 640
10.7	**Vol. 3:** 233–234
10.8	**Vol. 3:** 263
10.9 f	**Vol. 1:** 539
10.9	**Vol. 2:** 798
10.10 f	**Vol. 2:** 299
10.10	**Vol. 2:** 798 **Vol. 3:** 761
10.11 f	**Vol. 1:** 102
10.11	**Vol. 2:** 197
10.12	**Vol. 1:** 333, 382
10.14	**Vol. 2:** 799
10.15	**Vol. 2:** 298
10.24	**Vol. 2:** 842
11.1–12.5	**Vol. 2:** 602
11.2 f	**Vol. 2:** 651
11.3	**Vol. 3:** 210
11.5–7	**Vol. 3:** 735
11.6 f	**Vol. 2:** 495
11.6	**Vol. 2:** 558 **Vol. 3:** 650

War Scroll (1QM) *(cont'd)*

11.7	**Vol. 2:** 337	
11.8 f	**Vol. 2:** 793	**Vol. 3:** 469
11.9	**Vol. 3:** 194	
11.12 ff	**Vol. 3:** 273	
11.13	**Vol. 2:** 799	
12	**Vol. 2:** 117	
12.1 f	**Vol. 2:** 298	
12.1	**Vol. 2:** 798	**Vol. 3:** 961
12.2	**Vol. 2:** 651	
12.3	**Vol. 2:** 480, 595, 779	
12.4	**Vol. 2:** 699	
12.5	**Vol. 2:** 818	
12.7 f	**Vol. 1:** 102	
12.7	**Vol. 1:** 296	
12.8	**Vol. 1:** 333	**Vol. 2:** 161, 512
12.9	**Vol. 1:** 102	**Vol. 2:** 602
12.11	**Vol. 2:** 792	
12.12 ff	**Vol. 1:** 735	
12.13	**Vol. 2:** 355	
12.14	**Vol. 2:** 793	
12.18	**Vol. 2:** 512	
13.1–5	**Vol. 1:** 452	
13.1	**Vol. 1:** 197	
13.2–5	**Vol. 2:** 298	
13.4 f	**Vol. 3:** 469	
13.5 f	**Vol. 2:** 608	
13.7	**Vol. 2:** 651, 798	
13.8	**Vol. 3:** 250	
13.9	**Vol. 2:** 298, 798	
13.10	**Vol. 1:** 102 **Vol. 2:** 492 **Vol. 3:** 704	
13.11 f	**Vol. 1:** 423, 452	
13.12 ff	**Vol. 2:** 355	
13.12 f	**Vol. 2:** 357	
13.12	**Vol. 3:** 469	
13.14	**Vol. 2:** 893	**Vol. 3:** 194
14.4 f	**Vol. 3:** 210	
14.4	**Vol. 1:** 735 **Vol. 2:** 71, 357, 595, 651	
14.5 f	**Vol. 3:** 193	
14.5	**Vol. 1:** 273, 296 **Vol. 2:** 707, 798 **Vol. 3:** 193, 211, 250, 801	
14.6	**Vol. 3:** 761	
14.7	**Vol. 2:** 793, 824	
14.8 f	**Vol. 2:** 595 **Vol. 3:** 250	
14.8	**Vol. 2:** 651	
14.9	**Vol. 2:** 608 **Vol. 3:** 469	
14.10	**Vol. 3:** 194	
14.12	**Vol. 2:** 228, 651	
14.14 ff	**Vol. 3:** 503	
14.15	**Vol. 1:** 102	
14.16	**Vol. 2:** 71	
15.1 f	**Vol. 3:** 211	
15.1	**Vol. 2:** 808 **Vol. 3:** 194	
15.2 f	**Vol. 2:** 893	
15.3	**Vol. 3:** 469	
15.4	**Vol. 2:** 34	
15.5	**Vol. 3:** 487	
15.9	**Vol. 1:** 296	
15.14	**Vol. 1:** 102	
16.1	**Vol. 2:** 799	
16.3 ff	**Vol. 1:** 646	
16.7	**Vol. 2:** 799	
16.10 ff	**Vol. 1:** 646	
17	**Vol. 2:** 34	
17.1	**Vol. 2:** 779,	
17.2	**Vol. 3:** 233–234	
17.5 f	**Vol. 2:** 608	
17.6	**Vol. 3:** 194	
17.7 f	**Vol. 1:** 102 **Vol. 2:** 355	
17.9	**Vol. 1:** 735	
18	**Vol. 2:** 34	
18.1	**Vol. 3:** 469	
18.3	**Vol. 3:** 469	
18.5	**Vol. 2:** 893	
18.6	**Vol. 2:** 71, 651	
18.7 f	**Vol. 2:** 608	
18.7	**Vol. 3:** 210	
18.8	**Vol. 2:** 357, 651	
18.11	**Vol. 2:** 595 **Vol. 3:** 194, 211	
18.14	**Vol. 2:** 109	
19.1	**Vol. 2:** 72	
19.4	**Vol. 2:** 298	
19.6	**Vol. 2:** 793	

Words of Moses (1Q22)

1.1	**Vol. 2:** 640
1.7	**Vol. 2:** 285
1.11	**Vol. 2:** 640
2.5	**Vol. 2:** 640
2.8	**Vol. 1:** 333
2.11	**Vol. 2:** 640
4.3	**Vol. 2:** 640

Jewish Hellenistic Writers

The following references to the works of Josephus reflect the Loeb Classical Library numbering system. For the few articles that cite the Whiston numbering system, the Loeb equivilant of the Whiston citation is used to list the reference while the citation actually found in the article is given in parentheses following the page number.

Josephus, *Against Apion (Ap.)*

1.1	**Vol. 1:** 711
1.8	**Vol. 3:** 485
1.21	**Vol. 3:** 419
1.31 ff	**Vol. 3:** 491
1.31	**Vol. 3:** 36
1.42	**Vol. 1:** 330
1.114 f	**Vol. 2:** 756
1.119	**Vol. 3:** 279
1.155	**Vol. 3:** 570
1.167	**Vol. 2:** 43
1.199	**Vol. 2:** 570
1.219–2.150	**Vol. 2:** 310
1.224	**Vol. 2:** 659
1.282	**Vol. 3:** 996
1.289	**Vol. 3:** 480
1.290	**Vol. 3:** 479
1.292	**Vol. 3:** 380
2.29	**Vol. 1:** 264
2.121–124	**Vol. 2:** 310, 792 (2.10)
2.145–150	**Vol. 2:** 310
2.169	**Vol. 1:** 599
2.190–219	**Vol. 3:** 931
2.190	**Vol. 3:** 572
2.193	**Vol. 3:** 789
2.211	**Vol. 1:** 264
2.218	**Vol. 1:** 185
2.255–261	**Vol. 2:** 792 (2.36)
2.256	**Vol. 1:** 599
2.273	**Vol. 2:** 660
2.275	**Vol. 2:** 660
2.282	**Vol. 1:** 627

Josephus, *Jewish Antiquities (Ant.)*

1.33	**Vol. 3:** 407
1.40–51	**Vol. 3:** 638 (1.1.4)
1.43	**Vol. 1:** 334
1.49	**Vol. 1:** 87
1.60	**Vol. 3:** 98
1.74	**Vol. 2:** 682
1.75–79	**Vol. 2:** 660 (1.3.2)
1.85	**Vol. 3:** 265
1.98	**Vol. 3:** 952
1.104–108	**Vol. 3:** 638 (1.3.9)
1.116	**Vol. 1:** 529

1.155	**Vol. 1:** 387
1.179	**Vol. 2:** 779
1.180 f	**Vol. 3:** 36
1.215–219	**Vol. 1:** 698 (1.12.3)
1.222	**Vol. 3:** 1202
1.255	**Vol. 3:** 318
1.331	**Vol. 3:** 324
1.333	**Vol. 3:** 324
2.9	**Vol. 3:** 681
2.63	**Vol. 1:** 511
2.72	**Vol. 1:** 580
2.136–159	**Vol. 3:** 638 (2.6.8)
2.138	**Vol. 1:** 363
2.205	**Vol. 3:** 480
2.209	**Vol. 3:** 876
2.243–253	**Vol. 2:** 381 (2.10.2)
2.275 f	**Vol. 2:** 651 (2.12.4 f)
2.275	**Vol. 3:** 785
2.277–280	**Vol. 2:** 309 (2.13.1)
2.301	**Vol. 2:** 798
2.315–317	**Vol. 2:** 463 (2.15.1)
2.339	**Vol. 3:** 318
3.8	**Vol. 2:** 899
3.26–32	**Vol. 1:** 252 (3.1.6)
3.96	**Vol. 3:** 265
3.100	**Vol. 3:** 789
3.122–133	**Vol. 2:** 659 (3.6.4)
3.123	**Vol. 3:** 789
3.133	**Vol. 3:** 27
3.139–143	**Vol. 1:** 586 (3.6.6)
3.144–146	**Vol. 2:** 258 (3.6.7)
3.151 ff	**Vol. 1:** 204 (3.7.1 ff)
3.166–171	**Vol. 3:** 396
3.172–178	**Vol. 2:** 651 (3.7.6)
3.179–187	**Vol. 2:** 659 (3.7.7)
3.180 ff	**Vol. 3:** 789
3.189	**Vol. 3:** 37
3.202	**Vol. 2:** 899 **Vol. 3:** 789
3.212	**Vol. 3:** 324
3.234	**Vol. 3:** 919
3.237–254	**Vol. 1:** 627
3.252 ff	**Vol. 2:** 783
3.252 f	**Vol. 2:** 461
3.252	**Vol. 2:** 783
3.255–257	**Vol. 1:** 586 (3.10.7)
3.259–260	**Vol. 1:** 221 (3.11.2)
3.290	**Vol. 3:** 789

Josephus, Jewish
Antiquities (Ant.) *(cont'd)*

3.310	**Vol. 3:** 318
3.312	**Vol. 3:** 721
3.317–322	**Vol. 2:** 827 (3.15.3)
4.6	**Vol. 2:** 677
4.24	**Vol. 2:** 608
4.73	**Vol. 2:** 43
4.114	**Vol. 2:** 796
4.188	**Vol. 1:** 419
4.207	**Vol. 2:** 235 (4.8.10), 651 (4.8.10)
4.209	**Vol. 3:** 813
4.228	**Vol. 2:** 742 **Vol. 3:** 1160, 1164
4.231–239	**Vol. 1:** 163 (4.8.21) **Vol. 2:** 696 (4.8.21)
4.238	**Vol. 2:** 96
4.244–259	**Vol. 2:** 696 (4.8.23)
4.267–270	**Vol. 2:** 659 (4.8.26)
4.270	**Vol. 3:** 721
4.320–326	**Vol. 2:** 659 (4.8.48)
4.326	**Vol. 3:** 265
5.5	**Vol. 3:** 126
5.39	**Vol. 3:** 571, 594
5.93–99	**Vol. 3:** 638 (5.1.25)
5.109	**Vol. 2:** 608
5.166–174	**Vol. 2:** 258 (5.2.12)
5.205–209	**Vol. 2:** 659 (5.5.4)
5.214	**Vol. 3:** 952
5.215–217	**Vol. 2:** 659 (5.6.3)
5.249	**Vol. 1:** 515
5.264	**Vol. 3:** 1202
6.7–12	**Vol. 2:** 258 (6.1.2)
6.92	**Vol. 1:** 700
6.123	**Vol. 2:** 879
6.126 ff	**Vol. 2:** 677
6.156–165	**Vol. 2:** 815 (6.8.1)
6.170–174	**Vol. 2:** 659 (6.9.1)
6.185	**Vol. 1:** 143
6.225	**Vol. 3:** 875–876
6.237 f	**Vol. 3:** 92
6.240	**Vol. 3:** 218
6.262–268	**Vol. 2:** 806 (6.12.7)
6.309	**Vol. 3:** 1164
6.328	**Vol. 2:** 879
6.347	**Vol. 3:** 744
6.374	**Vol. 3:** 785
7.110	**Vol. 3:** 480
7.117–121	**Vol. 2:** 258 (7.6.1)
7.130–140	**Vol. 2:** 660 (7.7.1)
7.169	**Vol. 1:** 511
7.209	**Vol. 3:** 721
7.244	**Vol. 2:** 33
7.319	**Vol. 3:** 480
7.332	**Vol. 3:** 572
7.338	**Vol. 1:** 334
7.342	**Vol. 1:** 334
7.365	**Vol. 2:** 34
7.380	**Vol. 1:** 387, 618
8.23	**Vol. 3:** 125
8.44–49	**Vol. 3:** 651
8.45 ff	**Vol. 3:** 476
8.45	**Vol. 3:** 996
8.71	**Vol. 3:** 795, 948
8.88	**Vol. 3:** 418
8.94	**Vol. 1:** 334
8.100	**Vol. 3:** 813
8.102	**Vol. 3:** 789
8.106	**Vol. 3:** 789
8.107	**Vol. 3:** 789
8.111–117	**Vol. 2:** 651 (8.4.3)
8.114	**Vol. 3:** 789
8.115	**Vol. 3:** 210
8.117	**Vol. 3:** 789
8.120	**Vol. 1:** 334
8.123	**Vol. 3:** 813
8.124–129	**Vol. 1:** 345 (8.4.6)
8.131	**Vol. 3:** 789
8.141–149	**Vol. 3:** 279 (8.5.3)
8.165 f	**Vol. 2:** 381 (8.6.5 f)
8.167	**Vol. 1:** 577
8.230	**Vol. 3:** 418
8.251–255	**Vol. 3:** 575 (8.10.2)
8.256–262	**Vol. 1:** 345 (8.10.3)
8.280	**Vol. 2:** 61
8.318	**Vol. 3:** 125
8.335–342	**Vol. 2:** 659 (8.13.5)
8.337	**Vol. 1:** 334
8.355–362	**Vol. 1:** 345 (8.13.8)
8.360	**Vol. 3:** 876
8.376	**Vol. 1:** 513
8.404	**Vol. 2:** 33
8.405	**Vol. 2:** 779
9.34	**Vol. 2:** 879
9.43	**Vol. 3:** 721
9.55	**Vol. 2:** 899
9.60	**Vol. 3:** 318
9.176	**Vol. 3:** 744
9.208–214	**Vol. 2:** 679 (9.10.2)
9.214	**Vol. 1:** 700
9.239–242	**Vol. 2:** 679 (9.11.3)
9.240	**Vol. 3:** 681
9.258–262	**Vol. 2:** 659 (9.13.1)
9.280	**Vol. 3:** 456
9.287	**Vol. 3:** 460
10.2	**Vol. 3:** 756
10.24–29	**Vol. 2:** 628 (10.2.1)
10.51	**Vol. 3:** 772
10.70	**Vol. 3:** 102
10.75	**Vol. 3:** 51
10.81–83	**Vol. 2:** 659 (10.5.2)
10.142	**Vol. 2:** 659 (10.8.3)
10.155	**Vol. 3:** 756
10.184	**Vol. 3:** 450
10.195	**Vol. 1:** 511
10.209 f	**Vol. 2:** 899
10.216	**Vol. 2:** 557
10.267	**Vol. 2:** 899
10.276	**Vol. 2:** 899
10.281	**Vol. 3:** 923

**Josephus, Jewish
Antiquities (Ant.)** *(cont'd)*

11.3   **Vol. 3:** 570
11.28   **Vol. 1:** 341
11.47   **Vol. 2:** 136
11.63   **Vol. 3:** 147
11.66   **Vol. 1:** 185
11.88–94   **Vol. 3:** 610 (11.4.4)
11.88   **Vol. 3:** 450
11.97–103 **Vol. 3:** 610 (11.4.6)
11.114   **Vol. 1:** 700
11.128   **Vol. 3:** 478
11.133   **Vol. 3:** 871
11.154   **Vol. 3:** 813
11.159–167 **Vol. 1:** 151 (11.5.6)
11.169   **Vol. 1:** 694
11.192   **Vol. 1:** 574
11.213   **Vol. 3:** 248
11.216   **Vol. 2:** 779
11.240   **Vol. 3:** 681
11.261   **Vol. 1:** 394
11.266 f   **Vol. 1:** 394
11.291   **Vol. 3:** 451
11.302–347 **Vol. 3:** 451
11.303   **Vol. 3:** 450
11.306 ff **Vol. 3:** 451
11.312   **Vol. 3:** 451
11.321–324 **Vol. 3:** 451
11.327   **Vol. 3:** 39
11.329–339 **Vol. 1:** 207 (11.8.5)   **Vol. 2:** 651
           (11.8.5)
11.340   **Vol. 3:** 450–451
11.341   **Vol. 3:** 451
11.344   **Vol. 3:** 450
11.345   **Vol. 3:** 453
11.346   **Vol. 3:** 451, 465
12.7–10   **Vol. 3:** 453
12.7   **Vol. 1:** 580
12.10   **Vol. 3:** 450, 460
12.18   **Vol. 2:** 882
12.23   **Vol. 1:** 387
12.40 ff   **Vol. 1:** 196 (12.2.5 ff)
12.40–50   **Vol. 2:** 697 (12.2.5)
12.57–59   **Vol. 2:** 697 (12.2.7)
12.99   **Vol. 2:** 879
12.129–144 **Vol. 1:** 406 (12.3.3)
12.136   **Vol. 3:** 318
12.138–153 **Vol. 3:** 756
12.141   **Vol. 3:** 756
12.142   **Vol. 3:** 478
12.176   **Vol. 3:** 758
12.186 ff **Vol. 2:** 578
12.258–262 **Vol. 3:** 450
12.258–261 **Vol. 3:** 452
12.258   **Vol. 3:** 450
12.259   **Vol. 3:** 461
12.261   **Vol. 3:** 455, 461
12.262   **Vol. 3:** 450
12.278   **Vol. 2:** 33

12.322   **Vol. 2:** 899
12.323–325 **Vol. 1:** 627
12.378   **Vol. 3:** 191
12.387 f   **Vol. 3:** 451
12.413–419 **Vol. 2:** 332 (12.10.6)
13.49–57   **Vol. 3:** 756
13.62–73   **Vol. 3:** 451
13.74–79   **Vol. 3:** 453, 460
13.76   **Vol. 3:** 461
13.78 f   **Vol. 3:** 461
13.117 ff **Vol. 3:** 439
13.173   **Vol. 3:** 439
13.242   **Vol. 3:** 813
13.252   **Vol. 2:** 783
13.254–258 **Vol. 1:** 309 (13.9.1)
13.255 f   **Vol. 3:** 452
13.255   **Vol. 3:** 456
13.256   **Vol. 3:** 451
13.257   **Vol. 3:** 872
13.288–292 **Vol. 2:** 815 (13.10.5)
13.293–298 **Vol. 2:** 811 (13.10.6)
13.293 ff **Vol. 3:** 439
13.293   **Vol. 3:** 439
13.297 f   **Vol. 3:** 488
13.297   **Vol. 3:** 439, 772
13.299   **Vol. 3:** 39
13.311 ff **Vol. 3:** 80
13.318   **Vol. 3:** 872
13.372   **Vol. 3:** 813
13.380   **Vol. 2:** 578
13.409   **Vol. 3:** 772
14.19–24   **Vol. 2:** 463 (14.2.1)
14.71 f   **Vol. 3:** 815
14.91   **Vol. 1:** 363
14.107   **Vol. 3:** 196
14.110–118 **Vol. 2:** 309 (14.7.2)
14.158–162 **Vol. 2:** 308 (14.9.2)
14.192   **Vol. 1:** 363
14.202   **Vol. 3:** 191
14.255   **Vol. 1:** 615
14.267   **Vol. 3:** 1211
14.285   **Vol. 3:** 745
14.302   **Vol. 2:** 607
14.337   **Vol. 2:** 783
14.411   **Vol. 3:** 452
14.415   **Vol. 3:** 380
14.450   **Vol. 3:** 441
14.468   **Vol. 3:** 452
14.480   **Vol. 3:** 716
15.22   **Vol. 3:** 443
15.39–41   **Vol. 3:** 443
15.50   **Vol. 3:** 813
15.98   **Vol. 1:** 419
15.118 ff **Vol. 3:** 789
15.127–146 **Vol. 1:** 102 (15.5.3)
15.200   **Vol. 3:** 952
15.253   **Vol. 3:** 37
15.259   **Vol. 1:** 505   **Vol. 3:** 189, 534
15.320–322 **Vol. 3:** 443
15.403 ff **Vol. 3:** 789

**Josephus, Jewish
Antiquities (Ant.)** *(cont'd)*

15.410–416 **Vol. 3:** 789
15.416   **Vol. 3:** 783
15.417   **Vol. 3:** 486, 789
15.421   **Vol. 1:** 627
16.10   **Vol. 2:** 33
16.11   **Vol. 3:** 1164
16.27–30 **Vol. 2:** 651 (16.2.3)
16.93   **Vol. 3:** 681
16.151   **Vol. 1:** 89
16.162–165 **Vol. 3:** 752 (16.6.2)
16.163   **Vol. 1:** 363   **Vol. 3:** 408
16.167 f   **Vol. 3:** 752 (16.6.4 f)
16.170   **Vol. 2:** 882
16.172   **Vol. 3:** 415
16.187   **Vol. 3:** 36
16.244   **Vol. 3:** 996
16.301   **Vol. 3:** 681
17.19 f   **Vol. 2:** 578
17.99   **Vol. 3:** 570
17.130   **Vol. 3:** 925
17.140   **Vol. 1:** 342
17.149   **Vol. 1:** 574
17.199   **Vol. 1:** 342
17.213–223 **Vol. 2:** 699 (17.9.3)
17.226   **Vol. 3:** 486
17.254   **Vol. 2:** 783
17.289   **Vol. 3:** 923
17.295–298 **Vol. 3:** 530 (17.10.10)
17.295   **Vol. 1:** 394
17.299–303 **Vol. 1:** 127 (17.11.1)
17.319   **Vol. 3:** 449
17.320   **Vol. 3:** 756
18   **Vol. 2:** 320
18.1   **Vol. 2:** 565
18.4   **Vol. 3:** 756
18.6   **Vol. 3:** 1167
18.11   **Vol. 3:** 439, 1035
18.12–25   **Vol. 2:** 810 (18.1.3–6)
18.12–15   **Vol. 2:** 811 (18.1.3)
18.14   **Vol. 2:** 207
18.16 f   **Vol. 3:** 439
18.16   **Vol. 3:** 439
18.17   **Vol. 3:** 439
18.18   **Vol. 3:** 681
18.21   **Vol. 3:** 545
18.23–25   **Vol. 1:** 270 (18.1.6)
18.24   **Vol. 1:** 710
18.25   **Vol. 3:** 996
18.29 f   **Vol. 3:** 452
18.35   **Vol. 3:** 39
18.59   **Vol. 3:** 1029
18.65–80   **Vol. 2:** 521 (18.3.4)
18.65   **Vol. 3:** 785
18.81   **Vol. 1:** 574
18.82   **Vol. 3:** 1029
18.85 ff   **Vol. 1:** 396
18.85–89   **Vol. 3:** 452

18.85   **Vol. 3:** 147
18.90   **Vol. 3:** 756
18.95   **Vol. 3:** 39
18.116–119 **Vol. 3:** 1006
18.135   **Vol. 1:** 428
18.167   **Vol. 3:** 452, 456
18.266   **Vol. 3:** 925
18.284   **Vol. 2:** 899
18.293   **Vol. 3:** 439
18.310–317 **Vol. 3:** 752 (18.9.1), 853 (18.9.1)
18.356   **Vol. 2:** 136
19.96   **Vol. 1:** 546
19.110   **Vol. 1:** 342
19.294   **Vol. 3:** 796
19.317–325 **Vol. 2:** 521 (19.7.1)
19.328–331 **Vol. 2:** 258 (19.7.3)
20.38–48   **Vol. 2:** 792 (20.2.4)
20.40   **Vol. 3:** 1052
20.49–53   **Vol. 2:** 827 (20.2.5)
20.83   **Vol. 3:** 681
20.97 ff   **Vol. 1:** 396, 629
20.100–104 **Vol. 2:** 827 (20.5.2)
20.102   **Vol. 1:** 394
20.103   **Vol. 3:** 40
20.106 f   **Vol. 1:** 629
20.118–136 **Vol. 3:** 454
20.118–124 **Vol. 3:** 452
20.118   **Vol. 3:** 452
20.124   **Vol. 2:** 33
20.129   **Vol. 1:** 394
20.131 ff   **Vol. 3:** 40
20.132   **Vol. 1:** 341
20.142   **Vol. 2:** 557
20.161   **Vol. 1:** 394
20.169 ff   **Vol. 1:** 396, 532, 629
20.179–181 **Vol. 2:** 467 (20.8.8)
20.181   **Vol. 3:** 853
20.193   **Vol. 2:** 608
20.197–203 **Vol. 2:** 331 (20.9.1)
20.199   **Vol. 3:** 439
20.205 ff   **Vol. 3:** 40
20.206 f   **Vol. 3:** 853

Josephus, *The Jewish War (War)*

1.19   **Vol. 2:** 688
1.27   **Vol. 1:** 503
1.33   **Vol. 3:** 451
1.63   **Vol. 3:** 452
1.76   **Vol. 3:** 993
1.97   **Vol. 2:** 578
1.139   **Vol. 3:** 441
1.152 f   **Vol. 3:** 815
1.170   **Vol. 1:** 363
1.204–207 **Vol. 2:** 660 (1.10.5)
1.213   **Vol. 3:** 452
1.253   **Vol. 2:** 783
1.302 f   **Vol. 3:** 452
1.352   **Vol. 3:** 716
1.355   **Vol. 3:** 452

Josephus, The Jewish War (War) *(cont'd)*

1.430	Vol. 3: 681
1.488	Vol. 1: 560
1.493	Vol. 3: 681
1.511	Vol. 2: 578
1.540	Vol. 2: 879
1.562	Vol. 2: 578
1.625	Vol. 3: 486
1.649	Vol. 1: 574
1.666	Vol. 2: 839
2.8	Vol. 2: 565
2.10	Vol. 2: 463
2.20	Vol. 1: 513
2.42	Vol. 1: 330 Vol. 2: 783
2.55–65	Vol. 2: 313 (2.4.1–3)
2.97	Vol. 3: 756
2.112	Vol. 1: 511
2.117–166	Vol. 2: 811 (2.8)
2.117–118	Vol. 2: 659 (2.8.1)
2.118	Vol. 3: 1029, 1168
2.119–166	Vol. 2: 810 (2.8.2–14)
2.119–161	Vol. 1: 641
2.119–121	Vol. 2: 579 (2.8.2)
2.119	Vol. 3: 439, 1035
2.120	Vol. 1: 495
2.122–123	Vol. 2: 842 (2.8.3)
2.125	Vol. 3: 978
2.129–131	Vol. 1: 630
2.129	Vol. 3: 989
2.134–136	Vol. 3: 740 (2.8.6)
2.135	Vol. 2: 779
2.137–142	Vol. 1: 102 (2.8.7), 554 (2.8.7) Vol. 2: 651 (2.8.7) Vol. 3: 740 (2.8.7)
2.138	Vol. 1: 495
2.140	Vol. 2: 608
2.149	Vol. 3: 989
2.150	Vol. 1: 495
2.151 ff	Vol. 3: 1042
2.151	Vol. 2: 49 Vol. 3: 572
2.154	Vol. 3: 681
2.155	Vol. 3: 229
2.159 f	Vol. 1: 145 (2.8.12 f)
2.160–161	Vol. 1: 152 (2.8.13) Vol. 2: 579 (2.8.13)
2.162 ff	Vol. 3: 439
2.163	Vol. 2: 207 Vol. 3: 681
2.164	Vol. 3: 439
2.165	Vol. 3: 439
2.166	Vol. 3: 439
2.170 f	Vol. 3: 1168
2.175	Vol. 2: 43 Vol. 3: 430
2.196	Vol. 3: 721
2.232–246	Vol. 3: 452, 454
2.232	Vol. 3: 452
2.258–263	Vol. 3: 1006
2.260	Vol. 1: 377
2.261 ff†	Vol. 1: 396
2.261	Vol. 1: 532

2.313 f	Vol. 2: 160
2.350	Vol. 2: 608
2.367	Vol. 2: 776
2.385	Vol. 1: 511
2.420	Vol. 2: 109
2.425	Vol. 1: 627
2.427	Vol. 3: 1168
2.441	Vol. 3: 40
2.454	Vol. 3: 1168
2.515	Vol. 3: 813
2.517–522	Vol. 2: 309 (2.19.2)
2.549	Vol. 1: 342
2.624	Vol. 3: 51
3.9	Vol. 3: 1168
3.92	Vol. 3: 51
3.110–114	Vol. 3: 528 (3.6.1)
3.164	Vol. 3: 229
3.228	Vol. 1: 515
3.241	Vol. 3: 229
3.307–315	Vol. 3: 452
3.352	Vol. 3: 39
3.361–382	Vol. 2: 659 (3.8.5)
3.375	Vol. 2: 207
3.398	Vol. 1: 663
3.419–427	Vol. 2: 660 (3.9.3)
3.436	Vol. 1: 688
3.516–521	Vol. 3: 754 (3.10.8)
4.188	Vol. 3: 839
4.224	Vol. 3: 1168
4.236–269	Vol. 2: 660 (4.4.3)
4.326 f	Vol. 3: 1168
4.334–344	Vol. 3: 82 (4.5.4)
4.406	Vol. 1: 230
4.414	Vol. 3: 248
4.449	Vol. 3: 457
4.503–508	Vol. 3: 608 (4.9.3)
4.508	Vol. 3: 1168
4.514	Vol. 3: 1168
4.528	Vol. 2: 839
4.544	Vol. 3: 1168
4.567	Vol. 3: 1168
4.656	Vol. 2: 109
5.1–10	Vol. 2: 313 (5.1.1–2)
5.5	Vol. 3: 185, 788–789
5.31	Vol. 3: 229
5.193	Vol. 3: 949
5.199	Vol. 3: 1058
5.200	Vol. 3: 796
5.210	Vol. 3: 921
5.212–217	Vol. 3: 789
5.233–235	Vol. 3: 396
5.250	Vol. 3: 1168
5.262	Vol. 3: 952
5.264	Vol. 3: 952
5.375–419	Vol. 1: 345 (5.9.4)
5.405	Vol. 3: 756
5.415	Vol. 1: 700
5.429–438	Vol. 2: 651 (5.10.3)
5.449 ff	Vol. 1: 394
5.469 ff	Vol. 3: 952

Josephus, The Jewish War (War) *(cont'd)*

5.480	**Vol. 3:** 210
5.510	**Vol. 2:** 136
5.532	**Vol. 3:** 480
5.565	**Vol. 3:** 1162
6.4 ff	**Vol. 3:** 789
6.50	**Vol. 2:** 563
6.68–80	**Vol. 3:** 847 (6.1.7)
6.105	**Vol. 1:** 683
6.130	**Vol. 1:** 742
6.142	**Vol. 1:** 262
6.170	**Vol. 3:** 131
6.190	**Vol. 1:** 89
6.196	**Vol. 1:** 513
6.282	**Vol. 3:** 796
6.285	**Vol. 3:** 210
6.288–309	**Vol. 3:** 634 (6.5.3)
6.291	**Vol. 3:** 480
6.299	**Vol. 2:** 783
6.310–315	**Vol. 2:** 921 (6.5.4)
6.313	**Vol. 2:** 899
6.351	**Vol. 3:** 1006
6.435–442	**Vol. 2:** 591 (6.10.1)
6.438	**Vol. 3:** 36
7.8	**Vol. 2:** 565
7.67	**Vol. 3:** 210
7.123	**Vol. 3:** 785
7.132–152	**Vol. 2:** 660 (7.5.5)
7.171–177	**Vol. 2:** 659 (7.6.2)
7.203	**Vol. 1:** 392
7.216–218	**Vol. 3:** 753 (7.6.6)
7.325 f	**Vol. 1:** 435
7.330	**Vol. 2:** 140
7.337–388	**Vol. 2:** 480 (7.8.7)
7.340	**Vol. 1:** 435
7.341 ff	**Vol. 1:** 435 **Vol. 3:** 681
7.341	**Vol. 1:** 435
7.349	**Vol. 2:** 762
7.372	**Vol. 1:** 435
7.388	**Vol. 1:** 435
7.405	**Vol. 3:** 109
7.418	**Vol. 1:** 345
7.420–736	**Vol. 3:** 451
7.447	**Vol. 2:** 140
7.450	**Vol. 3:** 92
7.453	**Vol. 1:** 694

**Josephus, *Life of
Flavius Josephus* (Life)**

1†	**Vol. 3:** 871
7	**Vol. 1:** 152 (2)
10 ff	**Vol. 2:** 311
10	**Vol. 3:** 439
72	**Vol. 2:** 607–608
80–83	**Vol. 2:** 467 (15)
112	**Vol. 2:** 607
198	**Vol. 3:** 36
258	**Vol. 3:** 737

Philo, *De Abrahamo* (Abr.)

5	**Vol. 2:** 660
17 f	**Vol. 3:** 266
26	**Vol. 2:** 61
27	**Vol. 2:** 681
32	**Vol. 3:** 1118
35	**Vol. 2:** 681
42–44	**Vol. 1:** 80
44	**Vol. 3:** 126
51	**Vol. 2:** 651
56	**Vol. 3:** 37
87	**Vol. 2:** 659 **Vol. 3:** 531
90	**Vol. 3:** 744
103	**Vol. 3:** 575
116	**Vol. 1:** 342
153	**Vol. 2:** 756
157	**Vol. 2:** 659
163	**Vol. 3:** 1157
167	**Vol. 3:** 369
198	**Vol. 3:** 35
201–207	**Vol. 2:** 357
208	**Vol. 2:** 659
223	**Vol. 2:** 169
235	**Vol. 2:** 757
248	**Vol. 2:** 659
261	**Vol. 2:** 377
268 ff	**Vol. 1:** 598
272 ff	**Vol. 1:** 598
275	**Vol. 2:** 169

**Philo, *De Aeternitate Mundi*
(Aet. Mund.)**

2	**Vol. 1:** 512
8	**Vol. 1:** 178
9	**Vol. 1:** 178
28	**Vol. 2:** 659
34	**Vol. 2:** 659
84	**Vol. 3:** 681
88	**Vol. 1:** 711
89 ff	**Vol. 1:** 184
92	**Vol. 1:** 711
112	**Vol. 3:** 570
116	**Vol. 3:** 570
143	**Vol. 1:** 468

Philo, *De Agricultura* (Agric.)

16	**Vol. 1:** 577
40	**Vol. 3:** 98
63	**Vol. 3:** 681
95–99	**Vol. 1:** 509
136	**Vol. 3:** 1120
160	**Vol. 3:** 716

Philo, *De Cherubin* (Cher.)

14	**Vol. 3:** 533
40–47	**Vol. 3:** 642
52	**Vol. 3:** 522

Philo, De Cherubin (Cher.) *(cont'd)*

87	Vol. 3: 407
88	Vol. 3: 842
94 f	Vol. 3: 789
115	Vol. 3: 716
125 ff	Vol. 3: 1117

Philo, De Confusione Linguarum (Conf. Ling.)

8	Vol. 2: 740
63	Vol. 3: 639
101	Vol. 3: 716
103	Vol. 3: 716
109	Vol. 3: 486
134 ff	Vol. 1: 734
152	Vol. 3: 522, 526
161	Vol. 3: 681

Philo, De Congressu Eruditionis Gratia (Congr.)

34	Vol. 3: 486	
90	Vol. 2: 681	Vol. 3: 486
99	Vol. 2: 590–591	Vol. 3: 36
109	Vol. 3: 194	
159	Vol. 3: 877	
161 ff	Vol. 1: 627	

Philo, De Decalogo (Decal.)

25	Vol. 2: 658	
30 f	Vol. 3: 842	
33	Vol. 2: 784	
41	Vol. 2: 658	
46	Vol. 2: 784	
47	Vol. 3: 1120	
49	Vol. 2: 496	
87	Vol. 1: 349	Vol. 2: 659
93 f	Vol. 2: 651	
100	Vol. 3: 407	
101	Vol. 2: 659	Vol. 3: 842
102	Vol. 2: 192	
121 f	Vol. 2: 583	
124	Vol. 2: 583	
126	Vol. 2: 583	
129	Vol. 2: 583	
131	Vol. 2: 583	
149	Vol. 3: 716	
160	Vol. 2: 783	
165 ff	Vol. 3: 931	

Philo, Quod Deterius Potiori Insidiari Soleat (Det. Pot. Ins.)

13	Vol. 3: 533
20	Vol. 3: 789
29	Vol. 3: 125
56	Vol. 3: 595
57	Vol. 3: 533
59	Vol. 3: 681

83	Vol. 2: 288
84	Vol. 3: 681
86	Vol. 3: 125
175	Vol. 2: 763

Philo, Quod Deus Sit Immutabilis (Deus Imm.)

20	Vol. 2: 833	
29	Vol. 1: 695	
31	Vol. 1: 523	
35	Vol. 2: 658	
37	Vol. 2: 658	
52–56	Vol. 1: 674	
54	Vol. 3: 769	
60 f	Vol. 3: 1166	
76	Vol. 3: 98	
91	Vol. 2: 833	
131 ff	Vol. 3: 35	
135	Vol. 2: 493	Vol. 3: 789
143	Vol. 3: 126	

Philo, De Ebrietate (Ebr.)

30	Vol. 1: 523	
44	Vol. 2: 496	
65	Vol. 3: 36	
72	Vol. 3: 210	
75	Vol. 3: 716	
76	Vol. 3: 35	
97	Vol. 2: 779	
98	Vol. 1: 409	
105	Vol. 3: 716	
111	Vol. 3: 210	
126	Vol. 3: 36	
133	Vol. 2: 288	
137	Vol. 2: 288	Vol. 3: 126
142	Vol. 1: 468	

Philo, De Exsecrationibus (Exsec.)

6	Vol. 3: 867, 869

Philo, In Flaccum (Flacc.)

1	Vol. 3: 479
4	Vol. 3: 479
41–96	Vol. 2: 310
45 f	Vol. 2: 309
111	Vol. 2: 689
164	Vol. 1: 511

Philo, De Fuga et Inventione (Fug.)

72	Vol. 2: 659
79	Vol. 2: 830
108	Vol. 3: 36
109	Vol. 3: 35
165	Vol. 3: 533

Philo, *De Gigantibus (Gig.)*

22	**Vol. 2:** 187
31 ff	**Vol. 3:** 692
51	**Vol. 3:** 963
52	**Vol. 1:** 330
54	**Vol. 3:** 760

Philo, *De Josepho (Jos.)*

1	**Vol. 3:** 769
2	**Vol. 1:** 89
39	**Vol. 1:** 89
57	**Vol. 2:** 779
67	**Vol. 2:** 608
68	**Vol. 2:** 493
145	**Vol. 2:** 493

Philo, *Legum Allegoriae (Leg. All.)*

1.10	**Vol. 2:** 588	
1.20	**Vol. 3:** 842	
1.31 f	**Vol. 1:** 520	
1.39	**Vol. 3:** 681	
1.44	**Vol. 1:** 734	
1.52	**Vol. 1:** 228	
1.54 f	**Vol. 1:** 330	
1.73	**Vol. 3:** 716	
1.80	**Vol. 3:** 522	
1.86	**Vol. 3:** 926	
1.95	**Vol. 2:** 608	
1.100	**Vol. 3:** 716	
1.105 ff	**Vol. 1:** 435	
1.107	**Vol. 1:** 435	
2.23	**Vol. 2:** 658	
2.28†	**Vol. 1:** 341	
2.31	**Vol. 3:** 126	
2.34	**Vol. 1:** 465	
2.57	**Vol. 2:** 480, 763	
2.70	**Vol. 3:** 126	
2.79–81	**Vol. 1:** 509	
2.81	**Vol. 1:** 87	
2.89	**Vol. 1:** 599	**Vol. 2:** 659
2.98	**Vol. 3:** 939	
2.106 f	**Vol. 1:** 412	
3.4	**Vol. 1:** 734	
3.21	**Vol. 2:** 480	**Vol. 3:** 194
3.25 f	**Vol. 3:** 451	
3.26	**Vol. 3:** 458	
3.27	**Vol. 3:** 639	
3.32 f	**Vol. 3:** 377	
3.36	**Vol. 1:** 468	
3.78	**Vol. 2:** 115	
3.79 ff	**Vol. 3:** 36	
3.79	**Vol. 2:** 590, 592	
3.81	**Vol. 2:** 590	
3.82	**Vol. 3:** 922	
3.84	**Vol. 3:** 533	
3.92	**Vol. 3:** 716	
3.95–104	**Vol. 2:** 288	
3.96	**Vol. 3:** 1117	
3.98 f	**Vol. 3:** 842	
3.99 f	**Vol. 3:** 554	
3.100–103	**Vol. 3:** 515	
3.102	**Vol. 2:** 290	**Vol. 3:** 904
3.103 f	**Vol. 3:** 554	
3.105	**Vol. 2:** 830	
3.108	**Vol. 2:** 290	
3.151	**Vol. 2:** 480	
3.152	**Vol. 1:** 674	
3.159	**Vol. 2:** 61	
3.162	**Vol. 2:** 659	
3.171 f	**Vol. 2:** 493	
3.185	**Vol. 3:** 522	
3.203 ff	**Vol. 3:** 41	
3.211	**Vol. 3:** 996	
3.228	**Vol. 3:** 369	
3.229	**Vol. 3:** 877	
3.234	**Vol. 3:** 125	
4.108	**Vol. 3:** 939	

Philo, *Legatio ad Gaium (Leg. Gai.)*

26	**Vol. 2:** 608
53	**Vol. 3:** 779
54	**Vol. 2:** 608
120–139	**Vol. 2:** 310
137 f	**Vol. 3:** 598
155	**Vol. 3:** 598
156 f	**Vol. 3:** 598
190	**Vol. 2:** 608
281–283	**Vol. 2:** 309
293	**Vol. 3:** 526
353	**Vol. 1:** 580

Philo, *De Migratione Abrahami (Migr. Abr.)*

2	**Vol. 3:** 210	
18	**Vol. 3:** 681	
34 f	**Vol. 2:** 397, 762	
34	**Vol. 3:** 681	
39 f	**Vol. 2:** 493	
71	**Vol. 2:** 289	
97	**Vol. 2:** 377	
122–125	**Vol. 3:** 210	
124	**Vol. 3:** 210	
133	**Vol. 3:** 946	
170	**Vol. 3:** 939	
171	**Vol. 3:** 939	
176 f	**Vol. 3:** 465	
192	**Vol. 2:** 659	**Vol. 3:** 126
195	**Vol. 3:** 939	
204	**Vol. 3:** 946	
218	**Vol. 3:** 1029	

Philo, *De Mutatione Nominum (Mut. Nom.)*

4	**Vol. 1:** 428
11 f	**Vol. 2:** 651
29–32	**Vol. 1:** 387

Philo, De Mutatione Nominum (Mut. Nom.) *(cont'd)*

121	Vol. 2: 332
181	Vol. 2: 289
197	Vol. 1: 428 Vol. 3: 1157
269	Vol. 3: 526

Philo, Quod Omnis Probus Liber Sit (Omn. Prob. Lib.)

12 f	Vol. 1: 641
12	Vol. 3: 545
62	Vol. 2: 659
81 f	Vol. 3: 487
87	Vol. 3: 545
114	Vol. 3: 194
160	Vol. 2: 659

Philo, De Opificio Mundi (Op. Mund.)

3	Vol. 2: 660 Vol. 3: 332
10	Vol. 1: 387
16	Vol. 1: 523 Vol. 3: 904
17	Vol. 2: 608
19	Vol. 3: 904
23	Vol. 1: 89
25	Vol. 1: 523
26	Vol. 3: 842
29	Vol. 2: 192 Vol. 3: 904
31	Vol. 1: 580
36	Vol. 2: 659 Vol. 3: 904
60	Vol. 3: 843
79	Vol. 3: 769
80	Vol. 3: 92
82	Vol. 2: 192
89	Vol. 1: 618, 627
117	Vol. 2: 192
129	Vol. 3: 904
132	Vol. 1: 377
134 ff	Vol. 1: 520
135	Vol. 3: 125
137	Vol. 3: 789
143	Vol. 3: 486
146	Vol. 2: 289
155 f	Vol. 2: 480
155	Vol. 3: 681
165	Vol. 1: 89
171	Vol. 1: 694

Philo, De Plantatione (Plant.)

14	Vol. 3: 681
18	Vol. 2: 288
48	Vol. 3: 522
50	Vol. 2: 289
91	Vol. 2: 659
93	Vol. 2: 61

Philo, De Posteritate Caini (Post. C.)

38	Vol. 3: 942
42	Vol. 3: 716
57 f	Vol. 2: 493
124	Vol. 1: 185
143	Vol. 1: 742
150	Vol. 2: 659
154	Vol. 3: 939
233	Vol. 3: 942

Philo, De Praemiis et Poenis (Praem.)

13	Vol. 2: 659
16	Vol. 2: 899
17	Vol. 3: 266
65	Vol. 2: 659
72	Vol. 1: 695
79	Vol. 1: 334
91–97	Vol. 2: 899
101	Vol. 1: 334
117	Vol. 1: 342 Vol. 3: 939
123	Vol. 2: 798
125	Vol. 2: 798
153	Vol. 1: 627

Philo, Quis Rerum Divinarum Heres Sit (Rer. Div. Her.)

5–29	Vol. 2: 736
8	Vol. 1: 334
38	Vol. 2: 288
44	Vol. 3: 194
55	Vol. 3: 681
70	Vol. 2: 187
75	Vol. 1: 523
76	Vol. 2: 830
94	Vol. 3: 369
98	Vol. 2: 99
124	Vol. 3: 194
133	Vol. 1: 387
166	Vol. 3: 98
182	Vol. 3: 36
186	Vol. 3: 194
205 f	Vol. 3: 36
263 ff	Vol. 3: 491
265	Vol. 3: 126
269	Vol. 3: 716
293	Vol. 3: 147
302	Vol. 2: 659
315	Vol. 2: 355, 357

Philo, De Sacrificiis Abelis et Caini (Sacr.)

5	Vol. 3: 681
6 f	Vol. 2: 798
22	Vol. 3: 926
27	Vol. 3: 926

Philo, De Sacrificiis Abelis et Caini (Sacr.) *(cont'd)*

49	**Vol. 2:** 377
60	**Vol. 2:** 608
63	**Vol. 1:** 674
67	**Vol. 1:** 734
69	**Vol. 3:** 838
95	**Vol. 1:** 468
100	**Vol. 2:** 658
114	**Vol. 3:** 194
117 ff	**Vol. 3:** 194

Philo, *De Sobrietate (Sobr.)*

42	**Vol. 3:** 575
55	**Vol. 3:** 210
56	**Vol. 3:** 639
66	**Vol. 3:** 37

Philo, *De Somniis (Som.)*

1.6	**Vol. 3:** 459
1.33	**Vol. 2:** 659
1.36	**Vol. 2:** 762
1.71	**Vol. 2:** 289
1.75	**Vol. 2:** 493
1.76	**Vol. 1:** 387
1.86	**Vol. 3:** 210
1.115	**Vol. 2:** 289
1.135	**Vol. 3:** 681
1.139	**Vol. 2:** 187
1.149	**Vol. 3:** 789
1.163	**Vol. 2:** 512
1.181	**Vol. 3:** 681
1.206	**Vol. 2:** 290 **Vol. 3:** 904
1.214 f	**Vol. 3:** 36
1.215	**Vol. 3:** 35
1.239	**Vol. 2:** 290
1.256	**Vol. 3:** 925
2.23	**Vol. 3:** 526
2.31	**Vol. 2:** 744
2.175	**Vol. 1:** 334
2.226	**Vol. 2:** 397
2.244	**Vol. 2:** 377
2.248	**Vol. 3:** 789
2.253	**Vol. 2:** 779
2.354	**Vol. 2:** 651

Philo, *De Specialibus Legibus (Spec. Leg.)*

1	**Vol. 1:** 89
1.1–11	**Vol. 1:** 309
1.18	**Vol. 3:** 126
1.20†	**Vol. 3:** 515
1.32–35	**Vol. 3:** 515
1.44	**Vol. 1:** 742
1.58	**Vol. 2:** 573
1.59	**Vol. 3:** 760
1.65	**Vol. 3:** 491

1.66	**Vol. 3:** 681	
1.77 ff	**Vol. 3:** 752	
1.77	**Vol. 3:** 194	
1.81	**Vol. 3:** 1117	
1.82–97	**Vol. 3:** 36	
1.96	**Vol. 1:** 618	
1.135	**Vol. 3:** 194	
1.149	**Vol. 1:** 495	**Vol. 2:** 99
1.169–189	**Vol. 1:** 627	
1.173	**Vol. 1:** 495	
1.190	**Vol. 1:** 700	
1.199	**Vol. 1:** 230	
1.209	**Vol. 3:** 925	
1.212	**Vol. 3:** 422	
1.221	**Vol. 2:** 518	
1.224	**Vol. 3:** 422	
1.243	**Vol. 3:** 35	
1.269	**Vol. 1:** 330	
1.271	**Vol. 3:** 422	
1.285 ff	**Vol. 3:** 418	
1.288	**Vol. 2:** 493	
1.290	**Vol. 3:** 418	
1.300	**Vol. 1:** 334	
1.302	**Vol. 2:** 192	
1.333	**Vol. 1:** 228	
1.345	**Vol. 3:** 531	
2.2–38	**Vol. 3:** 740	
2.6	**Vol. 1:** 618	**Vol. 2:** 659
2.8	**Vol. 2:** 651	
2.27	**Vol. 2:** 659	
2.41	**Vol. 1:** 627	
2.42–55	**Vol. 1:** 627	
2.42	**Vol. 2:** 659	
2.54 f	**Vol. 2:** 357	
2.95	**Vol. 3:** 194	
2.116	**Vol. 3:** 194	
2.121 f	**Vol. 3:** 194	
2.159	**Vol. 1:** 574	
2.164	**Vol. 3:** 36	
2.176 ff	**Vol. 2:** 785	
2.176–188	**Vol. 2:** 783	
2.176	**Vol. 2:** 783	
2.185	**Vol. 2:** 462	
2.192	**Vol. 2:** 782	
2.195	**Vol. 1:** 495	
2.196	**Vol. 3:** 98	
2.201	**Vol. 2:** 266	
2.225	**Vol. 2:** 659	
3.1 f	**Vol. 2:** 762	
3.40	**Vol. 3:** 785	
3.54	**Vol. 2:** 140	
3.63	**Vol. 3:** 926	
3.145	**Vol. 3:** 194	
3.189	**Vol. 1:** 694	
3.209	**Vol. 3:** 575	
4.40	**Vol. 2:** 651	
4.49	**Vol. 3:** 491	
4.112	**Vol. 1:** 495	
4.123	**Vol. 2:** 289, 659	
4.147	**Vol. 2:** 99	

Philo, De Specialibus Legibus (Spec. Leg.) *(cont'd)*

4.150	**Vol. 3:** 772
4.170	**Vol. 1:** 228
4.176–179	**Vol. 2:** 738
4.180	**Vol. 3:** 416
4.203	**Vol. 2:** 742 **Vol. 3:** 1160, 1164
4.231	**Vol. 2:** 497
5.741d	**Vol. 1:** 589

Philo, *De Virtutibus (Virt.)*

5	**Vol. 2:** 659
18	**Vol. 2:** 659
57	**Vol. 3:** 125
90	**Vol. 2:** 821
188	**Vol. 3:** 789
215 f	**Vol. 2:** 396
217	**Vol. 3:** 68 i

Philo, *De Vita Contemplativa (Vit. Cont.)*

25	**Vol. 1:** 641	**Vol. 3:** 669
28	**Vol. 1:** 580	**Vol. 2:** 744
31	**Vol. 1:** 580	
65 f	**Vol. 2:** 785	
75	**Vol. 1:** 577	
78	**Vol. 1:** 574	

Philo, *De Vita Mosis (Vit. Mos.)*

1.23	**Vol. 3:** 772
1.48	**Vol. 3:** 877
1.54	**Vol. 2:** 677
1.75	**Vol. 2:** 651

1.95	**Vol. 3:** 570
1.156	**Vol. 2:** 757
1.158	**Vol. 1:** 639–640 **Vol. 3:** 126, 486
1.187	**Vol. 1:** 513
1.235	**Vol. 3:** 875
1.279	**Vol. 3:** 522
1.287	**Vol. 3:** 486
1.295 ff	**Vol. 2:** 677
2.4	**Vol. 2:** 792
2.7	**Vol. 2:** 792
2.14	**Vol. 2:** 659
2.20–24	**Vol. 1:** 627
2.29	**Vol. 2:** 757
2.65	**Vol. 1:** 185
2.74 ff	**Vol. 3:** 904
2.76	**Vol. 2:** 290
2.101–104	**Vol. 3:** 789
2.109–135	**Vol. 3:** 36
2.122–135	**Vol. 3:** 396
2.125	**Vol. 1:** 578
2.134	**Vol. 1:** 89, 523
2.138	**Vol. 3:** 989
2.141	**Vol. 3:** 904
2.147	**Vol. 1:** 700
2.160–173	**Vol. 3:** 871
2.167	**Vol. 3:** 875
2.185	**Vol. 1:** 514
2.196	**Vol. 3:** 418
2.203	**Vol. 3:** 486
2.238	**Vol. 1:** 734
2.284	**Vol. 3:** 877
2.290	**Vol. 3:** 486
2.291	**Vol. 3:** 345
2.292	**Vol. 3:** 486
3.171	**Vol. 1:** 469

Early Christian Literature

Barnabas, Letter of (Barn.)

4.6	**Vol. 2:** 316
4.9	**Vol. 1:** 204
4.11	**Vol. 1:** 339
4.14	**Vol. 2:** 316
6.6	**Vol. 2:** 299
6.7	**Vol. 2:** 316
8.1–3	**Vol. 2:** 316
8.7	**Vol. 2:** 316
9.3	**Vol. 1:** 411
9.9	**Vol. 3:** 770
10.12	**Vol. 2:** 316
11.1	**Vol. 2:** 316

12.2	**Vol. 2:** 316	
12.5 ff	**Vol. 1:** 510	
12.5	**Vol. 2:** 316	
12.8 ff	**Vol. 2:** 332	
12.10	**Vol. 3:** 653	
15.3–9	**Vol. 2:** 701	
15.4–5	**Vol. 2:** 697	
15.8–9	**Vol. 2:** 692	
15.9	**Vol. 1:** 631	
16.5	**Vol. 2:** 316	
18–20	**Vol. 3:** 929	
18.1	**Vol. 2:** 481	**Vol. 3:** 940
19 ff	**Vol. 1:** 339	

Barnabas, Letter of (Barn.) *(cont'd)*

19.12	**Vol. 2:** 776
20.1	**Vol. 1:** 204

1 Clement

1.2	**Vol. 2:** 94
1.3	**Vol. 2:** 539
3.2	**Vol. 3:** 963
4.8	**Vol. 1:** 619
4.13	**Vol. 2:** 316
6.1	**Vol. 3:** 856
7.6	**Vol. 2:** 682
8.3	**Vol. 1:** 618 **Vol. 2:** 316
9.3	**Vol. 3:** 265
9.4	**Vol. 2:** 682
13.3	**Vol. 1:** 339
16.17	**Vol. 3:** 1163
18.10	**Vol. 2:** 673
20.11	**Vol. 1:** 387
21.6–8	**Vol. 3:** 929
22.6	**Vol. 3:** 516
23.2 ff	**Vol. 3:** 687
25.2	**Vol. 2:** 725
29.2 f	**Vol. 2:** 316
30.1	**Vol. 3:** 346
30.3	**Vol. 3:** 346
31.2–4	**Vol. 2:** 316
31.2	**Vol. 1:** 619
32.4	**Vol. 2:** 81
33.5	**Vol. 2:** 570
33.6	**Vol. 2:** 130
34.7	**Vol. 3:** 1194
35.5	**Vol. 3:** 346, 931
40.5	**Vol. 2:** 457
41.1	**Vol. 3:** 931
42.1 f	**Vol. 3:** 548
43	**Vol. 2:** 316
43.4	**Vol. 3:** 37
46.5	**Vol. 1:** 535 **Vol. 3:** 963
47.3	**Vol. 3:** 383
49.5	**Vol. 2:** 214
50.5	**Vol. 1:** 339
55.3 ff	**Vol. 3:** 962
55.6	**Vol. 2:** 316
59.2 ff	**Vol. 3:** 611
59.2–4	**Vol. 3:** 611
59.4	**Vol. 3:** 319
60.3	**Vol. 3:** 319
60.4	**Vol. 1:** 619
62.2	**Vol. 3:** 931

2 Clement

2.1 f	**Vol. 1:** 411
2.4	**Vol. 3:** 492
4	**Vol. 3:** 929
4.5	**Vol. 1:** 339
6.1	**Vol. 2:** 838
6.7	**Vol. 1:** 339

7.6	**Vol. 3:** 499
8.2	**Vol. 3:** 912
8.4	**Vol. 1:** 339
8.6	**Vol. 3:** 499
11.2 ff	**Vol. 3:** 687
13.1	**Vol. 2:** 817
14.2	**Vol. 2:** 570
16.3	**Vol. 3:** 180
16.4	**Vol. 2:** 214
17.1	**Vol. 3:** 772
17.7	**Vol. 3:** 856
19.2	**Vol. 3:** 687

Didache (Did.)

1–5	**Vol. 3:** 929
1.1	**Vol. 2:** 481 **Vol. 3:** 940
1.3	**Vol. 1:** 613
2.1	**Vol. 3:** 770
4.3	**Vol. 2:** 776
6.1	**Vol. 3:** 770
6.3	**Vol. 2:** 284
7.1–3	**Vol. 3:** 648
7.3	**Vol. 3:** 648
8.1	**Vol. 1:** 630 **Vol. 3:** 408
8.2	**Vol. 2:** 870
9 f	**Vol. 3:** 611
9	**Vol. 1:** 117 **Vol. 2:** 896
9.2	**Vol. 1:** 641
9.5	**Vol. 3:** 395
10	**Vol. 2:** 896
10.5 f	**Vol. 3:** 245
10.5	**Vol. 2:** 531
10.6†	**Vol. 2:** 531, 895–896
10.7	**Vol. 3:** 89
11.2	**Vol. 3:** 770
11.3	**Vol. 3:** 84
11.7–12	**Vol. 3:** 89
13	**Vol. 1:** 198
13.1–7	**Vol. 3:** 89
13.1	**Vol. 3:** 349
13.2	**Vol. 3:** 768
14.1	**Vol. 1:** 631
15.1 f	**Vol. 3:** 84
16.3	**Vol. 2:** 130
16.5	**Vol. 1:** 656
16.6	**Vol. 3:** 634

Epistle to Diognetus (Ep. Diog.)

2.2	**Vol. 3:** 913
2.7	**Vol. 3:** 913
3.1	**Vol. 2:** 85
5	**Vol. 2:** 804
6.3	**Vol. 3:** 1188
7.2	**Vol. 1:** 387
9.2	**Vol. 3:** 1196
9.5	**Vol. 3:** 1196

Gospel of Thomas (Gos. Thom.)

6	**Vol. 1:** 92
7	**Vol. 2:** 752
8	**Vol. 2:** 751
10	**Vol. 3:** 697
16	**Vol. 3:** 697
17	**Vol. 2:** 219
20	**Vol. 2:** 751, 926
22	**Vol. 1:** 284
24	**Vol. 2:** 706
25	**Vol. 2:** 752
27	**Vol. 2:** 751
37	**Vol. 2:** 926
38	**Vol. 3:** 634
47	**Vol. 2:** 838
64	**Vol. 2:** 751
65	**Vol. 2:** 751
66	**Vol. 2:** 751
82	**Vol. 2:** 752 **Vol. 3:** 697
90	**Vol. 3:** 640
94	**Vol. 2:** 752
95	**Vol. 2:** 752
104	**Vol. 2:** 752

Hermas, *Commandments* or *Mandates* (*Com.* or *Man.*)

2.2 f	**Vol. 3:** 346
3 f	**Vol. 3:** 983
4.1	**Vol. 3:** 316
4.3	**Vol. 3:** 316
6.1	**Vol. 3:** 929
8.3	**Vol. 3:** 346
8.8	**Vol. 3:** 316
8.12	**Vol. 1:** 339
11.1 ff	**Vol. 3:** 687

Hermas, *Similitudes* (*Sim.*)

5.3.1	**Vol. 1:** 577
5.3.2	**Vol. 1:** 577
5.4.2	**Vol. 1:** 577
5.5.1	**Vol. 1:** 577
5.6.8	**Vol. 1:** 577
6.5.5	**Vol. 3:** 345
8.6.3	**Vol. 3:** 499
8.11.1	**Vol. 1:** 577
9.11.9	**Vol. 1:** 577
9.12.3 f	**Vol. 2:** 31
10.4.1†	**Vol. 1:** 339

Hermas, *Visions* (*Vis.*)

3.5.3	**Vol. 1:** 339
3.9.7	**Vol. 1:** 666
3.10.6	**Vol. 3:** 515
4.3.3	**Vol. 2:** 836
5.5 ff	**Vol. 1:** 339

Ignatius, *Letter to the Ephesians* (*Eph.*)

4.1 f	**Vol. 3:** 675
5.3	**Vol. 3:** 1194
7.2	**Vol. 3:** 724
9.2	**Vol. 1:** 339
10.3	**Vol. 3:** 529
13.1	**Vol. 3:** 1194
18.2	**Vol. 3:** 653
20	**Vol. 2:** 271
20.2	**Vol. 3:** 653

Ignatius, *Letter to the Magnesians* (*Mag.*)

2.1	**Vol. 3:** 548
5	**Vol. 3:** 929
6.1	**Vol. 3:** 548
7.1	**Vol. 3:** 1194
8	**Vol. 2:** 316
9.1	**Vol. 1:** 631 **Vol. 3:** 411
10.3	**Vol. 2:** 316

Ignatius, *Letter to the Philadelphians* (*Phil.*)

6	**Vol. 2:** 677
6.2	**Vol. 3:** 1194
9.1	**Vol. 2:** 31
10.1	**Vol. 3:** 1194

Ignatius, *Letter to Polycarp* (*Pol.*)

3.2	**Vol. 3:** 724
4.1–6.2	**Vol. 3:** 929
4.2	**Vol. 3:** 724

Ignatius, *Letter to the Romans* (*Rom.*)

7.3	**Vol. 3:** 653
9.2	**Vol. 1:** 183

Ignatius, *Letter to the Smyrnaeans* (*Smy.*)

1.1	**Vol. 3:** 653, 661
4.2	**Vol. 3:** 724
8.2	**Vol. 2:** 547

Ignatius, *Letter to the Trallians* (*Trall.*)

2.1	**Vol. 3:** 548
6.1	**Vol. 1:** 535
9.1	**Vol. 3:** 653
11	**Vol. 2:** 677
13.2	**Vol. 1:** 339

Martyrdom of Polycarp

2.2	**Vol. 3:** 257
2.3	**Vol. 3:** 856
14.1 ff	**Vol. 3:** 611
14.1	**Vol. 3:** 611
14.3	**Vol. 3:** 611

Polycarp, *To the Philippians*
(Polycarp)

4.2 – 6.1	**Vol. 3:** 929
4.2	**Vol. 2:** 539
8.1	**Vol. 2:** 40

Rabbinic Writings

Mishnah

Aboth (= Pirke Aboth)

1.1	**Vol. 3:** 772
1.3	**Vol. 2:** 191 **Vol. 3:** 1149
1.5	**Vol. 3:** 536, 1058
1.9	**Vol. 3:** 1154
1.10	**Vol. 2:** 608
1.11	**Vol. 2:** 191
1.12	**Vol. 2:** 779
1.17	**Vol. 3:** 1121
2.1	**Vol. 3:** 614
2.3	**Vol. 2:** 608 **Vol. 3:** 614
2.12 f	**Vol. 2:** 481 **Vol. 3:** 940
2.12	**Vol. 2:** 837
2.16	**Vol. 3:** 140
3.5	**Vol. 3:** 1161 – 1162
3.14 ff	**Vol. 2:** 812
3.14	**Vol. 2:** 798 **Vol. 3:** 773
3.15 f	**Vol. 2:** 608
3.16	**Vol. 3:** 140
4.11	**Vol. 1:** 83
4.17	**Vol. 1:** 405
4.22	**Vol. 3:** 1154
5.19	**Vol. 3:** 942
5.21	**Vol. 2:** 261
6.2	**Vol. 3:** 488, 769, 1162
6.5	**Vol. 1:** 405
6.6	**Vol. 2:** 34, 652
6.10	**Vol. 2:** 310
6.11	**Vol. 3:** 140

Arakhin

7.3 ff	**Vol. 3:** 194
9.1 – 4	**Vol. 3:** 194

Baba Bathra

6.8	**Vol. 3:** 381

Baba Kamma

3.5	**Vol. 2:** 608
5.3	**Vol. 2:** 608
10.1	**Vol. 3:** 756
10.2	**Vol. 3:** 754

Berakoth

1.4	**Vol. 2:** 864
3.3	**Vol. 3:** 1058
5.5	**Vol. 1:** 128
6.1	**Vol. 2:** 521
7.2	**Vol. 3:** 1058
7.3	**Vol. 1:** 212 **Vol. 2:** 521
9.2	**Vol. 3:** 1154

Erubin

6.2	**Vol. 3:** 439

Gittin

1.1	**Vol. 3:** 498
1.3	**Vol. 3:** 498
4.9	**Vol. 3:** 194

Hagigah

2.1	**Vol. 2:** 397 **Vol. 3:** 502, 748
2.7	**Vol. 3:** 105

Hallah

3.3	**Vol. 3:** 194

Hullin

3.6	**Vol. 1:** 172

313

Kelim

13.6	Vol. 3: 498
13.7	Vol. 3: 479

Ketuboth

4.3	Vol. 1: 159
4.6	Vol. 3: 921
9.5	Vol. 2: 608
9.9	Vol. 1: 159

Kiddushin

1.10	Vol. 3: 761
4.9	Vol. 2: 608

Kilaim

8.2	Vol. 3: 1160

Makkoth

1.6	Vol. 3: 439
3.16	Vol. 3: 140

Megillah

4.4	Vol. 3: 485

Menahoth

10.3	Vol. 2: 785

Middoth

1.2	Vol. 1: 314
2.6	Vol. 3: 1162
3	Vol. 3: 419
3.8	Vol. 3: 921

Moed Katan

3.7 ff	Vol. 1: 329

Nazir

1.3	Vol. 2: 61

Nedarim

1	Vol. 2: 43
3	Vol. 2: 43
3.2	Vol. 2: 43
3.4	Vol. 3: 757
8	Vol. 2: 43
9	Vol. 2: 43
9.1	Vol. 2: 43
10.2-4	Vol. 2: 608
11	Vol. 2: 43

Niddah

4.2	Vol. 3: 439

Oholoth

17.5	Vol. 3: 498

Parah

3.3	Vol. 3: 439
3.7	Vol. 3: 439

Peah

2.6	Vol. 3: 772
4.7	Vol. 3: 194
8.9	Vol. 1: 219

Pesahim

2.5	Vol. 3: 194
8.8	Vol. 1: 155
10.2-7	Vol. 2: 522
10.5 f	Vol. 3: 194
10.5	Vol. 2: 313

Rosh ha-Shanah

1.1	Vol. 1: 628
3.8	Vol. 1: 509

Sanhedrin

3.2	Vol. 1: 203 Vol. 2: 159 Vol. 3: 741
4.1	Vol. 1: 630
4.5	Vol. 3: 498
6.1	Vol. 3: 51
7.4	Vol. 3: 227
7.5	Vol. 3: 341-343
9.1	Vol. 1: 235
10.1	Vol. 2: 798, 811
11.1-4	Vol. 1: 196
11.1	Vol. 2: 311, 313 Vol. 3: 227
11.3	Vol. 3: 479

Shabbath

3.1	Vol. 2: 811
6.5	Vol. 3: 444
7.2	Vol. 3: 408
8.5	Vol. 3: 498
14.4	Vol. 2: 798
16.2	Vol. 3: 408

Shebuoth

6.13	Vol. 3: 741

Shekalim

1.7	Vol. 2: 823
2.5	Vol. 2: 823
5.3	Vol. 3: 498
5.4	Vol. 3: 498

Sotah

1.7	**Vol. 3:** 402
3.4	**Vol. 3:** 1058
7.7 f	**Vol. 2:** 158
9.9	**Vol. 1:** 724
9.14	**Vol. 2:** 126
9.15	**Vol. 1:** 544, 724 **Vol. 2:** 811

Sukkah

4.9	**Vol. 3:** 814
5.2 ff	**Vol. 1:** 629
5.2–5	**Vol. 3:** 814

Taanith

2.1 f	**Vol. 3:** 389

Terumoth

6.5	**Vol. 3:** 194

Tohoroth

3.6	**Vol. 1:** 155
7.6	**Vol. 3:** 756
7.7	**Vol. 3:** 498

Yadaim

4.6	**Vol. 3:** 439
4.7	**Vol. 3:** 439

Yebamoth

1.1	**Vol. 2:** 61
2.29	**Vol. 1:** 145
4.11	**Vol. 2:** 608
8.5	**Vol. 2:** 311
9.3	**Vol. 3:** 1121
11.2	**Vol. 1:** 159

Yoma

2.4	**Vol. 2:** 294
3.8	**Vol. 3:** 159
3.9b	**Vol. 3:** 233
4.2	**Vol. 3:** 159
6.2	**Vol. 3:** 159
8.8 f	**Vol. 3:** 428
8.9	**Vol. 3:** 173, 428

Yom Tob (= Betzah)

3.1	**Vol. 2:** 811

Zabim

2.1	**Vol. 1:** 155

Babylonian Talmud

Abodah Zarah

17a	**Vol. 2:** 833

Baba Bathra

14b	**Vol. 3:** 485
16a	**Vol. 1:** 83 **Vol. 3:** 469
73a	**Vol. 3:** 983
75a	**Vol. 3:** 396

Baba Kamma

38a	**Vol. 2:** 309
113a	**Vol. 3:** 756

Baba Metzia

59b	**Vol. 2:** 687

Bekhoroth

30b	**Vol. 3:** 756

Berakoth

3a	**Vol. 3:** 448
5a	**Vol. 3:** 447
8b	**Vol. 1:** 230 **Vol. 3:** 1121
17a	**Vol. 3:** 105
27b	**Vol. 2:** 608
28b–29a	**Vol. 2:** 312
31a	**Vol. 2:** 433
32b	**Vol. 3:** 396
34b	**Vol. 3:** 638
35a	**Vol. 1:** 212
40a	**Vol. 1:** 614
46a	**Vol. 2:** 521
47b	**Vol. 1:** 485
50a	**Vol. 2:** 521
51a	**Vol. 3:** 921
55a	**Vol. 2:** 480
55b	**Vol. 1:** 116
60b	**Vol. 2:** 313 **Vol. 3:** 1152
61b	**Vol. 2:** 720, 837
2.2	**Vol. 3:** 1161
60 ff	**Vol. 1:** 231

Erubin

| 13b | Vol. 3: 1121 |
| 53b | Vol. 3: 1058 |

Gittin

| 60b | Vol. 3: 488 |
| 88a | Vol. 2: 730 |

Hagigah

12b	Vol. 3: 35
13 ff	Vol. 1: 527
14b	Vol. 1: 216
15a	Vol. 1: 175 Vol. 2: 608

Hullin

92a	Vol. 2: 309
106a	Vol. 2: 608
131	Vol. 2: 467

Kiddushin

29b	Vol. 3: 445
76a	Vol. 3: 455
81a	Vol. 3: 536

Makkoth

22a–22b	Vol. 2: 696
23b–24a	Vol. 2: 442
23b	Vol. 3: 367
24a–24b	Vol. 2: 310

Megillah

10b	Vol. 3: 656
12b–13a	Vol. 2: 310
13b	Vol. 2: 310
14b	Vol. 3: 656
23a	Vol. 3: 1058
27b	Vol. 2: 479
29a	Vol. 2: 310
31a	Vol. 2: 350

Menahoth

20b	Vol. 3: 445
65a–66a	Vol. 1: 627
85a	Vol. 2: 557
93b	Vol. 1: 223
104b	Vol. 3: 422
110a	Vol. 3: 422

Nedarim

| 32b | Vol. 2: 591 |
| 41a | Vol. 2: 824 |

Niddah

| 23a | Vol. 3: 1121 |

| 31a | Vol. 3: 1121 |

Ketuboth

50a	Vol. 2: 738
66b	Vol. 3: 445
67a–67b	Vol. 2: 738

Pesahim

3a	Vol. 1: 641
13a	Vol. 1: 641
54a	Vol. 3: 487
68b	Vol. 2: 784
87b	Vol. 2: 309
91b	Vol. 1: 145
112b	Vol. 2: 608
174b	Vol. 3: 195
7	Vol. 1: 641
27	Vol. 3: 195
68	Vol. 3: 408

Rosh ha-Shanah

10b–11a	Vol. 1: 628
21a	Vol. 3: 51
12	Vol. 1: 628

Sanhedrin

5a	Vol. 2: 608
19b	Vol. 1: 180 Vol. 2: 738
21b	Vol. 2: 141
25b	Vol. 3: 756
38a	Vol. 2: 608, 730 Vol. 3: 392
39a	Vol. 3: 447
40b	Vol. 3: 183
41a	Vol. 3: 538
43a	Vol. 1: 630 Vol. 2: 28, 295 Vol. 3: 51, 472
46b	Vol. 1: 265
56a–56b	Vol. 2: 309
59a	Vol. 2: 34
70b	Vol. 1: 614
88b	Vol. 2: 880
90b	Vol. 3: 274
91a	Vol. 1: 674 Vol. 3: 682
93b	Vol. 2: 314
94b	Vol. 3: 1161
97a–97b	Vol. 2: 698
97a	Vol. 2: 712 Vol. 3: 575
98a–98b	Vol. 3: 610
98b	Vol. 2: 314
99a	Vol. 2: 696
99b	Vol. 1: 180
102b	Vol. 1: 455
107b	Vol. 3: 472
108b	Vol. 2: 591
111b	Vol. 3: 1161

Shabbath

4a	**Vol. 3:** 183
12b	**Vol. 2:** 313
17b	**Vol. 3:** 1121
31a–31b	**Vol. 2:** 730
31a	**Vol. 1:** 485 **Vol. 2:** 311, 442, 811 **Vol. 3:** 488
33b	**Vol. 3:** 756
63a	**Vol. 2:** 314
88b	**Vol. 3:** 1121
104a	**Vol. 3:** 488
116a	**Vol. 1:** 455
119a	**Vol. 3:** 408, 753
129a	**Vol. 3:** 1121
132a	**Vol. 1:** 310
137b	**Vol. 1:** 309

Sotah

12b	**Vol. 1:** 598
22a	**Vol. 3:** 463
28b	**Vol. 3:** 1121
33a	**Vol. 3:** 39
47a	**Vol. 3:** 472
47b	**Vol. 3:** 1161
48b	**Vol. 1:** 597
49a	**Vol. 2:** 712
49b	**Vol. 2:** 126
47	**Vol. 3:** 227

Sukkah

45b	**Vol. 3:** 161

52a	**Vol. 1:** 178
52b	**Vol. 3:** 36

Taanith

8a	**Vol. 1:** 597
19a	**Vol. 3:** 638
19b–20a	**Vol. 3:** 638
20b	**Vol. 2:** 479–480
21a	**Vol. 3:** 1152
23b	**Vol. 1:** 614 **Vol. 3:** 639
24a	**Vol. 2:** 823

Yebamoth

15b	**Vol. 2:** 579
22a	**Vol. 1:** 180
62b	**Vol. 2:** 562
63a	**Vol. 3:** 867
63b	**Vol. 2:** 579
86	**Vol. 2:** 467

Yoma

5a	**Vol. 1:** 223
9a	**Vol. 1:** 555
22b	**Vol. 3:** 170
53b	**Vol. 3:** 39
72b	**Vol. 1:** 405

Zebahim

6a	**Vol. 1:** 223

Errata

(Line numbers in parentheses are counted from the bottom of the page)

Page	Line	Instead of	Read
Volume 1			
86	(8)	1 Cor. 14:45 ff.	1 Cor. 15:45 ff.
109	18	Wis. 11:90	Wis. 11:9
115	(6)	2 Tim. 5:18	1 Tim. 5:18
116	9	Jud. 6:25a, 28a	Jdg. 6:25a, 28a
165	32	Ezek 9:27	Ezek. 7:27
175	(4)	Rev. 8:17	Rev. 8:13
184	(5)	Isa. 60:31	Isa. 60:21
280	13	Ki. 19:15	2 Ki. 19:15
339	(9)	Hermas, *Sim.* 10, 3, 9	Hermas, *Sim.* 10, 4, 1
341	23	*Leg. All.* 2; 28	*Leg. All.* 2, 28
367	(11)	Jos. 23:24	Jos. 24:24
396	19	*War* 2,2,261 ff.	*War* 2,261 ff.
409	12	54:16	55:16
415	20	Deut. 20:27	Deut. 20:17
415	21	Deut. 20:27	Deut. 20:17
451	1	1 Sam. 28:36	1 Sam. 28:9
490	9	Jn. 61:66	Jn. 6:66
503	(14)	Joel 4:2	Joel 3:2
513	(25)	Ezek. 22:33	Ezek. 23:33
520	14	Jer. 14:51	Jer. 14:5
559	2	3 Ki. 2:29	1 Ki. 2:29
626	(10)	Lev. 23:32–32	Lev. 23:26–32
634	11	Lk. 22–19 f.	Lk. 22:19 f.
648	3	Tim. 4:6	2 Tim. 4:6
666	20	Rom. 29:9, 10	Rom. 2:9, 10
683	3	Ps. 104:41	Ps. 105:41
685	(10)	Test. Ass. 7:2	Test. Ash. 7:2
710	(16)	4 Esd. 8:36	4 Ezra 8:36
733	17	Acts 6:17	Acts 7:17
Volume 2			
63	11	Lk. 16:36	Lk. 6:36
69	12	Gen. 20:28	Gen. 20:18
69	27	Amos 3:18	Amos 3:13
80	2	cf. 31:5 f.	cf. 3:15 f.
113	22	1 Pet. 23–25	1 Pet. 1:23–25
150	37	Acts 7:78	Acts 7:48
211	16	4 Ki. 19:26	2 Ki. 19:26
248	18	Matt. 7:27–7	Matt. 7:24–27
253	(9)	1 Cor. 3:10–4	1 Cor.3:10–14
268	(8)	1 God. 8:8	1 Cor. 8:8
268	(15)	66:27, 55	6:27, 55

Page	Line	Instead of	Read
295	14	Lk. 28:56	Lk. 23:56
303	(13)	Pos. 50[49]:18	Pss. 50[49]:18
306	19	Gen. 40:50 ff.	Gen. 41:50 ff.
314	(1)	Acts 41:1	Acts 14:1
316	26	4:15	4:14
363	(5)	Joel 4:2	Joel 3:2
381	(5)	19:34	19:24
403	7	Rom. 6:3–3	Rom. 6:3–13
403	9	Phil. 3;10	Phil. 3:10
404	(5)	Jn. 5:69	Jn. 6:69
417	(4)	1 Ki. 25:1; 28:3	1 Sam. 25:1; 28:3
431	5	Ezr. 23:32	Ezek. 23:32
433	(5)	Lk. 16:23–37	Lk. 16:23–31
448	11	Deut. 19:15; 10:34	Deut. 19:15; Jn. 10:34
458	(18)	Job 12:33	Job 12:16
459	7	1 Jn. 2:66	1 Jn. 2:26
498	26	Wis. 7:3 6	Wis. 7:3, 6
535	(8)	Jn. 13; 14, 20	Jn. 13:14, 20
555	23	Mal. 5:5	Mal. 3:5
565	15	IQS 3:13–4:26	IQS 3:13–4:26
577	15	Lev. 12:12–18	Lev. 18:6–18
580	16	Mk. 10:2–2	Mk. 10:2–12
581	(17)	Lk. 20:20:34 f.	Lk. 20:34 f.
602	17	Sam. 22:32 ff.	2 Sam. 22:32 ff.
605	18	1 Cor. 12:10; 28;	1 Cor. 12:10, 28;
629	12	Jn. 2:11; 18, 23	Jn. 2:11, 18, 23
630	11	15:1 ff., 19:7	15:1 ff.; Lk. 19:7
630	(1)	26:51 ff.; 27:39 ff.	Matt. 26:51 ff.; 27:39 ff.
636	(5)	Exod. 2:27–31	Exod. 4:27–31
641	25	2 Cor. 2:9	2 Cor. 3:9
650	2	Ezek. 34:50	Ezek. 34:30
660	5	*Ap.* 273, 275	*Ap.* 2, 273; 275
675	5	Gen. 19:31, 34 f., 39	Gen. 19:31, 34 f., 38
679	3	*Ant.* 9, 10, 21	*Ant.* 9, 10, 2
688	18	*War* 1, 7, 19	*War* 1, 19
691	(19)	8:2–40:1	8:2 ff.
695	9	2 Chron. 6:60–80	1 Chr. 6:61–81
696	(8)	4, 8 23 (248)	4, 8, 23 (248)
709	16	1 Pet. 2:66	1 Pet. 2:6
711	3	18:4, 51	18:4; 28:51
714	20	Lk. 5:56 f.	Lk. 5:36 f.
722	15	Gal. 2:28	Gal. 3:28

319

Page	Line	Instead of	Read
739	16	except 16:12	except 19:37
767	23	Ezek. 26:28	Ezek. 26:2 f.
771	26	Pss. 10:38	Pss. 10:18
778	(4)	Pss. 4:8 29[28]:10	Pss. 4:8; 29[28]:10
793	7	1Qflor 1:4	4Qflor 1:4
793	(19)	Isa. 8:23	Isa. 9:1
803	10	Isa. 32:28	Isa. 32:18
842	10	Est. 10:10	Est. 10:3
854	9	1 Sam. 59:7	1 Sam. 25:3
863	6	2 Macc. 20:10	2 Macc. 2:10
863	(11)	Gen. 28:22–23	Gen. 18:22–23
874	8	1 Cor. 15, 26	1 Cor. 15:26
874	(1)	2 Tim. 16, 18	2 Tim. 1:16, 18
875	9	Cor. 1:3, 9–14	Col. 1:3, 9–14
890	12	Eccl. 11:19	Eccl. 11:9
890	19	Joel 4:14	Joel 3:14
893	17	1Q 14:7 ff.	1QM 14:7 ff.
893	(13)	Exod. 34:38	Exod. 34:28
896	8	Did. 10, 6	Did. 10:6

Volume 3

Page	Line	Instead of	Read
28	3	Mk. 11:45	Lk. 11:45
33	(5)	1 Sam. 21:27	1 Sam. 21:1
35	15	Neh. 13:4–9:28	Neh. 13:4–9, 28
45	(5)	Ps. 71:[70]:17	Ps. 71[70]:17
46	17	3:18);	3:18;
69	(3)	Exod. 3:24 f.	Exod. 2:24 f.
110	15	Matt. 12:18:21	Matt. 12:18, 21
110	(13)	Jdt. 16:17	Jdg. 16:17
137	24	Tit. 1:17	Tit. 1:7
161	(10)	Isa. 55:15	Isa. 54:14
165	25	Rom. 3:35	Rom. 3:25
181	(10)	Mk. 10:1–12:	Mk. 10:1–12;
192	25	Ps. 49(48)7	Ps. 49(48):7
193	(13)	Ps. 130(129);7	Ps. 130(129):7
207	12	Ps. 74(73);12	Ps. 74(73):12
207	29	2 Sam. 11:13	1 Sam. 11:13
225	11	1 Cor. 13:15	1 Cor. 13:13
238	(10)	Ezek. 21:37[32]:25:10	Ezek. 21:37[32];25:10
257	10	Ps. 95,11	Ps. 95:11
272	(19)	cf. 95:33 ff.	cf. 95:3 ff.
287	24	Heb. 13:20;ff.	Heb. 13:20 ff.
310	(1)	Ezek. 16:36 f., 57:	Ezek. 16:36 f., 57;
331	16	Matt. 6:16 ff., 45	Matt. 6:16 ff.; 5:45
342	27	2 Macc. 9:4, 12, 38	2 Macc. 9:4, 12, 28
342	(9)	2 Pet:10 ff.	2 Pet. 2:10 ff.
346	(5)	Prov. 20:31	Prov. 20:3
354	(25)	Num. 30:17	Num. 30:16
355	3	Joel 4:19	Joel 3:19
365	2	Heb. 8:38	Heb. 10:38
402	20	2 Chr. 23:29	1 Chr. 23:29
433	7	1 Cor. 19:19	1 Cor. 10:19

Page	Line	Instead of	Read
444	14	Zeph. 2:19	Zeph. 2:9
448	12	Deut. 25:22	Deut. 25:12
455	9	Lk. 10:51, 53	Lk. 9:51, 53
470	23	Mk. 8:53	Mk. 8:33
487	4	Deut. 35:10	Deut. 25:10
509	(12)	Mk. 15:61	Mk. 14:61
515	10	*Spec. Leg.* 1 20,	*Spec. Leg.* 1, 20,
515	17	Matt. 28:27	Matt. 28:7
517	8	1 Jn. 1:11	1 Jn. 1:1
532	34	2 Tim. 2:33	2 Tim. 2:23
589	22	Matt. 10:46	Mk. 10:46
595	4	Ps. 119[118],17	Ps. 119[118]:17
613	10	Acts 15:47	Acts 13:47
614	(16)	Dan. 18:26 f.	Dan. 8:26 f.
629	17	Matt. 19:38	Matt. 19:28
651	(19)	Ps. 16:20	Ps. 16:10
669	(13)	Matt. 16:30	Matt. 26:30
686	(4)	Ps. 39[38]:14	Ps. 39[38]:13
691	(8)	1 Sam. 11:16	1 Sam. 11:6
703	6	Rom. 1:11, 1; Cor. 12:8–11	Rom. 1:11; 1 Cor. 12:8–11
711	(16)	4 Macc. 8; 24;	4 Macc. 8:24;
714	30	2 Thess. 1:19	2 Thess. 1:9
722	16	1QH3:5–18	1QH 3:5–18
732	(10)	Acts 2:38, 40; 3; 19, 23	Acts 2:38, 40; 3:19, 23
733	(4)	Isa. 60; 19	Isa. 60:19
760	(6)	Ezr. 44:23	Ezek. 44:23
760	(11)	Ps. 94(93); 10, 12;	Ps. 94(93):10, 12;
760	(12)	Ps. 34(33) 11;	Ps. 34(33):11;
786	15	1 Ki. 17:7, 50	1 Ki. 7:50; 17:7
786	17	Hos. 8:16	Hos. 8:14
786	(9)	Ezek. 9:6, 23, 38	Ezek. 9:6; 23:38
799	(1)	Exod. 29:49 f.	Exod. 29:45 f.
817	1	2 Chr. 16:27	1 Chr. 16:27
823	(18)	4 Macc. 2:2–34	4 Macc. 2:2–24
871	17	(*Life* 1, 1)	(*Life* 1)
924	7	Ps. 37(36), 18	Ps. 37(36):18
939	29	Test. Ash. 8:9	Test. Ash. 1:9
964	(16)	Amos 5:27 ff.	Amos 5:25 ff.
983	23	Job 7:82	Job 7:12
989	21	Ezek. 26:25 ff.	Ezek. 36:25 ff.
1006	21	Isa. 35:15 f.	Isa. 35:5 f.
1010	3	1 Sam. 19:25	1 Sam. 9:25
1024	(13)	Ps. 94(93):8;	Ps. 94(93):8;
1024	(21)	Prov. 9:6 (4, 16)	Prov. 9:6 (4:16)
1024	(23)	2 Sam. 25:25	1 Sam. 25:25
1024	(24)	Eccl. 4:17, 25	Eccl. 4:17; 7:25
1041	2	1 Sam. 8:24	1 Sam. 9:24
1065	(5)	1 Tim. 5:39	1 Tim. 5:9
1074	3	Zech. 7:20	Zech. 7:10
1095	(5)	Jer. 2:4:5	Jer. 2:1–4:5
1099	(8)	Ezek. 26:28	Ezek. 26:2 f.
1157	(10)	Gal. 5:69 ff.	Gal. 5:19 ff.